personal ^{14e}
Financial Planning

Randall S. Billingsley
Virginia Tech

Lawrence J. Gitman
San Diego State University

Michael D. Joehnk
Arizona State University

CENGAGE
Learning·

Australia • Brazil • Mexico • Singapore • United Kingdom • United States

Personal Financial Planning, Fourteenth Edition
Randall S. Billingsley, Lawrence J. Gitman,
Michael D. Joehnk

Vice President, General Manager Science, Math and
Quantitative Business: Balraj Kalsi

Product Director: Mike Schenk

Senior Product Manager: Mike Reynolds

Content Developer: Conor Allen

Senior Product Assistant: Adele Scholtz

Marketing Manager: Nate Anderson

Marketing Coordinator: Eileen Corcoran

Associate Media Producer: Mark Hopkinson

Manufacturing Planner: Kevin Kluck

Art and Cover Direction, Production Management,
and Composition: Lumina Datamatics, Inc.

Cover Images: Macrovector/Shutterstock.com,
©graphixmania/Shutterstock.com, ©Incomible/
Shutterstock.com

Intellectual Property

Analyst: Christina Ciaramella, Brittani Morgan

Project Manager: Erika Mugavin

For product information and technology assistance, contact us at
Cengage Learning Customer & Sales Support, 1-800-354-9706

For permission to use material from this text or product,
submit all requests online at **www.cengage.com/permissions**
Further permissions questions can be emailed to
permissionrequest@cengage.com

Library of Congress Control Number: 2015950159

Student Edition:
ISBN: 978-1-305-63661-3

Loose-leaf Edition:
ISBN: 978-1-305-86233-3

Cengage Learning
20 Channel Center Street
Boston, MA 02210
USA

Cengage Learning is a leading provider of customized learning
solutions with employees residing in nearly 40 different countries
and sales in more than 125 countries around the world. Find your
local representative at **www.cengage.com**.

Cengage Learning products are represented in Canada by Nelson Education, Ltd.

To learn more about Cengage Learning Solutions, visit **www.cengage.com**

Purchase any of our products at your local college store or at our
preferred online store **www.cengagebrain.com**

Unless otherwise noted, all items are © Cengage Learning

Printed in the United States of America

Print Number: 01   Print Year: 2015

For Bonnie, Lauren, and Evan
RSB

For our children:
Zachary, Jessica, and Caren
LJG

For Colwyn,
Grace, and Rhett
MDJ

Brief Contents

Contents

Preface, ix
About the Authors, xviii

ARIEL SKELLEY/JUPITER IMAGES

ALIKEYOU/SHUTTERSTOCK.COM

©SEYOMEDO/SHUTTERSTOCK.COM

© STOCKLITE/SHUTTERSTOCK.COM

©WAVEBREAKMEDIA/SHUTTERSTOCK.COM

©DEAN MITCHELL/SHUTTERSTOCK.COM

Preface

- Why can't I budget more effectively and what should I do about it?
- How much money should I set aside for emergencies?
- How do I pick the best credit card and best manage it?
- Would I be better off renting or buying a home?
- How much of a mortgage can I afford?
- What are the implications of the Affordable Care Act for my health insurance?
- What features do I need in car and homeowner's insurance and how do I get the best prices?
- What do I need to know about stocks and bonds to make good investments?
- How do I choose the best mutual funds and exchange traded funds (ETFs)?
- How do I plan for retirement?
- How do tax-deferred investment vehicles work and what should I do about them?
- Do I really need a will if I'm young and just getting started?
- Isn't estate planning just for rich people?

So many questions about managing our personal finances—and the stakes are so high! *Personal Financial Planning*, 14th edition, provides a framework for answering these questions and more. Careful planning allows us to best adapt to changes in the financial environment and the associated changes in our own lives. This book provides tools for preparing personal financial plans that serve as road maps for achieving goals. It emphasizes the dynamics of the financial planning process by considering the impact of life changes—birth, marriage, divorce, job and career, and death.

Personal Financial Planning addresses all of the major financial planning issues and problems that individuals and families encounter. It links together all of the major elements of effective money management. All of the latest financial planning tools and techniques are discussed. This comprehensive text is written in a personal style that uses state-of-the-art pedagogy to present the key concepts and procedures used in sound personal financial planning and effective money management. The roles of various financial decisions in the overall personal financial planning process are clearly delineated.

The book serves individuals who are, or will be, actively developing their own personal financial plans. It meets the needs of instructors and students in a first course in personal financial planning (often called "personal finance") offered at colleges and universities, junior and community colleges, professional certification programs, and continuing education courses. The experiences of individuals and families are used to demonstrate successes and failures in various aspects of personal financial planning. A conversational style and liberal use of examples and worksheets guide students through the material and emphasize important points. The benefits of the book's readability accrue not only to students but also to their instructors.

ORGANIZATION OF THE BOOK

Personal Financial Planning is divided into six parts. Part 1 presents the foundations of personal financial planning, beginning with the financial planning process and then covering financial statements and budgets and also taxes. Part 2 concerns the management of basic assets, including cash and savings instruments, automobiles, and housing. Part 3 covers credit management, including the various types of open account borrowing and consumer loans. Part 4 deals with managing insurance needs and considers life insurance, health care insurance, and property insurance. Part 5 covers investments—including stocks, bonds, mutual funds, ETFs, and real estate—and how to make transactions in securities markets. Part 6 is devoted to retirement and estate planning.

Pedagogy

Each chapter opens with six learning goals that link the material covered to specific learning outcomes and anchor the text's *integrated learning system*. The learning goal numbers are tied to major chapter headings and restated and reviewed point by point in the end-of-chapter summary. New to the 14th edition, each chapter also opens with a series of statements presented as *Financial Fact or Fantasy* in the related chapter material. Each statement is critically evaluated as fact or fantasy in the context of the relevant material. Then, at the end of each of the major sections, *Test Yourself* questions allow readers to reinforce their understanding of the material before moving on to the next section. As students read through the chapters, these *Test Yourself* questions allow them to test their understanding of the material in each section. Students can find the answers to the *Test Yourself* questions on the book's companion website by going to www.cengagebrain.com and searching for this book by its author or ISBN, and then adding it to the dashboard. They're also found in the instructor's manual. Also new to the 14th edition, at the end of select chapters is a summary of all key financial relationships along with a problem set illustrating their application.

Each chapter contains several *Financial Planning Tips* and *Financial Road Signs*, which provide important hints or suggestions to consider when implementing certain parts of a financial plan. *Worksheets* are included to simplify demonstration of various calculations and procedures and to provide students with helpful materials that they can use in managing their own personal finances. The worksheets are numbered for convenient reference in end-of-chapter problems, and they include descriptive captions. Numerous exhibits, each including a descriptive caption, are used throughout to more fully illustrate key points in the text. Also included in each chapter is a *running glossary* that appears in the margin and provides brief definitions of all highlighted terms in the accompanying text. Most chapters discuss how the Internet can be used in various phases of personal financial planning. End-of-chapter material includes a *Summary*, which restates each learning goal and follows it with a brief paragraph that summarizes the material related to it. The next element is the new *Financial Impact of Personal Choices* feature, which presents a personal financial planning decision related to an important topic in each chapter and evaluates the outcome. Selected chapters also provide a new feature, *Key Financial Relationships*, which concisely summarizes the analytical frameworks used and provides related practice problems and their solutions. Then each chapter provides *Financial Planning Exercises*, which include questions and problems that students can use to test their grasp of the material. Following this feature is *Applying Personal Finance*, which generally involves some type of outside project or exercise. Two *Critical Thinking Cases* that highlight the important analytical topics and concepts are also provided.

Major Changes in the 14th Edition

The 14th edition has been thoroughly updated to consider the most up-to-date techniques of contemporary personal financial planning. We emphasize that the key principles of personal financial planning remain valid: save, diversify your investments, watch your expenditures, and borrow carefully. This edition reflects feedback from past users, practicing financial planners, finance industry experts, students, and our own research. It provides helpful new approaches, expanded coverage in certain areas, streamlined coverage in others, and enhanced pedagogy anchored by a state-of-the-art integrated learning system. The basic organizational structure, topical coverage, superior readability, and useful instructional aids that marked the success of the first 13 editions have been retained and extended. Important changes in this edition are described below, first as general changes and then as specific chapter-by-chapter changes.

General Changes and Hallmark Features

- The 14th edition includes in each chapter a series of highlighted practical examples illustrating everyday applications of the covered material. The featured examples include "The Sooner You Start an IRA, the Better" (Chapter 1), "Determining the Value of an Investment" and Keeping Track of Loans" (Chapter 2), "Applying Tax Rates" and "Determining the Amount Owed or Refunded" (Chapter 3), "Determining the Extent of FDIC Insurance Protection" (Chapter 4), "Calculating the Maximum Affordable Mortgage Loan" (Chapter 5), "Credit Card Choice Trade-offs" and "Paying Only the Minimum on Your Credit Card" (Chapter 6), "Calculating the Total Finance Charge and Payment on a Simple Interest Loan" (Chapter 7), "Appropriate Use of Term Life Insurance" and "Using Low-Load Whole Life Insurance—Building Cash Value" (Chapter 8), "Effect of Per-Illness, Per-Accident Deductible" (Chapter 9), "Effect of Co-insurance," and "Homeowner's Policy Coverage Limits" (Chapter 10), "Limit Orders" and "Using Margin Trades to Magnify Returns" (Chapter 11), "Inflation-Adjustment of TIPS Bonds" and "Calculating the Approximate Yield to Maturity" (Chapter 12), "Calculating a Mutual Fund's NAV" and "Calculating the Value of Income-Producing Property" (Chapter 13), "Effect of Inflation on Future Retirement Needs" and "Measuring the Benefits of a Roth IRA Over a Taxable Account" (Chapter 14), and "Disadvantage of Joint Tenancy with the Right of Survivorship" and "Use of Life Insurance in an Estate" (Chapter 15).
- The 14th edition includes a new feature in each chapter, *You Can Do It Now*, which allows the reader to act on the presented material on the spot. The *You Can Do It Now* features include "Start a List of Your Financial Goals" and "Recognize that YOU are Your Most Important Asset" (Chapter 1), "Track Your Expenses" and "Save Automatically" (Chapter 2), "Tax Planning" (Chapter 3), "Shop for the Best Short-Term Rates" and "Reconcile Your Checkbook" (Chapter 4), "What's Your Car Worth?" and "Rent vs. Buy a Home?" (Chapter 5), "How Does Your Credit Report Look?" and "Is Your Credit Card a Good Deal?" (Chapter 6), "Current Auto Loan Rates" (Chapter 7), "Shop for a Customized Life Insurance Policy" and "Check Out the Best Life Insurance Companies" (Chapter 8), "Compare Policies on an ACA Health Insurance Exchange" (Chapter 9), "Check Out the Best Homeowner's Insurance Companies" and "Evaluate the Best Auto insurance Companies" (Chapter 10), "How's the Market Doing Right Now?" and "Get a Quick Perspective on Your Asset Allocation" (Chapter 11), "What's the Market P/E Ratio Telling You?" and "How Do Stock and Bond Market Returns Compare This Year?" (Chapter 12), "Objective Mutual Fund Resources" and "How to Choose the Best ETF for You" (Chapter 13), "Get a Rough Estimate of Your Future Social Security Benefits" and "Calculating the Benefits of a Traditional IRA" (Chapter 14), and "Estate Planning Conversations" and "Importance of Naming Alternative Beneficiaries" (Chapter 15).
- New to the 14th edition is the *Financial Impact of Personal Choices* feature, which presents a personal financial planning decision related to an important topic in each chapter and evaluates the outcome. The *Financial Impact of Personal Choices* feature includes "Bob Cuts Back on Lunch Out and Lattes" (Chapter 1), "No Budget, No Plan: Sean Bought a Boat!" (Chapter 2), "Angela and Tim's Tax Management Strategy" (Chapter 3), "Stella Likes Cash—Too Much?" (Chapter 4), "Vivian Wants to Buy a House but Doesn't Want a Roommate Now" (Chapter 5), "Stan Has Had It and Files for Bankruptcy" (Chapter 6), "John and Mary Calculate Their Auto Loan Backwards" (Chapter 7), "Matt and Jan Consider 'Buying Term and Investing the Rest'" (Chapter 8), "Josh Expands His Health Insurance

Coverage" (Chapter 9), "Wade Saves on His Car Insurance" (Chapter 10), "Trey and April Get Serious About Their Retirement Asset Allocation" (Chapter 11), "Landon and Kirsten Like High Flying Stocks" (Chapter 12), "Virginia Finds a Simple Retirement Investment Plan" (Chapter 13), "Carl and Brian's Different Approaches to a Traditional IRA" (Chapter 14), and "The (Un)intended Effects of Corbin's Beneficiary Designations" (Chapter 15).

- The 14th edition adds a summary of *Key Financial Relationships* at the end of selected chapters. Practice problems illustrating the application of these key analytical frameworks are also provided.

- The highly regarded *Worksheets* are provided in a user-friendly Excel® format that students can download from the book's companion Internet site. Students have the option of using the Worksheets multiple times and having some of the calculations within the Worksheets completed electronically.

- The book has been *completely updated and redesigned* to allow improved presentation of each of the text's pedagogical features.

- The 14th edition continues to place emphasis on *using the Internet*. Included are a number of features that either link students to relevant Internet sites or describe how the Internet can be incorporated into the personal financial planning process.

- Step-by-step *use of a handheld financial calculat*or to make time value calculations continues to be integrated into relevant discussions in this edition. To improve understanding, relevant keystrokes are highlighted in these demonstrations. Basics of the time value of money are introduced in Chapter 2, "Using Financial Statements and Budgets," and Appendix E now explains how financial calculators can be used to make time value calculations. The use of a financial calculator is reinforced in later chapters, where the time value techniques are applied. For example, using a calculator to find the future value of a deposit given various compounding periods is shown in Chapter 4, "Managing Your Cash and Savings," and calculating estimates of future retirement needs is demonstrated in Chapter 14, "Planning for Retirement." The inclusion of calculator keystrokes should help the reader learn how to develop financial plans more effectively by using this important tool of the trade.

- The 14th edition continues and updates the well-received *Behavior Matters*, which relates each chapter's topic to the reader's everyday behavior and shows how readers might adapt their behavior to become more financially savvy. The *Behavior Matters* features show how all-too-common behavioral biases can adversely affect how we process financial information and make financial decisions. The feature helps link the text discussions to actual financial planning ideas, experiences, and practices—all intended to fully engage readers in the personal financial planning process. The *Behavior Matters* features include "Practicing Financial Self-Awareness" (Chapter 1), "Don't Fool Yourself...Pessimistic Budgeting Wins" (Chapter 2), "Do We Really Value Paying Taxes After All?" (Chapter 3), "Why Can't I Save More—And What Can I Do About It?" (Chapter 4), "Watch Out for 'Anchoring': The Case of the Used Car Salesperson Strategy," (Chapter 5), "Behavioral Biases and Credit Card Use" (Chapter 6), "The Paradox of More Financial Choices" (Chapter 7), "Whole Life vs. Term Life Insurance and Behavioral Biases" (Chapter 8), "Behavioral Biases in Making Health Insurance Decisions" (Chapter 9), "Behavioral Tips in Buying Property Insurance" (Chapter 10), "Do We Live in the Present Too Much? Looking for Patterns That Aren't There..." (Chapter 11), "Dealing with Investor Overreaction" (Chapter 12), "Behavioral Biases in Mutual Fund Investing" (Chapter 13), "Behavioral Biases in Retirement Planning" (Chapter 14), and "Recognizing and Overcoming Aversion to Ambiguity in Estate Planning" (Chapter 15).

- Exhibits and Worksheets, and end-of-chapter *Financial Planning Exercises* and *Critical Thinking Cases*—have been retained and improved as part of the integrated learning system. The *Planning Over a Lifetime* feature continues to highlight how the chapter's topic is important to readers in different life stages.

Specific Chapter-by-Chapter Changes and Summaries

Because instructors often like to know where new material appears, the significant changes that have been made in the 14th edition are summarized next.

Chapter 1 on understanding the financial planning process, has been carefully revised to focus on the most important themes in the book. Emphasis is placed on setting realistic goals for your finances, helpful ways to save money by changing everyday habits, and being more financially self-aware.

Chapter 2 on using your financial statements and budgeting has been restructured, streamlined, and updated. Calculator keystrokes and time lines continue to appear in discussions of the time value of money. There are new discussions on setting realistic budgeting plans and avoiding potential budgeting mistakes, how to choose the right personal finance software, and practical ways to change your behavior to spend less.

Chapter 3 on preparing your taxes has been updated to reflect the changes in tax laws, rates, procedures, and forms in effect at the time we revised the chapter. The material emphasizes current tax practices and explains the nature of progressive tax rates, average tax rates, itemized deductions, individual retirement accounts (IRAs), and other types of tax issues. The chapter continues to provide readers with sidebar advice on finding commonly missed tax deductions, avoiding common tax-form errors, tax tips, and audit triggers. There are new features about what documents you'll need to collect to prepare for tax time, effective ways to reduce your tax liability, and tips for choosing the most appropriate tax preparer for you.

Chapter 4 on managing your cash and savings, has been revised to reflect up-to-date capital market conditions. The potential use of I bonds to manage inflation risk is emphasized. There are practical explanations of why you should start saving *now*, what to look for when choosing a new bank, planning tips for when and when not to use your debit card, and tips for what you should and shouldn't store in a safety deposit box.

Chapter 5 on making automobile and housing decisions considers new market developments and sources of information. The chapter discusses when it makes sense to lease a car, when to buy versus rent a house, how to know when it's time to buy your first home, how to tell what kind of house you need (prioritizing your needs and being practical), and the top ten home improvement projects based on the percentage of the investment recovered at the sale of a home.

Chapter 6 on consumer credit and credit cards, focuses on the positive aspects of using credit and what it takes to build and maintain a strong credit history. The chapter explores the dangers of making only the minimum payment on your credit cards and why "mental accounting" can be dangerous, tips for choosing the right credit card, risky situations for using your debit card, protecting yourself from identity theft, and how to use credit through the different stages of your life.

Chapter 7 on using consumer loans, analyzes the benefits and uses of consumer credit for both single-payment and installment loans. The discussion concentrates on the key issues surrounding loan provisions, finance charges, and other credit considerations. There are suggested questions to ask before you loan money to family and friends, a discussion about 0 percent annual percentage rate (APR) loans and their potential limitations, and a discussion of what lenders are looking at when you submit a loan application—your credit report, debt history, employment history, and savings.

Chapter 8 on insuring your life, discusses how to choose the right life insurance, the benefits of buying a whole-life policy, the differences between whole life and term life insurance, knowing what to expect during your life insurance medical exam, potential conflicts of interest in dealing with insurance agents, and key considerations for life insurance use in each stage of life.

Chapter 9 on insuring your health, has been updated and includes a discussion of the new rules and guidelines for student health care, Medicare Advantage plans, how to save on health insurance, and how to choose the right plan for you. There's also a new discussion about the rationale for health-care reform and the controversy over the Affordable Health Care Act of 2010. The chapter also includes tips on buying disability income insurance, buying long-term care insurance, and health-care apps for your smart phone.

Chapter 10 on protecting your property, discusses behavioral biases when buying property insurance, how to handle a denied insurance claim, and buying auto insurance—getting multiple quotes, how the car itself affects the price of the policy, and how much auto insurance you need. We continue to emphasize practical advice for reducing homeowner's insurance premiums, filing auto insurance claims, preventing auto theft, strategies to avoid liability, and obtaining discounts for auto safety and good driving.

Chapter 11 on investment planning has been revised and updated with discussions of why people are more likely to make short-term investments (and why you might want to avoid this tendency), the importance of saving for retirement, and how to begin investing online.

Chapter 12 on investing in stocks and bonds continues to emphasize the risk–return characteristics of these securities. As part of the revision process, we present new information on successful stock and bond investing, analysis of Apple's financial performance and valuation, tips for avoiding common investing mistakes, properly interpreting overly optimistic equity analysis, how accrued interest affects bond prices, and how to invest in stocks and bonds at each stage of life.

Chapter 13 on investing has been updated and discusses target-date mutual funds, choosing the best mutual funds, avoiding "dog" funds, choosing between exchange traded funds (ETFs) and mutual funds, and a lengthy new discussion and exhibit about how to evaluate ETF performance. There's also a *Behavior Matters* feature about behavioral biases in mutual fund investing—how educating yourself can help you break harmful investing tendencies.

Chapter 14 on planning for retirement, has several valuable features discussing behavioral biases in retirement planning, an app for your smart phone that will help you plan for retirement, a discussion about protecting private-sector defined benefit retirement plans, tips for managing your 401(k) account, and coverage about converting a traditional IRA to a Roth IRA and the implications of doing so.

Chapter 15 on preserving your estate, has been updated to reflect the most recent estate tax laws and tax rates. The chapter discusses online estate planning resources, the details of choosing a suitable guardian for minor children in case of death, tips for writing a will, reasons to use a trust, and a feature about recognizing and overcoming aversion to ambiguity in estate planning.

SUPPLEMENTARY MATERIALS

Because we recognize the importance of outstanding support materials to the instructor and the student, we have continued to improve and expand our supplements package.

Instructor Supplements

CengageNOW

CengageNOW is a powerful course management and online homework tool that provides robust instructor control and customization to optimize the student learning experience and meet desired outcomes. CengageNOW offers:

- Auto-graded homework (static and algorithmic varieties), a test bank, and an eBook, all in one resource.
- Easy-to-use course management options offering flexibility and continuity from one semester to another.
- New! Expanded post-submission feedback explains each problem to students. The instructor decides when this solution is delivered to the students. The 14th edition of *Personal Financial Planning* is the first to offer post-submission feedback to students using CengageNOW.
- The most robust and flexible assignment options in the industry.
- The ability to analyze student work from the gradebook and generate reports on learning outcomes. Each problem is tagged to Business Program (AACSB) and Bloom's Taxonomy outcomes so that you can measure student performance.
- Contact your sales representative for more details if you are interested in offering CengageNOW to your students.

Instructor's Manual and Test Bank

A comprehensive *Instructor's Manual* has been prepared to assist the instructor. For each chapter, the manual includes:

- An outline
- Discussion of major topics
- A list of key concepts
- Solutions to all *Test Yourself* questions, end-of-chapter *Financial Planning Exercises*, and *Critical Thinking Cases*

The *Test Bank* has been revised, updated, and expanded, and all solutions have been checked for accuracy. It includes true–false and multiple-choice questions, as well as four to six short problems for nearly every chapter. Each question is tagged with the corresponding learning objective and learning outcomes. The *Instructor's Manual* has been revised by Professor Sam Hicks, CPA, of VirginiaTech.

Testing with Cognero

Cengage Learning Testing Powered by Cognero is a flexible, online system that allows you to author, edit, and manage test bank content, create multiple test versions in an instant, and deliver tests from your LMS, in your classroom or through CengageNOW.

Microsoft PowerPoint®

Enhance lectures and simplify class preparation. Chapter PowerPoint® presentations are available to instructors both on the Instructor's Resource CD and on the text's instructor Web site. Each presentation consists of a general outline of key concepts from the book. The PowerPoints were revised by Professor Sam Hicks, CPA, of VirginiaTech.

STUDENT SUPPLEMENTS

Interactive Worksheets

Interactive *Worksheets* identical to those presented in the text can be downloaded from this text's student companion Internet site. Each Worksheet provides a logical format for dealing with some aspect of personal financial planning, such as preparing a cash budget, assessing home affordability, or deciding whether to lease or purchase an automobile. Providing worksheets electronically in Excel® format allows students to complete them multiple times for mastery, and many of the worksheets can actually be used to calculate figures needed to make financial decisions.

ACKNOWLEDGMENTS

In addition to the many individuals who made significant contributions to this book by their expertise, classroom experience, guidance, general advice, and reassurance, we also appreciate the students and faculty who used the book and provided valuable feedback, confirming our conviction that a truly teachable personal financial planning text could be developed.

Of course, we are indebted to all the academicians and practitioners who have created the body of knowledge contained in this text. We particularly wish to thank several people who gave the most significant help in developing and revising it. They include Professor John Brozovsky, CPA, of VirginiaTech, for assistance in the chapter on taxes; Professor Sam Hicks, CPA, of VirginiaTech, for his thorough review of the entire book; Thomas C. Via Jr., CLU, for his help in the chapters on life and property insurance; Kent Dodge for his help in the chapter on health insurance; Professor Hongbok Lee, of Western Illinois University, for helpful observations, and Marlene Bellamy of Writeline Associates for her help with the real estate material.

Cengage Learning shared our objective of producing a truly teachable text and relied on the experience and advice of numerous excellent reviewers for the 14th edition:

Ed Anthony, Trevecca Nazarene University
John Bedics, DeSales University
Omar Benkato, Ball State University
Ross E. Blankenship, State Fair Community College
Tim Chesnut, Mt. Vernon Nazarene University
Joseph C. Eppolito, Syracuse University
Jonathan Fox, Ohio State University
Laurie Hensley, Cornell University
John Guess, Delgado Community College
Dianne Morrison, University of Wisconsin—La Crosse
Kathy Mountjoy, Illinois State University
Eric Munshower, University of Dubuque
Muhammad Mustafa, South Carolina State University
Thomas Paczkowski, Cayuga Community College
Ohaness Paskelian, University of Houston—Downtown
Joan Ryan, Clackamas Community College
Amy Scott, DeSales University
Donna Scarlett, Iowa Western Community College—Clarinda Campus
Rahul Verma, University of Houston—Downtown

We also appreciate the many suggestions from previous reviewers, all of whom have had a significant impact on the earlier editions of this book. Our thanks go to the following: Linda Afdahl, Micheal J. Ahern III, Robert J. Angell, H. Kent Baker, Harold David Barr, Catherine L. Bertelson, Steve Blank, Kathleen K. Bromley, D. Gary

Carman, Dan Casey, P. R. Chandy, Tony Cherin, Larry A. Cox, Maurice L. Crawford, Carlene Creviston, Rosa Lea Danielson, William B. Dillon, David Durst, Jeanette A. Eberle, Mary Ellen Edmundson, Ronald Ehresman, Jim Farris, Stephen Ferris, Sharon Hatten Garrison, Wayne H. Gawlick, Alan Goldfarb, Carol Zirnheld Green, Joseph D. Greene, C. R. Griffen, John L. Grimm, Chris Hajdas, James Haltman, Vickie L. Hampton, Forest Harlow, Eric W. Hayden, Henry C. Hill, Kendall B. Hill, Darrell D. Hilliker, Arlene Holyoak, Marilynn E. Hood, Frank Inciardi, Ray Jackson, Kenneth Jacques, Dixie Porter Johnson, Ted Jones, William W. Jones, Judy Kamm, Gordon Karels, Peggy Keck, Gary L. Killion, Earnest W. King, Karol Kitt, George Klander, Xymena S. Kulsrud, Carole J. Makela, Paul J. Maloney, David Manifold, Charles E. Maxwell, Charles W. McKinney, Robert W. McLeod, George Muscal, Robert Nash, Ed Nelling, Charles O'Conner, Albert Pender, Aaron L. Phillips, Armand Picou, Franklin Potts, Fred Power, Alan Raedels, Margaret P. Reed, Charles F. Richardson, Arnold M. Rieger, Vivian Rippentrop, Gayle M. Ross, Kenneth H. St. Clair, Brent T. Sjaardema, Thomas M. Springer, Frank A. Thompson, Dick Verrone, Rosemary Walker, Peggy Bergmeier Ward, Tom Warschauer, Gary Watts, Grant J. Wells, Brock Williams, Janet Bear Wolverton, Betty Wright, and R. R. Zilkowski.

Because of the wide variety of topics covered in this book, we called on many experts for whose insight on recent developments we are deeply grateful. We would like to thank them and their firms for allowing us to draw on their knowledge and resources, particularly Robert Andrews, Willis M. Allen Co. Realtors; Bill Bachrach, Bachrach & Associates; Mark D. Erwin, Commonwealth Financial Network; Robin Gitman, Willis M. Allen Co. Realtors; Craig Gussin, CLU, Auerbach & Gussin; Frank Hathaway, CFA, Chief Economist, NASDAQ; John Markese, former President of the American Association of Individual Investors; Mark Nussbaum, CFP®, Wells Fargo Advisors, Inc.; Sherri Tobin, Farmers Insurance Group; and Deila Mangold, Ideal Homes Realty.

The editorial staff of Cengage Learning has been most helpful in our endeavors. We wish to thank Joe Sabatino, Senior Product Team Manager; Mike Reynolds, Senior Product Manager; Conor Allen, Content Developer; and Adele Scholtz, Senior Product Assistant.

Finally, our wives—Bonnie, Robin, and Charlene—have provided needed support and understanding during the writing of this book. We are forever grateful to them.

Randall S. Billingsley, FRM, CFA
VirginiaTech

Lawrence J. Gitman, CFP®
San Diego State University

Michael D. Joehnk, CFA
Arizona State University

About the Authors

Randall S. Billingsley is a finance professor at VirginiaTech. He received his bachelor's degree in economics from Texas Tech University and received both an M.S. in economics and a Ph.D. in finance from Texas A&M University. Professor Billingsley holds the Chartered Financial Analyst (CFA), Financial Risk Manager (FRM), and Certified Rate of Return Analyst (CRRA) professional designations. An award-winning teacher at the undergraduate and graduate levels, his research, consulting, and teaching focus on investment analysis and issues relevant to practicing financial advisors. Formerly a vice president at the Association for Investment Management and Research (now the CFA Institute), Professor Billingsley's published equity valuation case study of Merck & Company was assigned reading in the CFA curriculum for several years. In 2006 the Wharton School published his book, *Understanding Arbitrage: An Intuitive Approach to Financial Analysis*. In addition, his research has been published in refereed journals that include the *Journal of Portfolio Management*, the *Journal of Banking and Finance*, *Financial Management*, the *Journal of Financial Research*, and the *Journal of Futures Markets*. Professor Billingsley advises the Student-Managed Endowment for Educational Development (SEED) at Virginia Tech, which manages an equity portfolio of about $5 million on behalf of the Virginia Tech Foundation.

Professor Billingsley's consulting to date has focused on two areas of expertise. First, he has acted extensively as an expert witness on financial issues. Second, he has taught seminars and published materials that prepare investment professionals for the CFA examinations. This has afforded him the opportunity to explore and discuss the relationships among diverse areas of investment analysis. His consulting endeavors have taken him across the United States and to Canada, Europe, and Asia. A primary goal of Professor Billingsley's consulting is to apply the findings of academic financial research to practical investment decision making and personal financial planning.

Lawrence J. Gitman is an emeritus professor of finance at San Diego State University. He received his bachelor's degree from Purdue University, his M.B.A. from the University of Dayton, and his Ph.D. from the University of Cincinnati. Professor Gitman is a prolific textbook author and has more than 50 articles appearing in various finance journals.

His other major textbooks include *Fundamentals of Investing*, 12th edition, which is co-authored with Scott B. Smart and Michael D. Joehnk; and *Principles of Managerial Finance*, 7th Brief edition, and *Principles of Managerial Finance*, 14th edition, both co-authored with Chad J. Zutter.

An active member of numerous professional organizations, Professor Gitman is past president of the Academy of Financial Services, the San Diego Chapter of the Financial Executives Institute, the Midwest Finance Association, and the FMA National Honor Society. In addition, he is a Certified Financial Planner® (CFP®). Gitman formerly served as a director on the CFP® Board of Governors, as vice-president–financial education for the Financial Management Association, and as director of the San Diego MIT Enterprise Forum. He has two grown children and lives with his wife in La Jolla, California, where he is an avid bicyclist.

Michael D. Joehnk is an emeritus professor of finance at Arizona State University (ASU). In addition to his academic appointments at ASU, Professor Joehnk spent a year (1999) as a visiting professor of finance at the University of Otago in New Zealand. He received his bachelor's and Ph.D. degrees from the University of Arizona and his M.B.A. from Arizona State University. A Chartered Financial Analyst (CFA), he has served as a member of the Candidate Curriculum Committee and of the Council of Examiners of the Institute of Chartered Financial Analysts. He has also served as a director of the Phoenix Society of Financial Analysts and as secretary-treasurer of the Western Finance Association, and he was elected to two terms as a vice-president of the Financial Management Association. Professor Joehnk is the author or co-author of some 50 articles, five books, and numerous monographs. His articles have appeared in *Financial Management*, the *Journal of Finance*, the *Journal of Bank Research*, the *Journal of Portfolio Management*, the *Journal of Consumer Affairs*, the *Journal of Financial and Quantitative Analysis*, the *AAII Journal,* the *Journal of Financial Research*, the *Bell Journal of Economics*, the *Daily Bond Buyer*, *Financial Planner,* and other publications.

In addition to co-authoring several books with Lawrence J. Gitman, Professor Joehnk was the author of a highly successful paperback trade book, *Investing for Safety's Sake*. In addition, Dr. Joehnk was the editor of *Institutional Asset Allocation*, which was sponsored by the Institute of Chartered Financial Analysts and published by Dow Jones–Irwin. He also was a contributor to the *Handbook for Fixed Income Securities* and to *Investing and Risk Management*, volume 1 of the Library of Investment Banking. In addition, he served a six-year term as executive co-editor of the *Journal of Financial Research*. He and his wife live in Flagstaff, Arizona, where they enjoy hiking and other activities in the nearby mountains and canyons.

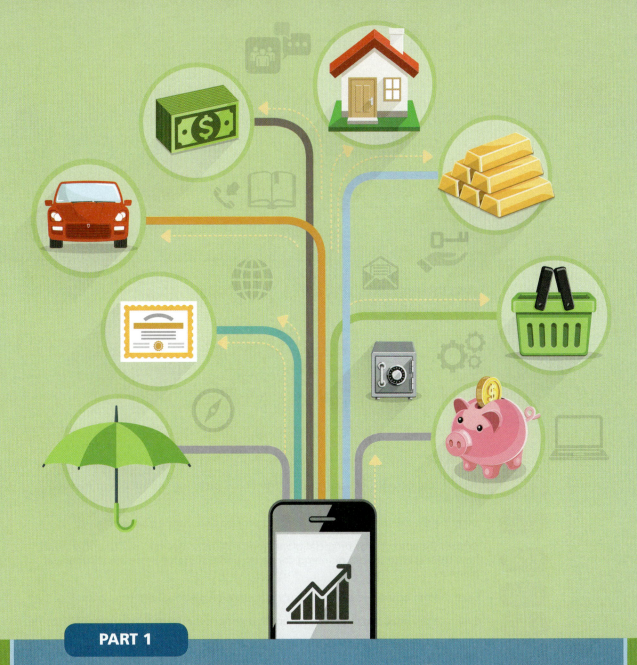

PART 1

Foundations of Financial Planning

CHAPTERS

1 Understanding the Financial Planning Process

2 Using Financial Statements and Budgets

3 Preparing Your Taxes

CHAPTER 1

Understanding the Financial Planning Process

LEARNING GOALS

LG1   Identify the benefits of using personal financial planning techniques to manage your finances.

LG2   Describe the personal financial planning process and define your goals.

LG3   Explain the life cycle of financial plans, their role in achieving your financial goals, how to deal with special planning concerns, and the use of professional financial planners.

LG4   Examine the economic environment's influence on personal financial planning.

LG5   Evaluate the impact of age, education, and geographic location on personal income.

LG6   Understand the importance of career choices and their relationship to personal financial planning.

How Will This Affect Me?

The heart of financial planning is making sure your values line up with how you spend and save. That means knowing where you are financially and planning on how to get where you want to be in the future no matter what life throws at you. For example, how should your plan handle the projection that Social Security costs may exceed revenues by 2037? And what if the government decides to raise tax rates to help cover the federal deficit? An informed financial plan should reflect such uncertainties and more.

This chapter overviews the financial planning process and explains its context. Topics include how financial plans change to accommodate your current stage in life and the role that financial planners can play in helping you achieve your objectives. After reading this chapter you will have a good perspective on how to organize your overall personal financial plan.

Financial Fact or Fantasy?

Are the following statements Financial Facts (true) or Fantasies (false)? Consider these statements as you read through this chapter.

- An improved standard of living is one of the payoffs of sound personal financial planning.
- A savings account is an example of a tangible asset because it represents something on deposit at a bank or other financial institution.
- Personal financial planning involves translating personal financial goals into specific plans and strategies that put these plans into action.
- Over the long-run, gaining only an extra percent or two on an investment makes little difference in the amount of earnings generated.
- Inflation generally has little effect on personal financial planning.
- Your income level depends on your age, education, and career choice.

1-1 THE REWARDS OF SOUND FINANCIAL PLANNING

What does living "the good life" mean to you? Does it mean having the flexibility to pursue your dreams and goals in life? Is it owning a home in a certain part of town, starting a company, being debt free, driving a particular type of car, taking luxury vacations, or having a large investment portfolio? Today's complex, fast-paced world offers a bewildering array of choices. Rapidly changing economic, political, technological, and social environments make it increasingly difficult to develop solid financial strategies that will improve your lifestyle consistently. Moreover, the recent financial crisis dramatizes the need to plan for financial contingencies. Today, a couple may need two incomes just to maintain an acceptable standard of living, and they may have to wait longer to buy a home. Clearly, no matter how you define it, the good life requires sound planning to turn financial goals into reality.

The best way to achieve financial objectives is through *personal financial planning,* which helps define financial goals and develop appropriate strategies to reach them. We should not depend solely on employee or government benefits—such as steady salary increases or adequate funding from employer-paid pensions or Social Security—to retire comfortably. Creating flexible plans and regularly revising them is the key to building a sound financial future. Successful financial planning also brings rewards that include greater flexibility, an improved standard of living, wise spending habits, and increased wealth. Of course, planning alone does not guarantee success; but having an effective, consistent plan can help you use your resources wisely. Careful financial planning increases the chance that your financial goals will be achieved and that you will have sufficient flexibility to handle such contingencies as illness, job loss, and even financial crises.

The goal of this book is to remove the mystery from the personal financial planning process and replace it with the tools you need to take charge of your personal finances and your life. To organize this process, the text is divided into six parts as follows.

- Part 1: Foundations of Financial Planning
- Part 2: Managing Basic Assets
- Part 3: Managing Credit
- Part 4: Managing Insurance Needs
- Part 5: Managing Investments
- Part 6: Retirement and Estate Planning

FINANCIAL PLANNING TIPS

Be SMART in Planning Your Financial Goals

Success is most likely if your goals are:

Specific: What do I want to achieve? What is required of me and what are my constraints?

Measurable: How much money is needed? How will I know if I am succeeding?

Attainable: How can I do this? Is this consistent with my other financial goals?

Realistic: Am I willing and able to do this?

Timely: What is my target date? What short-term goals must be achieved along the way to achieve my longer term goals?

Source: Inspired by Paul J. Meyer's, *Attitude Is Everything*, The Meyer Resource Group, 2003.

Each part explains a different aspect of personal financial planning, as shown in Exhibit 1.1. This organizational scheme revolves around financial decision making that's firmly based on an operational set of financial plans. We believe that sound financial planning enables individuals to make decisions that will yield their desired results. Starting with Part 1—where we look at personal financial statements, plans, and taxes—we move through the various types of decisions you'll make when implementing a financial plan.

1-1a Improving Your Standard of Living

standard of living
The necessities, comforts, and luxuries enjoyed or desired by an individual or family.

With personal financial planning we learn to acquire, use, and control our financial resources more efficiently. It allows us to gain more enjoyment from our income and thus to improve our **standard of living**—the necessities, comforts, and luxuries we have or desire.

Americans view standards of living, and what constitute necessities or luxuries, differently depending on their level of affluence. For example, 45 percent of Americans consider a second or vacation home the ultimate symbol of affluence, while others see taking two or more annual vacations or living in an exclusive neighborhood as an indicator of wealth.

So our quality of life is closely tied to our standard of living. Although other factors—geographic location, public facilities, local cost of living, pollution, traffic, and population density—also affect quality of life, wealth is commonly viewed as a key determinant. Material items such as a house, car, and clothing, as well as money available for health care, education, art, music, travel, and entertainment, all contribute to our quality of life. Of course, many so-called wealthy people live "plain" lives, choosing to save, invest, or support philanthropic organizations with their money rather than indulge themselves with luxuries.

One trend with a profound effect on our standard of living is the *two-income family*. What was relatively rare in the early 1970s has become commonplace today, and the incomes of millions of families have risen sharply as a result. About 75 percent

Financial Fact or Fantasy?

An improved standard of living is one of the payoffs of sound personal financial planning. **Fact:** The heart of sound financial planning and effective money management is the greater enjoyment of the money one makes by improving one's standard of living.

EXHIBIT 1.1 **Organizational Planning Model**

This text emphasizes making financial decisions regarding assets, credit, insurance, investments, and retirement and estates.

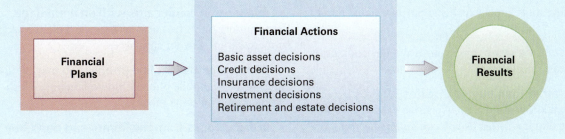

of married adults say that they and their mate share all their money, while some partners admit to having a secret stash of cash. Two incomes buy more, but they also require greater responsibility to manage the money wisely.

1-1b Spending Money Wisely

Using money wisely is a major benefit of financial planning. Whatever your income, you can either spend it now or save some of it for the future. Determining your current and future spending patterns is an important part of personal money management. The goal, of course, is to spend your money so that you get the most satisfaction from each dollar.

Current Needs

average propensity to consume
The percentage of each dollar of income, on average, that a person spends for current needs rather than savings.

Your current spending level is based on the necessities of life and your **average propensity to consume**, which is the percentage of each dollar of income, on average, that is spent for current needs rather than savings. A minimum level of spending would allow you to obtain only the necessities of life: food, clothing, and shelter. Although the quantity and type of food, clothing, and shelter purchased may differ among individuals depending on their wealth, we all need these items to survive. Some people with high average propensities to consume earn low incomes and spend a large portion of it on basic necessities. On the other hand, many "ultra-consumers" choose to splurge on a few items and scrimp elsewhere; these people also exhibit high average propensities to consume. Conversely, individuals earning large amounts quite often have low average propensities to consume, in part because the cost of necessities represents only a small portion of their income.

Still, two people with significantly different incomes could have the same average propensity to consume because of differences in their standard of living. The person making more money may believe it is essential to buy better-quality items or more items and will thus, on average, spend the same percentage of each dollar of income as the person making far less.

Future Needs

A carefully developed financial plan should set aside a portion of current income for deferred, future spending. Placing these funds in various savings and investment vehicles allows you to generate a return on your funds until you need them. For example, you may want to build up a retirement fund to maintain a desirable

FINANCIAL PLANNING TIPS

Ways to Save More Money

You can save more money by being purposeful in your spending.

• **Cook at home more.** Ease your way in by cooking at home at least once a week.

• **Make rather than buy your coffee.** While a latte is great, we all know that it's an expensive habit. Don't stop cold—just skip it as often as you can and make your coffee at home instead.

• **Take your lunch to work.** Lunch with coworkers may be the norm and a wise way to build helpful relationships. So it may not be practical to take your lunch all of the time. But it will save you money to take your lunch at least occasionally.

• **Avoid late fees by paying your bills on time.** You can have many bills like utilities paid automatically so there is no reason to pay late fees.

• **Avoid ATM fees.** Many banks do not waive ATM withdrawal fees. Be sure to use ATMs that do not charge a fee.

• **Avoid using credit cards with an annual fee.** The number of no-fee cards with reward plans makes it unnecessary to pay an annual fee.

• **Disconnect the landline phone.** You may do just fine with you mobile phones and no landline, which would save you some money.

• **Borrow books from the library and don't buy them.** Library cards are free and the book and media selection is usually up-to-date.

• **Don't buy bottled water, bottle your own.** Buy bottled water only occasionally just so you can get the bottle to fill with your own water.

• **Drive your car a long time.** Keep your car until the repair costs and questionable reliability make it necessary to find a replacement.

Source: Adapted from Sam Baker of GradMoneyMatters.com, republished June 19, 2011, http://www.dumblittleman.com/2008/01/30-easy-ways-to-save-money-and-no-you.html, accessed July 2015.

---

standard of living in your later years. Instead of spending the money now, you defer actual spending until the future when you retire. Nearly 35 percent of Americans say retirement planning is their most pressing financial concern. Other examples of deferred spending include saving for a child's education, a primary residence or vacation home, a major acquisition (such as a car or home entertainment center), or even a vacation.

The portion of current income we commit to future needs depends on how much we earn and also on our average propensity to consume. About two-thirds of affluent Americans say they need at least $5 million to feel rich. The more we earn and the less we devote to current spending, the more we can commit to meeting future needs. In any case, some portion of current income should be set aside regularly for future use. This practice creates good saving habits.

1-1c Accumulating Wealth

In addition to using current income to pay for everyday living expenses, we often spend it to acquire assets such as cars, a home, or stocks and bonds. Our assets largely determine how wealthy we are. Personal financial planning plays a critical role in the accumulation of wealth by directing our financial resources to the most productive areas.

Financial Fact or Fantasy?

A savings account is an example of a tangible asset because it represents something on deposit at a bank or other financial institution. **Fantasy: A savings account, like stocks, bonds, and mutual funds, is an example of a financial asset—an intangible, a "paper" asset. Real assets, in contrast, refer to tangibles— physical items like houses, cars, and appliances.**

EXHIBIT 1.2   The Average American, Financially Speaking

This financial snapshot of the "average American" gives you an idea of where you stand in terms of income, net worth, and other measures. It should help you set some goals for the future.

	Income and Assets
What Do We Earn? (*median*)	
All families	$ 46,700
What Are We Worth? (*median*)	
All families	81,200
Home Ownership (*median*)	
Value of primary residence	170,000
Mortgage on primary residence	115,000
How Much Savings Do We Have? (*median*)	80,000
Pooled investment funds (excluding money market)	27,000
Individual stocks	94,500
Bonds	20,100
Bank accounts/CDs	
Retirement accounts	59,000

Source: Adapted from Jesse Bricker, Lisa J. Dettling, Alice Henriques, Joanne W. Hsu, Kevin B. Moore, John Sabelhaus, Jeffrey Thompson, and Richard A.Windle, "Changes in U.S. Family Finances from 2010 to 2013: Evidence from the Survey of Consumer Finances," Board of Governors of the Federal Reserve System, Washington, DC, (October 24, 2014, data is for 2013), http://www.federalreserve.gov/pubs/bulletin/2014/pdf/scf14.pdf, Tables 1–4, accessed July 2015.

wealth
The total value of all items owned by an individual, such as savings accounts, stocks, bonds, home, and automobiles.

financial assets
Intangible assets, such as savings accounts and securities, that are acquired for some promised future return.

tangible assets
Physical assets, such as real estate and automobiles that can be held for either consumption or investment purposes.

One's **wealth** is the net total value of all the items the individual owns. Wealth consists of financial and tangible assets. **Financial assets** are intangible, paper assets, such as savings accounts and securities (stocks, bonds, mutual funds, and so forth). They are *earning assets* that are held for the returns they promise. **Tangible assets**, in contrast, are physical assets, such as real estate and automobiles. These assets can be held for either consumption (e.g., your home, car, artwork, or jewelry) or investment purposes (e.g., a duplex purchased for rental income). In general, the goal of most people is to accumulate as much wealth as possible while maintaining current consumption at a level that provides the desired standard of living. To see how you compare with the typical American in financial terms, check out the statistics in Exhibit 1.2.

TEST YOURSELF

1-1 What is a *standard of living*? What factors affect the quality of life?

1-2 Are consumption patterns related to quality of life? Explain.

1-3 What is *average propensity to consume*? Is it possible for two people with very different incomes to have the same average propensity to consume? Why?

1-4 Discuss the various forms in which wealth can be accumulated.

personal financial planning
A systematic process that considers important elements of an individual's financial affairs in order to fulfill financial goals.

Many people mistakenly assume that personal financial planning is only for the wealthy. However, nothing could be further from the truth. Whether you have a lot of money or not enough, you still need personal financial planning. If you have enough money, planning can help you spend and invest it wisely. If your income seems inadequate, taking steps to plan your financial activities will lead to an improved lifestyle. **Personal financial planning** is a systematic process that considers the important elements of an individual's financial affairs and is aimed at fulfilling his or her financial goals.

Everyone—including recent college graduates, single professionals, young married couples, single parents, mid-career married couples, and senior corporate executives—needs to develop a personal financial plan. Knowing what you need to accomplish financially, and how you intend to do it, gives you an edge over someone who merely reacts to financial events as they unfold. Just think of the example provided by the recent financial crisis. Do you think that a financial plan would have helped in weathering the financial storm?

Purchasing a new car immediately after graduation may be an important goal for you. But buying a car is a major expenditure involving a large initial cash outlay and additional consumer debt that must be repaid over time. It therefore warrants careful planning. Evaluating (and possibly even arranging) financing before your shopping trip, as opposed to simply accepting the financing arrangements offered by an auto dealer, could save you a considerable amount of money. Moreover, some dealers advertise low-interest loans but charge higher prices for their cars. Knowing all your costs in advance can help you find the best deal. Using personal financial planning concepts to reach all your financial goals will bring similar positive benefits.

Behavior Matters

Practicing Financial Self-Awareness

Are you aware of your financial behavior, its causes, and its consequences? For example, are you routinely relying too heavily on your credit card, which puts you more in debt? Are you saving enough to buy a new car or to fund your retirement? And the bottom line: Are you continuing the same financial behavior you have in the past and yet expecting different results?

The first decisive step in taking control of your life is to be aware of what you're thinking, feeling, and doing. Be financially self-aware: observe your own thoughts, feelings, and behavior concerning your finances. Take notes on things that affect how you feel and what you do about financial decisions. Watch yourself and be honest about your feelings concerning money and your future.

Then ask yourself two critically important questions:

- **Is the way I spend money consistent with what I believe?** Financial planning that works is taking the time to develop a plan that purposely lines up your values and your use of money.

- **Have I clearly stated the financial goals that are important to me and, if so, what am I doing today to make sure I achieve them?** The heart of financial planning is determining where you are today and where you want to be in the future. This implies the need for a financial plan: limited resources sometimes bring painful trade-offs.

Source: Adapted from Carl Richards, "Practicing Radical Self-Awareness," Behaviorgap.com. http://us2.campaign-archive1.com/?u=23ce2ac179e8158f 7583c4e3f&id=86f42577bc&e=b50e826a9e, accessed July 2015.

EXHIBIT 1.3   **The Six-Step Financial Planning Process**

The financial planning process translates personal financial goals into specific financial plans and strategies, implements them, and then uses budgets and financial statements to monitor, evaluate, and revise plans and strategies as needed. This process typically involves the six steps shown in sequence here:

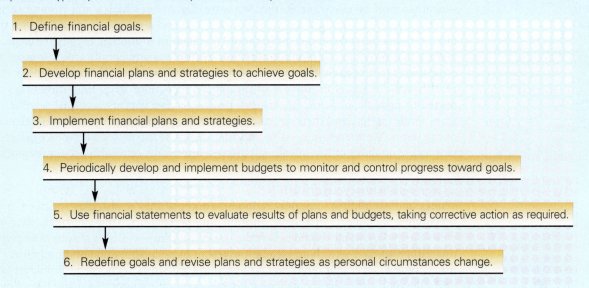

1. Define financial goals.

2. Develop financial plans and strategies to achieve goals.

3. Implement financial plans and strategies.

4. Periodically develop and implement budgets to monitor and control progress toward goals.

5. Use financial statements to evaluate results of plans and budgets, taking corrective action as required.

6. Redefine goals and revise plans and strategies as personal circumstances change.

1-2a Steps in the Financial Planning Process

If you take a closer look at financial planning, you'll see that the process translates personal financial goals into specific financial plans, which then helps you implement those plans through financial strategies. The financial planning process involves the six steps shown in Exhibit 1.3.

The financial planning process runs full circle. You start with financial goals, formulate and implement financial plans and strategies to reach them, monitor and control progress toward goals through budgets, and use financial statements to evaluate the plan and budget results. This leads you back to redefining your goals so that they better meet your current needs and to revising your financial plans and strategies accordingly.

Let's now look at how goal setting fits into the planning process. In Chapters 2 and 3, we'll consider other information essential to creating your financial plans: personal financial statements, budgets, and taxes.

1-2b Defining Your Financial Goals

financial goals
Results that an individual wants to attain, such as buying a home, building a college fund, or achieving financial independence.

Financial goals are the results that an individual wants to attain. Examples include buying a home, building a college fund, or achieving financial independence. What are your financial goals? Have you spelled them out? It's impossible to effectively manage your financial resources without financial goals. We need to know where we are going, in a financial sense, to effectively meet the major financial events in our lives. Perhaps achieving financial independence at a relatively early age is important to you. If so, then saving, investing, and retirement planning will be an important part of your financial life. Your financial goals or preferences must be stated in monetary terms because money and the satisfaction it can bring are an integral part of financial planning.

The Role of Money

money
The medium of exchange used as a measure of value in financial transactions.

About 75 percent of Americans believe that money is freedom. **Money** is the medium of exchange used to measure value in financial transactions. It would be difficult to set specific personal financial goals and to measure progress toward achieving them without the standard unit of exchange provided by the dollar. Money, as we know it today, is the key consideration in establishing financial goals. Yet it's not money, as such, that most people want. Rather, we want the **utility**, which is the amount of satisfaction received from buying quantities of goods and services of a given quality that money makes possible. People may choose one item over another because of a special feature that provides additional utility. For example, many people will pay more for a car with satellite radio than one with only an audio player. The added utility may result from the actual usefulness of the special feature or from the "status" it's expected to provide, or both. Regardless, people receive varying levels of satisfaction from similar items, and their satisfaction isn't necessarily directly related to the cost of the items. We therefore need to consider utility along with cost when evaluating alternative qualities of life, spending patterns, and forms of wealth accumulation.

utility
The amount of satisfaction received from purchasing certain types or quantities of goods and services.

The Psychology of Money

Money and its utility are not only economic concepts; they're also closely linked to the psychological concepts of values, emotion, and personality. Your personal value system—the important ideals and beliefs that guide your life—will also shape your attitude toward money and wealth accumulation. If you place a high value on family life, you may choose a career that offers regular hours and less stress or choose an employer who offers flextime rather than a higher-paying position that requires travel and lots of overtime. You may have plenty of money but choose to live frugally and do things yourself rather than hire someone to do them for you. Or you may spend a high proportion of your current income on acquiring luxuries. Financial goals and decisions should be consistent with your personal values. You can formulate financial plans that provide the greatest personal satisfaction and quality of life by identifying your values.

Money is an important motivator of personal behavior because it has a strong effect on self-image. Each person's unique personality and emotional makeup determine the importance and role of money in his or her life. Depending on timing and circumstances, emotional responses to money may be positive (love, happiness, security) or negative (fear, greed, insecurity). For example, some people feel satisfaction in their work when they receive a paycheck. Others feel relief in knowing that they can pay past-due bills. You should become aware of your own attitudes toward money because they are the basis of your "money personality" and money management style. Exhibit 1.4 explores attitudes toward money.

Some questions to ask yourself include: How important is money to me? Why? What types of spending give me satisfaction? Am I a risk taker? Do I need large financial reserves to feel secure? Knowing the answers to these questions is a prerequisite for developing realistic and effective financial goals and plans. For example, if you prefer immediate satisfaction, then you will find it more difficult to achieve long-term net worth or savings goals than if you are highly disciplined and primarily concerned with achieving a comfortable retirement at an early age. Trade-offs between current and future benefits are strongly affected by values, emotions, and personality. Effective financial plans are both economically and psychologically sound. They must not only consider your wants, needs, and financial resources, but must also realistically reflect your personality and emotional reactions to money.

1-2c Money and Relationships

The average couple spends between 250 and 700 hours planning their wedding. While most couples spend less than $10,000 on the big day, the average cost has risen to almost $30,000, depending on where they live. But with all the hoopla surrounding the wedding day, many couples overlook one of the most important aspects

EXHIBIT 1.4 | **What's Your Attitude Toward Money?**

Our attitudes toward money influence how we spend, save, and invest. Which of the following attitudes toward money best describes you? You may be predominately one type or a combination of types.

The Spender: You only live once
Spenders see shopping as entertainment. They would rather have something tangible than something intangible like savings or an investment. Spenders have a hard time saving money.

The Builder: Make it so
Builders see money as a tool. They use money to achieve their goals and dreams. Examples include self-made millionaires, entrepreneurs, corporate leaders, and dedicated hobbyists. Builders can miscalculate risks or ignore the need for a margin of error. They may start projects simply for the challenge but not finish them as the next new thing beckons.

The Giver: It's better to give than to receive
Givers enjoy taking care of other people. They volunteer and give to charities. Givers commit their time, energy, and money to their beliefs. Most givers simply enjoy making other people happy and doing good deeds. Givers sometimes ignore their own needs, and their long-term financial plans can suffer as a result.

The Saver: A bird in the hand is worth two in the bush
Savers can accumulate significant wealth even on a modest income. They tend to be organized and to avoid money-wasting activities. Although savers can be good investors, they can be too risk averse and prefer holding too much cash. Such conservatism means that their investments often grow too slowly.

Source: Adapted from Diane McCurdy, CFP, *How Much Is Enough?* (John Wiley & Sons, 2005). Copyright © 2005 by John Wiley & Sons. All rights reserved. Reproduced by permission.

of marriage: financial compatibility. Money can be one of the most emotional issues in any relationship, including that with a partner, your parents, or children. Most people are uncomfortable talking about money matters and avoid such discussions, even with their partners. However, differing opinions on how to spend money may threaten the stability of a marriage or cause arguments between parents and children. Learning to communicate with your partner about money is a critical step in developing effective financial plans.

Your parents should play an important role in your financial planning. As they age, you may have to assume greater responsibility for their care. Do you know what health care coverage and financial plans they have in place? Where do they keep important financial and legal documents? What preferences do they have for health care should they become incapacitated? Asking these questions may be difficult, but having the answers will save you many headaches.

The best way to resolve money disputes is to be aware of your partner's financial style, consistently communicate openly, and be willing to compromise. It's unlikely that you can change your partner's style, but you can work out your differences. Financial planning is an especially important part of the conflict resolution process.

1-2d Types of Financial Goals

Financial goals cover a wide range of financial aspirations: controlling living expenses, meeting retirement needs, setting up a savings and investment program, and minimizing your taxes. Other important financial goals include having enough money to live as well as possible now, being financially independent, sending children to college, and providing for retirement.

EXHIBIT 1.5 Check Your Financial Planning Assumptions

It's important to make sure that your financial planning assumptions are realistic. Consider these common assumptions.

Assumption 1: Saving a few thousand dollars a year should provide enough to fund my child's college education.

Reality: The College Board reports that the average increase in tuition and fees over the last decade has been 5 percent, which is about twice the rate of inflation. If this rate of increase continues, the average 4-year cost of tuition and fees for a child born in 2014 will be about $323,900 for a private school and $94,800 for an in-state public education. And that doesn't consider the cost of room and board. That's more than a few thousand dollars to save each year!

Assumption 2: An emergency fund lasting 3 months should be adequate.

Reality: Tell that to the average unemployed person in the United States in 2011 who looked for work for over 9 months. While this is the longest average duration of unemployment since 1948, it would be wise to keep an emergency fund that covers 6 to 9 months.

Assumption 3: I will be able to retire at 65 and should have plenty to live on in retirement.

Reality: The average 65-year old man can expect to live to about 84 and a 65-year old woman can expect to live to about 87. That planning horizon could easily leave you short on funding. So it would be wise to determine how much you need to set aside to fund a realistic life expectancy horizon. This might imply saving more now, retiring later, or working part-time after retirement.

Assumption 4: I'm relying on the rule of thumb that I will need only 70 percent of my pre-retirement income to manage nicely in retirement.

Reality: Like all rules of thumb, one size does not necessarily fit all. While it's true that you won't have work-related expenses in retirement, you're likely to have much higher health care costs. And it's important to consider long-term care insurance to protect against such high costs. So betting on 70 percent could leave you short.

Sources: Adapted from http://www.savingforcollege.com/tutorial101/the_real_cost_of_higher_education.php, http://economix.blogs.nytimes.com/2011/06/03/average-length-of-unemployment-at-all-time-high/, accessed July 2015.

Financial goals should be defined as specifically as possible. Saying that you want to save money next year is not a specific goal. How much do you want to save, and for what purpose? A goal such as "save 10 percent of my take-home pay each month to start an investment program" states clearly what you want to do and why.

Because they are the basis of your financial plans, your goals should be realistic and attainable. If you set your savings goals too high—for example, 25 percent of your take-home pay when your basic living expenses already account for 85 percent of it—then your goal is unattainable and there's no way to meet it. But if savings goals are set too low, you may not accumulate enough for a meaningful investment program. If your goals are unrealistic, they'll put the basic integrity of your financial plan at risk and be a source of ongoing financial frustration. You must also use realistic assumptions when setting goals. Exhibit 1.5 will help you do a reality check.

It's important to involve your immediate family in the goal-setting process. When family members "buy into" the goals, it eliminates the potential for future conflicts and improves the family's chances for financial success. After defining and approving your goals, you can prepare appropriate cash budgets. Finally, you should assign priorities and a time frame to financial goals. Are they short-term goals for the next year, or are they intermediate or long-term goals that will not be achieved for many

EXHIBIT 1.6 **How Financial Goals Change with a Person's Life Situation**

Financial goals are not static; they change continually over a lifetime. Here are some typical long-term, intermediate, and short-term goals for a number of different personal situations.

Personal Situation	Long-Term Goals (6+ years)	Intermediate Goals (2–5 years)	Short-Term Goals (1 year)
College senior	Begin an investment program Buy a townhouse Earn a master's degree	Repay college loans Trade in car and upgrade to a nicer model Buy new furniture	Find a job Rent an apartment Get a bank credit card Buy a new stereo
Single, mid-20s	Begin law school Build an investment portfolio Save enough for a down payment on a home	Begin regular savings program Take a Caribbean vacation Buy life insurance Start a retirement fund	Prepare a budget Buy a new flat-screen television Get additional job training Build an emergency fund Reduce expenses by 10 percent
Married couple with children, late 30s	Diversify investment portfolio Buy a larger home	Buy a second car Increase college fund contributions Increase second income from part-time to full-time	Repaint house Get braces for children Review life and disability insurance
Married couple with grown children, mid-50s	Decide whether to relocate when retired Retire at age 62 Travel to Europe and the Far East	Take cruise Shift investment portfolio into income-producing securities Sell house and buy smaller residence	Buy new furniture Review skills for possible career change

more years? For example, saving for a vacation might be a medium-priority short-term goal, whereas buying a larger home may be a high-priority intermediate goal and purchasing a vacation home a low-priority long-term goal. Normally, long-term financial goals are set first, followed by a series of corresponding short-term and intermediate goals. Your goals will continue to change with your life situation, as Exhibit 1.6 demonstrates.

1-2e Putting Target Dates on Financial Goals

goal dates
Target dates in the future when certain financial objectives are expected to be completed.

Financial goals are most effective when they are set with goal dates. **Goal dates** are target points in the future when you expect to have achieved or completed certain financial objectives. They may serve as progress checkpoints toward some longer-term financial goals and/or as deadlines for others.

EXAMPLE: Target Dates for Financial Goals

Jim and Stacy Thompson are both 28 and have been married for one year. They have set financial goals of buying a boat for $3,000 in 2018, accumulate a net worth of $10,000 by 2022, and accumulate a net worth of $50,000 by 2030.

Long-Term Goals

Long-term financial goals should indicate wants and desires for a period covering about 6 years out to the next 30 or 40 years. Although it's difficult to pinpoint exactly what you will want 30 years from now, it's useful to establish some tentative long-term financial goals. However, you should recognize that long-term goals will change over time and that you'll need to revise them accordingly. If the goals seem too ambitious, you'll want to make them more realistic. If they're too conservative, you'll want to adjust them to a level that encourages you to make financially responsible decisions rather than squander surplus funds.

Short-Term Goals and Intermediate Goals

Short-term financial goals are set each year and cover a 12-month period. They include making substantial, regular contributions to savings or investments in order to accumulate your desired net worth. Intermediate goals bridge the gap between short- and long-term goals, and both intermediate and short-term goals should be consistent with those long-term goals. Short-term goals become the key input for the cash budget, a tool used to plan for short-term income and expenses. To define your short-term goals, consider your immediate goals, expected income for the year, and long-term goals. Short-term planning should also include establishing an emergency fund with at least 6 to 9 months' worth of income. This special savings account serves as a safety reserve in case of financial emergencies such as a temporary loss of income.

Unless you attain your short-term goals, you probably won't achieve your intermediate or long-term goals. It's tempting to let the desire to spend now take priority over the need to save for the future. But by making some short-term sacrifices now, you're more likely to have a comfortable future. If you don't realize this for another 10 or 20 years, then you may discover that it's too late to reach some of your most important financial goals.

Worksheet 1.1 is a convenient way to summarize your personal financial goals. It groups them by time frame (short-term, intermediate, or long-term) and lists a priority for each goal (high, medium, or low), a target date to reach the goal, and an estimated cost.

We have filled out the form showing the goals that Simon and Meghan Kane set in December 2016. The Kanes were married in 2017, own a condominium in a Midwestern suburb, and have no children. Because Simon and Meghan are 28 and 26 years old, respectively, they have set their longest-term financial goal 33 years from now, when they want to retire. Simon has just completed his fifth year as an electrical engineer. Meghan, a former elementary school teacher, finished her MBA in May

Financial Fact or Fantasy?

Personal financial planning involves translating personal financial goals into specific plans and arrangements that put these plans into action.
Fact: Personal financial plans are based on the specific financial goals that you set for yourself and your family. Once in place, the plans are put into action using the various financial strategies explained in this book.

Do It Now

Start a List of Your Financial Goals

Yogi Berra summed it up: "If you don't know where you're going, you might not get there." And so it is with your financial goals. Pick up some paper now and start a list of your financial goals. May be it's as simple as saving $25 by the end of the month or as lofty as saving $200,000 for retirement by the time you're 50. You'll never achieve your goals if you don't know what they are, much less know whether they're realistic. Go ahead and dream. List your goals (short-term, intermediate, and long-term) and start laying out how you'll get there. You can do it now.

2015 and began working at a local advertising agency. Simon and Meghan love to travel and ski. They plan to start a family in a few years, but for now they want to develop some degree of financial stability and independence. Their goals include purchasing assets (clothes, stereo, furniture, and car), reducing debt, reviewing insurance, increasing savings, and planning for retirement.

WORKSHEET 1.1 **Summary of Personal Financial Goals**

Set financial goals carefully and realistically, because they form the basis for your personal financial plans. Each goal should be clearly defined and have a priority, time frame, and cost estimate.

Personal Financial Goals

Name(s) _Simon and Meghan Kane_   Date _December 27, 2016_

Short-Term Goals (1 year or less)

Goal	Priority	Target Date	Cost Estimate $
Buy new tires and brakes for Ford Focus	High	Feb. 2017	500
Take Colorado ski trip	Medium	Mar. 2017	1,800
Buy career clothes for Meghan	High	May 2017	1,200
Buy new work cloths for Simon	Medium	June 2017	750
Replace stereo components	Low	Sept. 2017	1,100

Intermediate Goals (2 to 5 years)

Goal	Priority	Target Date	Cost Estimate $
Start family	High	2018	–
Take 2-week Hawaiian vacation	Medium	2018 – 19	5,000
Repay all loans except mortgage	High	2019	7,500
Trade Focus and buy larger car	High	2019	10,500
Review insurance needs	High	2019	–
Accumulate $10,000 net worth	High	2019	–
Buy new bedroom furniture	Low	2021	4,000

Long-Term Goals (61 years)

Goal	Priority	Target Date	Cost Estimate $
Begin college fund for children	High	2022	? /year
Diversify/increase investment portfolio	High	2023	Varies
Take European vacation	Low	2024	10,000
Increase college fund contributions	High	2024	–
Accumulate $50,000 net worth	High	2024	–
Buy larger home	High	2025	250,000
Accumulate $100,000 net worth	High	2034	–
Retire from jobs	High	2049	?

TEST YOURSELF

1-5 What is the role of money in setting financial goals? What is the relationship of money to utility?

1-6 Explain why financial plans must be psychologically as well as economically sound. What is the best way to resolve money disputes in a relationship?

1-7 Explain why it is important to set realistically attainable financial goals. Select one of your personal financial goals and develop a brief financial plan for achieving it.

1-8 Distinguish between long-term, intermediate, and short-term financial goals. Give examples of each.

1-3 FROM GOALS TO PLANS: A LIFETIME OF PLANNING

How will you achieve the financial goals you set for yourself? The answer, of course, lies in the financial plans you establish. Financial plans provide the roadmap for achieving your financial goals. The six-step financial planning process (introduced in Exhibit 1.3) results in separate yet interrelated components covering all the important financial elements in your life. Some elements deal with the more immediate aspects of money management, such as preparing a budget to help manage spending. Others focus on acquiring major assets, controlling borrowing, reducing financial risk, providing for emergency funds and future wealth accumulation, taking advantage of and managing employer-sponsored benefits, deferring and minimizing taxes, providing for financial security when you stop working, and ensuring an orderly and cost-effective transfer of assets to your heirs.

In addition to discussing your financial goals and attitudes toward money with your partner, you must allocate responsibility for money management tasks and decisions. Many couples make major decisions jointly and divide routine financial decision-making on the basis of expertise and interest. Others believe it is important for their entire family to work together as a team to manage the family finances. They hold family financial meetings once every few months to help their children understand how the household money is spent. These meetings also serve as a forum for children to request a raise in allowance, a new bike, or funds for a school trip. The entire family is involved in the decision-making process on how surplus funds will be allocated.

Giving children an allowance is a good way to start teaching them to budget and save. By setting their own financial goals and taking steps to reach them, they will develop their own money management skills.

ARIEL SKELLEY/JUPITER IMAGES

1-3a The Life Cycle of Financial Plans

Financial planning is a dynamic process. As you move through different stages of your life, your needs and goals will change. Yet certain financial goals are important regardless of age. Having extra resources to fall back on in an economic downturn or period of unemployment should be a priority whether you are 25, 45, or 65. Some changes—a new job, marriage, children, moving to a new area—may be part of your original plan.

More often than not, you'll face unexpected "financial shocks" during your life: loss of a job, a car accident, divorce or death of a spouse, a long illness, or the need to support adult children or aging parents. With careful planning, you can get through tough times and prosper in good times. You need to plan ahead and take steps to weather life's financial storms successfully. For example, setting up an emergency fund or reducing monthly expenses will help protect you and your family financially if a setback occurs.

As we move from childhood to retirement age, we traditionally go through different life stages. Exhibit 1.7 illustrates the various components of a typical *personal financial planning life cycle* as they relate to these different life stages. This exhibit presents the organizing framework of the entire financial planning process. We will refer to it in every chapter of the book—as we suggest that you do for the rest of your life. As we pass from one stage of maturation to the next, our patterns of income, home ownership, and debt also change. From early childhood, when we rely on our parents for support, to early adulthood, when we hold our first jobs and start our families, we can see a noticeable change in income patterns. For example, those in the 45–64 age range tend to have higher income than those younger than age 45. Thus, as our emphasis in life changes, so do the kinds of financial plans we need to pursue.

Today, new career strategies—planned and unplanned job changes—are common and may require that financial plans be revised. Many young people focus on their careers and building a financial base before marrying and having children. The families of women who interrupt their careers to stay home with their children, whether for

EXHIBIT 1.7   The Personal Financial Planning Life Cycle

As you move through life and your income patterns change, you'll typically have to pursue a variety of financial plans. For instance, after graduating from college your focus likely will be on buying a car and a house, and you'll be concerned about health and automobile insurance to protect against loss.

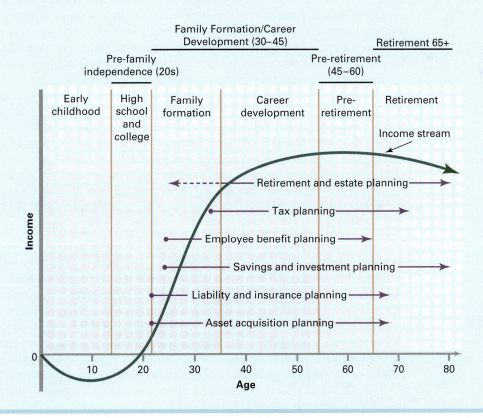

6 months or 6 years, will experience periods of reduced income. A divorce, a spouse's death, or remarriage can also drastically change your financial circumstances. Many people in their 40s and 50s find themselves in the "sandwich generation," supporting their elderly parents while still raising their own children and paying for college. And some people must cope with reduced income due to jobs lost because of corporate downsizing or early retirement. We'll look at these and other special planning concerns next.

1-3b Plans to Achieve Your Financial Goals

As discussed earlier, financial goals can range from short-term goals such as saving for a new stereo to long-term goals such as saving enough to start your own business. Reaching your particular goals requires different types of financial planning. Let's take a brief look at what each major plan category includes.

Asset Acquisition Planning

One of the first categories of financial planning is asset acquisition. We accumulate *assets*—things we own—throughout our lives. These include *liquid assets* (cash, savings accounts, and money market funds) used to pay everyday expenses, *investments* (stocks, bonds, and mutual funds) acquired to earn a return, *personal property* (movable property such as automobiles, household furnishings, appliances, clothing, jewelry, home electronics, and similar items), and *real property* (immovable property; land and anything fixed to it, such as a house). Chapters 4 and 5 focus on important considerations for managing liquid assets and other major assets such as automobiles and housing.

Liability and Insurance Planning

Another category of financial planning is liability planning. A *liability* is something we owe, which is measured by the amount of debt we incur. We create liabilities by borrowing money. By the time most of us graduate from college, we have debts of some sort: education loans, car loans, credit card balances, and so on. Our borrowing needs typically increase as we acquire other assets such as a home, furnishings, and appliances. Whatever the source of credit, such transactions have one thing in common: *the debt must be repaid at some future time*. How we manage our debt burden is just as important as how we manage our assets. Managing credit effectively requires careful planning, which is covered in Chapters 6 and 7.

Obtaining adequate *insurance coverage* is also essential. Like borrowing money, obtaining insurance is generally introduced relatively early in our life cycle (usually in the family formation stage). Insurance is a way to reduce financial risk and protect both income (life, health, and disability insurance) and assets (property and liability insurance). Most consumers regard insurance as absolutely essential—and for good reason. One serious illness or accident can wipe out everything you have accumulated over many years of hard work. But having the wrong amount of insurance can be costly. We'll examine how to manage your insurance needs in Chapters 8, 9 and 10.

Savings and Investment Planning

As your income begins to increase, so does the importance of savings and investment planning. Initially, people save to establish an emergency fund for meeting unexpected expenses. Eventually, however, they devote greater attention to investing excess income as a means of accumulating wealth, either for major expenditures (such as a child's college education) or for retirement. Individuals build wealth through savings and the subsequent investing of funds in various investment vehicles: common or preferred stocks, government or corporate bonds, mutual funds, real estate, and so on. The higher the returns on the investment of excess funds, the greater wealth they accumulate.

Exhibit 1.8 shows the impact of alternative rates of return on accumulated wealth. The graph shows that if you had $1,000 today and could keep it invested at

EXHIBIT 1.8   How a $1,000 Investment Grows Over Time

Four percent or 6 percent: How big a deal is a 2 percent difference? The deal is more than twice the money over a 40-year period! Through the power of compound interest, a higher return means dramatically more money as time goes on.

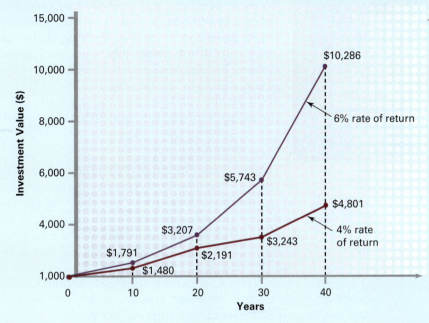

4 percent, then you would accumulate a considerable sum of money over time. For example, at the end of 40 years, you'd have about $4,801 from your original $1,000. Earning a higher rate of return provides even greater rewards. Some might assume that earning, say, only 2 percentage points more (i.e., 6 percent rather than 4 percent) would not matter much. But it certainly would! Observe that if you could earn 6 percent over the 40 years, then you'd accumulate $10,286, or *more than twice as much* as you'd accumulate at 4 percent. This powerful observation is important to keep in mind when comparing competing investment and savings alternatives.

As we'll explore in Part 5 on managing investments, seemingly small differences in various investment management fees can translate into significant differences in net investment returns over long periods of time. The length of time you keep your money invested is just as important as the rate of return you earn on your investments. You can accumulate more than twice as much capital by investing for 40 rather than 30 years with either rate of return (4 percent or 6 percent). This is the magic of compound interest, which explains why it's so important to create strong savings and investment habits early in life. We'll examine compounding more fully in Chapter 2, savings in Chapter 4, and investments in Chapters 11, 12, and 13.

Employee Benefit Planning

Your employer may offer a wide variety of employee benefit plans, especially if you work for a large firm. These could include life, health, and disability insurance; tuition reimbursement programs for continuing education; pension and profit-sharing plans, and 401(k) retirement plans; flexible spending accounts for child care and health care expenses; stock options; sick leave, personal time, and vacation days; and miscellaneous benefits such as employee discounts and subsidized meals or parking. Employee benefit plans are described more fully in later chapters.

Managing your employee benefit plans and coordinating them with your other plans are an important part of the overall financial planning process. For example, tax-deferred retirement plans and flexible spending accounts offer tax advantages. Some retirement plans allow you to borrow against them. Employer-sponsored insurance programs may need to be supplemented with personal policies. In addition, in today's volatile labor market, you can no longer assume that you'll be working at the same company for many years. If you change jobs, your new company may not offer the same benefits. Your personal financial plans should include contingency plans to replace employer-provided benefits as required. We'll discuss employee benefits in greater detail in Chapters 2 (planning); 3 (taxes); 8, 9, and 10 (insurance); and 14 (retirement).

Tax Planning

Despite all the talk about tax reform, our tax code remains highly complex. Income can be taxed as active (ordinary), portfolio (investment), passive, tax-free, or tax-deferred. Then there are tax shelters, which use various aspects of the tax code (such as depreciation expenses) to legitimately reduce an investor's tax liability. Tax planning considers all these factors and more. It involves looking at your current and projected earnings and then developing strategies that will defer and minimize taxes. Tax plans are closely tied to investment plans and will often specify certain investment strategies. Although tax planning is most common among individuals with high incomes, people with lower incomes can also obtain sizable savings. We'll examine taxes and tax planning in Chapter 3.

Retirement and Estate Planning

While you're still working, you should be managing your finances to attain those goals you feel are important after you retire. These might include maintaining your standard of living, extensive travel, visiting children, frequent dining at better restaurants, and perhaps a vacation home or boat. Retirement planning should begin long before you retire. Most people don't start thinking about retirement until well into their 40s or 50s. This is unfortunate, because it usually results in a substantially reduced level of retirement income. The sooner you start, the better off you'll be. Take, for instance, the IRA (individual retirement account), whereby certain wage earners were allowed to invest up to $6,500 per year in 2015. We'll look at IRAs and other aspects of retirement planning in Chapter 14.

EXAMPLE: The Sooner You Start an IRA, the Better

If you start investing for retirement at age 40 and put only $2,000 a year in an IRA earning 5 percent for 25 years, you will have $95,454 at age 65. However, if you start the same retirement plan 10 years earlier at age 30, you'll have $180,641 at age 65!

Accumulating assets to enjoy in retirement is only part of the long-term financial planning process. As people grow older, they must also consider how they can most effectively pass their wealth on to their heirs, an activity known as *estate planning*. We'll examine this complex subject—which includes such topics as wills, trusts, and the effects of gift and estate taxes—in Chapter 15.

1-3c Special Planning Concerns

Students may not spend much time on financial planning. Yet the sooner you start, the better prepared you'll be to adapt your plans to changing personal circumstances. Such changes include changing or losing a job, relocating to a new state,

FINANCIAL ROAD SIGN

Common Misconceptions About Financial Planning

- **A professional financial planner is an unnecessary expense.** The answer depends on you. A lot of good financial planning can be done on your own. But honestly ask yourself: Do I have the discipline, time, and financial experience to manage these complicated tasks effectively and confidently? If the answer is no, see a financial planner to get a decent idea of the planning process.
- **A little credit card debt is just fine.** Define "a little." A modest amount of credit card debt is OK. The problem is that for all too many people, "a little" leads to a lot. As discussed in Part 3 of this book, "Managing Credit," credit card debt is often one of the biggest problems in managing your personal finances. Just consider the high interest rates on credit cards and how easy it is to build up a big balance.
- **I don't need a budget because I have a general idea of what I earn and spend.** There is a natural tendency to overspend because expenses are easy to underestimate without a formal budget. And if you spend first and only save what's left over, the probability of achieving your financial goals is much lower. Sticking to a budget is the key.
- **Retirement is a lifetime away.** While that may be true, that doesn't justify focusing only on short-term goals, like coming up with the down payment on a house. When retirement is a "lifetime away," that's the time to exploit the compounding of returns over a long period of time by taking full advantage of retirement investments in your employer's 401(k) plan and in IRAs. An early start can put you well ahead.

Source: Adapted from Kimberly J. Howard, CFP®, CRPC, "Financial Fiascos Every Young Couple with Debts Should Avoid," NAPFA Planning Perspectives, volume 6, issue 5, Sept./Oct. 2011, www.NAPFA.org, accessed July 2015.

getting married, having children, being in a serious accident, getting a chronic illness, losing a spouse through divorce or death, retiring, or taking responsibility for dependent parents. These and other stressful events are "financial shocks" that require reevaluation of your financial goals and plans.

It is important not to rush to make major financial decisions at these times, when you're most vulnerable. Postpone any action until you have had time to recover from the event and evaluate all your options carefully. This can be difficult because some financial salespeople will rush to contact you in these circumstances. For example, when you have a child, you will find that insurance agents, financial planners, and stockbrokers actively encourage you to buy insurance and start investing in a college fund. Although these are valid objectives, don't be pushed into any expensive decisions. People who get large sums of money—from severance packages, retirement benefits, or insurance policies when a loved one dies—are also likely to hear from financial salespeople eager to help them invest the funds. This is another time to wait. Face it—some professionals may have a greater interest in selling their own products than advising you on the best strategy for your needs.

Managing Two Incomes

Did you know that the earnings of the average dual-income family will add up to more than $1 million over the wage earners' lives? Today, two-income couples account for the majority of U.S. households and many depend on the second income to make ends meet. For others, it provides financial security and a way to afford "extras." Often, however, a second income doesn't add as much as expected to the bottom line. Higher expenses such as child care, taxes, clothing, dry cleaning, transportation, and lunches may consume a large part of the second paycheck. And two-income families tend to spend what they earn rather than save it.

When Alicia Cisneros was offered a job as a credit analyst, she and her husband, Luis, filled out Worksheet 1.2 to assess the net monthly income from her paycheck, both with and without the impact of employer-paid benefits. Alicia had been staying home with their three children, but now two were in school all day. The couple listed only those expenses that *directly related to the second job* and made sure not to

WORKSHEET 1.2

Analyzing the Benefit of a Second Income

Use this worksheet to estimate the contribution of a second paycheck. Without the employer-paid benefits of $1,632 (line 2), the Cisneros family would realize a net monthly income of $1,808 (line 1 - line 3); with those benefits, their net monthly income would be $3,440 (line 4).

Second Income Analysis

Name(s) _Alicia and Luis Cisneros_   Date _December 27, 2016_

MONTHLY CASH INCOME

Gross pay	$5,000
Pretax employer contributions (401(k) plans, dependent-care reimbursement account(s))	400
Additional job-related income (bonuses, overtime, commissions)	0
(1) Total Cash Income	**$5,400**

EMPLOYER-PAID BENEFITS

Health insurance	$550
Life insurance	100
Pension contributions	600
Thrift-plan contributions	0
Social Security	382
Profit sharing	0
Other deferred compensation	0
(2) Total Benefits	**$1,632**

MONTHLY JOB-RELATED EXPENSES

Federal income tax	$1,500
Social Security tax	382
State income tax	250
Child care	640
Clothing; personal care; dry cleaning	400
Meals away from home	200
Public transportation	0
Auto-related expenses (gas, parking, maintenance)	220
Other	0
(3) Total Expenses	**$3,592**
(4) Net Income (Deficit) = Total Cash Income + Total Benefits − Total Expenses	**$3,440**

include personal expenses that would exist even without the second job. Alicia's job offer included good employer-paid benefits, with a better health insurance plan than the one Luis' employer offered. Taking these benefits and the job-related expenses into account, the Cisneros family's net monthly income would increase by $3,440 a month, or $41,280 a year. Without benefits, this amount drops to $1,808, or $21,696 a year. These numbers provided the information that the Cisneros family needed to discuss the pros and cons of Alicia's job offer. They took into account not just the higher total income and out-of-pocket costs, but also the intangible costs (additional demands on their lives, less time with family, and higher stress) and benefits (career development, job satisfaction, and sense of worth). They decided that the timing was right and agreed that they'd use the second income to increase their college savings accounts and build up their other investments. This would provide greater financial security in these uncertain times if Luis were laid off from his research job at a bio-technology company.

Like the Cisneros family, partners in two-income households need to approach discussions on financial matters with an open mind and be willing to compromise. Spouses need to decide together how to allocate income to household expenses, family financial goals, and personal spending goals. Will you use a second income to meet basic expenses, afford a more luxurious lifestyle, save for a special vacation, or invest in retirement accounts? You may need to try several money management strategies to find the one that works best for you. Some couples place all income into a single joint account. Others have each spouse contribute *equal* amounts into a joint account to pay bills, but retain individual discretion over remaining income. Still others contribute a *proportional* share of each income to finance joint expenses and goals. In any case, both spouses should have money of their own to spend without accountability.

Managing Employee Benefits

As we've already discussed, if you hold a full-time job, then your employer probably provides various employee benefits, ranging from health and life insurance to pension plans. As we saw when analyzing the Cisneros family's case, these benefits can have a major financial impact on family income. Most American families depend solely on employer-sponsored group plans for their health insurance coverage and also for a big piece of their life insurance coverage and retirement needs.

Today's well-defined employee benefits packages cover a full spectrum of benefits that may include:

- Health and life insurance
- Disability insurance
- Long-term care insurance
- Pension and profit-sharing plans
- Supplemental retirement programs, such as 401(k) plans
- Dental and vision care
- Child care, elder care, and educational assistance programs
- Subsidized employee food services

Each company's benefit package is different. Some companies and industries are known for generous benefit plans; others offer far less attractive packages. In general, large firms can afford more benefits than small ones can. Because employee benefits can increase your total compensation by 30 percent or more, you should thoroughly investigate your employee benefits to choose those appropriate for your personal situation. Be sure to coordinate your benefits with your partner's to avoid paying for duplicate coverage. Companies change their benefit packages often and today are shifting more costs to employees. Although an employer may pay for some benefits in full, typically employees pay for part of the cost of group health insurance, supplemental life insurance, long-term care insurance, and participation in voluntary retirement programs.

Due to the prevalence of two-income families and an increasingly diverse workforce, many employers today are replacing traditional programs, where the company sets the type and amounts of benefits, with **flexible-benefit (cafeteria) plans**. In flexible-benefit programs, the employer allocates a certain amount of money to each employee and then lets the employee "spend" that money for benefits that suit his or her age, marital status, number of dependent children, level of income, and so on. These plans usually cover everything from child care to retirement benefits, offer several levels of health and life insurance coverage, and have some limits on the minimum and maximum amounts of coverage. Within these constraints, you can select the benefits that do you the most good. In some plans, you can even take part of the benefits in the form of more take-home pay or extra vacation time!

Managing Your Finances in Tough Economic Times

Tough economic times can be due to broad macroeconomic trends like a recession, or they can be brought on by more personal, local developments. The effects of recessions and financial crises divide people into three groups: (1) those who are directly and severely hurt through job loss, (2) those who are marginally hurt by reduced income, and (3) those who are not directly hurt. If you are in either of the first two groups, you must make significant lifestyle changes to reduce spending. Even if you are in the last group, a recession affects you indirectly. For example, retirement accounts typically drop in value and financial plans must be revised. And everyone's expectations are at least temporarily affected, which causes most people to be more cautious about their expenditures during a recession or crisis.

The financial crisis of 2008 and 2009 and the subsequent long period of high unemployment was a macroeconomic challenge of historic global proportions. It drives home the benefits of having a sound financial plan—and dramatized the cost of not having one. The precipitous decline in stock and home prices and the many people laid off from their jobs made everyone think a lot more about financial planning in general and how to survive a financial crisis in particular. Although we all hope that such broad crises will be rare, it is important to plan for a possible recurrence. All of the financial planning principles explained in this book remained valid during the recent global financial crisis and should continue to serve us well in any future similar situations.

So how do you best plan to survive a broad-based financial crisis? First, you remind yourself of the key principles of financial planning presented in this book:

- Spend less than you earn.
- Keep investing so your money continues to work toward your goals.
- Know where you are and plan for the unexpected. You cannot know where you are financially unless you carefully, and frequently, update your family's budget. And it is important to set aside money for an emergency fund. As discussed earlier in this chapter, you should set aside enough cash to last at least 6 to 9 months.

Second, don't panic when financial markets crash! This means that you shouldn't try to time the market by buying when the experts say it's at a low or by selling when they say it's at a high. Continue to invest for the long-term but keep in mind how close you are to achieving your financial objectives. For example, if you pull all of your

---

Do It Now

Start Building an Emergency Fund

What would happen if you lost your job, got hurt, or had an unexpected big expense? Even if you're not making much money now, you could start building an emergency fund by putting aside even $10 a month. As this chapter points out, your goal is to eventually set aside enough to last at least 6 to 9 months. Considering the risk of not doing so, you can do it now.

money out of the stock market when it has fallen, you will not be positioned to take advantage of its eventual recovery. Part 5 of the book focuses on investment management.

You can take specific actions in your day-to-day life to deal effectively with a financial crisis or recession. Consider the following ways to manage expenses in times of stress:

- Postpone large expenses. For example, hold on to your old car rather than buying a new one. And you could wait on that new refrigerator or big-screen TV.
- Cut back on the number of times you eat out.
- Take your vacation at or around home.
- If you rely mostly on a cell phone, consider canceling your landline phone and/or the extras like caller ID.
- Cancel nonessential magazine subscriptions.

Recessions and financial crises can be challenging. A financial plan that considers such contingencies will help you weather the storm.

Adapting to Other Major Life Changes

Economic hardships are not always the result of adverse macroeconomic developments. Even in the best of times, people can lose their job or face other hardships. Situations that require special consideration include changes in marital status and the need to support grown children or elderly relatives. Marriage, divorce, or the death of a spouse results in the need to revise financial plans and money management strategies.

FINANCIAL PLANNING TIPS

Planning for Critical Life Events

Just like you, financial plans go through stages and must adapt to changes over your lifetime. Here are some of the critical life events that may make you reconsider and possibly revise an existing financial plan:

- **Marriage.** Finances must be merged, and there may be a need for life insurance.

- **Children.** It's time to start a college savings plan and revise your budget accordingly. A will is needed that makes provisions for guardianship if both parents die while the children are minors.

- **Divorce.** Financial plans based on two incomes are no longer applicable. Revised plans must reflect any property settlements, alimony, and/or child support.

- **Moving into middle age.** Although having started a savings and investing plan early in life should be paying off, the number of working years is declining, along with future earning ability. The shorter horizon implies that you may want to take less risk and keep less money in the stock market. While the greater safety is appealing, the reduced expected returns are also sobering. In addition, this could be the time to consider long-term-care insurance for possible use in retirement.

- **Death of a parent.** The estate must be settled, and you may need help managing a possible inheritance.

- **Retirement.** If you set it up right, your financial plan generated the amount needed to fund your retirement. During retirement, you will try to preserve your capital, relying as much as possible on the income generated by your investments to fund your living expenses. Although investment risk should be reduced greatly, it cannot be eliminated because inflation risk must be managed. Money can be withdrawn from tax-deferred retirement accounts beginning at age 59 1/2 without penalty, but taxes will be due. You *must* start taking out such money at age 70 1/2 at a rate that is based on the average life expectancy for that age. The risk of increases in future tax rates can be managed, in part, with Roth IRAs, which are retirement accounts where your original contributions are not tax-deductible. However, there is no requirement that you take out the money and it is not taxed when you do. Estate planning and long-term care issues must also be addressed.

As we mentioned previously, couples should discuss their money attitudes and financial goals and decide how to manage joint financial affairs *before* they get married. Take an inventory of your financial assets and liabilities, including savings and checking accounts; credit card accounts and outstanding bills; auto, health, and life insurance policies; and investment portfolios. You may want to eliminate some credit cards. Too many cards can hurt your credit rating, and most people need only one or two. Each partner should have a card in his or her name to establish a credit record. Compare employee benefit plans to figure out the lowest-cost source of health insurance coverage, and coordinate other benefits. Change the beneficiary on your life insurance policies as desired. Adjust withholding amounts as necessary based on your new filing category.

In the event of divorce, income may decrease because alimony and child-support payments may cause one salary to be divided between two households. Single parents may have to stretch limited financial resources further to meet added expenses such as child care. Remarriage brings additional financial considerations, including decisions involving children from prior marriages and managing the assets that each spouse brings to the marriage. Some couples develop a prenuptial contract that outlines their agreement on financial matters, such as the control of assets, their disposition in event of death or divorce, and other important money issues.

The death of a spouse is another change that greatly affects financial planning. The surviving spouse is typically faced with decisions on how to receive and invest life insurance proceeds and manage other assets. In families where the deceased made most of the financial decisions with little or no involvement of the surviving spouse, the survivor may be overwhelmed by the need to take on financial responsibilities. Advance planning can minimize many of these problems.

Couples should regularly review all aspects of their finances. Each spouse should understand what is owned and owed, participate in formulating financial goals and investment strategies, and fully understand estate plans (covered in detail in Chapter 15).

1-3d Technology in Financial Planning

Using personal computers and the Internet streamlines the number crunching and information gathering involved in budgeting, tax planning, and investment management. Many reasonably priced, user-friendly programs are available for personal financial planning and money management, including the popular Microsoft Money and Quicken packages. And the number of free and reasonably priced online and smart-phone apps for this purpose continues to grow at an amazing rate.

The Internet puts a wealth of financial information literally at your fingertips. Comprehensive sites that consistently get good reviews include Yahoo! Finance (**http://finance.yahoo.com**), Microsoft's MSN MoneyCentral (**http://moneycentral.msn.com**), and Intuit's Quicken.com (**http://www.quicken.com**). Where applicable, we'll point out ways to use the computer and Internet resources to simplify and reduce the time required to manage your personal finances.

1-3e Using Professional Financial Planners

professional financial planners
An individual or firm that helps clients establish financial goals and develop and implement financial plans to achieve those goals.

Does developing your own financial plans seem like an overwhelming task? Help is at hand! **Professional financial planners** will guide you through establishing goals, plan preparation, and the increasingly complex maze of financial products and investment opportunities. This field has experienced tremendous growth, and there are now more than 300,000 financial planners in the United States.

Financial planners offer a wide range of services, including preparing comprehensive financial plans that evaluate a client's total personal financial situation or abbreviated plans focusing on a specific concern, such as managing a client's assets and investments and retirement planning. Where once only the wealthy used professional planners, now financial firms such as H&R Block's Financial Advisors and the Personal Advisors of Ameriprise Financial compete for the business of middle-income people as well.

Why do people turn to financial advisors? Surveys indicate that retirement needs motivated 50 percent, while 23 percent were unhappy with the results of trying to manage their own finances. Estate and inheritance planning caused another 13 percent to seek help; saving for college and tax issues were also mentioned as reasons.

1-3f Types of Planners

Most financial planners fall into one of two categories based on how they are paid: commissions or fees. *Commission-based planners* earn commissions on the financial products they sell, whereas *fee-only planners* charge fees based on the complexity of the plan they prepare. Many financial planners take a hybrid approach and charge fees and collect commissions on products they sell, offering lower fees if you make product transactions through them.

Insurance salespeople and securities brokers who continue to sell the same financial products (life insurance, stocks, bonds, mutual funds, and annuities) often now call themselves "financial planners." Other advisors work for large, established financial institutions that recognize the enormous potential in the field and compete with the best financial planners. Still others work in small firms, promising high-quality advice for a flat fee or an hourly rate. Regardless of their affiliation, full-service financial planners help their clients articulate their long- and short-term financial goals, systematically plan for their financial needs, and help implement various aspects of the plans. Exhibit 1.9 provides a guide to some of the different planning designations.

EXHIBIT 1.9	Financial Planning Designations

Confused about what the letters after a financial advisor's name signify? Here's a summary of the most common certifications so you can choose the one that best suits your needs.

Credential	Description	Internet Address
Chartered Financial Analyst (CFA)	Focuses primarily on securities analysis not financial planning	http://www.cfainstitute.org
Certified Financial Planner® (CFP®)	Requires a comprehensive education in financial planning	http://www.cfp.net
Chartered Financial Consultant (ChFC)	Financial planning designation for insurance agents	http://www.theamerican college.edu/
Certified Trust & Financial Advisor (CTFA)	Estate planning and trusts expertise, found mostly in the banking industry	http://aba.com/ICB/CTFA.htm
Personal Financial Specialist (PFS)	Comprehensive planning credential only for CPAs	http://www.pfp.aicpa.org
Chartered Life Underwriter (CLU)	Insurance agent designation, often accompanied by the ChFC credential	http://www.theamerican college.edu
Certified Investment Management Analyst	Consulting designation for professional investment managers	http://www.imca.org/
Registered Financial Associate (RFA)	Designation granted only to recent graduates of an approved academic curriculum in financial services	http://www.iarfc.org

Source: Adapted from http://apps.finra.org/DataDirectory/1/prodesignations.aspx, accessed July 2015.

In addition to one-on-one financial planning services, some institutions offer computerized financial plans. Merrill Lynch/Bank of America, Ameriprise Financial, T. Rowe Price, and other major investment firms provide these computerized plans on the Internet to help clients develop plans to save for college or retirement, reduce taxes, or restructure investment portfolios.

Personal finance programs such as Quicken and Microsoft Money also have a financial planning component that can help you set a path to your goals and do tax and retirement planning. As you'll see in later chapters, some Internet sites provide planning advice on one topic, such as taxes, insurance, or estate planning. Although these plans are relatively inexpensive or even free, they are somewhat impersonal. However, they are a good solution for those who need help getting started and for do-it-yourself planners who want some guidance.

The cost of financial planning services depends on the type of planner, the complexity of your financial situation, and the services you want. The cost may be well worth the benefits, especially for people who have neither the time, inclination, discipline, nor expertise to plan on their own. Remember, however, that the best advice is worthless if you're not willing to change your financial habits.

1-3g Choosing a Financial Planner

Planners who have completed the required course of study and earned the Certified Financial Planner® (CFP®) or Chartered Financial Consultant (ChFC) designation are often a better choice than the many self-proclaimed "financial planners." Of course, CPAs, attorneys, investment managers, and other professionals without such certifications in many instances also provide sound financial planning advice.

FINANCIAL ROAD SIGN

Potential Financial Advisor Conflicts of Interest

When interviewing a prospective financial advisor, keep in mind the following and ask questions.

How is the advisor paid? Financial advisors can be paid by product sale commissions and/or by client-paid fees. Client-paid fees can include an hourly fee, an annual retainer, a fee that is based on the amount invested with the advisor, or a flat fee for each service provided. And some advisors are paid using a combination of commissions and fees. While most advisors are honest, opportunities for conflicts of interest abound. Advisors who get a commission have an incentive to sell you the products that generate the most money for them, but those are not necessarily the best products for you. Advisors who are paid an hourly fee have an incentive to add hours to your bill. And advisors who earn a fee based on the amount of assets under management tend to encourage you to invest more with them.

Good questions to ask: Ask a prospective advisor how he or she is paid. If an advisor receives commissions, ask for a description of the commissions on the company's products. Alternatively, ask a fee-paid advisor for a schedule of fees for each type of service provided. Consider using the questionnaire provided on the National Association of Personal Financial Advisors (NAPFA) Internet site, which is **www.napfa. org**. The questionnaire has good questions to ask when interviewing a prospective advisor and provides a form that your advisor can use to disclose the commissions that he or she receives.

Source: Adapted from Jennifer Lane, CFP, with Bill Lane, "Advisor Fees and Conflicts," http://www.netplaces.com/money-for-40s-50s/do-you-need-an-advisor/advisor-fees-and-conflicts.htm, accessed July 2015.

Unlike accounting and law, the field is still largely unregulated, and almost anyone can call himself or herself a financial planner. Most financial planners are honest and reputable, but there have been cases of fraudulent practice. So it's critical to thoroughly check out a potential financial advisor—and preferably to interview two or three.

The way a planner is paid—commissions, fees, or both—should be one of your major concerns. Obviously, you need to be aware of potential conflicts of interest when using a planner with ties to a brokerage firm, insurance company, or bank. Many planners now provide clients with disclosure forms outlining fees and commissions for various transactions. In addition to asking questions of the planner, you should also check with your state securities department and the Securities and Exchange Commission (for planners registered to sell securities). Ask if the planner has any pending lawsuits, complaints by state or federal regulators, personal bankruptcies, or convictions for investment-related crimes. However, even these agencies may not have accurate or current information; simply being properly registered and having no record of disciplinary actions don't guarantee that an advisor's track record is good. You may also want to research the planner's reputation in the local financial community. Clearly, you should do your homework before engaging the services of a professional financial planner.

TEST YOURSELF

1-9 What types of financial planning concerns does a complete set of financial plans cover?

1-10 Discuss the relationship of life-cycle considerations to personal financial planning. What are some factors to consider when revising financial plans to reflect changes in the life cycle?

1-11 Don Smitham's investments over the past several years have not lived up to his full return expectations. He is not particularly concerned, however, because his return is only about 2 percentage points below his expectations. Do you have any advice for Don?

1-12 Describe employee benefit and tax planning. How do they fit into the financial planning framework?

1-13 "There's no sense in worrying about retirement until you reach middle age." Discuss this point of view.

1-14 Discuss briefly how the following situations affect personal financial planning:

a. Being part of a dual-income couple
b. Major life changes, such as marriage or divorce
c. Death of a spouse

1-15 What is a *professional financial planner?* Does it make any difference whether the financial planner earns money from commissions made on products sold as opposed to the fees he or she charges?

1-4 THE PLANNING ENVIRONMENT

Financial planning takes place in a dynamic economic environment created by the actions of government, business, and consumers. Your purchase, saving, investment, and retirement plans and decisions are influenced by both the present and future state of the economy. Understanding the economic environment will allow you to make better financial decisions.

Consider that a strong economy can lead to high returns in the stock market, which in turn can positively affect your investment and retirement programs. The economy also affects the interest rates you pay on your mortgage and credit cards as well as those you earn on savings accounts and bonds. Periods of high inflation can lead to rapid price increases that make it difficult to make ends meet. Here we look at two important aspects of the planning environment: the major financial planning players and the economy.

1-4a The Players

The financial planning environment contains various interrelated groups of players, each attempting to fulfill certain goals. Although their objectives are not necessarily incompatible, they do impose some constraints on one another. There are three vital groups: government, business, and consumers. Exhibit 1.10 shows the relationships among these groups.

Government

Federal, state, and local governments provide us with many essential public goods and services, such as police and fire protection, national defense, highways, public education, and health care. The federal government plays a major role in regulating economic activity. Government is also a customer of business and an employer of consumers, so it's a source of revenue for business and of wages for consumers. The two major constraints from the perspective of personal financial planning are taxation and regulation.

EXHIBIT 1.10	The Financial Planning Environment

Government, business, and consumers are the major players in our economic system. They interact with one another to produce the environment in which we carry out our financial plans.

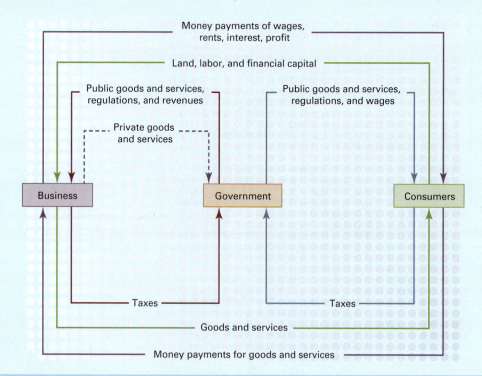

Taxation The federal government levies taxes on income, state governments levy taxes on sales and income, and local governments levy taxes primarily on real estate and personal property. The largest tax bite for consumers is federal income taxes, which are *progressive* in that (up to a point) the greater the taxable income, the higher the tax rate. Changes in tax rates and procedures will increase or decrease the amount of income consumers have to spend, so you should factor the effects of taxes into your personal money management activities. Because of tax structure constraints and the potential magnitude of taxes, financial decisions should be evaluated on an after-tax basis. Taxes are discussed in Chapter 3.

Regulation Federal, state, and local governments place many regulations on activities that affect consumers and businesses. Aimed at protecting the consumer from fraudulent and undesirable actions by sellers and lenders, these regulations require certain types of businesses to have licenses, maintain specified hygiene standards, adequately disclose financial charges, and warrant their goods and services. Other laws protect sellers from adverse activities such as shoplifting and nonpayment for services rendered. Decisions related to achieving personal financial goals should consider the legal requirements that protect consumers and those that constrain their activities.

Business

As Exhibit 1.10 shows, business provides consumers with goods and services and, in return, receives payment in the form of money. Firms must hire labor and use land and financial capital (economists call these *factors of production*) to produce these goods and services. In return, firms pay out wages, rents, interest, and profits to the various factors of production. Thus, businesses are an important part of the circular flow of income that sustains our free enterprise system. In general, they create a competitive environment in which consumers may select from an array of goods and services. As noted previously, all businesses are limited in some way by federal, state, and local laws.

Consumers

The consumer is the central player in the financial planning environment. Consumer choices ultimately determine the kinds of goods and services that businesses will provide. The consumer's choice of whether to spend or save also has a direct impact on present and future circular flows of money. Cutbacks in consumer spending are usually associated with a decline in economic activity, whereas increases in consumer spending help the economy to recover.

Consumers are often thought to have free choices in the marketplace, but they must operate in an environment that includes government and business. Although they can affect these parties by voting and by their purchasing actions, consumers need lobbyists and consumer groups in order to have a significant impact. The individual consumer should not expect to change government or business and instead plan transactions within the existing financial environment.

1-4b The Economy

Our economy is influenced by interactions among government, business, and consumers, as well as by world economic conditions. Through specific policy decisions, the government's goal is to manage the economy to provide economic stability and a high level of employment. Government decisions have a major impact on the economic and financial planning environment. The federal government's *monetary policy*—programs for controlling the amount of money in circulation (the money supply)—is used to stimulate or moderate economic growth. For example, increases in the money supply tend to lower interest rates. This typically leads to a higher level of consumer and business borrowing and spending that increases overall economic activity. The reverse is also true. Reducing the money supply raises interest rates, which reduces consumer and business borrowing and spending and thus slows economic activity. The historically low interest rates in the wake of the financial crisis of 2008 and 2009 and beyond reflect efforts by the Federal Reserve (Fed) to bolster the sagging economy and decrease unemployment.

The government's other principal tool for managing the economy is *fiscal policy*—its programs of spending and taxation. Increased spending for social services, education, defense, and other programs stimulates the economy, while decreased spending slows economic activity. Increasing taxes, on the other hand, gives businesses and individuals less to spend and, as a result, negatively affects economic activity. Conversely, decreasing taxes stimulates the economy. The importance of fiscal policy is illustrated by the government's massive spending to stimulate the U.S. economy in 2008 and 2009 as a way to address the greatest financial crisis since the Great Depression of the 1930s in the United States.

Economic Cycles

Although the government uses monetary and fiscal policy to manage the economy and provide economic stability, the level of economic activity changes constantly. The upward and downward movement creates *economic cycles* (also called *business cycles*), which vary in length and in extent. An economic cycle typically contains four stages: *expansion, peak, contraction,* and *trough.*

Exhibit 1.11 shows how each of these stages relates to real (inflation-adjusted) **gross domestic product (GDP)**, which is an important indicator of economic activity. The stronger the economy, the higher the levels of real GDP and employment. During an **expansion**, real GDP increases until it hits a **peak**, which usually signals the end of the expansion and the beginning of a **contraction**. During a contraction (also known as a *recession*), real GDP falls into a **trough**, which is the end of a contraction and the beginning of an expansion. For about 75 years, the government has been reasonably successful in keeping the economy out of a depression, although we have experienced periods of rapid expansion and high inflation, followed by periods of deep recession. And some would argue that the financial crisis of 2008 and 2009 came close to precipitating a depression.

Economic growth is measured by changes in GDP, the total of all goods and services produced within the country. The broadest measure of economic activity, GDP is reported quarterly and is used to compare trends in national output. A rising GDP means that the economy is growing. The *rate* of GDP growth is also important. Although the long-term trend in nominal GDP typically is positive, the annual rate of GDP growth varies widely. For example, while nominal GDP grew an average of about 6.6 percent between 1950 and 2014, its minimum value was –2 percent and its maximum value was 15.7 percent. And real GDP only grew about 3.3 percent over that time period, with a minimum of 2.8 percent and a maximum of 8.7 percent. Another important measure of economic health is the *unemployment rate*. The swings in unemployment from one phase of the cycle to the next can be substantial. For example, between 1950 and 2014, the civilian unemployment rate fluctuated between a low of 2.9 percent and a high of 9.7 percent. In addition to GDP growth and the unemployment rate, numerous economic statistics such as inflation, interest rates, bank failures, corporate profits, taxes, and government deficits directly and profoundly affect our financial well-being. These factors affect our financial plans: our level of income, investment returns, interest earned and paid, taxes paid, and prices paid for goods and services we buy.

Inflation, Prices, and Planning

As we've discussed, our economy is based on the exchange of goods and services between businesses and their customers—consumers, government, and other businesses—for a medium of exchange called money. The mechanism that facilitates

gross domestic product (GDP)
The total of all goods and services produced in a country; used to monitor economic growth.

expansion
The phase of the economic cycle when levels of employment and production are high and the economy is growing, generally accompanied by rising prices for goods and services.

peak
The phase of the economic cycle when an expansion ends and a contraction begins.

contraction
The phase of the economic cycle when real GDP falls.

trough
The phase of the economic cycle when a contraction ends and an expansion begins.

EXHIBIT 1.11	The Business Cycle

The business cycle consists of four stages: expansion, peak, contraction, and trough.

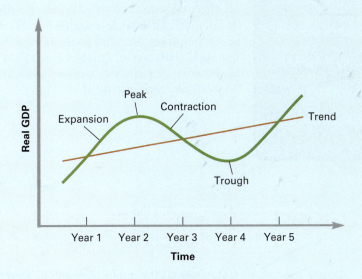

Source: Adapted from William Boyes and Michael Melvin, *Economics*, 8th ed. (Cengage, 2011), p. 35.

inflation
A state of the economy in which the general price level is increasing.

consumer price index (CPI)
A measure of inflation based on changes in the cost of consumer goods and services.

this exchange is a system of *prices*. Technically speaking, the price of something is *the amount of money the seller is willing to accept in exchange for a given quantity of some good or service*—for instance, $3 for a pound of meat or $10 for an hour of work. The economy is said to be experiencing a period of **inflation** when the general level of prices *increases* over time. The most common measure of inflation, the **consumer price index (CPI)**, is based on changes in the cost of consumer goods and services. At times, the rate of inflation has been substantial. In 1980, for instance, prices went up by 13.6 percent. Fortunately, inflation has dropped dramatically in this country, and the annual rate of inflation has remained below 5 percent every year since 1983, except in 1990, when it was 5.4 percent. While there was mild deflation of –0.34 percent during the financial crisis in 2009, inflation moved up to about 3.2 percent in 2011 and fell below 2 percent for the next few years.

Inflation is of vital concern to financial planning. It affects not only what we pay for our goods and services but also what we earn in our jobs. Inflation tends to give an illusion of something that doesn't exist. That is, though we seem to be making more money, we really aren't. As prices rise, we need more income because our purchasing power—the amount of goods and services each dollar buys at a given time—declines. So be sure to look at what you earn in terms of its purchasing power, not just in absolute dollars.

EXAMPLE: Impact of Inflation on Financial Planning

Carla earned $48,000 in 2015 and expected to receive annual raises so that her salary would be $52,000 by 2018. While the annual growth rate in her salary is 2.7 percent, assume that inflation averaged 3 percent per year. Carla's salary needed to growth to $52,451 just to keep pace with inflation. So her real salary declined.

Financial Fact or Fantasy?

Inflation generally has little effect on personal financial planning.
Fantasy: Inflation is a vital concern in financial planning. This is because inflation affects not only the prices we pay for the goods and services we consume but also the amount of money we make. If ignored, inflation can wreak havoc on our budgets and financial plans.

Inflation also directly affects interest rates. High rates of inflation drive up the cost of borrowing money as lenders demand compensation for their eroding purchasing power. Higher interest rates mean higher mortgage payments, higher monthly car payments, and so on. High inflation rates also have a detrimental effect on stock and bond prices. Finally, sustained high rates of inflation can have devastating effects on retirement plans and other long-term financial goals. Indeed, for many people it can put such goals out of reach. Clearly, low inflation is good for the economy, for interest rates and stock and bond prices, and for financial planning in general.

TEST YOURSELF

1-16 Discuss the following statement: "The interactions among government, business, and consumers determine the environment in which personal financial plans must be made."

1-17 What are the stages of an economic cycle? Explain their significance for your personal finances.

1-18 What is *inflation*, and why should it be a concern in financial planning?

1-5 WHAT DETERMINES YOUR PERSONAL INCOME?

LG5, LG6

An obvious and important factor in determining how well we live is the amount of income we earn. In the absence of any inheritance or similar financial windfall, your income will largely depend on such factors as your age, marital status, education, geographic location, and choice of career. A significant level of income—whether derived from your job, your own business, or your investments—is within your reach if you have the necessary dedication, a commitment to hard work, and a well-thought-out set of financial plans. The data in Exhibit 1.12 show how income changes with age and education.

1-5a Demographics and Your Income

Typically, people with low incomes fall into the very young or very old age groups, with the highest earnings generally occurring between the ages of 45 and 64. Those below age 45 are developing careers or beginning to move up in their jobs, and many over 64 are working only part time or are retired. In the 35–44 age group, the median annual income of household heads is about $60,900, and then falls to about $28,500 in the 75 or older age group. Your own income will vary over time, too, so you should incorporate anticipated shifts in earnings into your financial plans.

1-5b Your Education

Your level of formal education is a controllable factor that significantly affects your income. As Exhibit 1.12 illustrates, individuals who have more formal education earn higher annual incomes than do those with lesser degrees. Specifically, the average

EXHIBIT 1.12 **How Age and Education Affect Annual Income**

The amount of money you earn is closely tied to your age and education. Generally, the closer you are to middle age (45–65) and the more education you have, the greater your income will be.

ANNUAL INCOME (HEAD OF HOUSEHOLD)

Age	Median Income ($)*
Less than 35	35,300
35–44	60,900
45–54	60,900
55–64	55,100
65–74	45,900
75 or older	28,500

Education	Median Income ($)**
No high school diploma	20,150
High school diploma	29,770
Bachelor's degree	50,280
Master's degree	61,040
Professional degree	97,200
Dr. degree	82,880

*Data for 2013.
** Data for 2012.

Source: Adapted from Jesse Bricker, Lisa J. Dettling, Alice Henriques, Joanne W. Hsu, Kevin B. Moore, John Sabelhaus, Jeffrey Thompson, and Richard A. Windle, "Changes in U.S. Family Finances from 2010 to 2013: Evidence from the Survey of Consumer Finances," Board of Governors of the Federal Reserve System, Washington, DC, http://www.federalreserve.gov/pubs/bulletin/2014/pdf/scf14.pdf, Table 1, accessed July 2015; and Institute of Education Statistics, National Center for Education Statistics, Digest of Education Statistics: 2013, http://nces.ed.gov/programs/digest/d13/tables/dt13_502.40.asp, Table 502.40, Table 440, accessed July 2015.

(median) salary of a high school graduate in 2013 was about $29,770, compared to $50,280 for the holder of a bachelor's degree. Add a master's or other professional degree and earnings rise substantially. Over a lifetime, these differences really add up! Education alone cannot guarantee a high income, but these statistics suggest that a solid formal education greatly enhances your earning power. And it makes sense to consider the cost of getting a degree while making your decision to get one.

> **Do It Now**
>
> *Recognize That YOU Are Your Most Important Asset*
>
> Your greatest asset is YOU. So it's important to build the value of your best asset by investing in your education and career. The amount you can consume, save, and invest is directly related to your earning ability. Consider that over an entire career, the average bachelor's degree holder will earn $1.19 million, which is about twice what the typical high school grad earns and $335,000 more than the typical associate degree holder. (For additional motivating information, see the source of these statistics: The Hamilton Project at the Brookings Institution, http://hamiltonproject.org/earnings_by_major/). It's so important to realize you're your greatest asset and act on it—you can do it now.

1-5c Where You Live

Geographic factors can also affect your earning power. Salaries vary regionally, tending to be higher in the Northeast and West than in the South. Typically, your salary will also be higher if you live in a large metropolitan area rather than a small town or rural area. Such factors as economic conditions, labor supply, and industrial base also affect salary levels in different areas.

Living costs also vary considerably throughout the country. You'd earn more in Los Angeles than in Memphis, Tennessee, but your salary would probably not go as far because of the much higher cost of living in Los Angeles. Like many others, you may decide that lifestyle considerations take priority over earning potential. Your local chamber of commerce or the Internet can provide an intercity cost-of-living index that shows living costs in major cities and serves as a useful resource for comparing jobs in different areas. The overall index is developed by tracking costs in six major categories: groceries, housing, utilities, transportation, health care, and miscellaneous goods and services.

1-5d Your Career

A critical determinant of your lifetime earnings is your career. The career you choose is closely related to your level of education and your particular skills, interests, lifestyle preferences, and personal values. Social, demographic, economic, and technological trends also influence your decision as to what fields offer the best opportunities for your future. It's not a prerequisite for many types of careers (e.g., sales, service, and certain types of manufacturing and clerical work), but a formal education generally leads to greater decision-making responsibility—and consequently increased income potential—within a career. Exhibit 1.13 presents a list of average salaries for various careers.

EXHIBIT 1.13	Representative Salaries for Selected Careers

Professional and managerial workers, who typically have a college degree, tend to earn the highest salaries.

Career	Average Annual Salary ($)
Accountants and auditors	73,760
Architects and engineers	81,520
Computer programmer	82,690
Family and general practice physicians	186,320
Financial analyst	92,250
Human resources manager	114,140
Lawyer	133,470
Paralegal	51,840
Pharmacist	118,470
Police officer	59,530
Psychiatrist	182,700
Registered nurse	69,790
Teacher, elementary school	56,830

Source: "Occupational Employment and Wages - May 2014," News Release, March 25, 2015, Table 1, U.S. Department of Labor, Bureau of Labor Statistics, http://www.bls.gov/news.release/ocwage.nr0.htm, accessed July 2015.

1-5e Planning Your Career

Career planning and personal financial planning are closely related activities, so the decisions you make in one area affect the other. Like financial planning, career planning is a lifelong process that includes short- and long-term goals. Since your career goals are likely to change several times, you should not expect to stay in one field, or to remain with one company, for your whole life.

You might graduate with a computer science degree and accept a job with a software company. Your financial plan might include furnishing your apartment, saving for a vacation or new car, and starting an investment program. If five years later, you decide to attend law school, you'll have to revise your financial plan and include strategies to cover living expenses and finance your tuition. You may decide that you need to go to school at night while earning a living during the day.

The average American starting a career today can expect to have at least ten jobs with five or more employers, and many of us will have three, four, or even more careers during our lifetimes. Some of these changes will be based on personal decisions; others may result from layoffs or corporate downsizing. For example, a branch manager for a regional bank who feels that bank mergers have reduced her job prospects in banking may start her own business and become her own boss. Job security is practically a thing of the past, and corporate loyalty has given way to a more self-directed career approach that requires new career strategies.

Through careful career planning, you can improve your work situation to gain greater personal and professional satisfaction. Some of the steps are similar to the financial planning process described earlier.

- Identify your interests, skills, needs, and values.
- Set specific long- and short-term career goals.
- Develop and use an action plan to achieve those goals.
- Review and revise your career plans as your situation changes.

Your action plan depends on your job situation. For example, if you're unemployed then it should focus on your job search. If you have a job but want to change careers, your action plan might include researching career options, networking to develop a broad base of contacts, listing companies to contact for information, and getting special training to prepare for your chosen career.

A personal portfolio of skills, both general and technical, will protect your earning power during economic downturns and advance it during prosperous times. It's important to keep your skills current with on-the-job training programs and continuing education. Adding proficiency in technology or languages puts you ahead of the pack in keeping up with changing workplace requirements.

Good job-hunting skills will serve you well throughout your career. Learn how to research new career opportunities and investigate potential jobs, taking advantage of online resources as well as traditional ones. Develop a broad base of career resources, starting with your college placement office, the public library, and personal contacts such as family and friends. Know how to market your qualifications to your advantage in your résumé and cover letters, on the phone, and in person during a job interview.

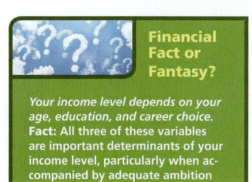

Financial Fact or Fantasy?

Your income level depends on your age, education, and career choice.
Fact: All three of these variables are important determinants of your income level, particularly when accompanied by adequate ambition and disciplined work habits.

TEST YOURSELF

1-19   "All people who have equivalent formal education earn similar incomes." Do you agree or disagree with this statement? Explain your position.

1-20   Discuss the need for career planning throughout the life cycle and its relationship to financial planning. What are some of your personal career goals?

Financial Impact of Personal Choices
Bob Cuts Back on Lunch Out and Lattes

Bob buys lunch out most days and buys a latte every morning. He believes he could cut back a bit and save $5 a day, which is $35 a week and $140 a month. So what's the impact of this seemingly modest cutback?

If Bob invests his $35 savings a week every month at 5 percent, he will have the following in the future:

20 years: $ 57,545
30 years: $116,516
40 years: $213,643

So the seemingly small act of investing only $5 a day would have a dramatic long-term effect on Bob's future accumulated wealth.

Summary

LG1   Identify the benefits of using personal financial planning techniques to manage your finances. p. 3
Personal financial planning helps you marshal and control your financial resources. It should allow you to improve your standard of living, to enjoy your money more by spending it wisely, and to accumulate wealth. By setting short- and long-term financial goals, you'll enhance your quality of life both now and in the future.

LG2   Describe the personal financial planning process and define your goals. p. 8
Personal financial planning is a six-step process that helps you achieve your financial goals: (1) define financial goals; (2) develop financial plans and strategies to achieve those goals; (3) implement financial plans and strategies; (4) periodically develop and implement budgets to monitor and control progress toward goals; (5) use financial statements to evaluate results of plans and budgets, taking corrective action as required; and (6) redefine goals and revise plans and strategies as personal circumstances change. It is critical to realistically spell out your short-term, intermediate, and long-term financial goals. Your goals, which reflect your values and circumstances, may change owing to personal circumstances.

LG3   Explain the life cycle of financial plans, their role in achieving your financial goals, how to
deal with special planning concerns, and the use of professional financial planners. p. 16
In moving through various life-cycle stages, you must revise your financial plans to include goals and strategies appropriate to each stage. Income and expense patterns change with age. Changes in your life due to marriage, children, divorce, remarriage, and job status also necessitate adapting financial plans to meet current needs. Although these plans change over time, they are the road map you'll follow to achieve your financial goals. After defining your goals, you can develop and implement an appropriate personal financial plan. A complete set of financial plans covers asset acquisition, liability and insurance, savings and investments, employee benefits, taxes, and retirement and estate planning. Review these plans regularly and revise them accordingly. Situations that require special attention include managing two incomes, managing employee benefits, and adapting to changes in your personal situation, such as marital status or taking responsibility for elderly relatives' care. Professional financial planners can help you with the planning process.

LG4   Examine the economic environment's influence on personal financial planning. p. 29
Financial planning occurs in an environment where government, business, and consumers are all influential participants. Personal financial decisions are affected by economic cycles (expansion, recession,

depression, and recovery) and the impact of inflation on prices (purchasing power and personal income).

LG5 **Evaluate the impact of age, education, and geographic location on personal income. p. 34**
Demographics, education, and career are all important factors affecting your income level. People between 45 and 64 years old tend to earn more than others, as do those who are married. Equally important, statistics show that income generally increases with the level of education. Where you live is an additional consideration, because salaries and living costs are higher in some areas than in others. Career choices also affect your level of income: those in professional and managerial positions tend to earn the highest salaries.

LG6 **Understand the importance of career choices and their relationship to personal financial planning. p. 34**
Career planning is a lifetime process that involves goal setting as well as career development strategies. A career plan should be flexible enough to adapt to new workplace requirements. When making career plans, identify your interests, skills, needs, and values; set specific long- and short-term career goals; develop and use an action plan to achieve your goals; and review and revise your career plans as your situation changes. Coordinate your career plans with your personal financial plans.

Key Terms

average propensity to consume, 5

consumer price index (CPI), 33

contraction, 32

expansion, 32

financial assets, 7

financial goals, 9

flexible-benefit (cafeteria) plan, 24

goal dates, 13

gross domestic product (GDP), 32

inflation, 33

money, 10

peak, 32

personal financial planning, 8

professional financial planner, 26

standard of living, 4

tangible assets, 7

trough, 32

utility, 10

wealth, 7

Answers to Test Yourself

You can find answers to these questions on this book's companion website. Look for it at *www.cengagebrain.com*. Search for this book by its title, and then add it to your dashboard.

Financial Planning Exercises

LG1, p. 3 1. ***Benefits of Personal Financial Planning.*** How can using personal financial planning tools help you improve your financial situation? Describe changes you can make in at least three areas.

LG2, 3 p. 8, 16 2. ***Personal Financial Goals and the Life Cycle. Use Worksheet 1.1.*** Describe your current status based on the personal financial planning life cycle shown in Exhibit 1.7. Fill out Worksheet 1.1, "Summary of Personal Financial Goals," with goals reflecting your current situation and your expected life situation in 5 and 10 years. Discuss the reasons for the changes in your goals and how you'll need to adapt your financial plans as a result. Which types of financial plans do you need for your current situation, and why?

LG2, p. 8 3. ***Personal Financial Goals.*** Recommend three financial goals and related activities for someone in each of the following circumstances:
  * A junior in college
  * A 30-year-old computer programmer who plans to earn an MBA degree

- A couple in their 30s with two children, ages 3 and 6
- A divorced 52-year-old man with a 16-year-old child and a 78-year-old father who is ill

LG3, p. 16 4. *Life Cycle of Financial Plans.* Ben Saunders and Ashley Tinsdale are planning to get married in six months. Both are 30 years old have been out of college for several years. Ben uses three credit cards and has a bank account balance of $7,500 while Ashely only uses one credit card and has $9,500 in her bank account. What financial planning advice would you give the couple?

LG4, p. 29 5. *Impact of Economic Environment on Financial Planning.* Summarize current and projected trends in the economy with regard to GDP growth, unemployment, and inflation. How should you use this information to make personal financial and career planning decisions?

LG5, p. 34 6. *Financial Impact of Career Decisions.* Alice Reynolds and Tricia Bostwick, both freshman and friends at a major university, are interested in going into a health sciences career. While they're not just interested in the money they can make, they do want to have a sense of the compensation in different health sciences careers. What do the data in Exhibit 1.13 tell Alice and Tricia?

LG6, p. 34 7. *Career Choices and Financial Planning.* Assume that you graduated from college with a major in marketing and took a job with a large consumer products company. After three years, you are laid off when the company downsizes. Describe the steps you'd take to "repackage" yourself for another field.

Applying Personal Finance

Watch Your Attitude!

Many people's *attitude* toward money has as much or more to do with their ability to accumulate wealth as it does with the *amount* of money they earn. As observed in Exhibit 1.4, your attitude toward money influences the entire financial planning process and often determines whether financial goals become reality or end up being pipe dreams. This project will help you examine your attitude toward money and wealth so that you can formulate realistic goals and plans.

Use the following questions to stimulate your thought process.

a. Am I a saver, or do I spend almost all the money I receive?
b. Does it make me feel good just to spend money, regardless of what it's for?
c. Is it important for me to have new clothes or a new car just for the sake of having them?
d. Do I have clothes hanging in my closet with the price tags still on them?
e. Do I buy things because they are a bargain or because I need them?
f. Do I save for my vacations, or do I charge everything and take months paying off my credit card at high interest?
g. If I have a balance on my credit card, can I recall what the charges were for without looking at my statement?
h. Where do I want to be professionally and financially in 5 years? In 10 years?
i. Will my attitude toward money help get me there? If not, what do I need to do?
j. If I dropped out of school today or lost my job, what would I do?

Does your attitude toward money help or hinder you? How can you adjust your attitude so that you are more likely to accomplish your financial goals?

CRITICAL THINKING CASES

LG1, 2, 3, 4, p. 3, 8, 16, 29 ## 1.1 *Jim's Need to Know: Personal Finance or Golf?*

During the Christmas break of his final year at the University of Maryland (UMD), Jim Malone plans to put together his résumé in order to seek full-time employment as a software engineer during the spring semester. To help Jim prepare for the job interview process, his older brother has arranged for him to meet with a friend, Lisa Bancroft, who has worked as a software engineer since her graduation from UMD two years earlier. Lisa gives him numerous pointers on résumé preparation, the interview process, and possible job opportunities.

After answering Jim's many questions, Lisa asks Jim to update her on what he's up to at UMD. As they discuss courses, Lisa indicates that of all the electives she took, the personal financial planning course was most useful. Jim says that, although he had considered personal financial planning for his last elective, he's currently leaning toward a beginning golf course. He feels that the course will be fun because some of his friends are taking it. He points out that he doesn't expect to get rich and already knows how to balance his checkbook. Lisa tells him that personal financial planning involves much more than balancing a checkbook, and that the course is highly relevant regardless of income level. She strongly believes that the personal financial planning course will benefit Jim more than beginning golf—a course that she also took while at UMD.

Critical Thinking Questions

1. Describe to Jim the goals and rewards of the personal financial planning process.
2. Explain to Jim what is meant by the term *financial planning* and why it is important regardless of income.
3. Describe the financial planning environment to Jim. Explain the role of the consumer and the impact of economic conditions on financial planning.
4. What arguments would you present to convince Jim that the personal financial planning course would benefit him more than beginning golf?

LG5, 6, p. 34

1.2 Brad's Dilemma: Finding a New Job

Brad Thomas, a 53-year-old retail store manager earning $75,000 a year, has worked for the same company during his entire 28-year career. Brad was recently laid off and is still unemployed 10 months later, and his severance pay and 6 months' unemployment compensation have run out. Because he has consistently observed careful financial planning practices, he now has sufficient savings and investments to carry him through several more months of unemployment.

Brad is actively seeking work but finds that he is overqualified for available lower-paying jobs and under-qualified for higher-paying, more desirable positions. There are no openings for positions equivalent to the manager's job he lost. He lost his wife several years earlier and is close to his two grown children, who live in the same city.

Brad has these options:

- Wait out the recession until another retail store manager position opens up.
- Move to another area of the country where store manager positions are more plentiful.
- Accept a lower-paying job for two or three years and then go back to school evenings to finish his college degree and qualify for a better position.
- Consider other types of jobs that could benefit from his managerial skills.

Critical Thinking Questions

1. What important career factors should Brad consider when evaluating his options?
2. What important personal factors should Brad consider when deciding among his career options?
3. What recommendations would you give Brad in light of both the career and personal dimensions of his options noted in Questions 1 and 2?
4. What career strategies should today's workers employ in order to avoid Brad's dilemma?

CHAPTER 2

Using Financial Statements and Budgets

LEARNING GOALS

LG1 Understand the relationship between financial plans and statements.

LG2 Prepare a personal balance sheet.

LG3 Generate a personal income and expense statement.

LG4 Develop a good record-keeping system and use ratios to evaluate personal financial statements.

LG5 Construct a cash budget and use it to monitor and control spending.

LG6 Apply time value of money concepts to put a monetary value on financial goals.

How Will This Affect Me?

Recent polls show that up to 70 percent of Americans do not prepare a detailed household budget and about 75 percent do not have enough savings to cover 6 to 9 months of expenses.* These are scary numbers … and this chapter shows what you can do to avoid being part of these alarming statistics.

Everyone knows it's hard to get where you need to go if you don't know where you are. Financial goals describe your destination, and financial statements and budgets are the tools that help you determine exactly where you are in the journey. This chapter helps you define your financial goals and explains how to gauge your progress carefully over time.

*Gallup's annual Economy and Personal Finance poll, June 2013, and CNNMoney, 2013.

2-1 MAPPING OUT YOUR FINANCIAL FUTURE

personal financial statements
Balance sheets and income and expense statements that serve as essential planning tools for developing and monitoring personal financial plans.

balance sheet
A financial statement that describes a person's financial position at a *given point* in time.

income and expense statement
A financial statement that measures financial performance *over* time.

On your journey to financial security, you need navigational tools to guide you to your destination: namely, the fulfillment of your financial goals. Operating without a plan is like traveling without a road map. Financial plans, financial statements, and budgets provide direction by helping you work toward specific financial goals. Financial plans are the road maps that show you the way, whereas personal financial statements let you know where you stand. Budgets, detailed short-term financial forecasts that compare estimated income with estimated expenses, allow you to monitor and control expenses and purchases in a manner that is consistent with your financial plans. All three tools are essential to sound personal financial management and the achievement of goals. They provide control by bringing the various dimensions of your personal financial affairs into focus.

2-1a The Role of Financial Statements in Financial Planning

Before you can set realistic goals, develop your financial plans, or effectively manage your money, you must take stock of your current financial situation. You'll also need tools to monitor your progress. **Personal financial statements** are planning tools that provide an up-to-date evaluation of your financial well-being, help you identify potential financial problems, and help you make better-informed financial decisions. They measure your financial condition so you can establish realistic financial goals and evaluate your progress toward those goals. Knowing how to prepare and interpret personal financial statements is a cornerstone of personal financial planning.

Two types of personal financial statements—the balance sheet and income and expense statement—are essential to developing and monitoring personal financial plans. They show your financial position as it *actually* exists and report on financial transactions that have *really* occurred.

The **balance sheet** describes your financial position—the assets you hold, less the debts you owe, equal your net worth (general level of wealth)—at a *given point in time*. This planning tool helps you track the progress you're making in building up your assets and reducing your debt.

budgets
A detailed financial report that looks *forward*, based on expected income and expenses.

In contrast, the **income and expense statement** measures financial performance *over* time. It tracks income earned, as well as expenses made, during a given period (usually a month or a year). You use this tool to compare your actual expenses and purchases with the amounts budgeted and then make the necessary changes to correct discrepancies between the actual and budgeted amounts. This information helps you control your future expenses and purchases so you'll have the funds needed to carry out your financial plans.

Budgets, another type of financial report, are *forward* looking. Budgets allow you to monitor and control spending because they are based on expected income and expenses.

Exhibit 2.1 summarizes the various financial statements and reports and their relationship to each other in the personal financial planning process. Note that financial plans provide direction to annual budgets, whereas budgets directly affect both your balance sheet and your income and expense statement. As you move from plans to budgets to actual statements, you can compare your actual results with your plans. This will show you how well you are meeting your financial goals and staying within your budget.

EXHIBIT 2.1   The Interlocking Network of Financial Plans and Statements

Personal financial planning involves a network of financial reports that link future goals and plans with actual results. Such a network provides direction, control, and feedback.

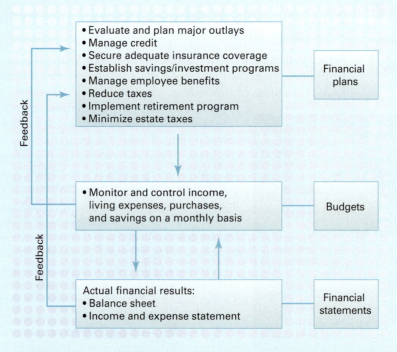

FINANCIAL ROAD SIGN

How to Have a Realistic Budget

- **So what if it's on sale?** Don't buy it if you wouldn't have bought it anyway.
- **Spend less than you earn.** You'll need to pay off debt, design a realistic budget, and save some of your income each month.
- **Make more and buy less.** Make your own lunches, coffee, and anything else you can without great effort. Why spend the money if you can make it yourself without spending a lot of time?
- **Live one raise behind.** When you get a raise, continue living and spending as you did before and put that additional income into savings.
- **Make 30-day lists.** When you see something you really want to buy, put it on a 30-day list and only buy it if you still want it in 30 days.

Source: http://www.careeroverview.com/blog/2010/the-psychology-of-spending-money-25-tricks-you-need-to-know/, accessed July 2015.

2-1b Assessing Your Financial Situation, Plans, and Goals

As you learned in Chapter 1, the financial planning process includes six steps that translate personal financial goals into specific financial plans and the strategies to achieve these goals. In addition to clearly defining your financial goals in measurable terms, you need to put target dates and a monetary value on your short-term, intermediate, and long-term goals. We'll discuss the various types of financial statements and plans in this chapter. Then we'll look at how to use "time value of money" concepts to calculate the value of a financial goal that occurs years into the future.

TEST YOURSELF

2-1 What are the two types of personal financial statements? What is a budget, and how does it differ from personal financial statements? What role do these reports play in a financial plan?

2-2 THE BALANCE SHEET: HOW MUCH ARE YOU WORTH TODAY?

Because you should track your progress toward your financial goals, you need a starting point that shows how much you're worth today. Preparing a personal balance sheet, or statement of financial position, will give you this important information. This financial statement represents a person's (or family's) financial condition at a given point in time. Think of a balance sheet as a snapshot taken of your financial position on one day out of the year.

A balance sheet has three parts that, taken together, summarize your financial picture:

- **Assets:** What you own
- **Liabilities, or debts:** What you owe
- **Net worth:** The difference between your assets and liabilities

The accounting relationship among these three categories is called the balance sheet equation and is expressed as follows:

$$\text{Total Assets} = \text{Total Liabilities} + \text{Net Worth}$$

or

$$\text{Net Worth} = \text{Total Assets} - \text{Total Liabilities}$$

> **EXAMPLE: The Balance Sheet Identity**
>
> Courtney has total liabilities of $150,000 and a net worth of $75,000. This implies that she has total assets of $325,000 (total liabilities of $150,000 + net worth of $75,000 = $325,000 in total assets).

Let's now look at the components of each section of the balance sheet.

2-2a Assets: The Things You Own

Assets are the items you own. An item is classified as an asset whether it was purchased with cash or financed using debt. In other words, even if you haven't fully paid for an asset, you should list it on the balance sheet. In contrast, an item that's leased is not shown as an asset because someone else actually owns it.

A useful way to group assets is on the basis of their underlying characteristics and uses. This results in four broad categories: liquid assets, investments, real property, and personal property.

- **Liquid assets:** Low-risk financial assets held in the form of cash or instruments that can be converted to cash quickly, with little or no loss in value. They are used to meet the everyday needs of life and provide for emergencies and unexpected opportunities. Cash on hand or in a checking or savings account, money market deposit accounts, money market mutual funds, or certificates of deposit that mature within 1 year are all examples of liquid assets.
- **Investments:** Assets acquired to earn a return rather than provide a service. These assets are mostly intangible financial assets (stocks, bonds, mutual funds, and other types of securities), typically acquired to achieve long-term personal financial goals. Business ownership, the cash value of life insurance and pensions, retirement funds such as IRAs and 401(k) plans, and other investment vehicles such as commodities, financial futures, and options represent still other forms of investment assets. (For retirement fund accounts, only those balances that are eligible to be withdrawn should be shown as an asset on the balance sheet. Alternatively, those balances could be shown on an after-tax basis.) They vary in marketability (the ability to sell quickly) from high (stocks and bonds) to low (real estate and business ownership investments).
- **Real and personal property:** Tangible assets that we use in our everyday lives. **Real property** refers to immovable property: land and anything fixed to it, such as a house. Real property generally has a relatively long life and high cost, and it may appreciate, or increase in value. **Personal property** is movable property, such as automobiles, recreational equipment, household furnishings and appliances, clothing, jewelry, home electronics, and similar items. Most types of personal property depreciate, or decline in value, shortly after being put into use.

About 40 percent of the average household's assets consists of financial assets (liquid assets and investments); nearly half is real property (including housing); and the rest is other nonfinancial assets. The left side of Worksheet 2.1 lists some of the typical assets you'd find on a personal balance sheet.

assets
Items that one owns.

liquid assets
Assets that are held in the form of cash or that can readily be converted to cash with little or no loss in value.

investments
Assets such as stocks, bonds, mutual funds, and real estate that are acquired in order to earn a return rather than provide a service.

real property
Tangible assets that are immovable: land and anything fixed to it, such as a house.

personal property
Tangible assets that are movable and used in everyday life.

fair market value
The actual value of an asset, or the price for which it can reasonably be expected to sell in the open market.

All assets, regardless of category, should be recorded on the balance sheet at their current **fair market value**, which may differ considerably from their original purchase price. Fair market value is either the actual value of the asset (such as money in a checking account) or the price for which the asset can reasonably be expected to sell in the open market (as with a used car or a home).

If you've taken an accounting course, you will notice a difference between the way assets are recorded on a personal balance sheet and a business balance sheet. Under generally accepted accounting principles (GAAP), the accounting profession's guiding rules, assets appear on a company's balance sheet at cost, not at fair market value. One reason for the disparity is that in business, an asset's value is often subject to debate and uncertainty. The users of the statements may have different goals, and accountants like to be conservative in their measurements. For purposes of personal financial planning, the user and the preparer of the statement are one and the same. Besides, most personal assets have market values that can be estimated easily.

Financial Fact or Fantasy?

A leased car should be listed as an asset on your personal balance sheet. **Fantasy:** You are only "using" the leased car and do not own it. Consequently, it should not be included as an asset on the balance sheet.

2-2b Liabilities: The Money You Owe

liabilities
Debts such as credit card charges, loans, and mortgages.

Liabilities represent an individual's or family's debts. They could result from department-store charges, bank credit card charges, installment loans, or mortgages on housing and other real estate. A liability, regardless of its source, is something that you owe and must repay in the future.

Liabilities are generally classified according to maturity.

current (short-term) liability
Any debt due within 1 year of the date of the balance sheet.

open account credit obligations
Current liabilities that represent the balances outstanding against established credit lines.

long-term liability
Any debt due 1 year or more from the date of the balance sheet.

- **Current, or short-term, liability:** Any debt currently owed and due within 1 year of the date of the balance sheet. Examples include charges for consumable goods, utility bills, rent, insurance premiums, taxes, medical bills, repair bills, and total **open account credit obligations**—the outstanding balances against established credit lines (usually through credit card purchases).
- **Long-term liability:** Debt due 1 year or more from the date of the balance sheet. These liabilities typically include real estate mortgages, most consumer installment loans, education loans, and margin loans used to purchase securities.

You must show all types of loans on your balance sheet. Although most loans will fall into the category of long-term liabilities, any loans that come due within a year should be shown as current liabilities. Examples of short-term loans include a 6-month, single-payment bank loan and a 9-month consumer installment loan for a refrigerator.

Regardless of the type of loan, only the latest outstanding loan balance should be shown as a liability on the balance sheet, because at any given time, it is the balance still due that matters, not the initial loan balance. Another important and closely related point is that only the outstanding principal portion of a loan or mortgage should be listed as a liability on the balance sheet. In other words, you should not include the interest portion of your payments as part of your balance sheet debt. The **principal** is the amount of debt you owe at a given time, and future interest payments are not accounted for separately as long-term liabilities on the balance sheet.

Lenders evaluate a prospective borrower's liabilities carefully. High levels of debt and overdue debts are both viewed with disfavor. You'll find the most common categories of liabilities on Worksheet 2.1.

Financial Fact or Fantasy?

Only the principal portion of a loan should be recorded on the liability side of a balance sheet. **Fact:** The principal portion of a loan represents the unpaid balance and is the amount of money you owe. In contrast, interest is a charge that will be levied over time for the use of the money.

A balance sheet is set up to show what you own on one side (your assets) and how you pay for them on the other (debt or net worth). As you can see, the Kanes have more assets than liabilities.

BALANCE SHEET

Name(s) _Simon and Meghan Kane_   Date _December 31, 2017_

ASSETS			LIABILITIES		
Liquid Assets			**Current Liabilities**		
Cash on hand	$	150	Utilities	$	175
In checking		575	Rent		
Savings accounts		760	Insurance premiums		
Money market funds and deposits		800	Taxes		
Certificates of deposit			Medical/dental bills		125
Total Liquid Assets	$	2,285	Repair bills		
			Bank credit card balances		425
Investments			Dept. store credit card balances		165
Stocks		3,750	Travel and entertainment card balances		135
Bonds		1,000	Gas and other credit card balances		
Certificates of deposit			Bank line of credit balances		
Mutual funds		2,250	Other current liabilities		45
Real estate			**Total Current Liabilities**	$	1,070
Retirement funds, IRA		4,000			
Other			**Long-Term Liabilities**		
Total Investments	$	11,000	Primary residence mortgage	$160,000	
			Second home mortgage		
Real Property			Real estate investment mortgage		
Primary residence	$225,000		Auto loans		4,350
Second home			Appliance/furniture loans		800
Other			Home improvement loans		
Total Real Property	$	225,000	Single-payment loans		
			Education loans		3,800
Personal Property			Margin loans		
Auto(s): '12 Toyota Corolla	$	10,600	Other long-term loans (from parents)		4,000
Auto(s): '10 Ford Focus		7,400	**Total Long-Term Liabilities**	$	172,950
Recreational vehicles			**(II) Total Liabilities**	$	174,020
Household furnishings		3,700			
Jewelry and artwork		1,500	Net Worth [(I) – (II)]	$	87,465
Other					
Other					
Total Personal Property	$	23,200			
(I)Total Assets	$	261,485	Total Liabilities and Net Worth	$	261,485

2-2c Net Worth: A Measure of Your Financial Worth

net worth
An individual's or family's actual wealth; determined by subtracting total liabilities from total assets.

equity
The actual ownership interest in a specific asset or group of assets.

Now that you've listed what you own and what you owe, you can calculate your **net worth**, the amount of actual wealth or **equity** that an individual or family has in owned assets. It represents the amount of money you'd have left after selling all your owned assets at their estimated fair market values and paying off all your liabilities (assuming there are no transaction costs). As noted earlier, every balance sheet must "balance" so that total assets equal total liabilities plus net worth. Rearranging this equation, we see that net worth equals total assets minus total liabilities. Once you establish the fair market value of assets and the level of liabilities, you can easily calculate net worth by subtracting total liabilities from total assets. If net worth is less than zero, the family is technically insolvent. Although this form of **insolvency** doesn't necessarily mean that the family will end up in bankruptcy proceedings, it likely shows insufficient financial planning.

Net worth typically increases over the life cycle of an individual or family, as Exhibit 2.2 illustrates. For example, the balance sheet of a college student will probably be fairly simple. Assets would include modest liquid assets (cash, checking, and savings accounts) and personal property, which may include a car. Liabilities might include utility bills, perhaps some open account credit obligations, and automobile and education loans. At this point in life, net worth would typically be low because assets are small in comparison with liabilities. In contrast, a 32-year-old single schoolteacher would have more liquid assets and personal property, may have started an investment program, and may have purchased a condominium. Net worth would be rising but may still be low due to the increased liabilities associated with real and personal property purchases. The higher net worth of a two-career couple in their late 30s with children reflects a greater proportion of assets relative to liabilities as they save for college expenses and retirement.

The level of net worth is important in the long-term financial planning process. Once you have established a goal of accumulating a certain level and type of wealth, you can track progress toward that goal by monitoring net worth.

EXAMPLE: Calculating Net Worth

A family has total assets of $225,000 and total liabilities of $175,000. Net worth is total assets of $225,000 less total liabilities of $175,000, which equals $50,000. This is effectively the amount of assets the family "owns" after paying off its liabilities.

2-2d Balance Sheet Format and Preparation

You should prepare your personal balance sheet at least once a year, preferably every 3 to 6 months. Here's how to do it, using the categories in Worksheet 2.1 as a guide.

1. **List your assets at their fair market value as of the date you are preparing the balance sheet.** You'll find the fair market value of liquid and investment assets on checking and savings account records and investment account statements. Estimate the values of homes and cars using published sources of information, such as advertisements for comparable homes and the *Kelley Blue Book* for used car values. Certain items—for example, homes, jewelry, and artwork—may appreciate, or increase in value, over time. The values of assets like cars and most other types of personal property will depreciate, or decrease in value, over time.
2. **List all current and long-term liabilities.** Show all outstanding charges, even if you haven't received the bill, as current liabilities on the balance sheet. For example, assume that on April 25, you used your MasterCard to charge $600 for a set of tires. You typically receive your MasterCard bill around the 10th of the following month. If you were preparing a balance sheet dated April 30, you should include the $600 as a current liability, even though the bill won't arrive until May 10. Remember to list only the principal balance of any loan obligation.
3. **Calculate net worth.** Subtract your total liabilities from your total assets. This is your net worth, which reflects the equity you have in your total assets.

2-2e A Balance Sheet for Simon and Meghan Kane

What can you learn from a balance sheet? Let's examine a hypothetical balance sheet as of December 31, 2017, prepared for Simon and Meghan Kane, the young couple (ages 28 and 26) we met in Chapter 1 (see Worksheet 2.1). Assets are listed on the left side, with the most liquid first; liabilities are on the right, starting with the most recent. The net worth entry is at the bottom right of the statement, just below the

EXHIBIT 2.2   Median Net Worth by Age

Net worth starts to build in the younger-than-35 age bracket and continues to climb, peaking at the 65–74 age bracket. As indicated for the 75 and older age bracket, net worth declines after a person has been retired for a few years and has consequently used some of his or her assets to meet living expenses.

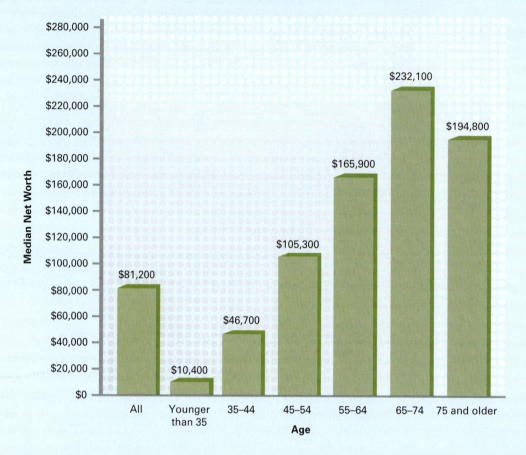

Source: Adapted from Jesse Bricker, Lisa J. Dettling, Alice Henriques, Joanne W. Hsu, Kevin B. Moore, John Sabelhaus, Jeffrey Thompson, and Richard A. Windle, "Changes in U.S. Family Finances from 2010 to 2013: Evidence from the Survey of Consumer Finances," Board of Governors of the Federal Reserve System, Washington, DC (October 24, 2014; data are for 2013), http://www.federalreserve.gov/pubs/bulletin/2014/pdf/scf14.pdf, Table 2, accessed July 2015.

liabilities. The statement should balance: total assets should equal the sum of total liabilities and net worth, as in the balance sheet equation on page 46. Here's what this financial statement tells us about the Kanes' financial condition:

- **Assets:** Given their ages, the Kanes' asset position looks quite good. The dominant asset is their house. They also have $11,000 in investments, which include retirement funds and appear to have adequate liquid assets to meet their bill payments and cover small, unexpected expenses.
- **Liabilities:** The Kanes' primary liability is the $160,000 mortgage on their house. Their equity, or actual ownership interest, in the house is approximately $65,000 ($225,000 market value minus the $160,000 outstanding mortgage loan). Their current liabilities are $1,070, with other debts of $12,950 representing auto, furniture, and education loans, as well as a loan from their parents to help with the down payment on their home.
- **Net worth:** The Kanes' net worth ($261,485 in total assets minus total liabilities of $174,020) is $87,465—a respectable amount that is enviably above the median for their age group shown in Exhibit 2.2.

Comparing the Kanes' total liabilities to their total assets gives a more realistic view of their current wealth position than merely looking at assets or liabilities alone. By calculating their net worth periodically, the Kanes can measure their progress toward achieving their financial goals.

TEST YOURSELF

2-2 Describe the balance sheet, its components, and how you would use it in personal financial planning. Differentiate between investments and real and personal property.

2-3 What is the balance sheet equation? Explain when a family may be viewed as technically insolvent.

2-4 Explain two ways in which net worth could increase (or decrease) from one period to the next.

2-3 THE INCOME AND EXPENSE STATEMENT: WHAT WE EARN AND WHERE IT GOES

When confronted with a lack of funds, the first question people ask themselves is, "Where does all the money go?" Preparing an income and expense statement would answer this question. Whereas the balance sheet describes a person's or family's financial position at a given time, the income and expense statement captures the various financial transactions that have occurred over the stated period of time, which is usually a year or a month. Think of this statement as a motion picture that not only shows actual results over time but also lets you compare them with budgeted financial goals. Equally important, the statement allows you to evaluate the amount of saving and investing during the period it covers.

Like the balance sheet, the income and expense statement has three major parts: income, expenses, and cash surplus (or deficit). A cash surplus (or deficit) is merely the difference between income and expenses. The statement is prepared on a **cash basis**, which means that only transactions involving actual cash inflows or actual cash outlays are recorded. The term cash is used in this case to include not only coin and currency but also checks and debit card transactions drawn against checking and certain types of savings accounts.

Income and expense patterns change over the individual's or family's life cycle. Income and spending levels typically rise steadily to a peak in the 45–54 age bracket. On average, people in this age group, whose children are typically in college or no longer at home, have the highest level of income. They also spend more than other age groups on entertainment, dining out, transportation, education, insurance, and charitable contributions. Families in the 35–44 age range have slightly lower average levels of income and expenses and very different spending patterns. Because they tend to have school-age children, they spend more on groceries, housing, clothing, and other personal needs. Yet the average percentage of pre-tax income spent is about the same—at around 75 percent to 80 percent—for all age ranges through age 64. It rises sharply to about 97 percent, however, for persons age 65 and over.

cash basis
A method of preparing financial statements in which only transactions involving actual cash receipts or actual cash outlays are recorded.

2-3a Income: Cash In

Common sources of **income** include earnings received as wages, salaries, self-employment income, bonuses, and commissions; interest and dividends received from savings and investments; and proceeds from the sale of assets such as stocks

income
Earnings received as wages, salaries, bonuses, commissions, interest and dividends, or proceeds from the sale of assets.

and bonds or an auto. Other income items include pension, annuity, and Social Security income; rent received from leased assets; alimony and child support; scholarships or grants; tax refunds; and miscellaneous types of income. Worksheet 2.2, Income and Expense Statement for Simon and Meghan Kane, has general categories for recording income.

Note also that the proper figure to use is *gross* wages, salaries, and commissions, which constitute the amount of income you receive from your employer *before* taxes and other payroll deductions. The gross value is used because the taxes and payroll deductions will be itemized and deducted as expenses later in the income and expense statement. Therefore, you should not use take-home pay, because it understates your income by the amount of these deductions.

2-3b Expenses: Cash Out

expenses
Money spent on living costs and to pay taxes, purchase assets, or repay debt.

Expenses represent money used for outlays. Worksheet 2.2, Income and Expense Statement for Simon and Meghan Kane categorizes them by the types of benefits they provide: (1) living expenses (such as housing, utilities, food, transportation, medical, clothing, and insurance); (2) tax payments; (3) asset purchases (such as autos, stereos, furniture, appliances, and loan payments on them); and (4) other payments for personal care, recreation and entertainment, and other expenses. Some are **fixed expenses**—usually contractual, predetermined, and involving equal payments each period (typically each month). Examples include mortgage and installment loan payments, insurance premiums, professional or union dues, club dues, monthly savings or investment programs, and cable TV fees. Others (such as food, clothing, utilities, entertainment, and medical expenses) are **variable expenses**, because their amounts change from one time period to the next.

fixed expenses
Contractual, predetermined expenses involving equal payments each period.

variable expenses
Expenses involving payment amounts that change from one time period to the next.

Exhibit 2.3 shows the average annual expenses by major category as a percentage of after-tax income. It's a useful benchmark to see how you compare with national averages. However, your own expenses will vary according to your age, lifestyle, and where you live. For example, it costs considerably more to buy a home in San Diego than in Charlotte. Similarly, if you live in the suburbs, your commuting expenses will be higher than those of city dwellers.

2-3c Cash Surplus (or Deficit)

The third component of the income and expense statement shows the net result of the period's financial activities. Subtracting total expenses from total income gives you the cash surplus (or deficit) for the period. At a glance, you can see how you did financially over the period. A positive figure indicates that expenses were less than income, resulting in a **cash surplus**. A value of zero indicates that expenses were exactly equal to income for the period, while a negative value means that your expenses exceeded income and you have a **cash deficit**.

cash surplus
An excess amount of income over expenses that results in *increased* net worth.

cash deficit
An excess amount of expenses over income, resulting in insufficient funds as well as in *decreased* net worth.

You can use a cash surplus for savings or investment purposes, to acquire assets, or to reduce debt. Adding to savings or investments should increase your future income and net worth, and making payments on debt affects cash flow favorably by reducing future expenses. In contrast, when a cash deficit occurs, you must cover the shortfall from your savings or investments, reduce assets, or borrow. All of these strategies will reduce net worth and negatively affect your financial future.

> **EXAMPLE: Calculating a Cash Surplus or Deficit**
>
> Will had cash income this year of $50,000 and cash expenses of $47,500. Consequently, his cash surplus is $2,500, which is income of $50,000 less expenses of $47,500. Had Will's expenses been $51,200 while earning the same income, he would have generated a cash deficit of $1,200, which is $50,000 minus $51,200.

The income and expense statement shows what you earned, how you spent your money, and how much you were left with (or, if you spent more than you took in, how much you went "in the hole").

INCOME AND EXPENSE STATEMENT

Name(s) _Simon and Meghan Kane_

For the _Year_ Ended _December 31, 2017_

INCOME

Wages and salaries	Name: _Simon Kane_	$	65,000
	Name: _Meghan Kane_		18,350
	Name:		
Self-employment income			
Bonuses and commissions	_Simon—sales commissions_		3,050
Investment income	Interest received		195
	Dividends received		120
	Rents received		
	Sale of securities		
	Other		
Pensions and annuities			
Other income			
	(I) Total Income	$	86,715

EXPENSES

Housing	Rent/mortgage payment (include insurance and taxes, if applicable)	$	11,820
	Repairs, maintenance, improvements		1,050
Utilities	Gas, electric, water		1,750
	Phone		480
	Cable TV and other		240
Food	Groceries		2,425
	Dining out		3,400
Transportation	Auto loan payments		2,520
	License plates, fees, etc.		250
	Gas, oil, repairs, tires, maintenance		2,015
Medical	Health, major medical, disability insurance (payroll deductions or not provided by employer)		2,250
	Doctor, dentist, hospital, medicines		305
Clothing	Clothes, shoes, and accessories		1,700
Insurance	Homeowner's (if not covered by mortgage payment)		1,200
	Life (not provided by employer)		1,865
	Auto		1,780
Taxes	Income and social security		18,319
	Property (if not included in mortgage)		2,100
Appliances, furniture, and other major purchases	Loan payments		800
	Purchases and repairs		450
Personal care	Laundry, cosmetics, hair care		700
Recreation and entertainment	Vacations		2,000
	Other recreation and entertainment		2,630
Other items	_Tuition and books: Meghan_		1,400
	Gifts		215
	Loan payments: Education loans		900
	Loan payments: Parents		600
	(II) Total Expenses	$	65,164
	CASH SURPLUS (OR DEFICIT) [(I) − (II)]	$	21,551

EXHIBIT 2.3   How We Spend Our Income

Almost three-quarters of expenditures made with pre-tax income fall into one of four categories: housing, transportation, food, and personal insurance and pensions.

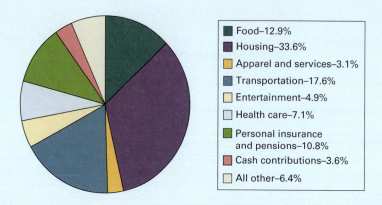

- Food–12.9%
- Housing–33.6%
- Apparel and services–3.1%
- Transportation–17.6%
- Entertainment–4.9%
- Health care–7.1%
- Personal insurance and pensions–10.8%
- Cash contributions–3.6%
- All other–6.4%

Source: "Consumer Expenditures—2013," Washington, DC: U.S. Department of Labor, Bureau of Labor Statistics, News Release, USDL-14-1671, based on Table A, September 9, 2014.

It is important to keep in mind that a cash surplus does not necessarily mean that funds are simply lying around waiting to be used. The actual disposition of the surplus (or deficit) is shown in the asset, liability, and net worth accounts on the balance sheet. For example, if you used the surplus to make investments, this would increase the appropriate asset account. If you used the surplus to pay off a loan, the payment would reduce that liability account. Of course, if you used the surplus to increase cash balances, you'd have the funds to use. In each case, your net worth *increases*. Surpluses *increase* net worth; deficits *decrease* it, whether the shortfall is financed by reducing an asset (e.g., drawing down a savings account) or by borrowing.

2-3d Preparing the Income and Expense Statement

As shown in Worksheet 2.2, the income and expense statement is dated to define the period covered. To prepare the statement, follow these steps.

1. **Record your income from all sources for the chosen period.** Use your paycheck stubs to verify your gross pay for the period, and be sure to include bonuses, commission checks, and overtime pay. You'll find interest earned, securities bought and sold, interest and dividends received, and other investment matters on your bank and investment account statements. Keep a running list of other income sources, such as rents, tax refunds, and asset sales.
2. **Establish meaningful expense categories.** Those shown on Worksheet 2.2 are a good starting point. Information on monthly house (or rent) payments, loan payments, and other fixed payments (such as insurance premiums and cable TV) is readily available from either the payment book or your checkbook (or, in the case of payroll deductions, your check stubs). (Be careful with adjustable-rate loans because the amount of monthly loan payments will eventually change when the interest rate changes.)
3. **Subtract total expenses from total income to get the cash surplus (a positive number) or deficit (a negative number).** This "bottom line" summarizes the net cash flow resulting from your financial activities during the period.

You'll probably pay for most major variable expenses by check, debit card, or credit card, so it's easy to keep track of them. It's harder to keep tabs on all the items in a month that you pay for with cash, such as parking, lunches, movies, and incidentals. Try to remember what you spent during the week, and write it down on your calendar to the nearest $5. If you can't remember, then try the exercise over shorter and shorter periods of time until you can.

Just as you show only the amounts of cash actually received as income, record only the amounts of money you actually pay out in cash as expenses. If you borrow to buy an item, particularly an asset, include only the actual cash payment—purchase price minus amount borrowed—as an expense, as well as payments on the loan in the period you actually make them. You show credit purchases of this type as an asset and corresponding liability on the balance sheet. Record only the cash payments on loans, not the actual amounts of the loans themselves, on the income and expense statement.

EXAMPLE: Keeping Track of Loans

Carter bought a car for $20,000 in September. He made a down payment of $3,000 and financed the remaining $17,000 with a 4-year, 5.5 percent loan, payable monthly.

On Carter's September 30th income and expense statement he showed a cash expenditure of $3,000, and each subsequent monthly statement would show a loan payment expense of $395. Carter's September 30th balance sheet would show the car as an asset worth $20,000 and the $17,000 loan as a long-term liability. The values of the car and the loan will be adjusted going forward.

Finally, when making your list of expenses for the year, remember to include the amount of income tax and Social Security taxes withheld from your paycheck, as well as any other payroll deductions (health insurance, savings plans, retirement and pension contributions, and professional/union dues). These deductions (from gross wages, salaries, bonuses, and commissions) represent personal expenses, even if they don't involve a direct cash payment.

You might be shocked when listing what's taken out of your paycheck. Even if you're in a fairly low federal income tax bracket, your paycheck could easily be reduced by more than 25 percent for taxes alone. Your federal tax could be withheld at 15 percent, your state income tax could be withheld at 5 percent, and your Social Security and Medicare tax could be withheld at 7.65 percent. That doesn't even count health and disability income insurance.

Preparing income and expense statements can involve a lot of number crunching. Fortunately, some good computer software packages, such as Quicken and Microsoft Money, can simplify the job of preparing personal financial statements and doing other personal financial planning tasks.

2-3e An Income and Expense Statement for Simon and Meghan Kane

Simon and Meghan Kane's balance sheet in Worksheet 2.1 shows us their financial condition *as of* December 31, 2017. Worksheet 2.2, their income and expense statement for the *year ended* December 31, 2017, was prepared using the background material presented earlier, along with the Kanes' balance sheet. This statement shows how money flowed into and out of their "pockets."

- **Income:** Total income for the year ended December 31, 2017, is $86,715. Simon's wages represent the family's chief source of income, although Meghan has finished her MBA and will now be making a major contribution. Other sources of income include $195 in interest on their savings accounts and bond investments and $120 in dividends from their common stock holdings.

- **Expenses:** Total expenses for this year of $65,164 include their home mortgage, food, auto loan, clothing, and income and Social Security taxes. Other sizable expenses during the year include home repairs and improvements, gas and electricity, auto license and operating expenses, insurance, tuition, and education loan payments.
- **Cash surplus:** The Kanes end the year with a cash surplus of $21,551 (total income of $86,715 minus total expenses of $65,164).

The Kanes can use their surplus to increase savings, invest in stocks, bonds, or other vehicles, or make payments on some outstanding debts. The best strategy depends on their financial goals. If they had a cash deficit, the Kanes would have to withdraw savings, liquidate investments, or borrow an amount equal to the deficit to meet their financial commitments (i.e., to "make ends meet"). With their surplus of $21,551, the Kanes have made a positive contribution to their net worth.

TEST YOURSELF

2-5   What is an income and expense statement? What role does it serve in personal financial planning?

2-6   Explain what cash basis means in this statement: "An income and expense statement should be prepared on a cash basis." How and where are credit purchases shown when statements are prepared on a cash basis?

2-7   Distinguish between fixed and variable expenses, and give examples of each.

2-8   Is it possible to have a cash deficit on an income and expense statement? If so, how?

2-4 USING YOUR PERSONAL FINANCIAL STATEMENTS

Whether you're just starting out and have a minimal net worth or are farther along the path toward achieving your goals, your balance sheet and income and expense statement provide insight into your current financial status. You now have the information you need to examine your financial position, monitor your financial activities, and track the progress you're making toward your financial goals. Let's now look at ways to help you create better personal financial statements and analyze them to better understand your financial situation.

2-4a Keeping Good Records

Although record keeping doesn't rank high on most "to do" lists, a good record-keeping system helps you manage and control your personal financial affairs. With organized, up-to-date financial records, you'll prepare more accurate personal financial statements and budgets, pay less to your tax preparer, not miss any tax deductions, and save on taxes when you sell a house or securities or withdraw retirement funds. Also, good records make it easier for a spouse or relative to manage your financial affairs in an emergency. To that end, you should prepare a comprehensive list of these records, their locations, and your key advisors (financial planner, banker, accountant, attorney, doctors) for family members.

Prepare your personal financial statements at least once each year, ideally when drawing up your budget. Many people update their financial statements every 3 or

6 months. You may want to keep a **ledger**, or financial record book, to summarize all your financial transactions. The ledger has sections for assets, liabilities, sources of income, and expenses; these sections contain separate accounts for each item. Whenever any accounts change, make an appropriate ledger entry. For example, if you bought headphones for $100 in cash, you'd show the headphones on your balance sheet as an asset (at its fair market value) and as a $100 expenditure on your income and expense statement. If you borrowed to pay for the headphones, the loan amount would be a liability on the balance sheet, and any loan payments made during the period would be shown on the income and expense statement. You'd keep similar records for asset sales, loan repayments, income sources, and so on.

Managing Your Financial Records

Your system doesn't have to be fancy to be effective. You'll need the ledger book just described and a set of files with general categories such as banking and credit cards, taxes, home, insurance, investments, and retirement accounts. An expandable file, with a dozen or so compartments for incoming bills, receipts, paycheck stubs, or anything you might need later, works well. You can easily keep a lot of this kind of information in a computer spreadsheet—but if so, be sure to back it up from time to time. Also, keep in mind that a bank safe-deposit box is a great place to store important documents and files.

Start by taking an inventory. Make a list of everything you own and owe. Check it at least once a year to make sure it's up-to-date and to review your financial progress. Then, record transactions manually in your ledger or with financial planning software. Exhibit 2.4 offers general guidelines for keeping and organizing your personal financial records.

You'll want to set up separate files for tax planning records, with one for income (paycheck stubs, interest on savings accounts, etc.) and another for deductions, as well as for individual mutual fund and brokerage account records. Once you set up your files, be sure to go through them at least once a year and throw out unnecessary items.

2-4b Tracking Financial Progress: Ratio Analysis

Each time you prepare your financial statements, you should analyze them to see how well you're doing on your financial goals. For example, with an income and expense statement, you can compare actual financial results with budgeted figures to make sure that your spending is under control. Likewise, comparing a set of financial plans with a balance sheet will reveal whether you're meeting your savings and investment goals, reducing your debt, or building up a retirement reserve. You can compare current performance with historical performance to find out if your financial situation is improving or getting worse.

Calculating certain financial ratios can help you evaluate your financial performance over time. What's more, if you apply for a loan, the lender probably will look at these ratios to judge your ability to carry additional debt. Four important money management ratios are (1) solvency ratio, (2) liquidity ratio, (3) savings ratio, and (4) debt service ratio. The first two are associated primarily with the balance sheet, the last two with the income and expense statement. Exhibit 2.5 defines these ratios and illustrates their calculation for Simon and Meghan Kane.

Balance Sheet Ratios

When evaluating your balance sheet, you should be most concerned with your net worth at a given time. As explained earlier in this chapter, you are technically insolvent when your total liabilities exceed your total assets—that is, when you have a

EXHIBIT 2.4 Managing Your Financial Records

Here are some key steps to managing your financial records effectively.

Keep a list of key financial documents. These include records of all bank accounts, credit cards, investment accounts, home deed, vehicle registrations, all insurance policies, will and all legal documents, tax records, birth certificate, driver's license copy, passport, marriage and death certificates, and car titles. Store these in a safe place like a fireproof box or a safe-deposit box at a bank.

Renew key documents. Many important documents have an expiration date. Make sure you don't miss important renewal dates for your driver's license, passport, and automobile and homeowners insurance.

Save records for tax and insurance purposes. The Internal Revenue Service requires you to keep most tax records and related receipts for 3 to 7 years. Don't throw away any financial documents without checking whether you'll need them in the future. For example, receipts for home renovations can be needed to support insurance claims. Scanning important documents is a great way to reduce clutter.

Review your financial plans. Review how your investments are doing at least once a quarter and evaluate whether you are well on your way to meeting key financial goals like retirement. Organize your records so that you can complete the financial statements discussed in this chapter, making sure to calculate your net worth.

Ensure your family can locate important documents. If you are injured or die, your family will appreciate being able to find your insurance records or will easily. Electronic records can be saved online with services such as www.assetlock. net and www.legacylocker.com, which can be accessed by your family. It's also important to keep up-to-date records of important computer accounts and passwords in a secure location. Consider a safe-deposit box at a bank.

Dispose of documents safely. Shred unneeded documents that have identifying and/or financial information on them.

Re-organize your finances at least once a year. This is not a one-time event. Schedule a date that's easy to remember.

---

solvency ratio
Total net worth divided by total assets; measures the degree of exposure to insolvency.

negative net worth. The **solvency ratio** shows, as a percentage, your degree of exposure to insolvency, or how much "cushion" you have as a protection against insolvency. Simon and Meghan's solvency ratio is 33.4 percent, which means that they could withstand about a 33 percent decline in the market value of their assets before they would be insolvent. Consider that the stock market, as measured by the S&P 500 index, fell about 37 percent during the financial crisis of 2008. Also, the average home's value fell about 18 percent during that crisis year, as measured by the S&P/Case-Shiller U.S. National Home Price Index. The value of Simon and Meghan's solvency ratio suggests that they are in good shape for now, but they may want to consider increasing it a bit in the future to manage a potential decline in the value of their assets even better.

Although the solvency ratio indicates the potential to withstand financial problems, it does not deal directly with the ability to pay current debts. This issue is addressed with the **liquidity ratio**, which shows how long you could continue to pay current debts (any bills or charges that must be paid within 1 year) with existing liquid assets in the event of income loss.

liquidity ratio
Total liquid assets divided by total current debts; measures the ability to pay current debts.

The calculated liquidity ratio indicates that the Kanes can cover only about 13 percent of their existing 1-year debt obligations with their current liquid assets. In other words, they have 1½ months of coverage (a month is one-twelfth, or 8.3 percent, of a year). If an unexpected event cut off their income, their liquid reserves would quickly be exhausted. Although there's no hard-and-fast rule for what this ratio should be, it seems too low for the Kanes. They should consider strengthening it along with their solvency ratio. They should be able to add to their cash surpluses now that Meghan is working full-time.

EXHIBIT 2.5   Ratios for Personal Financial Statement Analysis

Ratio	Formula	2017 Calculation for the Kanes
Solvency ratio	$\dfrac{\text{Total net worth}}{\text{Total assets}}$	$\dfrac{\$87,465}{\$261,485} = 0.334$, or 33.4%
Liquidity ratio	$\dfrac{\text{Total liquid assets}}{\text{Total current debts}}$	$\dfrac{\$2,285}{\$17,710^{(a)}} = 0.129$, or 12.90%
Savings ratio	$\dfrac{\text{Cash surplus}}{\text{Income after taxes}}$	$\dfrac{\$21,551}{\$86,715 - \$18,319} = \dfrac{\$21,551}{\$68,396} = 0.315$, or 31.5%
Debt service ratio	$\dfrac{\text{Total monthly loan payments}}{\text{Monthly gross (before-tax) income}}$	$\dfrac{\$1,387^{(b)}}{\$7,226^{(c)}} = 0.192$, or 19.2%

(a) You'll find the Kanes' total liquid assets ($2,285) and total current liabilities ($1,070) on Worksheet 2.1. The current debt totals $17,710: current liabilities of $1,070 (from Worksheet 2.1) plus loan payments due within 1 year of $16,640 (from Worksheet 2.2). Note that loan payments due within 1 year consist of $11,820 in mortgage payments, $2,520 in auto loan payments, $800 in furniture loan payments, $900 in education loan payments, and $600 in loan payments to parents.

(b) On an annual basis, the Kanes' debt obligations total $16,640 ($11,820 in mortgage payments, $2,520 in auto loan payments, $800 in furniture loan payments, $900 in education loan payments, and $600 in loan payments to parents; all from Worksheet 2.2). The Kanes' total monthly loan payments are about $1,387 ($16,640 ÷ 12 months).

(c) Dividing the Kanes' annual gross income (also found in Worksheet 2.2) of $86,715 by 12 equals $7,226 per month.

The amount of liquid reserves will vary with your personal circumstances and "comfort level." Another useful liquidity guideline is to have a reserve fund equal to at least 6 to 9 months of after-tax income available to cover living expenses. The Kanes' after-tax income for 2017 was $5,700 per month [($86,715 total income − $18,319 income and Social Security taxes) ÷ 12]. Therefore, this guideline suggests that they should have at least $34,200 in total liquid assets—considerably more than the $2,285 on their latest balance sheet. If you feel that your job is secure or you have other potential sources of income, you may be comfortable with three or four months in reserve. In troubled economic times, such as the recent recession, you may want to keep more than six to nine months of income in this fund as protection in case you lose your job.

Income and Expense Statement Ratios

When evaluating your income and expense statement, you should be concerned with the bottom line, which shows the cash surplus (or deficit) resulting from the period's activities. You can relate the cash surplus (or deficit) to income by calculating a **savings ratio**, which is done most effectively with after-tax income.

Simon and Meghan saved about 31 percent of their after-tax income, which is excellent (American families, on average, save about 5 percent to 8 percent). How much to save is a personal choice. Some families would plan much higher levels, particularly if they're saving to achieve an important goal, such as buying a home.

Although maintaining an adequate level of savings is obviously important to personal financial planning, so is the ability to pay debts promptly. In fact, debt payments have a higher priority. The **debt service ratio** allows you to make sure you can comfortably meet your debt obligations. This ratio excludes current liabilities and considers only mortgage, installment, and personal loan obligations.

Monthly loan payments account for about 19 percent of Simon and Meghan's monthly gross income. This relatively low debt service ratio indicates that the

savings ratio
Cash surplus divided by net income (after tax); indicates relative amount of cash surplus achieved during a given period.

debt service ratio
Total monthly loan payments divided by monthly gross (before-tax) income; provides a measure of the ability to pay debts promptly.

Kanes should have little difficulty in meeting their monthly loan payments. In your financial planning, try to keep your debt service ratio somewhere under 35 percent or so, because that's generally viewed as a manageable level of debt. Of course, the lower the debt service ratio, the easier it is to meet loan payments as they come due.

TEST YOURSELF

2-9 How can accurate records and control procedures be used to ensure the effectiveness of the personal financial planning process?

2-10 Describe some of the areas or items you would consider when evaluating your balance sheet and income and expense statement. Cite several ratios that could help in this effort.

2-5 CASH IN AND CASH OUT: PREPARING AND USING BUDGETS

LG5 Many of us avoid budgeting as if it were the plague. After all, do you really want to know that 30 percent of your take-home pay is going to restaurant meals? Yet preparing, analyzing, and monitoring your personal budget are essential steps for successful personal financial planning.

After defining your short-term financial goals, you can prepare a cash budget for the coming year. Recall that a budget is a short-term financial planning report that helps you achieve your short-term financial goals. By taking the time to evaluate your current financial situation, spending patterns, and goals, you can develop a realistic budget that is consistent with your personal lifestyle, family situation, and values. A cash budget is a valuable money management tool that helps you:

- Maintain the necessary information to monitor and control your finances
- Decide how to allocate your income to reach your financial goals
- Implement a system of disciplined spending—as opposed to just existing from one paycheck to the next
- Reduce needless spending so you can increase the funds allocated to savings and investments
- Achieve your long-term financial goals

Just as your goals will change over your lifetime, so too will your budget as your financial situation becomes more complex. Typically, the number of income and expense categories increases as you accumulate more assets and debts and have more family responsibilities. For example, the budget of a college student should be quite simple, with limited income from part-time jobs, parental contributions, and scholarships and grants. Expenses might include room and board, clothes, books,

FINANCIAL PLANNING TIPS

Tips on Budgeting

• **Gather every financial statement and receipt you can find.** This includes bank statements, investment accounts, recent utility bills, and any documents on income or expenses. The purpose of collecting this information is to create a monthly average of income and expenses.

• **Record all of your sources of income.** Record your total income as a monthly amount.

• **Create a list of usual monthly expenses.** This should include any mortgage payments, car payments, auto insurance, groceries, utilities, entertainment, dry cleaning, auto insurance, retirement or college savings, and anything else you spend money on.

• **Categorize expenses as fixed or variable.** Fixed expenses stay about the same each month. Examples include your mortgage or rent, car payments, cable and/or Internet service, and trash pickup. Variable expenses change from month to month and include groceries, gasoline, entertainment, eating out, gifts and

credit card payments. Variable expenses provide some room to maneuver when trying to balance your budget.

• **Total your monthly income and monthly expenses and project them over the next year.** If you have more income than expenses, then you're well on your way. You can allocate this excess to areas of your budget such as saving for retirement or paying more on credit cards to pay off outstanding debt. If your expenses exceed your income, changes have to be made.

• **Make adjustments to expenses if necessary.** The overall goal of your budget is to have your income equal your expenses, which should include your savings expense allocation.

• **Review your budget monthly.** It is important to review your budget on a regular basis to make sure you know how things are going. At the end of each month, compare the actual expenses with what you budgeted.

Source: Adapted from Jerry Vohwinkle, http://financialplan.about.com/od/budgetingyourmoney/ht/createbudget.htm, accessed July 2015.

auto expenses, and entertainment. Once a student graduates and goes to work full-time, his or her budget will include additional expenses, such as rent, insurance, work clothes, and commuting costs. For most people, this process does not become simpler until retirement.

2-5a The Budgeting Process

Like the income and expense statement, a budget should be prepared on a cash basis; thus, we call this document a **cash budget** because it deals with estimated cash receipts and cash expenses, including savings and investments, that are expected to occur in the coming year. Because you receive and pay most bills monthly, you'll probably want to estimate income as well as expenses on a monthly basis.

The cash budget preparation process has three stages: forecasting income, forecasting expenses, and finalizing the cash budget. When you're forecasting income and expenses, take into account any anticipated changes in the cost of living and their impact on your budget components. If your income is fixed—not expected to change over the budgetary period—then increases in various expense items will probably decrease the purchasing power of your income. Worksheet 2.3, the Kanes' Annual Cash Budget by Month, has separate sections to record income (cash receipts) and expenses (cash expenses) and lists the most common categories for each.

cash budget
A budget that takes into account estimated monthly cash receipts and cash expenses for the coming year.

The Kanes' annual cash budget shows several months in which substantial cash deficits are expected to occur; they can use this information to develop plans for covering those monthly shortfalls.

ANNUAL CASH BUDGET BY MONTH

Name(s) Simon and Meghan Kane

For the Year   Ended December 31, 2017

	Jan.	Feb.	Mar.	April	May	June	July	Aug.	Sep.	Oct.	Nov.	Dec.	Total for the Year
INCOME													
Take-home pay	$4,800	$4,800	$4,800	$4,800	$4,800	$5,200	$5,200	$5,200	$5,200	$5,200	$5,200	$5,200	$60,400
Bonuses and commissions						1,350						1,300	2,650
Pensions and annuities													
Investment income			50			50			50			50	200
Other income													
(I) Total Income	$4,800	$4,800	$4,850	$4,800	$4,800	$6,600	$5,200	$5,200	$5,250	$5,200	$5,200	$6,550	$63,250
EXPENSES													
Housing (rent/mortgage, repairs)	$1,185	$1,485	$1,185	$1,185	$1,185	$1,185	$1,185	$1,185	$1,185	$1,185	$1,185	$1,185	$14,520
Utilities (phone, elec., gas, water)	245	245	245	175	180	205	230	245	205	195	230	250	2,650
Food (home and away)	696	696	1,200	696	696	696	696	696	696	696	696	696	8,856
Transportation (auto/public)	375	620	375	355	375	375	575	375	375	425	375	375	4,975
Medical/dental, incl. insurance	50	50	50	50	50	75	50	50	50	50	50	50	625
Clothing	150	150	670	200	200	200	300	600	200	300	300	300	3,570
Insurance (life, auto, home)				660	1,598					660	1,598		4,516
Taxes (property)		550							550				1,100
Appliances, furniture, and other (purchases/loans)	60	60	60	60	60	60	60	60	60	60	60	60	720
Personal care	100	100	100	100	100	100	100	100	100	100	100	100	1,200
Recreation and entertainment	250	300	3,200	200	200	400	300	200	200	200	200	2,050	7,700
Savings and investments	575	575	575	575	575	575	575	575	575	575	575	575	6,900
Other expenses	135	200	175	135	510	180	135	235	235	135	405	325	2,805
Fun money	200	200	230	130	200	200	200	200	200	200	200	230	2,390
(II) Total Expenses	$4,021	$5,231	$8,065	$4,521	$5,929	$4,251	$4,406	$5,071	$4,081	$4,781	$5,974	$6,196	$62,527
CASH SURPLUS (OR DEFICIT) [(I)-(II)]	$779	($431)	($3,215)	$279	($1,129)	$2,349	$794	$129	$1,169	$419	($774)	$354	$723
CUMULATIVE CASH SURPLUS (OR DEFICIT)	$779	$348	($2,867)	($2,588)	($3,717)	($1,368)	($574)	($445)	$724	$1,143	$369	$723	$723

Forecasting Income

The first step in preparing your cash budget is to forecast your income for the coming year. Include all income expected for the year: the take-home pay of both spouses, expected bonuses or commissions, pension or annuity income, and investment income—interest, dividend, rental, and asset (particularly security) sale income. When estimating income, keep in mind that any amount you receive for which repayment is required is not considered income. For instance, loan proceeds are treated not as a source of income but as a liability for which scheduled repayments are required.

Unlike the income and expense statement, in the cash budget you should use take-home pay (rather than gross income). Your cash budget focuses on those areas that you can control—and most people have limited control over things like taxes withheld, contributions to company insurance and pension plans, and the like. In effect, take-home pay represents the amount of disposable income you receive from your employer.

Forecasting Expenses

The second step in the cash budgeting process is by far the most difficult: preparing a schedule of estimated expenses for the coming year. This is usually done using actual expenses from previous years (as found on income and expense statements and in supporting information for those periods), along with predetermined short-term financial goals. Good financial records, as discussed earlier, make it easier to develop realistic expense estimates. If you do not have past expense data, you could reexamine old checkbook registers and credit card statements to approximate expenses, or take a "needs approach" and attach dollar values to projected expenses. Pay close attention to expenses associated with medical disabilities, divorce and child support, and similar special circumstances.

When preparing your budget, be aware of your expenditure patterns and how you spend money. After tracking your expenses over several months, study your spending habits to see if you are doing things that should be eliminated. For example, you may become aware that you are going to the ATM too often or using credit cards too freely.

You'll probably find it easier to budget expenses if you group them into several general categories rather than trying to estimate each item. Worksheet 2.3 is an example of one such grouping scheme, patterned after the categories used in the income and expense statement. You may also want to refer to the average expense percentages given in Exhibit 2.3. Choose categories that reflect your priorities and allow you to monitor areas of concern.

Your expense estimates should include the transactions necessary to achieve your short-term goals. You should also quantify any current or short-term contributions toward your long-term goals and schedule them into the budget. Equally important are scheduled additions to savings and investments, because planned savings should be high on everyone's list of goals. If your budget doesn't balance with all these items, you will have to make some adjustments in the final budget.

Base estimated expenses on current price levels and then increase them by a percentage that reflects the anticipated rate of inflation. For example, if you estimate the current monthly food bill at $500 and expect 4 percent inflation next year, you should budget your monthly food expenditure next year at $520, or $500 + $20 (4 percent × $500).

Do It Now

Track Your Expenses

It's easy for spending to become so automatic that we're not aware we're doing it. So where does your money go? The only way to find out is to keep track of it. Writing down what you spend in a paper journal or using an app like Expensify (www.expensify.com) is simple and will make you more aware of where your money goes. Knowing where you are will probably make you feel better too—so do it now.

Behavior Matters

Pessimistic Budgeting Works

People tend to be overly optimistic when budgeting for a few months than for longer time periods. They tend to underestimate short-term expenses, but they are more realistic with longer-term budgets. We are likely less confident about longer periods and adjust our expenses upward to be safe. So win by being *purposely pessimistic* in short-term budgeting.

Don't forget an allowance for "fun money," which family members can spend as they wish. This gives each person some financial independence and helps form a healthy family budget relationship.

Finalizing the Cash Budget

After estimating income and expenses, finalize your budget by comparing projected income to projected expenses. Show the difference in the third section as a surplus or deficit. In a balanced budget, the total income for the year equals or exceeds total expenses. If you find that you have a deficit at year end, you'll have to go back and adjust your expenses. If you have several months of large surpluses, you should be able to cover any shortfall in a later month, as explained later. Budget preparation is complete once all monthly deficits are resolved and the total annual budget balances.

Admittedly, there's a lot of number crunching in personal cash budgeting. As discussed earlier, personal financial planning software can greatly streamline the budget preparation process.

2-5b Dealing with Deficits

Even if the annual budget balances, in certain months expenses may exceed income, causing a monthly budget deficit. Likewise, a budget surplus occurs when income in some months exceeds expenses. Two remedies exist:

- Shift expenses from months with budget deficits to months with surpluses (or, alternatively, transfer income, if possible, from months with surpluses to those with deficits).
- Use savings, investments, or borrowing to cover temporary deficits.

FINANCIAL ROAD SIGN

Biggest Budgeting Mistakes

- **Failing to plan for inevitable expenses.** While some expenses are unexpected, most aren't. Plan for your car to need maintenance and put it in your budget. Include property, auto, health and life insurance, taxes, clothing, and gifts. Spread infrequent but significant expenses over your annual budget.
- **No emergency fund.** A real emergency—not just something unexpected—includes loss of income, severe illness, or death in the family.
- **Putting savings last.** It's important to budget your savings rather than just save when there just happens to be something left over. Pay yourself first!

Because the budget balances for the year, the need for funds to cover shortages is only temporary. In months with budget surpluses, you should return funds taken from savings or investments or repay loans. Either remedy is feasible for curing a monthly budget deficit in a balanced annual budget, although the second is probably more practical.

What can you do if your budget shows an annual budget deficit even after you've made a few expense adjustments? You have three options, as follows:

- **Liquidate enough savings and investments or borrow enough to meet the total budget shortfall for the year.** Obviously, this option is not preferred, because it violates the objective of budgeting: to set expenses at a level that allows you to enjoy a reasonable standard of living *and* progress toward achieving your long-term goals. Reducing savings and investments or increasing debt to balance the budget reduces net worth. People who use this approach are *not* living within their means.
- **Cut low-priority expenses from the budget.** This option is clearly preferable to the first one. It balances the budget without using external funding sources by eliminating expenses associated with your least important short-term goals, such as flexible or discretionary expenses for nonessential items (e.g., recreation, entertainment, some types of clothing).
- **Increase income.** Finding a higher-paying job or perhaps a second, part-time job is the most difficult option; it takes more planning and may result in significant lifestyle changes. However, people who can't liquidate savings or investments or borrow funds to cover necessary expenses may have to choose this route to balance their budgets.

2-5c A Cash Budget for Simon and Meghan Kane

Using their short-term financial goals (Worksheet 1.1 in Chapter 1) and past financial statements (Worksheets 2.1 and 2.2), Simon and Meghan Kane have prepared their cash budget for the 2018 calendar year. Worksheet 2.3 shows the Kanes' estimated total 2018 annual take-home income and expenses by month, as well as their monthly and annual cash surplus or deficit.

The Kanes list their total 2018 take-home income of $63,250 by source for each month. By using take-home pay, they eliminate the need to show income-based taxes, Social Security payments, and other payroll deductions as expenses. The take-home pay reflects Simon and Meghan's expected salary increases.

In estimating annual expenses for 2018, the Kanes anticipate a small amount of inflation and have factored some price increases into their expense projections.

They have also allocated $6,900 to savings and investments, a wise budgeting strategy, and included an amount for fun money to be divided between them.

During their budgeting session, Simon and Meghan discovered that their first estimate resulted in expenses of $63,877, compared with their estimated income of $63,250. To eliminate the $627 deficit to balance their budget and allow for unexpected expenses, Simon and Meghan made these decisions:

- Omit some low-priority goals: spend less on stereo components, take a shorter Hawaiian vacation instead of the Colorado ski trip shown in Worksheet 1.1.

- Reschedule some of the loan repayment to their parents.
- Reduce their fun money slightly.

These reductions lower Simon and Meghan's total scheduled expenses to $62,527, giving them a surplus of $723 ($63,250 − $62,527) and balancing the budget on an annual basis with some money left over. Of course, the Kanes can reduce other discretionary expenses to further increase the budget surplus and have a cushion for unexpected expenses.

The Kanes' final step is to analyze monthly surpluses and deficits and determine whether to use savings, investments, or borrowing to cover monthly shortfalls. The bottom line of their annual cash budget lists the cumulative, or running, totals of monthly cash surpluses and deficits. Despite their $723 year-end cumulative cash surplus, they have cumulative deficits from March to August, primarily because of their March Hawaiian vacation and insurance payments. To help cover these deficits, Simon and Meghan have arranged an interest-free loan from their parents. If they had dipped into savings to finance the deficits, they would have lost some interest earnings, which are included as income. They could delay clothing and recreation and entertainment expenses until later in the year to reduce the deficits more quickly. If they weren't able to obtain funds to cover the deficits, they would have to reduce expenses further or increase income. At year end, they should use their surplus to increase savings or investments or to repay part of a loan.

2-5d Using Your Budgets

In the final analysis, a cash budget has value only if (1) you use it and (2) you keep careful records of actual income and expenses. These records show whether you are staying within your budget limits. Record this information in a budget record book or an Excel spreadsheet often enough that you don't overlook anything significant, yet not so often that it becomes a nuisance. A loose-leaf binder with separate pages for each income and expense category works quite well. So does a well-organized spreadsheet. Rounding entries to the nearest dollar simplifies the arithmetic.

At the beginning of each month, record the budgeted amount for each category and enter income received and money spent on the appropriate pages. At month's end, total each account and calculate the surplus or deficit. Except for certain income accounts (such as salary) and fixed expense accounts (such as mortgage or loan payments), most categories will end the month with a positive or negative variance, indicating a cash surplus or deficit. You can then transfer your total spending by category to a **budget control schedule** that compares actual income and expenses with the various categories and shows the **budget variance**,

budget control schedule
A summary that shows how actual income and expenses compare with the various budget categories and where variances (surpluses or deficits) exist.

budget variance
The difference between the budgeted and actual amount paid out or received.

Behavior Matters

How to Really Spend Less

Spending less means changing your behavior, which is hard to do. These concrete steps will help.

- **Make a budget and use it to help set financial goals.** Decide how much less you want to spend and set a savings goal.

- **Use your savings account first and your checking account last.** Set up two bank accounts so that money can be transferred between them. Deposit your income into savings and transfer your budgeted amount into checking—not the other way around.

- **Spend cash—don't rely on credit cards.** It's harder to use cash for everything, so you'll spend less.

- **Have someone hold you accountable.** Let someone you trust—your spouse, friend, or parent, for instance—know your goals and have them follow your progress.

- **Before you buy, consider the alternatives.** Always wait at least two days before making a big purchase. Think about how it fits into your budget. Really think about your alternatives.

Source: Adapted from Brian Reed, "6 New Behavioral Strategies to Curb Your Spending in 2012," http://www.investinganswers.com/personal-finance/savings-budget/6-new-behavioral-strategies-curb-your-spending-2012-3963, accessed July 2015.

which is the difference between the budgeted and actual amount paid out or received.

This monthly comparison makes it easy to identify major budget categories where income falls far short of—or spending far exceeds—desired levels (variances of 5 percent to 10 percent or more). After pinpointing these areas, you can take corrective action to keep your budget on course. Don't just look at the size of the variances. Analyze them, particularly the larger ones, to discover *why* they occurred. An account deficit that occurs in only one period is obviously less of a problem than one that occurs in several periods. If recurring deficits indicate that an account was underbudgeted, you may need to adjust the budget to cover the outlays, reducing over-budgeted or nonessential accounts. Only in exceptional situations should you finance budget adjustments by using savings and investments or by borrowing.

EXAMPLE: Calculating Budget Variance

Angie budgeted $125 last month for transportation but actually spent $150. She consequently had a variance that was a budget deficit of $25. Had Angie actually spent only $115, the variance would have been a $10 budget surplus.

Looking at the Kanes' budget control schedule for a representative month in Worksheet 2.4, you can see that actual income and expense levels are reasonably close to their targets and have a net positive variance for the month shown. The biggest variances were in medical/dental and recreation and entertainment, which presumably occurred because these expenses are paid unevenly over the months of the year.

The monthly budget provides important feedback on how the actual cash flow stacks up against the forecasted monthly cash budget. If the variances are significant enough and/or continue month after month, the Kanes should consider altering either their spending habits or their cash budget.

MONTHLY BUDGET

Name(s) _Simon and Meghan Kane_

	Budgeted Amount (1)	Actual Amount (2)	Variance (3)*
INCOME			
Take-home pay	$4,800	$4,817	$17
Bonuses and commissions			0
Pensions and annuities			0
Investment income			0
Other income			0
(I) Total Income	$4,800	$4,817	$17
EXPENSES			
Housing (rent/mtge, repairs)	$1,185	1,185	0
Utilities (phone, elec., gas, water)	245	237	(8)
Food (home and away)	696	680	(16)
Transportation (auto/public)	375	385	10
Medical/dental, incl. insurance	50	0	(50)
Clothing	150	190	40
Insurance (life, auto, home)	0	0	0
Taxes (property)	0	0	0
Appliances, furniture, and other (purchases/loans)	60	60	0
Personal care	100	85	(15)
Recreation and entertainment	250	210	(40)
Savings and investments	575	575	0
Other expenses	135	118	(17)
Fun money	200	200	0
(II) Total Expenses	$4,021	$3,925	($96)
CASH SURPLUS (OR DEFICIT) [(I)-(II)]	$779	$892	$113

* Col. (3) = Col. (2) – Col. (1).

TEST YOURSELF

2-11   Describe the cash budget and its three parts. How does a budget deficit differ from a budget surplus?

2-12   The Rivera family has prepared their annual cash budget for 2018. They have divided it into 12 monthly budgets. Although only 1 monthly budget balances, they have managed to balance the overall budget for the year. What remedies are available to the Rivera family for meeting the monthly budget deficits?

2-13   Why is it important to analyze budget variances and their implied surpluses or deficits at the end of each month?

2-6 THE TIME VALUE OF MONEY: PUTTING A DOLLAR VALUE ON FINANCIAL GOALS

Assume that one of your financial goals is to buy your first home in 6 years. Then your first question is how much you want to spend on that home. Let's say you've done some "window shopping" and feel that, taking future inflation into consideration, you can buy a condominium for about $200,000 in 6 years. Of course, you won't need the full amount, but assuming that you'll make a 20 percent down payment of $40,000 (0.20 × $200,000 = $40,000) and pay $5,000 in closing costs, you'll need $45,000. You now have a well-defined long-term financial goal: To accumulate $45,000 in 6 years to buy a home costing about $200,000.

The next question is how to get all that money. You'll probably accumulate it by saving or investing a set amount each month or year. You can easily estimate how much to save or invest each year if you know your goal and what you expect to earn on your savings or investments. In this case, if you have to start from scratch (i.e., if nothing has already been saved) and estimate that you can earn about 5 percent on your money, you'll have to save or invest about $6,616 per year for each of the next 6 years to accumulate $45,000 over that time. Now you have another vital piece of information: You know what you must do over the next 6 years to reach your financial goal.

time value of money
The concept that a dollar today is worth more than a dollar received in the future.

How did we arrive at the $6,616 figure? We used a concept called the **time value of money**, the idea that a dollar today is worth more than a dollar received in the future. With time value concepts, we can correctly compare dollar values occurring at different points in time. So long as you can earn a positive rate of return (interest rate) on your investments (ignoring taxes and other behavioral factors), in a strict financial sense, you should always prefer to receive equal amounts of money sooner rather than later. The two key time value concepts, future value and present value, are discussed separately next. We'll use **timelines**, graphical representations of cash flows, to visually depict the time value calculations. They will appear in the text margin near the related discussion. (*Note:* The time value discussions and demonstrations initially rely on the use of financial tables. Appendix E explains how to use financial calculators, which have tables built into them, to conveniently make time value calculations.) The calculator keystrokes for each calculation are shown in the text margin near the related discussion. Because of rounding in the tables, the calculator values will always be more precise.

timeline
A graphical presentation of cash flows.

2-6a Future Value

future value
The value to which an amount today will grow if it earns a specific rate of interest over a given period.

To calculate how much to save to buy the $200,000 condominium, we used **future value**, the value to which an amount today will grow if it earns a specific rate of interest over a given period. Assume, for example, that you make annual deposits of $2,000 into a savings account that pays 5 percent interest per year. At the end of 20 years, your deposits would total $40,000 (20 × $2,000). If you made no withdrawals, your account balance would have increased to $66,132! This growth in value occurs not only because of earning interest but also because of **compounding**—the interest earned each year is left in the account and becomes part of the balance (or principal) on which interest is earned in subsequent years.

compounding
When interest earned each year is left in an account and becomes part of the balance (or principal) on which interest is earned in subsequent years.

Future Value of a Single Amount

To demonstrate future value, let's return to the goal of accumulating $45,000 for a down payment to buy a home in 6 years. You might be tempted to solve this problem by simply dividing the $45,000 goal by the 6-year period: $45,000/6 = $7,500. This procedure would be incorrect, however, because it fails to take into account the time value of money. The correct way to approach this problem is to use the **future value**

I = 5%

0 1 2 3 4 5

6

$5,000 $6,700

End of Year

INPUTS	FUNCTIONS
5000	PV
6	N
5	I
	CPT
	FV
	SOLUTION
	6,700.48

See Appendix E for details.

concept. For instance, if you can invest $100 today at 5 percent, you will have $105 in a year. You will earn $5 on your investment (0.05 × $100 = $5) and get your original $100 back. Once you know the length of time and rate of return involved, you can find the future value of any investment by using the following simple formula:

$$\text{Future Value} = \text{Amount Invested} \times \text{Future Value Factor}$$

Tables of future value factors simplify the computations in this formula (see Appendix A). The table is easy to use; simply find the factor that corresponds to a given year and interest rate.

EXAMPLE: Calculating the Future Value of a Single Amount

You've saved $5,000 toward the down payment for the purchase of a home. You plan to invest this single amount at 5 percent for 6 years. The interest factor in Appendix A is 1.340. In 6 years you should have:

$$\text{Future Value} = \$5,000 \times 1.340 = \$6,700$$

In 6 years, then, you will have about $6,700 if you invest the $5,000 at 5 percent. Because you feel you are going to need $45,000, you are still $38,300 short of your goal.

Future Value of an Annuity

How are you going to accumulate the additional $38,300? You'll again use the future value concept, but this time you'll use the future value annuity factor. An **annuity** is a fixed sum of money that occurs annually, for example, a deposit of $1,000 per year for each of the next 5 years, with payment to be made at the end of each year. To find out how much you need to save each year in order to accumulate a given amount, use this equation:

annuity
A fixed sum of money that occurs annually.

$$\text{Yearly Savings} = \frac{\text{Future Amount of Money Desired}}{\text{Future Value Annuity Factor}}$$

When dealing with an annuity, you need to use a different table of factors, such as that in Appendix B. Note that it's very much like the table of future value factors and, in fact, is used in exactly the same way: the proper future value annuity factor is the one that corresponds to a given year *and* interest rate.

I = 5%

$38,300

1   2   3   4   5

0   6

$5,631 $5,631 $5,631 $5,631 $5,631 $5,631

End of Year

INPUTS	FUNCTIONS
38,300	FV
6	N
5	I
	CPT
	PMT
	SOLUTION
	5,630.77

See Appendix E for details.

EXAMPLE: Calculating the Future Value of an Annuity

You want to make equal annual investments that will grow to the additional $38,300 needed for the down payment on a home in 6 years while earning 5 percent a year. Appendix B provides an annuity factor of 6.802. The needed equal annual investment is:

$$\text{Yearly Savings} = \frac{\$38,300}{6.802} = \$5,630.70$$

You'll need to save about $5,630.70 a year to reach your goal. Note in this example that you must add $5,630.70 each year to the $5,000 you initially invested in order to build up a pool of $45,000 in 6 years. At a 5 percent rate of return, the $5,630.70 per year will grow to $38,300 and the $5,000 will grow to about $6,700, so in 6 years you'll have $38,300 + $6,700 = $45,000.

Timeline

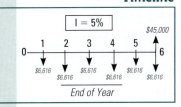

I = 5%

$45,000

0 — 1 — 2 — 3 — 4 — 5 — 6

$6,616 $6,616 $6,616 $6,616 $6,616 $6,616

End of Year

Calculator

INPUTS	FUNCTIONS
45,000	FV
6	N
5	I
	CPT
	PMT
	SOLUTION
	6,615.79

See Appendix E for details.

rule of 72
A useful formula for estimating about how long it will take to double a sum at a given interest rate.

present value
The value today of an amount to be received in the future; it's the amount that would have to be invested today at a given interest rate over a specified time period to accumulate the future amount.

discounting
The process of finding present value; the inverse of *compounding* to find future value.

How much, you may ask, would you need to save each year if you didn't have the $5,000 to start with? In this case, your goal would still be the same (to accumulate $45,000 in 6 years), but because you'd be starting from scratch, the full $45,000 would need to come from yearly savings. Assuming you can still earn 5 percent over the 6-year period, you can use the same future value annuity factor (6.802) and compute the amount of yearly savings as follows:

$$\text{Yearly Savings} = \frac{\$45,000}{6.802} = \$6,615.70$$

or approximately $6,616. Note that this amount corresponds to the $6,616 figure cited at the beginning of this section.

Using the future value concept, you can readily find either the future value to which an investment will grow over time or the amount that you must save each year to accumulate a given amount of money by a specified future date. In either case, the procedures allow you to put monetary values on long-term financial goals.

2-6b The Rule of 72

Suppose that you don't have access to time value of money tables or a financial calculator but want to know how long it takes for your money to double. There's an easy way to approximate this using the **rule of 72**. Simply divide the number 72 by the percentage rate you're earning on your investment:

$$\text{Number of Years to Double Money} = \frac{72}{\text{Annual Compound Interest Rate}}$$

EXAMPLE: Applying the Rule of 72

You recently opened a savings account with $1,000 that earns 4.5 percent annually. Its value will double to $2,000 in 16 years (72 ÷ 4.5 = 16).

The rule of 72 also applies to debts. Your debts can quickly double with high interest rates, such as those charged on most credit card accounts. So keep the rule of 72 in mind whether you invest or borrow!

2-6c Present Value

Lucky you! You've just won $100,000 in your state lottery. You want to spend part of it now, but because you're 30 years old, you also want to use part of it for your retirement fund. Your goal is to accumulate $300,000 in the fund by the time you're age 55 (25 years from now). How much do you need to invest if you estimate that you can earn 5 percent annually on your investments during the next 25 years?

Using **present value**, the value today of an amount to be received in the future, you can calculate the answer. It represents the amount you'd have to invest today at a given interest rate over the specified time period to accumulate the future amount. The process of finding present value is called **discounting**, which is the inverse of compounding to find future value.

Present Value of a Single Amount

Assuming you wish to create the retirement fund (future value) by making a single lump-sum deposit today, you can use this formula to find the amount you need to deposit:

Present Value = Future Value × Present Value Factor

Tables of present value factors make this calculation easy (see Appendix C).

Timeline

I = 5%

$300,000

0 | 1 | 2 | ... | 24 | 25

$88,500

End of Year

EXAMPLE: Calculating the Present Value of a Single Amount

You want to have a retirement fund of $300,000 in 25 years by making a lump-sum deposit today that will earn 5 percent a year. Appendix C provides a present value factor of 0.295. Your deposit will be:

$$\text{Present Value} = \$300,000 \times 0.295 = \$88,500$$

Calculator

INPUTS	FUNCTIONS
300000	FV
25	N
5	I
	CPT
	PV
	SOLUTION
	88,590.83

See Appendix E for details.

The $88,500 is the amount you'd have to deposit today into an account paying 5 percent annual interest in order to accumulate $300,000 at the end of 25 years.

Present Value of an Annuity

You can also use present value techniques to determine how much you can withdraw from your retirement fund each year over a specified time horizon. This calls for the **present value annuity factor**. Assume that at age 55 you wish to begin making equal annual withdrawals over the next 30 years from your $300,000 retirement fund. At first, you might think you could withdraw $10,000 per year ($300,000/30 years). However, the funds still on deposit would continue to earn 5 percent annual interest. To find the amount of the equal annual withdrawal, you again need to consider the time value of money. Specifically, you would use this formula:

$$\text{Annual Withdrawal} = \frac{\text{Initial Deposit}}{\text{Present Value Annuity Factor}}$$

Timeline

I = 5%

0 | 1 | 2 | ... | 29 | 30

$300,000 | $19,515 | $19,515 | | $19,515 | $19,515

End of Year

EXAMPLE: Calculating the Present Value of an Annuity

You've successfully accumulated $300,000 for retirement and want to make equal annual withdrawals over the next 30 years while earning 5 percent. Using the present value annuity factor of 15.373 in Appendix D, the equal annual withdrawal is:

$$\text{Annual Withdrawal} = \frac{\$300,000}{15.372} = \$19,514.73$$

Calculator

INPUTS	FUNCTIONS
300000	PV
30	N
5	I
	CPT
	PMT
	SOLUTION
	19,515.43

See Appendix E for details.

Therefore, you can withdraw $19,514.73 each year for 30 years. This value is clearly much larger than the $10,000 annual withdrawal mentioned earlier.

Other Applications of Present Value

You can also use present value techniques to analyze investments. Suppose you have an opportunity to purchase an annuity investment that promises to pay $700 per year for 5 years. You know that you'll receive a total of $3,500 ($700 × 5 years) over the 5-year period. However, you wish to earn a minimum annual return of 5 percent on your investments. What's the most you should pay for this annuity today? You can answer this question by rearranging the terms in the formula to get:

$$\text{Initial Deposit} = \text{Annual Withdrawal} \times \text{Present Value Annuity Factor}$$

Adapting the equation to this situation, "initial deposit" represents the maximum price to pay for the annuity, and "annual withdrawal" represents the annual annuity payment of $700.

Timeline

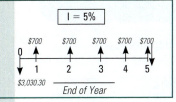

I = 5%

$700 $700 $700 $700 $700
0
  1   2   3   4   5
$3,030.30
End of Year

Calculator

INPUTS	FUNCTIONS
700	PMT
5	N
5	I
	CPT
	PV
	SOLUTION
	3,030.63

See Appendix E for details.

EXAMPLE: Determining the Value of an Investment

What should you be willing to pay up front for an investment that will pay $700 a year for 5 years when you want to earn at least a 5 percent return?

This is calculated as the present value of an annuity, which Appendix D shows to have a factor of 4.329.

Initial Deposit = $700 × 4.329 = $3,030.30

The most you should pay for the $700, 5-year annuity, given your 5 percent annual return, is about $3,031. At this price, you'd earn 5 percent on the investment.

Using the present value concept, you can easily determine the present value of a sum to be received in the future, equal annual future withdrawals available from an initial deposit, and the initial deposit that would generate a given stream of equal annual withdrawals. These procedures, like future value concepts, allow you to place monetary values on long-term financial goals.

EXAMPLE: Comparing the Value of Money Over Time

Why would you be willing to pay about $9,524 for the right to receive $10,000 in about a year when the interest rate is 5 percent a year? You'd pay $9,542 today because, if invested at 5%, it would grow to $10,000 in a year. Alternatively viewed, $9,542 is the *present value* of the $10,000 *future value* to be received in a year given that you can invest at 5 percent. Thus, monetary values at different points in time may be compared by considering the present amount that would need to be invested to produce the given future amount.

TEST YOURSELF

2-14 Why is it important to use time value of money concepts in setting personal financial goals?

2-15 What is compounding? Explain the rule of 72.

2-16 When might you use future value? Present value? Give specific examples.

Planning Over a Lifetime: *Budgeting*

While budgeting is important across all stages of the life cycle, here are some key considerations in each stage.

Independent Lifestyle (20s)	Family and Career Development (30s–40s)	Mature Lifestyle (50s–60s)	Retirement (65+)
✓ Develop financial record-keeping system.	✓ Revise budget in light of family and career financial changes.	✓ Revise budget to reflect typically higher income relative to expenses.	✓ Revise budget to adapt to retirement living expenses, health costs, insurance needs, and income.
✓ Develop a budget and carefully track expenses.	✓ Budget amount to save for children's education.	✓ Evaluate projected expenses and housing for retirement planning.	✓ Draw on retirement income sources and accumulated assets.
✓ Budget savings each month and build up an emergency fund.	✓ Determine and set aside retirement contribution.	✓ More aggressively budget to increase retirement contributions.	✓ Spend to meet previously determined long-term financial goals.
✓ Develop personal balance sheet and income statement, and calculate net worth at least annually.	✓ Spend to meet previously determined short- and medium-term financial goals.	✓ Spend to meet previously determined medium-term financial goals.	✓ Update personal balance sheet and income statement, and calculate net worth at least annually.
✓ Develop short-, medium-, and long-term financial goals.	✓ Update personal balance sheet and income statement, and calculate net worth at least annually.	✓ Update personal balance sheet and income statement, and calculate net worth at least annually.	

Financial Impact of Personal Choices
No Budget, No Plan: Sean Bought a Boat!

Sean is 28 and has a good job as a sales rep. He's always found budgeting boring and has been intending to start a financial plan for years.

Recently Sean went out with some friends on a rented boat to fish. He had a great time and saw a boat sale on his way home. Before he knew it, the salesman convinced Sean that the deal was just too good to pass up. So Sean bought a $10,000 boat and financed 80 percent of the cost for the next 5 years. Sean now finds himself relying more on his credit card to get by each month.

What if Sean had kept track of his money, used a budget, and had a set of financial goals? Knowing where his money went and having a financial plan would have increased the chance that Sean would make more deliberate, informed financial decisions.

Summary

Key Terms

Answers to Test Yourself

You can find answers to these questions on this book's companion website. Look for it at *www.cengagebrain.com*. Search for this book by its title, and then add it to your dashboard.

Key Financial Relationships

Concept	Financial Relationship	Page Number
Balance Sheet Identity	Total Assets = Total Liabilities + Net Worth	46
Income & Expenditures Identity	Income − Expenses = Cash Surplus (or Deficit)	51
Future Value of a Single Amount	Future Value = Amount Invested × Future Value Factor	70
Future Value of an Annuity	Yearly Savings = Future Amount of Money Desired/Future Value Annuity Factor	70
Rule of 72	Number of Years to Double Money = 72/Annual Compound Interest Rate	71
Present Value of a Single Amount	Present Value = Future Value × Present Value Factor	71
Present Value of an Annuity	Annual Withdrawal = Initial Deposit/Present Value Annuity Factor	72

Key Financial Relationship Problem Set

1. ***Balance Sheet Identity.*** David Allen would like to better understand where he stands financially. He has total assets of $175,000 and total liabilities of $95,000. What is David's net worth?

   Solution: Total Assets = Total Liabilities + Net Worth, which implies that Net Worth = Total Assets − Total Liabilities = $175,000 − $95,000 = $80,000.

2. ***Income & Expenditures Identity.*** Ashley Warren earned $48,500 last year while paying $12,000 in housing expenses, $2,400 on utilities, $2,000 on food, $15,000 in miscellaneous expenses, and $7,663 in taxes. What cash surplus or deficit did Ashley earn last year?

   Solution: Income − Expenses = Cash Surplus (or Deficit). In Ashley's case, Income = $48,500 and Expenses = $12,000 + $2,400 + $2,000 + $15,000 + $7,663 = $39,063. Thus, Ashley generated a cash surplus of $48,500 − $39,063 = $9,437.

3. **Future Value of a Single Amount.** Stan Davis has saved $8,000 and wants to invest this single amount for the next 10 years. He believes that he can earn a 7 percent annual return in a moderately risky portfolio. How much should Stan's portfolio be worth in 10 years?

   Solution: Future value = Amount Invested × Future Value Factor. The future value interest factor for 10 years and 7 percent in Appendix A is 1.967. Thus, in 10 years Stan's portfolio is expected to be worth $8,000 × 1.967 = $15,736.

4. **Future Value of an Annuity.** Alice Tobias is 30 years of age and wants to know how much she needs to invest every year to have $100,000 in her account by the time she turns 60. She expects to earn 6 percent per year. What answer can you provide to Alice?

   Solution: Yearly Savings = Future Amount of Money Desired/Future Value Annuity Factor. The future value annuity factor for 30 years and 6 percent in Appendix B is 79.058. Alice should invest a yearly amount of $100,000/79.058 = $1,264.89 if she wants to have $100,000 in her account at the age of 60.

5. **Rule of 72.** Carla Martinez has saved $6,500. How long will it take for Carla's savings to double if she is able to earn 4 percent a year?

   Solution: Number of Years to Double Money = 72/Annual Compound Interest Rate. Carla's savings should double to $13,000 in 72/4 = 18 years.

6. **Present Value of a Single Amount.** Van Tran would like to have $150,000 in his investment account in 20 years. He would like to invest a single sum that will grow to that goal at 4 percent a year. What amount should Van invest?

   Solution: Present Value = Future Value × Present Value Factor. The present value interest factor for 20 years and 4 percent in Appendix C is 0.456. Van would consequently need to invest $150,000 × 0.456 = $68,400 in order for this sum to grow to $150,000 in 20 years.

7. **Present Value of an Annuity.** Lee Zorn wants to help his parents plan for their retirement. They're about to retire and have built up a nest egg of $425,000. Lee would like to let his parents know how much they could plan to withdraw from this fund each year over the next 25 years of retirement if they can earn 6 percent.

   Solution: Annual Withdrawal = Initial Deposit/Present Value Annuity Factor. The present value annuity factor for 25 years and 6 percent in Appendix D is 12.783. Lee can tell his parents that they should be able to withdraw $425,000/12.873 = $33,014.84 per year for the next 25 years.

Financial Planning Exercises

LG2, 3, p. 45, 51

1. **Preparing financial statements.** Chad Livingston is preparing his balance sheet and income and expense statement for the year ending June 30, 2017. He is having difficulty classifying six items and asks for your help. Which, if any, of the following transactions are assets, liabilities, income, or expense items?
   a. Chad rents a house for $1,350 a month.
   b. On June 21, 2017, Chad bought diamond earrings for his wife and charged them using his MasterCard. The earrings cost $900, but he hasn't yet received the bill.
   c. Chad borrowed $3,500 from his parents last fall, but so far, he has made no payments to them.
   d. Chad makes monthly payments of $225 on an installment loan; about half of it is interest, and the balance is repayment of principal. He has 20 payments left, totaling $4,500.
   e. Chad paid $3,800 in taxes during the year and is due a tax refund of $650, which he hasn't yet received.
   f. Chad invested $2,300 in some common stock.

2. ***Projecting financial statements.*** Put yourself 10 years into the future. Construct a fairly detailed and realistic balance sheet and income and expense statement reflecting what you would like to achieve by that time.

3. ***Preparing personal balance sheet. Use Worksheet 2.1.*** Denise Fisher's banker has asked her to submit a personal balance sheet as of June 30, 2017, in support of an application for a $6,000 home improvement loan. She comes to you for help in preparing it. So far, she has made the following list of her assets and liabilities as of June 30, 2017:

Cash on hand	$70	
Balance in checking account	180	
Balance in money market deposit account with		
Southwest Savings	650	
Bills outstanding:		
Telephone	$20	
Electricity	70	
Charge account balance	190	
Visa	180	
MasterCard	220	
Taxes	400	
Insurance	220	1,300
Condo and property		68,000
Condo mortgage loan		52,000
Automobile: 2012 Honda Civic		12,000
Installment loan balances:		
Auto loans	3,000	
Furniture loan	500	3,500
Personal property:		
Furniture	1,050	
Clothing	900	1,950
Investments:		
U.S. government savings bonds	500	
Stock of Harvester Corp.	3,000	3,500

From the data given, prepare Denise Fisher's balance sheet, dated June 30, 2017 (follow the balance sheet form shown in Worksheet 2.1). Then evaluate her balance sheet relative to the following factors: (a) solvency, (b) liquidity, and (c) equity in her dominant asset.

4. ***Preparing income and expense statement. Use Worksheet 2.2.*** Bill and Nancy Ballinger are about to construct their income and expense statement for the year ending December 31, 2017. Bill is finishing up college and currrently has no income. They have put together the following income and expense information for 2017:

Nancy's salary	$47,000
Reimbursement for travel expenses	1,950
Interest on:	
Savings account	110
Bonds of Alpha Corporation	70
Groceries	4,150
Rent	9,600
Utilities	960

Gas and auto expenses	650
Bill's tuition, books, and supplies	3,300
Books, magazines, and periodicals	280
Clothing and other miscellaneous expenses	2,700
Cost of photographic equipment purchased with charge card	2,200
Amount paid to date on photographic equipment	1,600
Nancy's travel expenses	1,950
Purchase of a used car (cost)	9,750
Outstanding loan balance on car	7,300
Purchase of bonds in Alpha Corporation	4,900

Using the information provided, prepare an income and expense statement for the Ballingers for the year ending December 31, 2017 (follow the form shown in Worksheet 2.2).

LG5, p. 60

5. **Preparing cash budget.** Richard and Elizabeth Walker are preparing their cash budget. Help the Walkers reconcile the following differences, giving reasons to support your answers.
   a. Their only source of income is Richard's salary, which amounts to $5,000 a month before taxes. Elizabeth wants to show the $5,000 as their monthly income, whereas Richard argues that his take-home pay of $3,917 is the correct value to show.
   b. Elizabeth wants to make a provision for fun money, an idea that Richard cannot understand. He asks, "Why do we need fun money when everything is provided for in the budget?"

LG5, p. 60

6. **Identifying missing budget items.** Here is a portion of Chuck Schwartz's budget record for a recent month. Fill in the blanks in columns 5 and 6.

Item (1)	Amount Budgeted (2)	Amount Spent (3)	Beginning Balance (4)	Surplus (Deficit) (5)	Cumulative Surplus (Deficit) (6)
Rent	$550	$575	$50	$ _____	$ _____
Utilities	150	145	15	_____	_____
Food	510	475	−45	_____	_____
Auto	75	95	−25	_____	_____
Recreation and entertainment	100	110	−50	_____	_____

LG5, p. 60

7. **Personal cash budget. Use Worksheet 2.3.** Prepare a record of your income and expenses for the last 30 days; then prepare a personal cash budget for the next three months. (Use the format in Worksheet 2.3, but fill out only three months and the Total column.) Use the cash budget to control and regulate your expenses during the next month. Discuss the impact of the budget on your spending behavior, as well as any differences between your expected and actual spending patterns.

LG6, p. 69

8. **Calculating present and future values.** Use future or present value techniques to solve the following problems.
   a. Starting with $15,000, how much will you have in 10 years if you can earn 6 percent on your money? If you can earn only 4 percent?
   b. If you inherited $45,000 today and invested all of it in a security that paid a 7 percent rate of return, how much would you have in 25 years?
   c. If the average new home costs $275,000 today, how much will it cost in 10 years if the price increases by 5 percent each year?
   d. You think that in 15 years, it will cost $212,000 to provide your child with a 4-year college education. Will you have enough if you take $70,000 today and invest it for the next 15 years at 5 percent? If you start from scratch, how much will you have to save each year to have $212,000 in 15 years if you can earn a 4 percent rate of return on your investments?

e. If you can earn 4 percent, how much will you have to save each year if you want to retire in 35 years with $1 million?

f. You plan to have $750,000 in savings and investments when you retire at age 60. Assuming that you earn an average of 8 percent on this portfolio, what is the maximum annual withdrawal you can make over a 25-year period of retirement?

LG6, p. 69

9. **Evaluating a savings goal.** Over the past several years, Catherine Lee has been able to save regularly. As a result, she has $54,188 in savings and investments today. She wants to establish her own business in 5 years and feels she will need $100,000 to do so.

a. If she can earn 4 percent on her money, how much will her $54,188 in savings/investments be worth in 5 years? Will Catherine have the $100,000 she needs? If not, how much more money will she need?

b. Given your answer to part **a,** how much will Catherine have to save each year over the next 5 years to accumulate the additional money? Assume that she can earn interest at a rate of 4 percent.

c. If Catherine can afford to save only $4,000 a year, then given your answer to part a, will she have the $100,000 she needs to start her own business in 5 years?

LG6, p. 69

10. **Funding a retirement goal.** Chris Jones wishes to have $800,000 in a retirement fund 20 years from now. He can create the retirement fund by making a single lump-sum deposit today.

a. If he can earn 6 percent on his investments, how much must Chris deposit today to create the retirement fund? If he can earn only 4 percent on his investments? Compare and discuss the results of your calculations.

b. If, upon retirement in 20 years, Chris plans to invest the $800,000 in a fund that earns 4 percent, what is the maximum annual withdrawal he can make over the following 15 years?

c. How much would Chris need to have on deposit at retirement to annually withdraw $35,000 over the 15 years if the retirement fund earns 4 percent?

d. To achieve his annual withdrawal goal of $35,000 calculated in part **c,** how much more than the amount calculated in part **a** must Chris deposit today in an investment earning 4 percent annual interest?

LG6, p. 69

11. **Funding a college goal.** Dan Weaver wants to set up a fund to pay for his daughter's education. In order to pay her expenses, he will need $23,000 in four years, $24,300 in five years, $26,000 in six years, and $28,000 in seven years. If he can put money into a fund that pays 4 percent interest, what lump-sum payment must Dan place in the fund today to meet his college funding goals?

LG6, p. 69

12. **Calculating expected future value of investments.** Jessica Wright has always been interested in stocks. She has decided to invest $2,000 once every year into an equity mutual fund that is expected to produce a return of 6 percent a year for the foreseeable future. Jessica is really curious how much money she can reasonably expect her investment to be worth in 20 years. What would you tell her?

Applying Personal Finance

What's Your Condition?

Financial statements reflect your financial condition. They help you measure where you are now. Then, as time passes and you prepare your financial statements periodically, you can use them to track your progress toward financial goals. Good financial statements are also a must when you apply for a loan. This project will help you to evaluate your current financial condition.

Look back at the discussion in this chapter on balance sheets and income and expense statements, and prepare your own. If you're doing this for the first time, it may not be as easy as it sounds! Use the following questions to help you along.

80   Part 1 | Foundations of Financial Planning

1. Have you included all your assets at fair market value (not historical cost) on your balance sheet?

2. Have you included all your debt balances as liabilities on your balance sheet? (Don't take your monthly payment amounts multiplied by the number of payments you have left—this total includes future interest.)

3. Have you included all items of income on your income and expense statement? (Remember, your paycheck is income and not an asset on your balance sheet.)

4. Have you included all debt payments as expenses on your income and expense statement? (Your phone bill is an expense for this month if you've already paid it. If the bill is still sitting on your desk staring you in the face, it's a liability on your balance sheet.)

5. Are there occasional expenses that you've forgotten about, or hidden expenses such as entertainment that you have overlooked? Look back through your checkbook, spending diary, or any other financial records to find these occasional or infrequent expenses.

6. Remember that items go on either the balance sheet or the income and expense statement, but not on both. For example, the $350 car payment you made this month is an expense on your income and expense statement. The remaining $15,000 balance on your car loan is a liability on your balance sheet, while the fair market value of your car at $17,500 is an asset.

After completing your statements, calculate your solvency, liquidity, savings, and debt service ratios. Now, use your statements and ratios to assess your current financial condition. Do you like where you are? If not, how can you get where you want to be? Use your financial statements and ratios to help you formulate plans for the future.

CRITICAL THINKING CASES

2.1 The Beckers' Version of Financial Planning

Terry and Evelyn Becker are a married couple in their mid-20s. Terry has a good start as an electrical engineer and Evelyn works as a sales representative. Since their marriage four years ago, Terry and Evelyn have been living comfortably. Their income has exceeded their expenses, and they have accumulated an enviable net worth. This includes $10,000 that they have built up in savings and investments. Because their income has always been more than enough for them to have the lifestyle they desire, the Beckers have done no financial planning.

Evelyn has just learned that she's pregnant. She's concerned about how they'll make ends meet if she quits work after their child is born. Each time she and Terry discuss the matter, he tells her not to worry because "we've always managed to pay our bills on time." Evelyn can't understand his attitude because her income will be completely eliminated. To convince Evelyn that there's no need for concern, Terry points out that their expenses last year, but for the common stock purchase, were about equal to his take-home pay. With an anticipated promotion and an expected 10 percent pay raise, his income next year should exceed this amount. Terry also points out that they can reduce luxuries (trips, recreation, and entertainment) and can always draw down their savings or sell some of their stock if they get in a bind. When Evelyn asks about the long-run implications for their finances, Terry says there will be "no problems" because his boss has assured him that he has a bright future with the engineering firm. Terry also emphasizes that Evelyn can go back to work in a few years if necessary.

Despite Terry's arguments, Evelyn feels that they should carefully examine their financial condition in order to do some serious planning. She has gathered the following financial information for the year ending December 31, 2017:

Salaries	Take-Home Pay	Gross Salary
Terry	*$52,500*	*$76,000*
Evelyn	*29,200*	*42,000*

Item	Amount
Food	$5,902
Clothing	2,300
Mortgage payments, including property taxes of $1,400	11,028
Travel and entertainment card balances	2,000
Gas, electric, water expenses	1,990
Household furnishings	4,500
Telephone	640
Auto loan balance	4,650
Common stock investments	7,500
Bank credit card balances	675
Federal income taxes	22,472
State income tax	5,040
Social security contributions	9,027
Credit card loan payments	2,210
Cash on hand	85
2012 Nissan Sentra	10,500
Medical expenses (unreimbursed)	600
Homeowner's insurance premiums paid	1,300
Checking account balance	485
Auto insurance premiums paid	1,600
Transportation	2,800
Cable television	680
Estimated value of home	185,000
Trip to Europe	5,000
Recreation and entertainment	4,000
Auto loan payments	2,150
Money market account balance	2,500
Purchase of common stock	7,500
Addition to money market account	500
Mortgage on home	148,000

Critical Thinking Questions

1. Using this information and Worksheets 2.1 and 2.2, construct the Beckers' balance sheet and income and expense statement for the year ending December 31, 2017.
2. Comment on the Beckers' financial condition regarding (a) solvency, (b) liquidity, (c) savings, and (d) ability to pay debts promptly. If the Beckers continue to manage their finances as described, what do you expect the long-run consequences to be? Discuss.
3. Critically evaluate the Beckers' approach to financial planning. Point out any fallacies in Terry's observations, and be sure to mention (a) implications for the long term, as well as (b) the potential impact of inflation in general and specifically on their net worth. What procedures should they use to get their financial house in order? Be sure to discuss the role that long- and short-term financial plans and budgets might play.

2.2 Brooke Stauffer Learns to Budget

Brooke Stauffer recently graduated from college and moved to Atlanta to take a job as a market research analyst. She was pleased to be financially independent and was sure that, with her $45,000 salary, she could cover her living expenses and have plenty of money left over to furnish her studio apartment and enjoy the wide variety of social and recreational activities available in Atlanta. She opened several department-store charge accounts and obtained a bank credit card.

For a while, Brooke managed pretty well on her monthly take-home pay of $2,893, but by the end of 2017, she was having trouble fully paying all her credit card charges each month. Concerned that her spending had gotten out of control and that she was barely making it from paycheck to paycheck, she decided to list her expenses for the past calendar year and develop a budget. She hoped not only to reduce her credit card debt but also to begin a regular savings program.

Brooke prepared the following summary of expenses for 2017:

Item	Annual Expenditure
Rent	$12,000
Auto insurance	1,855
Auto loan payments	3,840
Auto expenses (gas, repairs, and fees)	1,560
Clothing	3,200
Installment loan for stereo	540
Personal care	424
Phone	600
Cable TV	440
Gas and electricity	1,080
Medical care	120
Dentist	70
Groceries	2,500
Dining out	2,600
Furniture purchases	1,200
Recreation and entertainment	2,900
Other expenses	600

After reviewing her 2017 expenses, Brooke made the following assumptions about her expenses for 2018:

1. All expenses will remain at the same levels, with these exceptions:
   a. Auto insurance, auto expenses, gas and electricity, and groceries will increase 5 percent.
   b. Clothing purchases will decrease to $2,250.
   c. Phone and cable TV will increase $5 per month.
   d. Furniture purchases will decrease to $660, most of which is for a new television.
   e. She will take a one-week vacation to Colorado in July, at a cost of $2,100.
2. All expenses will be budgeted in equal monthly installments except for the vacation and these items:
   a. Auto insurance is paid in two installments due in June and December.
   b. She plans to replace the brakes on his car in February, at a cost of $220.
   c. Visits to the dentist will be made in March and September.
3. She will eliminate his bank credit card balance by making extra monthly payments of $75 during each of the first six months.
4. Regarding her income, Brooke has just received a small raise, so her take-home pay will be $3,200 per month.

Critical Thinking Questions

1. a. Prepare a preliminary cash budget for Brooke for the year ending December 31, 2018, using the format shown in Worksheet 2.3.
    b. Compare Brooke's estimated expenses with her expected income and make recommendations that will help her balance his budget.
2. Make any necessary adjustments to Brooke's estimated monthly expenses, and revise her annual cash budget for the year ending December 31, 2018, using Worksheet 2.3.
3. Analyze the budget and advise Brooke on her financial situation. Suggest some long-term, intermediate, and short-term financial goals for Brooke, and discuss some steps she can take to reach them.

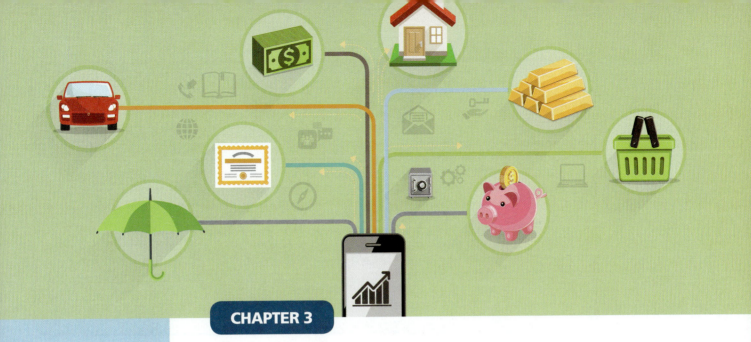

CHAPTER 3

Preparing Your Taxes

LEARNING GOALS

LG1 Discuss the basic principles of income taxes and determine your filing status.

LG2 Describe the sources of gross income and adjustments to income, differentiate between standard and itemized deductions and exemptions, and calculate taxable income.

LG3 Prepare a basic tax return using the appropriate tax forms and rate schedules.

LG4 Explain who needs to pay estimated taxes, when to file or amend your return, and how to handle an audit.

LG5 Know where to get help with your taxes and how software can make tax return preparation easier.

LG6 Implement an effective tax planning strategy.

How Will This Affect Me?

There's an old joke that people who complain about taxes can be divided into two groups: men and women. This chapter helps you pursue the tax-planning goal of maximizing the money that you get to keep by legally minimizing the taxes you have to pay. Income, various adjustments to income, deductions, and credits are considered in computing taxes. The chapter walks through the steps in completing representative tax returns. The impact of Social Security taxes and tax shelters are considered. And a framework for choosing a professional tax preparer or tax preparation software is provided. After reading this chapter you should be able to prepare your own taxes or to better understand and evaluate how your taxes are prepared by software or a tax professional.

Jose Luis Pelaez Inc/Blend Images/Jupiter Images

3-1 UNDERSTANDING FEDERAL INCOME TAX PRINCIPLES

taxes
The dues paid for membership in our society; a cost of living in this country.

Taxes are dues that we pay for membership in our society; they're the cost of living in this country. Federal, state, and local tax receipts fund government activities and a wide variety of public services, from national defense to local libraries. Administering and enforcing federal tax laws is the responsibility of the Internal Revenue Service (IRS), a part of the U.S. Department of Treasury.

Because federal income tax is generally the largest tax you'll pay, you are wise to make tax planning an important part of personal financial planning. A typical American family currently pays *more than one-third of its gross income in taxes:* federal income and Social Security taxes and numerous state and local income, sales, and property taxes. You may think of tax planning as an activity to do between the beginning of the year and April 15, the usual filing deadline, but you should make tax planning a year-round activity. It's always wise to consider tax consequences when preparing and revising your financial plans and making major financial decisions, such as buying a home and making any investment decisions at all.

The overriding objective of tax planning is simple: *to maximize the amount of money that you can keep legally by minimizing the amount of taxes you pay.* So long as it's done honestly and within the tax codes, there is nothing immoral, illegal, or unethical about trying to minimize your tax bill. Most tax planning focuses on ways to minimize income and estate taxes. In this chapter, we concentrate on *income taxes paid by individuals*—particularly the federal income tax, the largest and most important tax for most taxpayers. Although you may currently pay little or no taxes, we use a mid-career couple to demonstrate the key aspects of individual taxation. This approach will give you a good understanding of your future tax situation and allow you to develop realistic financial plans.

In addition to federal income tax, there are other forms of taxes to contend with. For example, additional federal taxes may be levied on self-employment or outside consulting income and on certain types of transactions. At the state and local levels, sales transactions, income, property ownership, and licenses may be taxed. Because most individuals have to pay many of these other types of taxes, you should evaluate their impact on your financial decisions. Thus, a person saving to purchase a new automobile costing $25,000 should realize that the state and local sales taxes, as well as the cost of license plates and registration, may add another $2,000 or more to the total cost of the car.

Behavior Matters

Do We Really Value Paying Taxes After All?

Surprisingly, your brain may like paying taxes! Recent research suggests that people can feel good about paying taxes that improve others' well-being. While most people would prefer to keep their money rather than pay taxes, paying taxes still is not the same thing as throwing the money away. Taxes can be viewed, even if only subconsciously, as a social good. And people don't like inequality and seek to preserve a positive self-image, which means that most are unlikely to cheat on their taxes. Interestingly, there is evidence that many people work harder when they realize they will be taxed. In a recent experiment, participants worked harder when paid $100 and there was a $10 tax than when they were paid $90 with no taxes due.

So what could explain this? It's important for people to feel that their taxes actually do some good. When people clearly know what their taxes are used for—and if it appears to be for the common good—they can actually find paying taxes somewhat satisfying. This challenges governments everywhere to make their tax systems fully transparent and to explicitly show that the money is being spent in a positive way. Doing so makes sense in a democracy and creates the right incentives for taxpayers.

Source: Adapted from Patrick Temple-West, "Surprise, Your Brain Might Value Paying Taxes," http://blogs.reuters.com/unstructuredfinance/2012/04/02/surprise-your-brain-might-value-paying-taxes/, accessed July 2015; based on a research article by Iwan Djanali and Damien Sheehan-Connor, "Tax affinity hypothesis: Do we really hate paying taxes?" *Journal of Economic Psychology*, August 2012.

Because tax laws are complicated and subject to frequent revision, we'll present key concepts and show how they apply to common tax situations. Provisions of the tax code may change annually for tax rates, amounts and types of deductions and personal exemptions, and similar items. The tax tables, calculations, and sample tax returns presented in this chapter are based on the tax laws applicable to the calendar year 2014. Nonetheless, *although tax rates and other provisions will change, the basic procedures will remain the same.* Before preparing your tax returns, be sure to review the current regulations; IRS publications and other tax preparation guides may be helpful.

3-1a The Economics of Income Taxes

Unsurprisingly, most people simply don't like paying taxes. Some of this feeling likely stems from the widely held perception that a lot of government spending amounts to little more than bureaucratic waste. But a good deal of this feeling is probably because taxpayers don't always perceive that they receive tangible benefits for their money. After all, paying taxes isn't like spending $7,000 on a European vacation. We too often tend to overlook or take for granted the many services provided by the taxes we pay—public schools and state colleges, roads and highways, and parks and recreational facilities, not to mention police and fire protection, retirement benefits, and many other health and social services.

Income taxes are the major source of revenue for the federal government. Personal income taxes are scaled on progressive rates. To illustrate how this **progressive tax structure** works, consider the following data for single taxpayers filing 2014 returns:

income taxes
A type of tax levied on taxable income by the federal government and by many state and local governments.

progressive tax structure
A tax structure in which the larger the amount of taxable income, the higher the rate at which it is taxed.

Taxable Income	Tax Rate
$1 to $9,075	10%
$9,076 to $36,900	15%
$36,901 to $89,350	25%
$89,351 to $186,350	28%
$186,351 to $405,100	33%
$405,101 to $406,750	35%
Over $406,750	39.6%

Of course, any nontaxable income can be viewed as being in the 0 percent tax bracket. As taxable income moves from a lower to a higher bracket, the higher rate applies *only to the additional taxable income in that bracket,* not to the entire taxable income.

EXAMPLE: Applying Tax Rates

Two single brothers, Finn and Connor, have taxable incomes of $50,000 and $100,000, respectively. They calculate their tax liabilities as follows:

Name	Taxable Income	Tax Calculation	Tax Liability
Finn	$50,000	= [($50,000 − $36,900) × 0.25]	
		+ [($36,900 − $9,075) × 0.15]	
		+ [$9,075 × 0.10]	
		= $3,275 + $4,173.75 + $907.50 =	$8,356.25
Connor	$100,000	= [($100,000 − $89,350) × 0.28]	
		+ [(89,350 − $36,900) × 0.25]	
		+ [(36,900 − $9,075) × 0.15]	
		+ [$9,075 × 0.10]	
		= $2,982 + $13,112.5 + $4,173.75 + $907.5	$21,175.75

Note that Finn pays the 25 percent rate only on the portion of his $50,000 taxable income that exceeds $36,900. Due to this kind of progressive scale, the more money you make, the progressively more you pay in taxes. Although Connor's taxable income is twice that of Finn's, his income tax is about 2½ times higher than his brother's.

The tax rate for each bracket—10 percent, 15 percent, 25 percent, 28 percent, 33 percent, 35 percent, and 39.6 percent—is called the **marginal tax rate**, or the rate applied to the next dollar of taxable income. When you relate the tax liability to the level of taxable income earned, the tax rate, called the **average tax rate**, drops considerably.

marginal tax rate
The tax rate that you pay on the next dollar of taxable income.

average tax rate
The rate at which each dollar of taxable income is taxed on average; calculated by dividing the tax liability by taxable income.

EXAMPLE: Calculating an Average Tax Rate

Finn paid taxes of $8,356.25 on taxable income of $50,000, which implies an average tax rate of $8,356.25/$50,000 = 16.7 percent. His brother, Connor, paid taxes of $21,175.75 on income of $100,000 for an average tax rate of $21,175.75/$100,000) = 21.2 percent. While taxes are progressive, the average size of the bite is not as bad as the stated tax rate might suggest.

3-1b Your Filing Status

The taxes you pay depend in part on your *filing status,* which is based on your marital status and family situation on the last day of your tax year (usually December 31). Filing status affects whether you're required to file an income tax return, the amount of your standard deduction, and your tax rate. If you have a choice of filing status, you should calculate your taxes both ways and choose the status that results in the lower tax liability.

There are five different filing status categories:

- **Single taxpayers:** Unmarried or legally separated from their spouses by either a separation or final divorce decree.
- **Married filing jointly:** Married couples who combine their income and allowable deductions and file one tax return.
- **Married filing separately:** Each spouse files his or her own return, reporting only his or her income, deductions, and exemptions.
- **Head of household:** A taxpayer who is unmarried or considered unmarried and pays more than half of the cost of keeping up a home for himself or herself and an eligible dependent child or relative.
- **Qualifying widow or widower with dependent child:** A person whose spouse died within two years of the tax year (e.g., in 2012 or 2013 for the 2014 tax year) and who supports a dependent child may use joint return tax rates and is eligible for the highest standard deduction. (After the two-year period, such a person may file under the head of household status if he or she qualifies.)

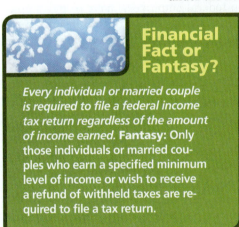

Financial Fact or Fantasy?

Every individual or married couple is required to file a federal income tax return regardless of the amount of income earned. **Fantasy:** Only those individuals or married couples who earn a specified minimum level of income or wish to receive a refund of withheld taxes are required to file a tax return.

The tax brackets (rates) and payments for married couples filing separately are now typically close to the same as for joint filers. However, because the spouses rarely account for equal amounts of taxable income and deductions, it may be advantageous in some cases for spouses to file separate returns. For instance, if one spouse has a moderate income and substantial medical expenses and the other has a low income and no medical expenses, then filing separately may provide a tax savings. It's worth your time to calculate your taxes using both scenarios to see which results in the lower amount.

Every individual or married couple who earns a specified level of income is required to file a tax return. For example: for those under 65, a single person who earned more than $10,150 and a married couple with a combined income of more than $20,300 must file a tax return (for 2014). Like the personal tax rates, these minimums are adjusted annually based on the annual rate of inflation, and they're published in the instructions accompanying each year's tax forms. If your income falls below the current minimum levels, you're not required to file a tax return. But if you had any income tax withheld during the year, you must file a tax return—even if your income falls *below* the minimum filing amount—to receive a refund of the income tax withheld.

3-1c Your Take-Home Pay

Although many of us don't give much thought to taxes until April 15 approaches, we actually are required to pay taxes as we earn income throughout the year. Under this *pay-as-you-go* system, your employer withholds (deducts) a portion of your income every pay period and sends it to the IRS to be credited to your own tax account. Self-employed persons must also prepay their taxes by forwarding part of their income to the IRS at four dates each year (referred to as quarterly estimated tax payments). The amounts withheld are based on a taxpayer's estimated tax liability. After the close of the taxable year, you calculate the actual taxes you owe and file your tax return. When you file, you receive full credit for the amount of taxes withheld (including estimated tax payments) from your income during the year and either (1) receive a refund from the IRS (if too much tax was withheld from your paycheck and/or pre-paid in estimated taxes) or (2) pay additional taxes (if the amount withheld/prepaid didn't cover your tax liability). Your employer normally withholds funds not only for federal income taxes but also for **Federal Insurance Contributions Act (FICA,** or **Social Security** and **Medicare)** taxes and, if applicable, state and local income taxes. In addition to taxes, you may have other tax deductions for items such as life and health insurance, savings plans, retirement programs, professional or union dues, or charitable

Federal Insurance Contributions Act (FICA) or social security tax
The law establishing the combined Old-Age, Survivor's, Disability, and Hospital Insurance tax levied on both employer and employee.

contributions—all of which lower your take-home pay. Your *take-home pay* is what you're left with after subtracting the amount withheld from your *gross earnings*.

Federal Withholding Taxes

The amount of **federal withholding taxes** deducted from your gross earnings each pay period depends on both the level of your earnings and the number of withholding allowances you have claimed on a form called a *W-4*, which you must complete for your employer. Withholding allowances reduce the amount of taxes withheld from your income. A taxpayer is entitled to one allowance for himself or herself, one for a nonworking spouse (if filing jointly), and one for each dependent claimed (children or parents being supported mainly by the taxpayers). In addition, you may qualify for a *special allowance* or *additional withholding allowances* under certain circumstances. Taxpayers may have to change their withholding allowances during the tax year if their employment or marital status changes.

Financial Fact or Fantasy?

The amount of federal income tax withheld depends on both your level of earnings and the number of withholding allowances claimed. **Fact:** The more you make and the fewer withholding allowances you claim, the more will be withheld from your paycheck.

FICA and Other Withholding Taxes

In addition to income tax withholding on earnings, all employed workers (except certain federal employees) have to pay a combined old-age, survivor's, disability, and hospital insurance tax under provisions of the FICA. Known more commonly as the Social Security tax, it is paid equally by employer and employee. In 2014, the total Social Security tax rate was 15.3 percent, allocating 12.4 percent to Social Security and 2.9 percent to Medicare. The 12.4 percent applies only to the first $117,000 of an employee's earnings (this number rises with national average wages), whereas the Medicare component is paid on all earnings. In 2014, self-employed persons pay the full 15.3 percent tax but can deduct 50 percent of it on their tax returns.

Most states have their own income taxes, which differ from state to state. Some cities assess income taxes as well. These state and local income taxes will also be withheld from earnings. They are deductible on federal returns, but deductibility of federal taxes on the state or local return depends on state and local laws.

TEST YOURSELF

3-1 What is a *progressive tax structure* and the economic rationale for it?

3-2 Briefly define the five filing categories available to taxpayers. When might married taxpayers choose to file separately?

3-3 Distinguish between *gross earnings* and *take-home pay*. What does the employer do with the difference?

3-4 What two factors determine the amount of federal withholding taxes that will be deducted from gross earnings each pay period? Explain.

3-2 IT'S TAXABLE INCOME THAT MATTERS

As you've no doubt gathered by now, paying your income taxes is a complex process involving several steps and many calculations. Exhibit 3.1 depicts the procedure to compute your **taxable income** and total tax liability. It looks simple enough—just subtract certain adjustments from your gross income to get your adjusted gross income; then subtract either the standard deduction or your itemized deductions and your total personal exemptions to get taxable income; and finally, calculate your taxes, subtract any tax credits from that amount, and add any other taxes to it to get your

EXHIBIT 3.1   **Calculating Your Taxable Income and Total Tax Liability Owed**

To find taxable income, you must first subtract all adjustments from gross income and then subtract deductions and personal exemptions. Your total tax liability owed includes tax on this taxable income amount, less any tax credits, plus other taxes owed.

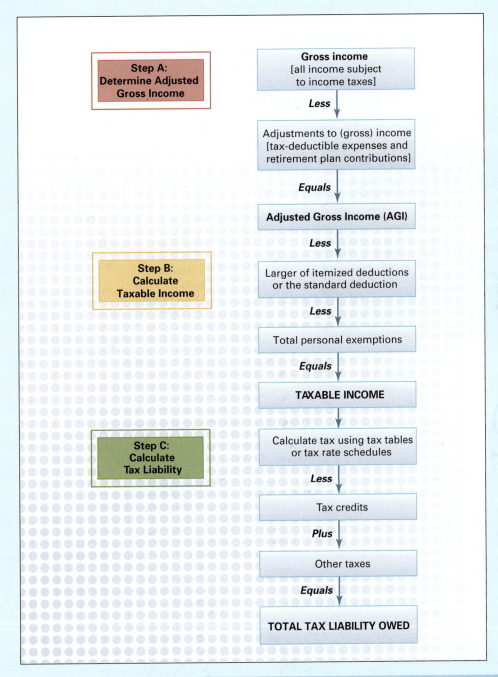

total tax liability. This isn't as easy as it sounds, however! Various sections of the Internal Revenue Code place numerous conditions and exceptions on the tax treatment and deductibility of certain income and expense items and also define certain types of income as tax exempt. As we'll see, some problems can arise in defining what you may subtract.

3-2a Gross Income

gross income
The total of all of a taxpayer's income (before any adjustments, deductions, or exemptions) subject to federal taxes; it includes active, portfolio, and passive income.

Gross income essentially includes any and all income subject to federal taxes. Here are some common forms of gross income:

- Wages and salaries
- Bonuses, commissions, and tips
- Interest and dividends received
- Alimony received
- Business and farm income
- Gains from the sale of assets
- Income from pensions and annuities
- Income from rents and partnerships
- Prizes, lottery, and gambling winnings

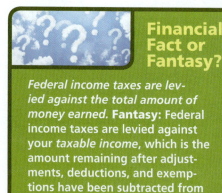

Financial Fact or Fantasy?

Federal income taxes are levied against the total amount of money earned. **Fantasy:** Federal income taxes are levied against your *taxable income*, which is the amount remaining after adjustments, deductions, and exemptions have been subtracted from gross income.

In addition to these sources of income, there are others that are considered *tax exempt* and consequently are excluded—totally or partially—from gross income. Common types of tax-exempt income include child-support payments; municipal bond interest payments; certain types of employee fringe benefits; compensation from accident, health, and life insurance policies; federal income tax refunds; gifts, inheritances, scholarships, and fellowships (limited as to amount and time); and veterans' benefits.

Three Kinds of Income

Individual income falls into one of three basic categories:

- **Active income:** Income *earned* on the job, such as wages and salaries, bonuses and tips; most other forms of *noninvestment* income, including pension income and alimony
- **Portfolio income:** Earnings (interest, dividends, and capital gains [profits on the sale of investments]) generated from most types of investment holdings; includes savings accounts, stocks, bonds, mutual funds, options, and futures
- **Passive income:** A special category that includes income derived from real estate, limited partnerships, and other forms of tax shelters

These categories limit the amount of deductions and write-offs that taxpayers can take. Specifically, the amount of allowable, deductible expenses associated with portfolio and passive income *is limited to the amount of income derived from these two sources.* For deduction purposes, you cannot combine portfolio and passive income with each other or with active income. *Investment-related expenses can be used only with portfolio income,* and with a few exceptions, *passive investment expenses can be used only to offset the income from passive investments.* All the other allowances and deductions we'll describe later are written off against the total amount of *active* income the taxpayer generates.

Capital Gains

Technically, a *capital gain* occurs whenever a capital asset (such as a stock, a bond, or real estate) is sold for more than its original cost. So, if you purchased stock for $50 per share and sold it for $60, you'd have a capital gain of $10 per share.

Capital gains are taxed at different rates, depending on the holding period. Exhibit 3.2 shows the different holding periods and applicable tax rates based on the 2014 tax brackets. As a rule, taxpayers include most capital gains as part of *portfolio income*. They will add any capital gains to the amount of dividends, interest, and rents they generate to arrive at total investment income. In addition to the rates shown in Exhibit 3.2, some higher income earners may also have to pay a 3.8 percent Medicare surtax.

Although there are no limits on the amount of capital gains taxpayers can generate, the IRS imposes some restrictions on the amount of capital losses taxpayers can take in a given year. Specifically, a taxpayer can write off capital losses, dollar for dollar, against any capital gains. After that, he or she can write off a maximum of $3,000

| EXHIBIT 3.2 | Capital Gains Tax Categories as of 2014 |

Capital gains tax rates are as low as 0 percent for low-income levels or as high as 28 percent for higher income levels and certain types of assets, so long as the holding period is more than 12 months.

Holding Period	Tax Brackets/Asset Sold (2014)	Tax on Capital Gains
Less than 12 months	All (10%, 15%, 25%, 28%, 33%, 35%, and 39.6%) - any asset sold	Same as ordinary income
Over 12 months	10% and 15% - assets other than real estate and collectibles	0%,
	25%, 33%, 35%, 39.6%	15%, or 20% (later only if in 39.6% tax bracket)
	Sale of depreciable real estate	25% on gain up to depreciation amount
	Collectibles	28% all gains from collectibles

in additional capital losses against other (active, earned) income. For example, if a taxpayer had $10,000 in capital gains and $18,000 in capital losses in 2014, only $13,000 could be written off on 2014 taxes: $10,000 against the capital gains generated in 2014 and another $3,000 against active income. The remainder—$5,000 in this case—will have to be written off in later years, in the same order as just indicated: first against any capital gains and then up to $3,000 against active income.

Financial Fact or Fantasy?

Gains on the sale of investments such as stocks, bonds, and real estate are always taxed at the lower capital gains tax rate to encourage such investment.

Fantasy: Only capital gains on investments held for longer than 12 months (long-term) qualify for tax rates lower than those on ordinary income. Short-term capital gains are taxed at ordinary income rates.

Selling Your Home: A Special Case Homeowners, for various reasons, receive special treatment in the tax codes, including the taxation of capital gains on the sale of a home. Under current law, single taxpayers can exclude from income the first $250,000 of gain on the sale of a principal residence. Married taxpayers can exclude the first $500,000. To get this favorable tax treatment, the taxpayer must own and occupy the residence as a principal residence for at least two of the five years prior to the sale. This exclusion is available on only one sale every two years. A loss on the sale of a principal residence is not deductible. This law is generally quite favorable to homeowners.

EXAMPLE: Taxes on the Sale of a Home

The Jacobs are married taxpayers who just sold their principal residence for $475,000. They had purchased their home four years earlier for $325,000. They may exclude their $150,000 gain ($475,000 − $325,000) from their income because they occupied the residence for more than two years, and the gain is less than $500,000.

3-2b Adjustments to (Gross) Income

adjustments to (gross) income
Allowable deductions from gross income, including certain employee, personal retirement, insurance, and support expenses.

Now that you've totaled your gross income, you can deduct your **adjustments to (gross) income**. These are allowable deductions from gross income, including certain employee, personal retirement, insurance, and support expenses. Most of these deductions are nonbusiness in nature.

Here are some items that can be treated as adjustments to income:

- Educator expenses (limited)
- Higher education tuition costs (limited)
- IRA contributions (limited)

- Self-employment taxes paid (limited to 50 percent of the amount paid)
- Self-employed health insurance payments
- Penalty on early withdrawal of savings
- Alimony paid
- Reimbursed moving expenses (some limits)

(*Note:* The limitations on deductions for self-directed retirement plans, such as individual retirement accounts (IRAs) and Simplified Employee Pensions (SEPs), are discussed in Chapter 14.)

After subtracting the total of all allowable adjustments to income from your gross income, you're left with **adjusted gross income (AGI)**. AGI is an important value, because it's used to calculate limits for certain itemized deductions.

adjusted gross income (AGI)
The amount of income remaining after subtracting all allowable adjustments to income from gross income.

3-2c Deductions: Standard or Itemized?

As we see from Exhibit 3.1, the next step in calculating your taxes is to subtract allowable deductions from your AGI. This may be the most complex part of the tax preparation process. You have two options: take the *standard deduction,* a fixed amount that depends on your filing status, or list your *itemized deductions* (specified tax-deductible personal expenses). Obviously, you should use the method that results in larger allowable deductions.

Standard Deduction

standard deduction
A blanket deduction that depends on the taxpayer's filing status, age, and vision and can be taken by a taxpayer whose total itemized deductions are too small.

Instead of itemizing personal deductions, a taxpayer can take the **standard deduction**, a blanket deduction that includes the various deductible expenses that taxpayers normally incur. People whose total itemized deductions are less than the standard

FINANCIAL PLANNING TIPS

Ways to Reduce Your Taxes

It is all too common for some taxpayers to overlook the following tax deductions and credits that would decrease their tax bill. While there are qualifications and limitations on these tax deductions and credits, it's worth your time to be aware of these opportunities. Keep in mind that all of these deductions are reduced by 2 percent of AGI before adding them to the other itemized deductions.

- **Medical travel expenses.** The costs of traveling to visit health care providers to receive medical care are deductible if the visits are recommended by a doctor. There is a standard mileage deduction if you drive, and you can deduct direct expenses like taxis, parking fees, and tolls.

- **Health insurance and medical expenses.** Health insurance premiums are deductible. Similarly, the cost of prescriptions and separate charges for medical coverage included in a dependent child's college fees are deductible. Medical bills that you pay for a person who is your dependent are also deductible.

- **Real estate taxes and home sale costs.** Real estate taxes paid are deductible, as are any "point" fees associated with a mortgage. Annual maintenance fees for a

condo also may be deducted because they are your share of the overall property's real estate taxes.

- **Volunteer and donation-related expenses.** When you donate to a charity or volunteer your time, the associated expenses are tax-deductible. For example, if you donate cookies to be sold by a charity, you can deduct the cost of baking them. Transportation costs can also be deducted.

- **Job search expenses.** The costs associated with looking for a new job are generally deductible. So you can write off employment placement agency fees, resume printing costs, and related travel expenses.

- **Tax and investment-related expenses.** The expenses paid for preparing your tax return are deductible. Further, any expenses associated with managing your investments are generally deductible. For example, you can write off financial advisors' fees and investment publication subscription costs.

- **College tuition tax credit.** You can get up to a $2,500 tax credit in college tuition for family members if your adjusted gross income falls within certain limits.

deduction take the standard deduction, which varies depending on the taxpayer's filing status (single, married filing jointly, and so on), age (65 or older), and vision (blind). In 2014, the standard deduction ranged from $6,200 to $17,200. For single filers, it is $6,200, and for married people filing jointly, it is $12,400. Those over 65 and those who are blind are eligible for a higher standard deduction. Each year, the standard deduction amounts are usually adjusted in response to any changes in the cost of living.

Itemized Deductions

itemized deductions
Personal expenditures that can be deducted from AGI when determining taxable income.

Itemized deductions allow taxpayers to reduce their AGI by the amount of their allowable personal expenditures. The Internal Revenue Code defines the types of nonbusiness items that can be deducted from AGI. Here are some of the more common ones:

- Medical and dental expenses (*in excess* of 10 percent of AGI for those under the age of 65)
- State, local, and foreign income and property taxes; state and local personal property taxes
- Residential mortgage interest and investment interest (limited)
- Charitable contributions (limited to 50 percent, 30 percent, or 20 percent of AGI depending on certain factors)
- Casualty and theft losses (in excess of 10 percent of AGI; reduced by $100 per loss)
- Job, investment, and other expenses (in excess of 2 percent of AGI)
- Moving expenses (some restrictions; also reimbursed expenses are deductible for those who don't itemize)

Read the instructions accompanying the tax forms for detailed descriptions of allowable deductions in each category and of qualifying factors such as distance from previous residence.

Choosing the Better Option

Your decision to take the standard deduction or itemize deductions may change from year to year, or even in the same year. Taxpayers who find they've chosen the wrong option and paid too much may recalculate their tax using the other method and claim a refund for the difference. For example, suppose that you computed and paid your taxes, which amounted to $2,450, using the standard deduction. A few months later you find that had you itemized your deductions, your taxes would have been only $1,950. Using the appropriate forms, you can file an *amended return (Form 1040X)* showing a $500 refund ($2,450 − $1,950). To avoid having to file an amended return because you used the wrong deduction technique, estimate your deductions using both the standard and itemized deduction amounts and then choose the one that results in lower taxes. Most taxpayers use the standard deduction, but homeowners who pay home mortgage interest and property taxes generally itemize because those expenses alone typically exceed the allowable standard deduction.

3-2d Exemptions

exemptions
Deductions from AGI based on the number of persons supported by the taxpayer's income.

There's one more calculation for determining your taxable income. Deductions from AGI based on the number of persons supported by the taxpayer's income are called **exemptions**. A taxpayer can claim an exemption for himself or herself, his or her spouse, and any *dependents*. A dependent must be either a qualified child or a qualified relative. A major requirement for a qualified child is the age test—the child must less than 18 or, if a full-time student, 24. A major requirement for a qualified relative is the gross income test—gross income must be less than the amount of the exemption, which was $3,950 in 2014. All dependents must have a social security number, which can be a problem in the year of adoption for parents of adopted children.

MONKEY BUSINESS IMAGES/SHUTTERSTOCK.COM

So a college student, for example, could be 20 years old and still be claimed as an exemption by her parents, so long as all other dependency requirements are met. In 2014, each exemption claimed was worth $3,950. The personal exemption amount is tied to the cost of living and changes annually based on the prevailing rate of inflation.

A personal exemption can be claimed only once. If a child is *eligible* to be claimed as an exemption by her parents, then she doesn't have the choice of using a personal exemption on her own tax return, regardless of whether the parents use her exemption.

In 2014, a family of four could take total exemptions of $15,800—that is, 4 × $3,950. Subtracting the amount claimed for itemized deductions (or the standard deduction) and exemptions from AGI results in the amount of *taxable income,* which is the basis on which taxes are calculated. A taxpayer who makes $50,000 a year may have only, say, $25,000 in taxable income after adjustments, deductions, and exemptions. It is the *lower,* taxable income figure that determines how much tax an individual must pay.

TEST YOURSELF

3-5   Define and differentiate between *gross income* and *AGI.* Name several types of tax-exempt income. What is *passive income?*

3-6   What is a *capital gain,* and how is it treated for tax purposes?

3-7   If you itemize your deductions, you may include certain expenses as part of your itemized deductions. Discuss five types of itemized deductions and the general rules that apply to them.

3-8   Dan Caldwell was married on January 15, 2014. His wife, Catherine, is a full-time student at the university and earns $625 a month working in the library. How many personal exemptions will Dan and Catherine be able to claim on their joint return? Would it make any difference if Catherine's parents paid for more than 50 percent of her support? Explain.

3-3   CALCULATING AND FILING YOUR TAXES

LG3   Now that we've reviewed the general principles of federal income taxes and the components of taxable income, we can direct our attention to calculating the amount of income tax due. To do this, we need to address several key aspects of measuring taxable income and taxes: (1) the tax rates applicable to various types of personal income, (2) tax credits, (3) the basic tax forms and schedules, and (4) the procedures for determining tax liability.

3-3a Tax Rates

As we saw earlier in this chapter, to find the amount of *taxable income,* we subtract itemized deductions (or the standard deduction for non-itemizers) *and* personal exemptions from AGI. *Both itemizers and non-itemizers* use this procedure, which is a key calculation in determining your tax liability. It is *reported taxable income* that determines the amount of income subject to federal income taxes. Once you know the amount of your taxable income, you can refer to *tax rate tables* to find the amount of taxes you owe. (When actually filing a tax return, taxpayers with taxable income of more than $100,000 must instead use the tax rate schedules.)

Tax rates vary not only with the amount of reported taxable income but also with filing status. Thus, different tax rate schedules apply to each filing category, as shown in Exhibit 3.3. The vast majority of taxpayers fall into the first three brackets and are subject to tax rates of either 10 percent, 15 percent, or 25 percent.

EXHIBIT 3.3   **Sample Tax Rate Schedules**

Tax rates levied on personal income vary with the amount of reported taxable income and the taxpayer's filing status.

2014
Tax Rate
Schedules

Schedule X—If your filing status is **Single**

If your taxable income is: Over—	But not over—	The tax is:	of the amount over—
$0	$9,075	------ 10%	$0
9,075	36,900	$907.50 + 15	9,075
36,900	89,350	5,081.25 + 25	36,900
89,350	186,350	18,193.75 + 28	89,350
186,350	405,100	45,353.75 + 33	186,350
405,100	406,750	117,541.25 + 35	405,100
406,750	------	118,118.75 + 39.6	406,750

Schedule Y-1—If your filing status is **Married filing jointly** or **Qualifying widow(er)**

If your taxable income is: Over—	But not over—	The tax is:	of the amount over—
$0	$18,150	------ 10%	$0
18,150	73,800	$1,815.00 + 15	18,150
73,800	148,850	10,162.50 + 25	73,800
148,850	226,850	28,925.00 + 28	148,850
226,850	405,100	50,765.00 + 33	226,850
405,100	457,600	109,587.50 + 35	405,100
457,600	------	127,962.50 + 39.6	457,600

Schedule Y-2—If your filing status is **Married filing separately**

If your taxable income is: Over—	But not over—	The tax is:	of the amount over—
$0	$9,075	------ 10%	$0
9,075	36,900	$907.50 + 15	9,075
36,900	74,425	5,081.25 + 25	36,900
74,425	113,425	14,462.50 + 28	74,425
113,425	202,550	25,382.50 + 33	113,425
202,550	228,800	54,793.75 + 35	202,550
228,800	------	63,981.25 + 39.6	228,800

Schedule Z—If your filing status is **Head of household**

If your taxable income is: Over—	But not over—	The tax is:	of the amount over—
$0	$12,950	------ 10%	$0
12,950	49,400	$1,295.00 + 15	12,950
49,400	127,550	6,762.50 + 25	49,400
127,550	206,600	26,300.00 + 28	127,550
206,600	405,100	48,434.00 + 33	206,600
405,100	432,200	113,939.00 + 35	405,100
432,200	------	123,424.00 + 39.6	432,200

Source: Internal Revenue Service.

To see how the tax rates in Exhibit 3.3 work, consider two single taxpayers: one has taxable income of $12,500; the other, $38,600. Here's how we would calculate their respective tax liabilities:

- For taxable income of $12,500: $907.50 + [($12,500−$9,075) × 0.15] = $907.50 + $513.75 = $1,421.25
- For taxable income of $38,600: $5,081.25 + [($38,600−$36,900) × 0.25] = $5,081.25 + $425.00 = $5,506.25

The income of $12,500 is partially taxed at the 10 percent rate and partially taxed at the 15 percent rate. The first $9,075 of the $38,600 is taxed at 10 percent, the next $27,825 at 15 percent, and the remaining $1,700 at 25 percent. Keep in mind that taxpayers use the same procedures at this point whether they itemize or not. To show how the amount of tax liability will vary with the level of taxable income, Exhibit 3.4 lists the taxes due on a range of taxable incomes, from $1,500 to $460,000, for individual and joint returns.

Returning to our example involving the taxpayer with an income of $38,600, we see that this individual had an average tax rate of 14.3 percent ($5,506.25/$38,600), which is considerably less than the stated tax rate of 25 percent. Actually, the 25 percent represents the taxpayer's *marginal tax rate*—the rate at which the next dollar

| EXHIBIT 3.4 | Taxable Income and the Amount of Income Taxes Due (2014) |

Given the progressive tax structure used in this country, it follows that the larger your income, the more you can expect to pay in taxes.

| | Taxes Due (Rounded) | |
Taxable Income	Individual Returns	Joint Returns
$ 1,500	$ 150[a]	$ 150[a]
8,000	800[a]	800[a]
15,000	1,796[b]	1,500[a]
30,000	4,046[b]	3,592[b]
60,000	10,856[c]	8,902[b]
100,000	21,176[c]	16,712[c]
200,000	49,858[d]	43,247[d]
410,000	119,256[f]	111,302[f]
460,000	139,206[g]	128,913[f]

[a] Income is taxed at 10 percent.
[b] 15 percent tax rate now applies.
[c] 25 percent tax rate now applies.
[d] 28 percent tax rate now applies.
[e] 33 percent tax rate now applies.
[f] 35 percent tax rate now applies.
[g] 39.6 percent tax rate now applies.

Source: Internal Revenue Service.

of taxable income is taxed. Notice in our calculations that the marginal 25 percent tax rate applies only to that portion of the single person's income that exceeds $ 36,900, which is $1,700 in this example.

Some taxpayers are subject to the *alternative minimum tax (AMT)*, currently 26 percent of the first $182,500 and 28 percent of the excess. A taxpayer's tax liability is the higher of the AMT or the regular tax. The AMT is designed to ensure that high-income taxpayers with many deductions and tax shelter investments that provide attractive tax write-offs are paying their fair share of taxes. The AMT includes in alternative minimum taxable income certain types of deductions otherwise allowed, such as state and local income and property taxes, miscellaneous itemized deductions, unreimbursed medical expenses, and depreciation. Therefore, taxpayers with moderate levels of taxable income, including those living in states with high tax rates and self-employed persons with depreciation deductions, may be subject to the AMT calculation and additional tax.

3-3b Tax Credits

After determining amount of taxes some taxpayers are allowed to reduce their tax using **tax credits**, directly from their tax liability.

A tax credit is much more valuable than a deduction or an exemption because it directly reduces, dollar for dollar, the amount of *taxes due*, whereas a deduction or an exemption merely reduces the amount of *taxable income*. In Exhibit 3.5, we see how this difference affects the tax liability of two single taxpayers with $34,000 of gross income and $6,000 of other deductions/exemptions (in the 15 percent tax bracket). One has $1,000 in deductions, and the other has a $1,000 tax credit. Look at what happens to the amount of taxes due. In effect, the tax credit in this example has reduced taxes (and therefore *increased* after-tax income) by $850.

tax credits
Deductions from a taxpayer's tax liability that directly reduce his or her *taxes due* rather than *taxable income*.

EXHIBIT 3.5	How Deductions and Tax Credits Affect Taxes Due

As this example shows, a $1,000 tax credit reduces taxes due by far more than a $1,000 tax deduction.

Calculation	$1,000 Deduction	$1,000 Tax Credit
Gross income	$34,000	$34,000
Less: Other deductions/exemptions	6,000	6,000
Less: $1,000 deduction	1,000	—
Taxable income	$27,000	$28,000
Tax liability*	3,596	3,746
Less $1,000 tax credit	—	1,000
Taxes due	$ 3,596	$ 2,746

*Tax liability is figured as follows: the first $9,075 of taxable income is taxed at 10 percent, the balance at 15 percent.

An often-used tax credit is for *child and dependent care expenses*. This credit is based on the amount spent for dependent care while a taxpayer (and spouse, if married) works or goes to school. An *adoption tax credit* of up to $13,190 is available for the qualifying costs of adopting a child under age 18. Here are some other common tax credits:

- Credit for the elderly or the disabled
- Foreign tax credit
- Credit for prior year minimum tax
- Retirement savings credit
- Credit for qualified electric vehicle

To receive one of these credits, the taxpayer must file a return along with a separate schedule in support of the tax credit claimed.

3-3c Tax Forms and Schedules

The IRS requires taxpayers to file their returns using specified tax forms. As noted earlier, these forms and various instruction booklets on how to prepare them are available to taxpayers free of charge. Generally, all persons who filed tax returns in the previous year are automatically sent a booklet containing tax forms and instructions for preparing returns for the current year. Inside the booklet is a form that can be used to obtain additional tax forms for filing various tax-related returns and information. Tax forms and instructions can be downloaded from **http://www.irs.gov.**

Variations of Form 1040

All individuals use some variation of Form 1040 to file their tax returns. *Form 1040EZ* is a simple, one-page form. You qualify to use this form if you are single or married filing a joint return; under age 65 (both if filing jointly); not blind; do not claim any dependents; have taxable income of less than $100,000 from only wages, salaries, tips, or taxable scholarships or grants; have interest income of less than $1,500; and do not claim any adjustments to income, itemize deductions, or claim any tax credits. Worksheet 3.1 shows the Form 1040EZ filed in 2014 by Anna Bhatia, a full-time graduate student at State University. Keep in mind that the tax form only shows dollar amounts and not cents, which is permissible in filing the form with the IRS. Her sources of income include a $12,500 scholarship, of which $4,900 was used for room and board; $7,600 earned from part-time and summer jobs; and $50 interest earned on a savings account deposit. Because scholarships used for tuition and fees are not taxed, she should include as income only the portion used for room and board. She had a total of $475 withheld for federal income taxes during the year. Although Anna would also complete a Salaries & Wages Report form, it is omitted for simplicity because it only lists the $4,900 of her scholarship that went toward her room and board, her part-time income of $7,600, and the details of her withholdings.

To use *Form 1040A*, a two-page form, your income must be less than $100,000 and be derived only from specified sources. Using this form, you may deduct certain IRA contributions and claim certain tax credits, but you cannot itemize your deductions. If your income is over $100,000 or you itemize deductions, you must use the standard Form 1040 along with appropriate schedules.

The use of these schedules, which provide detailed guidelines for calculating certain entries on the first two pages of *Form 1040*, varies among taxpayers depending on the relevance of these entries to their situations. Pages 1 and 2 of Form 1040, which summarize all items of income and deductions detailed on the accompanying schedules, are used to determine and report the taxable income and associated tax liability.

Form 1040EZ is easy to use, and most of the instructions are printed on the form itself. Anna Bhatia qualifies to use it because she is single, under age 65, not blind, and meets its income and deduction restrictions.

Department of the Treasury—Internal Revenue Service

Form 1040EZ

Income Tax Return for Single and Joint Filers With No Dependents (99) **2014**

OMB No. 1545-0074

Your first name and initial	Last name	Your social security number
Anna	Bhatia	123 45 6789

If a joint return, spouse's first name and initial	Last name	Spouse's social security number

Home address (number and street). If you have a P.O. box, see instructions.   Apt. no.
1000 State University Drive

▲ Make sure the SSN(s) above are correct.

City, town or post office, state, and ZIP code. If you have a foreign address, also complete spaces below (see instructions).
Anytown, Anystate 10001

Presidential Election Campaign
Check here if you, or your spouse if filing jointly, want $3 to go to this fund. Checking a box below will not change your tax or refund. ☑ You ☐ Spouse

Foreign country name	Foreign province/state/county	Foreign postal code

Income

Attach Form(s) W-2 here.

Enclose, but do not attach, any payment.

1	Wages, salaries, and tips. This should be shown in box 1 of your Form(s) W-2. Attach your Form(s) W-2.	**1** 12,500
2	Taxable interest. If the total is over $1,500, you cannot use Form 1040EZ.	**2** 50
3	Unemployment compensation and Alaska Permanent Fund dividends (see instructions).	**3**
4	Add lines 1, 2, and 3. This is your **adjusted gross income**.	**4** 12,550
5	If someone can claim you (or your spouse if a joint return) as a dependent, check the applicable box(es) below and enter the amount from the worksheet on back. ☐ **You** ☐ **Spouse** If no one can claim you (or your spouse if a joint return), enter $10,150 if **single**; $20,300 if **married filing jointly**. See back for explanation.	**5** 10,150
6	Subtract line 5 from line 4. If line 5 is larger than line 4, enter -0-. This is your **taxable income**. ▶	**6** 2,400

Payments, Credits, and Tax

7	Federal income tax withheld from Form(s) W-2 and 1099.	**7** 495
8a	**Earned income credit (EIC)** (see instructions)	**8a**
b	Nontaxable combat pay election. 8b	
9	Add lines 7 and 8a. These are your **total payments and credits**. ▶	**9** 495
10	**Tax.** Use the amount on **line 6 above** to find your tax in the tax table in the instructions. Then, enter the tax from the table on this line.	**10** 241
11	Health care: individual responsibility (see instructions) Full-year coverage ☑	**11**
12	Add lines 10 and 11. This is your **total tax.**	**12** 254

Refund

Have it directly deposited! See instructions and fill in 13b, 13c, and 13d, or Form 8888.

13a	If line 9 is larger than line 12, subtract line 12 from line 9. This is your **refund.** If Form 8888 is attached, check here ▶ ☐	**13a** 254
▶ b	Routing number	▶ c Type: ☐ Checking ☐ Savings
▶ d	Account number	

Amount You Owe

14	If line 12 is larger than line 9, subtract line 9 from line 12. This is the **amount you owe.** For details on how to pay, see instructions. ▶	**14**

Third Party Designee

Do you want to allow another person to discuss this return with the IRS (see instructions)? ☐ **Yes.** Complete below. ☐ **No**

Designee's name ▶	Phone no. ▶	Personal identification number (PIN) ▶

Sign Here

Under penalties of perjury, I declare that I have examined this return and, to the best of my knowledge and belief, it is true, correct, and accurately lists all amounts and sources of income I received during the tax year. Declaration of preparer (other than the taxpayer) is based on all information of which the preparer has any knowledge.

Joint return? See instructions.

Keep a copy for your records.

Your signature	Date	Your occupation	Daytime phone number
Anna Bhatia	4/14/15	Student	(555) 555-1212
Spouse's signature. If a joint return, **both** must sign.	Date	Spouse's occupation	If the IRS sent you an Identity Protection PIN, enter it here (see inst.)

Paid Preparer Use Only

Print/Type preparer's name	Preparer's signature	Date	Check ☐ if self-employed	PTIN
Firm's name ▶			Firm's EIN ▶	
Firm's address ▶			Phone no.	

For Disclosure, Privacy Act, and Paperwork Reduction Act Notice, see instructions. Cat. No. 11329W FORM **1040EZ** (2014)

(Continued)

FINANCIAL PLANNING TIPS

Best Ways to Spend Your Tax Refund

While it may be tempting to celebrate your tax refund by just spending it all on stuff, consider how a refund could constructively enter into your overall financial plan.

- **Add to an emergency fund.** Who knows when an emergency will happen? Consider starting a new fund or adding to your present emergency fund.

- **Pay off some debt.** Using your refund to pay off some debt will save you interest charges. Start with any credit card debt because it carries the highest rates.

- **Add to your retirement savings.** Consider putting some of your refund into an IRA.

- **Invest in your career.** Your refund could help pay for going back to school or taking some courses that will upgrade your skills.

- **Get healthier.** You could use your refund to buy a gym membership or to pay for needed dental work, which is often not fully covered by health insurance.

- **Do house repairs.** Your refund could help pay for needed repairs or upgrades, such as painting or plumbing.

- **Improve your home's energy efficiency.** You could make your house more energy-efficient by putting in energy-efficient appliances, installing double-paned windows, or by replacing traditional light bulbs with light-emitting diodes (LEDs) or fluorescent bulbs.

- **Buy life insurance.** If you don't already own some life insurance, use your tax refund to protect your loved ones if you die prematurely. Term life insurance policies are usually the cheapest to buy.

- **Save for family vacations.** While they can be expensive, vacations can bring a family closer. Consider adding your refund to a vacation savings account.

- **Donate to charity.** Donating at least part of your refund to a charity will help others. And it's also tax-deductible!

Source: Adapted from Rose Kivi, "10 Tips on How to Spend Your Tax Refund Money," http://www.candofinance.com/taxes/how-to-spend-your-tax-refund-money/, accessed July 2015.

Despite detailed instructions that accompany the tax forms, taxpayers still make a lot of mistakes when filling them out. Common errors include missing information and arithmetic errors. So check and recheck your forms *before submitting them to the IRS*.

3-3d The 2014 Tax Return of Terry and Evelyn Becker

Let's now put all the pieces of the tax preparation puzzle together to see how Terry and Evelyn Becker calculate and file their income taxes. The Beckers own their own home and are both 35 years old. Married for 11 years, they have three children—Thomas (age 9), Richard (age 7), and Harriet (age 3). Terry is a manager for an insurance company headquartered in their hometown. Evelyn works part-time as a sales clerk in a retail store. During 2014, Terry's salary totaled $60,415, while Evelyn earned $9,750. Terry's employer withheld taxes of $6,260, and Evelyn's withheld $1,150. During the year, the Beckers earned $800 interest on their joint savings account and realized $1,250 in capital gains on the sale of securities that they had owned for 11 months. In addition, Terry kept the books for his brother's car dealership, from which he netted $5,800 during the year. Because no taxes were withheld from any of their outside income, during the year they made estimated tax payments totaling $1,000. The Beckers' records indicate that they had $14,713 of potential itemized deductions during the year. Finally, the Beckers plan to contribute $4,000 to Evelyn's traditional IRA account. Beginning next year, the Beckers plan to switch Terry's account to a Roth IRA (see Chapter 14 for more information about that topic).

Finding the Beckers' Tax Liability: Form 1040

Looking at the Beckers' 2014 tax return (Worksheet 3.2), we can get a feel for the basic calculations required in the preparation of a Form 1040. Although we don't include the supporting schedules here, we illustrate the basic calculations that they require. As in the above example, keep in mind that the tax form only shows dollar amounts and not cents, which is permissible in filing the form with the IRS. The Beckers have detailed records of their income and expenses, which they use not only for tax purposes, but as important input to their budgeting process. Using this information, the Beckers intend to prepare their 2014 tax return so that their total tax liability is as low as possible. Like most married couples, the Beckers file a *joint return*.

Gross Income The Beckers' gross income in 2014 amounted to $78,015—the amount shown as "total income" on line 22 of their tax return. They have both active income and portfolio income, as follows:

Active Income	
Terry's earnings	$60,415
Evelyn's earnings	9,750
Terry's business income (Net)	5,800
Total active income	$75,965

Portfolio Income	
Interest from savings account	$ 800
Capital gains realized*	1,250
Total portfolio income	$ 2,050
Total income ($75,965 + $2,050)	$78,015

* Because this gain was realized on stock held for less than 12 months, the full amount is taxable as ordinary income.

They have no investment expenses to offset their portfolio income, so they'll be liable for taxes on the full amount of portfolio income. Although they have interest income, the Beckers don't have to file Schedule B (for interest and dividend income) with the Form 1040, because the interest is less than $1,500 and they earned no dividends. (If they receive dividends on stock in the future, they will have to complete a Qualified Dividends and Capital Gains Tax Worksheet, provided in the Form 1040 instruction booklet. Qualified dividends are taxed at the lower capital gains rates.) In addition, Terry will have to file Schedule C, detailing the income earned and expenses incurred in his bookkeeping business, and Schedule D to report capital gains income.

Adjustments to Gross Income The Beckers have only two adjustments to income: Evelyn's IRA contribution and 50 percent of the self-employment tax on Terry's net business income. Since Evelyn isn't covered by a retirement plan and since Terry's and her combined modified AGI is below $181,000, they can deduct her entire $4,000 contribution (the maximum contribution to an IRA is $5,500 or, depending on age, $6,500 in 2014) to an IRA account even though Terry is already covered by a company-sponsored retirement program (see Chapter 14). Terry's self-employment tax will be 15.3 percent of 0.9235 of his $5,800 net business income, and he will be able to deduct one-half that amount—$409.76 [(0.153 × 0.9235 × $5,800) ÷ 2], which is rounded to $410 on line 27. As noted in working through the prior tax return example for an individual, keep in mind that the tax form in Worksheet 3.2 only shows dollar amounts and not cents, which is permissible in filing the form with the IRS.

Because they itemize deductions, the Beckers use standard Form 1040 to file their tax return. When filed with the IRS, their return will include not only Form 1040, but also other schedules and forms detailing many of their expenses and deductions.

Form **1040**

Department of the Treasury—Internal Revenue Service   (99)

U.S. Individual Income Tax Return   **2014**   OMB No. 1545-0074   IRS Use Only—Do not write or staple in this space.

For the year Jan. 1–Dec. 31, 2014, or other tax year beginning _____, 2014, ending _____, 20 ____   See separate instructions.

Your first name and initial **Terry S.** Last name **Becker**	Your social security number 1 2 3	4 5	6 7 8 9
If a joint return, spouse's first name and initial **Evelyn M.** Last name **Becker**	Spouse's social security number 9 8 7	6 5	4 3 2 1

Home address (number and street). If you have a P.O. box, see instructions.   **1234 Success Circle**   Apt. no.

▲ Make sure the SSN(s) above and on line 6c are correct.

City, town or post office, state, and ZIP code. If you have a foreign address, also complete spaces below (see instructions).   **Anytown, Anystate 10001**

Presidential Election Campaign
Check here if you, or your spouse if filing jointly, want $3 to go to this fund. Checking a box below will not change your tax or refund. ☑ You ☐ Spouse

Foreign country name   Foreign province/state/county   Foreign postal code

Filing Status

Check only one box.

1 ☐ Single
2 ☑ Married filing jointly (even if only one had income)
3 ☐ Married filing separately. Enter spouse's SSN above and full name here. ▶
4 ☐ Head of household (with qualifying person). (See instructions.) If the qualifying person is a child but not your dependent, enter this child's name here. ▶
5 ☐ Qualifying widow(er) with dependent child

Exemptions

6a ☑ **Yourself.** If someone can claim you as a dependent, **do not** check box 6a
b ☑ **Spouse**

Boxes checked on 6a and 6b   **2**

c **Dependents:**

(1) First name Last name	(2) Dependent's social security number	(3) Dependent's relationship to you	(4) ✓ if child under age 17 qualifying for child tax credit (see instructions)
Thomas C. Becker	0 6 5 0 1 2 3 4 7	Son	☑
Richard E. Becker	0 1 2 3 4 5 6 7 8	Son	☑
Harriet G. Becker	0 3 4 6 5 1 2 3 4	Daughter	☑
			☐

No. of children on 6c who:
• lived with you   **3**
• did not live with you due to divorce or separation (see instructions)
Dependents on 6c not entered above

If more than four dependents, see instructions and check here ▶ ☐

d Total number of exemptions claimed

Add numbers on lines above ▶   **5**

Income

Attach Form(s) W-2 here. Also attach Forms W-2G and 1099-R if tax was withheld.

If you did not get a W-2, see instructions.

7	Wages, salaries, tips, etc. Attach Form(s) W-2	7	70,165 00
8a	**Taxable** interest. Attach Schedule B if required	8a	800 00
b	**Tax-exempt** interest. **Do not** include on line 8a 8b		
9a	Ordinary dividends. Attach Schedule B if required	9a	
b	Qualified dividends 9b		
10	Taxable refunds, credits, or offsets of state and local income taxes	10	
11	Alimony received	11	
12	Business income or (loss). Attach Schedule C or C-EZ	12	5,800 00
13	Capital gain or (loss). Attach Schedule D if required. If not required, check here ▶ ☐	13	1,250 00
14	Other gains or (losses). Attach Form 4797	14	
15a	IRA distributions 15a b Taxable amount	15b	
16a	Pensions and annuities 16a b Taxable amount	16b	
17	Rental real estate, royalties, partnerships, S corporations, trusts, etc. Attach Schedule E	17	
18	Farm income or (loss). Attach Schedule F	18	
19	Unemployment compensation	19	
20a	Social security benefits 20a b Taxable amount	20b	
21	Other income. List type and amount _____	21	
22	Combine the amounts in the far right column for lines 7 through 21. This is your **total income** ▶	22	78,015 00

Adjusted Gross Income

23	Educator expenses	23	
24	Certain business expenses of reservists, performing artists, and fee-basis government officials. Attach Form 2106 or 2106-EZ	24	
25	Health savings account deduction. Attach Form 8889	25	
26	Moving expenses. Attach Form 3903	26	
27	Deductible part of self-employment tax. Attach Schedule SE	27	410 00
28	Self-employed SEP, SIMPLE, and qualified plans	28	
29	Self-employed health insurance deduction	29	
30	Penalty on early withdrawal of savings	30	
31a	Alimony paid b Recipient's SSN ▶	31a	
32	IRA deduction	32	4,000 00
33	Student loan interest deduction	33	
34	Tuition and fees. Attach Form 8917	34	
35	Domestic production activities deduction. Attach Form 8903	35	
36	Add lines 23 through 35	36	4,410 00
37	Subtract line 36 from line 22. This is your **adjusted gross income** ▶	37	73,605 00

For Disclosure, Privacy Act, and Paperwork Reduction Act Notice, see separate instructions.   Cat. No. 11320B   Form **1040** (2014)

Tax and Credits

38	Amount from line 37 (adjusted gross income)	38	73,605	00

39a Check if: ☐ **You** were born before January 2, 1950, ☐ Blind. ☐ **Spouse** was born before January 2, 1950, ☐ Blind. } Total boxes checked ▶ 39a [ ]

b If your spouse itemizes on a separate return or you were a dual-status alien, check here ▶ 39b ☐

Standard Deduction for—
- People who check any box on line 39a or 39b **or** who can be claimed as a dependent, see instructions.
- All others:
Single or Married filing separately, $6,200
Married filing jointly or Qualifying widow(er), $12,400
Head of household, $9,100

40	**Itemized deductions** (from Schedule A) **or** your **standard deduction** (see left margin)	40	12,978	00
41	Subtract line 40 from line 38	41	60,627	00
42	**Exemptions.** If line 38 is $152,525 or less, multiply $3,950 by the number on line 6d. Otherwise, see instructions	42	19,750	00
43	**Taxable income.** Subtract line 42 from line 41. If line 42 is more than line 41, enter -0-	43	40,877	00
44	**Tax** (see instructions). Check if any from: **a** ☐ Form(s) 8814 **b** ☐ Form 4972 **c** ☐ _____	44	5,224	00
45	**Alternative minimum tax** (see instructions). Attach Form 6251	45		
46	Excess advance premium tax credit repayment. Attach Form 8962	46		
47	Add lines 44, 45, and 46 ▶	47	5,224	00

48	Foreign tax credit. Attach Form 1116 if required	48			
49	Credit for child and dependent care expenses. Attach Form 2441	49			
50	Education credits from Form 8863, line 19	50			
51	Retirement savings contributions credit. Attach Form 8880	51			
52	Child tax credit. Attach Schedule 8812, if required	52	3,000		
53	Residential energy credits. Attach Form 5695	53			
54	Other credits from Form: **a** ☐ 3800 **b** ☐ 8801 **c** ☐ ____	54			

55	Add lines 48 through 54. These are your **total credits**	55	3,000	00
56	Subtract line 55 from line 47. If line 55 is more than line 47, enter -0- ▶	56	2,224	00

Other Taxes

57	Self-employment tax. Attach Schedule SE	57	819	00
58	Unreported social security and Medicare tax from Form: **a** ☐ 4137 **b** ☐ 8919	58		
59	Additional tax on IRAs, other qualified retirement plans, etc. Attach Form 5329 if required	59		
60a	Household employment taxes from Schedule H	60a		
b	First-time homebuyer credit repayment. Attach Form 5405 if required	60b		
61	Health care: individual responsibility (see instructions) Full-year coverage ☑	61		
62	Taxes from: **a** ☐ Form 8959 **b** ☐ Form 8960 **c** ☐ Instructions; enter code(s) ____	62		
63	Add lines 56 through 62. This is your **total tax** ▶	63	3,043	00

Payments

If you have a qualifying child, attach Schedule EIC.

64	Federal income tax withheld from Forms W-2 and 1099	64	7,410	00	
65	2014 estimated tax payments and amount applied from 2013 return	65	1,000	00	
66a	**Earned income credit (EIC)**	66a			
b	Nontaxable combat pay election	66b			
67	Additional child tax credit. Attach Schedule 8812	67			
68	American opportunity credit from Form 8863, line 8	68			
69	Net premium tax credit. Attach Form 8962	69			
70	Amount paid with request for extension to file	70			
71	Excess social security and tier 1 RRTA tax withheld	71			
72	Credit for federal tax on fuels. Attach Form 4136	72			
73	Credits from Form: **a** ☐ 2439 **b** ☐ Reserved **c** ☐ Reserved **d** ☐ ____	73			

74	Add lines 64, 65, 66a, and 67 through 73. These are your **total payments** ▶	74	8,410	00

Refund

75	If line 74 is more than line 63, subtract line 63 from line 74. This is the amount you **overpaid**	75	5,367	00
76a	Amount of line 75 you want **refunded to you.** If Form 8888 is attached, check here ▶ ☐	76a	5,367	00

Direct deposit? See instructions.
▶ b Routing number |_|_|_|_|_|_|_|_|_| ▶ c Type: ☐ Checking ☐ Savings
▶ d Account number |_|_|_|_|_|_|_|_|_|_|_|_|_|_|_|_|_|

77	Amount of line 75 you want **applied to your 2015 estimated tax** ▶	77	

Amount You Owe

78	**Amount you owe.** Subtract line 74 from line 63. For details on how to pay, see instructions ▶	78	
79	Estimated tax penalty (see instructions)	79	

Third Party Designee

Do you want to allow another person to discuss this return with the IRS (see instructions)? ☐ **Yes.** Complete below. ☐ **No**

Designee's name ▶ _____   Phone no. ▶ _____   Personal identification number (PIN) ▶ _____

Sign Here

Joint return? See instructions. Keep a copy for your records.

Under penalties of perjury, I declare that I have examined this return and accompanying schedules and statements, and to the best of my knowledge and belief, they are true, correct, and complete. Declaration of preparer (other than taxpayer) is based on all information of which preparer has any knowledge.

Your signature	Date	Your occupation	Daytime phone number
Terry S. Becker	4/10/15	Manager	(555) 555-1234

Spouse's signature. If a joint return, **both** must sign.	Date	Spouse's occupation	If the IRS sent you an Identity Protection PIN, enter it here (see inst.)
Evelyn M. Becker	4/10/15	Sales Clerk	

Paid Preparer Use Only

Print/Type preparer's name	Preparer's signature	Date	Check ☐ if self-employed	PTIN

Firm's name ▶ _____   Firm's EIN ▶ _____
Firm's address ▶ _____   Phone no. _____

Source : Internal Revenue Service.

Adjusted Gross Income (AGI) After deducting the $410 self-employment tax and Evelyn's $4,000 IRA contribution from their gross income, the Beckers are left with an AGI of $73,605, as reported on line 37.

Itemized Deductions or Standard Deduction? The Beckers are filing a joint return, and neither is over age 65 or blind; so according to the box on page 2 of Form 1040, they are entitled to a standard deduction of $12,400. However, they want to evaluate their itemized deductions before deciding which type of deduction to take—obviously they'll take the higher deduction because it will result in the lowest amount of taxable income and keep their tax liability to a minimum. Their preliminary paperwork resulted in the following deductions:

Medical and dental expenses	$ 1,223
State income and property taxes paid	2,560
Mortgage interest	8,893
Charitable contributions	475
Job and other expenses	2,522
Total	$15,673

The taxes, mortgage interest, and charitable contributions are deductible in full; so at the minimum, the Beckers will have itemized deductions amounting to $11,928 ($2,560 + $8,893 + $475). However, to be deductible, the medical and dental expenses and job and other expenses must exceed stipulated minimum levels of AGI—only that portion exceeding the specified minimum levels of AGI can be included as part of their itemized deductions. For medical and dental expenses, the minimum is 10 percent of AGI, and for job and other expenses, it is 2 percent of AGI. Because 10 percent of the Beckers' AGI is about $7,360 (0.10 × $73,605), they fall short of the minimum and cannot deduct any medical and dental expenses. In contrast, because 2 percent of the Beckers' AGI is about $1,472 (0.02 × $73,605), they can deduct any job and other expenses exceeding that amount, or $2,522 − $1,472 = $1,050. Adding that amount to their other allowable deductions ($11,928) results in total itemized deductions of $12,978. This amount exceeds the standard deduction of $12,400, so the Beckers should strongly consider itemizing their deductions. They would enter the details of these deductions on Schedule A and attach it to their Form 1040. (The total amount of the Beckers' itemized deductions is listed on line 40 of Form 1040.)

The Beckers are entitled to claim two exemptions for themselves and another three for their three dependent children, for a total of five (see line 6d). Because each exemption is worth $3,950, they receive a total personal exemption of $19,750 (5 × $3,950), which is the amount listed on line 42 of their Form 1040.

The Beckers' Taxable Income and Tax Liability Taxable income is found by subtracting itemized deductions and personal exemptions from AGI. In the Beckers' case, taxable income (rounded) amounts to $73,605 − $12,978 − $19,750 = $40,877, as shown on line 43. Given this information, the Beckers can now refer to the tax rate schedule (like the one in Exhibit 3.3) to find their appropriate tax rate and, ultimately, the amount of taxes they'll have to pay. (Because the Beckers' taxable income is less than $100,000, they could use the *tax tables* [not shown in this chapter] to find their tax. For clarity and convenience, we use the schedules here.) As we can see, Beckers' $40,877 in taxable income places them in the 15 percent marginal tax bracket. Using the schedule in Exhibit 3.3, they calculate their tax as follows: $1,815 + [0.15 × ($40,877− $18,150] = $5,224. They enter this amount on line 44.

The Beckers also qualify for the child tax credit: $1,000 for each child under age 17. They enter $3,000 on lines 52 and 55 and subtract that amount from the tax on line 47, entering $2,224 on line 56. In addition, the Beckers owe self-employment

(Social Security) tax on Terry's $5,800 net business income. This will increase their tax liability by $819 (0.153 × .9235 × $5,800) and would be reported on Schedule SE and entered on line 57 of Form 1040. (Recall that the Beckers deducted 50 percent of this amount, or $410, on line 27 as an adjustment to income.) The Beckers enter their total tax liability on line 63: $3,043 ($2,224 + 819).

Do They Get a Tax Refund? Because the total amount of taxes withheld of $7,410 ($6,260 from Terry's salary and $1,150 from Evelyn's wages) shown on line 64 plus estimated tax payments of $1,000 shown on line 65 total $8,410, as shown on line 74, the Beckers total tax payments exceed their tax liability. As a result, they are entitled to a refund of $ 5,367: the $8,410 withholding less their $3,043 tax liability. (Over 75 percent of all taxpayers receive refunds each year.) Instead of paying the IRS, they'll be getting money back. (Generally, it takes 1 to 2 months after a tax return has been filed to receive a refund check or electronic deposit. If filed electronically, it usually takes about three weeks to get a refund.)

All the Beckers have to do now is sign and date their completed Form 1040 and send it, along with any supporting forms and schedules, to the nearest IRS Center that serves their state on or before April 15, 2015.

One reason for the Beckers' large refund was the child tax credit. With such a sizable refund, the Beckers may want to stop making estimated tax payments because their combined withholding more than covers the amount of taxes they owe. Another option is to change their withholding to reduce the amount withheld.

Note that if total tax payments had been less than the Beckers' tax liability, they would have owed the IRS money—the amount owed is found by subtracting total tax payments made from the tax liability. If they owed money, they would include a check in the amount due with Form 1040 when filing their tax return.

TEST YOURSELF

3-9 Define and differentiate between the *average tax rate* and the *marginal tax rate*. How does a *tax credit* differ from an *itemized deduction*?

3-10 Explain how the following are used in filing a tax return: (a) Form 1040, (b) various schedules that accompany Form 1040, and (c) tax rate schedules.

3-4 OTHER FILING CONSIDERATIONS

LG4, LG5

Preparing and filing your tax returns involves more than merely filling out and filing a form on or before April 15th (the traditional date for filing taxes, although as the example in this chapter shows, that date sometimes changes, for various reasons). Other considerations include the need to pay estimated taxes, file for extensions, or amend the return; the possibility of a tax audit; and whether to use a tax preparation service or computer software to assist you in preparing your return.

3-4a Estimates, Extensions, and Amendments

Like Terry Becker, who provided accounting services to his brother's business, you may have income that's not subject to withholding. You may need to file a declaration of estimated taxes with your return and to pay quarterly taxes. Or perhaps you are unable to meet the normal filing deadline or need to correct a previously filed return. Let's look at the procedures for handling these situations.

Estimated Taxes

estimated taxes
Tax payments required on income not subject to withholding that are paid in four installments.

Because federal withholding taxes are regularly taken only from employment income, such as that paid in the form of wages or salaries, the IRS requires certain people to pay **estimated taxes** on income earned from other sources. This requirement allows the pay-as-you-go principle to be applied not only to employment income subject to withholding, but also to other sources of income. Four payments of estimated taxes are most commonly required of investors, consultants, lawyers, business owners, and various other professionals who are likely to receive income in a form that is not subject to withholding. Generally, if all your income is subject to withholding, you probably do not need to make estimated tax payments.

The declaration of estimated taxes (Form 1040-ES) is not filed with the tax return. Estimated taxes must be paid in four installments on April 15, June 15, and September 15 of the current year, and January 15 of the following year. Failure to estimate and pay these taxes in accordance with IRS guidelines can result in a penalty levied by the IRS.

April 15th: Filing Deadline

As we've seen from the Becker family example, at the end of each tax year, those taxpayers required to file a return must determine the amount of their *tax liability*—the amount of taxes they owe due to the past year's activities. The tax year corresponds to the calendar year and covers the period January 1 through December 31. Taxpayers may file their returns any time after the end of the tax year and *must* file no later than April 15th of the year immediately following the tax year (or by the first business day after that date if it falls on a weekend or federal holiday). If you have a computer, an Internet connection, and tax preparation software, you can probably use the IRS's *e-file* and *e-pay* to file your return and pay your taxes electronically either by using a credit card or by authorizing an electronic withdrawal from your checking or savings account. You can use an "Authorized *e-file* Provider," who may charge a fee to file for you, or do it yourself using commercial tax preparation software. (We'll discuss computer-based tax returns in greater detail later.)

Depending on whether the total of taxes withheld and any estimated tax payments is greater or less than the computed tax liability, the taxpayer either receives a refund or must pay additional taxes. Taxpayers can pay their taxes using a credit card; however, because the IRS cannot pay credit card companies an issuing fee, taxpayers must call a special provider and pay a service charge to arrange for the payment.

EXAMPLE: Determining the Amount Owed or Refunded

Ashok had $2,000 withheld and paid estimated taxes of $1,200 during the year. After filling out the appropriate tax forms, he had a tax liability of only $2,800. Consequently, Ashok overpaid his taxes by $400 ($2,000 + $1,200 − $2,800) and will receive a $400 refund from the IRS. On the other hand, if Ashok's tax liability had been $4,000, then he would owe the IRS an additional $800 ($4,000 − $2,000 − $1,200).

Filing Extensions and Amended Returns

It's possible to receive an extension of time for filing your federal tax return. You can apply for an automatic six-month filing extension, which makes the due date October 15, simply by submitting Form 4868. In filing for an extension, however, the taxpayer must estimate the taxes due and remit that amount with the application. The extension does *not* give taxpayers more time to pay their taxes.

amended return
A tax return filed to adjust for information received after the filing date of the taxpayer's original return or to correct errors.

After filing a return, you may discover that you overlooked some income or a major deduction or made a mistake, so you paid too little or too much in taxes. You can easily correct this by filing an **amended return** (Form 1040X) showing the corrected amount of income or deductions and the amount of taxes you should have paid, along with the amount of any tax refund or additional taxes owed. You generally have three years from the date you file your original return or two years from the date you paid the taxes, whichever is later, to file an amended return. If you prepare and file your amended return properly and it reflects nothing out of the ordinary, it generally won't trigger an audit. By all means, don't "correct" an oversight in one year by "adjusting" the following year's tax return—the IRS frowns on that.

3-4b Audited Returns

tax audit
An examination by the IRS to validate the accuracy of a given tax return.

Because taxpayers themselves provide the key information and fill out the necessary tax forms, the IRS has no proof that taxes have been correctly calculated. In addition to returns that stand out in some way and warrant further investigation, the IRS also randomly selects some returns for a **tax audit**—an examination to validate the return's accuracy. Despite the traditionally scary aura that surrounds the audit concept, the outcome of an audit is not *always* additional tax owed to the IRS. In fact, about 5 percent of all audits result in a refund to the taxpayer, and in 15 percent of all audits, the IRS finds that returns are correctly prepared.

FINANCIAL PLANNING TIPS

Watch Out for Tax Audit Red Flags

While the IRS typically only audits about 1 percent of tax returns, there are some practices that significantly increase your chance of being audited. It's wise to be aware of the following possible triggers:

- **High income.** The more income you make, the more likely you are to experience an audit. For example, if you make more than $200,000, you chance is about 3 percent, and if you make $1 million or more, your chance rises to about 11 percent.

- **Unreported taxable income.** If your 1099s and W-2s add up to more than the income reported on your tax return, expect a bill from the IRS—and a possible audit.

- **Higher-than-average deductions.** If your deductions are large relative to your income, the IRS can flag your return for a potential audit. Make sure that you know the IRS regulations for deductions and donations and keep all supporting documents and receipts.

- **Home office deductions.** A home office is supposed to be used exclusively for business. The IRS

has found that this requirement is frequently not met, and the deduction is consequently denied. Thus, this is a red flag for an audit. If you take this deduction, be ready to prove it.

- **Business meals, travel, and entertainment.** IRS experience shows that the self-employed are responsible for most of the underreporting of income and overstating of deductions. Large deductions for meals, travel, and entertainment are an audit flag. Make sure to keep good records if you plan to take these kinds of deductions.

- **Business use of a vehicle.** Claiming 100 percent business use of a car is a red flag to the IRS because it's rare for an individual to really use a car exclusively for business. Make sure that you keep detailed mileage logs.

- **Unreported foreign bank account.** You are required to disclose offshore accounts. If the IRS finds an unreported account, it's an audit flag.

Source: Adapted from Joy Taylor, "IRS Audit Red Flags: The Dirty Dozen," http://www.kiplinger.com/article/taxes/T054-C000-S001-irs-audit-red-flags-the-dirty-dozen.html, accessed July 2015.

Typically, audits question (1) whether all income received has been properly reported and (2) if the deductions claimed are legitimate and the correct amount. The IRS can take as many as three years—and in some cases, six years—from the date of filing to audit your return, so you should retain records and receipts used in preparing returns for about seven years. Severe financial penalties, even prison sentences, can result from violating tax laws.

In summary, you should take advantage of all legitimate deductions to minimize your tax liability, but you must also be sure to properly report all items of income and expense as required by the Internal Revenue Code.

3-4c Tax Preparation Services: Getting Help on Your Returns

Many people prepare their own tax returns. These "do-it-yourselfers" typically have fairly simple returns that can be prepared without much difficulty. Of course, some taxpayers with quite complicated financial affairs may also invest their time in preparing their own returns. The IRS offers many informational publications to help you prepare your tax return. You can order them directly from the IRS by mail, from the IRS Web site (**http://www.irs.gov**), or by calling the IRS toll-free number (800-829-3676, or special local numbers in some areas). An excellent (and free) comprehensive tax preparation reference book is *Your Federal Income Tax*. Other publications cover special topics, such as the earned income credit, self-employment taxes, and business use of your home. Each form and schedule comes with detailed instructions to guide you, step-by-step, in completing the form accurately.

Help from the IRS

The IRS, in addition to issuing various publications for use in preparing tax returns, also provides direct assistance to taxpayers. The IRS will compute taxes for those whose taxable income is less than $100,000 and who do not itemize deductions. Persons who use this IRS service must fill in certain data, sign and date the return, and send it to the IRS on or before April 15 of the year immediately following the tax year. The IRS attempts to calculate taxes to result in the "smallest" tax bite. It then sends taxpayers a refund (if their withholding exceeds their tax liability) or a bill (if their tax liability is greater than the amount of withholding). People who either fail to qualify for or do not want to use this total tax preparation service can still obtain IRS assistance in preparing their returns from a toll-free service. Consult your telephone directory for the toll-free number of the IRS office closest to you.

Private Tax Preparers

More than half of all taxpayers believe that the complexity of the tax forms makes preparation too difficult and time-consuming. They prefer to use professional *tax preparation services* to improve accuracy and minimize their tax liability as much as possible. The fees charged by professional tax preparers can range from at least $100 for simple returns to $1,000 or more for complicated returns that include many itemized deductions, partnership income or losses, or self-employment income. You can select from the following types of tax preparation services.

- **National and local tax services:** These include national services such as H&R Block and independent local firms. These services are best for taxpayers with relatively common types of income and expenditures.
- **Certified public accountants (CPAs):** Tax professionals who prepare returns and can advise taxpayers on planning.
- **Enrolled agents (EAs):** Federally licensed individual tax practitioners who have passed a difficult, 2-day, IRS-administered exam. They are fully qualified to handle tax preparation at various levels of complexity.
- **Tax attorneys:** Lawyers who specialize in tax planning.

The services of CPAs, EAs, and tax attorneys can be expensive and are best suited to taxpayers with relatively complicated financial situations.

Always check your own completed tax returns carefully before signing them. Remember that *taxpayers themselves must accept primary responsibility for the accuracy of their returns*. The IRS requires professional tax preparers to sign each return as the preparer, enter their own Preparers Tax Identification Number (PTIN), firm's Employer Identification number (EIN), and give the taxpayer a copy of the return being filed. Tax preparers with the necessary hardware and software can electronically file their clients' tax returns so that eligible taxpayers can receive refunds more quickly.

There's no guarantee that your professional tax preparer will correctly determine your tax liability. To reduce the chance of error, you should become familiar with the basic tax principles and regulations, check all documents (such as *W-2s* and *1099s*) for accuracy, maintain good communication with your tax preparer, and request an explanation of any entries on your tax return that you don't understand.

3-4d Computer-Based Tax Returns

Many people use their computers to help with tax planning and preparing tax returns. Several good tax software packages will save hours when you're filling out the forms and schedules involved in filing tax returns. The programs often identify tax-saving opportunities you might otherwise miss. These computer programs aren't for everyone, however. Simple returns, like the *Form 1040EZ*, don't require them. And for complex returns, there's no substitute for the skill and expertise of a tax accountant or attorney. Tax preparation software will be most helpful for taxpayers who itemize deductions but don't need tax advice.

There are two general kinds of software: tax planning and tax preparation. Planning programs such as Quicken let you experiment with different strategies to see their effects on the amount of taxes you must pay. The other category of tax software focuses on helping you complete and file your tax return. These programs take much of the tedium out of tax preparation, reducing the time you spend from days to hours. If you file the *Form 1040* and some supporting forms, invest in the stock market, own real estate, or have foreign income or a home-based business, you'll probably benefit from using tax preparation programs.

The two major software players are Intuit's TurboTax and H&R Block's TaxCut, both available for either Windows or Macintosh. TurboTax also has a Web-based version that lets you work on your returns from any computer. Both major companies also offer an add-on program that accurately assigns fair market value to the household items most commonly donated to charity. Both programs feature a clean interface and guide you through the steps in preparing your return by asking you the questions that apply to your situation. In addition to the primary tax-form preparation section, they include extensive resources and links to additional Internet references, video clips to make tricky concepts easier to understand, tax planning questionnaires, deduction finders, and more. State tax return packages cost more. All major software providers have free online versions for preparing federal taxes for people who meet specific requirements, which vary by provider. See **http://apps.irs.gov/app/freeFile/jsp/index.jsp** for a listing of providers of free federal software with their individual restrictions.

The IRS has "fill-in forms," which allow you to enter information while the form is displayed on your computer by Adobe Acrobat Reader. After entering the requested information, you can print out the completed form. Fill-in forms give you a cleaner, crisper printout for your records and for filing with the IRS. Unlike tax preparation software, these fill-in forms have no computational capabilities, so you must do all your calculations before starting. These forms are labeled "Fill-in forms" at the IRS Internet site.

FINANCIAL PLANNING TIPS

Working with the Best Tax Preparer

As already stated, you are legally responsible for your tax returns, even if someone else prepared them. Thus, it's important to choose the right person or firm to prepare them for you. Keep in mind the following tips in making this major decision and working with your preparer:

• **Qualifications.** All paid tax return preparers are required to have a Preparer Tax Identification Number (PTIN). Make sure that a prospective preparer has a PTIN.

• **Preparer's history.** Check with the Better Business Bureau for the preparer's history of problems. Make sure that there have been no disciplinary actions, and check the status of any CPA's license through the state boards of accountancy. The same check should be made for state bar associations for attorneys and with the IRS Office of Enrollment for Enrolled Agents (EAs).

• **Understand the fees that the preparer will charge you.** Make sure that you understand and accept the fee for services rendered and compare

preparers' fees. It does not make sense to use preparers who ask for a percentage of your refund.

• **Electronic filing.** Be certain that the prospective preparer offers IRS e-file. You can opt to file a paper return instead, but it is typically easiest to file electronically—and if you're getting a refund, you'll get it faster that way.

• **Accessibility.** Make sure that you can get hold of the tax preparer easily in case you have questions *before* or *after* the return is filed.

• **Requests for records and receipts.** Good preparers will ask to see your records and receipts. They will also ask questions about your total income, tax-deductible expenses, and more. It's best to avoid preparers who are willing to file your return electronically without seeing your W-2 form and other records.

• **Return signature.** Never use a preparer who asks you to sign a blank tax form. Similarly, review the entire return, verify its accuracy, and make sure that preparer has supplied his or her PTIN before you sign it.

Source: Adapted from Internal Revenue Publication, "Tips for Choosing a Tax Return Preparer," http://www.irs.gov/newsroom/article/0,,id=251962,00.html, accessed July 2015.

TEST YOURSELF

3-11 Define *estimated taxes,* and explain under what conditions such tax payments are required.

3-12 What is the purpose of a *tax audit*? Describe some things you can do to be prepared if your return is audited.

3-13 What types of assistance and tax preparation services does the IRS provide?

3-14 What are the advantages of using tax preparation software?

3-5 EFFECTIVE TAX PLANNING

LG6 *Tax planning* is a key ingredient of your overall personal financial planning. The overriding objective of effective tax planning is to maximize total after-tax income by reducing, shifting, and deferring taxes to as low a level as legally possible.

Keep in mind that *avoiding taxes* is one thing, but *evading* them is another matter altogether. By all means, don't confuse tax avoidance with tax evasion, which includes such illegal activities as omitting income or overstating deductions. **Tax evasion**, in effect, involves a failure to accurately report income or deductions and, in extreme cases, a failure to pay taxes altogether. Persons found guilty of tax evasion are subject to severe financial penalties—and even prison terms. **Tax avoidance**, in contrast, focuses on reducing taxes in ways that are legal and compatible with the intent of Congress.

3-5a Fundamental Objectives of Tax Planning

Tax planning involves the use of various investment vehicles, retirement programs, and estate distribution procedures to (1) reduce, (2) shift, and (3) defer taxes. You can *reduce* taxes, for instance, by using techniques that create tax deductions or credits, or that receive preferential tax treatment—such as investments that produce depreciation (such as real estate) or that generate tax-free income (such as municipal bonds). You can *shift* taxes by using gifts or trusts to transfer some of your income to other family members who are in lower tax brackets and to whom you intend to provide some level of support anyway, such as a retired, elderly parent.

The idea behind *deferring* taxes is to reduce or eliminate your taxes today by postponing them to some time in the future, when you may be in a lower tax bracket. Perhaps more important, *deferring taxes gives you use of the money that would otherwise go to taxes*—thereby allowing you to invest it to make even more money. Deferring taxes is usually done through various types of retirement plans, such as IRAs, or by investing in certain types of annuities, variable life insurance policies, or even Series EE bonds (U.S. savings bonds).

The fundamentals of tax planning include making sure that you take all the deductions to which you're entitled and also take full advantage of the various tax provisions that will minimize your tax liability. Thus, comprehensive tax planning is an ongoing activity with both an immediate and a long-term perspective. *It plays a key role in personal financial planning.* In fact, a major component of a comprehensive personal financial plan is a summary of the potential tax impacts of various recommended financial strategies. Tax planning is closely interrelated with many financial planning activities, including investment, retirement, and estate planning.

3-5b Some Popular Tax Strategies

Many tax strategies are fairly straightforward and can be used by the average middle-income taxpayer. For example, the interest income on Series EE bonds is free from state income tax, and the holder can elect to delay payment of federal taxes until (1) the year the bonds are redeemed for cash or (2) the year in which they finally mature, whichever occurs first. This feature makes Series EE bonds an excellent vehicle for earning tax-deferred income.

There are other strategies that can cut your tax bill. Accelerating or bunching deductions into a single year may permit itemizing deductions. Shifting income from one year to another is one way to cut your tax liability. If you expect to be in the same or a higher-income tax bracket this year than you will be next year, defer income until next year and shift expenses to this year so you can accelerate your deductions and reduce taxes this year.

Maximizing Deductions

Review a comprehensive list of possible deductions for ideas, because even small deductions can add up to big tax savings. Accelerate or bunch deductions into one tax year if this allows you to itemize rather than take the standard deduction. For example, make your fourth-quarter estimated state tax payment before December 31 rather than on January 15 to deduct it in the current taxable year. Group miscellaneous expenses—and schedule unreimbursed elective medical procedures—to fall into one tax year so that they exceed the required "floor" for deductions (2 percent of AGI for miscellaneous expenses; 10 percent of AGI for medical expenses). Increase discretionary deductions such as charitable contributions.

Income Shifting

income shifting
A technique used to reduce taxes in which a taxpayer shifts a portion of income to relatives in lower tax brackets.

One way of reducing income taxes is to use a technique known as **income shifting**. Here, the taxpayer shifts a portion of his or her income, and thus taxes, to relatives in lower tax brackets. This can be done by creating trusts or custodial accounts or by making outright gifts of income-producing property to family members. For instance, parents with $125,000 of taxable income (28 percent marginal tax rate) and $18,000 in corporate bonds paying $2,000 in annual interest might give the bonds to their 15-year-old child—with the understanding that such income is to be used ultimately for the child's college education. The $2,000 would then belong to the child, who would probably be assumed to be able to pay $100 [0.10 × ($2,000 – $1,000 minimum standard deduction for a dependent)] in taxes on this income, and the parents' taxable income would be reduced by $2,000, thereby reducing their taxes by $560 (0.28 × $2,000).

Unfortunately, this strategy is not as simple as it might seem. A number of restrictions surround the strategy for children under 19, so it's possible to employ such techniques with older children (and with other older relatives, such as elderly parents). Parents need to be aware that shifting assets into a child's name to save taxes could affect the amount of college financial aid for which the child qualifies. Additional tax implications of gifts to dependents are discussed in Chapter 15.

> **YOU CAN DO IT NOW**
>
> ### Tax Planning
>
> Consider whether you expect your tax rate to be lower, the same, or higher next year. Then do some simple but effective tax planning:
>
> - If your tax rate is expected to be lower or the same next year, if you can, delay receiving income until next year so it will be taxed at the lower rate—or just later at the same rate.
> - If your tax rate is expected to be higher next year, try to speed up the receipt of income so it will be taxed at the currently lower rate. And consider waiting to take some deductions until next year when the higher rate will shield you better from the higher rate.

Tax-Free and Tax-Deferred Income

Some investments provide tax-free income; in most cases, however, the tax on the income is only deferred (or delayed) to a later day. Although there aren't many forms of tax-free investments left today, probably the best example would be the *interest* income earned on *municipal bonds*. Such income is free from federal income tax and possibly state income taxes. No matter how much municipal bond interest income you earn, you don't have to pay any federal taxes on it. (Tax-free municipal bonds are discussed in Chapter 12.) Income that is **tax deferred**, in contrast, only delays the payment of taxes to a future date. Until that time arrives, however, tax-deferred investment vehicles allow you to *accumulate tax-free earnings*. This results in much higher savings than would occur in a taxed account. A good example of tax-deferred income would be income earned in a *traditional IRA*. Chapter 14 provides a detailed discussion of this and other similar arrangements.

tax deferred
Income that is not subject to taxes immediately but that will be subject to taxes later.

Most any wage earner can open an IRA and contribute up to $5,500 (or possibly $6,500, depending on age) each year to the account (in 2014). So why have an IRA? *Because all the income that you earn in your IRA accumulates tax free.*

Financial Fact or Fantasy?

An easy way to earn tax-deferred income is to invest in Series EE savings bonds. **Fact:** The interest income from a Series EE savings bond can be tax deferred. The holder can elect to delay payment of taxes until the earlier of the year the bonds are redeemed for cash or the year in which they finally mature.

This is a *tax-deferred* investment, so you'll eventually have to pay taxes on these earnings, but not until you start drawing down your account. *Roth IRAs* provide a way for people to contribute after-tax dollars. Not only do earnings grow tax free, but so do withdrawals if the account has been open for five or more years and the individual is over 59 ½. However, keep in mind that using after-tax dollars for a Roth IRA means that the contribution is not tax-deductible. In addition to IRAs, tax-deferred income can also be obtained from other types of pension and retirement plans and annuities. See Chapter 14 for more information on these financial products and strategies.

TEST YOURSELF

3-15 Differentiate between *tax evasion* and *tax avoidance*.

3-16 Explain each of the following strategies for reducing current taxes: (a) maximizing deductions, (b) income shifting, (c) tax-free income, and (d) tax-deferred income.

Planning Over a Lifetime: *Tax Preparation and Planning*

Here are some key considerations for life insurance use in each stage of the life cycle.

Pre-family Independence: 20s	Family Formation/ Career Development: 30–45	Pre-Retirement: 45–65	Retirement: 65 and Beyond
✓ Manage your withholding amount so that it is about equal to your tax bill. Avoid large amounts owed or refunded.	✓ When you marry and/or have family changes, revise your withholding amount accordingly.	✓ As your income grows, consider tax-exempt investments like municipal bonds.	✓ Estimate Social Security benefits and plan when you will start receiving payments.
✓ Maintain a careful record of income and tax-deductible expenses.	✓ Acquire tax shelters like a mortgage, which has tax-deductible interest expenses.	✓ Consider increasing your average contributions to tax-sheltered retirement plans.	✓ Plan orderly withdrawals from tax-sheltered retirement accounts and associated tax bill.
✓ Consider using tax preparation software.	✓ Make regular contributions to your employer's tax-sheltered retirement plan and consider IRAs.	✓ Consider "catch up" larger retirement plan contributions.	✓ Consider the use of life insurance to manage potential estate taxes. This is covered in more detail in Chapter 15.

Financial Impact of Personal Choices
Angela and Tim's Tax Management Strategy

Angela and Tim are a married couple in their late 20s. Angela is an electrical engineer and Tim is a freelance computer programmer. They recently saw a newscast about the budget deficit in the United States and believe it's likely tax rates will increase significantly by the time they retire. Tim expects to finish a large programming job toward the end of this year and is preparing to bill his client. The couple expects their marginal tax rate to increase from 15 percent to 25 percent next year. What tax management strategies should they pursue?

Angela and Tim decided that they should get more serious about retirement planning given the prospect of a larger tax bite next year and going forward. So they each invested $3,000 in an IRA this year and plan to invest the maximum next year. Angela invested in a traditional IRA that reduces their taxable income by $3,000 this year. Her plan to invest more next year will provide even more of a benefit given their higher expected tax rate. Tim invested in a Roth IRA, which provides no tax benefit this year but will shield the future value of the IRA from ever being taxed. This addresses their long-term concerns. Finally, Tim decided to bill his client immediately to speed the receipt of the consulting income to this year when their tax rate is expected to be lower than next year. Tim and Angela are well on their way to managing their taxes effectively.

Summary

LG1 Discuss the basic principles of income taxes and determine your filing status, p. 86

The dominant tax in our country today is the federal income tax, a levy that provides the government with most of the funds it needs to cover its operating costs. Federal income tax rates are progressive, so that your tax rate increases as your income rises. Other types of taxes include state and local income taxes, sales taxes, and property taxes. The administration and enforcement of federal tax laws is the responsibility of the IRS, a part of the U.S. Department of the Treasury. The amount of taxes that you owe depends on your filing status—single, married filing jointly, married filing separately, head of household, or qualifying widow(er) with dependent child—and the amount of taxable income that you report. Because the government collects taxes on a pay-as-you-go basis, employers are required to withhold taxes from their employees' paychecks.

LG2 Describe the sources of gross income and adjustments to income, differentiate between standard and itemized deductions and exemptions, and calculate taxable income, p. 90

Gross income includes active income (such as wages, bonuses, pensions, alimony), portfolio income (dividends, interest, and capital gains), and passive income (income derived from real estate, limited partnerships, and other tax shelters). You must decide whether to take the standard deduction or itemize your various deductions. Some allowable deductions for those who itemize include mortgage interest, medical expenses, and certain job-related expenses. To calculate taxable income, deduct allowable adjustments, such as IRA contributions and alimony paid, from gross income to get AGI; then subtract from AGI the amount of deductions and personal exemptions claimed.

LG3 Prepare a basic tax return using the appropriate tax forms and rate schedules, p. 96

After determining your taxable income, you can find the amount of taxes owed using either the tax rate tables or, if your taxable income is over $100,000, the tax rate schedules. Tax rates vary with the level of taxable income and filing status. Personal tax returns are filed using one of these forms: *1040EZ*, *1040A*, or *1040*. Certain taxpayers must include schedules with their *Form 1040*.

LG4 **Explain who needs to pay estimated taxes, when to file or amend your return, and how to handle an audit, p. 107**
Persons with income not subject to withholding may need to file a declaration of estimated taxes and make tax payments in four installments. Annual returns must usually be filed on or before April 15, unless the taxpayer requests an automatic 6-month filing extension. The IRS audits selected returns to confirm their validity by carefully examining the data reported in them.

LG5 **Know where to get help with your taxes and how software can make tax return preparation easier, p. 107**
Assistance in preparing returns is available from the IRS and private tax preparers such as national and local tax firms, certified public accountants, enrolled agents, and tax attorneys. Computer programs can help do-it-yourselfers with both tax planning and tax preparation.

LG6 **Implement an effective tax planning strategy, p. 112**
The objectives of tax planning are to reduce, shift, or defer taxes so that the taxpayer gets maximum use of and benefits from the money he or she earns. Some of the more popular tax strategies include maximizing deductions, shifting income to relatives in lower tax brackets, investing in tax-exempt municipal bonds, setting up IRAs, and using other types of pension and retirement plans and annuities to generate tax-deferred income.

Key Terms

adjusted gross income (AGI), 94

adjustments to (gross) income, 93

amended return, 109

average tax rate, 88

estimated taxes, 108

exemptions, 95

Federal Insurance Contributions Act (FICA, or social security), 89

federal withholding taxes, 90

gross income, 92

income shifting, 114

income taxes, 87

itemized deductions, 95

marginal tax rate, 88

progressive tax structure, 87

standard deduction, 94

taxable income, 90

taxes, 86

tax audit, 109

tax avoidance, 113

tax credits, 99

tax deferred, 114

tax evasion, 113

Answers to Test Yourself

You can find answers to these questions on this book's companion website. Look for it at *www. cengagebrain.com*. Search for this book by its title, and then add it to your dashboard.

Financial Planning Exercises

LG2, 3, p. 90, 96

1. ***Estimating taxable income, tax liability, and potential refund.*** Sophia Johnson is 24 years old and single, lives in an apartment, and has no dependents. Last year she earned $55,000 as a sales assistant for Office Furniture Rentals, $6,910 of her wages were withheld for federal income taxes. In addition, she had interest income of $142. She takes the standard deduction. Calculate her taxable income, tax liability, and tax refund or tax owed.

LG2, p. 90

2. ***Calculating gross income and tax exempt income.*** Emma Williams received the following items and amounts of income during 2014. Help her calculate (a) her gross income and (b) that portion (dollar amount) of her income that is tax exempt.

Salary	$33,500
Dividends	800
Gift from mother	500
Child support from ex-husband	3,600
Interest on savings account	250
Rent	900
Loan from bank	2,000
Interest on state government bonds	300

LG2, p. 90

3. ***Calculating taxes on security transactions.*** If Olivia Garcia is single and in the 28 percent tax bracket, calculate the tax associated with each of the following transactions. (Use the IRS regulations for capital gains in effect in 2014.)
   a. She sold stock for $1,200 that she purchased for $1,000 5 months earlier.
   b. She sold bonds for $4,000 that she purchased for $3,000 3 years earlier.
   c. She sold stock for $1,000 that she purchased for $1,500 15 months earlier.

LG2, p. 90

4. ***Effect of tax credit vs. tax exemption.*** Explain and calculate the differences resulting from a $2,000 tax credit versus a $2,000 tax deduction for a single taxpayer in the 25 percent tax bracket with $40,000 of pre-tax income.

LG3, p. 96

5. ***Choosing and preparing an individual's tax form. Use Worksheets 3.1 and 3.2***. Henry Zhao graduated from college in 2014 and began work as a systems analyst in July 2014. He is preparing to file his income tax return for 2014, and has collected the following financial information for calendar year 2014:

Tuition, scholarships, and grants	$ 5,750
Scholarship, room, and board	1,850
Salary	30,250
Interest income	185
Deductible expenses, total	3,000
Income taxes withheld	2,600

   a. Prepare Henry's 2014 tax return, using a $6,200 standard deduction, a personal exemption of $3,950, and the tax rates given in Exhibit 3.3. Which tax form should Henry use, and why?
   b. Prepare Henry's 2014 tax return using the data in part a, along with the following information:

IRA contribution	$5,000
Cash dividends received	150

   Which tax form should he use in this case? Why?

LG2, 3,
p. 90, 96

6. ***Calculating taxable income for a married couple filing jointly.*** Ethan and Zoe Wilson are married and have one child. Ethan is putting together some figures so that he can prepare the Wilson's joint 2014 tax return. He can claim three personal exemptions (including himself). So far, he's been able to determine the following with regard to income and possible deductions:

Total unreimbursed medical expenses incurred	$ 1,155
Gross wages and commissions earned	50,770
IRA contribution	5,000
Mortgage interest paid	5,200
Capital gains realized on assets held less than 12 months	1,450
Income from limited partnership	200
Job expenses and other allowable deductions	875
Interest paid on credit cards	380
Dividend and interest income earned	610
Sales taxes paid	2,470
Charitable contributions made	1,200
Capital losses realized	3,475
Interest paid on a car loan	570
Alimony paid by Ethan to his first wife	6,000
Social Security taxes paid	2,750
Property taxes paid	700
State income taxes paid	1,700

Given this information, how much taxable income will the Wilsons have in 2014? (*Note:* Assume that Ethan is covered by a pension plan where he works, the standard deduction of $12,400 for married filing jointly applies, and each exemption claimed is worth $3,950.)

LG4, p. 107

7. ***Preparing for a tax audit.*** Jacob and Mia Davis have been notified that they are being audited. What should they do to prepare for the audit?

Applying Personal Finance

Tax Relief

Even though many were eliminated by the Tax Reform Act of 1986, tax shelters are still around. Beware, however, because some are legitimate, while others are not. American taxpayers have the right to lower their tax burdens, so long as they do it by legal means. This project will help you to learn about any tax shelters currently allowed by law.

Where can you go to find tax shelter opportunities? First, try the financial section of your newspaper. There may be advertisements or articles on tax shelters, such as tax-free bond funds. A bank is another source. Simply ask at the "new accounts" department for tax shelter information. Another major source of new tax shelters is the brokerage houses that sell stocks, bonds, and other securities to the investing public. If you have access to a brokerage house, ask them for tax shelter information. Also, you might want to search for "tax shelters" on the Internet.

List the tax shelters you've found. Do any apply to you now, or are there any that you'd like to use in the future? Finally, pull up the IRS Web site at **http://www.irs.gov** and search for "abusive tax shelters" to determine if the tax shelters you have found are allowed by current tax laws.

LG1, 2, 3,
p. 86, 90, 96

3.1 The Andersons Tackle Their Tax Return

Noah and Olivia Anderson are a married couple in their early 20s living in Dallas. Noah Anderson earned $73,000 in 2014 from his sales job. During the year, his employer withheld $9,172 for income tax purposes. In addition, the Andersons received interest of $350 on a joint savings account, $750 interest on tax-exempt municipal bonds, and dividends of $400 on common stocks. At the end of 2014, the Andersons sold two stocks, A and B. Stock A was sold for $700 and had been purchased four months earlier for $800. Stock B was sold for $1,500 and had been purchased three years earlier for $1,100. Their only child, Logan, age 2, received (as his sole source of income) dividends of $200 from Hershey stock.

Although Noah is covered by his company's pension plan, he plans to contribute $5,000 to a traditional deductible IRA for 2014. Here are the amounts of money paid out during the year by the Andersons:

Medical and dental expenses (unreimbursed)	$ 200
State and local property taxes	831
Interest paid on home mortgage	4,148
Charitable contributions	1,360
Total	$6,539

In addition, Noah incurred some unreimbursed travel costs for an out-of-town business trip:

Airline ticket	$250
Taxis	20
Lodging	60
Meals (as adjusted to 50 percent of cost)	36
Total	$366

Critical Thinking Questions

1. Using the Andersons' information, determine the total amount of their itemized deductions. Assume that they'll use the filing status of married filing jointly, the standard deduction for that status is $12,400, and each exemption claimed is worth $3,950. Should they itemize or take the standard deduction? Prepare a joint tax return for Noah and Olivia Anderson for the year ended December 31, 2014, that gives them the smallest tax liability. Use the appropriate tax rate schedule provided in Exhibit 3.3 to calculate their taxes owed.
2. How much have you saved the Andersons through your treatment of their deductions?
3. Discuss whether the Andersons need to file a tax return for their son.
4. Suggest some tax strategies that the Andersons might use to reduce their tax liability for next year.

3.2 Kendra Thayer: Waitress or Tax Expert?

Kendra Thayer, who is single, goes to graduate school part-time and works as a waitress at the Backwater Grill in New York. During the past year (2014), her gross income was $18,700 in wages and tips. She has decided to prepare her own tax return because she cannot afford the services of a tax expert. After preparing her return, she comes to you for advice. Here's a summary of the figures that she has prepared thus far:

Gross income:	
Wages	$10,500
Tips	+8,200
Adjusted gross income (AGI)	$18,700
Less: Itemized deductions	−2,300
	$16,400
Less: Standard deduction	−6,200
Taxable income	$10,600

Kendra believes that if an individual's income falls below $20,350, the federal government considers him or her "poor" and allows both itemized deductions and a standard deduction.

Critical Thinking Questions

1. Calculate Kendra Thayer's taxable income, being sure to consider her exemption. Assume that the standard deduction for a single taxpayer is $6,200, and that each exemption claimed is worth $3,950.
2. Discuss Kendra's errors in interpreting the tax laws, and explain the difference between itemized deductions and the standard deduction.
3. Kendra has been dating Joe Keating for nearly four years, and they are seriously thinking about getting married. Joe has income and itemized deductions that are identical to Kendra's. How much tax would they pay as a married couple (using the filing status of married filing jointly and a standard deduction of $12,400) versus the total amount the two would pay as single persons (each using the filing status of single)? Strictly from a tax perspective, does it make any difference whether Kendra and Joe stay single or get married? Explain.

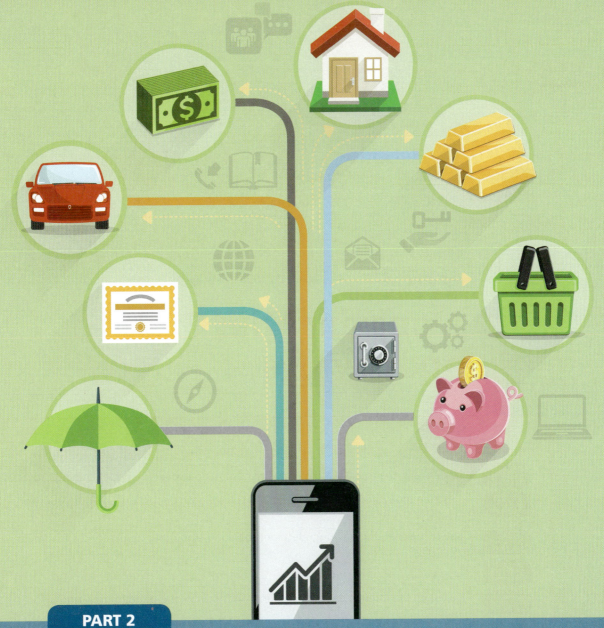

Managing Basic Assets

CHAPTERS

Managing Your Cash and Savings

How Will This Affect Me?

Finding the best mix of alternative cash management accounts and assets requires careful cost/benefit analysis based on your personal objectives and constraints.

This chapter presents a variety of different alternatives and focuses on key characteristics that include minimum balances, interest rate returns and costs, liquidity, and safety. Cash management alternatives examined include checking and savings accounts, money market deposit accounts, certificates of deposit (CDs), money market mutual funds, U.S. Treasury bills, U.S. Series EE bonds, and U.S. Series I bonds. After reading this chapter you should be able to design an effective cash management strategy, which is an integral part of your comprehensive financial plan.

4-1 THE ROLE OF CASH MANAGEMENT IN PERSONAL FINANCIAL PLANNING

cash management
The routine, day-to-day administration of cash and near-cash resources, also known as *liquid assets,* by an individual or family.

Establishing good financial habits involves managing cash as well as other areas of personal finance. In this chapter we focus on **cash management**—the routine, day-to-day administration of cash and near-cash resources, also known as *liquid assets,* by an individual or family. These assets are considered liquid because they're either held in cash or can be readily converted into cash with little or no loss in value.

In addition to cash, there are several other kinds of liquid assets, including checking accounts, savings accounts, money market deposit accounts, money market mutual funds, and other short-term investment vehicles. As a rule, near-term needs are met using cash on hand, and unplanned or future needs are met using some type of savings or short-term investment vehicle. Exhibit 4.1 briefly describes some popular types of liquid assets and the representative rates of return they earned in mid-2015. The rates reflect the Federal Reserve's (the Fed's) policy goal of keeping rates low to help stimulate the economy during the fragile period following the global financial crisis of 2008–2009. As detailed below, these low interest rates pose difficult problems for some consumers.

In personal financial planning, efficient cash management ensures adequate funds for both household use and an effective savings program. The success of your financial plans depends on your ability to develop and follow cash budgets like those discussed in Chapter 2.

EXHIBIT 4.1   **Where to Stash the Cash**

The wide variety of liquid assets available meets just about any savings or short-term investment need. Rates vary considerably both by type of asset and point in time, so shop around for the best interest rate.

REPRESENTATIVE RATES OF RETURN

Type	Mid-2015	Description
Cash	0%	Pocket money; the coin and currency in one's possession.
Checking account	0%–0.37%	A substitute for cash. Offered by commercial banks and other financial institutions such as savings and loans and credit unions.
Savings account/ Money market deposit	0.05%–1.25%	Savings accounts are available at any time, but funds cannot be withdrawn by check. Money market deposit accounts (MMDAs) require a fairly large (typically $1,000 or more) minimum deposit, and offer check-writing privileges.
Certificate of deposit (CD)	0.33%–1.25% (1-year)	A savings instrument where funds are left on deposit for a stipulated period (1 week to 1 year or more); imposes a penalty for withdrawing funds early. Market yields vary by size and maturity; no check-writing privileges.
U.S. Treasury bill (T-bill)	0.06% (3-month)	Short-term, highly marketable security issued by the U.S. Treasury (originally issued with maturities of 13 and 26 weeks); smallest denomination is $100.
U.S. savings bond (EE)	0.30%	Issued at a discount from face value by the U.S. Treasury; rate of interest is tied to U.S. Treasury securities. Long a popular savings vehicle (widely used with payroll deduction plans). Matures to face value in approximately 5 years; sold in denominations of $25 and more.

A good way to keep your spending in line is to make all household transactions (even fun money or weekly cash allowances) using a tightly controlled *checking account*. Write checks only at certain times of the week or month and, just as important, avoid carrying your checkbook (or debit card) when you might be tempted to write checks (or make debits) for unplanned purchases. If you're going shopping, set a maximum spending limit beforehand—an amount consistent with your cash budget. This system not only helps you avoid frivolous, impulsive expenditures but also documents how and where you spend your money. If your financial outcomes aren't consistent with your plans, you can better identify causes and take corrective actions.

Another aspect of cash management is establishing an ongoing savings program, which is an important part of personal financial planning. Savings are not only a cushion against financial emergencies but also a way to accumulate funds to meet future financial goals. You may want to put money aside so you can go back to school in a few years to earn a graduate degree, or buy a new home, or take a vacation. Savings will help you meet these specific financial objectives.

4-1a The Problem with Low Interest Rates

Just how low did interest rates fall in the wake of the financial crisis under the Fed's policies? Consider how some key interest rates in mid-2015 compare with their historical averages from 1980 to

Financial Fact or Fantasy?

An asset is considered liquid only if it is held in the form of cash.

Fantasy: A liquid asset is one that is held in cash or can be readily converted to cash with little or no loss in value. Thus, liquid assets include checking accounts, savings accounts, money market accounts and funds, and other short-term investment vehicles.

mid-2015. The average interest rates on 5- and 10-year Treasury bonds over this time period were 6.03 percent and 6.50 percent, respectively. In mid-2015, these rates had fallen to only 1.68 percent and 2.36 percent! And a prudent saver looking for a short-term return on a 3-month negotiable CD could only get less than 1 percent in mid-2015!

These massive drops in interest rates have important implications for your personal finances. For a sense of the significance of the drop in interest rates, consider the effect of investing $25,000 for 5 years at the low rate of only 1.68 percent in mid-2015 vs. investing at the historical average rate of 6.03 percent. After 5 years, you would have earned about $33,503 at the average rate and only about $28,982 at the lower rate.

There are benefits and costs to the unprecedentedly low interest rates that have persisted for years after the financial crisis of 2008–2009. Whether they are a net benefit or a net cost depends on your perspective. While financial markets generally reacted positively to this low rate policy by pushing up asset prices, low interest rates also tend to signal sluggish economic growth and the risk of deflation. The benefits of lower interest rates include the reduced costs of financing the massive federal budget deficit, which is a significant savings given that interest on the federal debt was $430.8 billion in 2014. And lower rates have helped support the "too big to fail" banks. Indeed, the Fed's low interest rate policy has allowed banks to pay less than 1 percent interest on savings. But the costs are equally impressive. Low interest rates reduce income to retirees and to pension funds. Some retirees have had to dip into their principal, which could put more stress on welfare programs for the elderly and may prompt the government to increase its financial support of underfunded pension funds.

The recent extremely low interest rates favor borrowers and dampen the incentive to save. While keeping big banks afloat has advantages, many argue that low interest rates have helped protect banks from absorbing the consequences of their actions and redistribute wealth away from prudent savers. Indeed, the inflation-adjusted real interest rate has been negative, which means that savers are not keeping up with inflation and will either have to tap into their principal or cut their spending. This is bad for retirees and for the overall economy. People are also giving less to charity as they seek to cover income shortfalls resulting from lower interest rates. The percentage of savings out of income is decreasing. It has fallen from a high of 8.2 percent in 1985 to a low of only 1.5 percent in 2005 and settled around 4.9 percent in late 2014.

Low interest rates also create economic distortions, especially when real, inflation-adjusted interest rates are negative. Low rates discourage savings and discourage the reduction of overall debt levels in the economy. Low interest rates also encourage investors to search for investments that pay higher income, which increases the demand for stocks paying high dividends and for lower-grade, riskier bonds. Low interest rates imply low opportunity costs for holding assets that pay no income. Investors consequently hope for asset price increases, which push up demand for commodities like gold and alternative assets (such as art) and can encourage the mispricing of risk and thereby create asset bubbles. Unfortunately, low interest rates do not seem to increase the supply of credit. Being fearful of taking much risk during and after the financial crisis, banks have tended to invest more in government securities and less in risky loans.

So what's a prudent saver to do in a low-interest-rate environment? Unfortunately, the search for higher current returns has led many people to make higher risk investments. Some move into higher-quality corporate bonds. But when rates are so low, they are likely to go up. And bond prices fall when rates rise, which poses substantial risk to longer-term bonds. More moderate strategies involve buying stocks that pay higher dividends and buying preferred stocks, which will be discussed more in Chapter 12. But stocks are generally riskier than bonds, so the pursuit of higher returns in a low-interest-rate environment must be tempered by careful consideration of the suitability of the higher risk.

TEST YOURSELF

4-1   What is *cash management,* and what are its major functions?

4-2   Give at least two reasons for holding liquid assets. Identify and briefly describe the popular types of liquid assets.

4-3   Explain the effects that historically low interest rates have on borrowers, lenders, savers, and retirees.

4-2 TODAY'S FINANCIAL SERVICES MARKETPLACE

LG2 Emily Davis hasn't been inside her bank for years. Her company pays her salary into her checking account each month by direct deposit, and she regularly does all her banking from her home computer: with the click of a mouse, she can check her account balances, pay her bills, even search for the best rates on savings instruments. And by pushing a few buttons, she is able to withdraw money from her U.S. bank account using an automated teller machine (ATM) in Geneva!

Financial Fact or Fantasy?

Today's financial marketplace offers consumers a full range of financial products and services, many times all under one roof.
Fact: The financial marketplace offers financial products such as checking and savings accounts, credit cards, loans and mortgages, insurance, and mutual funds, and financial services concerned with financial planning, taxes, real estate, trusts, retirement, and estate planning. Such products and services are offered by banks and savings institutions, insurance companies, brokerage firms, mutual funds, and even nonfinancial companies like Kroger and General Motors.

The pace of change in the financial services industry is accelerating, thanks to advanced technology and less restrictive regulations. Consumers can now choose from many financial institutions competing for their business. No longer must you go to one place for your checking accounts, another for credit cards or loans, and yet another for stock brokerage services. Today, financial institutions are expanding services and are competitively pricing products by bundling different accounts. For example, if you have $25,000 in Bank of America/Merrill Lynch accounts, you're eligible for reduced or zero-cost commissions on stock trades, free checking, free bill-pay, a credit card, and free ATM debit card transactions. And online banking allows you to easily access all of these services. It's your choice: you can choose an institution like Bank of America that provides "one-stop shopping," or you can have accounts with a variety of financial service providers, depending on what's best for you.

The *financial services industry,* comprises all institutions that market various kinds of *financial products* (such as checking and savings accounts, credit cards, loans and mortgages, insurance, and mutual funds) and *financial services* (such as financial planning, securities brokerage, tax filing and planning, estate planning, real estate, trusts, and retirement). What 30 years ago were several distinct (though somewhat related) industries is now, in essence, one industry in which firms are differentiated more by organizational structure than by name or product offerings.

4-2a Types of Financial Institutions

Financial institutions can be classified into two broad groups—depository and nondepository—based on whether or not they accept deposits as traditional banks do.

Depository Financial Institutions

The vast majority of financial transactions take place at *depository financial institutions*—commercial banks (both brick-and-mortar and Internet), savings and loan associations

Behavior Matters

Why Can't I Seem to Save More—and What Can I Do about It?

There's a well-worn joke about meaning to read a book about procrastination … but you just can't get around to it. Similarly, procrastination is a common behavioral bias that often keeps us from saving more because we just keep putting it off. People are most likely to procrastinate when they make decisions that are perceived as complex. For example, if you view the saving decision more broadly as a set of complex investment decisions, you're more likely to put off the decision to save more. So what's the best way to save more? Simplify the decision by adopting an easy plan, like saving 10 percent of your income by directing your bank to automatically transfer the money each month from your checking to savings account. Putting basic decisions like this on autopilot combats our natural tendency to procrastinate. That's a start that you can build on before approaching more complex investing decisions. But no savings means nothing to invest … it's best to act now and not worry about specific savings decisions every month.

VLADGRIN/SHUTTERSTOCK.COM

(S&Ls), savings banks, and credit unions. Although they're regulated by different agencies, depository financial institutions are commonly referred to as "banks" because of their similar products and services. What sets these institutions apart from others is their ability to accept deposits; most people use them for checking and savings account needs. These depository financial institutions are briefly described in Exhibit 4.2.

EXHIBIT 4.2   Depository Financial Institutions

Depository financial institutions differ from their nonbank counterparts, such as stock brokerages and mutual funds, in their ability to accept deposits. Most consumers use these institutions to meet their checking and savings account needs.

Institution	Description
Commercial bank	Offers checking and savings accounts and a full range of financial products and services; the only institution that can offer *non-interest-paying checking accounts (demand deposits)*. The most popular of the depository financial institutions. Most are traditional *brick-and-mortar banks,* but **Internet banks**—online commercial banks—are becoming more popular because of their convenience, lower service fees, and higher interest paid on account balances.
Savings and loan association (S&L)	Channels the savings of depositors primarily into mortgage loans for purchasing and improving homes. Also offers many of the same checking, saving, and lending products as commercial banks. Often pays slightly higher interest on savings than do commercial banks.
Savings bank	Similar to S&Ls, but located primarily in the New England states. Most are *mutual* associations—their depositors are their owners and thus receive a portion of the profits in the form of interest on their savings.
Credit union	A nonprofit, member-owned financial cooperative that provides a full range of financial products and services to its *members,* who must belong to a common occupation, religious or fraternal order, or residential area. Generally small institutions when compared with commercial banks and S&Ls. Offer interest-paying checking accounts—called **share draft accounts**—and a variety of saving and lending programs. Because they are run to benefit their members, they pay higher interest on savings and charge lower rates on loans than do other depository financial institutions.

internet banks
An online commercial bank.

share draft account
An account offered by credit unions that is similar to interest-paying checking accounts offered by other financial institutions.

deposit insurance
A type of insurance that protects funds on deposit against failure of the institution; can be insured by the FDIC and the NCUA.

Nondepository Financial Institutions

Other types of financial institutions that offer banking services, but don't accept deposits like traditional banks, are considered *nondepository institutions*. Today you can hold a credit card issued by a stock brokerage firm or have an account with a mutual fund that allows you to write a limited number of checks.

- *Stock brokerage firms* offer several cash management options, including money market mutual funds that invest in short-term securities and earn a higher rate of interest than bank accounts, special "wrap" accounts, and credit cards.
- *Mutual funds,* discussed in detail in Chapter 13, provide yet another alternative to bank savings accounts. Like stockbrokers, mutual fund companies offer money market mutual funds.

Other nondepository financial institutions include life insurance and finance companies.

4-2b How Safe Is Your Money?

Today, the main reason that a bank goes out of business is its purchase by another bank. Almost all commercial banks, S&Ls, savings banks, and credit unions are federally insured by U.S. government agencies. The few that are not federally insured usually obtain insurance through either a state-chartered or private insurance agency. Most experts believe that these privately insured institutions have less protection against loss than those that are federally insured. Exhibit 4.3 lists the insuring agencies and maximum insurance amounts provided under the various federal deposit insurance programs.

Deposit insurance protects the funds you have on deposit at banks and other depository institutions against institutional failure. In effect, the insuring agency stands behind the financial institution and guarantees the safety of your deposits up to a specified maximum amount. The ordinary amount covered per depositor by federal insurance was $100,000 prior to the financial crisis, and it was increased to $250,000 in 2009. Deposit insurance is provided to the *depositor* rather than a *deposit account.* Thus, the checking *and* savings accounts of each depositor are insured and, *as long as the maximum insurable amount is not exceeded,* the depositor can have any number of accounts and still be fully protected. This is an important feature to keep in mind because many people mistakenly believe that the maximum insurance applies to *each* of their accounts.

EXHIBIT 4.3 Federal Deposit Insurance Programs

If your checking and savings accounts are at a federally insured institution, you are covered up to $250,000.

Savings Institution	Insuring Agency	Insurance Amounts
Commercial bank	Federal Deposit Insurance Corporation (FDIC)	$250,000/depositor through the Bank Insurance Fund (BIF)
Savings and loan association	FDIC	$250,000/depositor through the Savings Association Insurance Fund (SAIF)
Savings bank	FDIC	$250,000/depositor through the BIF
Credit union	National Credit Union Administration (NCUA)	$250,000/depositor through the National Credit Union Share Insurance Fund (NCUSIF)

Now that banks are offering a greater variety of products, including mutual funds, it's important to remember that only deposit accounts, including CDs, are covered by deposit insurance. *Securities purchased through your bank are not protected by any form of deposit insurance.*

As a depositor, it's possible to increase your $250,000 of deposit insurance if necessary by opening accounts in different depositor names at the same institution. For example, a married couple can obtain $1,500,000 or more in coverage, apart from the coverage of CDs noted below, by setting up several accounts:

- One in the name of each spouse ($500,000 in coverage)
- A *joint* account in both names (good for $500,000, which is $250,000 per account owner)
- *Separate trust or self-directed retirement (IRA, Keogh, etc.) accounts* in the name of each spouse (good for an additional $250,000 per spouse)

In this case, each depositor name is treated as a separate legal entity, receiving full insurance coverage—the husband alone is considered one legal entity, the wife another, and the husband and wife as a couple a third. The trust and self-directed retirement accounts are also viewed as separate legal entities. The Certificate of Deposit Account Registry Service (CDARS) allows a bank to provide customers with full FDIC insurance on CDs up to $50 million. This is available to businesses, nonprofit companies, public funds, and consumers.

TEST YOURSELF

4-4 Briefly describe the basic operations of—and the products and services offered by—each of the following financial institutions: (a) commercial bank, (b) savings and loan association, (c) savings bank, (d) credit union, (e) stock brokerage firm, and (f) mutual fund.

4-5 What role does the FDIC play in insuring financial institutions? What other federal insurance program exists? Explain.

4-6 Would it be possible for an *individual* to have, say, six or seven checking and savings accounts at the same bank and still be fully protected under federal deposit insurance? Explain. Describe how it would be possible for a *married couple* to obtain $1,500,000 in federal deposit insurance coverage at a single bank.

4-3 A FULL MENU OF CASH MANAGEMENT PRODUCTS

After meeting with an officer at his local bank, Raul Rodriguez was confused. As a student on a tight budget, working to pay his way through college, Raul knew how important it was to plan his saving and spending, and he wanted to make the right decisions about managing his financial resources. By using a checking account comparison chart, like to the one in Exhibit 4.4, Raul could compare information on daily balance requirements, service fees, interest rates, and the services his bank offers to college students and others. As Exhibit 4.4 demonstrates, banks offer a variety of convenient checking account services.

4-3a Checking and Savings Accounts

People hold cash and other forms of liquid assets, such as checking and savings accounts, for the convenience they offer in making purchase transactions, meeting normal living expenses, and providing a safety net, or cushion, to meet unexpected expenses or take advantage of unanticipated opportunities. Financial institutions compete to offer a wide array of products meeting every liquid-asset need.

The federal *Truth-in-Savings Act of 1993* helps consumers evaluate the terms and costs of banking products. Depository financial institutions must clearly disclose fees, interest rates, and terms—of both checking and savings accounts. The Act places strict controls on bank advertising and on what constitutes a "free" account. For example, banks cannot advertise free checking if there are minimum balance requirements or

EXHIBIT 4.4	Checking Accounts Comparison Chart

Most banks offer a variety of checking account options, typically differentiated by minimum balances, fees, and other services.

REPRESENTATIVE BANK USA

Features	College Checking	Custom Checking	Advantage Checking	Advantage Plus Checking
Minimum daily balance (to waive monthly service fee)	None	$750 in checking	$5,000 in checking	$7,500 combined balance
Monthly service fee	$5.95	$9 with direct deposit	$11 without direct deposit; no fee with Homeowner's Option	$12 ($2 discount with direct deposit)
Interest	No	No	Yes	Yes
Online statements	Free	Free	Free	Free
Check safekeeping	Free	Free	Free	Free
Monthly check return	$3.00	$3.00	$3.00	Free
ATM and check card	Free	Free	Free	Free
Bank by phone	Free automated calls	Free automated calls	Free automated calls	Free banker-assisted calls
Overdraft protection	Credit card	Credit card	Credit card, line of credit account, and select deposit accounts	Credit card, line of credit account, and select deposit accounts
Direct deposit advance service	Not available	Yes, with a direct deposit of $100 a month or more	Yes, with a direct deposit of $100 a month or more	Yes, with a direct deposit of $100 a month or more

per-check charges. Banks must use a standard *annual percentage yield (APY)* formula that considers compounding (discussed later) when stating the interest paid on accounts. This makes it easier for consumers to compare each bank's offerings. The law also requires banks to pay interest on a customer's full daily or monthly average deposit balance. Banks are prohibited from paying interest on only the lowest daily balance and from paying no interest if the account balance falls below the minimum balance for just 1 day. In addition, banks must notify customers 30 days in advance before lowering rates on deposit accounts or CDs.

Checking Accounts

demand deposit
An account held at a financial institution from which funds can be withdrawn on demand by the account holder; same as a *checking account*.

A checking account held at a financial institution is a **demand deposit**, meaning, that the bank must permit these funds to be withdrawn whenever the account holder demands. You put money into your checking account by *depositing* funds; you withdraw it by *writing a check, using a debit card,* or *making a cash withdrawal.* As long as you have sufficient funds in your account, the bank, when presented with a valid check or an electronic debit, must immediately pay the amount indicated by deducting it from your account. Money held in checking accounts is liquid, so you can easily use it to pay bills and make purchases.

Regular checking is the most common type of checking account. Traditionally, it pays no interest, and any service charges can be waived if you maintain a minimum balance (usually between $500 and $1,500). Many banks are moving away from such minimum balance requirements. Technically, only commercial banks can offer non-interest-paying regular checking accounts. Savings banks, S&Ls, and credit unions also offer checking accounts; but these accounts, which must pay interest, are called *negotiable order of withdrawal (NOW) accounts* or, in the case of credit unions, *share draft accounts.* Demand deposit balances are an important type of cash balance, and using checks to pay bills or electronic debits to make purchases gives you a convenient payment record.

Savings Accounts

time deposits
A savings deposit at a financial institution; remains on deposit for a longer time than a demand deposit.

A savings account is another type of liquid asset available at commercial banks, S&Ls, savings banks, credit unions, and other types of financial institutions. Savings deposits are referred to as **time deposits** because they are expected to remain on deposit for longer periods of time than demand deposits. Because savings deposits earn higher rates of interest, savings accounts are typically preferable to checking accounts when the depositor's goal is to accumulate money for a future expenditure or to maintain balances for meeting unexpected expenses. Most banks pay higher interest rates on larger savings account balances. For example, a bank might pay 0.5 percent on balances up to $2,500, 0.65 percent on balances between $2,500 and $10,000, and 0.75 percent on balances of more than $10,000. As noted above, current interest rates are extremely low by historical standards due to the Fed's post-crisis policy initiatives.

Although financial institutions generally have the right to require a savings account holder to wait a certain number of days before receiving payment of a withdrawal, most are willing to pay withdrawals immediately. In addition to withdrawal policies and deposit insurance, the stated interest rate and the method of calculating interest paid on savings accounts are important considerations when choosing the financial institution in which to place your savings.

Interest-Paying Checking Accounts

Depositors can choose from NOW accounts, money market deposit accounts, and money market mutual funds.

negotiable order of withdrawal (NOW) account
A checking account on which the financial institution pays interest; NOWs have no legal minimum balance.

Now Accounts Negotiable order of withdrawal (NOW) accounts are checking accounts on which the financial institution pays interest. There is no legal minimum balance for a NOW, but many institutions impose their own requirement, often between $500 and $1,000. Some pay interest on any balance in the account, but most institutions pay a higher rate of interest for balances above a specified amount.

Money Market Deposit Accounts Money market deposit accounts (MMDAs) are a popular offering at banks and other financial institutions and compete for deposits with money market mutual funds. MMDAs are popular with savers and investors because of their convenience and safety, because deposits in MMDAs (unlike those in money funds) are *federally insured*. Most banks require a minimum MMDA balance of $1,000 or more.

Depositors can use check-writing privileges or ATMs to access MMDA accounts. They receive a limited number (usually six) of free monthly checks and transfers but pay a fee on additional transactions. Although this reduces the flexibility of these accounts, most depositors view MMDAs as savings rather than convenience accounts and do not consider these restrictions a serious obstacle. Moreover, MMDAs pay the highest interest rate of any bank account on which checks can be written.

A major problem with the growing popularity of interest-paying checking accounts has been a rise in monthly bank charges, which can easily amount to more than the interest earned on all but the highest account balances. So the higher rates of interest offered by MMDAs can be misleading.

Money Market Mutual Funds Money market mutual funds have become the most successful type of mutual fund ever offered. A money market mutual fund (MMMF) pools the funds of many small investors to purchase high-return, short-term marketable securities offered by the U.S. Treasury, major corporations, large commercial banks, and various government organizations. (Mutual funds are discussed in greater detail in Chapter 13.)

MMMFs have historically paid interest at rates of 1 percent to 3 percent above those paid on regular savings accounts. Moreover, investors have instant access to their funds through check-writing privileges, although these must be written for a stipulated minimum amount (often $500). The checks look like, and are treated like, any other check drawn on a demand deposit account. As with all interest-bearing checking accounts, you continue to earn interest on your money while the checks make their way through the banking system.

Asset Management Accounts

Perhaps the best example of a banking service also offered by a nondepository financial institution is the asset management account (AMA), or *central asset account*. The AMA is a comprehensive deposit account that combines checking, investing, and borrowing activities and is offered primarily by brokerage houses and mutual funds. AMAs appeal to investors because they can consolidate most of their financial transactions at one institution and on one account statement.

A typical AMA account includes an MMDA with unlimited free checking, a Visa or MasterCard debit card, use of ATMs, and brokerage and loan accounts. Annual fees and account charges, such as a per-transaction charge for ATM withdrawals, vary; so it pays to shop around. AMAs have increased in popularity as more institutions have lowered minimum balance requirements to $5,000, and they pay higher interest rates on checking account deposits than banks do. Their distinguishing feature is that they automatically "sweep" excess balances—for example, those more than $500—into a higher-return MMMF daily or weekly. When the account holder needs funds to purchase securities or cover checks written on the MMDA, the funds are transferred back to the MMDA. If the amount of securities purchased or checks

---

money market deposit account (MMDA)
A federally insured savings account, offered by banks and other depository institutions that competes with money market mutual funds.

money market mutual fund (MMMF)
A mutual fund that pools the funds of many small investors and purchases high-return, short-term marketable securities.

Financial Fact or Fantasy?

Unlike money market mutual funds, money market deposit accounts are federally insured. **Fact**: Money market deposit accounts are funds deposited in special, higher-paying savings accounts at banks, S&Ls, and other depository institutions and thus are covered by the same federal deposit insurance as any other checking or savings account. Money market mutual funds don't have this coverage.

asset management account (AMA)
A comprehensive deposit account, offered primarily by brokerage houses and mutual funds.

presented for payment exceeds the account balance, the needed funds are supplied automatically through a loan.

Although AMAs are an attractive alternative to a traditional bank account, they have some drawbacks. Compared with banks, there are fewer "branch" locations. However, AMAs are typically affiliated with ATM networks, making it easy to withdraw funds. Yet ATM transactions are more costly; checks can take longer to clear; and some bank services, such as traveler's and certified checks, may not be offered. AMAs are not covered by deposit insurance, although these deposits are protected by the *Securities Investor Protection Corporation* (explained in Chapter 11) and the firm's private insurance.

4-3b Electronic Banking Services

The fastest-changing area in cash management today is electronic banking services. Whether you're using an ATM or checking your account balance online, electronic banking services make managing your money easier and more convenient. Electronic funds transfer systems allow you to conduct many types of banking business at any hour of the day or night.

Electronic Funds Transfer Systems

electronic funds transfer systems (EFTSs)

Systems using the latest telecommunications and computer technology to electronically transfer funds into and out of customers' accounts.

Electronic funds transfer systems (EFTSs) use the latest telecommunications and computer technology to electronically transfer funds into and out of your account. For example, your employer may use an EFTS to electronically transfer your pay from the firm's bank account directly into your personal bank account at the same or a different bank. This eliminates the employer's need to prepare and process checks and the employee's need to deposit them. Electronic transfer systems make possible such services as debit cards and ATMs, preauthorized deposits and payments, bank-by-phone accounts, and online banking.

debit cards

Specially coded plastic cards used to transfer funds from a customer's bank account to the recipient's account to pay for goods or services.

Debit Cards and Automated Teller Machines This form of EFTS uses specially coded plastic cards, called **debit cards**, to transfer funds from the customer's bank account (a debit) to the recipient's account. A debit card may be used to make purchases at any place of business set up with the point-of-sale terminals required to accept debit card payments. The personal identification number (PIN) issued with your debit card verifies that you are authorized to access the account.

Visa and MasterCard issue debit cards linked to your checking account that give you even more flexibility. In addition to using the card to purchase goods and services, you can use it at ATMs, which have become a popular way to make banking transactions. **Automated teller machines (ATMs)** are remote computer terminals that customers of a bank or other depository institution can use to make deposits, withdrawals, and other transactions such as loan payments or transfers between accounts—24 hours a day, 7 days a week. Most banks have ATMs outside their offices, and some place freestanding ATMs in shopping malls, airports, and grocery stores; at colleges and universities; and in other high-traffic areas to enhance their competitive position. If your bank belongs to an EFTS network, such as Cirrus, Star, or Interlink, you can get cash from the ATM of any bank in the United States or overseas that is a member of that network. (In fact, the easiest way to get foreign currency when you travel overseas is through an ATM on your bank's network! It

automated teller machines (ATM)

A remote computer terminal that customers of depository institutions can use to make basic transactions 24 hours a day, 7 days a week.

ALIKEYOU/SHUTTERSTOCK.COM

also gives you the best exchange rate for your dollar.) Banks charge an average per-transaction fee of $2.60 for using the ATM of another bank, and some also charge when you use your ATM card to pay certain merchants. However, to be more competitive some banks now reimburse the fees associated with using the ATMs of other banks.

The total dollar volume of purchases made using Visa's branded debit cards surpassed credit-card purchases for the first time late in 2008. This is likely related to more cautious use of credit cards during a recession. Yet the trend was becoming clear before this because combined credit- and debit-card purchases of retail goods and services exceeded purchases via checks in 2003. Thus, plastic is growing more popular among U.S. consumers in general, with debit cards starting to overtake credit cards.

Security concerns are increasing pressure for financial institutions to replace the common magnetic strip on credit cards with EMV chips, named for its developers—Europay, MasterCard, Visa. The cardholder information is entered on a chip embedded in the card in an encrypted form. Card issuers hope to require use of EMV cards by late 2015. However, many ATMs and merchants' credit card readers are not expected to be converted by that time. In the interim, cards with both a magnetic strip and the EMV chip are being offered by issuers.

Debit card use is increasing because these cards are convenient both for retailers, who don't have to worry about bounced checks, and for consumers, who don't have to write checks and can often get cash back when they make a purchase. ATM and other debit cards are accepted by supermarkets, gas stations, and convenience stores as well as many other retail and service outlets. The convenience of debit cards may, in fact, be their biggest drawback: it can be easy to overspend. To avoid problems, make sure to record all debit card purchases immediately in your checkbook ledger and deduct them from your checkbook balance. Also be aware that if there's a problem with a purchase, you can't stop payment—an action you could take if you had paid by check or credit card.

Preauthorized Deposits and Payments Two related EFTS services are *preauthorized deposits and payments*. They allow you to receive automatic deposits or make payments that occur regularly. For example, you can arrange to have your paycheck or monthly pension or Social Security benefits deposited directly into your account. Regular, fixed-amount payments, such as mortgage and consumer loan payments or monthly retirement fund contributions, can be preauthorized to be made automatically from your account. You can also preauthorize regular payments of varying amounts such as monthly utility bills. In this case, each month you would specify by phone the amount to be paid.

Charges for preauthorized payments vary from bank to bank. Typically, customers must maintain a specified minimum deposit balance and pay fees ranging from nothing to less than $1 per transaction. This system better allows the customer to earn interest on deposits used to pay bills, and it's a convenient payment method that eliminates postage costs.

Bank-by-Phone Accounts Bank customers can make various banking transactions by telephone, either by calling a customer service operator who handles the transaction or by using the keypad on a touch-tone telephone to instruct the bank's computer. After the customer provides a passcode to access the account, the system provides the appropriate prompts to perform various transactions, such as obtaining an account balance, finding out what checks have cleared, transferring funds to other accounts, and dispatching payments to participating merchants. To encourage banking by phone, many banks today charge no fee on basic account transactions or allow a limited number of free transactions per month. However, online banking options are replacing bank-by-phone accounts.

Online Banking and Bill Payment Services

The Pew Internet & American Life Project found that over 61 percent of Internet users rely on some form of *online banking* services. The number has grown steadily as banks make online services easier to use and as people become more comfortable using the Internet for financial transactions. Many individuals just check their balances, but more than half use the Internet to transfer funds as well. Thanks to improved security procedures, most online bank services are delivered through the Internet, although some may use direct dial-up connections with the customer's bank. Today, most banks will compete for your online banking business because it's in their best financial interests to do so. A recent study showed that the cost of a full-service teller transaction is about $1, an ATM transaction is less than 30 cents, and an Internet transaction is less than 1 cent.

FINANCIAL PLANNING TIPS

Using a Debit Card Wisely

A debit card seems like a substitute for a credit card. But the way transactions are processed and the protections afforded the cardholder are significantly different. Remember that unlike a credit card, a debit card is a direct link to your bank account. You may want to use a credit card over a debit card in some situations, like the following:

- **Online and phone orders:** While your liability for fraudulent transactions is limited to $50 if you report it to your bank within two days and perhaps to zero under your bank's policies, you still face significant inconveniences. Getting money put back into your account is not easy, and your balance could drop and cause returned checks and extra fees.

- **Expensive items and delayed delivery:** While credit cards generally provide dispute rights if there is a problem with a purchase, debit cards do not generally do so. A credit card is safer to use for big purchases and items that will be delivered later. And you can sometimes get extended warranties and additional property insurance on car rentals with credit cards, which you can't for debit cards.

- **Required deposits:** Let's say that you are renting a power washer and a deposit is required. If you use a credit card to make the deposit, you retain access to the funds in your bank account and will hopefully never have to give up the money. You lose access to the money with a debit card.

- **Restaurants:** Many argue that you shouldn't let your debit card out of your sight, which always happens at a restaurant. And restaurants often authorize your card for more than the purchase amount because they expect you to add a tip. It may be for more than you actually pay, and you'll lose the use of that difference for a few days.

- **Recurring payments:** It's common to have problems stopping recurring payments like magazine subscriptions and fitness club memberships. Getting your money back is typically easier with credit cards than debit cards.

- **Future travel:** If you book airline and hotel reservations with a debit card, your money is paid out immediately. A credit card often will not be charged until close to the time you use the service (that is, when you arrive at the hotel or take the flight).

- **Hotels:** Upon check-in, some hotels place holds on your card to cover expenses for clients who may leave without settling the entire bill. This involves extra charges on a debit card that must be reversed. You probably won't even notice extra charges that will be voided on a credit card.

- **At ATMs:** Criminals are getting better at adding "skimmers" to ATMs, which read your debit card information. If you do decide to use your debit card at an ATM, make sure that the ATM looks like it's in good shape and that nothing unusual seems added.

Source: Adapted from Dana Dratch, "10 Places NOT to Use Your Debit Card," http://www.creditcards.com/credit-card-news/10-places-not-to-use-debit-card-1271.php, accessed July 2015.

Although computer-based bank-at-home systems and mobile banking don't replace the use of an ATM to obtain cash or deposit money, they can save both time and postage when you're paying bills. Other benefits include convenience and the potential to earn higher interest rates and pay lower fees. Customers like being able to check their account balances at any time of the day or night, not just when their printed statement comes once a month.

While some banks still charge for online bill payment services, they are now free at most banks. But online banking doesn't always live up to its promises. You can't make cash deposits, checks may get lost in the mail, and you don't know when the funds will reach your account. Most consumers prefer the security of a bank with a physical presence and a variety of other banking options such as branches, ATMs, and phone services. Your current "traditional" bank probably offers online and mobile banking services.

4-3c Regulation of EFTS Services

The federal *Electronic Fund Transfer Act of 1978* describes your rights and responsibilities as an EFTS user. Under this law, you cannot stop payment on a defective or questionable purchase, although individual banks and state laws have more lenient provisions. If there's an error, you must notify the bank within 60 days of its occurrence. The bank must investigate and tell you the results within 10 days. The bank can then take up to 45 more days to investigate the error but must return the disputed money to your account until the issue is resolved.

If you fail to notify the bank of the error within 60 days, the bank has no obligation under federal law to conduct an investigation or return your money. You must notify the bank immediately about the theft, loss, or unauthorized use of your EFTS card. Notification within 2 business days after you discover the card missing limits your loss to $50. After 2 business days, you may lose up to $500 (but never more than the amount that was withdrawn by the thief). If you don't report the loss within 60 days after your periodic statement was mailed, you can lose all the money in your account. When reporting errors or unauthorized transactions, it's best to notify your bank by telephone and follow up with a letter. Keep a copy of the letter in your file.

Many state regulations offer additional consumer protection regarding your use of EFTS. However, your best protection is to carefully guard the PIN used to access your accounts. Don't write the PIN on your EFTS card, and be sure to check your periodic statements regularly for possible errors or unauthorized transactions.

4-3d Other Bank Services

In addition to the services described earlier in this chapter, many banks offer other types of money management services, such as safe-deposit boxes and trust services.

- Safe-deposit boxes: A *safe-deposit* box is a rented drawer in a bank's vault. Boxes can be rented for an average of about $30 per year, depending on their size. When you rent a box, you receive one key to it, and the bank keeps another key. The box can be opened only when both keys are used. This arrangement protects items in the box from theft and serves as an excellent storage place for jewelry, contracts, stock certificates, titles, and other important documents. Keeping valuables in a safe-deposit box may also reduce your homeowner's insurance by eliminating the "riders" that are often needed to cover such items.

- Trust services: Bank trust departments provide investment and estate planning advice. They manage and administer the investments in a trust account or from an estate.

FINANCIAL PLANNING TIPS

Be Careful What You Store in a Safe-Deposit Box

- **What Should I Keep in a Safe-Deposit Box?**

Important papers include original deeds, titles, mortgages, contracts, and insurance policies. Family records, such as birth, marriage, and death certificates, can be time consuming to replace. Valuables that deserve space in a safe-deposit box include expensive jewels, medals, rare stamps, and other collectibles. It's important to keep videos or pictures of your home's contents to provide your insurance company in case of theft or damage to your house.

- **What Should I NOT Keep in a Safety Deposit Box?**

Don't keep anything in a safe-deposit box that you might need in an emergency when your bank is closed. Examples include the originals of a "power of attorney" (written authorization for another person to transact business on your behalf), passports (for an emergency trip), medical care directives if you become ill and incapacitated, and funeral or burial instructions. It's also reasonable to give the originals of important documents to your attorney and keep copies in your safe-deposit box.

- **Protect Your Property**

If a safe-deposit box is apparently unused for a number of years, your state can view it as abandoned and its contents as unclaimed property. And the majority of states do not return unclaimed property to the rightful owners. So it's important to make documented contact with your bank at least once a year and to make sure that it has your current address. Insure valuables even though they are in your safe-deposit box. This will assure that your valuables are protected even if the bank or state mistakenly takes your property or if a fire or flood destroys the contents of your box.

Source: Adapted from "Helpful Guide to Bank Safe-Deposit Boxes—Use, Access, and Safety of Safe-Deposit Boxes in U.S. Banks," http://foreignborn.com/self-help/banking/10-sd_boxes.htm, accessed July 2015; Elisabeth Leamy, "Not-So-Safe-Deposit Boxes: States Seize Citizens' Property to Balance Their Budgets," http://abcnews.go.com/GMA/story?id=4832471, accessed July 2015.

TEST YOURSELF

4-7 Distinguish between a checking account and a savings account.

4-8 Define and discuss (a) demand deposits, (b) time deposits, (c) interest-paying checking accounts.

4-9 Briefly describe the key characteristics of each of the following forms of interest-paying checking accounts: (a) NOW account, (b) MMDA, and (c) MMMF.

4-10 Describe the features of an AMA, its advantages, and its disadvantages.

4-11 Briefly describe (a) debit cards, (b) banking at ATMs, (c) preauthorized deposits and payments, (d) bank-by-phone accounts, and (e) online banking and bill-paying services.

4-12 What are your legal rights and responsibilities when using EFTSs?

4-4 MAINTAINING A CHECKING ACCOUNT

By the time Alison Brown started college, she had a thriving car-detailing business that earned her several hundred dollars per week. Some customers paid her in advance, some paid after the fact, and some forgot (or otherwise neglected) to pay at all. But by depositing each check or cash payment into her checking account, Alison was able to keep track of her earnings without complicated bookkeeping. A checking account is one of the most useful cash management tools you can have. It's a safe and convenient way to hold money and streamline point-of-sale purchases, debt payments, and other basic transactions. You can have regular or interest-paying checking accounts at commercial banks, S&Ls, savings banks, credit unions, and even brokerage houses through asset management accounts. For convenience, we'll focus on commercial bank checking accounts, although our discussion also applies to checking accounts maintained at other types of financial institutions.

4-4a Opening and Using Your Checking Account

Factors that typically influence the choice of where to maintain a checking account are convenience, services, and cost. Many people choose a bank based solely on convenience factors: business hours, location, number of drive-thru windows, and number and location of branch offices and ATMs. Ease of access is obviously an important consideration because most people prefer to bank near home or work. Although services differ from bank to bank, today most banks offer several types of accounts: debit, ATM, credit cards, and loans. Many banks also offer online and telephone banking and bill-paying services, safe-deposit box rental, provision for direct deposits and withdrawals, and mutual-fund sales.

After determining the banking services you need, evaluate the offerings of conveniently located, federally insured financial institutions. In addition to convenience and safety, consider interest rates, types of accounts (including special accounts that combine such features as credit cards, free checks, and reduced fees), structure and level of fees and charges, and quality of customer service.

The Cost of a Checking Account

Bank service charges have increased sharply owing to deregulation and the growth of interest-paying checking accounts. Today few, if any, banks and other depository institutions allow unlimited free check-writing privileges. Most banks levy monthly and per-check fees when your checking account balance drops below a required minimum, and some may charge for checking no matter how large a balance you carry.

Some banks are moving away from minimum balance requirements, but a common requirement is to maintain a minimum balance of $500 to $1,000 (or even more) to avoid service charges. Although some banks use the *average monthly* balance in an account to determine whether to levy a service charge, most use the *daily* balance procedure. This means that if your account should happen to fall just $1 below the minimum balance *just once* during the month, you'll be hit with the full service charge—even if your average balance is three times the minimum requirement.

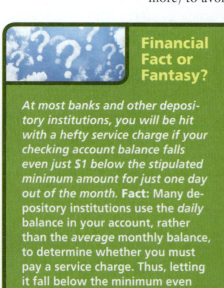

Financial Fact or Fantasy?

At most banks and other depository institutions, you will be hit with a hefty service charge if your checking account balance falls even just $1 below the stipulated minimum amount for just one day out of the month. **Fact:** Many depository institutions use the *daily* balance in your account, rather than the *average* monthly balance, to determine whether you must pay a service charge. Thus, letting it fall below the minimum even once can have a significant cost.

Service charges take two forms: (1) a base service charge of, say, $7.50 a month, and (2) additional charges of, say, 25 cents for each check you write and 10 cents for each ATM or bank-by-phone transaction. Using these fees as an illustration, assume you write 20 checks and make 7 ATM transactions in a given month. If your balance falls below the minimum, you'll have to pay a service charge of $7.50 + (20 × $0.25) + (7 × $0.10) = $13.20.

In addition to the service charges on checking accounts, banks have increased most other check-related charges and raised the minimum balances required for free checking and waivers of specified fees. The average charge on a returned check is between $25 and $30, and stop-payment orders typically cost $20 to $35. Some banks charge fees for ATM or bank-by-phone transactions that exceed a specified number. Most also charge for using the

FINANCIAL PLANNING TIPS

Choosing a Bank

If you're looking for a bank, here are some important factors to consider.

• **Convenient location, online, and mobile services.** Find a bank that is conveniently located *and* has online services, because online service providing banks tend to pay more competitive savings rates.

• **Free checking and free money transfers.** "Free checking" usually means that you aren't required to keep a minimum balance in your account and can write as many checks a month as you like. Even if it isn't labeled as such, look for free checking. Also look for banks that let you transfer funds between different accounts for free.

• **Convenient ATMs.** The average fee for using the ATM of another bank is over $4. Although some banks

are starting to refund such fees, by visiting only ATMs that belong to your bank, you can avoid all surcharges and the hassle of refunds. It is best to have an ATM close to your work and home.

• **Overdraft and FDIC protection.** Given that fees for bounced checks average about $35, it is important to know what the charges are and what kind of overdraft protection is offered. Also make sure that your deposits are insured by the FDIC.

• **Competitive interest income.** Find out if the bank pays interest on your balance. You can shop for the most competitive rates at **www.bankrate.com** and **www.bankingmyway.com**.

Source: Adapted from Farnoosh Torabi, "Back to Basics: Choosing a New Bank," http://www.mainstreet.com/article/back-to-basics-choosing-a-new-bank, accessed July 2015.

ATM of another bank that is not a member of the same network. It's not surprising that smart consumers use cost as the single most important variable when choosing where to set up a checking account.

Individual or Joint Account

Two people wishing to open a checking account may do so in one of three ways:

1. They can each open individual checking accounts (on which the other cannot write checks).
2. They can open a joint account that requires both signatures on all checks.
3. They can open a joint account that allows either one to write checks (the most common type of joint account).

One advantage of the joint account over two individual accounts is lower service charges. In addition, the account has rights of survivorship: for a married couple, this means that if one spouse dies, the surviving spouse, after fulfilling a specified legal requirement, can draw checks on the account. If account owners are treated as tenants in common rather than having rights of survivorship, then the survivor gets only his or her share of the account. Thus, when you're opening a joint account, be sure to specify the rights you prefer.

General Checking Account Procedures

After you select the bank that meets your needs and has the type of account you want, it's a simple matter to open the account. The application form asks for basic personal information such as name, date of birth, Social Security number, address, phone, and place of employment. You'll also have to provide identification, sign signature cards, and make an initial deposit. The bank will give you a supply of checks to use until your personalized checks arrive.

After opening a checking account, follow these basic procedures:

- Always write checks in ink.
- Include the name of the person being paid, the date, and the amount of the check—written in both numerals and words for accuracy.
- Sign the check the same way as on the signature card you filled out when opening the account.
- Note the check's purpose on the check—usually on the line provided in the lower left corner. This information is helpful for both budgeting and tax purposes.

Make sure to enter all checking account transactions—checks written, deposits, point-of-sale debit purchases, ATM transactions, and preauthorized automatic payments and deposits—in the **checkbook ledger** provided with your supply of checks. Then, subtract the amount of each check, debit card purchase, ATM cash withdrawal, or payment, and add the amount of each deposit to the previous balance to keep track of your current account balance. Good transaction records and an accurate balance prevent overdrawing the account.

With each deposit, write a deposit slip (generally included with your checks and also available at your bank) listing the currency, coins, and checks being deposited. List checks by the *transit ID number* printed on the check, usually at the top right. Also properly endorse all checks that you're depositing. Federal regulations require your endorsement to be made in black or blue ink, within 1½ inches of the check's trailing edge (left end of the check when viewed from the front) so as not to interfere with bank endorsements. If you don't comply, you'll still get your money but it may take longer.

To protect against possible loss of endorsed checks, it is common practice to use a special endorsement, such as "Pay to the order of XYZ Bank," or a restrictive endorsement, such as "For deposit only." If the way your name is written on the check differs from the way that you signed the signature card, you should sign your correct signature below your endorsement. To further ensure that the deposit is properly entered into your account, write your account number below your endorsement.

When depositing checks, you may encounter a delay in funds' availability that is due to the time required for them to clear. To avoid overdrawing your account, know your bank's "hold" policy on deposits, which are capped by federal maximum funds-availability delays. It generally takes between 1 and 5 business days for funds to become available. For example, on a check drawn on another local bank, funds must be made available no later than the second business day after deposit. An out-of-town check, however, may take up to 5 business days to clear. Longer holds—up to 9 business days—can be applied by banks under special circumstances, such as when large amounts (over $5,000) are deposited in a single day or when the depositor has repeatedly overdrawn his or her account during the immediately preceding 6 months.

Overdrafts

When a check is written for an amount greater than the current account balance, the result is an **overdraft**. If the overdraft is proven to be intentional, the bank can initiate legal proceedings against the account holder. The action taken by a bank on an overdraft depends on the strength of its relationship with the account holder and the amount involved. In many cases, the bank stamps the overdrawn check with the words "insufficient balance (or funds)" and returns it to the party to whom it was written. This is often called a "bounced check." The account holder is notified of this action, and the holder's bank deducts an average overdraft fee of $35 from his checking account. The depositor of a "bad check" may also be charged by her bank, which explains why merchants typically charge customers who give them bad checks $15 to $25 or more and often refuse to accept future checks from them.

When you have a good relationship with your bank or arrange **overdraft protection**, the bank will pay a check that overdraws the account. In cases where overdraft protection has not been prearranged but the bank pays the check, the account holder is

checkbook ledger
A booklet, provided with a supply of checks, used to maintain accurate records of all checking account transactions.

overdraft
The result of writing a check for an amount greater than the current account balance.

overdraft protection
An arrangement between the account holder and the depository institution wherein the institution automatically pays a check that overdraws the account.

usually notified by the bank and charged a penalty fee for the inconvenience. However, the check does not bounce, and the check writer's creditworthiness is not damaged.

There are several ways to arrange overdraft protection. Many banks offer an overdraft line of credit, which automatically extends a loan to cover the amount of an overdraft. In most cases, however, the loans are made only in specified increments, such as $50 or $100, and interest (or a fee) is levied against the loan amount, not the actual amount of the overdraft. This can be an expensive form of protection, particularly if you do not promptly repay such a loan.

For example, if you had a $110 overdraft and the bank made overdraft loans in $100 increments, it would automatically deposit $200 in your account. If the bank charged 12 percent annually (or 1 percent per month) and you repaid the loan within a month, you would incur total interest of $2 ([$200 × 12%]/12). But remember, you paid interest on $90 ($200 – $110) that you didn't need, and the annualized rate of interest on this overdraft loan is *21.8 percent* ([$2/$110] × 12)!

Another way to cover overdrafts is with an *automatic transfer program*, which automatically transfers funds from your savings account into your checking account in the event of an overdraft. Under this program, some banks charge both an annual fee and a fee on each transfer. Of course, the best form of overdraft protection is to use good cash management techniques and regularly balance your checking account.

Stopping Payment

stop payment
An order made by an account holder instructing the depository institution to refuse payment on an already issued check.

Occasionally it's necessary to **stop payment** on a check that has been issued because a good or service paid for by check is found to be faulty (though some states prohibit you from stopping payment on faulty goods or services) or on a check issued as part of a contract that is not carried out. If your checks or checkbook are lost or stolen, there's no need to stop payment on them because you have no personal liability. Stopping payment in this case only incurs expense; it doesn't change your personal liability.

To stop payment on a check, you must notify the bank and fill out a form indicating the check number and date, amount, and the name of the person to whom it was written. You can initiate stop-payment orders online or by phone. Once you place a stop-payment order, the bank refuses payment on the affected check, and the check will be rejected if another bank presents it in the check-clearing process. Banks typically charge a fee ranging from $20 to $35 to stop payment on a check.

4-4b Monthly Statements

Once a month, your bank provides a statement—an itemized listing of all transactions in your checking account (checks written, ATM transactions, debit purchases, automatic payments, and deposits made). Also included are bank service charges and interest earned (see Jackson Smith's May 2017 bank statement in Exhibit 4.5). Some banks include your original canceled checks with your bank statement, although most are abandoning this practice as we move closer to a "paperless society." Many banks now let you view canceled checks online, free of charge. It's important to review your monthly bank statement to verify the accuracy of your account records and to reconcile differences between the statement balance and the balance shown in your checkbook ledger. The monthly statement is also a valuable source of information for your tax records.

Account Reconciliation

account reconciliation
Verifying the accuracy of your checking account balance in relation to the bank's records as reflected in the bank statement, which is an itemized listing of all transactions in the checking account.

You should reconcile your bank account as soon as possible after receiving your monthly statement. The **account reconciliation** process, or *balancing the checkbook*, can uncover errors in recording checks or deposits, in addition or subtraction, and, occasionally, in the bank's processing of a check. It can also help you avoid overdrafts by forcing you to verify your account balance monthly. Assuming that neither you nor the bank has made any errors, discrepancies between your checkbook ledger account balance and your bank statement can be attributed to one of four factors:

EXHIBIT 4.5   A Bank Statement

Each month, you receive a statement from your bank or depository financial institution that summarizes the month's transactions and shows your latest account balance. This sample statement for Jackson Smith not only shows the checks that have been paid, but it also lists all ATM transactions, point-of-sale transactions using his ATM card (e.g., the Interlink payments at Lucky Stores), and direct payroll deposits.

```
        YOUR BANK                          #240
        P.O. BOX 516   ANY CITY, USA    90000-0000

            JACKSON G. SMITH
            1765 SHERIDAN DRIVE              N        CALL (800) 222-0000
            YOUR CITY, STATE 12091          21        24 HOURS/DAY, 7 DAYS/WEEK
                                                      FOR ASSISTANCE WITH
                                                      YOUR ACCOUNT.

    PAGE 1 OF 1       THIS STATEMENT COVERS: 4/30/2017 THROUGH 5/29/2017
    _____
    PREMIUM           SUMMARY
    ACCOUNT
                      PREVIOUS BALANCE        473.68    MINIMUM BALANCE    21.78
    0123-45678        DEPOSITS              1,302.83+
                      WITHDRAWALS           1,689.02-
                      SERVICE CHARGES           7.50-
                      DIRECT DEPOSIT DISCOUNT   1.00+
                      NEW BALANCE              80.99

    CHECKS AND        CHECK    DATE PAID    AMOUNT    CHECK    DATE PAID   AMOUNT
    WITHDRAWALS       203        5/01        10.00     213       5/08       40.00
                      204        4/30        15.00     214       5/09        9.58
                      205        5/10       635.00     215       5/20       66.18
                      206        5/08        25.00     216       5/20       64.92
                      207        5/07        19.00     217       5/21       25.03
                      208        5/07        50.00     218       5/21       37.98
                      209        5/08        15.00     219       5/22       35.00
                      210        5/10        83.00     220       5/22      105.00
                      211        5/10        10.00     222*      5/22      100.00
                      212        5/08        70.00     223       5/21       40.00
                                                       224       5/29       40.82

                      PREMIUM ACCOUNT FEE LESS $1.00 DISCOUNT    4/30        6.50
    ATM
    TRANSACTIONS      INTERLINK PURCHASE #572921 ON 04/30 AT     5/01       50.00
                      LUCKY STORE NO 043
                      WITHDRAWAL #08108 AT 00165A ON 05/04       5/06       20.00
                      INTERLINK PURCHASE #807409 ON 05/11 AT     5/13       12.51
                      LUCKY STORE NO 056
                      WITHDRAWAL #01015 AT 00240C ON 05/17       5/17       20.00
                      WITHDRAWAL #04792 AT 00167C ON 05/20       5/20       20.00
                      WITHDRAWAL #04386 AT 00240D ON 05/21       5/21       40.00
                      INTERLINK PURCHASE #880318 ON 05/28 AT     5/29       30.00
                      LUCKY STORE #043
    _____
    DEPOSITS                                            DATE POSTED       AMOUNT
                      AVS RNT CAR SYST PAYROLL G2 000000035382   5/03      618.69
                      AVS RNT CAR SYST PAYROLL G2 000000035382   5/17       83.39
                      AVS RNT CAR SYST PAYROLL G2 000000035382   5/17      600.75
    _____
    ATM               00165A: 249 PRIMROSE RD, ANY CITY, USA
    LOCATIONS USED    00240C: 490 BROADWAY, ANY CITY, USA
                      00167C: 1145 BROADWAY, ANY CITY, USA
                      00240D: 490 BROADWAY, ANY CITY, USA
    _____
```

1. Checks that you've written, ATM withdrawals, debit purchases, or other automatic payments subtracted from your checkbook balance haven't yet been received and processed by your bank and therefore remain outstanding.
2. Deposits that you've made and added to your checkbook balance haven't yet been credited to your account.
3. Any service (activity) charges levied on your account by the bank haven't yet been deducted from your checkbook balance.
4. Interest earned on your account (if it's a NOW or an MMDA account) hasn't yet been added to your checkbook balance.

Exhibit 4.6 lists the steps to reconcile your checkbook each month.

The reverse side of your bank statement usually provides a form for reconciling your account along with step-by-step instructions. Worksheet 4.1 includes an account reconciliation form that Jackson Smith completed for the month of May 2017 using the reconciliation procedures we have described. You can use the form to reconcile either regular or interest-paying checking accounts such as NOWs or MMDAs.

4-4c Special Types of Checks

In some circumstances, sellers of goods or services may not accept personal checks because they can't be absolutely sure that the check is good. This is common for large purchases or when the buyer's bank is not located in the same area where the purchase is being made. A form of check that guarantees payment may be required instead: cashier's checks, traveler's checks, or certified checks.

- **Cashier's check:** Anyone can buy a cashier's check from a bank. These checks are often used by people who don't have checking accounts. They can be purchased

cashier's check
A check payable to a third party that is drawn by a bank on itself in exchange for the amount specified plus, in most cases, a service fee (of about $5).

EXHIBIT 4.6	**Make That Checkbook Balance!**

Take the following steps to reconcile your account:

1. On receipt of your bank statement, arrange all canceled checks in ascending numerical order based on their sequence numbers or issuance dates. (Skip this step if your bank doesn't return canceled checks.)

2. Compare each check or its bank statement information with the corresponding entry in your checkbook ledger to make sure there are no recording errors. Mark off in your checkbook ledger each check and any other withdrawals such as from ATMs, point-of-sale debit transactions, or automatic payments.

3. List the checks and other deductions (ATM withdrawals or debit purchases) still *outstanding*—that is, those deducted in your checkbook but not returned with your bank statement (see Step 2). Total their amount.

4. Compare the deposits indicated on the statement with deposits shown in your checkbook ledger. Total the amount of deposits still outstanding—that is, those shown in your checkbook ledger but not yet received by the bank. Be sure to include all automatic deposits and deposits made at ATMs in your calculations.

5. *Subtract* the total amount of checks outstanding (from Step 3) from your bank statement balance, and *add* to this balance the amount of outstanding deposits (from Step 4). The resulting amount is your *adjusted bank balance*.

6. Deduct the amount of any bank service charges from your checkbook ledger balance, and add any interest earned to that balance. Make sure that you include all service charges for the period, including those for any returned checks, stop payments, or new checks ordered. The resulting amount is your *new checkbook balance*. This amount should equal your adjusted bank balance (from Step 5). If it doesn't, check all addition and subtraction in your checkbook ledger, because you've probably made an error.

Jackson Smith used this form to reconcile his checking account for the month of May 2017. Because line A equals line B, he has fully reconciled the difference between the $80.99 bank statement balance and his $339.44 check-book balance. Accounts should be reconciled each month—as soon as possible after receiving the bank statement.

CHECKING ACCOUNT RECONCILIATION

For the Month of ____May____ , 20 _17_

Accountholder Name (s) ___Jackson Smith___

Type of Account ___Regular Checking___

1. Ending balance shown on bank statement _____ $ 80.99

Add up checks and withdrawals still outstanding:

Check Number or Date	Amount	Check Number or Date	Amount
221	$ 81.55		
225	196.50		
Lucky—5/28	25.00		
ATM—5/29	40.00		
	TOTAL $ 343.05		

2. Deduct total checks/withdrawals still outstanding from bank balance _____ – $343.05

Add up deposits not shown on bank statement:

Date	Amount	Date	Amount
5/29/17	$ 595.00		
	TOTAL $ 595.00		

3. Add total deposits still outstanding to bank balance _____ + $595.00

A **Adjusted Bank Balance (1 – 2 + 3)** _____ $332.94

4. Ending balance shown in checkbook _____ $339.44

5. Deduct any bank service charges for the period ___(–$7.50 + $1.00)___ – $ 6.50

6. Add interest earned for the period _____ + $ 0

B **New Checkbook Balance (4 – 5 + 6)** _____ $332.94

Note: Your account is reconciled when line A equals line B.

for the face amount of the check plus a service fee that averages around $9, although under some circumstances they're issued at no charge to bank customers. The bank issues a check payable to a third party and drawn on itself, not you—the best assurance you can give that the check is good.

MONKEY BUSINESS IMAGES/DREAMSTIME.COM

traveler's check
A check sold (for a fee of about 1 to 2 percent) by many large financial institutions, typically in denominations ranging from $20 to $100, that can be used for making purchases and exchanged for local currencies in most parts of the world.

- **Traveler's check:** Some large financial organizations—such as Citibank, American Express, MasterCard, Visa, and Bank of America—issue **traveler's checks**, which can be purchased at commercial banks and most other financial institutions, typically in denominations ranging from $20 to $100. A fee of 1 to 2 percent or more can be charged on the purchase.

  Properly endorsed and countersigned traveler's checks are accepted by most U.S. businesses and can be exchanged for local currencies in most parts of the world. Because they're insured against loss or theft by the issuing agency, they provide a safe, convenient, and popular form of money for travel. However, the large number of counterfeit traveler's checks has made them less popular with many businesses, which is making them less commonly used.

certified check
A personal check that is guaranteed by the bank on which it is drawn.

- **Certified check:** A **certified check** is a personal check that the bank certifies, with a stamp, to guarantee that the funds are available. The bank immediately deducts the amount of the check from your account. There's usually only a minimal or no charge for this service if you are the bank's customer.

TEST YOURSELF

4-13 What are the key factors to consider when opening a checking account? Discuss the advantages and disadvantages of individual versus joint accounts.

4-14 Is it possible to bounce a check because of insufficient funds when the checkbook ledger shows a balance available to cover it? Explain what happens when a check bounces. Can you obtain protection against overdrafts?

4-15 Describe the procedure used to stop payment on a check. Why might you wish to initiate this process?

4-16 What type of information is found in the monthly bank statement, and how is it used? Explain the basic steps involved in reconciling an account.

4-17 Briefly describe each of these special types of checks:

  a. Cashier's check

  b. Traveler's check

  c. Certified check

4-5 ESTABLISHING A SAVINGS PROGRAM

LG5, LG6

The vast majority of American households have some money put away in savings, making it clear that most of us understand the value of saving for the future. In the wake of the recent financial crisis, the U.S. personal saving rate increased to an average of almost 5 percent of after-tax income, after hitting a low of around 1 percent in 2005. The act of saving is a deliberate, well-thought-out activity designed to preserve the value of money, ensure liquidity, and earn a competitive rate of return. Almost by definition, *smart savers are smart investors*. They regard saving as more than putting loose change into a piggy bank; rather, they recognize the importance of saving and know that savings must be managed as astutely as any security.

After all, what we normally think of as "savings" is really a form of investment—a short-term, highly liquid investment—that's subject to minimal risk. Establishing and maintaining an ongoing savings program is a vital element of personal financial planning. To get the most from your savings, however, you must understand your options and how different savings vehicles pay interest.

4-5a Starting Your Savings Program

Careful financial planning dictates that you hold a portion of your assets to meet liquidity needs and accumulate wealth. Although opinions differ as to how much you should keep as liquid reserves, the post-crisis consensus is that most families should have an amount equal to at least 6 to 9 months of after-tax income. Therefore, if you take home $3,000 a month, you should have between $18,000 and $27,000 in liquid reserves. If your employer has a strong salary continuation program covering extended periods of illness, or if you have a sizable line of credit available, then a somewhat lower amount is probably adequate.

A specific savings plan should be developed to accumulate funds. Saving should be a priority item in your budget, not something that occurs only when income happens to exceed expenditures. Some people manage this by arranging to have savings directly withheld from their paychecks. Not only do direct deposit arrangements help your savings effort, but they also enable your funds to earn interest sooner. Or you can transfer funds regularly to other financial institutions such as commercial banks, savings and loans, savings banks, credit unions, and even mutual funds. But the key to success is to establish a *regular* pattern of saving.

You should make it a practice to set aside an amount you can comfortably afford *each month*, even if it's only $50 to $100. (Keep in mind that $100 monthly deposits earning 4 percent interest will grow to more than $36,500 in 20 years!) Exhibit 4.7 lists some strategies that you can use to increase your savings and build a nest egg.

You must also decide which savings products best meet your needs. Many savers prefer to keep their emergency funds in a regular savings or money market deposit account at an institution with federal deposit insurance. Although these accounts are safe, convenient, and highly liquid, they tend to pay relatively low rates of interest. Other important considerations include your risk preference, the length of time you can leave your money on deposit, and the level of current and anticipated interest rates.

Suppose that one year from now, you plan to use $5,000 of your savings to make the down payment on a new car, and you expect interest rates to drop during that period. You should lock in today's higher rate by purchasing a 1-year CD. On the other hand, if you're unsure about when you'll actually need the funds or believe that interest rates will rise, then you're better off with an MMDA or MMMF because their rates change with market conditions, and you can access your funds at any time without penalty.

Short-term interest rates generally fluctuate more than long-term rates, so it pays to monitor interest rate movements, shop around for the best rates, and place your funds in savings vehicles consistent with your needs. If short-term interest rates drop, you won't be able to reinvest the proceeds from maturing CDs at comparable rates. You'll need to reevaluate your savings plans and may choose to move funds into other savings vehicles with higher rates of interest but greater risk.

Many financial planning experts recommend keeping a minimum of 10 percent to 25 percent of your investment portfolio in savings-type instruments in addition to the 6 to 9 months of liquid reserves noted earlier. Someone with $50,000 in investments should probably have a minimum of $5,000 to $12,500—and possibly more—in short-term vehicles such as MMDAs, MMMFs, or CDs. At times, the amount invested in short-term vehicles could far exceed the recommended minimum, approaching 50 percent or more of the portfolio. This generally depends on expected interest rate movements. If interest rates are relatively high and you expect them to fall, you would invest in longer-term vehicles in order to lock in the attractive interest rates. On the other hand, if rates are relatively low and you expect them to rise, you might invest in shorter-term vehicles so you can more quickly reinvest when rates do rise.

4-5b Earning Interest on Your Money

Interest earned is the reward for putting your money in a savings account or short-term investment vehicle, and it's important for you to understand how that interest is earned. But unfortunately, even in the relatively simple world of savings, not all interest rates are created equal.

The Effects of Compounding

Interest can be earned in one of two ways. First, some short-term investments are sold on a *discount basis*. This means the security is sold for a price that's lower than its redemption value; the difference is the amount of interest earned. Treasury bills, for instance, are issued on a discount basis. Another way to earn interest on short-term investments is by *direct payment*, which occurs when interest is applied to a regular savings account. Although this is a simple process, determining the actual rate of return can be complicated.

EXHIBIT 4.7	Strategies to Build Up Your Savings

Having trouble getting your savings program started? Here are some strategies to begin building up your savings:

- **Pay yourself first, then pay your bills.** Write a check to yourself each month as if it were another invoice and deposit it in a savings account.
- **Examine your spending habits** for places to cut back. Bring your lunch to work or school. Comparison shop. Carpool. Cut back on trips to the ATM.
- **Set up a payroll deduction** and have your employer deduct money from your paycheck to be deposited directly into your savings account. It's painless because you never see the money in your checking account.
- **Save your raise or bonus.** Keep your lifestyle where it is and put the difference in your savings account.
- **Keep making those loan payments,** and you'll feel rich when those obligations finally end. When the loans are paid off, deposit the same amount to your savings account.
- **Be aware of the return paid on your savings account.** You might do a bit better by moving your money to an asset management account at a brokerage firm.
- **Reinvest interest and dividends.** You won't miss the money, and your account will grow more rapidly. If you have a savings account, make sure the interest is reinvested rather than paid into your non-interest-bearing checking account. If you own stocks or mutual funds, virtually all offer dividend reinvestment plans.
- **Set up a retirement plan** to make sure you contribute to your company's retirement program. Your contributions are tax-deductible, and many employers match your contributions. Check out available individual retirement account options such as IRAs and 401(k)s (see Chapter 14).
- **Splurge once in a while**—the boost you get will make saving money a little easier. All work and no play makes for a dull life, so once you've reached a savings goal, take some money and enjoy yourself.

Glossary (margin)

compound interest
When interest earned in each subsequent period is determined by applying the *nominal (stated) rate of interest* to the sum of the initial deposit and the interest earned in each prior period.

simple interest
Interest that is paid only on the initial amount of the deposit.

nominal (stated) rate of interest
The promised rate of interest paid on a savings deposit or charged on a loan.

effective rate of interest
The annual rate of return that is *actually earned* (or *charged*) during the period the funds are held (or borrowed).

The first complication is in the method used to set the amount and rate of **compound interest** earned annually. You've probably read or seen advertisements by banks or other depository institutions declaring that they pay daily, rather than annual, interest. Consider an example to understand what this means. Assume that you invest $1,000 in a savings account advertised as paying annual **simple interest** at a rate of 5 percent. The interest is paid only on the initial amount of the deposit with simple interest. This means that if you leave the $1,000 on deposit for 1 year, you'll earn $50 in interest, and the account balance will total $1,050 at year's end. In this case, the **nominal (stated) rate of interest** (the promised rate of interest paid on a savings deposit or charged on a loan) is 5 percent.

In contrast, the **effective rate of interest** is the annual rate of return that's *actually earned* (or *charged*) during the period the funds are held (or borrowed). You can calculate it with the following formula:

$$\text{Effective Rate of Interest} = \frac{\text{Amount of Interest Earned}}{\text{Amount of Money Invested or Deposited}}$$

In our example, because $50 was earned during the year on an investment of $1,000, the effective rate is $50/$1,000 or 5 percent, which is the same as the nominal rate of interest. (Notice in the preceding formula that it's interest earned during the *year* that matters; if you wanted to calculate the effective rate of interest on an account held for 6 months, you'd double the amount of interest earned.)

Calculator

INPUTS	FUNCTIONS
1000	PV
365	N
7	÷
365	=
	I
	CPT
	FV
	SOLUTION
	1,072.50

See Appendix E for details.

EXAMPLE: Calculating Earnings When Interest Is Compounded Semiannually

Suppose Ramon can invest $1,000 at 5 percent, compounded *semiannually*. Because interest is applied midyear, his dollar earnings will be:

First 6 months' interest = $1,000 × 0.05 × 6/12 = **$25.00**

Second 6 months' interest = $1,025 × 0.05 × 6/12 = $25.63

Total annual interest = $50.63

Interest is generated on a larger investment in the second half of the year because the amount of money on deposit has increased by the amount of interest earned in the first half ($25). Although the nominal rate on this account is still 5 percent, the effective rate is 5.06 percent ($50.63/$1,000). As you may have guessed, *the more frequently interest is compounded, the greater the effective rate for any given nominal rate*. Exhibit 4.8 shows these relationships for a sample of interest rates and compounding periods. Note, for example, that with a 7 percent nominal rate, daily compounding adds one-fourth of a percent to the total return—not a trivial amount.

You can calculate the interest compounded daily by using a financial calculator similar to that described in Appendix E. Let's assume you want to invest $1,000 at 7 percent interest compounded daily. How much money will you have in the account at the end of the year? Using a calculator, we get $1,072.50. This value is clearly greater than the $1,070 that annual compounding would return. The effective interest rate would have been 7.25 percent ($72.50 interest earned ÷ $1,000 initially invested), as noted in Exhibit 4.8.

Financial Fact or Fantasy?

In all but a few cases, the nominal (stated) interest rate on a savings account is the same as its effective rate of interest. **Fantasy:** In only a few cases are the two rates the same. Because the nominal (stated) interest rate paid by a bank or other depository institution typically compounds during the year, the effective rate is greater than the nominal rate.

EXHIBIT 4.8   The Magic of Compounding

The effective rate of interest you earn on a savings account will exceed the nominal (stated) rate if interest is compounded more than once a year (as are most savings and interest-paying accounts).

Nominal Rate	Effective Rate				
	Annually	Semiannually	Quarterly	Monthly	Daily
3%	3.00%	3.02%	3.03%	3.04%	3.05%
4	4.00	4.04	4.06	4.07	4.08
5	5.00	5.06	5.09	5.12	5.13
6	6.00	6.09	6.14	6.17	6.18
7	7.00	7.12	7.19	7.23	7.25
8	8.00	8.16	8.24	8.30	8.33
9	9.00	9.20	9.31	9.38	9.42
10	10.00	10.25	10.38	10.47	10.52
11	11.00	11.30	11.46	11.57	11.62
12	12.00	12.36	12.55	12.68	12.74

Compound Interest Generates Future Value

Compound interest is consistent with the *future value* concept introduced in Chapter 2. You can use the procedures described there to find out how much an investment or deposit will grow over time at a compounded rate of interest. You can use the same basic procedure to find the future value of an *annuity*.

Calculator

INPUTS	FUNCTIONS
1000	PV
4	N
5	I
	CPT
	FV
	SOLUTION
	1,215.51

See Appendix E for details.

EXAMPLE: Calculating the Future Value of a Savings Deposit

Brandon would like to know how much $1,000 will be worth in 4 years if he deposits it into a savings account paying 5 percent interest per year compounded annually. Using the future value formula and the future value factor from Appendix A (see Chapter 2 if you need a reminder):

$$\text{Future Value} = \text{Amount Deposited} \times \text{Future Value Factor}$$
$$= \$1,000 \times 1.216$$
$$= \$1,216$$

Calculator

INPUTS	FUNCTIONS
1000	PV
4	N
5	I
	CPT
	FV
	SOLUTION
	4,310.13

See Appendix E for details on calculator use.

EXAMPLE: Calculating the Future Value of Ongoing Savings

Caroline deposits $1,000 a year into a savings account paying 5% per year, compounded annually. Using the future value interest factor for an annuity in Appendix B, in 4 years Caroline will have:

$$\text{Future Value} = \text{Amount Deposited Yearly} \times \text{Future Value Annuity Factor}$$
$$= \$1,000 \times 4.310$$
$$= \$4,310$$

4-5c A Variety of Ways to Save

During the past decade or so, there has been a huge growth of savings and short-term investment vehicles, particularly for people of modest means. And because of the flexibility it provides, there'll always be a place in your portfolio for cash savings.

Today, investors can choose from savings accounts, money market deposit accounts, money market mutual funds, NOW accounts, CDs, U.S. Treasury bills, Series EE bonds, and asset management accounts. We examined several of these savings vehicles earlier in this chapter. Now let's look at the three remaining types of deposits and securities.

Certificates of Deposit

certificates of deposit (CDs)
A type of savings instrument issued by certain financial institutions in exchange for a deposit; typically requires a minimum deposit and has a maturity ranging from 7 days to as long as 7 or more years.

Certificates of deposit (CDs) differ from the savings instruments discussed earlier in that CD funds (except for CDs purchased through brokerage firms) must remain on deposit for a specified period (from 7 days to as long as 7 or more years). Although it's possible to withdraw funds prior to maturity, an interest penalty usually makes withdrawal somewhat costly. The bank or other depository institution is free to charge whatever penalty it likes, but most require you to forfeit some interest. Banks, S&Ls, and other depository institutions can offer any rate and maturity CD they wish. As a result, a wide variety of CDs are offered by most banks, depository institutions, and other financial institutions such as brokerage firms. Most pay higher rates for larger deposits and longer periods of time. CDs are convenient to buy and hold because they offer attractive and highly competitive yields plus federal deposit insurance protection.

U.S. Treasury Bills

U.S. Treasury bill (T-bill)
A short-term (3- or 6-month maturity) debt instrument issued at a discount by the U.S. Treasury in the ongoing process of funding the national debt.

The **U.S. Treasury bill (T-bill)** is considered the ultimate safe haven for savings and investments. T-bills are issued by the U.S. Treasury as part of its ongoing process of funding the national debt. They are sold on a discount basis in minimum denominations of $100 and are issued with 3-month (13-week) or 6-month (26-week) maturities. The bills are auctioned off every Monday. Backed by the full faith and credit of the U.S. government, T-bills pay an attractive and safe return that is free from state and local income taxes.

T-bills are almost as liquid as cash because they can be sold at any time (in a very active secondary market) with no interest penalty. However, should you have to sell before maturity, you may lose some money on your investment if interest rates have risen, and you'll have to pay a broker's fee. Treasury bills pay interest on a *discount basis* and thus are different from other savings or short-term investment vehicles—that is, their interest is equal to the difference between the purchase price paid and their stated value at maturity.

EXAMPLE: Interest Earned on a Treasury Bill

Kevin paid $980 for a Treasury bill that will be worth $1,000 at maturity. How much interest will Kevin earn?

Because a T-bill is a discount instrument, Kevin will earn interest of $1,000 − $980 = $20.

An individual investor may purchase T-bills directly by participating in the weekly Treasury auctions or indirectly through a commercial bank or a securities dealer who buys bills for investors on a commission basis. T-bills may now be purchased over the Internet (**www.treasurydirect.gov**) or by phone (call 800-722-2678 and follow the interactive menu to complete transactions).

Outstanding Treasury bills can also be purchased in the secondary market through banks or dealers. This approach gives the investor a much wider selection of maturities, ranging from less than a week to as long as 6 months.

Series EE Bonds

Series EE bond
A savings bond issued in various denominations by the U.S. Treasury.

Although they are issued by the U.S. Treasury on a discount basis and are free of state and local income taxes, **Series EE bonds** are quite different from T-bills. Savings bonds are *accrual-type securities,* which means that interest is paid when they're cashed in or before maturity, rather than periodically during their lives. The government does issue Series HH bonds; they have a 10-year maturity and are available in denominations of $50 to $10,000. Unlike EE bonds, HH bonds are issued at their full face value and pay interest semiannually at the current fixed rate.

Series EE savings bonds are backed by the full faith and credit of the U.S. government and can be replaced without charge in case of loss, theft, or destruction. Now also designated as "Patriot Bonds" in honor of September 11, 2001, they present an opportunity for all Americans to contribute to the government's efforts and save for their own futures as well. You can purchase them at banks or other depository institutions or through payroll deduction plans. Issued in denominations from $25 through $10,000, their purchase price is a uniform 50 percent of the face amount (thus a $100 bond will cost $50 and be worth $100 at maturity).

Series EE bonds earn interest at a fixed rate for 30 years. Their long life lets investors use them for truly long-term goals like education and retirement. The higher the rate of interest being paid, the shorter the time it takes for the bond to accrue from its discounted purchase price to its maturity value. Bonds can be redeemed any time after the first 12 months, although redeeming EE bonds in less than 5 years results in a penalty of the last 3 months of interest earned. The fixed interest rate is set every 6 months in May and November and changes with prevailing Treasury security market yields. EE bonds increase in value every month, and the fixed interest rate is compounded semiannually. To obtain current rates on Series EE bonds, it's easiest to use the Internet link for the savings bond site.

In addition to being exempt from state and local taxes, Series EE bonds give their holders an appealing tax twist: *Savers need not report interest earned on their federal tax returns until the bonds are redeemed.* Although interest can be reported annually (for example, when the bonds are held in the name of a child who has limited interest income), most investors choose to defer it. A second attractive tax feature allows partial or complete tax avoidance of EE bond earnings when proceeds are used to pay education expenses, such as college tuition, for the bond purchaser, a spouse, or another IRS-defined dependent. To qualify, the purchaser must be age 24 or older and must have income below a given maximum that is adjusted annually. The rationale for the later requirement is to provide tax relief only to low- and middle-income people.

I savings bonds
A savings bond, issued at face value by the U.S. Treasury, whose partially fixed rate provides some inflation protection.

Financial Fact or Fantasy?

U.S. Series EE and I savings bonds are not a very good way to save.
Fantasy: Investing in Series EE and I savings bonds are excellent ways to save. The bonds are safe because they are backed by the U.S. government, offer market rates of return, and offer several attractive features. Series I bonds are particularly attractive to those wanting protection against inflation.

I Savings Bonds

I savings bonds are similar to Series EE bonds in numerous ways. Both are issued by the U.S. Treasury and are accrual-type securities. I bonds are available in denominations between $25 and $10,000. Interest compounds semiannually for 30 years on both securities. Like Series EE bonds, I savings bonds' interest remains exempt from state and local income taxes but does face state and local estate, inheritance, gift, and other excise taxes. Interest earnings are subject to federal income tax but may be excluded when used to finance education, with some limitations.

There are some significant differences between the two savings vehicles. Whereas Series EE bonds are sold at a discount, I bonds are sold at face value. I savings bonds differ from Series EE bonds in that their annual interest rate combines a fixed rate that remains the same for the life of the bond with a semi-annual inflation rate that changes with the Consumer Price Index for all Urban Consumers (CPI-U). In contrast, the rate on Series EE bonds is based on the 6-month averages of 5-year Treasury security market yields. Thus, the key

FINANCIAL ROAD SIGN

Determining How Much Interest You Will Earn

Before opening a deposit account, investigate the following factors, which determine the amount of interest you'll earn on your savings or interest-bearing checking account:

- **Frequency of compounding.** The more often interest is compounded, the higher your return.
- **Balance on which interest is paid.** For balances that qualify to earn interest, most banks now use the *actual balance, or day of deposit to day of withdrawal,* method. The actual balance method is fairest because it pays depositors interest on all funds on deposit for the actual amount of time they remain there.
- **Interest rate paid.** As mentioned earlier, the Truth in Savings Act standardized the way that banks calculate the rate of interest they pay on deposit accounts. This makes it easy to compare each bank's annual percentage yield (APY) and to choose the bank offering the highest APY.

difference between Series EE bonds and I bonds is that I bond returns are adjusted for inflation. Note in particular that the earnings rate cannot go below zero and that the value of I bonds cannot drop below their redemption value. Like Series EE bonds, I bonds can be bought on the Internet or via phone. I bonds offer the opportunity to "inflation-protect" your savings somewhat. I bonds cannot be bought or sold in the secondary market; transactions are only with the U.S. Treasury.

TEST YOURSELF

4-18 In general, how much of your annual income should you save in the form of liquid reserves? What portion of your investment portfolio should you keep in savings and other short-term investment vehicles? Explain.

4-19 Define and distinguish between the *nominal (stated) rate of interest* and the *effective rate of interest.* Explain why a financial institution that pays a nominal rate of 4.5 percent interest, compounded daily, actually pays an effective rate of 4.6 percent.

4-20 What factors determine the amount of interest you will earn on a deposit account? Which combination provides the best return?

4-21 Briefly describe the basic features of each of the following savings vehicles: (a) CDs, (b) U.S. Treasury bills, (c) Series EE bonds, and (d) I savings bonds.

Planning Over a Lifetime: *Managing Cash and Savings*

Here are some key considerations for managing your cash and savings in each stage of the life cycle.

Pre-family Independence: 20s	Family Formation/ Career Development: 30–45	Pre-Retirement: 45–65	Retirement: 65 and Beyond
✓ Build up savings in general and emergency fund in particular.	✓ Increase savings to fund future financial goals.	✓ Maintain emergency fund.	✓ Maintain list of bank accounts that are easily accessible by spouse and family.
✓ Pay off any outstanding college loans.	✓ Broaden variety of cash management vehicles and reliance on financial planners for strategy development.	✓ Relate savings strategies more directly to retirement planning.	✓ Take advantage of bank accounts with senior discounts on fees.
✓ Find best mix of financial institution accounts based on fees, returns, and convenience. Make comparisons across banks.	✓ Carefully relate savings program to funding children's future educational needs.	✓ Start being sensitive to the presence of "senior" discounts.	✓ Integrate cash management and savings with retirement spending and estate plan.
		✓ Get an estimate of your Social Security benefits based on your expected retirement date.	

WILLIAM HUBER/PHOTONICA/GETTY IMAGES

Financial Impact of Personal Choices
Stella Likes Cash—Too Much?

Stella has a good job that pays $65,000 a year. She invests the maximum amount allowable in her work-based retirement plan. During the financial crisis a few years ago her retirement investments fell about 40 percent in value! While her investments have more than recovered, Stella is very risk conscious and has consequently built up an emergency fund of $60,000, which she keeps in a savings account that pays 0.5 percent, compounded monthly. Is Stella's approach to handling her emergency funds the best way to go?

Stella has done a great job setting aside a $60,000 emergency fund. And contributing the maximum will serve her well. However, the recommended emergency fund for 6 to 9 months of income for her $65,000 annual income is only $32,500 to $48,750. So Stella has set aside much more than is recommended. Further, Stella is leaving it in a savings account only paying 0.5 percent a year, which generates interest income of only about $325 a year. It would make sense for Stella to invest more aggressively—even a CD would provide a higher return with comparable risk. And she should at least shop around for a better savings rate than 0.5 percent for her hopefully reduced emergency fund. Stella could find another savings vehicle with a rate of at least 1 percent a year, which would about double her annual return. Stella is doing great—but she likes cash too much for her own good. She could do even better.

Summary

LG1 **Understand the role of cash management in the personal financial planning process. p.125**
Cash management plays a vital role in personal financial planning. It involves the administration and control of liquid assets—cash, checking accounts, savings, and other short-term investment vehicles. With good cash management practices, you'll have the necessary funds to cover your expenses and establish a regular savings program.

LG2 **Describe today's financial services marketplace, both depository and nondepository financial institutions. p.128**
Today's financial services marketplace is highly competitive and offers consumers expanded product offerings at attractive prices. Individuals and families continue to rely heavily on traditional depository financial institutions for most of their financial services needs. Nondepository financial institutions also offer some banking services such as credit cards and money market fund accounts with check-writing privileges. You should make sure your bank has federal deposit insurance and is financially sound. Most depository institutions are federally insured for up to $250,000 per depositor name.

LG3 **Select the checking, savings, electronic banking, and other bank services that meet your needs. p.131**
Financial institutions provide a variety of accounts to help you manage your cash: regular checking accounts; savings accounts; and interest-paying checking accounts, such as NOW accounts, money market deposit accounts, and money market mutual funds. Asset management accounts offered by brokerage firms and mutual funds combine checking, investment, and borrowing activities and pay higher interest on deposits than do other, more traditional, checking accounts. Other money management services include electronic funds transfer systems (EFTSs) that use telecommunications and computer technology to electronically transfer funds. Popular EFTS services include debit cards, ATMs, preauthorized deposits and payments, bank-by-phone accounts, and online banking and bill-paying services. Many banks also provide safe-deposit boxes, which serve as a storage place for valuables and important documents.

LG4 **Open and use a checking account. p.139**
A checking account is a convenient way to hold cash and pay for goods and services. The sharp increase in bank service charges makes it important to evaluate different types of checking accounts and their service charges, minimum balance requirements, and other fees. You should understand how to write and endorse checks, make deposits, keep good checking account records, prevent overdrafts, and stop payment on checks. The account reconciliation, or checkbook balancing, process confirms the accuracy of your account records and monthly bank statement. Other special types of checks that you may occasionally use include cashier's, traveler's, and certified checks.

LG5 **Calculate the interest earned on your money using compound interest and future value techniques. p.148**
Once you know the interest rate, frequency of compounding, and how the bank determines the balance on which interest is paid, you can calculate how much interest you'll earn on your money. Use future value and future value of an annuity formulas to find out how your savings will grow. The more often interest is compounded, the greater the effective rate for a given nominal rate of interest. Most banks use the actual balance (or "day of deposit to day of withdrawal") method to determine which balances qualify to earn interest, which is the fairest method for depositors.

LG6 **Develop a cash management strategy that incorporates a variety of savings plans. p.148**
Your cash management strategy should include establishing a regular pattern of saving with liquid reserves equal to at least 6 to 9 months of after-tax income. The choice of savings products depends on your needs, your risk preference, the length of time you plan to leave money on deposit, and current and expected interest rates. You may wish to put some of your savings into vehicles that pay a higher rate of interest than savings or NOW accounts, such as CDs, U.S. Treasury bills, Series EE bonds, and I savings bonds.

Key Terms

account reconciliation, 143

asset management account (AMA), 134

automated teller machines (ATMs), 135

cash management, 125

cashier's check, 145

certificates of deposit (CDs), 152

certified check, 147

checkbook ledger, 142

compound interest, 150

debit cards, 135

demand deposit, 133

deposit insurance, 130

effective rate of interest, 150

electronic funds transfer systems (EFTSs), 135

I savings bonds, 153

internet banks, 130

money market deposit account (MMDA), 134

money market mutual fund (MMMF), 134

negotiable order of withdrawal (NOW) account, 133

nominal (stated) rate of interest, 150

overdraft, 142

overdraft protection, 142

series EE bonds, 153

share draft accounts, 130

simple interest, 150

stop payment, 143

time deposits, 133

traveler's checks, 147

U.S. Treasury bill (T-bill), 152

Answers to Test Yourself

You can find answers to these questions on this book's companion website. Look for it at *www. cengagebrain.com*. Search for this book by its title, and then add it to your dashboard.

Key Financial Relationships

Concept	Financial Relationship	Page Number
Effective Rate of Interest	$\text{Effective Rate of Interest} = \dfrac{\text{Amount of Interest Earned}}{\text{Amount of Money Invested or Deposited}}$	150
Future Value of a Savings Deposit	Future Value = Amount Deposited × Future Value Factor	151
Future Value of Ongoing Savings	Future Value = Amount Deposited Yearly × Future Value Annuity Factor	151

Key Financial Relationships Problem Set

1. ***Effective Rate of Interest.*** Hannah Reed invested $5,000 in a short-term investment that yielded interest of $203.71 after one year. What effective rate of interest did Hannah earn?

   Solution:

   $$\text{Effective Rate of Interest} = \frac{\text{Amount of Interest Earned}}{\text{Amount of Money Invested or Deposited}} = \frac{\$203.71}{\$5,000.00} = 4.07 \text{ percent}$$

2. ***Future Value of a Savings Deposit.*** Nolan Adams just got a $7,500 bonus and plans to invest it in a CD paying 6 percent interest compounded annually. What value can Nolan expect his investment to grow to after five years?

   Solution: Future Value = Amount Deposited × Future Value Factor. The future value interest factor for 5 years and 6 percent in Appendix A is 1.338. Thus, in 5 years Nolan's CD is expected to be worth $7,500 × 1.338 = $10,035.

3. **Future Value of Ongoing Savings.** Abigail Lewis deposits $2,500 a year into a savings account paying 4 percent per year, compounded annually. Her goal is to accumulate an emergency fund of $20,000 in 8 years. Is Abigail likely to achieve her financial goal?

   Solution: Future Value = Amount Deposited Yearly × Future Value Annuity Factor. The future value interest factor for an annuity for 8 years and 4 percent in Appendix B is 9.214. In 8 years Abigail should consequently have accumulated $2,500 × 9.214 = $23,035.57.

Financial Planning Exercises

LG1, p. 125
1. **Adapting to a low interest rate environment.** Your parents are retired and have expressed concern about the really low interest rates they're earning on their savings. They've been approached by an advisor who says he has a "sure-fire" way to get them higher returns. What would you tell your parents about the low-interest-rate environment, and how would you advise them to view the advisor's new prospective investments?

LG2, 3, 4, p. 128, 131, 139
2. **Comparing banks online.** What type of bank serves your needs best? Visit the Internet sites of the following institutions and prepare a chart comparing the services offered, such as traditional and online banking, investment services, and personal financial advice. Which one would you choose to patronize, and why?
   a. Wells Fargo (**https://www.wellsfargo.com**)—a nationwide full-service bank
   b. A leading local commercial bank in your area
   c. A local savings institution
   d. A local credit union

LG3, p. 131
3. **Exposure from stolen ATM card.** Suppose that someone stole your ATM card and withdrew $950 from your checking account. How much money could you lose according to federal legislation if you reported the stolen card to the bank: (a) the day the card was stolen, (b) 6 days after the theft, (c) 65 days after receiving your periodic statement?

LG2, 3, 4, p. 128, 131, 139
4. **Choosing a new bank.** You're getting married and are unhappy with your present bank. Discuss your strategy for choosing a new bank and opening an account. Consider the factors that are important to you in selecting a bank—such as the type and ownership of new accounts and bank fees and charges.

LG4, p. 139
5. **Calculating the net costs of checking accounts.** Determine the annual net cost of these checking accounts:
   a. Monthly fee $4, check-processing fee of 20 cents, average of 23 checks written per month
   b. Annual interest of 2.5 percent paid if balance exceeds $750, $8 monthly fee if account falls below minimum balance, average monthly balance $815, account falls below $750 during 4 months

LG4, p. 139
6. **Checking account reconciliation. Use Worksheet 4.1.** Carlos Perez has a NOW account at the First National Bank. His checkbook ledger lists the following checks:

Check Number	Amount
654	$206.05
658	55.22
662	103.00
668	99.00
670	6.10
671	50.25
672	24.90
673	32.45

Check Number	Amount
674	44.50
675	30.00
676	30.00
677	111.23
678	38.04
679	97.99
680	486.70
681	43.50
682	75.00
683	98.50

Carlos also made the following withdrawals and deposits at an ATM near his home:

Date	Amount	Transaction
11/1	$50.00	Withdrawal
11/2	$525.60	Deposit
11/6	$100.00	Deposit
11/14	$75.00	Withdrawal
11/21	$525.60	Deposit
11/24	$150.00	Withdrawal
11/27	$225.00	Withdrawal
11/30	$400.00	Deposit

Carlos' checkbook ledger shows an ending balance of $286.54. He has just received his bank statement for the month of November. It shows an ending balance of $622.44; it also shows that he earned interest for November of $3.28, had a check service charge of $8 for the month, and had another $12 charge for a returned check. His bank statement indicates the following checks have cleared: 654, 662, 672, 674, 675, 676, 677, 678, 679, and 681. ATM withdrawals on 11/1 and 11/14 and deposits on 11/2 and 11/6 have cleared; no other checks or ATM activities are listed on his statement, so anything remaining should be treated as outstanding. Use a checking account reconciliation form like the one in Worksheet 4.1 to reconcile Carlos' checking account.

LG5, 6, p. 148

7. ***Determining the right amount of short-term, liquid investments.*** Owen and Audrey Nelson together earn approximately $82,000 a year after taxes. Through an inheritance and some wise investing, they also have an investment portfolio with a value of almost $150,000.
   a. How much of their annual income do you recommend they hold in some form of liquid savings as reserves? Explain.
   b. How much of their investment portfolio do you recommend they hold in savings and other short-term investment vehicles? Explain.
   c. How much, in total, should they hold in short-term liquid assets?

LG5, 6, p. 148

8. ***Calculating interest earned and future value of savings account.*** If you put $6,000 in a savings account that pays interest at the rate of 4 percent, compounded annually, how much will you have in 5 years? (*Hint:* Use the *future value* formula.) How much interest will you earn during the 5 years? If you put $6,000 *each* year into a savings account that pays interest at the rate of 4 percent a year, how much would you have after 5 years?

LG6, p. 148

9. ***Short-term investments and inflation.*** Describe some of the short-term investment vehicles that can be used to manage your cash resources. What would you focus on if you were concerned that inflation will increase significantly in the future?

Manage Your Cash!

What difference does it make where you keep your money? The returns are so low on checking and savings accounts that you certainly won't grow rich on their earnings! It's no wonder that many people tend to overlook the importance of managing their cash and liquid assets. This project will help you evaluate your cash management needs and the various financial service providers available so that you can select the one best suited to your needs.

First, spend some time making a list of your needs and preferences. Do you like to visit your banking institution in person, or would you rather do your banking electronically or by mail? Is a high yield important to you, or is your typical balance usually pretty low so that any earnings would be minimal? What other services might you need, such as a safe-deposit box, brokerage account, trust services, or financial and estate planning?

Next, go back through this chapter and review all the types of financial institutions and the services they provide. Then, beside each need on your list, write down the institutions that would best meet that need. Is there one banking institution that would meet all your needs, or do you think you'd require several? After identifying the type or types that are appropriate for you, survey your community via the phone book, interviews with finance professionals, and other methods to identify the various financial institutions in your area. Look beyond your area as well, and consider what services are available over the Internet or from other regions of the country. Make a list of your top choices and find out more information concerning their services, products, and fees charged to help you decide where you'd like to do business. Bring your findings to class to compare and discuss with your classmates.

CRITICAL THINKING CASES

LG4, 5, 6,
p. 139, 148

4.1 June Xu's Savings and Banking Plans

June Xu is a registered nurse who earns $3,250 per month after taxes. She has been reviewing her savings strategies and current banking arrangements to determine if she should make any changes. June has a regular checking account that charges her a flat fee per month, writes an average of 18 checks a month, and carries an average balance of $795 (although it has fallen below $750 during 3 months of the past year). Her only other account is a money market deposit account with a balance of $4,250. She tries to make regular monthly deposits of $50–$100 into her money market account but has done so only about every other month.

Of the many checking accounts June's bank offers, here are the three that best suit her needs.

- *Regular checking, per-item plan*: Service charge of $3 per month plus 35 cents per check.
- *Regular checking, flat-fee plan (the one* June *currently has)*: Monthly fee of $7 regardless of how many checks written. With either of these regular checking accounts, she can avoid any charges by keeping a minimum daily balance of $750.
- *Interest checking*: Monthly service charge of $7; interest of 3 percent, compounded daily (refer to Exhibit 4.8). With a minimum balance of $1,500, the monthly charge is waived.

June's bank also offers CDs for a minimum deposit of $500; the current annual interest rates are 3.5 percent for 6 months, 3.75 percent for 1 year, and 4 percent for 2 years.

Critical Thinking Questions

1. Calculate the annual cost of each of the three accounts, assuming that June's banking habits remain the same. Which plan would you recommend and why?
2. Should June consider opening the interest checking account and increasing her minimum balance to at least $1,500 to avoid service charges? Explain your answer.
3. What other advice would you give June about her checking account and savings strategy?

4.2 Reconciling the Campbells' Checking Account

Caleb and Eva Campbell are college students who opened their first joint checking account together at the American Bank on September 14, 2017. They've just received their first bank statement for the period ending October 5, 2017. The statement and checkbook ledger are shown in the table following the *Critical Thinking Questions*.

Critical Thinking Questions

1. From this information, prepare a bank reconciliation for the Campbells as of October 5, 2017, using a form like the one in Worksheet 4.1.
2. Given your answer to Question 1, what, if any, adjustments will the Campbells need to make in their checkbook ledger? Comment on the procedures used to reconcile their checking account and their findings.
3. If the Campbells earned interest on their idle balances because the account is a money market deposit account, what impact would this have on the reconciliation process? Explain.

CALEB AND EVA CAMPBELL 2128 E. ARBOR ST. DENVER, COLORADO				THE AMERICAN BANK 800-000-0000 STATEMENT PERIOD SEPT. 6—OCT. 5, 2017

	Opening Balance	Total Deposits for Period	Total Checks/With-drawals for Period	Ending Balance
	$ 0.00	$569.25	$473.86	$95.39

Date	Withdrawals (Debits)			Deposits (Credits)	Balance
Sept. 14				$360.00	$360.00
Sept. 15				97.00	457.00
Sept. 25	$45.20			9.25	421.05
Oct. 1				103.00	524.05
Oct. 1	3.00 BC				521.05
Oct. 4	65.90	$49.76	$45.00		360.39
Oct. 5	265.00				95.39
RT = Returned Check	DM = Debit Memo		BC = Bank Charges		
FC = Finance Charges	CM = Credit Memo				

Checkbook Ledger						
Check Number	Date 2017	Details	✓	Check Amount	Deposit Amount	Account Balance
—	Sept. 14	Cash—gift from birthday			$360.00	$360.00
—	Sept. 15	Scott's wages			97.00	457.00
101	Sept. 24	Kroger's—groceries		$45.20		411.80
102	Sept. 27	Telephone bill		28.40		383.40
—	Oct. 1	Scott's wages			103.00	486.40
103	Oct. 1	Univ. Bk. Sto.—college books		65.90		420.50

Checkbook Ledger						
Check Number	Date 2017	Details	✓	Check Amount	Deposit Amount	Account Balance
104	Oct. 1	Walmart—sewing material		16.75		403.75
105	Oct. 1	B. Hadley—apartment rent		265.00		138.75
106	Oct. 2	Anthem—health insurance		17.25		121.50
107	Oct. 3	Kroger's—groceries		49.76		71.74
108	Oct. 4	Cash: gas, entertain., laundry		45.00		26.74
—	Oct. 5	Angela's salary			450.00	476.74

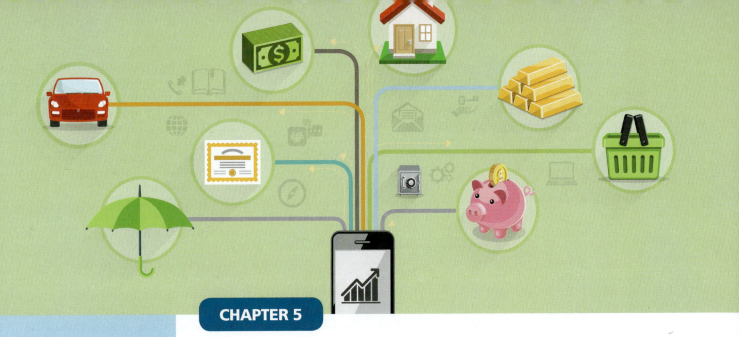

CHAPTER 5

Making Automobile and Housing Decisions

LEARNING GOALS

LG1 Design a plan to research and select a new or used automobile.

LG2 Decide whether to buy or lease a car.

LG3 Identify housing alternatives, assess the rental option, and perform a rent-or-buy analysis.

LG4 Evaluate the benefits and costs of homeownership and estimate how much you can afford to pay for a home.

LG5 Describe the home-buying process.

LG6 Choose mortgage financing that meets your needs.

How Will This Affect Me?

A home is typically the largest single investment you'll ever make, and a car is usually the second largest. As a result, the decisions to buy and finance these assets are important, personal, and complicated.

This chapter presents frameworks for deciding when to buy a first home, how to finance a home, and when to rent rather than to purchase a home. It also discusses the best way to go about buying a new or a used car and how to decide between leasing and purchasing a car. Given the large costs of such assets, the frameworks provided in this chapter can significantly improve your short- and long-term financial well-being. After reading this chapter you should be able to make more informed decisions in purchasing and financing your home and car.

5-1 BUYING AN AUTOMOBILE

LG1 Buying an automobile is probably the first major expenditure that many of us make. The car purchase is second only to housing in the amount of money the typical consumer spends. Because you'll buy a car many times during your life—most people buy one every two to five years—a systematic approach to selecting and financing a vehicle can mean significant savings. Before making any major purchase—whether it's a car, house, or large appliance—consider some basic guidelines to wise purchasing decisions.

- *Research* your purchase thoroughly, considering not only the market but also your personal needs and preferences.
- *Select* the best item for your needs and preferences.
- *Buy* the item after negotiating the best price and arranging financing on favorable terms. Be sure you understand all the terms of the sale before signing any contracts.
- *Maintain* your purchase and make necessary repairs promptly.

Exhibit 5.1 summarizes the steps in the car-buying process.

5-1a Choosing a Car

Hybrid, diesel, or gas? Sport utility vehicle (SUV) or pickup truck? Sedan, convertible, or coupe? Car buyers today have more choices than ever before, so more than one category of vehicle may be of interest. A good way to start your research is by tapping into the many available sources of information about cars, their prices, features, and reliability. Industry resources include manufacturers' brochures and dealer personnel. Car magazines, such as *Car and Driver*, *Motor Trend*, and *Road and Track*, and consumer magazines, such as *Consumer Reports* and *Consumer Guide*, regularly compare and rate cars. In addition, *Consumer Reports* and *Kiplinger's Personal Finance* magazine publish annual buying guides that include comparative statistics and ratings on most domestic and foreign cars. Kiplinger's Personal Finance also has an online Find the Right Car Tool at **http://www.kiplinger.com** (go to the "Spending section," then "Car Buying Guide"). *Consumer Reports* includes information on used cars in its guide

Financial Fact or Fantasy?

For most people, an automobile will be their second largest purchase. **Fact:** A car ranks second only to housing with respect to the amount of money spent.

EXHIBIT 5.1 | Key Steps in Buying a New Car

These steps summarize the car-buying process discussed in this chapter:

- Research which car best meets your needs and determine how much you can afford to spend on it. Choose the best way to pay for your new car—cash, financing, or lease. Ask your insurance agent for annual premium quotes for insuring various cars, as auto insurance is another significant expense of owning a car.
- Check Internet sites like Edmunds.com and TV and newspapers for incentives and rebates on the car you would like to buy. This could include a cash rebate or low-cost financing.
- Decide on a price based on the dealer's cost for the car and options, plus a markup for the dealer's profit, minus rebates and incentives.
- Find the exact car for you in terms of size, performance, safety, and styling. Choose at least three "target cars" to consider buying. Get online quotes from multiple car dealers.
- Test-drive the car—and the car salesperson. Test-drive the car at least once, both on local streets and on highways. Determine if the car salesperson is someone you want to do business with. Is he or she relaxed, open, and responsive to your questions?
- If you are trading in your old car, you are not likely to get as high a price as if you sell it yourself. Look up your car's trade-in-value at Edmunds.com or kkb.com. Get bids from several dealers.
- Negotiate the lowest price on your new car by getting bids from at least three dealers. Hold firm on your target price before closing the deal.
- Close the deal after looking not just at the cost of the car but also the related expenses. Consider the sales tax and various fees. Get the salesperson to fax you a worksheet and invoice before you go to the dealership.
- Review and sign the paperwork. If you have a worksheet for the deal, the contract should match it. Make sure the numbers match and there are no additional charges or fees.
- Inspect the car for scratches and dents. If anything is missing—like floor mats, for example—ask for a "Due Bill" that states it in writing.

Source: Adapted from Philip Read, "10 Steps to Buying a New Car," http://www.edmunds.com/car-buying/10-steps-to-buying-a-new-car.html, accessed August 2015.

and offers a fee-based service called the *Consumer Reports* New & Used Car Price Service (for more information, see **http://www.consumerreports.org**), which provides the list price and dealer cost on a new car, and its available options.

The Internet has made it especially easy to do your homework before ever setting foot in a dealer's showroom. In addition to finding online versions of automotive magazines, you can visit one of the many comprehensive Internet sites for car shoppers, offering pricing and model information, as well as links to other useful sites. And don't forget the Internet sites of the automobile companies themselves. For example, Ford Motor Company is online at **http://www.ford.com**, and Toyota is at **http://www.toyota.com**. Once you've done the research, you'll be in a better position to negotiate with the dealer. Knowing what you want and can afford before purchasing either a new or used car will prevent a persuasive auto salesperson from talking you into buying a car you don't need.

5-1b Affordability

Before shopping for a car, determine how much you can afford to spend. You'll need to calculate two numbers unless you can pay cash for the entire cost of the car.

- Amount of down payment: This money will come from savings, so be sure not to deplete your emergency fund.
- Size of the monthly loan payment you can afford: Analyze your available resources—for example, your other expenses, including housing—and your transportation requirements. Don't forget to include insurance. Your monthly car payment should be no more than 20 percent of your monthly net income.

EXAMPLE: Calculating How Much of a Car Loan You Can Afford

You can use the your available down payment and monthly payment amount to calculate the total amount that you can afford for a car. For example, suppose that you have $3,000 for a down payment, you can pay $500 a month, and your bank is offering 4-year (48-month) car loans at a 5 percent annual interest rate. How much of a loan can you afford? Using a calculator and keystrokes shown in the margin, you'll find that you can pay off a loan of about $21,711. Add that to the $3,000 down payment, and you'll be able to afford a car costing about $24,700. It pays to shop around for loans because their rates can differ by as much as 2 percent!

Calculator

INPUTS	FUNCTIONS
48	N
5	I
500	PMT
	CPT
	PV
	SOLUTION
	21,711.48

See Appendix E for details.

depreciation
The loss in the value of an asset, such as an automobile, that occurs over its period of ownership; calculated as the difference between the price initially paid and the subsequent sale price.

Operating Costs

The out-of-pocket cost of operating an automobile includes not only car payments but also insurance, license, fuel, oil, tires, and other operating and maintenance outlays. Some of these costs are *fixed* regardless of how much you drive; others are *variable*, depending on the number of miles you drive. The biggest fixed cost is likely to be the *installment payments* associated with the loan or lease used to acquire the car; the biggest variable cost will probably be fuel.

Another purchase cost is **depreciation**, which is the loss in value that occurs over its period of ownership. In effect, depreciation is the difference between the price you paid for the car and what you can sell it for. If you paid $20,000 for an automobile that can be sold 3 years later for $14,000, the car will cost you $6,000 in depreciation. Although depreciation may not be a recurring out-of-pocket cost, it's an important operating expense that shouldn't be overlooked.

Gas, Diesel, or Hybrid?

Given the cost of fuel, it's important to determine the type of fuel you prefer. If you're a "green" who's concerned about the environmental impact of the fuel your car uses, you may be interested only in a hybrid or an electric car. In this case, price differences may not matter. Although you'll want to consider fuel economy when car shopping, comparable gas-fueled, internal combustion engines and diesel-powered cars have similar fuel economy. Generally diesels are a bit noisier, accelerate slower but have more power, and have longer engine lives than do traditional gas-powered cars.

Hybrids, which blend gas and battery power, have experienced rapid sales growth due to historically increasing gas prices, improved technology and availability, and greater public awareness of environmental issues. Although they're more economical and less polluting than gas- and diesel-powered vehicles, hybrids do have some disadvantages: high cost of battery replacement, generally higher repair costs, and typically

FINANCIAL ROAD SIGN

Where Can You Find Used Cars?

In addition to trade-ins and privately sold vehicles, here are some other sources of used cars.

- **Certified used ("pre-owned") cars.** Near-new cars that are inspected, certified, and warrantied by the dealer.
- **Off-lease cars.** Typically single-driver, fully equipped cars that have been inspected after lease return and prior to resale.
- **Rental cars ("program cars").** Attractive rental cars, often with some remaining factory warranty, relatively high miles, and limited options.
- **Corporate fleet cars.** Typically well-maintained, high-mileage cars that are two to three years old.

EXHIBIT 5.2   Pros and Cons of Buying a Used Car

Thinking of buying a used car? Consider both the advantages and disadvantages. Here are some of the *advantages.*

- It's less expensive than a comparable new car, and the recent popularity of short-term car leases has increased the availability of late-model, attractively priced used cars.
- It won't depreciate in value as quickly as a new car—purchasing a used car that is fewer than 18 months old often means saving the 20 percent to 25 percent depreciation in value typically experienced during that part of a car's life.
- Because used cars are less expensive, buyers don't have to put down as much money as they would for a new car.
- Today's used cars are more reliable. The quality and durability of well-maintained 2- to 4-year-old cars makes them more reliable and less expensive to maintain than the new cars of 10 years ago.
- The *federal odometer disclosure law*, requiring sellers to give buyers a signed statement attesting that the mileage shown on the odometer of their used cars is accurate, protects consumers. Penalties for violating this law are stringent.

The main *disadvantage* of buying a used car is the uncertainty about its mechanical condition. It might look good and have low mileage, but it could still have mechanical problems requiring future maintenance and repair expenditures. Having your prospective used car purchase checked out by a reputable mechanic or independent inspection service is money well spent that could save you hundreds of dollars and much aggravation later on.

a higher initial purchase price. It's important to consider the differences between the costs and performance of differently fueled vehicles and decide on the vehicle you want before shopping for a specific new or used car.

New, Used, or "Nearly New"?

One decision you must make is whether to buy a new, used, or "nearly new" car. If you can't afford to buy a new car, the decision is made for you. Some people who can afford to buy a new car choose to buy a used car so they can have a better model—a used luxury car such as a BMW, Lexus, or Mercedes—rather than a less-expensive brand of new car such as a Ford. With the increasing popularity of used cars, car dealers are trying to dispel the negative image associated with buying a used, or "pre-owned," car. You'll find used cars advertised in local or nearby city newspapers, publications like *AutoTrader,* and their Web sites. These provide an excellent source of information on used cars for sale. Exhibit 5.2 offers advice for buying a used car.

Once you know what you want, shop at these places.

- **Franchise dealerships:** Offer the latest-model used cars, provide financing, and will negotiate on price. Be sure to research values before shopping.
- **Superstores:** AutoNation, CarMax, and similar dealers offer no-haggle pricing and a large selection. They certify cars and may offer a limited short-term warranty. May cost slightly more than at a dealer who will negotiate.
- **Independent used car lots:** Usually offer older (four- to six-year-old) cars and have lower overhead than franchise dealers do. There are no uniform industry standards, so be sure to check with the Better Business Bureau before buying.
- **Private individuals:** Generally cost less because there's no dealer overhead; may have maintenance records. Be sure that the seller holds the title of the car.

Size, Body Style, and Features

Your first consideration should be what type of car you need. More than one style category may work for you. For example, a family of five can buy a mid-size or full-size sedan, station wagon, minivan, or compact or full-size SUV. When considering size, body style, and features, think about your needs, likes, and dislikes, as well as

Behavior Matters

Watch out for "Anchoring": The Case of the Used Car Salesperson Strategy

While we try to be logical and objective in making purchases, psychologists find that people make estimates of the appropriate price of an item by starting from an initial estimate. We tend to make biased decisions because we often **anchor** on that initial value and have a hard time moving away from it in negotiating transactions.

Consider a common strategy of used car salespersons. Why do you think that they start negotiating with a high price and then work their way down? Salespeople are trying to get the consumer anchored on the initial high price so that when a lower price is offered, the consumer views the lower price as a good value, even if that is not the case. Combine this behavioral bias with our tendency to be a bit too overconfident about our negotiating skills, and you have a potential problem.

So what should you do about the anchoring behavioral bias? Recognize the tendency, do your homework about a reasonable price for a used car, and take into account the used car salesperson's strategy.

anchoring
A behavioral bias in which an individual tends to allow an initial estimate (of value or price) to dominate one's subsequent assessment (of value or price) regardless of new information to the contrary.

the cost. In most cases, there's a direct relationship between size and cost: In general, the larger the car, the more expensive it will be to purchase and to operate. Also consider performance, handling, appearance, fuel economy, reliability, repair problems, and the resale value of the car. And don't try to adapt your needs to fit the car you want—a two-passenger sports car may not be appropriate if you need the car for business or if you have children.

By listing all of the options you want before shopping for a new car, you can avoid paying for features you really don't need. Literally hundreds of options are available, ranging in price from a few dollars up to $2,000 or more, including automatic transmission, a bigger engine, air conditioning, high-performance brakes, an audio system, clock, power windows, power seats, electric door locks, leather seats, navigation systems, a rear window defroster, and special suspension. Some appearance-related options are two-tone or metallic paint, electric sunroof, special tires, sport wheels, and various interior and exterior trim packages.

Most cars have at least some options, but you can select additional optional features that provide a broad range of conveniences and luxuries—for a price. On new cars, a window sticker details each option and its price, but on used cars, only close observation serves to determine the options. Window stickers quite often list standard features that might be considered optional on other models, and vice versa. When shopping for a new car, it's important to be sure that you're comparing comparably equipped models.

Reliability and Warranties

Assess the *reliability* of a car by talking with friends who own similar cars and reading objective assessments published by consumer magazines and buying guides such as *Consumer Reports*. Study the *warranty* offered by new car manufacturers, comparing those for cars that interest you. Significant differences may exist. Be sure to read the warranty booklet included with a new car to understand the warranty terms. Most warranties are void if the owner has not performed routine maintenance or has somehow abused the car.

On new cars, the manufacturer guarantees the general reliability and quality of construction of the vehicle for a specified period in a written warranty, obligating it to repair or replace, at little or no cost to the owner, any defective parts and/or flaws in workmanship. Today, most new car warranties cover a minimum of the first three years of ownership or 36,000 miles, whichever comes first, and some provide coverage for as long as seven years or 70,000 miles. However, most warranties have limitations. For example, longer warranty periods may apply to only the engine and drive train. Auto manufacturers and private insurers also sell extended warranties and service contracts, sometimes called "buyer protection plans." Most experts consider these unnecessary and not worth their cost, given the relatively long initial warranty periods now being offered by most manufacturers.

Other Considerations

Here are some other factors that affect affordability:

- **Trading in or selling your existing car:** Although trading in is convenient, it's generally a better deal to sell your old car outright. If you're willing to take the time, you can usually sell your car for more than the wholesale price typically offered by a dealer on a trade-in.
- **Fuel economy:** The *Environmental Protection Agency (EPA) mileage ratings* are especially useful on new vehicles, which carry a sticker indicating the number of miles per gallon each model is expected to get (as determined by EPA tests) for both city and highway driving. You can check out those ratings at **http://www. fueleconomy.gov.**
- **Safety features:** Government regulations ensure that these features are likely to be similar in new cars, but older used cars may not have some features, such as side-impact airbags. Don't forget to include *auto insurance costs,* which vary depending on make, model, safety features, and other factors (and are discussed in detail in Chapter 10).

5-1c The Purchase Transaction

Once you've determined what you can afford to spend and the features that you want, you're ready to begin car shopping. If you plan to buy a new car, visit all

Image Source/Getty Images

dealers with cars that meet your requirements. Look the cars over and ask questions—but don't make any offers until you've found two or three cars with the desired features that are priced within your budget. Also, if you can be flexible about the model and options you want, you can sometimes negotiate a better deal than if you're determined to have a particular model and options. Make an appointment to test-drive the cars you're interested in. Drive—then leave! You need time to evaluate the car without pressure to buy from the salesperson.

Comparison shopping is essential, because a dealer selling the same brand as another may give you a better deal. Be aware of the sales technique called *lowballing,* where the salesperson quotes a low price for the car to get you to make an offer, and then negotiates the price upward prior to your signing the sales contract. Exhibit 5.3 lists some other factors to consider once you begin looking at cars.

Because lowballing, price haggling, and other high-pressure sales tactics can make car buying an unpleasant experience, many dealers have refocused their sales practices to emphasize customer satisfaction. Some manufacturers offer firm prices, so if you buy today, you can be sure that no one will get a better deal tomorrow. However, you should still research prices, as described in the next section, because a firm selling price doesn't guarantee the lowest cost.

EXHIBIT 5.3   Finding the Best Car for You

Start by inspecting the key points of the car. Don't overlook the obvious.

1. *How easy is it to get people and things into and out of the car?*
   - Do the doors open easily?
   - Is the trunk large enough for your needs?
   - Does the car offer a pass-through or fold-down rear seat to accommodate larger items?

2. *Comfort and visibility.*
   - Are the seats comfortable?
   - Can you adjust the driver's seat and steering wheel properly?
   - What are the car's blind spots for a person of your height?
   - Can you see all the gauges clearly?
   - Can you reach the controls for the radio, audio player, heater, air conditioner, and other features easily while driving?
   - Does it have the options you want?

Then take the car for a test drive.

1. Set aside at least 20 minutes and drive it on highways and local roads.

2. To test acceleration, merge into traffic getting onto the freeway and try passing another car.

3. If possible, drive home and make sure the car fits into your garage—especially if you're interested in a larger SUV or truck!

4. For a used car, test the heater and air conditioner. Then turn the fan off and listen for any unusual engine noises.

5. Check out overall handling. Parallel park, make a U-turn, brake hard, and so on. Do the gears shift smoothly? If testing a standard transmission, try to determine if the clutch is engaging too high or too low, which might indicate excessive wear or a problem.

As soon as you return to the car lot, take notes on how well the car handled and how comfortable you felt driving it.

This is especially important if you are test driving several cars.

Negotiating Price

Choosing among various makes, models, and options can make comparisons difficult. The price you pay for a car, whether new or used, can consequently vary widely. The more you narrow your choices to a particular car, the easier it is to get price quotes from dealers to make an "apples-to-apples" comparison.

The "sticker price" on a new car represents the manufacturer's *suggested retail price* for that particular car with its listed options. This price means very little. The key to negotiating a good price is knowing the *dealer's cost* for the car. The easiest and quickest way to find the dealer's invoice cost is going to the Edmunds and Kelley Blue Book Internet sites mentioned in this chapter or by checking car-buying guides available at your library or bookstore.

Before making an offer, prepare a worksheet with the cost versus the list price for the exact car you want. This will help you avoid high pressure by the salesperson and paying for options you don't want or need. Try to negotiate the lowest acceptable markup (3 percent to 4 percent for cars priced under $20,000; 6 percent to 7 percent for higher-priced models), push for a firm quote, and make it clear that you are comparison shopping. Don't let the salesperson pressure you into signing a sales contract or leaving a deposit until you're sure that you have negotiated the best deal. Good cost information will improve your bargaining position and possibly allow you to negotiate a price that is only several hundred dollars above the dealer's cost.

If you want to avoid negotiating entirely, you can buy your car through a buying service, either by phone or over the Internet. These include independent companies—such as AutoVantage (**http://www.autovantage.com**), Autobytel (**http://www.autobytel.com**), and AutoWeb (**http://www.autoweb.com**)—or services offered through credit unions, motor clubs, and discount warehouses such as Costco. Buying services work in a variety of ways. They may have an arrangement with a network of dealers to sell cars at a predetermined price above invoice, provide you with competitive bids from several local dealers, find the car you want and negotiate the price with the dealer, or place an order with the factory for a made-to-order car. You'll get a good price through a service—although you can't assume that it will be the best price.

It's best not to discuss your plan to finance the purchase or the value of your trade-in until you've settled the question of price. These should be separate issues. Salespeople will typically want to find out how much you can afford monthly and then offer financing deals with payments close to that amount. In the case of trade-ins, the dealer might offer you a good price for your old car and raise the price of the new car to compensate. The dealer may offer financing terms that sound attractive, but be sure to compare them with the cost of bank loans. Sometimes dealers increase the price of the car to make up for a low interest rate, or attractive financing may apply only to certain models. Often financing charges include unneeded extras such as credit life insurance, accident insurance, an extended warranty, or a service package.

Manufacturers and dealers often offer buyers special incentives, such as rebates and cut-rate financing, particularly when car sales are slow. (Deduct rebates from the dealer's cost when you negotiate price.) You may have a choice between a rebate and low-cost financing. To determine which is the better deal, calculate the difference between the monthly payments on a market-rate bank loan and the special dealer loan for the same term. Multiply the payment difference by the loan maturity, in months, and compare it with the rebate.

EXAMPLE: Is That Rebate a Good Deal?

A car dealer offers either a $1,000 rebate or a 4 percent interest rate on a $10,000, 4-year loan. Your monthly payments would be $226 with dealer financing and $234 on a 6 percent bank loan with similar terms. The payment savings over the life of the loan are $384 ($8 per month 3 48 months), which is less than the $1,000 rebate. So in this case you would be better off with the rebate.

Closing the Deal

Whether you're buying a new or used car, to make a legally binding offer, you must sign a **sales contract** that specifies the offering price and all the conditions of your offer. The sales contract also specifies whether the offer includes a trade-in. If it does,

sales contract
An agreement to purchase an automobile that states the offering price and all conditions of the offer; when signed by the buyer and seller, the contract legally binds them to its terms.

You Can Do It Now

What's Your Car Worth?

If you have a car, it's good to know what it's worth from time-to-time. That way you'll have a better sense of your net worth and you'll know how much your car is depreciating over time. Just go to the Kelley Blue book site at **http://www.kbb.com** and go to the "Price New/Used Cars"—you can do it now.

the offering price will include both the payment amount and the trade-in allowance. Because this agreement contractually binds you to purchase the car at the offering price, be sure that you want and can afford the car before signing this agreement. You may be required to include a deposit of around $200 or more with the contract to show that you're making an offer in good faith.

Once the dealer accepts your offer, you complete the purchase transaction and take delivery of the car. If you're not paying cash for the car, you can arrange financing through the dealer, at your bank, a credit union, or a consumer finance company. The key aspects of these types of installment loans, which can be quickly negotiated if your credit is good, are discussed in Chapter 7. Prior to delivery, the dealer is responsible for cleaning the car and installing any optional equipment. It's a good idea to make sure that all equipment you are paying for has been installed and that the car is ready for use before paying the dealer. When you pay for the car in full, you should receive a title or appropriate evidence that you own the car.

Refinancing Your Auto Loan

Refinancing your auto loan can pay off—but only under particular circumstances. First, you need to have enough equity in the car to serve as collateral for what is essentially a used car loan. If you made a large down payment or are well into a loan, then you may be a candidate for refinancing. If you can cut your interest rate by at least 2 percentage points without stretching the final payment date of your current loan, you could enjoy substantial savings.

Banks generally aren't interested in refinancing car loans, so online lenders such as E-Loan (**http://www.eloan.com**) and HSBC Auto Finance (**http://www.auto-loan-center.com/lenders-hsbc.php**) get most of that business. If you're a member of a credit union, see what it can do for you. If you own a home, consider tapping a home equity line of credit to pay off a high-interest auto loan. Unlike consumer loans, the interest paid on a home equity loan is tax deductible. Wherever you choose to refinance, you'll probably have to pay $5 to $50 for a title change listing the new lien holder. And forget about refinancing your auto loan if you have bad credit.

Traditionally, car loans were for three or four years, but loan terms are lengthening as buyers stretch to afford cars that can top $40,000 or even $50,000. These loans typically carry higher interest rates. It is common for six-year loan rates to exceed four-year loan rates by 0.75 percent or more. However, the monthly payments are smaller than those on the shorter-term loans. So far, only a handful of banks and credit unions are offering eight-year loans, but many now offer seven-year loans. Today, five-year and longer loans account for over half of all new car loans. Long-term loans are most commonly used to buy high-end luxury vehicles and are not available for all vehicles. By the end of the loan term, you'll still be making payments on a vehicle that has used up most of its life and is practically worthless—a major downside of longer-term car loans.

5-1 Briefly discuss how each of these purchase considerations would affect your choice of a car:

a. Affordability

b. Operating costs

c. Gas, diesel, hybrid, or electric?

d. New, used, or "nearly new"?

e. Size, body style, and features

f. Reliability and warranty protection

5-2 Describe the purchase transaction process, including shopping, negotiating price, and closing the deal on a car.

5-2 LEASING A CAR

lease
An arrangement in which the lessee receives the use of a car (or other asset) in exchange for making monthly lease payments over a specified period.

Don't worry about temperamental engines or transmissions—you could just get a new car every few years using a leasing arrangement. Put a small amount down, make easy payments. No wonder leasing is popular, accounting for about 25 percent of all new vehicles delivered. When you **lease**, you (the lessee) receive the use of a car in exchange for monthly lease payments over a specified period, usually two to four years. Leasing appeals to a wide range of car buyers, even though the total cost of leasing is generally more than buying a car with a loan, and at the end of the lease, you have nothing. The car—and the money you paid to rent it—are gone. So why do so many car buyers lease their cars? Reasons include rising new car prices, the nondeductibility of consumer loan interest, lower monthly payments, driving a more expensive car for the same monthly payment, and minimizing the down payment to preserve cash.

closed-end lease
The most popular form of automobile lease; often called a *walk-away lease*, because at the end of its term the lessee simply turns in the car (assuming the preset mileage limit has not been exceeded and the car hasn't been abused).

With all the advertisements promising low monthly lease payments, it's easy to focus on only the payment. Unlike a loan purchase, with a lease you're paying not for the whole car but only for its use during a specified period. Leasing is a more complex arrangement than borrowing money to buy a car. Until you understand how leasing works and compare lease terms with bank financing, you won't know if leasing is the right choice for you.

5-2a The Leasing Process

open-end (finance) lease
An automobile lease under which the estimated *residual value* of the car is used to determine lease payments; if the car is actually worth less than this value at the end of the lease, the lessee must pay the difference.

The first step is the same for leasing and purchasing: research car types and brands, comparison shop at several dealers, and find the car you want at the best price. Don't ask the dealer about leasing or any financing incentives until *after* you've negotiated the final price. Then compare the lease terms offered by the dealer to those of at least one independent leasing firm. As with a purchase, try to negotiate lower lease payments—a payment reduction of $20 a month saves nearly $1,000 on a four-year lease. And don't reveal what you can afford to pay per month; doing so can lead you to a poor lease deal. Once you agree on leasing terms, be sure to get everything in writing.

residual value
The remaining value of a leased car at the end of the lease term.

The majority of car lessees choose the **closed-end lease**, often called the *walk-away lease*, because at the end of its term you simply turn in the car, assuming that you have neither exceeded the preset mileage limit nor abused the car. This is the dominant type of lease used by consumers. Under the less popular **open-end** or **finance lease**, if the car is worth less than the estimated **residual value**—the remaining value of the car at the end of the lease term—then you must pay the difference. These leases are used primarily for commercial business leasing.

A commonly cited benefit of leasing is the absence of a down payment. However, most leases require a "capital cost reduction," which is a down payment that lowers the potential depreciation and therefore your monthly lease payments. You may be able to negotiate a lower capital cost reduction or find a lease that doesn't require one.

The lease payment calculation is based on four variables:

capitalized cost
The price of a car that is being leased.

money factor
The financing rate on a lease; similar to the interest rate on a loan.

1. The **capitalized cost** of the car (the price of the car you are leasing)
2. The forecast *residual value* of the car at the end of the lease
3. The **money factor**, or financing rate on the lease (similar to the interest rate on a loan)
4. The *lease term*

The *depreciation* during the lease term (which is what you are financing) is the capitalized cost minus the residual value. Dividing the sum of the depreciation and the sales tax (on the financed portion only) by the number of months in the lease term and then adding the lessor's required monthly return (at the money factor) results in the monthly payment. (To convert the money factor to an annual percentage rate, multiply it by 2,400; for example, a money factor of 0.0025 is the equivalent of paying 6 percent interest on a loan.) The lower the capitalized cost and higher the residual value, the lower your payment. Residual values quoted by different dealers can vary, so check several sources to find the highest residual value to minimize depreciation.

Lease terms typically run two to four years. Terminating a lease early is often difficult and costly, so be reasonably sure that you can keep the car for the full lease term. The lease contract should outline any costs and additional fees associated with early termination. Early termination clauses also apply to cars that are stolen or totaled in an accident. Some leases require "gap insurance" to cover the lost lease payments that would result from early termination caused by one of these events.

Under most leases, you are responsible for insuring and maintaining the car. At the end of the lease, you are obligated to pay for any "unreasonable wear and tear." A good lease contract should clearly define what is considered unreasonable. In addition, most leases require the lessee to pay a disposition fee of about $150 to $250 when the car is returned.

purchase option
A price specified in a lease at which the lessee can buy the car at the end of the lease term.

Most auto leases include a **purchase option** (either a fixed price, the market price at the end of the lease term, or the residual value of the car) that specifies the price at which the lessee can buy the car at the end of the lease term. A lower residual results in a lower purchase price but raises monthly payments. Experts recommend negotiating a fixed-price purchase option, if possible.

The annual mileage allowance—typically, about 10,000 to 15,000 miles per year for the lease term—is another important lease consideration. Usually the lessee must pay between 10 and 25 cents per mile for additional miles. If you expect to exceed the allowable mileage, you would be wise to negotiate a more favorable rate for extra miles before signing the lease contract.

FINANCIAL ROAD SIGN

Auto Leasing Checklist

Smart buyers will know the following figures before attempting to negotiate a car lease:

- List price for the car and options
- Capitalized cost (the value on which monthly payments are based)
- Money factor (interest rate assumption)
- Total interest paid
- Total sales tax
- Residual value for which the car can be purchased at the lease's end
- Depreciation (the capitalized cost minus the residual value)
- Lease term (period)

5-2b Lease versus Purchase Analysis

To decide whether it is less costly to lease rather than purchase a car, you need to perform a *lease versus purchase analysis* to compare the total cost of leasing to the total cost of purchasing a car over equal periods. In this analysis, the purchase is assumed to be financed with an installment loan over the same period as the lease.

For example, assume that Mary Dixon is considering either leasing or purchasing a new Toyota Prius costing $29,990. The four-year, closed-end lease that she is considering requires a $2,900 down payment (capital cost reduction), a $500 security deposit, and monthly payments of $440, including sales tax. If she purchases the car, she will make a $4,500 down payment and finance the balance with a four-year, 4 percent loan requiring monthly payments of about $576. She will also have to pay 5 percent sales tax ($1,500) on the purchase, and she expects the car to have a residual value of $16,500 at the end of 4 years. Mary can earn 3 percent interest on her savings with short-term CDs. After filling in Worksheet 5.1, Mary concludes that purchasing is better because its *total cost* of $17,665.42 is $6,762.58 less than the $24,428.00 total cost of leasing—even though the monthly lease payment is about $136 lower. Clearly, all else being equal, the least costly alternative of purchasing is preferred to leasing.

If you're fortunate enough to be able to pay cash for your car, you may still want to investigate leasing. Sometimes dealers offer such good lease terms that you can come out ahead by leasing and then investing the money you would have paid for the car. The decision to make a cash purchase rather than to finance it depends on the cost of the car, the financing cost, the rate of return that could be earned on investing the purchase price, and the trade-in value of the car at the end of the lease period. More specifically, to compare the total cost of a cash purchase, simply take the cost of the car (including sales tax), add to it the opportunity cost of using all cash, and deduct the car's value at the end of the lease or loan period. At 3 percent per year on her savings, Mary's total cost of the car is as follows: $31,489.50 cost + $3,778.74 lost interest (4 × 0.03 × $31,489.50) − $16,500 trade-in value = $18,768.24. Compare this with the previously determined cost of buying the car using financing, which is $17,665.42. Thus, in this case, the cost of purchasing the car for cash is about $1,102.82 more than its purchase cost with financing. So Mary would be better off using the financing.

5-2c When the Lease Ends

At the end of the lease, you'll be faced with a major decision. Should you return the car and walk away, or should you buy the car? If you turn in the car and move on to a new model, you may be hit with "excess wear and damage" and "excess mileage" charges and disposition fees. To minimize these, replace worn tires, get repairs done yourself,

FINANCIAL ROAD SIGN

When Does It Make Sense to Lease a Car?

The most important question to ask yourself is why you need a new car every few years. Leasing may make sense if:

- **You value purchasing flexibility.** A lease allows you to put off the purchasing decision while using the car. It's like having a test drive that lasts several years instead of a few minutes.
- **You value the convenience of not having to deal with significant auto repairs.**
- **You're self-employed and can take the leasing payment as a tax-deductible business expense.**
- **You want to drive a luxury car for less, but you don't want to put up that much money.**

The key is being honest about why you want to lease and being informed about the costs and benefits of a leasing arrangement.

This worksheet illustrates Mary Dixon's lease versus purchase analysis for a new Toyota Prius costing $29,990. The four-year closed-end lease requires an initial payment of $3,400 ($2,900 down payment + $500 security deposit) and monthly payments of $440. Purchasing requires a $4,500 down payment, sales tax of 5 percent ($1,499.50), and 48 monthly payments of $575.45. The trade-in value of the new car at the end of four years is estimated to be $16,500. *Because the total cost of leasing of $24,428 is greater than the $17,665.42 total cost of purchasing, Mary should purchase rather than lease the car.*

AUTOMOBILE LEASE VERSUS PURCHASE ANALYSIS*

Name ___Mary Dixon___   Date ___Sep 11, 2017___

Item Description		Amount
LEASE		
1	Initial payment:	
	a. Down payment (capital cost reduction): $ 2,900.00	
	b. Security deposit: 500.00	$ 3,400.00
2	Term of lease and loan (years)*	4
3	Term of lease and loan (months) (Item 2 × 12)	48
4	Monthly lease payment	$ 440.00
5	Total payments over term of lease (Item 3 × Item 4)	$ 21,120.00
6	Interest rate earned on savings (in decimal form)	$ 0.030
7	Opportunity cost of initial payment (Item 1 × Item 2 × Item 6)	$ 408.00
8	Payment/refund for market value adjustment at end of lease ($0 for closed-end leases) and/or estimated end-of-term charges	$ 0.00
9	**Total cost of leasing (Item 1a + Item 5 + Item 7 + Item 8)**	**$ 24,428.00**
PURCHASE		
10	Purchase price	$ 29,990.00
11	Down payment	$ 4,500.00
12	Sales tax rate (in decimal form)	$ 0.50
13	Sales tax (Item 10 × Item 12)	$ 1,499.50
14	Monthly loan payment (Terms: _25,490.00_ , _48_ months, _4_ %)	$ 575.54
15	Total payments over term of loan (Item 3 × Item 14)	$ 27,625.92
16	Opportunity cost of down payment (Item 2 × Item 6 × Item 11)	$ 540.00
17	Estimated value of car at end of loan	$ 16,500.00
18	**Total cost of purchasing (Item 11 + Item 13 + Item 15 + Item 16 − Item 17)**	**$ 17,665.42**

DECISION

If the value of Item 9 is less than the value of Item 18, leasing is preferred; otherwise, the *purchase alternative is preferred.*

**Note:* This form is based on assumed equal terms for the lease and the installment loan, which is assumed to be used to finance the purchase.

and document the car's condition before returning it. You may be able to negotiate a lower disposition fee. If you can't return the car without high repair charges or greatly exceeded mileage allowances, you may come out ahead by buying the car.

Whether the purchase option makes sense depends largely on the residual value. With popular cars, the residual value in your lease agreement may be lower than the car's trade-in value. Buying the car then makes sense. Even if you want a different car, you can exercise the purchase option and sell the car on the open market to net the difference, which could be $1,000 or more. If the reverse is true and the residual is higher than the price of a comparable used car, just let the lease expire. Find your car's market value by looking in used car price guides and newspaper ads and comparing it with the residual value of your car in the lease agreement.

TEST YOURSELF

5-3 What are the advantages and disadvantages of leasing a car?

5-4 Given your personal financial circumstances, if you were buying a car today, would you probably pay cash, lease, or finance it, and why? Which factors are most important to you in making this decision?

5-3 MEETING HOUSING NEEDS: BUY OR RENT?

LG3

5-3a Housing Prices and the Recent Financial Crisis

Before considering how and when to buy or rent a home, it is important to consider the recent rough history of housing prices during and after the financial crisis of 2008–2009. After examining this context in which housing decisions are made, we'll consider how to know when you should buy your first home. There are many factors to consider before taking on such a large financial responsibility. In the remainder of this chapter, we'll explore some of these factors and discuss how to approach the home-buying and renting process.

From early 2001 through 2006, home prices in the United States rose rapidly. The median nominal sales price of existing homes rose from $141,600 to $230,400. Existing home prices started dropping and fell to a median price of $154,600 in early 2012. Prices had fallen because the real estate bubble had popped and the financial crisis of 2008–2009 had vastly depressed home sales. This period of recession was characterized by high unemployment, low consumer confidence, and tighter credit. Indeed, about 1 in 7 American homeowners had *negative equity:* owing more on their mortgage than their homes were worth.

The bubble in real estate prices had several important side effects. It encouraged a massive increase in construction and the extraction of a lot of home equity through home equity loans and refinancings, about two-thirds of which went into increased consumption. Net worth increased with home prices as well. Yet those side effects went in the opposite direction during the financial crisis. Between 2007 and 2009, the crisis reduced the average family's net worth by about 23 percent and dampened consumption, which slowed the macroeconomy. Home **foreclosures**, the process whereby lenders attempt to recover loan balances from borrowers who have quit making payments by forcing the sale of the home pledged as collateral, increased significantly.

foreclosure
The process whereby lenders attempt to recover loan balances from borrowers who have quit making payments by forcing the sale of the home pledged as collateral.

Although housing prices and the number of home sales result from a variety of economic and behavioral factors, it's generally agreed that increasing interest rates tend to slow the volume (and prices) of home sales. Conversely, declines in mortgage rates tend to increase the volume of home sales (and prices). However, as shown in Exhibit 5.4, prices vary widely from one part of the country to another.

5-3b What Type of Housing Meets Your Needs?

Because you have your own unique set of likes and dislikes, the best way to start your search for housing is to list your preferences and classify them according to whether their satisfaction is essential, desirable, or merely a "plus." This exercise is important for three reasons. First, it screens out housing that doesn't meet your minimum

Behavior Matters

Did the Real Estate Bubble Result from Behavioral Biases?

There's a tendency for us to sometimes exhibit herding behavior. Well-known Yale behavioral economist and Nobel laureate Robert Shiller argues that after the rapid run-up in real estate prices between 2001 and 2006, a "social epidemic" encouraged the belief that housing was a critical investment opportunity that shouldn't be missed. And there is a behavioral bias, known as the *conservatism bias*, which encourages us to rely too heavily on past experience and to revise our expectations for the future too slowly in light of new, relevant information. These psychological biases only fed additional housing price increases apart from the underlying real estate investment fundamentals, which supported the development of the real estate bubble.

Others argue that households generally have trouble distinguishing between real (inflation-adjusted) and nominal (unadjusted for inflation) changes in interest rates and rents. Thus, when expected inflation drops, consumers buy homes to take advantage of apparently low nominal financing costs, without realizing that future home price and rent appreciation rates will fall by comparable amounts. The falling inflation and the associated "inflation illusion" in the early 2000s consequently brought unjustified real estate price spikes, which culminated in the housing bubble and it's subsequent dramatic pop.

EXHIBIT 5.4 | **Home Prices in Different Regions of the U.S.**

The median sales price of existing homes varies widely from one part of the country to another—$299,600 in the Western states, $159,100 in the Midwest, $184,100 in the South, and $246,600 in the Northeast.

West: median price $299,600

Midwest: median price $159,100

Northeast: median price $246,600

South: median price $184,100

National Median Homes	Single-Family Homes	Condos and Co-ops
Price: $209,500	Price: $210,200	Price: $204,000

Source: National Association of Realtors, "Infographic: December 2014 Existing-Home Sales," http://www.realtor.org/infographics/infographic-december-2014-existing-home-sales, accessed August 2015.

requirements. Second, it helps you recognize that you may have to make trade-offs, because seldom will you find a single home that meets all your needs. Third, it will help you focus on those needs for which you are willing and able to pay.

One of the first decisions you'll have to make is the type of housing unit that you want and need. Several of the following may be suitable:

- **Single-family homes:** These are the most popular choice. They can be stand-alone homes on their own legally defined lots or *row houses* or *townhouses* that share a common wall. As a rule, single-family homes offer buyers privacy, prestige, pride of ownership, and maximum property control.

condominium (condo)
A form of direct ownership of an individual unit in a multiunit project in which lobbies, swimming pools, and other common areas and facilities are jointly owned by all property owners in the project.

- **Condominiums:** The term **condominium**, or **condo**, describes a form of ownership rather than a type of building. Condominiums can be apartments, townhouses, or cluster housing. The condominium buyer receives title to an individual residential unit and joint ownership of common areas and facilities such as lobbies, swimming pools, lakes, and tennis courts. Buyers arrange their own mortgages and pay their own taxes for their units. They are assessed a monthly *homeowner's fee* for their proportionate share of common facility maintenance costs. The *home-owners' association* elects a board of managers to supervise the buildings and grounds. Condominiums generally cost less than single-family detached homes because they're designed for more efficient land use and lower construction costs. Many home buyers are attracted to condominiums because they don't want the responsibility of maintaining and caring for a property. Exhibit 5.5 lists some of the key things to check before buying a condominium.

cooperative apartment (co-op)
An apartment in a building in which each tenant owns a share of the nonprofit corporation that owns the building.

- **Cooperative apartments:** In a **cooperative apartment**, or **co-op**, building, each tenant owns a share of the nonprofit corporation that owns the building. Residents lease their units from the corporation and pay a monthly assessment in proportion to ownership shares, based on the space they occupy. These assessments cover the cost of services, maintenance, taxes, and the mortgage on the entire building and are subject to change, depending on the actual costs of operating the building and the actions of the board of directors, which determines the corporation's policies. The cooperative owner receives the tax benefits resulting from interest and property taxes attributable to his or her

---

EXHIBIT 5.5 | Condo Buyer's Checklist

It pays to carefully check out the various operating and occupancy features of a condo before you buy.

- Thoroughly investigate the developer's reputation—through local real estate brokers, banks, or the Better Business Bureau—whether the building is brand new, under construction, or being converted.
- Investigate the condo homeowners' association, the restrictions on condo owners, and the quality of the property management. Read the rules of the organization.
- Check the construction of the building and its physical condition. If the building is being converted to condos, ask to see an independent inspection firm's report on the building's condition.
- Insist that any planned changes to the property be detailed in writing.
- Talk to the current occupants to see if they are satisfied with the living conditions.
- Determine how many units are rented; generally, owner-occupied units are better maintained.
- Determine if there is sufficient parking space.
- Watch for unusually low maintenance fees that may have to be increased soon.
- Consider the resale value.

For new developments, compare the projected monthly homeowner's fees with those of similar buildings already in operation. For older developments, check to see when capital improvements such as exterior painting and roof replacement were last made. Special assessments are usually levied on all unit owners for major costly improvements.

proportionate ownership interest. Drawbacks of co-op ownership include difficulty in obtaining a mortgage (because many financial institutions don't like taking shares of a corporation rather than property as collateral), rent increases to cover maintenance costs of vacant units, and the need to abide by the capital improvement decisions of the co-op board of directors, which can increase the monthly assessment.

- **Rental units:** Some individuals and families choose to *rent* or *lease* their place of residence rather than own it. They may be just starting out and have limited funds for housing, or they may be uncertain where they want to live. Perhaps they like the short-term commitment and limited maintenance responsibilities. The cost and availability of rental units varies from one geographic area to another. Rental units range from duplexes, fourplexes, and even single-family homes to large, high-rise apartment complexes containing several hundred units. Renting does come with restrictions, however. For example, you may not be allowed to have a pet or make changes to the unit's appearance.

5-3c The Rental Option

Many people choose to rent rather than buy their home. For example, young adults usually rent for one or more of the following reasons: (1) they don't have the funds for a down payment and closing costs, (2) they're unsettled in their jobs and family status, (3) they don't want the additional responsibilities associated with homeownership, or (4) they believe they can afford a nicer home later by renting now because housing market conditions or mortgage rates are currently unattractive. A big drawback of renting is that the payments are *not* tax deductible.

The Rental Contract (Lease Agreement)

When you rent an apartment, duplex, house, or any other type of residence, you'll be required to sign a **rental contract** or **lease agreement**. Although oral agreements are generally binding, a written contract is a legal instrument that better protects both the *lessor* (the person who owns the property) and the *lessee* (the person who leases the property). Because the rental contract binds you, the lessee, to various actions, be sure that you fully understand it before signing it. As a rule, the contract specifies the *amount* of the monthly payment, the payment *due date, penalties* for late payment, the *length* of the lease agreement, security and/or advance rent (*deposit*) requirements, *fair wear and tear* definitions and provisions, the distribution of *expenses, lease renewal* options and *early termination penalties,* and any *restrictions* on children, pets, subleasing, or using the facilities.

Most leases have a minimum term of either six months or one year and require payments at the beginning of each month. They may initially require a security deposit and/or payment of the last month's rent in advance as security against damages or violation of the lease agreement. If there's no serious damage, most of the deposit should be refunded to the lessee shortly after the lease expires. A portion of the deposit is sometimes retained by the lessor to cover the cost of cleaning and minor repairs, regardless of how clean and well kept the unit was. Because the landlord controls the deposit, a written statement describing any preexisting damage, *prior to* occupancy, may help the lessee avoid losing their entire deposit. Renters should also clarify who bears expenses such as utilities and trash collection and exactly what, if any, restrictions are placed on the use of the property. It's also a good idea for renters to check the renter–landlord laws in their state to fully understand their *rights* and responsibilities.

rental contract lease agreement

A legal instrument that protects both the *lessor* and the *lessee* from an adverse action by the other party; it specifies the *amount* of the monthly payment, the payment *due date, penalties* for late payment, the *length* of the lease agreement, *deposit* requirements, *fair wear and tear* definitions and provisions, the distribution of *expenses, renewal* options and *early termination penalties,* and any *restrictions* on children, pets, subleasing or using the facilities.

Evaluating the General Attractiveness of Renting versus Buying a Home

rent ratio
The ratio of the average house price to the average annual rent, which provides insight into the relative attractiveness of buying a house versus renting in a given area of potential interest.

You can get a general sense of the relative cost of renting versus buying a home by considering the so-called **rent ratio**, which is the ratio of the average house price to the average annual rent in the area that you are considering. Given the bursting of the housing bubble in the late 2000s, the inflation-adjusted rent ratio steadily fell to around late-1990 levels. Thus, the relative attractiveness of renting has decreased in recent years. Exhibit 5.6 shows the nominal rent ratios for major U.S. cities, which differ significantly in the relative attractiveness of buying versus renting. Rent ratios between 31 and 35 indicate that it is more attractive to rent than to buy. At the other extreme, a rent ratio between 6 and 10 indicates that it is more attractive to buy than to rent. And a moderate rent ratio (between 16 and 20) suggests that while renting is expensive, it may still be better to buy. Exhibit 5.6 shows that nationally in late 2014 it was generally 38 percent cheaper to buy than to rent. However, the decision

---

EXHIBIT 5.6   Relative Attractiveness of Renting versus Buying a House

The Trulia Rent vs. Buy Index portrays the average list price of homes versus the average annual rent on two-bedroom apartments, condos, and townhomes in America's 50 largest cities by population listed on Trulia.com. Note the highlighted mortgage rate, tax bracket, and expected home holding period assumptions.

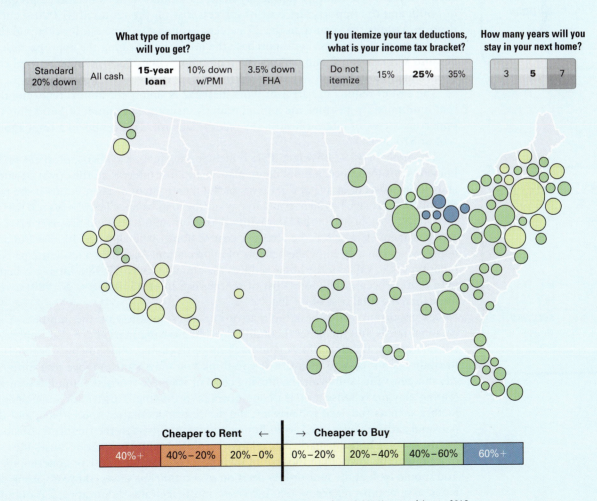

Source: "Rent vs. Buy: Which Is Cheaper for You?" http://www.trulia.com/trends/vis/rentvsbuy-q3-2014/, accessed August 2015.

was closer in California and New York City. The gap between the benefits of buying vs. renting was widest in the Midwest and the South. You may want to consider the rent ratio when considering where to relocate or to form some basic expectations if you've decided where to move.

Analyzing the Rent-or-Buy Decision

Owning a home is not always more costly on a monthly basis than renting, although there are many other factors to consider before making this important decision. The economics of renting or buying a place to live depends on four main factors: (1) housing prices and mortgage interest rates, (2) tax write-offs for homeowners, (3) the expected increase or decrease in home values over time, and (4) how many years you expect to stay in your home.

To choose the lowest-cost alternative, compare the cost of renting with the cost of buying, as illustrated by the rent-or-buy analysis in Worksheet 5.2. Note that because the interest deduction nearly always exceeds the amount of the standard deduction ($6,300 for single and $12,600 for married filing jointly in 2015), the form assumes that the taxpayer will itemize deductions. Suppose that you must decide between renting an apartment for $850 a month or buying a similar-sized condominium for $150,000. Purchasing the condo involves a $30,000 down payment; a $120,000, 6 percent, 30-year mortgage with monthly mortgage payments of $719; $4,500 in closing costs; and property taxes, insurance, and maintenance. With renting, the only costs are the $850 monthly rental payment, an annual renter's insurance premium of $600, and the opportunity cost of interest lost on the required $1,000 security deposit. Assume that you're in the 25 percent ordinary income tax bracket and that you'll itemize deductions if you purchase the home. Substituting the appropriate values into Worksheet 5.2 and making the required calculations results in the total cost of each alternative.

The cost of renting in Part A of Worksheet 5.2 is simply the annual rent (monthly rent multiplied by 12) plus the annual renter's insurance premium of $600 plus the opportunity cost of interest lost on the security deposit. This results in a total annual cost of $10,840.

The annual cost of buying in Part B includes mortgage payments, property taxes, homeowner's insurance, annual maintenance, and lost interest on the down payment and closing costs to arrive at total costs of $14,964 in Item 6. Then, subtract the portion of the mortgage payment going to pay off the loan balance because it's not part of the interest cost. Subtract the tax savings derived from interest and property taxes to arrive at Item 11, which is the after-tax cost of homeownership of $10,980. But as a homeowner, you also enjoy the benefits of appreciation. Assuming a modest 2 percent inflation in the value of the home reduces the annual cost to $7,980. Buying is better than renting because the total cost of renting is $2,860 ($10,840 − $7,980) a year more than the total cost of buying.

It's important *not* to base the rent-or-buy decision solely on the numbers. Your personal needs and the general condition of the housing market are also important considerations. Renting allows you much more flexibility than buying a home—but flexibility is not easy to quantify. If you think you may want to move to a different city in a few years and incur the moving costs or if you're worried about job security, renting may make sense even if the numbers favor buying. Further, for some people, factors such as the need for privacy, the desire to personalize one's home, and the personal satisfaction gained from homeownership outweigh the financial considerations. In some housing markets, a relative surplus of rental properties causes the cost of renting to be lower than the cost of owning a comparable house or condominium. You should look at the rent-or-buy decision over a timeline of several years, using different assumptions regarding rent increases, mortgage rates, home appreciation rates in the area, and the rate of return that you can earn on the funds you could invest (if you rent) rather than use toward a down payment on a house (if you buy).

Calculator

INPUTS	FUNCTIONS
120000	PV
360	N
6	÷
12	=
	I
	CPT
	PMT
	SOLUTION
	719.46

See Appendix E for details.

Calculator

INPUTS	FUNCTIONS
180000	PV
360	N
6	÷
12	=
	I
	CPT
	PMT
	SOLUTION
	1079.19

See Appendix E for details.

With this procedure for making the rent-or-buy decision, you should *rent* if the total cost of renting is less than the total cost of buying, or *buy* if the total cost of renting is more than the total cost of buying. In this example, the rental option requires monthly payments of $850. The purchase option is a $150,000 condo, financed with a $30,000 down payment and a $120,000, 6 percent, 30-year mortgage, with additional closing costs of $4,500.

RENT-OR-BUY ANALYSIS

A. COST OF RENTING

1. Annual rental costs
   (12 × monthly rental rate of $ 850) .... $ 10,200
2. Renter's insurance 600
3. Opportunity cost of security deposit: $ 1,000 × after-tax savings rate 0.040 40
   Total cost of renting (line A.1 + line A.2 + line A.3) .... $ 10,840

B. COST OF BUYING

1. Annual mortgage payments (Terms: $ 120,000 , 360 months, 6 %) $ 8,634
   (12 × monthly mortgage payment of $ 719)
2. Property taxes 3,000
   (2.0% of price of home)
3. Homeowner's insurance 750
   (0.5% of price of home)
4. Maintenance 1,200
   (0.8% of price of home)
5. After-tax cost of interest on down payment and closing costs 1,380
   ($ 34,500 × 4.0 % after-tax rate of return)
6. Total costs (sum of lines B.1 through B.5) .... $ 14,964

Less:

7. Principal reduction in loan balance (see note below) .... $ 1,434
8. Tax savings due to interest deductions* 1,800
   (Interest portion of mortgage payments $ 7,200 × tax rate of 25 %)
9. Tax savings due to property tax deductions* 750
   (line B.2 × tax rate of 25 %)
10. Total deductions (sum of lines B.7 through B.9) 3,984
11. Annual after-tax cost of homeownership .... $ 10,980
    (line B.6 − line B.10)
12. Estimated annual appreciation in value of home 3,000
    (2 % of price of home)
    Total cost of buying (line B.11 − line B.12) .... $ 7,980

Note: Find monthly mortgage payments using a calculator or from Exhibit 5.9. An easy way to approximate the portion of the annual loan payment that goes to interest (line B.8) is to multiply the interest rate by the size of the loan (in this case, $120,000 × 0.06 = $7,200). To find the principal reduction in the loan balance (line B.7), subtract the amount that goes to interest from total annual mortgage payments ($8,634 − $7,200 = $1,434).

*Tax-shelter items.

TEST YOURSELF

5-5 In addition to single-family homes, what other forms of housing are available in the United States? Briefly describe each of them.

5-6 What type of housing would you choose for yourself now, and why? Why might you choose to rent instead of buy?

5-7 Why is it important to have a written lease? What should a rental contract include?

5-4 HOW MUCH HOUSING CAN YOU AFFORD?

LG4 Buying a home obviously involves lots of careful planning and analysis. Not only must you decide on the kind of home you want (its location, number of bedrooms, and other features), you must also consider its cost, what kind of mortgage to get, how large a monthly payment you can afford, what kind of homeowner's insurance coverage to have, and so forth.

Buying a home (or any other major, big-ticket item) touches on many elements of personal financial planning. The money you use for a down payment will likely be drawn from your *savings program*; the homeowner's policy you choose is a part of your *insurance planning*; and your monthly mortgage payments will have an enormous impact on your *cash budget* and *tax plans*.

Sound financial planning dictates caution when buying a home or any other major item. Knowing how much housing you can afford goes a long way toward helping you achieve balanced financial goals.

5-4a Benefits of Owning a Home

Homeownership is important to most people, whether they own a detached home or a condominium. It offers the security and peace of mind derived from living in one's own home and the feeling of permanence and sense of stability that ownership brings. This so-called psychological reward is not the only reason people enjoy owning their home. There are also financial payoffs from homeownership.

- **Tax shelter:** As noted in Chapter 3, you can deduct both mortgage interest and property taxes when calculating your federal and, in most states, state income taxes, reducing your taxable income and thus your tax liability. The only requirement is that you itemize your deductions. This tax break is so good that people who have never itemized usually begin doing so after they buy their first house. Also keep in mind that, for the first 15 to 20 years of ownership (assuming a 30-year mortgage), most of your monthly mortgage payment is made up of interest and property taxes—in fact, during the first 5 to 10 years or so, these could well account for *85 percent to 90 percent of your total payment.* This allows you to write off nearly all of your monthly mortgage payment.

- **Inflation hedge:** Homeownership usually provides an inflation hedge because your home appreciates in value at a rate equal to or greater than the rate of inflation. For example, from 2001 through 2006, a home became one of the best investments that you could make, generating a far better return than stocks, bonds, or mutual funds. However, housing values on average dropped by around a third between 2006 and 2012. Whether a real estate market is "hot" or "cold" is literally a matter of supply and demand. For long-term planning purposes, it makes sense to expect that housing prices will roughly keep pace with the rate of inflation.

5-4b The Cost of Homeownership

Although there definitely are some strong emotional and financial reasons for owning a home, there's still the question of whether you can afford to own one. There are two important aspects to the consideration of affordability: You must come up with the down payment and other closing costs, and you must be able to meet the cash-flow requirements associated with monthly mortgage payments and home maintenance expenses. In particular, you should consider these five costs of homeownership in determining how much home you can afford: the down payment, points and closing costs, mortgage payments, property taxes and insurance, and maintenance and operating expenses.

The Down Payment

The first major hurdle is the **down payment**. Most buyers finance a major part of the purchase price of the home, but they're required by lenders to invest money of their own, called *equity*. The actual amount of down payment required varies among lenders, mortgage types, and properties. To determine the amount of down payment required in specific instances, lenders use the **loan-to-value ratio**, which specifies the maximum percentage of the value of a property that the lender is willing to loan. For example, if the loan-to-value ratio is 80 percent, the buyer will have to come up with a down payment equal to the remaining 20 percent.

Most first-time home buyers spend several years accumulating enough money to afford the down payment and other costs associated with a home purchase. You can best accumulate these funds if you plan ahead, using future value techniques (presented in Chapters 2, 4, 11, and 14) to determine the monthly or annual savings necessary to have the needed amount by a specified future date. A detailed demonstration of this process is included in Chapter 11 (see Worksheet 11.1, part B). A disciplined savings program is the best way to obtain the funds needed to purchase a home or any other big-ticket item requiring a sizable down payment or cash outlay.

If you don't have enough savings to cover the down payment and closing costs, you can consider several other sources. You may be able to obtain some funds by withdrawing (subject to legal limitations) your contributions from your company's profit-sharing or thrift plan. Your IRA is another option; first-time home buyers are permitted to withdraw $10,000 without penalty before age 59½. However, using retirement money should be a last resort because you must still pay income tax on retirement distributions. Thus, if you're in the 25 percent income tax bracket, your $10,000 IRA withdrawal would net you only $7,500 ($10,000 – $2,500) for your down payment. And you would be reducing your retirement funds.

The Federal National Mortgage Association ("Fannie Mae") has programs to help buyers who have limited cash for a down payment and closing costs. The "Fannie 3/2" Program is available from local lenders to limit required down payments for qualified buyers. "Fannie 97" helps the home buyer who can handle monthly mortgage payments but doesn't have cash for the down payment. It requires only a 3 percent down payment from the borrower's own funds, and the borrower needs to have only one month's mortgage payment in cash savings, or reserves, after closing. Programs have also developed to help banks liquidate homes owned by Fannie Mae because of the foreclosures resulting from the financial crisis

down payment
A portion of the full purchase price provided by the purchaser when a house or other major asset is purchased; often called *equity*.

loan-to-value ratio
The maximum percentage of the value of a property that the lender is willing to loan.

in 2008–2009. The HomePath Mortgage Financing program is available from local and national lenders. Borrowers who meet certain income criteria may qualify for a 97 percent loan-to-value mortgage and may obtain their down payment from a gift, grant, or loan from a nonprofit organization, state or local government, or employer. The HomePath Renovation Mortgage Financing program is a comparable program available only on homes that will be a primary residence that are in need of light renovations.

When the down payment is less than 20 percent, the lender usually requires the buyer to obtain **private mortgage insurance (PMI)**, which protects the lender from loss if the borrower defaults on the loan. Usually PMI covers the lender's risk above 80 percent of the house price. Thus, with a 10 percent down payment, the mortgage will be a 90 percent loan, and mortgage insurance will cover 10 percent of the home's price. The average cost of mortgage insurance is about 0.50 percent, ranging between 0.20 percent and 0.80 percent of the loan balance each year, depending on the size of your down payment. It can be included in your monthly payment, and the average cost ranges from about $40 to $70 per month. You should contact your lender to cancel the mortgage insurance once the equity in your home reaches 20 to 25 percent. However, under federal law, PMI on most loans made after mid-1999 ends automatically once the mortgage is paid down to 78 percent of the home's original value.

private mortgage insurance (PMI)
An insurance policy that protects the mortgage lender from loss in the event the borrower defaults on the loan; typically required by lenders when the down payment is less than 20 percent.

mortgage points
Fees (one point equals 1 percent of the amount borrowed) charged by lenders at the time they grant a mortgage loan; they are related to the lender's supply of loanable funds and the demand for mortgages.

Points and Closing Costs

A second hurdle to homeownership relates to mortgage points and closing costs. **Mortgage points** are fees charged by lenders at the time that they grant a mortgage loan. In appearance, points are like interest in that they are a charge for borrowing money. They're related to the lender's supply of loanable funds and the demand for mortgages; the greater the demand relative to the supply, the more points you can expect to pay. One point equals 1 percent of the amount borrowed.

> **EXAMPLE: Calculating Mortgage Points**
>
> If you borrow $100,000 and loan fees equal 3 points, the amount of money you'll pay in points is:
>
> $100,000 \times 0.03 = $3,000$.

Lenders typically use points as an alternative way of charging interest on their loans. They can vary the interest rate along with the number of points they charge to create loans with comparable effective rates. For example, a lender might be willing to give you a 5 percent rather than a 6 percent mortgage if you're willing to pay more points; that is, you choose between a 6 percent mortgage rate with 1 point or a 5 percent mortgage rate with 3 points. If you choose the 5 percent loan, you'll pay a lot more *at closing* (although the amount of interest paid *over the life of the mortgage* may be considerably less).

Points increase the *effective rate of interest* or APR on a mortgage. The amount you pay in points and the length of time you hold a mortgage determine the increase in the effective interest rate. For example, on an 8 percent, 30-year, fixed-rate mortgage, each point increases the annual percentage rate by about 0.11 percent if the loan is held for 30 years, 0.17 percent if held 15 years, 0.32 percent if held 7 years, and 0.70 percent if held 3 years. You pay the same amount in points regardless of how long you keep your home. So, the longer you hold the mortgage, the longer the period over which you spread out (amortize) the fixed cost of the points and the smaller the effect of the points on the effective annual interest rate.

According to IRS rulings, the points paid on a mortgage at the time a home is originally purchased are usually considered immediately tax deductible. The same points are *not* considered immediately tax deductible if they're incurred when *refinancing* a mortgage; in this case, the amount paid in points must be written off (*amortized*) over the life of the new mortgage loan.

closing costs
All expenses (including mortgage points) that borrowers ordinarily pay when a mortgage loan is closed and they receive title to the purchased property.

Closing costs are all expenses that borrowers ordinarily pay when a mortgage loan is closed and they receive title to the purchased property. Closing costs are like down payments: they represent money you must come up with *at the time you buy the house*. Closing costs are made up of such items as loan application and loan origination fees paid to the lender, mortgage points, title search and insurance fees, attorneys' fees, appraisal fees, and other miscellaneous fees for things such as mortgage taxes, filing fees, inspections, credit reports, and so on. As Exhibit 5.7 shows, these costs can total 50 percent or more of the down payment amount. For example, with a 10 percent down payment on a $200,000 home, the closing costs, as shown in Exhibit 5.7, are about 56 percent of the down payment, or $11,130. The exhibit indicates that this buyer will need about $31,130 to buy the house (the $20,000 down payment plus another $11,130 in closing costs).

EXHIBIT 5.7   **Closing Costs: The Hidden Costs of Buying a Home**

The closing costs on a home mortgage loan can be substantial—as much as 5 percent to 7 percent of the price of the home. Except for the real estate commission (generally paid by the seller), the buyer incurs the biggest share of the closing costs and must pay them—in addition to the down payment—when the loan is closed and title to the property is conveyed.

	SIZE OF DOWN PAYMENT	
Item	**20%**	**10%**
Loan application fee	$300	$300
Loan origination fee	1,600	1,800
Points	4,160	5,400
Mortgage and homeowner's insurance	—	675
Title search and insurance	665	665
Attorneys' fees	400	400
Appraisal fees	425	425
Home inspection	350	350
Mortgage tax	665	725
Filing fees	80	80
Credit reports	35	35
Miscellaneous	200	200
Total closing costs	$9,530	$11,130

Note: Typical closing costs for a $200,000 home—2.6 points charged with 20 percent down, 3 points with 10 percent down. Actual amounts will vary by lender and location.

Mortgage Payments

Each mortgage payment is made up partly of principal repayment on the loan and partly of interest charges on the loan. However, as Exhibit 5.8 shows, for much of the life of the mortgage, the vast majority of each monthly payment goes to *interest*. The loan illustrated in the exhibit is a $100,000, 30-year, 5 percent mortgage with monthly payments of $536.82, for a total of $6,441.84 per year. Note that it is not until the 16th year of this 30-year mortgage that the principal portion of the monthly loan payment exceeds the amount that goes to interest.

In practice, most mortgage lenders and realtors use their calculator to obtain monthly payments. Some of them still use *comprehensive mortgage payment tables*, which provide monthly payments for virtually every combination of loan size, interest rate, and maturity. Exhibit 5.9 provides an excerpt from one such comprehensive mortgage payment table (with values rounded to the nearest cent). It lists the *monthly payments* associated with a $10,000, fixed-rate loan for selected maturities of 10 to 30 years and for various interest rates ranging from 5 percent to 10 percent. This table can be used to find the monthly payment for a loan of any size. Preferably, you can use a business calculator to quickly and precisely calculate monthly mortgage payments.

EXHIBIT 5.8 **Typical Principal and Interest Payment Patterns on a Mortgage Loan**

For much of the life of a fixed rate mortgage loan, the majority of each monthly payment goes to interest and only a small portion goes toward repaying the principal. Over the 30-year life of the 5 percent, $100,000 mortgage illustrated here, the homeowner will pay about $93,255 in interest.

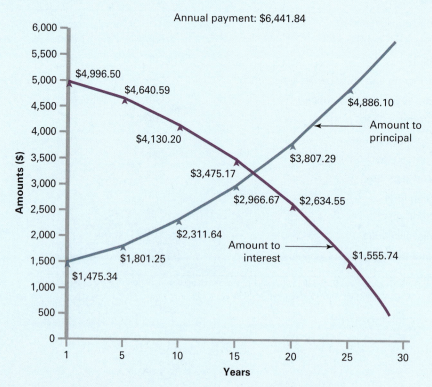

Note: Dollar amounts in the graph represent the amount of principal repaid and interest from the $6,441.84 annual payment made during the given year.

EXAMPLE: Calculating Monthly Mortgage Payment

You'd like to use the mortgage payment tables to find the monthly loan payment on an $180,000, 6 percent, 30-year mortgage.

Divide the amount of the loan ($180,000) by $10,000 and then multiply this factor (18.0) by the payment amount shown in Exhibit 5.9 for a 6 percent, 30-year loan ($59.96):

$$\text{Mortgage Payment} = \frac{\text{Amount of Loan}}{\$10,000} \times \text{Monthly Payment on } \$10,000 \text{ Loan}$$

$$= \frac{\$180,000}{\$10,000} \times \$59.96 = \$1,079.28$$

The resulting monthly mortgage payment is thus $1,079.28.

The calculator keystrokes shown in the margin can be used to more easily calculate mortgage payments in the above example. Note that the mortgage payment of $1,079.19 generated by the calculator is considered to be more precise than the value calculated using the table of monthly mortgage payments but they're close.

Affordability Ratios. The key issue regarding mortgage payments is *affordability*: How large a monthly mortgage payment can you afford, given your budget? This amount determines how much you can borrow to finance the purchase of a home.

To obtain a mortgage, a potential borrower must be "qualified"—demonstrate that he or she has adequate income and an acceptable credit record to reliably make

---

EXHIBIT 5.9	A Table of Monthly Mortgage Payments (Monthly Payments Necessary to Repay a $10,000 Loan)

The monthly loan payments on a mortgage vary not only by the amount of the loan, but also by the rate of interest and loan maturity.

	LOAN MATURITY				
Rate of Interest	**10 Years**	**15 Years**	**20 Years**	**25 Years**	**30 Years**
5.0%	$106.07	$79.08	$66.00	$58.46	$53.68
5.5	108.53	81.71	68.79	61.41	56.79
6.0	111.02	84.39	71.64	64.43	59.96
6.5	113.55	87.11	74.56	67.52	63.21
7.0	116.11	89.88	77.53	70.68	66.53
7.5	118.71	92.71	80.56	73.90	69.93
8.0	121.33	95.57	83.65	77.19	73.38
8.5	123.99	98.48	86.79	80.53	76.90
9.0	126.68	101.43	89.98	83.92	80.47
9.5	129.40	104.43	93.22	87.37	84.09
10.0	132.16	107.47	96.51	90.88	87.76

Instructions: (1) Divide amount of the loan by $10,000; (2) find the loan payment amount in the table for the specific interest rate and maturity; and (3) multiply the amount from step 1 by the amount from step 2.
Example: Using the steps just described, the monthly payment for a $98,000, 5.5 percent, 30-year loan would be determined as: (1) $98,000/$10,000 5 9.8; (2) the payment associated with a 5.5 percent, 30-year loan, from the table, is $56.79; (3) the monthly payment required to repay a $98,000, 5.5 percent, 30-year loan is 9.8 × $56.79 = $556.54.

scheduled loan payments. Federal and private mortgage insurers and institutional mortgage investors have certain standards they expect borrowers to meet to reduce the borrower's risk of default.

The most important affordability guidelines relate both *monthly mortgage payments* and *total monthly installment loan payments* (including the monthly mortgage payment and monthly payments on auto, furniture, and other consumer installment loans) to *monthly borrower gross income*. Customary ratios for a *conventional mortgage* stipulate that monthly mortgage payments cannot exceed 25 to 30 percent of the borrower's monthly *gross* (before-tax) income, and the borrower's total monthly installment loan payments (including the mortgage payment) cannot exceed 33 percent to 38 percent of monthly gross income. Because both conditions stipulate a range, the lender has some leeway in choosing the most appropriate ratio for a particular loan applicant.

Let's look at how these affordability ratios work. Assume that your monthly gross income is $4,500. Applying the lower end of the ranges (i.e., 25 and 33 percent), we see that this income level supports mortgage payments of $1,125 a month ($4,500 × 0.25 = $1,125) *so long as total monthly installment loan payments do not exceed $1,485* ($4,500 × 0.33 = $1,485). If your nonmortgage monthly installment loan payments exceeded $360 (the difference between $1,485 and $1,125), then your mortgage payment would have to be reduced accordingly or the other installment loan payments reduced or paid off. For instance, if you had $500 in other installment payments, your maximum monthly mortgage payment would be $1,485 − $500 = $985.

Property Taxes and Insurance

Aside from loan costs, mortgage payments often include property tax and insurance payments. The mortgage payment therefore consists of *p*rincipal, *i*nterest, property *t*axes, and homeowner's *i*nsurance (or **PITI** for short). Actually, that portion of the loan payment that goes for taxes and insurance is paid into an *escrow account*, where it accumulates until the lender pays property taxes and homeowner insurance premiums that are due. Some lenders pay interest—typically at no higher than the regular savings rate—on escrow account balances. However, it's preferable to pay insurance and taxes yourself, if you have the financial discipline. This strategy provides greater cash flexibility and an opportunity to earn a higher rate of return on funds than the escrow account pays.

The level of **property taxes** differs from one community to another because they're local taxes levied to fund schools, law enforcement, and other local services. In addition, within a given community, individual property taxes will vary according to the *assessed value* of the real estate—the larger and/or more expensive the home, the higher the property taxes, and vice versa. Annual property taxes typically vary from less than 0.5 percent to more than 2 percent of a home's approximate market value. Thus, the property taxes on a $100,000 home could vary from about $500 to more than $2,000 a year, depending on location and geographic area.

The other component of the monthly mortgage payment is **homeowner's insurance**. Its cost varies with such factors as the age of the house, location, materials used in construction, and geographic area. Homeowner's insurance is required by mortgage lenders and covers only the replacement value of the home and its contents, not the land. Annual insurance costs usually amount to approximately 0.25 percent to 0.5 percent of the home's market value, or from $500 to $1,000 for a $200,000 house. The types, characteristics, and features of homeowner's insurance policies are discussed in more detail in Chapter 10.

Maintenance and Operating Expenses

In addition to monthly mortgage payments, homeowners incur maintenance and operating expenses. Maintenance costs should be anticipated even on new homes. Painting, mechanical and plumbing repairs, and lawn maintenance, for example, are inescapable facts of homeownership. Such costs are likely to be greater for larger, older homes. Thus, although a large, established home may have an attractive purchase price, a new, smaller home may be a better buy in view of its lower

PITI
Acronym that refers to a mortgage payment including stipulated portions of *p*rincipal, *i*nterest, property *t*axes, and homeowner's *i*nsurance.

property taxes
Taxes levied by local governments on the *assessed value* of real estate for the purpose of funding schools, law enforcement, and other local services.

homeowner's insurance
Insurance that is required by mortgage lenders and covers the replacement value of a home and its contents.

maintenance and operating costs. Also consider the cost of operating the home, specifically the cost of utilities such as electricity, gas, water, and sewage. These costs have skyrocketed over the past 20 years and today are a large part of home ownership costs, so obtain estimates of utilities when evaluating a home for purchase.

5-4c Performing a Home Affordability Analysis

Worksheet 5.3 helps you determine your maximum price for a home purchase based on your monthly income and down payment amount after meeting estimated closing costs. In our example, Rene and Pierre Goulet have a combined annual income of $75,200 and savings of $30,000 for a down payment and closing costs. They estimate monthly property taxes and homeowner's insurance at $375 and expect the mortgage lender to use a 28 percent monthly mortgage payment affordability ratio, to lend at an average interest rate of 6 percent on a 30-year (360-month) mortgage, and to require a 10 percent minimum down payment. The Goulets' analysis shows that they can afford to purchase a home for about $201,000.

Worksheet 5.3 walks us through the steps that the Goulet family took to reach this conclusion. The maximum purchase price is determined from two perspectives: the maximum based on monthly income and the maximum based on the minimum acceptable down payment. The lower of the two estimates determines the maximum purchase price. Based on their monthly income and the 28 percent affordability ratio, their monthly payment could be $1,755 ($6,267 × 0.28), shown as Item 4. After deducting taxes and insurance, the maximum monthly mortgage payment amount is $1,380 (Item 6).

Calculator

INPUTS	FUNCTIONS
1380	PMT
360	N
6	÷
12	=
	I
	CPT
	PV
	SOLUTION
	230172.43

See Appendix E for details.

EXAMPLE: Calculating the Maximum Affordable Mortgage Loan

The Goulets want to determine the maximum loan they can carry given that they can afford a maximum monthly mortgage payment of $1,380. Exhibit 5.9 indicates that a $10,000 loan for 30 years at 6 percent would result in a monthly payment of $59.96, as indicated in Item 9 of Worksheet 5.3. This would support loan of:

$$\text{Maximum Mortgage Loan} = \$10,000 \times \frac{\text{Maximum Monthly Payment}}{\text{Present Value Interest Factor}}$$

$$= \$10,000 \times \frac{\$1,380}{\$59.96} = \$230,153.44$$

The calculator result in the margin indicates a maximum purchase price of $230,172.43, which is more precise than the approximation provided using Exhibit 5.9.

By using the following variables in the home affordability analysis form, the Goulets estimate a maximum home pur-chase price of $201,000: their combined annual income of $75,200; the $30,000 available for a down payment and pay-ing all closing costs; estimated monthly property taxes and homeowner's insurance of $375; the lender's 28 percent monthly mortgage payment affordability ratio; an average interest rate of 6 percent and expected loan maturity of 30 years; and a minimum down payment of 10 percent.

HOME AFFORDABILITY ANALYSIS*

Name _Rene and Pierre Goulet_   Date _August 14, 2017_

Item	Description	Amount
1	Amount of annual income	$ 75,200
2	Monthly income (Item 1 ÷ 12)	$ 6,267
3	Lender's affordability ratio (in decimal form)	0.28
4	Maximum monthly mortgage payment (PITI) (Item 2 × Item 3)	$ 1,755
5	Estimated monthly prop tax and homeowner's insurance payment	$ 375
6	Maximum monthly loan payment (Item 4 − Item 5)	$ 1,380
7	Approximate average interest rate on loan	6 %
8	Planned loan maturity (years)	30
9	Monthly mortgage payment per $10,000 (using Item 7 and Item 8 and Table of Monthly Mortgage Payments in Exhibit 5.9)	$ 59.96
10	Maximum loan based on monthly income ($10,000 × Item 6 ÷ Item 9)	$230,000
11	Funds available for making a down payment and paying closing costs	$ 30,000
12	Funds available for making a down payment (Item 11 × .67)	$ 20,100
13	Maximum purchase price based on available monthly income (Item 10 + Item 12)	$250,100
14	Minimum acceptable down payment (in decimal form)	0.10
15	Maximum purchase price based on down payment (Item 12 ÷ Item 14)	$201,000
16	Maximum home purchase price (lower of Item 13 and Item 15)	$201,000

*Note: This analysis assumes that one-third of the funds available for making the down payment and paying closing costs are used to meet closing costs and that the remaining two-thirds are available for a down payment. This means that closing costs will represent an amount equal to 50 percent of the down payment.

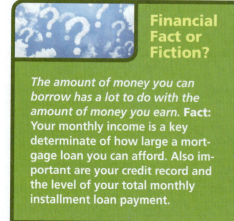

Financial Fact or Fiction?

The amount of money you can borrow has a lot to do with the amount of money you earn. **Fact:** Your monthly income is a key determinate of how large a mort-gage loan you can afford. Also im-portant are your credit record and the level of your total monthly installment loan payment.

With a down payment of $30,000 and monthly income of $6,267, the Goulet family can afford a home costing $250,100 (Item 13). The Goulets then look at the maximum purchase price based on their $30,000 down payment, or $150,000 (Item 15). Their maximum home purchase price is the lower of Items 13 and 15, or $201,000 (Item 16), and is limited by the amount available for a down payment.

You can use Exhibit 5.10 to quickly estimate the size of mortgage you can afford based on various assumptions about interest rates and the monthly mortgage payment. First, deter-mine the maximum monthly mortgage payment you can handle, then follow that line across to find the approximate size of the mortgage your payment will buy at each mortgage interest rate.

EXHIBIT 5.10 | How Much Mortgage Will Your Payment Buy?

This table lets you quickly estimate the size of the mortgage that you can afford based on the monthly mortgage payment and mortgage interest rate. It assumes a 30-year, fixed-rate loan. Remember that this amount is only for mortgage principal and interest; you must have funds available for paying property taxes and homeowner's insurance as well.

Monthly Mortgage Payment	Mortgage Interest Rate					
	5%	6%	7%	8%	9%	10%
$ 500	$ 93,141	$ 83,396	$ 75,154	$68,142	$ 62,141	$ 56,975
600	111,769	100,075	90,185	81,770	74,569	68,370
700	130,397	116,754	105,215	95,398	86,997	79,766
800	149,025	133,433	120,246	109,027	99,425	91,161
900	167,653	150,112	135,277	122,655	111,854	102,556
1,000	186,282	166,792	150,308	136,283	124,282	113,951
1,100	204,910	183,471	165,338	149,912	136,710	125,346
1,200	223,538	200,150	180,369	163,540	149,138	136,741
1,300	242,166	216,829	195,400	177,169	161,566	148,136
1,400	260,794	233,508	210,431	190,797	173,995	159,531
1,500	279,422	250,187	225,461	204,425	186,423	170,926

Instructions: (1) Find the amount of monthly mortgage payment you can afford, to the nearest $100. Then find the current mortgage interest rate to the nearest percent. The approximate mortgage amount will be at the intersection of the two columns. (2) To estimate the mortgage size if the interest rate ends in ".5," add the mortgage amounts for the lower and higher mortgage interest rates and divide by 2. (3) To estimate the mortgage size for a payment ending in "50," add the mortgage amounts for the lower and higher monthly mortgage payments and divide by 2.

Example: (1) The estimated mortgage size if you have a monthly mortgage payment of $900 on a 30-year, 6% loan is $150,112. (2) To find the estimated mortgage size if you have a monthly mortgage payment of $900 and the mortgage interest rate is 5.5%, add the mortgage sizes for $900 at 5% and at 6% and divide by 2: ($167,653 + $150,112) ÷ 2 = $317,765 ÷ 2 = $158,882. (3) To find the estimated mortgage size if you have a monthly mortgage payment of $950 and the mortgage interest rate is 6%, add the mortgage sizes for $900 and $1,000 at 6% and divide by 2: ($150,112 + $166,792) ÷ 2 = $316,904 ÷ 2 = $158,402.

(This figure assumes a 30-year, fixed-rate loan and does *not* include property taxes and homeowner's insurance.) For example, if you estimate that you have $1,000 available per month and the prevailing mortgage interest rate is 6 percent, you can afford a mortgage of about $166,792.

TEST YOURSELF

5-8 Briefly describe the various benefits of owning a home. Which one is most important to you? Which is least important?

5-9 What does the *loan-to-value ratio* on a home represent? Is the down payment on a home related to its loan-to-value ratio? Explain.

5-10 What are *mortgage points?* How much would a home buyer have to pay if the lender wanted to charge 2.5 points on a $250,000 mortgage? When would this amount have to be paid? What effect do points have on the mortgage's rate of interest?

5-11 What are *closing costs,* and what items do they include? Who pays these costs, and when?

5-12 What are the most common guidelines used to determine the monthly mortgage payment one can afford?

5-13 Why is it advisable for the prospective home buyer to investigate property taxes?

5-5 THE HOME-BUYING PROCESS

Buying a home requires time, effort, and money. You'll want to educate yourself about available properties and prevailing prices by doing a systematic search and careful analysis. And you'll also need a basic understanding of the role of a real estate agent, the mortgage application process, the real estate sales contract, and other documents required to close a deal.

5-5a Shop the Market First

Most people who shop the housing market rely on real estate agents for information, access to properties, and advice. Many of them also shop via the Internet, visiting various real estate sites to learn about available properties. Other sources of information, such as newspaper ads, are also widely used to find available properties. Occasionally a person seeking to buy or rent property will advertise his or her needs and wait for sellers to initiate contact.

Buying a home involves many factors, both financial and emotional, and the emotional factors often carry the greatest weight. As noted earlier, you must begin your home search project by figuring out what *you* require for your particular lifestyle needs—in terms of living space, style, and other special features. The property's location, neighborhood, and school district are usually important considerations as well. It's helpful to divide your list into *necessary* features, such as the number of bedrooms and baths, and *optional*—but desirable—features, such as fireplaces, whirlpool tubs, and so on. And of course, an affordability analysis is a critical part of the housing search.

Keep an open mind as you start looking. Be flexible and look at a variety of homes in your price range. This can be invaluable in helping to define your wants and needs more clearly.

If you already own a house but want or need a larger or different type of home, you can either trade up or remodel it. You may choose to remodel it if you like your neighborhood and can make the desired changes to your current home. In some cases, the cost to remodel will be less than the transaction costs of buying another house. The best remodeling projects are those whose costs you can recover when you sell the house. Kitchen improvements, additional bathrooms, and family rooms tend to best enhance a home's market value. Although a swimming pool may give you pleasure, you may not recover its cost when you sell the house.

Real Estate Short Sales

real estate short sale
Sale of real estate property in which the proceeds are less than the balance owed on a loan secured by the property sold.

The bursting of the real estate bubble associated with the financial crisis of 2008–2009 increased the use of real estate short sales. A **real estate short sale** is the sale of property in which the proceeds are less than the balance owed on a loan secured by the property sold. This procedure is an effort by mortgage lenders to come to terms with homeowners who are about to default or are defaulting on their mortgage loans. A broker's price opinion or an appraisal is obtained to estimate the probable selling price of the property for the purposes of the short sale. The short sale typically occurs to prevent home foreclosure by finding the most economic means for the mortgage lender—often a bank—to recover as much of the loan balance owed on the property as possible. In a **foreclosure**, the borrower typically cannot make scheduled mortgage payments and the lender repossesses the property in an effort to recover the loan balance owed. Mortgage holders will agree to a short sale only if they believe that the proceeds generated by the sale will bring a smaller loss than foreclosing on the property. A real estate short sale may consequently be viewed as a negotiated effort to mitigate the losses of the mortgage lender.

foreclosure
A borrower typically cannot make scheduled mortgage payments and the lender repossesses the property in an effort to recover the loan balance owed.

You may be wondering if a short sale works only for the benefit of the mortgage lender. Although it certainly can reduce a lender's losses, it can also be beneficial for the homeowner. A real estate short sale will avoid having a foreclosure appear on the

FINANCIAL PLANNING TIPS

Top Home Remodeling Projects

The National Association of Realtors found that the value of home remodeling projects declined by only about half as much as home prices during the recent financial crisis. While it's best to expect that you will not get all of your money back from home improvements when you sell your home, keep in mind that you will likely enjoy the improvements until that time and will probably recover most of the money if you stay in your home for some years to come. Here's a list of the top remodeling projects in terms of the percentage of the investment recovered at the sale of the home.

Midrange Project	Cost Recovered
Entry door replacement (steel)	101.8%
Manufactured stone veneer	92.2%
Garage door replacement	88.4%
Siding replacement (vinyl)	80.7%
Deck addition (wood)	80.5%
Minor kitchen remodel	79.3%
Window replacement (wood)	78.8%
Attic bedroom	77.2%
Window replacement (vinyl)	72.9%
Basement remodel	72.8%
Entry door replacement (fiberglass)	72.0%
Roofing replacement	71.6%

Source: Adapted from "Cost vs. Value Report: 2015," http://www.remodeling.hw.net/cost-vs-value/2015/, accessed August 2015.

homeowner's credit history. Short sales should also help homeowners manage the costs that got them into trouble in the first place. Finally, a short sale is usually faster and cheaper for the homeowner than a foreclosure. Most short sales fully satisfy the debt owed, but this is not always the case, so homeowners should confirm this in the settlement.

5-5b Using an Agent

Most home buyers rely on real estate agents because they're professionals who are in daily contact with the housing market. Once you describe your needs to an agent, he or she can begin to search for appropriate properties. Your agent will also help you negotiate with the seller, obtain satisfactory financing, and, although not empowered to give explicit legal advice, prepare the real estate sales contract.

Most real estate firms belong to a local **Multiple Listing Service (MLS)**, a comprehensive listing, updated daily, of properties for sale in a given community or metropolitan area. A brief description of each property and its asking price are included, with a photo of the property. Only realtors who work for an MLS member firm have access to this major segment of the market.

Multiple Listing Service (MLS)
A comprehensive listing, updated daily, of properties for sale in a given community or metropolitan area; includes a brief description of each property with a photo and its asking price but can be accessed only by realtors who work for an MLS member.

Buyers should remember that *agents typically are employed by sellers*. Unless you've agreed to pay a fee to a sales agent to act as a buyer's agent, a realtor's primary responsibility, by law, is to sell listed properties at the highest possible prices. Agents are paid only if they make a sale, so some might pressure you to "sign now or miss the chance of a lifetime." But most agents will listen to your needs and work to match you with the right property and under terms that will benefit both you and the seller. Good agents recognize that their interests are best served when all parties to a transaction are satisfied.

Real estate commissions generally range from 5 percent to 6 percent for new homes and from 6 percent to 7 percent for previously occupied homes or *resales*. It may be possible to negotiate a lower commission with your agent or to find a discount broker or one who charges a flat fee. Commissions are typically paid only by the seller, but because the price of a home is often inflated by the size of the real estate commission—many builders are believed to factor commission costs into the prices of their new homes—it follows that the buyer probably absorbs some or even all of the commission. Of course, you may be able to find a suitable property that is "for sale by owner" and therefore eliminate the need for a realtor. This approach is generally not recommended, however, because of the many legal and financial complexities of the real estate transaction.

Whereas traditional agents represent the seller's interests, *buyer's agents,* as the term implies, are hired by buyers to negotiate on their behalf. Commissions to buyer's agents are negotiated and may ultimately be paid by the seller. A *facilitator,* on the other hand, represents neither the buyer nor the seller but is typically paid by both parties to serve as a neutral intermediary between them.

5-5c Prequalifying and Applying for a Mortgage

prequalification
The process of arranging with a mortgage lender, in advance of buying a home, to obtain the amount of mortgage financing the lender deems affordable to the home buyer.

Before beginning your home search, you may want to meet with one or more mortgage lenders to prearrange a mortgage loan. **Prequalification** can work to your advantage in several ways. You'll know ahead of time the specific mortgage amount that you qualify for—subject, of course, to changes in rates and terms—and can focus your search on homes within an affordable price range.

Prequalification also provides estimates of the required down payment and closing costs for different types of mortgages. It identifies in advance any problems, such as credit report errors, that might arise from your application and allows you time to correct them. Finally, prequalification enhances your bargaining power with the seller of a house you want by letting her or him know that the deal won't fall through because you can't afford the property or obtain suitable financing. And since you will have already gone through the mortgage application process, the time required to close the sale should be relatively short.

There are many sources of mortgage loans, and you should begin investigating them while looking for a house. When you actually apply for a mortgage loan on a particular home, you'll need to give the lender information on your income, assets, and outstanding debts. Documents the lender may request include proof of your monthly income (paycheck stubs, W-2 forms, etc.), statements showing all debt balances (credit cards, car and education loans, bank lines of credit, and so on), lists of financial assets such as savings accounts and securities, several months' bank account statements, and at least two years' income tax returns. Financing your home is covered in detail later in this chapter.

5-5d The Real Estate Sales Contract

After selecting a home to buy, you must enter into a sales contract. State laws generally specify that, to be enforceable in court, real estate buy–sell agreements must be in writing and contain certain information, including: (1) the names of buyers and sellers, (2) a description of the property sufficient for positive identification, (3) specific price and other terms, and (4) usually the signatures of the buyers and sellers.

Real estate sales transactions often take weeks and sometimes months to complete. Because they involve a fair amount of legal work, they require expert assistance in preparation. Contract requirements help keep the facts straight and reduce the chance for misunderstanding, misrepresentation, or fraud.

Although these requirements fulfill the minimums necessary for court enforcement, in practice real estate sales contracts usually contain several other contractual clauses relating to earnest money deposits, contingencies, personal property, and closing costs. An **earnest money deposit** is the money that you pledge to show good faith when you make an offer. If, after signing a sales contract, you withdraw from the transaction without a valid reason, you might have to forfeit this deposit. A valid reason for withdrawal would be stated in the contract as a contingency clause. With a **contingency clause**, you can condition your agreement to buy on such factors as the availability of financing, a satisfactory termite inspection or other physical inspection of the property, or the advice of a lawyer or real estate expert. Your lawyer should review and approve all agreements before you sign them.

5-5e Closing the Deal

After you obtain financing and your loan is approved, the closing process begins. Although closing costs may climb into the thousands of dollars, home buyers can often save significant amounts if they shop for financing, insurance, and other closing items rather than merely accepting the costs quoted by any one lender or provider of closing services.

The **Real Estate Settlement Procedures Act (RESPA)** governs closings on owner-occupied houses, condominiums, and apartment buildings of four units or fewer. This act reduced closing costs by prohibiting kickbacks made to real estate agents and others from lenders or title insurance companies. It also requires clear, advance disclosure of all closing costs to home buyers. Lenders must give potential borrowers a U.S. Department of Housing and Urban Development booklet entitled *Settlement Costs and You: A HUD Guide for Homebuyers*. The booklet sets forth the specific requirements of RESPA, and can take much of the mystery out of the closing process. An overview of these closing requirements may be found on HUD's Web site (go to the "Homes" section of **http://www.hud.gov**). Exhibit 5.11 provides some tips to help you sail smoothly through the home-buying process in general and the closing process in particular.

Title Check

Numerous legal interests can exist in real estate simultaneously: for example, those of the owners, lenders, lien holders (such as an unpaid roofing contractor), and easement holders. Before taking title to a property, make sure that the seller (who is conveying title to you) actually has the legal interest he or she claims and that the title is free of all liens and encumbrances (except those specifically referred to in the sales contract).

Although it's up to you to question the integrity of the title to the property you're buying, in most cases, an attorney or title insurance company performs a **title check**, consisting of the necessary research of legal documents and courthouse records. The customary practices and procedures and costs vary widely throughout the country. Regardless of the specific custom in your area, be sure to make some form of title check an essential part of your closing process.

Closing Statement

A *closing statement*, provided to both buyer and seller at or before the actual closing, accounts for monies that change hands during the transaction. The statement reconciles the borrower's and seller's costs and shows how much the borrower owes and the seller receives from the transaction. Before closing a home purchase, you should be given an opportunity to review the closing statement and have your questions

earnest money deposit
Money pledged by a buyer to show good faith when making an offer to buy a home.

contingency clause
A clause in a real estate sales contract that makes the agreement conditional on such factors as the availability of financing, property inspections, or obtaining expert advice.

Real Estate Settlement Procedures Act (RESPA)
A federal law requiring mortgage lenders to give potential borrowers a government publication describing the closing process and providing clear, advance disclosure of all closing costs to home buyers.

title check
The research of legal documents and courthouse records to verify that the seller conveying title actually has the legal interest he or she claims and that the title is free of all liens and encumbrances.

EXHIBIT 5.11   Effective Home-Buying Strategies

Keeping in mind the following pitfalls will improve your chances of becoming a happy, successful homeowner:

- **Don't wipe out your savings.** While it makes sense to put down the largest down payment that you can afford, it is important to keep your emergency reserves intact, hold money for closing costs, and set aside funds to handle possible repairs and future maintenance.
- **Pick the right neighborhood.** You've heard that the three most important factors in valuing real estate are location, location, and location. This is no joke. Drive through a neighborhood, ask the police department about crime statistics, and talk to neighbors before you buy. If they don't want to talk, that tells you something too!
- **Stay away from the most expensive home in the neighborhood.** While having the largest and most expensive home in the neighborhood might be appealing, it doesn't bode well for resale value. If you need three bedrooms, don't consider a five-bedroom that looks good but costs more and meets your needs less.
- **Interview your agent and ask hard questions.** Make sure that he or she is experienced. Consider signing a buyer's broker agreement, which gives both you and the broker responsibilities and reasonable performance expectations.
- **Rely on professional advice.** Pay attention to what your agent or mortgage broker tells you. Look up information on the Internet, read real estate books, and ask for a second opinion. Lawyers and accountants are excellent resources.
- **Use traditional financing.** One of the biggest lessons of the financial crisis a few years ago is that real estate prices don't always go up. And what you don't know about your mortgage can hurt you! Don't sign off on your mortgage until you understand every detail. Terms like indexes, margins, caps, and negative amortization should make you nervous.
- **Don't change the financial picture before closing.** While waiting for loan funding, there is no need to buy a new car to match your new home. Your excellent credit report does not give you free rein to buy whatever you want. Borrowing too much more at this time could adversely affect the funding of a mortgage.
- **Be sure to do the home inspection.** Home inspections are *not* a waste of time and money. Qualified home inspectors can find problems that most of us would miss.
- **Be careful about taking on additional debt after closing.** After you become a homeowner, you'll be offered many deals on a home equity loan. Although it may be tempting to pull out all your equity and use this newfound money to buy all sorts of new toys, you should stick to a reasonable financial plan. It is critically important to cover the contingency of losing a job or an emergency by setting aside some money.

answered. Carefully and critically review the statement to make sure that it is accurate and consistent with the contractual terms of the transaction; if not, have the statement corrected before closing the deal.

TEST YOURSELF

5-14 Describe some of the steps home buyers can take to improve the home-buying process and increase their overall satisfaction with their purchases.

5-15 What role does a real estate agent play in the purchase of a house? What is the benefit of the *MLS?* How is the real estate agent compensated, and by whom?

5-16 Describe a real estate short sales transaction. What are the potential benefits and costs from the perspective of the homeowner?

5-17 Why should you investigate mortgage loans and prequalify for a mortgage early in the home-buying process?

5-18 What information is normally included in a real estate sales contract? What is an *earnest money deposit?* What is a *contingency clause?*

5-19 Describe the steps involved in closing the purchase of a home.

5-6 FINANCING THE TRANSACTION

mortgage loan
A loan secured by the property: If the borrower defaults, the lender has the legal right to liquidate the property to recover the funds it is owed.

Earlier in the chapter, we saw that mortgage terms can dramatically affect the amount you can afford to spend on a home. The success of a real estate transaction often hinges on obtaining a mortgage with favorable terms. A **mortgage loan** is secured by the property: If the borrower defaults, the lender has the legal right to liquidate the property to recover the funds it is owed. Before you obtain such a loan, it's helpful to understand the sources and types of mortgages and their underlying economics.

5-6a Sources of Mortgage Loans

The major sources of home mortgages today are commercial banks, thrift institutions, and mortgage bankers or brokers; also, some credit unions make mortgage loans available to their members. Commercial banks are also an important source of *interim construction loans,* providing short-term financing during the construction process for individuals who are building or remodeling a home. After the home is completed, the homeowner obtains *permanent financing,* in the form of a standard mortgage loan, and then uses the proceeds from it to repay the construction loan.

mortgage banker
A firm that solicits borrowers, originates primarily government-insured and government-guaranteed loans, and places them with mortgage lenders; often uses its own money to initially fund mortgages that it later resells.

Another way to obtain a mortgage loan is through a mortgage banker or mortgage broker. Both solicit borrowers, originate loans, and place them with traditional mortgage lenders, as well as life insurance companies and pension funds. Whereas **mortgage bankers** often use their own money to initially fund mortgages they later resell, **mortgage brokers** take loan applications and then seek lenders willing to grant the mortgage loans under the desired terms. Mortgage bankers deal primarily in government-insured and government-guaranteed loans, whereas mortgage brokers concentrate on finding conventional loans for consumers. Most brokers also have ongoing relationships with different lenders, thereby increasing your chances of finding a loan even if you don't qualify at a commercial bank or thrift institution. Brokers can often simplify the financing process by cutting through red tape, negotiating more favorable terms, and reducing the amount of time to close the loan. Mortgage brokers earn their income from commissions and origination fees paid by the lender, costs that are typically passed on to the borrower in the points charged on a loan. The borrower must often pay application, processing, and document preparation fees to the lender at closing. Exhibit 5.12 offers advice for finding a good mortgage broker. You may prefer to shop for a mortgage on your own or with your realtor, who is knowledgeable about various lenders and is legally prohibited from collecting fees or kickbacks for helping to arrange financing.

mortgage broker
A firm that solicits borrowers, originates primarily conventional loans, and places them with mortgage lenders; the broker merely takes loan applications and then finds lenders willing to grant the mortgage loans under the desired terms.

5-6b Online Mortgage Resources

Shopping for the best mortgage rate and terms has become easier thanks to the Internet. Many sites allow you to search for the best fixed-rate or adjustable-rate mortgage in your area. HSH Associates, a mortgage consulting firm with a Web site at **http://www.hsh.com**, lists mortgages offered by banks, mortgage companies, and brokerage firms across the country, along with information on prevailing interest rates, terms, and points. Bankrate (**http://www.bankrate.com**) and similar sites also offer mortgage comparisons. Shopping via the Internet gives you great leverage when dealing with a lender. For example, if a local mortgage lender offers a three-year adjustable-rate mortgage (ARM) with 1.20 points and a 5.75 percent rate, while a lender in a different state offers the same terms with the same rate and only 1 point, you can negotiate with your local lender to get a better deal.

Although the Internet is still primarily a source of comparative information, online lenders such as E-Loan (**http://www.eloan.com**), a large online-only mortgage bank, hope that home buyers will choose to apply for and close a loan online. Or submit your information to LendingTree at **http://www.lendingtree.com**; within 24 hours you'll receive bids from four lenders interested in making your loan. You can also visit MSN Real Estate at **http://realestate.msn.com** for loan and general home-buying information.

| EXHIBIT 5.12 | Should I Use a Mortgage Broker or My Bank? |

You've decided to buy a home and it's time to shop for a mortgage. Is it better to get your mortgage from your bank or from a mortgage broker? Here's how to best approach the decision.

It is common to find the best deal at the bank where you have your checking and savings accounts. Importantly, this is not the same as a mortgage company with the same name as your local bank. This is because your bank tends to do a volume business, is lending out its own money, and doesn't have as many middlemen who charge for dealing with your loan. Banks also tend to be cheaper than mortgage brokers because they focus on borrowers with good credit, established jobs with decent income, and long-term residence in the area. By implication, mortgage brokers tend to attract prospective borrowers with less appealing creditworthiness. That usually brings higher fees and mortgage interest rates.

So how should you organize your search for a mortgage?

Focus on finding a mortgage broker when you:
- don't have the best credit history
- are self-employed and/or can't document your income
- have just changed professions
- have a large amount of debt

Focus on your bank when you:
- have a good credit history
- have an established job and lengthy work history
- have a modest amount of debt
- are self-employed but can provide at least two years of income tax returns and other documents that prove your income

Even in light of the above general rules, some mortgage brokers may have rates and fees that compare favorably with your bank. So it's important to compare the deals that you can get with your bank vs. at least a couple of mortgage brokers.

Source: Adapted from "Mortgage Broker or My Bank—Which Is Better?" http://www.creditinfocenter.com/mortgage/brokeRbank.shtml, accessed August 2015.

5-6c Types of Mortgage Loans

There is no single way to classify mortgages. For our purposes, we'll group them in two ways: (1) terms of payment and (2) whether they're conventional, insured, or guaranteed.

There are literally dozens of different types of home mortgages from which to choose. The most common types of mortgage loans made today are fixed-rate and adjustable-rate mortgages. Let's take a closer look at their features, advantages, and disadvantages.

Fixed-Rate Mortgages

fixed-rate mortgage
The traditional type of mortgage, in which both the rate of interest and the monthly mortgage payment are fixed over the full term of the loan.

The **fixed-rate mortgage** still accounts for a large portion of all home mortgages. Both the rate of interest and the monthly mortgage payment are fixed over the full term of the loan. The most common type of fixed-rate mortgage is the *30-year fixed-rate* loan, although *10- and 15-year loans* are becoming more popular as homeowners recognize the advantages of paying off their loan over a shorter period of time. Because of the risks that the lender assumes with a 30-year loan, it's usually the most expensive form of home financing.

Gaining in popularity is the *15-year fixed-rate* loan. Its chief appeal is that it is repaid twice as fast (15 years versus 30) and yet the monthly payments don't increase twofold. To pay off a loan in less time, the homeowner must pay more each month, but the monthly payment on a 15-year loan is generally only about 20 percent larger than the payment on a 30-year loan. The following table shows the difference in monthly payment and total interest paid for 30- and 15-year fixed-rate mortgages. In both cases, the purchaser borrows $160,000 at a 5 percent fixed rate of interest:

Term of Loan	Regular Monthly Payment	Total Interest Paid over Life of Loan
30 years	$ 858.91	$149,209.25
15 years	$1,265.27	$ 67,748.56

Perhaps the most startling feature is the substantial difference in the total amount of interest paid over the term of the loan. In effect, you can save *about $81,460* just by financing your home with a 15-year mortgage rather than over the traditional 30 years! Note that this amount of savings is possible even though monthly payments differ by only about $406. In practice, the difference in the monthly payment would be even less, because 15-year mortgages are usually available at interest rates that are about half a percentage point below comparable 30-year loans.

Although the idea of paying off a mortgage in 15 years instead of 30 may seem like a good one, you should consider how long you plan to stay in the house. While paying off the loan faster always increases your home equity faster, you might not feel as motivated to do this if you plan to sell the house in a few years. In addition, the tax deductibility of mortgage interest makes a mortgage one of the least expensive sources of borrowing. If you can earn a higher rate of return than the rate of interest on a 30-year loan, then you'd be better off taking the 30-year loan and investing the difference in the payment between it and the comparable 15-year loan.

Another way to shorten the mortgage term without committing to an initially shorter term is by making extra principal payments regularly or when you have extra funds. If you can earn exactly the mortgage interest rate (5 percent annually, in our example), then you could take the 30-year loan and invest the $406 that you save each month over the 15-year mortgage; then, at any time, subtracting the sum of the saved mortgage payments and the interest earned on them from the outstanding 30-year mortgage balance would exactly equal the outstanding balance on the 15-year loan. In other words, you could use the 30-year loan to exactly replicate the 15-year loan. Because of this relationship, some people recommend "taking the 30-year loan and investing the savings over a comparable 15-year loan." However, the success of this strategy depends on (1) sufficient discipline for you to invest the difference every month and, more importantly, (2) an ability to consistently earn the mortgage interest rate on your investments. Because both of these conditions are unlikely, you're best off taking the mortgage that most closely meets your financial needs.

balloon-payment mortgage
A mortgage with a single large principal payment due at a specified future date.

Some lenders offer other types of fixed-rate loans. **Balloon-payment mortgages** offer terms of 5, 7, or 10 years where the interest rate is fixed, typically at 0.25 to 0.5 percent below the 30-year fixed rate. The monthly payments are the same as for a 30-year loan at the given rate. When the loan matures, the remaining principal balance comes due and must be refinanced. Although the lower rate results in lower monthly payments, these loans do carry some risk because refinancing may be difficult, particularly if rates have risen.

You Can Do It Now

Current Mortgage Rates

If you're considering buying a home, you need to know current mortgage rates to determine prospective monthly payments and what price you can pay for the home. Up-to-date market rates for different maturities of fixed and adjustable rate mortgages are available at **http://www.bankrate.com**. And you can also obtain refinancing rates there when you already have a mortgage and are considering refinancing it. It's so accessible—you can do it now.

Calculator

INPUTS	FUNCTIONS
100000	PV
360	N
6.5	÷
12	=
	/
	CPT
	PMT
	SOLUTION
	632.07

See Appendix E for details.

Adjustable-Rate Mortgages (ARMs)

Another popular form of home loan is the **adjustable-rate mortgage (ARM)**. The rate of interest, and therefore the size of the monthly payment, is adjusted based on market interest rate movements. The mortgage interest rate is linked to a specific *interest rate index* and is adjusted at specific intervals (usually once or twice a year) based on changes in the index. When the index moves up, so does the interest rate on the mortgage and, in turn, the size of the monthly mortgage payment increases. The new interest rate and monthly mortgage payment remain in effect until the next adjustment date.

The term of an ARM can be 15 or 30 years. Because the size of the monthly payments will vary with interest rates, there's no way to tell what your future payments will be. However, because the borrower assumes most or all of the interest rate risk in these mortgages, the *initial rate of interest* on an adjustable-rate mortgage is normally well below—typically by 2 to 3 percentage points—the rate of a standard 30-year fixed-rate loan. Of course, whether the borrower actually ends up paying less interest depends on the behavior of market interest rates during the term of the loan.

Features of ARMs. It's important for home buyers to understand the following basic features of an ARM:

- **Adjustment period:** Although the period of time between rate or payment changes is typically six months to one year, adjustment periods can range from three months to three or five years.
- **Index rate:** A baseline rate that captures the movement in interest rates, tied to six-month U.S. Treasury securities, six-month CDs, or the average cost of funds to savings institutions as commonly measured by the 11th Federal Home Loan Bank District Cost of Funds.
- **Margin:** The percentage points that a lender adds to the index to determine the rate of interest on an ARM, usually a fixed amount over the life of the loan. Thus, the rate of interest on an ARM equals the index rate plus the margin.
- **Interest rate caps:** Limits on the amount the interest rate can increase over a given period. *Periodic caps* limit interest rate increases from one adjustment to the next (typically, lenders cap annual rate adjustments at 1 to 2 percentage points), and *overall caps* limit the interest rate increase over the life of the loan (lifetime interest rate caps are typically set at 5 to 8 percentage points). Many ARMs have both periodic and overall interest rate caps.
- **Payment caps:** Limits on monthly payment increases that may result from a rate adjustment—usually a percentage of the previous payment. If your ARM has a 5 percent payment cap, your monthly payments can increase no more than 5 percent from one year to the next—regardless of what happens to interest rates.

Because most ARMs are 30-year loans (360 payments), you can determine the initial monthly payment in the same manner as for any other 30-year mortgage. For example, for a $100,000 loan at 6.5 percent (4.5 percent index rate + 2 percent margin), we can use a calculator as shown in the margin to find the first-year monthly payments of $632.07. Assuming a 1-year adjustment period, if the index rate rises to 5.5 percent, then the interest rate for the second year will be 7.5 percent (5.5 percent + 2 percent = 7.5 percent). The size of the monthly payment for the next 12 months will then be adjusted upward to about $697.83. This process is repeated each year thereafter until the loan matures.

Beware of Negative Amortization. Some ARMs are subject to **negative amortization**—an increase in the principal balance resulting from monthly loan payments that are lower than the amount of monthly interest being charged. In other words, you could end up with a larger mortgage balance on the next anniversary of your loan than on the previous one. This occurs when the payment is intentionally set below the interest charge, or when the ARM has interest rates that are adjusted monthly—with monthly payments that adjust annually. In the latter case, when rates are rising on these loans, the current monthly payment can be less than the interest being charged, and the difference is added to the principal, thereby increasing the size of the loan.

ARMs with a cap on the dollar amount of monthly payments can also lead to negative amortization. For example, assume that the monthly payment on a 5.5 percent, 30-year, $100,000 loan is $568, with its next annual adjustment in 10 months. If rising interest rates cause the mortgage rate to increase to 7 percent, therefore increasing the monthly payment to $663, then negative amortization of $95 per month would occur. If no other interest rate change occurred over the remaining 10 months until its next adjustment, then the mortgage balance would be $100,950, with the increase of $950 attributable to the $95 per month negative amortization over 10 months.

When considering an ARM, be sure to learn whether negative amortization is allowed in the mortgage document. Generally, loans without the potential for negative amortization are available, although they tend to have slightly higher initial rates and interest rate caps.

Here are other types of ARMs lenders may offer.

convertible ARM
An adjustable-rate mortgage loan that allows borrowers to convert from an adjustable-rate to a fixed-rate loan, usually at any time between the 13th and the 60th month.

two-step ARM
An adjustable-rate mortgage with just two interest rates: one for the first five to seven years of the loan, and a higher one for the remaining term of the loan.

- **Convertible ARMs** allow borrowers to convert from an adjustable-rate to a fixed-rate loan during a specified time period, usually any time between the 13th and 60th month. Although these loans seldom provide the lowest initial rate, they allow the borrower to convert to a fixed-rate loan if interest rates decline. A conversion fee of about $500 is typical, and the fixed rate is normally set at 0.25 percent to 0.5 percent above the going rate on fixed-rate loans at the time you convert.
- **Two-step ARMs** have just two interest rates, the first for an initial period of 5 to 7 years and a higher one for the remaining term of the loan.

Implications of the ARM Index. The index on your ARM significantly affects the level and stability of your mortgage payments over the term of your loan. Lenders use short-term indexes such as the Six-Month Treasury Bill; the *London Interbank Offered Rate*, or LIBOR, a base rate similar to the prime rate and used in the international marketplace; CD-based indexes; and the 11th Federal Home Loan Bank District Cost of Funds.

The most important difference between the indexes is their volatility. LIBOR and CD rates are volatile because they quickly respond to changes in the financial markets. The 11th Federal Home Loan Bank District Cost of Funds index is less volatile because it represents an average of the cost of funds to S&Ls in the district. It tends to lag other short-term rate movements, both up and down, and exhibits a fairly smooth pattern over time. You may want to compare index rates over the past several years to more fully understand how one index behaves relative to another.

So what does this mean for the home buyer considering an ARM? If your mortgage is tied to a LIBOR or CD index, you can expect sharper and more frequent upward and downward interest rate movements compared to cost of funds indexes, which move more slowly in both directions. To see which index is better for you, consider the annual rate cap on the mortgage, the level of interest rates, and future interest rate expectations. If you have a low rate cap of 1 to 2 percentage points and you think that rates might go down, you may be comfortable with a more volatile index.

Some lenders offer special first-year "teaser" rates that are below the index rate on the loan. Be wary of lenders with very low rates. Ask them if the first-year rate is based on the index and verify the rate yourself. Be sure you can comfortably make the monthly mortgage payment when the interest rate steps up to the indexed rate.

Monitoring Your Mortgage Payments. You should carefully monitor your mortgage over its life. Always verify the calculation of your loan payment when rate or payment adjustments are made. To verify your payment amount, you need to know the index rate, the margin, and the formula used to adjust the loan; all are found in the loan agreement. Interest rates for the most commonly used indexes are readily available in the financial press and are published weekly in the real estate section of most newspapers. The loan formula tells you when the rate is set—for example, 45 days before the adjustment date—and the margin on the loan. You can use a handheld business calculator (as demonstrated earlier) to calculate the payment once you know the new

Financial Fact or Fantasy?

In an adjustable-rate mortgage, payment will change periodically, along with prevailing interest rates. **Fact:** In this popular form of home mortgage loan, the term of the loan is fixed (usually at 15 or 30 years), but the rate of interest, and therefore the size of the monthly mortgage payment, is adjusted up and down in line with movements in interest rates.

rate, the number of years until the loan is paid off, and the current principal balance.

If you suspect you're being overcharged, call your lender and ask for an explanation of the rate and payment calculations. Special mortgage-checking services will review your ARM for a fee of about $70 to $100.

Fixed Rate or Adjustable Rate?

Fixed-rate mortgages are popular with home buyers who plan to stay in their homes for at least 5 to 7 years and want to know what their payments will be. Of course, the current level of interest rates and your expectations about future interest rates will influence your choice of a fixed-rate or adjustable-rate mortgage. When the average interest rate on a 30-year mortgage loan is high, people choose ARMs to avoid being locked into prevailing high rates. When interest rates are low, many home buyers opt for fixed-rate mortgages to lock in these attractive rates. In such situations, many homeowners with existing ARMs refinance them with fixed-rate loans to take advantage of favorable current fixed rates.

Other Mortgage Payment Options

In addition to standard fixed-rate and adjustable-rate mortgage loans, some lenders offer variations designed to help first-time home buyers.

- **Interest-only mortgages** are loans requiring the borrower to pay only the interest. The popularity of these mortgages increased in response to the rapidly rising prices of the real estate boom between 2001 and 2006. Rather than amortizing the loan into equal monthly payments over the term of the loan, the borrower merely pays the accrued interest each month. These mortgages allow the borrower, typically on more expensive properties, to make lower payments that are fully tax deductible. Most interest-only mortgages are offered as ARMs.
- **Graduated-payment mortgages** are loans offering low payments for the first few years, gradually increasing until year 3 or 5 and then remaining fixed. The low initial payments appeal to people who are just starting out and expect their income to rise. If this doesn't occur, however, it could result in a higher debt load than the borrower can handle.
- **Growing-equity mortgages** are fixed-rate mortgages with payments that increase over a specific period. The extra funds are applied to the principal, so a conventional 30-year loan is paid off in about 20 years. However, you can accomplish the same thing without locking yourself into a set schedule by taking a fixed-rate mortgage that allows prepayments.
- **Shared-appreciation mortgages** are loans that have a below-market interest rate because the lender or other party shares from 30 percent to 50 percent of the appreciated value when the home is sold. This can be a useful tool if you absolutely can't afford the higher rates of a conventional loan; but keep in mind that, with appreciation of only 2 percent per year for just five years, such a loan could cost you up to $5,000 in shared equity on a $100,000 property.
- **Biweekly mortgages** are loans on which payments equal to half of a regular monthly payment are made every two weeks rather than once a month. Because you make 26 payments (52 weeks ÷ 2), which is the equivalent of 13 monthly payments, the principal balance declines faster and you pay less interest over the life of the loan. Once again, with most 30-year mortgages, you can make extra principal payments at any time without penalty. This may be preferable to committing to a biweekly loan that can charge an additional processing fee.
- **Buydowns** are a type of seller financing sometimes offered on new homes. A builder or seller arranges for mortgage financing with a financial institution at

interest-only mortgage
A mortgage that requires the borrower to pay only interest; typically used to finance the purchase of more expensive properties.

graduated-payment mortgage
A mortgage that starts with unusually low payments that rise over several years to a fixed payment.

growing-equity mortgage
Fixed-rate mortgage with payments that increase over a specific period. Extra funds are applied to the principal so that the loan is paid off more quickly.

shared-appreciation mortgage
A loan that allows a lender or other party to share in the appreciated value when the home is sold.

biweekly mortgage
A loan on which payments equal to half the regular monthly payment are made every two weeks.

buydown
Financing made available by a builder or seller to a potential new-home buyer at well below market interest rates, often only for a short period.

interest rates well below market rates. For example, a builder may offer 5 percent financing when the market rate of interest is around 6 percent or 6.5 percent. Typically, the builder or seller subsidizes the loan for the buyer at a special low interest rate. However, the reduced interest rate may be for only a short period, or the buyer may pay for the reduced interest in the form of a higher purchase price.

Conventional, Insured, and Guaranteed Loans

A **conventional mortgage** is a mortgage offered by a lender who assumes all the risk of loss. To protect themselves, lenders usually require a down payment of at least 20 percent of the value of the mortgaged property. For lower down payments, the lender usually requires *PMI*, as described earlier in the chapter. High borrower equity greatly reduces the likelihood of default on a mortgage and subsequent loss to the lender. However, a high down payment requirement makes home buying more difficult for many families and individuals.

To promote homeownership, the federal government, through the Federal Housing Administration (FHA), offers lenders mortgage insurance on loans with a high loan-to-value ratio. These loans usually feature low down payments, below-market interest rates, few if any points, and relaxed income or debt-ratio qualifications.

The **FHA mortgage insurance** program helps people buy homes even when they have very little money available for a down payment and closing costs. As of mid-2015, the up-front mortgage insurance premium for a 15- or 30-year mortgage was 1.75 percent of the loan amount—paid by the borrower at closing or included in the mortgage—plus another 0.80 to 1.05 percent annual renewal premium, paid monthly, depending on the maturity of the loan and the amount of the down payment. The FHA agrees to reimburse lenders for losses up to a specified maximum amount if the buyer defaults. The interest rate on an FHA loan is generally about 0.5 percent to 1 percent lower than that on conventional fixed-rate loans. The affordability ratios that are used to qualify applicants for these loans are typically less stringent than those used for conventional loans. The maximum mortgage amount that the FHA can insure is based on the national *median* price of homes and varies depending on location. To learn more about FHA mortgages, visit **http://www.fha.com.**

Guaranteed loans are similar to insured loans, but better—if you qualify. **VA loan guarantees** are provided by the U.S. Veterans Administration to lenders who make qualified mortgage loans to eligible veterans of the U.S. armed forces and their unmarried surviving spouses. This program, however, does not require lenders or veterans to pay a premium for the guarantee. In many instances, an eligible veteran must pay only closing costs; in effect, under such a program, a veteran can buy a home with no down payment. (This can be done *only once* with a VA loan.) The mortgage loan—subject to a maximum of about $417,000 for a no-money-down loan (or more in high-cost areas as of 2015)—can amount to as much as 100 percent of a purchased property's appraised value. It is important to note that there are some regional differences in VA loan requirements. VA loans include a funding fee of about 2.15 percent on first-time, no-down-payment loans for regular military members (the fee is lower if the down payment is 10 percent or more). The VA sets the maximum interest rate, which (as with FHA loans) is usually about 0.5 percent below the rate on conventional fixed-rate loans. To qualify, the veteran must meet VA credit guidelines. You can find more information at **http://www.homeloans.va.gov.**

5-6d Refinancing Your Mortgage

After you've purchased a home and closed the transaction, interest rates on similar loans may drop. If rates drop by 1 percent to 2 percent or more, then you should consider the economics of refinancing after carefully comparing the terms of the old and new mortgages, the anticipated number of years you expect to remain in the home, any prepayment penalty on the old mortgage, and closing costs associated with the new mortgage.

Worksheet 5.4 provides a form for analyzing the impact of refinancing. The data for the Varela family's analysis is shown. Their original $80,000, 10-year-old,

---

conventional mortgage
A mortgage offered by a lender who assumes all the risk of loss; typically requires a down payment of at least 20 percent of the value of the mortgaged property.

FHA mortgage insurance
A program under which the Federal Housing Administration (FHA) offers lenders mortgage insurance on loans having a high loan-to-value ratio; its intent is to encourage loans to home buyers who have very little money available for a down payment and closing costs.

VA loan guarantee
A guarantee offered by the U.S. Veterans Administration to lenders who make qualified mortgage loans to eligible veterans of the U.S. armed forces and their unmarried surviving spouses.

8 percent mortgage has a current balance of $70,180 and monthly payments of $587 for 20 more years. If they refinance the $70,180 balance at the prevailing rate of 5 percent then, over the remaining 20-year life of the current mortgage, the monthly payment would drop to $463. The Varelas plan to live in their house for at least five more years. They won't have to pay a penalty for prepaying their current mortgage, and closing and other costs associated with the new mortgage are $2,400 after taxes. Entering these values into Worksheet 5.4 reveals (in Item 7) that it will take the Varelas 26 months to break even with the new mortgage. Because 26 months is considerably less than their anticipated minimum five years (60 months) in the home, the economics easily support refinancing their mortgage under the specified terms.

There are two basic reasons to refinance—to reduce the monthly payment or to reduce the total interest cost over the term of the loan. If a lower monthly payment is the objective, then the analysis is relatively simple: determine how long it will take for the monthly savings to equal your closing costs (see Worksheet 5.4).

If your objective is to reduce the total interest cost over the life of the loan, then the analysis is more complex. The term of the new loan versus the existing loan is a critical element. If you refinance a 30-year loan that's already 10 years old with another 30-year loan, you're extending the total loan maturity to 40 years. Consequently, even with a lower interest rate, you may pay more interest over the life of the newly extended loan. So you should refinance with a shorter-term loan, ideally one that matures no later than the original loan maturity date. (The example in Worksheet 5.4 is prepared on this basis.)

Many homeowners want to pay off their loans more quickly to free up funds for their children's college education or for their own retirement. By refinancing at a lower rate and continuing to make the same monthly payment, a larger portion of each payment will go toward reducing the principal, so the loan will be paid off more quickly. Alternately, the borrower can make extra principal payments whenever possible. Paying only an additional $25 per month on a 30-year, 6 percent, $100,000 mortgage reduces the term to about 26 years and saves about $18,500 in interest.

WORKSHEET 5.4 Mortgage Refinancing Analysis for the Varela Family

Using this form, the Varelas find that—by refinancing the $70,180 balance on their 10-year-old, $80,000, 8 percent, 30-year mortgage (which has no prepayment penalty and requires payments of $587 per month) with a 5 percent, 20-year mortgage requiring $463 monthly payments and $2,400 in total after-tax closing costs—it will take 26 months to break even. Because the Varelas plan to stay in their home for at least 60 more months, the refinancing is easily justified.

MORTGAGE REFINANCING ANALYSIS

Name _Demi and Nicholas Varela_   Date _October 8, 2017_

Item	Description		Amount
1	Current monthly payment (Terms: $ _80,000, 8%, 30 years_)		$ 587
2	New monthly payment (Terms: $ _70,180, 5%, 20 years_)		463
3	Monthly savings, pretax (Item 1 − Item 2)		$ 124
4	Tax on monthly savings [Item 3 × tax rate (_25_ %)]		31
5	Monthly savings, after-tax (Item 3 − Item 4)		$ 93
6	Costs to refinance:		
	a. Prepayment penalty	$ 0	
	b. Total closing costs (after-tax)	2,400	
	c. Total refinancing costs (Item 6a + Item 6b)		$2,400
7	Months to break even (Item 6c ÷ Item 5)		26

Some people consider the reduced tax deduction associated with a smaller mortgage interest deduction as a disadvantage of refinancing. Although the interest deduction may indeed be reduced because of refinancing, the more important concern is the amount of the actual after-tax cash payments. In this regard, refinancing with a lower-interest-rate mortgage (with all other terms assumed unchanged) will always result in lower after-tax cash outflows and is therefore economically appealing. Of course, as demonstrated in Worksheet 5.4, the monthly savings should be compared with the refinancing costs before making the final decision.

Remember that when you refinance, most lenders require you to have at least 20 percent equity in your home, based on a current market appraisal. Many financial institutions are willing to refinance their existing loans, often charging fewer points and lower closing costs than a new lender would charge, so be sure to check with your existing lender first.

TEST YOURSELF

5-20 Describe the various sources of mortgage loans. What role might a *mortgage broker* play in obtaining mortgage financing?

5-21 Briefly describe the two basic types of mortgage loans. Which has the lowest initial rate of interest? What is *negative amortization*, and which type of mortgage can experience it? Discuss the advantages and disadvantages of each mortgage type.

5-22 Differentiate among conventional, insured, and guaranteed mortgage loans.

Planning Over a Lifetime: *Auto and Housing Decisions*

Here are some key considerations in making auto and housing decisions in each stage of the life cycle.

Pre-family Independence: 20s	Family Formation/ Career Development: 30–45	Pre-Retirement: 45–65	Retirement: 65 and Beyond
✓ Start saving for a down payment on a house.	✓ Compare current mortgage rates with yours and evaluate the value of refinancing.	✓ Periodically re-evaluate the attractiveness of refinancing your mortgage.	✓ Re-evaluate housing choices and location. Consider downsizing but watch transactions costs.
✓ Compare renting vs. buying a house.	✓ Budget to make additional payments on your mortgage to gain greater financial flexibility in the future.	✓ Budget to pay off your mortgage prior to retirement.	✓ Pay off your mortgage.
✓ Familiarize yourself with the various types of mortgages.	✓ Save to finance the replacement of your current car.	✓ Consider whether a different type of car(s) is (are) appropriate.	✓ Consider whether more than one family car is needed in retirement.

Financial Impact of Personal Choices
Vivian Wants to Buy a House but Doesn't Want a Roommate Now

Vivian has saved $10,000 toward a $20,000 down payment on buying a home. She puts aside $300 a month in her house fund and is currently renting a one-bedroom apartment on her own for $1,300 a month. If she rented a two-bedroom apartment with a roommate, she could reduce her rent to $900 a month. While having a roommate is not Vivian's favorite solution, she'd be able to build up her down payment for buying a house a lot faster if she were able to save an extra $400 a month. If Vivian stays on her own and her finances remain the same, it will take her about 2¾ years to put aside the needed additional $10,000. In contrast, if she set aside the rent saved by getting a roommate, she would have the needed $10,000 in about only 14 months. Doing without a roommate at this stage in Vivian's life is costly.

Summary

LG1 Design a plan to research and select a new or used automobile. p. 164

The purchase of an automobile should be based on thorough market research and comparison shopping. Important purchase considerations include affordability; operating costs; whether to buy a gas-, diesel-, or hybrid-fueled car; whether to buy a new versus a used or nearly new car; the type of car and its features; and its reliability and warranties. Knowing the dealer's cost is the key to negotiating a good price.

LG2 Decide whether to buy or lease a car. p. 173

Before leasing a vehicle you should consider all the terms of the lease, including the annual mileage allowance and early termination penalties. The economics of leasing versus purchasing a car with an installment loan should not be considered until the price is set. The four components of the lease payment are the capitalized cost, residual value, money factor, and lease term.

LG3 Identify housing alternatives, assess the rental option, and perform a rent-or-buy analysis. p. 177

In addition to single-family homes, there are condominiums, cooperative apartments, and rental units. Evaluate the advantages and disadvantages of each for your current lifestyle. Many people rent because they can't afford to buy a home; others rent because it's more convenient for their lifestyle and economic situation. The rental contract, or lease agreement, describes the terms under which you can rent the property, including the monthly rental amount, lease term, restrictions, and so forth. The rent ratio—the relationship between renting and buying a comparable house—quantifies the relative attractiveness of renting versus buying. A rent-or-buy analysis will identify the least costly alternative. Also consider qualitative factors, such as how long you plan to stay in an area, and perform the analysis over a several-year timeline.

LG4 Evaluate the benefits and costs of homeownership and estimate how much you can afford to pay for a home. p. 184

In addition to the emotional rewards, other benefits of homeownership are the tax shelter and inflation hedge it provides. Homeownership costs include the down payment, points and closing costs, monthly mortgage payments, property taxes and insurance, and normal home maintenance and operating expenses. Carefully consider all of these costs when estimating how much you can afford to spend on a home.

LG5 Describe the home-buying process. p. 194

Most people shopping for a home seek the help of a real estate agent to obtain access to properties and to provide needed information and advice. The agents involved in the transaction usually split a commission of 5 percent to 7 percent, paid by the seller, when the transaction is closed. Today, the Internet is a valuable resource that allows home buyers to conveniently search for the best available properties. It's a good idea to prequalify yourself for a mortgage before starting to house-hunt. A real estate sales contract is used to confirm in writing all terms of the transaction between buyer and seller. After a mortgage loan is approved, the loan is closed. A closing statement shows how much the borrower owes and the seller receives in the transaction.

LG6 **Choose mortgage financing that meets your needs. p. 199**
Mortgage loans can be obtained from commercial banks, from thrift institutions, or through a mortgage banker or mortgage broker. Although many types of mortgage loans are available, the most widely used are 30- and 15-year fixed-rate mortgages and adjustable-rate mortgages (ARMs). Sometimes interest rates will drop several years after closing, and mortgage refinancing will become attractive. The refinancing analysis considers the difference in terms between the old and new mortgages, any prepayment penalty on the old mortgage, closing costs, and how long you plan to stay in the home.

Key Terms

You can find answers to these questions on this book's companion website. Look for it at *www.cengagebrain.com*. Search for this book by its title, and then add it to your dashboard.

Key Financial Relationships

Concept	Financial Relationship	Page Number
Mortgage Payment	$\text{Mortgage Payment} = \dfrac{\text{Amount of Loan}}{\$10,000} \times \text{Monthly Payment on \$10,000 Loan}$	189
Maximum Affordable Mortgage Loan	$\text{Maximum Mortgage Loan} = \$10,000 \times \dfrac{\text{Maximum Monthly Payment}}{\text{Present Value Interest Factor}}$	191

Key Financial Relationships Problem Set

1. **Mortgage Payment.** Evelyn Ward wants to find the monthly payment on a $150,000, 5 percent, 30-year mortgage.

   Solution: Using the monthly mortgage payments provided in Exhibit 5.9 to repay a $10,000, 5 percent, 15-year loan:

   $$\text{Mortgage Payment} = \frac{\text{Amount of Loan}}{\$10,000} \times \text{Monthly Payment on \$10,000 Loan}$$

   $$= \frac{\$150,000}{\$10,000} \times \$79.08 = 15 \times \$79.08 = \$1,186.20$$

   Evelyn could also use a financial calculator with the following key strokes:

Inputs	Functions
15000	*PV*
180	*N*
5	÷
12	=
	I
	CPT
	PMT
	SOLUTION
	1186.19

2. **Maximum Affordable Mortgage Loan.** Alex and Lucy Riley have saved a $25,000 down payment and are considering buying a home. Based on their monthly income and affordability analysis, the Rileys can handle a maximum mortgage payment of $1,500 a month. The Riley's want to determine the amount of the maximum 30-year, 6 percent mortgage they can obtain.

   Solution: Using the monthly mortgage payments provided in Exhibit 5.9 to repay a $10,000, 6 percent, 30-year loan:

   $$\text{Maximum Mortgage Loan} = \$10,000 \times \frac{\text{Maximum Monthly Payment}}{\text{Monthly Payment on \$10,000 Loan}}$$

   $$= \$10,000 \times \frac{\$1,500}{\$59.96} = \$250,166.78$$

Alex and Lucy Riley could also use a financial calculator with the following key strokes:

Inputs	Functions
1500	*PMT*
360	*N*
6	*÷*
12	*=*
	I
	CPT
	PV
	SOLUTION
	250187.42

Further, the quick estimate provided in Exhibit 5.10 indicates a maximum mortgage of $250,187.

Thus, given their $25,000 down payment, the Riley's could afford to pay about $280,000 mortgage.

Financial Planning Exercises

LG1, 2, p. 164, 173

1. *Planning a new car purchase.* Janet Wilhite has just graduated from college and needs to buy a car to commute to work. She estimates that she can afford to pay about $450 per month for a loan or lease and has about $2,000 in savings to use for a down payment. Develop a plan to guide her through her first car-buying experience, including researching car type, deciding whether to buy a new or used car, negotiating the price and terms, and financing the transaction.

LG2, p. 173

2. *Lease vs. purchase car decision. Use Worksheet 5.1.* Chris Svenson is trying to decide whether to lease or purchase a new car costing $18,000. If he leases, he'll have to pay a $600 security deposit and monthly payments of $425 over the 36-month term of the closed-end lease. On the other hand, if he buys the car then he'll have to make a $2,400 down payment and will finance the balance with a 36-month loan requiring monthly payments of $515; he'll also have to pay a 6 percent sales tax ($1,080) on the purchase price, and he expects the car to have a residual value of $6,500 at the end of 3 years. Chris can earn 4 percent interest on his savings. Use the automobile lease versus purchase analysis form in Worksheet 5.1 to find the total cost of both the lease and the purchase and then recommend the best strategy for Chris.

LG3, p. 177

3. *Interpreting the rent ratio.* Art Patton has equally attractive job offers in Miami and Los Angeles. The rent ratios in the cities are 8 and 20, respectively. Art would really like to buy rather than rent a home after he moves. Explain how to interpret the rent ratio and what it tells Art about the relative attractiveness of moving to Miami rather than Los Angeles, given his stated goal.

LG3, 4, p. 177, 184

4. *Rent vs. buy home. Use Worksheet 5.2.* Denise Green is currently renting an apartment for $725 per month and paying $275 annually for renter's insurance. She just found a small townhouse that she can buy for $185,000. She has enough cash for a $10,000 down payment and $4,000 in closing costs. Her bank is offering 30-year mortgages at 6 percent per year. Denise estimated the following costs as a percentage of the home's price: property taxes, 2.5 percent; homeowner's insurance, 0.5 percent; and maintenance, 0.7 percent. She is in the 25 percent tax bracket and has an after-tax rate of return on invested funds of 4 percent. Using Worksheet 5.2, calculate the cost of each alternative and recommend the less costly option—rent or buy—for Denise.

LG4, p. 184

5. *Calculating required down payment on home purchase.* How much would you have to put down on a house costing $100,000 if the house had an appraised value of $105,000 and the lender required an 80 percent loan-to-value ratio?

LG4, p. 184

6. *Determining maximum affordable mortgage.* Using the maximum ratios for a conventional mortgage, how big a monthly payment could the Danforth family afford if their gross (before-tax) monthly income amounted to $4,000? Would it make any difference if they were already making monthly installment loan payments totaling $750 on two car loans?

LG4, p. 184

7. **Changes in mortgage principal and interest over time.** Explain how the composition of the principal and interest components of a fixed-rate mortgage change over the life of the mortgage. What are the implications of this change?

LG4, p. 184

8. **Calculating monthly mortgage payments.** Find the *monthly* mortgage payments on the following mortgage loans using either your calculator or the table in Exhibit 5.8:
    a. $80,000 at 6.5 percent for 30 years
    b. $105,000 at 5.5 percent for 20 years
    c. $95,000 at 5 percent for 15 years

LG4, p. 184

9. **Home affordability analysis. Use Worksheet 5.3.** Selma and Rodney Jackson need to calculate the amount that they can afford to spend on their first home. They have a combined annual income of $47,500 and have $27,000 available for a down payment and closing costs. The Jacksons estimate that homeowner's insurance and property taxes will be $250 per month. They expect the mortgage lender to use a 30 percent (of monthly gross income) mortgage payment affordability ratio, to lend at an interest rate of 6 percent on a 30-year mortgage, and to require a 15 percent down payment. Based on this information, use the home affordability analysis form in Worksheet 5.3 to determine the highest-priced home that the Jacksons can afford.

LG4, 5, p. 184, 194

10. **Estimating closing costs on home purchase.** How much might a home buyer expect to pay in closing costs on a $220,000 house with a 10 percent down payment? How much would the home buyer have to pay at the time of closing, taking into account closing costs, down payment, and a loan fee of 3 points?

LG6, p. 199

11. **Conventional vs. ARM mortgage payments.** What would the monthly payments be on a $150,000 loan if the mortgage were set up as:
    a. A 15-year, 6 percent fixed-rate loan?
    b. A 30-year ARM in which the lender adds a margin of 2.5 to the index rate, which now stands at 4.5 percent? Find the monthly mortgage payments for the first year only.

LG6, p. 199

12. **Adding to monthly mortgage payments.** What are the pros and cons of adding $100 a month to your fixed-rate mortgage payment?

LG6, p. 199

13. **Refinancing a mortgage. Use Worksheet 5.4.** Latha Yang purchased a condominium four years ago for $180,000, paying $1,250 per month on her $162,000, 8 percent, 25-year mortgage. The current loan balance is $152,401. Recently, interest rates have dropped sharply, causing Latha to consider refinancing her condo at the prevailing rate of 6 percent. She expects to remain in the condo for at least four more years and has found a lender that will make a 6 percent, 21-year, $152,401 loan requiring monthly payments of $1,065. Although there is no prepayment penalty on her current mortgage, Latha will have to pay $1,500 in closing costs on the new mortgage. She is in the 15 percent tax bracket. Based on this information, use the mortgage refinancing analysis form in Worksheet 5.4 to determine whether she should refinance her mortgage under the specified terms.

Applying Personal Finance

How's Your Local Housing Market?

What's the best source of information about available housing in your community? The answer is a well-informed professional real estate agent whose business is helping buyers find and negotiate the purchase of the most suitable property at the best price. However, there's another readily available source of information: the local newspaper—in paper or online. Almost anything you want to know about the local housing scene can be found in the real estate section of the paper. For this project, you'll gather information concerning your local housing market.

Review recent issues of your local newspaper and describe the market for both purchased homes and rental units. Look for useful information such as location, size of property, price or rent, lease requirements, and so forth. You should observe that the housing market is very fragmented, which makes good purchase and rent decisions more difficult. See if you can answer questions such as: What is the average size of a house or apartment in your community? What is the typical sales price or monthly rent per square foot? Is the purchase market competitive? How about the rental market? How great a difference exists in prices and rents between the most and least desirable areas of the community? Also check online for other sources of information, such as the county tax office, and try to find out how much property taxes and homeowner's insurance premiums average in your area. From your study of the local market, summarize its conditions and be prepared to participate in a class discussion of the local housing market.

CRITICAL THINKING CASES

LG1, 2, p. 164, 173

5.1 The Newtons' New Car Decision: Lease vs. Purchase

Farrah and Sam Newton, a dual-income couple in their late 20s, want to replace their seven-year-old car, which has 90,000 miles on it and needs some expensive repairs. After reviewing their budget, the Newtons conclude that they can afford auto payments of not more than $350 per month and a down payment of $2,000. They enthusiastically decide to visit a local dealer after reading its newspaper ad offering a closed-end lease on a new car for a monthly payment of $245. After visiting with the dealer, test-driving the car, and discussing the lease terms with the salesperson, they remain excited about leasing the car but decide to wait until the following day to finalize the deal. Later that day, the Newtons begin to question their approach to the new car acquisition process and decide to reevaluate their decision carefully.

Critical Thinking Questions

1. What are some basic purchasing guidelines that the Newtons should consider when choosing which new car to buy or lease? How can they find the information they need?
2. How would you advise the Newtons to research the lease-versus-purchase decision before visiting the dealer? What are the advantages and disadvantages of each alternative?
3. Assume that the Newtons can get the following terms on a lease or a bank loan for the car, which they could buy for $17,000. This amount includes tax, title, and license fees.
   - **Lease:** 48 months, $245 monthly payment, 1 month's payment required as a security deposit, $350 end-of-lease charges; a residual value of $6,775 is the purchase option price at the end of the lease.
   - **Loan:** $2,000 down payment, $15,000, 48-month loan at 5 percent interest requiring a monthly payment of $345.44; assume that the car's value at the end of 48 months will be the same as the residual value and that sales tax is 6 percent.

   The Newtons can currently earn interest of 3 percent annually on their savings. They expect to drive about the same number of miles per year as they do now.
   a. Use the format given in Worksheet 5.1 to determine which deal is best for the Newtons.
   b. What other costs and terms of the lease option might affect their decision?
   c. Based on the available information, should the Newtons lease or purchase the car? Why?

LG4, 6, p. 184, 199

5.2 Evaluating a Mortgage Loan for the Gerrards

Ben and Marie Gerrard, both in their mid-20s, have been married for four years and have two pre-school-age children. Ben has an accounting degree and is employed as a cost accountant at an annual salary of $62,000. They're now renting a duplex but wish to buy a home in the suburbs of their rapidly developing city. They've decided they can afford a $215,000 house and hope to find one with the features they desire in a good neighborhood.

The insurance costs on such a home are expected to be $800 per year, taxes are expected to be $2,500 per year, and annual utility bills are estimated at $1,440—an increase of $500 over those they pay in the duplex. The Gerrards are considering financing their home with a fixed-rate, 30-year, 6 percent mortgage. The lender charges 2 points on mortgages with 20 percent down and 3 points if less than 20 percent is put down (the commercial bank that the Gerrards will deal with requires a minimum of 10 percent down). Other closing costs are estimated at 5 percent of the home's purchase price. Because of their excellent credit record, the bank will probably be willing to let the Gerrards' monthly mortgage payments (principal and interest portions) equal as much as 28 percent of their monthly gross income. Since getting married, the Gerrards have been saving for the purchase of a home and now have $44,000 in their savings account.

Critical Thinking Questions

1. How much would the Gerrards have to put down if the lender required a minimum 20 percent down payment? Could they afford it?
2. Given that the Gerrards want to put only $25,000 down, how much would their closing costs be? Considering only principal and interest, how much would their monthly mortgage payments be? Would they qualify for a loan using a 28 percent affordability ratio?
3. Using a $25,000 down payment on a $215,000 home, what would the Gerrards' loan-to-value ratio be? Calculate the monthly mortgage payments on a PITI basis.
4. What recommendations would you make to the Gerrards? Explain.

LG3, 4,
p. 177, 184

5.3 Julie's Rent-or-Buy Decision

Julie Brown is in her late 20s. She is renting an apartment in the fashionable part of town for $1,200 a month. After much thought, she's seriously considering buying a condominium for $175,000. She intends to put 20 percent down and expects that closing costs will amount to another $5,000; a commercial bank has agreed to lend her money at the fixed rate of 6 percent on a 15-year mortgage. Julie would have to pay an annual condominium owner's insurance premium of $600 and property taxes of $1,200 a year (she's now paying renter's insurance of $550 per year). In addition, she estimates that annual maintenance expenses will be about 0.5 percent of the price of the condo (which includes a $30 monthly fee to the property owners' association). Julie's income puts her in the 25 percent tax bracket (she itemizes her deductions on her tax returns), and she earns an after-tax rate of return on her investments of around 4 percent.

Critical Thinking Questions

1. Given the information provided, use Worksheet 5.2 to evaluate and compare Julie's alternatives of remaining in the apartment or purchasing the condo.
2. Working with a friend who is a realtor, Julie has learned that condos like the one that she's thinking of buying are appreciating in value at the rate of 3.5 percent a year and are expected to continue doing so. Would such information affect the rent-or-buy decision made in Question 1? Explain.
3. Discuss any other factors that should be considered when making a rent-or-buy decision.
4. Which alternative would you recommend for Julie in light of your analysis?

Managing Credit

CHAPTERS

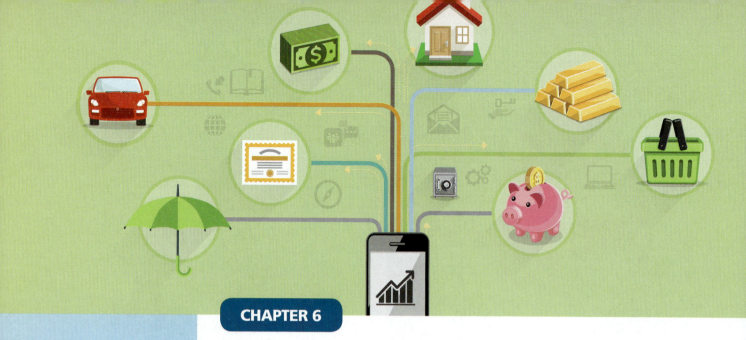

CHAPTER 6

Using Credit

LEARNING GOALS

LG1 Describe the reasons for using consumer credit, and identify its benefits and problems.

LG2 Develop a plan to establish a strong credit history.

LG3 Distinguish among the different forms of open account credit.

LG4 Apply for, obtain, and manage open forms of credit.

LG5 Choose the right credit cards and recognize their advantages and disadvantages.

LG6 Avoid credit problems, protect yourself against credit card fraud, and understand the personal bankruptcy process.

How Will This Affect Me?

The ability to borrow funds to buy goods and services is as convenient as it is seductive. It is important to understand how to get and maintain access to credit and convenient transactions via credit cards, debit cards, lines of credit, and other means. This chapter reviews the common sources of consumer credit and provides a framework for choosing among them. It also discusses the importance of developing a good credit history, achieving and maintaining a good credit score, and protecting against identity theft and credit fraud. The chapter will help you understand the need to use credit intentionally, in a way that is consistent with your overall financial objectives.

6-1 THE BASIC CONCEPTS OF CREDIT

LG1, LG2

It's so easy. Just slide that credit card through the reader and you can buy gas for your car, have a gourmet meal at an expensive restaurant, or furnish an apartment. It happens *several hundred million times a day* across the United States. Credit, in fact, has become an entrenched part of our everyday lives, and we as consumers use it in one form or another to purchase just about every type of good or service imaginable. Indeed, because of the ready availability and widespread use of credit, our economy is often called a "credit economy." And for good reason: as of the end of 2014, households in this country had run up almost *$11.83 trillion dollars* in debt—and that doesn't even include home mortgages.

Consumer credit is important in the personal financial planning process because of the impact it can have on (1) attaining financial goals and (2) cash budgets. For one thing, various forms of consumer credit can help you reach your financial objectives by enabling you to acquire some of the more expensive items in a systematic fashion, without throwing your whole budget into disarray. But there's another side to consumer credit: it has to be paid back! Unless credit is used intelligently, the "buy now, pay later" attitude can quickly turn an otherwise orderly budget into a budgetary nightmare and lead to some serious problems—even bankruptcy! So, really, the issue is one of moderation and affordability.

In today's economy, consumers, businesses, and governments alike use credit to make transactions. Credit helps businesses supply the goods and services needed to satisfy consumer demand. Business credit also provides higher levels of employment and helps raise our overall standard of living. Local, state, and federal governments borrow for various projects and programs that also increase our standard of living and create additional employment opportunities. Clearly, borrowing helps fuel our economy and enhance the overall quality of our lives. Consequently, *consumers in a credit economy need to know how to establish credit and how to avoid the dangers of using it improperly.*

6-1a Why We Use Credit

People typically use credit as a way to pay for goods and services that cost more than they can afford to pay out of their current income. This is particularly true for those in the 25–44 age group, who simply have not had time to accumulate the liquid assets required to pay cash outright for major purchases and expenditures. As people begin to approach their mid-40s, however, their savings and investments start to build up and their debt loads tend to decline, which is really not too surprising when you consider that the median household net worth for those in the 45–54 age group is considerably higher than for those aged 35–44.

Whatever their age group, people tend to borrow for several major reasons.

- **To avoid paying cash for large outlays:** Rather than pay cash for large purchases such as houses and cars, most people borrow part of the purchase price and then repay the loan on some scheduled basis. Spreading payments over time makes big-ticket items more affordable, and consumers get the use of an expensive asset right away. In their minds, at least, the benefits of current consumption outweigh the interest costs on the loan. Unfortunately, while the initial euphoria of the purchase may wear off over time, the loan payments remain—perhaps for many more years to come.
- **To meet a financial emergency:** For example, people may need to borrow to cover living expenses during a period of unemployment or to purchase plane tickets to visit a sick relative. As indicated in Chapter 4, however, using savings is preferable to using credit for financial emergencies.
- **For convenience:** Merchants as well as banks offer a variety of charge accounts and credit cards that allow consumers to charge just about anything—from gas or clothes and stereos to doctor and dental bills and even college tuition. Further, in many places—restaurants, for instance—using a credit card is far easier than writing a check. Although such transactions usually incur no interest (at least not initially), these credit card purchases are still a form of borrowing. This is because payment is not made at the time of the transaction.
- **For investment purposes:** As we'll see in Chapter 11, it's relatively easy for an investor to partially finance the purchase of many different kinds of investments with borrowed funds.

Financial Fact or Fantasy?

One of the benefits of using credit is that it allows you to purchase expensive goods and services while spreading the payment for them over time. **Fact:** One of the major benefits of buying on credit is that expensive purchases are made more affordable because the consumer is able to pay for them systematically over time.

6-1b Improper Uses of Credit

Many people use consumer credit to live beyond their means. For some people, overspending becomes a way of life, and it is perhaps the biggest danger in borrowing—especially because it's so easy to do. And nowhere did that become more apparent than in the wake of the credit crisis of 2007–2009. Indeed, as credit became more readily available and easier to obtain, it also became increasingly clear that many consumers were, in fact, severely overusing it. All this resulted in a credit meltdown unlike anything this country had ever seen.

Once hooked on "plastic," people may use their credit cards to make even routine purchases and all too often don't realize they have overextended themselves until it's too late. And by making only the minimum payment, borrowers pay a huge price in the long run. Exhibit 6.1 shows the amount of time and interest charges required to repay credit card balances if you make only minimum payments of 3 percent of the outstanding balance. Paying only the minimum balance is a costly decision.

EXAMPLE: Paying Only the Minimum on Your Credit Card

If you carry a $3,000 balance—which is about *one-fifth* of the national average—on a credit card that charges 15.0 percent annually and only pay the minimum amount due, it would take you 14 years to retire the debt, and your interest charges would total some $2,000—*or more than 66 percent of the original balance!*

EXHIBIT 6.1   **Minimum Payments Mean Maximum Years**

Paying off credit card balances at the minimum monthly amount required by the card issuer will take a long time and cost you a great deal of interest, as this table demonstrates. *The calculations here are based on a minimum 3 percent payment and 15 percent annual interest rate.*

Original Balance	Years to Repay	Interest Paid	Total Interest Paid, as Percentage of Original Balance
$5,000	16.4	$3,434	68.7%
4,000	15.4	2,720	68.0
3,000	14.0	2,005	66.8
2,000	12.1	1,291	64.5
1,000	8.8	577	57.7

Some cards offer even lower minimum payments of just 2 percent of the outstanding balance. Although such small payments may seem like a good deal, clearly they don't work to your advantage and only increase the time and amount of interest required to repay the debt. For example, by making minimum 2 percent payments, it would take *more than 32 years* to pay off a $5,000 balance on a credit card that carries a 15 percent rate of interest. In contrast, as can be seen in Exhibit 6.1, that same $5,000 balance could be paid off in *just 16.4 years* if you had made 3 percent minimum payments. Just think, making an additional 1 percent payment can save you nearly 16 years of interest! That's why the federal banking regulators issued guidelines stating that minimum monthly credit card payments should now cover at least 1 percent of the outstanding balance, plus all monthly finance charges and any other fees.

Avoid the possibility of future repayment shock by keeping in mind the following types of transactions for which you should *not* (routinely, at least) use credit: (1) to meet basic living expenses; (2) to make impulse purchases, especially expensive ones; and (3) to purchase nondurable (short-lived) goods and services. Except in situations where credit cards are used occasionally for convenience (such as for gasoline, groceries, and entertainment) or where payments on recurring credit purchases are built into the monthly budget, a good rule to remember when considering the use of credit is that *the product purchased on credit should outlive the amount of time it takes to pay it off.*

Unfortunately, people who overspend eventually must choose to either become delinquent in their payments or sacrifice necessities, such as food and clothing. If payment obligations aren't met, the consequences are likely to be a damaged credit rating, lawsuits, or even personal bankruptcy. Exhibit 6.2 lists some common signals that indicate it may be time to stop buying on credit. *Ignoring the telltale signs that you are overspending can only lead to more serious problems.*

6-1c Establishing Credit

The willingness of lenders to extend credit depends on their assessment of your creditworthiness—that is, your ability to promptly repay the debt. Lenders look at various factors in making this decision, such as your present earnings and net worth. Equally important, they look at your current debt position and your credit history. Thus, it's worth your while to do what you can to build a strong credit rating.

EXHIBIT 6.2 | **Watch for Credit Danger Signs**

If one or more of these signs exist, it's time to proceed with caution in your credit spending. Be prepared to revise and update your spending patterns, cut back on the use of credit, and be alert for other signs of overspending.

Serious trouble may be ahead if you:

- Regularly use credit cards to buy on impulse
- Postdate checks to keep them from bouncing
- Regularly exceed the borrowing limits on your credit cards
- Never add up all your bills, to avoid facing grim realities
- Now take 60 or 90 days to pay bills that you once paid in 30
- Have to borrow just to meet normal living expenses
- Often use one form of credit—such as a cash advance from a credit card—to make payments on other debt
- Can barely make the minimum required payments on bills
- Are using more than 20 percent of your take-home income to pay credit card bills and personal loans (excluding mortgage payments)
- Have little or no savings
- Are so far behind on credit payments that collection agencies are calling you

First Steps in Establishing Credit

First, open checking and savings accounts. They signal stability to lenders and indicate that you handle your financial affairs in a businesslike way. Second, use credit: open one or two charge accounts and use them periodically, even if you prefer paying cash. For example, get a *MasterCard* and make a few credit purchases each month (don't overdo it, of course). You might pay an annual fee or interest on some (or all) of your account balances, but in the process, you'll build a record of being a reliable credit customer. Third, obtain a small loan, even if you don't need one. If you don't actually need the money, put it in a liquid investment, such as a money market account or certificate of deposit. The interest you earn should offset some of the interest expense on the loan; you can view the difference as a cost of building good credit. You should repay the loan promptly, perhaps even a little ahead of schedule, to minimize the difference in interest rates. However, don't pay off the loan too quickly because lenders like to see how you perform over an extended period of time. Keep in mind that your ability to obtain a large loan in the future will depend, in part, on how you managed smaller ones in the past.

Build a Strong Credit History

From a financial perspective, maintaining a strong credit history is just as important as developing a solid employment record! Don't take credit lightly, and don't assume that getting the loan or the credit card is the toughest part. It's not. That's just the first step; servicing it (i.e., making payments) in a timely fashion—month in and month out—is the really tough part of the consumer credit process. By using credit wisely and repaying it on time, you're establishing a *credit history* that tells lenders you're a dependable, reliable, and responsible borrower.

The consumer credit industry watches your credit and your past payment performance closely (more on this when we discuss *credit bureaus* later in this chapter). So the more responsible you are as a borrower, the easier it will be to get credit when and where you want it. The best way to build a strong credit history and maintain your creditworthiness is to *consistently make payments on time*, month after month. Being late occasionally—say, two or three times a year—might label you a "late payer." When you take on credit, you have an *obligation* to live up to the terms of the loan, including how and when the credit will be repaid.

If you foresee difficulty in meeting a monthly payment, let the lender know. Usually arrangements can be made to help you through the situation. This is especially true with installment loans that require fixed monthly payments. If you have one or two of these loans and see a month coming that's going to be really tight, the first thing you should try to do (other than trying to borrow some money from a family member) is get an extension on your loan. Don't just skip a payment, because that's going to put your account into *late status until you make up the missed payment*. In other words, until you make a *double* payment, your account/loan will remain in a late status, which is subject to a monthly late penalty. Trying to work out an extension with your lender obviously makes a lot more sense.

Here's what you do. Explain the situation to the loan officer and ask for an extension of one (or two) months on your loan. In most cases, so long as this hasn't occurred before, the extension is almost automatically granted. The maturity of the loan is formally extended for a month (or two), and the extra interest of carrying the loan for another month (or two) is either added to the loan balance or, more commonly, paid at the time the extension is granted (such an extension fee generally amounts to a fraction of the normal monthly payment). Then, in a month or two, you pick up where you left off and resume your normal monthly payments on the loan. This is the most sensible way of making it through those rough times because it doesn't harm your credit record. Just don't do it too often.

How Much Credit Can You Handle?

Sound financial planning dictates that you need a good idea of how much credit you can comfortably tolerate. The easiest way to avoid repayment problems and ensure that your borrowing won't place an undue strain on your monthly budget is to *limit the use*

Financial Fact or Fantasy?

It's a good idea to contact your creditors immediately if, for some reason, you can't make payments as agreed. **Fact:** Let the lenders know and they'll often give you a credit extension. This is one of the smartest things you can do to build a sound credit history. However, except for those occasional tight spots, it's important to make credit payments on time consistently!

FINANCIAL ROAD SIGN

The 5 Cs of Credit

Lenders often look to the "5 Cs of Credit" as a way to assess the willingness and ability of a borrower to repay a loan.

1. **Character.** A key factor in defining the borrower's willingness to live up to the terms of the loan.
2. **Capacity.** The ability of the borrower to service the loan in a timely fashion.
3. **Collateral.** Something of value that's used to secure a loan and that the lender can claim in case of default.
4. **Capital.** The amount of unencumbered assets owned by the borrower, used as another indicator of the borrower's ability to repay the loan.
5. **Condition.** The extent to which prevailing economic conditions could affect the borrower's ability to service a loan.

Here are some things you can do to build a strong credit history:

- Use credit only when you can afford it and only when the repayment schedule fits comfortably into the family budget—in short, don't overextend yourself.
- Fulfill all the terms of the credit.
- Be *consistent* in making payments *promptly*.
- Consult creditors immediately if you cannot meet payments as agreed.
- Be truthful when applying for credit. Lies are not likely to go undetected.

debt safety ratio
The proportion of total monthly consumer credit obligations to monthly take-home pay.

of credit to your ability to repay the debt! A useful *credit guideline* (and one widely used by lenders) is to make sure your monthly repayment burden doesn't exceed 20 percent of your monthly *take-home pay*. Most experts, however, regard the 20 percent figure as the *maximum* debt burden and strongly recommend a **debt safety ratio** closer to 10 or 15 percent—perhaps even lower if you plan on applying for a new mortgage in the near future. Note that the monthly repayment burden here *does include* payments on your credit cards, but it *excludes* your monthly mortgage obligation.

To illustrate, consider someone who takes home $2,500 a month. Using a 20 percent ratio, she should have monthly consumer credit payments of no more than $500—that is, $2,500 × 0.20 = $500. This is the maximum amount of her monthly disposable income that she should need to pay off both personal loans and other forms of consumer credit (such as credit cards and education loans). This, of course, is not the maximum amount of consumer credit that she can have outstanding—in fact, her total consumer indebtedness can, and likely would, be considerably larger. The key factor is that with her income level, her *payments* on this type of debt should not exceed $500 a month. (*Caution:* This doesn't mean that credit terms should be lengthened just to accommodate this guideline; rather, in all cases, it's assumed that standard credit terms apply.)

Exhibit 6.3 provides a list of low (10 percent), manageable (15 percent), and maximum (20 percent) monthly credit payments for various income levels. Obviously, the closer your total monthly payments are to your desired debt safety ratio, the less future borrowing you can do. Conversely, *the lower the debt safety ratio, the better shape you're in, creditwise, and the easier it should be for you to service your outstanding consumer debt.*

You can compute the debt safety ratio as follows:

$$\text{Debt Safety Ratio} = \frac{\text{Total Monthly Consumer Credit Payments}}{\text{Monthly Take} - \text{Home Pay}}$$

EXHIBIT 6.3 **Credit Guidelines Based on Ability to Repay**

According to the debt safety ratio, the amount of consumer credit you should have outstanding depends on the monthly payments you can afford to make.

MONTHLY CONSUMER CREDIT PAYMENTS

Monthly Take-Home Pay	*Low* Debt Safety Ratio (10%)	*Manageable* Debt Safety Ratio (15%)	*Maximum* Debt Safety Ratio (20%)
$1,000	$100	$150	$200
1,250	125	188	250
1,500	150	225	300
2,000	200	300	400
2,500	250	375	500
3,000	300	450	600
3,500	350	525	700
4,000	400	600	800
5,000	500	750	1,000

This measure is the focus of Worksheet 6.1, which you can use for keeping close tabs on your own debt safety ratio. It shows the impact that each new loan you take out, or credit card you sign up for, can have on this important measure of creditworthiness. Consider, for example, Winston and Victoria Chang. As seen in Worksheet 6.1, they have five outstanding consumer loans, plus they're carrying balances on three credit cards. All told, these eight obligations require monthly payments of almost $740, which accounts for about one-fifth of their combined take-home pay and gives them a debt safety ratio of 18 percent. And note the information at the bottom of the worksheet that says if the Changs want to lower this ratio to, say, 15 percent, then they'll either have to reduce their monthly payments to $615 or increase their take-home pay to at least $4,927 a month.

6-2 CREDIT CARDS AND OTHER TYPES OF OPEN ACCOUNT CREDIT

open account credit
A form of credit extended to a consumer in advance of any transaction.

credit limit
A specified amount beyond which a customer may not borrow or purchase on credit.

credit statement
A monthly statement summarizing the transactions, interest charges, fees, and payments in a consumer credit account.

Open account credit is a form of credit extended to a consumer in advance of any transactions. Typically, a retail outlet or bank agrees to allow the consumer to buy or borrow up to a specified amount on open account. Credit is extended so long as the consumer does not exceed the established **credit limit** and makes payments in accordance with the specified terms. Open account credit issued by a retail outlet, such as a department store or oil company, is usually applicable only in that establishment or one of its locations. In contrast, open account credit issued by banks, such as *MasterCard* and *Visa* accounts, can be used to make purchases at a wide variety of businesses. For the rest of this chapter, we'll direct our attention to the various types and characteristics of open account credit; in Chapter 7, we'll look at various forms of single-payment and installment loans.

Having open account credit is a lot like having a personal line of credit—it's there when you need it. But unlike most other types of debt, consumers who use open forms of credit can often avoid paying interest charges *if they promptly pay the full amount of their account balance.* For example, assume that in a given month you charge $75.58 on an open account at a department store. Sometime within the next month or so, you'll receive a **credit statement** from the store that summarizes recent transactions on your account. Now, if there are no other charges and the total

A worksheet like this one will help a household stay on top of their monthly credit card and consumer loan payments, as well as their *debt safety ratio*—an important measure of creditworthiness. The key is to keep the debt safety ratio as low as (reasonably) possible, something that can be done by keeping monthly loan payments in line with monthly take-home pay.

MONTHLY CONSUMER LOAN PAYMENTS & DEBT SAFETY RATIO

Name Winston and Victoria Chang   **Date** June 21, 2017

■ Type of Loan*	Lender	Current Monthly (or Min.) Payment
• Auto and personal loans	Ford Motor Credit	$ 360.00
	Bank of America	115.00
• Education loans	U.S. Dept. of Education	75.00
• Overdraft protection line	Bank of America	30.00
• Personal line of credit		
• Credit cards	Bank of America Visa	28.00
	Fidelity MC	31.00
	JC Penney	28.00
• Home equity line	Bank of America	72.00
	TOTAL MONTHLY PAYMENTS	$ 739.00

***Note:** List only those loans that require regular monthly payments.

■ Monthly Take-Home Pay	1. Winston	$ 1,855.00
	2. Victoria	2,250.00
	TOTAL MONTHLY TAKE-HOME PAY	$ 4,105.00

■ **Debt Safety Ratio:**

$$\frac{\text{Total monthly payments}}{\text{Total monthly take-home pay}} \times 100 = \frac{\$\ 739.00}{\$4,105.00} \times 100 = \underline{18.0}\ \%$$

• **Changes needed to reach a new debt safety ratio**

1. New (Target) debt safety ratio: 15.0 %

2. At current take-home pay of $4,105.00 ,
   total monthly payments must equal:

   Total monthly take-home pay × Target debt safety ratio**

   $4,105.00 × 0.150 = $ 615.75

                         New Monthly Payments

   OR

3. With current monthly payments of $739.00 ,
   total take-home pay must equal:

$$\frac{\text{Total monthly payments}}{\text{New (target) debt safety ratio}} \times 100 = \frac{\$\ 739.00}{0.150} = \underline{\$4,926.67}$$

                                          New take-home pay

****Note:** Enter debt safety ratio as a decimal (e.g., 15% = 0.15).

account balance is $75.58, you can (usually) avoid any finance charges by paying the account in full before the next billing date.

Open account credit generally is available from two broadly defined sources: (1) financial institutions and (2) retail stores/merchants. *Financial institutions* issue general-purpose credit cards, as well as secured and unsecured revolving lines of credit and overdraft protection lines. Commercial banks have long been the major providers of consumer credit; and, since deregulation, so have S&Ls, credit unions, major stock-brokerage firms, and consumer finance companies. *Retail stores and merchants* make up the other major source of open account credit. They provide this service as a way to promote the sales of their products, and their principal form of credit is the charge (or credit) card. Let's now take a look at these two forms of credit, along with *debit cards* and *revolving lines of credit*.

6-2a Bank Credit Cards

bank credit card
A credit card issued by a bank or other financial institution that allows the holder to charge purchases at any establishment that accepts it.

Probably the most popular form of open account credit is the **bank credit card** issued by commercial banks and other financial institutions—*Visa* and *MasterCard* are the two dominant types. These cards allow their holders to charge purchases worldwide at literally millions of stores, restaurants, shops, and gas stations as well as at state and municipal governments, colleges and universities, medical groups, and mail-order houses—not to mention the Internet, where they've become the currency of choice. They can be used to pay for almost anything. The volume of credit and debit card purchases moved beyond cash and check transactions in 2003. Thousands of banks, S&Ls, credit unions, brokerage houses, and other financial services institutions issue *Visa* and *MasterCard*; and each issuer, within reasonable limits, can set its own credit terms and conditions.

Bank credit cards can be used to borrow money as well as buy goods and services on credit. Because of their potential for use in literally thousands of businesses and banks, they can be of great convenience and value to consumers. However, individuals who use them should be thoroughly familiar with their basic features.

The financial crisis in 2008–2009 brought tighter credit standards to the bank credit card business. This includes higher standards for personal credit history. Standards tend to tighten quickly in a crisis, and it can take several years before they move back to their pre-crisis levels. As a result, consumers find it harder to get new credit cards, and the limits on many existing cards are reduced markedly.

Line of Credit

line of credit
The maximum amount of credit a customer is allowed to have outstanding at any point in time.

The **line of credit** provided to the holder of a bank credit card is set by the issuer for each card. It's the maximum amount that the cardholder can owe at any time. The size of the credit line depends on both the applicant's request and the results of the issuer's investigation of the applicant's credit and financial status. Lines of credit offered by issuers of bank cards can reach $50,000 or more, but for the most part they range from about $500 to $2,500. Although card issuers fully expect you to keep your credit within the specified limits, most won't take any action unless you extend your account balance a certain percentage beyond the account's stated maximum. For example, if you had a $1,000 credit limit, you probably wouldn't hear from the card issuer until your outstanding account balance exceeded, say, $1,200 (i.e., 20 percent above the $1,000 line of credit). On the other hand, don't count on getting off for free, because most card issuers assess *over-the-limit* fees whenever you go over your credit limit.

Cash Advances

cash advance
A loan that can be obtained by a bank credit cardholder at any participating bank or financial institution.

In addition to purchasing merchandise and services, the holder of a bank credit card can obtain a **cash advance** from any participating bank. Cash advances are loans on which interest begins to accrue immediately. They're transacted in the same way as merchandise purchases, except that they take place at a commercial bank or some other financial institution and involve the receipt of cash (or a check) instead of goods and services. Another way to get a cash advance is to use the "convenience checks" that you receive from the card issuer to pay for purchases. You can even use your credit card to draw cash from an ATM, any time of the day or night. Usually, the size of the cash advance from an ATM is limited to some nominal amount (a common amount is $500 or less), although the amount you can obtain from the teller window at a bank is limited only by the unused credit in your account. Thus, if you've used only $1,000 of a $5,000 credit limit, you can take out a cash advance of up to $4,000.

Interest Charges

The average *annual rate of interest* charged on standard fixed-rate bank credit cards was 13.01 percent in mid-2015, while the average rate on standard variable-rate cards was 15.76 percent. You'll find that most bank cards have one rate for merchandise purchases and a much higher rate for cash advances. For example, the rate on merchandise purchases might be 12 percent, while the rate on cash advances could be 19 percent or 20 percent. And when shopping for a credit card, watch out for those *special low introductory rates* that many banks offer. Known as "teaser rates," they're usually only good for the first 6 to 12 months. Then, just as soon as the introductory period ends, so do the low interest rates.

base rate
The rate of interest a bank uses as a base for loans to individuals and small to midsize businesses.

Most of these cards have variable interest rates that are tied to an index that moves with market rates. The most popular is the prime or **base rate**: the rate a bank uses as a base for loans to individuals and small or midsize businesses. These cards adjust their interest rate monthly or quarterly and usually have minimum and maximum rates. Given the widespread use of variable interest rates, bank cardholders should be aware that—just as falling rates bring down interest rates on credit cards—rising market rates are guaranteed to lead to much higher interest charges!

> ### EXAMPLE: Bank Credit Card Index Interest Rates
>
> Consider a bank card whose terms are *prime plus 7.5 percent*, with a minimum of 10 percent and a maximum of 15.25 percent. If the prime rate is 3.25 percent, then the rate of interest charged on this card would be 3.25 percent + 7.5 percent = 10.75 percent.

Generally speaking, *the interest rates on credit cards are higher than any other form of consumer credit*. However, because competition has become so intense, a growing number of banks today are actually willing to negotiate their fees as a way to retain their customers. Whether this trend will have any significant impact on permanently reducing interest rates and fees remains to be seen, but at least most consumers would agree it's a step in the right direction.

grace period
A short period of time, usually 20 to 30 days, during which you can pay your credit card bill in full and not incur any interest charges.

Bank credit card issuers must disclose interest costs and related information to consumers *before* extending credit. In the case of purchases of merchandise and services, the specified interest rate may not apply to charges until after the **grace period**. During this short period, usually 20 to 30 days, you have historically been able to pay your credit card bill in full and avoid any interest charges. Once you carry a balance—that is, when you don't pay your card in full during the grace period—the interest rate is usually applied to any unpaid balances carried from previous periods, as well as to any new purchases made. Interest on cash advances, however, *begins the day that the advance is taken out*.

Those Other Fees

Besides the interest charged on bank credit cards, there are a few other fees you should be aware of. To begin with, many (though not all) bank cards charge *annual fees* just for the "privilege" of being able to use the card. In most cases, the fee is around $25 to $40 a year, though it can amount to much more for prestige cards. Sometimes, this annual fee is waived in the first year, but you'll be stuck with it for the second and every other year you hold the card. As a rule, the larger the bank or S&L, the more likely it is to charge an annual fee for its credit cards. What's more, many issuers also charge a *transaction fee* for each (non-ATM) cash advance; this fee usually amounts to about $5 per cash advance or 3 percent of the amount obtained in the transaction, whichever is more.

Historically, card issuers have come up with many ways to squeeze additional revenue from you. These have included late-payment fees, over-the-limit charges, foreign transaction fees, and balance transfer fees. For example, if you were a bit late in making your payment, then some banks will hit you with a late-payment fee, which is really a redundant charge because you were already paying interest on the unpaid balance. Similarly, if you happened to go over your credit limit, then you'd be hit with a charge for that, too (again, this is in addition to the interest you're already paying). The card issuers have justified these charges by saying it costs money to issue and administer these cards, so they have a right to charge these fees if you don't use their cards. Of course, you have the right to let the issuer know what you think of these charges by canceling your card! Regardless of when or why any of these fees are levied, the net effect is that *they add to the true cost of using bank credit cards.*

These onerous credit card issuer practices and extra fees led to the passage of the Credit Card Act of 2009. In the past, credit card companies could change interest rates and other aspects of the agreement without notice. They could even change terms retroactively such that they applied two months before you were notified. The new law requires credit card companies to give 45 days' notice before changing your agreement. Similarly, credit card companies previously could raise your interest rate if your credit report deteriorated or if you were late on even just one payment. The new law allows credit card companies to apply a new interest rate only to new balances after you are 60 days delinquent paying on your account. And just as important is that your old balance can only be charged your old interest rate. Exhibit 6.4 summarizes some of the key provisions of the law. In the year after the law went into effect in 2010, credit card balances fell, late payments dropped, payment defaults declined, and there was increased use of debit over credit cards.

Balance Transfers

balance transfer
A program that enables cardholders to readily transfer credit balances from one card to another.

One feature of bank credit cards that some users find attractive is the ability to transfer balances from one card to another. Known as **balance transfers**, the card issuers make a big deal out of allowing you to transfer the balances from one or more (old) cards to their (new) card. The idea is to dump the old card(s) by putting everything, including current balances, on the issuer's (new) card. There are two potential advantages to these balance transfer programs. First, there's the convenience of being able to consolidate your credit card payments. Second, there's the potential savings in interest that accompanies the transfer, since such deals usually come with very low (introductory) rates. But these transfers also have their drawbacks. For starters, although you may benefit (initially) from a low rate on all transferred funds, the issuer will often charge a much higher rate on new purchases. On top of that, your monthly payment is usually applied first to the transferred balance and not the *new purchases,* which incur the higher rate. In addition, some banks will charge a flat fee on all transferred funds.

EXAMPLE: Cost of Transferring a Credit Card Balance

Suppose you transfer a balance of $5,000 to a new credit card that imposes a 4 percent fee for the transfer. This would result in a charge of $200, and that's in addition to any other interest charges! Although many balance transfer programs offer relatively low introductory rates, those low rates usually don't last very long.

EXHIBIT 6.4 | How the Credit Card Act of 2009 Affects You

The Credit Card Act of 2009 provides sweeping and significant credit card reform. Its goal is to protect consumers from some of the harsher practices of credit card companies. While it provides some protection, it's no substitute for responsible credit card habits. Here are some of the major provisions of the new law:

Finance Charges and Interest Rate Increases

- Credit card companies must give you notice 45 days before increasing your interest rate or changing your agreement. Prior to passage of the new law, the requirement was only 15 days' notice. Promotional rates must last at least six months.
- Finance charges can no longer be calculated using the double-cycle billing approach, which takes into account not only the average daily balance of the current billing cycle, but also the average daily balance of the prior period. This billing approach can increase interest charges significantly for consumers whose average balance varies a lot from month to month.
- If your card company increases your rate, the new rate can be applied only to new balances, not to preexisting balances.

Payment Allocation and Fees

- Fees for making your credit card payment are prohibited unless you're making a last-minute payment by phone when your payment is due.
- If your balances have different interest rates, any payment above the minimum due must be allocated to your highest-interest rate balance first.
- Over-the-limit fees cannot be charged unless you direct the credit card company to process the over-the-limit transactions. Only one over-the-limit fee is allowed per billing cycle.

Billing Statements and Payment Processing

- Credit card statements must be sent out 21 days before the due date.
- Payments received the next business day after a holiday or a weekend are considered on time.

Credit Cards for Minors and College Students

- Minors under 18 cannot have credit cards unless they are emancipated or are authorized to use a parent's or guardian's account.
- College students without verifiable income cannot be issued credit cards.

Credit Card Disclosures

- Billing statements must include payoff information, including the number of months it will take to pay off the balance while making only minimum payments.
- Credit card solicitations must explain that numerous credit report inquiries can lower your credit score.

Source: Adapted from Miranda Marquit, "Credit Card Act of 2009: How It Affects You," http://personaldividends.com/credit-card-act-of-2009-how-it-affects-you/, accessed August 2015; LaToya Irby, "The Credit Cardholder's Bill of Rights Act of 2009: New Rules for the Credit Card Industry," http://credit.about.com/od/consumercreditlaws/a/creditbillright.htm, accessed August 2015.

6-2b Special Types of Bank Credit Cards

Today, in addition to standard, "plain vanilla" bank cards, you can obtain cards that offer rebates and special incentive programs, cards that are sponsored by nonprofit organizations, even credit cards aimed specifically at college and high-school students. We'll now look at several of these special types of bank credit cards, including reward cards, affinity cards, secured credit cards, and student credit cards.

Reward Cards

One of the fastest-growing segments of the bank card market is the **reward (co-branded) credit card**, which combines features of a traditional bank credit card

reward (co-branded) credit card
A bank credit card that combines features of a traditional bank credit card with an additional incentive, such as rebates and airline mileage.

with an incentive: cash, merchandise rebates, airline tickets, or even investments. About half of credit cards are rebate cards, and new types are introduced almost every day. Here are some of the many incentive programs.

- **Frequent flyer programs:** In this program, the cardholder earns free frequent flyer miles for each dollar charged on his or her credit card. These frequent flyer miles can then be used with airline-affiliated programs for free tickets, first-class upgrades, and other travel-related benefits. Examples include the Delta Sky Miles Card and United Airlines Mileage Plus *Visa* Card; with the American Express and Chase Travel Plus programs, the miles can be used on any one of numerous airlines.

- **Automobile rebate programs:** A number of credit cards allow the cardholder to earn annual rebates of up to 5 percent for new car purchases or leases and gas and auto maintenance purchases up to specified limits. For example, Citibank's ThankYou Preferred Card provides rebates that can be applied to the purchase of any vehicle brand, new or used. Cardholders can earn 1 percent on most all purchases (notably excluding gas) and 6 percent during the year. Most of the major car companies offer some kind of rewards-related credit card that can be used to buy a car or related items.

- **Other merchandise rebates:** An increasing number of companies are participating in bank card reward programs, including, for example, Norwegian Cruise Line, NASCAR, Starbucks, Marriott Hotels, and Hard Rock Café. Some major oil companies also offer rebate cards, where the cardholder earns credit that can be applied to the purchase of the company's gasoline. Several regional phone companies even offer rebates on phone calls. (A good site for finding information about these and other rebate card offers is **http://www.cardtrak.com**.)

Are rebate cards a good deal? Well, yes and no. To see if they make sense for you, evaluate these cards carefully by looking at your usage patterns and working out the annual cost of the cards before and after the rebate. Don't get so carried away with the gimmick that you lose sight of the total costs. Most incentive cards carry higher interest rates than regular bank cards do. These cards work best for those who can use the rebates, charge a lot, and don't carry high monthly balances.

Affinity Cards

affinity card
A standard bank credit card issued in conjunction with some charitable, political, or other nonprofit organization.

"Credit cards with a cause" is the way to describe **affinity cards**. These cards are nothing more than standard *Visa* or *MasterCard* that are issued in conjunction with a sponsoring group—most commonly some type of charitable, political, or professional organization. So-named because of the bond between the sponsoring group and its members, affinity cards are sponsored by such nonprofit organizations as Mothers Against Drunk Driving (MADD), the American Association of Individual Investors, the American Wildlife Fund, AARP, and the Special Olympics. In addition, they are issued by college and university alumni groups, labor organizations, religious and fraternal groups, and professional societies. In many cases, all you have to do is support the cause to obtain one of these cards (as in the case of MADD). In other cases, you'll

You Can Do It Now

Is Your Credit Card a Good Deal?

While your credit card might have been a good deal when you first got it, that may not still be the case. Go to a credit card Internet site like **http://www.creditcards.com**, which allows you to evaluate numerous credit cards by type. For example, you can focus on 0% APR, rewards, cash back, travel & airline, cards for students, and more types of cards. It's worth a look—you can do it now.

Behavior Matters

Behavioral Biases and Credit Card Use

Be wary of the minimum payment in your monthly credit card statement. Many people focus unduly or "anchor" on the stated minimum payment and as a result, pay a lower amount than they would otherwise. And the effect is obvious—they end up paying more interest.

Another tendency is to fall victim to "mental accounting," which refers to inappropriately viewing interdependent decisions as independent. For example, some people hold short-term, low-yield investments and costly credit card debt at the same time. It would obviously make sense to liquidate the investments and use the proceeds to pay off the credit card debt, which reduces interest charges. But many people don't do this because they view these as separate, unrelated transactions.

You should always consider how your financial decisions relate to one another and take into account common behavioral biases like anchoring and mental accounting, especially as they relate to managing credit card debt.

have to belong to a certain group in order to get one of their cards (for example, be a graduate of the school or member of a particular professional group to qualify).

Why even bother with one of these cards? Well, unlike traditional bank cards, affinity cards make money for the group backing the card as well as for the bank, because the sponsoring groups receive a share of the profits (usually 0.5 percent to 1 percent of retail purchases made with the card). So, for the credit cardholder, it's a form of "painless philanthropy." But to cover the money that goes to the sponsoring organization, the cardholder usually pays higher fees or higher interest costs. Even so, some may view these cards as a great way to contribute to a worthy cause. Others, however, may feel it makes more sense to use a traditional credit card and then write a check to their favorite charity.

Secured Credit Cards

secured (collateralized) credit cards
A type of credit card that's secured with some form of collateral, such as a bank CD.

You may have seen the ad on TV where the announcer says that no matter how bad your credit, you can still qualify for one of their credit cards. The pitch may sound too good to be true; and in some respects it is, because there's a catch. Namely, the credit is "secured"—meaning that you have to put up *collateral* in order to get the card! These are so-called **secured** or **collateralized credit cards**, where the amount of credit is determined by the amount of liquid collateral you're able to put up. These cards are targeted at people with no credit or bad credit histories, who don't qualify for conventional credit cards. Issued as *Visa* or *MasterCard*, they're like any other credit card except for the collateral. To qualify, a customer must deposit a certain amount (usually $500 or more) into a 12- to 18-month certificate of deposit that the issuing bank holds as collateral. The cardholder then gets a credit line equal to the deposit. If the customer defaults, the bank has the CD to cover its losses. By making payments on time, it's hoped that these cardholders will establish (or reestablish) a credit history that may qualify them for a conventional (unsecured) credit card. Even though fully secured, these cards still carry annual fees and finance charges that are equal to, or greater than, those of regular credit cards.

Student Credit Cards

student credit card
A credit card marketed specifically to college-students.

Some large banks, through their *Visa* and *MasterCard* programs, have special credit cards that target college students (in some cases, even high-school students). These **student credit cards** often come packaged with special promotional programs that

FINANCIAL PLANNING TIPS

Choosing a Credit Card

You'll get the best credit card for you by considering the following factors:

• **Spending habits.** How do you plan to use the card? If you'll pay off the card's balance every month, then the interest rate doesn't matter. Thus, just look for a card with no annual fee and a grace period that makes it easy to stay current. In contrast, if you're going to carry a balance, then find a card with the lowest interest rate *and* a low introductory rate. If you will use the card only for emergencies, get the lowest interest rate you can find and low or no fees.

• **Type of interest rate.** The annual percentage rate (APR) can be fixed or variable, which means adjusted relative to another rate such as prime. Are you comfortable with the prospect that the interest rate you pay could vary?

• **Credit limit.** Your credit history will determine how much the card will let you borrow. Be careful not to get a card with such a low credit limit that you could frequently max it out, which can hurt your credit score.

• **Fees and penalties.** Card issuers often charge fees for balance transfers, cash advances, exceeding your credit limit, or for making payments by phone. Compare the fees on cards to make sure that you get a card with reasonable charges. And don't pay extra for rewards programs, which often can be had for free.

• **Balance computation method.** If you plan to carry a balance, it's important to know how the finance charge is calculated. The most common approach is the average daily balance (ADB), which adds the daily balances and then divides by the number of days in the billing cycle. Avoid cards that compute the balance using two billing cycles because that approach increases financing fees.

• **Incentives.** Some card issuers offer reward programs to encourage their customers to use the card. If you plan to make the purchases anyway and don't have to pay extra for the card, this can be a useful benefit. Make sure the program offers flexibility, such as cash or travel, benefits that you will actually use, and benefits that are easy to earn and to redeem. Watch out for program restrictions, and note whether rewards expire and if there are limits on the benefits that you can earn.

Source: Adapted from Pat Curry, "6 Things to Consider before Choosing a Credit Card," http://www.creditcards.com/credit-card-news/help/6-consider-before-choosing-picking-credit-card-6000.php, accessed August 2015.

©SEYOMEDO/SHUTTERSTOCK.COM

are meant to appeal to this segment of the market—such as free music, movie tickets, and the like. Some even offer special discounts on pizzas, clothing, computer software, and so on. Except for these features, there's really nothing unusual about these cards or their terms. Most simply require that you be enrolled in a two- or four-year college or university and have some source of income, whatever that may be. In particular, they usually *do not require* any parental or guardian guarantees, nor do they require that you hold a full-time (or even a part-time) job.

So what's in it for the card issuers? While they know that most college students don't earn much money, they also know that's likely to change after they graduate—which is why they're so willing to offer the cards. Their logic seems to be that students obviously have some source of income and are going to be spending money anyway, so why not spend it with one of their credit cards? From the student's perspective, these cards not only offer convenience but are also great for building up a solid credit history. Just *remember to use them responsibly*; that's the way to get the most from these cards—or any other form of credit, for that matter!

6-2c Retail Charge Cards

Retail charge cards are the second-largest category of credit card and are issued by department stores, oil companies, car rental agencies, and so on. These cards are popular with merchants because they build consumer loyalty and enhance sales; consumers like them because they offer a convenient way to shop. These cards carry a preset credit limit—a line of credit—that varies with the creditworthiness of the cardholder.

This form of credit is most common in department and clothing stores and other high-volume outlets, where customers are likely to make several purchases each month. Most large oil companies also offer charge cards that allow customers to buy gas and oil products, *but they're expected to pay for such purchases in full upon receipt of the monthly bill.* However, to promote the sale of their more expensive products, oil companies frequently offer revolving credit for use in purchasing items such as tires, batteries, and accessories. Many families have—and regularly use—five or six different retail charge cards. Interest on most retail charge cards is typically fixed at 1.5 percent to 1.85 percent monthly, or 18 percent to 22 percent per year. These cards are generally more expensive than bank credit cards.

6-2d Debit Cards

It looks like a credit card, it works like a credit card, it even has the familiar *MasterCard* and *Visa* credit card markings. But it's not a *credit* card—rather, it's a *debit* card. Simply put, a debit card provides direct access to your checking account and thus *works like writing a check.* For example, when you use a debit card to make a purchase, the amount of the transaction is charged directly to your checking account. Using a debit card isn't the same thing as buying on credit. It may appear that you're charging it, but actually *you're paying with cash.* Accordingly, there are no finance charges to pay.

Debit cards are becoming more popular, especially with consumers who want the convenience of a credit card but not the high cost of interest that comes with them. In fact, in 2006, debit card use exceeded credit card use for the first time. Debit cards are accepted at most establishments displaying the *Visa* or *MasterCard* logo but function as an alternative to writing checks. If you use a debit card to make a purchase at a department store or restaurant, the transaction will show up on your next monthly *checking account* statement. Needless to say, to keep your records straight, you should enter debit card transactions directly into your checkbook ledger as they occur and treat them as withdrawals, or checks, by subtracting them from your checking account balance. Debit cards can also be used to gain access to your account through 24-hour teller machines or ATMs—which is the closest thing to a cash advance that these cards have to offer.

A big disadvantage of a debit card, of course, is that it doesn't provide a line of credit. In addition, it can cause overdraft problems if you fail to make the proper entries to your checking account or inadvertently use it when you think you're using a credit card. Also, some debit card issuers charge a transaction fee or a flat annual fee; and some *merchants* may even charge you just for using your debit card. On the plus side, a debit card enables you to avoid the potential credit problems and high costs of credit cards. Further, it's as convenient to use as a credit card. In fact, if convenience is the major reason you use a credit card, you might want to consider switching to a debit card for at least some transactions, especially at outlets such as gas stations that give discounts for cash purchases and consider a debit card to be as good as cash.

Another difference between debit and credit cards involves the level of protection for the user when a card is lost or stolen. When a credit card is lost or stolen, federal banking laws state that the cardholder is not liable for any fraudulent charges if the loss or theft is reported before that card is used. If reported after the card is used, the cardholder's maximum liability is $50. Unfortunately, *this protection does not extend to debit cards typically.* Instead, your liability resulting from a lost or stolen debit card is limited to between $50 and $500, "depending on the circumstances of the loss." In practice, most banks provide the same level of protection for debit cards as for credit cards, but check with your bank to be sure.

Prepaid Cards

prepaid card
A plastic card with a magnetic strip or microchip that stores the amount of money the purchaser has to spend and from which is deducted the value of each purchase.

Tired of fumbling for change to buy a candy bar from a vending machine or to use a pay phone? Buy a **prepaid card** and your pockets won't jingle with coins anymore. Or you can use a smartphone app that effectively provides a prepaid card for purchases at coffee shop chains and the like. These "smart cards" can now be used to purchase a variety of items—phone calls, coffee, meals in some employee cafeterias, vending machine snacks—and their use is increasing. You pay a fixed amount, which is then stored on either a magnetic strip or rechargeable microchip on the card. Each time you make a purchase, the amount is electronically deducted from the card. The popularity of these "electronic wallets" is increasing, as consumers and merchants alike find them convenient. And they're likely to become even more popular, since the microchips now being embedded in these smart cards can be used not only to execute

FINANCIAL PLANNING TIPS

Risky Places to Use Your Debit Card

Yes, debit cards are convenient to use and generally accepted by most establishments. But unlike credit cards, debit cards provide a thief with direct access to your checking account. If you find a fraudulent charge on your credit card bill, you can just decline or dispute the charge. In contrast, by the time you find a fraudulent charge on your debit card, your money—not the bank's money—is already gone, and it's up to *you* to get it back, not the bank. While it usually takes only a few days to deal with fraudulent credit card transactions, it can take months to get your money back from fraudulent debit transactions.

You are most vulnerable to debit card fraud in the following situations:

• **Be careful using outdoor ATMs.** "Skimming" is the capturing of card information by a magnetic strip reader. Such skimmers can be placed over the real card slots at ATMs. Watch for apparently beaten-up or old-looking ATMs, which might indicate that a skimmer has been added. Surprisingly, outdoor ATMs are one of the most dangerous places to use a debit card. Public places provide criminals with the ability to add skimmers, point cameras at the ATM, or to even watch transactions with

binoculars. It's much safer to use ATMs inside retail stores or other well-lighted, high-traffic areas.

• **Protect your personal identification number (PIN) at gas stations.** Gas stations are another vulnerable spot for using debit cards. Given that there's not much supervision, it's easy for a criminal to install a skimmer or to point a camera at the gas pump. Credit cards are much safer to use.

• **The Internet is a dangerous place to use a debit card.** Your debit card information is vulnerable to capture at many points: malware could be on your computer, your data could be intercepted by wireless eavesdropping on the way to the vendor, or your merchant's database could be compromised. The site may say it's safe, but so what? You have no idea how many people are handling your private debit card data, or who they are.

• **Some restaurants keep debit card data on file.** And restaurants routinely take your card out of your sight to process a transaction, which creates the opportunity for someone to inappropriately keep the information. Ethical or not, few small businesses take adequate steps to protect your private data.

Source: Adapted from Claes Bell, "4 Risky Places to Swipe Your Debit Card," http://www.bankrate.com/finance/checking/risky-places-swipe-debit-card-1.aspx, accessed August 2015.

transactions but also to store such things as electronic plane tickets or theater tickets. It's also easier to control Internet fraud, because the cards have electronic readers that plug easily into your computer for authenticity verification.

Prepaid cards and comparable smartphone apps are a lot like *debit cards.* Each time you use one, you're actually debiting the amount purchased to what you have stored on the card (or in your checking account). But don't confuse prepaid cards with prepaid *credit cards,* which you can use again and again. With prepaid cards, once the card is used up, you either toss it or get it recharged—there's no line of credit here, and no monthly bills with their minimum monthly payments.

6-2e Revolving Credit Lines

revolving lines of credit

A type of open account credit offered by banks and other financial institutions that can be accessed by writing checks against demand deposit or specially designated credit line accounts.

Revolving lines of credit are offered by banks, brokerage houses, and other financial institutions. These credit lines normally don't involve the use of credit cards. Rather, they're accessed by writing checks on regular checking accounts or specially designated credit line accounts. They are a form of open account credit and often represent a far better deal than credit cards, not only because they offer more credit but also because they can be a lot less expensive. And there may even be a tax advantage to using one of these other kinds of credit. These lines basically provide their users with ready access to borrowed money (i.e., cash advances) through revolving lines of credit. The three major forms of open (non-credit card) credit are overdraft protection lines, unsecured personal lines of credit, and home equity credit lines.

Overdraft Protection

overdraft protection line

A line of credit linked to a checking account that allows a depositor to overdraw the account up to a specified amount.

An **overdraft protection line** is simply a line of credit linked to a checking account that enables a depositor to overdraw his or her checking account up to a predetermined limit. These lines are usually set up with credit limits of $500 to $1,000, but they can be for as much as $10,000 or more. The consumer taps this line of credit by writing a check. If that particular check happens to overdraw the account, the overdraft protection line will automatically advance funds in an amount necessary to put the account back in the black. In some cases, overdraft protection is provided by *linking*

FINANCIAL PLANNING TIPS

Debit Card Signature Transactions: The Best of Both Worlds

When you put a debit card in the reader, you don't have to press the "debit" button and enter your PIN (a PIN transaction). Instead, you can choose "credit" and sign the receipt (a signature transaction). The benefits of doing so are:

• *Avoid fees.* While some banks charge for PIN transactions, they typically do not charge for signature transactions.

• *Reward points.* You're more likely to get reward points on a signature than on a PIN transaction.

• *Liability protection.* Signature transactions go through credit card networks that provide some fraud protection.

PIN transactions are processed through electronic funds transfer systems that don't provide liability protection.

If you use a debit transaction, your money will be taken out of your account the same day. However, if you use credit, your money will not be removed for two or three days.

So why would you ever do a debit PIN transaction? If you want cash back, you should use a debit PIN transaction rather than using the ATM of another bank. Otherwise, both the ATM and your bank will charge you more than enough to offset any benefit from signing for the transaction.

the bank's credit card to your checking account. These arrangements act like regular overdraft lines except that, when the account is overdrawn, the bank automatically taps your credit card line and transfers the money into your checking account. It's treated as a cash advance from your credit card, but the result is the same as a regular overdraft protection line; it automatically covers overdrawn checks.

If you're not careful, you can quickly exhaust this type of credit by writing a lot of overdraft checks. As with any line of credit, there's a limit to how much you can obtain. Be careful with such a credit line, and by all means, *Don't use it to routinely overdraw your account!* Doing so on a regular basis is a signal that you're probably mismanaging your cash and/or living beyond your budget. It's best to view an overdraft protection line strictly as an *emergency* source of credit—and any funds advanced should be repaid as quickly as possible.

Unsecured Personal Lines

Another form of revolving credit is the **unsecured personal credit line**, which basically makes a line of credit available to an individual on an as-needed basis. In essence, it's a way of borrowing money from a bank, S&L, credit union, savings bank, or brokerage firm any time you wish and without going through all the hassle of setting up a new loan.

Here's how it works. Suppose you apply for and are approved for a personal line of credit at your bank. Once you've been approved and the credit line is established, you'll be issued *checks* that you can write against it. If you need a cash advance, all you need to do is write a check (against your credit line account) and deposit it into your checking account. Or, if you need the money to buy some big-ticket item—say, an expensive personal electronics—you can just make the credit line check out to the dealer and, when it clears, it will be charged against your unsecured personal credit line as an advance. (While these credit line checks look and "spend" just like regular checks, they are not channeled through your normal checking account.) Personal lines of credit are usually set up for minimums of $2,000 to $5,000 and often amount to $25,000 or more. As with an overdraft protection line, once an advance is made, repayment is set up on a monthly installment basis. Depending on the amount outstanding, repayment is normally structured over a period of two to five years; to keep the monthly payments low, larger amounts of debt are usually given longer repayment periods.

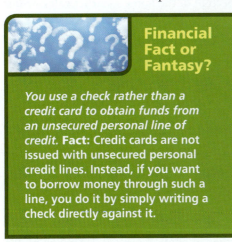

Financial Fact or Fantasy?

You use a check rather than a credit card to obtain funds from an unsecured personal line of credit. **Fact:** Credit cards are not issued with unsecured personal credit lines. Instead, if you want to borrow money through such a line, you do it by simply writing a check directly against it.

Although these credit lines do offer attractive terms to the consumer, they come with their share of problems, perhaps the biggest of which is how easily cash advances can be obtained. These lines also normally involve *substantial* amounts of credit and are nearly as easy to use as credit cards. This combination can have devastating effects on a family's budget if it leads to overspending or excessive reliance on credit. To be safe, these lines should be used only for emergency purposes or to make *planned credit expenditures.* Systematic repayment of the debt should be built into the budget, and every effort should be made to ensure that using this kind of credit will not overly strain the family finances.

Home Equity Credit Lines

Here's a familiar situation. A couple buys a home for $285,000; some 10 years later, it's worth $365,000. The couple now has an asset worth $365,000 on which all they owe is the original mortgage, which may now have a balance of, say, $220,000. The couple clearly has built up a substantial amount of equity in their home: $365,000 − $220,000 = $145,000. But how can they tap that equity without having to sell their home? The answer is a **home equity credit line**. Such lines are much like unsecured personal credit lines except that they're *secured with a second mortgage on the home.* These lines of credit allow you to tap up to 100 percent (or more) of the equity in your home by merely writing a check. Although some banks and financial institutions allow their customers to borrow up to 100 percent of the *equity* in their homes—or, in some cases, even more—most lenders set their maximum credit lines at 75 percent to 80 percent of the *market value* of the home, which reduces the amount of money they'll lend.

Here's how these lines work. Recall the couple in our example that has built up equity of $145,000 in their home—equity against which they can borrow through a home equity credit line. Assuming that they have a good credit record and using a 75 percent loan-to-market-value ratio, a bank would be willing to lend up to $273,750; that is, 75 percent of the value of the house is $0.75 \times \$365,000 = \$273,750$. Subtracting the $220,000 still due on the first mortgage, we see that our couple could qualify for a home equity credit line of $53,750. Note, in this case, that if the bank had been willing to lend the couple *100 percent of the equity* in their home, it would have given them a (much higher) credit line of $145,000, which is the difference between what the house is worth and what they still owe on it. Most lenders don't do this because it results in very large credit lines and, more importantly, it provides the lender with much less of a cushion should the borrower default. Even worse, from the borrowers' perspective, it provides access to a lot of relatively inexpensive credit, which can lead some homeowners to overextend themselves and thus encounter serious debt service problems down the road—even bankruptcy or loss of their home!

Home equity lines also have a tax feature that you should be aware of: the annual interest charges on such lines may be fully deductible for those who itemize. This is the only type of consumer loan that still qualifies for such tax treatment. According to the latest provisions of the tax code, a homeowner is allowed to *fully deduct the interest charges on home equity loans up to $100,000*, regardless of the original cost of the house or use of the proceeds. Indeed, the only restriction is that *the amount of total indebtedness on the house cannot exceed its fair market value*, which is highly unlikely because homeowners usually cannot borrow more than 75 percent to 80 percent of the home's market value anyway. (In effect, the interest on that portion of the loan that exceeds $100,000—or 100 percent of the home's market value, if this amount is lower—*cannot* be treated as a tax-deductible expense.)

> ### EXAMPLE: Tax Deductibility of Home Equity Credit Line Interest
>
> The homeowners in the prior discussion could take out the full amount of their credit line ($53,750), and every dime that they paid in interest would be tax deductible. If they paid, say, $3,225 in interest and if they were in the 28 percent tax bracket, then this feature would reduce their tax liability by some $903 (i.e., $3,225 $\times$ 0.28)—assuming, of course, that they itemize their deductions.

Not only do home equity credit lines offer shelter from taxes, they're also among *the cheapest forms of consumer credit*. For example, while the average rate on standard fixed rate credit cards in mid-2015 was about 13.01 percent, the average rate on home equity credit lines was considerably less than that, at about 4 percent depending on the amount of the line and the borrower's credit score. To see what that can mean to you as a borrower, assume you have $10,000 in consumer debt outstanding. If you had borrowed that money through a standard consumer loan at 13.01 percent, then you'd pay interest of $1,301 per year—none of which would be tax deductible. But borrow the same amount through a home equity credit line at 4.00 percent, and you'll pay only $400 in interest. And because that's all tax deductible, if you're in the 28 percent tax bracket, then the after-tax cost to you would be $400 \times (1 - 0.28) = \$288.00$. This is about a fifth of the cost of the other loan! So, which would you rather pay for a $10,000 loan: $1,301 or $288.00? That's really not a tough decision, and it explains why these lines have become so popular and are today one of the fastest-growing forms of consumer credit.

Home equity credit lines are offered by a variety of financial institutions, from banks and S&Ls to major brokerage houses. All sorts of credit terms and credit lines are available, and most of them carry repayment periods of 10 to 15 years, or longer. Perhaps most startling, however, is the maximum amount of credit available under these lines—indeed, $100,000 figures are not at all unusual. And it's precisely because of the enormous amount of money available that this form of credit should be used with caution. *The fact that you have equity in your home does not necessarily mean that you have the cash flow necessary to service the debt that such a credit line imposes.* Remember that your house is the collateral. If you can't repay the loan, you could lose your home! At the minimum, paying for major expenditures through a home equity credit line should be done only after you have determined that you can afford the purchase and the required monthly payments will fit comfortably within your budget. Equally important, don't be tempted to use a 15-year home equity credit line to finance, say, a new car that you may be driving for only 5 or 6 years—the last thing you want to be doing is paying for that car 8 to 10 years after you've traded it in. If a 15-year loan is the only way you can afford the car, then face it: you can't afford the car!

And Then There Are These Other Lenders ...

FINANCIAL ROAD SIGN

Various "shadow" lenders exist outside of the traditional banking system. They are most commonly used by low-income consumers who do not have good enough credit histories to borrow money from traditional lenders. These alternative lenders tend to have two sobering common characteristics: high interest rates and high fees. Here are some example loans:

- *Payday Loans*
  In the average loan, a consumer borrows $350 for 14 days and writes the lender a check for $402.50. The lender agrees to hold the check until the next payday in two weeks. While this might seem like a 15 percent interest rate, the annual percentage rate is actually almost 400 percent! The average borrower does this 10 times a year and is indebted to the lender for 199 days. So the average borrower is keeping the loan open rather than paying it off after the first two weeks. About 12 million households borrow money with payday loans.

- *Pawnshops*
  Pawnshops offer loans that are secured by personal property as collateral. Consumers who cannot get a loan from a bank will often borrow against jewelry, electronics, and precious metals. The loans are typically for 30 to 45 days and are often for less than $100. If the loan and fees are paid by the deadline, the property is returned. Yet the finance charges range from 5 to 25 percent *per month,* depending on state regulations. Annual interest rates of 100 percent are not unusual.

- *Car Title Loans*
  Car title loans use your car as collateral to secure a short-term loan for a fraction of the value of the car. If the borrower misses a payment, doesn't pay the fees, or doesn't pay the interest and principal on the loan by the end of the term, the car could be sold or repossessed. The average loan is for about 30 days and the annual percentage rate can approach 300 percent!

The high fees and interest rate costs make the above alternative loan sources extremely expensive. Proper planning and building a good credit history should allow you to avoid them.

Source: Payday loan statistics and example obtained from Consumer Financial Protection Bureau, http://files.consumerfinance.gov/f/201304_cfpb_payday-factsheet.pdf, accessed August 2015.

6-3 OBTAINING AND MANAGING OPEN FORMS OF CREDIT

Consumers love to use their charge cards. In 2014, *Visa* alone handled about $7.3 trillion in transactions. Consumers find credit and debit cards more convenient than cash or checks, and the number of other benefits (e.g., rebates and frequent flyer miles) continues to grow.

For the sake of convenience, people often maintain several different kinds of open credit. Nearly every household, for example, uses 30-day charge accounts to pay their utility bills, phone bills, and so on. In addition, most families have one or more retail charge cards and a couple of bank cards. And that's not all—families can also have revolving credit lines in the form of overdraft protection or a home equity line. When all these cards and lines are totaled together, a family conceivably can have tens of thousands of dollars of readily available credit. It's easy to see why consumer credit has become such a popular way of making relatively routine purchases. Although open account credit can increase the risk of budgetary overload, these accounts can also serve as a useful way of keeping track of expenditures.

6-3a Opening an Account

What do retail charge cards, bank credit cards, and revolving lines of credit all have in common? *Answer:* They all require you to go through a formal credit application. Let's now look at how you'd go about obtaining open forms of credit, including the normal credit application, investigation, and decision process. We'll focus our discussion on credit cards, but keep in mind that similar procedures apply to other revolving lines of credit as well.

The Credit Application

Credit applications are usually available at the store or bank involved. Sometimes they can be found at the businesses that accept these cards or obtained on request from the issuing companies. Exhibit 6.5 provides an example of a bank credit card application. As you can see, the type of information requested in a typical credit application covers little more than personal/family matters, housing, employment and income, and existing charge accounts. Such information is intended to give the lender insight about the applicant's creditworthiness. In essence, the lender is trying to determine whether the applicant has the *character* and *capacity* to handle the debt in a prompt and timely manner.

The Credit Investigation

Once the credit application has been completed and returned to the establishment issuing the card, it is subject to a **credit investigation**. The purpose is to evaluate the kind of credit risk that you pose to the lender (the party issuing the credit or charge card). So be

credit investigation An investigation that involves contacting credit references or corresponding with a credit bureau to verify information on a credit application.

EXHIBIT 6.5 **An Online Credit Card Application**

You can apply for many credit cards today right on the Internet. This credit application, like most, seeks information about the applicant's place of employment, monthly income, place of residence, credit history, and other financial matters that are intended to help the lender decide whether or not to extend credit.

Credit Card Application   YOUR BANK

Read Privacy Policy and Pricing and Terms for important information about rates, fees and other costs.

🔒 All application pages are secure.

* indicates a required field.

Application Information

Before completing the application, you should be able to answer "Yes" to the following statements by checking the boxes:

☐ Yes, my credit history is clear of bankruptcy.

☐ Yes, my credit history is clear of seriously delinquent accounts.

☐ Yes, I have NOT been denied credit within the last 6 months.

Personal Information

	Title	First* (Required)	M.I.	Last* (Required)

Name:

Residential Address Line 1:*   **Unit/Apt #:**

Residential Address Line 2:

City:*   **State:***

Zip Code:* -   **Home Phone:*** - -

Lived There:* [ ] Years [ ] Months

SSN:* - -

Date of Birth:* [ ] / [ ] / [ ] (MM/DD/YYYY)

Mother's Maiden Name:*

E-mail Address:

Employment Information

(If retired, note previous employer. If self-employed, note nature of business.)

Employer:*   **Position:***

Worked There:* [ ] years [ ] months

Work Phone:* - -

Financial Information

Alimony, child support, or separate maintenance income need not be revealed if you do not wish it to be considered as a basis for repaying this obligation.

Annual Household Income:* $ [ ] .00 (Please do not use commas.)

Please select the type(s) of bank account(s) you have:* [ ]

Select Residence:* [ ]

Monthly Rent or Mortgage:* $ [ ] .00 (Please do not use commas.)

JOHNNY LYE/SHUTTERSTOCK.COM

sure to fill out your credit application carefully. Believe it or not, they really do look at those things closely. The key items that lenders look at are how much money you make, how much debt you have outstanding and how well you handle it, and how stable you are (for example, your age, employment history, whether you own or rent a home, and so on). Obviously, the higher your income and the better your credit history, the greater the chance that your credit application will be approved.

During the credit investigation, the lender attempts to verify much of the information you've provided on the credit application. Obviously, false or misleading information will almost certainly result in outright rejection of your application. For example, the lender may verify your place of employment, level of income, current debt load, debt service history, and so forth. If you've lived in the area for several years and have established relations with a local bank, a call to your banker may be all it takes to confirm your creditworthiness. If you haven't established such bank relations—and most young people have not—the lender is likely to turn to the local credit bureau for a *credit report* on you.

The Credit Bureau

credit bureau
An organization that collects and stores credit information about individual borrowers.

A **credit bureau** is a type of reporting agency that gathers and sells information about individual borrowers. If, as is often the case, the lender doesn't know you personally, it must rely on a cost-effective way of verifying your employment and credit history. It would be far too expensive and time-consuming for individual creditors to confirm your credit application on their own, so they turn to credit bureaus that maintain fairly detailed credit files about you. Information in your file comes from one of three sources: creditors who subscribe to the bureau, other creditors who supply information at your request, and publicly recorded court documents (such as tax liens or bankruptcy records).

Contrary to popular opinion, your credit file does *not* contain everything anyone would ever want to know about you—there's nothing on your lifestyle, friends, habits, or religious or political affiliations. Instead, most of the information is pretty dull stuff and covers such things as name, social security number, age, number of dependents, employment record and salary data, public records of bankruptcies, and the names of those who have recently requested copies of your file.

Although one late credit card payment probably won't make much of a difference on an otherwise clean credit file, a definite pattern of delinquencies (consistently being 30 to 60 days late with your payments) or a personal bankruptcy certainly will. Unfortunately, poor credit traits will stick with you for a long time, because delinquencies remain on your credit file for as long as 7 years and bankruptcies for 10 years. An example of an actual credit bureau report (or at least a part of one) is provided in Exhibit 6.6. It shows the kind of information you can expect to find in one of these reports.

You Can Do It Now

How Does Your Credit Report Look?

When did you last check your credit report? It's a good idea to look at it at least once a year to know where you stand and to assure that there are no errors. The Fair Credit Reporting Act (FCRA) requires each of the national credit reporting firms—Experian, Equifax Credit Information Services, and TransUnion—to provide a free copy of your credit report once a year. These three companies have set up an Internet site where you can get your free annual report at **https://www.annualcreditreport.com**. Be careful about using other Internet sites that offer free credit reports, free credit monitoring, or free credit scores. Such sites are not authorized to meet the legal requirements of the FCRA and often have strings attached. Just go to the authorized site—you can do it now.

EXHIBIT 6.6   An Example of a Credit Bureau Report

Credit bureau reports have been revised and are now easier to understand. Notice that, in addition to some basic information, the report deals strictly with credit information—including payment records, past-due status, and types of credit.

Your Credit Report as of 04/09/2017

This Credit Report is available for you to view for 30 days. If you would like a current Credit Report, you may order another from MyEquifax.

ID # XXXXXXXXXXXX

• **Personal Data**

John Q. Public
2351 N 85th Ave
Phoenix, AZ 85037

Social Security Number: 022-22-2222
Date of Birth: 1/11/1980

• **Previous Address(es):**

133 Third Avenue
Phoenix, AZ 85037

• **Employment History**

Cendant Hospitality FR

	Location:	Employment Date:	Verified Date:
Cendant Hospitality FR	Phoenix, AZ	2/1/2005	1/3/2017

Previous Employment(s):

	Location:	Employment Date:	Verified Date:
SOFTWARE Support Hospitality Franch	Atlanta, GA	1/3/2003	1/3/2004

• **Public Records**

No bankruptcies on file
No liens on file
No foreclosures on file

• **Collection Accounts**

No collections on file.

• **Credit Information**

Company Name	Account Number and Whose Account	Date Opened	Last Activity	Type of Account and Status	High Credit	Items as of Date Reported Terms Balance		Past Due	Date Reported
Americredit Financial Services	40404XXXX JOINT ACCOUNT	03/2010	03/2016	Installment REPOSSESSION	$16933	$430	$9077	$128	3/2016

Prior Paying History
30 days past due 07 times; 60 days past due 05 times; 90+ days past due 03 times
INVOLUNTARY REPOSSESSION AUTO

Capital One	412174147128XXXXX INDIVIDUAL ACCOUNT	10/2014	01/2017	Revolving PAYS AS AGREED	$777	15	$514		01/2017

Prior Paying History
30 days past due 02 times; 60 days past due 1 times; 90+ days past due 00 times
CREDIT CARD

Desert Schools FCU	423325003406XXXXX INDIVIDUAL ACCOUNT	07/2003	06/2013	Revolving PAYS AS AGREED	$500		$0		07/2013

Prior Paying History
30 days past due 02 times; 60 days past due 00 times; 90+ days past due 00 times
ACCOUNT PAID   CLOSED ACCOUNT

• **Credit Inquiries**

Companies that Requested your Credit File

04/09/2017 EFX Credit Profile Online
06/30/2016 Automotive
01/18/2014 Desert Schools Federal C.U.
07/02/2013 Time Life, Inc.

Local credit bureaus (there are about a thousand of them) are established and mutually owned by local merchants and banks. They collect and store credit information on people living within the community and make it available, for a fee, to members who request it. Local bureaus are linked together nationally through one of the "big three" national bureaus—TransUnion, Equifax Credit Information Services, and Experian—each of which provides the mechanism for obtaining credit information from almost any place in the United States. Traditionally, credit bureaus did little more than collect and provide credit information; they neither analyzed the information nor used it to make final credit decisions. In 2006, however, the three major credit bureaus announced that they had jointly developed a new credit-scoring system, called *VantageScore*, that would incorporate data from all three bureaus—Equifax, Experian, and TransUnion. Thus, for the first time, each of the three national bureaus began assigning uniform credit ratings to individual credit files. The VantageScore system is supposed to simplify and enhance the credit-granting process, because all three bureaus will now be reporting, among other things, the same credit score—although they're still obligated to report other credit scores, such as the widely used FICO scores. Of course, whether adding still another credit score to the four or five that already exist actually simplifies matters or not remains to be seen. (We'll examine credit scores and FICO scores in more detail later in this text.)

Credit bureaus in the past were heavily criticized because of the large numbers of reporting errors they made and their poor record in promptly and efficiently correcting these errors. Fortunately, things have changed dramatically in recent years as the major credit bureaus have taken a more consumer-oriented approach. According to the amended Fair Credit Reporting Act, credit bureaus must provide you with low-cost copies of your own credit report and they must have toll-free phone numbers. Disputes must be resolved in 30 days and must take the consumer's documentation into account, not just the creditor's.

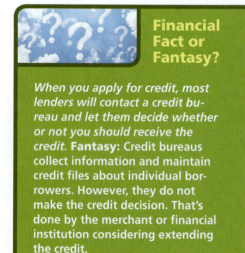

All Americans are entitled to receive *a free copy of their credit report once a year*. To get your free report, go to the Internet site set up by the Federal Trade Commission (FTC) at **http://www.annualcreditreport.com**. You should ensure that your credit report accurately reflects your credit history. The best way to do that is to obtain a copy of your own credit report and then go through it carefully. If you do find a mistake, let the credit bureau know immediately—and by all means, put it in writing. *Then request a copy of the corrected file to make sure that the mistake has been eliminated.* Most consumer advisors recommend that you review your credit files annually. Here are the Internet sites for the three national credit bureaus:

- Equifax Credit Information Services
  http://www.equifax.com
- TransUnion LLC Consumer Disclosure Center
  http://www.tuc.com
- Experian National Consumer Assistance Center
  http://www.experian.com

6-3b The Credit Decision

credit scoring
A method of evaluating an applicant's creditworthiness by assigning values to such factors as income, existing debts, and credit references.

Using the data provided by the credit applicant, along with any information obtained from the credit bureau, the store or bank must decide whether to grant credit. Very likely, some type of **credit scoring** scheme will be used to make the decision. An overall credit score is developed for you by assigning values to such factors as your annual income, whether you rent or own your home, number and types of credit cards you hold, level of your existing debts, whether you have savings accounts, and general credit references. Fifteen or 20 different factors may be considered, and each characteristic receives a score based on some predetermined standard. For example, if you're 26 years old, single, earn $32,500 a year (on a job that you've had for only two years), and rent an apartment, you might receive the following scores:

1. Age (25–30)	5 points
2. Marital status (single)	−2 points
3. Annual income ($30–35,000)	12 points
4. Length of employment (2 years or less)	4 points
5. Rent or own a home (rent)	0 points
	19 points

Based on information obtained from your credit application, similar scores would be assigned to another 10 to 15 factors.

In all cases, the stronger your personal traits or characteristics, the higher the score you'll receive. For instance, if you were 46 years old (rather than 26), you might receive 18 points for your age factor, being married rather than single would give you 9 points, and earning $75,000 a year would obviously be worth a lot more than earning $32,500! The idea is that the more stable you are *perceived* to be, the more income you make, the better your credit record, and so on, the higher the score you should receive. In essence, statistical studies have shown that certain personal and financial traits can be used to determine your creditworthiness. Indeed, the whole credit scoring system is based on extensive statistical studies that identify the characteristics to look at and the scores to assign.

The largest provider of credit scores is, by far, Fair Isaac & Co.—the firm that produces the widely used *FICO scores*. Unlike some credit score providers, *Fair Isaac uses only credit information in its calculations*. There's nothing in them about your age, marital status, salary, occupation, employment history, or where you live. Instead, FICO scores are derived from the following five major components, which are listed along with their respective weights: payment history (35 percent), amounts owed (30 percent), length of credit history (15 percent), new credit (10 percent), and types of credit used (10 percent). FICO scores, which are reported by all three of the major credit bureaus, range from a low of 300 to a max of 850. A representative reported distribution of FICO scores is as follows:

300–499	5.8%
500–549	8.4%
550–599	9.8%
600–649	10.2%
650–699	12.7%
700–749	16.3%
750–799	18.4%
800–850	18.6%

FICO scores are meant to be an indication of a borrower's credit risk; the higher the score, the lower the risk. While few, if any, credit decisions are based solely on FICO scores, you can be sure that higher scores are likely to result in lower interest rates on loans and, as a result, lower loan payments. For example, in mid-2015, if you were taking out a 30-year fixed-rate mortgage, you could expect to borrow at an interest rate of around 3.664 percent if you had a FICO score of 760–850, compared with 5.253 percent if your score was in the range of 620–639. That translates

into monthly mortgage payments of around $1,375 a month versus $1,657 a month. Granted, a lot more goes into a credit decision than a simple credit score. But as you can see, it definitely pays to keep your FICO score as high as possible.

6-3c Computing Finance Charges

Because card issuers don't know in advance how much you'll charge on your account, they cannot specify the dollar amount of interest you will be charged. But they can—and must, according to the Truth in Lending Act—disclose the *rate of interest* that they charge and their method of computing finance charges. This is the **annual percentage rate (APR)**, the true or actual rate of interest paid, which must include all fees and costs and be calculated as defined by law. Remember, it's your right as a consumer to know—and it is the lender's obligation to tell you—the dollar amount of charges (where applicable) and the APR on any financing you consider.

The amount of interest you pay for open credit depends partly on the method the lender uses to calculate the balances on which they apply finance charges. Most bank and retail charge card issuers use one of two variations of the **average daily balance (ADB) method**, which applies the interest rate to the ADB of the account over the billing period. The most common method (used by an estimated 95 percent of bank card issuers) is the *ADB, including new purchases*. Card issuers can also use an ADB method that *excludes* new purchases. Balance calculations under each of these methods are as follows:

- **ADB, including new purchases:** For each day in the billing cycle, take the outstanding balance, including new purchases, and subtract payments and credits; then divide by the number of days in the billing cycle.
- **ADB, excluding new purchases:** Same as the first method, but excluding new purchases.

These different calculations can obviously affect a card's credit balance, and therefore the amount of finance charges you'll have to pay. Also be aware that the finance charges on two cards with the same APR but different methods of calculating balances may differ dramatically. It's important to know the method your card issuer uses. The comparisons in Exhibit 6.7 show how the method used to calculate the ADB affects the amount of finance charges you pay. In the situation illustrated here, monthly finance charges are between $66 and $132. It is clear that carrying a balance on a credit card can be expensive and that the way in which the finance charge is calculated can be important.

annual percentage rate (APR)
The actual or true rate of interest paid over the life of a loan; includes all fees and costs.

average daily balance (ADB) method
A method of computing finance charges by applying interest charges to the ADB of the account over the billing period.

Consider how to calculate balances and finance charges under the most popular method, *the ADB including new purchases*. Assume that you have a FirstBank *Visa* card with a monthly interest rate of 1.5 percent. Your statement for the billing period extending from October 10, 2017, through November 10, 2017—a total of 31 days—show, that your beginning balance was $1,582, you made purchases of $750 on October 15 and $400 on October 22, and you made a $275 payment on November 6. Therefore, the outstanding balance for the first 5 days of the period (October 11 through 15) was $1,582; for the next 7 days (October 16 through 22), it was $2,332 ($1,582 + $750); for the next 15 days (October 23 through November 6), it was $2,732 ($2,332 + $400); and for the last 4 days (November 7 through November 10), it was $2,457 ($2,732 minus the $275 payment). We can now calculate the ADB using the procedure shown in Exhibit 6.8. Note that the outstanding balances are weighted by the number of days that the balance existed and then averaged (divided) by the number of days in the billing period. By multiplying the ADB of $2,420.71 by the 1.5 percent interest rate, we get a finance charge of $36.31.

Financial Fact or Fantasy?

Credit card issuers are required by truth-in-lending laws to use the average daily balance in your account when computing the amount of finance charges you owe. **Fantasy:** Truth in lending laws require only that lenders fully disclose the effective rate of interest being charged and the method used to compute finance charges. Lenders can choose the specific method used to calculate the balances on which they apply finance charges. The average daily balance method is the most widely used.

6-3d Managing Your Credit Cards

Congratulations! You have applied for and been granted a bank credit card, as well as a retail charge card from your favorite department store. You carefully reviewed the terms of the credit agreement and have at least a basic understanding of how finance charges are computed for each account. Now you must manage your accounts efficiently, which involves using the monthly statement to help you make the required payments on time, as well as to track purchases and returned items.

The Statement

If you use a credit card, you'll receive monthly statements similar to the sample bank card statement in Exhibit 6.9, showing billing cycle and payment due dates, interest rate, minimum payment, and all account activity during the current period. Retail charge cards have similar monthly statements, but without a section for cash advances. (Revolving line of credit lenders will also send you a monthly statement showing the amount borrowed, payments, and finance charges.) The statement summarizes your account activity: the previous balance (the amount of credit outstanding at the beginning of the month—not to be confused with past-due, or late, payments); new charges made (four, in this case) during the past month; any finance charges (interest) on the unpaid balance; the preceding period's payment; any other credits (such as those for returns); and the new balance (previous balance plus new purchases and finance charges, less any payments and credits).

Although merchandise and cash transactions are separated on the statement, the finance charge in each case is calculated at the rate of 1.5 percent per month (18 percent annually). This procedure works fine for illustration but it's a bit out of the ordinary, because most card issuers charge a higher rate for cash advances than for purchases. Note that the ADB method is used to compute the finance charge in this statement.

You should review your statements promptly each month. Save your receipts and use them to verify statement entries for purchases and returns *before* paying. If you find any errors or suspect fraudulent use of your card, first use the issuer's toll-free number to report any problems. Then always follow up *in writing* within 60 days of the postmark on the bill.

The way a credit card issuer calculates the ADB on which the consumer pays finance charges has a big effect on the amount of interest you actually pay, as this table demonstrates. Note that the Credit Card Act of 2009 prohibits the use of the two-cycle method.

Example: A consumer starts the first month with a zero *balance* and charges $1,000, of which he pays off only the minimum amount due (1/36 of balance due). The next month, he charges another $1,000. He then pays off the entire balance due. This same pattern is repeated three more times during the year. The interest rate is 19.8 percent.

	Annual Finance Charges
ADB (including new purchases):	$132.00
ADB (excluding new purchases):	$66.00

Source: Based on "How Do Credit Card Companies Determine the Balance on Which Interest Is Charged?" http://www.extension.org/faq/29098, accessed August 2015.

The average daily balance including new purchases is the method most widely used by credit card issuers to determine the monthly finance charge on an account.

	Number of Days (1)	**Balance (2)**	**Calculation (1) × (2) (3)**
	5	$1,582	$7,910
	7	$2,332	$16,324
	15	$2,732	$40,980
	4	$2,457	$9,828
Total	31		$75,042

$$\text{Average daily balance} = \frac{\$75,042}{31} = \$2,420.71$$

Finance charge: $2,420.71 × .015 = $36.31

Payments

minimum monthly payment
In open account credit, a minimum specified percentage of the new account balance that must be paid in order to remain current.

Credit card users can avoid *future* finance charges by paying the total new balance shown on their statement each month. For example, if the $534.08 total new balance shown in Exhibit 6.9 is paid by the due date of September 21, 2017, then no additional finance charges will be incurred. (The cardholder, however, is still liable for the $4.40 in finance charges incurred to date.) If cardholders cannot pay the total new balance, they can pay any amount that is equal to or greater than the **minimum monthly payment** specified on the statement. If they do this, however, they will incur

EXHIBIT 6.9	A Bank Credit Card Monthly Statement

Each month, a bank credit cardholder receives a statement that provides an itemized list of charges and credits, as well as a summary of previous activity and finance charges.

Please detach the above portion and return it with your payment to insure proper credit.

Bank Card Statement

Retain this statement for your records.

Account Number 123-XYZ-45678	Name(s) Mr. Scott Lataste Mrs. Emily Lataste	8-24-17 Statement Date	09-21-17 Payment Due Date

ACCOUNT ACTIVITY

			FINANCE CHARGE CALCULATION			This Month's Charge	
Previous Balance	203.64	Credit Status Your Credit Limit is:	Amounts Subject to Finance Charge			ENTIRE BAL.	
Payments −	119.89		A. *Average Daily Balance	293.25	4.40	1.5%	18.00%
Credits −	.00		B. *Cash Advance	.00	.00	Monthly Periodic Rate	Nominal Annual Rate
Subtotal	83.75	2000.00	C. *Loan Advance	.00	.00		
New Transaction +	445.93	Your Available Credit is:			4.40	18.00%	
Finance Charge +	4.40						
Late Charge +	.00		*Finance Charges explained on reverse side			Annual	
NEW BALANCE	534.08	1465.92			Finance Charge	Percentage Rate	

Mail Billing Inquiries to: Post Office Box 7890, Van Niles, California, 85258, or call 800/000-0000
For Inquiries on Past Due Accounts, Overlimits or Credit Line Increase, call 800/000-0000

Posted Mo./Day	Transaction Description or Merchant Name and Location		Purchase Mo./Day	Bank Reference Number	Purchases/ Advances/Debits	Payments Credits
8-08	AMERICA WEST AIRLINES	LOS ANGELES	07-25	850000008823395192	42.00	
8-13	HACIENDA MOTORS	COSTA MESA	08-05	015400018537022316	166.86	
8-15	RICOS RESTAURANT	PALM SPRG	08-10	114500018856161722	132.47	
8-12	PAYMENT—THANK YOU		08-11	4501000182MD02139		119.89
8-24	RENEES RESTAURANT	NEWPORT	08-13	114500068201632483	104.60	

Notice See reverse side for important information

					Total Debits	Total Credits
MIN. PAYMENT:	27.00	NEW BALANCE:	534.08		445.93	119.89

additional finance charges in the following month. Note that the account in Exhibit 6.9 has a minimum payment of 5 percent of the new balance, rounded to the nearest full dollar. As shown at the bottom of the statement, this month's minimum payment is $27.00 (i.e., $534.08 × 0.05 = $26.70 ≈ $27.00). This $27.00 works out to be a *principal payment* of $22.60; that is, $27.00 − $4.40 (interest charges) = $22.60. That's actually about 4.25 percent of the "new balance." Now if the new balance had been less than $200, the bank would have required a payment of $10 (which is the absolute minimum dollar payment) or of the total new balance, if less than $10. Cardholders who fail to make the minimum payment are considered to be in default on their account, and the bank issuing the card can take whatever legal action it deems necessary.

6-4 USING CREDIT WISELY

LG5, LG6

As we've discussed, credit cards and revolving lines of credit can simplify your life financially. Unfortunately, you can also get into real trouble unless you use them wisely. That's why you should carefully shop around to choose the right credit cards for your personal situation, understand the advantages and disadvantages of credit cards, learn how to resolve credit problems, and know how to avoid the ultimate cost of credit abuse—bankruptcy.

6-4a Shop Around for the Best Deal

They say it pays to shop around, and when it comes to credit cards, that's certainly true. With all the fees and high interest costs, it pays to get the best deal possible. So, where do you start? Most credit experts suggest the first thing you should do is step back and take a look at yourself. What kind of "spender" are you, and how do you pay your bills? In fact, no single credit card is right for everyone. If you pay off your card balance each month, then you'll want a card that's different from the one that's right for someone who carries a credit balance from month to month and may pay only the minimum due.

Regardless of which category you fall into, there are basically four card features to look for:

- Annual fees
- Rate of interest charged on account balance
- Length of the grace period
- Method of calculating balances

Now, if you normally pay your account balance in full each month, get a card with *no annual fees and a long grace period*. The rate of interest on the card is irrelevant, since you don't carry account balances from month to month anyway. In contrast, if you don't pay your account in full, then look for cards that charge *a low rate of interest on unpaid balances*. The length of the grace period isn't all that important here, but obviously, other things being equal, you're better off with low (or no) annual fees.

Sometimes, however, "other things aren't equal," and you have to decide between interest rates and annual fees. If you're not a big spender and don't build up big balances on your credit card (i.e., the card balance rarely goes above $400 or $500), then *avoid* cards with annual fees and get one with as *low* a rate of interest as possible. This situation often applies to college students. On the other hand, if you do carry big balances (say, $1,000 or more), then you'll probably be better off *paying an annual fee* (even a relatively high one) *to keep the rate of interest on the card as low as possible.*

The bottom line is: don't take the first credit card that comes along. Instead, get the one that's right for you. To do that, learn as much as you can about the credit cards you've been offered or are considering. Be sure to read (or at least review) the credit agreement, and look for information about annual fees, grace periods, interest rates, and how finance charges are calculated. Don't overlook all those other charges and fees you may be assessed if you're ever late with a payment or go over your credit limit. Also, if local credit card deals aren't great, you might consider cards that are offered nationally. To help you do that, look at publications like *Money* magazine and *Kiplinger's Personal Finance* magazine, whose respective Internet sites are located at **http://www.money.com** and **http://www.kiplinger.com**. These magazines and Internet sites regularly publish information about banks and other financial institutions that offer low-cost credit cards nationally; an example is given in Exhibit 6.10.

One final point: Some people spend a lot of time and energy shopping for deals, jumping from one card to another to take advantage of low introductory rates. Although a strategy like this may result in lower interest payments, it can backfire if the low rates rise significantly after the introductory period or if you miss a payment. A wiser approach is to shop around, check for better deals from time to time, and then *direct the rest of your energy toward working to reduce (or even eliminate) any monthly balances*.

6-4b Avoiding Credit Problems

As more places accept credit cards, and as shopping online becomes more widely accepted, the volume of credit card purchases has grown tremendously—and so has the level of credit card debt. As a result, it's not unusual to find people using credit cards to solve cash-flow problems. Even the most careful consumers occasionally find themselves with mounting credit card debt, especially after the year-end holiday buying season. The real problems occur when the situation is no longer temporary and the debt continues to increase. If overspending is not curtailed, then the size of the unpaid balance may seriously strain the budget. Essentially, people who let their credit balances build up are *limiting their future flexibility*. By using credit, they're actually committing a part of their future income to make payments on the debt.

Should You Switch Credit Cards?

Shopping for a better deal on a credit card can be confusing because card issuers frequently change their offers. Here's how to figure out if it's time to switch.

- Review your card terms about every six months. Visit the Internet site of the card issuer to learn of current offers for new customers. If it's better than what you have, call the company and ask for the better deal. They may be willing to offer you the same terms to keep your business.
- Compare offers from competing companies at one of the credit card sites mentioned in the chapter, such as **http://www.bankrate.com**.
- Know what you need. If you carry balances, you'll want a lower introductory rate; if you pay in full each month, look for ways to reduce fees or earn rewards.

EXHIBIT 6.10 | **Average Interest Rates for Different Types of Credit Cards**

Information about low-cost credit cards is readily available in the financial media. Pay particular attention to the *cards with the lowest rates* (probably best for people who regularly carry an account balance) and *no-fee cards with the lowest rates* (probably best for people who pay their accounts in full each month).

Type of Credit Card	Average Annual Percentage Rate (APR)
Balance transfer cards	14.12%
Cash back cards	15.27%
Low interest cards	11.62%

These rates are as of August 5, 2015; rates are adjustable. Banks sometimes offer lower introductory rates, many charge no annual fee, and the cards vary in credit score requirements. Most of these cards have variable rates. Data compiled from http://www.bankrate.com, accessed August 2015.

The best way to avoid credit problems is to be disciplined when using credit. Reduce the number of cards you carry, and don't rush to accept the tempting preapproved credit card offers filling your mailbox. A wallet full of cards can work against you in two ways. Obviously, the ready availability of credit can tempt you to overspend and incur too much credit card debt. But there's another, less obvious, danger: when you apply for a loan, lenders look at the *total amount* of credit you have available as well as at the outstanding balances on your credit cards. If you have a lot of unused credit capacity, it may be harder to get a loan because of lender concerns that you could become overextended. Two cards is the most that financial advisors suggest you carry: perhaps one rebate card, if you charge enough to make the benefit worthwhile, and a low-rate card for purchases you want to repay over time. And should you decide to start using a new card (because their offer was just too good to pass up), then *get rid of one of your old cards*—physically cut up the old card and inform the issuer in writing that you're canceling your account.

Suppose that, despite all your efforts, you find that your credit card balances are higher than you'd like and you anticipate having problems reducing them to a more manageable level. The first thing you can do is stop making any new charges until you pay off (or pay down) the existing balances. Then, commit to a repayment plan. One good strategy is to pay off the highest-interest cards first, keeping the original payment rather than reducing it as your balance drops. Or, even better, pay more than the minimum—even if it's just $10 more. You'd be surprised how much difference that makes.

You may also want to consider transferring your balances to a card with a low introductory rate and paying off as much as possible before the rate increases. Another option is to consolidate all your credit card debt and pay it off as quickly as possible using a lower-rate loan, such as a revolving personal line of credit. This can be a risky strategy, however. If you continue to be undisciplined about repaying your debts, then you could end up with one big credit problem instead of a bunch of small ones! Even worse, cleaning up your credit card debt may tempt you to start the credit card borrowing cycle all over again, putting you even farther behind than you were before.

6-4c Credit Card Fraud

Despite the efforts of law enforcement officials, plastic has become the vehicle of choice among crooks as a way of defrauding and stealing from both you and the merchants who honor credit cards. No doubt about it: credit card crime is a big business, with estimated losses in the United States at billions of dollars a year. Stolen account numbers are the biggest source of credit card fraud. Be especially careful where you use your credit card on the Internet. Most, if not all, of the big-name sites are about as secure as they can get, but when you go to one of the less reputable sites, you could be asking for trouble by giving them your credit card number!

Basically, "it's us against them," and the first thing you have to understand is that the credit card you're carrying around is a powerful piece of plastic. To reduce your chances of being defrauded, here are some suggestions:

- Never, ever, give your account number to people or organizations *who call you*. No matter how legitimate it sounds, if you didn't initiate the call then don't give out the information!
- If you initiated the call, it's acceptable to give your account number over the phone when ordering or purchasing something from a major catalog house, airline, hotel, and so on, but don't do it for any other reason.
- Use the same precautions *when purchasing something over the Internet* with your credit card—don't do it *unless* you're dealing at the site of a major retailer who uses state-of-the-art protection against fraud and thievery.
- When paying for something *by check*, don't put your credit card account number on the check and don't let the store clerk do it—show the clerk a check guarantee card (if you have one), a driver's license, or some other form of identification—but *not* your Social Security number.
- Don't put your phone number or address (and certainly not your Social Security number) on credit/charge slips, even if the merchant asks for it—they're *not* entitled to it.
- When using your card to make a purchase, *always keep your eye on it* (so the clerk can't make an extra imprint). If the clerk makes a mistake and wants to make another imprint, ask for the first imprint, and tear it up on the spot.
- Always draw a line on the credit slip through any blank spaces above the total, so the amount can't be altered.
- *Destroy* all old credit slips. And when you receive your monthly statement, be sure to *go over it promptly* to make sure there are no errors. If you find a mistake, call or send a letter immediately, detailing the error.
- If you lose a card or it's stolen, *report it to the card issuer immediately*—the most you're ever liable for with a lost or stolen card is $50 (per card), but if you report the loss *before* the card can be used, you won't be liable for any unauthorized charges (the phone number to call is listed on the back of your statement).
- Destroy old cards or those that you no longer use.

6-4d Bankruptcy: Paying the Price for Credit Abuse

It certainly isn't an overstatement to say that during the 1980s and 1990s, *debt was in*! In fact, the explosion of debt that has occurred since 1980 is almost incomprehensible. The national debt rose from less than a trillion dollars when the 1980s began to about $18.7 trillion by mid-2015. Businesses also took on debt rapidly. Not to be outdone, consumers were using credit like there was no tomorrow. So it should come as no surprise that when you couple this heavy debt load with a serious economic recession like that in 2009, you have all the ingredients of a real financial crisis. In 2014 about 910,000 people filed for **personal bankruptcy**.

When too many people are too heavily in debt, a recession (or some other economic reversal) can come along and push many of them over the edge. But let's face it, the recession is not the main culprit here; the only way a recession can push you over the edge is if you're already sitting on it! The real culprit is excess debt. Some people simply abuse credit by taking on more than they can afford. Maybe they're pursuing a lifestyle beyond their means, or perhaps an unfortunate event—like the loss of a job—occurs.

Whatever the cause, sooner or later, these debtors start missing payments and their credit rating begins to deteriorate. Unless corrective actions are taken, this is followed by repossession of property and, eventually, even bankruptcy. These people

personal bankruptcy
A form of legal recourse open to insolvent debtors, who may petition a court for protection from creditors and arrange for the orderly liquidation and distribution of their assets.

FINANCIAL PLANNING TIPS

Protect Against Identity Theft

Watch out for the following methods that thieves use to get your information:

- **Dumpster diving.** Don't leave bills or anything with personal information in your trash. Shredding such documents is a good idea.

- **Skimming.** Watch for unusual "additions" to credit and debit card readers that can steal your numbers.

- **Phishing.** Thieves can pretend to be financial institutions or companies and can use Internet pop-ups or send e-mail messages that ask you to disclose personal information.

- **Changing your address.** Thieves can re-route your bills to them by completing a change of address form.

- **Old-fashioned stealing.** Simple still works. Thieves continue to steal wallets and purses, mail, and new checks or tax information. Also, they sometimes bribe store employees to provide access to your personal information.

- **Pretexting.** Thieves can obtain your personal information from financial institutions, telephone companies, and other sources under false pretenses.

So what should you do? The FTC recommends the following:

- **Deter** thefts by protecting your information. Be aware of the above mentioned ways in which information is stolen.

- **Detect** suspicious activity by consistently checking your financial and billing statements.

- **Defend** against identity theft as soon as you suspect a possible problem. Place a "fraud alert" on your credit reports by contacting one of the consumer reporting companies noted earlier in this chapter (Experian, TransUnion, or Equifax). Contact the security departments of each company where an unauthorized account was opened.

Source: Adapted from http://www.finra.org/web/groups/sai/@sai/documents/sai_original_content/p036799.pdf, accessed August 2015.

have reached the end of a long line of deteriorating financial affairs. Households that cannot resolve serious credit problems on their own need help from the courts. Two of the most widely used legal procedures (employed by well over 95 percent of those who file for bankruptcy) are (1) the Wage Earner Plan and (2) straight bankruptcy.

Wage Earner Plan

Wage Earner Plan
An arrangement for scheduled debt repayment over future years that is an alternative to straight bankruptcy; used when a person has a steady source of income and there is a reasonable chance of repayment within 3 to 5 years.

The **Wage Earner Plan** (as defined in *Chapter 13* of the U.S. Bankruptcy Code) is a workout procedure involving some type of debt restructuring—usually by establishing a debt repayment schedule that's more compatible with the person's income. It may be a viable alternative for someone who has a steady source of income, not more than $1,149,525 in secured debt and $383,175 in unsecured debt, and a reasonably good chance of being able to repay the debts in three to five years. A majority of creditors must agree to the plan, and interest charges, along with late-payment penalties, are waived for the repayment period. Creditors usually will go along with this plan because they stand to lose more in a straight bankruptcy. After the plan is approved, the individual makes periodic payments to the court, which then pays off the creditors. Throughout the process, the individual retains the use of, and keeps title to, all of his or her assets.

Straight Bankruptcy

Straight bankruptcy, which is allowed under Chapter 7 of the bankruptcy code, can be viewed as a legal procedure that results in "wiping the slate clean and starting anew." *About 70 percent of those filing personal bankruptcy choose this route.* However, straight bankruptcy does not eliminate all the debtor's obligations, nor does the debtor necessarily lose all of his or her assets. For example, the debtor must make certain tax payments and keep up alimony and child-support payments but is allowed to retain certain payments from Social Security, retirement, veterans', and disability benefits. The debtor also may retain the equity in a home (based on established exemptions), a car (once again, based on established exemptions), and some other personal assets. Minimum values of what you can keep are established by federal regulations, though state laws are generally much more generous regarding the amount the debtor is allowed to keep. The choice of filing for bankruptcy under federal versus state regulations depends on the debtor's assets.

6-4e Using Credit Counselor Services

Filing for bankruptcy is a serious step that should be taken only as a last resort. For one thing, it's going to stick with you for a long time (it will stay in your credit file for up to 10 years) and certainly won't help your chances of getting credit in the future. It often makes more sense to work problems out before they get so bad that bankruptcy is the only option. Some people can do that on their own, but in many cases, it may be a good idea to seek the help of a qualified *credit counselor.*

credit counselor
A professional financial advisor who assists overextended consumers in repairing budgets for both spending and debt repayment.

Credit counselors work with a family to set up a budget and may even negotiate with creditors to establish schedules for repaying debts. The counseling service will often go so far as to collect money from the debtor and distribute it to creditors. Some private firms will, for a fee, act as intermediaries between borrowers and creditors and provide counseling services. These counselors generally try to reduce the size of payments, the size of outstanding debt, or both. However, their fees can run as much as 20 percent of the amount owed.

Another option is a nonprofit agency, such as those affiliated with the nationwide network of Consumer Credit Counseling Services (CCCS) (**http://credit.org/cccs/**). You'll get many of the services that private agencies provide, but at a lower cost. Of course, as with any financial advisor, you should check out a credit counselor's credentials, fees, services provided, and track record *before* using his or her services. But before even going to a credit counselor, try contacting your creditors yourself. You may be able to work out a deal on your own, especially if you have just a few lenders and need only two to three months to catch up. If, however, you have six or more creditors, then you should probably see a credit counselor. Make sure to ask your counselor for several *debt-reduction options* appropriate for your financial situation. More important, face up to credit and debt problems as soon as they occur, and do everything possible to avoid ruining your credit record.

TEST YOURSELF

6-16 What are some key factors that you should consider when choosing a credit card?

6-17 Discuss the steps that you would take to avoid and/or resolve credit problems.

6-18 What's the biggest source of credit card fraud? List at least five things you can do to reduce your chances of being a victim of credit card fraud.

6-19 Distinguish between a Wage Earner Plan and straight bankruptcy.

Planning Over a Lifetime: *Using Credit*

Here are some key considerations for using credit in each stage of the life cycle.

Pre-family Independence: 20s	Family Formation/Career Development: 30–45	Pre-Retirement: 45 –65	Retirement: 65 and Beyond
✓ Obtain a credit card to start building a credit history. Consider a secured card first.	✓ Watch consumer credit use carefully to avoid overspending.	✓ Re-evaluate use of consumer credit in light of revised expenditures and income.	✓ Budget to eliminate reliance on consumer credit in retirement.
✓ Plan to pay all consumer credit bills in full.	✓ Periodically evaluate credit card costs, and change cards if you are not getting the best deal.	✓ Check your credit score periodically.	✓ Maintain credit score to assure credit access.
✓ Carefully monitor all charges and financial statements for unauthorized transactions.	✓ Continue to monitor all accounts for unauthorized transactions and possible identity theft.	✓ Continue to watch for unauthorized transactions and identity theft.	✓ Be particularly careful about releasing personal financial information.

Financial Impact of Personal Choices
Stan Has Had It and Files for Bankruptcy

Stan Thompson is overwhelmed by his bills. While making $60,000 a year, he has amassed credit card debt of $24,000, has an $80,000 college loan, holds a $150,000 mortgage, and pays monthly on his leased Jetta. He's having trouble paying the mortgage monthly and can never seem to pay more than the minimum on his credit card debt. Stan's wife, Zoe, is currently unemployed. Stan has heard that declaring bankruptcy can eliminate some of his debt commitments and give him extra time to deal with others. He's had it and just filed for bankruptcy. What can Stan look forward to as a result of his decision?

Stan can expect some short-term cash flow relief and filing for bankruptcy will likely prevent or at least delay foreclosure on his home. However, the bankruptcy filing will adversely affect his credit report for up to the next 10 years. Stan will probably have trouble getting a loan or a new credit card. And if he can borrow money or get a new credit card, he'll probably have to pay the highest allowable interest rate. By not having managed his family's indebtedness, Stan has exercised the bankruptcy "nuclear option." This provides short-term relief at the expense of longer-term access to credit on reasonable terms.

Summary

LG1 **Describe the reasons for using consumer credit, and identify its benefits and problems. p. 217**
Families and individuals use credit as a way to pay for relatively expensive items and, occasionally, to deal with a financial emergency. Consumer credit is also used because it's so convenient. Finally, it's used to partially finance the purchase of various types of investments. Consumer credit can be misused to the point where people live beyond their means by purchasing goods and services that they simply can't afford. Such overspending can get so bad that it eventually leads to bankruptcy.

LG2 **Develop a plan to establish a strong credit history. p. 217**
Establishing a strong credit history is an important part of personal financial planning. Opening checking and savings accounts, obtaining one or two credit cards and using them judiciously, and taking out a small loan and repaying it on schedule are ways to show potential lenders that you can handle credit wisely. Be sure to use credit only when you're sure you can repay the obligation, make payments promptly, and notify a lender immediately if you can't meet payments as agreed. The debt safety ratio is used to calculate how much of your monthly take-home pay is going toward consumer credit payments. One widely used credit capacity guideline is that total monthly consumer credit payments (exclusive of your mortgage payment) should not exceed 20 percent of your monthly take-home pay.

LG3 **Distinguish among the different forms of open account credit. p. 223**
Open account credit is one of the most popular forms of consumer credit; it's available from various types of financial institutions and from many retail stores and merchants. Major types of open account credit include bank credit cards; retail charge cards; and revolving lines of credit such as overdraft protection lines, home equity credit lines, and unsecured personal lines of credit. Many financial institutions issue special types of credit cards, such as rewards cards, affinity cards, or secured credit cards. Instead of using only credit cards, a growing number of consumers are turning to debit cards, which give their users a way to "write checks" with plastic.

LG4 **Apply for, obtain, and manage open forms of credit. p. 238**
Most types of revolving credit require formal application, which generally involves an extensive investigation of your credit background and an evaluation of your creditworthiness. This usually includes checking credit bureau reports. You should verify the accuracy of these reports regularly and promptly correct any errors. The amount of finance charges, if any, due on consumer credit depends largely on the technique used to compute the account balance; the ADB method that includes new purchases is the most common today. Managing your accounts involves understanding the monthly statement and making payments on time.

LG5 **Choose the right credit cards and recognize their advantages and disadvantages. p. 248**
With so many different types of credit cards available, it pays to shop around to choose the best one for your needs. Consider your spending habits and then compare the fees, interest rates, grace period, and any incentives. If you pay off your balance each month, you'll want a card with low annual fees; if you carry a balance, a low interest rate is your best bet. Advantages of credit cards include interest-free loans, simplified record-keeping, ease of making returns and resolving unsatisfactory purchase disputes, convenience and security, and use in emergencies. The disadvantages are the tendency to overspend and high interest costs on unpaid balances.

LG6 **Avoid credit problems, protect yourself against credit card fraud, and understand the personal bankruptcy process. p. 248**
Avoiding credit problems requires self-discipline. Keep the number of cards you use to a minimum, and be sure you can repay any balances quickly. When credit card debt gets out of control, adopt a payment strategy to pay off the debt as fast as possible by looking for a low-rate card, paying

more than the minimum payment, and not charging any additional purchases until the debt is repaid or substantially paid down. Another option is a consolidation loan. To protect yourself against credit card fraud, don't give out your card number unnecessarily; destroy old cards and receipts, verify your credit card transactions, and report a lost card or suspicious activity immediately. A solution to credit abuse, albeit a drastic one, is personal bankruptcy. Those who file for bankruptcy work out a debt restructuring program under Chapter 13's Wage Earner Plan or Chapter 7's straight bankruptcy. If you have serious problems in managing personal credit, a credit counselor may be able to help you learn to control spending and work out a repayment strategy.

Key Terms

affinity card, 229

annual percentage rate (APR), 244

average daily balance (ADB) method, 244

balance transfer, 227

bank credit card, 225

base rate, 226

cash advance, 225

credit bureau, 240

credit counselor, 253

credit investigation, 238

credit limit, 223

credit scoring, 242

credit statement, 223

debt safety ratio, 222

grace period, 226

home equity credit line, 235

line of credit, 225

minimum monthly payment, 246

open account credit, 223

overdraft protection line, 234

personal bankruptcy, 251

prepaid card, 233

retail charge card, 232

revolving lines of credit, 234

reward (co-branded) credit card, 228

secured (collateralized) credit cards, 230

straight bankruptcy, 252

student credit card, 230

unsecured personal credit line, 235

Wage Earner Plan, 252

Answers to Test Yourself

You can find answers to these questions on this book's companion website. Look for it at *www.cengagebrain.com.* Search for this book by its title, and then add it to your dashboard.

Financial Planning Exercises

LG1, p. 217   1. ***Establishing credit history.*** After graduating from college last fall, Nicole Butler took a job as a consumer credit analyst at a local bank. From her work reviewing credit applications, she realizes that she should begin establishing her own credit history. Describe for Nicole several steps that she could take to begin building a strong credit record. Does the fact that she took out a student loan for her college education help or hurt her credit record?

LG2, p. 217   2. ***Evaluating debt burden.*** Isaac Wright has a monthly take-home pay of $1,685; he makes payments of $410 a month on his outstanding consumer credit (excluding the mortgage on his home). How would you characterize Isaac's debt burden? What if his take-home pay was $850 a month and he had monthly credit payments of $150?

LG2, p. 217
3. **Calculating and interpreting personal debt safety ratio.** Calculate your own debt safety ratio. What does it tell you about your current credit situation and your debt capacity? Does this information indicate a need to make any changes in your credit use patterns? If so, what steps should you take?

LG2, p. 217
4. **Evaluating debt safety ratio. Use Worksheet 6.1.** Alyssa Clark is evaluating her debt safety ratio. Her monthly take-home pay is $3,320. Each month, she pays $380 for an auto loan, $120 on a personal line of credit, $60 on a department store charge card, and $85 on her bank credit card. Complete Worksheet 6.1 by listing Alyssa's outstanding debts, and then calculate her debt safety ratio. Given her current take-home pay, what is the maximum amount of monthly debt payments that Alyssa can have if she wants her debt safety ratio to be 12.5 percent? Given her current monthly debt payment load, what would Alyssa's take-home pay have to be if she wanted a 12.5 percent debt safety ratio?

LG2, p. 217
5. **Implications of Credit Card Act.** What are the main features and implications of the Credit Card Act of 2009?

LG4, p. 238
6. **Using overdraft protection line.** Isabella Harris has an overdraft protection line. Assume that her October 2017 statement showed a latest (new) balance of $862. If the line had a minimum monthly payment requirement of 5 percent of the latest balance (rounded to the nearest $5 figure), then what would be the minimum amount that she'd have to pay on her overdraft protection line?

LG3, p. 223
7. **Home equity line interest.** Sean and Amy Anderson have a home with an appraised value of $180,000 and a mortgage balance of only $90,000. Given that an S&L is willing to lend money at a loan-to-value ratio of 75 percent, how big a home equity credit line can Sean and Amy obtain? How much, if any, of this line would qualify as tax-deductible interest if their house originally cost $100,000?

LG4, p. 238
8. **Calculating credit card interest.** Ryan Gray, a student at State College, has a balance of $380 on his retail charge card; if the store levies a finance charge of 21 percent per year, how much monthly interest will be added to his account?

LG4, p. 238
9. **Choosing between credit cards.** Wyatt Collins recently graduated from college and is evaluating two credit cards. Card A has an annual fee of $75 and an interest rate of 9 percent. Card B has no annual fee and an interest rate of 16 percent. Assuming that Wyatt intends to carry no balance and to pay off his charges in full each month, which card represents the better deal? If Wyatt expected to carry a significant balance from one month to the next, which card would be better? Explain.

LG4, p. 238
10. **Balance transfer credit cards.** Martina Lopez has several credit cards, on which she is carrying a total current balance of $14,500. She is considering transferring this balance to a new card issued by a local bank. The bank advertises that, for a 2 percent fee, she can transfer her balance to a card that charges a 0 percent interest rate on transferred balances for the first nine months. Calculate the fee that Martina would pay to transfer the balance, and describe the benefits and drawbacks of balance transfer cards.

LG4, p. 238
11. **Calculating credit card finance charge.** Parker Young recently received his monthly *MasterCard* bill for the period June 1–30, 2017, and wants to verify the monthly finance charge calculation, which is assessed at a rate of 15 percent per year and based on ADBs, including new purchases. His outstanding balance, purchases, and payments are as follows:

Previous Balance:

Purchases:	$386	Payments:	
June 4	$137	June 21	$35
June 12	78		
June 20	98		
June 26	75		

What are his ADB and finance charges for the period? (Use a table like the one in Exhibit 6.8 for your calculations.)

LG3, p. 223

12. **Credit vs. debit card.** Henry Stewart is trying to decide whether to apply for a credit card or a debit card. He has $8,500 in a savings account at the bank and spends his money frugally. What advice would you have for Henry? Describe the benefits and drawbacks of each type of card.

LG5, p. 248

13. **Credit card liability.** Christine Lin was reviewing her credit card statement and noticed several charges that didn't look familiar to her. Christine is unsure whether she should pay the bill in full and forget about the unfamiliar charges, or "make some noise." If some of these charges aren't hers, is she still liable for the full amount? Is she liable for any part of these charges, even if they're fraudulent?

LG2, p. 217

14. **Evaluating loan request.** Carter Hall recently graduated from college and wants to borrow $50,000 to start a business, which he believes will produce a cash flow of at least $10,000 per year. As a student, Carter was active in clubs, held leadership positions, and did a lot of community service. He currently has no other debts. He owns a car worth about $10,000 and has $6,000 in a savings account. Although the economy is currently in a recession, economic forecasters expect the recession to end soon. If you were a bank loan officer, how would you evaluate Carter's loan request within the context of the "5 C's of Credit"? Briefly describe each characteristic and indicate whether it has *favorable or unfavorable* implications for Carter's loan request.

Applying Personal Finance

How's Your Credit?

Establishing credit and maintaining your creditworthiness are essential to your financial well-being. Good credit allows you to obtain loans and acquire assets that you otherwise might not be able to attain. This project will help you to examine your credit.

If you've already established credit, get a copy of your credit report from one of the credit bureaus mentioned in this chapter. (If you've applied for a loan recently, your lender may already have sent you a copy of your credit report.) Carefully examine your report for any inaccuracies, and take the necessary steps to correct them. Then look over your report and evaluate your creditworthiness. If you feel you need to improve your creditworthiness, what steps do you need to take?

If you haven't yet established credit, find an application for a card such as *Visa*, *MasterCard*, or a department store or gasoline company credit card. Places to look might be at a department store, banking institution, gas station, or the Internet. Take the application home and fill it out. Then look it over and try to do a self-evaluation of your creditworthiness. Based on the information that you've provided, do you think you would qualify for the credit card? What do you see as your major strengths? What are your major weaknesses? Is there anything you can do about them?

CRITICAL THINKING CASES

LG2, 4, p. 217, 238

6.1 The Ramirez Family Seeks Some Credit Card Information

Felipe and Lucia Ramirez are a newly married couple in their mid-20s. Felipe is a senior at a state university and expects to graduate in the summer of 2017. Lucia graduated last spring with a degree in marketing and recently started working as a sales rep for the Fulcrum Systems Corporation. She supports both of them on her monthly salary of $4,250 after taxes. The Ramirez family currently pay all their expenses by cash or check. They would, however, like to use a bank credit card for some of their transactions. Because neither Felipe nor Lucia has ever applied for a credit card, they approach you for help.

Critical Thinking Questions

1. Advise the couple on how to fill out a credit application.
2. Explain to them the procedure that the bank will probably follow in processing their application.

3. Tell them about credit scoring and how the bank will arrive at a credit decision.
4. What kind of advice would you offer the Ramirez family on the best use of their card? What would you tell them about building a strong credit record?

LG2, 3, 4, p. 217, 223, 238

6.2 June Starts Over After Bankruptcy

A year after declaring bankruptcy and moving with her daughter back into her parents' home, June Maffeo is about to get a degree in nursing. As she starts out in a new career, she also wants to begin a new life—one built on a solid financial base. June will be starting out as a full-time nurse at a salary of $52,000 a year, and she plans to continue working at a second (part-time) nursing job with an annual income of $10,500. She'll be paying back $24,000 in bankruptcy debts and wants to be able to move into an apartment within a year and then buy a condo or house in five years.

June won't have to pay rent for the time that she lives with her parents. She also will have child care at no cost, which will continue after she and her daughter are able to move out on their own. While the living arrangement with her parents is great financially, the accommodations are "tight," and June's work hours interfere with her parents' routines. Everyone agrees that one more year of this is about all the family can take. However, before June is able to make a move—even into a rented apartment—she'll have to reestablish credit over and above paying off her bankruptcy debts. To rent the kind of place she'd like, she needs to have a good credit record for a year; to buy a home she must sustain that credit standing for at least three to five years.

Critical Thinking Questions

1. In addition to opening checking and savings accounts, what else might June do to begin establishing credit with a bank?
2. Although June is unlikely to be able to obtain a major bank credit card for at least a year, how might she begin establishing credit with local merchants?
3. What's one way she might be able to obtain a bank credit card? Explain.
4. How often should June monitor her credit standing with credit reporting services?
5. What general advice would you offer for getting June back on track to a new life financially?

CHAPTER 7

Using Consumer Loans

LEARNING GOALS

LG1 Know when to use consumer loans, and be able to differentiate between the major types.

LG2 Identify the various sources of consumer loans.

LG3 Choose the best loans by comparing finance charges, maturity, collateral, and other loan terms.

LG4 Describe the features of, and calculate the finance charges on, single payment loans.

LG5 Evaluate the benefits of an installment loan.

LG6 Determine the costs of installment loans, and analyze whether it is better to pay cash or take out a loan.

How Will This Affect Me?

Consumer loan sources abound, and their terms vary significantly. The primary types are single-payment and installment consumer loans. It's important to understand when to use each credit source, to be able to calculate and compare their costs, and to determine the circumstances in which it is best to take out a loan or pay cash. Practical examples considered in this chapter include taking out a car loan and borrowing to pay for a college education. The chapter provides you with an applied framework for evaluating the best ways to choose among and obtain consumer loans.

7-1 BASIC FEATURES OF CONSUMER LOANS

LG1, LG2

In previous chapters, we've discussed the different types of financial goals that individuals and families can set for themselves. These goals often involve large sums of money and may include such things as a college education or the purchase of a new car. One way to reach these goals is to systematically save the money. Another is to use a loan to at least partially finance the transaction. Consumer loans are important to the personal financial planning process because they can help you reach certain types of financial goals. The key, of course, is to successfully manage the credit by keeping the amount of debt used and debt-repayment burden *well within your budget!*

7-1a Using Consumer Loans

As we saw in Chapter 6, using open or revolving credit can be helpful to those who plan and live within their personal financial budgets. More important to the long-term achievement of personal financial goals, however, are single-payment and installment consumer loans. These long-term liabilities are widely used to finance the purchase of goods that are far too expensive to buy from current income, to help fund a college education, or to pay for certain types of nondurable items, such as expensive vacations. Of course, the extent to which this type of borrowing is used should be governed by personal financial plans and budgets.

These loans differ from open forms of credit in several ways, including the formality of their lending arrangements. That is, while open account credit results from a rather informal process, **consumer loans** are *formal, negotiated contracts* that specify both the terms for borrowing and the repayment schedule. Another difference is that an open line of credit can be used again and again, but consumer loans are one-shot transactions made for specific purposes. Because there's no revolving credit with a consumer loan, no more credit is available (from that particular loan) once it's paid off. Furthermore, no credit cards or checks are issued with this form of credit. Finally, whereas open account credit is used chiefly to make repeated purchases of relatively low-cost *goods and services*, consumer loans are used mainly to *borrow money* to pay for big-ticket items.

consumer loans
Loans made for specific purposes using formally negotiated contracts that specify the borrowing terms and repayment.

FINANCIAL PLANNING TIPS

Arranging an Auto Loan

It's important to do the following things *before* you go to the car dealership:

• Review your credit report and correct any errors that could increase your borrowing costs. Bring your credit report to the dealership when it's time to talk about financing.

• Know the maximum amount that you can spend on the car. Work backward from the maximum monthly payment to the implied maximum car price.

• Visit the car manufacturer's Internet site to see available special incentives or other deals. Print them out and take to the dealer when negotiating.

• Visit the Web sites of Kelley Blue Book (**http://kbb.com**) and Edmunds (**http://edmunds.com**) to get the value of your current car. Sell the car yourself if the dealer won't give you a fair trade-in price.

• Print out all of the pricing information on the car you want from the Internet and take it with you to the dealership.

• Get loan quotes from banks, credit unions, and online financial institutions and take the information with you to the dealership. Compare rates, application fees, loan terms, and prepayment penalties. If the terms look better, get the best loan and go to the dealership as a cash buyer.

• Increasing your down payment with rebate money to reduce the financed amount is often a better deal than 0 percent financing.

• Ask to have any rebates mailed directly to you. Don't let the dealership apply them to your down payment. Make the down payment yourself and then deposit the rebate in your account when you receive the check in the mail from the manufacturer.

Source: Adapted from Lee Anne Obringer, "How Car Financing Works," http://auto.howstuffworks.com/buying-selling/car-financing2.htm, accessed August 2015.

7-1b Different Types of Loans

Although they can be used for just about any purpose imaginable, most consumer loans fall into one of the following categories.

collateral
An item of value used to secure the principal portion of a loan.

• **Auto loans:** Financing a new car, truck, SUV, or minivan is the single most common reason for borrowing money through a consumer loan. Indeed, auto loans account for about 35 percent of all consumer credit outstanding. Typically, about 80 percent to 90 percent of the cost of a new vehicle (somewhat less with used cars) can be financed with credit. The buyer must provide the rest through a *down payment.* The loan is *secured* with the auto, meaning that the vehicle serves as **collateral** for the loan and can be repossessed by the lender should the buyer fail to make payments. These loans generally have maturities ranging from 36 to 60 months.

> **You Can Do It Now**
>
> *Current Auto Loan Rates*
>
> If you're considering buying a car, you need to know current auto loan rates to estimate prospective monthly payments and what price you can afford to pay for an auto. Up-to-date market rates are available at **http://www.bankrate.com**. You'll see how much higher used auto loan rates are than new auto loan rates. And you'll get a sense of the trade-off between auto loan rates and maturity, for example, between 48- and 60-month loan rates. Getting familiar with auto loan rates will help you be a more informed shopper–you can do it now.

- **Loans for other durable goods:** Consumer loans can also be used to finance other kinds of *costly durable goods*, such as furniture, home appliances, TVs, home computers, recreational vehicles, and even small airplanes and mobile homes. These loans are also secured by the items purchased and generally require some down payment. Maturities vary with the type of asset purchased: 9- to 12-month loans are common for less costly items, such as TVs and audio equipment, whereas 10- to 15-year loans (or even longer) are normal with mobile homes.
- **Education loans:** Getting a college education is another important reason for taking out a consumer loan. Such loans can be used to finance either undergraduate or graduate studies, and special government-subsidized loan programs are available to students and parents. We'll discuss student loans in more detail in the following section.
- **Personal loans:** These loans are typically used for nondurable expenditures, such as an expensive European vacation or to cover temporary cash shortfalls. Many personal loans are *unsecured*, which means there's no collateral with the loan other than the borrower's good name.
- **Consolidation loans:** This type of loan is used to straighten out an unhealthy credit situation. When consumers overuse credit cards, credit lines, or consumer loans and can no longer promptly service their debt, a consolidation loan may help control this deteriorating credit situation. By borrowing money from one source to pay off other forms of credit, borrowers can replace, say, five or six monthly payments that total $400 with one payment amounting to $250. *Consolidation loans are usually expensive, and people who use them must be careful to stop using credit cards and other forms of credit until they repay the loans. Otherwise, they may end up right back where they started.*

Student Loans

The recent average annual budget for tuition, fees, books and supplies, and room and board ranges from $23,410 at four-year public colleges for state residents to over $46,000 at private colleges. Alarmingly, after adjusting for inflation, students are paying about 3 times what they paid 30 years ago for a public college education and about 2.5 times what they paid for a private college education. Many families, even those who started saving for college when their children were young, are faced with higher-than-expected bills. Fortunately, there are many types of financial aid programs available, including some federal programs described later in this chapter, as well as state, private, and college-sponsored programs.

Paying for a college education is one of the most legitimate reasons for going into debt. Although you could borrow money for college through normal channels—that is, take out a regular consumer loan from your bank and use the proceeds to finance an education—there are better ways to go about getting education loans. That's because the federal government (and some state governments) have available several different types of subsidized educational loan programs. The federally sponsored programs are:

- Stafford loans (Direct and Federal Family Education Loans—FFELs)
- Perkins loans
- Parent Loans (PLUS)

The Stafford and Perkins loans have the best terms and are the foundation of the government's student loan program. In contrast, PLUS (which stands for *Parent Loans for Undergraduate Students*) loans are *supplemental loans* for *undergraduate students* who demonstrate a need but, for one reason or another, don't qualify for Stafford or Perkins loans or need more aid than they're receiving. Under this program, parents can take out loans to meet or

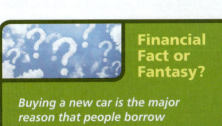

Financial Fact or Fantasy?

Buying a new car is the major reason that people borrow money through consumer loans. **Fact:** Buying a new car accounts for about 35 percent of all consumer loans outstanding, which is the single most common reason for taking out a consumer loan.

©SYDA PRODUCTIONS/SHUTTERSTOCK.COM

supplement the costs of their children's college education, *up to the full cost of attendance*. Whereas Stafford and Perkins loans are made directly to students, PLUS loans are made to the parents or legal guardians of college students. Probably the best place to look for information about these and other programs is the Internet. For example, look up FASTWEB (which stands for *Financial Aid Search Through the WEB*). This site, which is free, not only provides details on all the major, and some of the not-so-major, student loan programs but also has a service that matches individuals with scholarships and loans, even going so far as to provide form letters to use in requesting more information. (The address for this Internet site is **http://www.fastweb.com.**)

Let's look at the Stafford loan program to see how student loans work. There are two types of Stafford loans. In the subsidized loan program, the U.S. Department of Education pays interest while the student is in school and also during grace and deferment periods. In the unsubsidized program, the borrower is responsible for all interest, whether in or out of school. (Except where noted, the other two federally subsidized programs have much the same standards and follow the same procedures as discussed here.) Stafford loans carry low, possibly government-subsidized interest rates; most major banks, as well as some of the bigger S&Ls and credit unions, participate in the program. Actually, the loans are made directly by one of the participating financial institutions (in the case of the Stafford FFEL loan program), although the student has no direct contact with the lending institution. Instead, the whole process—which really is quite simple—begins with a visit to the school's financial aid office, where a financial aid counselor will help you determine your eligibility.

To be eligible, you must demonstrate a *financial need*, where the amount of your financial need is defined as the cost of attending school *less* the amount that can be paid by you or your family. Thus, in these programs, students are expected to contribute something to their educational expense regardless of their income. You must also be making *satisfactory progress in your academic program*, and you cannot be in default on any other student loans. Each academic year, you'll have to fill out a Free Application for Federal Student Aid (FAFSA) statement to attest that these qualifications are being met. The financial aid office will have the forms available in hard copy, or you can complete and submit the form on the Internet at **http://www.fafsa.ed.gov**. In short, so long as you can demonstrate a financial need and are making satisfactory academic progress, you'll probably qualify for a Stafford loan.

Obtaining a Student Loan. All you have to do to obtain a Stafford loan is complete a simple application form, which is then submitted to *your school's financial aid office*. You do *not* have to deal with the bank (your school will submit all the necessary papers to the institution actually making the loan in the case of an FFEL loan, or directly to the federal government in the case of a Stafford Direct loan), and you won't be subject to credit checks—although with PLUS loans, the borrower (parent) may be subject to a credit judgment by the lender. The latest innovation in this procedure involves transmitting the application electronically to the necessary parties, thus reducing paperwork and speeding up the processing (see, for example, **http://www.staffordloan.com**). Most schools are converting to this method, if they haven't already done so.

Each program has specific loan limits. For example, with subsidized Stafford loans for dependent students, you can borrow up to $3,500 per academic year for first-year studies, $4,500 for the second year, and $5,500 per academic year thereafter, up to a subsidized loan maximum of $23,000 for undergraduate studies—you can obtain even more if you can show that you're no longer dependent on your parents; in other words, that you're an *independent* undergraduate student paying for your college education on your own. Graduate students can qualify for up to $8,500 per academic year for independent students. The maximum for both undergraduate and graduate subsidized loans combined is $65,500 (or $224,000 for health professionals). There's no limit on the *number* of loans you can have, only on the maximum dollar amount that you can receive annually from each program. Exhibit 7.1 compares the major loan provisions (borrower, interest rates, guarantee and/or origination fees, borrowing limits, and loan terms) of the three federally sponsored student loan programs—Stafford, Perkins, and PLUS loans.

Each year, right on through graduate school, a student can take out a loan from one or more of these government programs. Over time, that can add up to a lot of loans. Indeed, the average graduating senior leaves school about $30,000 in debt—all of which must be repaid. But here's another nice feature of these loans: in addition to carrying low (government-subsidized) interest rates, loan repayment doesn't begin until after you're out of school (for the Stafford and Perkins programs only—repayment on PLUS loans normally begins within 60 days of loan disbursement). In addition, interest doesn't begin accruing until you get out of school (except, of course, with PLUS loans, where interest starts accumulating with the first disbursement). While you're in school, the lenders will receive interest on their loans, but it's paid by the federal government! Once repayment begins, you start paying interest on the loans, which may be tax deductible, depending on your income.

Student loans are usually amortized with monthly (principal and interest) payments over a period of 5 to 10 years. To help you service the debt, if you have several student loans outstanding, then you can *consolidate* the loans, at a single blended rate, and extend the repayment period to as long as 20 years. You also can ask for

| EXHIBIT 7.1 | Federal Government Student Loan Programs at a Glance |

More and more college students rely on loans subsidized by the federal government to finance all or part of their educations. There are three types of federally subsidized loan programs, the basic loan provisions of which are listed here. These loans all have low interest rates and provide various deferment options and extended repayment terms. (*Note: Loan rates and terms shown here are for the 2015–2016 school year.*)

	TYPE OF FEDERAL LOAN PROGRAM		
Loan Provisions	**Stafford Loans***	**Perkins Loans**	**PLUS Loans**
Borrower	Student	Student	Parent
Interest rate	4.29% (undergrad) 5.84% (grad/professional)	5%	7.21%
Cumulative borrow limits	*Dependent and independent undergraduate students:* $23,000; *Grad/professional students:* $138,500 (including a max of $65,500 in subsidized loans) or $224,000 for medical school/health professionals	$27,500 (undergrad) $60,000 (grad/professional)	*No total dollar limit:* Cost of attendance minus any other financial aid received.
Loan fees	1.073% of loan origination fee	None	4.272% of loan amount
Loan term	Up to 10 years	10 years	10 years

*Data are for subsidized Stafford loans and unsubsidized graduate or professional Stafford loans, and interest rates are as of mid-2015. Stafford loans can be subsidized and unsubsidized and the lifetime limits can differ. Subsidized Stafford loans also have annual borrowing limits. Perkins loans have annual limits of $5,550 per year of undergraduate study and $8,000 per year of graduate school.

Source: http://www.fastweb.com and http://www.staffordloan.com; accessed August 2015.

either an *extended repayment* for a longer term of up to 30 years; a *graduated repayment schedule*, which will give you low payments in the early years and then higher payments later on; or an *income-contingent repayment plan*, with payments that fluctuate annually according to your income and debt levels. But no matter what you do, *take the repayment provisions seriously, because defaults will be reported to credit bureaus and become a part of your credit records!* What's more, due to recent legislation, you can't get out of repaying your student loans by filing for bankruptcy: whether you file under Chapter 7 or Chapter 13, *student loans are no longer dischargeable in a bankruptcy proceeding.*

In addition to the government programs just described, there are other ways to pay for a college education. One of the most innovative is the so-called **529 College Savings Plan**. These plans aren't based on borrowing money to pay for college but rather on using a special tax-sheltered *savings and investment program*.

529 college savings plan
A government-sponsored investment vehicle that allows earnings to grow free from federal taxes, so long as they are used to meet college education expenses.

Are Student Loans "Too Big to Fail"? During the recent financial crisis, some banks were deemed "too big to fail" by virtue of their importance to the operation of the entire financial system. Their size consequently became the rationale for providing massive public financial assistance. Education is important to the economy, and, as discussed in this chapter, the federal government provides loans to finance undergraduate and graduate education. The financial crisis obviously put more pressure on households seeking to pay the increasing cost of college educations. So how large have student loans grown? Student loans now total more than $1.2 trillion! So the federal government has taken on a significant liability to support higher education that is important to the overall economy. This recently prompted a representative of the newly created Consumer Finance Protection Bureau (CFPB) to observe that the student loan program has possibly become "too big to fail" as well.

While this chapter discusses the limits on public loans, there is no limit on private student loans. While the average student debt is about $30,000, around 5 percent of student borrowers owe more than $100,000. And about 25 percent of all student borrowers have a past-due balance! Exhibit 7.2 portrays the distribution of loan balances for young families. These balances take on particular significance given that the average starting salary of a recent college graduate is about $48,700.

EXHIBIT 7.2 | **Distribution of Education Loan Balances for Young Families**

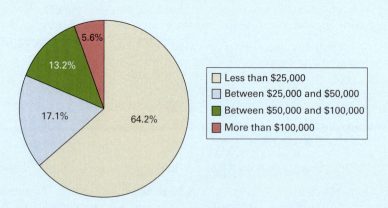

- Less than $25,000
- Between $25,000 and $50,000
- Between $50,000 and $100,000
- More than $100,000

5.6%
13.2%
17.1%
64.2%

Source: Jesse Bricker, Lisa J. Dettling, Alice Henriques, Joanne W. Hsu, Kevin B. Moore, John Sabelhaus, Jeffrey Thompson, and Richard A. Windle, "Changes in U.S. Family Finances from 2010 to 2013: Evidence from the Survey of Consumer Finances," Board of Governors of the Federal Reserve System, Washington, DC, (October 24, 2014, data is for 2013), http://www.federalreserve.gov/pubs/bulletin/2014/pdf/scf14.pdf, Box 10, Figure B, accessed August 2015.

A survey by the Young Invincibles, a nonprofit group focusing on issues affecting 18- to 34-year-olds (**http://www.younginvincibles.org**), found that about two-thirds of student borrowers with private loans did not understand the differences between public and private student loans. This is significant because public lenders are often more flexible than private lenders in providing financial relief when borrowers are under pressure. For example, federal programs provide public service loan forgiveness, income-based repayment, and loan repayment assistance programs. Public service loan forgiveness allows those who borrowed under the previously discussed FFEL program to make no more than 120 payments on their loans if they work for a federal, state, or local government agency, entity, or organization. The remaining balance is forgiven.

Strategies for Reducing Student Loan Costs. It's important to borrow as little as possible to cover college costs. This common-sense goal can be quantified by borrowing in light of the student's expected future salary. Based on that expected future salary, figure out what monthly payment the student will be able to afford and then use a loan repayment calculator to determine the maximum amount that can be borrowed at the expected interest rate on the loan. For example, consider using the following online student loan calculator: **http://www.bankrate.com/calculators/college-planning/loan-calculator.aspx**. The analysis should also include looking for the lowest interest rate. Before borrowing, it makes sense to explore all possibly available grants and scholarships and to apply for federal student aid. And upon graduation, it is wise to explore the Public Service Loan Forgiveness and Loan Repayment Assistance programs. There could also be the option to consolidate federal student loans and to participate in an income-based repayment program.

Single-Payment or Installment Loans

Consumer loans can also be broken into categories based on the type of repayment arrangement—single-payment or installment. **Single-payment loans** are made for a specified period of time, at the end of which payment in full (principal plus interest) is due. They generally have maturities ranging from 30 days to a year; rarely do these loans run for more than a year. Sometimes single-payment loans are made to finance purchases or pay bills when the cash to be used for repayment is known to be forthcoming in the near future; in this case, they serve as a form of **interim financing**. In other situations, single-payment loans are used by consumers who want to avoid being strapped with monthly installment payments and choose instead to make one large payment at the end of the loan.

Installment loans, in contrast, are repaid in a series of fixed, scheduled payments rather than in one lump sum. The payments are almost always set up on a monthly basis, with each installment made up partly of principal and partly of interest. For example, out of a $75 monthly payment, $50 might be credited to principal and the balance to interest. These loans are typically made to finance the purchase of a good or service for which current resources are inadequate. The repayment period can run from six months to six years or more. Installment loans have become a way of life for many consumers. They're popular because they provide a convenient way to "buy now and pay later" in fixed monthly installments that can be readily incorporated into a family budget.

Fixed- or Variable-Rate Loans

Most consumer loans are made at fixed rates of interest—that is, the interest rate charged and the monthly payment remain the same over the life of the obligation. However, variable-rate loans are also being made with increasing frequency, especially on *longer-term installment loans*. As with an adjustable-rate home mortgage, the rate of interest charged on such loans changes periodically in keeping with prevailing market conditions. If market interest rates go up, the rate of interest on the loan goes up accordingly, as does the monthly loan payment. These loans have periodic

single-payment loan
A loan made for a specified period, at the end of which payment is due in full.

interim financing
The use of a single-payment loan to finance a purchase or pay bills in situations where the funds to be used for repayment are known to be forthcoming in the near future.

installment loan
A loan that is repaid in a series of fixed, scheduled payments rather than a lump sum.

adjustment dates (for example, monthly, quarterly, or semiannually), at which time the interest rate and monthly payment are adjusted as necessary. Once an adjustment is made, the new rate remains in effect until the next adjustment date (sometimes the payment amount remains the same, but the number of payments changes). Many variable-rate loans have caps on the maximum increase per adjustment period as well as over the life of the loan. Generally speaking, variable-rate loans are desirable *if interest rates are expected to fall* over the course of the loan. In contrast, fixed-rate loans are preferable *if interest rates are expected to rise*.

Whether the loans are fixed or variable, their cost tends to vary with market conditions. As a rule, when interest rates move up or down in the market, so will the cost of consumer loans. Inevitably, there will be times when *the cost of credit simply becomes too high to justify borrowing* as a way of making major purchases. So when market rates start climbing, you should ask yourself whether the cost is really worth it. Financially, you may be far better off delaying the purchase until rates come down.

7-1c Where Can You Get Consumer Loans?

Consumer loans can be obtained from a number of sources, including commercial banks, consumer finance companies, credit unions, S&Ls, sales finance companies, and life insurance companies—even brokerage firms, pawnshops, or friends and relatives. *Commercial banks* dominate the field and provide nearly half of all consumer loans. Second to banks are *consumer finance companies* and then *credit unions*. Together, about 75 percent of all consumer loans are originated by these three financial institutions! The S&Ls are not much of a force in this market since they tend to focus on mortgage loans rather than consumer loans. Selection of a lender often depends on both the rate of interest being charged and how easily the loan can be negotiated. Of course, today it's becoming easier than ever to obtain consumer loans online. Just go to Google and search for "installment loans," and you'll get hundreds of Internet sites. Some of these sites will actually accept applications online; others offer a brief description of their services along with a toll-free phone number.

Commercial Banks

Because they offer various types of loans at attractive rates of interest, commercial banks are a popular source of consumer loans. Commercial banks typically charge lower rates than most other lenders, largely because they take only the best credit risks and are able to obtain relatively inexpensive funds from their depositors. The demand for their loans is generally high, and they can be selective in making consumer loans. Commercial banks usually lend only to customers with good credit ratings who can readily demonstrate an ability to repay a loan according to the specified terms. They also give preference to loan applicants who are account holders. Although banks prefer to make loans secured by some type of collateral, they also make unsecured loans to their better customers. The interest rate charged on a bank loan may be affected by the loan's size, terms, and whether it's secured by some type of collateral.

Consumer Finance Companies

consumer finance company
A firm that makes secured and unsecured personal loans to qualified individuals; also called a *small loan company*.

Sometimes called *small loan companies*, **consumer finance companies** make secured and unsecured (signature) loans to qualified individuals. These companies do not accept deposits but obtain funds from their stockholders and through open market borrowing. Because they don't have the inexpensive sources of funds that banks and other deposit-type institutions do, their interest rates are generally quite high. Actual rates charged by consumer finance companies are regulated by interest-rate ceilings (or usury laws) set by the states in which they operate. The maximum allowable interest rate may vary with the size of the loan, and the state regulatory authorities may also limit the length of the repayment period. Loans made by consumer finance companies typically are for $5,000 or less and are secured by some type of collateral. Repayment is required in installments, usually within five years or less.

Consumer finance companies specialize in small loans to high-risk borrowers. These loans are quite costly, but they may be the only alternative for people with poor credit ratings. Because of the high rates of interest charged, individuals should consider this source only after exhausting other alternatives.

Credit Unions

A credit union is a cooperative financial institution that is owned and controlled by the people ("members") who use its services. Only the members can obtain installment loans and other types of credit from these institutions, but credit unions can offer membership to just about anyone they want, not merely to certain groups of people. Because they are nonprofit organizations with minimal operating costs, credit unions charge relatively low rates on their loans. They make either unsecured or secured loans, depending on the size and type of loan requested. Membership in a credit union generally provides the most attractive borrowing opportunities available because their interest rates and borrowing requirements are usually more favorable than other sources of consumer loans.

Financial Fact or Fantasy?

An S&L is the only type of financial institution that is prohibited from making consumer loans. **Fantasy:** Financial deregulation opened up the consumer loan market to S&Ls and they are an important source of such credit.

S&L Associations

S&L associations (as well as savings banks) primarily make mortgage loans. While they aren't major players in the consumer loan field, S&Ls can make loans on such consumer durables as automobiles, televisions, refrigerators, and other appliances. They can also make certain types of home improvement and mobile-home loans, as well as some personal and educational loans. Rates of interest on consumer loans at S&Ls are fairly close to the rates charged by commercial banks; if anything, they tend to be a bit more expensive. Like their banking counterparts, the rates charged at S&Ls will, in the final analysis, depend on such factors as type and purpose of the loan, duration and type of repayment, and the borrower's overall creditworthiness.

Sales Finance Companies

Businesses that sell relatively expensive items—such as automobiles, furniture, and appliances—often provide installment financing to their customers. Because dealers can't afford to tie up their funds in installment contracts, they sell them to a **sales finance company** for cash. This procedure is often called "selling paper" because the merchants are, in effect, selling their loans to a third party. When the sales finance company purchases these notes, customers are usually notified to make payments directly to it.

The largest sales finance organizations are the **captive finance companies** owned by the manufacturers of big-ticket items—automobiles and appliances. General Motors Acceptance Corporation (GMAC) and General Electric Credit Corporation (GECC) are just two examples of captive finance companies that purchase the installment loans made by the dealers of their products. Also, most commercial banks act as sales finance companies by buying paper from auto dealers and other businesses. The cost of financing through a sales finance company is generally higher than the rates charged by banks and S&Ls, particularly when you let the dealer do all the work in arranging the financing. This is because dealers normally get a cut of the finance income, so it's obviously in their best interest to secure as high a rate as possible. That's certainly not true in all cases, however; automakers today will frequently use interest rates on new car loans (or leases) as a marketing tool. They do

sales finance company
A firm that purchases notes drawn up by sellers of certain types of merchandise, typically big-ticket items.

captive finance company
A sales finance company that is owned by a manufacturer of big-ticket merchandise. GMAC is a captive finance company.

this by dropping the rate of interest (*usually for selected models*) to levels that are well below the market—even 0 percent financing! Auto manufacturers use these loan rates (along with rebates) to stimulate sales by keeping the cost of buying a new car down. Clearly, cutting the cost of borrowing for a new car can result in big savings.

Life Insurance Companies

Life insurance policyholders may be able to obtain loans from their insurance companies. That's because certain types of policies not only provide death benefits but also have a savings function, so they can be used as collateral for loans. (*Be careful with these loans, however, as they could involve a tax penalty if certain conditions are not met*. A detailed discussion of life insurance is presented in Chapter 8.) Life insurance companies are required by law to make loans against the **cash value**—the amount of accumulated savings—of certain types of life insurance policies. The rate of interest on this type of loan is stated in the policy and usually carries a variable rate that goes up and down with prevailing market conditions. Although you'll be charged interest for as long as the policy loan is outstanding, these loans don't have repayment dates—in other words, *you don't have to pay them back*. When you take out a loan against the cash value of your life insurance policy, you're really borrowing from yourself. Thus, the amount of the loan outstanding, plus any accrued interest,

cash value (of life insurance)
An accumulation of savings in an insurance policy that can be used as a source of loan collateral.

FINANCIAL PLANNING TIPS

Lending to Family and Friends

Before you lend money to family or friends, it's helpful to answer the following questions:

- **Has your friend or family member explored other funding sources?** Starting with a bank or a credit union makes sense. If that doesn't work, non-financial-institution, peer-to-peer lending organizations like Prosper (**http://prosper.com**) or Lending Club (**http://lending-club.com**) are worth looking into. Every other resource should be exhausted before you consider giving a loan to friends or relatives.

- **Can you help other than with money?** For example, if a friend or relative is out of work, perhaps you could help by providing an introduction or by arranging an interview.

- **Will the loan be repaid?** It's a cliché for a reason: Don't lend any money that you can't afford to lose. If you really think repayment is unlikely, you may want to consider just offering cash as a gift, without any obligation to repay.

- **What will happen to your relationship if the loan isn't repaid?** How hard would you push your friend or relative for repayment, and how far would you be willing to go? Could you just forget about the money without

bearing a grudge? Is the risk of losing a friend worth any interest that you might earn on the loan?

- **What if the loan is not used as you'd hoped?** Resist the urge to direct how the money is used. While you should be repaid, you have no control over how the money is used. Don't lend the money if you have concerns about how it will be used.

- **Is the interest rate fair?** It is sometimes awkward to charge interest to a relative or friend. If you do decide to do that, though, a good rule is to charge interest at a rate comparable to that on a high-yield savings account. If you didn't make the loan, it's likely you'd keep it in a savings account anyway. If you charge interest, it should be a fair, legal rate.

- **Should this be a formal, legal transaction?** Even though this is your friend or relative, it's wise to formalize the loan with a contract. A contract shows that you're serious about the arrangement and expect to be repaid. Search online for "promissory note" and you'll find Internet sites where you can buy one at a reasonable price. If you wouldn't consider taking legal action against a friend or a relative, consider just giving some money instead of extending a loan.

Source: Adapted from Luke Landes, "Lending Money to Friends and Family," *Consumerism Commentary*, http://www.consumerismcommentary.com/lending-money-to-friends-and-family/, accessed August 2015.

is deducted from the amount of coverage provided by the policy—*effectively lowering your insurance coverage* and endangering your beneficiaries with a lower payout should you die before repayment. The chief danger in life insurance loans is that they don't have a firm maturity date, so *borrowers may lack the motivation to repay them*. Also, many insurers put borrowed policies in a different (less attractive) investment return category, based on the lower cash value in the policy.

Friends and Relatives

Sometimes, rather than going to a bank or some other financial institution, you may know of a close friend or relative who's willing to lend you money. Such loans often are attractive because little or no interest is charged. The terms will, of course, vary depending on the borrower's financial needs; but they should be specified in some type of loan agreement that states the costs, conditions, and maturity date of the loan as well as the obligations of both borrower and lender. Not only does a written loan agreement reduce opportunities for disagreement and unhappiness, it also protects both borrower and lender should either of them die or if other unexpected events occur. *Still, given the potential for disagreement and conflict, borrowing from friends or relatives is not advisable.* Consider doing so only when there are no other viable alternatives. Remember, a loan to or from a friend or family member is far more than a run-of-the-mill banking transaction: the interest is emotional, and the risks are the relationship itself!

TEST YOURSELF

7-1   List and briefly discuss the five major reasons for borrowing money through a consumer loan.

7-2   Identify several different types of federally sponsored student loan programs.

7-3   As a college student, what aspects of these student loan programs appeal to you the most?

7-4   Explain some strategies for reducing the cost of student loans.

7-5   Define and differentiate between (a) fixed- and variable-rate loans and (b) a *single-payment loan* and an *installment loan*.

7-6   Compare the consumer lending activities of (a) *consumer finance companies* and (b) *sales finance companies*. Describe a *captive finance company*.

7-7   Discuss the role in consumer lending of (a) credit unions and (b) savings and loan associations. Point out any similarities or differences in their lending activities. How do they compare with commercial banks?

7-2 MANAGING YOUR CREDIT

LG3   Borrowing money to make major purchases—and, in general, using consumer loans—is a sound and perfectly legitimate way to conduct your financial affairs. From a financial planning perspective, you should ask yourself two questions when considering the use of a consumer loan: (1) does making this purchase fit into your financial plans; and (2) do the required debt payments on the loan fit into your monthly cash budget? Indeed, when *full consideration is given not only to the need for the asset or item in question but also to the repayment of the ensuing debt*, sound credit management is the result. In contrast, if the expenditure in question will seriously jeopardize your financial plans or if repaying of the loan is likely to strain your cash budget, then you should definitely reconsider the purchase! Perhaps it can be postponed, or you can liquidate some assets in order to come up with more down payment.

You may even have to alter some other area of your financial plan in order to work in the expenditure. Whatever route you choose, the key point is to make sure that the debt will be fully compatible with your financial plans and cash budget *before* the loan is taken out and the money spent.

7-2a Shopping for Loans

Once you've decided to use credit, it's equally important that you shop around and evaluate the various costs and terms available. You may think the only thing you need do to make a sound credit decision is determine which source offers the lowest finance charge. But this could not be farther from the truth—as we'll see below, finance charges are just one of the factors to consider when shopping for a loan.

Finance Charges

What's it going to cost me? That's one of the first things most people want to know when taking out a loan. And that's appropriate, because borrowers should know what they'll have to pay to get the money. Lenders are required by law to explicitly disclose *all* finance charges and other loan fees. Find out the effective (or true) *rate* of interest you'll have to pay on the loan as well as whether the loan carries a fixed or variable rate. Obviously, *as long as everything else is equal*, it's in your best interest to secure the least expensive loan. In this regard, ask the lender what the *annual rate of interest* on the loan will be, because it's easier (and far more relevant) to compare percentage rates on alternative borrowing arrangements than the dollar amount of the loan charges. This rate of interest, known as the *APR* (annual percentage rate), includes not only the basic cost of money but also any additional fees that might be required on the loan (APR is more fully discussed later). Also, if it's a variable-rate loan, find out what the interest rate is pegged to, how many "points" are added to the base rate, how often the loan rate can be changed, and if rate caps exist. Just as important is how the lender makes the periodic adjustments: will the *size* of the monthly payment change or the *number* of monthly payments? To avoid any future shock, it's best to find out these things before making the loan.

Behavior Matters

The Paradox of More Financial Choices

More choices are better than fewer choices, right? That sounds like common sense. Yet behavioral finance studies show that when presented with too many financial choices, people tend to get overwhelmed and fall back on what they already know or to just make the simplest choice by default. This is called the *paradox of choice*. Complexity can overwhelm the average consumer. Our brains are just not wired to analyze lots of choices. The best defense is to be financially literate: do your homework, develop a framework for making such decisions, and be prepared to ask for help.

Consider the complicated choice among various mortgage types and terms. You have to choose between 15- and 30-year maturities and between fixed- and adjustable-rate mortgages; decide on the amount of the down payment, the amount of "points" (percent of the loan amount) to pay in order to reduce your mortgage rate, and when to "lock in" your rate; and you must choose the best array of up-front mortgage-related fees. Some consumers, when facing so many decisions, wind up making bad ones, borrowing too much, or holding mortgages that are inconsistent with their best interests. And research shows that lower financial literacy and analytical abilities are directly related to higher mortgage default rates.

This book in general, and the chapters on managing credit in particular, should help prepare you to make these complicated financial decisions.

Loan Maturity

Try to make sure that the size and number of payments will fit comfortably into your spending and savings plans. As a rule, the cost of credit increases with the length of the repayment period. Thus, to lower your cost, you should consider shortening the loan maturity—but only to the point where doing so won't place an unnecessary strain on your cash flow. Although a shorter maturity may reduce the cost of the loan, it also increases the size of the monthly loan payment. Indeed, finding a monthly loan payment you'll be comfortable with is a critical dimension of sound credit management. Altering the loan maturity is just one way of coming up with an affordable monthly payment; there are scores of Internet sites where you can quickly run through all sorts of alternatives to find the monthly payment that will best fit your monthly budget. (The "tools" section of most major financial services sites on the Internet have "calculators" that enable you to quickly and easily figure interest rates and monthly loan payments for all sorts of loans; generally, all you need to do is plug in a few key pieces of information—such as the interest rate and loan term—and then hit "calculate" and let the computer do the rest. For example, go to **http://www .finaid.org** and try out their "Loan Payments Calculator.")

Total Cost of the Transaction

When comparison shopping for credit, always look at the total cost of both the price of the item purchased *and* the price of the credit. Retailers often manipulate both sticker prices and interest rates, so you really won't know what kind of deal you're getting until you look at the total cost of the transaction. Along this line, comparing *monthly payments* is a good way to get a handle on total cost. It's a simple matter to compare total costs: *just add the amount put down on the purchase to the total of all the monthly loan payments;* other things being equal, the one with the lowest total is the one you should pick.

Collateral

Make sure you know up front what collateral (if any) you'll have to pledge on the loan and what you stand to lose if you default on your payments. Actually, if it makes no difference to you and if it's not too inconvenient, using collateral often makes sense. It may result in *lower* finance charges—perhaps half a percentage point or so.

Other Loan Considerations

In addition to following the guidelines just described, here are some questions that you should also ask. Can you choose a *payment date* that will be compatible with your spending patterns? Can you obtain the loan *promptly and conveniently?* What are the charges for late payments, and are they reasonable? Will you receive a refund on credit charges if you prepay your loan, or are there prepayment penalties? Taking the time to look around for the best credit deal will pay off, not only in reducing the cost of such debt but also in keeping the burden of credit in line with your cash budget and financial plans. In the long run, you're the one who has the most to gain (or lose). Thus, *you should see to it that the consumer debt you undertake does, in fact, have the desired effects on your financial condition.* You're paying for the loan, so you might as well make the most of it!

7-2b Keeping Track of Your Consumer Debt

To stay abreast of your financial condition, it's a good idea to periodically take inventory of the consumer debt you have outstanding. Ideally you should do this every three or four months, but at least once a year. To take inventory of what you owe, simply list all your outstanding consumer debt. Include *everything except your home*

FINANCIAL PLANNING TIPS

Is a 0 Percent APR Loan Really a Great Deal? Watch the Rebate …

Many 0 percent APR loan deals also give you the alternative of a cash-back rebate. You can have one or the other, but not both. Taking the cash-back rebate means that you finance your loan at a normal interest rate. Accepting the rebate will allow you to borrow less, although you pay a higher interest rate.

Consider an example in which you buy a car and finance $15,000 for 48 months at a 6.7 percent APR interest rate, which requires a monthly payment of $357.11. Your total payments over the life of the loan are $17,141. Interest is $17,141 − $15,000 = $2,141. Alternatively, a 0 percent APR loan deal for the same car at the same price would cost you only $312.50 per month, which is a savings of $2,141 over the life of the

loan. Assume that both loans are for 48 months and that your down payment is the same.

Now, assume that the car dealer offers a $2,000 cash-back rebate as an alternative to the 0 percent APR loan deal. This would reduce the loan amount to $13,000, which would mean a monthly payment of $309.49 at 6.7 percent APR. So the cash-back rebate provides a lower monthly payment than the 0 percent APR loan!

So what can we take away from this example? If you have the choice, it is almost always better to accept a rebate than a 0 percent APR loan. This is especially the case if you don't have much down payment money, because the rebate effectively acts as a down payment.

Source: Adapted from "0 percent APR Loan Deals—Good Deal or Not?" http://best-car-deals.buyerreports.org/0-apr-loan-deals, accessed August 2015.

mortgage—installment loans, single-payment loans, credit cards, revolving credit lines, overdraft protection lines, even home equity credit lines.

Worksheet 7.1 should be helpful in preparing a list of your debts. To use it, simply list the current monthly payment and the latest balance due for each type of consumer credit outstanding; then, total both columns to see how much you're paying each month and how large a debt load you have built up. Hopefully, when you've totaled all the numbers, you won't be surprised to learn just how much you really do owe.

A way to assess your debt position quickly is to compute your *debt safety ratio* (we discussed this ratio in Chapter 6) by dividing the total monthly payments (from the worksheet) by your monthly take-home pay. If 20 percent or more of your take-home pay is going to monthly credit payments, then you're relying too heavily on credit; but if your debt safety ratio works out to 10 percent or less, you're in a strong credit position. *Keeping track of your credit and holding the amount of outstanding debt to a reasonable level is the surest way to maintain your creditworthiness.*

TEST YOURSELF

7-8 What two questions should be answered before taking out a consumer loan? Explain.

7-9 List and briefly discuss the different factors to consider when shopping for a loan. How would you determine the total cost of the transaction?

7-3 SINGLE-PAYMENT LOANS

Unlike most types of consumer loans, a single-payment loan is repaid in full with a single payment on a given due date. The payment usually consists of principal and all interest charges. Sometimes, however, interim interest payments must be made (e.g., every quarter), in which case the payment at maturity is made up of principal plus any unpaid interest. Although installment loans are far more popular, single-payment loans still have their place in the consumer loan market.

WORKSHEET 7.1	Tracking Your Consumer Debt

Use a worksheet like this one to keep track of your outstanding credit along with your monthly debt service requirements. Such information is a major component of sound credit management.

AN INVENTORY OF CONSUMER DEBT

Name: Dan and Rebecca Watson   Date: June 14, 2017

Type of Consumer Debt	Creditor	Current Monthly Payment*	Latest Balance Due
Auto loans	Ford	$ 342.27	$13,796.00
Education loans	U.S. Dept of Education	117.00	7,986.00
Personal installment loans	Chase Bank	183.00	5,727.00
	Bank of America	92.85	2,474.00
Home improvement loan			
Other installment loans			
Single-payment loans			
Credit cards (retail charge cards, bank cards, etc.)	CapitalOne Visa	42.00	826.00
	Amex	35.00	600.00
	Sears	40.00	1,600.00
Overdraft protection line	Smith County Schools Credit Union	15.00	310.00
Personal line of credit			
Home equity credit line	Wells Fargo	97.00	9,700.00
Loan on life insurance			
Margin loan from broker			
Other loans	Mom & Dad		2,500.00
	Totals	$ 964.12	$ 45,519.00

$$\text{Debt safety ratio} = \frac{\text{Total monthly payments}}{\text{Monthly take-home pay}} \times 100 = \frac{\$ \ 964.12}{\$ 5,200.00} \times 100 = \underline{18.5}\%$$

*Leave the space blank if there is **no** monthly payment required on a loan (e.g., as with a single-payment or education loan).

Single-payment loans can be secured or unsecured and can be taken out for just about any purpose, from buying a new car to paying for a vacation. They're perhaps most useful when the funds needed for a given purchase or transaction are temporarily unavailable but are expected to be forthcoming in the near future. By helping you cope with a temporary cash shortfall, these loans can serve as a form of interim financing until more permanent arrangements can be made.

Single-payment loans can also be used to help establish or rebuild an individual's credit rating. Often a bank will agree to a single-payment loan for a higher-credit-risk customer if an equal amount is deposited into an account at the bank, where both the loan and deposit have the same maturity. In this way, the bank has the principal of the loan fully secured and need only be concerned about the difference between the rate charged for the loan and the rate paid on the deposit.

7-3a Important Loan Features

When applying for either a single-payment or installment loan, you must first submit a **loan application**, an example of which is shown in Exhibit 7.3. The loan application gives the lending institution information about the purpose of the loan, whether it will be secured or unsecured, and the applicant's financial condition. The loan officer uses this document, along with other information (such as a credit report from the local credit bureau and income verification) to determine whether you should be granted the loan. Here again, some type of *credit scoring* (as discussed in Chapter 6) may be used to make the decision. As part of the loan application process, you should also consider various features of the debt, the three most important of which are loan collateral, loan maturity, and loan repayment.

loan application
An application that gives a lender information about the purpose of the loan as well as the applicant's financial condition.

Loan Collateral

Most single-payment loans are secured by certain specified assets. For *collateral*, lenders prefer items they feel are readily marketable at a price that's high enough to cover the principal portion of the loan—for example, an automobile, jewelry, or stocks and bonds. If a loan is obtained to purchase some personal asset, then that asset may be used to secure it. In most cases, lenders don't take physical possession of the collateral but instead file a **lien**, which is a legal claim that permits them to liquidate the collateral to satisfy the loan if the borrower defaults. The lien is filed in the county courthouse and is a matter of public record. If the borrowers maintain possession or title to *movable* property—such as cars, TVs, and jewelry—then the instrument that gives lenders title to the property in event of default is called a **chattel mortgage**. If lenders hold title to the collateral—or actually take possession of it, as in the case of stocks and bonds—then the agreement giving them the right to sell these items in case of default is a **collateral note**.

lien
A legal claim permitting the lender, in case the borrower defaults, to liquidate the items serving as collateral to satisfy the obligation.

chattel mortgage
A mortgage on personal property given as security for the payment of an obligation.

collateral note
A legal note giving the lender the right to sell collateral if the borrower defaults on the obligation.

Loan Maturity

As indicated previously, the maturity (or term) on a single-payment loan is usually for a period of one year or less; it very rarely extends to two years or longer. When you request a single-payment loan, be sure that the term is long enough to allow you to obtain the funds for repaying the loans *but* not any longer than necessary. Don't stretch the maturity out too far, since the amount of the finance charges paid will increase with time. Because the loan is retired in a single payment, the lender must be assured that you'll be able to repay it even if unexpected events occur in the future. So, the term of your single-payment loan must be consistent with your budget and your ability to pay. If the money you plan to use for repayment will be received periodically over the term of the loan, then an installment-type loan may be more suitable.

EXHIBIT 7.3 | **A Consumer Loan Credit Application**

A typical loan application, like this one, contains information about the persons applying for the loan, including source(s) of income, current debt load, and a brief record of employment.

CONSUMER CREDIT APPLICATION

LOAN INFORMATION

Amount Requested $	Purpose		Application Type ☐Individual ☐Joint

COLLATERAL INFORMATION

☐Motor Vehicle: Year_____Make_____Model_____ Miles_____
☐Personal Property ☐Other (Describe)

APPLICANT INFORMATION

Name (Last, First, M.I.)		E-mail Address
Social Security # - -	Date of Birth / /	☐Married ☐Unmarried ☐Separated	# of Dependents

CO-APPLICANT INFORMATION

Name (Last, First, M.I.)		E-mail Address
Social Security # - -	Date of Birth / /	☐Married ☐Unmarried ☐Separated	# of Dependents

APPLICANT RESIDENCE INFORMATION

Address (Number, St, and Apt. or Lot # if applicable)	Telephone #
City, State, Zip Code	Time At Residence Years / Months /
Previous Address	Time At Residence Years / Months /
☐Rent ☐Live with Parents ☐Own ☐Other_____	Landlord or Mortgage Holder Name: Phone #:	Monthly Payment $

CO-APPLICANT RESIDENCE INFORMATION

Address (Number, St, and Apt. or Lot # if applicable)	Telephone #
City, State, Zip Code	Time At Residence Years / Months /
Previous Address	Time At Residence Years / Months /
☐Rent ☐Live with Parents ☐Own ☐Other_____	Landlord or Mortgage Holder Name: Phone #:	Monthly Payment $

APPLICANT EMPLOYMENT INFORMATION

Employer	Employer Telephone
Employer Address	Position
Gross Income: $	☐Weekly ☐Bi-weekly ☐Monthly	Time At Job Years / Months /
Other Income: $ Source	
Previous Employer & location	Previous Emp. Phone #
Position	Time At Job Years / Months /

CO-APPLICANT EMPLOYMENT

Employer	Employer Telephone
Employer Address	Position
Gross Income: $	☐Weekly ☐Bi-weekly ☐Monthly	Time At Job Years / Months /
Other Income: $ Source	Alimony, Child support, or separate maintenance income need not be revealed ifyou do not wish to have it considered as abasis for repaying this obligation.
Previous Employer & Location	Previous Emp. Phone #
Position	Time At Job Years / Months /

APPLICANT CREDIT REFERENCES

Creditor	Payment	Balance

☐Checking Bank Name_____ Acct#_____
☐Savings Bank Name_____ Acct#_____

CO-APPLICANT CREDIT REFERENCES

Creditor	Payment	Balance

☐Checking Bank Name_____ Acct#_____
☐Savings Bank Name_____ Acct#_____

AUTHORIZATION AND SIGNATURES

By signing this application, you promise that all information provided is true and complete. You also promise that you have revealed any pending lawsuits or unpaid judgements against you. You intend the lender and/or assignee to rely upon these promises in deciding whether to extend credit to you. You authorize a full investigation of your credit record and your employment history. You also authorize the seller and/or assignee to release information about your credit experience with them. You understand that the lender will retain this application whether or not it is approved. I understand that if the application is for a secured loan additional information may be required.

Applicant Signature	Date	Co-Applicant Signature	Date

Loan Repayment

Repayment of a single-payment loan is expected at a single point in time: on its maturity date. Occasionally, the funds needed to repay this type of loan will be received prior to maturity. Depending on the lender, the borrower might be able to repay the loan early and thus reduce the finance charges. Many credit unions permit early repayment of these loans with *reduced* finance charges. However, commercial banks and other single-payment lenders may not accept early repayments or, if they do, may charge a **prepayment penalty**. This penalty normally amounts to a set percentage of the interest that would have been paid over the remaining life of the loan. The Truth in Lending Act requires lenders to disclose in the loan agreement whether, and in what amount, prepayment penalties are charged on a single-payment loan.

Occasionally, an individual will borrow money using a single-payment loan and then discover that he or she is short of money when the loan comes due—after all, making one big loan payment can cause a real strain on one's cash flow. Should this happen to you, don't just let the payment go past due; instead, *inform the lender in advance so that a partial payment, loan extension, or some other arrangement can be made*. Under such circumstances, the lender will often agree to a **loan rollover**, in which case the original loan is paid off by taking out another loan. The lender will usually require that all the interest, and at least part of the principal, be paid at the time of the rollover. So if you originally borrowed $5,000 for 12 months, then the bank might be willing to lend you a lower amount, such as $3,500, for another 6 to 9 months as part of a loan rollover. In this case, you'll have to "pay down" $1,500 of the original loan, along with all interest due. However, you can expect the interest rate on a rollover loan to go up a bit; that's the price you pay for falling short on the first loan. Also, you should not expect to get more than one, or at the most two, loan rollovers—a bank's patience tends to grow short after a while!

ISTOCKPHOTO.COM/JULIE BIRCH

7-3b Finance Charges and the Annual Percentage Rate

As indicated in Chapter 6, lenders are required to disclose both the dollar amount of finance charges and the APR of interest. A sample **loan disclosure statement** applicable to either a single-payment or installment loan is in Exhibit 7.4. Note that such a statement discloses not only interest costs but also other fees and expenses that may be tacked onto the loan. Although disclosures like this one allow you to compare the various borrowing alternatives, you still need to understand the methods used to compute finance charges, because similar loans with the same *stated* interest rates may have different finance charges and APRs. The two basic procedures used to calculate the finance charges on single-payment loans are the *simple interest method* and the *discount method*.

Simple Interest Method

Interest is charged only on the *actual loan balance outstanding* in the **simple interest method**. This method is commonly used on revolving credit lines by commercial banks, S&Ls, and credit unions. To see how it's applied to a single-payment loan, assume that you borrow $1,000 for two years at an 8 percent annual rate of interest. On a single-payment loan, the actual loan balance outstanding for the two years will be the full $1,000 because no principal payments will be made until this period ends.

prepayment penalty
An additional charge you may owe if you pay off your loan prior to maturity.

loan rollover
The process of paying off a loan by taking out another loan.

loan disclosure statement
A document, which lenders are required to supply borrowers, that states both the dollar amount of finance charges and the APR applicable to a loan.

simple interest method
A method of computing finance charges in which interest is charged on the actual loan balance outstanding.

EXHIBIT 7.4	A Loan Disclosure Statement

The loan disclosure statement informs the borrower of all charges (finance and otherwise) associated with the loan and the APR. It also specifies the payment terms, as well as the existence of any balloon payments.

FEDERAL TRUTH IN LENDING DISCLOSURE STATEMENT

Creditor: YOUR FAVORITE MORTGAGE CORPORATION
Borrower(s):

Account Number: 1111111

ANNUAL PERCENTAGE RATE	FINANCE CHARGE	Amount Financed	Total of Payments
The cost of your credit as a yearly rate	The dollar amount the credit will cost you	The amount of credit provided to you or on your behalf	The amount you will have paid after you have made all payments as scheduled
7.337 %	$ 205,017.52	$ 138,796.50	$ 343,814.02

Your payment schedule will be:

NUMBER OF PAYMENTS	AMOUNT OF PAYMENTS	WHEN PAYMENTS ARE DUE
359	$955.05	Monthly beginning 09/01/17
1	951.07	Monthly beginning 08/01/48

Variable Rate: If checked, your loan contains a variable rate feature. Disclosures about the variable rate feature have been provided to you earlier.

Demand Feature: If checked, this obligation has a demand feature.

Insurance: You may obtain property insurance from anyone you want that is acceptable to the creditor.

If checked, you can get insurance through Your Favorite Mortgage Corporation. You will pay $____ for 12 months hazard insurance coverage. You will pay $ ____ for 12 months flood insurance coverage.

Security: You are giving a security interest in   property being purchased   property located at
1234 118TH STREET, NW, WASHINGTON, DC 20009
   Assignment of brokerage account and pledge of securities   Personal property: stocks and lease
   Assignment of life insurance policy   Other:
Late Charges: If a payment is late, you will be charged **5.000 %** of the payment.

Prepayment: If you pay off early, you   may   will not have to pay a penalty. You   may   will not be entitled to a refund of part of the finance charge.

Assumption: Someone buying your house   may, subject to conditions, be allowed to   cannot assume the remainder of the mortgage on the original terms.

See your contract documents for any additional information about nonpayment, default, any required repayment in full before the scheduled date, prepayment refunds and penalties and assumption policy.

ACKNOWLEDGMENT

By signing below you acknowledge that you have received a completed copy of this Federal Truth in Lending Statement prior to the execution *of* any closing documents.

_____
Borrower/Date of Acknowledgment

_____
Borrower/Date of Acknowledgment

Source: Adapted from http://www.entitledirect.com/sites/default/files/fed_truth_in_lending.pdf, accessed August 2015.

With simple interest, the finance charge is obtained by multiplying the outstanding *principal* by the stated annual rate of interest and then multiplying this amount by the term of the loan:

$$\text{Finance Charge (Simple Interest)} = \text{Amount of Loan} \times \text{Interest Rate} \times \text{Term of Loan}$$

Note that the term of the loan is stated in years. For example, the term would equal 0.5 for a 6-month loan, 1.25 for a 15-month loan, and 2.0 for a 2-year loan.

> **EXAMPLE: Calculating the Total Finance Charge and Payment on a Simple Interest Loan**
>
> You have taken out a $1,000, 8 percent, two-year simple interest loan. Using the above equation, the total finance charge on the loan equals $160 (i.e., $1,000 × 0.08 per year × 2 years). With this type of credit arrangement, the loan payment is found by adding the finance charges to the principal amount of the loan, so you'd have to make a loan payment of $1,000 + $160 = $1,160 at maturity to pay off this debt.

> **EXAMPLE: Calculating the Annual Percentage Rate on a Simple Interest Loan**
>
> Continuing the prior simple loan method example, the true, or annual, percentage rate of interest is the average annual finance charge divided by the average loan balance outstanding, as follows:
>
> $$\text{APR} = \frac{\text{Average Annual Finance Charge}}{\text{Average Loan Balance Outstanding}}$$
>
> The average annual finance charge is found by dividing the total finance charge by the life of the loan (in years), which is $80 in this example ($160/2). Because the loan

FINANCIAL PLANNING TIPS

How Do Lenders Look at Your Loan Application?

When you're planning to take out a loan for a purchase (large or small), it helps to understand how lenders will evaluate your loan application. Here are the items they look at and what you can do to make them as good as possible:

• **Credit report.** Lenders will review your credit report from two or three of the credit reporting companies (Experian, Equifax, and TransUnion) to assure that they have all the facts. Make sure to check at least one of your reports so you'll know what the lender is seeing and can fix any potential errors that could delay or prevent approval of your loan.

• **Debt history.** When looking over your credit report, the lender will consider how much debt you already owe, how much unused credit is available to you, how promptly you pay your bills, and whether you've applied

for more credit lately. Be prepared to answer questions about these points.

• **Job history.** Lenders will look at your job history in order to evaluate your financial stability and associated capacity to repay the loan.

• **Savings.** The lender will want to know if you have enough money for a down payment, funds to cover an emergency, and where these funds are (e.g., savings account, checking account, and mutual funds).

Keep in mind that whether you're hoping to finance a house or a new car, you'll be in the best bargaining position when shopping if you have obtained a pre-approval (pre-qualification) for a specific loan amount. Knowing the above points should help your loan application move along smoothly.

balance outstanding remains at $1,000 over the life of the loan, the average loan balance is $1,000. Thus, the APR is:

$$\$80/\$1{,}000 = 8 \text{ percent}$$

The APR and the stated rate of interest are equivalent: they both equal 8 percent. *This is always the case when the simple interest method is used to calculate finance charges, regardless of whether loans are single-payment or installment.*

Discount Method

discount method
A method of calculating finance charges in which interest is computed and then subtracted from the principal, with the remainder being disbursed to the borrower.

The **discount method** calculates total finance charges on the full principal amount of the loan, which is then subtracted from the amount of the loan. The difference between the amount of the loan and the finance charge is then paid to the borrower. In other words, finance charges are paid in advance and represent a discount from the principal portion of the loan. The finance charge on a single-payment loan using the discount method is calculated in exactly the same way as for a simple interest loan:

$$\text{Finance Charge (Discount Method)} = \text{Amount of Loan} \times \text{Interest Rate} \times \text{Term of Loan}$$

Using this formula, the finance charge on the $1,000, 8 percent, 2-year, single-payment discount method loan is (of course) the same $160 we calculated earlier. However, in sharp contrast to simple interest loans, the loan payment with a discount loan is based on the original amount of the loan, and the finance charges on the loan are deducted up front from the loan proceeds. Thus, the discount method yields a much higher APR on single-payment loans than does the simple interest method. Exhibit 7.5 contrasts the results from both methods for the single-payment loan example discussed here.

Financial Fact or Fantasy?

Using the discount method to calculate interest is one way of lowering the effective cost of a consumer loan. **Fantasy:** Because the interest is paid in advance on discount loans, the net effect is to substantially raise the cost of borrowing. Specifically, a discount loan results in a true interest rate (APR) that is much higher than the stated rate.

EXAMPLE: Calculating the Annual Percentage Rate on a Discount Loan

You have taken out a $1,000, 8 percent, two-year discount loan. To find the APR on this discount loan, substitute the appropriate values into the APR equation shown previously. For this 2-year loan, the average annual finance charge is $80 ($160 ÷ 2). However, because this is a discount loan, the borrower will receive only $840. And because this is a single-payment loan, the average amount of debt outstanding is also $840. When these figures are used in the APR equation, we find the true rate for this 8 percent discount loan is:

$$\$80/\$840 = 9.52\%.$$

EXHIBIT 7.5	Finance Charges and APRs for a Single-Payment Loan ($1,000 Loan for Two Years at 8 percent Interest)

Sometimes what you see is not what you get—such as when you borrow money through a discount loan and end up paying quite a bit more than the quoted rate.

Method	Stated Rate on Loan	Finance Charges	APR
Simple interest	8.0%	$160	8.00%
Discount	8.0	160	9.52

TEST YOURSELF

7-10   What is a *lien*, and when is it part of a consumer loan?

7-11   When might you request a *loan rollover*?

7-12   Describe the two methods used to calculate the finance charges on a single-payment loan. As a borrower, which method would you prefer? Explain.

7-4   INSTALLMENT LOANS

LG5, LG6

Installment loans differ from single-payment loans in that they require the borrower to repay the debt in a series of installment payments (usually monthly) over the life of the loan. Installment loans have long been one of the most popular forms of consumer credit—right up there with credit cards! Much of this popularity is due to how conveniently the loan repayment is set up. Unsurprisingly, most people find it easier on their checkbooks to make a series of small payments than one big one.

7-4a   A Real Consumer Credit Workhorse

As a source of financing, there are few things that installment loans can't do—which explains, in large part, why this form of consumer credit is so widely used. They can be used to finance just about any type of big-ticket item imaginable. New car loans are the dominant type of installment loan, but this form of credit is also used to finance home furnishings, appliances and entertainment centers, camper trailers and other recreational vehicles, and even expensive vacations. Also, more and more college students are turning to this type of credit as the way to finance their education.

Not only can installment loans be used to finance all sorts of things, they can also be obtained at many locations. You'll find them at banks and other financial institutions, as well as at major department stores and merchants that sell relatively expensive products. These loans can be taken out for just a few hundred dollars, or they can involve thousands of dollars—indeed, installment loans of $25,000 or more are common. In addition, installment loans can be set up with maturities as short as 6 months or as long as 7 to 10 years—or even 15 years.

Most installment loans are secured with some kind of collateral. For example, the car or home entertainment center you purchased with the help of an installment loan usually serves as collateral on the loan. Even personal loans used to finance things like expensive vacations can be secured—in these cases, the collateral could be securities, CDs, or some other type of financial asset. One rapidly growing segment of this market is installment loans secured by second mortgages. These so-called *home equity loans* are similar to the home equity credit lines discussed in Chapter 6, except they involve a set amount of money loaned over a set period of time (often as long as 15 years) rather than a revolving credit line from which you can borrow, repay, and reborrow. For example, if a borrower needs $25,000 to help pay for an expensive new boat, he can simply take out a loan in that amount and *secure it with a second mortgage on his home.* This loan would be like any other installment loan in the sense that it's for a set amount of money and is to be repaid over a set period of time in monthly installments. Besides their highly competitive interest rates, a big attraction of *home equity loans* is that the interest paid on them usually can be taken as a tax deduction. Thus, borrowers get the double benefit of *low interest rates* and *tax deductibility.* However, as with home equity credit lines, failure to repay could result in the loss of your home.

7-4b Finance Charges, Monthly Payments, and the APR

We previously discussed the simple interest and discount methods of determining finance charges on single-payment loans. In this section, we look at the use of simple and add-on interest to compute finance charges and monthly payments for installment loans (technically, discount interest can also be used with installment loans; but because this is rare, we ignore it here). To illustrate, we'll use an 8 percent, $1,000 installment loan that is to be paid off in 12 monthly payments. As in the earlier illustration for single-payment loans, we assume that interest is the only component of the finance charge; there are no other fees and charges.

Using Simple Interest

When simple interest is used with installment loans, interest is charged only on the outstanding balance of the loan. Thus, as the loan principal declines with monthly payments, the amount of interest being charged also decreases. Because finance charges change each month, the procedure used to find the interest expense is mathematically complex. Fortunately, this isn't much of a problem in practice because of the widespread use of computers, handheld financial calculators (which we'll illustrate later), and preprinted finance tables—an example of which is provided in Exhibit 7.6. The tables show the *monthly payment* required to retire an installment loan carrying a given simple rate of interest with a given term to maturity. Because

EXHIBIT 7.6	A Table of Monthly Installment Loan Payments to Repay a $1,000, Simple Interest Loan

You can use a table like this to find the monthly payments on a wide variety of simple interest installment loans. Although it's set up to show payments on a $1,000 loan, with a little modification, you can easily use it with any size loan (the principal can be more or less than $1,000).

LOAN MATURITY

Rate of Interest	6 Months	12 Months	18 Months	24 Months	36 Months	48 Months	60 Months
6.0	$169.60	$86.07	$58.23	$44.32	$30.42	$23.49	$19.33
6.5	169.84	86.30	58.46	44.55	30.65	23.71	19.57
7.0	170.09	86.53	58.68	44.77	30.88	23.95	19.80
7.5	170.33	86.76	58.92	45.00	31.11	24.18	20.05
8.0	170.58	86.99	59.15	45.23	31.34	24.42	20.28
8.5	170.82	87.22	59.37	45.46	31.57	24.65	20.52
9.0	171.07	87.46	59.60	45.69	31.80	24.89	20.76
9.5	171.32	87.69	59.83	45.92	32.04	25.13	21.01
10.0	171.56	87.92	60.06	46.15	32.27	25.37	21.25
11.0	172.05	88.50	60.64	46.73	32.86	25.97	21.87
12.0	172.50	88.85	60.99	47.08	33.22	26.34	22.25
13.0	173.04	89.32	61.45	47.55	33.70	26.83	22.76
14.0	173.54	89.79	61.92	48.02	34.18	27.33	23.27
15.0	174.03	90.26	62.39	48.49	34.67	27.84	23.79
16.0	174.53	90.74	62.86	48.97	35.16	28.35	24.32
17.0	175.03	91.21	63.34	49.45	35.66	28.86	24.86
18.0	175.53	91.68	63.81	49.93	36.16	29.38	25.40

these tables (sometimes referred to as *amortization schedules*) have interest charges built right into them, the monthly payments shown cover both principal and interest.

Notice that the loan payments shown in Exhibit 7.6 cover a variety of interest rates (from 6 percent to 18 percent) and loan maturities (from 6 to 60 months). The table values represent the monthly payments required to retire a $1,000 loan. Although it's assumed that you're borrowing $1,000, you can use the table with any size loan. For example, if you're looking at a $5,000 loan, just multiply the monthly loan payment from the table by 5 (since $5,000/$1,000 = 5); or, if you have a $500 loan, multiply the loan payment by 0.5 ($500/$1,000 = 0.5). In many respects, this table is just like the mortgage loan payment schedule introduced in Chapter 5, except we use much shorter loan maturities here than with mortgages.

> ## EXAMPLE: Determining Installment Loan Payment Amounts Using Financial Tables
>
> Suppose you want to find the monthly installment payment required on our example $1,000, 8 percent, 12-month loan using Exhibit 7.6. Looking under the 12-month column and across from the 8 percent rate of interest, we find a value of $86.99. That is the monthly payment it will take to pay off the $1,000 loan in 12 months. When we multiply the monthly payments ($86.99) by the term of the loan in months (12), the result is total payments of $86.99 × 12 = $1,043.88. The difference between the total payments on the loan and the principal portion represents the *total finance charges on the loan*—in this case, $1,043.88 − $1,000 = $43.88 in interest charges.

Calculator

INPUTS	FUNCTIONS
12	N
8	I/Y
−1000	PV
	CPT
	PMT
	SOLUTION
	86.99

See Appendix E for details.

Calculator Keystrokes. Instead of using a table like the one in Exhibit 7.6, you could just as easily have used a handheld financial calculator to *find the monthly payments on an installment loan.* Here's what you'd do. First, set the payments per year (P/Y) key to 12 to put the calculator in a monthly payment mode. Now, to find the monthly payment needed to pay off an 8 percent, 12-month, $1,000 installment loan, use the keystrokes shown here, where

> N = length of the loan, *in months*
> I/Y = the *annual* rate of interest being charged on the loan
> PV = the amount of the loan, entered as a *negative* number

As seen, to pay off this installment loan, you'll have to make payments of $86.99 per month for the next 12 months.

From each monthly payment (of $86.99), a certain portion goes to interest and the balance is used to reduce the principal. Because the principal balance declines with each payment, the amount that goes to interest also *decreases* while the amount that goes to principal *increases*. Exhibit 7.7 illustrates this cash-flow stream. Because *monthly* payments are used with the loan, the interest column in Exhibit 7.7 is also based on a *monthly* rate of interest—that is, the annual rate is divided by 12 to obtain a monthly rate (8 percent per year ÷ 12 months per year = 0.67 percent per month). This monthly rate is then applied to the outstanding loan balance to find the monthly interest charges in column 3. Because interest is charged only on the outstanding balance, *the annual percentage rate (APR) on a simple interest installment loan will always equal the stated rate*—in this case, 8 percent.

add-on method
A method of calculating interest by computing finance charges on the original loan balance and then adding the interest to that balance.

Add-on Method

Some installment loans, particularly those obtained directly from retail merchants or made at finance companies and the like, are made using the **add-on method**. Add-on

EXHIBIT 7.7

Monthly Payment Analysis for a Simple Interest Installment Loan (Assumes a $1,000, 8%, 12-Month Loan)

Part of each monthly payment on an installment loan goes to interest and part to principal. As the loan is paid down over time, less and less of each payment goes to interest and more and more goes to principal.

Month	Outstanding Loan Balance at Beginning of Month (1)	Monthly Payment (2)	Interest Charges [(1) × 0.00667] (3)	Principal [(2) − (3)] (4)
1	$1,000.00	$86.99	$6.67	$80.32
2	919.68	86.99	6.13	80.86
3	838.82	86.99	5.59	81.40
4	757.42	86.99	5.05	81.94
5	675.49	86.99	4.50	82.49
6	593.00	86.99	3.95	83.03
7	509.97	86.99	3.40	83.59
8	426.38	86.99	2.84	84.15
9	342.23	86.99	2.28	84.71
10	257.52	86.99	1.72	85.27
11	172.25	86.99	1.15	85.84
12	86.41	86.99	0.58	86.41
Total		$1,043.88	$43.88	$1,000.00

Note: The monthly interest rate is 0.08/12 = 0.00667. Column 1 values for months 2 through 12 are obtained by subtracting the principal payment shown in column 4 for the preceding month from the outstanding loan balance shown in column 1 for the preceding month; thus, $1,000 − $80.32 = $919.68, which is the outstanding loan balance at the beginning of month 2.

loans generally rank as one of the most costly forms of consumer credit, with APRs that are often well above the rates charged even on many credit cards. With add-on interest, the finance charges are calculated using the *original* balance of the loan; this amount (of the total finance charges) is then added on to the original loan balance to determine the total amount to be repaid. Thus, the amount of finance charges on an add-on loan can be found by using the familiar simple interest formula:

$$\text{Finance Charge (Add-on Method)} = \text{Amount of Loan} \times \text{Interest Rate} \times \text{Term of Loan}$$

Given the $1,000 loan we've been using for illustrative purposes, the total finance charges on an 8 percent, 1-year add-on loan would be

$$\text{Finance Charge (Add-on Method)} = \$1,000 \times 0.08 \times 1 = \$80$$

Compared to the finance charges for the same installment loan on a simple interest basis ($43.88), an add-on installment loan is a lot more expensive—a fact that also shows up in monthly payments and in the APR. Keep in mind that both of these loans would be quoted as "8 percent" loans. Thus, you may think you're getting an 8 percent loan, but looks can be deceiving—especially when you're dealing with add-on interest! So, when you're taking out an installment loan, be sure to find out whether simple or add-on interest is being used to compute finance charges. (And if it's add-on, you might want to consider looking elsewhere for the loan.)

To find the monthly payments on an add-on loan, add the finance charge to the original principal amount of the loan and then divide this sum by the number of monthly payments to be made:

$$\text{Monthly Payment} = \frac{(\text{Amount of Loan} + \text{Finance Charge})}{\text{Number of Payments}}$$

EXAMPLE: Calculating Monthly Payments on an Add-On Installment Loan

You want to calculate the monthly payments a $1,000, 8 percent, 12-month add-on interest loan. The previously-calculated finance charge is $80. Applying the above expression:

$$\text{Monthly Payment} = \frac{(\$1,000 + \$80)}{12} = \$90$$

As expected, these monthly payments are higher than those on an otherwise comparable simple interest installment loan.

Because the actual rate of interest with an add-on loan is considerably higher than the stated rate, it's particularly important to calculate the loan's APR. That can easily be done with a financial calculator, as shown below. As you can see, the APR on this 8 percent add-on loan is more like 14.45 percent. Clearly, when viewed from an APR perspective, the add-on loan is an expensive form of financing! (A rough but reasonably accurate rule of thumb is that the APR on an add-on loan is about *twice* the stated rate. Thus, if the loan is quoted at an add-on rate of 9 percent, you'll probably be paying a true rate that's closer to 18 percent.) This is because when add-on interest is applied to an installment loan, the interest included in each payment is charged on the *initial principal* even though the outstanding loan balance declines as installment payments are made. A summary of comparative finance charges and APRs for simple interest and add-on interest methods is presented in Exhibit 7.8.

Calculator

INPUTS	FUNCTIONS
12	N
–1000	PV
90.00	PMT
	CPT
	I/Y
	SOLUTION
	14.45

See Appendix E for details.

Calculator Keystrokes. Here's how you *find the APR on an add-on installment loan* using a financial calculator. First, make sure the payments per year (P/Y) key is set to 12, so the calculator is in the monthly payment mode. Then, to find the APR on a $1,000, 12-month, 8 percent add-on installment loan, use the following keystrokes, where

N = Length of the loan, in months
PV = Size of the loan, entered as a negative number
PMT = Size of the monthly installment loan payments

You'll find that the APR on the 8 percent add-on loan is a whopping 14.45 percent!

EXHIBIT 7.8 **Comparative Finance Charges and APRs on a $1,000, 8 Percent, 12-Month Installment Loan**

In sharp contrast to simple interest loans, the APR with add-on installment loans is much higher than the stated rate.

	Simple Interest	Add-on Interest
Stated rate on loan	8%	8%
Finance charges	$43.88	$80.00
Monthly payments	$86.99	$90.00
Total payments made	$1,043.88	$1,080.00
APR	8%	14.45%

Federal banking regulations require that the exact APR (accurate to the nearest 0.25 percent) must be disclosed to borrowers. And note that not only interest but also any other fees required to obtain a loan are considered part of the finance charges and must be included in the computation of APR.

Prepayment Penalties

Another type of finance charge that's often found in installment loan contracts is the *prepayment penalty*, an additional charge you may owe if you decide to pay off your loan prior to maturity. When you pay off a loan early, you may find that you owe quite a bit more than expected, especially if the lender uses the **Rule of 78s** (or sum-of-the-digits method) to calculate the amount of interest paid and the principal balance to date. You might think that paying off a $1,000, 8 percent, 1-year loan at the end of 6 months would mean that you've paid about half of the principal and owe somewhere around $500 to the lender. That's just not so with a loan that uses the Rule of 78s! This method charges more interest in the early months of the loan on the theory that the borrower has use of more money in the loan's early stages and so should pay more finance charges in the early months and progressively less later. There's nothing wrong with that, of course; it's how all loans operate. But what's wrong is that the Rule of 78s front-loads an inordinate amount of interest charges to the early months of the loan, thereby producing a much higher principal balance than you'd normally expect (remember: the more of the loan payment that goes to interest, the less that goes to the repayment of principal).

Let's assume that we want to pay off the $1,000, 8 percent, 1-year add-on loan after six months. Using the Rule of 78s, you would owe $518.46. So, even though you've made payments for half of the life of the loan, you still owe more than half of the principal. In contrast, with the same loan under simple interest, you'd owe only $509.97 in principal after six months. Thus, the Rule of 78s benefits the lender at the expense of the borrower.

Credit Life Insurance

Sometimes, as a condition of receiving an installment loan, a borrower is required to buy **credit life insurance** and possibly **credit disability insurance**. Credit life (and disability) insurance is tied to a particular installment loan and provides insurance that the loan will be paid off if the borrower dies (or becomes disabled) before the loan matures. These policies insure the borrower for an amount sufficient to repay the outstanding loan balance. The seller's (or lender's) ability to dictate the terms of these insurance requirements is either banned or restricted by law in many states. If this type of insurance is required as a condition of the loan, then its cost must be added to the finance charges and included as part of the APR. From the borrower's perspective, credit life and disability insurance is not a good deal: *It's very costly and does little more than give lenders an additional lucrative source of income.* Unsurprisingly, because it's so lucrative, some lenders aggressively push it on unsuspecting borrowers and, in some cases, even require it as a condition for granting a loan. The best advice is to avoid it if at all possible!

Financial Fact or Fantasy?

The Rule of 78s is a regulation that grew out of the Consumer Credit Enhancement Act of 1978 and mandates how installment loans will be set up. **Fantasy:** The Rule of 78s is a procedure that is used to find the monthly finance charges on add-on loans.

7-4c Buy on Time or Pay Cash?

When buying a big-ticket item, you often have little choice but to take out a loan—the purchase (perhaps it's a new car) is just so expensive that you can't afford to pay cash. And even if you do have the money, you may still be better off using something like an installment loan *if the cash purchase would end up severely depleting your liquid reserves.* But don't just automatically take out a loan. Rather, take the time to find out if that is, in fact, the best thing to do. Such a decision can easily be made by using Worksheet 7.2, which considers the cost of the loan relative to the after-tax earnings generated from having your money in some type of short-term investment. It's assumed that the consumer has an adequate level of liquid reserves and that these reserves are being held in some type of savings account. (Obviously, if this is not the case, then there's little reason to go through the exercise because you have no choice but to borrow the money.) Essentially, it all boils down to this: *If it costs more to borrow the money than you can earn in interest, then withdraw the money from your savings to pay cash for the purchase; if not, you should consider taking out a loan.*

Consider this situation: You're thinking about buying a second car (a nice, low-mileage used vehicle) but, after the normal down payment, you still need to come up with $12,000. This balance can be taken care of in one of two ways: (1) you can take out a 36-month, 8 percent installment loan (for a monthly payment of $376.04), or (2) you can pay cash by drawing the money from a money fund (paying 4 percent interest today and for the foreseeable future). We can now run the numbers to decide whether to buy on time or pay cash—see Worksheet 7.2 for complete details. In this case, we assume the loan is a standard installment loan (where the interest does not qualify as a tax deduction) and that you're in the 28 percent tax bracket. The worksheet shows that, by borrowing the money, you'll end up paying about $1,537 in interest (line 4), none of which is tax deductible. In contrast, by leaving your money on deposit in the money fund, you'll receive only $1,038 in interest, after taxes (see line 11). Taken together, we see the net cost of borrowing (line 12) is nearly $500—so you'll be paying $1,537 to earn only $1,038, which certainly doesn't make much sense! Clearly, it's far more cost-effective in this case to take the money from savings and pay cash for the car, because you'll save nearly $500.

Although saving $500 is a convincing reason for avoiding a loan, sometimes the actual dollar spread between the cost of borrowing and interest earned is very small, perhaps only $100 or less. Being able to deduct the interest on a loan can lead to a relatively small spread, but it can also occur, for example, if the amount being financed is relatively small—say, you want $1,500 or $2,000 for a ski trip to Colorado. In this case—and so long as the spread stays small enough—you may decide it's still worthwhile to borrow the money in order to maintain a higher level of liquidity. Although this decision is perfectly legitimate when very small spreads exist, it makes less sense as the gap starts to widen.

TEST YOURSELF

7-13   Briefly describe the basic features of an installment loan.

7-14   What is a home equity loan, and what are its major advantages and disadvantages?

7-15   Explain why a borrower is often required to purchase *credit life* and *disability insurance* as a condition of receiving an installment loan.

7-16   Define simple interest as it relates to an installment loan. Are you better off with add-on interest? Explain.

7-17   When does it make more sense to pay cash for a big-ticket item than to borrow the money to finance the purchase?

Using a worksheet like this, you can decide whether to buy on time or pay cash by comparing the after-tax cost of interest paid on a loan with the after-tax interest income lost by taking the money out of savings and using it to pay cash for the purchase.

BUY ON TIME OR PAY CASH

Name __Glen Bronson_____ Date __2/28/2017_____

■ **Cost of Borrowing**		
1. Terms of the loan		
a. Amount of the loan	$ 12,000.00	
b. Length of the loan (in years)	3.00	
c. Monthly payment	$ 376.04	
2. Total loan payments made (monthly loan payment × length of loan in months) $376.04 per month × 36 months		$ 13,537.44
3. Less: Principal amount of the loan		$ 12,000.00
4. Total interest paid over life of loan (line 2 — 3)		$ 1,537.44
5. Tax considerations:		
• Is this a home equity loan (where interest expenses can be deducted from taxes)?	☐ yes ☑ no	
• Do you itemize deductions on your federal tax returns?	☑ yes ☐ no	
• If you answered yes to BOTH questions, then proceed to line 6; if you answered no to *either one* or *both* of the questions, then proceed to *line 8* and use *line 4* as the after-tax interest cost of the loan.		
6. What federal tax bracket are you in? (use either 10, 15, 25, 28, 33, or 35%)	28 %	
7. Taxes saved due to interest deductions (line 4 × tax rate, from line 6: $_____ × _____ %)		$ 0.00
Total after-tax interest cost on the loan (line 4 — line 7) 8.		$ 1,537.44
■ **Cost of Paying Cash**		
9. Annual interest earned on savings (annual rate of interest earned on savings × amount of loan: 4 % × 12,000.00)		$ 480.00
10. Annual after-tax interest earnings (line 9 × [1 — tax rate] — e.g., 1 — 28% = 72%: $480.00 × 72 %)		$ 346.00
11. Total after-tax interest earnings over life of loan (line 10 × line 1b: $346.00 × 3 years)		$ 1,038.00
■ **Net Cost of Borrowing**		
12. Difference in cost of borrowing vs. cost of paying cash (line 8 minus line 11)		$ 499.44

BASIC DECISION RULE: *Pay cash* if line 12 is positive; *borrow the money* if line 12 is negative.

Note: For simplicity, compounding is ignored in calculating *both* the cost of interest and interest earnings.

Here are some key considerations for using credit in each stage of the life cycle.

Pre-family Independence: 20s	Family Formation/ Career Development: 30–45	Pre-Retirement: 45–65	Retirement: 65 and Beyond
✓ Make sure your emergency fund is adequate.	✓ Start selectively relying on savings rather than credit for large purchases.	✓ If you must make credit payments late, inform the lender.	✓ Consider a second mortgage or home equity line of credit to reduce borrowing costs.
✓ If you are married, maintain your individual credit history by not borrowing exclusively as a couple.	✓ Budget to keep credit account balances easy to pay each month.	✓ Monitor your credit card and bank statements for unauthorized transactions.	✓ Budget to limit dependence on consumer credit.
✓ Review your credit report at least once a year.	✓ Monitor your credit report at least once a year.	✓ Monitor your credit report at least once a year.	✓ Monitor your credit report at least once a year.

Financial Impact of Personal Choices

John and Mary Calculate their Auto Loan Backward

John and Mary Brunner budget and spend their money carefully. Their Honda CRV has over 150,000 miles and needs to be replaced. Because they drive their cars so long, John and Mary have decided to buy a new car and have saved a $5,000 down payment. They are willing to make a monthly car payment of about $350 while 48-month loans are at 3 percent. Before they choose a new car, they want to determine how much they can afford to spend.

John and Mary do their auto loan calculations backward to figure out the size of the auto loan implied by a 48-month maturity and 3 percent interest. Using a calculator and the approach explained in this chapter, that loan amount is about $15,813. Thus, given their down payment of $5,000, John and Mary can afford a car selling for about $20,813 net of tax, title and licensing fees ($15,813 + $5,000). They are indeed careful, if not "backward," car shoppers who explore the angles.

Summary

LG1 **Know when to use consumer loans, and be able to differentiate between the major types. p. 261**
Single-payment and installment loans are formally negotiated consumer loan arrangements used mainly to finance big-ticket items. Most of these consumer loans are taken out as auto loans, loans for other durable goods, education loans, personal loans, and consolidation loans.

LG2 **Identify the various sources of consumer loans. p. 261**
Consumer loans can be obtained from various sources, including commercial banks (the biggest providers of such credit), consumer finance companies, credit unions, S&Ls, sales finance (and captive finance) companies, life insurance companies (and other financial services organizations), and, as a last resort, your friends and relatives.

LG3 **Choose the best loans by comparing finance charges, maturity, collateral, and other loan terms. p. 271**
Before taking out a consumer loan, you should be sure the purchase is compatible with your financial plans and that you can service the debt without straining your budget. When shopping for credit, it's in your best interest to compare such loan features as finance charges (APRs), loan maturities, monthly payments, and collateral requirements; then choose loans with terms that are fully compatible with your financial plans and cash budget.

LG4 **Describe the features of, and calculate the finance charges on, single-payment loans. p. 275**
In a single-payment loan, the borrower makes just one principal payment (at the maturity of the loan), although there may be one or more interim interest payments. Such loans are usually made for one year or less, and they're normally secured by some type of collateral. A major advantage of the single-payment loan is that it doesn't require monthly payments and won't tie up the borrower's cash flow. Finance charges can be calculated in one of two ways: (1) the simple interest method, which applies the interest rate to the outstanding loan balance; or (2) the discount method, in which interest is calculated just as in the previous method but is then deducted from the loan principal, yielding a higher APR.

LG5 **Evaluate the benefits of an installment loan. p. 282**
In an installment loan, the borrower agrees to repay the loan through a series of equal installment payments (usually monthly) until the obligation is fully repaid; in this way, the borrower can receive a loan repayment schedule that fits neatly into his or her financial plans and cash budget. This highly popular form of consumer credit can be used to finance just about any type of big-ticket asset or expenditure. Many installment loans are taken out as home equity loans to capture tax advantages.

LG6 **Determine the costs of installment loans, and analyze whether it is better to pay cash or take out a loan. p. 282**
Most single-payment loans are made with either simple or discount interest, whereas most installment loans are made with either simple or add-on interest. When simple interest is used, the actual finance charge always corresponds to the stated rate of interest; in contrast, when add-on or discount rates are used, the APR is always more than the stated rate. In the end, whether it makes sense to borrow rather than to pay cash is a matter of which alternative costs less.

Key Terms

Answers Test Yourself

You can find answers to these questions on this book's companion website. Look for it at *www.cengagebrain.com*. Search for this book by its title, and then add it to your dashboard.

Key Financial Relationships

Concept	Financial Relationship	Page Number
Simple Interest Method Finance Charges on a Single-Payment Loan	Finance Charge (Simple Interest method) = Amount of Loan × Interest Rate × Term of Loan	280
Discount Method Finance Charges on a Single-Payment Loan	Finance Charge (Discount method) = Amount of Loan × Interest Rate × Term of Loan	281
Annual Percentage Rate (APR)	$\text{APR} = \dfrac{\text{Average Annual Finance Charge}}{\text{Average Loan Balance Outstanding}}$	280
Add-on Loan Monthly Payment	$\text{Monthly Payment (Add-on Method)} = \dfrac{\text{Amount of Loan} + \text{Finance Charge}}{\text{Number of Payments}}$	285

Key Financial Relationships Problem Set

1. ***Simple Interest Method Finance Charges.*** Todd Gardner wants to calculate the total finance charge on a 2-year, 4 percent simple interest, single-payment loan for $3,000.

   Solution: The total finance charge is calculated as:

   Finance Charge (Simple Interest) = Amount of Loan × Interest Rate × Term of Loan
   = $3,000 × 0.04 × 2 = $240.00

2. ***Discount Method Finance Charges.*** Nicole Holmes has taken out a 1 and a half-year, 3 percent discount, single-payment loan for $4,000. What is the total finance charge on the loan?

   Solution: The total finance charge is calculated as:

   Finance Charge (Discount method) = Amount of Loan × Interest Rate × Term of Loan
   = $4,000 × 0.03 × 1.5 = $180.00

   Notice that the approach to calculating the total finance charge is the same as that used for the simple interest approach.

3. ***Annual Percentage Rate (APR).*** Wayne Snyder is considering taking out a 2-year, 4 percent, single-payment discount loan for $3,500. He's heard that the APR for discount loans is greater than the stated rate and wants to confirm exactly how much higher it is before considering an otherwise comparable simple interest loan.

   Solution: Wayne must first determine the total finance charge, which is:

   Finance Charge (Discount method) = Amount of Loan × Interest Rate × Term of Loan

   $$= \$3{,}500 \times 0.04 \times 2 = \$280.00$$

   Because it's a discount loan, at the time the loan is extended Wayne will only receive $3,500 − $280.00 = $3,220. As a 2-year single-payment loan, the average amount of debt outstanding is also $3,220. The APR is calculated as:

   $$\text{APR} = \frac{\text{Average Annual Finance Charge}}{\text{Average Loan Balance Outstanding}} = \frac{\$280.00/2}{\$3{,}220.00} = 4.35 \text{ percent}$$

   Wayne is correct that the APR of the discount loan is somewhat higher than the rate on an otherwise comparable simple interest loan.

4. ***Add-on Loan Monthly Payment and APR.*** Craig Sims has decided to borrow $4,500 using a 1-year, 4 percent, monthly installment loan. He wants to calculate the amount of the monthly payments and the APR on the loan.

   Solution: Craig must first determine the total finance charge, which is:

   Finance Charge (Discount) = Amount of Loan × Interest Rate × Term of Loan

   $$= \$4{,}500 \times 0.04 \times 1 = \$180.00$$

   The monthly payments are calculated as:

   $$\text{Monthly Payment (Add- on Method)} = \frac{\text{Amount of Loan} + \text{Finance Charge}}{\text{Number of Payments}}$$

   $$= \frac{\$4{,}500 + \$180}{12} = \$390.00$$

   Craig could use a financial calculator with the following key strokes to estimate the APR on the add-on loan:

Inputs	Functions
12	N
−1450	PV
390	PMT
	CPT
	CPT
	I/Y
	SOLUTION
	7.30

   Thus, using a 4 percent add-on installment loan will really cost Craig about 7.3 percent while an otherwise comparable simple-interest installment loan would have a stated interest rate and an APR of 4 percent.

LG1, 2, p. 261 1. **Student loan options.** Marilyn Seacrest is a sophomore at State College and is running out of money. Wanting to continue her education, Marilyn is considering a student loan. Explain her options. How can she minimize her borrowing costs and maximize her flexibility?

LG3, 6, p. 271, 282 2. **Evaluating finance packages.** Assume that you've been shopping for a new car and intend to finance part of it through an installment loan. The car you're looking for has a sticker price of $18,000. The local dealership has offered to sell it to you for $3,000 down and finance the balance with a loan that will require 48 monthly payments of $333.67; Adventure Vehicles will sell you the exact same vehicle for $3,500 down, plus a 60-month loan for the balance, with monthly payments of $265.02. Which of these two finance packages is the better deal? Explain.

LG3, p. 271 3. **Calculating debt safety ratio. Use Worksheet 7.1.** Every six months, Larry Sun takes an inventory of the consumer debts that he has outstanding. His latest tally shows that he still owes $4,000 on a home improvement loan (monthly payments of $125); he is making $85 monthly payments on a personal loan with a remaining balance of $750; he has a $2,000, secured, single-payment loan that's due late next year; he has a $70,000 home mortgage on which he's making $750 monthly payments; he still owes $8,600 on a new car loan (monthly payments of $375); and he has a $960 balance on his *MasterCard* (minimum payment of $40), a $70 balance on his Exxon credit card (balance due in 30 days), and a $1,200 balance on a personal line of credit ($60 monthly payments). Use Worksheet 7.1 to prepare an inventory of Larry's consumer debt. Find his debt safety ratio given that his take-home pay is $2,500 per month. Would you consider this ratio to be good or bad? Explain.

LG4, p. 275 4. **Calculating single payment loan amount due at maturity.** Jim Grant plans to borrow $8,000 for five years. The loan will be *repaid with a single payment after five years*, and the interest on the loan will be computed using the simple interest method at an annual rate of 6 percent. How much will Jim have to pay in five years? How much will he have to pay at maturity if he's required to make *annual interest payments* at the end of each year?

LG4, p. 275 5. **Calculating the APR on simple interest and discount loans.** Find the finance charges on a 6.5 percent, 18-month, single-payment loan when interest is computed using the simple interest method. Find the finance charges on the same loan when interest is computed using the discount method. Determine the APR in each case.

LG4, p. 275 6. **Comparing the costs of single-payment discount and simple interest loans.** Sara Boquist needs to borrow $4,000. First State Bank will lend her the money for 12 months through a single-payment loan at 8 percent, discount; Home Savings and Loan will make her a $4,000, single-payment, 12-month loan at 10 percent, simple interest. From where should Sara borrow the money? Explain.

LG5, 6, p. 282 7. **Calculating monthly installment loan payments.** Using the simple interest method, find the monthly payments on a $3,000 installment loan if the funds are borrowed for 24 months at an annual interest rate of 6 percent. How much interest will be paid during the first year of this loan? (Use a monthly payment analysis similar to the one in Exhibit 7.7.)

LG5, 6, p. 282 8. **Calculating and comparing add-on and simple interest loans.** Chris Jenkins is borrowing $10,000 for five years at 7 percent. Payments are made on a monthly basis, which are determined using the add-on method.
   a.   How much total interest will Chris pay on the loan if it is held for the full five-year term?
   b.   What are Chris' monthly payments?
   c.   How much higher are the monthly payments under the add-on method than under the simple interest method?

LG5, 6, p. 282 9. **Calculating interest and APR of installment loan.** Assuming that interest is the only finance charge, how much interest would be paid on a $5,000 installment loan to be repaid in 36 monthly installments of $166.10? What is the APR on this loan?

LG5, 6, p. 282   10. ***Calculating payments, interest, and APR on auto loan.*** After careful comparison shopping, Bill Withers decides to buy a new Toyota Camry. With some options added, the car has a price of $23,558—including plates and taxes. Because he can't afford to pay cash for the car, he will use some savings and his old car as a trade-in to put down $8,500. Bill plans to finance the rest with a $20,000, 60-month loan at a simple interest rate of 4 percent.

    a.   What will his monthly payments be?

    b.   How much total interest will Bill pay in the first year of the loan? (Use a monthly payment analysis procedure similar to the one in Exhibit 7.7.)

    c.   How much interest will Bill pay over the full (60-month) life of the loan?

    d.   What is the APR on this loan?

LG5, 6, p. 282   11. ***Calculating and comparing APRs of competing financing alternatives.*** Lina Martinez wants to buy a new high-end audio system for her car. The system is being sold by two dealers in town, both of whom sell the equipment for the same price of $2,000. Lina can buy the equipment from Dealer A, with no money down, by making payments of $119.20 a month for 18 months; she can buy the same equipment from Dealer B by making 36 monthly payments of $69.34 (again, with no money down). Lina is considering purchasing the system from Dealer B because of the lower payment. Find the APR for each alternative. What do you recommend?

LG5, 6, p. 282   12. ***Calculating interest and APR of add-on loan.*** Sherman Jacobs plans to borrow $5,000 and to repay it in 36 monthly installments. This loan is being made at an annual add-on interest rate of 7.5 percent.

    a.   Calculate the finance charge on this loan, assuming that the only component of the finance charge is interest.

    b.   Use your finding in part (a) to calculate the monthly payment on the loan.

    c.   Using a financial calculator, determine the APR on this loan.

LG6, p. 282   13. ***Deciding whether to pay cash or finance a purchase.* Use Worksheet 7.2**. Elizabeth Ehrlich wants to buy a home entertainment center. Complete with a big-screen TV, DVD, and sound system, the unit would cost $4,500. Elizabeth has over $15,000 in a money fund, so she can easily afford to pay cash for the whole thing (the fund is currently paying 5 percent interest, and Elizabeth expects that yield to hold for the foreseeable future). To stimulate sales, the dealer is offering to finance the full cost of the unit with a 36-month installment loan at 5 percent, simple. (*Note:* Assume Elizabeth is in the 28 percent tax bracket and that she itemizes deductions on her tax returns.) Briefly explain your answer.

    a.   Should she pay cash for the entertainment center?

    b.   Rework the problem, assuming that Elizabeth has the option of using a 48-month, 6 percent *home equity loan* to finance the full cost of this entertainment center. Again, use Worksheet 7.2 to determine if Elizabeth should pay cash or buy on time. Does your answer change from the one you came up with in part (a)? Explain.

LG5, 6, p. 282   14. ***Comparing payments and APRs of financing alternatives.*** Because of a job change, Ben Hardesty has just relocated to the southeastern United States. He sold his furniture before he moved, so he's now shopping for new furnishings. At a local furniture store, he's found an assortment of couches, chairs, tables, and beds that he thinks would look great in his new two-bedroom apartment; the total cost for everything is $6,400. Because of moving costs, Ben is a bit short of cash right now, so he's decided to take out an installment loan for $6,400 to pay for the furniture. The furniture store offers to lend him the money for 48 months at an add-on interest rate of 6.5 percent. The credit union at Ben's firm also offers to lend him the money—they'll give him the loan at an interest rate of 6 percent simple, but only for a term of 24 months.

    a.   Compute the monthly payments for both of the loan offers.

    b.   Determine the APR for both loans.

    c.   Which is more important: low payments or a low APR? Explain.

Applying Personal Finance

Making the Payments!

For many of us, new cars can be so appealing! We get bitten by the "new car bug" and think how great it would be to have a new car. Then we tell ourselves that we *really need* a new car because our old one is just a piece of junk waiting to fall apart in the middle of the road. Of course, we don't have the money to purchase a new car outright, so we'll have to get a loan. That means car payments. The trouble is, car payments often turn out to be a lot less affordable *after* we actually get the loan than we thought they would be *before* we signed on the dotted line. And they last way beyond the time the new car aura wears off. This project will help you understand how loan payments are determined, as well as the obligation that they place on you as the borrower.

   Let's assume for this project that your parents have promised to make the down payment on a new car once you have your degree in hand. They have agreed to pay 30 percent of the cost of any car you choose, so long as you are able to obtain a loan and make the payments on the remainder. Find the price of the vehicle you would like by visiting a car dealership or pulling up a Web site such as **http://www.edmunds.com**. Add another 4 percent to the price for tax, title, license, and so on (or ask a dealer to estimate these costs for you). Take 70 percent of the total to determine how much you'll have to finance from your car loan. Then find out what the going rate is for car loans in your area by calling or visiting your bank or by consulting a Internet site such as **http://www.bankrate.com**. Calculate what your monthly payments would be at this rate if you financed the loan for three, five, and six years. How well do you think these car payments would fit into your budget? What kind of income would you have to make to afford such payments comfortably? If the payments are more than you thought they would be, what can you do to bring them down?

CRITICAL THINKING CASES

7.1 Financing Tessa's Education

At age 19, Tessa Trainor is in the middle of her second year of studies at a community college in Savannah. She has done well in her course work; majoring in pre-business studies, she currently has a 3.75 grade point average. Tessa lives at home and works part-time as a filing clerk for a nearby electronics distributor. Her parents can't afford to pay any of her tuition and college expenses, so she's virtually on her own as far as college goes. Tessa plans to transfer to the University of Tennessee next year. (She has already been accepted.) After talking with her counselor, Tessa feels she won't be able to hold down a part-time job and still manage to complete her bachelor's degree program at UT in two years. Knowing that on her 22nd birthday, she will receive approximately $35,000 from a trust fund left her by her grandmother; Tessa has decided to borrow against the trust fund to support herself during the next two years. She estimates that she'll need $25,000 to cover tuition, room and board, books and supplies, travel, personal expenditures, and so on during that period. Unable to qualify for any special loan programs, Tessa has found two sources of single-payment loans, each requiring a security interest in the trust proceeds as collateral. The terms required by each potential lender are as follows:

a. Tennessee State Bank will lend $30,000 at 6 percent discount interest. The loan principal would be due at the end of two years.

b. National Bank of Knoxville will lend $25,000 under a two-year note. The note would carry a 7 percent simple interest rate and would also be due in a single payment at the end of two years.

Critical Thinking Questions

1. How much would Tessa (a) receive in initial loan proceeds and (b) be required to repay at maturity under the Tennessee State Bank loan?
2. Compute (a) the finance charges and (b) the APR on the loan offered by Tennessee State Bank.

3. Compute (a) the finance charges and (b) the APR on the loan offered by the National Bank of Knoxville. How big a loan payment would be due at the end of two years?
4. Compare your findings in Questions 2 and 3, and recommend one of the loans to Tessa. Explain your recommendation.
5. What other recommendations might you offer Tessa regarding disposition of the loan proceeds?

7.2 Grant Gets His Outback

Grant Tyson, a 27-year-old living in Arlington, Virginia, has been a high-school teacher for five years. For the past four months, he's been thinking about buying a Subaru Outback, but he feels that he can't afford a brand-new one. Recently, however, his friend Martin Grubbs has offered to sell Grant his fully loaded Subaru Outback 3.6R. Martin wants $26,900 for his Outback, which has been driven only 8,000 miles and is in very good condition. Grant is eager to buy the vehicle but has only $10,000 in his savings account at Central Bank. He expects to net $8,000 from the sale of his Chevrolet Malibu, but this will still leave him about $8,900 short. He has two alternatives for obtaining the money:

a. Borrow $8,900 from the First National Bank of Arlington at a fixed rate of 6 percent per annum, simple interest. The loan would be repaid in equal monthly installments over a three-year (36-month) period.
b. Obtain an $8,900 installment loan requiring 36 monthly payments from the Arlington Teacher's Credit Union at a 4.5 percent stated rate of interest. The add-on method would be used to calculate the finance charges on this loan.

Critical Thinking Questions

1. Using Exhibit 7.6 or a financial calculator, determine the required monthly payments if the loan is taken out at First National Bank of Arlington.
2. Compute (a) the finance charges and (b) the APR on the loan offered by First National Bank of Arlington.
3. Determine the size of the monthly payment required on the loan from the Arlington Teacher's Credit Union.
4. Compute (a) the finance charges and (b) the APR on the loan offered by the Arlington Teacher's Credit Union.
5. Compare the two loans and recommend one of them to Grant. Explain your recommendation.

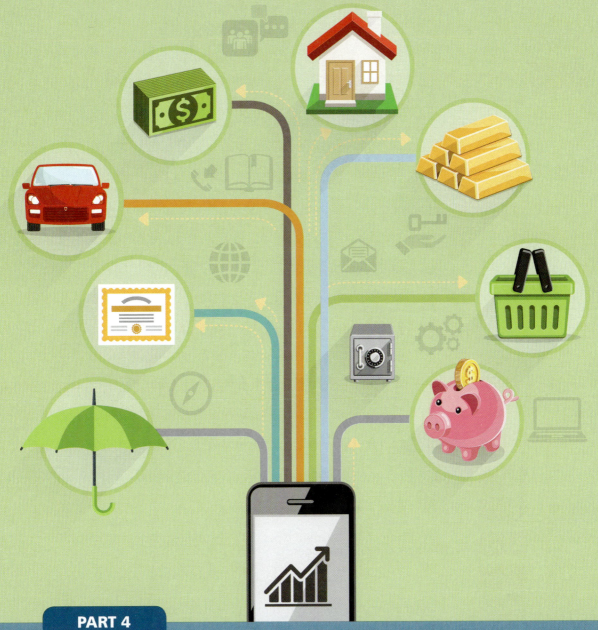

Managing Insurance Needs

CHAPTERS

CHAPTER 8

Insuring Your Life

LEARNING GOALS

LG1 Explain the concept of risk and the basics of insurance underwriting.

LG2 Discuss the primary reasons for life insurance and identify those who need coverage.

LG3 Calculate how much life insurance you need.

LG4 Distinguish among the various types of life insurance policies and describe their advantages and disadvantages.

LG5 Choose the best life insurance policy for your needs at the lowest cost.

LG6 Become familiar with the key features of life insurance policies.

How Will This Affect Me?

Insurance should be used only to protect against potentially catastrophic losses, not for small-risk exposures. It should cover losses that could derail your family's future. Insurance balances the relatively small, certain loss of ongoing premiums against low-probability, high-cost risks. This chapter focuses on how to buy life insurance. Premature death is a catastrophic loss that could endanger your family's financial future. We start by explaining how to determine the amount of life insurance that is right for you. Then we consider how to choose among key insurance products, which include term life, whole life, universal life, variable life, and group life policies. The key features of life insurance contracts are explained, and frameworks for choosing an insurance agent and an insurance company are presented. The chapter should prepare you to make informed life insurance decisions.

8-1 BASIC INSURANCE CONCEPTS

As most people discover, life is full of unexpected events that can have far-reaching consequences. Your car is sideswiped on the highway and damaged beyond repair. A family member falls ill and can no longer work. A fire or other disaster destroys your home. Your spouse dies suddenly. Although most people don't like to think about such events, protecting yourself and your family against unforeseen disasters is part of sound financial planning. Insurance plays a central role in providing that protection. *Auto and homeowner's insurance,* for example, reimburses you if your car or home is destroyed or damaged. *Life insurance* helps replace lost income if premature death occurs, providing funds so that your loved ones can keep their home, maintain an acceptable lifestyle, pay for education, and meet other needs. *Hospitalization and health insurance* covers medical costs when you get sick or injured, and *disability insurance* protects your income while you're ill.

All of these types of insurance are intended *to protect you and your family from the financial consequences of losing assets or income when an accident, illness, or death occurs.* By anticipating the potential risks to which your assets and income could be exposed and by weaving insurance protection into your financial plan, you lend a degree of certainty to your financial future. This chapter begins by introducing important insurance concepts, such as risk and underwriting, before focusing on how to make decisions regarding life insurance. In Chapters 9 and 10, we'll discuss other important types of insurance, including health insurance and property insurance.

8-1a The Concept of Risk

An important concept in any discussion of insurance is *risk*. In insurance terms, risk is defined as uncertainty concerning a potential economic loss. Whenever you and your family have a financial interest in something—whether it's your life, health, home, car, or business—there's a risk of significant financial loss if that item is lost or damaged. Because such losses can be devastating to your financial security, you must devise strategies for anticipating and dealing with such risk exposures, including risk avoidance, loss prevention and control, risk assumption, and insurance.

Risk Avoidance

The simplest way to deal with risk is to avoid the act that creates it. For example, people who are afraid they might lose everything they own because of a lawsuit resulting from an automobile accident could avoid driving. Or avid skydivers or bungee jumpers might choose another recreational activity to avoid life and health risks!

Although **risk avoidance** can be an effective way to handle some risks, it has its costs. People who avoid driving have to face considerable inconvenience as well, and the retired skydiver may find she now suffers *more* stress, which can lead to different types of health risks. Risk avoidance is an attractive way to deal with risk only when the estimated cost of avoidance is less than the estimated cost of handling it in some other way.

Loss Prevention and Control

Generally, **loss prevention** is any activity that reduces the probability that a loss will occur (such as driving within the speed limit to lessen the chance of being in a car accident). **Loss control**, in contrast, is any activity that lessens the severity of loss once it occurs (such as wearing a safety belt or buying a car with air bags). Loss prevention and loss control should be important parts of the risk management program of every individual and family. In fact, insurance is a reasonable way of handling risk only when people use effective loss prevention and control measures.

Risk Assumption

With **risk assumption**, you choose to accept and bear the risk of loss. Risk assumption can be an effective way to handle many types of potentially small exposures to loss when insurance would be too expensive. For example, the risk of having your *Personal Financial Planning* text stolen probably doesn't justify buying insurance. Risk assumption is also a reasonable approach for dealing with very large risks that you can't ordinarily prevent or secure insurance for (e.g., a nuclear holocaust). Unfortunately, people often assume risks unknowingly. They may be unaware of various exposures to loss or think that their insurance policy offers adequate protection when, in fact, it doesn't.

Insurance

An **insurance policy** is a contract between you (the insured) and an insurance company (the insurer) under which the insurance company agrees to reimburse you for the losses you suffer according to specified terms. From your perspective, *you are transferring your risk of loss to the insurance company.* You pay a relatively small *certain* amount (the insurance premium) in exchange for the insurance company's promise that they'll reimburse you if you suffer an *uncertain* loss covered by the insurance policy.

Why are insurance companies willing to accept this risk? They combine the loss experiences of large numbers of people and use statistical information, called *actuarial data*, to estimate the risk—frequency and magnitude—of loss for the given population. They set and collect premiums, which they invest and use to pay out losses and cover expenses. If they pay out less than the sum of the premiums and the earnings on them, they make a profit.

8-1b Underwriting Basics

Insurance companies take great pains to decide whom they will insure and the applicable premiums they will charge. This function is called **underwriting**. Underwriters design rate-classification schedules so that people pay premiums that reflect their chance of loss. Through underwriting, insurance companies try to guard against *adverse selection,* which happens when only high-risk clients apply for and get insurance coverage. Insurers are always trying to improve their underwriting capabilities in order to set premium rates that will adequately protect policyholders and yet be attractive and reasonable.

Because underwriting practices and standards also vary among insurance companies, you can often save money by shopping around for the company offering the most favorable underwriting policies for your specific characteristics and needs. The discussion of life insurance that follows in this chapter—and in succeeding chapters that discuss other types of insurance—will help you accomplish these goals.

risk avoidance
Avoiding an act that would create a risk.

loss prevention
Any activity that reduces the probability that a loss will occur.

loss control
Any activity that lessens the severity of loss once it occurs.

risk assumption
The choice to accept and bear the risk of loss.

insurance policy
A contract between the insured and the insurer under which the insurer agrees to reimburse the insured for any losses suffered according to specified terms.

underwriting
The process used by insurers to decide who can be insured and to determine applicable rates that will be charged for premiums.

8-2 WHY BUY LIFE INSURANCE?

Life insurance planning is an important part of every successful financial plan. Its primary purpose is *to protect your dependents from financial loss in the event of your untimely death*. It's an umbrella of protection for your loved ones, protecting the assets you've built up during your life and providing funds to help your family reach important financial goals even after you die. The key idea is that life insurance protects your family from the potentially catastrophic financial damage caused by the premature death of the major breadwinner(s).

8-2a Benefits of Life Insurance

Despite the importance of life insurance to sound financial planning, many people put off the decision to buy it. This happens partly because life insurance is associated with something unpleasant in most people's minds—namely, death. People don't like to think or talk about death or the things associated with it, so they often put off considering their life insurance needs. Life insurance is also intangible. You can't see, smell, touch, or taste its benefits—and those benefits mainly are realized after you've died. However, life insurance has some important benefits that should not be ignored in the financial planning process. These benefits include:

- **Financial protection for dependents:** If your family or loved ones depend on your income, what would happen to them after you die? Would they be able to maintain their current lifestyle, stay in their home, or afford a college education? Life insurance provides a financial cushion for your dependents, giving them a set amount of money after your death that they can use for many purposes. In short, the most important benefit of life insurance is providing financial protection for your dependents after your death.

> **EXAMPLE: Using Life Insurance to Protect Dependents**
> If you were to unfortunately die prematurely, your spouse could use your life insurance proceeds to pay off the mortgage on your home, so your family can continue living there comfortably, or set aside funds for your child's college education.

- **Protection from creditors:** A life insurance policy can be structured so that death benefits are paid directly to a named beneficiary rather than being considered as part of your estate. This means that even if you have outstanding bills and debts at the time of your death, creditors cannot claim the cash benefits from your life insurance policy, which provides further financial protection for your dependents.

- **Tax benefits:** Life insurance proceeds paid to your heirs, aren't generally subject to state or federal income taxes. Furthermore, if certain requirements are met, policy proceeds can pass to named beneficiaries free of any *estate taxes*.
- **Savings vehicle:** Some types of life insurance policies can serve as a savings vehicle, particularly for those who are looking for safety of principal. *Variable life policies*, which we'll discuss later in this chapter, are more investment vehicles than they are life insurance products. But don't assume that all life insurance products can be considered savings instruments. As we'll see later in this chapter, this is often inappropriate.

Just as with other aspects of personal financial planning, life insurance decisions can be made easier by following a step-by-step approach. You will need answers to the following questions:

- Do you need life insurance?
- If so, how much life insurance do you need?
- Which type of life insurance is best, given your financial objectives?
- What factors should you consider in making the final purchase decision?

8-2b Do You Need Life Insurance?

The first question to ask when considering the purchase of life insurance is whether you need it. Not everyone does. Many factors, including your personal situation and other financial resources, play a role in determining your need for life insurance. Remember, the major purpose of life insurance is to provide financial security for your dependents in the event of your death. As we've discussed, life insurance provides other benefits, but they're all a distant second to this one.

Who needs life insurance? In general, life insurance should be considered if you have dependents counting on you for financial support. Therefore, a single adult who doesn't have children or other relatives to support may not need life insurance at all. Children also usually don't require insurance on their life.

Once you marry, your life insurance requirements should be reevaluated, depending on your spouse's earning potential and assets—such as a house—that you want to protect. The need for life insurance increases the most when children enter the picture because young families stand to suffer the greatest financial hardship from the premature death of a parent. Even a non-wage-earning parent may require some life insurance to ensure that children are cared for adequately if the parent dies.

As families build assets, their life insurance requirements continue to change, both in terms of the amount of insurance needed and the type of policy necessary to meet their financial objectives and protect their assets. Other life changes will also affect your life insurance needs. For example, if you divorce or your spouse dies, you may need additional life insurance to protect your children. Once your children finish school and are on their own, the need for life insurance may end. In later years, life insurance needs vary depending on the availability of other financial resources, such as pensions and investments, to provide for your dependents.

TEST YOURSELF

8-4 Discuss some benefits of life insurance in addition to protecting family members financially after the primary wage earner's death.

8-5 Explain the circumstances under which a single college graduate would or would not need life insurance. What life-cycle events would change this initial evaluation, and how might they affect the graduate's life insurance needs?

8-3 HOW MUCH LIFE INSURANCE IS RIGHT FOR YOU?

multiple-of-earnings method
A method of determining the amount of life insurance coverage needed by multiplying gross annual earnings by some selected number.

After confirming your need for life insurance, you'll need to make more decisions to find the life insurance product that best fits your needs. First, you must determine how much life insurance you need for adequate coverage. Buying too much life insurance can be costly; buying too little may prove disastrous. To avoid these problems, you can use one of two methods to estimate how much insurance is necessary: the *multiple-of-earnings method* and the *needs analysis method*.

The **multiple-of-earnings method** takes your gross annual earnings and multiplies it by some selected (often arbitrary) number to arrive at an estimate of adequate life insurance coverage. The rule of thumb used by many insurance agents is that your insurance coverage should be equal to 5 to 10 times your current income. Although simple to use, the multiple-of-earnings method fails to fully recognize the financial obligations and resources of the individual and his or her family. Therefore, the multiple-of-earnings method should be used only to roughly approximate life insurance needs.

> **EXAMPLE: Determining the Amount of Life Insurance Using the Multiple-of-Earnings Method**
>
> You plan to rely on the rule that your life insurance coverage should be between 5 and 10 times your current income. Thus, if you currently earn $70,000 a year, using the multiple-of-earnings method you'd need between $350,000 and $700,000 worth of life insurance.

needs analysis method
A method of determining the amount of life insurance coverage needed by considering a person's financial obligations and available financial resources *in addition to life insurance*.

A more detailed approach is the **needs analysis method**. This method considers both the financial obligations and financial resources of the insured and his or her dependents. It involves three steps, as shown in Exhibit 8.1:

1. Estimate the total economic resources needed if the individual were to die.
2. Determine all financial resources that would be available after death, including existing life insurance and pension plan death benefits.
3. Subtract available resources from the amount needed to determine how much additional life insurance is required.

8-3a Step 1: Assess Your Family's Total Economic Needs

The first question that the needs analysis method asks is: *What financial resources will my survivors need should I die tomorrow?* When answering this question, you should consider the following five items:

Financial Fact or Fantasy?

The best way to figure out how much life insurance you need is to use a multiple of your earnings. **Fantasy:** While the multiple earnings approach is probably the simplest procedure, it suffers from a number of serious shortcomings. A better choice is the *needs approach.*

1. **Income needed to maintain an adequate lifestyle:** If you died, how much money would your dependents need each month in order to live a comfortable life? Estimate this amount by looking at your family's current monthly budget, including expenses for housing costs, utilities, food, clothing, and medical and dental needs. Other expenses to consider include property taxes, insurance, recreation and travel, and savings. Try to take into account that the amount needed may change over time. For example, once children are grown, monthly household expenses should decrease substantially, but the surviving spouse may still need monthly support. Therefore, the survivor's life expectancy and the income required should be considered.

EXHIBIT 8.1   How Much Life Insurance Do You Need?

The needs analysis method uses three steps to estimate life insurance needs.

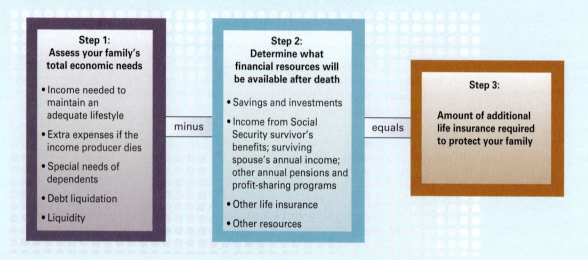

Step 1:
Assess your family's total economic needs

• Income needed to maintain an adequate lifestyle

• Extra expenses if the income producer dies

• Special needs of dependents

• Debt liquidation

• Liquidity

minus

Step 2:
Determine what financial resources will be available after death

• Savings and investments

• Income from Social Security survivor's benefits; surviving spouse's annual income; other annual pensions and profit-sharing programs

• Other life insurance

• Other resources

equals

Step 3:

Amount of additional life insurance required to protect your family

2. **Extra expenses if the primary income producer dies:** These expenses include funeral costs and any expenses that might be incurred to replace services that you currently provide. For example, a mother who doesn't work outside the home provides critically important child care, cooking, cleaning, and other services. If she were to die, or if her spouse died and she had to return to work, then these services likely would have to be replaced using the family's income. Because such expenses can stretch a family budget to the breaking point, include them when you're estimating insurance needs.

3. **Special needs of dependents:** In addition to daily economic needs, you may want to provide for special needs of your dependents. These needs might include long-term nursing care for a disabled or chronically ill dependent, an emergency fund for unexpected financial burdens, or a college education fund for your children.

4. **Debt liquidation:** In the event of their death, most breadwinners prefer to leave their families relatively debt free. To accomplish this, it's necessary to calculate the average amount due for outstanding bills. This amount would include the balances on credit cards, department store accounts, and other similar obligations. In addition, some will want to leave enough money to allow their dependents to pay off the home mortgage.

5. **Liquidity:** After your death, it may take time for your dependents to sell noncash assets. Real estate, for example, is difficult to convert into cash quickly. If a high percentage of your wealth is in illiquid assets, the cash proceeds from life insurance can be used to pay the bills until those assets can be sold at a fair market value.

8-3b Step 2: Determine What Financial Resources Will Be Available After Death

Once you've estimated the lifetime financial needs of dependents, the next step is to list all current resources that will be available for meeting those needs. For most families, money from savings, investments, and Social Security survivor's benefits make up the largest non–life insurance financial resources. Additional resources may include proceeds from employer-sponsored group life insurance policies and the death benefits payable from accumulated pension plans and profit-sharing programs. Another important source is income that can be earned by the surviving spouse or children. The earnings of a surviving spouse who is skilled and readily employable could be a family's largest available resource. After developing a complete list of available resources, you should make a reasonable estimate of their value. Although this step can be difficult because of the changing values of many assets, coming up with a set of reasonably accurate estimates is certainly within reach.

8-3c Step 3: Subtract Resources from Needs to Calculate How Much Life Insurance You Require

Finally, subtract the total available resources from the total needed to satisfy all of the family's financial objectives. If available resources are greater than anticipated needs, then no additional life insurance is required. If the resources are less than the needs—as is the case in most families with children—then the difference is the amount of life insurance necessary to provide the family with its desired standard of living.

FINANCIAL PLANNING TIPS

Buying the Right Life Insurance for You

The following tips will help you get the right insurance policy at the right price:

- **Don't let an insurance agent tell you how much insurance you need.** Use the methods in this chapter to determine the right amount of insurance for you. Agents often have a strong motivation to sell large policies—the larger, the better.

- **Consult an independent insurance broker.** Independent brokers have access to more products than the representative of any single company.

- **Just say no to one-meeting recommendations.** A broker who makes a recommendation in the first meeting is moving too fast and probably is not considering all of your best options.

- **Know how your agent is compensated.** Is he or she compensated by a commission-alone, fee-plus-commission, or fee-only structure? If you don't know how your broker is paid, you cannot recognize possible conflicts of interest.

- **Keep your insurance and investment decisions separate.** Term insurance provides protection against premature death alone, without a savings element. Whole life and universal life policies provide both insurance and savings; consequently, they cost much more. If you combine insurance and investing, make sure you understand why and the costs of doing so. Most people buy separate insurance and investment products.

- **Always do some comparison shopping.** There are lots of alternatives, with major price differences for essentially the same product.

- **Avoid replacing old whole-life insurance policies.** After holding a whole-life policy for years, you may lose the premiums that you've paid and pay more administration fees if you replace it. Just buy more insurance if your circumstances warrant doing so.

- **Avoid buying expensive riders.** Insurance agents often try to sell riders that provide special extra coverage. Make sure that you need any riders that you buy.

- **Consider your budget when buying insurance.** Make sure you understand and can afford new insurance before you buy it.

Source: Adapted from J. D. Roth, "14 Tips for Purchasing Life Insurance," http://www.getrichslowly.org/blog/2009/04/28/14-tips-for-purchasing-life-insurance/, accessed August 2015.

The needs analysis method may seem complex, but technology has made it simpler to use. Insurance companies now have computer software that can quickly determine the insurance needs of individuals and families. Many Internet sites and software programs also let you do your own analysis.

Regardless of the procedure you use, remember that *life insurance needs will likely change over time.* The amount and type of life insurance you need today will probably differ from the amount and type suitable for you 10 or 20 years from now. As with other areas of your personal financial plan, you should review and adjust life insurance programs (as necessary) at least every 5 years or after any major changes in the family (e.g., the birth of a child, the purchase of a home, or a job change).

Needs Analysis in Action: The Brewer Family

Let's take a closer look at how the needs analysis method works by considering the hypothetical case of Spencer and Erica Brewer. Spencer Brewer is 37 and the primary breadwinner in the family; his current earnings are $85,000. Spencer and his wife, Erica, want to be sure that his life insurance policy will provide enough proceeds to take care of Erica and their two children, ages 6 and 8, if he should die. You can follow their analysis of needs and resources in Worksheet 8.1.

Financial Resources Needed after Death (Step 1)

Spencer and Erica Brewer review their budget and decide that monthly living expenses for Erica and the two children would be about $3,500 in current dollars

© STOCKLITE/SHUTTERSTOCK.COM

while the children are still living at home (Period 1), or $42,000 annually. After both children leave home (Period 2), Erica, now 35, will need monthly income of $3,000—or $36,000 a year—until she retires at age 65. At that point (Period 3), the Brewers estimate that Erica's living expenses would fall to $2,750 a month, or $33,000 annually. The life expectancy of a woman Erica's age is 87 years, so the Brewers calculate that Erica will spend about 22 years in retirement. Therefore, as shown in the first section of the worksheet, the total income necessary to meet the Brewers' living expenses over the next 52 years is $1,878,000.

Although Erica previously worked as a stockbroker, they planned for her to stay home until the children graduated from high school. The Brewers are concerned that her previous education may be somewhat outdated at that point, so they include $25,000 for Erica to update her education and skills. Spencer and Erica also want to fund their children's college educations. After researching the current cost of their state's public university, they decide to establish a college fund of $100,000 for this purpose. Last, they estimate final expenses (e.g., funeral costs and estate taxes) of $15,000.

The Brewers use credit sparingly, so their outstanding debts are limited to a mortgage (with a current balance of $150,000), an automobile loan ($4,000), and miscellaneous charge accounts ($1,000). Spencer and Erica, therefore, estimate that $155,000 would pay off all of their existing debts.

All of these estimates are shown in the top half of Spencer and Erica's insurance calculations in Worksheet 8.1. Note that $2,173,000 is the total amount they estimate would be necessary to meet their financial goals if Spencer were to die.

Financial Resources Available After Death (Step 2)

If Spencer died, Erica would be eligible to receive **Social Security survivor's benefits** for both herself and her children. Social Security survivor's benefits are intended to provide basic, minimum support to families faced with the loss of their principal wage

Social Security survivor's benefits
Benefits under Social Security intended to provide basic, minimum support to families faced with the loss of a principal wage earner.

earner. The benefits are paid to unmarried children until age 18 (or 19 if they are still in high school) and to nonworking surviving spouses until their children reach age 16. The surviving spouse would also receive individual survivor's benefits upon turning 65. Limits are placed on the total amount of survivor's benefits that can be paid to a household, and if the surviving spouse returns to work, then the amount of benefits would be reduced if earnings exceed certain limits. We'll discuss Social Security and its benefits in more detail in Chapter 14.

Erica and Spencer visit the Social Security Administration's Internet site for an estimate of the survivor's benefits Erica will receive. Based on the number of years that Spencer has worked, his income, and the number of children they have, the Brewers estimate that Erica would receive approximately $3,200 a month, or $38,400 a year, in Social Security survivor's benefits for herself and the children until the youngest child graduates from high school in 12 years.

In the 18 years between when the children leave home and Erica retires, the Brewers expect Erica to be employed full-time and earn about $35,000 after taxes. After Erica turns 65, she'd receive approximately $2,250 a month ($27,000 a year) from Spencer's survivor's benefits, her own Social Security benefits, and her own retirement benefits. However, Erica will have some other resources available if Spencer should die prematurely. The couple has invested $65,000 in a mutual fund, and Spencer's employer provides a $100,000 life insurance policy for him. Adding these amounts to Erica's expected income means she'd have $1,849,800 in total resources available.

Additional Life Insurance Needed (Step 3)

How much life insurance should the Brewers buy for Spencer in order to be sure Erica and the children would be adequately cared for? To find out, the Brewers subtract the total financial resources available ($1,849,800) from the total financial resources needed ($2,173,000). The difference is $323,200, so the additional life insurance Spencer should buy to protect his family is about $325,000.

Of course, Spencer and Erica will need to examine their insurance situation periodically as their children grow and the family's financial circumstances change. But for now, they feel satisfied that they have a good estimate of the amount of additional life insurance they need to buy for Spencer. Next, they can begin to consider which type of policy is best.

8-3d Life Insurance Underwriting Considerations

As we discussed earlier, insurance companies use a process called *underwriting* to determine whom they will insure and what they will charge for insurance coverage. Underwriting policies are particularly important to understand when choosing life insurance products, so let's briefly examine some of the factors that life insurance underwriters consider.

Life insurance underwriting begins by asking potential insureds to complete an application designed to gather information about their risk potential. In other words, underwriters consider the likelihood the insured will die while the life insurance policy is in effect. Underwriters use life expectancy figures to look at overall longevity for various age groups. They also consider specific factors related to the applicant's health. Someone who smokes, is obese, has a history of heart disease, or has a dangerous job or hobby is considered a greater risk than someone who doesn't. Applicants who have been charged with driving under the influence of drugs or alcohol or who have had their driver's license suspended may also be viewed as riskier.

All these factors are then used to determine whether to accept you and, based on your risk factors, what premium to charge. For example, someone in excellent health

LIFE INSURANCE NEEDS ANALYSIS METHOD

Insured's Name Spencer and Erica Brewer   **Date** April 12, 2017

Step 1: Financial resources needed after death

1. Annual living expenses and other needs:

		Period 1	Period 2	Period 3	
a.	Monthly living expenses	$ 3,500	$ 3,000	$ 2,750	
b.	Net yearly income needed (a × 12)	$ 42,000	$ 36,000	$ 33,000	
c.	Number of years in time period	12	18	22	
d.	Total living need per time period (b × c)	$ 504,000	$ 648,000	$ 726,000	
TOTAL LIVING EXPENSES (add line d for each period):					$ 1,878,000

2. Special needs

a.	Spouse education fund		$ 25,000
b.	Children's college fund		$ 100,000
c.	Other needs		0
3. Final expenses (funeral, estate costs, etc.)			$ 15,000
4. Debt liquidation			
a.	House mortgage	$ 150,000	
b.	Other loans	5,000	
c.	Total debt (4 a + 4 b)		$ 155,000
5. Other financial needs			0
TOTAL FINANCIAL RESOURCES NEEDED (add right column)			$ 2,173,000

Step 2: Financial resources available after death

1. Income

		Period 1	Period 2	Period 3	
a.	Annual Social Security survivor's benefits	$ 38,400	0	0	
b.	Surviving spouse's annual income	0	$ 35,000	0	
c.	Other annual pensions and Social Security benefits	0	0	$ 27,000	
d.	Annual income	$ 38,400	$ 35,000	$ 27,000	
e.	Number of years in time period	12	18	22	
f.	Total period income (d × e)	$ 460,800	$ 630,000	$ 594,000	
g. TOTAL INCOME					$ 1,684,800
2.	Savings and investments				$ 65,000
3.	Other life insurance				$ 100,000
4.	Other resources				0
TOTAL FINANCIAL RESOURCES AVAILABLE (1g + 2 + 3 + 4)					$ 1,849,800

Step 3: Additional Life Insurance needed

Step 1: Total financial resources needed	$ 2,173,000
Step 2: Total financial resources available	$ 1,849,800

ADDITIONAL LIFE INSURANCE NEEDED	$ 323,200

is usually considered "preferred" and pays the lowest premium. Other typical categories include standard, preferred smoker, and smoker. Those with special medical conditions—high cholesterol or diabetes, for example—fall into rated categories and pay considerably higher premiums if they're accepted.

The bottom line: If you have any of the risks commonly considered in life insurance underwriting—such as obesity, heart disease, or a high-risk hobby or job—then it's especially important to shop carefully and compare the cost implications of different types of insurance policies and the underwriting standards used by different companies. For example, an overweight hang-gliding enthusiast with a history of heart disease who walks tightropes for a living should expect to pay more for life insurance.

TEST YOURSELF

8-6   Discuss the two most commonly used ways to determine a person's life insurance needs.

8-7   Name and explain the most common financial resources needed after the death of a family breadwinner.

8-8   What are some factors that underwriters consider when evaluating a life insurance application? Which, if any, apply to you or your family members?

8-4 WHAT KIND OF POLICY IS RIGHT FOR YOU?

After determining the amount of life insurance you need to cover your family's financial requirements and considering how various underwriting policies might affect you, your next step is to decide on the type of insurance policy. Although a variety of life insurance products are available, three major types account for 90 percent to 95 percent of life insurance sales: term life, whole life, and universal life.

8-4a Term Life Insurance

term life insurance
Insurance that provides only death benefits, for a specified period, and does not provide for the accumulation of cash value.

Term life insurance is the simplest type of insurance policy. You purchase a specified amount of insurance protection for a set period. If you die during that time, your beneficiaries will receive the full amount specified in your policy. Term insurance can be bought for many different time increments, such as 5 years, 10 years, even 30 years. Depending on the policy, premiums can be paid annually, semi-annually, or quarterly.

Types of Term Insurance
The most common types of term insurance are straight (or level) term and decreasing term.

straight term policy
A term insurance policy written for a given number of years, with coverage remaining unchanged throughout the effective period.

Straight Term. A straight term life insurance policy is written for a set number of years, during which time the amount of life insurance coverage remains unchanged. The *annual premium* on a **straight term policy** may increase each year, as with *annual renewable term policies,* or remain level throughout the policy period, as with *level premium term policies.* Due to the convenience of knowing the future premiums for at least a few years at a time, level premium term policies have become much more popular than annual renewable term policies in recent years.

Exhibits 8.2 and 8.3 list representative annual premiums for annual renewable term and level premium term life policies, respectively. (*Note:* The premiums

EXHIBIT 8.2

Representative Annual Renewable Term Life Insurance Premiums: $100,000 Policy, Preferred Nonsmoker Rates

When you buy term life insurance, you're buying a product that provides life insurance coverage and nothing more. This table shows representative rates for several age categories and selected policy years; actual premiums increase every year. As you can see, females pay less than males for coverage, and premiums increase sharply with age.

Policy Year	AGE 25 Male ($)	AGE 25 Female ($)	AGE 40 Male ($)	AGE 40 Female ($)	AGE 60 Male ($)	AGE 60 Female ($)
1	95	49	145	117	429	366
5	97	63	177	151	732	570
10	107	88	237	194	1,278	864
15	145	117	299	236	2,307	1,620
20	177	151	429	366	3,988	2,902

EXHIBIT 8.3

Representative Level Premium Term Life Rates: $100,000 Preferred Nonsmoker Policy

This table shows representative annual premiums for $100,000 of level premium term life insurance. Although level premium costs less than annual renewable term for the same period, you must requalify at the end of each term to retain the lower premium.

Age	10 YEAR Male/Female ($)	15 YEAR Male/Female ($)	20 YEAR Male/Female ($)	30 YEAR Male/Female ($)
25	106/102	116/110	128/116	161/143
35	108/102	117/112	134/125	175/152
40	122/115	135/129	157/145	222/185
50	203/171	250/199	298/233	475/341
60	403/300	539/373	669/502	Not Available

Financial Fact or Fantasy?

Term insurance provides nothing more than a stipulated amount of death benefits and, as a result, is considered the purest form of life insurance. **Fact:** Term insurance provides a given amount of life insurance (i.e., death benefits) for a stipulated period of time and nothing more—no investment feature or cash value.

are for nonsmokers; rates for similar smoker policies would be higher in view of the greater risk and shorter life expectancies of smokers.) Until recently, annual renewable term premiums were less expensive in the early years but increased rapidly over time. These policies, however, aren't popular today. Because people now live longer, the rates for level premium term have fallen sharply and are well below those on annual renewable term from year 1 on, so they're a better value and, as noted above, more popular.

Decreasing Term. Because the death rate increases with each year of life, the premiums on annual renewable straight term policies for each successive period of coverage will also increase. As an alternative, some term policies *maintain a level premium* throughout all periods of coverage *while the amount of protection*

decreasing term policy
A term insurance policy that *maintains a level premium* throughout all periods of coverage while *the amount of protection decreases.*

decreases. Such a policy is called a **decreasing term policy** because the amount of protection decreases over its life. Decreasing term is used when the amount of needed coverage declines over time. For example, decreasing term policies are popular with homeowners who want a level of life insurance coverage that will decline at about the same rate as the balances on their home mortgages. Families with young children use these policies to ensure a sufficient level of family income while the kids are growing up. As they grow older, the amount of coverage needed decreases until the last child becomes independent and the need expires.

Again, remember that the type and length of term policy you choose affects the amount of premiums you'll pay over time. For a given person, the annual premium for a specified initial amount of coverage, say $250,000, would be lowest for straight term, higher for decreasing term, and highest for annual renewable term. The only reason that the premium on decreasing term is higher than the premium on straight term is that most major insurance companies don't offer decreasing term policies, so the small number of companies offering these policies operate in a less competitive market that allows them to charge high premiums. Of course, the death benefit on the decreasing term policy will, by design, decline during the policy's term.

Advantages and Disadvantages of Term Life

One of the biggest advantages of term life is cost. Term life usually offers lower initial premiums than other types of insurance, especially for younger people. Term life is an economical way to buy a large amount of life insurance protection over a given, relatively short period, making it particularly advantageous for covering needs that will disappear over time.

> **EXAMPLE: Appropriate Use of Term Life Insurance**
>
> Term life insurance is particularly useful for covering needs that will disappear over time. For example, a family with young children can use term life insurance to provide coverage until the children are grown.

renewability
A term life policy provision allowing the insured to renew the policy at the end of its term without having to show evidence of insurability.

The main disadvantage, however, is that term insurance offers only temporary coverage. Once the policy term expires, you must renew the policy. This can be a problem if you develop underwriting factors in the future that make it difficult to qualify for insurance. Many term life policies overcome part of this drawback by offering a **renewability** provision that gives you the option to renew your policy at the end of its term without having to show evidence of insurability. A guaranteed renewal provision allows you to renew the policy even if you have become uninsurable because of an accident or other illness during the original policy period. Generally, term policies are renewable at the end of each term until the insured reaches age 65 or 70. However, the premium will still increase to reflect the greater chance of death at older ages.

convertibility
A term life policy provision allowing the insured to convert the policy into a comparable whole life policy.

Another option that can help overcome some of the limitations of term insurance is a **convertibility** provision. This lets you convert your term insurance policy into a comparable whole life policy at a future time. A whole life policy, as we'll discuss next, provides lifelong protection, eliminating the need to consistently renew your life insurance. Convertibility is particularly useful if you need a large amount of relatively low-cost, short-term protection immediately, but in the future, you expect to have greater income that will allow you to purchase permanent insurance. Convertibility options are standard on most term policies today, but many place specific limits on when the conversion can take place.

One way to overcome the drawback of having to pay increased premiums at the end of each term is to purchase a longer-term policy. The insurance industry offers 30-year straight term policies that lock in a set premium. For example, a 35-year-old man who qualifies for preferred rates could lock in a $250,000 death benefit for 30 years in a row and pay only a set premium of $360 a year. As with all insurance policies, however, make sure before signing up that the rate is fully locked in for the duration of the policy.

Who Should Buy Term Insurance?

For most young families on limited budgets, the need for death protection greatly exceeds their need to save. If you fall into this category, guaranteed renewable and convertible term insurance should account for the largest portion of your insurance protection. These policies provide the most life insurance coverage for the least cost, thereby preserving financial resources for meeting immediate and future consumption and savings goals. Healthy older people with many other financial resources may also prefer to use term policies to meet specific coverage needs.

A strategy used by some is to buy term insurance and invest in a retirement plan the difference between the premium for whole life and the premium for term insurance. The short name for this is "buy term and invest the difference." As the cost of term insurance increases, the value of the investment will also increase, hopefully to the level needed at that stage of life. That is, the investment replaces the need for lifetime insurance.

8-4b Whole Life Insurance

Unlike term insurance, which offers financial protection for only a certain period, **whole life insurance** is designed to provide ongoing insurance coverage during an individual's entire life. In other words, it's considered a permanent insurance product. In addition to death protection, whole life insurance has a *savings* feature, called **cash value**, that results from the investment earnings on paid-in insurance premiums. Thus, *whole life provides not only insurance coverage, but also a modest return on your investment*. The idea behind cash value is to provide the insurance buyer with a tangible return while also receiving insurance coverage; the savings rates on whole life policies are normally *fixed* and *guaranteed* to be more than a certain rate (historically, 4 to 6 percent). Exhibit 8.4 illustrates how the cash value in a whole life policy builds up over time. Obviously, the longer the insured keeps the policy in force, the greater the cash value. Whole life can be purchased through several different payment plans—including continuous premium, limited payment, and single premium—all of which provide for accumulating cash values.

The cash value of a policy increases over time to reflect the greater chance of death that comes with age. If a policyholder cancels his contract prior to death, then that portion of the assets set aside to provide payment for the death claim is available to him. This right to a cash value is termed the policyholder's **nonforfeiture right**. By terminating their insurance contracts, policyholders forfeit their rights to death benefits. Likewise, the company must forfeit its claim to the monies paid by these policyholders for a future death benefit that it is no longer required to pay.

Types of Whole Life Policies

Three major types of whole life policies are available: continuous premium, limited payment, and single premium. To develop a sense for the costs of these policies, look at the representative rates shown in Exhibit 8.5.

Continuous Premium. Under a *continuous premium whole life* policy—or *straight life,* as it's more commonly called—individuals pay a level premium each year until they either die or exercise a nonforfeiture right. The earlier in life the coverage is purchased, the lower the annual premium. Life insurance agents often use this as a selling point to convince younger people to buy now. Their argument is that the sooner you buy, the less you pay *annually*. Of course, the sooner people purchase whole life, the longer they have coverage in force, but (all other things being equal) the *more* they pay in total. There are good reasons (such as securing needed protection, savings, and insurability) for many young people to buy whole life insurance, but it should seldom be purchased by anyone simply because the *annual* premium will be lower now than if it's purchased later.

Of the various whole life policies available, continuous premium (straight life) offers the greatest amount of permanent death protection and the least amount of

whole life insurance
Life insurance designed to offer ongoing insurance coverage over the course of an insured's entire life.

cash value
The accumulated refundable value of an insurance policy; results from the investment earnings on paid-in insurance premiums.

nonforfeiture right
A life insurance feature giving the whole life policyholder, upon policy cancellation, the portion of those assets that were set aside to provide payment for the future death claim.

Here is an example of the projected cash value for an actual $200,000 whole life policy issued by a major life insurer to a male, age 30. For *each year* of the illustration, the difference between the $200,000 death benefit and the projected cash value represents the *death protection* offered by the insurer.

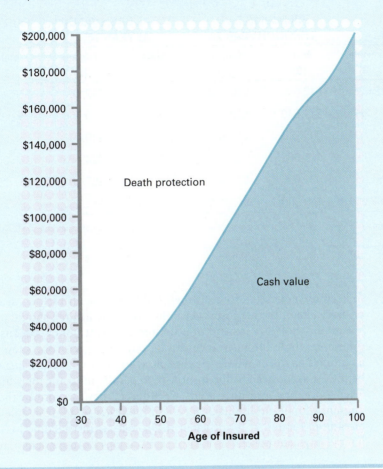

savings per premium dollar. This emphasis on *death protection* makes it the wisest choice to fill a permanent life insurance need.

Limited Payment. With a *limited payment whole life* policy, you're covered for your entire life, but the premium payment is based on a specified period—for example, so-called 20-pay life and 30-pay life require level premium payments for a period of 20 and 30 years, respectively. For stipulated age policies such as those paid up at age 55 or 65, you pay premiums until you reach the stated age. In all of these cases, on completion of the scheduled payments, *the insurance remains in force, at its face value, for the rest of the insured's life.*

Some insurance companies try to convince consumers to buy limited payment policies by stressing the "large" savings element that will develop and by emphasizing that the policyholder won't have to pay premiums for an entire lifetime. This logic fails on two counts. First, for most people, the primary purpose of whole life insurance is permanent protection against financial loss resulting from death, not the accumulation of savings. Second, even if people buy continuous premium whole life (straight life) policies, they need to pay the premium only so long as they wish

EXHIBIT 8.5

Like any life insurance product, whole life is more expensive the older you are. Also, whole life is more costly than term because you're getting an investment/savings account, represented by the "total cash value" column, in addition to life insurance coverage.

Age	ANNUAL PREMIUM		PREMIUMS PAID THROUGH YEAR 20		TOTAL CASH VALUE AT YEAR 20*		PAID UP INSURANCE AT YEAR 20	
	Male ($)	Female ($)	Male ($)	Female ($)	Male ($)	Female ($)	Male ($)	Female ($)
25	603	$ 525	$12,060	$10,580	$10,670	$12,360	$55,700	$56,200
30	727	$ 683	$14,540	$12,760	$13,518	$15,768	$57,500	$58,600
35	891	$ 775	$17,820	$15,500	$16,908	$19,842	$58,900	$60,600
40	1,078	$ 931	$21,560	$18,620	$20,518	$24,473	$60,000	$62,300
50	1,590	$1,367	$31,800	$27,340	$29,796	$35,382	$62,300	$65,300
60	2,418	$2,050	$48,360	$41,000	$41,796	$41,796	$66,260	$68,800

*The whole life policy in this example does not pay dividends, so the cash values and guaranteed paid-up insurance amounts are fixed (guaranteed).

to keep the policies in force at their full face value. If lifelong death protection is the primary aim of the life insurance policy, then the insured should purchase continuous premium whole life instead of a limited payment policy. Because more continuous premium whole life insurance can be purchased with the same number of dollars as limited payment whole life, people who need whole life insurance are probably better off using straight life insurance to get the most for their life insurance dollars. Then, once their insurance needs are reduced, they can convert the policy to a smaller amount of paid-up life insurance. On the other hand, if people have life insurance already in force that is sufficient to protect against income loss, then they can use limited payment policies as part of their savings or retirement plans.

Single Premium. Continuous premium and limited payment whole life policies represent methods of acquiring life insurance on an installment basis. In contrast, a *single premium whole life* policy is purchased with one cash premium payment at the inception of the contract, thus buying life insurance coverage for the rest of your life. The single premium policy has only limited usefulness in the life insurance programs of most families. However, because of its investment attributes, single premium life insurance, or *SPLI* for short, appeals to those looking for a *tax-sheltered investment vehicle*. Like any whole life insurance policy, interest/investment earnings within the policy are tax deferred. There is a catch, however: any cash withdrawals or loans taken against the SPLI cash value before you reach age 59 1/2 are not only taxed as capital gains, but also are subject to a 10 percent penalty for early withdrawal.

Advantages and Disadvantages of Whole Life

The most noteworthy advantage of whole life insurance is that premium payments contribute toward building an estate, regardless of how long the insured lives. The face value of the policy is paid on death; alternatively, the insured can borrow against it or withdraw cash value when the need for insurance protection has expired. As the final column of Exhibit 8.5 shows, the amount of this cash value can be significant.

A corresponding benefit of whole life (except SPLI) is that individuals who need insurance for an entire lifetime can budget their premium payments over a relatively long period. This eliminates the affordability and uninsurability problems often encountered with term insurance in later years.

Another benefit of whole life policies is shown in the "Paid Up Insurance at Year 20" column of Exhibit 8.5. This indicates how much insurance coverage the policyholder can retain if the policy premiums are no longer paid beyond that point and the total cash value at that time is exchanged for the indicated amount of coverage. For example, Exhibit 8.5 shows that a male buying insurance at the age of 40 would pay a premium of $1,078 a year. After 20 years, the cash value of the policy would be $20,518. If he decided to quit paying the premiums from then on, he could sacrifice the $20,518 cash value in return for life insurance coverage of $60,000 up to a maximum age specified in the policy, which is often 65. This flexibility of whole life policies is viewed as a benefit by some insurance buyers.

Some people like whole life policies because the periodic payments force them to save regularly and because favorable tax treatment is given to accumulated earnings. This is because your earnings build up on a tax-sheltered basis, which means that the underlying cash value of the policy increases at a much faster rate than it otherwise would. Insurance experts also point out that the whole life policy offers other potentially valuable options in addition to death protection and cash value. Some of these options include the continuation of coverage after allowing the policy to lapse because premiums were not paid (nonforfeiture option) and the ability to revive an older, favorably priced policy that has lapsed (policy reinstatement). These and other options are discussed in a later section on life insurance contract features.

One disadvantage of whole life insurance is its cost. It provides less death protection per premium dollar than term insurance does. Contrast the premiums paid for various whole life products with those paid for term insurance by comparing Exhibits 8.2, 8.3, and 8.5. You can readily see how much more expensive whole life is than term life. The reason for the difference is that you pay extra for the savings/investment feature included with whole life. Another disadvantage of whole life is that its investment feature provides lower yields than many otherwise comparable vehicles. The returns on most whole life insurance policies are just not very competitive. As with term insurance, the negative aspects of whole life often arise from misuse of the policy. In other words, a *whole life policy should not be used to obtain maximum return on investment*. However, if a person wishes to combine a given amount of death protection for the entire life of the insured (or until the policy is terminated) with a savings plan that provides a *moderate* tax-sheltered rate of return, then whole life insurance may be a wise purchase.

One way to keep the cost of whole life down is to consider purchasing *low-load* whole life insurance. Low-load products are sold directly by insurers to consumers, sometimes over the Internet or via a toll-free phone number, thereby eliminating sales agents from the transaction. With traditional whole life policies sold by an agent, sales commissions and marketing expenses account for between 100 percent and 150 percent of the first year's premium and from 20 percent to 25 percent of total premiums paid over the life of the policy. In comparison, only about 5 percent to 10 percent of low-load policy premiums go toward selling and marketing expenses. As a result, cash values grow much more quickly.

EXAMPLE: Using Low-Load Whole Life Insurance—Building Cash Value

Consider the case of a 50-year-old male who purchased a low-load policy with a $500,000 death benefit for an annual premium of $7,500. Within 5 years his cash surrender value was projected to be more than $36,000. In contrast, a comparable, fully-loaded policy was projected to produce a cash value of only $24,000.

Behavior Matters

Whole Life vs. Term Life Insurance and Behavioral Biases

A whole life insurance policy accumulates cash value over time based on the difference in the premiums on whole life and term life policies for a given individual. Whole life policies are consequently more expensive than term life. Let's consider how whole life insurance policies can be marketed to exploit behavioral biases.

Whole life insurance can be marketed to appeal to the mental accounting behavioral bias. Many people will think of life insurance and saving for retirement as separate though related "mental accounts," both of which have merit. Yet it's easy to confound the investment and life insurance components of a whole life policy when an agent pitches it as a mandated savings plan. Thus, the policy is marketed as offering protection for your family in the event of premature death, as well as providing a mandatory savings plan that will help you consistently pursue retirement savings goals. Some agents will even argue that the whole life policy will eventually be "free" when the cash value has grown large enough to cover the insurance premium. Many cannot resist the apparent appeal of protecting the family today in the event of premature death combined with embarking on a disciplined savings plan that helps save for retirement and will provide "free" insurance in the future.

A rational decision maker knows that there is no such thing as "free" insurance. And such a person would separate the need to have a savings plan from the need to have adequate life insurance coverage. So what causes people to confound these decisions? The concept of premature death, protecting one's family, and planning for retirement are emotional issues. A fully aware person would likely commit to a savings plan, buy term life insurance, and invest the difference between the whole life and term life premiums. Saving and investing for retirement are separate issues that need not be combined in a whole life insurance policy. This is not to say that there are no people for whom whole life insurance is appropriate. However, life insurance and investing for retirement should not be considered without separate analyses.

Source: Adapted from Justin Reckers and Robert Simon, "Behavioral Finance and Life Insurance," http://www.morningstar.com/advisor/t/42987554/behavioral-finance-and-life-insurance.htm#axzz2i25ZJlmG, accessed August 2015.

Who Should Buy Whole Life Insurance?

Most families also need some amount of permanent insurance and savings, which a continuous premium whole life policy can satisfy. Some financial advisors recommend that you use cash-value insurance to cover your *permanent need for insurance*—the amount your dependents will need regardless of the age at which you die. (Although term insurance is less expensive, you may not be able to buy term insurance as you grow older, or it may become too expensive.) Such needs may include final expenses and either the survivor's retirement need (Period 3 in Worksheet 8.1) or additional insurance coverage, whichever is less. This amount is different for every person. Using these guidelines, the Brewers in our earlier example would need about $147,000 in whole life insurance (in Worksheet 8.1: $15,000 final expenses [Step 1, line 3] plus about $132,000 of Period 3 living expenses [Period 3 resources needed vs. resources available, which is Step 1, line 1d for Period 3 minus Step 2, line 1f for Period 3—i.e., $726,000 − $594,000]) and another $176,200 (say $176,000 or $177,000) in term life (in Worksheet 8.1: $323,200 [Step 3] minus about $147,000 in permanent insurance just calculated). Limited payment whole life and single premium whole life policies should be purchased only when the primary goal is savings or additional tax-deferred investments and not protection against financial loss resulting from death.

Whole life may make sense in several other situations. For example, a family history of heart disease, cancer, or similar conditions may increase your risk of developing health problems and make it hard to qualify for term insurance at a later date. If you're already over 50, term life insurance may be too expensive. Or, perhaps you've "maxed out" your other tax-deferred savings options and want to buy cash-value insurance to accumulate additional retirement funds.

8-4c Universal Life Insurance

universal life insurance
Permanent cash-value insurance that combines term insurance (death benefits) with a tax-sheltered savings/investment account that pays interest, usually at competitive money market rates.

Universal life insurance is another form of permanent cash-value insurance that combines term insurance, which provides death benefits, with a tax-sheltered savings/investment account that pays interest, usually at competitive money market rates. The death protection (or pure insurance) portion and the savings portion are identified separately in its premium. This is referred to as *unbundling*. Exhibit 8.6 shows representative annual outlays, premiums, and cash values for a $100,000 universal life policy.

Traditionally, for whole life insurance, you pay a premium to purchase a stated face amount of coverage in a policy with a *fixed cash-value schedule*. With universal life, part of your premium pays administrative fees, and the remainder is put into the cash-value (savings) portion of the policy, where it earns a certain rate of return. This rate of earnings varies with market yields but is guaranteed to be more than some stipulated minimum rate (say, 3 percent). Then, each month the cost of 1 month's term insurance is withdrawn from the cash value to purchase the required death protection. So long as there's enough in the savings portion to buy death protection, the policy will stay in force. Should the cash value grow to an unusually large amount, the amount of insurance coverage must be increased in order for the policy to retain its favorable tax treatment (tax laws require that the death benefits in a universal life policy *must always exceed the cash value* by a stipulated amount).

The explicit separation of the protection and savings elements in universal policies has raised the question of whether this type of insurance is, in fact, whole life insurance. This question is important because the accumulation of cash values in whole life policies arises partly from the interest credited to them. Under

---

EXHIBIT 8.6	Representative Universal Life Insurance Annual Outlays: $100,000 Policy, Preferred Nonsmoker Rates

Universal life premiums are lower than whole life and can vary over the policy's life. After deducting the cost of the death benefit and any administrative fees from your annual contribution, the rest goes into an accumulation account and builds at a variable rate—in this example, the current rate is 3.5 percent. However, the guaranteed rate is only 3 percent, so your actual cash value may be less.

Age	ANNUAL OUTLAY Male ($)	Female ($)	PREMIUMS PAID THROUGH YEAR 20 Male ($)	Female ($)	CASH SURRENDER VALUE AT YEAR 20* Male ($)	Female ($)
25	701	628	14,027	12,574	16,206	14,495
30	830	742	16,590	14,833	19,480	17,302
35	995	885	19,896	17,702	23,169	20,481
40	1,205	1,067	24,108	21,340	27,366	24,234
50	1,806	1,579	36,127	31,573	38,468	34,368
60	2,808	2,402	56,155	48,034	56,365	47,912

*Based on an assumed annual rate of 3.5 percent.

today's tax laws, *this accumulation occurs tax-free so long as the cash value does not exceed the total premiums paid to the insurer*. However, if a whole life policy is surrendered for its cash value and that cash value exceeds the premiums paid, then *the gain* is taxed. Universal life policies enjoy the same favorable tax treatment as do other forms of whole life insurance: death benefits are tax-free and, prior to the insured's death, amounts credited to the cash value (including investment earnings) accumulate on a tax-deferred basis. The insurance company sends the insured an annual statement summarizing the monthly credits of interest and deductions of expenses.

A universal life insurance policy provides two types of death protection. The first type, known as Option A, provides a level death benefit. As the cash value increases, the amount of pure insurance protection *decreases*. The second type, Option B, provides a stated amount of insurance plus the accumulated cash value. Therefore, the death benefit at any time varies with the rate of earnings on the savings plan and will increase along with the accumulated cash value.

Advantages and Disadvantages of Universal Life

As with any insurance policy, universal life has its pros and cons. There are two principal advantages.

- **Flexibility:** The annual premium you pay can be increased or decreased from year to year, because the cost of the death protection *may be covered from either the annual premium or the accumulation account* (i.e., the cash value). If the accumulation account is adequate, you can use it to pay the annual premium. The death benefit also can be increased or decreased, and you can change from the level benefit type of policy to the cash value plus a stated amount of insurance. Note, however, that evidence of insurability is usually required if the death benefit is to be increased. This flexibility allows you to adapt the death benefit to your life-cycle needs—for example, increasing the death benefit when you have another child and decreasing it when your children are grown.
- **Savings feature:** A universal life insurance policy credits cash value at the "current" rate of interest, and this *current* rate of interest may well be higher than the guaranteed *minimum* rate. Find out what benchmark is used to determine the current rate of interest; the 90-day U.S. Treasury bill rate is often used.

Universal life's flexibility in making premium payments, although an attractive feature, is also one of its two major drawbacks.

- **Changing premiums and protection levels:** A policyholder who economizes on premium payments in early years may find that premiums must be higher than originally planned in later policy years to keep the policy in force. Indeed, some policyholders buy universal life expecting their premiums to vanish once cash value builds to a certain level. All too often, however, the premiums never disappear altogether. Or if they do, they reappear when interest rates fall below the rate in effect when the policy was purchased.
- **Charges or fees:** Universal life usually carries heavy fees compared to other policy types. These fees include the front-end load or commission on the first premium, the expense charge on each annual premium, investment expense charged by the insurer in determining the "current" rate of return, and other charges. Most states require the insurance company to issue an annual disclosure statement spelling out premiums paid, all expenses and mortality costs, interest earned, and beginning and ending cash values.

Who Should Buy Universal Life Insurance?

Universal life is a suitable choice if you're looking for a savings vehicle with greater potential returns than a whole life policy offers. Its flexible nature makes it particularly useful for people anticipating changes from their current need for death protection. For example, if you're recently married and expect to have children, a universal life policy will allow you to increase the death benefit as your family grows.

8-4d Other Types of Life Insurance

Besides term, whole life, and universal life, you can buy several other types of life insurance products, including variable life insurance, group life, and other special-purpose life policies such as credit life, mortgage life, and industrial life insurance. These insurance products serve diverse needs. Some may help you meet specific needs; others are simply comparable alternatives to traditional types of life insurance.

Variable Life Insurance

variable life insurance
Life insurance in which the benefits are a function of the returns being generated on the investments selected by the policyholder.

A **variable life insurance** policy goes further than whole and universal life policies in combining death benefits and savings. The policyholder decides how to invest the money in the savings (cash-value) component. The investment accounts are set up just like *mutual funds*, and most firms that offer variable life policies let you choose from a full menu of different funds, ranging from money market accounts and bond funds to international investments or aggressively managed stock funds. Unlike whole or universal life policies, however, variable life insurance policies do not guarantee a *minimum return*. Also, as the name implies, the amount of insurance coverage provided varies with the profits (and losses) generated in the investment account. Thus, the amount of death benefits payable in variable life insurance policies is, for the most part, related to the policies' investment returns. Exhibit 8.7 demonstrates how two possible investment return scenarios would affect the cash value and death benefits of a variable life insurance policy for a 45-year-old, nonsmoking male over a 20-year period.

Although all these features may sound great, variable life puts more emphasis on investments than any other life insurance product. Indeed, many observers view variable life more as an investment vehicle than a life insurance policy. It's an investment product wrapped around just enough life insurance coverage to make it legal. If you want the benefits of higher investment returns, then you must also be willing to assume the risks of reduced insurance coverage. So what does this mean for you? *It means you should use extreme care when buying variable life insurance.*

EXHIBIT 8.7	REPRESENTATIVE VARIABLE Life Insurance Values: $100,000 Policy, Preferred Nonsmoker, Male, Age 45

Variable life insurance pays a death benefit whose amount is tied to the policy's investment returns. The cash value created over the life of the policy is also related to investment returns. This table shows the effects of 6 percent and 12 percent annual returns over a 20-year period. Of course, a 12 percent return is quite optimistic. Lower returns result in lower cash value and death benefits; higher returns result in higher cash value and death benefits.

Policy Year	Total Premiums Paid	6% RETURN		12% RETURN	
		Cash Value	Death Benefit	Cash Value	Death Benefit
1	$1,575	$995	$100,995	$1,064	$101,064
5	8,705	5,244	105,244	5,705	105,705
10	19,810	10,592	110,592	15,365	115,365
15	33,986	15,093	115,093	27,688	127,688
20	52,079	17,080	117,080	43,912	143,912

Group Life Insurance

group life insurance
Life insurance that provides a master policy for a group; each eligible group member receives a certificate of insurance.

Under **group life insurance**, one master policy is issued and each eligible group member receives a certificate of insurance. Group life is nearly always term insurance, and the premium is based on the group's characteristics as a whole rather than the characteristics of any specific individual. Employers often provide group life insurance as a fringe benefit for their employees. However, just about any type of group (e.g., a labor union, a professional association, an alumni organization) can secure a group life policy as long as the insurance is only incidental to the reason for the group's existence.

Accounting for about one-third of all life insurance in the United States, group life insurance is one of the fastest-growing areas of insurance. Many group life policies now offer coverage for dependents as well as group members. What's more, group life policies generally provide that individual members who leave the group may continue the coverage by converting their protection to individually issued whole life policies. It is important to note that conversion normally doesn't require evidence of insurability as long as it occurs within a specified period. Of course, after conversion, the individual pays all premiums. Before buying additional coverage purchased through a group plan or converting a group policy to an individual one, it's important to compare rates. Often the premiums are more expensive than other readily available sources of term insurance.

As noted in Chapters 1 and 2, the availability of group coverage through employee benefit programs should be considered when developing a life insurance program. However, because of its potentially temporary nature and relatively low benefit amount (often equal to about 1 year's salary), it should be used only to fulfill low-priority insurance needs. Only in rare cases should a family rely solely on group life insurance to fulfill its primary income-protection requirements.

Other Special-Purpose Life Policies

Use caution before buying one of the following types of life insurance:

credit life insurance
Life insurance sold in conjunction with installment loans.

- **Credit life insurance:** Banks, finance companies, and other lenders generally sell credit life insurance in conjunction with installment loans. Usually, credit life is a term policy of less than five years with a face value corresponding to the outstanding balance on the loan. Although liquidating debts on the death of a family breadwinner is often desirable, it's usually preferable to do so through an individual's term or whole life insurance, rather than buying a separate credit life insurance policy. This is because credit life is one of the most expensive forms of life insurance—and one you should therefore avoid.

mortgage life insurance
A term policy designed to pay off the mortgage balance in the event of the borrower's death.

- **Mortgage life insurance:** Mortgage life insurance is a term policy designed to pay off the mortgage balance on a home in the event of the borrower's death. As in the case of credit life, this need can usually be met less expensively by shopping the market for a suitable decreasing term policy.

industrial life insurance (home service life insurance)
Whole life insurance issued in policies with relatively small face amounts, often $1,000 or less.

- **Industrial life insurance:** Sometimes called **home service life insurance**, this whole life insurance is issued in policies with small face amounts, often $1,000 or less. Agents call on policyholders weekly or monthly to collect the premiums. The term *industrial* became popular when the policies were first sold primarily to low-paid industrial wage earners. Industrial life insurance costs a good deal more per $1,000 of coverage than regular whole life policies, primarily because of its high marketing costs. Even so, some insurance authorities believe that industrial life insurance offers the only practical way to deliver coverage to low-income families.

8-9 What is *term life insurance?* Describe some common types of term life insurance policies.

8-10 What are the advantages and disadvantages of term life insurance?

8-11 Explain how *whole life insurance* offers financial protection to an individual throughout his or her life.

8-12 Explain how the "paid-up insurance" component of a whole life insurance policy works.

8-13 Describe the different types of whole life policies. What are the advantages and disadvantages of whole life insurance?

8-14 What is *universal life insurance?* Explain how it differs from whole life and *variable life insurance.*

8-15 Explain how *group life insurance* differs from standard term life insurance. What do employees stand to gain from group life?

8-16 Why should the following types of life insurance contracts be avoided? (a) *credit life insurance*, (b) *mortgage life insurance*, (c) *industrial life insurance (home service life insurance)*.

8-5 BUYING LIFE INSURANCE

Once you have evaluated your personal financial needs and have become familiar with the basic life insurance options, you're ready to begin shopping for a life insurance policy. Exhibit 8.8 summarizes the major advantages and disadvantages of the most popular types of life insurance discussed so far in this chapter.

Several factors should be considered when making the final purchase decision: (1) comparing the costs and features of competitive products, (2) selecting a financially healthy insurance company, and (3) choosing a good agent.

8-5a Compare Costs and Features

The cost of a life insurance policy can vary considerably from company to company, even for the same amount and type of coverage. By comparison shopping, you can save thousands of dollars over the life of your policy. For example, the total cost for a 10-year, $250,000, term life policy at preferred rates for a 25-year-old can range from $1,170 to more than $2,000. Exhibit 8.9 gives a quick overview of differences in the key features of various types of life insurance.

If you smoke or have a health problem such as high cholesterol or high blood pressure, then spending time to check out several companies can really pay off. Some companies are more willing to accept these risks than others. They may even give you preferred rates if you correct the problem within a certain period of time. But until you do your homework, you won't know which policy offers you the coverage that you need at the lowest cost. If you have an unusual health problem or some other type of complication, a policy bought through an agent may actually be the cheapest alternative.

It's not enough to look only at current rates. You'll also need to ask how long the rates are locked-in and to find out the maximum you can be charged when you renew. A guaranteed policy may cost another $20 a year, but you won't be hit with unexpected, larger rate increases later. Establish for how long you'll need the coverage, and then find the best rates for the total period; low premiums for a five-year policy may jump when you renew for additional coverage. Also be sure you're getting the features you need, like the convertibility of term policies.

EXHIBIT 8.8

Major Advantages and Disadvantages of the Most Popular Types of Life Insurance

Major advantages and disadvantages of the most popular types of life insurance are summarized here. They should be considered when shopping for life insurance.

Type of Policy	Advantages	Disadvantages
Term	• Low initial premiums: simple, easy to buy.	• Provides only temporary coverage for a set period. • May have to pay higher premiums when policy is renewed.
Whole life	• Permanent coverage • Savings vehicle: cash value builds as premiums are paid. • Some tax advantages on accumulated earnings.	• Cost: provides less death protection per premium dollar than term. • Often provides lower yields than other investment vehicles. • Sales commissions and marketing expenses can increase costs of fully loaded policy.
Universal life	• Permanent coverage • Flexible: allows insured adapt level of protection and cost of premiums. • Savings vehicle: cash value builds at current rate of interest. • Savings and death protection identified separately.	• Can be difficult to evaluate true cost at time of purchase; insurance carrier may levy costly fees and charges.
Variable life	• Investment vehicle: insured decides how cash value will be invested.	• Higher risk.

Finally, be sure the policies that you are comparing *have similar provisions and amounts*. In other words, don't compare a $100,000 term life policy from one company with a $150,000 universal life policy from another. Instead, *first decide how much and what kind of policy you want, and then compare costs*. For similar cash-value policies, you may find it useful to compare interest-adjusted cost indexes that are often shown on policy illustrations. The *surrender cost index* measures the policy's cost if you surrender it after a certain period, typically 10 or 20 years, assuming that premiums and dividends earn 5 percent interest. The *net payment cost index* is calculated in a similar way but assumes that the policy is kept in force.

It's easy to gather the information that allows you to compare costs and features. Term life quote services, available over the Internet or the phone, can streamline the selection process by providing you, free of charge, with the names of several companies offering the lowest-cost policies based on your specifications. Probably the fastest-growing source of life insurance quotes and policies in recent years is the Internet. You can not only obtain quick, real-time quotes but also can buy insurance electronically. Buying on the Internet allows you to avoid dealing with insurance salespeople, and you can purchase the policies (usually term insurance only) on cost-effective terms. For example, one major life insurer offers discounts of up to 20 percent for term life policies purchased online. Of course, you'll still need a physical exam, but often the insurance company will send a qualified technician/nurse to your home or office to take a blood sample and other basic readings. Efinancial (**http://www.efinancial.com**), Select Quote Insurance Services (**http://www.selectquote.com**), Insure.com (**http://www.insure.com**), and Matrix Direct Insurance Services (**http://matrixdirect.com**)

EXHIBIT 8.9 | **Key Features of Various Types of Life Insurance**

Differences in the key features of various types of life insurance are listed here. It's important to compare both costs and features when shopping for life insurance.

Feature	Term	Whole Life	Universal Life
Death protection	High	Moderate	Low to high
Coverage period	Temporary for set period	Ongoing	Ongoing
Costs	Low fixed premiums, no fees	High fixed premiums; may also be charged fees	Can vary from high to low; may also be charged fees
Return on investment?	None	Yes, moderate	Yes; return can vary
Tax advantages	No	Yes	Yes

maintain databases of life insurance policy costs for various companies and will also act as your agent to buy the policy if you wish. Insure.com and Matrix Direct provide quotes for both term insurance and whole life. Also, don't overlook companies that sell directly to the public or offer low-load policies, such as Ameritas, Lincoln Benefit, and USAA (for the military and their families).

8-5b Select an Insurance Company

Selecting a life insurance company is an important part of shopping for life insurance. Besides looking for a firm that offers reasonably priced products, attractive contract features, and good customer service, it's vital to consider the financial health of any insurance firm before buying a life insurance policy. You want to be sure that the company will be around and have the assets to pay your beneficiaries should you die. Even before you die, however, your insurance company's financial stability is important. If the company fails, you may be forced to buy a new policy at less favorable rates.

The age and size of insurance companies are useful indicators in narrowing your choices. Unless there's a good reason to do otherwise, you should probably limit the companies you consider to those that have been doing business for 25 years or more and that have annual premium volume of more than $100 million. These criteria will rule out a lot of smaller firms, but there are still plenty of companies left to choose from. You may also find that one company is preferable for your term protection and another for your whole life needs.

Factors to consider before making the final choice include the firm's reputation, financial history, commissions and other fees, and the specifics of its policy provisions. If you're choosing a company for a cash value life insurance policy, the company's investment performance and dividend history is also an important consideration.

> **You Can Do It Now**
> *Shop for a Customized Life Insurance Policy*
>
> Let's make life insurance more concrete and personal. You can easily get an insurance quote online. Go to the popular Internet site noted in this chapter, **http://www.insure .com/life-insurance/,** and provide the requested personal information. Then request a quote for, say, a 20-year, $200,000 term life insurance policy—you can do it now.

FINANCIAL PLANNING TIPS

Breezing through Your Life Insurance Medical Exam

You're more likely to pass your life insurance medical exam if you keep the following tips in mind:

• **Know what to expect.** The examiner will measure and record your height, weight, blood pressure, and pulse rate, and will collect blood and urine samples. Also, expect the examiner to confirm the answers that you provided on your life insurance application. The test results will be sent to the insurance company and the underwriter, which will assess your risk and determine your life insurance premiums.

• **Drink water before the exam.** This makes it easier to draw blood.

• **Fast before the exam.** Eating within four to eight hours before the exam could elevate your glucose levels.

• **Don't do a rigorous workout for at least 12 hours prior to the exam.** Take it easy, and avoid even a fast walk or a workout on an aerobic machine. Strenuous exercise before a physical can elevate the protein found in your urine to a point of concern.

• **Avoid alcohol for at least 12 hours before the exam.** Drinking too much alcohol can dehydrate you and possibly elevate liver function test flags, which can push you into a riskier category.

• **Avoid caffeine and nicotine for at least a couple of hours prior to the exam.** Caffeine and nicotine tend to elevate blood pressure. If you simply cannot make it without coffee, be sure to drink it black—no cream or sugar.

• **Bring a list of your medications.** Examiners typically take a medical history during the exam, which requires a list of your current prescriptions and over-the-counter medications.

• **Get to bed early the night before the exam.** While it might not directly affect your test results, you'll be more relaxed, and this should help moderate your blood pressure if you have "white coat anxiety."

Source: Adapted from Jeffrey Steele, "Ace Your Life Insurance Medical Exam," http://www.insurance.com/life-insurance/life-insurance-basics/life-insurance-medical-exam .aspx, accessed August 2015.

How do you find all of this information? Luckily, private rating agencies have done much of the work for you. The four most commonly used agencies are A. M. Best, Fitch, Moody's, and Standard & Poor's (see Exhibit 8-10). These agencies use publicly available financial data from insurance companies to analyze their debt structure, pricing practices, and management strategies in an effort to assess their financial stability. The purpose is to evaluate the insurance company's ability to pay future claims made by policyholders, which is known as its *claims paying ability*. In most cases, insurance firms pay ratings agencies a fee for this service. The ratings agencies then give each insurance firm a "grade" based on their analysis of the firm's financial data. Most public libraries and insurance agents have these ratings. Each rating firm has an Internet site where some insurance company ratings may also be found.

You Can Do It Now

Check Out the Best Life Insurance Companies

The ratings of the best life insurance companies and an overall ranking, known as the Comdex rank, are provided online at **http://toplifeinsurancereviews.com/ comdex-ranking-life-insurance/**. Go to the site and jot down the top five life insurance companies. Now you have a great start when you are ready to shop for life insurance—**you can do it now.**

FINANCIAL PLANNING TIPS

Potential Conflicts of Interest in Dealing with Insurance Agents

Most insurance agents are ethical and professional. However, in order to help you identify the others and protect yourself from the few who are not, it's important to keep in mind some potential conflicts of interest between you and insurance agents and brokers. Most have to do with sales commission incentives that can conflict with you getting the best advice.

• Agents only rarely disclose their commissions—and likely will do so only if you ask. Ask agents about the commissions that they receive on competing insurance products. If they balk at the request, it's time to find another agent.

• Agents have an incentive to recommend policies that provide the greatest commissions. Alternatively stated, agents have no financial incentive to recommend policies that pay no commissions.

• Agents often avoid bringing up the negative aspects of a policy because they don't want to blow the sale. This also tempts some agents to oversimplify policy features. You need to ask the hard questions.

• While some existing policies should be kept and some replaced, agents only get paid for giving advice when it leads to commissions. So agents can be unreliable sources of advice about the performance of an existing policy. Getting a second opinion from an agent with another firm is always a good idea.

• Watch out when agents present company illustrations and projections of future policy performance. Don't accept the projections and assumptions uncritically.

• Be aware that some lawyers, accountants, and financial planners don't ask hard questions about life insurance proposals because they depend on life insurance agents for business referrals. Thus, it can be hard to find objective sources of advice concerning life insurance proposals. Consider using a fee-only insurance advisor.

Notwithstanding these potential conflicts of interest, you can accomplish a lot by doing your own homework and by relying on recommended advisors who are true fiduciaries who put their clients first.

Source: Life Insurance Advisors, Inc., "Conflicts and Limitations of Life Insurance Agents," http://www.lifeinsuranceadvisorsinc.com/conflicts.html, accessed August 2015.

Most experts agree that it's wise to purchase life insurance only from insurance companies that are assigned ratings by at least two of the major rating agencies and are consistently rated in the top two or three categories (e.g., Aaa, Aa1, or Aa2 by Moody's) by each of the major agencies from which they received ratings. The easiest way to comprehensively evaluate an insurance company is to rely on the Comdex ranking, which considers the ratings established by A. M. Best, Standard & Poor's, Moody's Investors Services, and Fitch. (See **http://www.ebixlife.com/vitalsigns/comdexcalc.aspx** for more information.)

8-5c Choosing an Agent

There's an old axiom in the life insurance business that life insurance is sold, not bought. Life insurance agents play a major role in most people's decision to buy life insurance. Unless you plan to buy all of your life insurance via the Internet, selecting a good life insurance agent is important because you'll be relying on him or her for guidance in making some important financial decisions. Don't assume that just because agents are licensed, they are competent and will serve your best interests. Consider an agent's formal and professional level of educational attainment. Does the agent have a college degree with a major in business or insurance?

Financial Fact or Fantasy?

Selecting an insurance company is the first thing you should do when buying life insurance. **Fantasy:** The first thing you should do is determine the amount of life insurance you need and then select the type of policy that is best for you. Only after you have taken these steps should you address where you will buy the insurance.

EXHIBIT 8.10   Major Insurance Rating Agencies

The three biggest insurance rating agencies are A. M. Best Company, Moody's Investor Services, and Standard & Poor's Corporation. A smaller (but growing) agency is Fitch Inc. Contact information for each of these agencies is given here.*

A.M. Best Company
Internet address: **http://www.ambest.com**
Top three grades: A++, A+, and A

Moody's Investor Services
Internet address: **http://www.moodys.com**
Top three grades: Aaa, Aa1, and Aa2

Standard & Poor's Corporation
Internet address: **http://www.standardandpoors.com**
Top three grades: AAA, AA+, and AA

Fitch Inc.
Internet address: **http://www.fitchratings.com**
Top three grades: AAA, AA+, and AA

*The Comdex ranking shows how an insurance company compares to other companies based on the ratings assigned by the above four agencies. Internet address: http://www.ebixlife.com/vitalsigns/comdexcalc.aspx.

CORBIS/JUPITER IMAGES

Does the agent have a professional designation, such as Chartered Life Underwriter (CLU), Chartered Financial Consultant (ChFC), or Certified Financial Planner® (CFP®)? These designations are awarded only to those who meet certain experience requirements and pass comprehensive examinations in such fields as life and health insurance, estate and pension planning, investments, and federal income tax law.

Observe how an agent reacts to your questions. Does the agent use fancy buzzwords and generic answers, or does she really listen attentively and, after some thought, logically answer your questions? These and other personal characteristics should be considered. In most cases, you should talk with several agents and discuss the pros and cons of each agent with your spouse or other trusted person before committing yourself. Then, when you've decided, call the agent again and finish your business.

When seeking a good life insurance agent, try to obtain recommendations from other professionals who work with agents. Bankers in trust departments, attorneys, and accountants who are specialists in estate planning are usually good sources. In contrast, be a bit wary of selecting an agent simply because of the agent's aggressiveness in soliciting your patronage.

TEST YOURSELF

8-17   Briefly describe the steps to take when you shop for and buy life insurance.

8-18   Briefly describe the insurance company ratings assigned by A. M. Best, Moody's, Fitch, Standard & Poor's, and Comdex. Why is it important to know how a company is rated? What ratings would you look for when selecting a life insurance company? Explain.

8-19   What characteristics would be most important to you when choosing an insurance agent?

8-6 KEY FEATURES OF LIFE INSURANCE POLICIES

When buying a life insurance policy, you are entering into a contract with the insurance company. The provisions in this contract spell out the policyholder's and the insurer's rights and obligations as well as the features of the policy being purchased. Unfortunately, there's no such thing as a standard life insurance policy. Each insurance company uses its own wording. Policies can also vary from state to state, depending on the law of the state where the policy is sold. Even so, certain elements are common in most life insurance contracts.

8-6a Life Insurance Contract Features

Key features found in most life insurance contracts are the beneficiary clause, settlement options, policy loans, premium payments, grace period, nonforfeiture options, policy reinstatement, and change of policy.

Beneficiary Clause

beneficiary
A person who receives the death benefits of a life insurance policy after the insured's death.

The **beneficiary** is the person who will receive the death benefits of the policy on the insured's death. All life insurance policies should have one or more beneficiaries. Otherwise, death benefits are paid to the deceased's estate and are subject to the often lengthy and expensive legal procedure of going through probate. An insured person is able to name both a *primary beneficiary* and various *contingent beneficiaries*. The primary beneficiary receives the entire death benefit if he or she is surviving when the insured dies. If the primary beneficiary does not survive the insured, then the insurer will distribute the death benefits to the contingent beneficiary or beneficiaries. If neither primary nor contingent beneficiaries are living at the death of the insured, then the death benefits pass to the estate of the insured and are distributed by the probate court according to the insured's will or, if no will exists, according to state law.

The identification of named beneficiaries should be clear. For example, a man could buy a policy and simply designate the beneficiary as "my wife." But if he later divorces and remarries, there could be a controversy as to which "wife" is entitled to the benefits. Obviously, you should consider changing your named beneficiary if circumstances, such as marital status, change. The person you name as a beneficiary can be changed at any time as long as you didn't indicate an *irrevocable beneficiary* when you took out the policy. Thus, if your wishes change, all you need to do is notify the insurance company—easy to do, but also easy to forget.

Settlement Options

Insurance companies generally offer several ways of paying life insurance policy death proceeds. How the insurance benefits will be distributed can either be permanently established by the policyholder before death or left up to the beneficiary when the policy proceeds are paid out.

- **Lump sum:** This is the most common settlement option, chosen by more than 95 percent of policyholders. The entire death benefit is paid in a single amount, allowing beneficiaries to use or invest the proceeds soon after death occurs.
- **Interest only:** The insurance company keeps policy proceeds for a specified time; the beneficiary receives interest payments, usually at some guaranteed rate. This option can be useful when there's no current need for the principal. For example, proceeds could be left on deposit until children go to college, with interest supplementing family income. Typically, however, interest rates paid by insurers are lower than those available with other savings vehicles.
- **Fixed period:** The face amount of the policy, along with interest earned, is paid to the beneficiary over a fixed time period. For example, a 55-year-old beneficiary may need additional income until Social Security benefits start.

- **Fixed amount:** The beneficiary receives policy proceeds in regular payments of a fixed amount until the proceeds run out.
- **Life income:** The insurer guarantees to pay the beneficiary a certain payment for the rest of his or her life, based on the beneficiary's sex, age when benefits start, life expectancy, policy face value, and interest rate assumptions. This option appeals to beneficiaries who don't want to outlive the income from policy proceeds and so become dependent on others for support. An interesting variation of this settlement option is the *life-income-with-period-certain option,* whereby the company guarantees a specified number of payments that would pass to a secondary beneficiary if the original beneficiary dies before the period ends.

Policy Loans

An advance made by a life insurance company to a policyholder against a whole life policy is called a **policy loan**. These loans are secured by the cash value of the life insurance policy. Although these loans do *not* have to be repaid, any balance plus interest on the loan remaining at the insured's death is *subtracted from the proceeds of the policy.* Typically policies offer either a fixed-rate loan or a rate that varies with market interest rates on high-quality bonds. Some policies let the insured choose whether the loans will be at fixed or variable rates. Take out a policy loan only if your estate is large enough to cover the accompanying loss of death proceeds when the loan is not repaid. Remember that life insurance is intended to provide basic financial protection for your dependents, and spending those proceeds prematurely defeats the purpose of life insurance. A word of caution: *Be careful with these loans; unless certain conditions are met, the IRS may treat them as withdrawals, meaning they could be subject to tax penalties.* If you're in any way unsure, consult your insurance agent or a tax advisor.

Premium Payments

All life insurance contracts have a provision specifying when premiums, which are normally paid in advance, are due. With most insurers, the policyholder may elect to pay premiums annually, semiannually, quarterly, or monthly. In most cases, insurance companies charge a fee if you decide to pay more often than annually.

Grace Period

The *grace period* permits the policyholder to retain full death protection for a short period (usually 31 days) after missing a premium payment date. In other words, you won't lose your insurance protection just because you're a little late in making the premium payment. If the insured dies during the grace period, the face amount of the policy less the unpaid premium is paid to the beneficiary.

Nonforfeiture Options

As discussed earlier, a *nonforfeiture option* gives a cash value life insurance policyholder some benefits even when a policy is terminated before its maturity. State laws require that all permanent whole, universal, or variable life policies (and term contracts covering an extended period) contain a nonforfeiture provision. Rather than taking a check in the amount of the policy's cash value, insurance companies usually offer the two options—*paid-up insurance* and *extended term insurance*—described here.

- **Paid-up insurance:** The policyholder receives a policy exactly like the terminated one, but with a lower face value. In effect, the policyholder uses the cash value to buy a new, single premium policy. For example, a policy canceled after 10 years might have a cash value of $90.84 per $1,000 of face value, which could be used to buy $236 of paid-up whole life insurance. This paid-up insurance is useful, as the cash value continues to grow because of future interest earnings, even though the policyholder makes no further premium payments. This option is useful when a person's income and need for death protection decline—when he or she reaches age 60 or 65, for example—yet that person still wants some coverage.

- **Extended term insurance:** The insured uses the accumulated cash value to buy a term life policy for the same face value as the lapsed policy. The coverage period is based on the amount of term protection a single premium payment (equal to the total cash value) buys at the insured's present age. This option usually goes into effect automatically if the policyholder quits paying premiums and gives no instructions to the insurer.

Policy Reinstatement

So long as a whole life policy is under the reduced paid-up insurance option or the extended term insurance option, the policyholder may reinstate the original policy by paying all back premiums plus interest at a stated rate and by providing evidence that he or she can pass a physical examination and meet any other insurability requirements. *Reinstatement* revives the original contractual relationship between the company and the policyholder. Most often, the policyholder must reinstate the policy within a specified period (three to five years) after the policy has lapsed. However, before exercising a reinstatement option, a policyholder should determine whether buying a new policy (from the same or a different company) might be less costly.

Change of Policy

Many life insurance contracts contain a provision that permits the insured to switch from one policy form to another. For instance, a policyholder may decide that he'd rather have a policy that is paid up at age 65 rather than his current continuous premium whole life policy. A change-of-policy provision would allow this change without penalty. When policyholders change from high- to lower-premium policies, they may need to prove insurability. This requirement reduces the insurance company's exposure to adverse selection.

multiple indemnity clause
A clause in a life insurance policy that typically doubles or triples the policy's face amount if the insured dies in an accident.

disability clause
A clause in a life insurance contract containing a *waiver-of-premium benefit* alone or coupled with *disability income.*

8-6b Other Policy Features

Along with the key contractual features described earlier, here are some other policy features to consider:

- **Multiple indemnity clause:** Multiple indemnity clauses increase the face amount of the policy, most often doubling or tripling it, if the insured dies in an accident. This benefit is usually offered to the policyholder at a small additional cost. Many insurance authorities dismiss the use of a multiple indemnity benefit as irrational. This coverage should be ignored as a source of funds when determining insurance needs because it offers no protection if the insured's death is due to illness.

- **Disability clause:** A disability clause may contain a waiver-of-premium benefit alone or coupled with disability income. A *waiver-of-premium benefit* excuses the payment of premiums on the life insurance policy if the insured becomes totally and permanently disabled prior to age 60 (or sometimes age 65). Under the *disability income portion,* the insured not only is granted a waiver of premium but also receives a monthly income equal to $5 or $10 per $1,000 of policy face value. Some insurers will continue these payments for the life of the insured; others terminate them at age 65. Disability riders for a waiver of premium and disability income protection are relatively inexpensive and can be added to most whole life policies but generally not to term policies.

Financial Fact or Fantasy?

Because most life insurance policies are largely the same, you need not concern yourself with differences in specific contract provisions. **Fantasy:** All insurance policies are not the same. Thus, it is important to familiarize yourself with the provisions of the contract, including the beneficiary clauses and settlement options.

guaranteed purchase option
An option in a life insurance contract giving the policyholder the right to purchase additional coverage at stipulated intervals without providing evidence of insurability.

- **Guaranteed purchase option:** The policyholder who has a guaranteed purchase option may purchase additional coverage at stipulated intervals without providing evidence of insurability. This option is frequently offered to buyers of a whole life policy who are under age 40. Increases in coverage usually can be purchased every three, four, or five years in sums equal to the amount of the original policy or $10,000, whichever is lower. This option should be attractive to individuals whose life insurance needs and ability to pay are expected to increase over a 5- to 15-year period.

- **Suicide clause:** Nearly all life insurance policies have a *suicide clause* that voids the contract if an insured commits suicide within a certain period, normally two years after the policy's inception. In these cases, the company simply returns the premiums that have been paid. If an insured commits suicide after this initial period has elapsed, the policy proceeds are paid regardless.

- **Exclusions:** Although all private insurance policies exclude some types of losses, life policies offer broad protection. Other than the suicide clause, the only common exclusions are aviation, war, and hazardous occupation or hobby. However, a company would rarely be able to modify the premium charged or coverage offered should the insured take up, say, Formula One racing or hang gliding *after* a policy is issued.

participating policy
A life insurance policy that pays *policy dividends* reflecting the difference between the premiums that are charged and the amount of premium necessary to fund the actual mortality experience of the company.

- **Participation:** In a participating policy, the policyholder is entitled to receive *policy dividends* reflecting the difference between the premiums that are charged and the amount of premium necessary to fund the actual mortality experience of the company. When the base premium schedule for participating policies is established, a company estimates what it believes its mortality and investment experience will be and then adds a generous margin of safety to these figures. The premiums charged the policyholder are based on these conservative estimates.

- **Living benefits:** Also called *accelerated benefits*, this feature allows the insured to receive a percentage of the death benefit from a whole or universal life policy prior to death. Some insurers offer this option at no charge to established policyholders if the insured suffers a terminal illness that is expected to result in death within a specified period (such as six months to a year) or needs an expensive treatment (such as an organ transplant) to survive. These benefits can also be added as a *living benefit rider* that pays a portion of a policy's death benefit in advance, usually about 2 percent per month, for long-term health care such as nursing home expenses. This rider can add an extra 5 percent to 15 percent to the normal life insurance premium, and benefits are capped at some fixed percentage of the death benefit.

- **Viatical settlement:** Like a living benefits feature, this option allows a terminally ill insurance holder to receive a percentage of the insurance policy's death benefit for immediate use. But unlike the living benefits feature, this isn't handled through the insurance company but rather through a third-party investor. The insured sells an interest in the life insurance policy to the investor, who then becomes the policy's beneficiary, and then receives a cash amount from that investor—most commonly 60 percent of the policy value. After the insured dies, the investor receives the balance from the policy. Approach viatical settlements carefully, because they mean giving up all future claims on the life insurance policy and can also affect a patient's Medicare eligibility in some cases. Note also that some viatical settlement companies—the firms that arrange the transfer between insureds and investors—have been scrutinized by government agencies for unethical practices.

life insurance policy illustration
A hypothetical representation of a life insurance policy's performance that reflects the most important assumptions that the insurance company relies on when presenting the policy results to a prospective client.

8-6c Understanding Life Insurance Policy Illustrations

A **life insurance policy illustration** is a hypothetical representation of a policy's performance that reflects the most important assumptions that the company relies on when presenting the policy results to a prospective client. Insurance illustrations are complicated and often contain more than 20 pages of numbers and legal disclaimers. The insurance illustration specifies the inflows from premiums paid and interest credits, both of which increase the cash value of the policy. The illustration also states mortality charges and expenses, both of which decrease the cash value. An illustration typically consists of two main parts:

- **Guaranteed illustration:** The insurance company is required by law to disclose the worst-case scenario, which shows the effects of the insurer crediting the minimum interest and charging the maximum amount based on standard mortality tables. It's safe to assume that the benefits, cash surrender value, and accumulated values will never be lower than what this scenario presents.
- **Current illustration:** This is the insurance company's representation of policy performance based on the credit rates and mortality charges *currently* in effect.

When you look at an insurance illustration, focus first on the basic assumptions that the company used to compute it, including your age, sex, and underwriting health status. As noted above, the illustration will indicate the premiums, cash surrender value, and death benefits. Double-check all the information. Ask the insurance agent to provide an *inforce reprojection* that shows any changes in credits or charges that the insurance company has declared for the next policy year. These changes in credits and charges will affect premiums or benefits. Most agents will not provide this unless you ask them. Watch for any unanticipated premium increases.

Check to make sure that all the following sections are present in the narrative summary of the illustration and that no pages are missing:

- **Policy description, terms, and features:** This section overviews the main components of the policy. Double-check that the policy's premiums and benefit projections match your needs.
- **Underwriting discussion:** This provides a detailed description of the policy's benefits, premiums, and tax information.
- **Column definitions and key terms:** This defines the terms used in the illustration. Make sure that you understand all the definitions and terms.
- **Disclaimer:** This section informs the prospective client that the illustration's portrayal of future values could vary from actual results.
- **Signature page:** This section provides a numerical summary of the illustration in 5- and 10-year increments. The insurance agent's signature here acknowledges that he or she has explained that the nonguaranteed elements are subject to change, and your signature acknowledges that you understand this.

TEST YOURSELF

8-20 What is a *beneficiary*? A *contingent beneficiary*? Explain why it's essential to designate a beneficiary for your policy.

8-21 Explain the basic settlement options available for the payment of life insurance proceeds upon a person's death.

8-22 What do *nonforfeiture options* accomplish? Differentiate between *paid-up insurance* and *extended term insurance*.

8-23 Explain the following clauses often found in life insurance policies: (a) *multiple indemnity clause*, (b) *disability clause*, and (c) *suicide clause*. Give some examples of common exclusions.

8-24 Describe what is meant by a *participating policy*, and explain the role of *policy dividends* in these policies.

8-25 Describe the key elements of an *insurance policy illustration* and explain what a prospective client should focus on in evaluating an illustration.

Planning Over a Lifetime: *Life Insurance*

Here are some key considerations for life insurance use in each stage of the life cycle.

Pre-family Independence: 20s	Family Formation/ Career Development: 30–45	Pre-Retirement: 45–65	Retirement: 65 and Beyond
✓ Term life insurance is needed only if you have dependents relying on you financially.	✓ If you marry, add life insurance to cover the financial needs of your spouse and other dependents.	✓ Re-evaluate insurance coverage if you change jobs or move to a higher-paying job.	✓ Assure adequate financial protection of your surviving spouse.
	✓ Consider increasing insurance coverage as additional children are born.	✓ Consider reducing insurance coverage as children leave home and graduate from college. More insurance coverage may be needed if you are supporting aging parents. Consider possible use of life insurance in estate planning, which is covered in detail in Chapter 15.	✓ Consider possible use of life insurance in estate planning, which is covered in detail in Chapter 15.
		✓ Evaluate the magnitude of your accumulated assets relative to needs of dependents. Insurance may no longer be needed or could be dramatically decreased.	✓ It may be possible to discontinue coverage for grown dependents. May need to maintain some life insurance to help dependents with special needs.

Financial Impact of Personal Choices
Matt and Jan Consider "Buying Term and Investing the Rest"

Matt and Jan Horton have two young children and believe it's time to buy a life insurance policy to protect their family. They've both heard the life insurance advice to "buy term and invest the rest." In order to evaluate this advice they've collected quotes for 20-year term and whole life policies on Matt, both with a payoff of $250,000. The whole life policy premium is $347 a month while the term policy premium is only $23 a month. In 20 years the whole life policy will have a guaranteed cash value of $70,018 but at current rates would be worth $105,721. The death benefit will have grown to $326,352. If the Hortons buy the term policy and invest the $324 difference in monthly premiums at 8% for 20 years, they could have a portfolio worth about $190,843! The Hortons wonder about the financial consequences of their decision.

It looks like buying term and investing the difference leaves the Hortons better off. Yet the financial consequences can only be fully evaluated in light of the Hortons' objectives and attitude towards risk. The whole life insurance policy provides a *guaranteed* cash value in 20 years while the invested difference produces a higher expected but *risky*, unguaranteed payoff. And the Hortons must consider whether they will have the discipline to keep "investing the difference" over the next 20 years. Once the whole life policy's cash value builds up, they could stop paying the premium by accepting some trade-offs in the value of the policy. And in 20 years the term life insurance coverage will go away, which might be fine if the kids are independent and the mortgage is paid off. In contrast, the Hortons could stop paying the whole life policy premiums then and accept a reduced paid-up amount of coverage.

The personal financial consequences of "buy term and invest the rest" suggest the advice may well work for the Hortons. But the best decision depends on their objectives, discipline, and attitude towards the risks of "investing the rest."

Source: Adapted from Chris Arnold, "Life Insurance: Is Buying Term and Investing the Difference Your Best Approach?" http://www.nerdwallet.com/blog/finance/advisorvoices/difference-term-life-insuranc/, accessed August 2015.

Summary

LG1 Explain the concept of risk and the basics of insurance underwriting. p. 301
Adequate life insurance coverage is vital to sound personal financial planning because it not only protects what you've already acquired but also helps ensure the attainment of unfulfilled financial goals. The whole notion of insurance is based on the concept of risk and the different methods of handling it, including risk avoidance, loss prevention and control, risk assumption, and insurance (a cost-effective procedure that allows families to reduce financial risks by sharing losses). Through the underwriting process, insurance companies decide whom they consider an acceptable risk and the premiums to charge for coverage.

LG2 Discuss the primary reasons for life insurance and identify those who need coverage. p. 303
Life insurance fills the gap between the financial resources available to your dependents if you should die prematurely and what they need to maintain a given lifestyle. Some policies provide only a death benefit; others also have a savings component. If you have children or elderly relatives who count on your income to support them, you should include life insurance as one of several financial resources to meet their requirements. If you have no dependents, you probably don't need life insurance. Your life insurance needs change over your life cycle and should be reviewed regularly.

LG3 Calculate how much life insurance you need. p. 305
There are several ways to determine the amount of life insurance a family should have. Although the multiple-of-earnings method is simple to use, most experts agree that the needs analysis method is the better procedure. It systematically considers such variables as family income, household and other expenses, special needs, final expenses,

debt liquidation, and other financial needs, which are then compared with the financial resources available to meet these needs.

LG4   Distinguish among the various types of life insurance policies and describe their advantages and disadvantages. p. 311
The three basic types of life insurance policies are term life, whole life, and universal life. Term life insurance provides a stipulated amount of death benefits; whole life combines death benefits with a modest savings program; and universal life combines term insurance with a tax-sheltered savings/investment account that pays interest at competitive money market rates. Other types of life insurance include variable life, group life, credit life, mortgage life, and industrial life.

LG5   Choose the best life insurance policy for your needs at the lowest cost. p. 323
To get as much coverage as possible from your insurance dollar, it's important not only to compare costs but also to buy the proper amount of life insurance and pick the right type of insurance policy.

Beyond the cost and features of the insurance policy, carefully consider the financial stability of the insurer who offers it, paying special attention to the ratings assigned by major rating agencies. The Internet has become an excellent resource for comparison shopping. In addition to selecting a company, you must also choose an agent who understands your needs.

LG6   Become familiar with the key features of life insurance policies. p. 329
Some important contract features of life insurance policies you should become familiar with are the beneficiary clause, settlement options, policy loans, premium payments, grace period, nonforfeiture options, policy reinstatement, and change of policy. Other policy features include multiple indemnity and disability clauses, guaranteed purchase options, a suicide clause, exclusions, participation, living benefits, and viatical settlements. Life insurance policy illustrations provide insight into the assumptions relied on by an insurance company and the potential performance of the policy.

Key Terms

beneficiary, 329

cash value, 314

convertibility, 313

credit life insurance, 322

decreasing term policy, 313

disability clause, 331

group life insurance, 322

guaranteed purchase option, 332

industrial life insurance (home service life insurance), 322

insurance policy, 302

life insurance policy illustration, 332

loss control, 302

loss prevention, 302

mortgage life insurance, 322

multiple indemnity clause, 331

multiple-of-earnings method, 305

needs analysis method, 305

nonforfeiture right, 314

participating policy, 332

policy loan, 330

renewability, 313

risk assumption, 302

risk avoidance, 302

Social Security survivor's benefits, 308

straight term policy, 311

term life insurance, 311

underwriting, 302

universal life insurance, 319

variable life insurance, 321

whole life insurance, 314

Answers to Test Yourself

You can find answers to these questions on this book's companion website. Look for it at *www.cengagebrain.com*. Search for this book by its title, and then add it to your dashboard.

Financial Planning Exercises

LG2, 3, 4, p. 303, 305, 311

1. ***Estimating life insurance needs. Use Worksheet 8.1.*** Katie Holt is a 72-year-old widow who has recently been diagnosed with Alzheimer's disease. She has limited financial assets of her own and has been living with her daughter Laurie for two years. Her income is only $850 a month in Social Security survivor's benefits. Laurie wants to make sure her mother will be taken care of if Laurie should die. Laurie, 40, is single and earns $55,000 a year as a human resources manager for a small manufacturing firm. She owns a condo with a current market value of $100,000 and has a $70,000 mortgage. Other debts include a $5,000 auto loan and $500 in various credit card balances. Her 401(k) plan has a current balance of $24,500, and she keeps $7,500 in a money market account for emergencies. After talking with her mother's doctor, Laurie believes that her mother will be able to continue living independently for another two to three years. She estimates that her mother would need about $2,000 a month to cover her living expenses and medical costs during this time. After that, Laurie's mother will probably need nursing home care. Laurie calls several local nursing homes and finds that it will cost about $5,000 a month when her mother enters a nursing home. Her mother's doctor says it is difficult to estimate her mother's life expectancy but indicates that with proper care some Alzheimer's patients can live 10 or more years after diagnosis. Laurie also estimates that her personal final expenses would be around $5,000, and she'd like to provide a $25,000 contingency fund that would be used to pay a trusted friend to supervise her mother's care if Laurie were no longer alive. Use Worksheet 8.1 to calculate Laurie's total life insurance requirements and recommend the type of policy that she should buy.

LG2, 3, p. 303, 305

2. ***Deciding if life insurance is needed. Use Worksheet 8.1.*** Given your current personal financial situation, do you feel you need life insurance coverage? Why or why not? Use Worksheet 8.1 to confirm your answer and calculate how much additional insurance (if any) you might need to purchase.

LG2, 3, 4, p. 303, 305, 311

3. ***Deciding if additional life insurance is needed and, if so, appropriate type.*** Use Worksheet 8.1. Rudy Steele, 43, is a recently divorced father of two children, ages 9 and 7. He currently earns $95,000 a year as an operations manager for a utility company. The divorce settlement requires him to pay $1,500 a month in child support and $400 a month in alimony to his ex-wife, who currently earns $35,000 annually as a preschool teacher. Rudy is now renting an apartment, and the divorce settlement left him with about $100,000 in savings and retirement benefits. His employer provides a $75,000 life insurance policy. Rudy's ex-wife is currently the beneficiary listed on the policy. What advice would you give to Rudy? What factors should he consider in deciding whether to buy additional life insurance at this point in his life? If he does need additional life insurance, what type of policy or policies should he buy? Use Worksheet 8.1 to help answer these questions for Rudy.

LG4, p. 311

4. ***Life insurance premiums and comparison of types.*** Using the premium schedules provided in Exhibits 8.2, 8.3, and 8.5, how much in *annual* premiums would a 25-year-old male have to pay for $100,000 of annual renewable term, level premium term, and whole life insurance? (Assume a five-year term or period of coverage.) How much would a 25-year-old woman have to pay for the same coverage? Consider a 40-year-old male (or female): Using annual premiums, compare the cost of 10 years of coverage under annual renewable and level premium term options and whole life insurance coverage. Relate the advantages and disadvantages of each policy type to their price differences.

LG2, 3, 4, 5,
p. 303, 305,
311, 323

5. **Appropriateness of whole life insurance.** Ramona and Pablo Valdez are a dual-career couple who just had their first child. Pablo, age 29, already has a group life insurance policy, but Ramona's employer does not offer a life insurance benefit. A financial planner is recommending that the 25-year-old Ramona buy a $250,000 whole life policy with an annual premium of $1,670 (the policy has an assumed rate of earnings of 5 percent a year). Help Ramona evaluate this advice and decide on an appropriate course of action.

LG2, 3, 4, 6,
p. 303, 305,
311, 329

6. **Appropriateness of variable life insurance.** While at lunch with a group of coworkers, one of your friends mentions that he plans to buy a variable life insurance policy because it provides a good annual return and is a good way to build savings for his 5-year-old's college education. Another colleague says that she's adding coverage through the group plan's additional insurance option. What advice would you give them?

Applying Personal Finance

Insure Your Life!

Providing for our loved ones in the event of our death is a serious concern for most of us. The problem is that planning for such an event is not pleasant, and most of us would just as soon put off thinking about it. This project will help you determine your current and future life insurance needs.

Life insurance can be put in place to provide income for your family, educate your children, or pay off debt. Life insurance can also be used in estate planning or to benefit a cause that's important to you. Make a list of your present life insurance needs and another list of what you expect your needs to be 10 years down the road. Estimate the dollar amount for each of your needs. Use Worksheet 8.1 to determine the amount of life insurance you need now and in the future. Consider the features of different types of life insurance. Which type of life insurance would be most appropriate for you? What would the cost be to provide these amounts of life insurance? You may use the premium schedules in this chapter or obtain actual quotes from an agent or the Internet. Use these estimates to help you with your personal financial planning.

CRITICAL THINKING CASES

LG3, 4, 5,
p. 305, 311,
323

8.1 Jun Hsieh's Insurance Decision: Whole Life, Variable Life, or Term Life?

Jun Hsieh, a 38-year-old widowed mother of three children (ages 12, 10, and 4), works as a product analyst for Panama Hats. Although she's covered by a group life insurance policy at work, she feels, based on some rough calculations, that she needs additional protection. Phil Griffin, an insurance agent from Safety First Insurance, has been trying to persuade Jun to buy a $150,000, 25-year, limited payment whole life policy. However, Jun favors a variable life policy. To further complicate matters, Jun's father feels that term life insurance is more suitable to the needs of her young family.

Critical Thinking Questions

1. Explain to Jun the differences between (a) a whole life policy, (b) a variable life policy, and (c) a term life policy.
2. What are the major advantages and disadvantages of each type of policy?
3. In what way is a whole life policy superior to either a variable life or term life policy? In what way is a variable life policy superior? How about term life insurance?
4. Given the limited information in the case, which type of policy would you recommend for Ms. Hsieh? Defend and explain your recommendations.

8.2 The Jennings Want to Know: How Much Is Enough?

Darrell and Lena Jennings are a two-income couple in their early 30s. They have two children, ages 6 and 3. Darrell's monthly take-home pay is $3,600, and Lena's is $4,200. The Jennings feel that, because they're a two-income family, they both should have adequate life insurance coverage. Accordingly, they are now trying to decide how much *life insurance each one of them* needs.

To begin with, they'd like to set up an education fund for their children in the amount of $120,000 to provide college funds of $15,000 a year—in today's dollars—for four years for each child. Moreover, if either spouse should die, they want the surviving spouse to have the funds to pay off all outstanding debts, including the $210,000 mortgage on their house. They estimate that they have $25,000 in consumer installment loans and credit cards. They also project that if either of them dies, the other probably will be left with about $10,000 in final estate and burial expenses.

Regarding their annual income needs, Darrell and Lena both feel strongly that each should have enough insurance to replace her or his respective current income level until the youngest child turns 18 (a period of 15 years). Although neither Darrell nor Lena would be eligible for Social Security survivor's benefits because they both intend to continue working, both children would qualify in the (combined) amount of around $1,800 a month. The Jennings have accumulated about $75,000 in investments, and they have a decreasing term life policy on each other in the amount of $100,000, which could be used to partially pay off the mortgage. Darrell also has an $80,000 group life insurance policy at work and Lena a $100,000 group life insurance policy.

Critical Thinking Questions

1. Assume that Darrell's gross annual income is $54,000 and Lena's is $64,000. Their insurance agent has given them a multiple earnings table showing that the earnings multiple to replace 75 percent of their lost earnings is 8.7 for Darrell and 7.4 for Lena. Use this approach to find the amount of life insurance each should have if they want to replace 75 percent of their lost earnings.

2. Use Worksheet 8.1 to find the additional insurance needed on both Darrell's and Lena's lives. (Because Darrell and Lena hold secure, well-paying jobs, both agree that they won't need any additional help once the kids are grown; both also agree that they'll have plenty of income from Social Security and company pension benefits to take care of themselves in retirement. Thus, when preparing the worksheet, assume "funding needs" of zero in Periods 2 and 3.)

3. Is there a difference in your answers to Questions 1 and 2? If so, why? Which number do you think is more indicative of the Jennings' life insurance needs? Using the amounts computed in Question 2 (employing the needs approach), what kind of life insurance policy would you recommend for Darrell? For Lena? Briefly explain your answers.

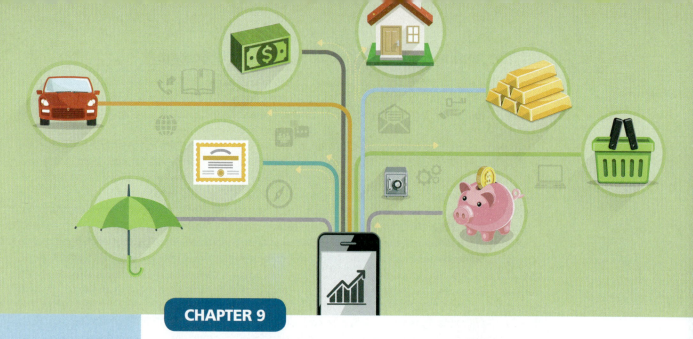

CHAPTER 9

Insuring Your Health

LEARNING GOALS

LG1 Discuss why having adequate health insurance is important and identify the factors contributing to the growing cost of health insurance.

LG2 Differentiate among the major types of health insurance plans and identify major private and public health insurance providers and their programs.

LG3 Analyze your own health insurance needs and explain how to shop for appropriate coverage.

LG4 Explain the basic types of medical expenses covered by and the policy provisions of health insurance plans.

LG5 Assess the need for and features of long-term-care insurance.

LG6 Discuss the features of disability income insurance and how to determine your need for it.

How Will This Affect Me?

Having adequate health insurance is critically important to your financial plan. Health care costs have grown dramatically in recent years, and a major illness or accident could wipe you and your family out financially if you are uninsured. Yet health insurance policies are complicated to price and to compare. This chapter explains the importance of health insurance and the key determinants of its costs. The various types of public and private health insurance are described and a framework for decision making is provided. This includes discussions of how to analyze your health insurance needs, how to make sense of common policy features, and policy buying tips. The implications of the Patient Protection and Affordable Care Act of 2010 are considered. This chapter also discusses how to determine whether you need long-term care insurance or disability income insurance. After reading this chapter, you should understand how to insure your health most effectively and economically.

9-1 THE IMPORTANCE OF HEALTH INSURANCE COVERAGE

The next best thing to good health is probably a good health insurance plan. In recent years, the price of medical treatment has risen dramatically. As a result, a serious illness or accident can involve not only physical pain from sickness and injury, but also economic pain. A major illness can easily cost tens (or even hundreds) of thousands of dollars once you consider hospitalization and medical expenses and the loss of income while you recover. Even routine medical care, such as doctors' office visits and health care screenings, can add up quickly. Health insurance helps you pay for the costs associated with both routine and major medical care so that your financial accomplishments and plans are not seriously damaged or even destroyed. Indeed, about 62 percent of all U.S. personal bankruptcies are due, at least in part, to medical costs.

Despite the financial importance of health insurance, many Americans remain underinsured or uninsured. About 13 percent of the population doesn't have health insurance. And about 6.5 percent of children are without health insurance. Exhibit 9.1 helps explain why so many are uninsured: health insurance premiums have skyrocketed between 1999 and 2014. The average annual premium for families has increased by about 290 percent! In 2014, the average annual premium was $6,025 for single coverage and $16,834 for family coverage. The average percentage of health care premiums paid by covered workers is 29 percent for family plans.

Costly advances in medical technology, an aging U.S. population, and a poor demand-and-supply distribution of health care facilities and services have fueled rapidly rising health care costs. In addition, administrative costs, excessive paperwork, increased regulation, and insurance fraud are contributing to rising health care costs.

Concerns over health care costs and the number of uninsured Americans has made health care reform a major priority of Congress and the administration. Policy

Financial Fact or Fantasy?

Health care insurance coverage should be viewed as an essential component of your personal financial plans. **Fact:** Health care insurance not only helps you meet the costs of illness or injury, but it also protects your existing assets and financial plans.

solutions concerning the proper mix between government-run and privately run health insurance programs continue to prompt vigorous debate even after the passage of the Patient Protection and Affordable Care Act and the Reconciliation Act of 2010, which is discussed in detail below. The high cost of public health insurance, the desire by most to preserve patient choices, and the effects of reform on competition make this issue as contentious as it is important. Becoming familiar with current health insurance options and the issues associated with the new legislation should help you make better decisions, as well as provide a useful perspective on the health care reform debate and how it could affect you.

EXHIBIT 9.1	Average Annual Health Insurance Premiums for Single and Family Coverage, 1999–2014

As the chart shows, health insurance premiums have risen dramatically in recent years.

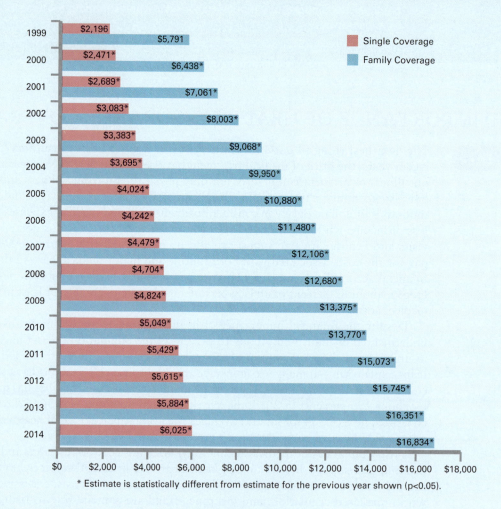

* Estimate is statistically different from estimate for the previous year shown (p<0.05).

Source: Kaiser/HRET Survey of Employer-Sponsored Health Benefits, 1999–2014.

TEST YOURSELF

9-1 Why should health insurance planning be included in your personal financial plan?

9-2 What factors have contributed to today's high costs of health care and health insurance?

9-2 HEALTH INSURANCE PLANS

Health insurance coverage is available from two main sources: private and government-sponsored programs. Regardless of the source of the plan, the Patient Protection and Affordable Care Act has significantly affected the expenses covered, the method of purchasing the plan, and the related taxes. In recent years, 28 percent of national health care expenditures were paid for by households, private businesses paid 21 percent, state and local governments paid 16 percent, the federal government paid 27 percent, and the rest was presumably paid by the self-insured.

9-2a Private Health Insurance Plans

group health insurance
Health insurance consisting of contracts written between a group (employer, union, etc.) and the health care provider.

Private companies sell a variety of health insurance plans to both groups and individuals. **Group health insurance** refers to health insurance contracts written between a group (such as an employer, union, credit union, or other organization) and the health care provider: a private insurance company, Blue Cross/Blue Shield plan, or a managed care organization. Typically, group plans provide comprehensive medical expense coverage and may also offer prescription drug, dental, and vision care service. The coverage provided by any given plan is subject to negotiation between the group and the insurer, and the group may offer several options for health insurance coverage.

If you work for an employer that has more than just a few employees, you'll probably have access to some type of group health plan. To control rising costs, many employers no longer provide universal coverage but merely underwrite employee applications, much as insurers do. Employers are also shifting a larger percentage of the cost to employees. As a result, you may want to compare group and individual policies before deciding which coverage to buy.

Most private health insurance plans fall into one of two categories: traditional *indemnity (fee-for-service) plans* and *managed care plans*, which include health maintenance organizations (HMOs), preferred provider organizations (PPOs), and similar plans. Both types of plans provide financial aid for the cost of medical care arising from illness or accidents, but they do so in somewhat different ways. Exhibit 9.2 compares some features of the three most common types of health plans.

Traditional Indemnity (Fee-for-Service) Plans

indemnity (fee-for-service) plan
A health insurance plan in which the health care provider is separate from the insurer, who pays the provider or reimburses you for a specified percentage of expenses after a deductible amount has been met.

With a traditional **indemnity (fee-for-service) plan**, the person or organization from which you obtain health care services is separate from your insurer. Your insurer either pays the health service provider directly or reimburses your expenses when you submit claims for medical treatment. Typically, indemnity plans pay 80 percent of the eligible health care expenses and the insured pays the other 20 percent. The health insurance company will begin paying its share after you pay a deductible amount of expenses. The deductible can range from $100 to over $2,000. The lower your deductible, the higher your premium.

The amount the insurance company pays is commonly based on the usual, customary, and reasonable (UCR) charges—what the insurer considers to be the prevailing fees within your area, not what your doctor or hospital actually charges. If your doctor charges more than the UCR, you may be responsible for the full amount

FINANCIAL PLANNING TIPS

Student Health Care Insurance in the New Era

Active students have a high injury rate, and viruses often move quickly through college campuses and dorms. It is essential to be insured, even when you are young and think you're healthy. No one knows when an expensive medical procedure may be required. For these reasons, colleges often require students to have health insurance. Under the new ACA, many parents can meet that requirement by keeping their children on their health insurance plan until the age of 26 (and this actually applies whether they are in school or not). Here are some key trends and issues to consider in arranging student health care insurance:

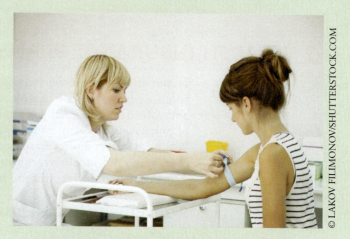

- **Escalating costs.** The ACA requires students to have a level of coverage that exceeds the plans historically offered by most colleges. Consequently, premiums are rising by several hundred dollars a year, to around $2,000 per student currently. Indeed, some colleges are dropping student health insurance plans due to their higher costs. Students who are not covered under their parents' health care plan should consider buying an individual health insurance plan. You can compare prices and coverage using an Internet provider like **http://www.eHealthInsurance.com** or **http://www.StudentHealthPlan.com**.

- **Network coverage.** If you are a student relying on your parents' policy, be careful if your college is in another state. Make sure that your plan's network of preferred doctors and hospitals extends there. If not, the highest level of coverage may not be available.

- **Parent policy choices.** Parents should choose a family plan that covers their children for all medical emergencies and associated care. Most plans have basic out-of-state coverage for children. However, if out-of-state coverage is limited, as noted above, consider a high-deductible student health plan. It makes sense for students to return home for all routine care and prescriptions.

- **Good effects of the new law.** The ACA may make some student health plans more appealing. It prohibits all plans from having "lifetime coverage limits" that could put a cap on the maximum coverage in the case of a serious illness or accident. The new law also prohibits insurers from excluding students under 19 for pre-existing conditions.

Source: Adapted from Quentin Fottrell, "How to Save on College Health Care," http://blogs.smartmoney.com/advice/2012/06/04/ how-to-save-on-college-health-care, accessed August 2015.

EXHIBIT 9.2	How the Most Common Types of Health Plans Compare

This table highlights some of the key differences among the three most common types of health plans.

Type	Choice of Service Providers	Premium Cost	Out-of-Pocket Costs	Annual Deductible
Indemnity	Yes	Low if high-deductible plan, high if low-deductible plan	Usually 20% of medical expenses plus deductible	Yes
HMO	No	Low	Low co-pay	No
PPO	Some	Higher than HMO	Low if using network providers, higher if provider is outside the network	No

© LAKOV FILIMONOV/SHUTTERSTOCK.COM

of the excess. UCR charges vary significantly among insurers, so you should compare your doctor's fees with what a plan pays. Many carriers offer indemnity plans wherein physicians who accept the insurance agree to accept the UCR payments set by the insurer. However, it should be noted that there are few indemnity plans left in the United States.

Managed Care Plans

Today, employers are moving away from traditional indemnity plans and adopting managed care plans. In a **managed care plan**, subscribers/users contract with and make monthly payments directly to the organization that provides the health care service. An insurance company may not even be involved, although today most major health insurance companies offer both indemnity and managed care plans. Managed care plan members receive comprehensive health care services from a designated group of doctors, hospitals, and other providers who must meet the managed care provider's specific selection standards.

With a managed care plan, the insured pays no deductibles and only a small fee, or co-payment, for office visits and medications. Most medical services—including preventive and routine care that indemnity plans may not cover—are fully covered when obtained from plan providers. Managed care plans include HMOs and PPOs (as already mentioned), exclusive provider organizations (EPOs), and point-of-service (POS) plans.

Health Maintenance Organizations. A **health maintenance organization (HMO)** is an organization of hospitals, physicians, and other health care providers who have joined to provide comprehensive health care services to its members. As an HMO member, you pay a monthly fee that varies according to the number of people in your family. You may also pay a co-payment typically of $5 to $40 each time that you use some of the services provided by the HMO or fill a prescription. The services provided to HMO members include doctors' office visits, imaging and laboratory services, preventive care, health screenings, hospital inpatient care and surgery, maternity care, mental health care, and drug prescriptions. The advantages of HMO membership include a lack of deductibles, few or no exclusions, and not having to file insurance claims. In the past, the primary disadvantage was that HMO members couldn't always choose their physicians and may have faced limitations if they needed care outside of the geographic area of their HMO. However, in recent years, many HMOs don't require members to pick one primary care physician, some don't require referrals, and almost all offer some flexibility to get out-of-network coverage.

There are two main types of HMOs: group and individual practice associations. A **group HMO** employs a group of doctors to provide health care services to members *from a central facility*. Group HMO members obtain medical care from the doctors and other medical personnel who practice there. Often, the group HMO's hospital facilities are located in the same building. Group HMOs are most prevalent in larger cities.

An **individual practice association (IPA)** is the most popular type of HMO. IPA members receive medical care from individual physicians practicing *from their own offices and from community hospitals* that are affiliated with the IPA. As a member of an IPA, you have some choice of which doctors and hospitals to use.

Preferred Provider Organizations. A **preferred provider organization (PPO)** is a managed care plan that has the characteristics of both an IPA and an indemnity plan. An insurance company or provider group contracts with a network of physicians and hospitals that agree to accept a negotiated fee for medical services provided to the PPO customers. Unlike the HMO, however, a PPO also provides insurance coverage for medical services not provided by the PPO network, so you can choose to go to other doctors or hospitals. However, you will pay a higher price for medical services provided by out-of-network doctors and hospitals.

managed care plan
A health care plan in which subscribers/users contract with the provider organization, which uses a designated group of providers meeting specific selection standards to furnish health care services for a monthly fee.

health maintenance organization (HMO)
An organization of hospitals, physicians, and other health care providers that have joined to provide comprehensive health care services to its members, who pay a monthly fee.

group HMO
An HMO that provides health care services *from a central facility*; most prevalent in larger cities.

individual practice association (IPA)
A form of HMO in which subscribers receive services from physicians practicing *from their own offices and from community hospitals* affiliated with the IPA.

preferred provider organization (PPO)
A health provider that combines the characteristics of the IPA form of HMO with an indemnity plan to provide comprehensive health care services to its subscribers within a network of physicians and hospitals.

exclusive provider organization (EPO)
A managed care plan that is similar to a PPO but reimburses members only when affiliated providers are used.

point-of-service (POS) plan
A hybrid form of HMO that allows members to go outside the HMO network for care and reimburses them at a specified percentage of the cost.

Other Managed Care Plans. Besides the plans just described, you may encounter two other forms of managed care plans. An **exclusive provider organization (EPO)** contracts with medical providers to offer services to members at reduced costs, but it reimburses members only when affiliated providers are used. Plan members who use a nonaffiliated provider must bear the entire cost. The **point-of-service (POS) plan** is a hybrid form of HMO that allows members to go outside of the HMO network for care. Payment for nonaffiliated physician services is similar to indemnity plan payments: the plan pays a specified percentage of the cost after your medical costs reach an annual deductible.

Blue Cross/Blue Shield Plans

In a technical sense, **Blue Cross/Blue Shield plans** are not insurance policies, but rather are prepaid hospital and medical expense plans. Today, there are about 38 independent local Blue Cross/Blue Shield organizations, all of them for-profit corporations, which collectively cover over 105 million people.

Blue Cross contracts with hospitals that agree to provide specified hospital services to members of groups covered by Blue Cross in exchange for a specified fee or payment. Blue Cross also contracts for surgical and medical services. Blue Cross serves as the intermediary between the groups that want these services and the physicians who contractually agree to provide them. Today, many Blue Cross and Blue Shield plans have combined to form one provider, and they compete for business with other private insurance companies. Because Blue Cross/Blue Shield is a producer cooperative, payments for health care services are seldom made to the subscriber but rather directly to the participating hospital or physician.

Financial Fact or Fantasy?

The difference between a health maintenance organization (HMO) and a preferred provider organization (PPO) is that the HMO offers a wider range of choices of physicians, hospitals, and so forth. **Fantasy:** One of the drawbacks of an HMO is that it is common to be treated at its central facility and by its own doctors. More options are, however, being offered. In a PPO, on the other hand, there are typically more opportunities to choose your health care providers from a network of designated physicians and hospitals.

Blue Cross/Blue Shield plans
Prepaid hospital and medical expense plans under which health care services are provided to plan participants by member hospitals and physicians.

Medicare
A health insurance plan administered by the federal government to help persons age 65 and over, and others receiving monthly Social Security disability benefits, to meet their health care costs.

9-2b Government Health Insurance Plans

In addition to health insurance coverage provided by private sources, federal and state agencies provide health care coverage to eligible individuals. About 34 percent of the U.S. population is covered by some form of government health insurance program. For example, prior to the implementation of the ACA, the government offered the Pre-Existing Condition Insurance Plan (PCIP), which provided health coverage to U.S. citizens or others residing in the United States legally who have been denied health insurance because of a pre-existing condition, so long as the person has been uninsured for at least six months. The program was administered by both the states and by the federal government. In addition, some states provide health insurance for children who do not qualify for Medicaid (discussed later), but whose family still has very low income.

Medicare

Medicare is a health insurance program administered under the Social Security Administration. It's primarily designed to help persons 65 and over meet their health care costs, but it also covers many people under 65 who receive monthly Social Security disability benefits. Funds for Medicare benefits come from Social Security taxes paid by covered workers and their employers. Traditionally, Medicare has provided two primary health care components, basic hospital insurance and supplementary medical insurance as well as prescription drug coverage.

- **Basic hospital insurance:** This coverage (commonly called *Part A*) provides inpatient hospital services such as room, board, and other customary inpatient service for the first 90 days of illness. A deductible is applied during the first 60 days of illness. Co-insurance provisions, applicable to days 61–90 of the hospital stay, can further reduce benefits. Medicare also covers all or part of the cost of up to 100 days in post-hospital extended-care facilities that provide skilled care, such as nursing homes. However, it doesn't cover the most common types of nursing home care—intermediate and custodial care. Medicare basic hospital insurance also covers some post-hospital medical services, such as intermittent nursing care, therapy, rehabilitation, and home health care. Medicare deductibles and co-insurance amounts are revised annually to reflect changing medical costs.

- **Supplementary medical insurance:** The **supplementary medical insurance (SMI)** program (commonly called *Part B*) covers the services of physicians and surgeons in addition to the costs of medical and health services such as imaging, laboratory tests, prosthetic devices, rental of medical equipment, and ambulance transportation. It also covers some home health services (such as in-home visits by a registered nurse) and limited psychiatric care. Unlike the basic Medicare hospital plan, SMI is a *voluntary program* for which participants pay premiums, which are then matched with government funds. Anyone age 65 or over can enroll in SMI.

- **Medicare Advantage plans:** Medicare Advantage (commonly called *Plan C*) plans provide Medicare benefits to eligible people, but they differ in that they are administered by private providers rather than by the government. Common supplemental benefits include vision, hearing, dental, general checkups, and health and wellness programs. These supplemental benefits are a major reason for interest in these plans. Medicare pays the private health plan a fixed amount every month for each member. The members may pay a monthly premium in addition to the Medicare Part B premium. However, many of the private providers don't charge a premium beyond the Medicare Part B premium, which the member pays directly to Medicare. Members usually pay a fixed amount (e.g., a co-payment of $30), every time they visit a doctor, rather than pay a deductible and buy co-insurance (typically 20 percent) under original Medicare. Private plans may use some of the excess payments that they receive from the government to offer supplemental benefits. Most of the plans also include Medicare prescription drug coverage, discussed next. Because Medicare Advantage plans cost the federal government more than standard Medicare, the subsidies paid to these plans will start to decline under the ACA, which may lead to higher premiums or reduced benefits. However, the benefits cannot be reduced if they could normally be received from standard Medicare.

- **Prescription drug coverage:** The **prescription drug coverage** program (commonly called *Part D*) is insurance covering both brand-name and generic prescription drugs at participating pharmacies. It's intended to provide protection for people who have very high drug costs. All Medicare recipients are eligible for this coverage, regardless of their income and resources, health status, or existing prescription expenses. There are several ways to obtain this coverage. Participants in this *voluntary program* pay a monthly fee and a yearly deductible, which vary by provider. In 2015, the national monthly fee was based on income and was the overall plan premium plus no more than $70.80. The average monthly premium was $33.13 and most plans had a deductible of $320. They also pay part of the cost of prescriptions, including a co-payment or co-insurance. The plan provides extra help—paying almost all prescription drug costs—for the 1 in 3 Medicare recipients who have limited income and resources.

Although Medicare pays for many health care expenses for the disabled and those over 65, there are still gaps in its coverage. Many Medicare enrollees buy private insurance policies to fill in these gaps.

Medicaid

Medicaid is a state-run public assistance program that provides health insurance benefits only to those who are unable to pay for health care. Each state has its own regulations about who is eligible for Medicaid coverage and the types of medical services that are covered. Although Medicaid is primarily funded by each state, the

---

supplementary medical insurance (SMI)

A voluntary program under Medicare (commonly called *Part B*) that provides payments for services not covered under basic hospital insurance (*Part A*).

Medicare Advantage plans

Commonly called *Plan C*, these plans provide Medicare benefits to eligible people, but they differ in that they are administered by private providers rather than by the government. Common supplemental benefits include vision, hearing, dental, general checkups, and health and wellness programs.

prescription drug coverage

A voluntary program under Medicare (commonly called *Part D*), insurance that covers both brand-name and generic prescription drugs at participating pharmacies. Participants pay a monthly fee and a yearly deductible and must also pay part of the cost of prescriptions, including a co-payment or co-insurance.

Medicaid

A state-run public assistance program that provides health insurance benefits only to those who are unable to pay for health care.

federal government also contributes funds. More than 65 million people are covered by Medicaid.

Workers' Compensation Insurance

Workers' compensation insurance is designed to compensate workers who are injured on the job or become ill through work-related causes. Although mandated by the federal government, each state is responsible for setting workers' compensation legislation and regulating its own program. Specifics vary from state to state, but typical workers' compensation benefits include medical and rehabilitation expenses, disability income, and scheduled lump-sum amounts for death and certain injuries, such as dismemberment. Employers bear nearly the entire cost of workers' compensation insurance in most states. Premiums are based on historical usage; employers who file the most claims pay the highest rates. Self-employed people are required to contribute to workers' compensation for themselves and their employees.

9-2c Rationale for Health Care Reform

The goal of health care reform is to provide more people access to needed services at affordable rates. Before considering the implications of the ACA, it's important to understand the problems in the U.S. health care system that prompted the development of the new legislation.

Historical cost-benefit analysis reveals that the U.S. health care system looks pretty anemic. The U.S. economy spends about 17 cents of every dollar on health care, which is about twice the average for other rich economies. And what do we get in return? Outcomes for infant mortality, life expectancy, and heart attack survival rates are all worse than the average for members of the Organization for Economic Cooperation and Development (OECD). And, about 41 million citizens were not covered by health insurance as recently as 2013.

Health care in the United States has been more expensive because of two significant economic distortions. First, the cost of employer-provided health care insurance is tax-deductible. This has encouraged overly generous programs in which the true costs are hard to determine. The tax deductibility of health care programs is estimated to cost the government at least $250 billion annually. Second, most U.S. physicians are compensated on a fee-for-service basis. This creates an incentive for excessive health care expenses that do not always lead to better outcomes. Although this problem is not unique to the United States, it is thought to be worse there than in any other rich country. Reducing unnecessarily expensive procedures and prescriptions could save from 10 percent to 30 percent on health care costs.

High health care costs hurt the United States in three important ways. First, taxpayer burdens are already high. More than half of the U.S. population relies on the government for health care, which presses federal and state budgets. Second, private insurance programs are costly for employers. Consider that the cost of health insurance has been prominent in the financial troubles of General Motors. And many small firms are being forced to give up funding employee health care insurance because of its cost. Third, high health care insurance premiums reduce workers' wages.

9-2d The Patient Protection and Affordable Care Act of 2010

Provisions of the Act

The **Patient Protection and Affordable Care Act (ACA)** is extensive and remains controversial. The ACA has significantly changed the offering of health insurance plans available to citizens of the United States. While its legality was contested, the U.S. Supreme Court affirmed the ACA's constitutionality in 2012. In making health care insurance decisions, it's important to understand the key provisions of the new law.

The ACA has two key goals:

- Reduce the number of uninsured citizens in the country.
- Reduce the increases in health care costs by providing a "state based" health insurance exchange in each state.

The ACA is designed to reach these goals by requiring the purchase of health insurance and by assuring that health insurance provides "essential health benefits." All individuals who are not covered by Medicaid or Medicare are required to purchase health insurance or pay a penalty that will amount to the greater of $695 per adult (and $347.50 per child) or 2.5% of the family income in 2016. Businesses that employ more than 50 full time employees must provide health insurance for their employees or pay a penalty of $2,000 times the number of employees less 30. For example, if a business has 130 full-time employees but does not provide insurance, the penalty would be $2,000 × (130 − 30) or $200,000 per year.

The essential health benefits required by the ACA include the following:

- Ambulatory patient services
- Emergency services
- Hospitalization
- Maternity and newborn care
- Mental health and substance use disorder services, including behavioral health treatment
- Prescription drugs
- Rehabilitative and habilitative services and devices
- Laboratory services
- Preventive and wellness services and chronic disease management
- Pediatric services, including oral and vision care

In addition, the ACA requires that health insurance plans provide the following features:

- Cover pre-existing conditions
- Parents must have the option to carry their children on their plan until age 26
- Life time dollar limits on total insurance coverage are prohibited
- Plans must cover preventive care and medical screenings
- Insurers must spend at least 80% of premiums on claims

Insurance Exchanges

Under the ACA health care insurance exchanges are available in each state. The exchanges are competitive marketplaces where health insurance may be purchased by individuals and small firms. All insurance plans listed on the insurance exchanges must provide the essential health benefits described above. Similarly, all plans offered by employers must provide the indicated essential health benefits. The ACA provides four levels of benefits, each of which are identified by a metal label.

Metal label	Percentage of benefit costs (%)
Bronze	60
Silver	70
Gold	80
Platinum	90

Financial Fact or Fantasy?

With health care insurance that covers the whole family, children may be included up to age 26 as long as they are full-time students. **Fantasy:** Under the Affordable Care Act a child may be covered in a family insurance plan so long as he or she is under 26 years of age. There is not a requirement that the child be a full-time student.

The areas where insurance companies can compete are quite limited. The rates that companies charge are allowed to vary largely upon whether or not the insured uses tobacco products and the geographical area. The hope is that by increasing the amount of competition among insurers, the cost of insurance will go down.

Premium Assistance and Taxes

The ACA provides a tax credit to assist low income consumers in the purchase of health insurance. The credit is based upon the federal poverty level in the rating area and the cost of the benchmark (bronze) plan. In order to help pay for the costs associated with the ACA, the law added some taxes. For example, those earning more than $250,000 who file joint returns are subject to a 0.9% Medicare tax and a net investment tax of 3.8% that is added to income from investments (e.g., dividends and capital gains). Beginning in 2018, there is also an excise tax levied on the insurance companies providing "Cadillac" plans, which are those plans that cost more than $27,500 for a family.

You Can Do It Now

Compare Policies on an ACA Health Insurance Exchange

It's worth taking the time to survey the policies and premiums available to you on an ACA health insurance marketplace. Just go to **https://www.healthcare.gov/see-plans**. All you have to do is put in your zip code and some basic information on yourself. If you're shopping, it provides useful information. And if you already have a plan through your job, it'll be interesting to see how it compares. It's easy and **you can do it now.**

TEST YOURSELF

9-3 What are the two main sources of health insurance coverage in the United States?

9-4 What is *group health insurance*? Differentiate between group and individual health insurance.

9-5 Describe the features of traditional *indemnity (fee-for-service) plans* and explain the differences between them and *managed care plans*.

9-6 Briefly explain how an HMO works. Compare and contrast group HMOs, IPAs, and PPOs.

9-7 Discuss the basics of the Blue Cross/Blue Shield plans.

9-8 Who is eligible for Medicare and Medicaid benefits? What do those benefits encompass?

9-9 What is the objective of workers' compensation insurance? Explain its benefits for employees who are injured on the job or become ill through work-related causes.

9-10 What are the key provisions of the ACA? How is it likely to affect your health care insurance?

9-3 HEALTH INSURANCE DECISIONS

With all these options, how can you systematically plan your health insurance purchases? As with other insurance decisions, you'll need to consider potential areas of loss, types of coverage and other resources available to you and your family, and any gaps in protection. Once you've done all three, you can choose a health insurance plan that's best for you.

9-3a Evaluate Your Health Care Cost Risk

Most people need protection against two types of losses that can result from illness or accidents: (1) expenses for medical care and rehabilitation and (2) loss of income or household services caused by an inability to work. The cost of medical care can't be estimated easily; but in cases of long-term, serious illness, medical bills and related expenses can easily run into hundreds of thousands of dollars. An adequate amount of protection against these costs for most people would be at least $300,000 and, with a protracted illness or disability, as high as $1 million. In contrast, lost income is relatively easy to calculate: it's a percentage of your (or your spouse's) current monthly earnings. Most experts believe that 60 percent to 75 percent is sufficient.

A good health insurance plan considers more than financing medical expenses, lost income, and replacement services. It should also incorporate other means of risk reduction. Recall from Chapter 8 that you can deal with risk in four ways: risk avoidance, loss prevention and control, risk assumption, and insurance. So, in deciding on health insurance, you should consider these other ways of minimizing your risk.

- **Risk avoidance:** Look for ways to avoid exposure to health care loss before it occurs. For example, people who don't take illegal drugs never have to worry about disability from overdose, people who refuse to ride on motorcycles avoid the risk of injury from this relatively dangerous means of transportation, and people who don't smoke in bed are a lot less likely to doze off and start a fire in their house.
- **Loss prevention and control:** People who accept responsibility for their own well-being and live healthier lifestyles can prevent illness and reduce high medical costs. Smoking, alcohol and drug dependency, improper diet, inadequate sleep, and lack of regular exercise contribute to more than 60 percent of all diagnosed illnesses. Eliminating some or all of these factors from your lifestyle can reduce your chances of becoming ill. Similarly, following highway safety laws, not driving while intoxicated, and wearing a seat belt help prevent injury from car accidents.
- **Risk assumption:** Consider the risks that you're willing to retain as you deal with health insurance decisions. Some risks pose relatively small loss potential; you can budget for them rather than insure against them. For example, choosing insurance plans with deductibles and waiting periods is a form of risk assumption because it's more economical to pay small losses from savings than to pay higher premiums to cover them.

9-3b Determine Available Coverage and Resources

Some employers offer employees a *flexible-benefit ("cafeteria") plan* offering a choice of benefits. Typically, the menu of benefits includes more than one health insurance option, as well as life insurance, disability income insurance, and other benefits. As we discussed in Chapter 2, the employer specifies a set dollar amount that it will provide, and employees choose a combination from these benefits, depending on their preferences and circumstances. If, after choosing your benefits from the menu offered, you decide you want or need additional insurance benefits, most employers will set up a salary reduction agreement with the employee. The employee agrees to reduce his or her salary by the amount of the additional cost of the desired benefit.

health reimbursement account (HRA)
An account into which employers place contributions that employees can use to pay for medical expenses. Usually combined with a high-deductible health insurance policy.

health savings account (HSA)
A tax-free savings account—funded by employees, employer, or both—to spend on routine medical costs. Usually combined with a high deductible policy to pay for catastrophic care.

flexible spending account (FSA)
Employee pre-tax contributions to an account that must be spent on qualified medical (or dependent care) expenses.

Some employers offer consumer-directed health plans that go one step beyond a flexible-benefit caféteria plan. Typically, these plans combine a high-deductible health insurance policy with a tax-free **health reimbursement account (HRA)**, a plan funded by employers for each participating employee. When the account is used up, you must pay the remaining deductible of the health insurance policy before insurance begins to pay. If you don't use the money by the end of the year, you can "roll over" the amount; after several years of rolling it over, you could accumulate quite a bit of cash to pay for medical expenses. If you change jobs, the money stays with the employer. The Internal Revenue Service (IRS) considers employer contributions to medical reimbursement accounts to be tax-free income.

Another similar type of account is the **health savings account (HSA)**. The HSA is also a tax-free account, but the money is funded by employees, employers, or both to spend on routine medical costs. An HSA is also combined with a high-deductible insurance policy to pay for catastrophic care in case of major accident or illness, and—as with an HRA—can be rolled over each year. If you change jobs, the money in your HSA belongs only to you and is yours to keep. In addition to the HSA and HRA, there are many other consumer-directed health plans. And there are also **flexible spending accounts (FSAs)** that allow employees to contribute pre-tax dollars to an account that must be spent on qualified medical (or dependent care) expenses. If the account balance is not spent during the year, it is not carried over to the next year.

If you're married and your spouse is employed, you should also evaluate his or her benefit package before making any decisions. You may, for example, already be covered under your spouse's group health insurance plan or be able to purchase coverage for yourself and family members at a cheaper rate than through your own employer's plan.

If you're laid off from or leave a job where you've had health benefits, then you are legally eligible to continue your coverage for a period of 18 months under federal COBRA regulations (discussed later in the chapter). You'll be responsible for paying the full cost of the insurance if you decide to continue your coverage during this time, but you'll still pay group insurance rates that are often less expensive than buying individual insurance. However, you must arrange to continue your coverage before leaving your former employer. Importantly, under the ACA losing your job triggers a "qualifying life event" that allows you to obtain health insurance under COBRA or you can buy a policy in the private health insurance market. But there are critical enrollment windows and policy coverage details to compare. You'll need to do the math to identify the best option for you.

Another important area of group coverage to consider is retiree benefits. The number of companies providing health insurance to retirees has decreased sharply, so you may not be able to count on receiving employer-paid benefits once you retire. Know what your options are to ensure continued coverage for both you and your family after you retire. Medicare will cover basic medical expenses, but you'll probably want to supplement this coverage with one of the 12 standard Medigap plans, which are termed plans "A" through "L."

There are several other possible sources of health care coverage. As we'll discuss in Chapter 10, homeowner's and automobile insurance policies often contain limited amounts of medical expense protections. Your automobile policy, for example, may cover you if you're involved in an auto accident regardless of whether you're in a car, on foot, or on a bicycle when the accident occurs. In addition to Social Security's Medicare program, various other government programs help pay medical expenses. For instance, medical care is provided for people who've served in the armed services and were honorably discharged. Public health programs exist to treat communicable diseases, handicapped children, and mental health disorders.

If you need or want to purchase additional medical insurance coverage on an individual basis, you can buy a variety of policies from private insurance companies such as Aetna, CIGNA, and United Healthcare. You should buy plans from an insurance agent who will listen to your needs and provide well-thought-out responses to your questions. You should also research the carrier that will be providing your

insurance. Look for a carrier that is rated highly by at least two of the major ratings agencies and that has a reputation for settling claims fairly and promptly. The National Committee for Quality Assurance (NCQA) is another source of information. This non-profit, unbiased organization issues annual "report cards" that rate the service quality of various health plans.

9-3c Choose a Health Insurance Plan

After familiarizing yourself with the different health insurance plans and providers and reviewing your needs, you must choose one or more plans to provide coverage for you and your dependents. If you're employed, first review the various health insurance plans that your company offers. If you can't get coverage from an employer, get plan descriptions and policy costs from several providers, including a group plan from a professional or trade organization, if available, for both indemnity and managed care plans. You should also check the state or federal insurance exchange available to you. Then take your time and carefully read the plan materials to understand exactly what is covered, and at what cost. Next, add up what you've spent on medical costs over the past few years and what you might expect to spend in the future, so you can see what your costs would be under various plans.

Before choosing a particular plan, you should ask yourself some important questions to decide whether you want an indemnity plan or a managed care plan.

- **How important is cost compared with having freedom of choice?** You may have to pay more to stay with your current doctor if he or she is not part of a managed care plan that you're considering. Also, you have to decide if you can tolerate the managed care plan's approach to health care.

  Some states have experimented in recent years with the **community rating approach to health insurance premium pricing**, which prohibits insurance companies from varying rates based on health status or claim history. The "community" is defined as the area in which the insurance is offered. In the "pure" approach, all policyholders in an area pay the same premium without regard to their personal health, age, gender, or other factors. Under the adjusted (modified) community rating approach, insurers can adjust premiums based only on your family size, where you live, whether you use tobacco, and your age. The ACA requires insurance companies to adhere to the adjusted community rating approach for individuals and small businesses.

- **Will you be reimbursed if you choose a managed care plan and want to see an out-of-network provider?** For most people, the managed care route is cheaper, even if you visit a doctor only once a year, because of indemnity plans' "reasonable charge" provisions.

- **What types of coverage do you need?** Everyone has different needs; one person may want a plan with good maternity and pediatric care, whereas another may want outpatient mental health benefits. Make sure the plans that you consider offer what you want.

- **How good is the managed care network?** Look at the participating doctors and hospitals to see how many of your providers are part of the plan. Check out the credentials of participating providers; a good sign is accreditation from the NCQA. Are the providers' locations convenient for you? What preventive medical programs does it provide? Has membership grown? Talk to friends and associates to see what their experiences have been with the plan.

- **How old are you, and how's your health?** Many financial advisors recommend buying the lowest-cost plan—which may be an indemnity plan with a high deductible—if you're young and healthy.

community rating approach to health insurance premium pricing
Policyholders in a community (area) pay the same premium without regard to their personal health, age, gender, or other factors.

FINANCIAL PLANNING TIPS

Saving on Health Insurance

Health insurance is not equally affordable by all people. And there are still plenty of decisions for you to make concerning health insurance. It's important to consider how to save on the cost of obtaining and using health insurance. Consider the following tips to manage your costs:

- **Stay in the network.** You can save a lot of money by staying within the insurer's network.

- **Check on alternative facilities.** Some physicians work at outpatient surgery centers as well as hospitals. And the charges can vary significantly by location. Ask your physician—you may be able to save by choosing a cheaper facility for surgery or treatment. This could save you thousands of dollars.

- **Look for lower-cost after-hours care.** Visiting a convenience care clinic, like a MinuteClinic at CVS, may well cost only a tenth of an emergency-room visit. If you don't really need an ER, consider this alternative.

- **Consider independent facilities.** The prices of X-rays and lab tests can vary a lot across different facilities. For example, having a magnetic resonance imaging (MRI) done at a hospital can easily cost twice as much as having the same procedure done at an independent radiology facility. The procedure is the same using a qualified radiologist—only the place differs.

- **Ask for generic drugs and buy your drugs through the mail.** Generic drugs are much cheaper than branded drugs, and mail-order pharmacies often offer a three-month supply of drugs for the same price as a one-month supply at a local pharmacy.

- **Know the fair prices of medical procedures.** Check out **http://www.healthcarebluebook.com**, which posts the average fee that providers in your area accept as payment from insurers for surgery, hospital stays, doctor visits, and medical tests.

Source: Adapted from Kimberly Lankford, "30 Ways to Cut Health Care Costs," http://www.kiplinger.com/article/spending/T027-C000-S002-30-ways-to-cut-health-care-costs.html, accessed August 2015.

FINANCIAL ROAD SIGN

Choosing a Health Insurance Plan

Ask the following questions when choosing among health care insurance plans:

- Can I choose to use any doctor, hospital, clinic, or pharmacy?
- What coverage, if any, is provided for seeing specialists like eye doctors and dentists?
- Does the plan cover special conditions or treatments like psychiatric care, pregnancy, and physical therapy?
- Does the plan cover home care or nursing home care?
- What kind of limitations are there on the coverage of prescribed medications?
- What are the deductible and any co-payment amounts?
- What is the maximum I would have to pay out of health care expenses, either in a calendar year or during my lifetime?
- How are billing or service disputes handled under the plan?

Source: Adapted from "Choosing a Health Insurance Plan," http://www.usa.gov/topics/health/health-insurance/choosing.shtml, accessed August 2015.

After considering all of the coverage and resources available to you, consider where gaps in your health insurance coverage may lie and how best to fill them. Doing this requires an understanding of the features, policy provisions, and coverage provided by various insurance carriers and policies. We'll discuss these in detail in the next section.

TEST YOURSELF

9-11	Explain four methods for controlling the risks associated with health care expenses.
9-12	Explain what factors should be considered in evaluating available employer-sponsored health insurance plans.
9-13	Discuss possible sources of health insurance available to supplement employer-sponsored health insurance plans.
9-14	Answer the key questions posed to help you choose a plan, based on your current situation. What type of plan do you think will best suit your needs?

9-4 MEDICAL EXPENSE COVERAGE AND POLICY PROVISIONS

So far, we've discussed the major types of health insurance plans, their providers, and the factors that should be considered in evaluating the need for health insurance. To evaluate different insurance plan options, however, you must be able to compare and contrast what they cover and how each plan's policy provisions may affect you and your family. By doing so, you can decide which health plan offers the best protection at the most reasonable cost. Worksheet 9.1 provides a convenient checklist for comparing the costs and benefits of competing health insurance plans. You may want to refer to it while reading the following sections.

9-4a Types of Medical Expense Coverage

The medical services covered vary from health plan to health plan. You can purchase narrowly defined plans that cover only what you consider to be the most important medical services or, if you can afford it and want the comfort of broader coverage, you can purchase insurance coverage to help you pay for most or all of your health care needs. Here are the medical expenses most commonly covered by health insurance.

Hospitalization

If you must spend time in the hospital, a *hospitalization insurance policy* will reimburse you for the cost of your stay. Hospitalization policies usually pay for a portion of: (1) the hospital's daily semiprivate room rate, which typically includes meals, nursing care, and other routine services; and (2) the cost of ancillary services, such as laboratory tests, imaging, and medications you receive while hospitalized. Many hospitalization plans also cover some outpatient and out-of-hospital services once you're discharged, such as in-home rehabilitation, diagnostic treatment, and preadmission testing. Some hospitalization plans simply pay a flat daily amount for each day the insured is in the hospital, regardless of actual charges. Most policies set a limit on the number of days of hospitalization and a maximum dollar amount on ancillary services that they will pay for.

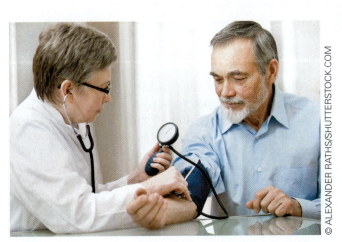

Surgical Expenses

Surgical expense insurance covers the cost of surgery in or out of the hospital. Usually, surgical expense coverage is provided as part of a hospitalization insurance policy or as a rider to such a

Here is a convenient checklist that you can use to compare the costs and benefits of competing health care plans. Check those services in the first column that are most important to you, determine how these services are handled in each policy, and then decide which policy best meets your needs. The most important covered service is hospitalization.

Service	Policy #1	Policy #2	Policy #3
Hospital care			
Surgery (inpatient and outpatient)			
Office visits to your doctor			
Maternity/well-baby care			
Pediatric care			
Immunizations			
Mammograms			
Medical tests, X-rays			
Mental health care			
Dental care, braces, and cleaning			
Vision care, eyeglasses, and exams			
Prescription drugs			
Home health care			
Nursing home care			
Services you need that are excluded			
Choice of doctors			
Location of doctors and hospitals			
Ease of getting an appointment			
Minimal paperwork			
Waiting period for coverage			
Copays and deductibles			
Premiums			
Totals			

Source: Adapted from http://www.pahealthoptions.com/docs/compare_coverage_checklist.pdf, accessed August 2015.

policy. Most plans reimburse you for *reasonable and customary* surgical expenses based on a survey of surgical costs during the previous year. They may also cover anesthesia, nonemergency treatment using imaging, and a limited allowance for diagnostic tests. Some plans still pay according to a *schedule of benefits*, reimbursing up to a fixed maximum for a particular surgical procedure. For example, the policy might state that you would receive no more than $1,500 for an appendectomy or $1,200 for diagnostic arthroscopic surgery on a knee. Scheduled benefits are often inadequate when compared with typical surgical costs. Most elective cosmetic surgeries, such as a "nose job" or "tummy tuck," are typically excluded from reimbursement unless they are deemed medically necessary.

Physician Expenses

Physicians expense insurance, also called *regular medical expense*, covers the cost of visits to a doctor's office or for a doctor's hospital visits, including consultation with a specialist. Also covered are imaging and laboratory tests performed outside of a hospital. Plans are offered on either a reasonable and customary or scheduled benefit basis. Sometimes, the first few visits with the physician for any single cause are excluded. This exclusion serves the same purpose as the deductible and waiting-period features found in other types of insurance. Often, these plans specify a maximum payment per visit as well as a maximum number of visits per injury or illness.

Major Medical Insurance

Major medical plans provide broad coverage for nearly all types of medical expenses resulting from either illnesses or accidents. In the past, it was common to have lifetime limits of $500,000 or $1,000,000. However, the ACA eliminates lifetime limits on total health care insurance payments by insurers. Because hospitalization, surgical, and physician coverage meets the smaller medical costs, major medical is used to finance more catastrophic medical costs. Many people use major medical with a high deductible to protect them in case they have a catastrophic illness.

Comprehensive Major Medical Insurance

A **comprehensive major medical insurance** plan combines basic hospitalization, surgical, and physician expense coverage with major medical protection into a single policy, usually with a low deductible. Comprehensive major medical insurance is often written under a group contract. However, some efforts have been made to make this type of coverage available to individuals.

Dental Services

Dental insurance covers necessary dental care and some dental injuries sustained through accidents. (Expenses for accidental damage to natural teeth are normally covered under standard surgical expense and major medical policies.) Depending on the policy, covered services may include examinations, X-rays, dental cleanings, fillings, extractions, dentures, root canal therapy, orthodontics, and oral surgery. The maximum limit on most dental policies is often low—$1,000 to $2,500 per patient—so these plans don't fully protect against unusually high dental work costs.

Limited Protection Policies

The types of health plans already discussed are sufficient to meet the protection needs of most individuals and families. But insurance companies offer other options that provide limited protection against certain types of perils:

- *Accident policies* that pay a specified sum to an insured injured in a certain type of accident
- *Sickness policies,* sometimes called *dread disease policies,* that pay a specified sum for a named disease, such as cancer
- *Hospital income policies* that promise to guarantee a specific daily, weekly, or monthly amount as long as the insured is hospitalized

Remember that sound insurance planning seldom dictates the purchase of such policies. Also, be aware that the extra cost of purchasing these insurance options typically outweighs the limited coverage that they provide. The problem with buying policies that cover only a certain type of accident, illness, or financial need is that

---

major medical plan
An insurance plan designed to supplement the basic coverage of hospitalization, surgical, and physician expenses; used to finance more catastrophic medical costs.

Financial Fact or Fantasy?

Hospital insurance is the most comprehensive type of medical insurance you can buy. **Fantasy:** Major medical or comprehensive major medical provides the most complete coverage, whereas hospital insurance covers only the costs incurred while confined to a hospital.

comprehensive major medical insurance
A health insurance plan that combines into a single policy the coverage for basic hospitalization, surgical, and physician expenses along with major medical protection.

PAUL BURNS/PHOTODISC/JUPITER IMAGES

major gaps in coverage will often occur. The financial loss can be just as great if the insured falls down a flight of stairs or if she contracts cancer, lung disease, or heart disease. Most limited-peril policies should be used only to supplement a comprehensive insurance program if the coverage is not overlapping.

9-4b Policy Provisions of Medical Expense Plans

To compare the health insurance plans offered by different insurers, evaluate whether they contain liberal or restrictive provisions. Generally, policy provisions can be divided into two groups: terms of payment and terms of coverage.

Terms of Payment

Four provisions govern how much your health insurance plan will pay: (1) deductibles, (2) the participation (co-insurance) clause, (3) the policy's internal limits, and (4) the coordination of benefits clause, if any.

Deductibles. Because major medical insurance plans are designed to supplement basic hospitalization, surgical, and physicians' expense plans, those offered under an indemnity (fee-for-service) plan often have a relatively large *deductible,* typically $500 or $1,000. The **deductible** represents the initial amount that's not covered by the policy and is thus the insured's responsibility. Comprehensive major medical plans tend to offer lower deductibles, sometimes $100 or less. Most plans offer a calendar-year, all-inclusive deductible. In effect, this allows a person to accumulate the deductible from more than one incident of use. Some plans also include a *carryover provision,* whereby any part of the deductible that occurs during the final three months of the year can be applied to the current year's deductible and can *also* be applied to the following calendar year's deductible. In a few plans, the deductible is on a per-illness or per-accident basis.

deductible
The initial amount *not* covered by an insurance policy and thus the insured's responsibility; it's usually determined on a calendar-year basis or on a per-illness or per-accident basis.

EXAMPLE: Effect of Per-Illness, Per-Accident Deductible

You're covered by a health insurance policy that has a $1,000 per-illness, per-accident deductible. How much would the policy pay if you suffered three separate accidents in one year, each requiring $1,000 of medical expenses? None! Unfortunately you wouldn't be eligible to collect any benefits from the major medical plan.

participation (co-insurance) clause
A provision in many health insurance policies stipulating that the insurer will pay some portion—say, 80 or 90 percent—of the amount of the covered loss in excess of the deductible.

Participation (Co-insurance). A **participation** or **co-insurance clause** stipulates that the company will pay some portion—say, 80 percent or 90 percent—of the amount of the covered loss in excess of the deductible rather than the entire amount. Co-insurance helps reduce the incentive for policyholders to fake an illness and discourages them from incurring unnecessary medical expenses. Many major medical plans also have a *stop-loss provision* that places a cap on the amount of participation required. Without a stop-loss provision, a $1 million medical bill would leave the insured with $200,000 of costs under an 80 percent plan. Often such provisions limit the insured's participation to less than $10,000 and sometimes to as little as $2,000.

internal limits
A feature commonly found in health insurance policies that limits the amounts that will be paid for certain specified expenses, even if the claim does *not* exceed overall policy limits.

Internal Limits. Most major medical plans are written with **internal limits** that control the amounts paid for certain specified expenses—even if the claim *doesn't* exceed overall policy limits. Charges commonly subject to internal limits are hospital room and board, surgical fees, mental and nervous conditions, and nursing services. If an insured chooses an expensive physician or medical facility, then he or she is responsible for paying the portion of the charges that are above a "reasonable and customary" level or beyond a specified maximum amount. The following example shows how deductibles, co-insurance, and internal limits constrain the amount a company is obligated to pay under a major medical plan.

Major Medical Policy: An Example. Assume that Fred Woods, a graduate student, has coverage under a major medical insurance policy that specifies a $500,000 lifetime limit of protection, a $1,000 deductible, an 80 percent co-insurance clause, internal limits of $350 per day on hospital room and board, and $6,000 as the maximum payable surgical fee. When Fred was hospitalized for three days to remove a small tumor, he incurred these costs:

Hospitalization: 3 days at $500 a day	$1,500
Surgical expense	5,800
Other covered medical expenses	3,800
Total medical expenses	$11,100

By the terms of the policy's co-insurance clause, the maximum that the company must pay is 80 percent of the covered loss in excess of the deductible. Without internal limits, the company would pay $8,080 [0.80 × ($11,100 − $1,000)]. The internal limits further restrict the payment. Even though 80 percent of the $500-per-day hospitalization charge is $400, the most the company would have to pay is $350 per day. Thus Fred, the insured, becomes liable for $50 per day for three days, or $150. The surgical expense is below the $6,000 internal limit, so the 80 percent co-insurance clause applies and the insurer will pay $4,640 (0.80 × $5,800). The company's total obligation is reduced to $7,930 ($8,080 − $150), and Fred must pay a total of $3,170 [$1,000 deductible + 0.20($11,100 − $1,000) co-insurance + $150 excess hospital room and board charges]. This example shows that, although major medical insurance can offer large amounts of reimbursement, you may still be responsible for substantial payments.

Coordination of Benefits. Health insurance policies are not contracts of *indemnity*. This means that the insured party can collect multiple payments for the same illness or accident unless health insurance policies include a **coordination of benefits provision**. This clause prevents you from collecting more than 100 percent of covered charges by collecting benefits from more than one policy. For example, many private health insurance policies coordinate benefit provisions with medical benefits paid under workers' compensation. In contrast, some companies widely advertise that their policies will pay claims regardless of other coverage the policyholder has. Of course, these latter types of insurance policies often charge more per dollar of protection. From the standpoint of insurance planning, using policies with coordination of benefits clauses can help you prevent coverage overlaps and, ideally, reduce your premiums.

Considering the complexity of medical expense contracts, the various clauses limiting payments, and coordination of benefits with other policies, one might expect that insurers often pay only partial claims and sometimes completely deny claims. However, if you make a claim and don't receive the payment you expected, don't give up. Exhibit 9.3 provides some guidelines on how you might go about getting your health insurance claims paid.

Terms of Coverage

Several contract provisions affect a health insurance plan's value to you. Some important provisions address (1) the persons and places covered, (2) cancellation,

coordination of benefits provision
A provision often included in health insurance policies to prevent the insured from collecting more than 100 percent of covered charges; it requires that benefit payments be coordinated if the insured is eligible for benefits under more than one policy.

EXHIBIT 9.3   **How to Get Paid on a Health Insurance Claim**

The following steps will help you to get paid for health insurance claims.

1. *Keep detailed records of all visits to physicians and medical professionals.* Even though medical facilities are supposed to keep medical records, it is also important for you to keep a copy for your own records. This includes all bills, dates of service, and insurance company approvals. Your records provide the proof you need when filing a claim with the insurance company.

2. *Contact the physician or medical professional's office yourself rather than waiting for the insurance company to do so.* Sometimes a claim is held up because the insurance company is waiting for documentation. Take the initiative and find out who needs what and make a call or two. This will reduce the wait for a claim to be paid.

3. *If the insurance company isn't paying the claim, ask them to explain why not.* Most companies will provide an explanation. This will allow you to quickly determine your next step in assuring that your claim is paid.

4. *If a claim is denied, make sure to call your physician or medical professional.* Such professionals deal with insurance companies frequently and can often cut to the essence of the problem quickly.

5. *Keep all documents provided by your insurance company.* This includes the company's Explanation of Benefits statement. Check them to make sure that you are contacting the proper departments at the company and asking the relevant questions. It may well be that your solution is buried in the fine print.

6. *If your claim is denied, it may be worthwhile to hire a private claims advocate.* Find one through the Alliance of Claims Assistance Professionals Web site, **http://www.claims.org.**

Sources: Adapted from "Choosing a Health Insurance Plan," http://www.usa.gov/topics/health/health-insurance/choosing.shtml, accessed August 2015; Sheila Guilloton, "What to Do If Your Health Insurance Company Won't Pay," http://www.examiner.com/article/what-to-do-if-your-health-insurance-company-won-t-pay, accessed August 2015.

(3) preexisting conditions, (4) pregnancy and abortion, (5) mental illness, (6) rehabilitation coverage, and (7) continuation of group coverage.

Persons and Places Covered. Under the ACA, family health care insurers must allow parents to retain their children on their health insurance policies up to the age of 26. Some policies protect you only while you're in the United States or Canada; others offer worldwide coverage but exclude named countries.

Cancellation. Many health insurance policies are written to permit *cancellation* at the insurer's option at any time. Some policies explicitly state this; others don't. To protect yourself against premature cancellation, buy policies that specifically state that the insurer won't cancel coverage so long as premiums are paid.

pre-existing condition clause

A clause that used to be included in most individual health insurance policies permitting permanent or temporary exclusion of coverage for any physical or mental problems the insured had at the time the policy was purchased; under the ACA, insurers now are prohibited from denying coverage for pre-existing conditions, making this clause moot.

Pre-existing Conditions. In the past, most health insurance policies sold to individuals (as opposed to group/employer-sponsored plans) contained a **pre-existing condition clause**. This means the policy might exclude coverage for physical or mental problems that you had at the time you bought it. In some policies, the exclusion was permanent; in others, it lasted only for the first year or two that the coverage is in force. Group insurance plans in the past may also have had pre-existing condition clauses, but they tended to be less restrictive than those in individually written policies. The ACA has changed this. The new legislation prohibits insurers from denying coverage due to the presence of pre-existing conditions.

Employees who have recently left a job or retired are covered by the *Health Insurance Portability and Accountability Act, or HIPAA*. This federal law, implemented in 1996, is designed to protect people's ability to obtain continued health insurance after they leave a job or retire, even if they have a serious health problem. Under HIPAA, if you've already been covered by a health plan without a break in coverage of more than 63 days and you apply for new insurance, insurers cannot turn you down, charge you higher premiums, or enforce an exclusionary period because of your health status. HIPAA doesn't guarantee you group coverage, but it does protect your ability to buy individual health insurance even if you have a preexisting health condition. HIPAA now applies only to "grandfathered" plans that existed when the ACA went into effect in March 2010 and have not been changed significantly since then. The ACA deals with some of the issues previously addressed by HIPAA.

Pregnancy and Abortion. Many individual and group health insurance plans include special clauses for medical expenses incurred through pregnancy or abortion. Some liberal policies pay for all related expenses, including sick-leave pay during the final months of pregnancy, whereas others pay for medical expenses that result from pregnancy or abortion complications, but not for routine procedure expenses. In the most restrictive cases, policies offer no coverage for any costs of pregnancy or abortion.

Mental Illness. Many health insurance plans omit or offer only reduced benefits for treatment of mental disorders. For example, a health insurance policy may offer hospitalization benefits that continue to pay so long as you remain hospitalized—except for mental illness. It may restrict payment for mental illness to one-half the normally provided payment amounts and for a period not to exceed 30 days. Unfortunately, mental illness is the number one sickness requiring long-term hospital care. Because coverage for mental illness is an important insurance protection, check your policies to learn how liberal—or how restrictive—they are regarding this feature.

Rehabilitation Coverage. In the past, health insurance plans focused almost exclusively on reasonable and necessary medical expenses. If an illness or accident left an insured partially or totally disabled, then normally no funds would be available to help the person retrain for employment and a more productive life. Now, though, many policies include *rehabilitation coverage* for counseling, occupational therapy, and even some educational or job training programs. This is a good feature to look for in major medical and disability income policies.

Consolidated Omnibus Budget Reconciliation Act (COBRA)
A federal law that allows an employee who leaves the insured group to continue coverage for up to 18 months by paying premiums to his or her former employer on time; the employee retains all benefits previously available, except for disability income coverage.

Continuation of Group Coverage. Under the **Consolidated Omnibus Budget Reconciliation Act (COBRA)** passed by Congress in 1986, an employee who leaves the insured group voluntarily or involuntarily (except in the case of "gross misconduct") may elect to continue coverage for up to 18 months by paying premiums to his or her former employer on time (up to 102 percent of the company cost). The employee retains all benefits previously available, except for disability income coverage.

Similar continuation coverage is available for retirees and their families for up to 18 months or until they become eligible for Medicare, whichever occurs first. An employee's dependents may be covered for up to 36 months under COBRA under special circumstances, such as divorce or death of the employee. After COBRA coverage expires, most states provide for conversion of the group coverage to an individual policy regardless of the insured's current health and without evidence of insurability. Premium charges and benefits of the converted policy are determined at the time of conversion. As noted above, under the ACA losing your job triggers a "qualifying life event" that allows you to obtain health insurance under COBRA or you can buy a policy in the private health insurance market.

9-4c Cost Containment Provisions for Medical Expense Plans

Considering the continued inflation in medical costs, it's hardly surprising that insurers, along with employers that sponsor medical expense plans, are looking for ways to limit their incurred costs. Today, various cost containment provisions are included in almost all medical expense plans, both indemnity and managed care policies. These cost containment provisions include the following.

- **Preadmission certification:** This requires you to receive approval from your insurer before entering the hospital for a scheduled stay. Such approval is not normally required for emergency stays.
- **Continued stay review:** To receive normal reimbursement, the insured must secure approval from the insurer for any stay that exceeds the originally approved limits.
- **Second surgical opinions:** Many plans require second opinions on specific non-emergency procedures and, in their absence, may reduce the surgical benefits paid. Most surgical expense plans now fully reimburse the cost of second opinions.
- **Waiver of co-insurance:** Because insurers can save money on hospital room-and-board charges by encouraging outpatient surgery, many now agree to waive the co-insurance clause and pay 100 percent of surgical costs for outpatient

Behavior Matters

Behavioral Biases in Making Health Insurance Decisions

Research in behavioral economics indicates that individuals have difficulty making decisions involving uncertainty, trade-offs between current and future benefits and costs, or significant complexity. These decisions require estimating the probabilities, financial costs, and quality of life and happiness associated with possible future health events such as having cancer or a heart attack. People find it hard to do this well.

Research shows that individuals tend to make systematic mistakes in estimating probabilities. For example, they are inclined to overestimate the likelihood of low-probability events, such as dying in a plane crash. And it's almost impossible for most people to estimate the financial costs associated with various health conditions. This is because, for the most part, there is no place to look up health service prices. And people tend to overestimate how much their quality of life and happiness will decline if they become sick.

Health care choices often require bearing costs today in the hope of future benefits. This is as much the case for preventative care as it is for more costly and invasive procedures designed to reduce the probability of cancer among high-risk patients. Yet research shows that people tend to invest too little in such activities because they put too much weight on current costs and too little weight on future benefits.

Health care insurance decisions can also be quite complex. Insurance policies include many facets such as deductibles, co-payments, and different levels of coverage for different providers. And health insurance includes trade-offs that many people don't seem to understand. For example, employees may not fully appreciate that they are sacrificing some wages in return for employer health care insurance premium subsidies.

What are the implications of the above biases?

- It's important to be aware of common behavioral biases when making health insurance decisions. For example, realize that most people don't pay sufficient attention to preventive health care measures.
- Most of us would be better off if our health insurance plans were mediated by some entity that would screen and restrict health insurance choices down to a manageable number. Research suggests that employers would perform this role better than the government or private insurance agents, which is a provocative finding in light of the ACA.

Source: "Lessons for Health Care from Behavioral Economics," http://www.nber.org/bah/2008no4/w14330.html (see referenced study by Jeffrey Liebman and Richard Zeckhauser, "Simple Humans, Complex Insurance, Subtle Subsidies," Working Paper 14330, http://www.nber.org/papers/w14330, 2008), accessed August 2015.

procedures. A similar waiver is sometimes applied to generic pharmaceuticals. For example, the patient may choose between an 80 percent payment for a brand-name pharmaceutical costing $35 or 100 percent reimbursement for its $15 generic equivalent.

- **Limitation of insurer's responsibility:** Many policies also have provisions limiting the insurer's financial responsibility to reimbursing only for costs that are considered "reasonable and customary." This provision can sometimes place limitations on the type and place of medical care for which the insurer will pay.

TEST YOURSELF

9-15 Explain the differences between hospitalization insurance and surgical expense insurance.

9-16 What are the features of a *major medical* plan? Compare major medical to *comprehensive major medical* insurance.

9-17 Describe these policy provisions commonly found in medical expense plans: (a) deductibles, (b) co-insurance, and (c) coordination of benefits.

9-18 What are the key provisions of COBRA? How do they relate to continuation of group coverage when an employee voluntarily or involuntarily leaves the insured group?

9-19 Explain the cost containment provisions commonly found in medical expense plans. How might the provision for second surgical opinions help an insurer contain its costs?

9-5 LONG-TERM-CARE INSURANCE

long-term care
The delivery of medical and personal care, other than hospital care, to persons with chronic medical conditions resulting from either illness or frailty.

Long-term care involves the delivery of medical and personal care, other than hospitalization, to persons with chronic medical conditions. Whether in a nursing home, in an assisted-living community, or through care provided in the patient's home, it can have a major financial impact. A year's stay in a private nursing home, for example, averages over $91,250, according to a 2015 cost-of-care survey by Genworth Financial. About 44 percent of men and 58 percent of women over 65 are expected to need long-term care at some time. And yet, less than 3 percent of American adults have purchased long-term care insurance. This is a potential concern because the average long-term stay is over one year.

Consumers pay about 25 percent of long-term care costs out of their own pockets. Government programs such as Medicare and Medicaid cover less than half of the total cost, and eligibility for their benefits is strictly defined. Major medical insurance plans also exclude most of the costs related to long-term care. When a person receiving nursing home care cannot afford to cover such a large personal expense out-of-pocket, the younger generation often ends up footing the bill.

The ACA has provisions that relate to long-term care. It includes the Community Living Assistance Services and Support Program (CLASS), which is a voluntary, consumer-financed insurance plan designed to cover long-term-care expenses. This is similar to long-term-care programs currently available in the private market. However, it differs in that the program will be administered by the government. Further, any working adult who is 18 or older will be able to enroll, regardless of any pre-existing medical condition. And the benefits will be good for as long as someone needs long-term care. However, the fate of the long-term-care parts of the ACA remain unclear. The U.S. Department of Health and Human Services has questioned the financial viability of implementing the long-term-care program presented in the ACA.

Fortunately, special insurance policies are available to cover long-term care. Most are indemnity policies that pay a fixed dollar amount for each day that you receive specified care either in a nursing home or at home. The decision to buy long-term-care insurance is an important part of health insurance and retirement financial planning.

Most people purchase individual long-term-care products either through organizations like the AARP or directly from the more than 100 insurance companies that offer them. Employer-sponsored long-term-care insurance is also growing in popularity. Many businesses now offer some type of long-term-care insurance to their employees. Usually, however, employees pay the full cost of premiums, although employer-sponsored plans can often cost less than purchasing long-term care on an individual basis. Whether you purchase long-term-care insurance as an individual or through an employer-sponsored plan, however, it's important to evaluate policy provisions and costs.

9-5a Do You Need Long-Term-Care Insurance?

The odds of needing more than a year of nursing home care before you reach age 65 are 1 in 33. And yet, the expense of a prolonged nursing home stay can cause severe financial hardship. How do you decide if you need long-term-care insurance? Answer the following questions.

- **Do you have many assets to preserve for your dependents?** Because you must deplete most of your assets before Medicaid will pay for nursing home care, some financial advisors recommend that people over 65 whose net worth is more than $100,000 and income exceeds $50,000 a year consider long-term-care

FINANCIAL PLANNING TIPS

Buying Long-Term-Care Insurance

Consider the following tips when shopping for a long-term-care insurance policy:

- **Buy the right amount and the right kind of coverage.** Long-term-care insurance benefits are usually stated as a fixed daily amount over a certain period, up to a given maximum amount of coverage. Access to the benefits is usually triggered by a "long-term-care event" like breaking a hip or having a stroke. The key is that physicians expect you to need help with daily living tasks for at least 90 days. Many salespeople will try to sell you a policy that covers the cost of several years of nursing home care. However, consider the more affordable alternative of a policy that includes time with a home health aide or adult day care, both of which are much cheaper than nursing home care.

- **Buy at the right time.** You'll save significantly over the lifetime of the policy if you buy a policy when you're under 60 and healthy. About 25 percent of people wait until they are much older and have health issues that can greatly increase the cost of obtaining a policy.

- **Be aware of the "restoration of benefits" rider, as well as the rest of the policy's fine print.** The "restoration of benefits" rider should be considered because it allows you to stop the clock on your policy. For example, assume that you fall down the stairs at the age of 83. The right policy will allow you to start spending the benefits immediately on a home health aide. And when you recover, a "restoration of benefits" rider allows you to stop the clock on the policy. If you stay well for six months, the overall total benefits are restored as if you never had fallen.

- **Take inflation into account.** It makes sense to buy a policy that provides at least 5 percent compound inflation protection.

Source: Adapted in part from Anya Kamenetz, "Tips for Buying Long-term Care Insurance," http://articles.chicagotribune.com/2012-04-24/business/sns-201204241730—tms—savingsgctnzy-a20120424apr24_1_long-term-care-insurance-home-health-affordable-policy, accessed August 2015.

insurance—*if* they can afford the premiums. The very wealthy, however, may prefer to self-insure.

- **Can you afford the premiums?** Premiums of many good-quality policies can be 5 percent to 7 percent of annual income, or even more. Such high premiums may cause more financial hardship than the cost of a potential nursing home stay. You may be better off investing the amount you'd spend in premiums; it would then be available for *any* future need, including long-term health care.
- **Is there a family history of disabling disease?** This factor increases your odds of needing long-term care. If there's a history of Alzheimer's, neurological disorders, or other potentially debilitating diseases, the need for long-term care insurance may increase.
- **Are you male or female?** Women tend to live longer and are more likely to require long-term care. They're also the primary caregivers for other family members, which may mean that when they need care, help won't be available.
- **Do you have family who can care for you?** The availability of relatives or home health services to provide care can reduce the cost of long-term care.

9-5b Long-Term-Care Insurance Provisions and Costs

Whether you purchase long-term-care insurance as an individual or through an employer-sponsored plan, it's important to understand what you're buying. Substantial variation exists between product offerings, so you must be especially careful to evaluate the provisions of each policy. Exhibit 9.4 summarizes the typical provisions of policies offered by leading insurers. Of course, policy provisions are important factors in determining the premium for each policy. Let's take a closer look at the most important policy provisions to consider in purchasing long-term-care insurance.

- **Type of care:** Some long-term-care policies offer benefits only for nursing home care, whereas others pay only for services in the insured's home, such as skilled or unskilled nursing care, physical therapy, homemakers, and home health aides. Because it's hard to predict whether a person might need to be in a nursing home, most financial planners recommend policies covering both. Many of these policies focus on nursing home care, and any expenses for health care in the insured's

---

| EXHIBIT 9.4 | **Typical Provisions in Long-Term-Care Insurance Policies** |

Long-term-care insurers offer a wide range of provisions in their policies. A typical policy includes the following:

Services covered	Skilled, intermediate, and custodial care; home health care; adult day care (often)
Benefit eligibility	Physician certification/medically necessary
Daily benefit	$100–$450/day, nursing home; $50–$250/day, home health care
Benefit period	3–4 years
Maximum benefit period	5 years; unlimited
Waiting period	0–100 days
Renewability	Guaranteed
Preexisting conditions	Conditions existing 6–12 months prior to policy coverage
Inflation protection	Yes, for an additional premium
Deductibility periods	0, 20, 30, 90, 100 days
Alzheimer's disease coverage	Yes
Age limits for purchasing	40–84

home are covered in a rider to the basic policy. Many policies also cover assisted living, adult day care and other community care programs, alternative care, and respite care for the caregiver.

- **Eligibility requirements:** Some important provisions determine whether the insured will receive payment for claims. These are known as *gatekeeper* provisions. The most liberal policies state that the insured will qualify for benefits so long as his or her physician orders the care. A common and much more restrictive provision pays only for long-term care that's medically necessary because of sickness or injury.

  One common gatekeeper provision requires the insured's inability to perform a given number of *activities of daily living (ADLs)* such as bathing, dressing, or eating. Some policies also provide care for cognitive impairment or when medically necessary and prescribed by the patient's physician. In the case of an Alzheimer's patient who remains physically healthy, inclusion of cognitive abilities as ADLs would be extremely important. Newer policies no longer require a certain period of nursing home care before covering home health care services.

- **Services covered:** Most policies today cover several levels of service in state-licensed nursing homes: skilled, intermediate, and custodial care. *Skilled care* is needed when a patient requires constant attention from a medical professional, such as a physician or registered nurse. *Intermediate care* is provided when the patient needs medical attention or supervision but not the constant attention of a medical professional. *Custodial care* provides assistance in the normal activities of daily living but no medical attention or supervision; a physician or nurse may be on call, however. Most long-term-care policies also cover home care services, such as skilled or unskilled nursing care, physical therapy, homemakers, and home health aides provided by state-licensed or Medicare-certified home health agencies. Newer policies no longer require a certain period of nursing home care before covering home health care services.

- **Daily benefits:** Long-term-care policies reimburse the insured for services incurred up to a daily maximum. For nursing home care policies, the daily maximums generally range from $100 to $450, depending on the amount of premium the insured is willing to pay. For combination nursing home and home care policies, the maximum home care benefit is normally half the nursing home maximum.

- **Benefit duration:** The maximum duration of benefits ranges from 1 year to the insured's lifetime. Lifetime coverage is expensive, however. Most financial planners recommend the purchase of a policy with a duration of three to six years to give the insured protection for a longer-than-average period of care.

- **Waiting period:** Even if the policy's eligibility requirements are met, the insured must pay long-term-care expenses during the **waiting** or **elimination period**. Typical waiting periods are 90 to 100 days. Although premiums are much lower for policies with longer waiting periods, the insured must have liquid assets to cover his or her expenses during that period. An insured individual who is still receiving care after the waiting period expires will begin to receive benefits for the duration of the policy so long as its eligibility requirements continue to be met.

- **Renewability:** Most long-term-care insurance policies now include a **guaranteed renewability** provision to ensure continued coverage for your lifetime as long as you continue to pay the premiums. This clause does not ensure a level premium over time, however. Nearly all policies allow the insurer to raise premiums if the claims experience for your peer group of policyholders is unfavorable. Watch out for policies with an **optional renewability** clause. These policies are renewable *only at the insurer's option*.

- **Pre-existing conditions:** Many long-term care policies include a *pre-existing conditions clause*, whose effect ranges from 6 to 12 months. On the other hand, many policies have no such clause, which effectively eliminates one important source of possible claim disputes. If someone has already been diagnosed with Parkinson's or Alzheimer's disease, takes memory drugs, uses any type of assistance in walking, has had a stroke, or has osteoporosis, an insurance company may well not be willing to sell that person a long-term insurance policy.

waiting (elimination) period
The period after an insured meets the policy's eligibility requirements, during which he or she must pay expenses out-of-pocket; when the waiting period expires, the insured begins to receive benefits.

guaranteed renewability
A policy provision ensuring continued insurance coverage for the insured's lifetime, so long as the premiums continue to be paid.

optional renewability
A contractual clause allowing the insured to continue insurance *only at the insurer's option.*

- **Inflation protection:** Many policies offer riders that, for an additional premium, let you increase your benefits over time so that benefits roughly match the rising cost of nursing home and home health care. Most inflation protection riders let you increase benefits by a flat amount, often 5 percent, per year. Others offer benefits linked to the rise in the consumer price index (CPI). Most policies discontinue inflation adjustments after either 10 or 20 years. Inflation protection riders can add between 25 percent and 40 percent to the basic premium for a long-term-care insurance policy.
- **Premium levels:** Long-term-care insurance is rather expensive, and premiums vary widely among insurance companies. For example, an average healthy 55-year-old male may pay about $5,100 per year for a policy that pays for three years of care at $250 per day for nursing home care with a 90-day waiting period and a 3 percent inflation rider. The cost of the same coverage drops substantially with the ages of the insured. Because of this marked rise in premium with age, some financial planners recommend buying long-term-care insurance when you are fairly young. But keep in mind that, although the annual premiums are lower, you'll be paying for a lot longer time before you are likely to actually need the benefits. And remember that insurance companies can and do get permission to increase premiums significantly over the life of a policy. So future premiums are uncertain, which is not comforting.

9-5c How to Buy Long-Term-Care Insurance

If you decide that you or a relative should have long-term-care insurance, be sure to buy from a financially sound company (based on ratings from the major ratings agencies) that has experience in this market segment. Here are some additional guidelines to help you choose the right policy:

- **Buy the policy when you're healthy:** Once you have a disease (such as Alzheimer's or multiple sclerosis) or have a stroke, you become uninsurable. The best time to buy is when you're in your mid-50s or 60s.
- **Buy the right types of coverage—but don't buy more coverage than you need:** Your policy should cover skilled, intermediate, and custodial care as well as adult day care centers and assisted living facilities. If you have access to family caregivers or home health services, opt for only nursing home coverage; if not, select a policy with generous home health care benefits. To reduce costs, increase the waiting period before benefits start; the longer you can cover the costs yourself, the lower your premiums. You may also choose a shorter benefit payment period; 3 years is a popular choice, but the average nursing home stay is about one year. Lifetime coverage increases the premium for a 65-year-old by as much as 40 percent.
- **Understand what the policy covers and when it pays benefits:** The amounts paid, benefit periods, and services covered vary among insurers. One rule of thumb is to buy a policy covering 80 percent to 100 percent of current nursing home costs in your area. Some policies pay only for licensed health care providers, whereas others include assistance with household chores. Know how the policy defines benefit eligibility.

TEST YOURSELF

9-20 Why should a consumer consider purchasing a long-term care insurance policy?

9-21 Describe the differences among long-term-care policies regarding (a) type of care, (b) eligibility requirements, and (c) services covered. List and discuss some other important policy provisions.

9-22 Discuss some of the questions one should ask before buying long-term-care insurance. What guidelines can be used to choose the right policy?

9-6 DISABILITY INCOME INSURANCE

When a family member becomes sick for an extended period, the effect on the family goes beyond medical bills. About one-third of people between the ages of 35 and 65 will be disabled for 90 days or longer before age 65, and about one in seven people between the ages of 35 and 65 will become disabled for five years or more. During the working years, becoming disabled is more likely than death. For a 35-year-old male, the odds are nearly 2 to 1, and for a 35-year-old female, the odds are nearly 3 to 1. Although most Americans have life insurance, few have taken steps to protect their family should a serious illness or accident prevent them from working for an extended period.

Disability income insurance
Insurance that provides families with weekly or monthly payments to replace income when the insured is unable to work because of a covered illness, injury, or disease.

The best way to protect against the potentially devastating financial consequences of a health-related disability is with disability income insurance. **Disability income insurance** provides families with weekly or monthly payments to replace income when the insured is unable to work because of a covered illness, injury, or disease. Some companies also offer disability income protection for a spousal homemaker; such coverage helps pay for the services that the spouse would normally provide.

Almost all employers offer disability income insurance at advantageous rates. However, coverage is often voluntary, and you may have to pay the entire premium yourself. Group coverage is usually a good buy, and premiums for employer-sponsored group coverage average $300 to $500 a year depending on age and income—about one-third less than the cost of comparable private coverage. A disadvantage is that if you change jobs, you may lose the coverage. The benefits from a group plan in which you pay the premiums are tax free (unless paid through a flexible spending account). As a safeguard, you'd be well advised to run a needs analysis, as described in the instructions for Worksheet 9.2, to be sure you have enough coverage for your needs.

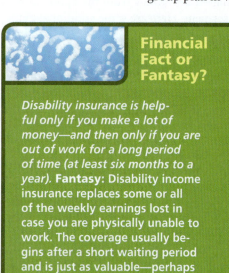

Financial Fact or Fantasy?

Disability insurance is helpful only if you make a lot of money—and then only if you are out of work for a long period of time (at least six months to a year). **Fantasy:** Disability income insurance replaces some or all of the weekly earnings lost in case you are physically unable to work. The coverage usually begins after a short waiting period and is just as valuable—perhaps more so—to the low-income family as it is to those with high incomes.

Social Security offers disability income benefits, but you must be unable to do *any* job whatsoever to receive benefits. Benefits are payable only if your disability is expected to last at least one year (or to be fatal), and they don't begin until you've been disabled for at least five months. The actual amount paid is a percentage of your previous monthly earnings, with some statistical adjustments. The percentage is higher for people with low earnings. Most recipients receive between $300 and $2,200 a month with a maximum monthly payment in 2015 of $2,663.

The need for disability income coverage is great but is generally ignored by the public. Although most workers receive some disability insurance benefits from their employer, in many cases, the group plan falls short and pays only about 60 to 70 percent of salary for a limited period. The first step in considering disability income insurance is to determine the dollar amount your family would need (typically monthly) if an earner becomes disabled. Then you can buy the coverage that you need or supplement existing coverage if necessary.

9-6a Estimating Your Disability Insurance Needs

The main purpose of disability income insurance is to replace all (or most) of the income—that is, earnings—that would be lost if you became disabled and physically unable to hold a job. In essence, it should enable you to maintain a standard of living at or near your present level. To help decide how much disability income insurance is right for you, use Worksheet 9.2 to estimate your monthly disability benefit needs. Here is all you have to do.

1. **Calculate take-home pay.** Disability benefits are generally, but not always, tax free, so you typically need to replace only your *take-home (after-tax) pay.* Benefits from employer-paid policies are fully or partially taxable. To estimate

Using a worksheet like this makes the job of estimating disability benefit insurance needs a lot easier.

DISABILITY BENEFIT NEEDS

Name(s) _____ Date _____

1. Estimate current monthly take-home pay $ _____

2. Estimate existing monthly benefits

   a. Social Security benefits $ _____

   b. Other government program benefits   _____

   c. Company disability benefits   _____

   d. Group disability policy benefits   _____

3. Total existing monthly disability benefits (2a + 2b + 2c + 2d) $ _____   _____

4. **Estimated monthly disability benefits needed ([1] – [3])** $ _____

---

take-home pay, subtract income and Social Security taxes paid from your gross earned income (salary only). Divide this total by 12 to calculate your monthly take-home pay.

2. **Estimate the monthly amounts of disability benefits from government or employer programs.**

   a. *Social Security benefits.* Obtain an estimate of your benefits by using the online calculators provided by the Social Security Administration on their Internet site. The average Social Security disability benefit is about $1,200 per month.

   b. *Other government program benefits* with disability benefits for which you qualify (armed services, Veterans Administration, civil service, the Federal Employees Compensation Act, state workers' compensation systems). There are also special programs for railroad workers, longshoremen, and people with black-lung disease.

   c. *Company disability benefits.* Ask your company benefits supervisor to help you calculate company-provided benefits, including sick pay or wage continuation plans (these are essentially short-term disability income insurance) and plans formally designated as disability insurance. For each benefit that your employer offers, check on its tax treatment.

   d. *Group disability policy benefits.* A private insurer provides the coverage, and you pay for it, often through payroll deduction.

3. **Add up your existing monthly disability benefits.**

4. **Subtract your existing monthly disability benefits from your current monthly take-home pay.** The result shows the estimated monthly disability benefits you'll need in order to maintain your present after-tax income. Note that investment income and spousal income (if the spouse is presently employed) are ignored because it's assumed this income will continue and is necessary to maintain your current standard of living. If your spouse is now unemployed but would enter the workforce if you ever became disabled, then his or her estimated monthly income (take-home pay) could be subtracted from item 4 of Worksheet 9.2 to determine your net monthly disability benefit needs.

9-6b Disability Income Insurance Provisions and Costs

The scope and cost of your disability income coverage depend on its contractual provisions. Although disability income insurance policies can be complex, certain features are important: (1) definition of disability, (2) benefit amount and duration, (3) probationary period, (4) waiting period, (5) renewability, and (6) other provisions.

Definition of Disability

Disability policies vary in the standards you must meet to receive benefits. Some pay benefits if you're unable to perform the duties of your customary occupation—the *own occupation* (or "Own Occ") definition—whereas others pay only if you can engage in no gainful employment at all—the *any occupation* (or "Any Occ") definition. Under the "Own Occ" definition, a professor who lost his voice—yet could still be paid to write or do research—would receive full benefits because he couldn't lecture, a primary function of his occupation. With a *residual benefit option,* you would be paid partial benefits if you can only work part-time or at a lower salary. The "Any Occ" definition is considerably less expensive because it gives the insurer more leeway in determining whether the insured should receive benefits.

Individual disability policies may contain a *presumptive disability* clause that supersedes the previously discussed definition of disability when certain types of

FINANCIAL PLANNING TIPS

Buying Disability Income Insurance

Consider the following tips in evaluating disability income insurance policies:

• **Know what the government can do for you.** Social Security disability benefits are available only to those with a condition that makes them unable to work of at least a year or that is terminal. The average benefit payout is only about 40 percent of pre-disability income. Qualified applicants should expect to wait between three and five months to get Social Security disability benefits. Only a few states provide additional benefits, although it's worth checking that. If you buy a private disability income insurance policy, be aware that most require you to apply for Social Security benefits, which will be subtracted from the benefit that you receive from the insurer.

• **Buying a policy at work is usually cheapest.** Many employers provide disability income insurance and pay part of the premiums. If you go this route, make sure that you have both short- and long-term coverage. Short-term coverage usually lasts for a few months, and long-term coverage often starts paying after 90 to 180 days. Make

sure that you're not exposed to a significant gap between the two. If you buy a policy through your employer, you may be able to pay the premiums directly out of your paycheck on a pretax basis. However, this means that your benefits would be taxable.

• **Determine if a policy purchased through your employer is portable.** It's good to know if you can keep the policy if you leave your current company.

• **Understand the circumstances in which the disability insurance benefit will be paid.** The best trigger is when you cannot do your current job. However, some policies only pay if you cannot do any comparable job, which is a much more complicated constraint.

• **Read the fine print.** It's important to know what percentage of pre-disability income is paid out by the policy. And does it include just base salary or additional compensation like commissions or bonuses? Are there limits on benefit payouts for certain conditions like mental illness? You'll want to know the ins and outs of each policy that you consider.

Source: Anna Wilde Mathews, "Just in Case: The Skinny on Buying Disability Insurance," http://www.wsj.com/articles/SB10001424052748704561004575013073100310794, accessed August 2015.

losses occur. Loss of both hands, sight in both eyes, and hearing in both ears are examples where the insured may be *presumed* totally disabled and may receive full benefits even though he or she still can be employed in some capacity.

Benefit Amount and Duration

Most individual disability income policies pay a flat monthly benefit, which is stated in the policy, whereas group plans pay a fixed percentage of gross income. In either case, insurers normally won't agree to amounts of more than 60 percent to 70 percent of the insured's gross income. Insurers won't issue policies for the full amount of gross income because this would give some people an incentive to fake a disability (e.g., "bad back") and possibly collect more in insurance benefits than they normally would receive as take-home pay.

Monthly benefits can be paid for a few months or a lifetime. If you're assured a substantial defined benefit pension, Social Security, or other benefits at retirement, then a policy that pays benefits until age 65 is adequate. Most people, however, will need to continue their occupations for many more years and should consider a policy offering lifetime benefits. Many policies offer benefits for periods as short as two or five years. Although these policies may be better than nothing, they don't protect against the major financial losses associated with long-term disabilities.

Probationary Period

Both group and individual disability income policies are likely to include a probationary period, usually 7 to 30 days, which is a time delay from the date the policy is issued until benefit privileges are available. Any disability stemming from an illness, injury, or disease that occurs during the probationary period is *not* covered—even if it continues beyond this period. This feature keeps costs down.

Waiting Period

The waiting, or elimination, period provisions in a disability income policy are similar to those discussed for long-term-care insurance. Typical waiting periods range from 30 days to a year. If you have an adequate emergency fund to provide family income during the early months of disability, you can choose a longer waiting period and substantially reduce your premiums, as shown in Exhibit 9.5.

With most insurers, you can trade off an increase in the waiting period—say, from 60 days to 90 days—for an increase in the duration of benefits from five years to age 65. In fact, as Exhibit 9.5 shows, the premium charged by this insurer for a

---

EXHIBIT 9.5 **Representative Disability Income Insurance Premium Costs**

The cost of disability income insurance varies with the terms of payment as well as the length of the waiting period. Women pay substantially higher rates than men do. This table shows representative premiums for basic disability income coverage for a 35-year-old that pays $2,000 per month in benefits, with guaranteed premiums to age 65. The policy also includes a 3 percent inflation rider.

Benefit Period	2 Years		5 Years		10 Years		To Age 65	
Waiting Period	Male	Female	Male	Female	Male	Female	Male	Female
60 days	$378	$486	$546	$740	$731	$1,122	$974	$1,575
90 days	294	357	412	532	552	828	747	1,189
6 months	269	317	393	487	519	758	713	1,136
One year	N/A	N/A	361	441	488	720	689	1,084

policy covering a 35-year-old male with a 60-day waiting period and two-year benefit period ($378) is about the same as one charged for a five-year benefit period with a six-month waiting period ($393). Accepting this type of trade-off usually makes sense because the primary purpose of insurance is to protect the insured against a catastrophic loss, not from smaller losses that are better handled through proper budgeting and saving.

Renewability

Most individual disability income insurance is either *guaranteed renewable* or *noncancelable*. As with long-term-care policies, guaranteed renewability ensures that you can renew the policy until you reach the age stated in the clause, usually age 65. Premiums can be raised over time if justified by the loss experience of all those in the same class (usually based on age, sex, and occupational category). Noncancelable policies offer guaranteed renewability, but they also guarantee that future premiums will remain the same as those stated in the policy at issuance. Because of this stable premium guarantee, noncancelable policies generally are more expensive than those with only a guaranteed renewability provision.

Other Provisions

The purchasing power of income from a long-term disability policy that pays, say, $2,000 per month could be severely affected by inflation. In fact, a 3 percent inflation rate would reduce the purchasing power of this $2,000 benefit to less than $1,500 in 10 years. To counteract such a reduction, many insurers offer a *cost-of-living adjustment (COLA)*. With a COLA provision, the monthly benefit is adjusted upward each year, often in line with the CPI, although these annual adjustments are often capped at a given rate (say, 8 percent). Although some financial advisors suggest buying COLA riders, others feel the 10 percent to 25 percent additional premium is too much to pay for it.

Although the COLA provision applies only once the insured is disabled, the *guaranteed insurability option (GIO)* can allow you to purchase additional disability income insurance in line with inflation increases while you're still healthy. Under the GIO, the price of this additional insurance is fixed at the contract's inception, and you don't have to prove insurability.

A *waiver of premium* is standard in disability income policies. If you're disabled for a minimum period, normally 60 or 90 days, then the insurer will waive any future premiums that come due while you remain disabled. In essence, the waiver of premium gives you additional disability income insurance in the amount of your regular premium payment.

Remember that disability income insurance is just one part of your overall personal financial plan. You'll need to find your own balance between cost and coverage.

TEST YOURSELF

9-23 What is disability income insurance? Explain the waiting-period provisions found in such policies.

9-24 Describe both the liberal and strict definitions used to establish whether an insured is disabled.

9-25 Why is it important to consider benefit duration when shopping for disability income coverage?

Planning Over a Lifetime: *Insuring Your Health*

Here are some key ideas concerning how insuring your health changes over the stages in the life cycle.

Independent Lifestyle (20s)	Family and Career Development (30s–40s)	Mature Lifestyle (50s–60s)	Retirement (65+)
✓ Assess your health and take steps to stay healthy: exercise, eat well, and avoid smoking and too much alcohol.	✓ Consider HMOs and PPOs to lower deductibles and to maximize flexibility of choices.	✓ Evaluate the need for long-term-care insurance.	✓ Consider the best way to get prescription benefits in light of Medicare options.
✓ While in school or unemployed, take advantage of your opportunity to stay on your parents' health insurance until the age of 26.	✓ Re-evaluate the need for disability income insurance.	✓ Re-evaluate the need for long-term-care insurance.	✓ Re-evaluate the need for long-term-care insurance.
✓ When employed, take out health care insurance coverage with your employer and/or check out policies available on an ACA insurance exchange.	✓ Re-evaluate your health insurance policy and its premiums.	✓ Familiarize yourself with Medicare benefits.	
✓ Evaluate the appropriateness of disability income insurance.			
✓ Consider pre-tax accounts like flexibility spending to save money.			

Financial Impact of Personal Choices
Josh Expands His Health Insurance Coverage

Josh Wallace is 27 years old. He works for a company with a good comprehensive major medical health insurance plan. Indeed, Josh has heard it's priced better than most plans and has consequently taken out the optional expanded dental and vision plans. While he doesn't currently wear glasses or contact lenses, he does go for an annual eye exam and wants the extra vision plan in case he ends up needing corrective lens or has any eye problems. His plan has a $40 co-payment for an annual eye exam and pays $100 toward eye glass frames plus 20 percent of the rest of the cost. Contact lenses have similar coverage. Josh pays just an additional $15 monthly premium for the vision plan. Josh feels more comfortable having expanded health insurance coverage.

While Josh feels better having expanded health insurance coverage in general and vision coverage in particular, it isn't currently a cost effective decision. Josh makes a $40 co-payment for an annual eye exam, which is probably cheaper than the full cost of an eye exam. But he doesn't wear glasses or contact lenses. His $15 monthly premium costs him $180 per year. It's extremely unlikely that he saves anywhere near that much on the cost of his exam under the vision plan. And if Josh has a significant medical problem with his eyes, his major medical insurance plan should cover the costs well. It could make sense for him to have such expanded vision coverage in the future if corrective lenses are needed. So it appears that Josh's comfort over having expanded vision coverage is costly.

Summary

LG1 **Discuss why having adequate health insurance is important and identify the factors contributing to the growing cost of health insurance. p. 341**
A serious illness or major injury can have devastating financial consequences, easily costing tens of thousands of dollars in medical care and lost income. Even routine medical care can be costly. Adequate health insurance protects you from having to pay all of these costs out of pocket. However, many Americans are uninsured or underinsured because the cost of health insurance has skyrocketed. Trends pushing medical expenses and health insurance higher include the growth of new drugs and treatments that save lives but also cost more to provide. Administrative costs, excessive paperwork, increased regulation, and insurance fraud are also contributing to rising costs.

LG2 **Differentiate among the major types of health insurance plans and identify major private and public health insurance providers and their programs. p. 343**
Health insurance is available from both private and government-sponsored programs. Private health insurance plans include indemnity (fee-for-service) plans and managed care plans. Indemnity plans pay a share of health care costs directly to a medical provider, who is usually separate from the insurer. The insured pays the remaining amount. In a managed care plan, subscribers contract with and make monthly payments directly to the organization providing the health services. Examples of managed care plans include health maintenance organizations (HMOs) and preferred provider organizations (PPOs). Blue Cross/Blue Shield plans are prepaid hospital and medical expense plans. Federal and state agencies also provide health insurance coverage to eligible individuals. Medicare, Medicaid, and workers' compensation insurance are all forms of government health insurance plans.

LG3 **Analyze your own health insurance needs and explain how to shop for appropriate coverage. p. 351**
From a health insurance perspective, most people need protection from two types of losses: (1) the cost of medical bills and other associated expenses, and (2) loss of income or household services caused by an inability to work. A good

health care plan should use risk avoidance, loss prevention and control, and risk assumption strategies to reduce risk and the associated need and cost of insurance. The best way to buy health insurance is to determine your current coverage and resources and then match your needs with the various types of coverage available. When shopping for health insurance, consider the cost of coverage, its availability as an employee benefit, the quality of both the agent and the insurer or managed care provider, and your own medical needs and care preferences.

LG4 **Explain the basic types of medical expenses covered by and the policy provisions of health insurance plans. p. 355**
The basic types of medical expenses covered by insurance are hospitalization, surgical expenses, physician expenses (nonsurgical medical care), and major medical insurance (which covers all types of medical expenses). Some health insurers offer comprehensive major medical policies that combine basic hospitalization, surgical, and physician expense coverage with a major medical plan to form a single policy.

The most important provisions in medical insurance policies pertain to terms of payment, terms of coverage, and cost containment. How much your plan will pay depends on deductibles, participation (co-insurance), internal limits, and coordination of benefits. Terms of coverage encompass the persons and places covered, cancellation, pregnancy and abortion, mental illness, rehabilitation, and group coverage continuation. The most common cost containment provisions are preadmission certification, continued stay review, second surgical opinions, waiver of co-insurance, and limitations of insurer's responsibility.

LG5 **Assess the need for and features of long-term-care insurance. p. 363**
Long-term-care insurance covers nonhospital expenses, such as nursing home care or home health care, caused by chronic illness or frailty. Coverage availability depends on provisions addressing type of care, eligibility requirements, services covered, renewability, and preexisting conditions. Terms-of-payment provisions include daily benefits, benefit duration, waiting period, and inflation protection. Premium levels result from differences in coverage and payment provisions, and they vary widely among insurance companies.

LG6 **Discuss the features of disability income insurance and how to determine your need for it. p. 368**
The loss of family income caused by the disability of a principal wage earner can be at least partially replaced by disability income insurance. Disability insurance needs can be estimated by subtracting the amount of existing monthly disability benefits from current monthly take-home pay. Important coverage terms include the definition of disability, probationary period, renewability, guaranteed insurability, and waiver of premium. Provisions pertaining to benefit amount and duration, waiting period, and cost-of-living adjustments define the terms of payment. Because these policies are expensive, you should choose as long a waiting period as possible given your other available financial resources.

Key Terms

Answers to Test Yourself

You can find answers to these questions on this book's companion website. Look for it at *www. cengagebrain.com*. Search for this book by its title, and then add it to your dashboard.

Financial Planning Exercises

LG2, 3, 4
p. 343, 351, 355

1. ***Choosing a health insurance plan.*** Joe and Whitney Alexander have two children, with ages of 6 years and 5 months. Their younger child, Nathan, was born with a congenital heart defect that will require several major surgeries in the next few years to correct fully. Joe is employed as a salesperson for a major pharmaceutical firm, and Whitney does not work outside the home. Joe's employer offers employees a choice between two health benefit plans:

   - A plan that allows the Alexanders to choose health services from a wide range of doctors and hospitals. The plan pays 80 percent of all medical costs, and the Alexanders are responsible for the other 20 percent. There's a deductible of $500 per person. Joe's employer will pay 100 percent of the cost of this plan for Joe, but the Alexanders will be responsible for paying $380 a month to cover Whitney and the children under this plan.
   - A group HMO. If the Alexanders choose this plan, the company still pays 100 percent of the plan's cost for Joe, but insurance for Whitney and the children will cost $295 a month. They'll also have to make a $20 co-payment for any doctor's office visits and prescription drugs. They will be restricted to using the HMO's doctors and hospital for medical services. Which plan would you recommend that the Alexanders choose? Why? What other health coverage options should the Alexanders consider?

LG2, 3, 4
p. 343, 351, 355

2. ***Out-of-pocket plan costs.*** John Chang was seriously injured in a snowboarding accident that broke both his legs and an arm. His medical expenses included five days of hospitalization at $900 a day, $6,200 in surgical fees, $4,300 in physician's fees (including time in the hospital and eight follow-up office visits), $520 in prescription medications, and $2,100 for physical therapy treatments. All of these charges fall within customary and reasonable payment amounts.
   a. If John had an indemnity plan that pays 80 percent of his charges with a $500 deductible and a $5,000 stop-loss provision, how much would he have to pay out of pocket?
   b. What would John's out-of-pocket expenses be if he belonged to an HMO with a $20 co-pay for office visits?
   c. Monthly premiums are $155 for the indemnity plan and $250 for the HMO. If he had no other medical expenses this year, which plan would have provided more cost-effective coverage for John? What other factors should be considered when deciding between the two plans?

LG2, 3, 4
p. 343, 351, 355

3. ***Comparing health insurance policies. Use Worksheet 9.1.*** Erika Willis, a recent college graduate, has decided to accept a job offer from a nonprofit organization. She'll earn $40,000 a year but will receive no employee health benefits. Erika estimates that her monthly living expenses will be about $2,000 a month, including rent, food, transportation, and clothing. She has no health problems and expects to remain in good health in the near future. Using the Internet or other

resources, gather information about three health insurance policies that Erika could purchase on her own. Use Worksheet 9.1 to compare the policies' features. Which of the three policies would you recommend Erika buy, and why?

LG5 p. 363

4. ***Pros and cons of long-term care insurance.*** Discuss the pros and cons of long-term care insurance. Does it make sense for anyone in your family right now? Why or why not? What factors might change this assessment in the future?

LG6 p. 368

5. ***Calculating need for disability income insurance. Use Worksheet 9.2.*** Ben West, a 35-year-old computer programmer, earns $72,000 a year. His monthly take-home pay is $3,750. His wife, Ashley, works part-time at their children's elementary school but receives no benefits. Under state law, Ashley's employer contributes to a workers' compensation insurance fund that would provide $2,250 per month for six months if Ben were disabled and unable to work.
   a. Use Worksheet 9.2 to calculate Ben's disability insurance needs, assuming that he won't qualify for Medicare under his Social Security benefits.
   b. Based on your answer in part **a**, what would you advise Ben about his need for additional disability income insurance? Discuss the type and size of disability income insurance coverage he should consider, including possible provisions he might want to include. What other factors should he take into account if he decides to purchase a policy?

LG6 p. 368

6. ***Calculating your need for disability income insurance. Use Worksheet 9.2.*** Do you need disability income insurance? Calculate your need using Worksheet 9.2. Discuss how you'd go about purchasing this coverage.

LG1, 2, 3, 4 p. 341, 343, 351, 355

7. ***Assess your health insurance situation.*** Do you have any health insurance now? What does your policy cover? What is excluded? Are there any gaps that you think need to be filled? Are there any risks in your current lifestyle or situation that might make additional coverage necessary? If you were to purchase health insurance for yourself in the near future, what type of plan would you select, and why? What steps can you take to keep your health costs down?

Applying Personal Finance

Insure Your Health!

Health care costs have increased dramatically in recent years, and many insurance providers have reduced their coverage, leaving the individual to foot more of the bill. In this project, you'll examine your health insurance needs and determine the coverage that's appropriate for you.

First, make a list of the possible health care needs you're likely to have during the year. Be sure to include the potential accident risks to which you're typically exposed in pursuit of your lifestyle activities. Then, if you currently have health insurance, make a list of the coverage it provides, including deductibles, co-insurance amounts, prescription coverage, policy limits and exclusions, and so forth. Is your coverage adequate in light of your needs? Are there ways you can reduce your costs? If you don't currently have health insurance, research possible providers. Can you obtain insurance through your university, place of employment, or through an organization to which you belong? What options are available to you on an ACA insurance exchange? Consider all of your feasible alternatives, the coverages that would be provided, and the cost of each.

CRITICAL THINKING CASES

LG2, 3, 4, 5, 6 p. 343, 351, 355, 363, 368

9.1 Evaluating Walter's Health Care Coverage

Walter Burton was a self-employed window washer earning approximately $700 per week. One day, while cleaning windows on the eighth floor of the Commercial Bank Building, he tripped and fell from the scaffolding to the pavement below. He sustained severe multiple injuries but miraculously survived the accident. He was immediately rushed to the local hospital for surgery. He remained there for 60 days of treatment, after which he was allowed to go home for further recuperation. During his hospital stay, he incurred the following expenses: surgeon, $2,500; physician, $1,000; hospital bill for room and board, $250 per day; nursing services, $1,200; anesthetics, $600; wheelchair rental, $100; ambulance, $150; and drugs, $350. Walter has a major medical policy that has a $3,000 deductible clause, an 80 percent co-insurance clause, internal limits of $180 per day on hospital room and board, and $1,500 as a maximum surgical fee. The policy provides no disability income benefits.

Critical Thinking Questions

1. Explain the policy provisions as they relate to deductibles, co-insurance, and internal limits.
2. How much should Walter recover from the insurance company? How much must he pay out of his own pocket?
3. Would any other policies have offered Walter additional protection? What about his inability to work while recovering from his injury?
4. Based on the information presented, how would you assess Walter's health care insurance coverage? Explain.

LG5 p. 363

9.2 Luis and Dora Barillas Evaluate Their Disability Income Needs

Luis Barillas and his wife, Dora, have been married for two years and have a 1-year-old son. They live in Charlotte, North Carolina, where Luis works for Advanced Marketing Analytics. He earns $3,200 per month, of which he takes home $2,300. Luis and his family are entitled to receive the benefits provided by the company's group health insurance policy. In addition to major medical coverage, the policy provides a monthly disability income benefit amounting to 20 percent of the employee's average monthly take-home pay for the most recent 12 months prior to incurring the disability. (*Note:* Luis' average monthly take-home pay for the most recent year is equal to his current monthly take-home pay.) In case of complete disability, Luis would also be eligible for Social Security payments of $700 per month.

Dora is also employed. She earns $700 per month after taxes by working part-time at a nearby grocery store. As a part-time employee, the store gives her no benefits. Should Luis become disabled, Dora would continue to work at her part-time job. If she became disabled, Social Security would provide monthly income of $400. Luis and Dora spend 90 percent of their combined take-home pay to meet their bills and provide for a variety of necessary items. They use the remaining 10 percent to fulfill their entertainment and savings goals.

Critical Thinking Questions

1. How much, if any, additional disability income insurance does Luis require to ensure adequate protection against his becoming completely disabled? Use Worksheet 9.2 to assess his needs.
2. Does Dora need any disability income coverage? Explain.
3. What specific recommendations regarding disability income insurance would you give Luis and Dora to provide adequate protection for themselves and their child?

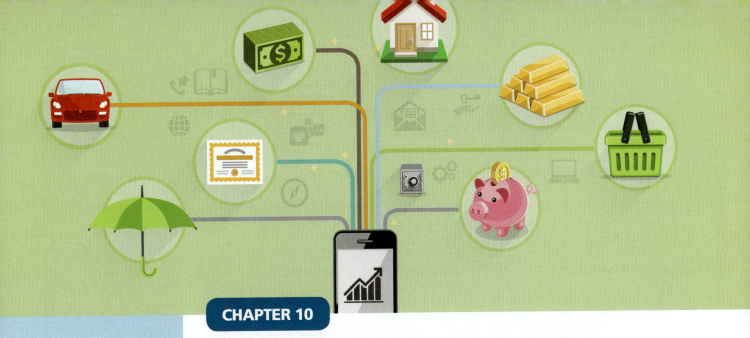

CHAPTER 10

Protecting Your Property

LEARNING GOALS

LG1 Discuss the importance and basic principles of property insurance, including types of exposure, indemnity, and co-insurance.

LG2 Identify the types of coverage provided by homeowner's insurance.

LG3 Select the right homeowner's insurance policy for your needs.

LG4 Analyze the coverage in a personal automobile policy (PAP) and choose the most cost-effective policy.

LG5 Describe other types of property and liability insurance.

LG6 Choose a property and liability insurance agent and company, and settle claims.

How Will This Affect Me?

The chapter explains the key property insurance concepts of indemnity, subrogation, and co-insurance. It then describes the common sources of property and liability risk exposures and the insurance coverage available to address them. The main characteristics of homeowner's and auto insurance are covered, as well as how to choose the version of each policy type that's best for you. Supplemental insurance to protect against floods and earthquakes and personal liability umbrella policies are also described. Especially practical tips can be found in the discussions of how to choose an insurance agent and how to settle property and liability insurance claims. When you finish this chapter, you should understand the best and most cost-effective ways to use insurance to protect your property and associated liability exposures.

10-1 BASIC PRINCIPLES OF PROPERTY INSURANCE

LG1 Suppose that a severe storm destroyed your home. Could you afford to replace it? Most people couldn't. To protect yourself from this and other similar types of property loss, you need property insurance. What's more, every day you face some type of risk of negligence. For example, you might be distraught over a personal problem and unintentionally run a red light, seriously injuring a pedestrian. Could you pay for the medical and other costs? Because consequences like this and other potentially negligent acts could cause financial ruin, having appropriate liability insurance is essential.

Property and liability insurance should be as much a part of your personal financial plans as life and health insurance. Such coverage protects the assets you've already acquired and safeguards your progress toward financial goals. **Property insurance** guards against catastrophic losses of real and personal property caused by such perils as fire, theft, vandalism, windstorms, and other calamities. **Liability insurance** offers protection against the financial consequences that may arise from the insured's responsibility for property loss or personal injuries to others.

People spend lots of money for insurance coverage, but few really understand what they're getting for their premium dollars. The vast majority of people consequently are totally unaware of any gaps, overinsurance, or underinsurance in their property and liability insurance policies. Ineffective insurance protection is at odds with the objectives of personal financial planning. It is thus important to become familiar with the principles of property and liability insurance. The basic principles of property and liability insurance pertain to types of exposure, indemnity, and co-insurance. We'll discuss each of these principles in the following sections.

property insurance
Insurance coverage that protects real and personal property from catastrophic losses caused by a variety of perils, such as fire, theft, vandalism, and windstorms.

liability insurance
Insurance that protects against the financial consequences that may arise from the insured's responsibility for property loss or injuries to others.

10-1a Types of Exposure

Most individuals face two types of exposure: physical loss of property and loss through liability.

Exposure to Property Loss

peril
A cause of loss.

Most property insurance contracts define the property covered and name the **perils**—the causes of loss—for which the insured will be compensated in case of a claim against their policy. As a rule, most property insurance contracts impose two obligations on the property owner: (1) developing a complete inventory of the property being insured; and (2) identifying the perils against which protection is desired. Some property contracts limit coverage by excluding certain types of property and perils, while others offer more comprehensive protection.

Property Inventory. Taking inventory of property is part of the financial planning process. It is especially important in the case of a total loss—if your home is destroyed by fire, for example. All property insurance companies require you to show *proof of loss* when making a claim. Your personal property inventory, along with corresponding values at the time of inventory, can serve as evidence to satisfy the company. A comprehensive property inventory not only helps you settle a claim when a loss occurs, but also serves as a useful guide for selecting the most appropriate coverage for your particular needs.

Most families have a home, household furnishings, clothing and personal belongings, lawn and garden equipment, and motor vehicles, all of which need to be insured. Fortunately, most homeowner's and automobile insurance policies provide coverage for these types of belongings. But many families also own such items as motorboats and trailers, various types of off-road vehicles, business property and inventories, jewelry, stamp or coin collections, musical instruments, guns, antiques, paintings, bonds, securities, and other items of special value, such as cameras, golf clubs, electronic equipment, and personal computers. Coverage for these belongings (and those that accompany you when you travel) often require special types of insurance.

Many insurance companies have easy-to-complete personal property inventory forms available to help policyholders prepare inventories. A partial sample of one such form is shown in Exhibit 10.1. These inventory forms can be supplemented with photographs or videos of household contents and belongings. For insurance purposes, a picture may truly be worth a thousand words. Regardless of whether inventory forms are supplemented with photographs or videotapes, *every effort should be made to keep these documents in a safe place*, where they can't be destroyed—such as a bank safe-deposit box. Also consider keeping a *duplicate copy* with a parent or trusted relative. Remember, you may need these photographs and inventories if something serious does happen and you have to come up with an authenticated list of property losses.

Identifying Perils. Many people feel a false sense of security after buying insurance because they believe they're safeguarded against all contingencies. However, certain *perils* cannot be reasonably insured. For example, most homeowner's or automobile insurance policies limit or exclude damage or loss caused by flood (remember Hurricane Katrina in New Orleans in 2005), earthquake, backing up of sewers and drains, mudslides, mysterious disappearance, war, nuclear radiation, and ordinary wear and tear. In addition, property insurance contracts routinely limit coverage based on the location of the property, time of loss, persons involved, and types of hazards to which the property is exposed.

Liability Exposures

We all encounter a variety of liability exposures daily. Driving a car, entertaining guests at home, volunteer activities, or being careless in performing professional duties are some common liability risks. Loss exposures result from negligence, which is failing to act in a reasonable manner or take necessary steps to protect others from harm. Even if you're never negligent and always prudent, someone might *believe* that you are the cause of a loss and bring a costly lawsuit against you. Losing the judgment could cost you thousands—or even millions—of dollars. A debt that size could force you into bankruptcy or financial ruin.

negligence
Failing to act in a reasonable manner or to take necessary steps to protect others from harm.

EXHIBIT 10.1 **A Personal Property Inventory Form**

Using a form like this will help you keep track of your personal property, including date of purchase, original purchase price, and replacement cost.

Living Room

Stereo System

Brand	
Model	
Serial #	Date purchased
Purchase price $	Replacement cost $

Large-Screen TV

Brand	
Model	
Serial #	Date purchased
Purchase price $	Replacement cost $

Personal Computer

Brand	
Model	
Serial #	Date purchased
Purchase price $	Replacement cost $

Home Theater System

Brand	
Model	
Serial #	Date purchased
Purchase price $	Replacement cost $

DVD Player

Brand	
Model	
Serial #	Date purchased
Purchase price $	Replacement cost $

Living Room

Article	Qty.	Date Purchased	Purchase Price	Replacement Cost
Air conditioners (window)				
Blinds/shades				
Bookcases				
Books				
Cabinets				
Carpets/rugs				
Chairs				
Chests				
Clocks				
Couches/sofas				
Curtains/draperies				
Fireplace fixtures				
Lamps/lighting fixtures				
Mirrors				
Pictures/paintings				
Audio recordings				
Planters				
Stereo equipment				
Tables				
Television sets				
Other				
Other				

Fortunately, *liability insurance* coverage will protect you against losses resulting from these risks, *including the high legal fees* required to defend yourself against suits that may, or may not, have merit. It's important to include adequate liability insurance in your overall insurance program, either through your homeowner's and automobile policies or through a separate umbrella policy.

10-1b Principle of Indemnity

principle of indemnity
An insurance principle stating that an insured may not be compensated by the insurance company in an amount exceeding the insured's economic loss.

The **principle of indemnity** states that the insured may not be compensated by the insurance company in an amount exceeding the insured's economic loss. Most property and liability insurance contracts are based on this principle—although, as noted in Chapters 8 and 9, this *principle does not apply to life and health insurance*. Several important concepts related to the principle of indemnity include actual cash value, subrogation, and other insurance.

Actual Cash Value versus Replacement Cost

actual cash value
A value assigned to an insured property that is determined by subtracting the amount of physical depreciation from its replacement cost.

The principle of indemnity limits the amount that an insured may collect to the **actual cash value** of the property: the replacement cost minus the value of physical depreciation. Some insurers pay replacement cost without taking depreciation into account—for example, most homeowner's policies will settle building losses on a replacement cost basis if the proper type and amount of insurance is purchased. Without a replacement-cost provision, it's common practice to deduct the amount of depreciation to obtain the actual cash value. If an insured property is damaged, then the insurer is obligated to pay no more than the property would cost new today (its replacement cost) less the amount of depreciation from wear and tear.

> **EXAMPLE: Recovery of Replacement Cost**
>
> A fire has destroyed two rooms of furniture that were 6 years old with an estimated useful life of 10 years. The replacement cost is $5,000. At the time of loss, the furniture was subject to an assumed physical depreciation of 60 percent (6 years ÷ 10 years)—in this case, $3,000. Because the actual cash value is estimated at $2,000 ($5,000 replacement cost minus $3,000 of depreciation), the maximum that the insurer would have to pay is $2,000. Importantly, the original cost of the property has no bearing on the settlement.

Subrogation

right of subrogation
The right of an insurer, who has paid an insured's claim, to request reimbursement from either the person who caused the loss or that person's insurer.

After an insurance company pays a claim, its **right of subrogation** allows it to request reimbursement from either the person who caused the loss or that person's insurance company. For example, assume you're in an automobile accident in which the other party damages your car. You may collect from your insurer or the at-fault party's insurer, but not from both (not for the same loss). Clearly, to collect the full amount of the loss from both parties would leave you better off after the loss than before it. However, this violates the principle of indemnity. Because the party who caused the accident (or loss) is ultimately responsible for paying the damages, your insurance company can go after the responsible party to collect its loss, which is the amount it paid out to you.

Other Insurance

Nearly all property and liability insurance contracts have an *other-insurance clause*, prohibiting insured persons from insuring their property with two or more insurance companies and collecting from multiple companies for the same loss. The other-insurance clause normally states that if a person has more than one insurance policy on a property, then each company need only pay an amount prorated for its share of all insurance covering the property. Without this provision, insured persons could use duplicate property insurance policies to profit from their losses.

10-1c Co-insurance

co-insurance
In property insurance, a provision requiring a policyholder to buy insurance of an amount equal to a specified percentage of the replacement value of their property.

Co-insurance, a provision commonly found in property insurance contracts, requires policyholders to buy insurance in an amount equal to a specified percentage of the replacement value of their property, or else the *policyholder* is required to pay for a proportional share of the loss. In essence, the co-insurance provision stipulates that if a property isn't sufficiently covered, the property owner will become the "co-insurer" and bear part of the loss. If the policyholder has the stipulated amount of coverage (usually 80 percent of the value of the property), then the insurance company will reimburse for covered losses, dollar-for-dollar, up to the amount of the policy limits.

Obviously, you should evaluate closely the co-insurance clause of any property insurance policy so you won't have an unexpected additional burden in the case of a loss.

> **EXAMPLE: Effect of Co-insurance**
>
> Joel and Anna have a fire insurance policy on their $300,000 home with an 80 percent co-insurance clause. The policy limits must equal or exceed 80 percent of the replacement value of their home. They ran short of money and decided to save by buying a $180,000 policy instead of $240,000 (80 percent of $300,000), as required by the co-insurance clause. If a loss occurs, then the company would be obligated to pay only 75 percent (180,000/240,000) of the loss, up to the amount of the policy limit. Thus, on damages of $40,000, the insurer would pay only $30,000 (75 percent of $40,000).

TEST YOURSELF

10-1 Briefly explain the fundamental concepts related to property and liability insurance.

10-2 Explain the principle of indemnity. Are any limits imposed on the amount that an insured may collect under this principle?

10-3 Explain the right of subrogation. How does this feature help lower insurance costs?

10-4 Describe how the co-insurance feature works.

10-2 HOMEOWNER'S INSURANCE

LG2, LG3

Although homeowner's insurance is often thought of as a single type of insurance policy, homeowners can choose from five different forms (HO-1, HO-2, HO-3, HO-5, and HO-8). Two other forms (HO-4 and HO-6) meet the needs of renters and owners of condominiums (see Exhibit 10.2). An HO-4 renter's policy offers essentially the same broad protection as an HO-2 homeowner's policy, but the coverage doesn't apply to the rented dwelling unit because tenants usually don't have a financial interest in the real property.

All HO forms are divided into two sections. Section I applies to the dwelling, accompanying structures, and personal property of the insured. Section II deals with comprehensive coverage for personal liability and for medical payments to others. The scope of coverage under Section I is least with an HO-1 policy and greatest with an HO-5 policy. HO-8 is a modified coverage policy for older homes, which is used to insure houses that have market values well below the cost to rebuild. The coverage in Section II is the same for all forms.

In the following paragraphs, we'll explain the important features of homeowner's forms HO-3 and HO-5, the most commonly sold policies. (As Exhibit 10.2 shows, HO-1 is a basic, seldom-used policy with relatively narrow coverage.) The coverage offered under the HO-3 and HO-5 forms is basically the same; the differences lie only in the number of perils against which protection applies to the personal property coverage.

comprehensive policy Property and liability insurance policy covering all perils unless they are specifically excluded.

named peril policy Property and liability insurance policy that individually names the perils covered.

10-2a Perils Covered

Some property and liability insurance agreements, called **comprehensive policies**, cover all perils except those specifically excluded, whereas **named peril policies** name particular, individual perils covered.

MELISSA BRANDES/SHUTTERSTOCK.COM

Section I Perils

The perils against which the home and its contents are insured are shown in Exhibit 10.2. Coverage on the dwelling is the same for the HO-3 and HO-5 forms, but coverage on the house itself and other structures (e.g., a detached garage) is comprehensive under HO-5 and a named peril in HO-3. An HO-5 provides comprehensive coverage on the personal property, where an HO-3 covers only named perils. Whether homeowners should buy an HO-3 or an HO-5 form depends primarily on how much they're willing to spend to secure the additional protection. The size of premiums for HO-3 and HO-5 policies can differ substantially among insurance companies. In some states, an HO-5 policy is the better buy because the premium differential is small. In other states, the HO-3 form has a much lower premium. Buying an HO-1 or HO-2 policy is not recommended because of its more limited coverage.

Note in Exhibit 10.2 that the types of Section I perils covered include just about every situation, from fire and explosions to lightning and wind damage to theft and vandalism. Although the list of perils is extensive, some are specifically excluded from most homeowner's contracts—in particular, *most policies (even HO-5 and HO-3 forms) exclude earthquakes and floods*. Many areas of the country are not susceptible to earthquakes and floods, and homeowners in those areas shouldn't have to pay premiums for coverage that they don't need. But even if you live in an area where the risk of an earthquake or a flood is relatively high, you'll find that *standard homeowner's policies do not provide protection against these perils* because the catastrophic nature of such events causes widespread and costly damage. As we'll see later in this chapter, you can obtain coverage for earthquakes and floods under a separate policy or a rider.

Section II Perils

The perils insured against under Section II of the homeowner's contract are the (alleged) negligence of an insured. The coverage is called *comprehensive personal liability coverage* because it offers protection against personal liability (major exclusions are noted later) resulting from negligence. It does not insure against other losses for which one may become liable, such as libel, slander, defamation of character, and contractual or intentional wrongdoing. For example, coverage would apply if you unintentionally knocked someone down your stairs. If you purposely struck and injured another person, however, or harmed someone's reputation either orally or in writing, homeowner's liability coverage would not protect you.

Section II also provides a limited amount of medical coverage for persons other than the homeowner's family in certain types of minor accidents on or off the insured's premises. This coverage helps homeowners to meet their moral obligations and helps deter possible lawsuits. The limited medical payment coverage pays irrespective of negligence or fault.

10-2b Factors Affecting Home Insurance Costs

Several factors affect premiums for home and property insurance.

- **Type of structure:** Do you live in a home made from wood or brick? The construction materials used in your home affect the cost of insuring it. A home built from brick costs less to insure than a similar home made of wood, yet the reverse is true when it comes to earthquake insurance—brick homes are more expensive

EXHIBIT 10.2 **A Guide to Homeowner's Policies**

The amount of insurance coverage you receive depends on the type of homeowner's (HO) policy you buy. You can also obtain coverage if you're a renter or a condominium owner.

Form	Coverages*	Covered perils
Basic Form (HO-1)	A—$15,000 minimum; B—10% of A; C—50% of A; D—10% of A; E—$100,000; F—$1,000 per person	Fire, smoke, lightning, windstorm, hail, volcanic eruption, explosion, glass breakage, aircraft, vehicles, riot or civil commotion, theft, vandalism or malicious mischief
Broad Form (HO-2)	Minimum varies; other coverages in same percentages or amounts except D—20% of A	Covers all basic-form risks plus weight of ice, snow, sleet; freezing; accidental discharge of water or steam; falling objects; accidental tearing, cracking, or burning of heating/cooling/sprinkler system or appliance; damage from electrical current
Special Form (HO-3)	Minimum varies; other coverages in same percentages or amounts except D—20% of A	Dwelling and other structures covered against risks of direct physical loss to property except losses specifically excluded; personal property covered by same perils as HO-2 plus damage by glass or safety glazing material, which is part of a building, storm door, or storm window
Renter's Form (HO-4)	Coverages A and B—Not applicable C—Minimum varies by company D—20% of C E—$100,000 F—$1,000 per person	Covers same perils covered by HO-2 for personal property
Comprehensive Form (HO-5)	Coverages A and B—Not applicable B—Not applicable C—Minimum varies by company D—40% of C E—$100,000 F—$1,000 per person	Covers same perils as HO-4, but covered perils are dwelling, other structures, and personal property covered against risks of direct physical loss except losses that are excluded specifically
Condominium Form (HO-6)	Coverage A—Minimum $1,000 B—Not applicable C—Minimum varies by company D—40% of C E—$100,000 F—$1,000 per person	Covers same perils covered by HO-2 for personal property
Modified Coverage Form (HO-8)	Same as HO-1, except losses are paid based on the amount required to repair or replace the property using common construction materials and methods	Same perils as HO-1, except theft coverage applies to losses only on the residential premises up to a maximum of $1,000; certain other coverage restrictions also apply

*Coverages:
A. Dwelling
B. Other structures
C. Personal Property

D. Loss of use
E. Personal liability
F. Medical Payments to Others

to insure. The style and age of the house also contribute to its potential insurance risk, thereby affecting insurance costs.

- **Credit score:** Research shows that people with lower credit scores tend to file more insurance claims. Credit scores affect premiums more than any other factor. If you have a poor credit score, you may pay two or three times more than an otherwise comparable person with an excellent credit score. So if your credit score improves, it's important to let your insurance company know because this could lower your premiums.
- **Location of home:** Local crime rates, weather, and proximity to a fire hydrant all affect your home's insurance premium costs. If many claims are filed from your area, insurance premiums for all the homeowners there will be higher. The local frequency of hailstorms and hurricanes will affect rates too.
- **Other factors:** If you have a swimming pool, trampoline, large dog, or other potentially hazardous risk factors on your property, your homeowner's premiums will be higher. Deductibles and the type and amount of coverage also affect the cost.

You Can Do It Now

Check Out the Best Homeowners Insurance Companies

When you're considering buying new homeowners insurance, it's good to know how the various insurance companies are rated. A good Internet site is **http://www.consumeraffairs.com/insurance/home.html#buyers-guide**, which summarizes industry ratings by A.M. Best, Standard & Poors, and J.D. Power & Associates. **You can do it now.**

10-2c Property Covered

The homeowner's policy offers property protection under Section I for the dwelling unit, accompanying structures, and personal property of homeowners and their families. Coverage for certain types of loss also applies to lawns, trees, plants, and shrubs. However, the policy excludes structures on the premises used for business purposes (except incidentally), animals (pets or otherwise), and motorized vehicles not used in maintaining the premises (such as autos, motorcycles, golf carts, or snowmobiles). *Business inventory* (e.g., goods held by an insured who is a traveling salesperson, or other goods held for sale) is not covered. Although the policy doesn't cover business inventory, it does cover *business property* (such as books, computers, copiers, office furniture, and supplies), typically up to a maximum of $2,500, while it is on the insured premises.

If you work at home, either full- or part-time, then you may need to increase your policy's limits to protect your home office. This insurance is critical because damage to your home affects not only where you live, but also your source of income. In many cases, adding a rider to your homeowner's policy can increase your home business limits to adequate levels for your computer and office equipment and provide additional limited liability coverage. The cost for these riders is low, often as low as $75 per year, depending on what coverage you include. If you need greater protection, you should investigate a separate business owner's policy that offers broader coverage for business liability, all-risk protection for equipment, and business income protection if damage to your home results in lost income.

personal property floater (PPF)
An insurance endorsement or policy providing either blanket or scheduled coverage of expensive personal property not adequately covered in a standard homeowner's policy.

10-2d Personal Property Floater

As we'll see later in this chapter, policies limit the type and amount of coverage provided. Your homeowner's policy may not protect your expensive personal property adequately. To overcome this deficiency, you can either add the **personal property floater (PPF)** as an endorsement to your homeowner's policy or take out a separate floater policy. *The PPF provides either blanket or scheduled coverage of items that are not covered adequately in a standard homeowner's policy.*

A *blanket*, or *unscheduled*, *PPF* provides the maximum protection available for virtually all the insured's personal property. *Scheduled PPFs* list the items to be covered and provide supplemental coverage under a homeowner's contract. This coverage is especially useful for expensive property and it includes loss, damage, and theft. Some popular uses of PPFs are for furs, jewelry, personal computers and peripheral equipment, photographic equipment, silverware, fine art and antiques, collections.

EXAMPLE: Personal Property Floaters

Angela owns a diamond ring valued at $7,500. She should itemize it under a personal property floater because it's worth more than the standard $1,000 coverage C (discussed later) allowance for all jewelry stolen. Generally, insurance companies require appraisals to determine value before scheduling items.

Financial Fact or Fantasy?

Homeowner's insurance provides protection not only on the home itself but also most of its contents. **Fact:** Homeowner's insurance covers the home itself and most of the contents in it, including furniture, stereos and TVs, computers, and clothing. On the other hand, cars, motorcycles, golf carts, high value jewelry, and the like usually are not covered under a homeowner's policy.

10-2e Renter's Insurance: Don't Move In Without It

If you live in an apartment (or some other type of rental unit), be aware that although the building you live in is likely to be fully insured, *your furnishings and other personal belongings are not.* As a renter (or even the owner of a condominium unit), you need a special type of HO policy to obtain insurance coverage on your personal possessions.

Consider, for example, Sally Caldwell's predicament. She never got around to insuring her personal possessions in the apartment that she rented in Chicago. One wintry night, a water pipe ruptured, and the escaping water damaged her furniture, rugs, and other belongings. When the building owner refused to pay for the loss, Sally hauled him into court—and lost. Why did she lose her case? Simple: *Unless a landlord can be proven negligent—and this one wasn't—he or she isn't responsible for a tenant's property.* The moral of this story is clear: once you've accumulated valuable personal belongings (from clothing and home furnishings to stereo equipment, TVs, computers, and video players), make sure that they're covered adequately by insurance, even if you're only renting a place to live! Otherwise, you could risk losing everything you own.

Apparently many tenants don't realize this, because surveys show that most of them aren't insured, even though renter's insurance is available at reasonable rates. The policy, called Renter's Form HO-4, is a scaled-down version of homeowner's insurance. It covers the contents of a house, apartment, or cooperative unit, but not the structure itself. Owners of condominium units need Form HO-6; it's similar, but it includes a minimum of $1,000 in protection for any building alterations, additions, and decorations paid for by the policyholder. Like regular homeowner's insurance, HO-4 and HO-6 policies include liability coverage and protect you at home and away. For example, if somebody is injured and sues you, the policy would pay for damages up to a specified limit, generally $100,000, although some insurers go as high as $500,000.

A standard renter's insurance policy covers furniture, carpets, appliances, clothing, and most other personal items for their cash value at the time of loss. Expect to pay around $150 to $250 a year for about $30,000 in personal property coverage and $100,000 in liability coverage, depending on where you live. For maximum protection, you can buy *replacement-cost insurance* (discussed again later in this chapter), which pays the actual cost of replacing articles with comparable ones, though some policies limit the payout to four times the cash value. You'll pay more

for this—perhaps as little as another 10 percent, but perhaps much more—depending on the insurer. Also, the standard renter's policy provides limited coverage of such valuables as jewelry, furs, and silverware. Coverage varies, although some insurers pay up to $1,000 for the loss of watches, gems, and furs and up to $2,500 for silverware. For larger amounts, you need an endorsement or a separate PPF policy, as discussed previously.

Renter's insurance pays for losses caused by fire or lightning, explosion, windstorms, hail, theft, civil commotion, aircraft, vehicles, smoke, vandalism and malicious mischief, falling objects, building collapse, and the weight of ice and snow. Certain damages caused by water, steam, electricity, appliances, and frozen pipes are covered as well. Plus, if your residence can't be occupied because of damage from any of those perils, the insurer will pay for any increase in living expenses resulting from staying at a hotel and eating in restaurants. The liability coverage also pays for damages and legal costs arising from injuries or damage caused by you, a member of your family, or a pet—either on or off your premises.

10-2f Coverage: What Type, Who, and Where?

We've discussed what types of property are covered by a homeowner's policy. These policies also define the types of losses that they cover and the persons and locations covered.

Types of Losses Covered

There are three types of property-related losses when misfortune occurs:

1. Direct loss of property
2. Indirect loss occurring due to loss of damaged property
3. Additional expenses resulting from direct and indirect losses

Homeowner's insurance contracts offer compensation for each type of loss.

Section I Coverage. When a house is damaged by an insured peril, the insurance company will pay reasonable living expenses that a family might incur. One such covered expense would be the cost of renting alternative accommodations while the insured's home is being repaired or rebuilt. Also, in many instances, the insurer will pay for damages caused by perils other than those mentioned in the policy if a named peril is determined to be the underlying cause of the loss. Assume, for instance, that lightning (a covered peril) strikes a house while a family is away and knocks out the power, causing $400 worth of food in the freezer and refrigerator to spoil. Insurance will pay for the loss even though temperature change (the direct cause) is not mentioned in the policy.

Section II Coverage. Besides paying successfully pursued liability claims against an insured, a homeowner's policy includes coverage for (1) the cost of defending the insured, (2) reasonable expenses incurred by an insured in helping the insurance company's defense, and (3) the payment of court costs. Because these costs apply even when the liability suit is found to be without merit, this coverage can save you thousands of dollars in attorney fees.

Persons Covered

A homeowner's policy covers the persons named in the policy and members of their families who are residents of the household. A person can be a resident of the household even while temporarily living away from home. For example, college students who live at school part of the year and at home during vacations are normally classified as household residents. Their parents' homeowner's policy may cover their belongings at school—including such items as stereo equipment, TVs, personal computers, and microwave ovens. But there could be limits and exceptions to the coverage, so check the policy to find out what's covered. For example, some companies may consider students living off-campus to be independent and therefore ineligible for coverage under their parents' insurance. The standard homeowner's contract also extends limited coverage to guests of the insured.

Locations Covered

Most homeowner's policies offer coverage worldwide. Consequently, an insured's personal property is fully covered even if it is lent to the next-door neighbor or kept in a hotel room in London. The only exception is property left at a second home (such as a beach house or resort condominium), where coverage is reduced to 10 percent of the policy limit on personal property unless the loss occurs while the insured is residing there.

Homeowners and their families have liability protection for their negligent acts wherever they occur. Excluded are negligent acts involving certain types of motorized vehicles (such as large boats and aircraft) or those occurring in the course of employment or professional practice. It does include golf carts (when used for golfing purposes) and recreational vehicles such as snowmobiles and "four-wheelers," provided that they're used on the insured's premises.

10-2g Limitations on Payment

In addition to the principle of indemnity, actual cash value, subrogation, and other insurance features restricting the amount paid out under a property and liability insurance contract, replacement-cost provisions, policy limits, and deductibles influence the amount an insurance company will pay for a loss.

Replacement Cost

replacement cost
The amount necessary to repair, rebuild, or replace an asset at today's prices.

The amount necessary to repair, rebuild, or replace an asset at today's prices is the **replacement cost**. When replacement-cost coverage is in effect, a homeowner's reimbursement for damage to a house or accompanying structures is based on the cost of repairing or replacing those structures. This means that the insurer will repair or replace damaged items without deducting for depreciation. Exhibit 10.3 illustrates a replacement-cost calculation for a 2,400-square-foot home with a two-car garage.

Homeowners are eligible for reimbursement on a full replacement-cost basis only if they keep their homes insured for at least 80 percent of the amount that it would cost to build them today, not including the value of the land. In periods of inflation, homeowners must either increase their coverage limits on the dwelling unit every

EXHIBIT 10.3	Calculating Replacement Cost

Here's a typical example of how an insurance company calculates replacement cost. It would take $374,400 to fully replace this home today.

Dwelling cost: 2,400 sq. ft. at $125 per sq. ft.	$300,000
Extra features: built-in appliances, mahogany cabinets, 3 ceiling fans	15,000
Porches, patios: screened and trellised patio	3,700
Two-car garage: 900 sq. ft. at $55 per sq. ft.	49,500
Other site improvements: driveway, storage, landscaping	6,200
Total replacement cost	$374,400

year or take a chance on falling below the 80 percent requirement. Alternatively, for a nominal cost, homeowners can purchase an inflation protection rider that automatically adjusts the amount of coverage based on prevailing inflation rates. Without the rider, maximum compensation for losses thus would be based on a specified percentage of loss. With the inflation protection rider, this won't happen.

Even if a home is in an excellent state of repair, its market value may be lessened by functional obsolescence within the structure—for example, when a house doesn't have enough electrical power to run a dishwasher, microwave, and hair dryer at the same time. The HO-8 homeowner's form (for older homes) was adopted as a partial response to this problem. A 2,200-square-foot home in an older neighborhood might have a market value (excluding land) of $195,000, yet the replacement cost might be $260,000. The HO-8 policy solves this problem so that homeowners don't have to buy more expensive coverage based on replacement cost. This policy covers property in full, up to the amount of the loss or up to the property's market value, whichever is less.

Although coverage on a house is often on a *replacement-cost basis*, standard coverage on its contents may be on an *actual cash-value basis*, which deducts depreciation from the *current replacement cost* for claims involving furniture, clothing, and other belongings. Some policies offer, for a slight increase in premium, replacement-cost coverage on contents. You should seriously consider this option—as well as an inflation protection rider on the dwelling—when buying homeowner's insurance.

FINANCIAL PLANNING TIPS

Lowering Your Homeowner's Insurance Premiums

Having the right amount of homeowner's insurance is important. But there's no need to overpay. Here are some ways to reduce your insurance premiums.

- **Increase your deductible.** A primary goal of insurance is to protect your family's financial resources from cataclysmic losses, not to totally insulate you from having to pay out much of anything under any circumstances. Think of your insurance as risk sharing, not risk elimination. Increasing your deductible from $500 to $1,000 could reduce your insurance premiums by 25 percent.

- **Bundle your homeowner's and auto insurance.** Buying your homeowner's and auto insurance from the same insurer can provide a discount of 5 percent to 15 percent. First, get quotes from separate companies for each policy, and then compare them with bundled quotes.

- **Check on the discounts that you may get from insurers.** Some relatively minor improvements to your home can earn you discounts. Examples include discounts for smoke detectors, deadbolt locks, security and fire alarms, and fire extinguishers. Often, seniors also can get an additional 10 percent discount.

- **Ask your insurance agent what you can do to reduce the risk of your home from the insurer's perspective.** For example, updating an old heating system or replacing old wiring can reduce your insurance premiums.

- **Avoid risks that insurers don't like to insure.** Owning dogs more frequently involved in claims (such as pit bulls) can limit or void your policy. Similarly, having a swimming pool or a trampoline can increase your insurance premium. You may have to buy additional coverage to protect yourself against certain risk exposures.

- **Manage your credit score.** Allowing your credit score to get too low can increase your insurance premiums.

- **Shop carefully for homeowner's insurance.** While it's worthwhile to shop around from time to time, keep in mind that you may be getting a longevity discount if you've been with your insurer for a few years. It's common to get a 5 percent discount if you've been with your company for three to five years and a 10 percent discount if you've been with the company for at least six years.

Source: Adapted from Deborah Fowles, "Ten Ways to Cut the Cost of Your Homeowner's Insurance," http://financialplan.about.com/od/homeownersinsurance/a/Homeowners.htm, accessed August 2015.

Policy Limits

In Section I of the homeowner's policy, the amount of coverage on the dwelling unit (coverage A) establishes the amounts applicable to the accompanying structures (coverage B), the unscheduled personal property (coverage C), and the temporary living expenses (coverage D). Generally, the limits under coverage B, C, and D are 10 percent, 50 percent, and 10 percent to 20 percent, respectively, of the amount of coverage under A.

> **EXAMPLE: Homeowner's Policy Coverage Limits**
>
> If a house is insured for $150,000, then the respective limits for coverage B, C, and D would be $15,000, $75,000, and $30,000 (i.e., 10 percent of $150,000, 50 percent of $150,000, and 20 percent of $150,000). These limits can be increased if either is considered insufficient to cover the exposure. Also, for a small reduction in premium, some companies will permit a homeowner to reduce coverage on unscheduled personal property to 40 percent of the amount on the dwelling unit.

Remember that homeowner's policies usually specify limits for certain types of personal property included under the coverage C category. These coverage limits are *within the total dollar amount* of coverage C and in no way act to increase that total. For example, the dollar limit for losses of money, bank notes, bullion, and related items is $200; securities, accounts, deeds, evidences of debt, manuscripts, passports, tickets, and stamps have a $1,000 limit. As mentioned earlier, loss from jewelry theft is limited to $1,000, and payment for theft of silverware, goldware, and pewterware has a $2,500 limit. Some policies also offer $5,000 coverage for home computer equipment. You can increase these limits by increasing coverage C.

In Section II the personal liability coverage (coverage E) often starts at $100,000, and the medical payments portion (coverage F) normally has a limit of $1,000 per person. Additional coverage included in Section II consists of claim expenses, such as court costs and attorney fees; first aid and medical expenses, including ambulance costs; and damage to others' property of up to $500 per occurrence.

Although these are the most common limits, most homeowners need additional protection, especially liability coverage. In these days of high damage awards by juries, a $100,000 liability limit may not be adequate. The cost to increase the liability limit with most companies is nominal. For example, the annual premium difference between a $100,000 personal liability limit and a $300,000 limit is likely to be only $20 to $30. You can also increase personal liability coverage with a personal liability umbrella policy, discussed later in the chapter.

Deductibles

Each of the preceding limits on recovery constrains the maximum amount an insurance company must pay under the policy. *Deductibles*, which limit what a company must pay for small losses, help reduce insurance premiums by doing away with the frequent small loss claims that are proportionately more expensive to administer. The standard deductible in most states is $250 on the physical damage protection covered in Section I. However, choosing higher deductible amounts of $500 or $1,000 results in considerable premium savings—as much as 10 percent to 20 percent in some states. Deductibles don't apply to liability and medical payments coverage because insurers want to be notified of all claims, no matter how trivial. Otherwise, they could be notified too late to investigate properly and prepare adequate defenses for resulting lawsuits.

10-2h Homeowner's Insurance Premiums

As you might expect, the size of insurance premiums varies widely depending on the insurance provider (company) and the location of the property (neighborhood/city/state). It pays to shop around! When you're shopping, be sure to state clearly the type of insurance you're looking for and to obtain and compare the cost, net of any discounts, offered by a number of agents or insurance companies. Remember, each type of property damage coverage is subject to a deductible of $250 or more.

Most people need to modify the basic package of coverage by adding an inflation rider and increasing the coverage on their homes to 100 percent of the replacement cost. Changing the contents protection from actual cash value to replacement cost and scheduling some items of expensive personal property may be desirable. Most insurance professionals also advise homeowners to increase their liability and medical payments limits. Each of these changes results in an additional premium charge.

At the same time, you can reduce your total premium by increasing the amount of your deductible. Because it's better to budget for small losses than to insure against them, larger deductibles are becoming more popular. You may also qualify for discounts for deadbolt locks, monitored security systems, and other safety features such as smoke alarms and sprinkler systems.

Behavior Matters

Behavioral Biases in Buying Property Insurance

What are the best property insurance policies for you? The answer to that question depends on your various risk exposures, your attitude toward risk, and the costs of competing insurance policies. There are some well-known behavioral biases that can lead you into making decisions that aren't in your best interest. It's a good idea to keep the following in mind when buying property insurance:

- **Don't just automatically renew your property insurance.** *Anchoring* is the behavioral bias in which people tend to rely unduly on past prices or estimates without considering new information. Just because your property insurance premiums were competitive in the past does not mean that they're still that way when your policy comes up for renewal. Be sure to shop around—don't just renew your current policy.

- **Be careful to weigh recent evidence properly before buying insurance.** The *representativeness bias* is the tendency to place too much weight on recent experience when making financial decisions. Guess what happens the day after an area is hit by an earthquake? Despite the fact that this is a relatively rare event almost everywhere, a lot of people run out to get it, and the price of earthquake insurance goes up! So be careful about buying insurance right after an adverse event occurs. Weigh the evidence carefully, assess your true risk exposures, and buy insurance deliberately and accordingly.

TEST YOURSELF

10-5 What are the *perils* that most properties are insured for under various types of homeowner's policies?

10-6 What types of property are covered under a homeowner's policy? When should you consider adding a PPF to your policy? Indicate which of the following are included in a standard policy's coverage: (a) an African parrot, (b) a motorbike, (c) Avon cosmetics held for sale, (d) Tupperware® for home use.

10-7 Describe (a) types of losses, (b) persons, and (c) locations that are covered under a homeowner's policy.

10-8 Describe *replacement-cost* coverage and compare this to *actual cash value* coverage. Which is preferable?

10-9 What are *deductibles?* Do they apply to either liability or medical payments coverage under the homeowner's policy?

10-3 AUTOMOBILE INSURANCE

Automobiles also involve risk because damage to them or negligence in their use can result in significant loss. Fortunately, insurance can protect individuals against a big part of these costs. Automobile insurance includes several types of coverage packaged together. We begin by describing the major features of a private passenger automobile policy. Then we explain no-fault laws, followed by discussions of auto insurance premiums and financial responsibility laws.

10-3a Types of Auto Insurance Coverage

personal automobile policy (PAP)

A comprehensive automobile insurance policy designed to be easily understood by the "typical" insurance purchaser.

The **personal automobile policy (PAP)** is a comprehensive, six-part automobile insurance policy designed to be easily understood by the "typical" insurance purchaser. The policy's first four parts identify the coverage provided.

- Part A: Liability coverage
- Part B: Medical payments coverage
- Part C: Uninsured motorists coverage
- Part D: Coverage for damage to your vehicle

Part E pertains to your duties and responsibilities if you're involved in an accident, and Part F defines basic provisions of the policy, including the policy coverage period and the right of termination. We'll focus mostly on the types of coverage in parts A through D of the policy.

You're almost sure to purchase liability, medical payments, and uninsured motorists protection. You may, however, choose *not* to buy protection against damage to your automobile if it's an older vehicle of relatively little value. On the other hand, if you have a loan against your car, then you'll probably be required to have physical damage coverage—part D—at least equal to the loan amount. Exhibit 10.4 illustrates how the four basic parts of a PAP might be displayed in a typical automobile insurance policy. The premiums shown are for a six-month period.

Part A: Liability Coverage

Most states require you to buy at least a minimum amount of liability insurance. As part of the liability provisions of a PAP, the insurer agrees to:

- Pay damages for bodily injury and/or property damage for which you are legally responsible as a result of an automobile accident
- Settle or defend any claim or suit asking for such damages

The provision for legal defense is important and could mean savings of thousands of dollars. Even if you're not at fault in an automobile accident, you may be compelled to prove your innocence in court, incurring expensive legal fees. The policy does *not* cover defense of criminal charges against the insured due to an accident (such as a drunk driver who's involved in an accident).

Part A of your insurance policy includes certain supplemental payments for items such as expenses incurred in settling the claim, reimbursement of premiums for appeal bonds, bonds to release attachments of the insured's property, and bail bonds required as a result of an accident. These supplemental payments are not restricted by the applicable policy limits.

Policy Limits. Although the insurance company provides both bodily injury and property damage liability insurance under part A, it typically sets *a dollar limit up to which it will pay for damages from any one accident*. Typical limits are $50,000, $100,000, $300,000, and $500,000. You'd be well advised to consider no less than $300,000 coverage in today's legal liability environment. Damage awards are increasing, and the insurer's duty to defend you *ends when the coverage limit has been exhausted*. It's easy to "exhaust" $50,000 or $100,000, leaving you to pay any

EXHIBIT 10.4   The Four Parts of a Personal Automobile Policy (PAP)

This automobile insurance statement for six months of coverage shows how the four major parts of a PAP might be incorporated. Notice that the premium for collision/comprehensive damage is relatively low because of the age and type of car (a 2012 Honda CRV); these drivers also enjoyed a premium reduction of more than $130 for the six months due to having other insurance with the same provider, a car alarm system, and a good driving record.

ANYSTATE INSURANCE COMPANIES   **AUTO RENEWAL**

Anystate Automobile Insurance Company
1665 West Anywhere Drive
Yourtown, CO 80209   2012 Honda CRV

POLICY NUMBER	PERIOD COVERED	DATE DUE	PLEASE PAY THIS AMOUNT
ABC-123-XYZ-456	MAY 26 2017 to NOV 26 2017	MAY 26 2017	$505

1 H -1582   A

Griffin, Nicholas S. and Allison B.
1643 Thunder Rd. #32
Yourtown, CO 80209

Coverages and Limits			Premiums
Part A	A	Liability	
		Bodily Injury 250,000/500,000	$219
		Property Damage 100,000	
Part B	M	Medical 5,000	19
Part C	U	Uninsured Motor Vehicle	
		Bodily Injury 100,000/300,000	71
Part D	G	500 Deductible Collision	140
	D-WG	500 Deductible Comprehensive	50
	H	Emergency Road Service	6
Amount Due			**$505**

Your premium has already been adjusted by the following:

Premium Reductions

Multiple Line	22
Antitheft devices	40
Good driver	70

Your premium is based on the following ...
If not correct, contact your agent.

2012 Honda CRV
Serial number: 4 ABCD12M3NP456789

Drivers of vehicle in your household ...
There are no male or unmarried female drivers under age 25.
Younger drivers included if rated on another car insured with us.

Ordinary use of vehicle ...
To and from work or school, more than 100 miles weekly.
Driven more than 7,500 miles annually. (National average is 10,000 miles annually.)

Source: Adapted from a major automobile insurance company quote.

---

additional costs above the policy limit. So be sure to purchase adequate coverage—*regardless of the minimum requirements in your state.* Otherwise, you place your personal assets at risk. As Exhibit 10.4 shows, the Griffin family obtained fairly high coverage limits.

Some insurers make so-called *split limits* of liability coverage available, with the first amount in each combination the per-individual limit and the second the per-accident limit. Some policy limit combinations for protecting individuals against claims made for **bodily injury liability losses** are $25,000/$50,000, $50,000/$100,000, $100,000/$300,000, $250,000/$500,000, and $500,000/$1,000,000. Because the

bodily injury liability losses
A PAP provision that protects the insured against claims made for bodily injury.

Griffins purchased the $250,000/$500,000 policy limits (Exhibit 10.4), the maximum amount any one person negligently injured in an accident could receive from the insurance company would be $250,000. Further, the total amount the insurer would pay to all injured victims in one accident would not exceed $500,000. If a jury awarded a claimant $80,000, the defendant whose insurance policy limits were $50,000/$100,000 could be required to pay $30,000 out of his or her pocket ($80,000 award minus $50,000 paid by insurance). For the defendant, this could mean loss of home, cars, bank accounts, and other assets. In many states, if the value of these assets is too little to satisfy a claim then the defendant's wages may be garnished (taken by the court and used to satisfy the outstanding debt).

property damage liability losses
A PAP provision that protects the insured against claims made for damage to property.

The policy limits available to cover **property damage liability losses** are typically $10,000, $25,000, $50,000, and $100,000. In contrast to bodily injury liability limits, property damage limits are stated as a per-accident limit, without specifying limits applicable on a per-item or per-person basis.

Persons Insured. Two basic definitions in the PAP determine who is covered under part A: insured person and covered auto. Essentially, an *insured person* includes you (the named insured) and any family member, any person using a covered auto, and any person or organization that may be held responsible for your actions. The *named insured* is the person named in the declarations page of the policy. The spouse of the person named is considered a named insured if he or she resides in the same household. Family members are persons related by blood, marriage, or adoption and residing in the same household. An unmarried college student living away from home usually is considered a family member. *Covered autos* are the vehicles shown in the declarations page of your PAP, autos acquired during the policy period, any trailer owned, and any auto or trailer used as a temporary substitute while your auto or trailer is being repaired or serviced. An automobile that you lease for an extended time can be included as a covered automobile.

The named insured and family members have part A liability coverage regardless of the automobile they are driving. However, for persons other than the named insured and family members to have liability coverage, they must be driving a covered auto.

When a motorist who is involved in an automobile accident is covered under two or more liability insurance contracts, the coverage *on the automobile* is primary and the other coverage is secondary. For example, if Dennis Ellis, a named insured in his own right, was involved in an accident while driving Kaitlin Wei's car (with permission), then a claim settlement exceeding the limits of Kaitlin's liability policy would be necessary before Dennis' liability insurance would apply. If Kaitlin's insurance had lapsed, Dennis' policy would then offer primary protection (but it would apply to Dennis only, not to Kaitlin.).

Part B: Medical Payments Coverage

Medical payments coverage insures a covered individual for reasonable and necessary medical expenses incurred within three years of an automobile accident in an amount not to exceed the policy limits. It provides for reimbursement even if other sources of recovery, such as health or accident insurance, also make payments. What's more, in most states, the insurer reimburses the insured for medical payments even if the insured proves that another person was negligent in the accident and receives compensation from that party's liability insurer.

A person need not be occupying an automobile when the accidental injury occurs to be eligible for benefits. Injuries sustained as a pedestrian, or on a bicycle in a traffic accident, are also covered. (Motorcycle accidents are normally not covered.) Part B insurance also pays on an excess basis. For instance, if you're a passenger in a friend's automobile during an accident and suffer $8,000 in medical expenses, you can collect under his medical payments insurance up to his policy limits. Further, you can collect (up to the amount of your policy limits) from your insurer the amount exceeding what the other medical payments provide.

Policy Limits. Medical payments insurance usually has per-person limits of $1,000, $2,000, $3,000, $5,000, or $10,000. Thus, an insurer could conceivably pay $60,000 or more in medical payments benefits for one accident involving a named insured and five passengers. Most families are advised to buy the $5,000 or $10,000 limit because, even though they may have other health insurance available, they can't be sure that their passengers are as well protected. Having automobile medical payments insurance also reduces the probability that a passenger in your auto will sue you and try to collect under your liability insurance coverage (in those states that permit it).

Persons Insured. Coverage under an automobile medical payments insurance policy applies to the named insured and to family members who are injured while occupying an automobile (whether owned by the named insured or not) or when struck by an automobile or trailer of any type. Part B also applies to any other person occupying a covered automobile.

Part C: Uninsured Motorists Coverage

Uninsured motorists coverage is available to meet the needs of "innocent" victims of accidents who are negligently injured by uninsured, underinsured, or hit-and-run motorists. Nearly all states require uninsured motorists insurance to be included in each liability insurance policy issued. The insured is allowed, however, to reject this coverage in most of these states. Because about 16 percent of drivers are uninsured and because many others meet only minimum insurance coverage requirements, rejecting uninsured motorists coverage is not a good idea. In many states, a person may also collect even if the negligent motorist's insurance company is insolvent. With uninsured motorists insurance, an insured is legally entitled to collect an amount equal to the sum that could have been collected from the negligent motorist's liability insurance, had such coverage been available, up to a maximum amount equal to the policy's stated *uninsured motorists limit*.

Three points must be proven to receive payment through uninsured motorists insurance: (1) another motorist must be at fault, (2) the motorist has no available insurance or is underinsured, and (3) damages were incurred. Because property damage is not included in this coverage in most states, with uninsured motorists coverage, you generally can collect only for losses arising from bodily injury.

Policy Limits. Uninsured motorists insurance is fairly low in cost (usually around $100 to $150 per year). Because the cost of this coverage is low compared to the amount of protection it provides, drivers should purchase at least the minimum available limits of uninsured motorists insurance. The Griffins purchased $100,000/$300,000 coverage for $71 per six months.

Persons Insured. Uninsured motorists protection covers the named insured, family members, and any other person occupying a covered auto.

Underinsured Motorists Coverage. In addition to *uninsured motorists*, in some states, for a nominal premium you can obtain **underinsured motorists coverage**, which protects the insured against damages caused by being in an accident with an underinsured motorist who is found liable. Underinsured motorists insurance has become increasingly popular and *can be purchased for both bodily injury and property damage*. If an at-fault driver causes more damage to you than the limit of her liability, your insurance company makes up the difference (up to the limits of your coverage) and then goes

uninsured motorists coverage
Automobile insurance designed to meet the needs of "innocent" victims of accidents who are negligently injured by uninsured, underinsured, or hit-and-run motorists.

underinsured motorists coverage
Optional automobile insurance coverage, available in some states, that protects the insured against damages caused by being in an accident with an underinsured motorist who is found liable.

after the negligent driver for the deficiency. If it's available in your state, you should consider purchasing this optional coverage.

EXAMPLE: Underinsured Motorists Coverage

If you have underinsured motorists coverage of $50,000 for bodily injury and incur medical expenses of $40,000 because of an accident caused by an at-fault insured driver with the minimum compulsory bodily injury limit of $25,000, then your insurer will cover the $15,000 gap ($40,000 medical expenses minus $25,000 liability limit of at-fault driver).

Part D: Coverage for Physical Damage to a Vehicle

This part of the PAP provides coverage for damage to your auto. The two basic types of coverage are collision and comprehensive (or "other than collision").

collision insurance
Automobile insurance that pays for collision damage to an insured automobile *regardless of who is at fault.*

Collision Insurance. Collision insurance is automobile insurance that pays for collision damage to an insured automobile *regardless of who is at fault.* The amount of insurance payable is the actual cash value of the loss in excess of your deductible. Remember that *actual cash value is defined as replacement cost less depreciation.* So, if a car is demolished, the insured is paid an amount equal to the car's depreciated value minus any deductible. Deductibles typically range between $50 and $1,000, and selecting a higher deductible, as did the Griffins, will reduce your premium.

LORAKS/SHUTTERSTOCK.COM

Lenders typically require collision insurance on cars they finance. In some cases, especially when the auto dealer is handling the financing, it will try to sell you this insurance. *Avoid buying automobile insurance from car dealers or finance companies.* It is best to buy such insurance from your regular insurance agent and include collision insurance as part of your full auto insurance policy (i.e., the PAP). A full-time insurance agent is better able to assess and meet your insurance needs. The collision provision of your insurance policy often fully protects you in a rental car, so be sure to check before purchasing supplemental collision insurance when renting a car. Also, when you charge your car rental to your credit card, collision insurance may be offered under the umbrella of the credit card.

comprehensive automobile insurance
Coverage that protects against loss to an insured automobile caused by any peril (with a few exceptions) *other than collision.*

Comprehensive Automobile Insurance. Comprehensive automobile insurance protects against loss to an insured automobile caused by any peril (with a few exceptions) *other than collision.* The maximum compensation provided under this coverage is the actual cash value of the automobile. This broad coverage includes, but is not limited to, damage caused by fire, theft, glass breakage, falling objects, malicious mischief, vandalism, riot, and earthquake. Contrary to popular belief, the automobile insurance policy normally does *not* cover the theft of personal property left in the insured vehicle. However, the off-premises coverage of the homeowner's policy may cover such a loss if the auto was locked when the theft occurred.

10-3b No-Fault Automobile Insurance

no-fault automobile insurance
Automobile insurance that reimburses the parties involved in an accident without regard to negligence.

No-fault automobile insurance is a system under which each insured party is compensated by his or her own company, regardless of which party caused the accident. In return, legal remedies and payments for pain and suffering are restricted. Under the concept of *pure* no-fault insurance, the driver, passengers, and injured pedestrians are reimbursed by the insurer of the car for economic losses stemming from bodily injury. The insurer doesn't have to cover claims for losses to other motorists who are covered by their own policies.

Advocates of no-fault automobile insurance apparently forget that the sole purpose of liability insurance is to protect the assets of the insured—not to pay losses, *per se*. State laws governing no-fault insurance vary widely as to both the amount of no-fault benefits provided and the degree to which restrictions for legal actions apply. Most states provide from $2,000 to $10,000 in personal injury protection and restrict legal recovery for pain and suffering to cases where medical or economic losses exceed some threshold level, such as $500 or $1,000. In all states, recovery based on negligence is permitted for economic losses exceeding the amount payable by no-fault insurance.

10-3c Automobile Insurance Premiums

The cost of car insurance depends on many things, including your age, where you live, the car you drive, your driving record, the coverage you have, and the amount of your deductible. Consequently, car insurance premiums—even for the same coverage—vary all over the map.

Factors Affecting Premiums

Factors that influence how auto insurance premiums are set include (1) rating territory, (2) amount of use the automobile receives, (3) personal characteristics of the driver, (4) type of automobile, and (5) insured's driving record.

- **Rating territory:** Rates are higher in geographic areas where accident rates, number of claims filed, and average cost of claims paid are higher. Rates reflect auto repair costs, hospital and medical expenses, jury awards, and theft and vandalism in the area. Even someone with a perfect driving record will be charged the going rate for the area where the automobile is garaged. Exhibit 10.5 gives some helpful tips for protecting your vehicle wherever you live. Some jurisdictions prohibit the use of rating territories, age, and gender factors because it's believed these factors unfairly discriminate against the urban, the young, and the male.
- **Use of the automobile:** Drive less, pay less! Low annual miles translate into a smaller probability of being in an accident, so you pay lower rates. Rates are also lower if the insured automobile isn't usually driven to work or is driven less than

---

EXHIBIT 10.5   Preventing Your Car from Being Stolen

You can help prevent your car from being stolen by taking the following precautions:
- Keep your car doors locked, even while driving. Close all windows.
- Never leave your keys in an unattended car.
- Never leave your car running and unattended.
- Avoid leaving valuables inside your car where they can be seen.
- Do not leave your vehicle title or proof of insurance in the car.
- Avoid high crime areas even if the alternate route takes more time.
- Install anti-theft devices like a burglar alarm or a steering wheel lock.
- Etch your car's vehicle identification number (VIN) on more than one of the windows.
- When parking on an incline, turn the wheels toward the curb and set the emergency brake.
- Do not resist a carjacker. You can't be replaced; your car can.

Sources: Adapted from "How to Prevent Your Car from Being Stolen," https://www.geico.com/information/safety/auto/preventing-auto-theft/, accessed August 2015.

3 miles one way. Premiums rise slightly if you drive more than 3 but fewer than 15 miles to work and increase if your commute exceeds 15 miles each way.

- **Drivers' personal characteristics:** The insured's age, sex, and marital status can also affect automobile insurance premiums. Insurance companies base premium differentials on the number of accidents involving certain age groups. For example, drivers aged 25 and under make up only about 15 percent of the total driving population, but they are involved in nearly 30 percent of auto accidents and in 26 percent of all fatal accidents. Male drivers are involved in a larger percentage of fatal crashes, so unmarried males under age 30 (and married males under 25) pay higher premiums than do older individuals. Females over age 24, as well as married females of any age, are exempt from the youthful operator classification and pay lower premiums.

- **Type of automobile:** Insurance companies charge higher rates for automobiles classified as intermediate-performance, high-performance, and sports vehicles and also for rear-engine models. Some states even rate four-door cars differently from two-door models.

- **Driving record:** The driving records—traffic violations and accidents—of those insured and the people who live with them affect premium levels. More severe traffic convictions—driving under the influence of alcohol or drugs, leaving the scene of an accident, homicide or assault arising from the operation of a motor vehicle, and driving with a revoked or suspended driver's license—result in higher insurance premiums. Any conviction for a moving traffic violation that results in the accumulation of points under a state point system also may incur a premium surcharge. In most states, accidents determined to be the insured's fault also incur points and a premium surcharge.

automobile insurance plan
An arrangement providing automobile insurance to drivers who have been refused regular coverage under normal procedures.

You Can Do It Now

Evaluate the Best Auto Insurance Companies

When you're considering buying new car insurance, it's helpful to know which insurance companies are considered the best. A good Internet site is **http://www.consumeraffairs.com/insurance/car.html**. The site discusses the key elements of auto insurance policies, which include liability, comprehensive coverage, uninsured motorist protection, collusion coverage, and personal injury protection. **You can do it now.**

Many states place drivers with multiple traffic violations in an **automobile insurance plan** (formerly called an *assigned-risk plan*), providing automobile insurance to those refused regular coverage. The automobile insurance plan generally offers less coverage for a higher premium. Even with high premiums, however, insurers lost billions of dollars on this type of business in a recent 5-year period.

Driving Down the Cost of Car Insurance

Comparison shopping for car insurance can really pay off, yet only about one-third of car owners shop around for auto coverage. One of the best ways to reduce the cost of car insurance is to take advantage of the discounts auto insurers offer. Taken together, such discounts can knock from 5 percent to 50 percent off your annual premium. Some give overall *safe-driving* (accident-free) discounts, and most give youthful operators lower rates if they've had *driver's training*. High school and college students may also receive *good-student* discounts for maintaining a B average or making the dean's list at their school.

Financial Fact or Fantasy?

The type of car you drive is a personal matter that has no bearing on how much you will have to pay for automobile insurance. **Fantasy:** The type of car you drive is one of the major determinants of auto insurance premiums. You can expect to pay a lot more for insurance on a sporty model than on a more " sedate" one.

Nearly all insurance companies give discounts to families with two or more automobiles insured by the same company (the *multicar* discount). Most insurers also offer discounts to owners who install *antitheft devices* in their cars. Likewise, some insurers offer *nonsmoker* and *nondrinker* discounts. And some insurers accept only persons who are educators or executives; others accept only government employees. Through more selective underwriting these companies are able to reduce losses and operating expenses, which results in lower premiums.

It's to your advantage to look for and use as many of these discounts as you can. Take another look at the auto insurance statement in Exhibit 10.4, and you'll see that the insured reduced his overall cost of coverage by 25 percent by qualifying for just three of the discounts (labeled "Premium Reductions"). Another effective way to drive down the cost of car insurance is to *raise your deductibles* (as discussed earlier in this chapter). This frequently overlooked tactic can affect the cost of your insurance premium dramatically. For example, the difference between a $100 deductible and a $500 deductible may be as much as 25 percent on collision coverage and 30 percent on comprehensive coverage; request a $1,000 deductible, and you may save as much as 50 percent on both collision and comprehensive coverage.

financial responsibility laws
Laws requiring motorists to buy a specified minimum amount of automobile liability insurance or to provide other proof of comparable financial responsibility.

10-3d Financial Responsibility Laws

Annual losses from automobile accidents in the United States run into billions of dollars. For this reason, most states have **financial responsibility laws**, whereby motorists *must buy a specified minimum amount of automobile liability insurance* or provide other proof of comparable financial responsibility. The required limits are low in most states—well below what you should carry.

FINANCIAL PLANNING TIPS

How to Buy Auto Insurance

The cost of auto insurance can vary greatly. It pays to keep the following in mind while shopping around:

- **Get at least a few quotes.** Start with the largest insurers, such as State Farm and Allstate. Then ask a couple of independent agents to provide quotes from more than one company. Finally, get quotes from direct marketers, GEICO (**http://www.geico.com**) and Progressive (**http://www.progressive.com**) being two of the most competitive. Make sure to ask for an itemized list of coverages and costs so that you can compare policies and prices.

- **The car you buy affects your premium.** The price of the car affects the replacement cost if it is stolen or destroyed in an accident. And the cost of repairing the car can affect your premium. Check the statistics on injury claims, collision repair costs, and theft rates by vehicle model available from the Highway Loss Data Institute (**http://www.carsafety.org/**) before making your final car purchase decision.

- **Decide how much insurance you need.** While it's risky to be underinsured, it's also costly to carry too much insurance. However, don't pay attention to the minimum amount of insurance required in your state—it's rarely enough. Think about the cost of plowing into a Mercedes-Benz! A common recommendation is to have liability coverage of at least $100,000 per person, $300,000 per accident, and $50,000 in property damage coverage.

- **Take advantage of available discounts.** When you get insurance quotes, ask what kind of discounts you can get. For example, a common discount is for those who drive less than 7,500 miles a year. And you can reduce your premium significantly if you increase your deductible for collision or if you drop the medical payments portion of your policy if your health insurance provides good coverage.

Source: Adapted from "5 Car Insurance Tips," http://auto.howstuffworks.com/buying-selling/cg-car-insurance-tips.htm, accessed August 2015.

Financial responsibility laws fall into two categories. *Compulsory auto insurance laws* require motorists to show evidence of insurance coverage *before* receiving their license plates. Penalties for not having liability insurance include fines and suspension of your driver's license. The second category requires motorists to show evidence of their insurance coverage only *after* being involved in an accident. If they then fail to demonstrate compliance with the law, their registrations and driver's licenses are suspended. Although motorists who aren't able to fulfill their financial responsibility lose their driving privileges, victims may never recover their losses.

TEST YOURSELF

10-10 Briefly explain the major types of coverage available under the personal auto policy (PAP). Which persons are insured under (a) automobile medical payments coverage and (b) uninsured motorists coverage?

10-11 Explain the nature of (a) automobile collision insurance and (b) automobile comprehensive insurance.

10-12 Define *no-fault insurance* and discuss its pros and cons.

10-13 Describe the important factors that influence the availability and cost of auto insurance.

10-14 Discuss the role of financial responsibility laws and describe the two basic types currently employed.

10-4 OTHER PROPERTY AND LIABILITY INSURANCE

LG5 Homeowner's and automobile insurance policies provide the basic protection needed by most families, but some need other, more specialized types of insurance. Popular forms of other insurance include supplemental property insurance—earthquake, flood, and other forms of transportation—as well as the personal liability umbrella policy.

10-4a Supplemental Property Insurance Coverage

Because homeowner's policies exclude certain types of damage, you may want to consider some of the following types of supplemental coverage.

- **Earthquake insurance:** In addition to California, areas in other states are also subject to this type of loss. Very few homeowners buy this coverage because these policies typically carry a 15 percent deductible on the replacement cost of a home damaged or destroyed by earthquake. So even though the premiums are relatively inexpensive, you have to pay a lot out of pocket before you can collect on the policy.
- **Flood insurance:** The federal government has established a subsidized flood insurance program in cooperation with private insurance agents, who can sell this low-cost coverage to homeowners and tenants living in designated communities. The flood insurance program also encourages communities to initiate land-use controls to reduce future flood losses.
- **Other forms of transportation insurance:** In addition to automobile insurance, you may wish to insure other types of vehicles, such as mobile homes, recreational vehicles, or boats.

10-4b Personal Liability Umbrella Policy

Persons with moderate to high levels of income and net worth may want to take out a **personal liability umbrella policy**. It provides added liability coverage for homeowner's and automobile insurance as well as additional coverage not provided by either of

personal liability umbrella policy
An insurance policy providing excess liability coverage for homeowner's and automobile insurance as well as additional coverage not provided by either policy.

those policies. Umbrella policies often include limits of $1 million or more. Some also provide added amounts of coverage for a family's major medical insurance.

The premiums are usually quite reasonable for the broad coverage offered—$150 to $300 a year for as much as $1 million in coverage. Although the protection is comprehensive, it does contain some exclusions. The insured party must already have relatively high liability limits ($100,000 to $300,000) on their homeowner's and auto coverage in order to purchase a personal liability umbrella policy.

Do you need the extra protection that a personal liability umbrella policy provides? The answer is yes if you have sizable assets that could be seized to pay a judgment against you that is not fully covered by your homeowner's and automobile policies. But you may also need this coverage if you rent your home to others, have house sitters, or hire unbonded help such as gardeners or babysitters because you're responsible for any injuries that they incur or cause. You may also need this coverage if you work from home and clients visit you at your home office.

TEST YOURSELF

10-15 Briefly describe the following supplemental property insurance coverage: (a) earthquake insurance, (b) flood insurance, and (c) other forms of transportation insurance.

10-16 What is a *personal liability umbrella policy?* Under what circumstances might it be a wise purchase?

10-5 BUYING INSURANCE AND SETTLING CLAIMS

The first step when buying property and liability insurance is to develop an inventory of exposures to loss and then arrange them from highest to lowest priority. Losses that lend themselves to insurance protection are those that seldom occur but are potentially substantial—for example, damage to a home and its contents or liability arising from a negligence claim. Somewhat less important, but still desirable, is insurance to cover losses that could disrupt a family's financial plans, even if the losses might not result in insolvency. Such risks include physical damage to automobiles, boats, and other personal property of moderate value. Lowest-priority exposures can be covered by savings or from current income.

10-5a Property and Liability Insurance Agents

A good property insurance agent can make the purchase process much easier. Most property insurance agents fall into either the captive or independent category. A **captive agent** represents only one insurance company and is more or less an employee of that company. Allstate, Nationwide, and State Farm are major insurance companies that market their products through captive agents. In contrast, **independent agents** typically represent from 2 to 10 different insurance companies. These agents may place your coverage with any of the companies with whom they have an agency relationship, so long as you meet the underwriting standards of that company. Some well-known companies that operate through independent agents

captive agent
An insurance agent who represents only one insurance company and who is, in effect, an employee of that company.

independent agent
An insurance agent who may place coverage with any company with which he or she has an agency relationship, as long as the insured meets that company's underwriting standards.

include The Hartford, Kemper, Chubb, and Travelers. Either type of agent can serve your needs well and should take the time to do the following:

- Review your total property and liability insurance exposures
- Inventory property and identify exposures
- Determine appropriate covered perils, limits, deductibles, and floater policies

Because of large variations in premiums and services, it pays to comparison shop.

Property insurance agents who meet various experiential and educational requirements, including passing a series of written examinations, qualify for the *Chartered Property and Casualty Underwriter (CPCU)* or *Certified Insurance Counselor (CIC)* designation. Another alternative to consider is companies that sell directly to the consumer through an 800 number or online. Generally, their premiums are lower. Examples of direct sellers are Amica, Erie, GEICO, and USAA.

10-5b Property and Liability Insurance Companies

Selecting an agent is an important step when purchasing property and liability insurance, but you should also ask questions about the company's financial soundness, its claims settlement practices, and the geographic range of its operations (this could be important if you're involved in an accident 1,000 miles from home). As with any form of insurance, you should check the company's ratings (see Chapter 8) and stick with those rated in the top categories. The agent should be a good source of information about the technical aspects of a company's operations; friends and acquaintances often can provide insight into its claims settlement policy. The Internet offers lots of information about various property and liability insurance products. Many insurance companies now have elaborate home pages on the Internet containing basic information about the provider and its products, directions to local agents, or calculators to crunch the numbers and generate sample premiums.

10-5c Settling Property and Liability Claims

Insurance companies typically settle claims promptly and fairly—especially life and health care claims. But in settling property and liability claims, there is often some claimant–insurer disagreement. In this section, we'll review the claims settlement process beginning with what you should do immediately following an accident.

First Steps Following an Accident

After an accident, record the names, addresses, and phone numbers of all witnesses, drivers, occupants, and injured parties, along with the license numbers of the automobiles involved. *Never leave the scene of an accident, even if the other party says it's acceptable to do so.* Immediately notify law enforcement officers and your insurance agent of the accident. Never discuss liability at the scene of an accident or with anyone other than the police and your insurer. The duty of the police is to assess the probability of a law violation and maintain order at the scene of an accident—not to make judgments about liability.

Steps in Claims Settlement

If you're involved in an accident, one of the first things to decide is whether you want to file a claim. Most experts agree that unless it's a very minor or insignificant accident, the best course of action is to file a claim. Be aware, though, that if you've made several claims, then your insurance company may decide to drop you after settling the current one. The claims settlement process typically involves these steps:

1. **Notice to your insurance company:** You must notify your insurance company that a loss (or potential for loss) has occurred. Timely notice is extremely important.
2. **Investigation:** Insurance company personnel may talk to witnesses or law enforcement officers and gather physical evidence to determine whether the claimed loss is

FINANCIAL PLANNING TIPS

How to Handle a Denied Insurance Claim

If your homeowner's or automobile insurance company refuses to pay all or part of your claim, that can be an upsetting. Here are some key steps to take if you decide to contest a denied claim:

- **Review the claim and the insurer's stated reason for denying it.** Determine whether there is a discrepancy between the terms stated in your policy and the rationale provided in the denial. Make sure that you know your policy maximums. You can't fight the denial effectively if you can't point out the discrepancy to your insurance company.

- **Document every step.** Obtain written copies of police or fire department reports and outside appraisals, and take lots of photos.

- **Request a review of the claim denial immediately.** Complain to your insurance company and ask for a review of your case. Do this as soon as possible, because some companies require you to file an appeal within one year of the date of the first decision.

- **If the insurance company does not honor your claim or takes weeks to respond, then go to your state's insurance department.** In most states, insurers have about six weeks to resolve a dispute.

- **Weigh the costs and the benefits carefully before you file a lawsuit.** The legal fees and hassle might be worth it if you have a homeowner's claim for $25,000 or $50,000. But a denied auto claim for a few thousand dollars may not be worth pursuing in light of the legal costs.

Source: Based, in part, on Kalen Smith, "What to Do If Your Homeowners Insurance Claim Is Denied," http://www.moneycrashers.com/homeowners-insurance-claim-denied/, accessed August 2015.

covered by the policy, and they'll check to make sure that the date of the loss falls within the policy period. If you delay filing your claim, you hinder the insurer's ability to check the facts. All policies specify the period within which you must give notice. Failure to report an accident can result in losing your right to collect on it.

3. **Proof of loss:** This proof requires you to give a sworn statement. You may have to show medical bills, submit an inventory, and certify the value of lost property (e.g., a written inventory, photographs, and purchase receipts). You may also have to submit an employer statement of lost wages and, if possible, physical evidence of damage (e.g., X-rays if you claim a back injury; show a broken window or pried door if you claim a break-in and theft at your home). After reviewing your proof of loss, the insurer may (1) pay you the amount you asked for, (2) offer you a lesser amount, or (3) deny that the company has any legal responsibility under the terms of your policy.

If the amount is disputed, most policies provide for some form of claims arbitration. You hire a third party, the company hires a third party, and these two arbitrators jointly select one more person. When any two of the three arbitrators reach agreement, their decision binds you and the company to their solution. When a company denies responsibility, you do not get the right of arbitration. In such cases, the company is saying that the loss does not fall under the policy coverage. You must then either forget the claim or bring in an attorney or, perhaps, a public adjustor (discussed next).

Claims Adjustment

Usually the first person to call when you need to file a claim is your insurance agent. If your loss is relatively minor, the agent

Financial Fact or Fantasy?

Filing a property or liability claim is quick and easy to do. Just call your agent, provide a few basic details, and look for your check in a few days. **Fantasy:** Filing a property or liability claim is often a detailed and time-consuming process wherein you must prove your loss. The insurance company can offer you an amount less than the loss you claim or deny your claim altogether.

claims adjustor
An insurance specialist who works for the insurance company, as an independent adjustor or for an adjustment bureau, to investigate claims.

can process it quickly and, in fact, often gives you a check right on the spot. If your loss is more complex, your company will probably assign a claims adjustor to the case. A **claims adjustor** is an insurance specialist who works for the insurance company either as an independent adjustor or for an adjustment bureau. The adjustor investigates claims, looking out for the company's interests—which might very well be to keep you, its customer, satisfied. However, many claimants are out to collect all they can from insurance companies, which they think have "deep pockets." Thus adjustors walk a fine line: they must diligently question and investigate while at the same time offering service to minimize settlement delays and financial hardship. To promote your own interest in the claim, cooperate with your adjustor and answer inquiries honestly—keeping in mind that the insurance company writes the adjustor's paycheck.

TEST YOURSELF

10-17 Differentiate between *captive* and *independent* insurance agents. What characteristics should you look for in an insurance agent and an insurance company when you're buying property or liability insurance?

10-18 Briefly describe key aspects of the claims settlement process, explaining what to do after an accident, the steps in claim settlement, and the role of claims adjustors.

Planning Over a Lifetime: *Protecting Your Property*

Here are some suggestions on how to insure your property and protect against liability exposures over the different stages of your life.

Independent Lifestyle (20s)	Family and Career Development (30s–40s)	Mature Lifestyle (50s–60s)	Retirement (65+)
✓ Evaluate renter's insurance to protect your personal property and to limit liability exposure.	✓ Buy homeowner's insurance with appropriate property and liability coverage.	✓ Review homeowner's insurance coverage. Keep in mind the possible need for riders on expensive, otherwise insufficiently uncovered personal items.	✓ Revise homeowner's and liability coverage in light of retirement situation.
✓ Make sure to get adequate auto insurance. Don't try to save by buying too little liability coverage.	✓ Document your personal items with photos and purchase receipts.	✓ Consider bundling your homeowner's and auto policies with the same insurer for a discount.	✓ Revise auto insurance in light of your retirement situation.
	✓ Re-evaluate auto insurance coverage.	✓ Consider getting policy discounts by buying anti-theft systems for your home and/or car.	

Financial Impact of Personal Choices
Wade Saves on His Car Insurance

Wade Bradley is a frugal and careful financial planner. One of his money-saving decisions is to continue driving his nine year-old car, which is now worth about $7,500. In order to save money on his car insurance, Wade increased his deductible from $500 to $1,000, which reduced his annual premium by $200. He has just decided that he no longer needs the collision coverage on his policy, which pays for the repair or replacement of his car if damaged. Wade has consequently decided that he should take the risk that he would have to pay for the repair or replacement of his low-value car rather than to continue taking the certain loss of the higher-priced insurance coverage. This decision will save him several hundred dollars a year.

Summary

LG1 **Discuss the importance and basic principles of property insurance, including types of exposure, indemnity, and co-insurance, p. 380.**
Property and liability insurance protects against the loss of real and personal property that can occur from exposure to various perils. Such insurance also protects against loss from lawsuits based on alleged negligence by the insured. The principle of indemnity limits the insured's compensation to the amount of economic loss. The co-insurance provision requires the policyholder to buy insurance coverage that equals a set percentage of the property's value in order to receive full compensation under the policy's terms.

LG2 **Identify the types of coverage provided by homeowner's insurance, p. 384.**
Most homeowner's insurance policies are divided into two sections. Section I covers the insured's dwelling unit, accompanying structures, and personal property. Section II provides comprehensive coverage for personal liability and medical payments to others. The most commonly sold homeowner's policies (Forms HO-2 and HO-3) cover a broad range of perils, including damage from fire or lightning, windstorms, explosions, aircraft, vehicles, smoke, vandalism, theft, freezing, and so on. Personal property coverage is typically set at 50 percent of the coverage on the dwelling.

LG3 **Select the right homeowner's insurance policy for your needs, p. 384.**
Everyone should have some form of homeowner's insurance, whether you own a single-family house or a condominium or rent an apartment. Renter's insurance covers your personal possessions. Except for the house and garage, which are covered on a replacement-cost basis, homeowner's or renter's insurance normally reimburses all losses on an actual cash-value basis, subject to applicable deductibles and policy limits. For an additional premium, you can usually obtain replacement-cost coverage on personal belongings. In Section I, internal limits are set for various classes of property. You may wish to increase these limits if you have valuable property. One way to do so is with a personal property floater (PPF). Because the standard Section II liability limit is only $100,000, it's a good idea to buy additional liability coverage, generally available at minimal cost. Choose a policy with a higher deductible to reduce premiums.

LG4 **Analyze the coverage in a personal automobile policy (PAP) and choose the most cost-effective policy, p. 394.**
Automobile insurance policies usually protect the insured from loss due to personal liability, medical payments, uninsured (and underinsured) motorists, collision (property damage to the vehicle), and comprehensive coverage (which applies to nearly any other type of noncollision damage a car might suffer, such as theft or vandalism). Where you live, the type of car, your driving record, how much you drive, and your personal characteristics influence the policy premium cost. Most automobile insurers offer discounts for good driving records, safety and antitheft devices, driver's training courses, and so on. Other ways to reduce premiums are through higher deductibles and eliminating collision coverage if your car is old.

LG5 **Describe other types of property and liability insurance, p. 402.**
Besides the major forms of homeowner's and automobile insurance, you can obtain other property and liability coverage, including supplemental property insurance coverage—earthquake insurance, flood insurance, and other forms of transportation insurance (mobile-home, recreational vehicle, and boat insurance)—and personal liability umbrella policies.

LG6 **Choose a property and liability insurance agent and company, and settle claims, p. 403.**
Before buying property and liability coverage, evaluate your exposure to loss and determine the coverage needed. Also, select your insurance agent and insurance company carefully to obtain appropriate coverage at a reasonable price. Equally important, make sure that the agent and company you deal with have reputations for fair claims settlement practices. Before filing a claim, decide whether the amount of damage warrants a claim. Document all claims properly and file promptly. If you have a complex loss claim, expect your insurer to assign a claims adjustor to the case.

Key Terms

actual cash value, 383

automobile insurance plan, 400

bodily injury liability losses, 395

captive agent, 403

claims adjustor, 406

co-insurance, 383

collision insurance, 398

comprehensive automobile insurance, 398

comprehensive policy, 384

financial responsibility laws, 401

independent agent, 403

liability insurance, 380

named peril policy, 384

negligence, 381

no-fault automobile insurance, 398

peril, 380

personal automobile policy (PAP), 394

personal liability umbrella policy, 402

personal property floater (PPF), 387

principle of indemnity, 382

property damage liability losses, 396

property insurance, 380

replacement cost, 390

right of subrogation, 383

underinsured motorists coverage, 397

uninsured motorists coverage, 397

Answers to Test Yourself

You can find answers to these questions on this book's companion website. Look for it at *www.cengagebrain.com*. Search for this book by its title, and then add it to your dashboard.

Financial Planning Exercises

LG1, p. 380   1.   *Co-insurance clauses.* Assume that Tina Walsh had a homeowner's insurance policy with $100,000 of coverage on the dwelling. Would a 90 percent co-insurance clause be better than an 80 percent clause in such a policy? Give reasons to support your answer.

LG2, p. 384   2.   *Evaluating homeowner's policy coverage.* Last year, Brett and Amber Walsh bought a home with a dwelling replacement value of $250,000 and insured it (via an HO-5 policy) for $210,000. The policy reimburses for actual cash value and has a $500 deductible, standard limits for coverage C items, and no scheduled property. Recently, burglars broke into the house and stole a two-year-old television set with a current replacement value of $600 and an estimated useful life of eight years. They also took jewelry valued at $1,850 and silver flatware valued at $3,000.

    a. If the Walsh's policy has an 80 percent co-insurance clause, do they have enough insurance?

    b. Assuming a 50 percent coverage C limit, calculate how much the Walshes would receive if they filed a claim for the stolen items.

    c. What advice would you give the Walshes about their homeowner's coverage?

LG3, p. 384   3. ***Payout on homeowner's insurance policy.*** Eva Stone's home in Chicago was recently gutted in a fire. Her living and dining rooms were destroyed completely, and the damaged personal property had a replacement price of $32,000. The average age of the damaged personal property was 5 years, and its useful life was estimated to be 15 years. What is the maximum amount the insurance company would pay Eva, assuming that it reimburses losses on an actual cash-value basis?

LG3, p. 384   4. ***Need for renter's insurance.*** Tyler and Sherry Hughes both graduate students, moved into an apartment near the university. Sherry wants to buy renter's insurance, but Tyler thinks that they don't need it because their furniture isn't worth much. Sherry points out that, among other things, they have some expensive computer and stereo equipment. To help the Hughes resolve their dilemma, suggest a plan for deciding how much insurance to buy and give them some ideas for finding a policy.

LG4, p. 394   5. ***Personal automobile policy coverage.*** Marc Rose has a PAP with coverage of $25,000/$50,000 for bodily injury liability, $25,000 for property damage liability, $5,000 for medical payments, and a $500 deductible for collision insurance. How much will his insurance cover in each of the following situations? Will he have any out-of-pocket costs?

    a. Marc loses control and skids on ice, running into a parked car and causing $3,785 damage to the unoccupied vehicle and $2,350 damage to his own car.

    b. Marc runs a stop sign and causes a serious auto accident, badly injuring two people. The injured parties win lawsuits against him for $30,000 each.

    c. Marc's 18-year old son borrows his car. He backs into a telephone pole and causes $450 damage to the car.

LG4, p. 394   6. ***Evaluating personal automobile policy features.*** Jose Ruiz is a single 40-year-old loan officer at large regional bank; he has a 16-year-old son. He has decided to use his annual bonus as a down payment on a new car. One Saturday afternoon in late September, he visits Unique Motors and buys a new car for $32,000. To obtain insurance on the car, Jose calls his agent, Carrie Ruffin, who represents Brown's Insurance Agency, and explains his auto insurance needs. Carrie says that she'll investigate the various options for him. Three days later, Jose and Carrie get together to review his coverage options. Carrie offers several proposals, including various combinations of the following coverages: (i) basic automobile liability insurance, (ii) uninsured motorists coverage, (iii) automobile medical payments insurance, (iv) automobile collision insurance, and (v) comprehensive automobile insurance.

    a. Describe the key features of these insurance coverages.

    b. Are there any limitations on these coverages? Explain.

    c. Indicate the persons who would be protected under each type of coverage.

    d. What kind of insurance coverages would you recommend that Jose purchase? Explain your recommendation.

LG5, p. 402   7. ***Supplemental property insurance.*** Chandler and Frances Cornett are a high-net worth couple. They have appropriate auto and homeowner's insurance but are concerned that they could be sued by someone visiting or working at their home. What type of supplemental insurance might be appropriate for the Cornetts in light of their expressed concern? Explain your answer.

LG6, p. 403   8. ***Auto insurance claims.*** Zach and Jane Rendon recently went out for dinner on a rainy night. When the traffic unexpectedly slowed down, they were rear-ended by an inexperienced driver. Describe what steps the Rendons should have taken after the accident to assure that their auto insurance claim would be settled properly.

Applying Personal Finance

Insure Your Property!

Adequate property insurance is a vital part of financial planning. It helps protect our hard-earned investments in a home, car, or other property. This project will help you determine your property insurance needs.

   List the property for which you'd need insurance coverage. Your list may include such things as a home, car, boat, motorcycle, or household items. Beside each entry, list the insurance that you currently have in place on each. Then examine the depth of coverage of your policies. Is this coverage adequate? What are its exclusions and limits? What are the costs? Can you do something to lower these costs? If you don't have coverage or if your coverage is inadequate, research various policies. If you rent a place to live, do you have renter's insurance? If not, tally up what it would cost you to replace all your household items, and then find several quotes for renter's insurance.

CRITICAL THINKING CASES

10.1 *The Perkins' Homeowners' Insurance Decision*

Calvin and Danielle Perkins, ages 30 and 28, were recently married in Kansas City. Calvin is an electrical engineer with Analytical Solutions, a computer component design firm. Danielle has a master's degree in education and teaches at a local middle school. After living in an apartment for six months, the Perkins have negotiated the purchase of a new home in a rapidly growing Kansas City suburb. Kansas City Savings and Loan Association has approved their loan request for $270,000, which represents 90 percent of the $300,000 purchase price. Before closing the loan, the Perkins must obtain homeowner's insurance for the home. The Perkins currently have an HO-4 renter's insurance policy, which they purchased from Calvin's bridge partner, Gene Patterson, who is an agent with the Roberts Insurance Company. To learn about the types of available homeowner's insurance, Calvin has discussed their situation with Gene, who has offered them several homeowner's policies for their consideration. He has recommended that the Perkins purchase an HO-5 policy because it would provide them with comprehensive coverage.

Critical Thinking Questions

1.   What forms of homeowner's insurance are available? Which forms should the Perkins consider?
2.   What are the perils against which the home and its contents should be insured?
3.   Discuss the types of loss protection provided by the homeowner's policies under consideration.
4.   What advice would you give the Perkins regarding Gene's suggestion? What coverage should they buy?

LG2, 3,
p. 384

10.2 *Auto Insurance for Dwight Fox*

Dwight Fox is a 40-year-old loan officer at a large regional bank; he has a 16-year-old son. He has decided to use his annual bonus as a down payment on a new car. One Saturday afternoon he visits Unique Motors and buys a new car for $32,000. To obtain insurance on the car, Dwight calls his agent, Carla Dawson, who represents Brown's Insurance Company, and explains his auto insurance needs. Carla says that she'll investigate the various options for him. Three days later, Dwight and carla get together to review his coverage options. carla offers several proposals, including various combinations of the following coverages: (a) basic automobile liability insurance, (b) uninsured motorist's coverage, (c) automobile medical payments insurance, (d) automobile collision insurance, and (e) comprehensive automobile insurance.

Critical Thinking Questions

1.   Describe the key features of these insurance coverages.
2.   Are there any limitations on these coverages? Explain.
3.   Indicate the persons who would be protected under each type of coverage.
4.   What kind of insurance coverages would you recommend that Dwight purchase? Explain your recommendation.

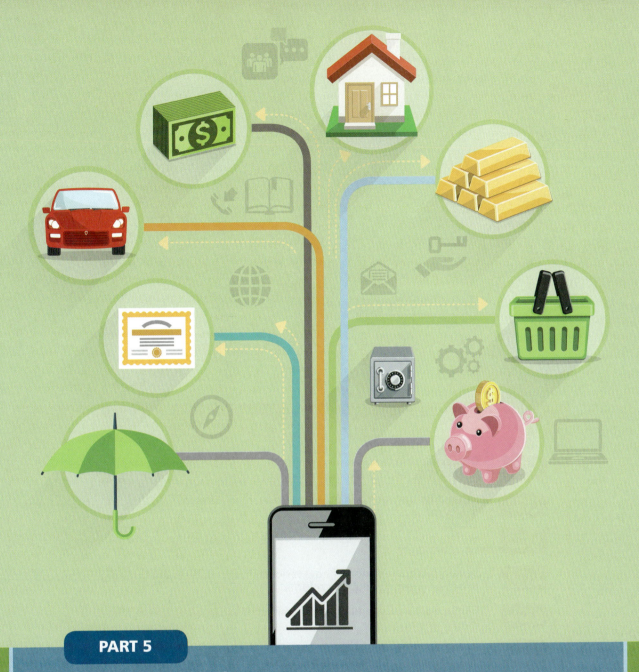

Managing Investments

CHAPTERS

411

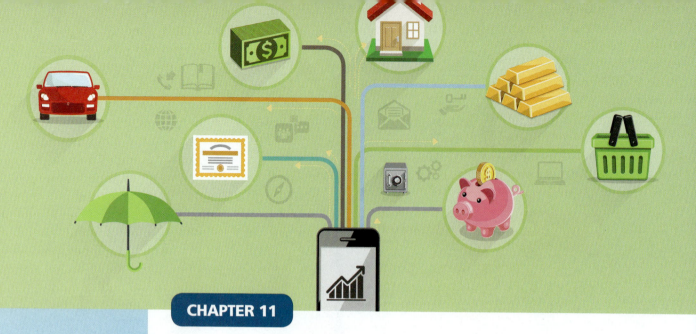

CHAPTER 11

Investment Planning

LEARNING GOALS

LG1 Discuss the role that investing plays in the personal financial planning-process and identify several different investment objectives.

LG2 Distinguish between primary and secondary markets, as well as between broker and dealer markets.

LG3 Explain the process of buying and selling securities and recognize the different types of orders.

LG4 Develop an appreciation of how various forms of investment information can lead to better investing skills and returns.

LG5 Gain a basic understanding of the impact of the Internet on the field of investments.

LG6 Describe an investment portfolio and how you'd go about developing, monitoring, and managing a portfolio of securities.

How Will This Affect Me?

Investing is the means by which many important financial goals in life are achieved. This chapter discusses how to determine the amount of investment capital needed to reach common financial goals and explains how to invest for retirement, to fund major expenditures, to earn needed income, and to establish tax shelters. The market context in which investing occurs is described, and how to buy and sell investments is explained. A framework for evaluating investments is also presented, which includes how to describe, monitor, and manage a portfolio. Sources of investment information are discussed, as well as some of the useful investing tools available online. After reading this chapter you should be able to plan your investments to better meet your financial goals.

11-1 THE OBJECTIVES AND REWARDS OF INVESTING

People invest their money for all sorts of reasons. Some do it as a way to accumulate the down payment on a new home; others do it as a way to supplement their income; still others invest to build up a nest egg for retirement. Actually, the term *investment* means different things to different people; that is, while millions of people *invest* regularly in securities like stocks, bonds, and mutual funds, others *speculate* in commodities or options. **Investing** is generally considered to take a long-term perspective and is viewed as a process of purchasing securities wherein stability of value and level of return are somewhat predictable. **Speculating**, on the other hand, is viewed as the short-term buying and selling of securities in which future value and expected return are highly uncertain. The average investor is **risk averse** and requires higher expected returns as compensation for taking on greater risk. Think of an investor as someone wearing a belt *and* suspenders, whereas the speculator might wear neither.

If you're like most investors, at first you'll probably keep your funds in some type of savings vehicle (as described in Chapter 4). Once you have *sufficient savings*—for emergencies and other purposes—you can start building up a *pool of invested capital*. This often means making sacrifices and doing what you can to *live within your budget*. Granted, it's far easier to spend money than to save it, but if you're really serious about getting into investments, you'll have to accumulate the necessary capital to invest! In addition to a savings and capital accumulation program, it's also important to have adequate *insurance coverage* to provide protection against the unexpected (we discussed different kinds of insurance in Chapters 8, 9, and 10). In this chapter we'll assume that you're adequately insured and that the cost of insurance coverage is built into your family's monthly cash budget. Ample insurance and liquidity (cash and savings) with which to meet life's emergencies are two *investment prerequisites* that are absolutely essential to developing a successful investment program. Once these conditions are met, you're ready to start investing.

11-1a How Do I Get Started?

Contrary to what you may believe, there's really nothing magical about the topic of investments. In fact, so long as you have the capital to do so, it's really quite easy to start investing. The terminology may seem baffling at times, and some of the procedures and techniques may seem quite complicated. But don't let that mislead you into

investing
The process of placing money in some medium such as stocks or bonds in the expectation of receiving some future benefit.

speculating
A form of investing in which future value and expected returns are highly uncertain.

risk averse
The average investor's attitude toward risk is such that, when presented with two investments having the same expected return, the one with the lowest risk will be chosen.

thinking there's no room for the small, individual investor. Nothing could be farther from the truth! As we'll see in this and the next two chapters, individual investors can choose from a wide array of securities and investment vehicles. What's more, opening an investment account is no more difficult than opening a checking account.

How, then, do you get started? First, you need some money—not a lot; $500 to $1,000 will do. And remember, this is *investment capital* we're talking about here—money you've accumulated above and beyond basic emergency savings. Besides the money, you need knowledge and know-how. Never invest in something you don't understand—that's the quickest way to lose money. Instead, learn as much as you can about the market, different types of securities, and various trading strategies. This course you're taking on personal finance is a good start, but you may want to do more, such as becoming a regular reader of publications such as *Money*, *The Wall Street Journal*, *Barron's*, and *Forbes*. We strongly suggest that, after you've learned a few things about stocks and bonds, you set up a portfolio of securities on paper and make *paper trades* in and out of your portfolio, for six months to a year, to get a feel for what it's like to make (and lose) money in the market. Start out with an imaginary sum of, say, $50,000 (if you're going to dream, you might as well dream big). Then keep track of the stocks and bonds you hold, record the number of shares bought and sold, dividends received, and so on. Throughout this exercise, be sure to use actual prices (as obtained from *The Wall Street Journal*, CNN.com, or your local newspaper) and keep it as realistic as possible. You might even want to use one of the *portfolio tracking* programs offered at such sites as **http://www.quicken.com** or **http://moneycentral.msn.com**.

You'll also need a way to invest—more specifically, a brokerage firm (person or online) and some investment vehicle in which to invest. As we'll see later in this chapter, the brokerage is the means whereby you'll be buying and selling stocks, bonds, and other securities. As a beginning investor with limited funds, it's probably best to confine your investment activity to the basics. Stick to stocks, bonds, mutual funds, and exchange-traded funds. Avoid getting fancy. Further, *be patient!* Don't expect the price of the stock to double overnight, and don't panic when things don't work out as expected in the short run (after all, security prices do occasionally go down). Finally, remember that you don't need spectacular returns in order to make a significant amount of money in the market. Instead, be consistent and let compound interest work for you. Do that and you'll find that just $2,000 a year invested at a fairly conservative rate of 5 percent will grow to over $66,000 in 20 years! Although the type of security you invest in is a highly personal decision, you might want to seriously consider some sort of mutual fund as your first investment (see Chapter 13). Mutual funds and exchange-traded funds provide professional management and diversification that individual investors—especially those with limited resources—can rarely obtain on their own.

11-1b The Role of Investing in Personal Financial Planning

Buy a car, build a house, enjoy a comfortable retirement—these are goals we'd all like to attain some day and, in many cases, they're the centerpieces of well-developed financial plans. As a rule, a financial goal such as building a house is not something we pay for out of our cash reserves. Instead, we must accumulate the funds over time, which is where investment planning and the act of investing enters into the personal financial planning process. By investing our money, we are letting it work for us.

It all starts with an objective: a particular financial goal that you'd like to achieve within a certain period of time. Take the case of the Dwyers. Shortly after the birth of their first child, they decided to start a college education fund. After doing some rough calculations, they concluded they'd need to accumulate about $330,000 over the next 18 years to have enough money for their daughter's education. Does that seem like a big number to you? Well, consider that public college tuition, fees, room, and board expenses are currently running around $24,000 a year. Then consider that college costs are expected to increase by more than the general level of inflation. Common estimates are between 5 percent and 7 percent a year for planning purposes.

Simply by setting that objective, the Dwyers created a well-defined, specific financial goal. The purpose is to meet their child's educational needs, and the amount of money involved is $330,000 in 18 years. But how do they reach their goal? First, they must decide where the money will come from. While part of it will come from the return (profit) on their investments, they still have to come up with the initial *investment capital*.

Coming Up with the Capital

So far, the Dwyers know how much money they want to accumulate ($330,000) and how long they have to accumulate it (18 years). The only other thing they need to determine at this point is the *rate of return* that they think they can earn on their money. Having taken a financial planning course in college, the Dwyers know that the amount of money they'll have to put into their investment program largely depends on *how much they can earn from their investments*: the higher their rate of return, the less they'll have to put up. Let's say they feel comfortable using a 6 percent rate of return. That's a fairly conservative number—one that won't require them to put all or most of their money into high-risk investments—and they're reasonably certain they can reach that level of return, *on average*, over the long haul. It's important to use some care in coming up with a projected rate of return. Don't saddle yourself with an unreasonably high rate because that will simply reduce the chance of reaching your targeted financial goal.

A reasonable way to project future returns is to look at what the market has done over the past and then use the average return performance over various historical periods as your estimates. To help you in this regard, take a look at the statistics in the following table; they show the average annual returns on stocks, bonds, and U.S. Treasury bills along with portfolios made up of two or three of these asset classes over holding periods of 5, 10, 15, and 87 years.

Holding Period	Stock Returns (S&P 500)	U.S. Treasury Bond Returns (10-year)	Stocks and Treasury Bonds Together (1/2, 1/2)	Returns on Short-Term U.S. Treasury Bills	Stocks, Bonds, and T-Bills Combined (1/3, 1/3, 1/3)
5 years: 2010–2014	15.69%	5.82%	10.75%	0.07%	7.19%
10 years: 2005–2014	9.37%	5.31%	7.34%	1.44%	5.38%
15 years: 2000–2014	6.00%	6.36%	6.18%	1.85%	4.73%
87 years: 1928–2014	11.53%	5.28%	8.40%	3.53%	6.78%

The average return on stocks over the 15-year period from 2000 to 2014 was 6 percent, and the average return from 1928 to 2014 was 11.53 percent. Thus, even in light of the financial crisis of 2008, long-term stock market performance suggests that average returns of at least 6 percent have not been unusual. The two portrayed portfolios of stocks and T-bonds and of stocks, T-bonds, and T-bills show the effect of diversification. When the stock market does well, its returns tend to exceed bond and bill returns. However, the relative stability of bonds and bills provides some protection when the stock market falters. Of course, there's no guarantee that these historical returns will occur again in the next 10 to 15 years, but the past does at least give us a basis for making projections into the future.

Now, returning to our problem at hand, there are two ways of coming up with the capital needed to reach a targeted sum of money: (1) you can make a lump-sum investment up front and let that amount grow over time; or (2) you can set up a systematic savings plan and put away a certain amount of money each year. Worksheet 11.1 is designed to help you find the amount of investment capital that you'll need to reach a given financial goal. It employs the *compound value* concept discussed in Chapter 2 and is based on a given financial target (line 1) and a projected average rate of return on your investments (line 2). By way of brief review of the chapter 2 framework, the yearly savings required to fund the target goal is computed as:

$$\text{Yearly Savings} = \frac{\text{Future Amount of Money Desired}}{\text{Future Value Annuity Factor}}$$

You can use this worksheet to find either a required lump-sum investment (part A) or an amount that will have to be put away each year in a savings plan (part B). We'll assume the Dwyers have $10,000 to start with (this comes mostly from gifts their daughter received from her grandparents). Since they know they'll need a lot more than that to reach their target, the Dwyers decide to use part B of the worksheet to find out how much they'll have to save annually.

Behavior Matters

Do We Live in the Present Too Much? Looking for Patterns That Aren't There …

Evidence indicates that frequent trading damages the average investor's wealth. A patient, long-term orientation works best. However, neuroscience researchers find that short-term thinking may well be hard-wired into our brains. Using a clever experiment that involved four slot machines with *random payoffs*, participants could choose among machines based on how much a given slot machine paid off. As soon as the payoffs changed, participants moved to the machine that had the most favorable *recent* payoffs. Thus, participants appeared to make choices largely by extrapolating from their most recent experience. This is consistent with so-called *recency cognitive bias*, in which undue emphasis is placed on recent experience in decision making. Thus, it appears that our brains are hard-wired to create patterns even when they don't exist in random data.

The random structure of the experiment is comparable to the returns in financial markets. Recent research finds that among the mutual funds that performed in the top half relative to the Standard & Poor's 500 index, only 49 percent were still in the upper half a year later. And a year after that, only 24 percent remained in the top half of mutual fund performers. Thus, the results seem to be no better than flipping a coin, which is a matter of pure luck. So if our brains are hard-wired to act on patterns that don't really exist, it's no surprise that most investors find it hard to pursue a long-term, buy-and-hold investing strategy.

Given this built-in bias, what should you do with your investments? Recognize that you may well have this bias yourself and be deliberate in your investment decision making. Make a list of criteria that every investment must meet before you buy or sell. Don't buy or sell only because of recent price moves. List three reasons for making the investment that have nothing to do with recent price performance. It's also critically important to follow the performance of an investment *after* you sell it as well. That lets you know if what you bought did better or worse than if you'd held the original investment. Understanding built-in behavioral biases is the start of more informed and consistent investing.

Source: Adapted from Jason Zweig, "Why We're Driven to Trade," http://professional.wsj.com/article/SB10000872396390444409790457753892403159182.html, accessed August 2015.

The first thing to do is find the future value of the $10,000 initial investment at the assumed 6 percent average rate of return. The specific question here is: How much will that initial lump-sum investment grow to over an 18-year period? Using the compound value concept and the appropriate "future value factor" (from Appendix A) for 6 percent and 18 years, we see in line 7 that this deposit will grow to about $28,540. That's only about 9 percent of the target amount of $330,000. Thus, by subtracting the terminal value of the initial investment (line 7) from our target (line 1), we find the amount that must be generated from some sort of annual savings plan—see line 8. (*Note:* If you were starting from scratch then you'd enter a zero in line 5, and the amount in line 8 would be equal to the amount in line 1.) Again, using the appropriate future value factor (this time from Appendix B), we find that the Dwyers will have to put away about $9,754 a year in order to reach their target of $330,000 in 18 years. That is, the $9,754 a year will grow to $301,460, and this amount plus $28,540 (the amount to which the initial $10,000 will grow) equals the Dwyers targeted financial goal of $330,000. (By the way, they can also reach their target by making an up-front lump-sum investment of $115,613—try working out part A of the worksheet on your own to see if you can come up with that number.) As you might have suspected, the last few steps in the worksheet can just as easily be done on a financial calculator. That is, after determining the size of the nest egg (as in step 8, for example), you can use a financial calculator to find the amount of money that must be put away each year to fund the nest egg.

Calculator

INPUTS	FUNCTIONS
18	N
6	I/Y
− 301,460	FV
	CPT
	PMT
	SOLUTION
	9,754.20

See Appendix E for details.

Calculator Keystrokes. You can use a financial calculator to *find the annual payments necessary to fund a target amount* by first putting the calculator in the *annual compounding* mode. Then, to determine the amount of money that must be put away each year, at a 6 percent rate of return, to accumulate $301,460 in 18 years, make the keystrokes shown here, where:

N = number of *years* in investment horizon
I/Y = expected average *annual* rate of return on investments
FV = the targeted amount of money you want to accumulate, entered as a *negative* number

The calculator should then display a value of $9,754.20 (net of the $ sign on most calculators), which is the amount of money that must be put away each year to reach the targeted amount of $301,460 in 18 years. (*Note:* The calculator keystrokes take you from steps 8 to 10 in Worksheet 11.1. You can also do steps 5 to 7 on the calculator by letting N = 18, I/Y = 6.0, and PV = −10000; then solve for (CPT) FV. Try it—you should come up with a number fairly close to the amount shown on line 7 of Worksheet 11.1.)

An Investment Plan Provides Direction

Now that the Dwyers know how much they have to save each year, their next step is deciding how they'll save it. For many investors, it's best to follow some type of *systematic routine*—for example, build a set amount of savings each month or quarter into the household budget and then stick with it. But whatever procedure is followed, keep in mind that all we're doing here is accumulating the required investment capital. That money still has to be put to work in some kind of investment program, and that's where an investment plan enters the picture. An **investment plan** is nothing

investment plan
A statement—preferably written—that specifies how investment capital will be invested to achieve a specified goal.

You can use a worksheet like this one to find out how much money you must come up with to reach a given financial goal. This worksheet is based on the same future value concepts we first introduced in Chapter 2

DETERMINING AMOUNT OF INVESTMENT CAPITAL

Financial goal: _To accumulate $330,000 in 18 years for the purpose of meeting the cost of daughter's college education._

1. Targeted Financial Goal (see Note 1)		$ 330,000
2. Projected Average Return on Investments		6%
A. Finding a Lump Sum Investment:		
3. Future Value Factor, from Appendix A ■ based on _____ years to target date and a projected average return on investment of ___%___		0.000
4. Required Lump Sum Investment ■ line 1 ÷ line 3		$ 0
B. Making a Series of Investments over Time:		
5. Amount of Initial Investment, if any (see Note 2)		$ 10,000
6. Future Value Factor, from Appendix A ■ based on _18_ years of target date and a projected average return on investment of _6%_		2.854
7. Terminal Value of Initial Investment ■ line 5 × line 6		$ 28,540
8. Balance to Come from Savings Plan ■ line 1 − line 7		$ 301,460.
9. Future Value Annuity Factor, from Appendix B ■ based on _18_ years to target date and a projected average return on investment of _6%_		30.906
10. Series of Annual Investments Required over Time ■ line 8 ÷ line 9		$ 9,754

Note 1: The "targeted financial goal" is the amount of money you want to accumulate by some target date in the future.

Note 2: If you're starting from scratch—that is, there is *no* initial investment—enter zero on line 5, *skip* lines 6 and 7, and then use the total targeted financial goal (from line 1) as the amount to be funded from a savings plan; now proceed with the rest of the worksheet.

more than a simple—preferably written—statement explaining how the accumulated investment capital will be invested in order to reach the targeted goal. In the Dwyers case, their capital accumulation plan calls for a 6 percent rate of return as a target they feel they can achieve. Now they need to find a way to obtain that 6 percent return on their money—meaning they have to specify, in general terms at least, the kinds of investment vehicles they intend to use. When completed, *an investment plan is a way of translating an abstract investment target* (in this case, a 6 percent return) *into a specific investment program.*

11-1c What Are Your Investment Objectives?

Some people buy securities for the protection they provide from taxes, which is what tax shelters are all about. Others want to have money put aside for that proverbial rainy day or, perhaps, to build up a nice retirement nest egg. *Your goals tend to set the tone for your investment program, and they play a major role in determining how conservative (or aggressive) you're likely to be in making investment decisions.* These goals define the purpose for your investments. Given that you have adequate savings and insurance to cover any emergencies, the most frequent investment objectives are to (1) accumulate funds for retirement, (2) save for a major purchase, (3) enhance current income, and (4) seek shelter from taxes.

©WAVEBREAKMEDIA/SHUTTERSTOCK.COM

Retirement

Accumulating funds for retirement is *the single most important reason for investing*. Too often, though, retirement planning occupies only a small amount of our time because we tend to rely too heavily on employers and Social Security for our retirement needs. As many people learn too late in life, that can be a serious mistake. A much better approach is to review the amounts of income you can realistically expect to receive from Social Security and your employee pension plan, and then decide, based on your retirement goals, *whether they'll be adequate to meet your needs.* You'll probably find that you'll have to supplement them through personal investing. (Retirement plans are discussed in Chapter 14.)

Major Expenditures

People often put money aside, sometimes for years, to save up enough to make just one major expenditure. Here are the most common ones:

- Down payment on a home
- Money for a child's college education
- Capital for going into business
- Expensive (perhaps once-in-a-lifetime) vacation
- Purchase of a special, expensive item
- Funds for retirement

Whatever your goal, the idea is to set your sights on something and then go about building your capital with that objective in mind. Once you know about how much money you're going to need to attain one of these goals (following a procedure like the one illustrated in Worksheet 11.1), you can specify the types of investment vehicles that you intend to use. For example, you might follow a low-risk approach by making a single lump-sum investment in a high-grade bond that matures the same year that you'll need the funds; or you could follow a riskier investment plan that calls for investing a set amount of money over time in something like a growth-oriented mutual fund (where there's little assurance of the investment's terminal value). Of course, for some purposes—such as the down payment on a home or a child's education—you'll probably want to take a lot less risk than for others, because attaining these goals should not be jeopardized by the types of investment vehicles that you choose to employ.

Current Income

The idea with current income is to put your money into investments that will enable you to supplement your income. In other words, it's for people who want to live off their investment income. A secure source of high current income, from dividends or interest, is the primary concern of such investors. Retired people, for example, often choose investments offering high current income at low risk. Another common reason for seeking supplemental income is that a family member requires extended, costly medical care. Even after insurance, such recurring costs can heavily burden a family budget without this vital income supplement.

Shelter from Taxes

As explained in Chapter 3, federal income taxes do not treat all sources of income equally. For example, if you own real estate then you may be able to take depreciation deductions against certain other sources of income, thereby reducing the amount of your taxable income. This tax write-off feature can make real estate an attractive investment vehicle for some investors, even though its pre-tax rate of return may not appear very high. The goal of sheltering income from taxes is a legitimate one that, for some investors, often goes hand in hand with the goals of saving for a major outlay or for retirement. If you can avoid paying taxes on the income from an investment then you will, all other things considered, have more funds available for reinvestment during the period.

11-1d Different Ways to Invest

After establishing your investment objectives, you can use a variety of investment vehicles to fulfill those goals. In this section, we'll briefly describe various types of investments that are popular with (and widely used by) individual investors.

Common Stock

Common stocks are a form of *equity*—as an investment, they represent an ownership interest in a corporation. Each share of stock symbolizes a fractional ownership position in a firm; for example, one share of common stock in a corporation that has 10,000 shares outstanding would denote a 1/10,000 ownership interest in the firm. A share of stock typically entitles the holder to equal participation in the corporation's earnings and dividends as well as an equal vote to elect the management of the corporation. From the investor's perspective, the return to stockholders comes from dividends and/or appreciation in share price. Common stock has no maturity date and, as a result, remains outstanding indefinitely (common stocks are discussed in Chapter 12).

Bonds

In contrast to stocks, *bonds* are *liabilities*—they're IOUs of the issuer. Governments and corporations issue bonds that pay a stated return, called *interest*. An individual who invests in a bond receives a stipulated interest income, typically paid every six months, plus the return of the principal (face) value of the bond at maturity. For example, if you purchased a $1,000 bond that paid 5 percent interest in semiannual installments, then you could expect to receive $25 every six months (i.e., 5 percent $\times$ 0.5 years $\times$ $1,000) and at maturity, recover the $1,000 face value of the bond. Of course, a bond can be bought or sold prior to maturity at a price that may differ from its face value because bond prices, like common stock prices, fluctuate in the marketplace (see Chapter 12).

Preferreds and Convertibles

These are forms of *hybrid securities* in that each has the characteristics of both stocks and bonds; they're a cross between the two. *Preferred securities* are issued as stock and, as such, represent an equity position in a corporation. But unlike common stock, preferreds have a stated (fixed) dividend rate that is paid before the dividends to holders of common stock are paid. Like bonds, preferred stocks are usually purchased for the current income (dividends) they pay. A *convertible security*, in contrast, is a fixed-income obligation (usually a bond, but sometimes a preferred stock) that carries a conversion feature permitting the investor to convert it into a specified number of shares of common stock. Thus convertible securities provide the fixed-income benefits (interest) of a bond while offering the price appreciation (capital gains) potential of common stock. (Convertibles are discussed in Chapter 12.)

Mutual Funds, Exchange-Traded Funds, and Exchange Traded Notes

An organization that invests in and professionally manages a diversified portfolio of securities is called a *mutual fund*. A mutual fund sells shares to investors, who then become part owners of the fund's securities portfolio. Most mutual funds issue and repurchase shares at a price that reflects the underlying value of the portfolio at the time the transaction is made. Mutual funds have become popular with individual investors because they offer a wide variety of investment opportunities and a full array of services that many investors find particularly appealing (these securities are discussed in Chapter 13).

Exchange-traded funds (ETFs) are similar to mutual funds in that they are portfolios of securities. They are commonly designed to track a basket or index of equity securities like the S&P 500 or a particular sector, such as telecommunications or utility stocks. They can also include other types of investments, which include bonds and real estate. Whereas mutual funds can be bought or sold only at the end of the day, investors can trade ETFs throughout the trading day just like individual shares of stock. ETFs offer certain advantages over mutual funds. For example, unlike mutual funds, they trade continuously throughout the trading day and can be purchased with borrowed money or sold short. Further, ETFs provide more favorable tax treatment than mutual funds.

Exchange-traded notes (ETNs) are more similar to ETFs than to mutual funds. They are senior, unsecured, unsubordinated debt securities issued by an underwriting bank. As such, ETNs are debt securities that have a maturity date and are backed only by the credit of the issuer. Like ETFs, most ETNs are designed to reproduce the returns on a market benchmark, net of investment management fees. Thus, the underwriting bank promises to pay an amount based on the value of the index, net of fees, upon maturity. It's important to realize that an ETN bears a different risk than an ETF. If the bank underwriting the ETN goes bankrupt, the ETN might lose value just as a senior debt security would. Consequently, ETFs only face the risk of market fluctuations, while ETNs face both market risk and the risk that the issuing bank will default. Unfortunately, this credit risk is hard for investors to evaluate. Like ETFs, ETNs are traded on an exchange and can be sold short. Also like ETFs, ETNs provide tax advantages over mutual funds. (More information on these advantages, and disadvantages, will be given in Chapter 13.)

Real Estate

Investments in *real estate* can take many forms, ranging from raw land speculation to limited-partnership shares in commercial property, even real estate mutual funds. The returns on real estate come from rents, capital gains, and certain tax benefits. (Various types of real estate investments are discussed in Chapter 13.)

TEST YOURSELF

11-1 Briefly discuss the relationship between investing and personal financial planning.

11-2 What's the difference between an investment plan and a capital accumulation plan?

11-3 Why is it important to have investment objectives when embarking on an investment program?

11-2 SECURITIES MARKETS

LG2

securities markets
The marketplace in which stocks, bonds, and other financial instruments are traded.

The term **securities markets** generally describes the arena where stocks, bonds, and other financial instruments are traded. Such markets can be physical places, but they can just as easily be *electronic networks* that allow buyers and sellers to come together to execute trades. Securities markets can be broken into two parts: capital markets and money markets. The *capital market* is where long-term securities like stocks and bonds are traded. The *money market* is the marketplace for short-term, low-risk credit instruments with maturities of 1 year or less; these include U.S. Treasury bills, commercial paper, negotiable certificates of deposit, and so on. Both types of markets provide a vital mechanism for bringing the buyers and sellers of securities together. Some of the more popular money market securities were discussed in Chapter 4, where we looked at short-term investment vehicles. In this chapter, we consider the capital markets.

11-2a Primary and Secondary Markets

Securities markets can also be divided into primary and secondary segments. In the *primary market*, new securities are sold to the public, and one party to the transaction is always the issuer. In contrast, old (outstanding) securities are bought and sold in the *secondary market*, where the securities are "traded" between investors. A security is sold in the primary market just once, when it's originally issued by a corporation or a governmental body (e.g., a state or municipality). Subsequent transactions, in which securities are sold by one investor to another, take place in the secondary market.

Primary Markets

When a corporation sells a new issue to the public, several financial institutions will participate in the transaction. To begin with, the corporation will probably use an *investment banking firm*, which specializes in *underwriting* (selling) new security issues. The investment banker will give the corporation advice on pricing and other aspects of the issue and will either sell the new security itself or arrange for a *selling group* to do so. The selling group is normally made up of several brokerage firms, each responsible for selling a certain portion of the new issue. On large issues, the originating investment banker will bring in other underwriting firms as partners and form an *underwriting syndicate* in order to spread the risks associated with underwriting and selling the new securities. A potential investor in a new issue must be given a **prospectus**, which is a document describing the firm and the issue. Certain federal agencies are responsible for ensuring that all the information included in a prospectus accurately represents the facts.

prospectus
A document made available to prospective security buyers that describes the firm and a new security issue.

Secondary Markets

The secondary markets permit investors to execute transactions among themselves; it's the marketplace where an investor can easily sell his or her holdings to someone else. Unlike primary market transactions, the secondary market does not generate cash for the underlying company (issuer). Included among the secondary markets are the various *securities exchanges*, in which the buyers and sellers of securities are brought together for the purpose of executing trades. Another major segment of the market is made up of those securities that are listed and traded on the *National Association of Securities Dealers Automated Quotation System (NASDAQ)* market, which employs an all-electronic trading platform to execute trades. Finally, the *over-the-counter (OTC)* market deals in smaller, unlisted securities.

11-2b Broker Markets and Dealer Markets

By far, the vast majority of trades made by small individual investors take place in the secondary market, so we'll focus on it for the rest of this chapter. When you look at the secondary market *on the basis of how securities are traded*, you'll find you can essentially divide the market into two segments: broker markets and dealer markets. Exhibit 11.1 shows the structure of the secondary market in terms of broker or dealer markets. As you can see, the *broker market* consists of national and regional "securities exchanges," while the *dealer market* is made up of both the NASDAQ market and the OTC market.

EXHIBIT 11.1 **Broker and Dealer Markets**

On a typical trading day, the secondary market is a beehive of activity, where literally billions of shares change hands. This market consists of two parts, the broker market and the dealer market. As can be seen, each of these markets is made up of various exchanges and trading venues.

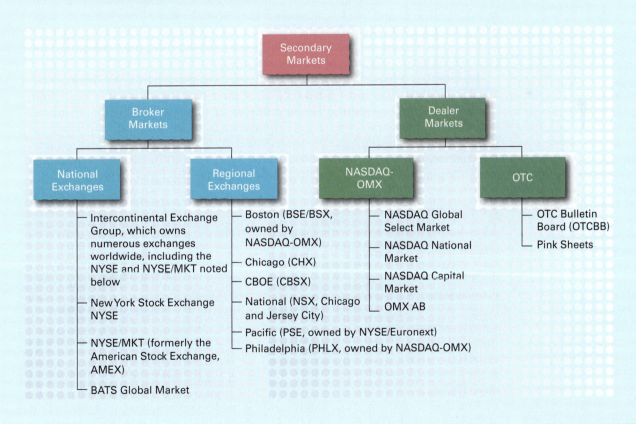

It's important to understand that a key *difference between the two markets is how the trades are executed*. That is, when a trade occurs in a *broker market* (on one of the so-called securities exchanges), the two sides to the transaction—the buyer and the seller—are brought together and the trade takes place at that point: Party A sells his securities directly to the buyer, Party B. In a sense, with the help of a *broker*, the securities change hands right there on the floor of the exchange. In contrast, when trades are made in one of the *dealer markets*, the buyer and seller are never brought together directly; instead, their buy/sell orders are executed separately through *securities dealers*, who act as *market makers*. Essentially, two separate trades are made: Party A sells his securities (in, say, the XYZ Corp.) to one dealer, and Party B buys her securities (in the same XYZ Corp.) from the same dealer or another dealer. Thus, there is always a dealer (market maker) on one side of the transaction.

Broker Markets

When you think of the stock market, if you're like most individual investors, then the first name to come to mind is the New York Stock Exchange (NYSE), which has been the largest stock exchange in the United States. In 2007, the NYSE combined with Euronext, which is the combination of stock exchanges in Amsterdam, Brussels, Lisbon, and Paris. The combined entity, NYSE Euronext, operates six cash equities exchanges in seven countries. And in late 2013 NYSE Euronext was acquired by the Intercontinental Exchange Group (ICE). ICE operates 11 regulated exchanges and numerous central clearing houses. In late 2014 its listings included companies with an aggregate market value in excess of $28 trillion. It includes about 90 percent of the firms in the Dow Jones Industrial Average (DJIA) and about 80 percent of the firms in the S&P 500 index. ICE also owns the American Stock Exchange (AMEX), which was formerly the second-largest U.S. exchange. The AMEX had less restrictive listing requirements than the NYSE, so the acquisition allowed the NYSE to broaden the types of companies falling under its umbrella. The organization is also referred to as NYSE MKT. In mid-2014 ICE spun off Euronext as a standalone European company. The ICE entity is a part of the broker market—indeed, it's their biggest player! BATS Global Market merged with Direct Edge in 2014. This created one of the largest stock exchange operators in the United States.

Besides ICE, a handful of *regional exchanges* are also a part of the broker market. The number of securities listed on each of these exchanges typically ranges from about 100 to 500 companies. The best known of these are the Boston, National, Pacific, and Philadelphia exchanges. These exchanges deal primarily in securities with local and regional appeal. Most are modeled after the NYSE, but their membership and listing requirements are considerably more lenient. To enhance their trading activity, regional exchanges often list securities that are also listed on the NYSE.

Dealer Markets

A key feature of the dealer market is that, unlike the NYSE, it doesn't have centralized trading floors. Instead, it's made up of many market makers who are linked together via a mass telecommunications network. Each market maker is actually a securities dealer who makes a market in one or more securities by offering to either buy or sell them at stated bid/ask prices. (The **bid price** and **ask price** represent, respectively, the highest price offered to purchase a given security and the lowest price at which the security is offered for sale; in effect, an investor pays the ask price when *buying* securities and receives the bid price when *selling* them.) Consisting of both the NASDAQ and OTC markets, dealer markets account for about 40 percent of all shares traded in the U.S. market—with NASDAQ accounting for the overwhelming majority of those trades.

The biggest dealer market, hands down, is made up of a select list of stocks that are listed and traded on the *NASDAQ*. Founded in 1971, NASDAQ had its origins in the OTC market, but today it is considered *a totally separate entity that's no longer*

bid price
The price at which one can sell a security.

ask price
The price at which one can purchase a security.

a part of the OTC market. In fact, in 2006, the Securities and Exchange Commission (SEC) formally recognized NASDAQ as a "listed exchange," giving it much the same stature and prestige as the NYSE. To be traded on NASDAQ, all stocks must have at least two market makers—although the bigger, more actively traded stocks (such as Apple) will have many more than that. These dealers electronically post all their bid/ask prices so that, when investors place (market) orders, they're immediately filled at the best available price. In 2008, NASDAQ combined its business with OMX AB, which owned and operated the largest securities market in northern Europe. It also acquired the Philadelphia and Boston stock exchanges. Across its markets, NASDAQ lists about 3,500 companies with an aggregate market value of $9.5 trillion from all over the world.

NASDAQ sets various listing standards, the most comprehensive of which are for the 2,000 or so stocks traded on the *NASDAQ National Market (NNM)* and the roughly 1,000 stocks traded on the *NASDAQ Global Select Market* (this market is reserved for the biggest and bluest NASDAQ stocks). Stocks included on these two markets are all actively traded and, in general, have a *national following.* These securities are widely quoted, and the trades, all executed electronically, are just as efficient as they are on the floor of the NYSE. Indeed, just as the NYSE has its list of big-name players (e.g., ExxonMobil, Wal-Mart, Pfizer, IBM, Coca-Cola, Home Depot, and UPS), so too does NASDAQ—including names like Apple, Microsoft, Intel, Cisco Systems, eBay, and Google.

The other part of the dealer market is made up of securities that trade in the *OTC market.* This market is separate from NASDAQ and includes mostly small companies that either can't or don't wish to comply with NASDAQ listing requirements. They trade on either the *OTC Bulletin Board (OTCBB)* or in the so-called *Pink Sheets.* The OTCBB is an electronic quotation system that links the market makers who trade the shares of small companies. The OTCBB is regulated by the SEC, which requires

(among other things) that all companies traded on this market file audited financial statements and comply with federal securities law. In sharp contrast, the OTC Pink Sheets represent the *unregulated* segment of the market, where the companies aren't even required to file with the SEC. Actually, this market is broken into two tiers. The larger (bottom) tier is populated by all those small and oftentimes questionable companies that provide little or no information about their operations, while the top (albeit smaller) tier is reserved for companies that choose to provide audited financial statements and other required information. Their name comes from the color of paper these quotes used to be printed on, but today the Pinks use an electronic quotation system. Even so, liquidity is often minimal or almost nonexistent; and the market, especially the bottom tier, is littered with scores of nearly worthless stocks—definitely not a market for the uninitiated!

11-2c Foreign Securities Markets

In addition to those in the United States, more than 100 other countries worldwide have organized securities exchanges. Indeed, actively traded markets can be found not only in the major industrialized nations like Japan, Great Britain, Germany, and Canada but also in emerging economies. In terms of market capitalization (total market value of all shares traded), the NYSE is the biggest stock market in the world, followed by the Tokyo stock market and then the NASDAQ market. After these three markets comes the London market, then Toronto and Frankfurt. Other major exchanges are located in Sydney, Zurich, Hong Kong, Singapore, Rome, and Amsterdam. Besides these markets, you'll find developing markets all over the globe—from Argentina and Armenia to Egypt and Fiji; from Iceland, Israel, and Malaysia to New Zealand, Russia, and Zimbabwe.

11-2d Regulating the Securities Markets

Several laws have been enacted to regulate the activities of various participants in the securities markets and to provide for adequate and accurate disclosure of information to potential and existing investors. State laws, regulating the sale of securities within state borders, typically establish procedures that apply to the sellers of securities doing business within the state. However, the most important and far-reaching securities laws are those enacted by the federal government.

Securities and Exchange Commission (SEC)
An agency of the federal government that regulates the disclosure of information about securities and generally oversees the operation of securities exchanges and markets.

- **Securities Act of 1933:** This act was passed by Congress to ensure full disclosure of information with respect to new security issues and to prevent a stock market collapse similar to the one that occurred during 1929–1932. The Act requires the issuer of a new security to file a registration statement containing information about the new issue with the **Securities and Exchange Commission (SEC)**, an agency of the U.S. government established to enforce federal securities laws.

- **Securities Exchange Act of 1934:** This act expanded the scope of federal regulation and formally established the SEC as the agency in charge of the administration of federal securities laws. The Act gives the SEC power to regulate organized securities exchanges and the OTC market by extending disclosure requirements to outstanding securities. It requires the stock exchanges and the stocks traded on them to be registered with the SEC.

- **Investment Company Act of 1940:** This act protects those purchasing investment company (mutual fund) shares. It established rules and regulations for investment companies and formally authorized the SEC to regulate the companies' practices and procedures. It requires investment companies to register with the SEC and to fulfill certain disclosure requirements. The Act was amended in 1970 to prohibit investment companies from paying excessive fees to their advisors and from charging excessive commissions to purchasers of company shares.

- **Sarbanes–Oxley Act of 2002:** The purpose of this act (known as "SOX" for short) is to eliminate corporate fraud as related to accounting practices and other information released to investors. Among other things, SOX requires an annual evaluation of internal controls and procedures for financial reporting; it also requires the top executives of the corporation, as well as its auditors, to certify the accuracy of its financial statements and disclosures. What's more, it prohibits audit/accounting firms from engaging in consulting activities with its clients and establishes ethical guidelines for financial officers and security analysts.

- **Dodd–Frank Wall Street Reform and Consumer Protection Act of 2010:** Prompted by the financial crisis of 2008–2009, this legislation is designed primarily to improve accountability and transparency in the U.S. financial system, to discontinue the "too big to fail" regulatory approach, to protect American taxpayers from costly government bailouts, and to protect consumers from exploitative financial services practices. The Act is the most significant change in financial regulation since the Great Depression. The legislation contains the so-called Volcker Rule, which prohibits depository banks from proprietary trading. Finally, the Act created new federal agencies, which include the Financial Stability Oversight Council, the Office of Financial Research, and the Bureau of Consumer Financial Protection.

National Association of Securities Dealers (NASD)
An agency made up of brokers and dealers in over-the-counter securities that regulates OTC market operations.

- **Other significant federal legislation:** The *Maloney Act of 1938* provided for the establishment of trade associations for the purpose of self-regulation within the securities industry. This act led to the creation of the **National Association of Securities Dealers (NASD)**, which is made up of all brokers and dealers who participate in the OTC market. The NASD is a self-regulatory organization that polices the activities of brokers and dealers to ensure that its standards are upheld. The SEC supervises NASD activities, thus further protecting investors from fraudulent activities. *The Securities Investor Protection Act of 1970* created the Securities

Investor Protection Corporation (SIPC), an organization that protects investors against the financial failure of brokerage firms, much as the Federal Deposit Insurance Corporation (FDIC) protects depositors against bank failures (we'll examine the SIPC later in this chapter).

11-2e Bull Market or Bear?

The general condition of the market is termed as either *bullish* or *bearish*, depending on whether securities prices are rising or falling over extended periods. Changing market conditions generally stem from changing investor attitudes, changes in economic activity, and certain governmental actions aimed at stimulating or slowing down the economy. Prices go *up* in **bull markets**; these favorable markets are normally associated with investor optimism, economic recovery, and growth. In contrast, prices go *down* in **bear markets**, which are normally associated with investor pessimism and economic slowdowns. These terms are used to describe conditions in the bond and other securities markets as well as the stock market. As a rule, investors can earn attractive rates of return during bull markets and only low (or negative) returns during bear markets. Exhibit 11.2 shows historical U.S. stock market performance going all the way back to 1825.

Look closely at the exhibit and you'll notice that, over the past 50 years or so, stock market behavior has been generally bullish, reflecting the growth and prosperity of the economy (the market was up about 75 percent of the last 50 years). Since World War II, the longest bull market lasted 125 months—from November 1990 through March 2000. This bull market is probably as well known for *how it ended* as it is for the returns it generated. That record-breaking bull market ended abruptly in the spring of 2000, when a nasty bear market took over. After recovering in October 2002, the market generally advanced until about October 2007, when the full effects of the financial crisis started to become apparent. The S&P 500 lost about 37 percent in 2008 yet rose by about 40 percent between March and May of 2009. The S&P 500 has varied significantly since, producing a low return of only about 2 percent in 2011 but a return in excess of 32 percent in 2013 and about 13.7 percent in 2014. The index produced a return of about 3 percent during the first six months of 2015.

Let's put recent developments in general and the financial crisis in particular in perspective. As Exhibit 11.2 shows, the 2008 decline was the second-worst stock market performance since 1825. Losses that bad occurred only in 1931 and 1937. Since 1825, returns increased in 134 years and decreased in 56 years.

bull market
A market condition normally associated with investor optimism, economic recovery, and expansion; characterized by generally rising securities prices.

bear market
A condition of the market typically associated with investor pessimism and economic slowdown; characterized by generally falling securities prices.

TEST YOURSELF

11-4 How does a primary market differ from a secondary market? Where are most securities traded: in the primary or the secondary market?

11-5 What is the difference between the broker and dealer markets?

11-6 What are regional exchanges, and what role do they play?

11-7 Describe the operations of the NASDAQ market. Compare it with an exchange, such as the NYSE.

11-8 Contrast the NASDAQ and National Market System with the OTCBB.

11-9 Explain the difference between a *bull* market and a *bear* market. Discuss the frequency with which returns as bad as those during 2008–2009 occur. How would you characterize the current state of the stock market?

This graphical portrayal of U.S. stock market performance since 1825 shows the variability in returns.

US stock market
Total return, %

Years
- 2000–2014
- 1900–1999
- 1825–1899

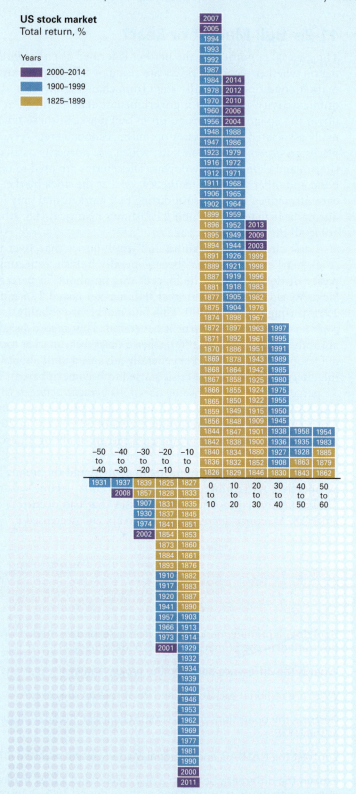

Source: Adapted from "U.S. Stockmarket Returns: Booms and Busts," http://www.economist.com/node/12811306. Based in part on data from Value Square Asset Management, "A New Historical Database of the NYSE 1815 to 1925: Performance and Predictability," Yale School of Management Working Paper, July 2000; data updated by authors.

11-3 MAKING TRANSACTIONS IN THE SECURITIES MARKETS

 In many respects, dealing in the securities markets almost seems like operating in another world, one with all kinds of unusual orders and strange-sounding transactions. Actually, making securities transactions is relatively simple once you understand the basics—in fact, you'll probably find it's no harder than using a checking account!

11-3a Stockbrokers

Stockbroker (account executive, financial consultant)
A person who buys and sells securities on behalf of clients and gives them investment advice and information.

Stockbrokers, or **account executives** and **financial consultants**, as they're also called, buy and sell securities for their customers. Although deeply ingrained in our language, the term *stockbroker* is really somewhat of a misnomer, as they help investors buy and sell not only stocks but also bonds, convertibles, mutual funds, options, and many other types of securities. Brokers must be licensed by the exchanges and must abide by the ethical guidelines of the exchanges and SEC regulations. They work for brokerage firms and in essence are there to execute the orders placed. As discussed earlier, procedures for executing orders in broker markets differ a bit from those in dealer markets; but you as an investor would never know the difference because you'd place your order in exactly the same way.

Selecting a Broker

If you decide to start investing with a *full-service broker*, it's important to select someone *who understands your investment objectives and who can effectively help you pursue them*. If you choose a broker whose own disposition toward investing is similar to yours, then you should be able to avoid conflict and establish a solid working relationship. A good place to start the search is to ask friends, relatives, or business associates to recommend a broker. It's not important to know your stockbroker

FINANCIAL PLANNING TIPS

Is It Time to Get a Robo Investment Advisor?

Robo investment advisers are Internet-based platforms that typically use algorithms to recommend portfolios of low-cost exchange-traded funds across multiple asset classes based on online questionnaires completed by investors. In the last few years, more than 200 companies have entered the market to help investors plan their portfolios online. These include fund giants Fidelity Investments, Vanguard Group, and brokerage firms such as Charles Schwab. While currently only a fraction of the wealth management market, digital wealth-management assets are projected to reach $60 billion soon.

The average robo-adviser customer is millennial, self-directed, and comfortable with technology. Robo-advisers charge annual management fees usually ranging between 0.25 percent and 0.75 percent of assets plus fund expenses. In contrast, traditional advisers tend to charge an average of 1 percent. The rationale for robo investment advisers is that investors are best served by low fees and broadly diversified portfolios.

Should you be tempted to use a robo-adviser? Low expenses and simplified investment management are positives. However, surveys indicate that investors with the same investment objectives can receive markedly different advice from the broad array of robo-advisers. Keep in mind that you can get a bit of hand-holding from companies like Vanguard's Personal Advisor Services (**https://investor.vanguard.com/advice/personal-advisor**) and Personal Capital (**https://www.personalcapital.com/**). It makes sense to sample a number of robo-advisors' platforms and read their reviews carefully. And it's wise to do your homework before putting your investment portfolio on (semi-) automatic pilot.

Source: Adapted, from Liz Moyer, "Putting Robo Advisers to the Test," *The Wall Street Journal*, **http://www.wsj.com/articles/putting-robo-advisers-to-the-test-1429887456**, accessed August 2015.

socially because most, if not all, of your transactions/orders will probably be placed online or by phone. But a broker should be far more than just a salesperson; *a good broker is someone who's more interested in your investments than in his or her own commissions*. Should you find you're dealing with someone who's always trying to get you to trade your stocks or who's pushing new investments on you, then by all means dump that broker and find a new one!

Full-Service, Discount, and Online Brokers

Just a few years ago, there were three distinct types of brokers—full-service, discount, and online—and each occupied a well-defined market niche. Today, the lines between these three types of brokers are blurred. Most brokerage firms, even the more traditional ones, now offer online services to compete with the increasingly popular online firms. And many discount brokers now offer services, such as research reports for clients, that once were available only from a full-service broker.

The traditional **full-service broker** offers investors a wide array of brokerage services, including investment advice and information, trade execution, holding securities for safekeeping, online brokerage services, and margin loans. Such services are fine for investors who want such help—and are willing to pay for it. In contrast, investors who simply want to execute trades and aren't interested in obtaining all those brokerage services should consider either a *discount broker* or *an online broker*. **Discount brokers** tend to have low-overhead operations and offer fewer customer services than do full-service brokers. Transactions are initiated by calling a toll-free number—or visiting the broker's Web site—and placing the desired buy or sell order. The brokerage firm then executes the order at the best possible price and confirms the transaction details by phone, e-mail, or regular mail. Depending on the transaction size, *discount brokers can save investors from 30 percent to 80 percent of the commissions charged by full-service brokers.*

With the technology that's available to almost everyone today, it's not surprising that investors can more easily trade securities online than on the phone. All you need is an **online broker** (also called *Internet* or *electronic brokers*) and you, too, can execute trades electronically. The investor merely accesses the online broker's Internet site to open an account, review the commission schedule, or see a demonstration of available transaction services and procedures. Confirmation of electronic trades can take as little as a few seconds, and most occur within a minute. Online investing is increasingly popular, particularly among young investors who enjoy surfing the Internet—so popular, in fact, that it has prompted virtually every traditional full-service broker (and many discount brokers) to offer online trading to their clients. Some of the major full-service, discount, and online brokers are shown below.

Brokerage Fees

Brokerage firms receive commissions for executing buy and sell orders for their clients. These commissions are said to be *negotiated*, meaning they're not fixed. In practice, however, most firms have *established fee schedules* that they use with small transactions. Fees definitely do differ from one brokerage firm to another, so it pays to shop around. If you're an "active trader" who generates a couple thousand dollars (or more) in annual commissions, then by all means try to negotiate a reduced commission schedule with your broker. Chances are, they'll probably agree to a deal with you: brokers much prefer active traders to buy-and-hold investors, because traders generate a lot more commissions. Generally speaking, brokerage fees on a round lot (100 shares) of common stock will amount to roughly 1 percent of the transaction value.

Because there are so many discount brokers today, there is significant variation in the fees charged and services offered. The way commissions are calculated also varies; some firms base them on the dollar value of the transaction, some on the number of shares, and some use both. Exhibit 11.3 ranks the best online brokers using

full-service broker
A broker who, in addition to executing clients' transactions, offers a full array of brokerage services.

discount broker
A broker with low overhead who charges low commissions and offers little or no services to investors.

online broker
Typically a discount broker through whom investors can execute trades electronically/online through a commercial service or on the Internet; also called *Internet broker* or *electronic broker*.

comprehensive criteria. The firms with higher commissions generally offer more services. Similarly, some discounters charge clients extra for their research services.

Brokerage commissions on *bond transactions* differ from those on stock transactions. Brokerage firms typically charge a minimum fee between $5 and $30, regardless of the number of bonds involved. For multiple bond transactions, the brokerage cost per $1,000 corporate bond typically drops to $10 or below. Commission schedules for other securities, such as mutual funds and options, differ from those used with stocks and bonds (we'll look at some of these in the next two chapters). The magnitude of brokerage commissions is obviously an important consideration when making security transactions, because these fees tend to raise the overall cost of purchasing securities and lower the overall proceeds from their sale. In recent years, competition and the increasing use of online brokers have decreased trading commissions significantly.

Type of Broker		
Full-Service	**Discount**	**Online**
Raymond James	Bank of America	AccuTrade
Edward Jones	Charles Schwab	TD Ameritrade
Morgan Stanley	J.D. Seibert	E*Trade
Merrill Lynch	Muriel Siebert	Fidelity Brokerage Services
Wachovia	Vanguard Brokerage Services	Scotttrade
UBS	York Securities	TD Waterhouse

odd lot
A quantity of fewer than 100 shares of a stock.

round lot
A quantity of 100 shares of stock, or multiples thereof.

Security transactions can be made in either odd or round lots. An **odd lot** consists of fewer than 100 shares of stock, while a **round lot** represents a 100-share unit or multiples thereof. The sale of 400 shares of stock would be considered a round-lot transaction, but the purchase of 75 shares would be an odd-lot transaction; trading 250 shares of stock would involve two round lots and an odd lot. Because the purchase or sale of odd lots requires additional processing, an added fee—known as an *odd-lot differential*—is often tacked on to the normal commission charge, driving up the costs of these small trades. Indeed, the relatively high cost of an odd-lot trade is why it's best to deal in round lots whenever possible.

Investor Protection

Securities Investor Protection Corporation (SIPC)
A nonprofit corporation, created by Congress and subject to SEC and congressional oversight, that insures customer accounts against the financial failure of a brokerage firm.

As a client, you're protected against the loss of securities or cash held by your broker by the **Securities Investor Protection Corporation (SIPC)**, a nonprofit corporation authorized by the Securities Investor Protection Act of 1970 to protect customer accounts against the financial failure of a brokerage firm. Although subject to SEC and Congressional oversight, the SIPC is *not* an agency of the U.S. government.

SIPC insurance covers each account for up to $500,000 (of which up to $100,000 may be in cash balances held by the firm). Note, however, that SIPC insurance does not guarantee that the dollar value of the securities will be recovered. It ensures only that *the securities themselves will be returned.* So what happens if your broker gives you bad advice and you lose a lot of money on an investment? The SIPC won't help you, because it's not intended to insure you against bad investment advice, stock market risk, or broker fraud. If you have a dispute with your broker, first discuss the situation with the managing officer at the branch where you do your business. If that doesn't help, then write or talk to the firm's compliance officer and contact the securities office in your home state. If you still aren't satisfied, you may have to take the case to **arbitration**, a process whereby you and your broker present the two sides of the argument before an arbitration panel, which then decides how the case will be resolved. If it's *binding* arbitration, and it usually is, then you have no choice but to

arbitration
A procedure used to settle disputes between a brokerage firm and its clients; both sides present their positions to a board of arbitration, which makes a final and often binding decision on the matter.

It's important to find the online broker that best meets your specific needs. Barron's ratings are based on the following criteria for an online broker's Internet site: 1) usability, availability, and quality of mobile trading; 2) range of investment offerings; 3) quality and accessibility of research, quotes, and charting; 4) timely and effectively organized portfolio analysis and reports; 5) customer service and education features like live chat capability, user guides, frequently-asked questions, and security features, and 6) costs, which include trading commissions and margin (borrowing) costs.

BEST FOR LONG-TERM INVESTING	STARS	BEST FOR INTERNATIONAL TRADERS	STARS
TD Ameritrade (Website)	★★★★½	Interactive Brokers	★★★★½
Fidelity	★★★★½	TradeStation	★★★★½
Charles Schwab	★★★★	Fidelity	★★★★
Merrill Edge	★★★★	E*Trade	★★★★
E*Trade	★★★★	Charles Schwab	★★★½

BEST FOR FREQUENT TRADERS	STARS	BEST FOR NOVICES	STARS
Interactive Brokers	★★★★½	TD Ameritrade (Website)	★★★★½
TradeStation	★★★★½	Fidelity	★★★★
Lightspeed Trading	★★★★½	E*Trade	★★★★
TD Ameritrade (thinkorswim)	★★★★	Capital One Sharebuilder	★★★★
Livevol	★★★★	Merrill Edge	★★★★

BEST FOR OPTIONS TRADERS	STARS	BEST FOR IN-PERSON SERVICE	STARS
OptionsHouse	★★★★½	Scottrade	★★★★
TD Ameritrade (thinkorswim)	★★★★½	Merrill Edge	★★★★
Interactive Brokers	★★★★½	Charles Schwab	★★★★
TradeStation	★★★★	Fidelity	★★★★
Livevol	★★★★	TD Ameritrade (firmwide)	★★★★

Source: Theresa W. Carey, "Barron's Best Online Broker Ranking of 2015," http://online.barrons.com/articles/SB51367578116875004693704580502703510707706, accessed August 2015.

accept the decision—you cannot go to court to appeal your case. In fact, many brokerage firms require that you resolve disputes using binding arbitration. So before you open an account, check the brokerage agreement to see if it contains a binding arbitration clause.

11-3b Executing Trades

For most individual investors, a securities transaction involves placing a buy or sell order, usually by phone or on the Internet, and later receiving confirmation that the order has been completed. These investors have no idea what happens to their orders. In fact, a lot goes on—and very quickly—once the order is placed. It has to, because on a typical day the NYSE alone executes *millions* of trades, and many more occur on the NASDAQ and the rest of the market. In most cases, if the investor places a market order (which we will explain later), then it should take *less than two minutes* to place, execute, and confirm a trade.

The process starts with a phone call to the broker or an online order. The order is then transmitted to the stock exchange floor, the NASDAQ market, or the OTCBB, where it's promptly executed. Confirmation that the order has been executed is transmitted to the originating broker and then to the customer. Once the trade takes place, the investor has three (business) days to "settle" his or her account with the broker—that is, to pay for the securities.

Financial Fact or Fantasy?

If you lose a lot of money because a broker gave you a poor investment recommendation, you can recover all or most of your loss by filing a claim with the Securities Investor Protection Corporation. **Fantasy:** SIPC insurance applies only if you are dealing with a *brokerage firm* that goes out of business. If the brokerage firm fails, you are protected against the loss of securities or cash held by the broker. Importantly, that has nothing to do with getting bad advice from a broker; the SIPC does not cover such situations.

In an online trade, your order goes via the Internet from your computer to the brokerage computer, which checks the type of order and confirms that it's in compliance with regulations. It is then transmitted to the exchange floor or a NASDAQ (or OTC) dealer for execution. The time for the whole process, including a confirmation that's sent back to your computer, is usually less than a minute.

11-3c Types of Orders

Investors may choose from several different kinds of orders when buying or selling securities. The type of order chosen normally depends on the investor's goals and expectations regarding the given transaction. The three basic types of orders are the market order, limit order, and stop-loss order.

Market Order

An order to buy or sell a security at the best price available at the time it's placed is a **market order**. It's usually the quickest way to have orders filled because market orders are executed as soon as they reach the trading floor. In fact, on small trades of less than a few thousand shares, it takes less than 10 seconds to fill a market order once it hits the trading floor. These orders are executed through a process that attempts to allow *buy orders* to be filled at the lowest price and *sell orders* at the highest, thereby providing the best possible deal to both the buyers and sellers of a security.

Limit Order

An order to buy at a specified price (or lower), or sell at a specified price (or higher) is known as a **limit order**. The broker transmits a limit order to a *specialist* dealing in the given security on the floor of the exchange. The order is executed as soon as the specified market price is reached and all other such orders with precedence have been filled. Although a limit order can be quite effective, it can also cost you money. If, for instance, you want to buy at $20 or less and the stock price moves from its current $20.50 to $32 while you're waiting, your limit order for $20 will have caused you to forgo an opportunity to make a profit of $11.50 ($32.00 − $20.50) per share. Had you placed a market order, this profit would have been yours.

> **EXAMPLE: Limit Orders**
>
> You've placed a limit order to buy 100 shares of a stock at a price of $20, even though the stock is currently selling at $20.50. Once the stock hits $20 and the specialist has cleared all similar orders received before yours, the specialist will execute the order.

Stop-Loss Order

An order to *sell a stock* when the market price reaches or drops below a specified level is called a **stop-loss**, or **stop order**. Used to protect the investor against rapid declines in stock prices, the stop order is placed on the specialist's book and activated when the stop price is reached. At that point, the stop order becomes a *market order* to sell. This means that the stock is offered for sale at the prevailing market price, which could be less than the price at which the order was initiated by the stop.

> **EXAMPLE: Stop-Loss Orders**
>
> Imagine that you own 100 shares of DEF, which is currently selling for $25. Because of the high uncertainty associated with the price movements of the stock, you decide to place a stop order to sell at $21. If the stock price drops to $21, your stop order is activated and the specialist will sell all your DEF stock at the best price available, which may be below $21 a share. Of course, if the market price increases, or stays at or about $25 a share, nothing will have been lost by placing the stop-loss order.

market order
An order to buy or sell a security at the best price available at the time it is placed.

limit order
An order to either buy a security at a specified or lower price or to sell a security at or above a specified price.

stop-loss (stop order)
An order to sell a stock when the market price reaches or drops below a specified level.

Types of Limit Orders

With a limit order, you set not only the price you want but also the time period you want the order to remain outstanding. Here are some choices.

- *Fill-or-kill order.* An order that is executed immediately (at the specified price or better), or else it is canceled.
- *Day order.* An order that expires at the end of the day, even if it hasn't been executed.
- *Good-till-canceled (GTC) order.* An order that will remain open until it's either executed or canceled.
- *All-or-none order.* An order to buy or sell a *specified quantity* of stocks (at a given price, or better), which remains open until executed or canceled.

11-3d Calculating Investment Returns

The reason you invest is to earn an expected rate of return that compensates you for the risk you take on. Indeed, the only way to earn a higher rate of return is to face higher risk, which involves a higher chance that you won't get the return you'd hoped for. So it's important to know how to determine the rate of return you earned over a given period of time. For example, perhaps you took your uncle's advice and invested $500 in a mutual fund two years ago. You should know how to calculate the rate of return on the investment so you can decide whether to keep it there or move it elsewhere.

The **rate of return** on an investment depends on the increase or decrease in the price of an investment as well as any income received over the investment period, both stated as a percentage of the initial investment. The rate of return is consequently the amount earned on an investment per dollar invested. It is calculated as:

rate of return
The increase or decrease in the price of an investment as well as any income received over the investment period, both stated as a percentage of the initial investment.

$$\text{Rate of Return} = \frac{\text{Ending Value} - \text{Beginning Value} + \text{Income}}{\text{Beginning Value}}$$

Thus, the rate of return on a stock is the change in the price of the stock plus any dividends received over the investment period, both divided by the original price paid for the stock.

> **EXAMPLE: Calculating the Rate of Return on a Stock Investment**
>
> You bought 100 shares of The Walt Disney Company (DIS) one year ago at $81.22 a share. The stock is currently selling at $111.40. Over the year Disney paid dividends of $1.15 per share. What rate of return did you earn?

$$\text{Rate of Return} = \frac{\text{Ending Value} - \text{Beginning Value} + \text{Income}}{\text{Beginning Value}}$$

$$= \frac{(100 \times \$111.40) - (100 \times \$81.22) + (100 \times \$1.15)}{(100 \times \$81.22)}$$

$$= 38.57 \text{ percent}$$

After you've calculated the return over the investment's time horizon, you can compare it with other investments of similar risk that you could have made. And you can also use this calculation approach to project future rates of return for competing investment alternatives.

11-3e Margin Trades and Short Sales

When you're ready to buy securities, you can do so by putting up your own money or by borrowing some of the money. *Buying on margin*, as it's called, is a practice that allows investors to use borrowed money to make security transactions. Margin trading is closely regulated and is carried out under strict *margin requirements* set by the Federal Reserve Board. These requirements specify the amount of *equity* that an investor must put up when buying stocks, bonds, and other securities. The most recent requirement is 50 percent for common stock, which means that at least 50 percent of each dollar invested must be the investor's own; the remaining 50 percent may be borrowed.

The use of margin allows you to increase the return on your investment when stock prices increase. A major attribute of margin trading is that it allows you to *magnify your returns*—that is, you can use margin to reduce your equity in an investment and thereby magnify the returns from invested capital when security prices go up. Importantly, the use of margin magnifies *both* profits and losses. And if the price of a margined stock continues to drop, you'll eventually reach the point where your equity in the investment will be so low that the brokerage house will liquidate the investment unless you provide more collateral (*margin call*).

EXAMPLE: Using Margin Trades to Magnify Returns

Assume you buy 100 shares of stock that increase from $50 to $70 a share—that's a $2,000 profit from a $5,000 investment, which translates into a 40 percent return on investment (i.e., $2,000 profit ÷ $5,000 investment = 40 percent). However, if that trade had been made on 50 percent margin (so you put up only $2,500 of the $5,000 and borrow the rest), then your return would be twice that amount, or a whopping 80 percent (i.e., $2,000 profit ÷ $2,500 investment = 80 percent). Now if the price of the stock had *fallen* $20, from $50 to $30 a share, then the return on your investment would have been a *negative* 40 percent (without the margin) or a *negative* 80 percent (with margin).

Investors can go long or short when they trade stocks. By far, the vast majority of trades are *long transactions*, like the margin trade just illustrated. That is, they're made in anticipation of *stock prices going up*, so the investor can make money by buying low and selling high. A **short sale** transaction, in contrast, is made in anticipation of a decline in the price of a stock. When an investor sells a security short, the broker borrows the security and then sells it on behalf of the short seller's account— short sellers actually *sell securities they don't own!* The borrowed shares must, of course, be replaced in the future, and if the investor can repurchase the shares at a lower price, then a profit will result.

The objective of a short sale is to take advantage of a *drop in price* by first selling high and then buying low—just like the adage, "buy low, sell high," except in reverse. Falling prices are good news to short-sellers, but the worst thing that can happen to them is for the price of the stock to go up. Make no mistake about it, *both margin trades and short sales involve a lot of risk, so it's important that you become thoroughly familiar with these techniques and their risk before using them.*

short sale
A transaction that involves selling borrowed securities with the expectation that they can be replaced at a lower price at some future date; made in anticipation of a decline in the security's price.

Financial Fact or Fantasy?

An aggressive investor would short sell a stock if he or she expects its price to go down. **Fact:** Short sales are made in anticipation of a drop in the price of a security; an investor makes money on a short sale when prices decline. However, selling short is quite risky and should only be done by risk-hardy, well-informed investors.

EXAMPLE: Short Sales

If an investor short-sells 100 shares of stock at $50 a share and then some time later, *after the price of the stock has dropped*, buys them back at, say, $30 a share, then she'll generate a profit of $20 a share, or $2,000 (i.e., ($50 − $30) × 100 shares = $2,000]. Of course, the investor will have to make a margin deposit equal to 50 percent of the value of the stock when the short sale was made. So a short transaction will require the investor to come up with some capital before the trade can be made.

FINANCIAL PLANNING TIPS

Understanding the Long and the Short of Investing

One of the best ways to understand an investment is to identify three factors:

- What's the most I could make?

- What's the most I could lose?

- At what price would I break even?

Consider the example of entering a stock investment at $60 per share. Let's compare the possible outcomes of long and short investments. To keep it simple, we'll ignore transaction costs and margin requirements. Graphs make it easier to understand what's going on.

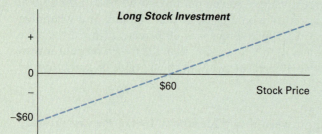

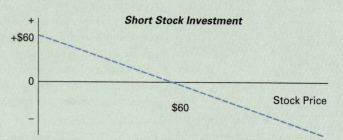

We can observe the following about these positions:

- **Long positions:** Maximum gain is unlimited; maximum loss is limited to the purchase price ($60), and the breakeven price is the purchase price ($60).

- **Short positions:** Maximum gain is limited to the purchase price ($60); maximum loss is unlimited, and the breakeven price is the short sale price ($60).

So what's the primary takeaway from this analysis? Determining these key price points is essential if you want to understand your potential investment gains and losses. And an unprotected short position can be very risky!

TEST YOURSELF

11-10 Describe the role that discount brokers play in carrying out security transactions. To whom are their services especially appealing?

11-11 What are *online brokers*, and what kinds of investors are most likely to use them?

11-12 What is the SIPC, and how does it protect investors?

11-13 What is *arbitration?* Does SIPC require the use of arbitration in investor disputes?

11-14 Name and describe three basic types of orders.

11-15 Why might an investor buy securities on margin?

11-16 Describe how the return on an investment is calculated.

11-17 What is a *short sale*? Explain the logic behind it. How much could be gained or lost on a short sale investment?

11-4 BECOMING AN INFORMED INVESTOR

Face it: Some people know more about investing than others. As a result, they may use certain investment vehicles or tactics that aren't even in another investor's vocabulary. Investor know-how, in short, defines the playing field. It helps determine how well you'll meet your investment objectives. Although being an informed investor can't guarantee you success, it can help you avoid unnecessary losses—as happens all too often when people put their money into investments they don't fully understand. These investors violate the first rule of investing: *Never start an investment program, or buy an investment vehicle, unless you thoroughly understand what you're getting into!* Thus, before making any major investment decision, thoroughly investigate the security and its merits. Formulate some basic expectations about its future performance, and gain an understanding of the sources of risk and return. This can usually be done by reading the popular financial press and referring to other print or Internet sources of investment information.

Here are the four types of investment information that you should follow on a regular basis:

- Economic developments and current events: To help you evaluate the underlying investment environment
- Alternative investment vehicles: To keep you abreast of market developments
- Current interest rates and prices: To monitor your investments and stay alert for developing investment opportunities
- Personal investment strategies: To help you hone your skills and stay alert for new techniques as they develop

11-4a Annual Stockholders' Reports

Every publicly traded corporation is required to provide its stockholders and other interested parties with **annual stockholders' reports**. These documents contain a wealth of information about the companies, including balance sheets, income statements, and other financial reports for the latest fiscal year, as well as for several prior years. Annual reports usually describe the firm's business activities, recent developments, and future plans and outlook. Financial ratios describing past performance are also included, along with other relevant statistics. In fact, annual reports offer a great deal of insight into the company's past, present, and future operations. You can obtain them for free directly from the companies, through a brokerage firm, or at most large libraries. And most companies also post their annual reports on the Internet, so you can obtain them online.

Here are some suggestions to help you get the most information when reading an annual report:

- Start with the highlights or selected financial data sections. These provide a quick overview of performance by summarizing key information, such as the past two years' revenues, net income, assets, earnings per share (EPS), and dividends.
- Read the chief executive's letter. But read it with a careful eye, looking for euphemisms like "a slowing of growth" to describe a drop in earnings.
- Move on to the discussion of operations in management's discussion and analysis. This section provides information on sales, earnings, debt, ongoing litigation, and so on.
   - Review the financial statements, including the notes. These will tell you about the company's financial condition and performance. Look for trends in sales, costs, profit, cash position, and net working capital.
   - Read the auditor's report. Look for phrases like "except for" or "subject to," as they mean just one thing: *there may be problems you need to understand.*

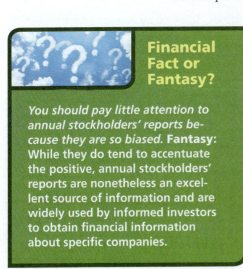

11-4b The Financial Press

The most common sources of financial news are the Internet and the local newspaper. Other common sources of financial news include *The Wall Street Journal, Barron's, Investor's Business Daily*, and the "Money" section of *USA Today*. These are all national publications that include articles on the behavior of the economy, the market, various industries, and individual companies. The most comprehensive and up-to-date coverage of financial news is provided Monday through

Saturday by *The Wall Street Journal*. Other excellent sources of investment information include magazines, such as *Money, Forbes, Fortune, Business Week*, and *Kiplinger's Personal Finance*. These publications are available online and as traditional hard copy publications.

Market Data

Usually presented in the form of averages, or indexes, *market data* describe the general behavior of the securities markets. The averages and indexes are based on the price movements of a select group of securities over an extended period. They're used to capture the overall performance of the market as a whole. You would want to follow one or more of these measures *to get a feel for how the market is doing over time* and, perhaps, an indication of what lies ahead. The absolute level of the index at a specific time (or on a given day) is far less important than *what's been happening to that index over a given period*. The most commonly cited market measures are those calculated by Dow Jones, Standard & Poor's, the NYSE, and NASDAQ. These measures are all intended to track the behavior of the stock market, particularly NYSE stocks (the Dow, S&P, and NYSE averages all follow stocks on the "big board," which is the NYSE).

Dow Jones Industrial Averages. The granddaddy of them all, and probably the most widely followed measure of stock market performance, is the **Dow Jones Industrial Average (DJIA)**. Actually, the Dow Jones averages, which began in 1896, are made up of four parts: (1) an industrial average, the DJIA, which is based on 30 stocks; (2) a transportation average based on 20 stocks; (3) a utility average based on 15 stocks; and (4) a composite average based on all 65 industrial, transportation, and utility stocks. Most of the stocks in the DJIA are picked from the NYSE; but a few NASDAQ shares, such as Intel and Microsoft, are included as well. Although these stocks are intended to represent a cross section of companies, there's a strong bias toward blue chips, which is a major criticism of the DJIA. However, the facts show that, as a rule, the DJIA behavior closely reflects that of other broadly based stock market measures—with the possible exception of NASDAQ. Exhibit 11.4 lists the 30 stocks in the DJIA.

Standard & Poor's Indexes. The **Standard & Poor's (S&P) indexes** are similar to the Dow Jones averages in that both are used to capture the overall performance of the market. However, some important differences exist between the two measures. For

Dow Jones Industrial Average (DJIA)
The most widely followed measure of stock market performance; consists of 30 blue-chip stocks listed mostly on NYSE.

Standard & Poor's (S&P) indexes
Indexes compiled by Standard & Poor's that are similar to the DJIA but employ different computational methods and consist of far more stocks.

EXHIBIT 11.4	The Dow Jones Industrial Average

The DJIA is made up of 30 of the bluest of blue-chip stocks and has been closely followed by investors for the past 100 years or so.

The 30 Stocks in the DJIA (as of August 2015)

American Express	General Electric	Minnesota M&M (3M)
Apple	Goldman Sachs	Nike
Boeing	Home Depot	Pfizer
Caterpillar	IBM	Procter & Gamble
Chevron	Intel	Travelers
Cisco	Johnson & Johnson	United Health
Coca-Cola	J.P. Morgan Chase	United Technologies
Disney	McDonald's	Verizon
DuPont	Merck	Visa
ExxonMobil	Microsoft	Wal-Mart

one thing, the S&P uses a lot more stocks: the popular S&P 500 composite index is based on 500 different stocks, whereas the DJIA uses only 30. What's more, the S&P index is made up of all large NYSE stocks in addition to some major AMEX and NASDAQ stocks, so there are not only more issues in the S&P sample but also a greater breadth of representation. Finally, there are some technical differences in the mathematical procedures used to compute the two measures; the Dow Jones is an *average*, whereas the S&P is an *index*. Despite the technical differences, movements in these two measures are, in fact, *highly correlated*. Even so, the S&P has a much lower value than the DJIA—for example, in August 2015, the Dow stood at almost 17,000, whereas the S&P index of 500 stocks was just around 2,000. Now, this doesn't mean that the S&P consists of less valuable stocks; rather, the disparity is due solely to the different methods used to compute the measures. In addition to the S&P 500, two other widely followed S&P indexes are the *MidCap 400* (made up of 400 medium-sized companies with market values ranging from about $1.4 billion to $5.9 billion.) and the *SmallCap 600* (consisting of companies with market caps of around $400 million to $1.8 billion).

The NYSE, NASDAQ, and Other Market Indexes. The most widely followed exchange-based indexes are those of the NYSE and NASDAQ. The **NYSE index** includes all the stocks listed on the "big board" and provides a measure of performance in that market. Behavior in the NASDAQ market is also measured by several indexes, the most comprehensive of which is the *NASDAQ Composite index*, which is calculated using virtually all the stocks traded on NASDAQ. In addition, there's the *NASDAQ 100 index*, which tracks the price behavior of the biggest 100 (nonfinancial) firms traded on NASDAQ—companies like Apple, Microsoft, Intel, Oracle, Cisco, Staples, and Dell. The NASDAQ Composite is often used as a benchmark in assessing the price behavior of *high-tech* stocks. This index is far more volatile than either the Dow or the S&P, which means that it tends to outperform those indices in up markets and to underperform them in down markets.

Besides these major indexes, there are a couple of other measures of market performance, one of which is the **Dow Jones Wilshire 5000 index**. It's estimated that the Wilshire index reflects the *total market value of 98 percent to 99 percent of all publicly traded stocks in the United States*. In essence, it shows what's happening in the stock market as a whole—the dollar amount of market value added or lost as the market moves up and down. Thus, the Wilshire can be used not only to track the behavior of the U.S. stock market but also to give you a pretty accurate reading on the size of that market on any given day. For example, in August 2015, the Wilshire index stood at about 21,200. That translates into a total market value over $24 *trillion!* Another widely followed measure is the *Russell 2000*, which tracks the behavior of 2,000 relatively small companies and is widely considered to be a fairly accurate measure of the small-cap segment of the market.

Industry Data

Local newspapers, *The Wall Street Journal*, *Barron's*, and various financial publications regularly contain articles and data about different industries. For example, Standard & Poor's *Industry Surveys* provides detailed descriptions and statistics for all the major industries; on a smaller scale, *Bloomberg Business Week* and other magazines regularly include indexes of industry performance and price levels.

Company Data

Articles about new developments and the performance of companies are included in local newspapers, *The Wall Street Journal*, *Barron's*, and most investment magazines—both online and in hard copy form. The prices of many securities are quoted daily in *The Wall Street Journal*, *Investor's Business Daily*, and *USA Today*, as well as weekly in *Barron's*. Many daily newspapers also contain stock price quotations, though in the smaller dailies the listing may be selective; in some cases, only stocks of local interest are included.

NYSE index
An index of the performance of all stocks listed on the New York Stock Exchange.

Dow Jones Wilshire 5000 index
An index of the total market value of the approximately 6,000–7,000 most actively traded stocks in the United States.

Stock Quotes

Stock price quotes appear daily online on many sites, which include Yahoo! Finance (**http://finance.yahoo.com**), the *Wall Street Journal* (**http://wsj.com**), and CNN (**www.cnn.com**). Most online quotations provide not only current prices but a great deal of additional information as well.

Consider representative information available on numerous Internet sites. Exhibit 11.5 shows that Apple's stock price was at $127.96 on the afternoon of May 1, 2015, which was an increase of $2.81 from the prior day's closing price. The shares are shown as listed on the NASDAQ market. We see that Apple's trading symbol is AAPL. Its annual cash dividend yield is 1.50 percent, which is found by dividing the annual dividend by the indicated market price. The firm's recent P/E ratio is also shown, which is the current market price divided by the per-share earnings for

---

EXHIBIT 11.5	Listed Stock Quote for Apple

This exhibit provides information on one day's trading activity and the price quote for Apple, which is traded on NASDAQ. Note that, in addition to the latest stock price, a typical online stock quote provides an array of other information.

Apple Inc (NASDAQ:AAPL)

127.96
Real-Time Quote

▲ **2.81 (2.24%)**
Today's Change

Today's Trading

Previous close	125.15
Today's open	126.10
Day's range	125.30 – 128.12
Volume	42,157,492
Average volume (3 months)	52,746,100
Market cap	$745.31B
Dividend and yield	$1.88 (1.50%)

Data as of 3:16 p.m. EDT, 5/1/2015

Growth & Valuation

Earnings growth (last 5 years)	28.39%
Earnings growth (this year)	38.90%
Earnings growth (next 5 years)	13.20%
P/E ratio	17.33
Price/Sales	3.65
Price/Book	5.91

Source: From http://finance.yahoo.com/q?s=AAPL, accessed May 1, 2015.

the most recent 12-month period. As can be seen, Apple is trading at a P/E of 17.33 times earnings. And the exhibit shows that Apple's overall market capitalization (stock price times the number of shares) is $745.31 billion. This makes it the largest company in the world, as measured by market capitalization.

11-4c Brokerage Reports

Reports produced by the research staffs of major (full-service) brokerage firms provide still another important source of investor information. These reports cover a wide variety of topics, from economic and market analyses to industry and company reports, news of special situations, and reports on interest rates and the bond market. Reports on certain industries or securities prepared by the house's research staff may be issued regularly and contain lists of securities within certain industries classified by the type of market behavior they are expected to exhibit. Brokerage houses also regularly issue reports, prepared by their security analysts, on specific securities; these reports include, among other things, recommendations for the type of investment returns expected and whether to buy, hold, or sell specific securities.

11-4d Advisory Services

Subscription advisory services provide information and recommendations on various industries and specific securities. The services normally cost from $50 to several hundred dollars a year, although you can usually review such materials (for free) at your broker's office, at university and public libraries, or online. Probably the best-known investment advisory services are those provided by Standard & Poor's, Moody's Investors Service, and Value Line. Both Standard & Poor's and Moody's publish manuals containing historical facts and financial data on thousands of corporations, broken down by industry groups. Standard & Poor's publishes a monthly stock guide and bond guide, each summarizing the financial conditions of a few thousand issues; Moody's also publishes stock and bond guides. And the *Value Line Investment Survey* is a popular source of firm and industry analysis. Some reports are also prepared weekly, like Standard & Poor's *Outlook*.

An example of a subscription service stock report is provided in Exhibit 11.6. Prepared by Standard & Poor's this report presents a concise summary of a company's financial history, current finances, and future prospects; similar stock reports are available from Value Line and Morningstar. Recommended lists of securities, broken down into groups based on investment objectives, constitute still another type of service. Besides these popular subscription services, many *investment letters*, which periodically advise subscribers on buying and selling securities, are available.

TEST YOURSELF

11-18   Briefly discuss the four basic types of information that you, as an investor, should follow.

11-19   What role do market averages and indexes play in the investment process?

11-20   Briefly describe the *DJIA, S&P 400, S&P 500, NASDAQ Composite, Russell 2000*, and *Dow Jones Wilshire 5000* indexes. Which segments of the market does each index track?

EXHIBIT 11.6 An S&P Stock Report

An S&P report like this one provides a wealth of information about the operating results and financial condition of the company and is an invaluable source of information to investors.

Stock Report | April 30, 2015 | NNM Symbol: **AAPL** | **AAPL** is in the S&P 500

Apple Inc

S&P CAPITAL IQ
McGRAW HILL FINANCIAL

S&P Capital IQ Recommendation	HOLD ★★★☆☆	Price $125.15 (as of Apr 30, 2015 4:00 PM ET)	12-Mo. Target Price $150.00	Report Currency USD	Investment Style Large-Cap Growth

S&P Capital IQ Equity Analyst Angelo Zino, CFA

UPDATE: PLEASE SEE THE ANALYST'S LATEST RESEARCH NOTE IN THE COMPANY NEWS SECTION

GICS Sector Information Technology
Sub-Industry Technology Hardware, Storage & Peripherals

Summary This company is a prominent provider of hardware including iPhone smartphones, iPad tablets, Mac computers and iPod digital media players.

Key Stock Statistics (Source S&P Capital IQ, Vickers, company reports)

52-Wk Range	$134.54–82.90	S&P Oper. EPS 2015E	8.95	Market Capitalization(B)	$728.967
Trailing 12-Month EPS	$8.05	S&P Oper. EPS 2016E	9.54	Yield (%)	1.66
Trailing 12-Month P/E	15.6	P/E on S&P Oper. EPS 2015E	14.0	Dividend Rate/Share	$2.08
$10K Invested 5 Yrs Ago	$35,573	Common Shares Outstg. (M)	5,824.7	Institutional Ownership (%)	61

Beta	0.81
S&P 3-Yr. Proj. EPS CAGR(%)	15
S&P Quality Ranking	B+

Price Performance

30-Week Mov. Avg. · · · 10-Week Mov. Avg. — GAAP Earnings vs. Previous Year   Volume Above Avg. ⎰⎱ STARS
12-Mo. Target Price — Relative Strength   ▲ Up ▼ Down ▶ No Change   Below Avg.

7-for-1

Past performance is not an indication of future performance and should not be relied upon as such.

Analysis prepared by Equity Analyst **Angelo Zino, CFA** on Apr 28, 2015 09:03 AM, when the stock traded at **$132.65**.

Highlights

➤ We project 39% revenue growth for FY 15 (Sep.) and a 6.6% gain for FY 16. AAPL's move to large screen iPhones (iPhone 6 at 4.7 inches and iPhone 6 Plus at 5.5 inches) is helping the company to capture share at the high-end of the smartphone market, we believe. We anticipate steady Mac sales, despite a challenging PC landscape, but lackluster iPad sales ahead of a new launch. In the March quarter, revenue was broken down as follows: 69% iPhone, 9% iPad, 10% Mac, 12% Services/Other. We positively view growth potential from the Apple Watch, but revenue contribution is likely to be minimal in the coming quarters.

➤ We see the annual gross margin widening to about 40% in FY 15 and FY 16, compared to a 39% margin in FY 14 and 38% margin in FY 13. iPhone and iPad margins will be aided by efficiencies, we think, offset somewhat by risks related to average selling prices. The Apple Watch commands higher margins than the corporate average, which could provide an upside in the coming years.

➤ We estimate operating EPS of $8.95 in FY 15 and $9.54 in FY 16. As of the end of March, AAPL had $194 billion in cash and investments.

Investment Rationale/Risk

➤ We note AAPL's significant market position in key areas, and high customer satisfaction and switching costs, in our view. Higher volumes, a focus on common components and a greater emphasis on software and services should aid profitability. AAPL's superior ecosystem and new product launches will be enough to sustain high iPhone customer retention rates, we think. The Apple Watch will see success over time, we believe, and we are optimistic about the potential for AAPL to expand its addressable market in the coming years. We positively view free cash flow generation, and believe the balance sheet will be increasingly employed for dividends and stock repurchases, as well as M&A.

➤ Risks to our recommendation and target price include weaker end-market demand, pricing pressures, competitive handset and tablet offerings gaining traction, carrier efforts to reduce or eliminate subsidy payments and less success with product launches/innovations.

➤ Our 12-month target price of $150 is based on a P/E of 15.7X our FY 16 EPS estimate, above hardware peers, but near the S&P 500 Technology sector.

Analyst's Risk Assessment

LOW	MEDIUM	HIGH

Our risk assessment reflects our view of a seemingly ever-evolving market for consumer-oriented technology products, potential challenges associated with the company's growing size and offerings and possible changes in the pace or success of product innovations following recent management changes.

Revenue/Earnings Data

Revenue (Million U.S. $)

	1Q	2Q	3Q	4Q	Year
2015	74,599	58,010	--	--	--
2014	57,594	45,646	37,432	42,123	182,795
2013	54,512	43,603	35,323	37,472	170,910
2012	46,333	39,186	35,023	35,966	156,508
2011	26,741	24,667	28,571	28,270	108,249
2010	15,683	13,499	15,700	20,343	65,225

Earnings Per Share (U.S. $)

2015	3.06	2.33	E1.74	E1.84	E8.95
2014	2.07	1.66	1.28	1.42	6.45
2013	1.97	1.44	1.07	1.18	5.68
2012	1.98	1.76	1.33	1.24	6.31
2011	0.92	0.91	1.11	1.01	3.95
2010	0.52	0.48	0.50	0.66	2.16

Fiscal year ended Sep. 30. Next earnings report expected: Late July. EPS Estimates based on S&P Capital IQ Operating Earnings; historical GAAP earnings are as reported in Company reports.

Dividend Data

Amount ($)	Date Decl.	Ex-Div. Date	Stk. of Record	Payment Date
0.470	Jul 22	Aug 7	Aug 11	Aug 14 '14
0.470	Oct 20	Nov 6	Nov 10	Nov 13 '14
0.470	Jan 27	Feb 5	Feb 9	Feb 12 '15
0.520	Apr 27	May 7	May 11	May 14 '15

Dividends have been paid since 2012. Source: Company reports.

Past performance is not an indication of future performance and should not be relied upon as such.

Please read the Required Disclosures and Analyst Certification on the last page of this report.

EXHIBIT 11.6 (Continued)

Stock Report | April 30, 2015 | NNM Symbol: **AAPL**

Apple Inc

Quantitative Evaluations

S&P Capital IQ   **5+**

1	2	3	4	5

Fair Value Rank

LOWEST   HIGHEST

Based on S&P Capital IQ's proprietary quantitative model, stocks are ranked from most overvalued (1) to most undervalued (5).

Fair Value Calculation   **$163.50**

Analysis of the stock's current worth, based on S&P Capital IQ's proprietary quantitative model suggests that AAPL is Undervalued by $38.35 or 30.6%.

Investability Quotient Percentile   **99**

LOWEST = 1   HIGHEST = 100

AAPL scored higher than 99% of all companies for which an S&P Capital IQ Report is available.

Volatility

LOW	AVERAGE	HIGH

Technical Evaluation   **BULLISH**

Since April, 2015, the technical indicators for AAPL have been BULLISH.

Insider Activity

UNFAVORABLE	NEUTRAL	FAVORABLE

For further clarification on the terms used in this report, please visit www.standardandpoors.com/stockreportguide

Expanded Ratio Analysis

	2014	2013	2012	2011
Price/Sales	3.70	3.06	3.21	3.50
Price/EBITDA	11.18	9.37	8.60	10.65
Price/Pretax Income	12.64	10.42	9.02	11.09
P/E Ratio	17.11	14.11	12.06	14.63
Avg. Diluted Shares Outstg (M)	6,122.7	6,521.6	6,617.5	6,556.5

Figures based on calendar year-end price

Key Growth Rates and Averages

Past Growth Rate (%)	1 Year	3 Years	5 Years	9 Years
Sales	6.95	18.06	35.01	36.91
Net Income	6.68	12.13	37.84	51.85

Ratio Analysis (Annual Avg.)

	1 Year	3 Years	5 Years	9 Years
Net Margin (%)	21.61	23.32	23.08	19.37
% LT Debt to Capitalization	20.63	10.90	6.54	3.63
Return on Equity (%)	33.61	35.70	37.16	32.76

Company Financials Fiscal Year Ended Sep. 30

Per Share Data (U.S. $)	2014	2013	2012	2011	2010	2009	2008	2007	2006	2005
Tangible Book Value	17.52	18.71	17.17	11.10	7.28	4.95	3.29	2.32	1.64	1.26
Cash Flow	7.75	6.72	6.80	4.23	2.32	1.41	0.84	0.61	0.36	0.25
Earnings	6.45	5.68	6.31	3.95	2.16	1.30	0.77	0.56	0.32	0.22
S&P Capital IQ Core Earnings	6.47	5.68	6.29	3.94	2.16	1.30	0.77	0.56	0.32	0.21
Dividends	Nil	1.63	0.38	Nil	Nil	Nil	Nil	Nil	Nil	Nil
Payout Ratio	Nil	29%	6%	Nil	Nil	Nil	Nil	Nil	Nil	Nil
Prices:High	119.75	82.16	100.72	60.96	46.67	30.56	28.61	28.99	13.31	10.78
Prices:Low	70.51	55.01	58.43	44.36	27.18	11.17	11.31	11.70	7.17	4.47
P/E Ratio:High	19	14	16	15	22	24	37	52	41	48
P/E Ratio:Low	11	10	9	11	13	9	15	21	22	20

Income Statement Analysis (Million U.S. $)	2014	2013	2012	2011	2010	2009	2008	2007	2006	2005
Revenue	182,795	170,910	156,508	108,249	65,225	42,905	32,479	24,006	19,315	13,931
Operating Income	60,449	55,756	58,518	35,604	19,412	12,474	6,748	4,726	2,645	1,829
Depreciation	7,946	6,757	3,277	1,814	1,027	734	473	317	225	179
Interest Expense	384	136	Nil	Nil	Nil	Nil	Nil	Nil	Nil	Nil
Pretax Income	53,483	50,155	55,763	34,205	18,540	12,066	6,895	5,008	2,818	1,815
Effective Tax Rate	26.1%	26.2%	25.2%	24.2%	24.4%	31.8%	29.9%	30.2%	29.4%	26.4%
Net Income	39,510	37,037	41,733	25,922	14,013	8,235	4,834	3,496	1,989	1,335
S&P Capital IQ Core Earnings	39,643	37,037	41,614	25,851	14,013	8,235	4,834	3,496	1,989	1,259

Balance Sheet & Other Financial Data (Million U.S. $)	2014	2013	2012	2011	2010	2009	2008	2007	2006	2005
Cash	25,158	40,590	29,129	25,952	25,620	23,464	24,490	9,352	6,392	3,491
Current Assets	68,531	73,286	57,653	44,988	41,678	31,555	34,690	21,956	14,509	10,300
Total Assets	231,839	207,000	176,064	116,371	75,183	47,501	39,572	25,347	17,205	11,551
Current Liabilities	63,448	43,658	38,542	27,970	20,722	11,506	14,092	9,299	6,471	3,484
Long Term Debt	28,987	16,960	Nil	Nil	Nil	Nil	Nil	Nil	Nil	Nil
Common Equity	111,547	123,549	118,210	76,615	47,791	31,640	21,030	14,532	9,984	7,466
Total Capital	140,534	140,509	118,210	76,615	47,791	31,640	21,705	15,151	10,365	7,466
Capital Expenditures	9,571	8,165	8,295	4,260	2,005	1,144	1,091	735	657	260
Cash Flow	47,456	43,794	45,010	27,736	15,040	8,969	5,307	3,813	2,214	1,514
Current Ratio	1.1	1.7	1.5	1.6	2.0	2.7	2.5	2.4	2.2	3.0
% Long Term Debt of Capitalization	20.6	12.1	Nil	Nil	Nil	Nil	Nil	Nil	Nil	Nil
% Net Income of Revenue	21.6	21.7	26.7	24.0	21.5	19.2	14.9	14.6	10.3	9.6
% Return on Assets	18.0	19.3	28.5	27.1	21.7	19.7	14.9	16.4	13.9	13.6
% Return on Equity	33.6	30.6	42.8	41.7	37.1	30.5	27.2	28.5	22.8	21.3

Data as originally reported in Company reports.; bef. results of disc opers/spec. items. Per share data adj. for stk. divs.; EPS diluted. E-Estimated. NA-Not Available. NM-Not Meaningful. NR-Not Ranked. UR-Under Review.

Source: Reprinted by permission of Standard & Poor's Financial Services LLC, a division of the McGraw-Hill Companies © 2015.

11-5 ONLINE INVESTING

The Internet is a major force in the investing environment. It has opened the world of investing to individual investors, leveling the playing field and providing access to tools and market information formerly restricted to professionals. Not only can you trade all types of securities online, you can also find a wealth of information, from real-time stock quotes to security analysts' research reports. However, online investing also carries risks. The Internet requires investors to exercise the same—and possibly more—caution as they would if they were getting information from and placing orders with a human broker. You don't have the safety net of a live broker suggesting that you rethink your trade. Online or off, the basic rules for smart investing are still the same: *know what you're buying, from whom, and at what level of risk.*

How can you successfully navigate through this cyberinvesting universe? Typically one site includes a combination of resources for novice and sophisticated investors alike. For example, the next time you're online, go to the home page for *E*Trade*, a major online brokerage firm (**http://www.etrade.com**). With a few clicks of the mouse, you can learn about E*Trade's services, open an account, or place an order to trade securities. You can also get a quick overview of recent market activity, obtain price quotes and research reports, or use their services to track a whole portfolio of securities. At their site you can select stocks, bonds, and mutual funds; get advice on retirement planning and saving for college; go to "Ideas, Education, and Guidance" under "Investing and Trading" to learn about the markets; and even do your banking at the *E*Trade Bank*.

11-5a Online Investor Services

As the E*Trade Internet site reveals, the Internet offers a full array of online investor services, from up-to-the-minute stock quotes and research reports to charting services and portfolio tracking. When it comes to investing, you name it and you can probably find it online! Unfortunately, although many of these are truly high-quality sites offering valuable information, many others are pure garbage, so be careful when entering the world of online investing. It takes time and effort to use the Internet wisely. Let's now review the kinds of investor services you can find online, starting with investor education sites.

Investor Education

The Internet offers a wide array of tutorials, online classes, and articles to educate the novice investor. Even experienced investors will find sites that expand their investing knowledge. Although most good investment-oriented Internet sites include many educational resources, here are a few good sites featuring *investment fundamentals*.

- *The Motley Fool* (**http://www.fool.com**) *Fool's School* has sections on fundamentals of investing, mutual fund investing, choosing a broker, investment strategies and styles, lively discussion boards, and more.
- Morningstar (**http://www.morningstar.com**) provides comprehensive information on stocks, mutual funds, ETFs, and more.
- Zacks Investment Research (**http://www.zacks.com**) is an excellent starting place to learn what the Internet can offer investors.
- NASDAQ (**http://www.nasdaq.com**) has an Investor Resource section that helps with financial planning and choosing a broker.

Other good educational sites include, as noted above, leading personal finance magazines like *Money* (**http://money.cnn.com**) and *Kiplinger's Personal Finance Magazine* (**http://www.kiplinger.com**).

Investment Tools

Once you're familiar with the basics of investing, you can use the Internet to develop financial plans and set investment goals, find securities that meet your investment objectives, analyze potential investments, and organize your portfolio. Many of these tools, once used only by professional money managers, are free to anyone who wants to go online. You'll find financial calculators and worksheets, screening and charting tools, and portfolio trackers at the Internet sites of large brokerage firms and on other financial sites. You can set up a personal calendar to notify you of forthcoming earnings announcements and receive alerts when one of your stocks hits a predetermined price target.

Investment Planning. Online calculators and worksheets can help you find answers to your financial planning and investing questions. With them, you can figure out how much to save each month for a particular goal, such as the down payment for your first home, a college education for your children, or to be able to retire by the time you reach 55. For example, Fidelity (**http://www.fidelity.com**) has a wide selection of planning tools that deal with such topics as investment growth, college planning, and retirement planning. One of the best sites for financial calculators is *Kiplinger's Personal Finance* (**http://www.kiplinger.com**). Go to their personal finance page, click on "Tools & Calculators," and you'll find over 100 calculators dealing with everything from stocks, bonds, and mutual funds to retirement planning, home buying, and taxes.

Investment Research and Screening. One of the best investor services offered online is the ability to conduct in-depth research on stocks, bonds, mutual funds, exchange-traded funds and other types of investment vehicles. Go to a site like **http://www.kiplinger.com**, click on "Investing," and you can obtain literally dozens of pages of financial and market information about a specific stock or mutual fund. For example, you can find historical and forecasted information about a firm's earnings, earnings per share, dividend yields, growth rates, and more in both tabular and graphic formats; you can also track the behavior of a specific stock relative to a market index or to one or more of its major competitors. Many of these sites have links to the company itself, so with a few mouse clicks you can obtain the company's annual report, detailed financial statements, and historical summaries of a full array of financial and market ratios. In addition, you'll find various *online screening tools*

FINANCIAL PLANNING TIPS

Starting Online Investing

• **Set aside some money to get started and choose a broker.** You don't need much—your initial deposit can be as little as $50. Choose an online broker with no minimum deposit. Consider the results of the Barron's online broker rankings provided in Exhibit 11.3 earlier in this chapter.

• **Learn the key investing jargon.** Some useful sources are Investopedia (**http://www.investopedia.com**) and InvestorWords (**http://www.investorwords.com**).

• **Practice with a paper account before investing real money.** Try out the Investing Simulator Center (**http://www.investingonline.org/isc/index.html**) and then practice with different investment strategies using online

trading simulators like Icarra (**http://www.icarra.com**) or paperTrade (**https://www.trademonster.com/Difference/Online-Paper-Trading.jsp**).

• **Gradually add more money to your brokerage account.** Add amounts regularly that are consistent with your investment goals.

• **Monitor your portfolio's performance.** Data can be obtained easily using Yahoo! Finance (**http://finance.yahoo.com/**) or Google Finance (**http://www.google.com/finance**).

• **Keep up with financial news.** In addition, read as much as you can on how to invest.

Source: Adapted from Matt Krantz, "How to Get Started Investing Online," http://www.dummies.com/how-to/content/investing-online-for-dummies-cheat-sheet.html, accessed August 2015.

that can be used to identify attractive and potentially rewarding investment vehicles. These tools (available at the Internet sites of Quicken, Morningstar, MSN Money Central, and elsewhere) enable you to sort quickly through huge databases of stocks and mutual funds to find those that meet specific characteristics, such as stocks with low or high P/E multiples, small market capitalizations, high dividend yields, specific revenue growth, and low debt-to-equity ratios. You answer a series of questions to specify the type of stock or fund you're looking for, performance criteria you desire, cost parameters, and so on. The screen then provides a list of stocks (or funds) that have met the standards that you've set.

Portfolio Tracking. Almost every investment-oriented Web site includes *portfolio tracking tools*. Simply enter the number of shares held and the symbol for those stocks or mutual funds you wish to follow, and the tracker automatically updates the value of your portfolio in real time. What's more, you can usually click on one of the provided links and quickly obtain detailed information about each stock or mutual fund in your portfolio. But be careful; the features, quality, and ease of using these portfolio trackers vary widely, so check several to find the one that meets your needs. Quicken.com, MSN MoneyCentral (**http://money.msn.com**), Google (**http://google.com/finance/portfolio**) and E*Trade (**http://www.etrade.com**) all have portfolio trackers that are easy to set up and use. For example, Quicken's tracker alerts you whenever an analyst changes the rating on one of your stocks or funds and tells you how well you're diversified among the major asset classes or sectors you hold.

Online Trading

As discussed earlier, trading stocks (and other securities) online has become popular among investors—if for no other reason than the rock-bottom cost of executing such trades. After all, it's an easy, convenient, and low-cost way of trading securities. But for some investors, the attraction of trading stocks online is so compelling that they become day traders. The opposite of buy-and-hold investors with a long-term perspective, **day traders** buy and sell stocks quickly throughout the trading day. They hope their stocks will continue to rise in value for the short time they own them—sometimes just seconds or minutes—so they can make quick profits. Day trading is neither illegal nor unethical, but *it is highly risky*. To compound their risk, day traders usually buy on margin to earn even higher returns. But as we've seen, margin trading also increases the risk of larger losses. Day traders typically incur major financial losses when they start trading. Some never reach profitability. Day traders also have high expenses for brokerage commissions, training, and computer equipment. By some estimates, they must make a 50 percent to 60 percent profit just to break even on fees and commissions.

day trader
An investor who buys and sells stocks (and other securities) rapidly throughout the trading day in hopes of making quick profits.

TEST YOURSELF

11-21   Describe the Internet's impact on the world of investing.

11-22   What are some products and services that you, as an individual investor, can now obtain online?

11-23   Briefly describe several types of online investment tools, and note how they can help you become a better investor.

11-24   What is *day trading*, and how is it different from the more traditional approach to investing?

11-6 MANAGING YOUR INVESTMENT HOLDINGS

portfolio
A collection of securities assembled for the purpose of meeting common investment goals.

diversification
The process of choosing securities with dissimilar risk–return characteristics in order to create a portfolio that provides an acceptable level of return and an acceptable exposure to risk.

Buying and selling securities is not difficult; the hard part is finding securities that will provide the kind of return that you're looking for. Like most individual investors, you too will be buying, selling, and trading securities with ease in time. Eventually, your investment holdings will increase to the point where you're managing a whole portfolio of securities. A **portfolio** is a collection of investment vehicles assembled to meet a common investment goal. But a portfolio is far more than a collection of investments. It breathes life into your investment program as it combines your personal and financial traits with your investment objectives to give some structure to your investments.

Seasoned investors often devote much attention to constructing diversified portfolios of securities. Such portfolios consist of stocks and bonds selected not only for their returns but also for their combined risk–return behavior. The idea behind **diversification** is that, by combining securities with dissimilar risk–return characteristics, you can produce a portfolio of reduced risk and more predictable levels of return. In recent years, investment researchers have shown that you can achieve a noticeable reduction in risk simply by diversifying your investment holdings. For the small investor with a moderate amount of money to invest, this means that *investing in several securities rather than a single one should be beneficial*. The payoff from diversification comes in the form of reduced risk without a significant impact on return. For example, Joanne Ortiz, who has all of her $30,000 portfolio invested in just one stock (Stock A), might find that—by selling two-thirds of her holdings and using the proceeds to buy equal amounts of Stocks B and C—she'll continue to earn the same level of return (say, 8 percent) while greatly decreasing the associated risk. Professional money managers emphasize that investors should not put all their eggs in one basket but instead should hold portfolios that are diversified across a broad segment of businesses.

11-6a Building a Portfolio of Securities

In developing a portfolio of investment holdings, it's assumed that diversification is a desirable investment attribute that leads to improved return and/or reduced risk. Again, as emphasized previously, holding a variety of investments is far more desirable than concentrating all your investments in a single security or industry. For example, a portfolio made up of nothing but drug stocks, such as Merck and Eli Lilly, would hardly be well diversified. As you build up your investment funds, your opportunities (and need) for diversification will increase dramatically. Certainly, by the time you have $10,000 to $15,000 to invest, you should make sure your holdings are well-diversified. To get an idea of the kind of portfolio diversification employed by investors, look at the following numbers, which show the types of investments held by average *individual investors*.

Type of Investment Product	Percentage of Portfolio (July 2015)
Stocks and stock funds	67%
Bonds and bond funds	16%
Short-term investments (CDs, money mkt. dep. accts., etc.)	17%
Total	100%

This portfolio reflects the results of a monthly asset allocation survey conducted by the *American Association of Individual Investors*. Whether this is what your portfolio should look like depends on various factors, including your own needs and objectives.

Investor Characteristics

To formulate an effective portfolio strategy, begin with an honest evaluation of your own financial condition and family situation. Pay particular attention to variables like these:

- Level and stability of income
- Family factors
- Investment horizon
- Net worth
- Investment experience and age
- Disposition toward risk

These are the variables that set the tone for your investments. They determine the kinds of investments you should consider and how long you can tie up your money. For your portfolio to work, it must be tailored to meet your personal financial needs. Your income, family responsibilities, relative financial security, experience, and age all enter into the delicate equation that yields a sound portfolio strategy.

For example, the size and predictability of an investor's employment income has a significant bearing on portfolio strategy. An investor with a secure job is more likely to embark on a more aggressive investment program than is an investor with a less secure position. Income taxes also bear on the investment decision. The higher an investor's income, the more important the tax ramifications of an investment program become. Consider that municipal bonds normally yield about 25 percent to 30 percent less in annual interest than corporate bonds, because the interest income on municipal bonds is tax-free. On an after-tax basis, however, municipal bonds may provide a superior return if an investor is in a tax bracket of 28 percent or higher.

In addition, an individual's investment experience also influences the type of investment strategy. Normally, investors assume higher levels of investment risk gradually over time. It's best to "get your feet wet" in the investment market by slipping into it slowly rather than leaping in head first. Investors who make risky initial investments often suffer heavy losses, damaging the long-run potential of the entire investment program. A cautiously developed investment program will likely provide more favorable long-run results than an impulsive, risky one. Finally, investors should carefully consider risk. High-risk investments have not only high return potential but also high risk of loss. Remember, when going for the home run (via a high-risk, high-return

FINANCIAL ROAD SIGN

Common Investing Mistakes

Avoiding these common mistakes will make you a better and more successful investor:

- Not defining objectives and priorities, which include risk tolerance, appropriate benchmarks, asset allocation, and diversification.
- Not rebalancing your portfolio every year or so to keep asset allocation percentages in line.
- Owning too many different stocks, bonds, exchange-traded funds, and mutual funds.
- Inefficient use of tax strategies.
- Paying too much in mutual fund fees.
- Not enough use of index funds, which are lower-cost and perform on average better than most actively-managed funds.
- Paying too much attention to financial media—almost nothing covered will help you achieve your goals.

Sources: Adapted, in part, from Jay Yoder, "7 common Investor Mistakes," http://www.investopedia.com/articles/stocks/07/mistakes.asp, accessed August 2015.

investment), the odds of striking out are much higher than when simply going for a base hit (a more conservative investment posture). A good rule to remember is that *an investor's exposure to risk should never exceed the ability to bear that risk.*

Investor Objectives

After developing a personal financial profile, the investor's next question is: "What do I want from my portfolio?" This seems like an easy question to answer. Ideally, we would all like to double our money every year by making low-risk investments. However, the realities of the highly competitive investment environment make this outcome unlikely, so the question must be answered more realistically. There's generally a trade-off between earning a high current income from an investment and obtaining significant capital appreciation from it. An investor must choose one or the other; it's hard to obtain both from a single investment vehicle. Of course, in a portfolio it's possible to have a *balance* of both income and growth (capital gains), but most often that involves "tilting" the portfolio in one direction (e.g., toward income) or the other (toward growth).

An investor's needs should determine which approach to choose. For instance, a retired investor whose income depends a lot on her portfolio will probably choose a lower-risk, current-income-oriented approach for financial survival. In contrast, a high-income, financially secure investor may be much more willing to take on risky investments in hopes of improving her net worth. Likewise, a young investor with a secure job may be less concerned about current income and more able to bear risk. This type of investor will likely be more capital gains oriented and may choose speculative investments. As an investor approaches age 60, the desired level of income likely rises as retirement approaches. The more senior investor is typically less willing to bear risk and will focus on preserving principal, because these investments will soon be needed as a source of retirement income.

11-6b Asset Allocation and Portfolio Management

A portfolio must be built around an individual's needs, which in turn depend on income, family responsibilities, financial resources, age, retirement plans, and ability to bear risk. These needs shape one's financial goals. But to create a portfolio geared to those goals, you need to develop an **asset allocation** strategy. Asset allocation is the decision on *how to divide your portfolio among different types of securities.* For example, what portion of your portfolio will be devoted to short-term securities, to long-term bonds and bond funds, and to individual common stocks and equity funds? In asset allocation, the emphasis is often on *preserving capital* using careful diversification. The idea is to position your assets in such a way that you can protect your portfolio from potential negative developments in the market while still taking advantage of potential positive developments. Asset allocation is one of the most overlooked yet most important aspects of investing. There's overwhelming evidence that, over the long run, *the total return on a portfolio is influenced far more by its asset allocation than by specific security selections.*

Asset allocation deals in broad categories and *does not tell you which individual securities to buy or sell.* It might look something like this:

asset allocation
A plan for dividing a portfolio among different classes of securities in order to preserve capital by protecting the portfolio against negative market developments.

Type of Investment	Asset Mix
Short-term securities	*5%*
Intermediate-term bonds (7- to 10-year maturities)	*20%*
Equity funds	*75%*
Total portfolio	*100%*

As you can see, all you're really doing here is deciding how to cut up the pie. You still have to decide which particular securities to invest in. Once you've decided that you want to put, say, 20 percent of your money into intermediate-term (7- to 10-year)

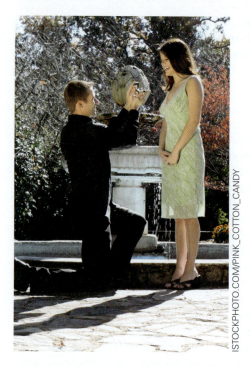

bonds, your next step is to select those specific securities. After establishing your asset allocation strategy, you should check it regularly for two reasons: first, to make sure that your portfolio is in line with your desired asset mix; and second, to see if that mix is still appropriate for your investment objectives. Here are some reasons to reevaluate your asset allocation:

- A major change in personal circumstances—marriage, birth of a child, loss of a spouse to divorce or death, child graduating from college, loss of job, or family illness—that changes your investment goals.
- The proportion of an asset category rises or falls considerably and thereby deviates from your target allocation for that class by more than, say, 5 percent.
- You're close to reaching a certain goal (such as saving for your child's college education or for your retirement).

Periodically, you'll likely find it necessary to *rebalance* your portfolio—that is, to reallocate the assets in your portfolio. For example, suppose that your asset allocation plan calls for 75 percent equities, but then the stock market falls, so stocks represent only 65 percent of your total portfolio value. If you're still bullish on the (long-term) market and if stocks are still appropriate for your portfolio, then you may view this as a good time to buy stocks and, in so doing, bring your portfolio back up to 75 percent in equities. If your personal goals change, or if you think the market may not recover in the near future, then you may decide to change your percentages so as to hold fewer stocks. But don't be too quick to rebalance every time your portfolio gets a little out of whack; you should allow for some variation in the actual allocations because market fluctuations will make it impossible to constantly maintain exact percentages. And don't forget to consider tax implications and the costs from trading commissions.

Portfolio management involves the buying, selling, and holding of various securities in order to meet a set of predetermined investment needs and objectives. To give you an idea of portfolio management in action, Exhibit 11.7 provides examples of four portfolios, each developed with a particular financial situation in mind. Notice that in each case, the asset allocation strategies and portfolio structures change with the different financial objectives. The first one is the *newlywed couple*; in their late 20s, they earn $65,000 a year and spend just about every cent. They have managed to put away some money, however, and are quickly beginning to appreciate the need to develop a savings program. Next is the *two-income couple*; in their early 40s, they earn $115,000 a year and are concerned about college costs for their children, ages

Financial Fact or Fantasy?

Coming up with a sound asset allocation plan will likely have more of an impact on long-term investment returns than the specific securities you hold in your portfolio. **Fact:** Research shows that, over the long-run, the total return on a portfolio is influenced more by its asset allocation plan—its mix of assets—than by specific security selections.

You Can Do It Now

Get a Quick Perspective on Your Asset Allocation

It's important to have a good perspective on your asset allocation decision. Good, rough recommendations can be found at **http://www.bankrate.com/calculators/retirement/asset-allocation.aspx** and **https://personal.vanguard.com/us/funds/tools/recommendation**. Just answer a few questions about your investment horizon and attitude towards risk and you're set—**you can do it now.**

EXHIBIT 11.7   Four Model Portfolios

The type of portfolio that you put together will depend on your financial and family situation as well as on your investment objectives. Clearly, what is right for one family may be totally inappropriate for another.

Family Situation	Portfolio
Newlywed couple	80 percent to 90 percent in common stocks, with three-quarters of that in mutual funds aiming for maximum capital gains and the rest in growth-and-income or equity-income funds
	10 percent to 20 percent in a money market fund or other short-term money market securities
Two-income couple	60 percent to 70 percent in common stocks, with three-quarters of that in blue chips or growth mutual funds and the rest in more aggressive issues or mutual funds aiming for maximum capital gains
	25 percent to 30 percent in discount Treasury notes whose maturities correspond with the bills for college tuition
	5 percent to 10 percent in money market funds or other short-term money market securities
Single parent	40 percent to 50 percent in money market funds or other short-term money market securities
	50 percent to 60 percent in growth and income mutual funds
Older couple	60 percent to 70 percent in blue-chip common stocks, growth funds, or value funds
	25 percent to 30 percent in municipal bonds or short- and intermediate-term discount bonds that will mature as the couple starts needing the money to live on
	5 percent to 10 percent in CDs and money market funds

17 and 12. Then there is the *single parent*; she is 34, has custody of her children, ages 7 and 4, and receives $50,000 a year in salary and child support. Finally, we have the *older couple*; in their mid-50s, they're planning for retirement in 10 years, when the husband will retire from his $95,000-a-year job.

11-6c Keeping Track of Your Investments

Just as you need investment objectives to provide direction for your portfolio, so too do you need to *monitor* it by keeping track of what your investment holdings consist of, how they've performed over time, and whether they've lived up to your expectations. Sometimes investments don't perform the way you thought they would. Their return may be well below what you'd like, or you may even have suffered a loss. In either case, it may be time to sell the investments and put the money elsewhere. A monitoring system should allow you to identify such securities in your portfolio. It should also enable you to stay on top of the holdings that are performing to your satisfaction. Knowing when to sell and when to hold can significantly affect the amount of return you're able to generate from your investments.

You can use a tool like Worksheet 11.2 to keep an inventory of your investment holdings. All types of investments can be included on this worksheet—from stocks, bonds, and mutual funds to real estate and savings accounts. To see how it works, consider the investment portfolio that has been built up since 2004 by Drew and Renee Porter, a two-income couple in their early 40s. Worksheet 11.2 shows that, as of May 1, 2015, Drew and Renee hold common stock in three companies, one bond exchange-traded fund, two equity mutual funds, and a savings account. While not shown, they also own a home that they bought in 2005, which has appreciated from an original cost of $280,000 to about $400,000. And they hold an emergency fund of $25,000 in an account that pays less than 1 percent a year. Using such a worksheet in conjunction with an online portfolio tracker would give an investor plenty of information about the performance of his or her portfolio—the *worksheet* providing long-term information from the date of purchase of an

A worksheet like this one will enable you to keep track of your investment holdings and to identify investments that aren't performing up to expectations.

AN INVENTORY OF INVESTMENT HOLDINGS

Name(s): Drew and Renee Porter   Date: May 1, 2015

Type of Investment	Description of Investment	Date Purchased	Amount of Original Investment	Latest Market Value	Cumulative Return
Common stock	250 shares–McDonalds	12/7/2005	$8,815.00	$24,450.00	+177.37%
Common stock	300 shares–Disney	10/19/2007	$10,143.00	$33,156.00	+226.89%
Common stock	150 shares–Intel	8/11/2010	$2,914.50	$5,013.00	+72.00%
Exchange-traded fund	400 shares–Vanguard Total International Bond ETF	8/12/2014	$20,444.00	$221,368.00	+ 4.52%
Mutual fund	200 shares–Vanguard Health Care	6/16/2004	$25,142.00	$45,426.00	+80.68%
Mutual fund	725 shares–Fidelity Contrafund	6/16/2004	$37,149.00	$73,384.50	+97.54%
	Portfolio Totals		**$104,607.50**	**$231,683.36**	**+93.87%**

asset, and the *online portfolio tracker* providing year-to-date or annual returns. Note that the Porters' holdings have grown from around $104,608 to about $231,683. A report like this should be prepared at least once a year. When completed, it provides a quick overview of your investment holdings and lets you know where you stand at a given point in time.

> ### You Can Do It Now
>
> ### *Track Your Portfolio for Free*
>
> You can track your portfolio for free. And you can track a "paper" portfolio as well just to test out investment ideas. Just go to **https://www.google.com/finance/portfolio?action=view** – you can do it now.

TEST YOURSELF

11-25   Explain why it might be preferable for a person to invest in a *portfolio* of securities rather than in a *single* security.

11-26   Briefly describe the concept of *asset allocation* and note how it works.

11-27   Discuss the role of asset allocation in portfolio management.

11-28   What, if anything, can be gained from keeping track of your investment holdings?

Planning Over a Lifetime: *Investing*

Here are some key considerations for investment planning in each stage of the life cycle.

Pre-family Independence: 20s	Family Formation/ Career Development: 30–45	Pre-Retirement: 45–65	Retirement: 65 and Beyond
✓ Describe specific, tangible investments goals concerning retirement, major purchases, ways to enhance current income, and tax shelters.	✓ Revise investment plan to focus more on retirement and funding children's education, if applicable.	✓ Revise investment plan in light of recent developments.	✓ Revise investment plan to include more conservative assets.
✓ Align your investment goals with an amount regularly set aside from your income.	✓ Consider rebalancing investment portfolio consistent with long-term strategy.	✓ Monitor portfolio performance and consider rebalancing asset exposures.	✓ Monitor portfolio performance and match current income to expenditures.
✓ Establish an emergency fund equal to six months of income.	✓ Gradually increase the amount set aside for investments and savings.	✓ Continue to gradually increase the amount you invest and save.	✓ Integrate investment strategy with estate planning.
✓ Make paying off college loans a priority. They limit your financial flexibility.			

Financial Impact of Personal Choices
Trey and April Get Serious About Their Retirement Asset Allocation

Trey and April Addison are married and are both 32 years old. While they want to save for their children's future college educations, they also want to be plan carefully for their retirement. They know it's important to be adequately diversified and to be properly positioned in the various asset categories in their 401(k) retirement plans and IRAs. So one recent Saturday afternoon they found a free online asset allocation calculator (**http://money.cnn.com/tools/assetallocwizard/assetallocwizard.html**) and got some initial guidance on their proper asset allocation.

The online survey asked them about their investment time horizon, how much risk they were comfortable with, the flexibility of their retirement date, and whether they're tempted to sell stocks during a downturn or buy more. They indicated a 20+ year investment time horizon, medium risk tolerance, flexible retirement dates, and an inclination to leave their investments alone during a downturn. The recommended asset allocation was:

10% bonds
50% large stocks
20% small stocks
20% foreign stocks

Given that this recommends they invest 90% of their money in stocks, Trey and April have decided to get some more recommendations for a broader perspective on their asset allocation decision. This recommendation strikes them as a bit too risky for their tastes. However, this recommendation confirms their interest in having a significant amount invested in stocks with decent international diversification for the long haul. Trey and April are well on their way to managing their retirement investments effectively.

Summary

LG1 **Discuss the role that investing plays in the personal financial planning process and identify several different investment objectives, p. 413**
Investing plays an important part in personal financial planning; it's the means of reaching many of your financial goals. Your investment activities should be based on a sound investment plan that's linked to an ongoing savings plan. Most people invest their money to enhance their current income, accumulate funds for a major expenditure, save for retirement, or shelter some of their income from taxes.

LG2 **Distinguish between primary and secondary markets as well as between broker and dealer markets, p. 422**
Stocks, bonds, and other long-term securities are traded in the capital, or long-term, markets. Newly issued securities are sold in the primary markets, whereas transactions between investors occur in the secondary markets; the secondary market can be further divided into broker and dealer markets. Broker markets are made up of various securities exchanges, like the NYSE as well as some smaller regional exchanges. In contrast, the dealer market is where you'll find both the NASDAQ markets (like the NASDAQ Global Select and National Markets) as well as the OTC markets.

LG3 **Explain the process of buying and selling securities, and recognize the different types of orders, p. 429**
The securities transaction process starts when you call and place an order with your broker, who then transmits it via sophisticated telecommunications equipment to the floor of the stock exchange or the OTC market, where it's promptly executed and confirmed. Investors can buy or sell securities in odd or round lots by simply placing one of the three basic types of orders: a market order, limit order, or stop-loss order.

LG4 **Develop an appreciation of how various forms of investment information can lead to better investing skills and returns, p. 436**
Becoming an informed investor is essential to developing a sound investment program. Vital information about specific companies and industries, the securities markets, the economy, and different investment vehicles and strategies can be obtained from such sources as annual stockholders' reports, brokerage and advisory service reports, the financial press, and the Internet. Various averages and indexes—such as the DJIA, the Standard & Poor's indexes, and the NYSE and NASDAQ indexes—provide information about daily market performance. These averages and indexes not only measure performance in the overall market but also provide standards of performance.

LG5 **Gain a basic understanding of the impact of the Internet on the field of investments, p. 444**
The computer and the Internet have empowered individual investors by providing information and tools formerly available only to investing professionals. The savings they offer in time and money are huge. Investors get the most current information, including real-time stock price quotes, market activity data, research reports, educational articles, and discussion forums. Tools such as financial planning calculators, stock screening programs, and portfolio tracking are free at many sites. Buying and selling securities online is convenient, simple, inexpensive, and fast.

LG6 **Describe an investment portfolio and how you'd go about developing, monitoring, and managing a portfolio of securities, p. 447**
An investment portfolio represents a collection of the securities/investments you hold, and it also gives focus and purpose to your investing activities. Developing a well-diversified portfolio of investment holdings enables an investor not only to achieve given investment objectives but also to enjoy reduced risk exposure and a more predictable level of return. To develop such a portfolio, the investor must carefully consider his or her level and stability of income, family factors, financial condition, experience and age, and disposition toward risk. Designing an asset allocation strategy, or mix of securities, that's based on these personal needs and objectives is also an important part of portfolio management. You should monitor your investment portfolio regularly to measure its performance and make changes as required by return data and life-cycle factors.

Key Terms

Answers to Test Yourself

You can find answers to these questions on this book's companion website. Look for it at *www.cengagebrain.com*. Search for this book by its title, and then add it to your dashboard.

Key Financial Relationships

Concept	Financial Relationship	Page Number
Payments to Fund Future Target Amount	Yearly Savings = Future Amount of Money Desired/Future Value Annuity Factor	416
Rate of Return	$\text{Rate of Return} = \dfrac{\text{Ending Value} - \text{Beginning Value} + \text{Income}}{\text{Beginning Value}}$	434

Key Financial Relationships Problem Set

1. ***Payments to Fund Future Target Amount.*** Liam and Tara Gleason want to have $275,000 available to fund their daughter's college education in 16 years. They are relatively conservative investors and expect to earn 5 percent per year on their portfolio. How much would the Gleason's need to invest every year to have the desired $275,000 available in 16 years?

   Solution: Yearly Savings = Future Amount of Money Desired/Future Value Annuity Factor. The future value annuity factor for 16 years and 5 percent in Appendix B is 23.657. Consequently, the

Gleasons should invest a yearly amount of $275,000/23.657 = $11,624.47 if they want to have $275,000 available to fund their daughter's education in 16 years

2. ***Rate of Return.*** Valerie Goldsmith bought a stock for $95 two years ago. Over this time period she received $3.00 in dividends while the price increased to $125. Valerie wants to find the rate of return on her investment.

   Solution: The rate of return is calculated as:

$$\text{Rate of Return} = \frac{\text{Ending Value} - \text{Beginning Value} + \text{Income}}{\text{Beginning Value}} = \frac{(\$125 - \$95) + \$3.000}{\$95.00}$$
$$= 34.74 \text{ percent}$$

Financial Planning Exercises

LG1, p. 413

1. ***Amount to invest to meet objectives. Use Worksheet 11.1*** Alison Conroy is early in her career and is now employed as the managing editor of a well-known business journal. Although she thoroughly enjoys her job and the people she works with, she would really like to be a literary agent. She would like to go on her own in about eight years and figures she'll need about $50,000 in capital to do so. Given that she thinks she can make about 10 percent on her money, use Worksheet 11.1 to answer the following questions.
   a. How much would Alison have to invest today, in one lump sum, to end up with $50,000 in eight years?
   b. If she's starting from scratch, how much would she have to put away annually to accumulate the needed capital in eight years?
   c. How about if she already has $10,000 socked away; how much would she have to put away annually to accumulate the required capital in eight years?
   d. Given that Alison has an idea of how much she needs to save, briefly explain how she could use an *investment plan* to help reach her objective.

LG2, p. 422

2. ***Rationale for stock exchange listings.*** Why do you suppose that large, well-known companies such as Apple, Starbucks, and Facebook prefer to have their shares traded on the NASDAQ rather than on one of the major listed exchanges, such as the NYSE (for which they'd easily meet all listing requirements)? What's in it for them? What would they gain by switching over to the NYSE?

LG3, p. 429

3. ***Market and limit orders.*** Suppose Gary Hooker places an order to buy 100 shares of The Gap. Explain how the order will be processed if it's a market order. Would it make any difference if it had been a limit order? Explain.

LG3, p. 429

4. ***Calculating profits on margined and unmargined investments.*** Claire Gerber wants to buy 300 shares of Google, which is selling in the market for $537.34 a share. Rather than liquidate all her savings, she decides to borrow through her broker at 5 percent a year. Assume that the margin requirement on common stock is 50 percent. If the stock rises to $625 a share over the next year, calculate the dollar profit and percentage return that Claire would earn if she makes the investment with 50 percent margin. Contrast these figures to what she'd make if she uses no margin.

LG3, p. 429

5. ***Calculating return on investment.*** Which of the following would offer the best return on investment? Assume that you buy $5,000 in stock in all three cases, and ignore interest and transaction costs in all your calculations.
   a. Buy a stock at $60 without margin, and sell it a year later at $90.
   b. Buy a stock at $20 with 50 percent margin, and sell it a year later at $30.
   c. Buy a stock at $40 with 75 percent margin, and sell it a year later at $55.

LG3, p. 429

6. ***Calculating short position profit.*** How much profit (if any) would Max Adler make if he short-sold 300 shares of a stock at $100 a share and the price of the stock suddenly tumbled to $70?

LG3, p. 429

7. *Calculating long and short position profits.* Given that Hometown Care, Inc.'s stock is currently selling for $40 a share, calculate the amount of money that Calvin Haskins will make (or lose) on each of the following transactions. Assume all transactions involve 100 shares of stock, and ignore brokerage commissions.
   a. He short-sells the stock and then repurchases the borrowed shares at $50.
   b. He buys the stock and then sells it some time later at $50.
   c. He short-sells the stock and then repurchases the borrowed shares at $25.

LG3, p. 429

8. *Calculating short position cash flows and returns.* Assume that an investor short-sells 500 shares of stock at a price of $85 a share, making a 50 percent margin deposit. A year later, she repurchases the borrowed shares at $50 a share.
   a. How much of her money did the short-seller have to put up to make this transaction?
   b. How much money did the investor make, or lose, on this transaction?
   c. What rate of return did she make on her *invested capital* (see part a)?

LG4, p. 436

9. *Interpreting stock quotes.* The following quote for The Walt Disney Company, a NYSE stock, appeared on May 1, 2015 (Friday) on Yahoo! Finance (**http://finance.yahoo.com/q?s=DIS&ql=1**):

The Walt Disney Company (DIS)—NYSE			
110.52 ↑ 1.80 (1.66%) May 1, 4:01 PM EDT			
Prev Close:	108.72	Day's Range:	109.27 – 110.67
Open:	109.79	52wk Range:	78.54 – 111.66
Bid:	110.81 × 400	Volume:	6,205,116
Ask:	110.95 × 500	Avg Vol (3m):	6,394,880
1y Target Est:	110.23	Market Cap:	187.84B
Beta:	1.1	P/E (ttm):	24.57
Next Earnings Date:	5-May-15	EPS (ttm):	4.50
		Div & Yield:	1.15 (1.10%)

Given this information, answer the following questions.
   a. At what price did the stock sell at the time of the quote?
   b. What is the stock's price/earnings ratio? What does that indicate?
   c. What is the last price at which the stock traded on the prior trading day?
   d. What is the stock's dividend yield?
   e. What are the highest and lowest prices at which the stock traded during the latest 52-week period?
   f. How large is the market capitalization of the company?

LG4, p. 436

10. *Finding and interpreting stock quotes.* Listed below are three pairs of stocks. Look at each pair and select the security you'd like to own, given that you want to *select the one with the highest market value.* Then, *after* making all three of your selections, use *The Wall Street Journal* or some other source to find the latest market value of the two securities in each pair.
    a. 50 shares of Berkshire Hathaway (stock symbol BRKA) or 150 shares of JP Morgan Chase (stock symbol JPM). (Both stocks are listed on the NYSE.)
    b. 100 shares of Home Depot (symbol HD), a NYSE stock; or 100 shares of Apple (symbol AAPL), a NASDAQ stock and a member of the Dow Jones Industrial Average.
    c. 150 shares of Wal-Mart (symbol WMT) or 50 shares of Facebook (symbol FB).

    How many times did you pick the one that was worth more money? Did the price of any of these stocks surprise you? If so, which one(s)? Does the price of a stock represent its value? Explain.

LG4, p. 436

11. *Finding and using market index quotes.* Using a resource like *The Wall Street Journal or Barron's* (either in print or online), find the latest values for each of the following market averages and indexes, and indicate how each has performed over the past six months:
    a. DJIA
    b. Dow Jones Global Titans 50
    c. S&P 500

d.   NYSE Composite

e.   NASDAQ Composite

f.   S&P MidCap 400

g.   Dow Jones Wilshire 5000

h.   Russell 2000

LG4, p. 436 12. **Finding stock quote information.** Using the Internet site for Yahoo! Finance (**http://finance.yahoo.com**), find the 52-week high and low for Coca-Cola's common stock (symbol KO). What is the stock's latest dividend yield? What was Coca-Cola's most recent closing price, and at what P/E ratio was the stock trading?

LG4, p. 436 13. **Interpreting stock report information.** Using the S&P report in Exhibit 11.6, find the following information for Apple.

a.   What was the amount of revenues (i.e., sales) generated by the company in 2014?

b.   What were the latest annual dividends per share and dividend yield?

c.   What were the earnings (per share) projections for 2015?

d.   How many common shareholders were there?

e.   What were the book value per share and earnings per share in 2014?

f.   Where is the stock traded?

g.   How much long-term debt did the company have in 2014?

h.   What was the company's effective tax rate in 2014?

LG6, p. 447 14. **Tracking portfolio performance. Use Worksheet 11.2** to help Clayton and Julie Grover, a married couple in their late 40s, evaluate their securities portfolio, which includes these holdings.

a.   *IBM.* (NYSE; symbol IBM): 100 shares bought in 2011 for $170.40 per share.

b.   *Verizon* (NYSE; symbol VZ): 250 shares purchased in 2007 for $40.62 per share.

c.   *Procter & Gamble* (NYSE; symbol PG): 150 shares purchased in 2010 at $61.85 per share.

d.   *Google* (NASDAQ; symbol, GOOG): 200 shares purchased in 2014 at $519.98 per share.

e.   The Grovers also have $8,000 in a bank savings account that pays 1.25 percent annual interest.

1.   Based on the latest quotes and portfolio tracking tools obtained from the Internet, complete Worksheet 11.2.

2.   What's the total amount the Grovers have invested in these securities, the annual income they now receive, and the latest market value of their investments?

Applying Personal Finance

Research Your Investments!

Investing involves making informed decisions, which means researching companies and industries *before* plunking down your hard-earned money! An excellent source of information about a company is the company itself, particularly its annual report to stockholders. In this project, you'll examine the annual stockholders' report of a company in which you are interested.

The annual report is a document that provides financial and operating information about a company to its owners, the stockholders. Obtain a copy of the latest annual report of the company you are researching. Copies can be found in many public and college libraries, at local brokerage offices, or on the company's Internet site. Carefully study the annual report and then prepare a corporate profile of the firm you selected. Your profile should include the following elements:

a.   Name of the company, its ticker symbol, and the exchange on which it trades

b.   Current market price of the stock and its percentage change from 1, 3, and 5 years ago (try to find a chart of its stock price)

c.   Location of its corporate headquarters, names of its officers, and percentage of inside ownership

d.   Brief description of the company, including its major products or services

e.   Brief history of the company

f.   Major competitors

g.   Sales and profit summaries
h.   Other relevant financial ratios and measures
i.   Recent developments and future plans

Based on your findings, would you consider this company for a potential investment? Why or why not?

CRITICAL THINKING CASES

LG6, p. 447   ### 11.1 The Woodsons Struggle with Two Investment Goals

Like many married couples, Damian and Brandi Woodson are trying their best to save for two important investment objectives: (1) an education fund to put their two children through college; and (2) a retirement nest egg for themselves. They want to set aside $100,000 per child by the time each one starts college. Given that their children are now 10 and 12 years old, Damian and Brandi have 6 years remaining for one child and 8 for the other. As far as their retirement plans are concerned, the Woodsons both hope to retire in 20 years, when they reach age 65. Both Damian and Brandi work, and together, they currently earn about $90,000 a year.

The Woodsons started a college fund some years ago by investing $6,000 a year in bank CDs. That fund is now worth $65,000. They also have $50,000 that they received from an inheritance invested in several mutual funds and another $20,000 in a tax-sheltered retirement account. Damian and Brandi believe that they'll be able to continue putting away $6,000 a year for the next 20 years. In fact, Brandi thinks they'll be able to put away even more, particularly after the children are out of school. The Woodsons are fairly conservative investors and feel they can probably earn about 6 percent on their money. (Ignore taxes for the purpose of this exercise.)

Critical Thinking Questions

1. **Use Worksheet 11.1** to determine whether the Woodsons have enough money right now to meet their children's educational needs. That is, will the $65,000 they've accumulated so far be enough to put their children through school, given they can invest their money at 6 percent? Remember, they want to have $100,000 set aside for each child by the time each one starts college.
2. Regarding their retirement nest egg, assume that no additions are made to either the $50,000 they now have in mutual funds or to the $20,000 in the retirement account. How much would these investments be worth in 20 years, given that they can earn 6 percent?
3. Now, if the Woodsons can invest $6,000 a year for the next 20 years and apply all of that to their retirement nest egg, how much would they be able to accumulate given their 6 percent rate of return?
4. How do you think the Woodsons are doing with regard to meeting their twin investment objectives? Explain.

LG6, p. 447   ### 11.2 Russ Alonzo Takes Stock of His Securities

Russ Alonzo is 42 years old, single, and works as a designer for a major architectural firm. He is well paid and has built up a sizable portfolio of investments. He considers himself an aggressive investor and, because he has no dependents to worry about, likes to invest in high-risk/high-return securities. His records show the following information.

1. In 2006, Russ bought 200 shares of eBay (NASDAQ; symbol EBAY) at $29.77 a share.
2. In 2013 he bought 250 shares of Facebook (NASDAQ; symbol FB) at $26.89 a share.
3. In 2008, Russ bought 200 shares of United Technologies Corp. (NYSE; symbol UTX) at $74.92 a share.
4. In early 2009, he bought 450 shares of JPMorgan Chase (NYSE; symbol JPM) at $16 a share.
5. Also in 2009, Russ bought 400 shares of PepsiCo (NYSE; symbol PEP) at $52.50 a share.
6. He has $12,000 in a 1 percent money market mutual fund.

Every three months or so, Russ prepares a complete, up-to-date report on his investment holdings.

Critical Thinking Questions

1. *Use a form like Worksheet 11.2* to prepare a complete inventory of Russ' investment holdings. (*Note*: Look in the latest issue of *The Wall Street Journal*, or pull up an online source such as **http://finance.yahoo.com**, to find the most recent closing price of the five stocks in Russ' portfolio.)

2. What is your overall assessment of Russ' investment portfolio? Does it appear that his personal net worth is improving because of his investments?

3. Based on the worksheet you prepared in Question 1, do you see any securities that you think Russ should consider selling? What other investment advice might you give Russ?

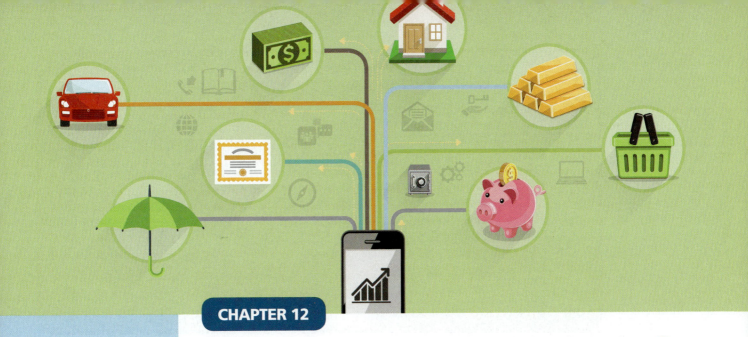

CHAPTER 12

Investing in Stocks and Bonds

LEARNING GOALS

LG1   Describe the various types of risks to which investors are exposed, as well as the sources of return.

LG2   Know how to search for an acceptable investment on the basis of risk, total return, and yield.

LG3   Discuss the merits of investing in common stock and be able to distinguish among the different types of stocks.

LG4   Become familiar with the various measures of performance and how to use them in placing a value on stocks.

LG5   Describe the basic issue characteristics of bonds, as well as how these securities are used as investment vehicles.

LG6   Distinguish between the different types of bonds, gain an understanding of how bond prices behave, and know how to compute different measures of yield.

How Will This Affect Me?

Once you've figured out how much you need to invest to meet important financial goals, it's time to decide which specific investments to buy. This chapter describes the basic characteristics of stocks and bonds, explains their potential returns and risks, and provides a framework for choosing among stocks and bonds to meet your financial objectives. Care is taken to explore how stock and bond prices behave and how to evaluate their performance over time. After reading this chapter you should be able to choose the most appropriate stocks and bonds for your portfolio in light of your goals and constraints.

12–1 THE RISKS AND REWARDS OF INVESTING

LG1, LG2

Most rational investors are motivated to buy or sell a security based on its expected return: buy if the return looks good, sell if it doesn't. But a security's return is just part of the story; you can't consider the return on an investment without also looking at its *risk*—the chance that the actual return from an investment may differ from what was expected (i.e., fall short—you wouldn't mind if it exceeded expectations, after all). Generally speaking, you expect riskier investments to provide higher levels of return. Otherwise, what incentive is there for an investor to risk his or her capital? This is referred to as the risk–return trade-off. The concepts of risk and return are of vital concern to investors, so, before taking up the issue of investing in stocks and bonds, let's look more closely at the risks of investing and the various components of return. Equally important, we'll see how these two components can be used together to find potentially attractive investments.

12–1a The Risks of Investing

Just about any type of investment is subject to some risk—some investment types more than others. The basic types of investment risk are business risk, financial risk, market risk, purchasing power risk, interest rate risk, liquidity risk, and event risk. Other things being equal, you'd like to reduce your exposure to these risks as much as possible.

Business Risk

When investing in a company, you accept the possibility that the firm will not be able to maintain sales and profits, or even to stay in business. Such failure is due either to economic or industry factors or, as is more often the case, to poor management decisions. **Business risk** is the variability surrounding the firm's cash flows and subsequent ability to meet operating expenses on time. Companies that are subject to high degrees of business risk may experience wide fluctuations in sales, may have widely erratic earnings, and can experience substantial operating losses every now and then.

Financial Risk

Financial risk concerns the amount of debt used to finance a firm, as well as the possibility that the firm will not have sufficient cash flows to meet these obligations on time.

business risk
The variability associated with a firm's cash flows and with its subsequent ability to meet its operating expenses on time.

financial risk
A type of risk associated with the amount of debt used to finance the firm and its ability to meet these obligations on time.

Look to the company's balance sheet in order to get a handle on a firm's financial risk. As a rule, companies that have little or no long-term debt are fairly low in financial risk. This is the case particularly if the company also has a healthy earnings picture. The problem with debt financing is that it creates principal and interest obligations that must be met regardless of how much profit the company is generating.

Market Risk

market risk
A type of risk associated with the price volatility of a security.

Market risk results from the behavior of investors in the securities markets that can lead to swings in security prices. These price changes can be due to underlying intrinsic factors, as well as to changes in political, economic, and social conditions or in investor tastes and preferences. Essentially, market risk is reflected in the *price volatility* of a security: the more volatile the price of a security relative to the overall market, the greater its market risk.

Purchasing Power Risk

purchasing power risk
A type of risk, resulting from possible changes in price levels, which can significantly affect investment returns.

Changes in the general level of prices within the economy also produce **purchasing power risk**. In periods of rising prices (inflation), the purchasing power of the dollar declines. This means that a smaller quantity of goods and services can be purchased with a given number of dollars. In general, investments (such as stocks and real estate) whose values tend to move with general price levels are most profitable during periods of rising prices, whereas investments (such as bonds) that pay fixed cash flows are preferred during periods of low or declining price levels.

Interest Rate Risk

fixed-income securities
Securities such as bonds, notes, and preferred stocks that offer purchasers fixed periodic income.

interest rate risk
A type of risk, resulting from changing market interest rates, that mainly affects fixed-income securities.

Fixed-income securities—which include notes, bonds, and preferred stocks—pay investors a fixed periodic cash flow and, as such, are most affected by **interest rate risk**. As interest rates change, the prices of these securities fluctuate, decreasing with rising interest rates and increasing with falling rates. The prices of fixed-income securities drop when interest rates increase because investors require rates of return that are competitive with securities offering higher levels of interest income.

Liquidity Risk

liquidity risk
A type of risk associated with the inability to liquidate an investment conveniently and at a reasonable price.

The risk of not being able to liquidate (i.e., sell) an investment conveniently and at a reasonable price is called **liquidity risk**. In general, investments traded in *thin markets*, where supply and demand are relatively small, tend to be less liquid than those traded in *broad markets*. However, to be liquid, an investment not only must be easy to sell, but also must be so *at a reasonable price*. The liquidity of an investment can generally be enhanced merely by cutting its price. For example, a security recently purchased for $1,000 wouldn't be viewed as highly liquid if it could be sold only at a significantly reduced price, such as $500. Vehicles such as mutual funds, common stocks, and U.S. Treasury securities are generally highly liquid; others, such as an isolated parcel of raw land, are not.

Event Risk

event risk
The risk that some major, unexpected event will occur that leads to a sudden and substantial change in the value of an investment.

Event risk occurs when something substantial happens to a company and that event, in itself, has a sudden impact on the company's financial condition. It involves an unexpected event that has a significant and usually immediate effect on the underlying value of an investment. A good example of event risk was the action by the Food and Drug Administration (FDA) years ago to halt the use of silicone breast implants. The share price of Dow Corning—the dominant producer of this product—quickly fell due to this single event! Another comparable example is the controversy over Vioxx, a drug produced by Merck, which was eventually withdrawn from the market and brought civil and criminal litigation that ultimately cost the company at least $5.8 billion. Fortunately, event risk tends to be confined to specific companies, securities, or market segments.

12–1b The Returns from Investing

Any investment—whether it's a share of stock, a bond, a piece of real estate, or a mutual fund—has two basic sources of return: *current income* and *capital gains*. Some investments offer only one source of return (for example, non-dividend-paying stocks provide only capital gains), but many others offer both income and capital gains, which together make up what's known as the *total return* from an investment. Of course, when both elements of return are present, the relative importance of each will vary among investments. For example, whereas current income is more important with bonds, capital gains are usually a larger portion of the total return from common stocks.

Current Income

Current income is generally received with some degree of regularity over the course of the year. It may take the form of dividends on stock, interest from bonds, or rents from real estate. People who invest to obtain income look for investments that will provide regular and predictable patterns of income. Preferred stocks and bonds, which are expected to pay established amounts at specified times (e.g., quarterly or semiannually), are usually viewed as good income investments.

Capital Gains

The other type of return available from investments is capital appreciation (or growth), which is reflected as an increase in the market value of an investment vehicle. Capital gains occur when you're able to sell a security for more than you paid for it. Investments that provide greater growth potential through capital appreciation normally have lower levels of current income, because the firm achieves its growth by reinvesting its earnings instead of paying dividends to the owners. Many common stocks, for example, are bought for their capital gains potential.

Earning Interest on Interest: Another Source of Return

When does a 4 percent investment end up yielding only 3 percent? Probably more often than you think! Obviously, it can happen when investment performance fails to live up to expectations. But it can also happen *even when everything goes right*. That is, so long as at least part of the return from an investment involves the periodic receipt of current income (such as dividends or interest payments), then that income must be *reinvested* at a given rate of return in order to achieve the yield you thought you had going into the investment. For example, consider an investor who buys a 4 percent U.S. Treasury bond and holds it to the maturity date in 20 years. Each year, the bondholder receives $40 in interest, and at maturity, the $1,000 in principal is repaid. There's no loss in capital, no default; everything is paid right on time. Yet this sure-fire investment ends up yielding only 3 percent. Why? Because the investor failed to reinvest the semiannual interest payments received at the original interest rate of 4 percent. By not plowing back all the investment earnings, the bondholder failed to earn any interest on interest.

Take a look at Exhibit 12.1. It shows the three elements of return for a 4 percent, 20-year bond: (1) the recovery of principal, (2) periodic interest income, and (3) the interest on interest earned from reinvesting the semiannual interest payments. Note that because the bond was originally bought at par ($1,000), you start off with a 4 percent investment. *Where you end up depends, in large part, on what you do with the interest earnings from this investment.* If you don't reinvest the interest income at the original 4 percent, then you could end up at the 3 percent line—or even lower.

You have to earn interest on interest from your investments in order to move to the 4 percent line. Specifically, because you started with a 4 percent investment, that's the rate of return that you need to earn when reinvesting your income. Keep in mind that, even though we used a bond in our illustration, *this same concept applies to any type of long-term investment* so long as current income is part of an

FINANCIAL PLANNING TIPS

Keys to Successful Stock and Bond Investing: Asset Allocation, Diversification, and Rebalancing

Here are some key concepts that will help you manage your portfolio successfully:

- **Asset allocation.** This is the decision on how to divide your investments among the different major asset classes, which include stocks, bonds, and cash. The best mix depends on your *tolerance for risk* and on your *time horizon*. Longer-term investors, like someone in their 20s saving for retirement, are often more comfortable investing in riskier assets like stocks. In contrast, shorter-term investors, like someone saving for a house down payment or a child's education, often will prefer less risk. Many such people will invest less in stocks and more in bonds. And most investors change their asset allocation as their time horizon changes—for instance, as they approach retirement. Thus, most investors tend to have less money in stocks and more money in bonds and cash as they get older.

- **Diversification.** This is the strategy of spreading your money among different investments so that losses on some investments will be offset, at least somewhat, by gains on other investments in your portfolio. Your portfolio should be diversified both *among* and *within* asset classes. This means that your asset allocation strategy

should spread out your money among stocks, bonds, and cash, and that your money should be spread out among different securities within *each* asset class. For example, within the equity asset class, it's important to identify stocks that perform distinctly under different equity market conditions. This often involves investing in stocks in different sectors and industries.

- **Rebalancing.** Over time, changes in market values could make your portfolio inconsistent with your financial goals. For example, what if you have decided that your portfolio should consist of 70 percent stocks, but a market turndown has reduced the value of your stock holdings to only 60 percent of your portfolio? In order to rebalance your holdings, you'll need to buy more equities or sell some bonds and/or use some cash to fund the additional exposure to stocks. But before you rebalance, you should consider carefully the transaction costs and any possible tax consequences. Many financial advisors suggest that you consider rebalancing your portfolio every 6 to 12 months, and whenever the asset allocation gets out of kilter by a significant percentage, like 5 percent or 10 percent.

Source: "Beginners' Guide to Asset Allocation, Diversification, and Rebalancing," http://www.sec.gov/investor/pubs/assetallocation.htm, accessed August 2015.

investment's return. In other words, it's just as relevant to common stocks and mutual funds as it is to long-term bond instruments. This notion of earning interest on interest is what the market refers to as a *fully compounded rate of return*. It's an important concept because you can't reap the full potential from your investments unless you earn a fully compounded return on your money.

If periodic investment income is a part of your investment return, then the reinvestment of that income and interest on interest are important matters. In fact, *interest on interest is a particularly important element of return for investment programs involving a lot of current income*. This is so because, in contrast to capital gains, current income must be reinvested by the individual investor. (With capital gains, the investment itself does all the reinvesting automatically.) It follows, then, that if your investment program tends to lean toward income-oriented securities, then interest on interest—and the continued reinvestment of income—will play an important role in defining the amount of investment success you have. Of course, *the length of your investment horizon* also plays a key role in defining the amount of interest on interest embedded in a security's return. In particular, *long-term investments* (e.g., 20-year bonds) are subject to a lot more interest on interest than are short-term investments (e.g., six-month T-bills or dividend-paying stocks that you hold for only 2 or 3 years).

EXHIBIT 12.1   Three Elements of Return for a 4 Percent, 20-Year Bond

As seen here, the long-term return from an investment (in this case, a bond) is made up of three parts: recovery of capital, current income, and interest on interest; of the three components, interest on interest is particularly important, *especially for long-term investments.*

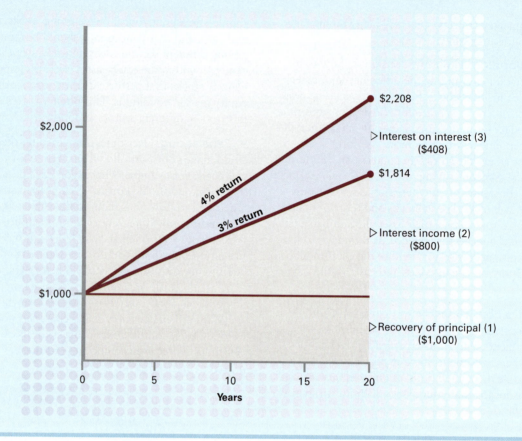

12–1c The Risk-Return Trade-off

The amount of risk associated with a given investment is directly related to its expected return. This universal rule of investing means that if you want a higher level of return, you'll probably have to accept greater exposure to risk. Yet, you can't invest in a high-risk security and earn a high rate of return automatically. Unfortunately, it doesn't work that way—risk isn't, by definition, that predictable!

Because most people are *risk averse* (they dislike taking risks), some incentive for taking risks must be offered. If a low-risk investment offered the same return as a high-risk one, then investors would naturally opt for the former; put another way, investors will choose the investment with the least risk for a given level of return. Exhibit 12.2 portrays the expected risk-return trade-off for some popular investment vehicles. Note that it's possible to receive a positive return for zero risk, such as at point A. This is referred to as the **risk-free rate of return**, which is often measured by the return on a short-term government security, such as a 90-day Treasury bill (T-bill).

12–1d What Makes a Good Investment?

In keeping with the preceding risk-return discussion, it follows that the value of any investment depends on the amount and timing of benefits it's expected to

risk-free rate of return
The rate of return on short-term government securities, such as Treasury bills, that is free from any type of risk.

EXHIBIT 12.2 | **The Risk–Return Relationship**

For investments, there's generally a direct relationship between risk and return: the more risk you face, the greater the return you should expect from the investment.

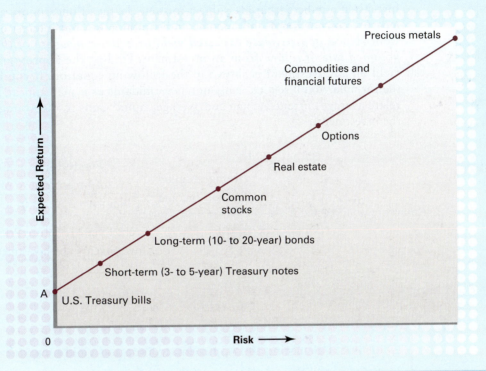

provide relative to the amount of perceived risk involved. This applies to all types of investments, including stocks, bonds, convertibles, options, real estate, and commodities.

Future Return

In investments, it's the *expected future return* that matters. Aside from the help that they can provide in getting a handle on future returns, past returns are of little value to investors. After all, it's not what the security did last year that matters, but rather, what it's expected to do next year.

To get an idea of the future return on an investment, we must *formulate expectations of its future income and future capital appreciation.* As an illustration, assume you're thinking of buying some stock in CTA Strategic Group, Inc. (CTA). After reviewing several financial reports, you've estimated the future dividends and price behavior of CTA as follows:

Expected average annual dividends, 2017–2019	$2.15 a share
Expected market price of the stock, 2019	$95.00 a share

Because the stock is now selling for $60 a share, the difference between its current and expected future market price ($95 − $60) represents the amount of *capital gains* that you expect to receive over the next three years—in this case, $35 a share. The projected future price, along with expected average annual dividends, gives you an estimate of the stock's *future income stream*; what you need now is a way to measure the *expected return.*

Approximate Expected Yield

Finding the exact rate of return on an investment involves an iterative mathematical procedure—one that's hard to solve without using a handheld financial calculator (which we'll demonstrate shortly). There is, however, a fairly easy way to obtain a reasonably close estimation of expected return, and that is to compute an investment's *approximate expected yield*. It's useful when dealing with forecasted numbers (that are subject to some degree of uncertainty anyway). The measure considers not only income and capital gains, but interest on interest as well. Hence, *approximate expected yield provides a measure of the fully compounded rate of return* from an investment. Finding the approximate expected yield on an investment is shown in the following equation. If you briefly study the formula, you'll see it's really not as formidable as it may appear. All it does is relate average current income and average capital gains to the average amount of the investment.

$$\text{Approximate Expected Yield} = \frac{\text{Average Annual Current Income} + \left[\dfrac{\text{Future Price of Investment} - \text{Current Price of Investment}}{\text{Number of Years in Investment Period}}\right]}{\left[\dfrac{\text{Current Price of Investment} + \text{Future Price of Investment}}{2}\right]}$$

EXAMPLE: Calculating the Approximate Expected Yield on a Stock

To illustrate, let's use the CTA example again. Given the average current income from annual dividends of $2.15, current stock price of $60, future stock price of $95, and an investment period of three years (you expect to hold the stock from the beginning of 2017 through the end of 2019), you can use this equation to find the approximate expected yield on CTA as follows:

$$\text{Approximate Yield} = \frac{\$2.15 + \left[\dfrac{\$95 - \$60}{3}\right]}{\left[\dfrac{\$60 + \$95}{2}\right]}$$

$$= \frac{\$2.15 + \left[\dfrac{\$35}{3}\right]}{\left[\dfrac{\$155}{2}\right]}$$

$$= \frac{\$2.15 + \$11.67}{\$77.50} = \frac{\$13.82}{\$77.50}$$

$$= \underline{17.8\%}$$

In this case, if your forecasts of annual dividends and capital gains hold up, an investment in CTA should provide a return of around 17.8 percent per year.

Calculator

INPUTS	FUNCTIONS
3	N
−60	PV
2.15	PMT
95.00	FV
	CPT
	I/Y
	SOLUTION
	19.66

See Appendix E for details.

Calculator Keystrokes. You can easily find the *exact* expected return on this example investment using a handheld financial calculator. Here's what you do. First, put the calculator in the *annual compounding* mode. Then—to find the expected return on a stock that you buy at $60 a share, hold for three years (during which time you receive average annual dividends of $2.15 a share), and then sell at $95—use the keystrokes shown in the margin, where:

N = number of *years* that you hold the stock
PV = the price that you pay for the stock (entered as a *negative* number)
PMT = *average* amount of dividends received *each year*
FV = the price that you expect to receive when you *sell* the stock (in three years)

You'll notice that there is a difference in the computed yield measures (17.8 percent with the approximate procedure, versus 19.66 percent here). That's to be expected because one is only an approximate measure of performance, whereas the calculator gives an exact measure.

required rate of return
The minimum rate of return an investor feels should be earned in compensation for the amount of risk assumed.

Financial Fact or Fantasy?

A good investment is one that offers a positive expected rate of return.
Fantasy: *A good investment is one that offers an expected return that equals or exceeds the investor's required rate of return, which is defined relative to the risk of the investment. Thus, what might be a good return in one case may be totally inadequate in another.*

Whether you should consider CTA a viable investment candidate depends on how the expected return stacks up to the amount of risk that you would assume. Suppose you've decided the stock is moderately risky. To determine whether the expected rate of return on this investment will be satisfactory, you can compare it to some benchmark. One of the best is the rate of return you can expect from a *risk-free* security, such as a *U.S. T-bill* or a *U.S. T-bond*. The idea is that the return on a *risky* security should be greater than that available on a risk-free security. If, for example, U.S. T-bonds are yielding 4 percent–5 percent, then you'd want to receive considerably more—perhaps 10 percent–12 percent—to justify your investment in a moderately risky security like CTA. In essence, the 10 percent to 12 percent is your **required rate of return**: the minimum rate of return you should receive in compensation for the amount of risk you must assume. *An investment is acceptable only if it's expected to generate a rate of return that meets (or exceeds) your required rate of return.* In the case of CTA, the stock *should be considered a viable investment candidate* because it provides more than the minimum or required rate of return.

TEST YOURSELF

12-1 Describe the various types of risk to which investors are exposed.

12-2 What is meant by the *risk-return trade-off?* What is the *risk-free rate of return?*

12-3 Briefly describe the two basic sources of return to investors.

12-4 What is *interest on interest,* and why is it such an important element of return?

12-5 What is the *desired rate of return,* and how would it be used to make an investment decision?

12–2 INVESTING IN COMMON STOCK

LG3, LG4

residual owners
Shareholders of the company; they are entitled to dividend income and a share of the company's profits only after all of the firm's other obligations have been met.

Common stocks appeal to investors for various reasons. To some, investing in stocks is a way to hit it big if the issue shoots up in price. To others, it's the level of current income that stocks offer. A share of common stock enables the investor to participate in the profits of the firm. Every shareholder is, in effect, a part owner of the firm and, as such, is entitled to a piece of its profit. Common stockholders are really the **residual owners** of the company, meaning that they're entitled to dividend income and a prorated share of the company's earnings, but only after all the firm's other obligations have been met.

12–2a Common Stocks as a Form of Investing

Given the nature of common stocks, if the market is strong, then investors can generally expect to benefit from steady price appreciation. A good example is the performance in 2013, when the market, as measured by the Dow Jones Industrial Average (DJIA), went up more than 26 percent. Unfortunately, when markets falter, so do investor returns. For example, over the three-year period from early 2000 through late 2002, the market (again, as measured by the DJIA) fell some 38 percent. Excluding dividends, that means a $100,000 investment would have declined in value to a little over $60,000. And in 2008, the Dow fell yet again, this time by almost 34 percent, while the S&P 500 Composite Index (S&P 500) fell by about 38 percent.

Make no mistake, the market does have its bad days, and sometimes those bad days seem to go on for months. It may not always seem that way, but those bad days *really are the exception, not the rule.* That was certainly the case from 1929 through 2015, when the Dow went down (for the year) just 21 times. That's only about 25 percent of the time; the other 75 percent the market was up—anywhere from around 2 percent to nearly 40 percent! True, there's some risk and price volatility (even in good markets), but that's the price you have to pay for all the upside potential. Consider, for example, the behavior of the market from 1982 through early 2000. Starting in August 1982, when the Dow stood at 777, this market saw the DJIA climb nearly 11,000 points to reach a high of 11,723 in January 2000. This turned out to be one of the longest bull markets in history, as the DJIA grew at an annual rate of nearly 17 percent.

Unfortunately, all that came to a screeching halt in early 2000, when each of the three major market measures peaked—the Dow at 11,723, the NASDAQ at 5,048, and the S&P 500 at 1,527. Over the course of the next 32 months, through September 2002, these market measures fell flat on their collective faces. While the Dow recovered from 2003 through mid-2007, it fell big time from that point on through early 2009. In fact, it fell from about 14,000 in July 2007 to around 6,500 in March 2009, with most of that loss occurring in 2008, when the Dow dropped by nearly 34 percent. Not to be outdone, the S&P 500 fell by 38 percent, which was the second-worst performance on record. Only 1931 was worse, when the S&P 500 fell by more than 49 percent.

Take a look at Exhibit 12.3, which tracks the behavior of the DJIA and the NASDAQ Composite from 2005 to mid-2015, and you'll quickly get a feel for just how volatile this market was! As the exhibit shows, despite all those market gyrations, both the Dow and the NASDAQ—which track two totally different segments of the market—ended up with decent returns (7.93 percent and 9.44 percent, respectively). Specifically, a $10,000 investment in the DJIA in January 2005 would have grown to about $22,031 by May 2015, while $10,000 invested in the NASDAQ would have grown to about $25,450. Given the high volatility of stock returns over time, investors who pull their money out of the market in bad times tend to lose the opportunity to make up their losses in good times. The possible effect of trying to time the market is discussed more fully later in this chapter.

The market entered one of the worst bear markets in history during 2007 and 2008, as the markets experienced the impact of the global financial crisis. Fortunately, the market recovered from 2009 to mid-2015. This graph shows how the value of a $10,000 investment changed between 2005 and mid-2015.

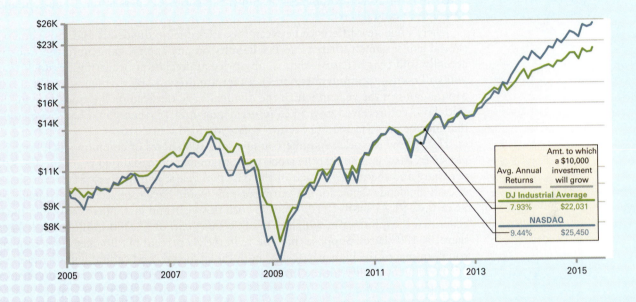

	Avg. Annual Returns	Amt. to which a $10,000 investment will grow
DJ Industrial Average	7.93%	$22,031
NASDAQ	9.44%	$25,450

Issuers of Common Stock

Shares of common stock can be issued by any corporation in any line of business. All corporations have stockholders, but not all of them have publicly traded shares. The stocks of interest to us in this book are the so-called *publicly traded issues*—the shares that are readily available to the general public and that are bought and sold in the open market. Aside from the initial distribution of common stock when the corporation is formed, subsequent sales of additional shares may be made through a procedure known as a *public offering*. In a public offering, the corporation, working with its underwriter, simply offers the investing public a certain number of shares of its stock at a certain price. When issued, the new shares are commingled with the outstanding shares (assuming they're all the same class of stock), and the net result will be an increase in the number of shares outstanding.

Voting Rights

The holders of common stock normally receive *voting rights*, which means that for each share of stock held, they receive one vote. In some cases, common stock may be designated as nonvoting at the time of issue, but this is the exception rather than the rule. Although different voting systems exist, small stockholders need not concern themselves with them because, regardless of the system used, their chances of affecting corporate control with their votes are quite slim.

proxy
A written statement used to assign a stockholder's voting rights to another person, typically one of the directors.

Corporations have annual stockholders' meetings, at which time new directors are elected and special issues are voted on. Because most small stockholders can't attend these meetings, they can use a proxy to assign their votes to another person, who will vote for them. A **proxy** is a written statement assigning voting rights to another party.

Basic Tax Considerations

Common stocks provide income in the form of dividends, usually paid quarterly, and/or capital gains, which occur when the price of the stock goes up over time. From a tax *rate* perspective, it really makes no difference whether the investment return comes in the form of dividends or long-term capital gains—in 2015, they're both taxed at 15 or 20 percent, or less (it's 0 percent for those filers in the 10 percent and 15 percent tax brackets).

There's one key difference between the taxes due on dividends and those due on capital gains: namely, there is no tax liability on any capital gains until the stock is actually sold (*paper gains*—that is, any price appreciation occurring on stock that you still own—accumulate tax free). Taxes are due on any dividends and realized capital gains in the year in which the dividends are received or the stock is actually sold. So if you received, say, $125 in dividends in 2015, then you'd have to include that income on your 2015 tax return when you filed it in 2016.

Here's how it works: Assume you just sold 100 shares of common stock for $50 per share. Also assume that the stock was originally purchased two years ago for $20 per share and that, during each of the past two years, you received $1.25 per share in cash dividends. Thus, for tax purposes, you would have received cash dividends of $125 (i.e., $1.25/share × 100 shares) *both* this year and last, plus you would have generated a capital gain, which is taxable this year, of $3,000 ($50/share − $20/share) × 100 shares. Suppose that you're in the 33 percent tax bracket. Even though you're in one of the higher brackets, both the dividends and capital gains earned on this investment qualify for the lower 15 percent tax rate. Therefore, on the dividends, you'll pay taxes of $125 × 0.15 = $18.75 (for each of the past two years), and on the capital gains, you'll owe $3,000 × 0.15 = $450 (for this year only). Therefore, your tax liability will be $18.75 (for the dividends last year), plus $468.75 (for the dividends and capital gains this year). Bottom line: out of the $3,250 you earned on this investment over the past two years, you keep $2,762.50 after taxes.

12–2b Dividends

Corporations pay dividends to their common stockholders in the form of cash and/or additional stock. *Cash dividends* are the most common. Cash dividends are normally distributed quarterly in an amount determined by the firm's board of directors. For example, if the directors declared a quarterly cash dividend of 50 cents a share and if you owned 200 shares of stock, then you'd receive a check for $100.

dividend yield
The percentage return provided by the dividends paid on common stock.

A popular way of assessing the amount of dividends received is to measure the stock's dividend yield. **Dividend yield** is a measure of common stock dividends on a relative (percentage) basis—that is, the dollar amount of dividends received is compared to the market price of the stock. As such, dividend yield measures the rate of current income being earned on the investment. It's computed as follows:

$$\text{Dividend Yield} = \frac{\text{Annual Dividend Received per Share}}{\text{Market Price per Share of Stock}}$$

For example, a company that pays $2 per share in annual dividends and whose stock is trading at $50 a share will have a dividend yield of 4 percent ($2/$50 = 0.04). Dividend yield is widely used by income-oriented investors looking for (reasonably priced) stocks with a long and sustained record of regularly paying higher-than-average dividends.

stock dividends
New shares of stock distributed to existing stockholders as a supplement to or substitute for cash dividends.

Occasionally, the directors may declare a stock dividend as a supplement to or in place of cash dividends. **Stock dividends** are paid in the form of additional shares of stock. That is, rather than receiving cash, shareholders receive additional shares of the company's stock—say, 1/10 of a share of new stock for each share owned (as in a *10 percent stock dividend*). For example, if you owned 100 shares of stock in a company that declared a 10 percent stock dividend, you'd receive 10 new shares of stock. Unfortunately, you'll be no better off after the stock dividend than you were before. That's because the total market value of the shares owned would be (roughly) the same after the stock dividend as before. This is because the price of the stock usually falls in direct proportion to the size of a stock dividend. Thus, in this example, a drop in price will bring the total market value of 110 shares (after the stock dividend) to about the same as the total market value of the 100 shares that existed before the dividend.

12–2c Some Key Measures of Performance

Seasoned investors use a variety of financial ratios and measures when making common stock investment decisions. Fortunately, most of the widely followed ratios can be found in published reports—like those produced by Morningstar or Standard & Poor's (see Exhibit 11.6 in Chapter 11 for an example of an S&P stock report)—so you don't have to compute them yourself. Even so, if you're thinking about buying a stock or already have some stocks, there are a few measures of performance you'll want to keep track of: dividend yield (mentioned earlier), book value (or book value per share), net profit margin, return on equity, earnings per share, price/earnings ratio, and beta.

Book Value

book value
The amount of stockholders' equity in a firm; determined by subtracting the company's liabilities and preferred stock from its assets.

The amount of stockholders' equity in a firm is measured by **book value**. This accounting measure is found by subtracting the firm's liabilities and preferred stock value from the value of its assets. Book value indicates the net amount of stockholder funds used to finance the firm. For instance, assume that our example company (CTA) had assets of $8 million, liabilities of $2 million, and preferred stock valued at $1 million. The book value of the firm's common stock would be $5 million ($8 million − $2 million − $1 million). If the book value is divided by the number of shares outstanding, the result is *book value per share*. So if CTA had 100,000 shares of common stock outstanding, then its book value per share would be $50 ($5,000,000/100,000 shares). Because it usually reflects attractive growth, you'd like to see book value per share steadily increasing over time. Also, look for stocks whose market prices are comfortably above their book values.

Net Profit Margin

net profit margin
A key measure of profitability that relates a firm's net profits to its sales; shows the rate of return the company is earning on its sales.

As a yardstick of profitability, **net profit margin** is one of the most widely followed measures of corporate performance. Measured as a firm's net profit divided by its sales, this ratio indicates how well the company translates sales into profits. It also captures how well the company manages its cost structure. The higher the net profit margin, the more money the company earns. Look for a relatively stable—or, even better, an increasing—net profit margin.

Return on Equity

return on equity (ROE)
A measure that captures the firm's overall profitability; it is important because of its impact on the firm's growth, profits, and dividends.

Another important and widely-followed measure, **return on equity (ROE)**, reflects the firm's overall profitability from the equityholders' perspective. Measured as net income divided by shareholders' equity, this captures how effectively the firm manages its assets, operations, and capital structure. ROE is important because it is significantly related to the profits, growth, and dividends of the firm. So long as a firm is not borrowing too much money, the better the ROE and the better the company's financial and competitive positions. Look for a stable or increasing ROE. Watch out for a falling ROE because that could spell trouble.

Earnings per Share

earnings per share (EPS)
The dollar return earned by each share of common stock; calculated by dividing all earnings remaining after paying preferred dividends by the number of common shares outstanding.

With stocks, the firm's annual earnings are usually measured and reported in terms of **earnings per share (EPS)**. EPS translates total corporate profits into profits on a per-share basis and provides a convenient measure of the amount of earnings available to stockholders. EPS is found by using this simple formula:

$$\text{EPS} = \frac{\text{Net Profit After Taxes} - \text{Preferred Dividends Paid}}{\text{Number of Shares of Common Stock Outstanding}}$$

For example, if CTA reported a net profit of $600,000, paid $100,000 in dividends to preferred stockholders, and had 100,000 shares of common outstanding, then it would have an EPS of $5.00 [($600,000 − $100,000)/100,000]. Note that preferred dividends are *subtracted* from profits because they must be paid before any monies can be distributed to common stockholders. Stockholders follow EPS closely because it represents the amount that the firm has earned on behalf of each outstanding share of common stock. Here, too, look for steady growth in EPS.

Price/Earnings Ratio

price/earnings (P/E) ratio
A measure of investors' confidence in a given security or the overall market; calculated by dividing market price per share by EPS.

When the prevailing market price of a share of common stock is divided by the annual EPS, the result is the **price/earnings (P/E) ratio**, which is viewed as an indication of investor confidence and expectations. The higher the P/E multiple, the more confidence that investors are presumed to have in a given security. In the case of CTA, whose shares are currently selling for $60, the P/E ratio is 12 ($60 per share/$5.00 per share). This means that CTA stock is selling for 12 times its earnings. P/E ratios are important to investors because they reveal how aggressively the stock is being priced in the market. Watch out for very high P/Es—that is, P/Es that are way out of line with the market—because that could indicate the stock is overpriced. P/E ratios tend to move with the market: when the market is soft, a stock's P/E will be lower when the market heats up, the stock's P/E will typically rise. For perspective, the long-term average P/E ratio for the S&P 500 index is about 15.

Beta

beta
An index of the price volatility for a share of common stock; a reflection of how the stock price responds to overall market forces.

A stock's **beta** is an indication of its *price volatility;* it shows how responsive the stock is to changes in the overall stock market. Published betas are available from most brokerage firms and investment services. The market (often measured by the S&P index of 500 stocks) is used as a benchmark of performance, which has a beta of 1.0. From there, everything is relative: low-beta stocks—those with betas of less than 1.0—have low price volatility (their prices are relatively stable), whereas high-beta stocks—those with betas of more than 1.0—are considered to be highly volatile. In short, the higher a stock's beta, the riskier the stock. Most stock betas are positive, which means the stocks move in the same general direction as the market.

Beta is an *index* of relative price performance. If CTA has a beta of, say, 0.8, then it should rise (or fall) only 80 percent as much as the market. Thus, if the market goes up by 10 percent, then CTA should go up only 8 percent (10 percent × 0.8). In contrast, if the stock had a beta of 1.8, then it would go up or down 1.8 times as fast—the price of the stock would rise higher and fall harder than the general market. Other things being equal, if you're looking for a relatively conservative investment, then you should stick with low-beta stocks; on the other hand, if it's potentially high capital gains and price volatility you're after, go with high-beta securities.

12–2d Types of Common Stock

Common stocks are often classified on the basis of their dividends or their rate of growth in EPS. Some popular types of common stock are blue-chip, growth, tech stocks, income, speculative, cyclical, defensive, large-cap, mid-cap, and small-cap stocks.

Blue-Chip Stocks

blue-chip stock
A stock generally issued by companies expected to provide an uninterrupted stream of dividends and good long-term growth prospects.

Blue-chip stocks are the cream of the common stock crop; these stocks are unsurpassed in quality and have a long and stable record of earnings and dividends. They're issued by large, well-established firms that have impeccable financial credentials—firms such as Apple, Nike, Wal-Mart, IBM, Microsoft, Merck, and ExxonMobil. These companies hold important, if not leading, positions in their industries, and they often determine the standards by which other firms are measured. Blue chips are particularly attractive to investors who seek high-quality investments offering decent dividend yields and respectable growth potential. Blue-chip stocks are popular with a large segment of the investing public and, as a result, are often relatively high priced, especially when the market is unsettled and investors become more quality-conscious.

Growth Stocks

growth stock
A stock whose earnings and market price have increased over time at a rate that is well above average.

Stocks that have experienced—and are expected to continue experiencing—consistently high rates of growth in operations and earnings are known as **growth stocks**. A good growth stock might exhibit a *sustained* rate of growth in earnings of 15 percent–20 percent (or more) over a period when common stocks are averaging only 6 percent–8 percent. In mid-2015, prime examples of large capitalization growth stocks include Apple, SAP, Intel, and Wal-Mart. Internet sites like Seeking Alpha (**http://seekingalpha.com**) try to predict the next growth stocks. For example, some of their mid-2015 projections of stocks that could prove to be the next crop of big growth stocks include: Monsanto, Gilead Sciences, Ensco, Michael Kors, and Matthews International. These stocks often pay little or nothing in dividends because the firms' rapid growth potential require them to retain and reinvest most, if not all, of their earnings. The high growth expectations for such stocks usually cause them to sell at relatively high P/E ratios, and they typically have betas in excess of 1.0. Because of their potential for dramatic price appreciation, they appeal mostly to investors who are seeking capital gains rather than dividend income.

Tech Stocks

tech stock
A stock from the technology sector of the market.

Tech stocks represent the technology sector of the market and include all those companies that produce or provide technology-based products and services such as computers, semiconductors, data storage devices, computer software and hardware, peripherals, Internet services, content providers, networking, and wireless communications. Thousands of companies fall into the tech stock category, including everything from very small firms providing some service on the Internet to huge multinational companies. These stocks often fall into either the *growth stock* category (described earlier) or the *speculative stock* class (discussed next), although some of them are legitimate *blue chips*. Tech stocks may offer the potential for attractive, even phenomenal, returns, but they also involve considerable risk and so are probably most suitable for investors with high tolerance for such risk. Included in the tech stock category are some big names—Microsoft, Cisco, Apple, and Google—as well as many not-so-big names, such as Infosonics, Freescale Semiconductor, and Amkor Technology.

Income Stocks versus Speculative Stocks

income stock
A stock whose primary appeal is the higher dividends it pays out; offers dividend payments that can be expected to increase over time.

Stocks whose appeal is based primarily on the dividends they pay are known as **income stocks**. They have a fairly stable stream of earnings, a large portion of which is

The Biggest Companies in the Market

The total market value of a company, defined as the price of the stock multiplied by the number of shares outstanding, is a measure of what investors think a company is worth. In May 2015, Apple topped the list of U.S.-based firms with a market value of about $725.1 billion, followed by Microsoft at $383 billion, Google at $367.6 billion, Exxon Mobile at $365 billion, Berkshire Hathaway at $357.6 billion, Wells Fargo at $286.4 billion, and China Mobile at $279.9 billion. These weren't necessarily the companies with the most assets or profits. Rather, what made these companies special—as far as investors were concerned—was their promise for the future!

distributed in the form of dividends. Income shares have relatively high dividend yields and thus are ideally suited for investors seeking a relatively safe and high level of current income from their investment capital. An added (and often overlooked) feature of these stocks is that, unlike bonds and preferred stock, holders of income stock can expect *the amount of dividends paid to increase over time*. Examples of income stocks include Philip Morris International, Johnson & Johnson, PepsiCo, and Proctor & Gamble. Reflecting their low risk, these stocks commonly have betas of less than 1.0.

Rather than basing their investment decisions on a proven record of earnings, investors in **speculative stocks** gamble that some new information, discovery, or production technique will favorably affect the firm's growth and inflate its stock price. For example, a company whose stock is considered speculative may recently have discovered a new drug or located a valuable resource, such as oil. They are also often small, not well-known firms in industries that could turn around. The value of speculative stocks and their P/E ratios tend to fluctuate widely as additional information about the firm's future is received. Betas for speculative stocks are nearly always well in excess of 1.0. Investors in speculative stocks should be prepared to experience losses as well as gains, since *these are high-risk securities*. In mid-2015, they include companies like Bona Film Group, Destination Maternity, Global Power Equipment Group, and Iridium Communications.

speculative stock
Stock that is purchased on little more than the hope that its price per share will increase.

cyclical stock
Stock whose price movements tend to parallel the various stages of the business cycle.

defensive stock
Stock whose price movements are usually *contrary* to movements in the business cycle.

Cyclical and Defensive Stocks

Stocks whose price movements tend to follow the business cycle are called **cyclical stocks**. This means that when the economy is in an expansionary stage, the prices of cyclical stocks tend to increase; during a contractionary stage (recession), they decline. Most cyclical stocks are found in the basic industries—automobiles, steel, and lumber, for example—which are generally sensitive to changes in economic activity. Investors try to purchase cyclical stocks just before an expansionary phase and to sell just before the contraction occurs. Because they tend to move with the market, these stocks always have positive betas. Alcoa, eBay, Kohl's, Goodyear Tire & Rubber, Dow Chemical, and Ford Motor are all examples of cyclical stocks.

The prices and returns from **defensive stocks**, unlike those of cyclical stocks, are expected to remain stable during periods of contraction in business activity. For this reason, they're often called *countercyclical*. The shares of consumer goods companies, certain public utilities, and gold mining companies are good examples of defensive stocks. Because they're basically income stocks, their earnings and dividends tend to keep their market prices up during periods of economic decline. Betas on these stocks are typically quite low. Coca-Cola, McDonald's, Wal-Mart, Procter & Gamble, and Merck are all examples of defensive stocks.

Financial Fact or Fantasy?

Income stocks have relatively high dividend yields and, as such, appeal to individuals who seek a high level of current income. **Fact:** Income shares are have a long and sustained record of regularly paying a much higher than average level of dividends. Because of this, they are highly sought after by investors seeking a safe and steady source of current income.

Large-Caps, Mid-Caps, and Small-Caps

In the stock market, a stock's size is based on its market value—or, more commonly, on what's known as its *market capitalization* or *market cap*. A stock's market cap is found by multiplying its market price by the number of shares outstanding. Generally speaking, the market can be broken into three major segments, as measured by a stock's market "cap":

Large-cap—Market caps of more than $10 billion
Mid-cap—Market caps of $2 to $10 billion
Small-cap—Stocks with market caps of less than $2 billion

In addition to these three segments, another is reserved for the *really small* stocks, known as *micro-caps*. Many of these stocks have market capitalizations of well below $250 million (some as low as $50 million); they should be purchased only by investors who fully understand the risks involved and can tolerate such risk exposure.

Of the three major categories, the **large-cap stocks** are the real biggies—the Apples, Wal-Marts, GEs, and Microsofts of the world—and many are considered to be blue-chip stocks. Although there are far fewer large-cap stocks than any of the other market cap categories, these companies account for about 80 percent–90 percent of the total market value of all U.S. equity markets. Just because they're big, however, doesn't mean they're better. Indeed, both the small- and mid-cap segments of the market tend to hold their own with, or even outperform, large stocks over time.

Mid-cap stocks offer investors some attractive return opportunities. They provide much of the sizzle of small-stock returns, but without all the price volatility. At the same time, because these are fairly good-sized companies and many have been around for a long time, they offer some of the safety of the big, established stocks. Among the ranks of the mid-caps are Accuity, Advance Auto Parts, Avery Dennison, Oshkosh, and USG. These securities offer a nice alternative to large cap stocks without all the drawbacks and uncertainties of small-caps, although they're probably most appropriate for investors who are willing to tolerate a bit more risk and price volatility.

Some investors consider small companies to be in a class by themselves. They believe these firms hold especially attractive return opportunities, and in many cases, this has turned out to be true. Known as **small-cap stocks**, these companies often have annual revenues of less than $250 million; because of their size, spurts of growth can dramatically affect their earnings and stock prices. Immunogen, Hecla Mining, Vaalco Energy, Western Refining, and Zynga are just a few of the interesting small-cap stocks out there. Although some small-caps are solid companies with equally solid financials, that's definitely not the case with most of them! Because many of these companies are so small, they don't have a lot of stock outstanding and their shares aren't widely traded. What's more, small-company stocks have a tendency to be "here today and gone tomorrow." These stocks may hold the potential for high returns, but investors should also be aware of the high risk exposure associated with many of them.

12–2e Market Globalization and Foreign Stocks

Besides investing in many of the different types of stocks already mentioned, a growing number of American investors are turning to foreign markets as a way to earn attractive returns. Ironically, as our world is becoming smaller, our universe of investment opportunities is growing by leaps and bounds! Consider, for example, that in 1970, the U.S. stock market accounted for fully *two-thirds of the world market*. In essence, our stock market was twice as big as the rest of the world's stock markets *combined*. That's no longer true; the U.S. share of the world equity market is now more like 36 percent.

Foreign stocks can offer investors not only attractive return opportunities but also attractive geographic diversification opportunities. Among the various ways of investing in foreign shares, three stand out: mutual funds, exchange-traded funds, and

large-cap stock
A stock with a total market value of equity of more than $10 billion.

mid-cap stock
A stock whose total market value falls somewhere between $2 billion and $10 billion.

small-cap stock
A stock with a total market value of equity of less than $2 billion.

Behavior Matters
Dealing with Investor Overreaction

Research shows that the average investor consistently earns below-average returns. For example, between about 1993 and 2013, the S&P 500 index earned an average return of about 9.22 percent a year, while the average equity fund investor earned a paltry return of just 5.02 percent. One likely explanation is that the average equity investor is just too emotional and tends to overreact to financial market developments.

Consider how investors tend to overreact. It's well known that when the stock market advances, many investors chase performance by moving money into equity mutual funds. Similarly, they tend to take their money out when the stock market is declining. This often leads to buying high and selling low—a recipe for disaster. Investors tend to overreact to both good and bad news.

What can you do to take into account the tendency to overreact to investment news? Consider the following guidelines:

- **Constructively decide to do nothing.** The evidence is that a long-term, buy-and-hold strategy is an effective, deliberate approach to investing. Take into account the tendency to overreact and purposely decide to do nothing in response to news in most cases. Doing nothing is an action.

- **Money is like soap.** The Nobel Prize–winning financial economist at the University of Chicago, Eugene Fama Jr., argues that "your money is like soap. The more you handle it, the less you'll have." Handling your money too often brings higher transaction costs and frequently results from overreacting to financial news.

- **Resist the urge to sell stocks in a declining market.** Patiently reevaluate your asset allocation and wait out the decline. Consider the analogy of putting your house up for sale when housing prices drop. Most people would not put their house up for sale as soon as the market drops. They would be more likely to wait it out. Why should managing your stocks be any different?

- **Discipline works.** The evidence supports the value of a consistent, unemotional, and disciplined approach to investing. Simply put, your risk-adjusted returns are likely to be higher over the long term if you don't overreact to financial news.

Source: Adapted from Dana Anspach, "Why Average Investors Earn Below-Average Market Returns," http://moneyover55.about.com/od/howtoinvest/a/averageinvestor.htm, accessed August 2015.

American Depositary Receipts (ADRs). Without a doubt, the best and easiest way to invest in foreign markets is through *international mutual funds or exchange-traded funds*—we'll discuss such funds in Chapter 13. An alternative to mutual funds is to buy ADRs, which are *denominated in dollars and are traded directly on U.S. markets* (such as the NYSE). They're just like common stock, except that each ADR represents a stated number of shares in a specific foreign company. The shares of more than 1,000 companies from some 50 foreign countries are traded on U.S. exchanges as ADRs; these companies include Honda Motor Co., Sony, Nestlé, Nokia, Ericsson, Tata Motors, and Vodafone, to mention just a few. ADRs are a great way to invest in foreign stocks because their prices are quoted in dollars, not in British pounds, Swiss francs, or euros. What's more, all dividends are paid in dollars.

12–2f Investing in Common Stock

There are three basic reasons for investing in common stock: (1) to use the stock as a warehouse of value, (2) to accumulate capital, and (3) to provide a source of income. Some investors are more concerned about storage of value than others, and they put safety of principal first in their stock selection process. These investors are more quality-conscious and tend to gravitate toward blue chips and other low-risk securities. Accumulation of capital generally is an important goal to individuals with long-term investment horizons. These investors use the capital gains and dividends that stocks provide to build up their wealth. Some use growth stocks for such purposes; others do it with income shares; still others use a little of both. Finally, some people use stocks as a source of income; to them, a dependable flow of dividends is essential. High-yielding, good-quality income shares are usually their preferred investment vehicle.

Advantages and Disadvantages of Stock Ownership

Ownership of common stock has both advantages and disadvantages. Its advantages are threefold. First, the potential returns, in the form of both dividend income and price appreciation, can be substantial. Second, many stocks are actively traded and so are a highly liquid form of investment, which means that they can be bought and sold quickly without having to take a significant price concession. Finally, they involve no direct management (or unusual management problems), and market/company information is usually widely published and readily available.

The disadvantages of owning common stock include risk, the problem of timing purchases and sales, and the uncertainty of dividends. Although potential common stock returns may be high, the risk and uncertainty associated with the actual receipt of that return is also great. Even though the careful selection of stocks may reduce the amount of risk to which the investor is exposed, a significant risk–return trade-off still exists. When it comes to common stock, not even dividends are guaranteed. If things turn bad, the company can always shut off the stream of dividends and suffer no legal ramifications. Finally, there's the timing of purchases and sales. Human nature being what it is, we don't always do it right. Unfortunately, all too many investors purchase a stock, hold it for a period of time during which the price drops, and then sell it below the original purchase price—that is, at a loss. The proper strategy, of course, is to buy low and sell high; but the problem of predicting price movements makes it difficult to implement such a plan.

12–2g Making the Investment Decision

The first step in investing is to know where to put your money; the second is to know when to make your moves. The first question basically involves matching your risk and return objectives with the available investment vehicles. *A stock (or any other investment vehicle) should be considered a viable investment candidate only as long as it looks likely to generate a sufficiently attractive rate of return* and, importantly, one that fully compensates for the risks you take. Thus, if you're considering the purchase of a stock, you should expect to earn more than what you can get from T-bills or high-grade corporate bonds. This is because stocks are riskier than bills or bonds and you consequently deserve a higher return from stocks. Indeed, if you can't get enough expected return from the security to offset the risk, then you shouldn't invest in the stock!

Putting a Value on Stock

Every investor faces one of the most difficult questions in the field of investments: *How much should you be willing to pay for a stock?* To answer this question, you must place a value on the stock. As noted earlier in this chapter, we know that the value of a stock depends on its expected stream of future earnings, expected future market price appreciation, and the associated risk. Once you have a handle on the expected stream of future earnings and price appreciation, you can use that information to find the *expected rate of return on the investment*. If the expected return from the investment exceeds your minimum required rate of return, then you should make the investment. If the return that you expect from the investment is less than your required rate of return, then you should not buy the stock because it's currently "overpriced," and thus you won't be able to earn your required rate of return.

FINANCIAL PLANNING TIPS

Recognize These Common Investing Myths

Here are some myths that you should be aware of when investing:

- **During volatile markets, it makes sense to sell your stocks and wait for calmer conditions.** While it sounds so reasonable, investors who remain in the market outperform those who move in and out to manage their market exposure. When trading in and out, you pay more commissions and, more importantly, you tend to miss the upturns in the market that can make you whole—or even more than whole—again.

- **Gold is a good addition to any portfolio.** It's true that gold can be a good asset to add because its returns tend to move opposite those of stocks, which is good for diversification. However, few advisors would recommend

allocating more than 5 or 10 percent of a portfolio to gold in most cases. There have been long periods when gold generated poor returns.

- **The S&P 500 is the best place for long-term stock investors.** The large stocks in the S&P 500 do not always pay the best returns. While riskier, small cap and value stocks tend to outperform the S&P 500 over the long haul.

- **Far less should be invested in stocks during retirement.** While it may make sense to reduce equity exposure as retirement *approaches*, there is evidence that gradually increasing equity exposure *during retirement* may best manage the risk of running out of money.

So, how do you go about finding a stock that's right for you? The answer is by doing a little digging and crunching a few numbers. Here's what you should do. First, find a company you like and then take a look at how it has performed *over the past three to five years*. Find out what kind of growth in sales it has experienced, if it has a strong ROE and has been able to maintain or improve its profit margin, and how much it has been paying out to stockholders in the form of dividends. This kind of information is readily available in publications like *Value Line Investment Survey* and *S&P Stock Reports* or from a number of Internet sites. The idea is to find stocks that are financially strong, have done well in the past, and continue to hold prominent positions in a given industry or market segment. But looking at the past is only the beginning; what's really important to stock valuation is the *future!*

So let's turn our attention to the expected future performance of a stock. The idea is to assess the *outlook* for the stock, thereby *gaining some insight into the benefits to be derived from investing in it*. The key benefits are future dividends and share price behavior. It usually doesn't make much sense to go out more than two

© ENDERMASALI / SHUTTERSTOCK.COM

or three years—five, at the most—because the accuracy of most forecasts begins to deteriorate rapidly after that. Thus, using a three-year investment horizon, you'd want to forecast annual dividends per share for each of the next three years *plus* the future price of the stock at the end of the three-year holding period. You can try to generate these forecasts yourself, or you can check such publications as *Value Line Investment Survey* to obtain projections (*Value Line* projects dividends and share prices three to five years into the future). After projecting dividends and share price, you can use the approximate expected yield equation or a handheld calculator to determine the expected return from the investment as discussed earlier in this chapter.

Consider the example of Apple, some data for which was provided in Exhibit 11.6. The calculations in the example below indicate that if Apple's stock performance lives up to the projections made by *Value Line Investment Survey* at the time this was written, it should provide a return between 13 and 14 percent. In today's market, that would be an attractive return and one that likely *exceeds* our risk-adjusted required rate of return (which probably should be around 8 or 9 percent under normal market conditions). If that's the case, then this should be considered a viable investment candidate. According to our standards, the stock is currently undervalued and thus should be seriously considered as a possible addition to our portfolio.

EXAMPLE: Calculating the Expected Return on Apple's Stock

To see how this can be done, consider the common shares of Apple, Inc., which provides hardware and software that includes Mac computers, iPod digital media players, iPhone smart phones, and iPad tablets. According to several financial reporting services, the company has strong financials; its sales have been growing at a bit more than 40 percent per year for the past five years, its recent net profit margin is almost 22 percent, and its ROE is around 28 percent. Thus, historically, the company has performed astoundingly well and is definitely a market leader in its field. Indeed, it's currently the largest company in the world! In April 2015, the stock was trading at around $127 a share and was expected to pay annual dividends of about $1.94 a share in 2015. Around that time Value Line was projecting dividends to grow to $2.10 per share the next year (2016), and to an average of about $4 a share between 2018 and 2020. It was also estimating that the price of the stock could rise to an average of $177.50 per share over that period. For simplicity, we'll look at these forecasts as applying to a planned holding period of about three years and average the data accordingly.

Because the approximate expected yield equation shown here uses "average annual current income" as one of the inputs, we use a rough average of our projected dividends ($2.68 a share) as a proxy for average annual dividends. Because this stock was trading at $127 a share and had a projected average future price of $177.50 per share, we can find the expected return (for our three-year investment horizon) as follows:

$$\text{Approximate Yield (Expected Return)} = \frac{\$2.68 + \left[\dfrac{\$177.50 - \$127.00}{3}\right]}{\left[\dfrac{\$177.50 + \$127.00}{2}\right]}$$

$$= \frac{\$2.68 + \$16.83}{\$152.25} = \underline{12.81\%}$$

Timing Your Investments

Once you find a stock that you think will give you the kind of return that you're looking for, then you're ready to deal with the matter of timing your investments. So long as the prospects for the market and the economy are positive, the time may be right to invest in stocks. On the other hand, sometimes investing in stocks makes no sense at all—in particular, *don't* invest in stocks under either of the following conditions:

- You believe *strongly* that the market is headed down in the short run. If you're confident the market's in for a big fall (or will continue to fall, if it's already doing so), then wait until the market drops and buy the stock when it's cheaper.

INPUTS	FUNCTIONS
3	N
−127.00	PV
2.68	PMT
177.50	FV
	CPT
	I/Y
SOLUTION	
13.70	

See Appendix E for details.

Calculator Keystrokes. You can use a handheld financial calculator—set in the *annual compounding mode*—to find the expected return on a stock that you purchase at $127.00 per share, hold for three years (during which time you receive average annual dividends of $2.68 per share), and then sell at an average of $177.50 per share. Simply use the keystrokes shown in the margin, where:

N = number of *years* you hold the stock
PV = the price you pay for the stock (entered as a *negative* value)
PMT = average amount of dividends received each *year*
FV = the price you expect to receive when you sell the stock (in three years)

The expected return (of 13.70 percent) is a bit higher here, but even so, it's still in the ballpark with the return (of 12.81 percent) that we computed using the approximate expected yield method. Of course, one would expect an approximation to be somewhat less precise, but it is nonetheless informative.

- You feel uncomfortable with the general tone of the market—it lacks direction, or there's way too much price volatility to suit you. Once again, wait for the market to settle down before buying stocks.

Research shows that most investors are better off investing steadily than trying to time the market. It is exceedingly difficult to buy consistently at market bottoms and sell at market tops. Many investors pulled out of the stocks during the financial crisis of 2008–2009. Yet as of mid-2015, the S&P 500 index had more than tripled since the worst of the stock market crisis in 2009. Consider the example of an investor who put $10,000 into the S&P 500 at the bottom of the market in 2009 and left

FINANCIAL PLANNING TIPS

Equity Analysts Are Too Optimistic—Invest with Caution!

Researchers at McKinsey & Company did a long-term study of the accuracy of equity analysts' forecasts. They find strong evidence that analysts are usually overly optimistic, far too slow to revise their forecasts in light of new economic developments, and likely to make even less accurate forecasts when the economy's growth is falling. This is particularly troubling given the numerous new rules and regulations developed over the last 10 years that are designed to improve the quality of analysts' forecasts, enhance investor confidence in these forecasts, and minimize conflicts of interest that could affect the forecasting process.

Consider analysts' earnings forecasts for the firms in the S&P 500 index. Analysts have been consistently too optimistic over the past 25 years. While their average earnings growth rate forecast was between 10 percent and 12 percent a year, actual earnings growth averaged only

about 6 percent. Indeed, during this time period, actual earnings growth exceed forecasts in only two cases, both of which were during the earnings recovery after a recession. Amazingly, analysts' average forecasts have been almost 100 percent too high!

So what's an investor to do? First, consider that long-term steady-state growth for the stock market as a whole is unlikely to differ much from growth in overall gross domestic product (GDP), which has historically been between 3 percent and 4 percent on average in nominal terms in the United States. Only firms with significant non-U.S. business should be able to sustain growth rates much beyond that. Second, recognize that overly optimistic analyst forecasts imply that analysts tend to overvalue stocks. Consequently, it makes sense to view analysts' forecasts as overly optimistic, particularly during an economic downturn, and to invest accordingly.

Source: Adapted from Marc Goedhart, Rishi Raj, and Abhishek Saxena, "Equity Analysts: Still Too Bullish," https://www.mckinseyquarterly.com/Equity_analysts_Still_too_bullish_2565, accessed August 2015. (Note that to gain full online access to the article, you'll have to register on the Internet site, which is free.)

it there untouched until the middle of 2015. The initial investment would have grown to about $34,000, which is an annualized return of about 22 percent. Indeed, even those who invested in the S&P 500 at the beginning of 2008 and early in 2009 had recouped their losses by the end of 2009. There's a high potential cost of being out of the equity market during its best-performing times. This is because pulling money out of the market exposes you to the significant risk that you'll miss the months of good returns that could help you recoup prior losses.

Be Sure to Plow Back Your Earnings

Unless you're living off the income, the basic investment objective with stocks is the same as it is with any other security: to earn an attractive, fully compounded rate of return. This requires regular reinvestment of dividend income. And there's no better way to accomplish such reinvestment than through a **dividend reinvestment plan (DRP)**. The investment philosophy at work here is this: if the company is good enough to invest in, then it's good enough to reinvest in. In a DRP, shareholders can sign up to have their cash dividends automatically reinvested in additional shares of the company's common stock—in essence, it's like taking your cash dividends in the form of more shares of common stock. Such an approach can have a tremendous impact on your investment position over time, as seen in Exhibit 12.4.

Today, many companies have DRPs, and each one gives investors a convenient and inexpensive way to accumulate capital. Stocks in most DRPs are acquired free of any brokerage commissions, and most plans allow *partial participation*. That is, rather than committing all of their cash dividends to these plans, participants may

dividend reinvestment plan (DRP)
A program whereby stockholders can choose to take their cash dividends in the form of more shares of the company's stock.

Financial Fact or Fantasy?

Putting your money into stocks that offer dividend reinvestment plans is a great way of building up your investment capital. **Fact:** In a dividend reinvestment plan, you receive additional shares of stock, rather than cash every time the company pays a dividend. It's a great way to reap the benefits of compounding and watch your money grow over time.

EXHIBIT 12.4	Cash or Reinvested Dividends

Participating in a dividend reinvestment plan is a simple yet highly effective way of building up capital over time. Over the long haul, it can prove to be a great way of earning a fully compounded rate of return on your money.

Situation: Buy 100 shares of stock at $25 a share (total investment $2,500); stock currently pays $1 a share in annual dividends. Price of the stock increases at 8 percent per year; dividends grow at 5 percent per year.

Investment Period	Number of Shares Held	Market Value of Stock Holdings	Total Cash Dividends Received
Take Dividends in Cash			
5 years	100	$3,672	$552
10 years	100	$5,397	$1,258
15 years	100	$7,930	$2,158
20 years	100	$11,652	$3,307
Participate in a DRP			
5 years	115.59	$4,245	$0
10 years	135.66	$7,322	$0
15 years	155.92	$12,364	$0
20 years	176.00	$20,508	$0

specify a portion of their shares for dividend reinvestment and receive cash dividends on the rest. Some plans even sell their shares in their programs at discounts of 3 percent to 5 percent. Most plans also credit fractional shares to the investors' accounts. There's a catch, however: even though these dividends take the form of additional shares of stock, *reinvested dividends are taxable in the year they're received, just as if they had been received in cash.*

TEST YOURSELF

12-6 From a tax perspective, would it make any difference to an investor whether the return on a stock took the form of dividends or capital gains? Explain.

12-7 What's the difference between a *cash* dividend and a *stock* dividend? Which would you rather receive?

12-8 Define and briefly discuss each of these common stock measures: (a) book value, (b) ROE, (c) EPS, (d) P/E ratio, and (e) beta.

12-9 Briefly discuss some of the different types of common stock. Which types would be most appealing to you, and why?

12-10 Summarize the evidence on the potential cost of being out of the stock market during its best months.

12-11 What are *DRPs*, and how do they fit into a stock investment program?

12–3 INVESTING IN BONDS

LG5, LG6

In contrast to stocks, *bonds are liabilities*—they're publicly traded IOUs where the bond-holders are actually *lending money* to the issuer. Bonds are often referred to as *fixed-income securities* because the debt service obligations of the issuer are usually fixed—that is, the issuing organization agrees to pay a *fixed amount of interest periodically and to repay a fixed amount of principal at or before maturity*. In the United States, bonds usually have face values of $1,000 or $5,000 and have maturities of 10 to 30 years or more.

12–3a Why Invest in Bonds?

Bonds provide investors with two kinds of income: (1) Most provide current income, and (2) they can generate substantial capital gains. The current income, of course, comes from the interest payments received periodically over the life of the issue. Indeed, this regular and predictable source of income is a key factor that draws investors to bonds. But these securities can also produce capital gains, which occur whenever market interest rates fall. A basic rule in the bond market is that *interest rates and bond prices move in opposite directions*: when interest rates rise, bond prices fall; conversely, when interest rates fall, bond prices rise. Thus, it's possible to buy bonds at one price and, if interest rate conditions are right, to sell them sometime later at a higher price. Taken together, the current income and capital gains earned from bonds can lead to competitive investor returns.

Bonds are also a versatile investment outlet. They can be used conservatively by those seeking high current income or aggressively by those actively seeking capital gains. And because of the high quality of many bond issues, they can also be used for the preservation and long-term accumulation of capital. In fact, some investors regularly commit all or a good deal of their investment funds to bonds because of this single attribute.

12–3b Bonds versus Stocks

Although bonds definitely do have their good points—lower risk and attractive levels of current income, along with *desirable diversification properties*. However, they also have a significant downside: their *comparative* returns. The fact is, *relative to stocks*, there's usually a big sacrifice in returns when investing in bonds—which, of course, is the price that you pay for the even bigger reduction in risk! But just because there's a deficit in long-term returns, it doesn't mean that bonds are always the underachievers. Consider, for example, what's happened over the past 20 years in general, and during and since the recent financial crisis of 2007–2009 in particular. Starting in the 1980s, fixed-income securities held their own and continued to do so through the early 1990s, only to fall far behind stocks for the rest of the decade. But then along came a couple of nasty bear markets in stocks (2000–2002 and 2007–2008) and the subsequent stock market recovery in 2009 and beyond. The net results of all this can be seen in Exhibit 12.5, which tracks the comparative returns of stocks (via the S&P 500 index) and bonds (using the BofA Merrill Lynch U.S. Treasuries 15+ year maturity total return index) from 1995 through mid-2015.

Over the roughly 20-year period from 1995 to mid-2015, the S&P 500 overperformed long-term Treasury bonds by 1.53 percent (9.83 percent versus 8.30 percent). The net result was that a $10,000 investment in 1995 would have generated a terminal value in mid-2015 of about $67,429 for stocks, compared with about $50,666 for bonds. Although historically, the long-term performance of stocks typically outstrips that of bonds, there have been times when that just wasn't so. And the margin was particularly small over this time period owing to the effects of the financial crisis.

EXHIBIT 12.5	Comparative Performance of Stocks and Bonds: 1995–mid-2015

This graph shows what happened to $10,000 invested in bonds over the (roughly) 20-year period from January 1995 through mid-2015, versus the same amount invested in stocks. While stocks held a commanding lead through early 2000 and then again in 2003–2006, the bear markets of 2000–2002 and 2008 limited the higher relative performance of stocks. Yet the strong bull market from 2009 to mid-2015 left stocks performing significantly better than bonds for the entire period.

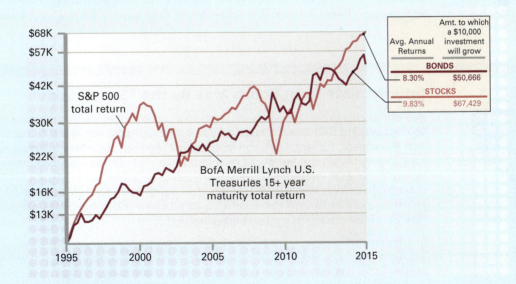

Source: Morningstar Direct, June 2015. © 2015 Morningstar, Inc. All rights reserved. The Morningstar data contained herein (1) is proprietary to Morningstar; (2) may not be copied or distributed without written permission; and (3) is not warranted to be accurate, complete, or timely. Morningstar is not responsible for any damages or losses arising from any use of this information and has not granted its consent to be considered or deemed an "expert" under the Securities Act of 1933.

12–3c Basic Issue Characteristics

A bond is a negotiable, long-term debt instrument that carries certain obligations on the part of the issuer. Unlike the holders of common stock, bondholders have no ownership or equity position in the issuing firm or organization. This is so because bonds are debt and thus the bondholders, in a roundabout way, are only lending money to the issuer.

YOU CAN DO IT NOW

How Do Stock and Bond Market Returns Compare This Year?

If you want a broad sense of how stock and bond returns compare so far this year, take a look at the returns on two broad-based exchange-traded funds (ETFs, which we discuss in detail in Chapter 13). Vanguard's Total Stock Market ETF (ticker VTI) seeks to track the overall performance of U.S. stocks traded on the New York Stock Exchange and NASDAQ. And Vanguard's Total Bond Market ETF (ticker BND) seeks to track investment grade U.S. bonds. Take a look at the year-to-date (YTD) returns, which were, for example, 3.61 percent for VTI and 0.78 percent for BND on July 1, 2015. Just go to http://finance.yahoo.com/ and type VTI and then BND into the Quote Lookup box. **You can do it now.**

---

coupon
Bond feature that defines the annual interest income the issuer will pay the bondholder.

U.S. bonds typically pay interest every six months. The amount of interest paid depends on the **coupon**, which defines the annual interest that the issuer will pay to the bondholder. For instance, a $1,000 bond with an 8 percent coupon would pay $80 in interest every year ($1,000 : 0.08 = $80), generally in the form of two $40 semiannual payments. The principal amount of a bond, also known as its *par value*, specifies the amount of capital that must be repaid at maturity—there's $1,000 of principal in a $1,000 bond.

Debt securities regularly trade at market prices that differ from their principal (or par) values. This occurs whenever an issue's coupon differs from the prevailing market rate of interest because the price of an issue will change until its yield is compatible with prevailing market yields. For example, such behavior explains why a 7 percent coupon issue will carry a market price of only $825 when the market yield is 9 percent. The drop in price is necessary to raise the yield on this bond from 7 percent to 9 percent. Issues with market values lower than par are known as *discount bonds*

Intermediate Term Bonds May Be the "Sweet Spot"

You can usually expect longer-term bonds to provide higher yields than shorter-term bonds. But that doesn't necessarily mean longer-term bonds are always the best investment. It's long been common knowledge that, for most individual investors, intermediate-term bonds are the place to be. The reason: *Intermediate-term bonds (those with maturities of 7–10 years) typically deliver about 80 percent or more of the returns obtained from long-term bonds (with maturities of 25–30 years), but at roughly half the risk.* This is an excellent risk–return trade-off: you give up a little return for a much bigger cut in risk.

In addition, bond returns are far more stable than stock returns and they possess *excellent portfolio diversification properties.* Adding bonds to a portfolio will generally—up to a point—have a much greater impact on (lowering) risk than it will on (reducing) returns. Face it: you don't buy bonds for high expected returns (except when you think interest rates are heading down). Rather, you buy them for their current income and the stability they bring to a portfolio.

and carry coupons that are less than those on new issues. In contrast, issues with market values above par are called *premium bonds* and have coupons greater than those currently being offered on new issues.

Types of Issues

In addition to their coupons and maturities, bonds can be differentiated from one another by the type of collateral behind them. In this regard, the issues can be viewed as having either junior or senior standing. *Senior bonds are secured obligations* because they're backed by a legal claim on some specific property of the issuer that acts as *collateral* for the bonds. Such issues include **mortgage bonds**, which are secured by real estate, and **equipment trust certificates**, which are backed by certain types of equipment and are popular with railroads and airlines. *Junior bonds*, on the other hand, are backed only with a promise by the issuer to pay interest and principal on a timely basis. There are several classes of *unsecured* bonds, the most popular of which is known as a **debenture**. Issued as either notes (with maturities of 2 to 10 years) or bonds (maturities of more than 10 years), debentures are totally unsecured in the sense that there's no collateral backing them up—other than the issuer's good name.

Sinking Fund

Another provision that's important to investors is the **sinking fund**, which describes how a bond will be paid off over time. Not all bonds have these requirements; but for those that do, a sinking fund specifies the annual repayment schedule to be used in paying off the issue and indicates how much principal will be retired each year. Sinking fund requirements generally begin one to five years after the date of issue and continue annually thereafter until all or most of the issue has been paid off. Any amount not repaid by maturity is then retired with a single balloon payment.

Call Feature

Every bond has a **call feature**, which stipulates whether a bond can be called (i.e., retired) before its regularly scheduled maturity date and, if so, under what conditions. Basically, there are three types of call features:

- A bond can be *freely callable*, which means the issuer can retire the bond prematurely at any time.
- A bond can be *noncallable*, which means the issuer is prohibited from retiring the bond prior to maturity.
- The issue could carry a *deferred call*, which means the issue cannot be called until after a certain length of time has passed from the date of issue. In essence, the issue is not callable during the deferment period and then becomes freely callable thereafter.

Call features are usually used to retire a bond prematurely and replace it with one that carries a lower coupon rate. In this way, the issuer benefits by being able to reduce its annual interest costs. In an attempt to at least partially compensate investors who have their bonds called out from under them, a *call premium* (usually equal to about six months to one year of interest) is tacked onto the par value of the bond and paid to investors, along with the issue's par value, at the time the bond is called. For example, if a company decides to call its 7 percent bonds some 15 years before they mature, then it might pay $1,052.50 for every $1,000 bond outstanding (i.e., a call premium equal to nine months' interest—$70 : 0.75 = $52.50—would be added to the par value of $1,000). Although this might sound like a good deal, it's really not for the investor. The bondholder may indeed get a few extra bucks when the bond is called; but in turn, she loses a source of high current income. For example, the investor may have a 7 percent bond called away at a time when the best she can do in the market is maybe 4 percent or 5 percent.

---

mortgage bond
A bond secured by a claim on real assets, such as a manufacturing plant.

equipment trust certificate
A bond secured by certain types of equipment, such as railroad cars and airplanes.

debenture
An unsecured bond issued on the general credit of the firm.

sinking fund
A bond provision specifying the annual repayment schedule to be used in paying off the issue.

call feature
Bond feature that allows the issuer to retire the security prior to maturity.

12–3d The Bond Market

One thing that really stands out about the bond market is its size—the U.S. bond market is huge and getting bigger almost daily. Indeed, from a $250 billion market in 1950 it has grown to the point where, in 2014, the dollar value of bonds outstanding in this country was around $39 *trillion!* Given such size, it's not surprising that today's bond market offers securities to meet just about any type of investment objective and suit virtually any type of investor, no matter how conservative or aggressive. The bond market is usually divided into four segments, according to type of issuer: Treasury, agency, municipal, and corporate.

Treasury Bonds

Treasury bond
A bond issued and backed up by the full faith and credit of the U.S. government.

Treasury bonds (sometimes called *Treasuries* or *governments*) are a dominant force in the bond market and, if not the most popular, are certainly the best known. The U.S. Treasury issues bonds, notes, and other types of debt securities (such as the T-bills discussed in Chapter 4) as a means of meeting the federal government's ever-increasing needs. All Treasury obligations are of the highest quality (backed by the full faith and credit of the U.S. government), a feature that, along with their liquidity, makes them extremely popular with individual and institutional investors both domestically and abroad. Indeed, U.S. Treasury securities are traded in all of the world's major markets, from New York to London to Tokyo.

Treasury notes are issued with maturities of 2, 3, 5, and 10 years, whereas *Treasury bonds* carry 20- and 30-year maturities. (Note that, although the Treasury is authorized to issue these securities, it hasn't issued any 20-year bonds since January 1986, and it did not resume issuing 30-year bonds until February 2006.) The Treasury issues its securities at regularly scheduled auctions. And it's through this auction process that the Treasury establishes the initial yields and coupons on the securities it issues. All Treasury notes and bonds are sold in minimum denominations of $1,000; although interest income is subject to normal federal income tax, *it is exempt from state and local taxes*. Also, the Treasury today issues only *noncallable* securities—the last time the U.S. Treasury issued callable debt was in 1984.

Treasury inflation-indexed bond
A bond, issued by the U.S. government, whose principal payments are adjusted to provide protection again inflation, as measured by the Consumer Price Index (CPI).

The newest type of Treasury issue is the **Treasury inflation-indexed bond** (or *TIPS*, which stands for Treasury Inflation-Protected Security). These securities—which are issued with maturities of 5, 10, or 20 years—give the investor the opportunity to keep up with inflation by periodically adjusting their returns for any

GOODLUZ/SHUTTERSTOCK.COM

inflation that has occurred. Unfortunately, the coupons on these securities are set very low because they're meant to provide investors with *real (inflation-adjusted) returns*. So one of these bonds might carry a coupon of only 1.5 percent (when regular T-bonds are paying, say, 3.5 percent or 4 percent). But there's an upside even to this: in the event of inflation, the actual *size of the coupon payment will increase over time as the par value on the bond increases*. For investors who seek protection against inflation, these securities may be just the ticket.

> ### EXAMPLE: Inflation-Adjustment of TIPS Bonds
>
> Assume that inflation is running at an annual rate of 3 percent. At the end of the year, the par (or maturity) value of your TIPS bond will increase by 3 percent (actually, adjustments to par value are made every six months). Thus, the $1,000 par value will grow to $1,030 at the end of the first year and, if the 3 percent inflation rate continues for the second year, the par value will once again move up, this time from $1,030 to $1,061 (or $1,030 × 1.03).

Agency and Mortgage-Backed Bonds

agency bond
An obligation of a political subdivision of the U.S. government.

Agency bonds are an important segment of the U.S. bond market. Although issued by political subdivisions of the U.S. government, *these securities are not obligations of the U.S. Treasury*. An important feature of these securities is that they customarily provide yields that are comfortably above the market rates for Treasuries and thus offer investors a way to increase returns with little or no real difference in risk. Some actively traded and widely quoted agency issues include those sold by the Federal Farm Credit Bank, the Federal National Mortgage Association (or "Fannie Mae," as it's more commonly known), the Federal Land Bank, the Student Loan Marketing Association, and the Federal Home Loan Mortgage Corporation (FHLMC, or Freddie Mac). Although various agencies issue traditional unsecured notes and bonds, they are perhaps best known for their **mortgage-backed securities**. Two of the biggest issuers of such securities are Fannie Mae and Freddie Mac, who package and issue bonds backed by mortgages that have no government guarantee.

mortgage-backed securities
Securities that are a claim on the cash flows generated by mortgage loans; bonds backed by mortgages as collateral.

Another participant in the mortgage market is the Government National Mortgage Association (GNMA, or Ginnie Mae). It is owned by the U.S. government and insures bonds that are backed by Veterans Administration (VA) and Federal Housing Administration (FHA) home loans. As a result, these GNMA-insured bonds are backed by the full faith and credit of the U.S. government. Some agency issues have unusual interest-payment provisions (i.e., interest is paid monthly in a few instances, and yearly in one case), and in some cases, the interest is exempt from state and local taxes.

Municipal Bonds

municipal bond
A bond issued by state or local governments; interest income is usually exempt from federal taxes.

Municipal bonds are the issues of states, counties, cities, and other political subdivisions, such as school districts and water and sewer districts. Historically, these have generally been considered high-grade securities. However, these days you should be careful when selecting municipal bonds because they can and sometimes do go into default. When a municipality goes into bankruptcy, you essentially end up holding a "junk" bond. While defaults are rare, there are more defaults than are reported by the rating agencies. Usually, only the most financially secure municipalities request bond ratings.

Municipal bonds are unlike other bonds in that their interest income is usually free from federal income tax (which is why they're known as *tax-free bonds*). However, this tax-free status does not apply to any capital gains that may be earned on these securities—such gains are subject to the usual federal taxes. A tax-free yield is probably the most important feature of municipal bonds and is certainly a major reason why individuals invest in them. Exhibit 12.6 shows what a taxable bond (such as a Treasury issue) would have to yield to equal the take-home yield of a tax-free municipal bond. It demonstrates how the yield attractiveness of municipal bonds varies with an investor's income level. The higher the individual's tax bracket, the more attractive municipal bonds become.

The yields on municipal bonds are usually lower than the returns available from fully taxable issues. So unless the tax effect is sufficient to raise the yield on a municipal to a level that equals or exceeds the yields on taxable issues, it obviously doesn't make sense to buy municipal bonds. You can determine the return that a fully taxable bond must provide in order to match the after-tax return on a lower-yielding tax-free bond by computing the municipal's **fully taxable equivalent yield**:

$$\text{Fully Taxable Equivalent Yield} = \frac{\text{Yield on Municipal Bond}}{1 - \text{Tax Rate}}$$

fully taxable equivalent yield
The return that a fully taxable bond must provide in order to match the after-tax return on a lower-yielding tax-free bond.

> **EXAMPLE: Calculating the Fully Taxable Equivalent Yield**
>
> If a municipal bond offered a yield of 6 percent, then an individual in the 35 percent federal tax bracket would have to find a fully taxable bond with a yield of more than 9 percent to reap the same after-tax return: 6 percent / (1 − 0.35) = 6 percent / 0.65 = 9.23 percent.

serial obligation
An issue that is broken down into a series of smaller bonds, each with its own maturity date and coupon rate.

Municipal bonds are generally issued as **serial obligations**, meaning that the issue is broken into a series of smaller bonds, each with its own maturity date and coupon rate. Thus, instead of the bond having just one maturity date 20 years from now, it will have a series of (say) 20 maturity dates over the 20-year time frame. Although it may not seem that municipal issuers would default on either interest or principal payments, it does occur! Investors should be especially cautious when investing in **revenue bonds**, which are municipal bonds serviced from the income generated by specific income-producing projects, such as toll roads. Unlike issuers of so-called **general obligation bonds**—which are backed by the full faith and credit of the municipality—the issuer of a revenue bond is obligated to pay principal and interest *only if a sufficient level of revenue* is generated. General obligation municipal bonds, in contrast, are required to be serviced in a prompt and timely fashion regardless of the level of tax income generated by the municipality.

revenue bond
A municipal bond serviced from the income generated by a specific project.

general obligation bond
A municipal bond backed by the full faith and credit of the issuing municipality.

Corporate Bonds

corporate bond
A bond issued by a corporation.

The major nongovernmental issuers of bonds are corporations. The market for **corporate bonds** is customarily subdivided into several segments, which include *industrials* (the most diverse of the group), *public utilities* (the dominant group in terms of the volume of new issues), *rail and transportation bonds*, and *financial issues* (such as banks and finance companies). In this market, you'll find the widest range of different types of issues, from *first-mortgage bonds and convertible bonds* (discussed below) to *debentures, subordinated debentures*, and *income bonds*. Interest on corporate bonds is paid semiannually, and sinking funds are common. The bonds usually come in $1,000 denominations, and maturities usually range from 5 to 10 years but can be up to 30 years or more. Many of the issues carry call provisions that prohibit prepayment of the issue during the first 5 to 10 years. Corporate issues are popular with individuals because of their relatively high yields.

The Special Appeal of Zero Coupon Bonds

zero coupon bond
A bond that pays no annual interest but sells at a deep discount to its par value.

In addition to the standard bond vehicles already described, investors can also choose from several types of *specialty issues*—bonds that, for the most part, have unusual coupon or repayment provisions. That's certainly the case with **zero coupon bonds**, which, as the name implies, are bonds issued without coupons. To compensate for their lack of coupons, these bonds are sold at a deep discount from their par values and then increase in value over time, at a compound rate of return, so at maturity they're worth much more than their initial investment. Other things being equal, the cheaper the bond, the greater the return you can earn. For example, whereas a 7 percent 15-year zero bond might sell for $362, a 15-year issue with a 5 percent yield will cost a lot more—say, $481.

EXHIBIT 12.6   Table of Taxable Equivalent Yields

Tax-exempt securities generally yield less than fully taxable obligations. As a result, you have to be in a sufficiently high tax bracket (25 percent or more) to make up for the yield shortfall.

	TO MATCH A TAX-FREE YIELD OF:					
	5%	6%	7%	8%	9%	10%
Tax Bracket*	You Must Earn This Yield on a Taxable Investment:					
10%	5.55%	6.66%	7.77%	8.88%	10.00%	11.11%
15	5.88	7.06	8.24	9.41	10.59	11.76
25	6.67	8.00	9.33	10.67	12.00	13.33
28	6.94	8.33	9.72	11.11	12.50	13.89
33	7.46	8.96	10.45	11.94	13.43	14.92
35	7.69	9.23	10.77	12.31	13.85	15.38
39.6	8.28	9.93	11.59	13.25	14.9	16.56

*Federal tax rates in effect in 2015.

Because they have no coupons, these bonds pay nothing to the investor until they mature. In this regard, zero coupon bonds are like the Series EE savings bonds discussed in Chapter 4. Strange as it may seem, this is the main attraction of zero coupon bonds. Investors need not worry about reinvesting coupon income twice a year because there are no interest payments. Instead, the fully compounded rate of return on a zero coupon bond is virtually guaranteed at the rate that existed when the issue was purchased as long as the investor holds it to full maturity. For example, in August 2015, U.S. Treasury zero coupon bonds with 10-year maturities were available at yields of about 2.16 percent. Thus, these bonds *lock in* a 2.16 percent compound rate of return on their investment capital for the full 10-year life of the issue. Because of their unusual tax exposure (even though the bonds don't pay regular yearly interest, the Internal Revenue Service treats the annually accrued interest as taxable income), zeros are best used in tax-sheltered investments, such as individual retirement accounts (IRAs), or held by minor children who are likely to be taxed at low rates, if at all.

Zeros are issued by corporations, municipalities, and federal agencies; you can even buy U.S. Treasury notes and bonds in the form of zero coupon securities. During the 1980s, major brokerage houses packaged U.S. Treasury securities as zeros and sold them to the investing public in the form of unit investment trusts. These securities became so popular with investors that the Treasury decided to eliminate the middleman and "issue" its own form of zero coupon bond, known as *Treasury STRIPS*, or *STRIP-Ts*, for short. Actually, the Treasury doesn't issue zero coupon bonds; instead, *they allow government securities dealers to take regular coupon-bearing notes and bonds in stripped form*, which can then be sold to the public as zero-coupon securities. Essentially, the coupons are stripped from the bond, repackaged, and then sold separately as zero coupon bonds. For instance, a 10-year Treasury bond has 20 semiannual coupon payments plus 1 principal payment—and each of these 21 cash flows can be repackaged and sold as 21 different zero coupon securities with maturities ranging from six months to 10 years.

Convertible Bonds

Another popular type of specialty issue is the convertible bond. Found only in the corporate market, these issues are a *hybrid security* that possess the features of both corporate bonds and common stocks. That is, though they're initially issued as debentures (unsecured debt), they carry a provision that enables them to *be converted into a certain number of shares of the issuing company's common stock.*

conversion privilege
The provision in a convertible issue that stipulates the conditions of the conversion feature, such as the conversion period and conversion ratio.

conversion ratio
A ratio specifying the number of shares of common stock into which a convertible bond can be converted.

conversion value
A measure of what a convertible issue would trade for if it were priced to sell based on its stock value.

conversion premium
The difference between a convertible security's market price and its conversion value.

The key element of any convertible issue is its **conversion privilege**, which describes the conditions and specific nature of the conversion feature. First, it states exactly when the bond can be converted. Sometimes there'll be an initial waiting period of six months to perhaps two years after the date of issue, during which time the issue cannot be converted. The *conversion period* then begins, after which the issue can be converted at any time. From the investor's point of view, the most important feature is the **conversion ratio**, which specifies the number of shares of common stock into which the bond can be converted. For example, one of these bonds might carry a conversion ratio of 20, meaning that you can exchange one convertible bond for 20 shares of the company's stock.

Given the significance of the price behavior of the underlying common stock to the value of a convertible security, one of the most important measures is conversion value. **Conversion value** indicates what a convertible issue would trade for *if it were priced to sell based only on its stock value*. Conversion value is easy to determine: simply multiply the conversion ratio of the issue by the current market price of the underlying common stock. Convertibles seldom trade precisely at their conversion value. Instead, they usually trade at **conversion premiums**, which means that the convertibles are priced in the market at more than their conversion values. Convertible securities appeal to investors who want *the price potential of a common stock along with the downside risk protection of a corporate bond*.

> **EXAMPLE: Calculating the Conversion Value of a Convertible Bond**
>
> A convertible bond carrying a conversion ratio of 20 would have a conversion value of $1,200 if the firm's stock traded at a current market price of $60 per share ($20 \times \$60 = \$1,200$).

12–3e Bond Ratings

Bond ratings are like grades: A letter grade is assigned to a bond, which designates its investment quality. Ratings are widely used and are an important part of the municipal and corporate bond markets. The two largest and best-known rating agencies are Moody's and Standard & Poor's. Every time a large, new corporate or municipal issue comes to the market, a staff of professional bond analysts determines its default risk exposure and investment quality. The financial records of the issuing organization are thoroughly examined and its future prospects assessed. The result of all this is the assignment of a bond rating at the time of issue that indicates *the ability of the issuing organization to service its debt in a prompt and timely manner*. Exhibit 12.7 lists the various ratings assigned to bonds by each of the two major agencies. Note that the top four ratings (Aaa through Baa, or AAA through BBB) designate *investment-grade bonds*—such ratings are highly coveted by issuers because they indicate

junk bond
Also known as *high-yield bonds*, these are highly speculative securities that have received low ratings from Moody's and/or Standard & Poor's.

financially strong, well-run companies or municipalities. The next two ratings (Ba/B or BB/B) are where you'll find most **junk bonds**. These ratings indicate that, although the principal and interest payments on the bonds are still being paid, the risk of default is relatively high because the issuers lack the financial strength found with investment-grade issues. Although junk bonds—or *high-yield bonds*, as they're also known—are popular with some investors, it should be understood that they involve substantial risk. In particular, there's a very real likelihood that the issue may encounter some difficulties.

Once a new issue is rated, the process doesn't stop there. Older, outstanding bonds are also regularly reviewed to ensure that their assigned ratings are still valid. Although most issues will carry a single rating to maturity, ratings can change over time as new information becomes available. Finally, although it may appear that the issuing

Financial Fact or Fantasy?

Convertible bonds are so named because they can be exchanged for a set number of shares of common stock. **Fact:** Convertible bonds carry the provision that they may, within a stipulated time period, be converted into a certain number of shares of the issuing company's common stock.

EXHIBIT 12.7 Moody's and Standard & Poor's Bond Ratings

Agencies like Moody's and Standard & Poor's rate corporate and municipal bonds; these ratings provide an indication of the bonds' investment quality (particularly regarding an issue's default risk exposure).

BOND RATINGS*

Moody's	S&P	Description
Aaa	AAA	*Prime-Quality Investment Bonds*—This is the highest rating assigned, denoting extremely strong capacity to pay.
AaA A	AA A	*High-Grade Investment Bonds*—These are also considered very safe bonds, though they're not quite as safe as Aaa/AAA issues; double-A-rated bonds (Aa/AA) are safer (have less risk of default) than single-A-rated issues.
Baa	BBB	*Medium-Grade Investment Bonds*—These are the lowest of the investment-grade issues; they're felt to lack certain protective elements against adverse economic conditions.
Ba B	BB B	*Junk Bonds*—With little protection against default, these are viewed as highly speculative securities.
Caa Ca C	CCC CC C D	*Poor-Quality Bonds*—These are either in default or very close to it; they're often referred to as "Zombie Bonds."

*Some ratings may be modified to show relative standing within a major rating category; for example, Moody's uses numerical modifiers (1, 2, 3), whereas S&P uses plus (+) or minus (–) signs.

firm or municipality is receiving the rating, it's actually the *individual* issue that is being rated. As a result, a firm (or municipality) can have different ratings assigned to its issues; the senior securities, for example, might carry one rating and the junior issues a slightly lower rating. Most investors pay careful attention to ratings, because they affect comparative market yields. Other things being equal, *the higher the rating, the lower the yield of an obligation.* Thus, whereas an A-rated bond might offer a 5 percent yield, a comparable AAA issue would probably yield something like 4.25 percent or 4.50 percent.

12–3f Pricing a Bond

Unlike stocks, bonds aren't widely quoted in the financial press, not even in *The Wall Street Journal.* So, rather than looking at how bonds are quoted, let's look at how they're priced in the marketplace. Regardless of the type, *all bonds are priced as a percentage of par,* meaning that a quote of, say, 85 translates into a price of 85 percent of the bond's par value. In the bond market, 1 point = $10, so a quote of 85 does not mean $85, but rather $850. This is so because market convention assumes that bonds carry par values of $1,000. Keep in mind that the price of any bond is always related to the issue's coupon and maturity—those two features are always a part of any listed price because of their effect on the price of a bond. (We'll explain more about the impact of coupons and maturities on bond price behavior in the section entitled "Bond Prices and Yields," later in this chapter.)

In the corporate and municipal markets, bonds are priced in decimals, using three places to the right of the decimal point. Thus, a quote of 87.562, as a percentage of a $1,000 par bond, converts to a price of $875.62. Similarly, a quote of 121.683 translates

Why Buy Junk?

Junk bonds are low-rated debt securities that carry a relatively high risk of default. You'd expect to find a bunch of no-name companies residing in this neighborhood but that's not always the case. Here's a list of some companies whose bonds were rated as junk in mid-2015:

- Caesars Entertainment (CCC−)
- Claire's Stores (CCC)
- Colt Defense (D)
- HCA Inc. (BB)
- H. J. Heinz Co. (BB−)
- Softbank Corp. (BB+)
- Sprint Corp. (B+)

These companies were slapped with low ratings because their operating earnings lacked the quality and consistency of high-grade bond issuers. So why invest in them? For their high returns! For example, in May of 2015, the average yield on junk bonds was about 4.5 percent higher than the yield on comparable maturity U.S. Treasury bonds. The attraction of junk bonds is clear—but junk bonds carry a higher chance of default and they're not for everyone.

*The rating is by Standard & Poor's.

into a price of 1.21683 × $1,000 = $1,216.83. In contrast, U.S. Treasury and agency bond quotes are stated in *32s of a point* (where, again, 1 point = $10). For example, you might see the price of a T-bond listed at "94:16." This means that the bond is being priced at $94^{16}/_{32}$, or 94.5 percent of par—in other words, it's being priced at $945.00. With government bonds, the figures to the right of the colon (:) show the number of 32s embedded in the price. Consider another bond that's trading at 141:08. This bond is being priced at $141^{8}/_{32}$, or 141.25% of par. Thus, if you wanted to buy 15 of these bonds (with a par value of $15,000), you'd have to pay $21,187.50 (i.e., 1.4125 × $15,000).

Bond Prices and Accrued Interest

The price of a bond quoted on your favorite financial Internet site is unlikely to be the price that you would actually pay as a buyer. This is because such quoted prices usually do not include the interest that accrues between the coupon payment dates of the bond. **Accrued interest** is the amount of interest that's been earned since the last coupon payment date by the bond holder/seller, but which will be received by the new owner/buyer of the bond at the next regularly scheduled coupon payment date. When a bond is sold between coupon payment dates, the buyer pays the seller for the accrued interest, which is the prorated share of the upcoming coupon payment.

Consider a specific example of how accrued interest affects the price paid for a bond between coupon payments. Assume that you're selling a corporate bond with $1,000 par value and paying a 4 percent coupon semiannually, which is $20 every six months. The bond is quoted on the Internet at $1,000, and it's three months after the last coupon payment. Because the bond is halfway between coupon payments, accrued interest is $20 × 3/6 = $10. Thus, the buyer's actual price paid to the seller will be the $1,000 quoted price plus the accrued interest of $10, for a total of $1,010.

In market jargon, how accrued interest is treated in bond pricing is the basis for the distinction between **clean price** and **dirty (full) price**. This can be summarized as:

Clean price = quoted price
Dirty (full) price = quoted price + accrued interest

So what's the significance of the distinction between dirty and clean prices for bond investors? It's important to realize that the commonly cited prices in the financial

accrued interest
The amount of interest that's been earned since the last coupon payment date by the bond holder/seller, but which will be received by the new owner/buyer of the bond at the next regularly scheduled coupon payment date.

clean price
The quoted price of a bond, which understates the true price of a bond by any accrued interest.

dirty (full) price
The quoted price of a bond plus accrued interest, the total of which is the relevant price to be paid by a bond buyer.

press and on the Internet are typically net of accrued interest and are so-called clean bond prices. The relevant sale or invoice price of a bond to the buyer is the dirty price, which adds the accrued interest to the quoted price. In terms of the earlier example, the buyer of the 4 percent coupon bond would pay the dirty price of $1,010, not the clean price of $1,000. In summary, the quoted clean price *understates* the true (dirty) price that must be paid to actually purchase the bond in the open market.

Bond Prices and Yields

premium bond
A bond whose market value is higher than par.

discount bond
A bond whose market value is lower than par.

The price of a bond depends on its coupon, maturity, and the movement of market interest rates. As previously noted, *when interest rates go down, bond prices go up, and vice versa*. The relationship of bond prices to market rates is captured in Exhibit 12.8. The graph serves to reinforce the *inverse* relationship between bond prices and market interest rates; note that *lower* rates lead to *higher* bond prices. The exhibit also shows the difference between premium and discount bonds. A **premium bond** is one that sells for more than its par value, which occurs whenever market interest rates drop below the coupon rate on the bond; a **discount bond**, in contrast, sells for less than par and is the result of market rates being greater than the issue's coupon rate. So the 4 percent bond in our illustration traded as a premium bond when market rates were at 2 percent but as a discount bond when rates stood at 6 percent.

When a bond is first issued, it's usually sold to the public at a price that equals (or is very close to) its par value. Likewise, when the bond matures—some 15, 20, or 30 years later—it will once again be priced at its par value. What happens to the price of the bond over time is of considerable concern to bond investors who may wish to trade the bond over its life. We know that how much bond prices move depends not only on the *direction* of interest rate changes but also on the *magnitude* of such changes. The greater the moves in interest rates, the greater the swings in bond prices. Bond prices will also vary according to the coupon and maturity of the issue. Bonds with *lower coupons* and/or *longer maturities* will respond more vigorously to changes in market rates and undergo *greater price swings*. Thus, if interest rates are moving up, then the investor should seek high coupon bonds with short maturities, because this will dampen price variation and *preserve as much capital as possible*. In contrast, if rates are heading down, that's the time to be in long-term bonds. If you're a speculator looking for lots of capital gains, then go with long-term, *low coupon bonds*. In contrast, if you're trying to lock in a high level of coupon (interest) income, then stick with long-term, *high coupon* bonds that offer plenty of call protection.

Financial Fact or Fantasy?

When interest rates go down, bond prices also go down because such securities become less valuable. **Fantasy:** Bond prices and interest rates move in the opposite direction. As a result, when interest rates go down, bond prices go up.

Current Yield and Yield to Maturity

Current yield
The amount of current income a bond provides relative to its market price.

The two most commonly cited bond yields are current yield and yield to maturity. **Current yield** reflects the amount of annual interest income the bond provides relative to its current market price. Here's the formula for current yield:

$$\text{Current Yield} = \frac{\text{Annual Interest Income}}{\text{Market Price of Bond}}$$

As you can see, the current yield on a bond is comparable to the dividend yield on a stock. This measure would be of interest to *investors seeking current income*. Other things being equal, the higher the current yield, the more attractive a bond would be to such an investor.

> **EXAMPLE: Calculating the Current Yield on a Bond**
>
> A 6 percent bond with a $1,000 face value is currently selling for $910. Because annual interest income is $60 (i.e., 0.06 × $1,000) and because the current market price of the bond is $910, its current yield would be 6.59 percent ($60/$910).

EXHIBIT 12.8   **Price Behavior** of a Bond with a 4 Percent Coupon

A bond sells at its par value so long as the prevailing market interest rate remains the same as the bond's coupon (for example, when both coupon and market rates equal 4 percent). But if market rates drop, then bond prices rise, and vice versa. Moreover, as a bond approaches its maturity, the issue price always moves toward its par value no matter what happens to interest rates.

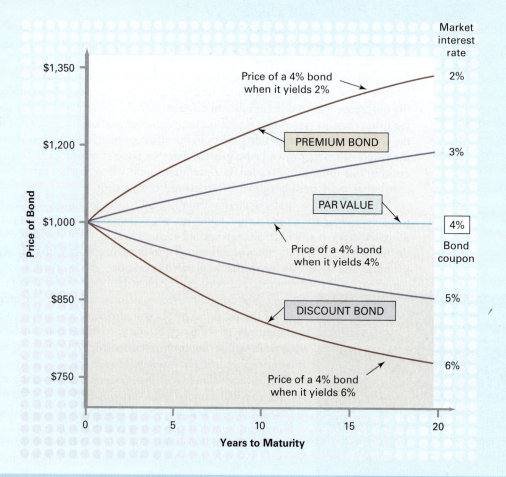

yield to maturity
The fully compounded rate of return that a bond would yield if it were held to maturity.

The annual rate of return that a bondholder would receive *if she held the issue to its maturity* is captured in the bond's **yield to maturity**. This measure captures both the annual interest income and the recovery of principal at maturity. It also includes the impact of interest on interest and therefore provides a fully compounded rate of return. If a bond is purchased at its face value, then its yield to maturity will equal the coupon, or stated, rate of interest. On the other hand, if the bond is purchased at a discount or a premium then its yield to maturity will vary according to the prevailing level of market yields.

You can find the yield to maturity on discount or premium bonds using the *approximate yield* formula introduced earlier in this chapter. Or you can use a hand-held financial calculator (which we'll demonstrate soon) to obtain a yield to maturity that's a bit more accurate and is, in fact, very close to the measure used in the market. The only difference is that market participants normally use semiannual compounding in their calculations, whereas we use annual compounding for simplicity to illustrate the basic concept. Bonds are normally priced in the market using semiannual compounding because the vast majority of U.S. bonds pay interest semiannually. The difference in yields using annual versus semiannual compounding usually amounts to no more than 5 or 6 basis points, where 1 basis point = 1/100 of 1 percent. Now that might be a big deal to institutional investors, but not to the small individual investor. So we'll stick with annual compounding here, though we'll show how you can use your handheld calculator to find yield to maturity on a semiannual basis. So, employing the approximate yield approach for now, by setting the future maturity value of the investment equal to the bond's face value ($1,000), you can use the following version of the equation to find the *approximate yield to maturity on a bond*:

$$\text{Approximate Yield to Maturity} = \frac{\text{Annual Coupon Income} + \left[\dfrac{\$1,000 - \text{Current Bond Price}}{\text{Number of Years to Maturity}}\right]}{\left[\dfrac{\text{Current Price of Bond} + \$1,000}{2}\right]}$$

EXAMPLE: Calculating the Approximate Yield to Maturity

Assume you're contemplating the purchase of a $1,000, 6 percent annual coupon income bond with 15 years remaining to maturity and that the bond currently is trading at a price of $910. The approximate yield to maturity on this bond will be:

$$\text{Approximate Yield to Maturity} = \frac{\$60 + \left[\dfrac{\$1,000 - \$910}{15}\right]}{\left[\dfrac{\$910 + \$1,000}{2}\right]}$$

$$= \frac{\$60 + \left[\dfrac{\$90}{15}\right]}{\left[\dfrac{\$1,910}{2}\right]} = \underline{6.91\%}$$

This is above both the 6 percent stated (coupon) rate and the 6.59 percent current yield. That's because the bond is trading at a discount to its face value.

Calculator

INPUTS	FUNCTIONS
15	N
−910	PV
60	PMT
1000	FV
	CPT
	I/Y
	SOLUTION
	6.99

See Appendix E for details.

Calculator Keystrokes. You can also *find the yield to maturity on a bond* by using a financial calculator; here's what you'd do. With the calculator in the *annual mode*, to find the yield to maturity on our 6 percent (annual pay coupon), 15-year bond that's currently trading at $910, use the keystrokes shown here, where:

N = number of *years* to maturity
PV = the current market price of the bond (entered as a negative)
PMT = the size of the annual coupon payments (in *dollars*)
FV = the par value of the bond

A value of 6.99 should appear in the calculator display, which is the bond's yield to maturity using annual compounding; note that it's very close to the approximate yield of 6.91 percent we just computed.

You can also use your handheld calculator to find the slightly more accurate *yield to maturity based on semiannual compounding*. Here's how: Keeping the calculator in the *annual mode, multiply* the number of years to maturity by 2 (to obtain the number of 6-month periods to maturity) and *divide* the coupon by 2 (to determine the size of the semiannual coupon payments). Now input the appropriate data: N = 15 × 2 = 30, PMT = 60/2 = 30, PV = −910; and FV = 1000; then hit CPT I/Y and you should end up with 3.49, which is the semiannual yield. Then double that value (3.49 × 2) and you'll have 6.98 percent, *the bond's yield to maturity using semiannual compounding*. Notice in this case that the difference in the annual (6.99 percent) versus semiannual (6.98 percent) yields to maturity is just 1 basis point!

Measures of yield to maturity are used by investors to assess the attractiveness of a bond. The higher the yield to maturity, the more attractive the investment, other things being equal. *If a bond provided a yield to maturity that equaled or exceeded an investor's desired rate of return, then it would be considered a worthwhile investment candidate* because it would promise a yield that should adequately compensate the investor for the perceived amount of risk involved.

Financial Impact of Personal Choices
Landon and Kirsten Like High Flying Stocks

Landon and Kirsten Malloy are both 33 years old and invest 15 percent of their after-tax annual income in stocks. They hate missing out on great returns when the stock of a company doing great things starts going through the roof. For example, Landon and Kirsten feel they should have invested in Electronic Arts in 2014 when it earned around a 60 percent return! So any time a company they know well earns more than 20 percent in a year, they try to invest in it. And because they believe in the stocks they buy, the Malloys always hold their stocks until they at least break-even. What do you make of the Malloys' approach to stock investing?

The Malloys decision to invest 15 percent of their after-tax income is great. However, Landon and Kirsten shouldn't invest just in stocks and should adopt an asset allocation strategy that provides diversified exposure to bonds, real estate, and more. Their current exclusive focus on stocks is likely too risky. Further, their rule to buy well-known stocks that earn more than 20 percent in a year likely leaves them insufficiently diversified. And their 20 percent return rule also focuses too much on *past* returns and not enough on a careful forecast of *future* returns. The Malloys could end up with overvalued stocks with their best performance behind them. Finally, their rule to not sell until they at least break-even suggests the behavioral bias of unduly "anchoring" on purchase prices. It could be that a company has changed for the worse and it's simply time to sell, even if it implies a loss. Investing 15 percent of their income is great, but the Malloys could do even better.

Planning Over a Lifetime: *Investing in Stocks and Bonds*

Here are some key considerations for investment planning in each stage of the life cycle.

Pre-family Independence: 20s	Family Formation/Career Development: 30–45	Pre-Retirement: 45–65	Retirement: 65 and Beyond
✓ Determine major investment goals and how much money needs to be invested each month to achieve them.	✓ Revise investment plan to focus more on retirement and funding children's education, if applicable.	✓ Revise investment plan in light of recent developments.	✓ Revise investment plan to lean more towards debt and cash instruments than to stocks.
✓ Determine your asset allocation among stocks, bonds, and cash based on your time horizon and attitude towards risk.	✓ Review your asset allocation and rebalance if it is inconsistent with your goals.	✓ Review your asset allocation and rebalance if it is inconsistent with your goals.	✓ Review your asset allocation and rebalance if it is inconsistent with your goals.
✓ Make sure to participate in any employer-sponsored 401(k) retirement plan and match your asset allocation plan.	✓ Gradually increase the amount invested in any employer-sponsored 401(k) retirement plan and reevaluate how it relates to your asset allocation plan.	✓ Continue to gradually increase the amount you invest in any employer sponsored 401(k) retirement plan and reevaluate how it relates to your asset allocation plan.	✓ Integrate investment asset allocation strategy with estate planning.
✓ Consider opening traditional and/or a Roth IRAs.	✓ Consider increasing your contribution to traditional and/or a Roth IRAs.	✓ Consider increasing your contribution to traditional and/or a Roth IRAs.	✓ Carefully plan for mandatory withdrawals from tax shelter accounts and associated tax consequences.

Summary

LG1 Describe the various types of risks to which investors are exposed, as well as the sources of return, p. 462

Although investing offers returns in the form of current income and/or capital gains, it also involves risk. The basic types of investment risk are business risk, financial risk, market risk, purchasing power risk, interest rate risk, liquidity risk, and event risk—all of which combine to affect the level of return from an investment.

LG2 Know how to search for an acceptable investment on the basis of risk, total return, and yield, p. 462

The value, and therefore the acceptability, of any investment depends on the return it's expected to produce relative to the amount of risk involved in the investment. Investors are entitled to be compensated for the risks that they must accept in an investment. Therefore, the more risk there is in an investment, the more return you should expect to earn. This risk–return trade-off is generally captured in the "desired rate of return," which is that rate of return you feel you should receive in compensation for the amount of risk you must assume. As long as the expected return on an investment (the return you *think* you'll earn) is greater than the desired rate of return (the return you *should* earn), it should be considered an acceptable investment candidate—one worthy of your attention.

LG3 **Discuss the merits of investing in common stock and be able to distinguish among the different types of stocks, p. 470**
Common stocks are a popular form of investing that can be used to meet just about any investment objective—from capital gains or current income to some combination of both. Investors can choose from blue chips, growth, or tech stocks; income, speculative, cyclical, or defensive stocks; and small- or mid-cap stocks. If they're so inclined, they can even buy foreign stocks by investing in American Depositary Receipts (ADRs).

LG4 **Become familiar with the various measures of performance and how to use them in placing a value on stocks, p. 470**
The value of a share of stock is largely based on performance measures: dividend yield, book value, net profit margin, return on equity (ROE), earnings per share, price/earnings (P/E) ratio, and beta. Investors look at these measures to gain insights about a firm's financial condition and operating results and ultimately to obtain the input needed to measure the expected return on the firm's stock.

LG5 **Describe the basic issue characteristics of bonds, as well as how these securities are used as investment vehicles, p. 484**
Bonds are a popular form of investing; they're often referred to as *fixed-income* securities because the debt service obligations of the issuer are fixed. The coupon that the bond carries defines the amount of annual interest income that the investor will receive over time, while the par value defines the amount of capital to be repaid at maturity. Bonds may be issued with or without collateral, and most bonds allow the issuer to retire the issue before its maturity. As investment vehicles, bonds can be used to generate either current income or capital gains (which occur when market rates go down).

LG6 **Distinguish between the different types of bonds, gain an understanding of how bond prices behave, and know how to compute different measures of yield, p. 484**
Bonds are the publicly issued debt of corporations and various types of government—from the U.S. Treasury and various agencies of the U.S. government to state and local (municipal) governments. Regardless of the issuer, the price of a bond moves inversely with market interest rates: the lower the market rate, the higher the price of the bond. There are basically two ways to measure the yield performance of a bond: one is current yield, which looks only at the coupon income on a bond; the other is yield to maturity, which provides a fully compounded rate of return that considers not only interest income but also capital gains (or loss) and interest on interest.

Key Terms

accrued interest, 494

agency bond, 489

beta, 474

blue-chip stock, 475

book value, 473

business risk, 462

call feature, 487

clean price, 494

conversion premium, 492

conversion privilege, 492

conversion ratio, 492

conversion value, 492

corporate bond, 490

coupon, 486

Current yield, 495

cyclical stock, 476

debenture, 487

defensive stock, 476

dirty (full) price, 494

discount bond, 495

dividend reinvestment plan (DRP), 483

dividend yield, 472

earnings per share (EPS), 473

equipment trust certificate, 487

event risk, 463

financial risk, 462

fixed-income securities, 463

fully taxable equivalent yield, 490

general obligation bond, 490

growth stock, 475

income stock, 475

interest rate risk, 463

Answers to Test Yourself

You can find answers to these questions on this book's companion website. Look for it at *www. cengagebrain.com*. Search for this book by its title, and then add it to your dashboard.

Key Financial Relationships

Concept	Financial Relationship	Page Number
Approximate Expected Yield	$$\text{Approximate Yield} = \frac{\text{Average Annual Current Income} + \left[\dfrac{\text{Future Price of Investment} - \text{Current Price of Investment}}{\text{Number of Years in Investment Period}}\right]}{\left[\dfrac{\text{Current Price of Investment} + \text{Future Price of Investment}}{2}\right]}$$	468
Dividend Yield	$$\text{Dividend Yield} = \frac{\text{Annual Dividend Received per Share}}{\text{Market Price per Share of Stock}}$$	472
Book Value per Share	$$\text{Book Value per Share} = \frac{\text{Total Assets} - \text{Total Liabilities} - \text{Preferred Stock}}{\text{Number of Shares of Common Stock Outstanding}}$$	473
Net Profit Margin	$$\text{Net Profit Margin} = \frac{\text{Net Profit}}{\text{Sales}}$$	473
Return on Equity	$$\text{Return on Equity} = \frac{\text{Net Profit}}{\text{Shareholders' Equity}}$$	473
Earnings per Share	$$\text{Earnings per Share} = \frac{\text{Net Profit} - \text{Preferred Dividends Paid}}{\text{Number of Shares of Common Stock Outstanding}}$$	474
Price/Earnings Ratio	$$\frac{\text{Price}}{\text{Earnings}} = \frac{\text{Market Price per Share of Common Stock}}{\text{Annual Earnings per Share}}$$	474

Concept	Financial Relationship	Page Number
Fully taxable Equivalent Yield	$\text{Fully Taxable Equivalent Yield} = \dfrac{\text{Yield on Municipal Bond}}{1 - \text{Tax Rate}}$	490
Current Yield	$\text{Current Yield} = \dfrac{\text{Annual Interest Income}}{\text{Market Price of Bond}}$	495
Approximate Yield to Maturity	$\text{Approximate Yield to Maturity} = \dfrac{\text{Annual Coupon Income} + \dfrac{\$1{,}000 - \text{Current Bond Price}}{\text{Number of Years to Maturity}}}{\left[\dfrac{\text{Current Price of Bond} + \$1{,}000}{2}\right]}$	**497**

Key Financial Relationships Problem Set

1. **Approximate expected yield.** Britney Cottrell is evaluating a small stock that's been recommended to her. The average annual dividend is $1.75, the current stock price is $72.50, the projected future stock price is $90.00, and she expects to hold the stock for four years. What is the expected approximate expected yield on the stock?

   Solution:

   $$\text{Approximate Yield} = \frac{\begin{array}{c}\text{Average Annual}\\ \text{Current Income}\end{array} + \dfrac{\begin{array}{c}\text{Future Price}\\ \text{of Investment}\end{array} - \begin{array}{c}\text{Current Price}\\ \text{of Investment}\end{array}}{\text{Number of Years in Investment Period}}}{\dfrac{\begin{array}{c}\text{Current Price}\\ \text{of Investment}\end{array} + \begin{array}{c}\text{Future Price}\\ \text{of Investment}\end{array}}{2}}$$

   $$= \frac{\$1.75 + \dfrac{\$90.00 - \$72.50}{4}}{\dfrac{\$72.50 + \$90.00}{2}}$$

   $$= 7.54 \text{ Percent}$$

2. **Dividend yield.** In mid-2015 Merck's stock was selling for $60.10 and had an annual dividend of $1.80. Kaleb Aleman is looking for stocks that pay attractive current income. The average dividend yield on dividend-paying S&P 500 stocks at the time was 2.31 percent. What is Merck's dividend yield and how attractive is it?

   Solution:

   $$\text{Dividend yield} = \frac{\text{Annual Dividend Received per Share}}{\text{Market Price per Share of Stock}}$$

   $$= \frac{\$1.80}{\$60.10}$$

   $$= 3 \text{ Percent}$$

   This is a bit above the average dividend yield for S&P 500 stocks, which may make Merck attractive to Kaleb.

3. **Book value per share.** At the end of 2014 Facebook had total assets of $40.184 billion and total liabilities of $4.088 billion. Given that the firm has 2.25 billion shares of common stock outstanding and no preferred stock, what is Facebook's book value per share?

   Solution:

   $$\text{Book Value per Share} = \frac{\text{Total Assets} - \text{Total Liabilities} - \text{Preferred Stock}}{\text{Number of Shares of Common Stock Outstanding}}$$

   $$= \frac{\$40.184 - \$4.088}{2.25}$$

   $$= \$16.04 \text{ per Share}$$

4. **Net profit margin.** In 2014 Facebook earned a net profit of $2.925 billion on sales of $12.466 billion. What was Facebook's net profit margin in 2014?

Solution:

$$\text{Net Profit Margin} = \frac{\text{Net Profit}}{\text{Sales}} = \frac{\$2.925}{\$12.466} = 23.46 \text{ Percent}$$

5. **Return on equity.** In 2014 Facebook had net income (net profit) of $2.925 billion and had stockholders' equity of $36.096 billion. What was Facebook's return on equity in 2014?

Solution:

$$\text{Return on Equity} = \frac{\text{Net Profit}}{\text{Shareholders' Equity}} = \frac{\$2.925}{\$36.096} = 8.1 \text{ Percent}$$

6. **Earnings per share.** In 2014 Facebook had net profit of $2.925 and 2.25 billion shares outstanding. What was Facebook's earnings per share in 2014?

Solution:

$$\text{Earnings per Share} = \frac{\text{Net Profit} - \text{Preferred Dividends Paid}}{\text{Number of Shares of Common Stock Outstanding}}$$
$$= \frac{\$2.925}{2.25}$$
$$= \$1.30 \text{ per Share}$$

7. **Price/Earnings ratio.** In 2014 Facebook had earnings per share of $1.30 and on May 21, 2015, its share price closed at $80.48 per share. What was its price/earnings ratio at that time using its 2014 earnings per share as the base?

Solution:

$$\text{Price/Earnings Ratio} = \frac{\text{Market Price per Share of Common Stock}}{\text{Annual Earnings per Share}}$$
$$= \frac{\$80.48}{\$1.30}$$
$$= 16.91$$

8. **Fully taxable equivalent yield.** A municipal bond is offering a yield of 5 percent. Darren Haskins is in the 35 percent marginal federal tax bracket. He is wondering what yield he would need to earn on a fully taxable corporate bond to earn the same after-tax return as that expected on the municipal bond. What should you tell Darren?

Solution:

$$\text{Fully Taxable Yield} = \frac{\text{Yield on Municipal Bond}}{1 - \text{Tax Rate}}$$
$$= \frac{5 \text{ Percent}}{1 - 35 \text{ Percent}}$$
$$= 7.69 \text{ Percent.}$$

Thus, you should tell Darren that he would have to earn more than 7.69 percent on a fully taxable corporate bond in order to earn an after tax return greater than the 5 percent return on the municipal bond.

9. **Current yield.** You're considering buying a bond that pays an annual interest (coupon) income of 4 percent that is selling for $925. What is the current yield on the bond?

Solution:

$$\text{Current Yield} = \frac{\text{Annual Interest Income}}{\text{Market Price of Bond}}$$
$$= \frac{\$40}{\$925}$$
$$= 4.32\%.$$

10. **Approximate yield to maturity.** Anna Schmidt is considering buying a bond that has a face value of $1,000, a 5% coupon, 12 years to maturity, and is trading at a price of $875. In order to decide on the purchase, Ann has asked you to calculate the bond's approximate yield to maturity. What should you tell Anna?

Solution:

$$\text{Approximate Yield to Maturity} = \frac{\text{Annual Coupon Income} + \dfrac{\$1,000 - \text{Current Bond Price}}{\text{Number of Years to Maturity}}}{\dfrac{\text{Current Bond Price} + \$1,000}{2}}$$

$$= \frac{\$50 + \dfrac{\$1,000 - \$875}{12}}{\dfrac{\$875 + \$1,000}{2}}$$

$$= 6.44 \text{ Percent}$$

Financial Planning Exercises

LG1,2, p. 462   1. **Ranking investments by expected returns.** What makes for a good investment? Use the approximate yield formula or a financial calculator to rank the following investments according to their expected returns.
   a.   Buy a stock for $30 a share, hold it for three years, and then sell it for $60 a share (the stock pays annual dividends of $2 a share).
   b.   Buy a security for $40, hold it for two years, and then sell it for $100 (current income on this security is zero).
   c.   Buy a one-year, 5 percent note for $1,000 (assume that the note has a $1,000 par value and that it will be held to maturity).

LG3,4, p. 470   2. **Calculating key financial ratios.** Selected financial information about Backpacking Resources, Inc. is as follows:

Total assets	$20,000,000
Total liabilities	$8,000,000
Total preferred stock	$3,000,000
Total annual preferred stock dividends	$240,000
Net profits after tax	$2,500,000
Number of shares of common stock outstanding	500,000 shares
Current market price of common stock	$50.00 a share
Annual common stock dividends	$2.50 a share

Using the company's financial information, compute the following:
   a.   Dividend yield
   b.   Book value per share
   c.   EPS
   d.   P/E ratio

LG3,4, p. 470   3. **Choosing appropriate stocks.** Assume that you've just inherited $500,000 and have decided to invest a big chunk of it ($350,000, to be exact) in common stocks. Your objective is to build up as much capital as you can over the next 15 to 20 years, and you're willing to tolerate a "good deal" of risk.
   a.   What *types* of stocks (blue chips, income stocks, and so on) do you think you'd be most interested in, and why? Select at least three types of stocks and briefly explain the rationale for selecting each.
   b.   Would your selections change if you were dealing with a smaller amount of money—say, only $50,000? What if you were a more risk-averse investor?

LG3,4, p. 470   4. **Effectiveness of stock market timing.** Discuss the evidence regarding the ability of most investors to effectively time getting in and out of the stock market. How sensitive are returns to being out of the market for just a few months of good stock market performance?

LG3,4, p. 470 5. ***Calculating expected return on investment.*** An investor is thinking about buying some shares of Health Monitoring, Inc., at $75 a share. She expects the price of the stock to rise to $115 a share over the next three years. During that time, she also expects to receive annual dividends of $4 per share. Given that the investor's expectations (about the future price of the stock and the dividends it pays) hold up, what rate of return can the investor expect to earn on this investment? (*Hint:* Use either the approximate yield formula or a financial calculator to solve this problem.)

LG3,4, p. 470 6. ***Calculating book value.*** A company has total assets of $2.5 billion, total liabilities of $1.8 billion, and $200 million worth of 8 percent preferred stock outstanding. What is the firm's total book value? What would its book value per share be if the firm had 100 million shares of common stock outstanding?

LG3,4, p. 470 7. ***Calculating key stock performance metrics.*** The Morton Company recently reported net profits after taxes of $15.8 million. It has 2.5 million shares of common stock outstanding and pays preferred dividends of $1 million a year. The company's stock currently trades at $60 per share.
   a. Compute the stock's EPS.
   b. What is the stock's P/E ratio?
   c. Determine what the stock's dividend yield would be if it paid $1.75 per share to common stockholders.

LG3,4, p. 470 8. ***Calculating expected return on a stock.*** The price of Green Mountain Homes, Inc. is now $85. The company pays no dividends. Trey Hamlin expects the price four years from now to be $125 a share. Should Trey buy Green Mountain Homes if he wants a 15 percent rate of return? Explain.

LG3,4,5,6, p. 470, 484 9. ***Collect key data on actual stocks, bonds, and convertible bonds.*** Using the resources available at your campus or public library, work the following problems. (*Note:* Show your work for all your calculations.)
   a. Select any two *common* stocks and then determine the dividend yield, EPS, and P/E ratio for each.
   b. Select any two *bonds* and then determine the current yield and yield to maturity of each.
   c. Select any two *convertible bonds* and then determine the conversion ratio, conversion value, and conversion premium for each.

LG5,6, p. 484 10. ***Tax treatment of bond returns.*** An investor in the 28 percent tax bracket is trying to decide which of two bonds to select: one is a 5.5 percent U.S. Treasury bond selling at par; the other is a municipal bond with a 4.25 percent coupon, which is also selling at par. Which of these two bonds should the investor select? Why?

LG5,6, p. 484 11. ***Calculating current yield and yield to maturity.*** Describe and differentiate between a bond's (a) current yield and (b) yield to maturity. Why are these yield measures important to the bond investor? Find the yield to maturity of a 20-year, 9 percent, $1,000 par value bond trading at a price of $850. What's the current yield on this bond?

LG5,6, p. 484 12. ***Calculating and comparing current yields.*** Which of these two bonds offers the highest current yield? Which one has the highest yield to maturity?
   a. A 6.55 percent, 22-year bond quoted at 52.000
   b. A 10.25 percent, 27-year bond quoted at 103.625

LG5,6, p. 484 13. ***Calculating and interpreting current yield and yield to maturity.*** Find the current yield of a 5.65 percent, 8-year bond that's currently priced in the market at $853.75. Now, use a financial calculator to find the yield to maturity on this bond (use annual compounding). What's the current yield and yield to maturity on this bond if it trades at $1,000? If it's priced at $750? Comment on your findings.

LG5,6, p. 484 14. ***Calculating current yield and yield to maturity.*** A 25-year, zero coupon bond was recently quoted at 6.500. Find the current yield and yield to maturity of this issue, given the bond has a par value of $1,000. (Assume annual compounding for the yield to maturity measure.)

LG5,6, p. 484 15. ***Calculating current yield and return on investment.*** Assume that an investor pays $850 for a long-term bond that carries a 7.5 percent coupon. During the next 12 months, interest rates drop sharply, and the investor sells the bond at a price of $962.50.
   a. Find the current yield that existed on this bond at the beginning of the year. What was it by the end of the one-year holding period?
   b. Calculate the return on this investment using the approximate yield formula and a one-year investment period.

LG5,6, p. 484 16. ***Calculating conversion value and conversion premium.*** Find the conversion value of a convertible bond that carries a conversion ratio of 24, given that the market price of the underlying common stock is $55 a share. Would there be any conversion premium if the convertible bond had a market price of $1,500? If so, how much?

LG5,6, p. 484 17. ***Calculate current yield, conversion ratio, conversion price, and yield to maturity.*** A 6 percent convertible bond (maturing in 20 years) is convertible into 25 shares of the company's common stock. The bond has a par value of $1,000 and is currently trading at $800; the stock (which pays a dividend of 95 cents a share) is currently trading in the market at $35 a share. Use this information to answer the following questions:

  a. What is the current yield on the convertible bond? What is the dividend yield on the company's common stock? Which provides more current income: the convertible bond or the common stock? Explain.
  b. What is the bond's conversion ratio? Its conversion price?
  c. What is the conversion value of this issue? Is there any conversion premium in this issue? If so, how much?
  d. What is the (approximate) yield to maturity on the convertible bond?

LG6, p. 484 18. ***Clean and dirty bond prices.*** You have decided to sell a 5 percent semiannual coupon bond two months after the last coupon payment. The bond is currently selling for $951.25. Answer the following questions about the bond:

  a. What is the clean price of the bond?
  b. What is the dirty (full) price of the bond?
  c. Explain how the clean and dirty prices of the bond are relevant to the buyer of the bond.

Applying Personal Finance

Choosing the Best Type of Stock

In this chapter, we learned that common stock is often placed into various categories—blue-chip, growth, income, and so forth—and referred to by its size, such as large-, mid-, or small-cap. In this project, you'll examine and compare the returns on various types of common stock.

Common comparisons include:

- Large-cap versus mid- or small-cap
- Blue-chip versus speculative
- Growth versus income
- Cyclical versus defensive

Pick any two combinations from the foregoing list, and then select a stock to represent each of the categories included in your choices. For all four of your stocks, obtain information on:

- The company's EPS
- Growth in dividends per share
- Dividend yield
- P/E ratio
- The stock's beta

In addition, use the formula given in this chapter to compute each stock's approximate yield for the past year, based on what the stock is trading for today versus the price it sold for a year ago. Be sure to include any dividends paid over the past 12 months. You can obtain this information from financial newspapers or from online sources, such as **http://finance.yahoo.com.**

Compare and contrast the performance and characteristics of the stocks you've chosen. Based on your findings, does the type of stock you own make a difference? Which type or types are the most suitable for your investment purposes?

**LG3,5,
p. 470, 484**

12.1 The Madsen's Problem: What to Do with "Extra" Money?

A couple in their early 30s, Rodney and Carly Madsen recently inherited $90,000 from a relative. Rodney earns a comfortable income as a sales manager for System Analytics, Inc., and Carly does equally well as an attorney with a major law firm. Because they have no children and don't need the money, they've decided to invest all of the inheritance in stocks, bonds, and perhaps even some money market instruments. However, because they're not very familiar with the market, they turn to you for help.

Critical Thinking Questions

1. What kind of investment approach do you think the Madsens should adopt—that is, should they be conservative with their money or aggressive? Explain.
2. What kind of stocks do you think the Madsens should invest in? How important is current income (i.e., dividends or interest income) to them? Should they be putting any of their money into bonds? Explain.
3. Construct an investment portfolio that you feel would be right for the Madsens and invest the full $90,000. Put actual stocks, bonds, and/or convertible securities in the portfolio; you may also put up to one-third of the money into short-term securities such as CDs, Treasury bills, money funds, or MMDAs. Select any securities you want, so long as you feel they'd be suitable for the Madsens. Make sure that the portfolio consists of six or more different securities, and use the latest issue of *The Wall Street Journal* or an online source such as **http://finance.yahoo.com** to determine the market prices of the securities you select. Show the amount invested in each security along with the amount of current income (from dividends and/or interest) that will be generated from the investments. Briefly explain why you selected these particular securities for the Madsens' portfolio.

**LG3,5,
p. 470, 484**

12.2 Natasha Explores Investing

Natasha Cormier is a 28-year-old management trainee at a large chemical company. She is single, has an annual salary of $34,000 (placing her in the 15 percent tax bracket), and her monthly expenditures come to approximately $1,500. During the past year or so, Natasha has managed to save around $8,000, and she expects to continue saving at least that amount each year for the foreseeable future. Her company pays the premium on her $35,000 life insurance policy. Because Natasha's entire education was financed by scholarships, she was able to save money from the summer and part-time jobs she held as a student. Altogether, she has a nest egg of nearly $18,000, out of which she'd like to invest about $15,000. She'll keep the remaining $3,000 in a bank CD that pays 3 percent interest and will use this money only in an emergency. Natasha can afford to take more risks than someone with family obligations can, but she doesn't wish to be a speculator; she simply wants to earn an attractive rate of return on her investments.

Critical Thinking Questions

1. What investment options are open to Natasha?
2. What chance does she have of earning a satisfactory return if she invests her $15,000 in (a) blue-chip stocks, (b) growth stocks, (c) speculative stocks, (d) corporate bonds, or (e) municipal bonds?
3. Discuss the factors you would consider when analyzing these alternate investment vehicles.
4. What recommendation would you make to Natasha regarding her available investment alternatives? Explain.

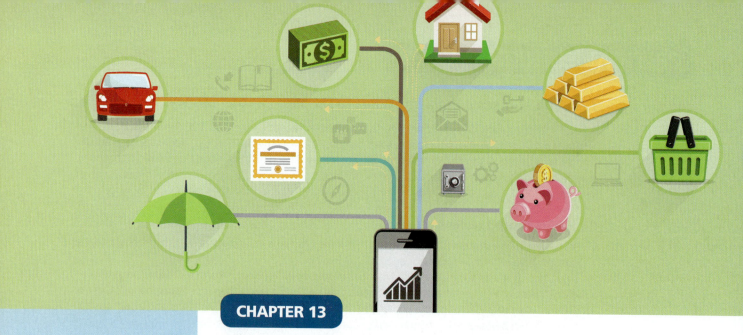

CHAPTER 13

Investing in Mutual Funds, ETFs, and Real Estate

LEARNING GOALS

LG1 Describe the basic features and operating characteristics of mutual funds and exchange-traded funds.

LG2 Differentiate between open- and closed-end mutual funds as well as exchange-traded funds, and discuss the various types of fund loads and charges.

LG3 Discuss the types of funds available to investors and the different kinds of investor services offered by mutual funds and exchange-traded funds.

LG4 Gain an understanding of the variables that should be considered when selecting funds for investment purposes.

LG5 Identify the sources of return and calculate the rate of return earned on an investment in a mutual fund, as well as evaluate the performance of an exchange-traded fund.

LG6 Understand the role that real estate plays in a diversified investment portfolio, along with the basics of investing in real estate, either directly or indirectly.

How Will This Affect Me?

Having a financial plan, and being aware that diversification is crucial is a great start to the task of investment planning. The next step is figuring out how to implement your plan by deciding what to invest in. For most people, diversification is best achieved using mutual funds and exchange-traded funds (ETFs). This chapter describes the key characteristics of each type of fund, sorts through the various options you have, shows how to calculate rates of return and evaluate performance, and explains how to choose among funds. The essential elements of investing in real estate and its role in diversifying your overall investment portfolio are also covered. After reading this chapter, you should be in a good position to invest in mutual funds, ETFs, and real estate in a way that will help you achieve your financial objectives.

Financial Facts or Fantasies?

Are the following statements Financial Facts (true) or Fantasies (false)? Consider the answers to the questions below as you read through this chapter.

- When a mutual fund is open-ended, it means there's no limit on the returns an investor can realize.
- Online and phone switching are services that enable you to move money from one fund to another, so long as you stay within the same family of funds.
- While exchange-traded funds (ETFs) offer many of the benefits of mutual funds, they have tax-timing disadvantages not present with otherwise comparable mutual funds.
- In many types of real estate investments, appreciation in the value of the property affects return more than annual rental income.
- A real estate investment trust (REIT) is a popular form of limited partnership that enables individuals to invest directly in income-producing property.

13-1 MUTUAL FUNDS AND EXCHANGE-TRADED FUNDS: SOME BASICS

LG1, LG2

Sound investment planning involves finding investments with risk–return characteristics that are compatible with your financial objectives. In this chapter, we'll look beyond stocks and bonds and consider other types of investment products that enjoy widespread use among individual investors: mutual funds, exchange-traded funds (ETFs), and real estate. These investment outlets offer risk–return opportunities that you may not be able to obtain from just buying stocks or bonds on your own. For example, investors interested in receiving the benefits of professional portfolio management, but who don't have the funds to purchase a diversified portfolio of securities, may find mutual funds attractive. ETFs, on the other hand, are similar to mutual funds but offer a degree of flexibility that standard mutual funds don't have. Still other investors may be drawn to real estate, either because of its perceived return potential or perhaps to obtain some preferential tax treatment. Let's now take a closer look at each of these investments.

mutual fund
A financial services organization that receives money from its shareholders and invests those funds on their behalf in a diversified portfolio of securities.

A **mutual fund** is a financial services organization that receives money from its shareholders and invests those funds on their behalf in a diversified portfolio of securities. An **exchange-traded fund (ETF)** is an investment company whose shares trade on stock exchanges. Unlike mutual funds, ETF shares can be bought or sold (or sold short) throughout the day. When investors buy shares in a mutual fund or an ETF, they usually become *part owners of a widely diversified portfolio of securities*. A mutual fund or an ETF share can be thought of as the *financial product* that's sold to the public by an investment company. That is, the investment company builds and manages a portfolio of securities and sells ownership interests—shares of stock—in that portfolio through a vehicle known as a mutual fund. This concept underlies the whole mutual fund structure and is depicted in Exhibit 13.1. For individual investors today, mutual funds are the investment vehicle of choice. In fact, more people invest in mutual funds than any other type of investment product.

exchange-traded fund (ETF)
An investment company whose shares trade on stock exchanges; unlike mutual funds, ETF shares can be bought or sold (or sold short) throughout the day. ETFs are usually structured as an index fund that's set up to match the performance of a certain market segment.

Mutual funds are popular because they offer not only a variety of interesting investment opportunities, but also a wide array of services that many investors find appealing. They're an easy and convenient way to invest—one that's especially suited to beginning investors and those with limited investment capital. And as we'll see later in the chapter, ETFs have become an increasingly popular alternative to mutual funds.

EXHIBIT 13.1 **Basic Mutual Fund Structure**

A mutual fund brings together the funds from many individual investors and uses this pool of money to acquire a diversified portfolio of stocks, bonds, and other securities.

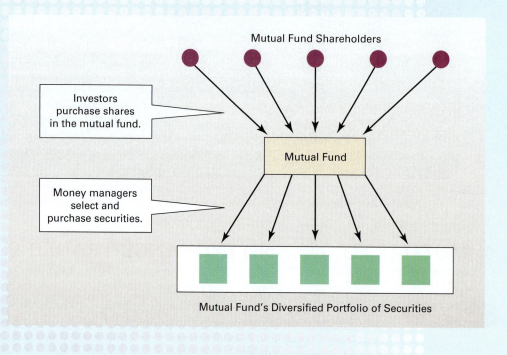

13-1a The Mutual Fund Concept

The first mutual fund in this country was started in Boston in 1924. By 1980, 564 mutual funds were in operation. But that was only the beginning—by the end of 2014, mutual fund assets under management grew to some $15.9 trillion in the United States. Indeed, in 2014, *there were nearly 8,000 publicly traded mutual funds in the United States*. Actually, counting duplicate or multiple fund offerings from the same investment company, there were closer to *30,000 funds* available; such duplication occurs because sometimes two or three versions of the same fund are offered, with each "fund" having a different type of load charge or fee structure. To put that number in perspective, *there are more mutual funds in existence today than there are stocks listed on all the stock exchanges in the United States!*

Mutual funds are big business in the United States and, indeed, all over the world. In 2014, registered investment companies managed 24 percent of households' financial assets, and about 53.2 million, or about 43 percent, of those households owned mutual funds. Mutual funds appeal to a lot of investors, who all share one view: they've decided, for one reason or another, to turn the problems of security selection and portfolio management over to professional money managers. Questions of which stock or bond to select, when to buy, and when to sell have plagued investors for about as long as there have been organized securities markets. Such concerns lie at the heart of the mutual fund concept and are largely behind the growth in funds. The fact is that many people simply lack the time, the know-how, or the commitment to manage their own securities, so they turn to others. And most often, that means mutual funds.

Pooled Diversification

The mutual fund concept is based on the simple idea of delegating security selection and portfolio management to professional money managers. A mutual fund combines the investment capital of many people with similar investment goals and invests those funds in a wide variety of securities. Investors receive shares of stock in the mutual fund and, through the fund, enjoy much wider investment diversification than they could otherwise achieve. Indeed, some mutual funds commonly hold hundreds of different stocks or bonds. For example, in the middle of 2015, the Fidelity Contrafund held about 319 different securities, and the Dreyfus GNMA bond fund had about 830 holdings. For all but the super-rich, that's far more diversification than most investors could ever hope to attain. Yet each investor who owns shares in a fund is, in effect, a part owner of that fund's diversified portfolio of securities.

Regardless of the fund size, as the securities held by it move up and down in price, the market value of the mutual fund shares moves accordingly. And when the fund receives dividend and interest payments, they too are passed on to the mutual fund shareholders and distributed on the basis of prorated ownership. For example, if you own 1,000 shares of stock in a mutual fund and that represents, say, 1 percent of all shares outstanding, then you would receive 1 percent of the dividends paid by the fund. When a security held by the fund is sold for a profit, the capital gain is also passed on to fund shareholders. The whole mutual fund idea, in fact, rests on the concept of **pooled diversification** and works much like insurance, whereby individuals pool their resources for the collective benefit of all contributors.

pooled diversification
A process whereby investors buy into a diversified portfolio of securities for the collective benefit of individual investors.

13-1b Why Invest in Mutual Funds or ETFs?

Mutual funds and ETFs can be used by individual investors in various ways. One investor may buy a fund because of the substantial capital gains opportunities that it provides; another may buy a totally different fund not for its capital gains, but instead for its current income. Whatever kind of income a fund provides, individuals tend to use these investment vehicles for one or more of these reasons: (1) to achieve diversification in their investment holdings, (2) to obtain the services of professional money managers, (3) to generate an attractive rate of return on their investment capital, and (4) for the convenience that they offer.

Diversification

As we just discussed, diversification is a primary motive for investing in mutual funds and ETFs. This ability to diversify allows investors to reduce their exposure to risk sharply by indirectly investing in several types of securities and numerous companies, rather than just one or two. If you have only $500 or $1,000 to invest, you obviously won't achieve much diversification on your own. But if you invest that money in a mutual fund or an ETF, you'll end up owning part of a well-diversified portfolio of securities.

Professional Management

While management is paid a fee for its services, the contributions of a full-time expert manager should be well worth the fee. These pros know where to look for return and how to avoid unnecessary risk; at the minimum, their decisions should result in better returns than the average individual investor can achieve.

Financial Returns

Although professional managers *may* be able to achieve better returns than small investors can generate, the relatively high purchase fees, coupled with the management and operating costs, tend to reduce the returns actually earned on mutual fund investments. But the mutual fund industry hasn't attracted millions of investors by generating substandard returns. Quite the contrary; over the long haul, mutual funds have provided relatively attractive returns. Exhibit 13.2 shows the average return performance on a

EXHIBIT 13.2

Comparative Performance of Selected Mutual Funds Categories by Holding Period: 2011–2015

The type of fund you invest in and your holding period have a lot to do with the kind of return you can expect. While the selected funds below are sorted by 5-year returns within each fund type, it is clear that the 1- and 3-year returns can be substantially different as well.

Fund Type	Average Annual Returns (%)		
	1 Year	3 Year	5 Year
Domestic Sector Stock Funds			
Consumer defensive	12.74	16.51	15.97
Health	40.62	33.25	25.80
Consumer cyclical	16.10	20.64	18.45
Technology	20.14	19.71	15.94
Real estate	12.72	12.04	14.12
Utilities	6.32	13.60	13.83
Industrials	7.50	20.67	16.26
Natural resources	−13.40	3.20	4.29
Equity energy	−18.81	5.57	4.92
Communications	7.15	15.14	13.24
Financial	10.27	19.40	11.48
Allocation Funds			
Convertibles	7.51	13.89	11.08
World allocation	2.97	8.92	8.68
International Stock Funds			
Pacific/Asia ex-Japan stock	10.80	11.98	9.39
Latin America stock	−20.34	−5.30	−2.85
Europe stock	0.51	15.96	11.86
Fixed-Income Funds			
Long-term government	8.00	1.59	6.56
High-yield bond	1.19	7.05	8.18
Inflation-protected bond	−1.54	−1.04	2.67
Intermediate-term bond	2.34	2.82	4.08
Short-term government	0.70	0.38	0.98

Source: Adapted from http://news.morningstar.com/fund-category-returns/, accessed May 2015. The Morningstar data contained herein (1) is proprietary to Morningstar; (2) may not be copied or distributed without written permission; and (3) is not warranted to be accurate, complete, or timely. Morningstar is not responsible for any damages or losses arising from any use of this information and has not granted its consent to be considered or deemed an "expert" under the Securities Act of 1933.

variety of mutual funds and suggests the kind of returns that investors were able to achieve over one-, three-, and five-year holding periods ending in May 2015. Given the range of returns across the different fund types and holding periods, it's clear that investors should do their homework before putting money into mutual funds.

Convenience

Mutual fund shares can be purchased from various sources, which is another reason for their appeal. Mutual funds make it easy to invest, and most don't require much capital to get started. They handle all the paperwork and recordkeeping, their prices are widely quoted, and it's usually possible to deal in fractional shares. Opening a mutual fund account is about as easy as opening a checking account. Just fill out an investor form, send in the minimum amount of money, and you're in business!

13-1c How Mutual Funds Are Organized and Run

Although it's tempting to think of a mutual fund as a monolithic entity, that's really not the case. Various functions—investing, recordkeeping, safekeeping, and others—are split among two or more companies. Besides the fund itself, which is organized as a separate corporation or trust and *is owned by the shareholders*, there are several other major players.

- The *management company* runs the fund's daily operations. These include the firms such as Fidelity, Vanguard, and T. Rowe Price. Usually, the management firm also serves as the investment advisor.
- The *investment advisor* buys and sells the stocks or bonds and otherwise oversees the portfolio. Three parties participate in this phase of the operation: the *portfolio manager*, who actually runs the portfolio and makes the buy and sell decisions; *securities analysts*, who analyze securities and look for attractive investment candidates; and *traders*, who try to buy and sell blocks of securities at the best possible price.
- The *distributor* sells the fund shares, either directly to the public or through certain authorized dealers (such as major brokerage houses and commercial banks).
- The *custodian* physically safeguards the securities and other assets of a fund, but without taking an active role in the investment decisions. To discourage foul play, an independent party (such as a bank) serves in this capacity.
- The *transfer agent* executes transactions, keeps track of purchase and redemption requests from shareholders, and maintains other shareholder records.

All this separation of duties is designed for just one thing—to protect the mutual fund investor/shareholder. Obviously, you can always lose money if your fund's stock or bond holdings go down in value. But that's really the only risk of loss you face, because the chance of ever losing money from fraud or a mutual fund collapse is almost nonexistent. Besides the separation of duties noted earlier, the only formal link between the mutual fund and the management company is a contract that must be regularly renewed—and approved by shareholders. The fund's assets *can never be in the hands of the management company*. As still another safeguard, each fund must have a board of directors, or trustees, who are elected by shareholders and charged with keeping tabs on the management company and renewing its contract.

13-1d Open-End versus Closed-End Funds

It may seem that all mutual funds are organized in roughly the same way, but investors should be aware of some major differences. One way that funds differ is in how they are structured. Funds can be set up either as *open-end companies*, which can sell an unlimited number of ownership shares, or as *closed-end companies*, which can issue only a limited number of shares.

Open-End Investment Companies

open-end investment company
A firm that can issue an unlimited number of shares that it buys and sells at a price based on the current market value of the securities it owns; also called a *mutual fund*.

The term *mutual fund* commonly denotes an **open-end investment company**. Such organizations are the dominant type of investment company and account for well over 95 percent of assets under management. In an open-end investment company, investors actually buy their shares from, and sell them back to, the mutual fund itself. When they buy shares in the fund, the fund issues new shares of stock and fills the purchase order with these new shares. There's no limit to the number of shares that the fund can issue, other than investor demand. Further, all open-end mutual funds stand behind their shares and buy them back when investors decide to sell. So there's never any trading among individuals. Many of these funds are huge and hold billions of dollars' worth of securities.

net asset value (NAV)
The current market value of all the securities the fund owns, less any liabilities, on a per-share basis.

Buy and sell transactions in an open-end mutual fund are carried out at prices based on the current value of all the securities held in the fund's portfolio. This is known as the fund's **net asset value (NAV)**; it is calculated at least once a day and represents the underlying value of a share of stock in a particular fund. NAV is found by taking the total market value of all securities held by the fund, subtracting any liabilities, and dividing the result by the number of shares outstanding. The NAV would be used to derive the price at which the fund's shares could be bought and sold. (As we'll see later, NAV is generally included in the fund's quoted price and indicates the price at which an investor can *sell shares*—or the price that an investor would pay to *buy no-load funds*.)

EXAMPLE: Calculating a Mutual Fund's NAV

On a recent day, the market value of all the securities held by the XYZ mutual fund equaled $10 million and XYZ had 500,000 shares outstanding. Consequently, the fund's NAV per share would be $20, which is calculated as:

$$\frac{\text{Total Market Value of All Securities} - \text{Liabilities}}{\text{Number of Shares Outstanding}} = \frac{\$10,000,000}{500,000}$$

Closed-End Investment Companies

closed-end investment company
An investment company that issues a fixed number of shares, which are themselves listed and traded like any other share of stock.

The term *mutual fund* is supposed to be used only with open-end funds, but as a practical matter, it's regularly used with closed-end investment companies as well. Basically, **closed-end investment companies** operate with a fixed number of shares outstanding and do *not* regularly issue new shares of stock. In effect, they are like any other corporation, except that the corporation's business happens to be investing in marketable securities. Like open-end funds, closed-end investment companies have enjoyed remarkable growth in the past decade or so. Only 34 of these funds existed in 1980. By the end of 2014, there were about 570 closed-end funds with total net assets of $289 billion—though still just a fraction of the $15.9 trillion invested in the mutual fund industry. Shares in closed-end investment companies are actively traded in the secondary market, just like any other common stock; but unlike open-end funds, *all trading is done between investors in the open market*. The fund itself plays no role in either buy or sell transactions; once the shares are issued, the fund is out of the picture.

There are some major differences that exist between open- and closed-end funds. Because closed-end funds have a fixed amount of capital to work with, they don't have to worry about stock redemptions or new money coming into the fund. So they don't have to be concerned about keeping cash on hand to meet redemptions. Equally important, because closed-end funds don't have new money flowing in all the time, they don't have to worry about finding new investments for that money. Instead, they can concentrate on a set portfolio of securities and do the best job they can in managing it. The share prices of closed-end companies are determined not only by their NAVs, but also by general supply-and-demand conditions in the market. Depending on the market outlook and investor expectations, closed-end companies generally trade at a *discount* or *premium* to their NAVs.

13-1e ETFs

Combine some of the operating characteristics of an open-end fund with some of the trading characteristics of a closed-end fund, and you'll end up with something called an *ETF*. As defined above, an ETF is an investment company whose shares trade on one of the stock exchanges. Most all ETFs are structured as *index funds*, set up to match the performance of a certain market segment. They do this by owning all or a representative sample of the stocks (or bonds) in a targeted market segment or index (we'll examine traditional index funds in more detail later in this chapter). Thus, ETFs offer the professional money management of traditional mutual funds and the liquidity of an exchange-traded stock.

However, the passive indexing of early ETFs is giving way to the creation of actively managed ETFs.

As pointed out in Chapter 11, *exchange-traded notes (ETNs)* are more similar to ETFs than to mutual funds. Like ETFs, most ETNs are designed to reproduce the returns on a market benchmark, net of investment management fees. Also like ETFs, ETNs provide tax advantages over mutual funds. However, they differ from ETFs in being senior, unsecured, unsubordinated debt securities issued by an underwriting bank. While our discussion in this chapter focuses on ETFs, ETNs are in many cases close, but not perfect substitutes for ETFs. ETNs should consequently be kept in mind when you choose among the different investments that can help you achieve your financial goals.

Even though ETFs are like closed-end funds (they're traded on listed exchanges), *they are actually open-end mutual funds* whose number of shares outstanding can be increased or decreased in response to market demand. That is, ETFs can be bought or sold like any other stock, and *the ETF distributor can also create new shares or redeem old shares*. This is done to prevent the fund from trading at (much of) a premium or discount to the underlying value of its holdings, thereby avoiding a pitfall of closed-end funds. In 1998, there were only 29 ETFs in the United States, with about $16 billion under management. By the end of 2014, there were over 1,400 ETFs in existence, with assets under management of nearly $2.0 trillion. ETFs have become more popular as institutional investors use them to exploit or hedge against broad movements in the stock market. It's estimated that about 4 percent (5.2 million) of U.S. households owned ETFs in 2014. About 9 percent of households that own mutual funds also own ETFs.

These funds cover a wide array of domestic and international stock indexes and submarkets as well as a handful of U.S. Treasury and corporate bond indexes. The biggest and oldest ETFs (dating back to 1993) are based on the S&P 500 and are known as *Spiders* (SPDRs). In addition, there are *Qubes* (based on the NASDAQ 100; this is the most actively traded ETF—in fact, it's the most actively traded stock in the world), *Diamonds* (based on the DJIA), and ETFs based on dozens of international markets (from Australia and Canada to Germany, Japan, and the United Kingdom). Just about every major U.S. index, in fact, has its own ETF, along with lots of minor indexes covering specialized market segments. The NAVs of ETFs are set at a fraction of the underlying index value at any given time. In June 2015, for example, when the S&P 500 index was 2,124.20, the ETF on that index traded at $212.04 (or about 1/10 of the index); likewise, the ETF on the Dow is set at about 1/100 of the DJIA (so when the Dow closed at 18,144.07 at this time, the ETF closed at $181.12).

ETFs combine many advantages of closed-end funds with those of traditional (open-end) index funds. That is, like closed-end funds, ETFs can be bought and sold at *any time of the day;* you can place an order through your broker (and pay a standard commission, just as you would with any other stock). In contrast, you *cannot* trade a traditional open-end fund on an intraday basis because all buy and sell orders for these funds are filled, at closing prices, at the end of the trading day. What's more, because most ETFs are passively managed, they offer all the advantages of any index fund: low costs, low portfolio turnover, and low taxes. The fund's tax liability is kept low because ETFs rarely distribute any capital gains to shareholders. However, actively managed ETFs could well have higher costs, portfolio turnover, and taxes than passively managed ETFs. It remains to be seen whether actively managed ETFs will take significant market share away from mutual funds.

There are many types of ETFs. The most common type tracks a major market index like the S&P 500 or the NASDAQ-100 index. Foreign market ETFs track non-U.S. market indexes, like Japan's Nikkei index or the MSCI index for Germany. Foreign-currency ETFs provide exposure to an individual foreign currency or to a basket to currencies. There are also sector and industry ETFs that allow investors access to specific segments of the market like high-tech or

pharmaceuticals. ETFs also provide exposure to commodities like gold or oil. You can even buy ETFs that invest in real estate, or are composed of derivatives like options and futures. *Style* ETFs typically follow either certain market capitalization stocks (small-, mid-, or large-cap) or value or growth stocks. The latter types of ETFs are often tied to style indexes developed by S&P, BARRA, or Frank Russell. There are also ETFs that track bonds. The trend toward customization of ETFs even provides inverse ETFs that effectively create short positions. These ETFs appreciate in value when the market falls, and vice versa. There are also a variety of new innovations that include actively managed ETFs and leveraged ETFs. As the name suggests, an actively managed ETF manages assets toward a goal of outperforming, rather than merely tracking, a given index. Leveraged ETFs seek to outperform a benchmark, which is usually achieved by using derivatives like options, futures, and swaps. If you're thinking that this can be extremely risky, you're right. Innovation continues in the ETF market to provide investors with more choices so that they can either moderate or enhance their risk exposure. Exhibit 13.3 lists some available ETFs.

13-1f Some Important Cost Considerations

When you buy or sell shares in a *closed-end* investment company, or in *ETFs* for that matter, you pay a commission just as you would with any other type of listed or over the counter (OTC) common stock transaction. This isn't so with *open-end* funds, however. In particular, the cost of investing in an open-end mutual fund depends on the types of fees and load charges that the fund levies on its investors.

Load Funds

load fund
A fund that charges a fee at time of purchase.

Most open-end mutual funds are so-called **load funds** because they charge a commission *when the shares are purchased* (such charges are often referred to as *front-end loads*). However, few funds today charge the maximum. Instead, many funds charge commissions of only 2 percent or 3 percent—such funds are known as **low-load funds**. The good news on front-end load funds is that there's normally no charge or commission to pay when you *sell* your shares! Occasionally, however, you'll run into funds that charge a commission—or a *redemption fee*—when you sell your shares. Known as **back-end load** funds, these charges tend to decline over time and usually disappear altogether after five or six years. The purpose of such charges is to discourage investors from trading in and out of the funds over short periods of time. According to the latest regulations, a mutual fund cannot charge more than 8.5 percent in *total sales charges and fees*, and that includes front- and back-end loads, as well as 12b-1 fees, which will be discussed later in the chapter. This means that, if a fund charges a 5 percent front-end load and a 1 percent 12b-1 fee, then it can charge a maximum of only 2.5 percent in back-end load charges—otherwise, it will violate the 8.5 percent cap.

low-load fund
A fund that has a low purchase fee.

back-end load
A commission charged for redeeming fund shares.

No-Load Funds

no-load fund
A fund on which no transaction fees are charged.

Some open-end investment companies charge you nothing at all to buy their funds; these are known as **no-load funds**. Less than half of the funds sold today are true no-loads; all the rest charge some type of load or fee. Even funds that don't have front-end loads (and so may be categorized as no-loads) can have back-end load charges that you must pay when selling your fund shares—or something called a 12b-1 fee, which you'd pay for as long as you hold your shares.

Behavior Matters

Behavioral Biases in Mutual Fund Investing

In theory, rational investors should pursue a simple investment strategy that involves well-diversified, low-expense mutual funds, accompanied by only minimal portfolio rebalancing. The time-tested approach is to choose index mutual funds with low fees and low portfolio turnover. In contrast, current research indicates that many individual investors exhibit the following puzzling behaviors:

- Investors tend to sell winners too quickly and hold losers too long.

- Investors often buy mutual funds with high fees and even pay high fees for index funds that passively hold the components of indexes like the S&P 500.

- Individual investors often chase funds with high past returns.

What does behavioral finance research have to say about the above biased behavior?

- **Disposition effect.** People dislike taking losses much more than they enjoy realizing gains. Consequently, they tend to hold assets that have lost value too long and tend to take gains too soon. In mutual fund investing, this bias may encourage some investors to overestimate their expected holding periods and mistakenly select high-expense (front-end load) funds, the effect of which declines with the expected holding period. This often leads to overly frequent trading.

- **Narrow framing.** It's possible that investors buy and sell mutual funds without adequately considering the effects of the costs on their *total* portfolio. Similarly, if investors tend to view mutual funds as much safer than buying individual stocks, they may spend less time than they should evaluating mutual fund performance and costs.

- **Representativeness.** There is evidence that investors view recent performance as overly representative of a mutual fund's future performance (despite those warning statements we've probably all seen if we've read a prospectus). This could cause them to buy mutual funds inappropriately, just because of their past records. This bias may be partially explained by investor services companies' ratings of funds based on *past* returns.

So what's the remedy for the above behavioral biases? The answer is clear: education! There is evidence that sophisticated investors are far less likely to fall into these behavioral traps. "Sophisticated" investors are better informed about key investment principles, understand these behavioral tendencies, are more experienced, and have higher incomes. They use mutual funds effectively, which means that they hold most funds for a long time, avoid high expense funds, and consequently enjoy relatively good performance. And based on what you now know, this could be you.

Source: Adapted from Warren Bailey, Alok Kumar, and David Ng, 2011, "Behavioral Biases of Mutual Fund Investors," *Journal of Financial Economics*, v. 102, pp. 1–27.

12b-1 Fees

12b-1 fee
An annual fee that's supposed to be used to offset promotion and selling expenses.

Also known as *hidden loads*, **12b-1 fees** are allowed by the Securities and Exchange Commission (SEC) and were originally designed to help no-load funds cover their distribution and marketing expenses. Unsurprisingly, the popularity of these fees spread rapidly among fund distributors, so they're now used by nearly 70 percent of all open-end mutual funds. The fees are assessed annually and can amount to as much as 1 percent of assets under management. In good markets and bad, the fee is paid right off the top—and that takes its toll. Consider, for instance, $10,000 in a fund that charges a 1 percent 12b-1 fee. That translates into an annual charge of *$100 a year*, which is a significant amount of money. The SEC set a 1 percent

Examples of Exchange-Traded Funds (ETFs)

The ETF market remains dominated by products that seek to track various domestic and international indexes. However, actively managed ETFs that focus on selecting and trading a dynamic mix of securities are growing. Below are representative examples of available ETFs.

Type of ETF	Ticker	Tracking Goal
U.S. Equity Indexes		
SPDR S&P 500 ETF	SPY	S&P 500 index.
PowerShares QQQ Trust, Ser 1	QQQ	Nasdaq-100 index.
SPDR Dow Jones Industrial Average ETF	DIA	Dow Jones Industrial Average index.
iShares Russell 2000	IWM	Russell 2000 index.
Vanguard Total Stock market ETF	VTI	Overall stock market.
U.S. Equity Sector Indexes		
Energy Select Sector SPDR ETF*	XLE	Energy Select Sector Index.
Financial Select Sector SPDR ETF	XLF	Financial Select Sector Index.
Technology Select Sector SPDR ETF	XLK	Technology Select Sector Index.
U.S. Bond Market		
iShares Core U.S. Aggregate Bond ETF	AGG	Index of U.S. investment-grade bond market.
Vanguard Short-Term Bond ETF	BSV	Market-weighted bond index with short-term dollar-weighted average maturity.
iShares Core 10+ Year USD Bond ETF	ILTB	Index of U.S. dollar-denominated, investment-grade U.S. corporate and government bonds with maturities of at least 10 years.
International Markets		
MSCI EAFE ETF	EFA	MSCI European, Australasian, and Far Eastern "EAFE" Index.
iShares MSCI Emerging Markets ETF	EEM	MSCI Emerging Markets Index.
Actively Managed Funds		
PIMCO Enhanced Short Maturity Active ETF	MINT	Seeks greater income and total return than money market funds.
PowerShares Active U.S. Real Estate ETF	PSR	Selects securities in the FTSE NAREIT Equity REIT index
iShares Enhanced U.S. Small-Cap ETF	IESM	Pursues long-term capital gains by investing in U.S. small cap stocks

*SPDRS are available on all of the S&P 500 sectors as well as on variously defined industries.

cap on annual 12b-1 fees and, perhaps more significantly, stated that true no-load funds cannot charge more than 0.25 percent in annual 12b-1 fees (otherwise, they must drop the "no-load" label in their sales and promotional material).

A trend in mutual fund fees is the *multiple-class sales charge*. You'll find such arrangements at firms like Dreyfus, Merrill Lynch, MFS, Scudder, Putnam, and others. The way it works is that the mutual fund will issue different classes of shares on the same fund or portfolio of securities. So, rather than having just one class of stock outstanding, there might be three of them: Class A shares might have normal (modest) front-end loads; Class B stock might have no front-end loads but substantial back-end loads along with maximum annual 12b-1 fees; and Class C shares might carry a small back-end load and modest 12b-1 fees. In other words, you pick your own poison.

Management Fees

management fee
A fee paid to the professional money managers who administer a mutual fund's portfolio.

The **management fee** is the cost that you incur to hire professional money managers to run the fund's portfolio of investments. These fees are also assessed annually and usually range from less than 0.5 percent to as much as 3 percent or 4 percent of assets under management. All funds—whether they're load or no-load, open- or closed-end—have these fees; and, like 12b-1 fees, they bear watching because high management fees will take their toll on performance. The size of the management fee is usually unrelated to the fund's performance. In addition to these management fees, some funds may charge an *exchange fee* whenever an investor transfers money from one fund to another within the same fund family and/or an *annual maintenance fee* to help defer the costs of providing service to low-balance accounts.

Keeping Track of Fund Fees and Loads

Fortunately, steps have been taken to bring fund fees and loads out into the open. For one thing, fund charges are more widely reported now than they were in the past. Most notably, today you can find detailed information about the types and amounts of fees and charges on just about any mutual fund by going to one of the dozens of Internet sites that report on mutual funds, including **Quicken.com, Kiplinger.com, Morningstar.com,** Yahoo! (at **http://finance.yahoo.com**), and a host of others. Or you could use the mutual fund quotes that appear daily in (most) major newspapers and in *The Wall Street Journal*. For example, take a look at *The Wall Street Journal*'s online quotations in Exhibit 13.4; right after the (abbreviated) name of the fund, you'll often find the letters *r*, *p*, or *t*. If you see an *r* after a fund's name, it means that the fund charges some type of redemption fee, or back-end load, when you sell your shares. The use of a *p* means the fund levies a 12b-1 fee. Finally, a *t* indicates funds that charge redemption fees *and* 12b-1 fees. The quotations, of course, tell you only *what kinds of fees* are charged by the funds; they don't tell you *how much* is charged. What's more, these quotes *tell you nothing about the front-end loads*, if any, charged by the funds. You can access Internet (or other) sources to find out whether a particular fund charges a front-end load or to obtain specifics on any amounts charged.

Mutual funds are required by the SEC to *disclose fully* all their fees and expenses in a standardized, easy-to-understand format. Every fund prospectus must contain, right up front, a fairly detailed *fee table*, much like the one illustrated in Exhibit 13.5. Notice that this table has three parts. The first specifies all *shareholder transaction costs*. This section tells you what it's going to cost to buy and sell shares in the mutual fund. The next section lists all *annual operating expenses* of the fund. Showing these expenses as a percentage of average net assets, the fund must break out management fees, those elusive 12b-1 fees, and any other expenses. The third section gives the *total*

EXHIBIT 13.4 Mutual Fund Quotes

Open-end mutual funds are listed separately from other securities and have their own quotation system; an example is shown here in online quotes from *The Wall Street Journal*. Note that these securities are also quoted in dollars and cents and that the quotes include not only the fund's NAV but also year-to-date (YTD) returns. Also included as part of the quotes is an indication of whether the fund charges redemption and/or 12b-1 fees.

Family/Fund	Symbol	NAV	Chg	YTD % return	3-year % chg
American Century A					
CorePls p	ACCQX	10.87	–0.01	0.9	2.2
EmgMktA t	AEMMX	9.31	0.04	11.9	9.6
Growth p	TCRAX	29.68	...	5.7	16.7
IntlBnd t	AIBDX	12.41	–0.10	–5.1	–3.5
LtTf	MMBAX	11.41	0.01	–0.5	0.01
Artisan Funds					
EmgMktsInv	ARTZX	13.03	0.04	8.9	13.03
EmgMktsInst	APHEX	12.93	0.03	8.7	5.3
IntlVal Inv	ARTKX	36.81	–0.21	7.6	18.8
MidCapInv	ARTMX	48.20	–0.01	6.1	17.9
MidCapVal Inv	ARTQX	25.61	–0.07	3.9	16.5
SmCapVal Inv	ARTVX	14.30	–0.09	1.1	8.0
ValueInv	ARTLX	13.87	–0.04	6.0	15.4

American Century Core Plus Fund, class A shares; a fund with a front-end load fee (p).

American Century Emerging Markets, class A shares; a fund with both 12b-1 and front-end load fees (t).

American Century International Bond Fund, class A shares; a fund with a front-end load fee and possible redemption fee (p).

American Century Long-Term Tax-Free Fund, class A shares; a fund with a front-end fee (p).

Artisan International Value Fund; a true no-load fund (no front-end, back-end, or 12b-1 fees)

p—Distribution costs apply, 12b-1.

r—Redemption charge may apply.

t—Footnotes p and r apply.

Source: The Wall Street Journal, http://online.wsj.com/mdc/public/page/2_3048-usmfunds_A-usmfunds.html, accessed May 22, 2015; NAV-net asset value. Chg-change in NAV from previous trading day. 3-year % chg-is trailing three-year annualized.

cost over time of buying, selling, and owning the fund. This part of the table contains both transaction and operating expenses and shows what the total costs would be over hypothetical 1-, 3-, 5-, and 10-year holding periods. To ensure consistency and comparability, the funds must follow a rigid set of guidelines when presenting the example costs.

13-1g Buying and Selling Funds

Buying and selling shares of closed-end investment companies or ETFs is no different from buying shares of common stock. The transactions are executed through brokers or dealers who handle the orders in the usual way. They're subject to the normal transaction costs, and because they're treated like any other listed or OTC stock, their shares can even be margined or sold short, which are discussed in Chapter 11.

The situation is considerably different, however, with *open-end funds*. Such funds can be bought through a discount or full-service broker or directly from the mutual fund company itself. And, of course, at most funds, you can open an account online. Once your account is open and the company has your initial deposit, you are ready to buy shares. Selling shares in a fund is a do-it-yourself affair that simply requires

EXHIBIT 13.5   Example of a Mutual Fund Fee Table

The SEC requires mutual funds to disclose fully load charges, redemption fees, and annual expenses in a three-part table like the one shown here. The table must be conspicuously placed near the front of the prospectus, not hidden somewhere in the back.

Fee table

The following table describes the fees and expenses that are incurred when you buy, hold, or sell shares of the fund.

Shareholder fees (paid by the investor directly)

Maximum sales charge (load) on purchases (as a % of offering price)	3.00
Sales charge (load) on reinvested distributions	None
Deferred sales charge (load) on redemptions	None
Exchange fees	None
Annual account maintenance fee (for accounts under $2,500)	$12.00

Annual fund operating expenses (paid from fund assets)

Management fee	0.45%
Distribution and service (12b-1) fee	None
Other expenses	0.20%
Total annual fund operating expenses	0.65%

Example

This example is intended to help an investor compare the cost of investing in different funds. The example assumes a $10,000 investment in the fund for 1, 3, 5, and 10 years and then redemption of all fund shares at the end of those periods. The example also assumes that an investment returns 5 percent each year and that the fund's operating expenses remain the same. Although actual costs may be higher or lower, based on these assumptions an investor's costs would be:

1 year	$ 364
3 years	$ 502
5 years	$ 651
10 years	$1,086

using an online account or an 800 telephone number. When selling, it is wise to see if your company offers the ability to switch funds. A common feature is the ability to go online (or pick up the phone) to move money from one fund to another—the only constraint is that the funds must be managed by the same "family" of funds. Most companies charge little or nothing for these shifts, although funds that offer free exchange privileges often limit the number of times you can switch each year. (We'll discuss this service in more detail when we cover *conversion privileges* later in the chapter.)

Should you want more information than what is provided in either the profile or prospectus, you can always request a copy of the fund's *Statement of Additional Information*, which contains detailed information on the fund's investment objectives, portfolio composition, management, and past performance. Whether it's the fund profile (which should be good enough for most investors), the fund's prospectus, or its Statement of Additional Information, the bottom line is these publications should be required reading for anybody who's thinking about investing in a mutual fund.

13-2 TYPES OF FUNDS AND FUND SERVICES

Categorizing mutual funds and ETFs according to their investment policies and objectives is widely practiced in the investment industry. This is because it tends to reflect similarities not only in how the funds manage their money, but also in their risk and return characteristics. Every fund has a particular stated investment objective, of which the most common are capital appreciation, income, tax-exempt income, preserving investment capital, or some combination thereof. Some popular types of mutual funds include growth, aggressive growth, value, equity-income, balanced, growth-and-income, bond, money market, index, sector, socially responsible, international, and asset allocation funds. Disclosure of a fund's investment objective is required by the SEC, and each fund is expected to conform to its stated investment policy and objective. Let's now look at these funds to see what they are and what they have to offer investors. After that, we'll look at the kinds of investor services these funds offer.

13-2a Types of Funds

Growth Funds

The objective of a *growth fund* is simple—capital appreciation. Long-term growth and capital gains are the primary goals of such funds, so they invest principally in common stocks with above-average growth potential. Because of the uncertainty concerning their future capital gains, growth funds involve a fair amount of risk exposure. They're usually viewed as long-term investment vehicles that are most suitable for the aggressive investor who wants to build capital and has little interest in current income.

Aggressive Growth Funds

Aggressive growth funds are highly speculative investments that seek large profits from capital gains; in many ways, they're really an extension of the growth fund concept. Many are fairly small with average assets under management of less than $300 million. Also known as "capital appreciation" funds, they often buy stocks of small, unseasoned companies; stocks with relatively high price/earnings multiples; and stocks whose prices are highly volatile. Some of these funds even go so far as to buy stocks on margin by borrowing part of the purchase price. Such leverage is designed to yield big returns. However, aggressive growth funds are perhaps the most volatile of all the fund types. When the markets are good, these funds do well; when the markets are bad, they typically experience substantial losses.

Value Funds

Value funds invest in stocks considered to be *undervalued* in the market. Consequently, the funds look for stocks that are fundamentally sound but have yet to be discovered, and as such, remain undervalued by the market. In stark contrast to growth funds, value funds look for stocks with relatively low price/earnings (P/E) ratios, high dividend yields, and moderate amounts of financial leverage. They prefer undiscovered companies that offer the *potential* for growth, rather than those that are already experiencing rapid growth. Value investing involves extensive evaluation of corporate financial statements and any other documents that will help fund managers *uncover value (i.e., investment opportunities) before the rest of the market does*—that's the key to getting low P/Es. And the approach seems to work. For even though value investing is generally regarded as being *less risky* than growth investing (lower P/Es, higher dividend yields, and fundamentally stronger companies all translate into reduced risk exposure), the long-term returns to investors in value funds are quite competitive with those earned from growth or even aggressive growth funds. Thus, value funds are often viewed as a viable alternative for relatively conservative investors who are looking for the attractive returns offered by common stocks, yet want to keep share price volatility and investment risk in check.

Equity-Income Funds

Equity-income funds emphasize current income, which they provide by investing primarily in high-yielding common stocks. Preserving capital is also a goal of these funds; so is increasing capital gains, although it's not their primary objective. These funds invest heavily in high-grade common stocks, some convertible securities and preferred stocks, and occasionally even junk bonds or certain types of high-grade foreign bonds. In general, because of their emphasis on dividends and current income, these funds tend to hold higher-quality securities that are subject to less price volatility than seen in the market as a whole. They're generally viewed as a fairly low-risk way of investing in stocks.

Balanced Funds

Balanced funds are so named because they tend to hold a balanced portfolio of both stocks and bonds, and they do so to generate a well-balanced return of current income and long-term capital gains. In many ways, they're like equity-income funds except that balanced funds usually put much more into fixed-income securities. Generally, they keep 30 percent to 40 percent (and sometimes more) of their portfolios in bonds. The bonds are used primarily to provide current income, and stocks are selected mainly for their long-term growth potential. The more the fund leans toward fixed-income securities, the more income-oriented it will be. Balanced funds tend to confine their investing mainly to high-grade securities and therefore are usually considered a relatively safe form of investing—one that can earn you a competitive rate of return without a lot of price volatility.

Growth-and-Income Funds

Like balanced funds, *growth-and-income funds* seek a balanced return made up of current income and long-term capital gains, but they put greater emphasis on growth of capital. Moreover, unlike balanced funds, growth-and-income funds put most of their money into equities—it's not unusual for these funds to have 80 percent to 90 percent of their capital in common stocks. They tend to confine most of their investing to high-quality issues, so you can expect to find lots of growth-oriented blue-chip stocks in their portfolios, along with a fair number of high-quality income stocks. These funds do involve a fair amount of risk, if for no other reason than their emphasis on stocks and capital gains. Growth-and-income funds are most suitable for investors who can tolerate their risk and price volatility.

Bond Funds

As their name implies, *bond funds* invest in various kinds of fixed-income securities. Income is their primary investment objective, although they don't ignore capital gains. There are three important advantages to buying shares in bond funds rather than investing directly in bonds. First, bond funds generally are more liquid; second, they offer a cost-effective way of achieving a high degree of diversification in an otherwise expensive investment (most bonds carry minimum denominations of $1,000 to $5,000 or more); and third, bond funds automatically reinvest interest and other income, thereby allowing the investor to earn fully compounded rates of return. Bond funds are considered a fairly conservative form of investment, but they're not totally without risk because the prices of the bonds held in the funds' portfolios will fluctuate with changing interest rates. In 2014, bond mutual funds had $3.46 trillion under management, while bond ETFs had about $296.4 billion under management.

No matter what your tastes, you'll find a full menu of bond funds available, including these:

- **Government bond funds,** which invest in U.S. Treasury and agency securities.
- **Mortgage-backed bond funds,** which put their money into various types of mortgage-backed securities issued by agencies of the U.S. government, such as Government National Mortgage Association (GNMA) issues. These funds appeal to investors because they provide diversification and a more affordable way to get into mortgage-backed securities. They also have a provision that allows investors (if they so choose) to reinvest the *principal* portion of the monthly cash flow—thereby enabling them to preserve, rather than consume, their capital.
- **High-grade corporate bond funds,** which invest chiefly in investment-grade securities rated BBB or better.
- **High-yield corporate bond funds,** which are risky investments that buy *junk bonds* for the yields that they offer, which can be higher than standard bonds.
- **Convertible bond funds,** which invest primarily in (domestic and possibly foreign) securities that can be converted or exchanged into common stocks. By investing in convertible bonds and preferred stocks, the funds offer investors some of the price stability of bonds, along with the capital appreciation potential of stocks.
- **Municipal bond funds,** which invest in tax-exempt securities and are suitable for investors looking for tax-free income. Like their corporate counterparts, municipals can also be in either high-grade or high-yield funds. A special type of municipal bond fund is the *single-state* fund, which invests in the municipal issues of only one state and so produces (for residents of that state) interest income that's *fully* exempt from federal taxes as well as state (and possibly even local/city) taxes.
- **Intermediate-term bond funds,** which invest in bonds with maturities of 7 to 10 years or less, and offer not only attractive yields but also relatively low price volatility. Shorter (2- to 5-year) funds are also available and can be used as substitutes for money market investments by investors looking for higher returns on their money, especially when short-term rates are way down.

Money Market Mutual Funds

Money market mutual funds invest in a widely diversified portfolio of short-term money market instruments. These funds are very popular with investors, and for good reason: They give investors with modest amounts of capital access to the higher-yielding end of the money market, where many instruments require minimum investments of $100,000 or more. Today, there are about 530 publicly traded money market funds that, together, hold nearly $2.73 *trillion* in assets.

There are several different kinds of money market mutual funds. **General-purpose money funds** invest in any and all types of money market investments, from Treasury bills to corporate commercial paper and bank certificates of deposit. They invest their

general-purpose money fund
A money fund that invests in virtually any type of short-term investment vehicle.

tax-exempt money fund
A money fund that limits its investments to short-term, tax-exempt municipal securities.

government securities money fund
A money fund that limits its investments to short-term securities of the U.S. government and its agencies.

money wherever they can find attractive short-term returns. Most money funds are of this type. The **tax-exempt money fund** limits its investments to tax-exempt municipal securities with very short (30- to 90-day) maturities. Because their income is free from federal income tax, they appeal predominantly to investors in high tax brackets. **Government securities money funds** were established as a way of meeting investors' need for safety. These funds eliminate any risk of default by confining their investments to Treasury bills and other short-term securities of the U.S. government or its agencies (such as the GNMA).

Money funds are highly liquid investment vehicles that are very low in risk because they're virtually immune to capital loss. However, the interest income they produce tends to follow interest rate conditions, so the returns to shareholders are subject to the ups and downs of market interest rates. (Money funds were discussed more fully in Chapter 4, along with other short-term investments.)

Index Funds

"If you can't beat 'em, join 'em." That's the idea behind the *index fund*, which is a type of fund that buys and holds a portfolio of stocks (or bonds) equivalent to those in a market index such as the S&P 500. An index fund that's trying to match the S&P 500, for example, would hold the same 500 stocks that are held in that index and in the same proportion. Rather than trying to beat the market, *index funds simply try to match the market*—that is, to match the performance of the index on which the fund is based. They do this through low-cost investment management. In many cases, the whole portfolio is run almost entirely by a computer that matches the fund's holdings with those of the targeted index. Besides the S&P 500, several other market indexes are used, including the S&P MidCap 400, Russell 2000, and Wilshire 5000, as well as value stock indexes, growth stock indexes, international stock indexes, and even bond indexes. While index funds form only a part of the overall mutual fund market, they comprise the vast majority of ETFs.

The approach of index funds is strictly buy and hold. About the only time there's a change to the portfolio of an index fund is when the targeted market index alters its "market basket" of securities. A pleasant by-product of this buy-and-hold approach is that the funds have low portfolio turnover rates and therefore little in *realized* capital gains. As a result, aside from a modest amount of dividend income, these funds produce little taxable income from year to year, which leads many high-income investors to view them as a type of tax-sheltered investment. But these funds provide something else—namely, they produce *highly competitive returns* for investors! It's tough to outperform the market consistently, so the index funds don't even try. The net result is that, on average, index funds tend to produce better returns than do most other types of stock funds. Granted, every now and then the fully managed funds will have a year (or two) when they outperform index funds, but those are the exception rather than the rule.

Sector Funds

As the name implies, a *sector fund* restricts its investments to a particular sector of the market. These funds concentrate their investment holdings in the one or more industries that make up the targeted sector. For example, a *health care* sector fund would confine its investments to those industries that make up this segment of the market: drug companies, hospital management firms, medical

DARREN BAKER/ DREAMSTIME.COM

suppliers, and biotech concerns. The underlying investment objective of most sector funds is *capital gains*. In many ways, they're similar to growth funds and should be considered speculative. The idea behind sector funds is that the really attractive returns come from small segments of the market. So, rather than diversifying the portfolio across wide segments of the market, you can put your money where the action currently is. Some popular sector funds concentrate their investments in real estate (real estate investment trusts, or REITs), technology, financial services, natural resources, electronics, telecommunications, and, of course, health care.

Socially Responsible Funds

socially responsible fund (SRF)
A fund that invests only in companies meeting certain moral, ethical, and/or environmental criteria.

For some investors, the security selection process doesn't end with bottom lines, P/E ratios, growth rates, and betas; rather, it also includes the *active, explicit consideration of moral, ethical, and environmental issues*. The idea is that social concerns should play just as big a role in the investment decision as profits and other financial matters. **socially responsible funds (SRFs)** consider only what they view as socially responsible companies for inclusion in their portfolios. If a company doesn't meet certain moral, ethical, or environmental tests, they simply won't consider buying the stock, no matter how good the bottom line looks. Generally speaking, these funds abstain from investing in companies that derive revenues from tobacco, alcohol, or gambling; that are weapons contractors; or that operate nuclear power plants. The funds also tend to favor firms that produce "responsible" products and services, have strong employee relations, have positive environmental records, and are socially responsive to the communities in which they operate. According to the Forum for Sustainable and Responsible Investment, SRF funds under management grew to about $6.6 trillion by early 2014.

International Funds

international fund
A mutual fund that does all or most of its investing in foreign securities.

In searching for higher returns and better diversification, American investors have shown increased interest in foreign securities, and the mutual fund industry has responded with a full array of **international funds**. In 1985, there were only about 40 of these funds; by 2015, that number had grown to several thousand. The fact is, many people would like to invest in foreign securities but simply don't have the experience or know-how. International funds may be just the ticket for such investors. Technically, the term *international fund* is used to describe a type of fund that *invests exclusively in foreign securities*, often confining the fund's activities to specific geographical regions (such as Mexico, Australia, Europe, or the Pacific Rim). In contrast, there's another class of international funds, known as *global funds*, that invests not only in foreign securities *but also in U.S. companies*—usually multinational firms. As a rule, global funds provide more diversity and, with access to both foreign and domestic markets, can go wherever the action is.

Asset Allocation Funds

Studies have shown that the most important decision an investor can make is where to allocate his or her investment assets. This is known as *asset allocation*, and (as we saw in Chapter 11) it involves deciding how you're going to divide your investments among different types of securities. For example, what portion of your money will be devoted to money market securities, what portion to stocks, and what portion to bonds? Asset allocation deals in broad terms and doesn't address individual security selection. Even so, as strange as it may sound, asset allocation has been found to be a far more important determinant of total returns on a well-diversified portfolio than has individual security selection.

Because a lot of individual investors have a tough time making asset allocation decisions, the mutual fund industry has created a product to do the job for them. Known as *asset allocation funds*, these funds spread investors' money across all different types of markets. That is, whereas most mutual funds concentrate on one type of investment—whether it is stocks, bonds, or money market securities—asset allocation funds put money into all these markets. Many of them also include foreign securities in their asset allocation scheme, and some may even include inflation-resistant investments such as gold or real estate.

These funds are designed for people who want to hire fund managers not only to select individual securities for them, but also to make the strategic decisions concerning asset allocation over time. The money manager will establish a desired allocation mix, which might look something like this: 50 percent of the portfolio goes to U.S. stocks, 10 percent to foreign securities, 30 percent to bonds, and 10 percent to money market securities. Securities are then purchased for the fund in this proportion, and the overall portfolio maintains the desired mix. Actually, each segment of the fund is managed almost as a separate portfolio, so that securities within (say) the stock portion are bought, sold, and held as the market dictates. *As market conditions change over time, the asset allocation mix also changes*. So, if the U.S. stock market starts to soften, then funds will be moved out of stocks to some other area. As a result, the stock portion of the portfolio may drop to 35 percent and the foreign securities portion may increase to 25 percent, for example. Of course, there's no assurance that the money manager will make the right moves at the right time, but that's the idea behind these funds.

FINANCIAL PLANNING TIPS

Target-Date Funds: One Size Does *Not* Fit All

Target-date mutual funds and ETFs are relatively new types of asset allocation funds. The funds select a year in which an investor expects to retire, and then gradually shift the asset allocation to become more conservative as that retirement date approaches and most investors' risk tolerance decreases. Notwithstanding their growing popularity, you should be aware of the following issues in using target-date funds:

- **Target-date funds don't suit every investor.** While they meet the needs of most investors, some people might want a different asset allocation depending on special circumstances. For example, if you have significantly different net worth than the average person your age, you might have different needs.

- **Asset classes can differ across funds.** Many target-date fund families use large-cap, small-cap, and mid-cap domestic equity funds; international and emerging markets equity funds; and domestic fixed-income funds. And yet others also include inflation-protected Treasury Inflation-Protected Securities (TIPs), high-yield bonds, international fixed-income, emerging-markets debt, real estate, commodities, and long or short funds. You need to know how the fund defines its asset classes because this has significant risk implications.

- **Different target-date fund companies can use different asset allocations for the same target date.** Let's say you're planning to retire in 2045. One 2045 target date fund might have 90 percent in stocks, while another company's 2045 fund might have only 60 percent in stocks. You have to look at the details and make sure that you're comfortable with the riskiness of a fund's underlying asset allocation.

- **Target-date fund costs vary significantly.** For example, one popular target-date fund provider has several versions of the same retirement-year fund. The catch is that the expense ratio varies from 0.42 percent to 1.5 percent for the same target retirement-year fund! And yet the comparable fund offered by Vanguard had an expense ratio of 0.18 percent. You need to shop around and make comparisons.

- **Target-date glide path.** The glide path is the point in time at which the allocation to stocks drops to steady-state retirement mode. Some funds go into the glide-path stage after the average investor hits age 65. In contrast, other funds assume that you will stay invested in their fund until you die. This assumption can have a big effect on the asset allocation and risk.

Source: Adapted from Daniel Solin, "The Hidden Dangers of Target-Date Funds," http://money.usnews.com/money/blogs/on-retirement/2012/06/21/the,-hidden-dangers-of-target-date-funds, accessed September 2015; and Roger Wohlner, "Evaluating Your Target-Date Fund Options," http://money.usnews.com/money/blogs/the-smarter-mutual-fund-investor/2012/03/07/evaluating-your-target-date-fund-options, accessed September 2015.

13-2b Services Offered by Mutual Funds

Ask most investors why they buy a particular mutual fund, and they'll probably tell you that the fund offers the kind of income and return that they're looking for. Now, no one would question the importance of return in the investment decision, but there are other reasons for investing in mutual funds, not the least of which are the valuable services they provide. Some of the most sought-after *mutual fund services* are automatic investment and reinvestment plans, regular income programs, conversion privileges, and retirement programs. Unfortunately, many of these services are not available with ETFs, as they are basically nothing more than shares of common stock, which customarily do not offer such programs.

Automatic Investment Plans

Mutual funds provide a program that makes savings and capital accumulation as painless as possible. The **automatic investment plan** allows fund shareholders to funnel fixed amounts of money *from their paychecks or bank accounts* automatically into a mutual fund. It's much like a payroll deduction plan that treats savings a lot like insurance coverage—that is, just as insurance premiums are automatically deducted from your paycheck (or bank account), so too are investments to your mutual fund.

Just about every major fund group offers some kind of automatic investment plan. To enroll, a shareholder simply fills out a form authorizing the fund to transfer a set amount (usually it must be a minimum of $25 to $100 per period) from your bank account or paycheck at regular intervals—typically monthly or quarterly. Once enrolled, you'll be buying shares in the funds of your choice every month or quarter (most funds deal in fractional shares). Of course, if it's a load fund, you'll still have to pay normal sales charges on your periodic investments. You can get out of the program anytime you like, without penalty, simply by contacting the fund. Convenience may be the chief advantage of these plans, but they make solid investment sense as well because one of the best ways of building up a sizable amount of capital is to *add funds to your investment program systematically over time.* The importance of making regular contributions to your investment program cannot be overstated—it ranks right up there with compound interest!

Automatic Reinvestment Plans

Automatic reinvestment is one of the real draws of mutual funds, and it's offered by just about every open-ended mutual fund. Whereas automatic investment plans deal with money shareholders put into a fund, **automatic reinvestment plans** deal with the dividends and other distributions that the funds pay to their shareholders. Much like the dividend reinvestment plans we looked at with stocks, the automatic reinvestment plans of mutual funds enable you to keep all your capital fully employed. Through this service, dividend and capital gains income is *used to buy additional shares in the fund automatically*, which enables the investor to earn a fully compounded rate of return. Keep in mind, however, that even though you reinvest your dividends and capital gains, the Internal Revenue Service (IRS) still treats them as cash receipts and taxes them in the year that they're paid.

The important point is that by plowing profits (reinvested dividends and capital gains distributions) back into a fund, investors can put this money to work generating even more earnings. Indeed, the effects of these plans on total accumulated capital over the long haul can be substantial. Exhibit 13.6 shows the long-term impact of one such plan, which provides the actual performance numbers for a real-life mutual fund, Fidelity Contrafund. In the illustration, we assume that the investor starts with $10,000 and, except for reinvesting dividends and capital gains distributions, *adds no new capital over time*. Even so, the initial investment of $10,000 grew to about $30,941 over the roughly 15-year period from 2000 to mid-2015 (which, by the way, amounts to a fully compounded rate of return of 7.6 percent). So long as care is taken

---

automatic investment plan
An automatic savings program that enables an investor to channel a set amount of money systematically into a given mutual fund.

automatic reinvestment plan
A plan that gives share owners the option of electing to have dividends and capital gains distributions reinvested in additional fund shares.

in selecting an appropriate fund, *attractive benefits can be derived from the systematic accumulation of capital offered by automatic reinvestment plans.*

Regular Income

systematic withdrawal plan
A plan offered by mutual funds that allows shareholders to be paid specified amounts of money each period.

Automatic reinvestment plans are great for the long-term investor, but how about the investor who's looking for a steady stream of income? Mutual funds also have a service to meet this need. It's called a **systematic withdrawal plan**, and it's offered by most open-ended funds. Once enrolled in one of these plans, you'll automatically receive a predetermined amount of money every month or quarter. To participate, shareholders are usually required to have a minimum investment of $5,000 to $10,000, and the size of the withdrawal must usually be $50 or more per month. Depending on how well the fund is doing, the annual return generated by the fund may actually be greater than the withdrawals, thus allowing the investor not only to receive regular income, but also to enjoy an automatic accumulation of *additional* shares in the plan. On the other hand, if the fund isn't performing well, then the withdrawals could eventually deplete the original investment.

EXHIBIT 13.6	Effects of Reinvesting Income

Reinvesting dividends and/or capital gains can have tremendous effects on your investment position. This graph shows the results of a hypothetical investor who initially invested $10,000 and, for a period of about 15 years, reinvested all dividends and capital gains distributions in additional fund shares. [No adjustment has been made for any fees or for any income taxes payable by the shareholder, which would be appropriate provided that the fund was held in a tax-deferred account like an individual retirement account (IRA) or a 401(k) account.] This example is for the Fidelity Contrafund.

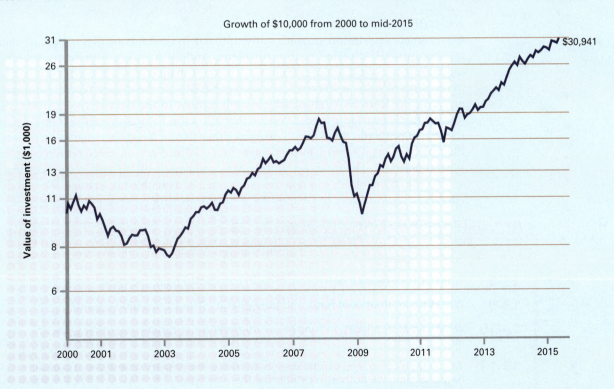

Growth of $10,000 from 2000 to mid-2015

Source: MorningstarDirect, May 2015. © 2015 Morningstar, Inc. All rights reserved. The Morningstar data contained herein (1) is proprietary to Morningstar; (2) may not be copied or distributed without written permission; and (3) is not warranted to be accurate, complete, or timely. Morningstar is not responsible for any damages or losses arising from any use of this information and has not granted its consent to be considered or deemed an "expert" under the Securities Act of 1933.

Conversion Privileges

conversion (exchange) privileges
A feature that allows investors to switch from one mutual fund to another within a family of funds.

Sometimes investors find it necessary to switch out of one fund and into another; for example, their investment objectives may change or the investment environment itself may have changed. **Conversion (or exchange) privileges** conveniently and economically meet the needs of these investors. Investment companies that offer a number of different funds to the investing public—known as *fund families*—usually provide conversion privileges that enable shareholders to move easily from one fund to another; this can be done either online or by phone. The only limitation is that the investor must confine the switches to the same *family* of funds. For example, an investor can switch from a Fidelity growth fund to a Fidelity money fund, or to its income fund, or to any other fund managed by Fidelity. Most fund families, especially the bigger ones, offer investors a full range of investment products as part of providing one-stop mutual fund shopping. Whether you want an equity fund, a bond fund, or a money fund, these fund families have something for you.

Conversion privileges are attractive because they permit investors to manage their holdings more aggressively by allowing them to move in and out of funds as the investment environment changes. Indeed, there is some evidence that stocks that have done well in one time period are likely to do well in the next period, all of which may be an effect of industry momentum. Regardless of what causes it, mutual fund families with conversion privileges make it easier and less costly to shift money across sectors and industries. Unfortunately, there's one major drawback; although you never see the cash, the exchange of shares from one fund to another is regarded, for tax purposes, as a sale followed by the purchase of a new security. As a result, if any capital gains exist at the time of the exchange, the investor is liable for the taxes on that profit.

Financial Fact or Fantasy?

Online and phone switching are services that enable you to move money from one fund to another, so long as you stay within the same family of funds. Fact: Online and phone switching are conversion (or exchange) privileges that allow you to sell one fund and buy another, with the only condition being that you confine your switches to the same family of funds.

Retirement Plans

Government legislation permits self-employed individuals to divert part of their income into self-directed retirement plans. And all working Americans, whether they're self-employed or not, are allowed to establish individual retirement accounts—in the form of either a standard, tax-deductible IRA or the newest type of retirement account, the Roth IRA (all of which we'll look at in the next chapter). Today, all mutual funds provide a special service that allows individuals to set up tax-deferred retirement programs quickly and easily as either IRA or Keogh accounts—or, through their place of employment, to participate in a qualified tax-sheltered retirement plan, such as a 401(k). The funds set up the plans and handle all the administrative details so that the shareholders can take full advantage of available tax savings. We will discuss these issues further in Chapter 14, which deals with retirement planning.

TEST YOURSELF

13-8 What's the difference between a growth fund and a balanced fund?

13-9 What's an international fund, and how does it differ from a global fund?

13-10 What's an asset allocation fund? How do these funds differ from other types of mutual funds?

13-11 If growth, income, and capital preservation are the primary objectives of mutual funds, why do we bother to categorize them by type?

13-12 What are fund families? What advantages do these families offer investors?

13-13 What are automatic reinvestment plans, and how do they differ from automatic investment plans?

13-3 MAKING MUTUAL FUND AND ETF INVESTMENTS

Suppose you have money to invest and are trying to select the right place to put it. You obviously want to pick an investment that not only meets your idea of an acceptable risk, but also generates an attractive rate of return. The problem is that you have to choose from literally thousands of investments. But perhaps if you approach the problem systematically, it may not be so formidable after all. For as we'll see, it is possible to whittle down the list of alternatives by matching your investment needs with the investment objectives of the funds.

13-3a The Selection Process

When it comes to mutual funds and ETFs, one question that every investor must answer is: Why invest in a mutual fund or an ETF to begin with; why not just go it alone (that is, buy individual stocks and bonds directly)? For beginning investors, or investors with little capital, the answer is pretty simple—mutual funds and ETFs provide far more diversification than such investors could ever get on their own, plus they get the help of professional money managers, and at a reasonable cost to boot.

Certainly, the diversification and professional money management come into play, but there are other reasons to invest in a mutual fund or an ETF. The competitive returns offered by mutual funds and ETFs have to be a factor with many investors, and so do the services they provide. A lot of well-to-do investors have decided that they can get better returns over the long haul by carefully selecting mutual funds than by trying to invest in individual stocks on their own. So they put all, or a big chunk, of their money into funds. Many of these investors will use part of their capital to buy and sell individual securities on their own, and they'll use the rest *to buy mutual funds or ETFs that invest in areas they don't fully understand or aren't well informed about.* For example, they'll use mutual funds or ETFs to get into foreign markets or as a way to buy mortgage-backed securities.

After deciding to use mutual funds or ETFs, the investor must then decide which funds to buy. The selection process itself (especially regarding the *types* of funds to purchase) obviously plays an important role in defining the amount of success you'll have with mutual funds or ETFs. It means putting into action all you know about investing in order to gain as much return as possible at an acceptable level of risk. Given that you have an asset allocation strategy in place and that you're trying to select funds compatible with your targeted mix, the selection process begins with an assessment of your own investment needs; this sets the tone for your investment program. Obviously, you'll want to select from those thousands of funds the one or two (or three or four) that will best meet your investment needs.

Objectives and Motives for Using Funds

The place to start is with your own investment objectives. In other words, why do you want to invest in a mutual fund or an ETF, and what are you looking for in a fund? Obviously, an attractive rate of return would be desirable, but there's also the matter of ensuring a tolerable amount of risk exposure. More than likely, when looking at your own risk temperament in relation to the various types of mutual funds and ETFs available, you'll discover that certain types of funds are more appealing to you than others. For instance, aggressive growth or sector funds will probably *not* be attractive to individuals wishing to avoid high exposure to risk.

Another important factor in the selection process is the intended use of the mutual fund or ETF. Do you want to invest in mutual funds or ETFs as a way of *accumulating capital* over an extended time, to *speculate* with your money in the hopes of generating high rates of return, or to *conserve your capital* by investing in low-risk securities where preservation of capital is no less important than return on capital. Finally, there's the matter of the services provided by the fund. If you're particularly interested in some services, be sure to look for them in the funds that you select.

FINANCIAL PLANNING TIPS

How to Choose the Best Mutual Funds

Choosing the best mutual funds to achieve your financial objectives is mostly about doing your homework and focusing on a few key elements. Here are the steps and the main considerations:

- **Decide how much money you want to invest in mutual funds.** That depends on how much money you need in the future, when you need it, and where your other money is invested. For example, are you hoping to fund a child's college education in 18 years, or are you investing for retirement?

- **Decide on your asset allocation.** This depends a lot on the length of time until you need the money, your capacity to take risk, and your risk tolerance. Let's say that you're investing for retirement. A reasonable starting point is the common rule of thumb that the percentage in bonds should equal your age, and the residual percentage should be in stocks. So if you're 25, it makes sense to have 25 percent of your money in bonds and 75 percent in stocks. You can fine-tune the percentages based on how comfortable you are with the risk implications of this rule-of-thumb allocation.

- **Diversify your investments over different types of mutual funds.** Research supports having some money invested in small-cap and value stocks, as well as in both domestic and foreign stocks. And you'll want to diversify your bond fund holdings at least across maturities, ratings, and possibly tax exposure. For many people,

the best choice in each fund category is a low-cost index fund, if available.

- **Put together a list of available mutual funds.** Compare each fund's historical performance with an appropriate benchmark. (**Morningstar.com** is a convenient source for such comparisons.) Then compare the expense ratios of each fund in the category that you are considering, which show how much the fund's returns are reduced by trading and operating expenses. Obviously, you would prefer the fund with the lowest expense ratio; over time, the higher net return will affect the amount of money in the fund significantly. Similarly, it's helpful to compare mutual funds' turnover ratios, which indicate the percentage of the assets held by the fund that were sold during the year. *Higher turnover ratios bring both higher expenses and higher taxes,* which will depress net returns in the same way as higher expense ratios.

- **Avoid "dog" funds.** Many people just pick the fund with the best historical performance and figure that's the star. Doesn't that make sense—who wouldn't want to reach for the stars? However, that strategy is often misguided. Although it's hard to identify the stars, past performance does appear to be a reliable way of identifying the true losers. The worst funds often stay at the bottom of their category in terms of performance for years. And that can be measured using their returns, expense ratios, and turnover. So here's the best approach: *Don't search for the stars—just avoid the dogs!*

Having assessed what you're looking for in a fund, now you can look at what the funds have to offer.

What Funds Have to Offer

The ideal mutual fund or ETF would achieve maximum capital growth when security prices rise, provide complete protection against capital loss when prices decline, and achieve high levels of current income at all times. Unfortunately, such funds don't exist. Instead, just as each individual has a set of investment needs, each fund has its own *investment objective,* its own *manner or style of operation,* and its own *range of services.* These three factors are useful in helping you assess investment alternatives. But where does the investor look for such information? One obvious place is the fund's *profile* (or its prospectus), where information on investment objectives, portfolio composition, management, and past performance can be obtained. In addition, publications such as *The Wall Street Journal, Barron's, Money, Fortune,* and *Forbes* provide all sorts of useful data and information about mutual funds. These sources publish a wealth of operating and performance statistics in a convenient, easy-to-read format. Services are also available that provide background information and assessments on a wide variety of funds. Among the best in this category are Morningstar's online (**http://morningstar.com**) and other vendors' software-based products (see Exhibit 13.7), *The Value Line Fund Advisor, and The Value Line ETF Survey* (these reports are similar to Value Line's stock reports, but they apply to mutual funds and ETFs). And, of course, all sorts of performance statistics are available on the Internet. For example, there are scores of free finance Internet sites, such as **http://finance.yahoo.com**, where you can obtain historical information on a fund's performance, security holdings, risk profile, load charges, and purchase information. Or you can buy, usually at reasonable prices, quarterly or annually updated software from organizations like Morningstar or the American Association of Individual Investors (AAII).

Whittling Down the Alternatives

At this point, fund selection becomes a process of elimination as you weigh your investment needs against the types of funds available. Many funds can be eliminated from consideration simply because they don't meet your needs. Some may be too risky; others may be unsuitable as a storehouse of value. So, rather than trying to evaluate thousands of different funds, you can use a process of elimination to narrow the list down to two or three *types* of funds that best match your investment (and asset allocation) needs.

From here, you can whittle the list down a bit more by introducing other constraints. For example, because of cost considerations, you may want to deal only in no-load or low-load funds (more on this later), or you may be seeking certain services that are important to your investment goals.

Now we're ready to introduce the final (but certainly not the least important) element in the selection process: *the fund's investment performance*. Useful information includes (1) how the fund has performed over the past five to seven years; (2) the type of return that it has generated in good markets as well as bad; (3) the level of dividend and capital gains distributions, which is an important indication not only of how much current income the fund distributes annually but also of the fund's *tax efficiency* (funds with low dividends and low asset turnovers typically expose their shareholders to lower taxes and consequently have higher tax-efficiency ratings); and (4) the level of investment stability the fund has enjoyed over time (or, put another way, the amount of volatility/risk in the fund's return). By evaluating such information, you can identify some of the more successful mutual funds—those that not only offer the investment objectives and services you seek but also provide the best payoffs. And while you're doing this, you might want to consider some of the fund facts listed in Exhibit 13.8.

Stick with No-Loads or Low-Load Mutual Funds

There's a longstanding "debate" in the mutual fund industry regarding load funds and no-load funds. The question is, do load funds add enough value to overcome the load fees? And if not, why pay the load charges? The evidence indicates that load fund returns generally aren't, on a risk-adjusted basis, any higher than the returns from no-load funds. In fact, the funds with abnormally high loads and 12b-1 fees often produce returns that are far *less* than what you can get from no-loads, after taking risk into account! Moreover, because of compounding, the differential returns tend to widen with longer holding periods.

That shouldn't be surprising, though, because big load charges and/or 12b-1 fees do nothing more than *reduce your invested capital*, thus reducing the amount of money you have working for you. In fact, the only way that a load fund can overcome this handicap is to *produce superior returns*—which is not easy to do year in

EXHIBIT 13.7 | **Mutual Fund Information**

Investors who want in-depth information about the operating characteristics, investment holdings, and market performance of mutual funds can usually find what they're looking for in Morningstar publications or, as shown here, from online and software-based information sources such as *MorningstarDirect*.

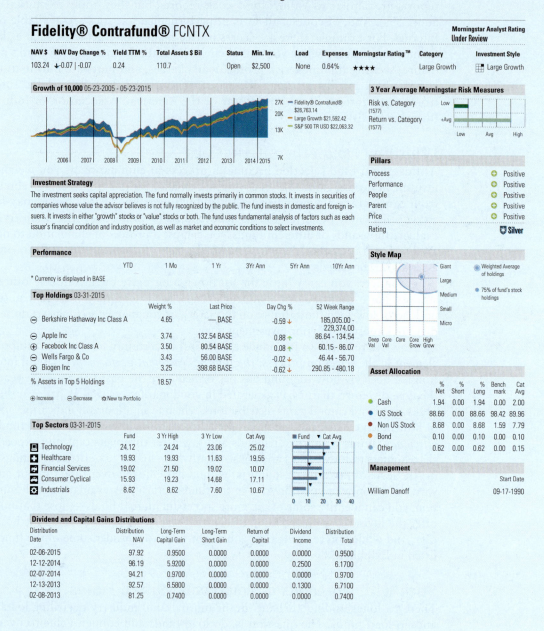

Source: MorningstarDirect, May 24, 2015. © 2012 Morningstar, Inc. All rights reserved. The Morningstar data contained herein (1) is proprietary to Morningstar; (2) may not be copied or distributed without written permission; and (3) is not warranted to be accurate, complete, or timely. Morningstar is not responsible for any damages or losses arising from any use of this information and has not granted its consent to be considered or deemed an "expert" under the Securities Act of 1933.

EXHIBIT 13.8	**Some Mutual Fund Facts Every Investor Should Know**

Mutual funds are meant to give investors a simple yet effective way of buying into the stock and bond markets. Unfortunately, fund investing isn't always as simple as it looks. Here are a few fund facts every investor should keep in mind when making mutual fund investments:

- Stock funds that get hit hard in market crashes aren't necessarily bad investments.
- Even great funds have bad years now and then.
- Most stock (and bond) funds fail to beat the market.
- You don't need a broker to buy mutual funds.
- A fund that doesn't charge a sales commission isn't necessarily a no-load fund. Watch out for 12b-1 charges.
- If you own a dozen or more funds, you probably own too many.
- Mutual fund names are often misleading. Look beyond the name to the actual performance. Morningstar-style categories are more useful than the fund's name. Consistency is important.
- Bond funds with high current yields don't necessarily produce high *total* returns.
- Money market funds are not risk-free (you never know what kind of return they'll earn).
- If the market crashes, it will be too late to sell your fund shares (the damage probably will already have been done).
- Even bad funds sometimes rank as top performers. And the same goes for good funds—sometimes they come in at the bottom of the pack. Once again, consistency is important.

and year out. Granted, a handful of load funds have produced attractive returns over extended periods, but they're the exception rather than the rule.

Obviously, it's in your best interest to pay close attention to load charges (and other fees) whenever you're considering an investment in a mutual fund. In order to maximize returns, *you should seriously consider sticking to no-load funds, or low-loads* (funds with total load charges, including 12b-1 fees, of 3 percent or less). At the very least, you should consider a more expensive load fund *only* if it has a much better performance record (and offers more return potential) than a less expensive fund. It shouldn't be all that hard to stick mostly with no-load funds because there are literally thousands of no-load and low-load funds to choose from, and they come in all types.

Choosing Between ETFs and Mutual Funds

The preceding discussion identifies the relative advantages and disadvantages of investing in funds. Yet this begs the question of how you choose between ETFs and mutual funds. The answer depends on what you want to invest in and how sensitive you are to taxes and costs. Consider the following criteria suggested by Morningstar:

- *Broad or narrow focus?* ETFs have been developed to accommodate investors pursuing narrow market segments. If you want to focus on a single market sector, industry, or geographic region, there's likely an ETF for you. Furthermore, there are far more ETFs that track single foreign countries than mutual funds that do so. The downside is that narrowly focused ETFs are not as well diversified as are many mutual funds. So, while there are mutual funds and ETFs for broad index investing, some ETFs offer more narrow, targeted investing.
- *Tax management.* ETFs are set up to protect investors from capital gains taxes better than most mutual funds can. Most ETFs are index funds that trade less than the average actively managed mutual fund, which means that they should generate fewer taxable gains.
- *Costs.* ETFs have lower overhead expenses than most mutual funds because they don't have to manage customer accounts or staff call centers. This means that ETFs tend to have lower expense ratios than mutual funds. ETFs are often the most cost-effective choice for investors using discount brokers, for those investing a large sum of money, and for those with a long-term horizon.

13-3b Getting a Handle on Fund Performance

If you were to believe all the sales literature, you'd think that there was no way you could go wrong by investing in mutual funds or ETFs. Just put your money into one of these funds and let the good times roll! Unfortunately, the hard facts of life are that, *when it comes to investing, performance is never guaranteed.* And that applies just as much to mutual funds as it does to any other form of investing—perhaps even more so, because with mutual funds, the single variable driving a fund's market price and return behavior is the performance of the fund's portfolio of securities.

Measuring Fund Performance

Any mutual fund (open- or closed-end) or any ETF has three potential sources of return: (1) dividend income, (2) capital gains distribution, and (3) change in the fund's share price. Depending on the type of fund, some will derive more income from one source than another. For example, we'd normally expect income-oriented funds to generate higher dividend income than capital gains-oriented funds do. Mutual funds regularly publish reports that recap investment performance. One such report is *The Summary of Income and Capital Changes;* an example of which is provided in Exhibit 13.9. This statement gives a brief overview of a fund's investment activities, including expense ratios and portfolio turnover rates. Of interest to us in this discussion is the top part of the report (from "Net asset value, beginning of period" through "Net asset value, end of period"—lines 1 to 10). This part reveals the amount of dividend income and capital gains distributed to the shareholders, along with any change in the fund's NAV.

Dividend income (see line 7 of Exhibit 13.9) is the amount derived from the dividend and interest income earned on the security holdings of the mutual fund. When the fund receives dividends or interest payments, it passes these on to shareholders in the form of dividend payments. The fund accumulates all the current income that it has received for the period and then pays it out on a prorated basis. Because the mutual fund itself is tax exempt, any taxes due on dividend earnings are payable by the individual investor. For funds that are not held in tax-deferred accounts [e.g., IRAs and 401(k)s], the amount of taxes due on dividends will depend on the source of such dividends. That is, *if these distributions are derived from dividends earned on the fund's common stock holdings, then they're subject to the preferential tax rate of 15 or 20 percent or less.* But, if these distributions are derived from interest earnings on bonds, dividends from REITs, or dividends from most types of preferred stocks, then such dividends *do not qualify for preferential tax treatment* and instead are taxed as ordinary income (see Chapter 3 for details).

Capital gains distributions (see line 8) work on the same principle as dividends, except that they're derived from the *capital gains actually earned* by the fund. (From a tax perspective, if the capital gains are long-term, then they qualify for the preferential tax rate of 15 or 20 percent or less; if not, they're treated as ordinary income.) Note that these (capital gains) distributions apply only to *realized* capital gains—that is, when the securities holdings are actually sold and capital gains actually earned. *Unrealized* capital gains (or "paper profits") make up the third

EXHIBIT 13.9 A Summary of Mutual Fund Income and Capital Changes

The return on a mutual fund is made up of (1) the (net) investment income the fund earns from dividends and interest and (2) the realized and unrealized capital gains the fund earns on its security transactions. Mutual funds provide such information to their shareholders in a standardized format (like the statement here) that highlights, among other things, income, expenses, and capital gains.

	2017	2016	2015
1. **Net asset value, beginning of period:**	$ 24.47	$ 27.03	$ 24.26
2. **Income from investment operations:**			
3. Net investment income	$ 0.60	$ 0.66	$ 0.50
4. Net gains on securities (realized and unrealized)	6.37	(1.74)	3.79
5. Total from investment operations	6.97	(1.08)	4.29
6. **Less distributions:**			
7. Dividends from net investment income	($0.55)	($0.64)	($0.50)
8. Distributions from realized gains	(1.75)	(.84)	(1.02)
9. Total distributions	(2.30)	(1.48)	(1.52)
10. **Net asset value, end of period:**	$ 29.14	$ 24.47	$ 27.03
11. **Total return:**	28.48%	(4.00%)	17.68%
12. **Ratios/supplemental data:**			
13. Net assets, end of period ($000)	$307,951	$153,378	$108,904
14. Ratio of expenses to average net assets	1.04%	0.85%	0.94%
15. Ratio of net investment income to average net assets	1.47%	2.56%	2.39%
16. Portfolio turnover rate*	85%	144%	74%

Portfolio turnover rate measures the number of shares bought and sold by the fund against the total number of shares held in the fund's portfolio; a high turnover rate (e.g., one exceeding 100%) would mean the fund has been doing a lot of trading.

and final element in a mutual fund's return, for *when the fund's securities holdings go up or down in price, its NAV moves accordingly.* This change (or movement) in the NAV is what makes up the unrealized capital gains of the fund. It represents the profit that shareholders would receive (and are entitled to) if the fund were to sell its holdings.

EXAMPLE: Calculating the Approximate Yield on a Mutual Fund

A simple but effective way of measuring performance is to describe mutual fund returns based on the three major sources of return noted above—dividends earned, capital gains distributions received, and change in share price. These payoffs can be converted to a convenient return figure by using the standard *approximate yield* formula that was first introduced in Chapter 12. The calculations necessary for finding such a return measure can be shown using the 2017 figures from Exhibit 13.9. Referring to the exhibit, we can see that this hypothetical no-load fund paid $0.55 per share in dividends and another $1.75 in capital gains distributions; also, its price (NAV) at the beginning of the year (that is, at the end of 2016) of $24.47 rose to $29.14 by the end of the year (see lines 1 and 10, respectively). Putting this data into the familiar approximate yield formula, we see that the hypothetical mutual fund provided an annual rate of return of 26 percent.

$$\text{Approximate Yield} = \frac{\text{Dividends and Capital Gains Distributions} + \left[\dfrac{\text{Ending} - \text{Beginning}}{\text{Length of Time Period}}\right]}{\left[\dfrac{\text{Ending Price} - \text{Beginning Price}}{2}\right]}$$

$$= \frac{(\$0.55 + \$1.75) + \left[\dfrac{\$29.14 - \$24.47}{1}\right]}{\left[\dfrac{\$29.14 - \$24.47}{2}\right]}$$

$$= \frac{\$2.30 + \$4.67}{\$26.80} = \frac{\$6.97}{\$26.80} = \underline{\underline{26.0\%}}$$

Calculator

INPUTS	FUNCTIONS
1	N
−24.47	PV
2.30	PMT
29.14	FV
	CPT
	I/Y
	SOLUTION
	28.48

See Appendix E for details.

Calculator Keystrokes. You can just as easily find the exact return on this investment with a handheld financial calculator. Here's what you'd do: Using *annual compounding*, to find the return on this mutual fund in 2017, we use the same input data as given before. Namely, we start with a price at the beginning of the year of $24.47; add in total dividends and capital gains distributions of $2.30 a share (i.e., $0.55 + $1.75); and then, using a year-end price of $29.14, punch the keystrokes shown in the margin, where:

N = number of *years* you hold the fund
PV = the *initial* price of the fund (entered as a *negative number*)
PMT = *total* amount of dividends and capital gains distributions received
FV = the *ending* price of the fund

Note that our computed return (of 28.48 percent) is exactly the same as the "Total Return" shown on line 11 of Exhibit 13.9—that's because this is basically the same procedure that the mutual funds must use to report their return performance. The approximate yield measure (26 percent) may be close to the actual return, but clearly it's not close enough for fund-reporting purposes.

Evaluating ETF Performance ETFs and mutual funds are similar in that their prices depend on the value of the funds' underlying investments. Both have NAVs and depend on dividends and capital gains to generate returns. So let's focus on the aspects that are particularly important in ETF performance evaluation. As discussed previously, while there are some actively managed ETFs, the vast majority are designed to replicate an index. Thus, for our purposes here, we'll consider the issues associated with evaluating the index-based form of ETF.

The primary reason for investing in an index-based ETF, of course, is to replicate the performance of the index. It follows that an important aspect of ETF performance is how well it tracks the performance of the underlying index. You can determine this by checking the so-called R-Squared (R^2) statistical measure, which shows how much of the variability in an ETF's total returns is explained by the variability in the total returns of the underlying index. The R^2 varies between 0 percent and a maximum of 100 percent. Obviously, the higher the R^2, the closer the relationship between the ETF and the associated target index. It also makes sense to know how the ETF's style is described and how consistently it pursues this style. Finally, it's wise to check how the ETF's performance compares to its peers and how the ETF's expense ratio compares with reasonable benchmarks.

Consider the Morningstar information on the PowerShares QQQ ETF (QQQ) in Exhibit 13.10. This ETF is designed to replicate the performance of the NASDAQ 100 index, which includes the 100 largest domestic and international non-financial firms trading on the NASDAQ stock exchange. The index includes companies from the following industries: health care, retail, transportation, telecommunications, biotechnology, technology, services, media, and industrial. The exhibit portrays various performance metrics for the ETF.

EXHIBIT 13.10 | Evaluating ETF Performance

Index-based ETF performance evaluation depends on how well the ETF's returns track the underlying index, the consistency with which it follows its investment style, its performance relative to its peers, and the competitiveness of its expenses. This example provides a page from a Morningstar report on the PowerShares QQQ ETF.

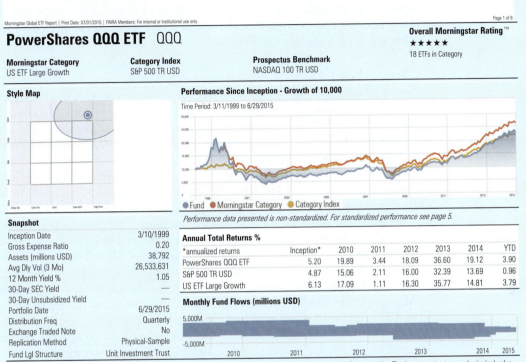

Morningstar Global ETF Report | Print Date: 07/01/2015 | FINRA Members: For internal or institutional use only.   Page 1 of 8

PowerShares QQQ ETF QQQ

Overall Morningstar Rating™
★★★★★
18 ETFs in Category

Morningstar Category	Category Index	Prospectus Benchmark
US ETF Large Growth	S&P 500 TR USD	NASDAQ 100 TR USD

Style Map

Performance Since Inception - Growth of 10,000

Time Period: 3/11/1999 to 6/29/2015

● Fund ● Morningstar Category ● Category Index

Performance data presented is non-standardized. For standardized performance see page 5.

Snapshot

Inception Date	3/10/1999
Gross Expense Ratio	0.20
Assets (millions USD)	38,792
Avg Dly Vol (3 Mo)	26,533,631
12 Month Yield %	1.05
30-Day SEC Yield	—
30-Day Unsubsidized Yield	—
Portfolio Date	6/29/2015
Distribution Freq	Quarterly
Exchange Traded Note	No
Replication Method	Physical-Sample
Fund Lgl Structure	Unit Investment Trust

Annual Total Returns %

*annualized returns	Inception*	2010	2011	2012	2013	2014	YTD
PowerShares QQQ ETF	5.20	19.89	3.44	18.09	36.60	19.12	3.90
S&P 500 TR USD	4.87	15.06	2.11	16.00	32.39	13.69	0.96
US ETF Large Growth	6.13	17.09	1.11	16.30	35.77	14.81	3.79

Monthly Fund Flows (millions USD)

5,000M

-5,000M

2010 2011 2012 2013 2014 2015

Performance Disclosure: *The performance data quoted represents past performance and does not guarantee future results. The investment return and principal value of an investment will fluctuate; thus an investor's shares, when sold, may be worth more or less than their original cost. Current performance may be lower or higher than return data quoted herein. For performance data current to the most recent month-end, please call +1 8009830903 or visit www.invescopowershares.com.*
The Overall Morningstar Rating is based on risk-adjusted returns, derived from a weighted average of the three-, five-, and 10-year (if applicable) Morningstar metrics.

Annual Income Return %

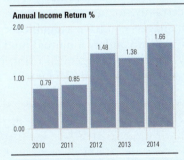

2010	2011	2012	2013	2014
0.79	0.85	1.48	1.38	1.66

Risk/Return Analysis (3 years)

	ETF	Cat Index	Cat Avg
Standard Deviation %	10.25	8.47	10.05
Arithmetic Mean %	1.76	1.54	1.56
Sharpe Ratio	2.06	2.17	—
R-Squared	71.10	—	—
Beta	1.02	—	—
Alpha %	2.28	—	—
Treynor Ratio	22.15	—	—
Sortino Ratio	4.67	4.97	—

Suitability

By Robert Goldsborough 5/11/2015

PowerShares QQQ ETF QQQ, the 11th most actively traded and sixth-largest U.S. exchange-traded fund offers a large helping of large-cap growth stocks with a strong tilt toward the technology sector. QQQ, which tracks the cap-weighted Nasdaq-100 Index of the 100 largest nonfinancial stocks in the Nasdaq Composite Index, also includes leading consumer discretionary (19.5% of assets) and biotech (15% of assets) firms. Given its focus on a few sectors, this ETF works best as a satellite holding in a diversified portfolio.

Given this fund's sector tilts, it is more volatile than a broad portfolio of large-cap stocks. For example, over the past 10 years, it has had a standard deviation of 17.9% compared with 14.7% for the S&P 500.

Many of the stocks in this fund are already in other more diversified funds. This ETF's tech holdings comprise almost the S&P 500's entire 20% tech component. Indeed, QQQ's performance correlates highly with the S&P 500 (90% over the past 10 years) and has an even higher correlation with Technology Select Sector SDPR XLK (97% over the past 10 years).

M⚙RNINGSTAR®

The Morningstar investment style category is "Large Growth." The exhibit shows that the ETF's performance compares favorably with other funds in its category. In addition, notice that the R^2 ("R-Squared" in the exhibit) of the QQQ ETF relative to the S&P 500 is 71.10 percent. The "alpha" of 2.28 percent shows that the QQQ ETF generated about 2.3 percent more than expected for its degree of market risk. While not shown in the exhibit, Morningstar indicates elsewhere that the net expense ratio for the QQQ ETF is only 0.20 percent. In summary, an investor wanting consistent exposure to the large non-financial growth stocks that characterize the NASDAQ 100 index can rest assured that the QQQ ETF replicates the performance of that index well with relatively low expenses.

What About Future Performance?

There's no question that approximate yield and return on investment are simple yet highly effective measures that capture all the important elements of mutual fund and ETF returns. Unfortunately, looking at past performance is one thing, but what about the future? Ideally, we'd want to evaluate the same three elements of return over the future much as we did for the past. Yet it's difficult—if not impossible—to get a handle on what the *future* holds for dividends, capital gains, and NAV. The reason is that a mutual fund's or ETF's future investment performance is directly linked to the future makeup of its securities portfolio, which is impossible to predict.

So where do you look for insight into the future? The key factors discussed here apply equally to the evaluation of both mutual funds and ETFs. First, carefully consider the *future direction of the market as a whole*. This is important because the behavior of a well-diversified mutual fund or ETF tends to reflect the general tone of the market. So, if the consensus forecast is that the market is going to be generally drifting up, that should bode well for the investment performance of mutual funds and ETFs. Second, take a hard look at the past performance of the mutual fund or ETF itself. It's a good way to see how successful the fund's investment managers have been. The success of a mutual fund or an ETF rests largely *on the investment skills of the fund managers*. So, when investing in a fund, look for consistently good performance in up as well as down markets, as well as over extended periods (five to seven years, or more). Most important, check to see whether the same key people are still running the fund. Although past success is certainly no guarantee of future performance, a strong, consistent team of money managers can have a significant bearing on the level of fund returns. Put another way, when you buy a mutual fund or ETF, you're buying a formula (investment policy + money management team) that has worked in the past, in the expectation that it will work again in the future.

TEST YOURSELF

13-14 What are the most common reasons for buying mutual funds and ETFs?

13-15 Briefly describe the steps in the mutual fund selection process.

13-16 Why does it pay to invest in no-load funds rather than load funds? Under what conditions might it make sense to invest in a load fund?

13-17 Identify three potential sources of return to mutual fund and ETF investors, and briefly discuss how each could affect total return to shareholders.

13-18 Which would you rather have: $100 in dividend income or $100 in capital gains distribution? $100 in realized capital gains or $100 in unrealized capital gains?

13-19 Describe how to evaluate the attractiveness of investing in an index-based ETF.

13-20 How important is the overall market in affecting the price performance of mutual funds and ETFs?

13-4 INVESTING IN REAL ESTATE

LG6

For many years, investing in real estate was quite lucrative. Real estate, it seemed, was one of the few investment vehicles that just couldn't go wrong. Of course, as with any investment, the market for real estate fluctuates over time, and investors must do their homework before making real estate investments. When the economy is growing and inflation is relatively high, as it was in the 1970s and early 1980s, real estate prices were also strong. But in the early 1990s, the market weakened, and prices started to level off. That didn't last long, however, as real estate values began to climb again in the latter part of the 1990s. One example of this behavior was housing prices, which rose rapidly—indeed, shot almost straight up—from 2001 through 2006. But then, from a market peak in 2006, housing prices fell almost as quickly as they had risen, with the average price

of a home plummeting nearly 33 percent by early 2011, which was the bottom when prices had fallen by more than during the Great Depression. Housing prices recovered significantly from 2012 to 2014. While still below 2006 peak levels in 2015, housing prices were expected to rise at an average rate of 4 to 5 percent in the near term.

Real estate includes everything from homes and raw land to different types of income-producing properties such as warehouses, commercial and retail space, office and apartment buildings, and condominiums. Investments in real estate can take several forms. For example, investors can buy land or property directly, or they may prefer to invest in various types of real estate securities such as real estate mutual funds (discussed earlier in this chapter), REITs, mortgages, stocks of real estate-related companies, or real estate limited partnerships. Adding real estate to your investment portfolio *provides greater diversification than does holding just stocks or bonds.* That's because *real estate typically exhibits less volatility than stocks and it doesn't usually move in tandem with stocks.* Before deciding to buy real estate for your portfolio, however, it's essential for you to evaluate such issues as the outlook for the national economy, interest rate levels, supply and demand for space, and regional considerations. Then you must choose the right properties or investment vehicles for your financial needs—and manage them well.

13-4a Some Basic Considerations

The attractiveness of a real estate investment depends on the expected cash flows over the planned holding period and the riskiness of those cash flows. The expected ongoing cash flows are determined by rent, depreciation, and taxes—and, of course, the all-important expected future sales price. The expected return on a real estate investment is determined by the relationship between the expected future cash flows relative to the initial investment, which is typically reduced by using a significant amount of borrowed funds. The value of the investment is assessed in light of the returns available on alternative investments of comparable risk (such as stocks, bonds, and mutual funds). Far more than with most other types of investment vehicles, financial leverage (borrowing) is a key determinant of real estate investment returns. We'll now briefly describe the basic factors affecting the value of real estate investments, including after-tax cash flows, appreciation in value, and the use of leverage.

Cash Flow and Taxes

The after-tax *cash flow* on a real estate investment depends on the revenues generated by the property, on any operating expenses, and on depreciation and taxes. Real estate typically provides large depreciation write-offs that tend to lower the taxable income of certain (*qualified*) investors. Depreciation gives the property owner an allowance for the decline in the physical condition of real estate over time. Although it's a book-keeping entry that's considered an expense for tax purposes, it involves no actual cash outflow. Depreciation can result in lower taxes; for this reason, it's viewed as a *tax shelter*. But there's a catch: depreciation can be used only up to a certain amount and only by investors who meet certain income qualifications, as we'll explain next.

Keep in mind that, for tax purposes, real estate is considered a *passive* investment. Therefore, the amount of expenses, *including depreciation*, that can be written off is generally limited to the amount of income generated by this and any other passive investments owned by the investor. For example, if you owned some apartments that generated $25,000 a year in rental income and if (in the absence of any other passive investments) you had mortgage interest and other operating expenses (such as property taxes and minor repairs) of $20,000 annually, then you might be able to write off up to $5,000 in depreciation ($25,000 income minus $20,000 other expenses). However, if your *adjusted gross income* (AGI) is less than $100,000 a year, then you may be able to write off even more depreciation—specifically, as much as $25,000 in losses on *rented real estate* can be used to offset the ordinary income of people who "actively participate" in the rental activity of the buildings *and* whose AGI is less than $100,000. (This provision is phased out at $150,000.) In this example, if you had $90,000 in AGI and $15,000 in depreciation expenses, then $5,000 of it could be written off against the remaining $5,000 of net rental income, as discussed before. The other $10,000 could be charged directly against your ordinary income, thereby reducing your taxable income and your taxes. Because of its effect on taxes, *depreciation is considered an important component of real estate investments*. Because depreciation and taxes are such important elements in measuring cash flow, an individual investor should have a tax consultant evaluate proposed real estate investments.

Appreciation in Value

An investment evaluation of a proposed piece of real estate should include not only the recurring cash flows from the property (e.g., rents), but also expected changes in property values. In many cases, such appreciation has a much greater impact on the rate of return than does the net annual cash flow from the property. Hence, if the market price of the real estate is expected to increase by $100,000, then that price appreciation should be treated as capital gains and included as part of the return from the investment (minus, of course, the capital gains taxes paid).

Use of Leverage

A big attraction for investing in real estate is the high degree of financial leverage that it permits. Leverage involves using borrowed money to magnify returns. Because real estate is a tangible asset, investors can borrow as much as 75 percent to 90 percent of its cost. As a result, if the profit rate on the investment is greater than the cost of borrowing, then the return on a leveraged investment will be *proportionally greater* than the return generated from an otherwise comparable unleveraged investment.

EXAMPLE: The Effect of Leverage on Real Estate Returns

You're considering a real estate investment costing $100,000—like the one in Exhibit 13.11. You can purchase the property in one of two ways: you can either pay cash for it or you can put up $20,000 of your own money and borrow the remaining $80,000 at 5 percent annual interest. If the property earns $13,000 per year after all expenses, including property taxes and depreciation but *before interest and income taxes are deducted*, then the leveraged investment will provide a much better rate of return than the cash deal, as seen in Exhibit 13.11. Observe that your return on investment in the no-leverage case will be 9.36 percent but that, with leverage, you stand to make a return of 32.40 percent! And the higher expected return is the compensation for taking on the higher risk implied by using leverage.

EXHIBIT 13.11   Using Leverage in Real Estate Investments

Although earnings after taxes are lower with the leveraged investment, the return on investment is considerably higher because the investor puts a lot less of his or her own money into the deal.

	No Leverage		Leverage
Owner investment	$100,000		$ 20,000
Borrowed money	0		80,000
Total investment	$100,000		$100,000
Earnings before interest and income taxes*	$ 13,000		$ 13,000
Less: Interest	0	(0.05)($80,000) =	4,000
Earnings before taxes	$ 13,000		$ 9,000
Less: Income taxes (assumed 28% rate)	3,640		2,520
Earnings after taxes	$ 9,360		$ 6,480

$$\text{Return on Investment} = \frac{\text{Earnings After Taxes}}{\text{Amount of Owner Investment}} = \frac{\$9,630}{\$100,000} = \underline{9.36\%} \qquad \frac{\$6,480}{\$20,000} = \underline{32.40\%}$$

*All expenses, including property taxes and depreciation, are assumed to have been deducted from earnings.

Financial Fact or Fantasy?

In many types of real estate investments, appreciation in the value of the property affects return more than annual rental income. Fact: Like most forms of investing, the biggest bang for your buck usually comes from capital gains. You'll find that's the way the really big money is made, and real estate is certainly no exception to that rule.

Because some of the leveraged investment is made with borrowed money, the return on investment in Exhibit 13.11 reflects *only the amount of money that you put up* to buy it. So, even though the leveraged investment provides *less in earnings after taxes*, it has a lower investment base. The net result is a *higher return on investment*. By leveraging your investment, you'll get a bigger bang from your investment bucks. However, when no borrowing is involved, you have no risk of default; on the other hand, when you use leverage, minimum earnings (before interest and taxes) of $4,000 are necessary to pay the interest and thereby avoid default. The risk that comes with leverage, therefore, must be considered along with the potential benefits. Indeed, many people have been driven into bankruptcy because they used too much leverage.

13-4b Speculating in Raw Land

Investing in real estate can take several forms. One approach that's popular with many investors is to *speculate in raw land*. In this approach, *which is often viewed as highly risky*, investors seek to generate high rates of return by investing in property that they *hope* will undergo dramatic increases in value. The key to such speculation is to isolate areas of potential population growth and/or real estate demand (ideally, before anyone else does) and purchase property in these areas in anticipation of their eventual development. Undeveloped acreage with no utilities or improvements is often purchased by land speculators either to hold for future development or to sell, as is, at a higher price later. Given the high degree of uncertainty involved, raw land speculation should be reserved for real estate investors who understand and can accept the inherent risks.

13-4c Investing in Income Property

One of the most popular forms of real estate investing is **income (or income-producing) property**, which includes commercial and residential properties. Investments in

income (income-producing) property
Real estate purchased for leasing or renting to tenants in order to generate ongoing monthly/annual income in the form of rent receipts.

income properties offer both attractive returns and tax advantages for investors. The purchased real estate is leased to tenants to generate income from rent. And although the primary purpose of investing in income property is to produce an attractive annual cash flow, certain types of strategically located income properties also offer attractive opportunities for appreciation in value. Before buying income property, be sure you know what you're getting into. The owner of income property is responsible for leasing the units and maintaining the property. This means fixing leaky roofs and appliances, painting and other repairs, cleaning after a tenant leaves, and similar responsibilities.

Calculating the value of income-producing property requires estimating the annual net operating income (NOI), which *equals gross rental income (less an allowance for vacancies and bad debts) minus all operating expenses, such as property (but not income) taxes, insurance, maintenance, and so on.* Once you have a property's NOI, you can apply a *cap rate* (the expected annual rate of return on the property) to arrive at an estimated value for the property. A typical cap rate for income property is around 9 percent or 10 percent.

EXAMPLE: Calculating the Value of Income-Producing Property

You're thinking about buying an office building that generates an estimated $50,000 per year in NOI. With a 9 percent cap rate, that property would have an estimated value of $555,556 = $50,000/0.09.

Commercial Properties

The commercial property category consists of many types of properties, including office buildings, industrial space, warehouses, retail space (from freestanding stores to strip shopping centers to malls), and hotels. The risks and returns on commercial real estate investments are tied to business conditions and location. The value of commercial property, especially retail businesses, is enhanced by a location in a high-traffic area. Because commercial properties call for professional management and involve significant expenses, investing in this category of income property is generally the domain of more seasoned (often professional) real estate investors.

Residential Properties

First-time investors often choose income-producing *residential properties* such as homes, apartments, and smaller multifamily buildings. This category of income property is available in various sizes, prices, and types ranging from single family homes, duplexes, and triplexes to large apartment buildings. Aside from the considerations of purchase and financing costs, major factors influencing the profitability of these investments are the occupancy rates—the percentage of available space rented over the year—and maintenance and management costs. Other factors to consider are the neighborhood where the units are located, local regulations regarding tenants, and supply and demand trends for the type of property.

13-4d Other Ways to Invest in Real Estate

What if the idea of owning and managing property doesn't appeal to you? Or perhaps you don't have enough money to buy income property outright. Another way to own real estate is by purchasing specialized securities. For example, you can buy shares in a *real estate mutual fund* (discussed earlier in this chapter). Or you can buy stock in *publicly traded real estate-related companies.* These include residential homebuilders, construction companies, mortgage lenders, home improvement retailers, property managers, real estate brokerage firms, and engineering companies. Let's now look at two other options: REITs and real estate limited partnerships (LPs; otherwise known as *limited liability companies,* or *LLCs*).

Real Estate Investment Trusts

real estate investment trust (REIT)

An investment company that accumulates money by selling shares to investors, in order to invest that money in various forms of real estate, including mortgages; this type of fund is similar to a mutual fund, but a REIT invests only in specific types of real estate or real estate-related firms.

Arguably, the best way for most individuals to invest in real estate is through a **real estate investment trust (REIT)**, which is a type of closed-end investment company that invests money in various types of real estate and real estate mortgages. A REIT is like a mutual fund in that it sells shares of stock to the investing public and uses the proceeds, along with borrowed funds, to invest in a portfolio of real estate investments. The investor therefore owns part of the real estate portfolio held by the REIT. REITs appeal to investors because they offer the benefits of real estate ownership—both capital appreciation and current income—without the headaches of property management.

REITs have become popular with investors seeking portfolio diversification because these trusts generally have relatively low correlations with other market sectors, such as common stocks and bonds. They also provide attractive dividend yields—well above the yields on common stocks. (In fact, about 65 percent of the total return from REITs comes from their dividends.) REITs have also produced competitive returns: the compound annual return from REITs (dividends plus stock price appreciation on the FTSE REIT U.S. Real Estate Index) for the last 30 years was 11.36 percent, compared with 12.51 percent for the S&P 500. The performance of REITs over this period is significantly influenced by the real estate losses resulting from the financial crisis of 2007–2009. However, the return on REITs was 27.15 percent in 2014 and the three-year return from 2012 to 2014 was 16.83 percent. REITs can be particularly attractive investments during periods of high inflation, which is projected by many to eventually result from the large deficit spending induced by the financial crisis of 2007–2009.

Like any investment fund, each REIT has stated investment objectives, which should be considered carefully before acquiring shares. There are three basic types of REITs:

- **Equity REITs:** They own and operate income-producing real estate such as apartments, office buildings, shopping centers, and hotels.
- **Mortgage REITs:** These make both construction and mortgage loans to real estate investors.
- **Hybrid REITs:** They invest in both income-producing properties and mortgage loans.

Equity REITs produce both attractive current yields and the potential to earn excellent capital gains as their properties appreciate in value. In contrast, mortgage REITs tend to be more income oriented; they emphasize the high current yields they generate by investing in debt. Listed equity REITs hold more than $1 trillion in U.S. real estate assets and constitute about 90 percent of the $700 billion listed REIT market. Most of the rest of the market involves mortgage REITs. The income earned by a REIT isn't taxed, but the income distributed to owners is designated and taxed as ordinary income. Whereas dividends on common stocks normally are taxed at preferential rates (of 15 or 20 percent or less), this is not the case with REITs, whose cash dividends are treated as ordinary income and taxed accordingly.

Financial Fact or Fantasy?

A real estate investment trust (REIT) is a popular form of limited partnership that enables individuals to invest directly in income-producing property. Fantasy: A REIT is a type of closed-end investment company (like a mutual fund) that issues stocks and invests the proceeds in various kinds of real estate properties, including mortgages.

Real Estate Limited Partnerships or Limited Liability Companies

Special-purpose syndicates organized to invest in real estate are another type of real estate investment. These can be structured as LPs or LLCs. With LPs, the managers assume the role of *general partner*, which means that their liability is unlimited and that the other investors are *limited partners* who are legally liable only for the amount of their initial investment. In recent years, the LLC has become a more popular way to form these entities. Rather than general and limited partners, the LLC has a managing member and other members—none of which have any liability. Investors buy *units* in an LP or LLC; a unit represents an ownership position, similar to a share of stock. Real estate LPs and LLCs are riskier investments than REITs, and they appeal to more affluent investors who can afford the typical unit cost of $100,000 or more.

TEST YOURSELF

13-21 Define and briefly discuss the role of each of these factors in evaluating a proposed real estate investment:

    a. Cash flow and taxes

    b. Appreciation in value

    c. Use of leverage

13-22 Why is speculating in raw land considered a high-risk venture?

13-23 Describe the major categories of income property, and explain the advantages and disadvantages of investing in income property. How can a single-family home be used to generate income?

13-24 Describe how the following securities allow investors to participate in the real estate market.

    a. Stock in real estate-related companies

    b. Real estate limited partnerships (LPs) or limited liability companies (LLCs)

13-25 Briefly describe the basic structure and investment considerations associated with a REIT. What are the three basic types of REITs?

Planning Over a Lifetime: *Investing in Mutual Funds, ETFs, and Real Estate*

Here are some key considerations for investment planning in each stage of the life cycle.

Pre-family Independence: 20s	Family Formation/ Career Development: 30–45	Pre-Retirement: 45–65	Retirement: 65 and Beyond
✓ Determine your major investment goals and how much money needs to be invested each month to achieve them.	✓ Revise investments in mutual funds, ETFs, and real estate to focus more on retirement and funding children's education, if applicable.	✓ Revise your investment plan in light of recent developments.	✓ Revise your investment plan to lean more toward debt and cash instruments than to stocks in your mutual funds and ETFs.
✓ Determine your asset allocation among stocks, bonds, real estate, and cash based on your time horizon and attitude towards risk. Choose mutual funds and ETFs accordingly.	✓ Review your asset allocation and rebalance it to be more consistent with your goals.	✓ Review your asset allocation and rebalance investments among mutual funds, ETFs, and real estate if it is inconsistent with your goals.	✓ Review your asset allocation, and rebalance it if it is inconsistent with your goals.

Here are some key considerations for investment planning in each stage of the life cycle.

Pre-family Independence: 20s	Family Formation/ Career Development: 30–45	Pre-Retirement: 45–65	Retirement: 65 and Beyond
✓ Match your investments in any employer-sponsored 401(k) retirement plan with your overall asset allocation plan.	✓ Gradually increase the amount invested in any employer-sponsored 401(k) retirement plan and reevaluate how it relates to your asset allocation plan.	✓ Continue to gradually increase the amount you invest in any employer-sponsored 401(k) retirement plan and reevaluate how it relates to your asset allocation plan.	✓ Integrate investment asset allocation strategy with estate planning.
✓ Consider investing in mutual funds and ETFs under a traditional IRA, a Roth IRA, or both.	✓ Consider increasing your contribution to traditional IRA, a Roth IRA, or both.	✓ Consider increasing your contribution to traditional and/or Roth IRAs using mutual funds and ETFs.	✓ Plan carefully for mandatory withdrawals from tax-sheltered accounts and associated tax consequences.

WILLIAM HUBER/PHOTONICA/GETTY IMAGES

Financial Impact of Personal Choices
Virginia Finds a Simple Retirement Investment Plan

Virginia Woodall, 27 years old, wants to get her retirement investing portfolio up and running. But she has a demanding job and little time to manage a portfolio closely. In doing some research, she read a short (16-page) booklet by William J. Bernstein, "If You Can" (www.etf.com/docs/IfYouCan.pdf). Bernstein argues that by age 25 it's important to invest at least 15 percent of your income annually in a 401(k), an IRA, or a taxable account (or all three) in just three mutual funds or ETFs:

- U.S. total stock market index fund
- International total stock market fund
- U.S. total bond market index fund

These funds will earn different rates of return over time, so once a year it makes sense to rebalance the amount in each account so they're equal. Bernstein convincingly argues that following this simple investment plan will beat most professional investors and would likely provide enough savings for Virginia to retire comfortably.

Virginia was indeed convinced and estimated that keeping the plan in place would take about 30 minutes a year. So she invested equal amounts in the following ETFs:

- Vanguard Total International Stock ETF (VXUS)
- Vanguard Total Stock Market ETF (VXUS)
- Vanguard Total Bond Market ETF (BND)

Virginia will invest 15 percent of her income each year in these ETFs and rebalance them annually. Her research and simple, systematic approach will no doubt serve her well.

Summary

LG1 **Describe the basic features and operating characteristics of mutual funds and exchange-traded funds, p. 509.**
Mutual fund shares represent ownership in a diversified, professionally managed portfolio of securities that do not trade on stock exchanges. In contrast, exchange-traded funds (ETFs) are investment company shares that trade throughout the day on stock exchanges. Many investors who lack the time, know-how, or commitment to manage their own money turn to these investments. By investing in mutual funds or ETFs, shareholders benefit from a level of diversification and investment performance that otherwise they might find difficult to achieve.

LG2 **Differentiate between open- and closed-end mutual funds as well as exchange-traded funds, and discuss the various types of fund loads and charges, p. 509.**
Investors can buy either open-end funds, which can issue an unlimited number of shares, or closed-end funds, which have a fixed number of shares outstanding and which trade in the secondary markets like any other share of common stock. Investors also can buy ETFs, which are typically structured like index funds and operate much like open-end funds but trade in the market like closed-end funds. There's a cost, however, to investing in mutual funds (and other types of professionally managed investment products). Mutual fund investors face a full array of loads, fees, and charges, including front-end loads, back-end loads, annual 12b-1 charges, and annual management fees. Some of these costs (e.g., front-end loads) are one-time charges, but others [such as 12b-1 and management fees] must be paid annually.

LG3 **Discuss the types of funds available to investors and the different kinds of investor services offered by mutual funds and exchange-traded funds, p. 522.**
Each fund has an established investment objective that determines its investment policy and identifies it as a certain type of fund. Some popular types of funds are growth, aggressive growth, value, equity-income, balanced, growth-and-income, bond, money market, index, sector, socially responsible, asset allocation, and international funds. The different categories of funds have different risk-return characteristics, which are important variables in the fund selection process. Many investors buy mutual funds not only for their investment returns, but also to take advantage of the various investor services that the funds offer, such as automatic investment and reinvestment plans, systematic withdrawal programs, low-cost conversion and phone or online switching privileges, and retirement programs.

LG4 **Gain an understanding of the variables that should be considered when selecting funds for investment purposes, p. 531.**
The fund selection process usually starts by assessing your own needs and wants. This sets the tone for your investment program and helps you decide on the types of funds to consider. Next, look at what the funds have to offer, particularly regarding their investment objectives and investor services; then, narrow down the alternatives by aligning your needs with the types of funds available. From this list of funds, conduct the final selection tests: fund performance and cost. Other things being equal, look for higher performance and lower costs.

LG5 **Identify the sources of return and calculate the rate of return earned on a mutual fund investment, as well as evaluate the performance of an exchange-traded fund, p. 531.**
The investment performance of mutual funds and ETFs largely depends on the returns that the money managers are able to generate from their securities portfolios. Strong markets usually translate into attractive returns for mutual fund and ETF investors. Mutual funds and ETFs have three basic sources of return: (1) dividends, (2) capital gains distributions, and (3) changes in the fund's NAV (accruing from unrealized capital gains). Both the approximate yield and total return measures recognize these three elements and provide simple yet effective ways of measuring the annual rate of return from a mutual fund or an ETF. Index-based ETF performance considers the fund's returns, as well as how closely it tracks the performance of its underlying index, how consistently it pursues its investment style, how its performance compares with its peers, and how the fund's expense ratio compares with reasonable benchmarks.

LG6 **Understand the role that real estate plays in a diversified investment portfolio along with the basics of investing in real estate, either directly or indirectly, p. 541.** Investing in real estate—be it raw land, income property (such as office buildings, apartments, and retail space), or even homes—provides an opportunity to earn attractive returns and further diversify an investment portfolio. Investors can buy property directly or invest in several types of real estate securities. Speculating in raw land is a high-risk type of real estate investment. Income-producing property, on the other hand, offers attractive returns from income and price appreciation as well as certain tax advantages. Investors not wishing to own real estate directly can invest indirectly through real estate mutual funds, as well as in the common shares of real estate-related companies, REITs, or real estate LPs or LLCs. REITs, which are closed-end investment companies that invest in real estate, are the most popular type of real estate security and have a track record of solid returns.

Key Terms

12b-1 fee, 517

automatic investment plan, 528

automatic reinvestment plan, 528

back-end load, 516

closed-end investment company, 514

conversion (exchange) privileges, 530

exchange-traded fund (ETF), 509

general-purpose money fund, 524

government securities money fund, 525

income (income-producing) property, 543

international fund, 526

load fund, 516

low-load fund, 516

management fee, 519

mutual fund, 509

net asset value (NAV), 513

no-load fund, 516

open-end investment company, 513

pooled diversification, 511

real estate investment trust (REIT), 545

socially responsible fund (SRF), 526

systematic withdrawal plan, 529

tax-exempt money fund, 525

Answers to Test Yourself

You can find answers to these questions on this book's companion website. Look for it at *www.cengagebrain.com*. Search for this book by its title, and then add it to your dashboard.

Key Financial Relationships

Concept	Financial Relationship	Page Number
Net Asset Value per Share	$$\text{Net Asset Value per Share} = \frac{\text{Total Market Value of All Securities} - \text{Liabilities}}{\text{Number of Fund Shares Outstanding}}$$	**514**
Approximate Yield	$$\text{Approximate Yield} = \frac{\text{Dividends and Capital Gains Distribution} + \dfrac{\text{Ending Price} - \text{Beginning Price}}{\text{Length of Time Period}}}{\dfrac{\text{Ending Price} + \text{Beginning Price}}{2}}$$	**537**

1. **Net asset value.** The market value of all of the securities held by a mutual fund is $5 billion. It's an open-end mutual fund with 750 million shares outstanding. What is the mutual fund's net asset value (NAV) per share?

   Solution:

   $$\text{Net Asset Value per Share} = \frac{\text{Total Market Value of All Securities} - \text{Liabilities}}{\text{Number of Fund Shares Outstanding}} = \frac{\$5 \text{ billion}}{\$750 \text{ million}}$$

   $$= \$6.67 \text{ per Share}$$

2. **Approximate yield.** Owen Chow wants to better understand how his mutual fund generated its return over the last year. The fund paid dividends of $0.85 per share, distributed capital gains of $3.25 per share and started the year with a net asset value of $32.25 per share and ended the year with a net asset value of $39.83 per share. What is the mutual fund's approximate yield and what is the primary source of its return?

   Solution:

   So Owen's mutual fund generated an attractive return. Most of the return was generated by the appreciation in the share price (NAV) of the fund. The NAV increased by $7.58 while dividends and capital gains distributed only contributed $4.10 to the return this year.

   $$\text{Approximate Yield} = \frac{\text{Dividends and Capital Gains Distribution} + \dfrac{\text{Ending Price} - \text{Beginning Price}}{\text{Length of Time Period}}}{\dfrac{\text{Ending Price} + \text{Beginning Price}}{2}}$$

   $$= \frac{(\$0.85 + \$3.25) + \dfrac{\$39.83 - \$32.25}{1}}{\dfrac{\$39.83 + \$32.25}{2}}$$

   $$= \frac{\$4.10 + \$7.58}{\$36.04} = 32.41\%$$

LG2, p. 509

1. **Estimating cost of mutual fund investments.** Using the mutual fund quotes in Exhibit 13.4, and assuming that you can buy these funds at their quoted NAVs, how much would you have to pay to buy each of the following funds?
   a. American Century Emerging Markets Fund, A shares (AEMMX)
   b. American Century Growth Fund, A shares (TCRAX)
   c. American Century International Bond Fund, A shares (AIBDX)
   d. Artisan Small Cap Value Fund Investor Shares (ARTVX)

   According to the quotes, which of these four funds have 12b-1 fees? Which have redemption fees? Are any of them no-loads? Which fund has the highest year-to-date return? Which has the lowest?

LG2,3,
p. 509, 522

2. ***Building a mutual fund portfolio.*** Imagine you've just inherited $40,000 from a rich uncle. Now you're faced with the problem of deciding how to spend it. You could make a down payment on a condo—or better yet, on that BMW that you've always wanted; or you could spend your windfall more profitably by building a mutual fund portfolio. Let's say that, after a lot of soul-searching, you decide to build a mutual fund portfolio. Your task is to develop a $40,000 mutual fund portfolio. Use actual funds and actual quoted prices, invest as much of the $40,000 as you possibly can, and be specific! Briefly describe the portfolio that you end up with, including the investment objectives that you're trying to achieve.

LG2,3,
p. 509, 522

3. ***Comparing ETF with mutual fund.*** Describe an ETF and explain how these funds combine the characteristics of open- and closed-end funds. Within the Vanguard family of funds, which would most closely resemble a "Spider" (SPDR)? In what respects are the Vanguard fund (that you selected) and SPDRs the same, and how are they different? If you could invest in only one of them, which would it be? Explain.

LG3, p. 522

4. ***Mutual fund family services.*** What investor service is most closely linked to the notion of a fund family? If a fund is not part of a family of mutual funds, can it still offer a full range of investor services? Explain. Using a source such as *The Wall Street Journal* or perhaps your local newspaper, find two examples of fund families and list some of the mutual funds that they offer.

LG3, p. 522

5. ***Comparing different types of mutual funds.*** Using a source like *Barron's, Forbes, Money,* or *Morningstar,* along with any related Internet sites, select five mutual funds—a growth fund, an index fund, a sector fund, an international fund, and a high-yield corporate bond fund—that you believe would make good investments. Briefly explain why you selected each of the funds.

LG4, p. 531

6. ***Contrasting direct and mutual fund or ETF investing.*** Contrast *mutual fund or ETF ownership* with *direct investment in stocks and bonds.* Assume that you've been asked to debate the merits of investing through mutual funds versus investing directly in stocks and bonds. Develop some pro and con arguments for this debate, and be prepared to discuss them. If you had to choose a side, which one would it be? Explain.

LG4, p. 531

7. ***Comparing risks of different mutual fund/ETF types.*** For *each pair* of funds listed below, select the fund that would be *less* risky and briefly explain your answer.
   a.   Growth versus growth-and-income
   b.   Equity-income versus high-grade corporate bonds
   c.   Intermediate-term bonds versus high-yield municipals
   d.   International versus balanced

LG4, 5, p. 531

8. ***Evaluating an ETF.*** Using the Morningstar information in Exhibit 13.10, evaluate the performance of the QQQ index-based ETF. Specifically, comment on how well it tracks the underlying index and how its performance compares with other similar ETFs.

LG5, p. 531

9. ***Calculating approximate yield on mutual fund.*** About a year ago, Ramon Navarrete bought some shares in the Sapphire Lake Mutual Fund. He bought the fund at $24.50 a share, and it now trades at $26. Last year, the fund paid dividends of 40 cents a share and had capital gains distributions of $1.83 a share. Using the approximate yield formula, what rate of return did Ramon earn on his investment? Repeat the calculation using a handheld financial calculator. What rate of return would he have earned if the stock had risen to $30 a share?

LG5, p. 531

10. ***Calculating mutual fund approximate rate of return.*** A year ago, the Stellar Growth Fund was being quoted at an NAV of $21.50 and an offer price of $23.35; today, it's being quoted at $23.04 (NAV) and $25.04 (offer). Use the approximate yield formula or a handheld financial calculator to find the rate of return on this load fund; it was purchased a year ago, and its dividends and capital gains distributions over the year totaled $1.05 a share. (*Hint:* As an investor, you buy fund shares at the offer price and sell at the NAV.)

LG5, p. 531

11. ***Calculating and evaluating mutual fund returns.*** Here is the per-share performance record of the Abacus Growth-and-Income fund for 2017 and 2016:

	2017	2016
1. **Net asset value, beginning of period:**	$58.60	$52.92
2. **Income from investment operations:**		
3. Net investment income	$1.39	$1.35
4. Net gains on securities (realized and unrealized)	8.10	9.39
5. Total from investment operations	$9.49	$10.74
6. **Less distributions:**		
7. Dividends from net investment income	($.83)	($1.24)
8. Distributions from realized gains	(2.42)	(3.82)
9. Total distributions	(3.25)	(5.06)
10. **Net asset value, end of period:**	$64.84	$58.60

Use this information to find the rate of return earned on this fund in 2016 and in 2017. What is your assessment of the investment performance of this fund for this time period?

LG6, p. 541

12. ***Different ways to invest in real estate.*** Assume you've just inherited $100,000 and want to use all or part of it to make a real estate investment.

   a. Would you invest directly in real estate, or indirectly through something like a REIT? Explain.
   b. Assuming that you decided to invest directly, would you invest in income-producing property or speculative property? Why? Describe the key characteristics of the types of income-producing or speculative property you would seek.
   c. What financial and nonfinancial goals would you establish before beginning the search for suitable property?
   d. If you decide to invest in real estate indirectly, which type(s) of securities would you buy, and why?

LG6, p. 541

13. ***Investing in residential income-producing property.*** Mallory Comer is thinking about investing in some residential income-producing property that she can purchase for $200,000. Mallory can either pay cash for the full amount of the property or put up $50,000 of her own money and borrow the remaining $150,000 at 5 percent interest. The property is expected to generate $30,000 per year after all expenses but *before* interest and income taxes. Assume that Mallory is in the 28 percent tax bracket. Calculate her annual profit and return on investment, assuming that she (a) pays the full $200,000 from her own funds or (b) borrows $150,000 at 5 percent. Then discuss the effect, if any, of leverage on her rate of return.

LG6, p. 541

14. ***Choosing a REIT.*** Choose two REITS from a list available at **https://www.reit.com/investing/investor-resources/reit-directory/reits-sp-indexes.** Using information you can find by clicking on the ticker symbol on this and other Internet sites, prepare a comparison that includes:
   a. The type of REIT that each represents (e.g., apartment, office, mortgage).
   b. The type and quality of the properties they hold.
   c. Each REIT's financial performance and management track record.

Based on your analysis, in which REIT would you invest? Explain why in terms of how it does or does not meet your investment objectives.

LG6, p. 541

15. ***Finding real estate stocks.*** Using Yahoo! Finance or another investor information Internet site, find three real estate-related stocks. Evaluate them as potential additions to your portfolio. Do you think they provide the same degree of diversification as other forms of real estate investments? Explain.

The Feeling's Mutual!

Mutual funds offer convenience, diversification, and the services of professional money managers and analysts. Mutual funds can be particularly appealing for small investors who don't have a lot of money and for those who are new to investing. This project will help you learn more about the various types of mutual funds and how to pick the funds that best suit your investment objectives.

Assume that you've just received a windfall of $25,000 and would like to invest it all in mutual funds. There are several ways to classify mutual funds, but for this project, we will consider the following eight categories:

- Growth
- Value
- Equity–income
- Bond
- Balanced
- Index
- Socially responsible
- International

Pick three or four categories that you believe best meet your financial needs and risk tolerance, and then select one fund from each category. You are strongly encouraged to use some of the online sources and other references mentioned in this chapter to help you make your selections. For each fund, find the following information:

a. Name of fund, its ticker symbol, the fund manager, and the tenure of the fund manager.
b. Category and size of the fund—try to find the *Morningstar* style box.
c. Loads, fees, and other charges; minimum investment required.
d. Performance of the fund over the past one, three, and five years. Compare the fund's performance to at least two or three other funds in its category and to an appropriate index over these same periods.
e. How much did the fund pay out last year in dividends and in distributions of short- and long-term capital gains?
f. What was the approximate yield on the fund last year? (You may have to compute this yourself; use the approximate yield formula or a handheld calculator after finding its price one year ago from a source such as **http://finance.yahoo.com**.)
g. What services does the fund offer, such as automatic reinvestment plans or phone switching?
h. Briefly explain why you selected the fund and how it meets your investment objectives.

CRITICAL THINKING CASES

13.1 Damon's Dilemma: Common Stocks, Mutual Funds, or ETFs?

Damon Bellamy has worked in the management services division of Niche Consultants for the past five years. He currently earns an annual salary of about $120,000. At 33, he's still a bachelor and has accumulated about $100,000 in savings over the past few years. He keeps his savings in a money market account, where it earns about 3 percent interest. Damon wants to get "a bigger bang for his buck," so he has considered withdrawing $50,000 from his money market account and investing it in the stock market. He feels that such an investment can easily earn more than 3 percent. Naomi Ladd, a close friend, suggests that he invest in mutual fund shares. Damon has approached you, his broker, for advice.

Critical Thinking Questions

1. Explain to Damon the key reasons for purchasing mutual fund or ETF shares.
2. What special fund features might help Damon achieve his investment objectives?
3. What types of mutual funds or ETFs would you recommend to Damon?
4. What recommendations would you make regarding Damon's dilemma about whether to go into stocks, mutual funds, or ETFs? Explain.
5. Explain to Damon the rationale for choosing ETFs over mutual funds.

13.2 Nichole Ponders Mutual Funds and ETFs

Nichole Whiting is the director of a major charitable organization in Charlotte, North Carolina. A single mother of one young child, she earns what could best be described as a modest income. Because charitable organizations aren't known for their generous retirement programs, Nichole has decided it would be best for her to do a little investing on her own. She'd like to set up a program to supplement her employer's retirement program and, at the same time, provide some funds for her child's college education (which is still 12 years away). Although her income is modest, Nichole believes that with careful planning, she could probably invest about $250 a quarter, and she hopes to increase this amount over time. Nichole now has about $15,000 in a bank savings account, which she's willing to use to start this program. In view of her investment objectives, she isn't interested in taking a lot of risk. Because her knowledge of investments extends no further than savings accounts, series EE bonds, and a little bit about mutual funds and ETFs, she approaches you for some investment advice.

Critical Thinking Questions

1. In view of Nichole's long-term investment goals, do you think mutual funds or ETFs are the more appropriate investment vehicle for her?
2. Do you think that Nichole should use her $15,000 savings to start a mutual fund or an ETF investment program?
3. What type of mutual fund or ETF investment program would you set up for Nichole? In your answer, discuss the types of funds you'd consider, the investment objectives you'd set, and any investment services (such as withdrawal plans) you'd seek. Would taxes be an important consideration in your investment advice? Explain.
4. Do you think some type of real estate investment would make sense for Nichole? If so, what type would you suggest? Explain.

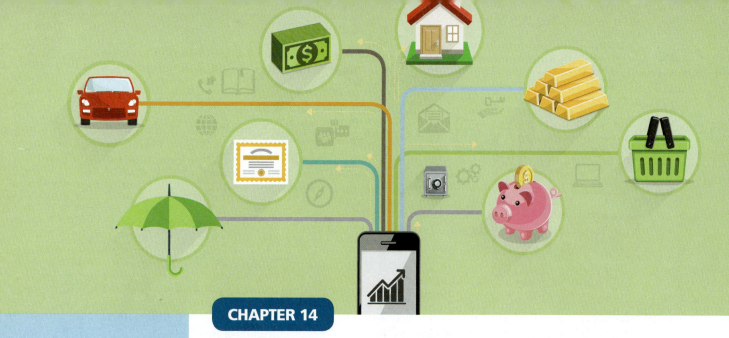

CHAPTER 14

Planning for Retirement

LEARNING GOALS

LG1 Recognize the importance of retirement planning, and identify the three biggest pitfalls to good planning.

LG2 Estimate your income needs in retirement and the level of retirement income you've estimated from various sources.

LG3 Explain the eligibility requirements and benefits of the Social Security program.

LG4 Differentiate among the types of basic and supplemental employer-sponsored pension plans.

LG5 Describe the various types of self-directed retirement plans.

LG6 Choose the right type of annuity for your retirement plan.

How Will This Affect Me?

While almost everyone understands that planning for retirement is important, far too few people actually implement a comprehensive plan, much less set aside enough savings to fund their retirement adequately. This chapter discusses the importance of retirement planning and encourages action by identifying the major pitfalls that you must overcome. In order to make the process more concrete and accessible, the steps for estimating your retirement income needs and the income that your investments will support are explained. Eligibility requirements to receive Social Security benefits and their amounts are detailed, as well as the key aspects of supplemental employer-sponsored pension plans and the potential benefits of self-directed retirement programs like traditional and Roth individual retirement accounts (IRAs). In addition, the usefulness of various annuity products in retirement planning is evaluated. After reading this chapter, you should understand how to develop and implement a financial plan that will help you achieve your long-term retirement objectives.

14-1 AN OVERVIEW OF RETIREMENT PLANNING

LG1, LG2

Do you know your life expectancy? Well, if you're in your late teens or early 20s, you'll probably live another 60 or 70 years. While this prospect may sound delightful, it also brings into focus the need for careful retirement planning. After all, you may work for only about 40 of those years and then spend 20 or more years in retirement. The challenge, of course, is to do it in style, the way you want—and that's where retirement planning comes into the picture! But to enjoy a comfortable retirement, you must *start now.* One of the biggest mistakes people make in retirement planning is waiting too long to begin.

Accumulating adequate retirement funds is a daunting task that takes careful planning. Like budgets, taxes, and investments, retirement planning is vital to your financial well-being and is a critical link in your personal financial plans. Even so, it's difficult for most people under the age of 30 to develop a well-defined set of retirement plans. There are just too many years to go until retirement and too many uncertainties to deal with: inflation, Social Security, family size, the type of pension you'll receive (if any), and how much money you will have when you're ready to retire. Yet it's just this kind of uncertainty that makes retirement planning so important. To cope with uncertainty, you must plan for various outcomes and then monitor and modify your plans as your hopes, abilities, and personal finances change.

14-1a Role of Retirement Planning in Personal Financial Planning

The financial planning process would be incomplete without *retirement planning.* Certainly no financial goal is more important than achieving a comfortable standard of living in retirement. In many respects, retirement planning captures the essence of financial planning. It is forward-looking (perhaps more so than any other aspect of financial planning), affects both your current and future standard of living, and, if successful, can be highly rewarding and contribute significantly to your net worth and quality of life.

As with most aspects of financial planning, you need a goal to get started. That is, the first step in retirement planning is to set *retirement goals* for yourself. Take some time to describe the things you want to do in retirement, the standard of living you hope to maintain, the level of income you'd like to receive, and any special retirement goals you may have (like buying a retirement home in Florida or taking

an around-the-world cruise). Such goals are important because *they give direction to your retirement planning*. Of course, like all goals, they're subject to change over time as the situations and conditions in your life change.

Once you know what you want out of retirement, the next step is to establish the *size of the nest egg* that you're going to need to achieve your retirement goals. In other words, at this point, you'll want to formulate an *investment program* that enables you to build up your required nest egg. This usually involves (1) creating a systematic savings plan in which you put away a certain amount of money each year and (2) identifying the types of investments that will best meet your retirement needs. This phase of your retirement program is closely related to investment and tax planning.

Investments and investment planning (see Chapters 11 through 13) are the vehicles for building up your retirement funds. They're the active, ongoing part of retirement planning in which you invest and manage the funds you've set aside for retirement. It's no coincidence that a major portion of most individual investor portfolios is devoted to building up a pool of funds for retirement. Tax planning (see Chapter 3) is also important because a major objective of sound retirement planning is to legitimately shield as much income as possible from taxes and, in so doing, maximize the accumulation of retirement funds.

14-1b The Three Biggest Pitfalls to Sound Retirement Planning

Human nature being what it is, people often get a little carried away with the amount of money they want to build up for retirement. Having a nest egg of $4 million or $5 million would be great, but it's really beyond the reach of most people. Besides, you don't need that much to live comfortably in retirement. So set a more realistic goal. But when you set that goal, remember: it's not going to happen by itself; you have to do something to bring it about. And this is precisely where things start to fall apart. Why? Because when it comes to retirement planning, people tend to make three big mistakes:

- Starting too late.
- Putting away too little.
- Investing too conservatively.

Many people in their 20s, or even their 30s, find it hard to put money away for retirement. Most often that's because they have other, more pressing financial concerns—such as buying a house, paying off a student loan, or paying for child care. The net result is that they *put off retirement planning until later in life*—in many cases, until they're in their late 30s or 40s. Unfortunately, the longer people put it off, the less they're going to have in retirement. Or they won't be able to retire as early as they'd hoped. Even worse, once people start a retirement program, *they tend to put away too little*. Although this may also be due to pressing financial needs, all too often it boils down to lifestyle choices. They'd rather spend today than save for tomorrow. So they end up putting maybe $1,000 a year into a retirement plan when, with a little more effective financial planning and family budgeting, they could afford to save two or three times that amount easily. So what's enough? While it all depends on your specific goals, start with a default amount of saving at least 15 percent of your pre-tax income and go from there.

On top of all this, many *people tend to be far too conservative* in the way they invest their retirement money. The fact is, they place way too much of their retirement money into *low-yielding*, fixed-income securities such as CDs and

Treasury notes. Although you should *never speculate* with something as important as your retirement plan, there's no need to avoid risk altogether. There's nothing wrong with following an investment program that involves a reasonable amount of risk, provided it results in a correspondingly higher level of expected return. Being overly cautious can be costly in the long run. Indeed, a low rate of return can have an enormous impact on the long-term accumulation of capital and, in many cases, may mean the difference between just getting by or enjoying a comfortable retirement.

Compounding the Errors

All three of these pitfalls become even more important when we introduce *compound interest*. That's because *compounding essentially magnifies the impact of these mistakes*. As an illustration, consider the first variable—starting too late. If you were to start a retirement program at age 35 by putting away $2,000 a year, it would grow to almost $160,000 by the time you're 65 if invested at an average rate of return of 6 percent. Not a bad deal, considering your total out-of-pocket investment over this 30-year period is only $60,000. But look at what you end up with if you start this investment program just 10 years earlier, at age 25: that same $2,000 a year will grow to over $309,000 by the time you're 65. Think of it—for another $20,000 ($2,000 a year for an extra 10 years), you can *nearly double* the terminal value of your investment! Of course, it's not the extra $20,000 that's doubling your money; rather, it's *compound interest* that's doing most of the work.

And the same holds true for the rate of return that you earn on the investments in your retirement account. Take the second situation just described—starting a retirement program at age 25. Earning 6 percent yields a retirement nest egg of over $309,000; increase that rate of return to 8 percent, and your retirement nest egg will be worth just over $518,000! *You're still putting in the same amount of money*, but because your money is working harder, you end up with a much bigger nest egg. Of course, when you seek higher returns (as you would when going from 6 percent to 8 percent), you should expect to take on more risk. But that may not be as much of a problem as it appears, because in retirement planning, *the one thing you have on your side is time* (unless, again, you start your plan later in life). And the more time you have, the easier it is to recover from those temporary market setbacks.

On the other hand, if you cannot tolerate the higher risks that accompany higher returns, then stay away from higher-risk investments. Rather, stick to safer, lower-yielding securities and find some other way to build up your nest egg. For instance, contribute more each year to your plan or extend the length of your investment period. The only other option—and not a particularly appealing one—is to accept the likelihood that you won't be able to build up as big a nest egg as you had thought and therefore will have to accept a lower standard of living in retirement. All else being the same, it should be clear that, the more you sock away each year, the more you're going to have at retirement. By putting away $4,000 a year rather than $2,000, you'll likely end up with at least twice as much money at retirement.

The combined impact of these three variables is seen in Exhibit 14.1. Note that *the combination of these three factors* determines the amount that you'll have at retirement. Consider the trade-offs among these factors. For example, you can offset the effects of earning a lower rate of return on your money by increasing the amount you put in each year or by lengthening the period over which you build up your retirement account—meaning that you start your program earlier in life or work longer and retire later in life. The table shows that *there are several ways of getting to roughly the same result;* that is, knowing the size of the nest egg you'd like to end up with, you can pick the combination of variables (period of accumulation, annual contribution, and rate of return) that you're most comfortable with.

EXHIBIT 14.1   Building Up Your Retirement Nest Egg

The size of your retirement nest egg will depend on when you start your program (period of accumulation), how much you contribute each year, and the rate of return that you earn on your investments. As this table shows, you can combine these variables in several ways to end up with a given amount at retirement.

AMOUNT OF ACCUMULATED CAPITAL FROM

Accumulation Period*	Contribution of $2,000/Year at These Average Rates of Return				Contribution of $5,000/Year at These Average Rates of Return			
	4%	6%	8%	10%	4%	6%	8%	10%
10 yrs. (55 yrs. old)	$ 24,010	$ 26,360	$ 28,970	$ 31,870	$ 60,030	$ 65,900	$ 72,440	$ 79,690
20 yrs. (45 yrs. old)	59,560	73,570	91,520	114,550	148,890	183,930	228,810	286,370
25 yrs. (40 yrs. old)	83,290	109,720	146,210	196,690	208,230	274,300	365,530	491,730
30 yrs. (35 yrs. old)	112,170	158,110	226,560	328,980	280,420	395,290	566,410	822,460
35 yrs. (30 yrs. old)	147,300	222,860	344,630	542,040	368,260	557,160	861,570	1,355,090
40 yrs. (25 yrs. old)	190,050	309,520	518,100	885,160	475,120	773,790	1,295,260	2,212,900

*Assumes retirement at age 65, so the age given in parentheses is the age at which the person would start his or her retirement program.

14-1c Estimating Income Needs

Retirement planning would be much simpler if we lived in a static economy. Unfortunately (or perhaps fortunately), we don't, so both your personal budget and the general state of the economy will change over time. This makes accurate forecasting of retirement needs difficult at best. Even so, it's a necessary task, and you can handle it in one of two ways. One strategy is to plan for retirement over *a series of short-run time frames*. A good way to do this is to state your retirement income objectives as a percentage of your present earnings. For example, if you want a retirement income equal to 80 percent of your final take-home pay, then you can determine the amount necessary to fund this need. Then, every 3 to 5 years, you can revise and update your plan.

Alternately, you can follow *a long-term approach* in which you estimate the level of income you'd like to receive in retirement; along with the amount of funds you must amass to achieve that desired standard of living. Rather than addressing the problem in a series of short-run plans, this approach goes 20 or 30 years into the future—to the time when you'll retire—in determining how much saving and investing you must do today in order to achieve your long-run retirement goals. Of course, if conditions or expectations should happen to change dramatically in the future (as they very likely could), then it may be necessary to make corresponding alterations to your long-run retirement goals and strategies. As emphasized in our planning examples below, it's critically important to consider the impact of inflation in implementing your retirement investment strategy.

Determining Future Retirement Needs

To illustrate how future retirement needs and income requirements can be formulated, let's consider the case of Leo and Frances Pendleton. In their mid-30s, they have two children and an annual income of about $80,000 before taxes. Until now, Leo and Frances have given only passing thought to their retirement. But even though it's still some 30 years away, they recognize it's now time to consider their situation seriously to see if they'll be able to pursue a retirement lifestyle that appeals to them.

A worksheet like this one will help you define your income requirements in retirement, the size of your retirement nest egg, and the amount that you must save annually to achieve your retirement goals.

PROJECTING RETIREMENT INCOME AND INVESTMENT NEEDS

Name(s) _Leo & Frances Pendelton_   Date _8/31/2017_

I. Estimated Household Expenditures in Retirement (Note 1):

A. Approximate number of years to retirement		30
B. Current level of annual household expenditures, excluding savings	$	56,000
C. Estimated household expenses in retirement as a *percent* of current expenses		70%
D. Estimated annual household expenditures in retirement (B × C)	$	39,200

II. Estimated Income in Retirement :

E. Social Security, annual income	$	24,000
F. Company/employer pension plans, annual amounts	$	9,000
G. Other sources, annual amounts	$	0
H. Total annual income (E + F + G)	$	33,000
I. Additional required income, or annual shortfall (D − H)	$	6,200

III. Inflation Factor :

J. Expected average annual rate of inflation over the period to retirement		5%
K. Inflation factor (in Appendix A): Based on _30_ years to retirement (A) and an expected average annual rate of inflation (J) of _5%_		4.322
L. Size of inflation-adjusted annual shortfall (I × K)	$	26,796

IV. Funding the Shortfall :

M. Anticipated return on assets held *after* retirement		8%
N. Amount of retirement funds required—size of nest egg (L ÷ M)	$	334,950
O. Expected rate of return on investments *prior* to retirement		6%
P. Compound interest factor (in Appendix B): Based on _30_ years to retirement (A) and an expected rate of return on investments of _6%_		79.058
Q. Annual savings required to fund retirement nest egg (N ÷ P)	$	4,237

Note: Parts I and II are prepared in terms of current (today's) dollars.

Worksheet 14.1 provides the basic steps to follow in determining retirement needs. This worksheet shows how the Pendletons have estimated their retirement income and determined the amount of investment assets they must accumulate to meet their retirement objectives.

Leo and Frances began by determining what their *household expenditures* will likely be in retirement. Their estimate is based on maintaining a "comfortable" standard of living—one that isn't extravagant but still allows them to do the things they'd like to in retirement. A simple way to derive an estimate of expected household expenditures is to base it on the current level of such expenses. Assume that the Pendletons' annual household expenditures (*excluding savings*) currently run about

Behavior Matters

Behavioral Biases in Retirement Planning

Rational investors should be good at forecasting retirement needs by considering expected future lifetime earnings, investment returns, tax rates, family and health situation, and expected longevity. However, research indicates that most people save too little, make questionable investment decisions, and spend their accumulated assets too quickly in retirement. Surveys indicate that about 40 percent of people have not calculated how much they need to retire, 30 percent haven't saved a significant amount, and only 20 percent feel confident they can live comfortably in retirement.

There are some behavioral biases that explain this disturbing lack of preparation for retirement. Recognizing them is more than half of the battle:

- **Self-control.** Most people *intend* to save and plan, but they do not get around to doing so. Commitment approaches like "pay yourself first" and automatic 401(k) deductions are helpful ways to encourage saving and planning follow-through.

- **Choice overload.** Faced with complex retirement investment choices, many people just give up and choose a default option or even decide not to participate in an employer-offered plan. Making the decision to ask for help can make all the difference.

- **Inertia in managing retirement investments.** Many people tend to "anchor" on their *initial* retirement account investment mix and don't revise it enough over their lives. Recognizing this tendency and scheduling periodic investment reviews with an advisor can limit any resulting damage to your retirement accounts.

- **Representativeness and availability biases.** People tend to view recent investment returns as overly representative of long-term returns and consequently tend to overweigh recent experience in their decision-making. For example, just because a mutual fund was a top performer last year does not mean that it will be next year. Similarly, many people tend to rely on the most readily available information in making investment decisions. Just because data are easy to get does not mean that they are sufficient to the task.

- **Overconfidence.** Many retirement investors are overconfident in their choices and consequently do not diversify their investments enough.

Source: Adapted from Olivia S. Mitchell and Stephen P. Utkus, "How Behavior Can Inform Retirement Plan Design," *Journal of Applied Corporate Finance,* Winter 2006, pp. 82–94.

$56,000 a year (this information can be readily obtained by referring to their most recent income and expenditures statement). After making some obvious adjustments for the different lifestyle they'll have in retirement—their children will no longer be living at home, their home will be paid for, and so on—the Pendletons estimate that they should be able to achieve the standard of living they'd like in retirement at an annual level of household expenses equal to about 70 percent of the current amount. Thus, *based on today's dollars*, their estimated household expenditures in retirement will be $56,000 × 0.70 = $39,200. (This process is summarized in steps A through D in Worksheet 14.1.)

Estimating Retirement Income

The next question is: Where will the Pendletons get the money to meet their projected household expenses of $39,200 a year? They've addressed this problem by estimating what their *income* will be in retirement—again *based on today's dollars*. Their two basic sources of retirement income are Social Security and employer-sponsored pension plans. They estimate that they'll receive about $24,000 a year from Social Security (as we'll see later in this chapter, you can obtain an estimate directly from the Social Security Administration of what your future Social Security benefits are likely to be when you retire) and another $9,000 from their employer pension plans, for a total projected annual income of $33,000. When comparing this figure to their projected household expenditures, it's clear the Pendletons will be facing an annual shortfall of $6,200 (see steps E through I in Worksheet 14.1). This is the amount of additional retirement income they must come up with; otherwise, they'll have to reduce their standard of living in retirement.

At this point, we need to introduce the *inflation factor* to our projections in order to put the annual shortfall of $6,200 in terms of retirement dollars. Here, we assume that both income and expenditures will undergo approximately the same average annual rate of inflation, which will cause the shortfall to grow by that rate over time. In essence, 30 years from now, the annual shortfall is going to amount to a lot more than $6,200. How large this number becomes will, of course, depend on what happens to inflation. Assume that the Pendletons expect inflation over the next 30 years to average 5 percent. While that's a bit on the high side by today's standards, the Pendletons are concerned that the ballooning of the federal deficit in response to the financial crisis of 2007–2009 will cause inflation to rise over the long term. Using the compound value table from Appendix A, we find that the *inflation factor* for 5 percent and 30 years is 4.322. Multiplying this inflation factor by the annual shortfall of $6,200 gives the Pendletons an idea of what that figure will be by the time they retire: $6,200 × 4.322 = $26,796 or nearly $27,000 a year (see steps J to L in Worksheet 14.1). Thus, based on their projections, the shortfall should amount to about $26,796 a year when they retire 30 years from now. *This is the amount they'll have to come up with through their own supplemental retirement program.*

EXAMPLE: Effect of Inflation on Future Retirement Needs

Renee expects to retire in 35 years. She's been told it's reasonable to expect long-term inflation to be 4 percent. Renee wants to have annual income of $80,000 in today's dollars. How much will she need in 35 years to have that much?

Using the future value interest factor for 4 percent and 35 years, Renee will need $80,000 × 3.946 = $315,680. While a daunting number, it's good Renee is planning for her retirement so carefully!

Funding a Projected Shortfall

The final two steps in the Pendletons estimation process are to determine (1) *how big their retirement nest egg must be* to cover the projected annual income shortfall, and (2) *how much to save each year* to accumulate the required amount by the time they retire. To find out how much money they need to accumulate by retirement, they must estimate the rate of return they think they'll be able to earn on their investments *after* they retire. This will tell them how big their nest egg will have to be by retirement in order to eliminate the expected annual inflation-adjusted shortfall of $26,796. Let's assume that this rate of return is estimated at 8 percent, in which case the Pendletons should accumulate $334,950 by retirement to cover the projected shortfall. This figure is found by *capitalizing* the estimated shortfall of $26,796 at an 8 percent rate of return: $26,796/0.08 = $334,950 (see steps M and N). Given an 8 percent rate of return, such a nest egg will yield $26,796 a year: $334,950 × 0.08 = $26,796. So long as the capital ($334,950) remains untouched, it will generate the same amount of annual income for as long as the Pendletons live and can eventually become a part of their estate.

Now that the Pendletons know how big their nest egg must be, the final question is: How are they going to accumulate such an amount by the time they retire? For most people, that means setting up a *systematic savings plan* and putting away a certain amount *each* year. To find out how much must be saved each year to achieve a targeted sum in the future, we can use the table of annuity factors in Appendix B. The appropriate interest factor depends on the rate of return one expects to generate and the length of the investment period. In the Pendletons' case, there are 30 years to go until retirement, meaning that the length of their investment period is 30 years. Suppose that they believe they can earn a 6 percent average rate of return on their investments over this 30-year period. From Appendix B, we see that the 6 percent, 30-year interest factor is 79.058. Because the Pendletons must accumulate $334,950 by the time they retire, *the amount they'll have to save each year* (over the next 30 years) can be found by *dividing* the amount they need to accumulate by the appropriate interest factor; that is, $334,950 ÷ 79.058 = $4,237 (see steps O to Q in Worksheet 14.1).

The Pendletons now know what they must do to achieve the kind of retirement that they want: *Put away $4,237 a year and invest it at an average annual rate of 6 percent over the next 30 years.* If they can do that, then they'll have their $334,950 retirement nest egg in 30 years. Of course, they could have been more aggressive in their investing and assumed an average annual rate of 8 percent, in which case they'd either end up with a bigger nest egg at retirement or could get away with saving less than $4,237 a year. How they actually invest their money so as to achieve the desired 6 percent (or 8 percent) rate of return will, of course, depend on the investment vehicles and strategies they use. All the worksheet tells them is how much money they'll need, not how they will get there; it's at this point that investment management enters the picture.

Calculator

INPUTS	FUNCTIONS
30	N
5.0	I/Y
−6200	PV
	CPT
	FV
SOLUTION	
26,796.04	

See Appendix E for details.

Calculator Keystrokes. As you might have suspected, the last few steps in the worksheet can just as easily be done on a handheld financial calculator. For example, consider Part III, *the inflation-adjusted annual projected shortfall*. With the calculator in the *annual mode*, you can determine how big the current annual shortfall of $6,200 will grow to in 30 years (given an average annual inflation rate of 5 percent) by using these keystrokes, where:

N = number of *years* to retirement
I/Y = *expected* annual rate of inflation
PV = additional required annual income (line I in Worksheet 14.1), entered as a *negative number*

Enter CPT (FV) and you should end up with an answer (FV) that is close to $26,796 (see step L in Worksheet 14.1); in this case, it's $26,796.04.

Now take a look at Part IV, *funding the projected shortfall* (step Q in Worksheet 14.1). Again, with the calculator in the *annual mode*, to find the amount that must be put away annually to fund a $334,950 retirement nest egg in 30 years (given an expected return of 6 percent), use the keystrokes shown here, where:

Calculator

INPUTS	FUNCTIONS
30	N
6.0	I/Y
−334950	FV
	CPT
	PMT
SOLUTION	
4,236.75	

See Appendix E for details.

N = number of *years* over which the retirement nest egg is to be accumulated
I/Y = *expected* annual return on invested capital
FV = the size of the targeted nest egg, entered as a *negative number*

Enter CPT (PMT) and a value of 4,236.75 should appear in the display, indicating the amount you must put away annually to reach a target of $334,950 in 30 years.

The procedure outlined here is admittedly a bit simplified, but in light of the uncertainty in the long-range projections being made, it provides a useful estimate of retirement income and investment needs. The procedure is far superior to the alternative of doing nothing! One important simplifying assumption in the procedure, though, is that it ignores the income that can be derived from the *sale of a house*. The sale of a house not only offers some special tax features (see Chapter 3), but also can generate a substantial amount of cash flow. If inflation does occur in the future (and it will!), it's likely to drive up home prices right along with the cost of everything else. Many people sell their homes around the time they retire and either move into smaller houses or decide to rent in order to avoid all the problems of homeownership. Of course, the cash flow from the sale of a house can substantially affect the size of the retirement nest egg. However, rather than trying to factor it into the forecast of retirement income and needs, we suggest that you *recognize* the existence of this cash-flow source in your retirement planning and consider it as a cushion against all the uncertainty inherent in retirement planning projections.

14-1d Online Retirement Planning

Like many other aspects of our lives, retirement planning has become easier with the Internet. Indeed, with the hundreds of sites that offer online retirement planning, the Internet has literally brought retirement planning to our doorsteps! You can find particularly helpful tools at **Quicken.com** and **Bloomberg.com**. At most of these Internet sites, all you do is answer a few key questions about expected inflation, desired rate of return on investments, and current levels of income and expenditures. Then the online app determines the size of any income shortfall, the amount of retirement funds that must be accumulated over time, and different ways to achieve the desired retirement nest egg. *An attractive feature of most of these Internet sites is the ability to run through "what-if" exercises easily.* By just punching a few buttons, you can change one or more key variables to see their effect on the amount of money that you must put away annually. For example, you can find out what would happen if you failed to achieve the desired rate of return on your investments.

14-1e Sources of Retirement Income

As seen in Exhibit 14.2, the principal sources of income for retired people are Social Security, earnings from income-producing assets (such as savings, stocks, and bonds), earnings from full- or part-time jobs, and pension plans. As of 2015, the largest source of income was Social Security, which represented about 38 percent of the average retiree's total income. In recent years, earned income has accounted for a growing amount of total retirement income as more and more people continue to work in retirement as a way to supplement their other sources of income. Keep in mind that these are percentage *sources* of retirement income and not dollar amounts. The *amount* of income retired individuals will receive, of course, will vary from amounts that are barely above the poverty line to six-figure incomes. Obviously, the more individuals make before they retire, the more they'll receive in Social Security benefits (up to a point) and from company-sponsored pension plans—and, very likely, the greater the amount of income-producing assets they'll hold. In this chapter, we examine Social Security and various types of pension plans and retirement programs. We'll also look briefly at an investment vehicle designed especially for retirement income: the *annuity*.

EXHIBIT 14.2   Sources of Income for the Average Retiree

Social Security is the single largest source of income for the average U.S. retiree. This source alone is larger than the amount the average retiree receives from pension plans and personal wealth/investment assets *combined*.

Income Sources as a Percent of total Income for People Aged 65 and Older

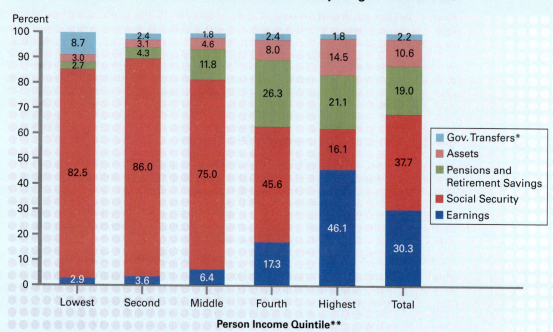

Income Sources as a Percent of total Income for People Aged 65 and Older

Note: Numbers do not sum to 100 percent because other cash income, such as family financial assistance, is not shown.

*Government cash transfers include unemployment compensation, workers' compensation, veterans' benefits, SSI, TANF, and education assistance.

**Income quintiles are based on personal total income. Quintile limits are as follows: $10,080, $16,043, $24,274, and $43,259.

Source: Adapted from Ke Bin Wu, "Sources of Income for Older Americans, 2012," AARP Public Policy Institute, Figure 1, p. 3, based on author tabulation of U.S. Bureau of the Census, March 2013 Current Population Survey, Annual Social and Economic Supplement, http://www.aarp.org/money/low-income-assistance/info-12-2013/sources-of-income-for-older-americans-2012-AARP-ppi-econ-sec.html, accessed September 2015.

TEST YOURSELF

14-1   Discuss the relationship of retirement planning to financial planning. Do investment and tax planning have a role in retirement planning?

14-2   Identify and briefly discuss the three biggest mistakes people tend to make when setting up retirement programs.

14-3   How do income needs fit into the retirement planning process?

14-4   What are the most important sources of retirement income?

14-2 SOCIAL SECURITY

The Social Security Act of 1935 was landmark legislation. It created a basic retirement program for working Americans at all income levels, and it established several other social programs, all administered under the auspices of the *Old Age, Survivor's,*

Disability, and Health Insurance (OASDHI) program. Some of the other services include supplementary security income (SSI), Medicare, unemployment insurance, public assistance, welfare services, and provision for black lung benefits. In this section, we give primary attention to the old age and survivor's portions of the act because they bear directly on retirement planning. We discussed the disability and health/Medicare benefits of Social Security in Chapter 9.

14-2a Coverage

As mandated by Congress, Social Security coverage today extends to nearly all gainfully employed workers. Only two major classes of employees are now exempt from *mandatory* participation in the Social Security system: (1) federal *civilian* employees who were hired before 1984 and are covered under the Civil Service Retirement System; and (2) employees of state and local governments who have chosen not to be covered (although most of these employees are covered through *voluntary participation* in Social Security). Certain employment positions, such as newspaper carriers under age 18 and full-time college students working for a university, are also exempt. By far, the largest group of workers in these excluded classes consists of employees of state and local governments. These people aren't compelled to participate because the federal government is not empowered to impose a tax on state and local governments.

To obtain Social Security benefits, an application must be filed with the Social Security Administration, which then determines the applicant's eligibility for benefits based on whether he or she has had enough quarters (three-month periods) of participation in the system. To qualify for full retirement benefits, nearly all workers today must be employed in a job covered by Social Security for at least 40 quarters, or 10 years. These quarters need not be consecutive. Once this 40-quarter requirement is met, the worker becomes fully insured and remains eligible for retirement payments even if he or she never works again in covered employment.

The surviving spouse and dependent children of a *deceased worker* are also eligible for monthly benefits if the worker was fully insured at the time of death or, in some special cases, if certain other requirements are met. Workers may be considered fully insured if they had 6 quarters of coverage during the three-year period preceding the time of death.

14-2b Social Security Payroll Taxes

The cash benefits provided by Social Security are derived from the payroll (FICA) taxes paid by covered employees and their employers. The tax rate in 2015 for employees was 6.2 percent for Social Security and 1.45 percent for Medicare, or a total of 7.65 percent. Self-employed people are also covered by Social Security; in 2015, they had to pay a Social Security rate of 12.4 percent and a Medicare rate of 2.9 percent for a total of 15.3 percent.

Whether the individual is an employee or self-employed, the indicated tax rate stays in effect only until the employee reaches a maximum *wage base*, which increases each year. For 2015, basic Social Security taxes were paid on the first $118,500 of wages earned or self-employed income. Thus, the maximum Social Security tax paid by an employee in 2015 was about $7,347 ($118,500 × 0.062) and by the *self-employed* was about $14,694 ($118,500 × 0.124). While the Social Security rate is paid up to taxable maximum, the Medicare rate is paid on all earnings. Further, individuals with earned income in excess of $200,000 ($250,000 for married couples filing jointly) pay an addition 0.9 percent in Medicare taxes. Thus, once the Social Security wage base is passed, employees become subject to a Medicare tax rate of 1.45 percent *on all earnings* over $118,500, whereas the added earnings of the self-employed are taxed at the rate of 2.9 percent. And, as previously noted, higher earners must also pay an additional 0.9 percent.

14-2c Social Security Retirement Benefits

Basic Social Security benefits that are important to retired people and their dependents include (1) old-age benefits and (2) survivor's benefits. Both programs provide extended benefits to covered workers and their spouses; in this section, we'll briefly describe the major provisions of each program.

Retirement Benefits

Workers who are fully covered (that is, who have worked the required 40 quarters under Social Security) may receive retirement benefits for life once they reach full retirement age. For anyone born in 1960 or later, the Social Security Administration defines "full retirement age" as age 67. (For our discussions here, we'll use 67 as the full retirement age.) Workers who elect to retire early—at age 62—will receive reduced benefits, currently 70 percent to 80 percent of the full amount (again, depending on when they were born). If the retiree has a spouse age 67 or older, the spouse may be entitled to benefits equal to one-half of the amount received by the retired worker. The spouse may also elect early receipt of reduced benefits at age 62. For retirement planning purposes, it seems reasonable to expect Social Security to provide the average retired wage earner (who is married) with perhaps 40 to 60 percent of the wages he or she was earning in the year before retirement—assuming, of course, that the retiree has had a full career working in covered employment. Social Security, therefore, should be viewed as *a foundation for your retirement income.* By itself, *it's insufficient to enable a worker and spouse to maintain their preretirement standard of living.*

In two-income families, both the husband and wife may be eligible for full Social Security benefits. When they retire, they can choose to receive their benefits in one of two ways: each can (1) take the full benefits to which each is entitled from his or her account or (2) take the husband and wife benefits of the higher-paid spouse. If each takes his or her own full share, there are no spousal benefits. If they take the husband and wife benefits of the higher-paid spouse, they effectively receive 1.5 shares. Obviously, two-income couples should select the option that provides the greater amount of benefits.

Survivor's Benefits

If a covered worker dies, the spouse can receive survivor's benefits from Social Security. These benefits include a small lump-sum payment of several hundred dollars, followed by monthly benefit checks. To be eligible for monthly payments, the surviving spouse generally must be at least 60 years of age or have a dependent and unmarried child of the deceased worker in his or her care. (To qualify for *full* benefits, the surviving spouse must be at least 67 years of age; reduced benefits are payable between ages 60 and 67.) If the children of a deceased worker reach age 16 before the spouse reaches age 60, the monthly benefits cease and do not resume until the spouse turns 60. This period during which survivor's benefits are not paid is sometimes called the *widow's gap.* (As we saw in Chapter 8, Social Security survivor's benefits play a key role in life insurance planning.)

Financial Fact or Fantasy?

In order to receive maximum social security retirement benefits, a worker must retire before his or her 66th birthday. **Fantasy:** To qualify for maximum benefits, a worker must be full retirement age and have career earnings (prior to retirement) that were equal to or greater than the maximum social security tax base for at least 10 years.

14-2d How Much Are Monthly Social Security Benefits?

The amount of Social Security benefits to which an eligible person is entitled is set by law and defined according to a fairly complex formula. But you don't need to worry about doing the math yourself. The Social Security Administration is required by law to provide all covered workers with a *Social Security Statement.* (You can also request a statement by going to the Social Security

Should You Depend on Social Security in Retirement Planning?

The old age and disability trust funds supporting Social Security benefits are projected to be unable to pay full benefits by 2034! This is because the birth rate is low, the ratio of workers to beneficiaries is declining, and people are living longer.

While the government will be unable to pay *full* benefits, it should be able to pay *some* benefits. Even if Congress does nothing to fix the problem, resources are expected to be sufficient to pay about 78 percent of the promised benefits. In order to pay full benefits the system will have to raise the full-retirement age, reduce benefits, increase payroll taxes, or pursue a combination of these options. It's unlikely that any cut in Social Security benefits would be applied uniformly to everyone. They would probably fall disproportionately on the young and higher earners.

How should your retirement planning take these issues into account? A conservative financial plan would reduce the amount of Social Security benefits that you can rely on by at least 20 percent.

Administration's Internet site: **http://www.ssa.gov**.) "Your Social Security Statement" lists the year-by-year Social Security earnings you've been credited with and shows (in today's dollars) what benefits you can expect under three scenarios: (1) if you retire at age 62 and receive 70 percent to 80 percent of the full benefit (depending on your age), (2) the full benefit at age 65 to 67 (depending on your year of birth), and (3) the increased benefit (of up to 8 percent per year) that's available if you delay retirement until age 70. The statement also estimates what your children and surviving spouse would get if you die and how much you'd receive monthly if you became disabled.

Range of Benefits

Using information provided by the Social Security Administration, the *current average level of benefits* (for someone who retired in 2015) is shown in Exhibit 14.3. The average benefits, as of mid-2015, are portrayed for a variety of beneficiaries. Keep in mind that the figures given in the exhibit represent amounts that the beneficiaries will receive in their *first year* of retirement. Those amounts will be adjusted upward each year with subsequent increases in the cost of living.

Note that the average benefits shown in Exhibit 14.3 reflect the fact that they *may be reduced* if the Social Security recipient is *under age 67 and still gainfully employed*—perhaps in a part-time job. In particular, given that full retirement age is now 67, retirees aged 62 through 66 are subject to an *earnings test* that effectively limits the amount of income they can earn before they start losing some (or all) of their Social Security benefits. In 2015, that limit was $15,720 per year (this earnings limit rises annually with wage inflation). The rule states that Social Security recipients aged 62 through 66 will lose $1 in benefits for every $2 they earn above the earnings test amount. So if you earned, say, $18,000 a year at a part-time job, you'd lose $1,140 in annual Social Security benefits—that is, $18,000 − $15,720 = $2,280, which is divided in two to yield $1,140. That's $95 a month you'd lose simply because you hold a job that pays you more than the stipulated maximum. Not a very fair deal! But at least it applies only to early retirees. *Once you reach "full retirement age," the earnings test no longer applies, so you can earn any amount without penalty.* In contrast to earned income, there never have been any limits on so-called unearned income derived from such sources as interest, dividends, rents, or profits

EXHIBIT 14.3 Average Monthly Social Security Benefits Paid in 2015

The Social Security benefits listed here are averages that include a variety of ages at which beneficiaries retired. As time passes, the beneficiary will receive correspondingly higher benefits as the cost of living goes up. However, these average benefits dramatize that you should not rely on such benefits too heavily in your retirement planning.

Type of Beneficiary	Average Monthly Benefit
Retired worker	$1,328
Retired couple	$2,176
Disabled worker	$1,165
Disabled worker with a spouse and child	$1,976
Widow or widower	$1,274
Young widow or widower with two children	$2,680

Source: "Understanding the Benefits," SSA Publication No. 05-10024, ICN 454930, http://www.socialsecurity.gov/pubs/EN-05-10024.pdf#page%031&zoom %03auto,0,576, accessed September 2015.

on securities transactions—a retiree can receive an unlimited amount of such income with no reduction in benefits.

You Can Do It Now

Get a Rough Estimate of Your Future Social Security Benefits

It's easy to get a rough estimate of your future Social Security benefits. While the Quick Calculator doesn't access your actual earnings history, it does provide a useful ballpark estimate: http://www.ssa.gov/oact/quickcalc/. Remember that this estimate does not consider that future Social Security benefits could be reduced somewhat. You can do it now.

Taxes on Benefits

Even though Social Security "contributions" are made in after-tax dollars, you may actually have to pay taxes (again) on at least some of your Social Security benefits. Specifically, as the law now stands, *Social Security retirement benefits are subject to federal income taxes if the beneficiary's annual income exceeds one of the following base amounts:* $25,000 for a single taxpayer, $32,000 for married taxpayers filing jointly, and zero for married taxpayers filing separately. In determining the amount of income that must be counted, the taxpayer starts with his or her *adjusted gross income (AGI)* as defined by current tax law (see Chapter 3) and then adds all nontaxable interest income (such as income from municipal bonds) plus a stipulated portion of the Social Security benefits received. Thus, if for single taxpayers the resulting amount is between $25,000 and $34,000, 50 percent of Social Security benefits are taxable. If income exceeds $34,000, 85 percent of Social Security benefits are subject to income tax for a single taxpayer. If the combined income of married taxpayers filing joint returns is between $32,000 and $44,000, then 50 percent of the Social Security benefits are taxable; the percentage of benefits taxed increases to 85 percent when their combined income exceeds $44,000.

Financial Fact or Fiction?

Social security retirement benefits should be sufficient to provide retired workers and their spouses with a comfortable standard of living. **Fantasy:** Social security is intended to be only a foundation for retirement income. By itself, these benefits will likely permit retirees to cover only a small fraction of their pre-retirement standard of living.

TEST YOURSELF

14-5   What benefits are provided under the Social Security Act, and who is covered?

14-6   What is the *earnings test,* and how does it affect Social Security retirement benefits?

14-7   Does Social Security coverage relieve you of the need to do some retirement planning on your own?

14-3 PENSION PLANS AND RETIREMENT PROGRAMS

LG4, LG5

Accompanying the expansion of the Social Security system has been a corresponding growth in employer-sponsored pension and retirement plans. In 1940, when the Social Security program was in its infancy, fewer than 25 percent of the workforce had the benefit of an employer-sponsored plan. Today, around 65 percent of all wage earners and salaried workers (in both the private and public sectors) are covered by some type of employer-sponsored retirement or profit-sharing plan.

Qualified pension plans (discussed later) allow firms to deduct, for tax purposes, their contributions to employee retirement programs. Even better, the employees can also deduct these contributions from their taxable income and can thus build up their own retirement funds on a tax-deferred basis. Of course, when the funds are eventually paid out as benefits, the employees will have to pay taxes on this income.

Government red tape, however, has taken a toll on pension plans. In particular, the **Employee Retirement Income Security Act (ERISA)** of 1974 (sometimes referred to as **ERISA** or the *Pension Reform Act*), which was established to protect employees participating in private employer retirement plans, has actually led to a reduction in the number of new retirement plans started among firms, especially the smaller ones. Indeed, the percentage of workers covered by company-sponsored plans has fallen dramatically since the late 1970s. It's estimated that today, *in the private sector, only about 40 percent of all full-time workers are covered by company-financed plans*— even worse, only about one-third (or less) of the part-time labor force is covered. In contrast, *there has been a significant increase in salary-reduction forms of retirement plans* (discussed later in this chapter). In addition to ERISA, the widespread availability of Keogh plans, Roth, traditional, and SEP IRAs, and other programs have lessened the urgency for small firms (and bigger ones as well) to offer their own company-financed pension plans.

Now fast-forward some 30 years after ERISA's enactment. In an attempt to curb some of the increasingly serious funding problems occurring in private pension plans, Congress passed, and President George W. Bush signed into law, the **Pension Protection Act** of 2006. One of the major provisions of this Act is that it forces those employers that provide traditional pension plans to their employees (with their defined monthly retirement benefits) to shore up these programs by pumping in tens of billions of dollars in *additional* contributions. At the same time, however, the law encourages employees to make use of various salary reduction (defined contribution) plans, like 401(k)s and IRAs, by setting higher contribution limits and, perhaps what is most important, by making it easier for companies to enroll workers automatically into company-sponsored savings plans (rather than relying on the current system, which leaves the option with the worker). Employees, of course, will still have the right to opt out of the programs if they so wish. This latter measure, which many believe could end up being the most significant part of the legislation, is aimed at substantially raising the participation rate among workers in various types

Employee Retirement Income Security act (ERISA)
A law passed in 1974 to ensure that workers eligible for pensions actually receive such benefits; also permits uncovered workers to establish individual tax-sheltered retirement plans.

Pension Protection Act
A federal law passed in 2006 intended to shore up the financial integrity of private traditional (defined benefit) plans and, at the same time, to encourage employees to make greater use of salary reduction (defined contribution) plans.

of corporate savings plans. There's still another provision of the law that's intended to help employees manage their retirement accounts by encouraging, rather than limiting, the amount and types of investment advice that mutual funds and other providers can give directly to employees.

14-3a Employer-Sponsored Programs: Basic Plans

Employers can sponsor two types of retirement programs—*basic plans*, in which employees automatically participate after a certain period of employment, and *supplemental plans*, which are mostly voluntary programs that enable employees to increase the amount of funds being set aside for retirement. We'll look first at some key characteristics of basic plans.

Participation Requirements

The vast majority of pension plans require that employees meet certain criteria before becoming eligible for participation. Most common are requirements relating to years of service, minimum age, level of earnings, and employment classification. Years of service and minimum age requirements are often incorporated into retirement plans in the belief that a much higher labor turnover rate applies to both newly hired and younger employees. Therefore, to reduce the administrative costs of the plans, employees in these categories are often excluded—at least initially—from participation. Once these (or any other) participation requirements are met, the employee automatically becomes eligible to participate in the program.

Not everyone who participates in a pension plan will earn *the right to receive retirement benefits*. Pension plans impose certain criteria that must be met before the employee can obtain a nonforfeitable right to a pension, known as **vested rights**. As the law now stands, *full vesting* rights are required after only three to six years of employment. More specifically, companies must now choose between two vesting schedules. One, the so-called *cliff vesting*, requires full vesting after no more than three years of service—but you obtain no vesting privileges until then. There are no vesting privileges at all for the first three years, and then suddenly you're fully vested. Once vested, you're entitled to everything that's been paid in so far (your contributions *plus* your employer's), as well as everything that will be contributed in the future. Under the alternate procedure, the so-called *graded schedule*, vesting takes place gradually over the first six years of employment. At the minimum, after two years you'd have a nonforfeiture right to at least 20 percent of the benefits, with an additional 20 percent each year thereafter until you're 100 percent vested after six years. Note, however, that these are minimum standards, and employers can grant more favorable vesting terms.

To illustrate the vesting process, assume a medium-sized firm offers a plan in which full vesting of benefits occurs after three years. The plan is contributory, with employees paying 3 percent of their salaries and the employer paying an amount equal to 6 percent of the salaries. Under this plan, employees cannot withdraw the contributions made by the employer until they reach retirement age, usually 65. The plan provides annual benefits in the amount of $11 per year of service for each $100 of an employee's final monthly earnings—the amount earned during the final month in the employ of the firm. Therefore, an employee who worked a minimum of three years for the firm would be eligible for a retirement benefit from that company, even if he or she left the company at, say, age 30.

Because of inflation, the value of the benefit for a worker who leaves the firm long before retirement age is typically very small. Consequently, the employee might be better off simply withdrawing his or her *own* contributions (which always vest immediately) and terminating participation in the plan at the same time he or she leaves the employer. Of course, any worker who leaves the firm before accumulating the required years of service would be entitled only to a return of his or her own contributions to the plan (plus nominal investment earnings). Whenever you terminate

vested rights
Employees' nonforfeitable rights to receive benefits in a pension plan based on their own and their employer's contributions.

noncontributory pension plan
A pension plan in which the employer pays the total cost of the benefits.

contributory pension plan
A pension plan in which the employee bears part of the cost of the benefits.

defined benefit plan
A pension plan in which the formula for computing benefits is stipulated in its provisions.

employment, *resist the urge to spend the money you have built up in your retirement account!* Over time, that can have a devastating effect on your ability to accumulate retirement capital. Instead, *when you take money out of one retirement account, roll it over into another one.*

What's Your Contribution?

Whether you, as an employee, must make payments toward your own pension depends on the type of plan you're in. If you belong to a noncontributory pension plan, then the employer pays the total cost of the benefits—you don't have to pay a thing. Under a contributory pension plan, the employer and the employee share the cost. Today the trend is toward contributory plans. In addition, nearly all plans for employees of federal, state, and local governments require a contribution from the employee. In contributory plans, the employee's share of the costs is often between 3 and 10 percent of annual wages and is typically paid through a payroll deduction. The most common arrangement is for the employer to match the employee's contribution—the employee puts up half the annual contribution and the employer puts up the other half. When employees who've participated in a contributory retirement plan terminate employment before retirement, they're legally entitled to a benefit that is based on the amount of their individual contributions. Usually this benefit is a cash lump sum, but in some cases, it can be taken as a monthly payment at retirement. Whether departing employees receive any benefit from the *employer's* contributions depends on the plan's benefit rights.

Defined Contributions or Defined Benefits

The two most commonly used methods to compute benefits at retirement are the defined contribution plan and the defined benefit plan. A defined contribution plan specifies the amount of contribution that both the employer and employee must make. At retirement, the worker is awarded whatever level of monthly benefits those contributions will purchase. Although such factors as age, income level, and the amount of contributions made to the plan have a great deal to do with the amount of monthly benefits received at retirement, probably no variable is more important than the level of *investment performance* generated on the contributed funds.

A defined contribution plan promises nothing at retirement except the returns the fund managers have been able to obtain. The only thing that's defined is the amount of contribution that the employee and/or employer must make (generally stated as a percentage of the employee's income). The benefits at retirement depend totally on investment results. Thus, the employee bears the risk of funding retirement. Of course, the investment managers follow a certain standard of care, so some protection is provided to the plan participants. Even so, that still leaves a lot of room for variability in returns.

Under a defined benefit plan, it's the formula for computing benefits, not contributions, that is stipulated in the plan provisions. These benefits are paid out regardless of how well (or poorly) the retirement funds are invested. If investment performance falls short, the employer must make up the difference in order to fund the benefits agreed to in the plan. Thus, the employer bears the risk of funding the employee's retirement. This type of plan allows employees to calculate, before retirement, how much their monthly retirement income will be. Often the number of years of service and amount of earnings are prime factors in the formula. For example, workers might be paid 2.5 percent of their final three-year average annual salary for each year of service. Thus, the *annual* benefit to an employee whose final three-year average annual salary was $85,000 and who was with the company for 20 years would be $42,500 (2.5% × $85,000 × 20 years).

Other types of defined benefit plans may simply pay benefits based on (1) a consideration of earnings excluding years of service, (2) a consideration of years of service excluding earnings, or (3) a flat amount with no consideration given to either earnings or years of service. Many defined benefit plans also increase retirement benefits periodically to help retirees keep up with the cost of living. In periods of high inflation, these increases are essential to maintain retirees' standards of living. About 65 percent of all private industry employees have some kind of retirement plan. Of those with retirement plans, about 60 percent of private industry workers have a defined contribution plan, and 20 percent have a defined benefit plan. In addition, most government workers have some kind of defined benefit plan. Even so, while the number of *people covered* by such plans continues to rise, the number of (private-sector) *defined benefit plans in existence* has steadily declined. In fact, there are now more assets held in defined contribution plans than there are in traditional (defined benefit) pension plans. And as noted previously (in discussing the Pension Protection Act of 2006), *it's very likely that this shift to defined contribution plans will only accelerate in the coming years.*

Regardless of the method used to calculate benefits, the employee's key concern should be with the percentage of final take-home pay that the plan is likely to produce

FINANCIAL ROAD SIGN

Be Aware of Potentially Damaging Retirement Planning Myths

Having a well-funded, secure retirement is an important financial goal. While useful information is abundant, there're also some myths that can get in the way of successfully reaching your retirement goals. Here are some of the most common retirement planning myths.

- **I just graduated from college and it's too early to start saving for retirement.** Consider that traditional pension funds are disappearing and future Social Security benefits are far from certain. Saving sooner allows you to gain the most from the compounding of your returns. Starting earlier will also reinforce good financial habits that will guide your financial life well.

- **For planning purposes, I'll need about 80 percent of my current income in retirement.** One size doesn't fit all. What if you want to spend a lot of time traveling in retirement? And what will health care cost when you retire? The future benefit levels of government programs like Medicare are unclear.

- **Social Security will provide no benefits by the time I retire.** As discussed earlier in this chapter, it's unlikely that Social Security will go away completely. However, future benefits may be reduced by 25 percent or so by 2034.

- **I have a lot of financial goals and can't afford to tie up so much money in a retirement plan.** It's true that especially when you're first getting started you're likely saving for emergencies, buying a home, and perhaps going back to school. If you're concerned about retaining access to some of your savings, consider a Roth IRA. As long as the account has been open for at least five years, you can withdraw your contributions any time and for any reason without tax or penalty.

- **I have a retirement plan at work and consequently cannot contribute to an IRA.** While there are income limits for traditional IRA contributions, you can make nondeductible, tax-deferred and possibly Roth IRA contributions.

- **I expect my tax rate to be the same in retirement so tax-deferred plans will provide no benefit.** Even if your *marginal* tax rate remains the same, some of the money in the plan will likely be taxed at lower rates. So the tax deferral feature could provide you with a lower *average* tax rate. And the tax deferral over time will have sheltered your earnings from taxes.

Source: Adapted from Erik Carter, "10 Common Myths That Could Be Hurting Your Retirement Planning," http://www.forbes.com/sites/financialfinesse/2012/08/22/10-common-myths-that-could-be-hurting-your-retirement-planning/, accessed September 2015.

at retirement. A pension is usually thought to be good if, when combined with Social Security, it will result in a monthly income equal to about 70 percent to 80 percent of preretirement net earnings. To reach this goal, however, today's employees must take some responsibility because *there's a growing trend for companies to switch from defined benefit plans to defined contribution programs.* Companies don't like the idea of facing uncertain future pension liabilities. So more and more of them are avoiding these problems altogether by changing to defined contribution plans. And in cases where the firms are sticking with their defined benefit plans, the benefits are often so meager that they don't come close to the desired 70 percent to 80 percent income target. The bottom line is that *the employee is now being forced to assume more responsibility for ensuring the desired level of retirement income.* This means that where you end up in retirement will depend, more than ever, on what *you've* done, rather than on what your employers have done. *Very likely, you're the one who is going to control not only how much goes into the company's retirement programs, but where it goes as well.*

Cash-Balance Plans

cash-balance plan
An employer-sponsored retirement program that combines features of defined contribution and defined benefit plans and is well suited for a mobile workforce.

One of the newest types of employer-sponsored retirement programs is the **cash-balance plan**. A cash-balance plan is much like a traditional defined benefit plan, but it also has features that are similar to those of defined contribution plans. As with traditional pension plans, the company funds the pension (the employee pays nothing into the plan). It also controls the investments and guarantees a benefit payout at retirement. And as with a defined contribution plan, the company contributions are based on a percentage (say, 4 percent or 5 percent) of the employee's current salary. Most important, the company sets up a separate "account" for each employee that shows how much has been accumulated in the account at any given time. In a cash-balance plan, the account is guaranteed by the company to earn a given minimum rate of return, which might be a fixed percentage rate (of perhaps 2 percent or 3 percent) or a variable rate of return that is linked to something like Treasury bills (T-bills). That's it; that's all the company guarantees. So, unlike traditional pension plans, your retirement benefits are in no way linked to the salary you'll be making when you retire. Instead, at retirement, you receive whatever the cash balance of your account happens to be, either in the form of a lump-sum payment or as a stream of fixed annuity payments over time.

Given the low guaranteed earnings rate, there's little doubt that the retirement benefits of cash-balance plans will turn out to be less—and perhaps substantially so—than what would have been paid under traditional plans (where the benefits are linked to how much the employee was making at the time of his or her retirement). But there's a big upside to these plans, particularly for younger employees: *the accounts are portable.* This means that, when employees leave a firm, they can roll their accounts into their new employer's cash-balance plans or into an IRA. Indeed, the portability of cash-balance plans makes them better suited than traditional pension plans to meet the needs of an increasingly mobile workforce.

Qualified Pension Plans

qualified pension plan
A pension plan that meets specified criteria established by the Internal Revenue Code.

The Internal Revenue Code permits a corporate employer making contributions to a **qualified pension plan** to deduct from taxable income its contributions to the plan. As a result, the employees on whose behalf the contributions are made don't have to include these payments as part of their taxable income until the benefits are actually received. Further, in contributory plans, *employees can also shelter their contributions from taxes.* In other words, such contributions aren't counted as part of taxable income in the year that they're made. They consequently act to reduce the amount of taxable income reported to the Internal Revenue Service (IRS) and therefore lead to lower taxes for the employee.

Still another tax advantage of these plans is that any and all investment income is allowed to accumulate tax free. As a result, investment capital can build up more quickly. Yet despite all these tax benefits, many firms still believe that the costs of regulation exceed any benefits that might result and therefore choose to forgo the procedures required for having a plan qualified. Probably the biggest disadvantage of nonqualified pension plans from the employee's perspective is that any contributions made to *contributory* plans are made on an after-tax basis and thus are *not* sheltered from taxes.

14-3b Employer-Sponsored Programs: Supplemental Plans

In addition to basic retirement programs, many employers offer supplemental plans. These plans are often *voluntary* and enable employees not only to increase the amount of funds being held for retirement, but also to enjoy attractive tax benefits. There are three basic types of supplemental plans: profit-sharing, thrift and savings, and salary reduction plans.

Profit-Sharing Plans

profit-sharing plan
An arrangement in which the employees of a firm participate in the company's earnings.

Profit-sharing plans enable employees to participate in the earnings of their employer. A **profit-sharing plan** may be qualified under the IRS and become eligible for essentially the same tax treatment as other types of pension plans. An argument supporting the use of profit-sharing plans is that they encourage employees to work harder because the employees benefit when the firm prospers. From the firm's perspective, a big advantage of profit-sharing plans is that they impose no specific levels of contribution or benefits by the employer. When profits are low, the firm makes smaller contributions to the plan, and when profits are high, it pays more.

Many employers establish minimum and maximum amounts to be paid as contributions to profit-sharing plans, regardless of how low or high corporate earnings are. Contributions to profit-sharing plans are invested in certain types of fixed-interest products, stocks and bonds, and in many cases securities issued by the employing firm itself. Employees who receive the firm's securities may actually benefit twice. When profits are good, larger contributions are made to the profit-sharing plan *and* the price of the shares already owned is likely to increase.

Some major firms offer *voluntary profit-sharing plans* that invest heavily in their own stock. It's common in many of these cases for long-term career employees to accumulate several hundred thousand dollars' worth of the company's stock. And we're not talking about highly paid corporate executives here; rather, these are just average employees who had the discipline to divert a portion of their salary consistently to the company's profit-sharing plan. However, *there is a real and significant downside to this practice*: if the company should hit hard times, then not only could you face salary cuts (or even worse, the loss of your job), but the value of your profit-sharing account will likely tumble as well. Just look at what happened to employees in the tech sector during the 2000–2002 bear market, and to employees in most sectors during the financial crisis of 2007–2009! Certainly, employees should seriously consider taking steps to diversify their pension portfolios more adequately if more than 30 percent to 40 percent of their portfolios is concentrated in their company's stock.

Thrift and Savings Plans

thrift and savings plans
A plan to supplement pension and other fringe benefits; the firm contributes an amount equal to a set proportion of the employee's contribution.

Thrift and savings plans were established to supplement pension and other fringe benefits. Most plans require the employer to make contributions to the savings plan in an amount equal to a set proportion of the amount contributed by the employee. For example, an employer might match an employee's contributions at the rate of 50 cents on the dollar up to, say, 6 percent of salary. Thus, an employee making $40,000 a year could pay $2,400 into the plan annually, and the employer would kick in another $1,200. These contributions are then deposited with a trustee, who invests the money in various types of securities, including stocks and bonds of the employing firm. With IRS-qualified thrift and savings plans, the *employer's* contributions and earnings on the savings aren't included in the *employee's* taxable income until he or she withdraws these sums. Unfortunately, this attractive tax feature doesn't extend to the employee's contributions, so any money put into one of these savings plans is still considered part of the employee's taxable income and subject to regular income taxes.

Thrift and savings plans usually have more liberal vesting and withdrawal privileges than do pension and retirement programs. Often the employee's right to the employer's contributions becomes nonforfeitable immediately upon payment, and the total savings in the plan can be withdrawn by giving proper notice. However, employees who terminate participation in such a plan are frequently prohibited from rejoining it for a specified period, such as one year. An employee who has the option should seriously consider participating in a thrift plan. The returns are usually pretty favorable, especially when you factor in the *employer's* contributions.

Salary Reduction Plans

salary reduction, or 401(k), plan
An agreement by which part of a covered employee's pay is withheld and invested in some form of investment; taxes on the contributions and the account earnings are deferred until the funds are withdrawn.

Another type of supplemental retirement program—and certainly the most popular, judging by employee response—is the salary reduction plan, or the 401(k) plan as it's more commonly known. Our discussion here centers on 401(k) plans, but similar programs are available for employees of public, nonprofit organizations. Known as *403(b) plans* or *457 plans*, they offer many of the same features and tax shelter provisions as 401(k) plans. (Workers at public schools, colleges, universities, nonprofit hospitals, and similar organizations have 403(b) plans; state or local government workers probably have a 457 plan, as do employees at some tax-exempt organizations.) Today, more and more companies are cutting back on their contributions to traditional (defined benefit) retirement plans. They're turning instead to 401(k) plans, a type of defined contribution plan.

According to Fidelity Investments, one of the largest 401(k) providers, the average 401(k) balance was around $91,800 in 2015. And the average balance was about $251,600 for employees having participated in a 401(k) for at least 10 years. Yet these averages are for those who participate in 401(k) programs. According to the National Institute on Retirement Security, more than 45 percent of households do not own any significant retirement account assets. When all households are considered, the median retirement account balance was a mere $3,000 and only $12,000 for those near retirement. Thus, up to 92 percent of households do not meet conservative retirement savings targets for their age and income levels! Thus, a retirement savings crisis is here and growing.

A 401(k) plan basically gives employees the option to divert part of their salary to a company-sponsored, tax-sheltered savings account. In this way, the earnings diverted to the savings plan accumulate tax free. Taxes must be paid eventually, but not until the employee starts drawing down the account at retirement, presumably when he or she is in a lower tax bracket. In 2015, an individual employee could put as much as $18,000 into a tax-deferred 401(k) plan. [Contribution limits for 403(b) and 457 plans are the same as those for 401(k) plans.] And for those over 50 years old, there is a "catch-up" provision that allows them to contribute up to $24,000 in 2015.

EXAMPLE: How Tax-Deferred Plans Work

Gabriela is under 50 years old with taxable income of $75,000 in 2015. She would like to contribute the maximum allowable mount—$18,000—to the 401(k) plan where she works. Doing so reduces her taxable income to $57,000 and, assuming she's in the 25 percent tax bracket, lowers her federal tax bill by $4,500 (i.e., $18,000 × 0.25). Such tax savings will offset a good portion—25 percent—of her contribution to the 401(k) savings plan. In effect, she'll add $18,000 to her retirement program with only $13,500 of her own money. The rest will come from the IRS via a reduced tax bill. What's more, all of the *earnings* on her investment account will accumulate tax free. However, the downside is that if she needs the money before she is 59½ she will have to pay the tax on the withdrawal *plus* a 10 percent penalty to the IRS.

FINANCIAL PLANNING TIPS

Managing Your 401(k) Retirement Account Effectively

A few basic ideas on managing your 401(k) account can take you a long way:

• **A reasonable asset allocation is more important than choosing the "right" funds for your 401(k) account money.** Research shows that over 90 percent of your investment performance will be determined by how much you allocate to cash, bonds, and equity funds. So less than 10 percent of performance is determined by choosing the right funds and by trying to time the market (which is never a good idea anyway). Remember that the conventional wisdom as a starting place: put 100 minus your age as the percentage in equities and the residual in bonds and cash. For example, if you're 30, start out with a plan to put 70 percent in equities and 30 percent in bonds and cash. Then adjust the mix to match your risk tolerance.

• **Invest enough in your 401(k) account.** Invest at least up to your company's matching amount, if you can possibly afford it. For example, if your company matches the first 6 percent of your annual contribution, then you should contribute at least that much or you're just throwing away money. A reasonable overall goal is to contribute at least 15 percent of your annual income to retirement investment accounts, which include 401(k)s, IRAs, and other investment vehicles.

• **Invest in your 401(k) consistently, regardless of its performance.** Some investors panic when their 401(k) accounts lose money and *reduce or even stop* making contributions in an effort to protect themselves from further losses. This is the opposite of what you should do. When you're losing money, it's time to grit your teeth and contribute more to your account, not less! This is because you've got to make up for your losses. If you stop or reduce your contributions, you'll be even less likely to achieve your retirement goal. And keep in mind that when investment values fall, you're buying more shares at lower prices (a principle known as "dollar-cost averaging"). In the long term, this should contribute positively to performance.

These plans are generally viewed as attractive *tax shelters* that offer not only substantial tax savings, but also a way to save for retirement. So long as you can afford to put the money aside, *you should seriously consider joining a 401(k)/403(b)/457 plan if one is offered at your place of employment.* This is especially true when one considers the matching features offered by many of these plans. Most companies that offer 401(k) plans have some type of matching contributions program, often putting up 50 cents (or more) for every dollar contributed by the employee. Such matching plans give both tax and savings incentives to individuals and clearly enhance the appeal of 401(k) plans. (Matching contributions by employers are far less common with 403(b) plans and virtually nonexistent with 457 plans.)

Another kind of 401(k) plan is being offered by a growing number of firms. This retirement savings option, which first became available in 2006, is the so-called *Roth 401(k)*. It's just like a traditional 401(k), except for one important difference: *All contributions to Roth 401(k) plans are made in after-tax dollars.* That means there are no tax savings to be derived from the annual employee contributions; if you earn, say, $75,000 a year and want to put $18,000 into your Roth 401(k), you'll end up paying taxes on the full $75,000. That's the bad news; now the good news. Because all contributions are made in after-tax dollars, *there are no taxes to be paid on plan withdrawals (in other words, they're tax free)*, provided you're at least 59½ and have held the account for five years or more. Like traditional 401(k) plans, Roth 401(k)s also have a contribution cap of $18,000 (in 2015, for those under 50). And that limit applies to *total contributions to both types of 401(k) plans combined*, so you can't put $18,000 into a traditional 401(k) plan and then put another $18,000 into a Roth 401(k). You can also have employer matches with the Roth plans, although those matches will accumulate in a separate account that will be taxed as ordinary income at withdrawal. Essentially, *employer* contributions represent tax-free income to employees, so they'll pay taxes on that income, and on any account earnings, when the funds are withdrawn, as is done with a traditional 401(k). A couple of final points: because of the tax differences in traditional versus Roth 401(k) plans, all earnings generated in the *employee's account* accumulate on a *tax-free basis* in Roth plans; they accumulate on a *tax-deferred basis* in traditional 401(k) plans. And the Roth 401(k) can offer an advantage to high-income individuals who aren't able to contribute to a Roth IRA. There are no income restrictions for using Roth 401(k) plans.

Both Roth and traditional 401(k) plans typically offer their participants various investment options, including equity and fixed-income mutual funds, company stock, and other interest-bearing vehicles such as bank CDs or similar insurance company products. Indeed, the typical 401(k) has about 10 choices, and some plans have as many as 20 or more. Today, the trend is toward giving plan participants more options and providing seminars and other educational tools to help employees make informed retirement plan decisions. As we've discussed throughout the book, behavioral finance research suggests that too many choices overwhelm most consumers.

14-3c Evaluating Employer-Sponsored Pension Plans

When participating in a company-sponsored pension plan, you're entitled to certain benefits in return for meeting certain conditions of membership, which may or may not include making contributions to the plan. Whether your participation is limited to the firm's basic plan or includes one or more of the supplemental programs, *it's vital that you take the time to acquaint yourself with the various benefits and provisions* of these retirement plans. And be sure to familiarize yourself not only with the basic plans (even though participation is mandatory, you ought to know what you're getting for your money) but also with any (voluntary) supplemental plans you may be eligible to join.

So, how should you evaluate these plans? Most experts agree that you can get a good handle on essential plan provisions and retirement benefits by getting answers to questions about the following features:

- **Eligibility requirements:** Precisely what are they, and if you're not already in the plan, when will you be able to participate?
- **Defined benefits or contributions:** Which one is defined? If it's the benefits, exactly what formula is used to define them? Pay particular attention to how Social Security benefits are treated in the formula. If it's a defined contribution program, do you have any control over how the money is invested? If so, what are your options? *What you'd like to have:* lots of attractive no-load stock/equity mutual funds to choose from. *What you don't need:* a bunch of low-yielding investment options, such as bank CDs, money market mutual funds, or fixed annuities.
- **Vesting procedures:** Does the company use a cliff or graded procedure, and precisely when do you become fully vested?
- **Contributory or noncontributory:** If the plan is contributory, how much comes from you and how much from the company; and what's the total of this contribution as a percentage of your salary? If it's noncontributory, what is the company's contribution as a percentage of your salary?
- **Retirement age:** What's the normal retirement age, and what provisions are there for *early* retirement? What happens if you leave the company before retirement? Are the pension benefits *portable*—that is, can you take them with you if you change jobs?
- **Voluntary supplemental programs:** How much of your salary can you put into one or more of these plans, and what—if anything—is matched by the company? Remember, these are like defined contribution plans, so nothing is guaranteed as far as benefits are concerned.

Finding answers to these questions will help you determine where you stand and what improvements are needed in your retirement plans. As part of this evaluation process, try to determine, as best as you can, *a rough estimate of what your benefits are likely to be at retirement*. You'll need to make some projections about future income levels, investment returns, and so on, but it's an exercise well worth taking (before you start cranking out the numbers, check with the people who handle employee benefits at your workplace; they'll often give you the help you need). Then, using a procedure similar to that followed in Worksheet 14.1, you can estimate what portion of your retirement needs will be met from your company's basic pension plan. If there's a shortfall—*and it's likely there will be*—it will indicate the extent to which you need to participate in some type of company-sponsored supplemental program, such as a 401(k) plan, or (alternatively) how much you'll need to rely on your own savings and investments to reach the standard of living you're looking for in retirement. *Such insights will enable you to dovetail more effectively the investment characteristics and retirement benefits of any company-sponsored retirement plans with the savings and investing that you do on your own.*

14-3d Self-Directed Retirement Programs

In addition to participating in company-sponsored retirement programs, individuals can set up their own tax-sheltered retirement plans. There are two basic types of self-directed retirement programs: *Keogh* and *SEP plans*, which are for self-employed individuals, and *IRAs*, which can be set up by almost anyone.

Keogh and SEP Plans

Keogh plans were introduced in 1962 as part of the Self-Employed Individuals Retirement Act, or simply the Keogh Act. Keogh plans allow self-employed individuals to set up tax-deferred retirement plans for themselves and their employees. Like contributions to 401(k) plans, payments to Keogh accounts may be taken as deductions from taxable income. As a result, they reduce the tax bills of self-employed individuals. The maximum contribution to this tax-deferred retirement plan in 2015 was $53,000 per year, or 25 percent of earned income, whichever is less.

Any individual who is self-employed, either full- or part-time, is eligible to set up a Keogh account. These accounts can also be used by individuals who hold full-time jobs and moonlight part-time—for instance, the engineer who has a small consulting business on the side, or the accountant who does tax returns on a freelance basis at night and on weekends. If the engineer, for example, earns $10,000 a year from his part-time consulting business, then he can contribute 25 percent of that income ($2,500) to his Keogh account and thereby reduce both his taxable income and the amount he pays in taxes. Further, he's still eligible to receive full retirement benefits from his full-time job and to have his own IRA (but as we'll see, contributions to his IRA may not qualify as a tax shelter).

Keogh accounts can be opened at banks, insurance companies, brokerage houses, mutual funds, and other financial institutions. Annual contributions must be made at the time the respective tax return is filed or by April 15 of the following calendar year (for example, you have until April 15, 2017, to contribute to your Keogh for 2016). Although a designated financial institution acts as custodian of all the funds held in a Keogh account, *actual investments held in the account are directed completely by the individual contributor*. These are self-directed retirement programs; the *individual* decides which investments to buy and sell (subject to a few basic restrictions).

Income earned from the investments must be reinvested in the account. This income also accrues tax free. All Keogh contributions and investment earnings must remain in the account until the individual turns 59½ unless he or she becomes seriously ill or disabled. Early withdrawals for any other reason are subject to 10 percent tax penalties. However, the individual is not *required* to start withdrawing the funds at age 59½; the funds can stay in the account (and continue earning tax-free income) until the

---

Keogh plan
An account to which self-employed persons may make specified payments that may be deducted from taxable income; earnings also accrue on a tax-deferred basis.

individual is 70½. The individual *must* then begin withdrawing funds from the account, unless he or she continues to be gainfully employed past the age of 70½. Of course, once an individual starts withdrawing funds (upon or after turning 59½), all such withdrawals are treated as ordinary income and subject to normal income taxes. Thus, the taxes on all contributions to and earnings from a Keogh account will eventually have to be paid—a characteristic of any tax-*deferred* (as opposed to tax-*free*) program.

A program that's similar in many ways to the Keogh account is something called a *simplified employee pension plan*—or SEP-IRA for short. It's aimed at small business owners, particularly those with *no employees*, who want a plan that's simple to set up and administer. SEP-IRAs can be used in place of Keoghs and, although simpler to administer, have the same annual contribution caps as a Keogh account: $53,000 per year or 25 percent of earned income (in 2015), whichever is less.

Individual Retirement Account (IRAs)

Some people mistakenly believe that an IRA is a specialized type of investment. It's not. An **individual retirement account (IRA)**, is virtually the same as any other investment account you open with a bank, credit union, stockbroker, mutual fund, or insurance company, except that it's clearly designated as an IRA. That is, you complete a form that designates the account as an IRA and makes the institution its trustee. That's all there is to it. Any gainfully employed person (and spouse) can have an IRA account, although the type of accounts that a person can have and the tax status of those accounts depend on several variables. All IRAs, however, have one thing in common: they're designed to encourage retirement savings for individuals.

Each individual now has three IRA types to choose from, as follows:

©DEAN MITCHELL/SHUTTERSTOCK.COM

- **Traditional (deductible) IRA**, which can be opened by anyone without a retirement plan at his or her place of employment, *regardless of income level*, or by couples filing jointly who—even if they are covered by retirement plans at their places of employment—have adjusted gross incomes of less than $98,000 (or single taxpayers with AGIs of less than $61,000). In 2015, individuals who qualify may make tax-deductible contributions of up to $5,500 a year to their accounts (an equal tax deductible amount can be contributed by a nonworking spouse). This maximum annual contribution increases to $6,500 for individuals age 50 or older. All account earnings grow tax free until withdrawn, when ordinary tax rates apply (though a 10 percent penalty normally applies to withdrawals made before age 59½).

- **Nondeductible (after-tax) IRA**, which is open to anyone regardless of their income level or whether they're covered by a retirement plan at their workplace. In 2015, contributions of up to $5,500 a year can be made to this account by those under 50 years of age and up to $6,500 for those over 50, but they're *made with after-tax dollars* (that is, the contributions are not tax deductible). However, *the earnings do accrue tax free and are not subject to tax until they are withdrawn*, after the individual reaches age 59½ (funds withdrawn before age 59½ may be subject to the 10 percent penalty).

- **Roth IRAs** are a lot like *Roth 401(k)s*, which we discussed earlier. Roth IRAs are the newest kid on the block and can be opened by couples filing jointly with adjusted gross incomes of up to $193,000 (singles up to $131,000), whether or not they have other retirement or pension plans. But the best part of the Roth IRA is its tax features—although the annual contributions of up to $6,500 a person in 2015 are made with nondeductible/after-tax dollars, all earnings in the account grow tax free. And *all withdrawals from the account are also tax free*, so long as the account has been open for at least five years and the individual is past the age of 59½. In other words, so long as these conditions are met, you won't have to pay taxes on any withdrawals you make from your Roth IRA!

Key features and provisions of all three of these IRAs are outlined in Exhibit 14.4.

EXAMPLE: Measuring the Benefits of a Roth IRA Over a Taxable Account

Roth IRAs provide no tax deduction for contributions. But all future earnings are sheltered from taxes under current law. So how much would you save over simply investing in a fully taxed fund if you're 25 years old and invested $5,500 a year at 6 percent until retirement at age 66?

Assuming you're in the 25 percent marginal tax bracket and you invested the money at the beginning of each year, you would have $962,228 in a Roth IRA and $648,586 in an unsheltered account at retirement (assuming, for simplicity, that all of your investment returns were taxed at your marginal tax rate). So the tax shelter afforded by the Roth IRA would be worth a whopping $313,642 more than the otherwise comparable but fully taxable account!

You Can Do It Now

Calculating the Value of a Traditional IRA

If you want to estimate the potential value of a traditional IRA at retirement, try the calculator at http://www.bankrate.com/calculators/retirement/traditional-ira-plan-calculator.aspx. You can do it now.

It is possible to convert a traditional IRA to a Roth IRA. If you convert, you will have to pay taxes on any earnings and pretax contributions. So why would you want to do that? It may make sense to convert if you expect your tax rate to remain the same or go up after retirement. Thus, converting to a Roth IRA could allow you to pay a lower amount of taxes on your IRA investments in the long run. However, it's important to be able to pay the taxes using money that doesn't come out of your IRA account. If you make a withdrawal from an IRA account before age 59½, you generally owe a 10 percent penalty on that amount. And you would also give up the opportunity for tax-free Roth IRA compounding on that amount—permanently. It usually makes less sense to convert a traditional IRA to a Roth IRA the older you are. This is because the older you are, the less time you have to make up for what you paid in taxes on the conversion. However, it can still be wise for an older person to convert a traditional to a Roth IRA for estate tax planning purposes. Conversions can be complicated, and it's best to consult a tax advisor.

Regardless of the type and notwithstanding the conditions just described, penalty-free withdrawals are generally allowed from an IRA so long as the funds are being used for first-time home purchases (up to $10,000), qualifying educational costs, certain major medical expenses, or other qualified emergencies. Also, with both the traditional/deductible and nondeductible IRAs, you must start making withdrawals from your account once you reach age 70½—although *this requirement does not apply to Roth IRAs*.

In addition to the three retirement-based IRAs, *Coverdell Education Savings Accounts* (or ESAs) can be set up and used to meet the future education (college) cost

EXHIBIT 14.4   **Qualifying for an IRA**

Individuals can now select from three types of individual retirement accounts.

Traditional Deductible IRA

- For 2015, if covered by a retirement plan at work, a taxpayer may make an annual contribution of up to $5,500 if under 50 years old and up to $6,500 if 50 years or older. A nonworking spouse can make the fully tax-deductible contribution if the couple's joint income is less than $183,000 and they file a joint return.
- If covered by a retirement plan at work, reduced tax-deductible contributions are available to joint filers with AGIs (in 2015) of $98,000 to $118,000, and to single filers with AGIs (in 2015) of $61,000 to $71,000—essentially, the deductible contribution is reduced at higher levels of AGI and phases out completely at an AGI of $71,000 for single taxpayers and $118,000 for joint returns. If one spouse is covered by a retirement plan at work and the other is not, then the deduction is phased out between AGIs of $183,000 and $193,000.

After-Tax IRA

- Working taxpayers who fail to qualify for deductible IRAs, and their nonworking spouses, each can make annual nondeductible IRA contributions of up to $5,500 (under 50 years old) or $6,500 (50 years or older) in 2015.

Roth IRA

- A working taxpayer with AGI of up to $116,000 on a single return, or $183,000 on a joint return, can make nondeductible contributions of up to $5,500 (younger than 50) or up to $6,500 (50 or older).
- A reduced contribution can be made by joint filers with AGIs (in 2015) of $183,000 to $193,000 and by single filers with AGIs of $116,000 to $131,000.
- A nonworking spouse can make after-tax contributions of up to $5,500 (younger than 50) or $6,500 (50 years or older) per year to a Roth IRA with AGI of $183,000 or less on a joint return.

of a child or grandchild. Specifically, these accounts, which were formerly known as *Education IRAs*, can be opened by couples with AGIs of up to $220,000 (or singles with AGIs up to $110,000) for the benefit of a child under the age of 18. *Nondeductible* annual contributions of up to $2,000 per child are allowed in 2015. As with Roth IRAs, the earnings grow tax free so long as they remain in the account, and all withdrawals (which must be made by the time the beneficiary reaches age 30) are also made tax free and penalty free, provided the funds are used for qualifying education expenses.

Similar to Coverdell ESAs are 529 plans, which are named after Section 529 of the Internal Revenue Code. A 529 plan is an education savings plan operated by a state or educational institution that is designed to help set aside money to fund future college costs. Every state offers at least one 529 plan and the student's chosen school does not have to be in the state in which the 529 plan is based. Savings plans invest your contributions in investments that grow tax deferred. It is also possible to prepay tuition in some states using a 529 plan. The savings plan contributions are not deductible at the federal level, but some states allow an up-front deduction. Distributions to pay for the student's college costs are not taxed. Although Coverdell ESAs and 529 plans are quite similar, they differ significantly in contribution limits, age limits for student use, and the type and level of schooling covered.

Self-Directed Accounts and Their Investment Vehicles

IRAs are like Keogh and SEP plans; they're *self-directed accounts*, which means that you are free to make almost any kind of investment decision you want. An individual can be conservative or aggressive in choosing securities for an IRA (or Keogh), though conventional wisdom favors funding your IRA (and Keogh) with *income-producing assets*. This would also suggest that, if you're looking for capital gains, it's best to do so *outside* your retirement account. The reasons are twofold: (1) growth-oriented securities are by nature *more risky*, and (2) you *cannot write off losses* from the sale of securities held in an IRA (or Keogh) account. This doesn't mean, however, that it would be totally inappropriate to place a good-quality growth stock or mutual fund in a Keogh or IRA. In fact, many advisors contend that growth investments should always have a place in your retirement account because of their often impressive performance and ability to protect against inflation. Such investments may pay off handsomely, as they can appreciate totally free of taxes. In the end, of course, *it's how much you have in your retirement account that matters, not how your earnings were made along the way.*

No matter what type of investment vehicle you use, keep in mind that once you place money in an IRA, it's meant to stay there for the long haul. Like most tax-sheltered retirement programs, there are restrictions on when you can withdraw the funds from an IRA. Specifically, as noted earlier, any funds withdrawn from an IRA prior to age 59½ are subject to a 10 percent tax penalty in addition to the regular tax paid on the withdrawal. (Note, however, that you can avoid the 10 percent tax penalty and still start

withdrawals before age 59½ by setting up a systematic withdrawal program that pays you equal amounts over the rest of your life expectancy. Of course, unless you have a substantial amount of money in your IRA, the annual payments under this program are likely to be pretty small.) Also, when you move your IRA account to a new firm (this is known as a *rollover*), the transfer is subject to a *20 percent withholding tax* if the proceeds from the transfer are paid to you directly. The rule is very clear on this: if you take possession of the funds (even for just a few days), you'll be hit with the withholding tax. So, the best way to handle IRA rollovers is to *arrange for the transfer of funds from one firm to another.*

So, should you contribute to an IRA or not? Obviously, so long as you qualify for either a traditional/tax-deductible IRA or a Roth IRA (see Exhibit 14.4), you should seriously consider making the maximum payments allowable. There are no special record-keeping requirements or forms to file, and the IRA continues to be an excellent vehicle for sheltering income from taxes. Probably the biggest decision you'll have to make is which IRA is right for you—the traditional or the Roth?

TEST YOURSELF

14-8 Which basic features of employer-sponsored pension plans should you be familiar with?

14-9 Under which procedure will you become fully vested most quickly—cliff or graded vesting?

14-10 What is the difference between a profit-sharing plan and a salary reduction, or 401(k), plan?

14-11 Why is it important to evaluate and become familiar with the pension plans and retirement benefits offered by your employer?

14-12 Briefly describe the tax provisions of 401(k) plans and Keogh plans.

14-13 Describe and differentiate between Keogh plans and individual retirement arrangements. What's the difference between a *nondeductible* IRA and a *Roth* IRA?

14-14 Under what circumstances would it make sense to convert your traditional IRA to a Roth IRA?

14-4 ANNUITIES

annuity
An investment product created by life insurance companies that provides a series of payments over time.

accumulation period
The period during which premiums are paid for the purchase of an annuity.

distribution period
The period during which annuity payments are made to an annuitant.

survivorship benefit
On an annuity, the portion of premiums and interest that has not been returned to the annuitant before his or her death.

single premium annuity contract
An annuity contract purchased with a lump-sum payment.

immediate annuity
An annuity in which the annuitant begins receiving monthly benefits immediately.

installment premium annuity contract
An annuity contract purchased through periodic payments made over time.

deferred annuity
An annuity in which benefit payments are deferred for a certain number of years.

An annuity is just the opposite of life insurance. As we pointed out in Chapter 8, life insurance is the systematic accumulation of an estate that is used for protection against financial loss resulting from premature death. In contrast, an **annuity** is the systematic *liquidation* of an estate in such a way that it provides protection against the economic difficulties that could result from outliving personal financial resources. The period during which premiums are paid toward the purchase of an annuity is called the **accumulation period**; correspondingly, the period during which annuity payments are made is called the **distribution period**.

Under a pure life annuity contract, a life insurance company will guarantee regular monthly payments to an individual for as long as he or she lives. These benefits are composed of three parts: principal, interest, and survivorship benefits. The *principal* consists of the premium amounts paid in by the *annuitant* (person buying the annuity) during the accumulation period. *Interest* is the amount earned on these funds between the time they're paid and distributed. The interest earnings on an annuity accrue (that is, accumulate) tax free—but note that, whereas the earnings in an annuity accumulate on a tax-sheltered basis, the amounts paid into an annuity are all made with *after-tax dollars* (that is, no special tax treatment is given to the capital contributions). The portion of the principal and interest that has not been returned to the annuitant before death is the **survivorship benefit**. These funds are available to those members of the annuity group who survive in each subsequent period.

14-4a Classification of Annuities

Annuities may be classified according to several key characteristics, including payment of premiums, disposition of proceeds, inception date of benefits, and method used in calculating benefits. Exhibit 14.5 illustrates this classification system.

Single Premium or Installments

There are two ways to pay the premiums when you purchase an annuity contract: you can make one large (lump-sum) payment up front or pay the premium in installments. The **single premium annuity contract** usually requires a *minimum investment* of anywhere from $2,500 to $10,000, with $5,000 the most common figure. These annuities have become popular primarily because of their attractive tax features. They're often purchased just before retirement as a way of creating a future stream of income. In these circumstances, the individual normally purchases an **immediate annuity**, in which case the stream of monthly benefits begins immediately—the first check arrives a month or so after purchase. Sometimes the cash value of a life insurance policy is used at retirement to acquire a single premium annuity. This is an effective use of a life insurance policy: you get the insurance coverage when you *need* it the most (while you're raising and educating your family) and then a regular stream of income when you can probably *use* it the most (after you've retired).

Although most *group* annuity policies are funded with single premiums, many *individuals* still buy annuities by paying for them in installments. With these **installment premium annuity contracts**, set payments, which can start as low as $100, are made at regular intervals (monthly, quarterly, or annually) over an extended period of time. Sometimes these annuities are set up with a fairly large initial payment (of perhaps several thousand dollars), followed by a series of much smaller installment payments (of, say, $250 a quarter). This approach would be used to purchase a **deferred annuity**, a type of contract in which cash benefits are deferred for several years (note that single premiums can also be used to purchase deferred annuities). A big advantage of *installment premium deferred annuities* is that your savings can build up over time *free of taxes*. With no taxes to pay, you have more money working for you and can build up a bigger retirement nest egg. You'll have to pay taxes on your earnings eventually, of course, but not until you start receiving benefit payments from your annuity.

EXHIBIT 14.5 | Types of Annuity Contracts

Annuity contracts vary according to how you pay for the annuity, how the proceeds are disbursed, how earnings accrue, and when you receive the benefits.

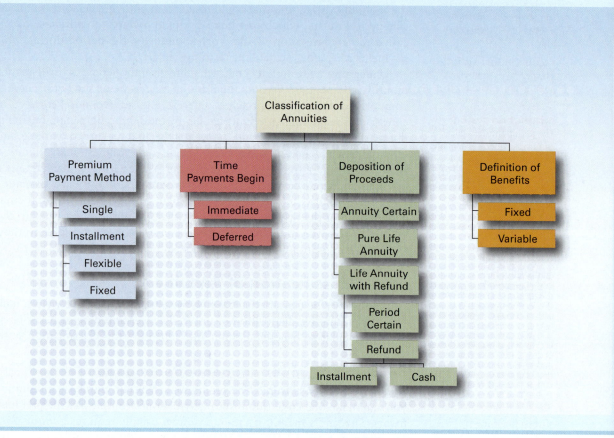

Installment premium contracts also carry an important *life insurance provision*, which stipulates that if an annuitant dies before the distribution period begins, then the annuitant's beneficiaries will receive the market value of the contract or the amount invested, whichever is greater (note that single-premium annuities contain similar life insurance provisions so long as the payout of benefits is deferred to some future date). In addition, the annuitant can terminate an installment premium contract at any time or simply stop paying the periodic installments and take a paid-up annuity for a reduced amount. One potential advantage of purchasing an installment-type annuity relatively early in life is that scheduled benefits are based on mortality rates in effect when the contract was purchased. Even if the mortality rate increases, as it normally does with the passage of time, the annuitant won't be required to pay the higher premium stipulated in contracts issued later.

Disposition of Proceeds

All annuities revolve around the basic concept of "pay now, receive later," so they allow individuals to prepare for future cash needs, such as planning for retirement, while obtaining significant tax benefits. When the annuity is distributed, you can take a lump-sum payment or, as is more often the case, you can *annuitize* the distribution by systematically parceling out the money into regular payments over a defined or open-ended period. Because most people choose to annuitize their proceeds (which is how an annuity is intended to be used), let's look at the most common annuity disbursement options:

- **Life annuity with no refund (pure life).** The annuitant receives a specified amount of income for life, whether the disbursement period turns out to be 1 year or 50 years. The estate or family receives no refunds when the annuitant dies. This results in the largest monthly payments of any of the distribution methods because the issuer (a life insurance company) doesn't have to distribute the principal, if any, to the annuitant's heirs.
- **Guaranteed-minimum annuity (life annuity with refund).** In this type of contract, the benefits (future cash flows) aren't limited to the annuitant only and may extend to named beneficiaries. There are two forms of this annuity. With a **life annuity, period certain**, the annuitant gets a guaranteed monthly income for life, with the added provision that the insurance company will pay the monthly benefits for a minimum number of years (5 or 10, for example). If the annuitant dies soon after the distribution begins, then his or her beneficiaries receive the monthly benefits for the balance of the "period certain." With a **refund annuity**, if the annuitant dies, then the designated beneficiary receives monthly payments (or in some cases a lump-sum cash refund) until the total purchase price of the annuity has been refunded.
- **Annuity certain.** This type of annuity pays a set amount of monthly income for a specified number of years, thereby filling a need for monthly income that will expire after a certain length of time. An annuitant selecting a 10-year annuity certain receives payments for 10 years after retirement, regardless of whether he or she lives for 2 or 20 more years. For example, a widow, age 52, could use a 10-year annuity certain contract to provide income until she reaches age 62 and can apply for Social Security benefits.

Fixed versus Variable Annuity

When you put your money into an annuity, the premium is invested on your behalf by the insurance company, much as a mutual fund invests the money you put into it. How that rate of return is figured on that investment determines whether you own a fixed or variable annuity. In a **fixed-rate annuity**, the insurance company safeguards your principal and agrees to pay a guaranteed minimum rate of interest over the life of the contract—which often amounts to little more than prevailing money market rates existing when you bought the contract. These are conservative, very low-risk annuity products that essentially promise to return *the original investment plus interest* when the money is paid out to the annuitant (or any designated beneficiaries). Unlike bond mutual funds, fixed annuities don't fluctuate in value when interest rates rise or fall; so your principal is always secure. These *interest-earning annuities*, as they're also called, are ideally suited for the cautious investor who likes the secure feeling of knowing what his or her monthly cash flow will be.

Imagine an investment vehicle that lets you move between stocks, bonds, and money funds and, at the same time, accumulate profits tax free. That, in a nutshell, is a variable annuity. With a **variable annuity** contract, the amount that's ultimately paid out to the annuitant varies with the investment results obtained by the insurance company—*nothing is guaranteed, not even the principal!* When you buy a variable annuity, *you decide* where your money will be invested, based on your investment objectives and tolerance for risk; you can usually choose from stocks, bonds, money market securities, real estate, alternative investments, or some combination thereof. As an annuity holder, you can stay put with a single investment for the long haul; or, as with most variable annuities, you can more aggressively play the market by switching from one fund to another. Obviously, when the market goes up, investors in variable annuities do well; but when the market falters, the returns on these policies will likewise be reduced.

life annuity with no refund (pure life)
An option under which an annuitant receives a specified amount of income for life, regardless of the length of the distribution period.

guaranteed-minimum annuity (life annuity with refund)
An annuity that provides a guaranteed minimum distribution of benefits.

life annuity, period certain
A type of guaranteed-minimum annuity that guarantees the annuitant a stated amount of monthly income for life; the insurer agrees to pay for a minimum number of years.

refund annuity
A guaranteed-minimum annuity that, on the annuitant's death, makes monthly payments to the beneficiary until the total price of the annuity is refunded.

annuity certain
An annuity that provides a specified monthly income for a stated number of years without consideration of any life contingency.

fixed-rate annuity
An annuity in which the insurance company agrees to pay a guaranteed rate of interest on your money.

variable annuity
An annuity in which the monthly income provided by the policy varies with the insurer's actual investment experience.

Although there's nothing to keep you from staying with market-sensitive variable annuities, in most cases *you can convert to a fixed annuity at distribution*. What you do, in effect, is use the cash value in your variable annuity to buy a paid-up fixed annuity. In this way, you use a *variable annuity during the accumulation period* to build up your capital as much as possible and then switch to a *fixed annuity for the distribution period* to obtain a certain, well-defined stream of future income.

14-4b Sources of Annuities

Annuities are administered by life insurance companies, so it's no surprise that they're also the leading sellers of these financial products. Annuities can also be purchased from stock brokers, mutual fund organizations, banks, and financial planners. When you buy an annuity, the cost will vary with the annuitant's age at issue, the annuitant's age when payments begin, the method used to distribute benefits, the number of lives covered, and the annuitant's gender. There can be substantial differences among the premiums charged by different companies. These differences confirm the need to shop around before making an annuity purchase. The cost to females is higher than the cost to males across all benefit levels because of the lower mortality rates among women.

> ### You Can Do It Now
>
> *What Do Annuities Cost?*
>
> Want to get a sense of what an annuity costs? Representative quotes based on state, age, and gender can be found at https://www.nylaarp.com/Annuities/Income-Example. You can do it now.

As with mutual funds, there are some annual fees that you should be aware of. In particular, be prepared to pay insurance fees of 1 percent or more—in addition to the annual management fees of perhaps 1 percent to 2 percent paid on variable annuities. That's a total of 2 percent to 3 percent or more taken right off the top, year after year. There is also a *contract charge* (or maintenance fee) that's deducted annually to cover various contract-related expenses; these fees usually run from about $30 to $60 per year. Obviously, these fees can drag down returns and reduce the advantage of tax-deferred income. Finally, most annuities charge hefty *penalties for early withdrawal*. This means that, in order to get out of a poorly performing annuity, you'll have to forfeit a chunk of your money.

14-4c Investment and Income Properties of Annuities

A major attribute of most types of annuities is that they're a source of income that can't be outlived. Although individuals might be able to create a similar arrangement by simply living off the interest or dividends from their investments, they'd find it difficult to liquidate their principal systematically so that the last payment would coincide closely (or exactly) with their death. Another advantage is that the income earned in an annuity is allowed to accumulate tax free, so it's a form of *tax-sheltered investment*. Actually, the income from an annuity is *tax deferred*, meaning that taxes on the earnings will have to be paid when the annuity is liquidated.

Shelter from taxes is an attractive investment attribute, but there's a hitch. You may be faced with a big tax penalty if you close out or withdraw money from an annuity before it's time. Specifically, the IRS treats annuity withdrawals like withdrawals from an IRA: except in cases of serious illness, *anyone who takes money out before reaching age 59½ will incur a 10 percent tax penalty*. So, if you're under age 59½ and in the 28 percent tax bracket, you'll end up paying a 38 percent tax rate on any funds withdrawn from an annuity. (The IRS views withdrawals *as taxable income*

FINANCIAL PLANNING TIPS

Does an Annuity Make Sense for You?

Most of us don't have a traditional defined benefit pension and have to manage with a 401(k) plan, along with careful investing, to fund our retirement. But we still long for the steady income that defined benefit plans provide. Annuities are designed to provide a monthly income for the rest of your life. You enter into an agreement with an insurer that provides that benefit for a predefined time period, after you pay in advance for this service. Annuities are designed to assure that you do not outlive your money.

So when does it make sense to buy an annuity? If you have guaranteed income from several different sources, you may not need an annuity. However, if you don't have a traditional pension plan and want the security of a fixed monthly payment in retirement, you may want to consider using some of your savings to purchase an annuity. Here is some more specific guidance.

A *deferred annuity* is worth considering when:

• You are making the maximum contribution to your employer-sponsored retirement plan and to your IRA (or if you're not eligible for an IRA).

• You don't expect to need the annuity funds until you are at least 59½ years old.

• You have an emergency fund that covers at least six months of living expenses.

An *immediate annuity* may be a good choice when:

• You want to convert part of your retirement savings into income now.

• You are in good health and expect to live at least another 20 years.

• You have sufficient assets to cover large expenses like medical bills.

Source: Adapted, in part, from Phil Taylor, "Do You Need an Annuity?" http://money.usnews.com/money/blogs/on-retirement/2012/01/06/do-you-need-an-annuity, accessed September 2015.

until the account balance falls to the amount of original paid-in principal, after which any further withdrawals are tax free.) Barring some type of serious illness, about the only way to tap your account without penalty before you're 59½ is to *annuitize*. Unfortunately, the annuity payments must be spread out over your estimated remaining life span, which means the size of each monthly payment could be pretty small. All of which only reinforces the notion that *an annuity should always be considered a long-term investment*. Assume that it's a part of your retirement program (after all, that's the way the IRS looks at it), and that you're getting in for the long haul.

From an investment perspective, the returns generated from an annuity can, in some cases, be a bit disappointing. For instance, as we discussed earlier, the returns on *variable annuities* are tied to returns in the money and capital markets; even so, they're still no better than what you can get from other investment vehicles—indeed, they're often lower, in part because of higher annuity fees. Keep in mind that these differential returns aren't due to tax features because in both cases, returns were measured on a before-tax basis. But *returns from annuities are tax sheltered*, so that makes those lower returns a lot more attractive.

If you're considering a variable annuity, go over it much as you would a traditional mutual fund: look for superior past performance, proven management talent/track record, and the availability of attractive investment alternatives that you can switch in and out of. And *pay particular attention to an annuity's total expense rate*. These products have a reputation for being heavily loaded with fees and charges, but it's possible to find annuities with both above-average performance and relatively low fee structures. That's the combination you're looking for.

One final point: If you're seriously considering buying an annuity, be sure to read the contract carefully and see what the guaranteed rates are, how long the initial rate applies, and if there's a bailout provision. (A *bailout provision* allows you to withdraw your money, free of any surrender fees, if the rate of return on your annuity falls below a specified minimum level. Of course, even if you exercise a bailout provision, you may still have to face a tax penalty for early withdrawal—unless you transfer the funds to another annuity through what's known as a *1035 exchange*.) Just as important, because *the annuity is only as good as the insurance company that stands behind it*, check to see how the company is rated by Best's, Standard & Poor's, or Moody's. It's important to make sure that the insurance company itself is financially sound before buying one of its annuity products. See Chapter 8 for more discussion on these insurance ratings and how they work.

TEST YOURSELF

14-15 What is an *annuity?* Briefly explain how an annuity works and how it differs from a life insurance policy.

14-16 Which one of the annuity distribution procedures will result in the highest monthly benefit payment?

14-17 What is a *fixed-rate* annuity, and how does it differ from a *variable* annuity? Does the type of contract (fixed or variable) have any bearing on the amount of money you'll receive at the time of distribution?

14-18 Which type of contract (fixed or variable) might be most suitable for someone who wants a minimum amount of risk exposure?

14-19 How do variable annuity returns generally compare to mutual fund returns? Can you explain why there would be any difference in returns?

Planning Over a Lifetime: *Retirement Planning*

Here are some key considerations for retirement planning in each stage of the life cycle.

Pre-family Independence: 20s	Family Formation/ Career Development: 30–45	Pre-Retirement: 45–65	Retirement: 65 and Beyond
✓ Estimate how much you will need to retire comfortably while taking inflation into account.	✓ Aim to invest between 10 and 15 percent of your income for retirement. The more you invest early on, the better off you'll be at retirement.	✓ Revise your retirement plan in light of recent developments. Try to save even more.	✓ Revise your retirement plan to weight your investments more toward debt and liquid instruments than stocks.
✓ Determine your asset allocation among stocks, bonds, real estate, and cash based on your time horizon and attitude toward risk. Most people are comfortable taking more risk earlier in life.	✓ Review your asset allocation and rebalance it to be more consistent with your goals. Most people are more comfortable reducing the risk of their investments a bit.	✓ Review your asset allocation and rebalance investments within and beyond your employer's retirement plan. Most people reduce the risk of their investments.	✓ Compare your spending rate to your assets and reassess how long your spending rate can be maintained. Consider how the current income produced by your portfolio relates to your day-to-day spending needs.
✓ Match your investments in any employer sponsored 401(k) retirement plan with your overall asset allocation plan.	✓ Gradually increase the amount invested in any employer-sponsored 401(k) retirement plan and re-evaluate how it relates to your asset allocation plan.	✓ Continue to increase the amount you invest in any employer sponsored 401(k) retirement plan gradually, and re-evaluate it periodically to see how it fits into your asset allocation plan.	✓ Integrate your investment asset allocation strategy with estate planning. Keep in mind that the equity in your home can be borrowed against if needed.
✓ Start setting aside money for investment outside your employer's retirement plan. Consider investing in mutual funds and exchange-traded funds (ETFs) under a traditional IRA, a Roth IRA, or both.	✓ Consider increasing your contribution to traditional IRA, a Roth IRA, or both.	✓ Consider increasing your contribution to traditional and Roth IRAs using mutual funds and exchange-traded funds (ETFs). Consider purchasing an annuity to supplement retirement income.	✓ Plan for mandatory withdrawals from tax-sheltered accounts and the associated tax consequences.

Financial Impact of Personal Choices
Carl and Brian's Different Approaches to a Traditional IRA

Carl Rowley and Brian Lyles, both 30 years old, are good friends who work together at a management consulting firm. They both take advantage of their firm's 401(k) plan. But they differ in how they set aside money in a traditional IRA. Carl has just started setting aside $5,500 a year in an IRA that he expects to earn 5 percent per year until he plans to retire at age 66. In contrast, while Brian also expects to retire at age 66, he believes it's too early in his career to bother investing in an IRA because it won't have that much impact in the long-term. He consequently plans to wait five years before following Carl's example.

At age 66 the pre-tax value of Carl's IRA should be about $553,455 while the value of Brian's account should be about $408,644. Carl will have invested $27,000 more than Brian but will end up with $144,811 more in his IRA account! That's because the IRA sheltered the earnings on Carl's investments from taxes and he also benefited handsomely from the compounding of returns on his money. So there's a moral here: invest early, often, and consider the impact of taxes on your investments.

Summary

LG1 **Recognize the importance of retirement planning, and identify the three biggest pitfalls to good planning, p. 557**
Retirement planning plays a vital role in the personal financial planning process. It's based on many of the same principles and concepts of effective financial planning, which include establishing financial goals and strategies, using savings and investment plans, and using certain insurance products such as annuities. The three biggest pitfalls to sound retirement planning are starting too late, not saving enough, and investing too conservatively.

LG2 **Estimate your income needs in retirement and the level of retirement income you've estimated from various sources, p. 557**
Rather than address retirement planning in a series of short-run (3- to 5-year) plans, it's best to take a long-term approach and look 20–30 years into the future to determine how much saving and investing you must do today in order to achieve the retirement goals you've set for tomorrow. Implementing a long-term retirement plan involves determining future retirement needs, estimating retirement income from known sources (such as Social Security and company pension plans), and

deciding how much to save and invest each year to build up a desired nest egg.

LG3 **Explain the eligibility requirements and benefits of the Social Security program, p. 566**
Social Security is the foundation for the retirement programs of most families; except for a few exempt classes (mostly government employees), almost all gainfully employed workers are covered by Social Security. Upon retirement, covered workers are entitled to certain monthly benefits as determined mainly by the employee's earning history and age at retirement.

LG4 **Differentiate among the types of basic and supplemental employer-sponsored pension plans, p. 571**
Employer-sponsored pension and retirement plans provide a vital source of retirement income to many individuals. Such plans can often spell the difference between enjoying a comfortable standard of living in retirement or a bare subsistence. In *basic* retirement programs, all employees participate after a certain period of employment. These plans can be defined contribution or defined benefit plans. There are also several forms of *supplemental* employer-sponsored programs,

including profit-sharing plans, thrift and savings plans, and perhaps most popular, salary reduction plans such as 401(k) plans.

LG5 Describe the various types of self-directed retirement plans, p. 571

In addition to company-sponsored retirement programs, individuals can set up their own self-directed tax-sheltered retirement plans; it's through such plans that most individuals can build up the nest eggs they'll need to meet their retirement objectives. The basic types of self-directed retirement programs are Keogh and SEP plans for self-employed individuals as well as various forms of IRAs, which any salary or wage earner can set up.

LG6 Choose the right type of annuity for your retirement plan, p. 585

Annuities are also an important source of income for retired people. An annuity is an investment vehicle that allows investment income to accumulate on a tax-deferred basis; it provides for the systematic liquidation (payout) of all invested capital and earnings over an extended period. There are many types of annuities, including single premium and installment premium, fixed and variable, and immediate and deferred; there are also different payout options.

Key Terms

accumulation period, 585

annuity, 585

annuity certain, 587

cash-balance plan, 575

contributory pension plan, 573

deferred annuity, 585

defined benefit plan, 573

distribution period, 585

employee retirement income security act (ERISA), 571

fixed-rate annuity, 587

guaranteed-minimum annuity (life annuity with refund), 587

immediate annuity, 585

individual retirement account (IRA), 581

installment premium annuity contract, 585

Keogh plan, 580

life annuity, period certain, 587

life annuity with no refund (pure life), 587

noncontributory pension plan, 573

Nondeductible (after-tax) IRA, 581

pension protection act, 571

profit-sharing plan, 576

qualified pension plan, 575

refund annuity, 587

salary reduction, or 401(k), plan, 577

single premium annuity contract, 585

survivorship benefit, 585

thrift and savings plans, 576

Traditional (deductible) IRA, 581

variable annuity, 587

vested rights, 572

Answers to Test Yourself

You can find answers to these questions on this book's companion website. Look for it at *www. cengagebrain.com*. Search for this book by its title, and then add it to your dashboard.

Financial Planning Exercises

LG2, p. 557   1. *Calculating amount available at retirement.* Marisa Gale, a 25-year-old personal loan officer at Second National Bank, understands the importance of starting early when it comes to saving for retirement. She has designated $3,000 per year for her retirement fund and assumes that she'll retire at age 65.

a.   How much will she have if she invests in CDs and similar money market instruments that earn 4 percent on average?

b.   How much will she have if instead she invests in equities and earns 10 percent on average?

c.   Marisa is urging her friend, Nolan Ransom, to start his plan right away because he's 35. What would his nest egg amount to if he invested in the same manner as Marisa and he, too, retires at age 65? Comment on your findings.

LG2, p. 557

2.   ***Calculating annual investment to meet retirement target.*** ***Use Worksheet 14.1*** to help Andy and Rachel Cutler, who'd like to retire in about 20 years. Both have promising careers, and both make good money. As a result, they're willing to put aside whatever is necessary to achieve a comfortable lifestyle in retirement. Their current level of household expenditures (excluding savings) is around $75,000 a year, and they expect to spend *even more* in retirement; they think they'll need about 125 percent of that amount. (*Note:* 125 percent equals a multiplier factor of 1.25.) They estimate that their Social Security benefits will amount to $20,000 a year in today's dollars and that they'll receive another $35,000 annually from their company pension plans. They feel that future inflation will amount to about 3 percent a year, and they think they'll be able to earn about 6 percent on their investments before retirement and about 4 percent afterward. Use Worksheet 14.1 to find out how big Andy and Rachel's investment nest egg will have to be and how much they'll have to save annually to accumulate the needed amount within the next 20 years.

LG2, p. 557

3.   ***Retirement planning.*** Use Worksheet 14.1 to assist Tara Easley with her retirement planning needs. She plans to retire in 15 years, and her current household expenditures run about $50,000 per year. Tara estimates that she'll spend 80 percent of that amount in retirement. Her Social Security benefit is estimated at $15,000 per year, and she'll receive $12,000 per year from her employer's pension plan (both in today's dollars). Additional assumptions include an inflation rate of 4 percent and a rate of return on retirement assets of 8 percent a year before retirement and 5 percent afterward. Use Worksheet 14.1 to calculate the required size of Tara's retirement nest egg and the amount that she must save annually over the next 15 years to reach that goal.

LG3, p. 566

4.   ***Critical evaluation of Social Security benefits.*** Many critics of the Social Security program feel participants are getting a substandard investment return on their money. Discuss why you agree or disagree with this viewpoint.

LG3, p. 566

5.   ***Average Social Security benefits and taxes.*** Use Exhibit 14.3 to estimate the average Social Security benefits for a retired couple. Assume that one spouse has a part-time job that pays $24,000 a year, and that this person also receives another $47,000 a year from a company pension. Based on current policies, would this couple be liable for any tax on their Social Security income?

LG3, p. 566

6.   ***Average Social Security benefits.*** Use Exhibit 14.3 to determine the annual Social Security benefit for Bob Lemus, assuming that he is an "average" retiree. Bob is 65 years old and earns $18,000 a year at a part-time job. (Note that Bob is already at "full retirement age," because he was born well before 1960.)

LG3, 4, p. 566, 571

7.   ***Retirement planning.*** At what age would you like to retire? Describe the type of lifestyle you envision—where you want to live, whether you want to work part-time, and so on. Discuss the steps you think you should take to realize this goal.

LG4, p. 571

8.   ***Comparing retirement plans.*** Ellen Honeycut has just graduated from college and is considering job offers from two companies. Although the salary and insurance benefits are similar, the retirement programs are not. One firm offers a 401(k) plan that matches employee contributions with 25 cents for every dollar contributed by the employee, up to a $10,000 limit. The other firm has a contributory plan that allows employees to contribute up to 10 percent of their annual salary through payroll deduction and matches it dollar for dollar; this plan vests fully after five years. Because Ellen is unfamiliar with these plans, explain the features of each to her so she can make an informed decision.

LG4, p. 571

9.   ***After-tax cost of 401(k) contribution.*** Brad Shin is an operations manager for a large manufacturer. He earned $72,500 in 2015 and plans to contribute the maximum allowed to the firm's 401(k) plan. Assuming that Brad is in the 25 percent tax bracket, calculate his taxable income and the

amount of his tax savings. How much did it actually cost Brad on an after-tax basis to make this retirement plan contribution?

LG4, p. 571   10. **Defined benefit vs. defined contribution pension plans.** Briefly describe the main characteristics of defined contribution and defined benefit pension plans, and discuss how they differ from cash-balance plans. In each of these plans, does the employee or employer bear the risk of poor investment performance?

LG5, p. 571   11. **Nature of different types of IRAs.** Describe the three basic types of IRAs (traditional, Roth, and nondeductible), including their respective tax features and what it takes to qualify for each. Which is most appealing to you personally? Explain.

LG5, p. 571   12. **Deciding between traditional and Roth IRAs.** Clint Crandall is in his early 30s and is thinking about opening an IRA. He can't decide whether to open a traditional/deductible IRA or a Roth IRA, so he turns to you for help.

a. To support your explanation, you decide to *run some comparative numbers on the two types of accounts;* for starters, use a 25-year period to show Clint what contributions of $4,000 per year will amount to (after 25 years), given that he can earn, say, 10 percent on his money. Will the type of account he opens have any impact on this amount? Explain.

b. Assuming that Clint is in the 28 percent tax bracket (and will remain there for the next 25 years), determine the annual and total (over 25 years) tax savings that he'll enjoy from the $4,000-a-year contributions to his IRA; contrast the (annual and total) tax savings he'd generate from a traditional IRA with those from a Roth IRA.

c. Now, fast-forward 25 years. Given the size of Clint's account in 25 years (as computed in part **a**), assume that he takes it all out in one lump sum. If he's still in the 30 percent tax bracket, how much will he have, after taxes, with a traditional IRA, as compared with a Roth IRA? How do the taxes computed here compare with those computed in part **b**? Comment on your findings.

d. Based on the numbers you have computed as well as any other factors, what kind of IRA would you recommend to Clint? Explain. Would knowing that maximum contributions are scheduled to increase to $7,000 per year make any difference in your analysis? Explain.

LG6, p. 585   13. **Comparing variable annuities and mutual funds.** Explain how buying a variable annuity is much like investing in a mutual fund. Do you, as a buyer, have any control over the amount of investment risk to which you're exposed in a variable annuity contract? Explain.

LG6, p. 585   14. **Tax shelter aspects of annuities.** Briefly explain how annuities are a type of tax-sheltered investment. Do you have to give up anything to obtain this tax-favored treatment? (*Hint:* Age 59½.)

LG6, p. 585   15. **Considerations in annuity purchase.** Why is it important to check an insurance company's financial ratings when buying an annuity? Why should you look at past performance when considering the purchase of a variable annuity?

LG6, p. 585   16. **Fixed vs. variable annuities.** What are the main differences between fixed and variable annuities? Which type is more appropriate for someone who is 60 years old and close to retirement?

Applying Personal Finance

Envisioning Your Ideal Retirement Plan!

Many people have little or no money set aside for their retirement. Those who do may find their retirement funds insufficient for maintaining their desired standard of living during retirement. In this project, you'll contemplate the type and features of a retirement program that would best meet your needs.

Looking back over this chapter, review the features of both employer-sponsored and self-directed retirement programs. Depending on your career, you may actually have both kinds. Develop an outline of your ideal retirement plan or plans (*be realistic*), being sure to consider the following issues:

1. Would the plan be contributory or noncontributory?
2. Stated as a *percentage* of your base salary, how much would be put into your retirement plan each year? Remember that there are certain allowable limits.

3. What would be the eligibility and vesting provisions? Would your plan be portable? Under what conditions?
4. What would be the earliest retirement age? Would there be provisions for early retirement?
5. Would your plan be a defined contribution or a defined benefit plan? You could also have a combination of the two types.
6. Would the plan be qualified?
7. Would you want a voluntary supplemental plan as part of your program? If you could have only one supplemental plan, what would it be?

What would be the advantages and disadvantages of your ideal plan? This research will help you understand the retirement benefits you may have with your current job or as part of the job offers you may receive in the future.

CRITICAL THINKING CASES

LG4, p. 571

14.1 Comparing Pension Plan Features

Linda Calloway and Meredith Perdue are neighbors in Charleston. Linda works as a software engineer for Progressive Apps Corporation, while Meredith works as an executive for Industrial Container Company. Both are married, have two children, and are well paid. Linda and Meredith are interested in better understanding their pension and retirement plans.

Progressive Apps Corporation, the company where Linda works, has a contributory plan in which 5 percent of the employees' annual wages is deducted to meet the cost of the benefits. The firm contributes an amount equal to the employee contribution. The plan uses a five-year graded vesting procedure; it has a normal retirement age of 60 for all employees, and the benefits at retirement are paid according to a defined contribution plan.

Industrial Container, where Meredith works, has a minimum retirement age of 60. Employees (full-time, hourly, or salaried) must meet participation requirements. Further, in contrast to the Progressive Apps plan, the Industrial Container program has a noncontributory feature. Annual retirement benefits are computed according to the following formula: 2 percent of the employee's final annual salary for each year of service with the company is paid upon retirement. The plan vests immediately.

Critical Thinking Questions

1. Discuss and contrast the features of the retirement plans offered by Progressive Apps and Industrial Container.
2. Which plan do you think is more desirable? Consider the features, retirement age, and benefit computations just described. Which plan do you think could be subject to a conversion to a cash-balance plan sometime in the future? Explain. Include in your answer the implications for the employee's future retirement benefits.
3. Explain how you would use each of these plans in developing your own retirement program.
4. What role, if any, could annuities play in these retirement programs? Discuss the pros and cons of using annuities as a part of retirement planning.

LG2, 4, 5, p. 557, 571

14.2 Evaluating Maria Sepulveda's Retirement Prospects

Maria Sepulveda is 57 years old. Never remarried, she has worked full-time since her husband died 13 years ago—in addition to raising her two children, the youngest of whom is now finishing college. After being forced to go back to work in her 40s, Maria's first job was in a fast-food restaurant. Eventually, she upgraded her skills sufficiently to obtain a supervisory position in the personnel department of a major corporation, where she's now earning $58,000 a year.

Although her financial focus for the past 13 years has, of necessity, been on meeting living expenses and getting her kids through college, she feels that now she can turn her attention to her retirement needs. Actually, Maria hasn't done too badly in that area, either. By carefully investing the proceeds from her husband's life insurance policy, Maria has accumulated the following investment assets:

Money market securities, stocks, and bonds	*$72,600*
IRA and 401(k) plans	*$47,400*

Other than the mortgage on her condo, the only other debt she has is $7,000 in college loans.

Maria would like to retire in eight years, and she recently hired a financial planner to help her come up with an effective retirement program. Her planner has estimated that, for her to live comfortably in retirement, she'll need about $37,500 a year (in today's dollars) in retirement income.

Critical Thinking Questions

1. After taking into account the income that Maria will receive from Social Security and her company-sponsored pension plan, the financial planner has estimated that her investment assets will need to provide her with about $15,000 a year to meet the balance of her retirement income needs. Assuming a 6 percent after-tax return on her investments, how big a nest egg will Maria need to earn that kind of income?
2. Suppose she can invest the money market securities, stocks, and bonds (the $72,600) at 5 percent after taxes and can invest the $47,400 accumulated in her tax-sheltered IRA and 401(k) at 7 percent. How much will Maria's investment assets be worth in eight years, when she retires?
3. Maria's employer matches her 401(k) contributions dollar for dollar, up to a maximum of $3,000 a year. If she continues to put $3,000 a year into that program, how much more will she have in eight years, given a 9 percent rate of return?
4. What would you advise Maria about her ability to retire in eight years, as she hopes to?

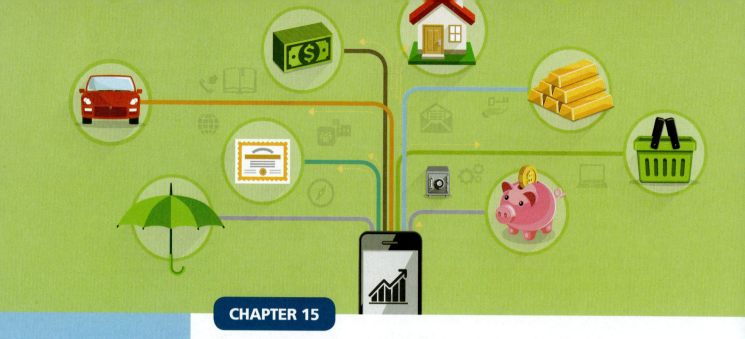

CHAPTER 15

Preserving Your Estate

LEARNING GOALS

LG1 Describe the role of estate planning in personal financial planning, and identify the seven steps involved in the process.

LG2 Recognize the importance of preparing a will and other documents to protect you and your estate.

LG3 Explain how trusts are used in estate planning.

LG4 Determine whether a gift will be taxable and use planned gifts to reduce estate taxes.

LG5 Calculate federal taxes due on an estate.

LG6 Use effective estate planning techniques to minimize estate taxes.

How Will This Affect Me?

No, you can't take it with you. But there's a next best thing: A carefully designed estate plan will allow your loved ones and family to keep as much of your accumulated wealth as possible. This chapter explains the role of estate planning and the importance of a will. It discusses the use and design of living wills, advance medical directives, and trusts. It also explains how federal estate taxes are calculated. After reading this chapter you should understand the key elements in handling and preserving your estate for your loved ones.

15-1 PRINCIPLES OF ESTATE PLANNING

Like it or not, no one lives forever. Safeguarding the future of the people you care about is one of the most important aspects of financial planning. Unless you develop an estate plan and take steps during your lifetime to accumulate, preserve, and distribute your assets upon your death, chances are that your heirs and beneficiaries will receive only part of your estate. The rest will be consumed (often unnecessarily) by poorly timed sales, sales at less-than-optimum prices, taxes, and various administrative costs. Planning the distribution of your assets to your heirs is necessary to maximize the wealth available to them. To be successful requires knowledge of your property, property law, wills, trusts, and taxes. This overall process is known as *estate planning*.

Understanding these components and their interrelationships will help you minimize estate shrinkage after your death and still allow you to achieve your lifetime personal financial goals. Also, keep in mind that not only wealthy people, but also individuals of modest or moderate means, need to plan their estates. While the amount of money in your estate may be small, planning the transfer of that property will help your heirs at a time of great stress and need.

estate planning
The process of developing a plan to administer and distribute your assets in a manner consistent with your wishes and the needs of your survivors, while minimizing taxes.

Estate planning is the process of developing a plan to administer and distribute your assets in a manner consistent with your wishes and the needs of your survivors. This process occurs over most of your adult life. Planning helps people accumulate enough capital to meet college education costs and other special needs, provide financial security for family members after the death of the head of household, take care of themselves and their family during a long-term disability, and provide for a comfortable retirement. However, estate planning goes beyond financial issues. It also includes plans to manage your affairs if you become disabled, manage your personal wishes for medical care, and make clear how you want your assets to be distributed among your heirs.

As with other financial planning activities, a major objective of estate planning is to legally eliminate or minimize tax exposure. With careful planning, estate taxes may be completely eliminated in most cases. Also, with planning, future income tax on the sale of inherited property may be minimized. Planning for the income and transfer tax increases the amount of your estate that ultimately is passed on to your heirs and beneficiaries. Estate planning also is closely related to insurance and retirement planning. Certainly, the most important reason for buying life insurance is to provide for your family in the event of your premature death. Likewise, a principal challenge of effective retirement planning is to achieve a comfortable standard of living in retirement while preserving as much of your accumulated wealth as possible. This not only

Financial Fact or Fantasy?

Estate planning is one of the key elements of personal financial planning. **Fact:** One of the principal objectives of financial planning is to transfer as much accumulated wealth to your heirs and designated beneficiaries as possible—a goal that is made easier through effective estate planning.

reduces the chances of you (or your spouse) outliving your financial resources but also leaves an estate that can be passed on to your heirs and designated beneficiaries according to your wishes.

Planning should occur in every estate. The estate owner and his or her professional counselors control the plan, but the plan or lack of a plan is subject to federal and state governments that will affect the plan. If an individual fails to plan, then state and federal laws will control the disposition of assets and determine who bears the burden of expenses and taxes. Indeed, the cost of administration and taxes may be higher because of lack of planning. People who wish to plan their estates must systematically uncover problems in several important areas and solve them. Exhibit 15.1 lists the major types of problems and their associated causes or indicators. In later sections, we'll discuss techniques to avoid or minimize these problems.

15-1a Who Needs Estate Planning?

Estate planning should be part of your financial plan, whether you're married or single and have five children or none. For example, married couples who own many assets jointly and have designated beneficiaries for assets such as retirement funds and life insurance policies may think that they don't need wills. However, a will covers many other important details, such as naming an executor to administer the estate and a guardian for children, clarifying how estate taxes will be paid, and distributing property that doesn't go directly to a joint owner.

EXHIBIT 15.1   Potential Estate Planning Problems

Careful estate planning can prevent many problems that arise when settling an estate. The first step toward preventing problems is an awareness and understanding of their major causes or indicators.

Potential Problem	Major Cause or Indicator
• Excessive transfer costs	Taxes and estate administrative expenses higher than necessary
• Lack of liquidity	Insufficient cash; not enough assets that are quickly and inexpensively convertible to cash within a short period of time to meet tax demands and other costs
• Improper disposition of assets	Beneficiaries receive the wrong asset, or the proper asset in the wrong manner or at the wrong time
• Inadequate income at retirement	Capital insufficient or not readily convertible to income-producing status
• Inadequate income, if disabled	High medical costs; capital insufficient or not readily convertible to income-producing status; difficulty in reducing living standards
• Inadequate income for family at estate owner's death	Any of the above causes
• Insufficient capital	Excessive taxes, inflation, improper investment planning
• Special problems	A family member with a serious illness or physical or emotional problem; children of a prior marriage; beneficiaries who have extraordinary medical or financial needs; beneficiaries who can't agree on how to handle various estate matters, business problems, or opportunities

Partners who aren't married and single persons will discover that estate planning is especially important, particularly if they own a home or other assets that they want to leave to specific individuals or to charity. Unmarried couples need to put extra effort into their estate plans. They may need to make special arrangements to be sure they can indeed leave assets to a partner.

The two main areas of estate planning are *people planning* and *asset planning*.

People Planning

People planning means anticipating the psychological and financial needs of those people you love and providing enough income or capital or both to ensure a continuation of their way of life. People planning gives guidance to your heirs who may need help managing assets. People planning also means keeping Mother's cameo brooch in the family and out of the pawnshop, or preserving the business that Great-Granddad started in the early 1900s. People planning is especially important for individuals with children who are minors; children who are exceptionally artistic or intellectually gifted; children or other dependents who are emotionally, mentally, or physically handicapped; and spouses who can't or don't want to handle money, securities, or a business.

Minor children cannot legally handle large sums of money or deal directly with real estate or securities. Custodial accounts, guardianships, or trusts will provide administration, security, financial advice, and the legal capacity to act on behalf of minors. Few children are exceptionally artistic or intellectually gifted, but those who are often need—or should have—special (and often expensive) schooling, travel opportunities, or equipment. Emotionally, mentally, or physically disabled children (and other relatives) may need nursing, medical, or psychiatric care. Outright gifts of money or property to those who can't care for themselves are inappropriate. These individuals may need more (or less) than other children. And an individual who gives all of his or her children equal shares may not be giving them equitable shares.

How many of us have handled hundreds of thousands of dollars? Think of the burden that we place on others when we expect that a spouse who can't—or doesn't want to—handle such large sums of money or securities to do so. This is particularly burdensome when the assets being handled are his or her only assets. Engaging in people planning demonstrates a high degree of caring. People planning also involves talking about estate planning with your loved ones.

Asset Planning

From the standpoint of wealth alone, estate planning is essential for anyone—single, widowed, married, or divorced—with an estate exceeding the "applicable exclusion amount," which is $5,430,000 for an individual in 2015. For a married couple, that number is doubled to $10,860,000. So it is not just about taxes. Your estate plan should match your assets with the people you wish to receive them.

> **You Can Do It Now**
>
> *Estate Planning Conversations*
>
> Talking about the prospect of each other's deaths in a family is never comfortable. But careful estate planning will assure that your intentions are best served in light of the family's needs. A useful perspective on how to have such a conversation may be found at: https://www.fidelity.com/estate-planning-inheritance/estate-planning/talking-estate-planning. The sooner the conversation happens, the more confident you can be that your estate plan will have the intended results. You can do it now.

When an estate involves a closely held business, estate planning is essential to stabilize and maximize its asset and income-producing values, both during the owner's lifetime and at the owner's death or disability. Likewise, estate planning is essential to

Behavior Matters

Recognizing and Overcoming Aversion to Ambiguity in Estate Planning

While many people recognize the need for an estate plan, they often have too little understanding of the process. Thus, too few of us take action at the right time. Why? Estate planning forces us to face and confirm our own mortality, which is hard to do. All too often, therefore, it takes a dramatic and serious health change to push the average American to plan for the worst. Consider how to overcome the *aversion to ambiguity* behavioral barrier so you can establish a timely and effective estate plan.

Estate planning can appear ambiguous to those who do not understand it. And most people dislike this ambiguity but fail to confront it. Two conflicting thoughts create this perceived ambiguity. First, we acknowledge that estate planning is important both for the planner and for the planner's family. Second, we often focus on living long and productive lives—a practice that is wrongly taken to imply that there is no hurry to start the estate planning process. The resulting conflicted feelings draw into question the importance of estate planning. Many, consequently, are paralyzed and do no planning.

So how do we move beyond the aversion to ambiguity and get the estate planning process going? We have to admit that life is too short and that we need to plan for the inevitable. After admitting this, the aversion to ambiguity barrier can be overcome by becoming more familiar with the basics of estate planning. This chapter should go a long way in addressing that issue. In summary, we must face our mortality, familiarize ourselves with the estate planning process, and decisively contact a professional to get the process moving forward.

Source: Adapted from Justin A. Reckers and Robert A. Simon, "Resolving the Aversion to Estate Planning," http://www.morningstar.com/advisor/t/42987539/resolving-the-aversion-to-estate-planning.htm, accessed September 2015.

avoid the special problems that occur when an estate owner holds title to property in more than one state. How you own your property (i.e., who is on the deed or title for the property) will affect your ability to plan for its transfer. The nature of the asset—whether it is cash, real property, cars, collectibles, stocks, or bonds—will also affect your ability to match your assets with the people you want to have them. Careful planning is needed to make sure that your assets will go to the desired beneficiaries.

15-1b Why Does an Estate Break Up?

Quite often, when people die, their estates die with them—not because they've done anything wrong, but because they have done nothing. There are numerous forces that, if unchecked, tend to shrink an estate, reduce the usefulness of its assets, and frustrate the objectives of the person who built it. These include death-related costs, inflation, lack of liquidity, improper use of vehicles of transfer, and disabilities.

1. **Death-related costs:** When someone dies, the estate incurs certain types of death-related costs. For example, medical bills for a final illness and funeral expenses are good examples of *first-level death-related costs. Second-level death-related costs* consist of fees for attorneys, appraisers, and accountants along with probate expenses (so-called administrative costs), federal estate taxes, and state death taxes. Most people also die with some current bills unpaid, outstanding long-term obligations (such as mortgages, business loans, and installment contracts), and unpaid income taxes and property taxes.

2. **Inflation:** Death-related costs are only the tip of the estate-impairment iceberg. Failure to continuously reappraise and rearrange an estate plan to counter the effects of inflation can impair the ability of assets—liquid, real, and personal property and investments—to provide steady and adequate levels of financial security.

FINANCIAL PLANNING TIPS

Common Excuses for Not Writing a Will

Two out of three people don't have a will! Consider the following common excuses, and why they don't hold up.

- **I'm too young to need a will.** There's a chance you won't live as long as you hope. Without a will, your heirs will have to figure it all out. A will can say who will get everything. Youth is no excuse—a will is needed at all ages.

- **My family knows what to do with my assets.** That may be true, but without a will, the state gets to decide who gets what. For example, even if you want your spouse to inherit all of your assets, your children will likely still be given a piece of your estate.

- **I don't have enough assets to need a will.** It's not just how much you have, it's who gets whatever you own. It's best to provide detailed instructions about who gets what and to update them often.

- **My mother would take care of the kids.** Perhaps she would, but what if your mother-in-law also decides she wants the kids? If there is no will, then a judge will decide who gets your children. So choose guardians carefully and put your choices in a will.

- **Writing a will is too expensive.** Not true. It doesn't cost much to write a will. Many state bar associations make available simple will forms. There's even reasonably priced software to do it.

- **My partner will get all of my assets.** A partner to whom you're not legally married may not get anything. While property and investments would likely go to your spouse or civil partner, without a will personal possessions might not go where you want. And what if you and your partner both die at the same time without a will?

- **I have no kids and I'm single, so there is no one to protect.** Single or married, if you have no will, then the state will leave everything to your relatives. And if you have no relatives, the state gets it all! A will can assure that your friends and favorite charities get something.

3. **Lack of liquidity:** Insufficient cash to cover death costs and other estate obligations has always been a major factor in estate impairment. Sale of the choicest parcel of farmland or a business that's been in the family for generations, for instance, often has undesirable psychological effects on the heirs. The outcome can be a devastating financial and emotional blow.

4. **Improper use of vehicles of transfer:** Assets are often put into the hands of beneficiaries who are unwilling or unable to handle them. Improper use of vehicles of transfer may pass property to unintended beneficiaries or to the proper beneficiaries in an improper manner or at an incorrect time. For example, spendthrift spouses or minors may be left large sums of money outright in the form of life insurance, through joint ownership of a savings account, or as the beneficiaries of an employee fringe benefit plan.

5. **Disabilities:** The prolonged and expensive disability of a family wage earner is often called a *living death*. Loss of income due to disability is often coupled with a massive financial drain caused by the illness itself. The financial situation is further complicated by inadequate management of currently owned assets. This not only threatens the family's financial security but also quickly diminishes the value of the estate.

15-1c What Is Your Estate?

Your estate is your property—whatever you own. Your **probate estate** consists of the real and personal property you own in your own name that can be transferred at death according to the terms of a will or, if you have no valid will, under *intestate* laws. The probate estate is distinct from the gross estate (a tax law term that may encompass a considerably larger amount of property). Your **gross estate** includes all

gross estate
All property that might be subject to federal estate taxes on a person's death.

EXHIBIT 15.2   **Steps in the Estate Planning Process**

The estate planning process consists of seven important steps, listed here in the order they would be performed.

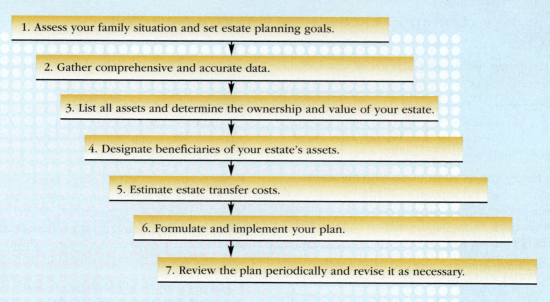

1. Assess your family situation and set estate planning goals.

2. Gather comprehensive and accurate data.

3. List all assets and determine the ownership and value of your estate.

4. Designate beneficiaries of your estate's assets.

5. Estimate estate transfer costs.

6. Formulate and implement your plan.

7. Review the plan periodically and revise it as necessary.

the property—both probate and nonprobate—that might be subject to federal estate taxes at your death. Life insurance, jointly held property with rights of survivorship, and property passing under certain employee benefit plans are common examples of nonprobate assets that might be subject to federal (and state) estate taxes.

You also may provide for property that's not probate property and won't be part of your estate for federal estate tax purposes yet will pass to your family and form part of their financial security program. There are two types of such assets. One is *properly arranged* life insurance. For instance, you could give assets to your daughter to allow her to purchase, pay the premiums for, and be the beneficiary of a policy on your life. At your death, the proceeds normally would not be included as part of your gross estate. The other type of financial asset that falls into this category is *Social Security*. Social Security payments to a surviving spouse and minor children generally are not probate assets and are not subject to any federal (or state) estate taxes. Because of the freedom from administrative costs and taxes, this category of assets provides unique and substantial estate planning opportunities.

15-1d The Estate Planning Process

The estate planning process consists of seven important steps, as summarized in Exhibit 15.2. First, you must assess your family situation, evaluating its strengths and weaknesses, and set estate planning goals. Here is where you focus on "people planning" to set your goals. Next, gather comprehensive and accurate data on all aspects of the family. Exhibit 15.3 summarizes the data that professionals require to prepare detailed estate plans. Most professional estate planners provide forms to help their clients compile this information. Then, you should take inventory and determine the ownership and value of your estate. Next, you must designate beneficiaries of your estate's assets, estimate estate transfer costs, and formulate and implement your plan. The final step is ongoing: review your estate plan periodically—at least every three to five years, and revise it as circumstances dictate.

EXHIBIT 15.3   **Data Needed for Estate Planning**

The second step in developing an effective estate plan involves gathering comprehensive and accurate data about you and your family. The types of data required by estate planners include the following:

Personal data:	Names, addresses, phone numbers, birth dates, marital status, marital agreements, wills, trusts, custodianships, trust beneficiary, gifts or inheritances, Social Security numbers, and military service
Property:	Classification, title, indebtedness, date and manner of acquisition, value of marketable securities and their locations
Life insurance:	Name of insured, kinds of policies, amounts, insurance companies, agents' names and addresses
Health insurance:	Medical insurance company, policy numbers and benefits; disability income insurance
Business interest:	Name, address, ownership, desired survivorship control; names, addresses, and phone numbers of business attorney and accountant
Employee benefits:	Group insurance plans, pension benefits
Family income:	Income of client, spouse, income tax information
Family finances:	Budget information, investment preferences, capital needs, other objectives
Other data:	Retirement: planned retirement age, potential sources of retirement income; disability: required amount, sources; upon death: expected sources of income for heirs
Liabilities:	Listing of liabilities, creditors, amounts, whether insured or secured
Authorization for information:	Life insurance, executor

The objective of estate plans, of course, is to maximize the usefulness of people's assets during their lives and to achieve their personal objectives after their deaths. Once the plan has been implemented, however, you must reevaluate it regularly. An estate plan is good only so long as it fits the needs, desires, and circumstances of the parties involved. As these elements change, you must modify your estate plan. Key events that should trigger an estate plan review include the death or disability of a spouse or other family member, moving to another state, changing jobs, getting married or divorced, having children, acquiring new assets, and substantial changes in income, health, or living standards. Even if none of these occur, you should automatically review life insurance needs at least once every two years and perform a full estate audit at least once every three to five years (or whenever there has been a major change in the federal or state death-tax laws). Because of the general complexity of the laws relating to estate transfer, it is often necessary to secure the assistance of estate planners, life insurance professionals, Certified Financial Planners® (CFPs®), accountants, and attorneys in the planning and evaluation process. Given the individual nature of estate planning, we cannot include specific guidelines in this chapter. We provide a general framework for considering the key estate planning issues.

TEST YOURSELF

15-1   Discuss the importance and goals of estate planning. Explain why estates often break up. Distinguish between the *probate estate* and the *gross estate*.

15-2   Briefly describe the steps involved in the estate planning process.

15-2 THY WILL BE DONE . . .

will
A written and legally enforceable document expressing how a person's property should be distributed on his or her death.

intestacy
The situation that exists when a person dies without a valid will.

Having an up-to-date will is an important aspect of personal financial planning and estate planning. Without it, you have no assurance that your assets will be divided according to your desires. A **will** is a written, legally enforceable expression or declaration of a person's wishes concerning the disposition of his or her property on death. Unfortunately, the majority of Americans do not have valid wills. The importance of a valid will becomes very apparent when we examine what happens when someone dies without one.

15-2a Absence of a Valid Will: Intestacy

Suppose that Stanley Laughlin died without a valid will, a situation called **intestacy**. State intestacy laws "draw the will the decedent failed to make" in order to determine the disposition of the probate property of persons who have died intestate. These statutes set forth certain preferred classes of survivors. Generally, the decedent's spouse is favored, followed by the children and then other offspring. If the spouse and children or other offspring (e.g., grandchildren or great-grandchildren) survive, then they will divide the estate, and other relatives will receive nothing. If no spouse, children, or other offspring survive, then the deceased's parents, brothers, and sisters will receive a share of the estate.

Exhibit 15.4 gives an example of how a typical intestate estate is distributed. After paying debts and taxes and deducting state-defined family exemptions, that individual's separately owned property would be distributed in the order and percentages shown. Where property goes to the state because there is no will, the property is said to *escheat to the state*. However, if a person without relatives dies with a valid will, then his or her property will go to friends or to charity, as the will directs, rather than to the state.

EXHIBIT 15.4 | **Distribution of a Typical Intestate Estate**

If a person dies intestate (without a valid will), then the estate is distributed according to established state laws of intestate succession. This summary is based on Utah's probate code.

Survivors	Distribution*
Spouse and offspring—children, grandchildren, etc.—not of the surviving spouse	The first $75,000 plus 50 percent of the balance to the surviving spouse and the other 50 percent of the balance to the decedent spouse's offspring by right of representation (the spouse's share is reduced by any nonprobate transfers to him or her)
Spouse and no offspring or decedent's offspring all by the surviving spouse	100 percent to surviving spouse
No spouse but offspring	To decedent's descendants per capita at each generation
No spouse and no offspring, but parent(s)	To parent or parents equally
No spouse, no offspring, no parents, but generation	To parents' descendants per capita at each offspring of parents
No spouse, no offspring, no parents, and no offspring of parents, but grandparents or offspring of grandparents	Divided half to maternal grandparents (or their offspring, if neither survives) and half to paternal grandparents (or their offspring, if neither survives). If one side predeceased and there are no offspring, the other side takes all.
None of the above	The intestate estate passes to the state for the benefit of the state school fund.

*Because intestate laws vary from state to state, the actual distribution of assets may differ from that shown here; however, the Utah probate code is based on the uniform probate code that has been adopted, at least in part, by many states.

Aside from having lost control of the disposition of the property, the person who dies intestate also forfeits the privileges of naming a personal representative to guide the disposition of the estate, naming a guardian for persons and property, and specifying which beneficiaries would bear certain tax burdens. Estate planning and a valid will may also minimize the amount of estate shrinkage through transfer taxes. Having a valid will—regardless of the estate size—is a critical element in the personal financial planning process.

15-2b Preparing the Will

testator

The person who makes a will that provides for the disposition of property at his or her death.

A will allows a person, called a **testator**, to direct the disposition of property at his or her death. The testator can change or revoke a will at any time; on the death of the testator, the will becomes operative.

Will preparation (or drafting) varies in difficulty and cost, depending on individual circumstances. In some cases, a two-page will costing $150 may be adequate; in others, a complex document costing $1,500 or more may be necessary. A will must effectively accomplish the objectives specified for distributing assets, while also taking into consideration income, gift, and estate tax laws. Will preparation also requires knowledge of corporate, trust, real estate, and securities laws. Note that a will, important as it is, may be ineffective or might misinterpret the testator's estate plan if it doesn't consider and coordinate assets passing outside its limits.

A properly prepared will should meet these three important requirements:

Financial Fact or Fantasy?

The wealthy are the only ones who need to make out wills. **Fantasy:** Nothing could be further from the truth! While the wealthy may have more motivation to do so, anyone who has accumulated an estate—no matter how small—should have a will drawn up that sets out how the estate is to be distributed to heirs and/or beneficiaries.

- Provide a plan for distributing the testator's assets according to his or her wishes, the beneficiaries' needs, and federal and state dispositive and tax laws
- Consider the changes in family circumstances that might occur after its execution
- Be concise and complete in describing the testator's desires

By following these general guidelines, the testator generally can develop a satisfactory will.

Will drafting, no matter how modest the estate size, should not be attempted by a layperson. The complexity and interrelationships of tax, property, domestic relations, and other laws make the homemade will a potentially dangerous document. Nowhere is the old adage, "He who serves as his own attorney has a fool for a client," more true. Few things may turn out more disastrous in the long run than the do-it-yourself will.

15-2c Common Features of the Will

LANE V. ERICKSON/SHUTTERSTOCK.COM

There's no absolute format that must be followed when preparing a will, but most wills contain similar distinct sections. Exhibit 15.5, which presents the will of Glenn Alfred Brannon, includes generalized examples of each of these clauses. Refer to the exhibit as you read these descriptions of the clauses. *These clauses must be tailored to individual needs and circumstances by an attorney familiar with the testator's situation.*

EXHIBIT 15.5   A Representative Will for Glenn Alfred Brannon

Glenn Alfred Brannon's will illustrates the eight distinct sections of most wills.

The Last Will and Testament of Glenn Alfred Brannon

Section 1 — Introductory Clause

I, Glenn Alfred Brannon, of the city of Chicago, state of Illinois, do, hereby make my last will and revoke all wills and codicils made prior to this will.

Section 2 — Direction of Payments

Article 1: Payment of Debts and Expenses

I direct payment out of my estate of all just debts and the expenses of my last illness and funeral.

Section 3 — Disposition of Property

Article 2: Disposition of Property

I give and bequeath to my wife, Karin Keyes Brannon, all my jewelry, automobiles, books, and photography equipment, as well as all other articles of personal and household use.

I give to the Chicago Historical Society the sum of $100,000.

All the rest, residue, and remainder of my estate, real and personal, wherever located, I give in equal one-half shares to my children, Bryant David and Casey Hanna, their heirs and assigns forever.

Section 4 — Appointment Clause

Article 3: Nomination of Executor and Guardian

I hereby nominate as the Executor of this Will my beloved wife, Karin Keyes Brannon, but if she is unable or unwilling to serve then I nominate my brother, Marshall Drake Brannon. In the event both persons named predecease me, or shall cease or fail to act, then I nominate as Executor in the place of said persons, the Midwestern Trust Bank of Chicago, Illinois.

If my wife does not survive me, I appoint my brother, Byron Franklin Brannon, Guardian of the person and property of my son, Bryant David, during his minority.

Section 5 — Tax Clause

Article 4: Payment of Taxes

I direct that there shall be paid out of my residuary estate (from that portion which does not qualify for the marital deduction) all estate, inheritance, and similar taxes imposed by a government in respect to property includable in my estate for tax purposes, whether the property passes under this will or otherwise.

Section 6 — Simultaneous Death Clause

Article 5: Simultaneous Death

If my wife and I shall die under such circumstances that there is not sufficient evidence to determine the order of our deaths, then it shall be presumed that she survived me. My estate shall be administered and distributed in all respects in accordance with such assumption.

Section 7 — Execution and Attestation Clause

In witness thereof, I have affixed my signature to this, my last will and testament, which consists of five (5) pages, each of which I have initialed, this 15th day of September, 2017.

Glenn Alfred Brannon

Section 8 — Witness Clause

Signed, sealed, and published by Glenn Alfred Brannon, the testator, as his last will, in the presence of us, who, at his request, and in the presence of each other, all being present at the same time, have written our names as witnesses.

(Note: Normally the witness signatures and addresses would follow this clause.)

- **Introductory clause:** An introductory clause, or preamble, normally states the testator's name and residence; this determines the county that will have legal jurisdiction and be considered the testator's domicile for tax purposes. The revocation statement nullifies old and forgotten wills and *codicils*—legally binding modifications of an existing will.
- **Direction of payments:** This clause directs the estate to make certain payments of expenses. As a general rule, however, the rights of creditors are protected by law, and therefore this clause might be left out of a professionally drafted will.

- **Disposition of property:** Glenn's will has three examples of clauses dealing with disposition of property:
  1. *Disposition of personal effects:* A testator may also make a separate detailed and specific list of personal property and carefully identify each item, and to whom it is to be given, as an informal guide to help the executor divide the property. (This list generally should not appear in the will itself, because it's likely to be changed frequently.)
  2. *Giving money to a specifically named party:* Be sure to use the correct legal title of a charity.
  3. *Distribution of residual assets after specific gifts have been made:* Bequests to close relatives (as defined in the statute) who die before the testator will go to the relative's heirs unless the will includes other directions. Bequests to nonrelatives who predecease the testator will go to the other residual beneficiaries.
- **Appointment clause:** Appointment clauses name the *executors* (the decedent's personal representatives who administer the estate), guardians for minor children, and trustees and their successors.
- **Tax clause:** In the absence of a specified provision in the will, the *apportionment statutes* of the testator's state will allocate the burden of taxes among the beneficiaries. The result may be an inappropriate and unintended reduction of certain beneficiaries' shares or other adverse estate tax effects. Earlier statutes tended to charge death taxes on the residual of the estate, but today the trend is toward statutes that charge each beneficiary based on his or her share of the taxable estate. Because the spouse's share and the portion going to a charity are deducted from the gross estate before arriving at the taxable estate, neither is charged with taxes.
- **Simultaneous death clause:** This clause describes what happens in the event of simultaneous death. The assumption that the spouse survives is used mainly to permit the marital deduction, which offers a tax advantage. Other types of clauses are similarly designed to avoid double probate of the same assets—duplication of administrative and probate costs. Such clauses require that the survivor live for a certain period, such as 30 or 60 days, to be a beneficiary under the will.
- **Execution and attestation clause:** Every will should be in writing and signed by the testator at its end as a precaution against fraud. Many attorneys suggest that the testator also initial each page after the last line or sign in a corner of each page.
- **Witness clause:** The final clause helps to affirm that the will in question is really that of the deceased. All states require two witnesses to the testator's signing of the will. Most states require witnesses to sign in the presence of one another after they witness the signing by the testator. Their addresses should be noted on the will. If the testator is unable to sign his or her name for any reason, most states allow the testator to make a mark and to have another person (properly witnessed) sign for him or her.

You Can Do It Now

Importance of Naming Alternative Beneficiaries

When you name beneficiaries on financial accounts or in your will, it's important to name alternate (contingent) beneficiaries as well. This will make clear what happens if your first choice beneficiary doesn't outlive you. See http://www.nolo.com/legal-encyclopedia/why-naming-alternate-beneficiaries-your-will-is-so-important.html for some useful tips on naming beneficiaries and related key issues. You can do it now.

15-2d Requirements of a Valid Will

To be valid, a will must be the product of a person with a sound mind, there must have been no *undue influence* (influence that would remove the testator's freedom of choice), the will itself must have been properly executed, and its execution must be free from fraud.

1. **Mental capacity:** You must be "of sound mind" to make a valid will. This means that you:

   a. Know what a will is and are aware that you are making and signing one.
   b. Understand your relationship with persons for whom you would normally provide, such as a spouse or children, and who would generally be expected to receive your estate (even though you might not be required to leave anything to them).
   c. Understand what you own.
   d. Are able to decide how to distribute your property.

   Generally, mental capacity is presumed. Setting aside a will requires clear and convincing proof of mental incapacity, and the burden of proof is on the person contesting the will.

2. **Freedom of choice:** When you prepare and execute your will, you must not be under the undue influence of another person. Threats, misrepresentations, inordinate flattery, or some physical or mental coercion employed to destroy the testator's freedom of choice are all types of undue influence.

3. **Proper execution:** To be considered properly executed, a will must meet the requirements of the state's wills act or its equivalent. It must also be demonstrable that it is, in fact, the will of the testator. Most states have statutes that spell out who may make a will (generally any person of sound mind, age 18 or older but 14 in Georgia and 16 in Louisiana), the form and execution the will must have (most states require a will to be in writing and to be signed by the testator at the logical end), and requirements for witnesses. Generally, a beneficiary should not serve as a witness. Although the will is otherwise valid, about 60 percent of the states penalize the beneficiary-witness in some way, such as limiting the beneficiary-witness' bequest to the intestate share that he or she would receive.

   Most states now provide for a *self-proving will* that indicates in the attestation clause that the correct formalities for will execution were observed. A self-proving will eliminates the need, after the testator's death, to have the witnesses sign a declaration verifying their signatures and that of the testator. This saves time and money and often avoids lots of inconvenience to the executor.

Financial Fact or Fantasy?

Due to recent changes in the law, a person no longer has to be mentally competent in order to draw up a valid will. **Fantasy:** A person still must be mentally competent in order to draw up (or have drawn up) a legally enforceable will.

15-2e Changing or Revoking the Will: Codicils

As life circumstances change, so should your will. Because a will is inoperative until the testator's death, the testator can change it at any time, so long as he or she has the mental capacity. In fact, periodic revisions should occur, especially on these events:

- His or her (or the beneficiaries') health or financial circumstances change significantly.
- Births, deaths, marriages, or divorces alter the operative circumstances.
- The testator moves to a state other than where the will was executed.
- An executor, trustee, or guardian can no longer serve.
- Substantial changes occur in the tax law.

Only the testator can change a will. By reviewing your will regularly, you can be sure that it accurately reflects your current wishes.

FINANCIAL PLANNING TIPS

Choosing a Guardian for Minor Children

Your estate plan will should make careful provisions for any minor children. One key issue is deciding who will take care of your children if you and your spouse die while they are minors. This requires you to choose a guardian or conservator for the children. Below are some important issues that should be considered in making the decision. The best approach is to prioritize these issues in light of what you think is most important and then put together a "pros and cons" list to come up with a list of good guardian prospects. Don't just line up one guardian; make sure you also have a backup plan.

- **Home.** Your children would probably be expected to move in with the guardian. So the size and location of the guardian's home are important considerations. You should be comfortable with both.

- **Religious, political, and moral beliefs.** You should make sure that you know and are comfortable with the potential guardian's religious, political, and moral beliefs. No guardian is likely to be a perfect match, but you should be comfortable with the extent and nature of any mismatches.

- **Parenting skills.** You want to make sure that you understand the potential guardian's parenting skills. What are the prospect's views on child discipline, education, sports, and other school activities? Does the prospect already have children? If so, will adding your children to the mix be too much for the potential guardian to handle?

- **Age of the potential guardian.** An older guardian may have better financial resources and more time to raise your children. On the other hand, an older prospect may not be up to date on current trends in education and parenting. You must also consider what would happen to your children if an older guardian became ill or died while the children were still minors. Alternatively, a younger guardian could be too involved in managing their own career and family to raise your children effectively.

- **Family situation.** It's important to think through the implications of the prospect's family situation. Is the potential guardian married with minor children, married with adult children, a single parent, married without children, or single without children? The potential guardian's family situation is closely related to how well your children would be raised.

- **Financial situation.** It's important to understand how well the potential guardian manages money, the stability of his or her job and that of the spouse, and whether the prospect's resources are sufficient to meet the costs of raising your children.

- **Willingness to serve as guardian.** It's important to ask and confirm explicitly that your prospect is willing to serve as your children's guardian. None of the above criteria matter if the prospect is simply unwilling to perform this critically important task for you. You need to have at least one discussion with this person about what the task would entail.

Source: Adapted from Julie Garber, "How to Choose a Guardian for Your Minor Children," http://wills.about.com/od/planningformino2/tp/howtochooseaguardianforminors.htm, accessed September 2015.

Changing the Will

codicil
A document that legally modifies a will without revoking it.

A **codicil** is a simple, often single-page document that provides a convenient legal means of making minor changes in a will. It reaffirms all the existing provisions in the will except the one to be changed, and it should be executed and witnessed in the same formal manner as a will.

When a will requires substantial changes, a new will is usually preferable to a codicil. In addition, if a gift in the original will is removed, it may be best to make a new will and destroy the old, even if substantial changes aren't required. This avoids offending the omitted beneficiary. Sometimes, however, the prior will should not be destroyed even after the new will has been made and signed. If the new will fails for some reason (because of the testator's mental incapacity, for example), then the prior will may qualify. Also, a prior will could help to prove a "continuity of testamentary purpose"—in other words, that the latest will (which may have provided a substantial gift to charity) continued an earlier intent and wasn't an afterthought or the result of an unduly influenced mind.

Revoking the Will

When he remarried, Stanley Laughlin might have wanted to change his will significantly. In that case, he'd have been better off revoking his old will and writing a new one, rather than doing a codicil. A will may be revoked either by the testator or automatically by the law. A testator can revoke a will in one of four ways:

1. Making a later will that expressly revokes prior wills
2. Making a codicil that expressly revokes all wills before the one being modified
3. Making a later will that is inconsistent with a former will
4. Physically mutilating, burning, tearing, or defacing the will with the intention of revoking it

Financial Fact or Fantasy?

Once a will is drawn up, it is relatively simple to make minor changes to it. **Fact:** As long as the changes are minor, a simple and convenient way to legally modify an existing will is a *codicil*, which is a short, legal document that specifies the changes.

The law automatically modifies a will under certain circumstances, which vary from state to state but generally center on divorce, marriage, birth or adoption, and murder. In many states, if a testator becomes divorced after making a will, then all provisions in the will relating to the spouse automatically become ineffective. If a testator marries after making a will, the spouse receives that portion of the estate that would have been received had the testator died without a valid will. If a testator did not provide for a child born or adopted after the will was made (unless it appears that such lack of provision was intentional), then the child receives that share of the estate not passing to the testator's spouse that would have been given to him or her had the deceased not had a will. Finally, almost all states have some type of slayer's statute that forbids a person who commits murder from acquiring property as the result of the deed.

15-2f Safeguarding the Will

In most cases, you should keep your original will in a safe-deposit box, with copies in an accessible and safe place at home and with the attorney who drafted it. Although some authorities and many attorneys recommend leaving the original will with the attorney who drafted it, this may make it awkward for the executor to exercise the right to choose his or her own attorney. Further, it may discourage the estate owner from changing the will or engaging a new attorney, even if he or she moves out of the state in which the will is drawn.

Worksheet 15.1 contains an executor's checklist of documents and information that should be kept in a safe-deposit box. If each spouse has a separate safe-deposit box, then the couple may want to keep their wills in each other's boxes. Some states provide for *lodging* of the will, a mechanism for filing and safekeeping it in the office of the probate court (also called *orphan's* or *surrogate's court*). In those states, this procedure satisfies the need to safeguard the will.

15-2g Letter of Last Instructions

letter of last instructions
An informal memorandum that is separate from a will and contains suggestions or recommendations for carrying out a decedent's wishes.

People often have thoughts they want to convey and instructions they wish others to carry out that aren't appropriate to include in their wills. For example, Stanley Laughlin might have explained why he chose Brenda as his executor rather than choosing her brother. A **letter of last instructions** is the best way to communicate these suggestions or recommendations. It's typically an informal memorandum that is separate from the will. (This letter of last instructions should contain no bequests

This checklist itemizes the various documents and information that the executor may need to carry out the terms of the will effectively. These items should be kept in a safe-deposit box.

CHECKLIST FOR EXECUTORS

Name (Testator) _____ Date _____

_____ 1. Marriage certificates
         (including prior marriages)
_____ 2. Your will and trust agreements
_____ 3. Life insurance policies
         or certificates
_____ 4. Your Social Security number
_____ 5. Military discharge papers

_____ 6. Bonds, stocks, and securities
_____ 7. Real estate deeds
_____ 8. Business agreements
_____ 9. Automobile titles and
         insurance policies
_____ 10. Property insurance policies
_____ 11. Tax information
_____ 12. Letter of last instructions

List all checking and savings account numbers, bank addresses, and locations of safe-deposit boxes:

_____ _____ _____

List names, addresses, and phone numbers of property and life insurance agents:

_____ _____ _____

List names, addresses, and phone numbers of attorney and accountant:

_____ _____ _____

List names, addresses, and phone numbers of (current or last) employer. State retirement date, if applicable. Include employee benefits booklets:

_____ _____ _____

List all debts owed to *and* by you, including names and account numbers:

_____ _____ _____

List the names, addresses, telephone numbers, and birth dates of your children and other beneficiaries (including charities):

_____ _____ _____

Source: Based on Stephan R. Leimberg, Stephen N. Kandell, Ralph Gano Miller, Morey S. Rosenbloom, and Timothy C. Polacek, *The Tools & Techniques of Estate Planning*, 14th ed. (Upper Saddle River, NJ: Prentice Hall, 2006); Metropolitan Life Insurance Company, Taking Legal Action: The Executor's Checklist, http://www.metlife.com/assets/cao/mmi/life-advice/finances/taking-legal-action/executors-check-list.pdf, accessed August 2015.

because it has no legal standing.) It's best to make several copies of the letter, keeping one at home and the others with the estate's executor or attorney, who can deliver it to beneficiaries at the appropriate time.

A letter of last instructions might provide directions regarding such items as:

- Location of the will and other documents
- Funeral and burial instructions (often a will is not opened until after the funeral)
- Suggestions or recommendations as to the continuation, sale, or liquidation of a business (it's easier to freely suggest a course of action in such a letter than in

a will—especially since, in many states, the will is placed in a probate court file that is open to the public)

- Personal matters that the testator might prefer not be made public in the will, such as statements (e.g., comments about a spendthrift spouse or a reckless son) that might sound unkind or inconsiderate but would be valuable to the executor
- Legal and accounting services (executors are free, however, to choose their own counsel—not even testators can bind them in that selection)
- An explanation of the actions taken in the will, which may help avoid litigation (for instance, "I left only $5,000 to my son, James, because . . . " or "I made no provisions for my oldest daughter, Patricia, because . . . ")
- Suggestions on how to divide the personal property

15-2h Administration of an Estate

When people die, they usually own property and owe debts. Often, they'll have claims (accounts receivable) against other persons. A process of liquidation called the **probate process**, similar to that used in dissolving a corporation, might be required. In this process, money owed the decedent is collected, creditors (including tax authorities) are satisfied, and what remains is distributed to the appropriate individuals and organizations. A local court generally supervises the probate process through a person designated as an **executor** in the decedent's will or, if the decedent died intestate (without a valid will), through a court-appointed **administrator**.

An executor or administrator, sometimes called the *decedent's personal representative*, must collect the decedent's assets, pay debts or provide for payment of debts that aren't currently due, and distribute any remaining assets to the persons entitled to them by will or by the intestate succession law of the appropriate state. Estate administration is important for many reasons. The executor or administrator becomes the decedent's legal representative, taking care of such matters as collecting bank accounts and other contracts, releasing liability, and creating clear title to make real estate marketable. Because of the importance of the estate administration process, you should select executors who are not only familiar with the testator's affairs but also can effectively handle the responsibilities of being an executor.

15-2i Other Important Estate Planning Documents

In addition to your will and the letter of last instructions, you should have several other documents to protect yourself and your family: a durable power of attorney for financial matters, a living will, a durable power of attorney for health care, and an ethical will.

Power of Attorney

If you're incapacitated by a serious illness, a **durable power of attorney for financial matters** allows you to name as your agent the person you consider best suited to take over your financial affairs—perhaps a spouse or other relative. Although this is a simple document, it transfers enormous power to your designated appointee, so be sure you can rely on the person you choose to manage your finances responsibly. If you have investments, your power of attorney should include language that covers powers of investment on your behalf. To make it durable—that is, effective even when you are incapacitated—the document must clearly state that your agent's authority to act on your behalf will continue during your incapacity. Just labeling the document a "durable power" is probably insufficient and, without a statement giving your agent authority to act on your behalf while you are incapacitated, his or her authority may cease just when it is needed most. You may want to clear your power of attorney with the brokerage firms and mutual funds where you have accounts.

probate process
The court-supervised disposition of a decedent's estate.

executor
The personal representative of an estate designated in the decedent's will.

administrator
The personal representative of the estate appointed by the court if the decedent died intestate.

durable power of attorney for financial matters
Legal document that authorizes another person to take over someone's financial affairs and act on his or her behalf.

Living Will

Had Stanley Laughlin lingered in a coma, with little or no hope of recovery, his family could have faced difficult decisions regarding his medical care. He hadn't prepared a *living will* or *durable power of attorney for health care* to guide them as to his preferences. These documents address another important aspect of estate planning: determining the medical care you wish to receive, or *not* receive, if you become seriously ill and are unable to give informed consent. The living will states, precisely, the treatments that you want and to what degree you wish them continued. You must be as specific as possible so that your wishes are clear; otherwise, a living will might be put aside because it is too vague. For example, you should define what you mean by "terminal illness." Each state has its own form for a living will, and you can usually complete it yourself.

Durable Power of Attorney for Health Care

Many experts prefer the durable power of attorney for health care, often called *advanced directives for health care*, instead of the living will; some advise having both to reinforce each other. Through the durable power of attorney for health care, you authorize an individual (your *agent*) to make health care decisions for you if you're unable to do so either temporarily or permanently. Unlike the living will, it applies in any case where you cannot communicate your wishes, not just when you're terminally ill. You can limit the scope of the durable power of attorney and include specific instructions for the desired level of medical treatment. You should spend some time making such decisions and then review your ideas and philosophy concerning these matters with your family and the person whom you designate as your agent. These documents, copies of which should be held by your designated agent and your doctor, can make it easier for your family to deal with these difficult issues.

Ethical Wills

Many people today also prepare ethical wills to leave family, friends, and community a personal statement of values, blessings, life's lessons, and hopes and dreams for the future. Sometimes called *legacy letters*, ethical wills are informal documents that are usually added to formal wills and read at the same time. An ethical will is not a legal document and consequently does not distribute your material wealth. An ethical will offers a way to share your morals, ethics, life experiences, family stories and history, and more with future generations. Ethical wills may be in the form of handwritten letters or essays, computer files, videos, or other electronic media.

Writing an ethical will can be a daunting project and may perhaps be even more difficult than writing a regular will. Experts suggest dividing it into smaller steps. You might prepare a list of questions about the impact of certain experiences on shaping your life and values, how you want to be remembered, the lessons that you wish to pass on to your family and friends, and any other important messages.

It's a good idea to review your ethical will with the lawyer who handles your estate planning. An ethical will that can be interpreted in a way that seems to contradict the intentions of the formal will could lead to a challenge of the formal will.

15-2j What about Joint Ownership?

Many people take title to property jointly, either through a *joint tenancy* or as *tenants by the entirety*. The two forms of joint ownership share the following characteristics:

1. The interest of a decedent passes directly to the surviving joint tenant(s)—that is, to the other joint owner(s)—by operation of the law and is free from the claims of the decedent's creditors, heirs, or personal representatives. This is called the right of survivorship.

joint tenancy
A type of ownership by two or more parties, with the survivor(s) continuing to hold all such property on the death of one or more of the owners.

tenancy by the entirety
A form of ownership by husband and wife, recognized in certain states, in which property automatically passes to the surviving spouse.

2. A **joint tenancy** may consist of any number of persons. The joint owners need not be related. A **tenancy by the entirety**, on the other hand, can exist only between husband and wife, and the right of survivorship is always included.
3. In joint tenancy, each joint tenant can unilaterally sever the tenancy. This is not the case with a tenancy by the entirety, which can be severed only by mutual agreement, divorce, or conveyance by both spouses to a third party. In some states, a tenancy by the entirety can exist only with respect to real property; other states don't recognize such tenancies at all.
4. The co-owners must have equal interests.

Joint tenancy with the right of survivorship, the more common form of joint ownership, offers a sense of family security, quick and easy transfer to the spouse at death, exemption of jointly owned property from the claims of the deceased's creditors, and avoidance of delays and publicity in the estate settlement process. The key disadvantage of joint tenancy with the right of survivorship is the inability to control jointly owned property by a will, so that the first joint owner to die cannot control the property's disposition and management on his or her death.

> **EXAMPLE: Disadvantage of Joint Tenancy with the Right of Survivorship**
>
> A father who has two unmarried children—a daughter with whom he has a good relationship and an estranged son—purchases property and places it in his own and his daughter's name as joint tenants. The father has a will that leaves everything he has to his daughter and specifically disinherits his son. The daughter has no estate planning documents. While traveling together, the father is killed outright in a car accident and the daughter is severely injured. She never fully recovers and dies two months later. At her death, intestate, her estate will likely pass to her brother. Had her father held the property in his name only, then he could have stipulated in his will a longer survivorship requirement (say, six months) with a provision that, in the event his daughter did not survive that period, there would be an alternative disposition (e.g., to a charity or to friends).

Creating a joint tenancy might also create a taxable gift. However, unless the donor's cumulative taxable gifts exceed $5,430,000 (the applicable exclusion amount for gifts in 2015), no gift tax must be paid. Yet a gift tax return must be filed if the annual exclusion amount is exceeded. Fortunately, because federal gift tax law doesn't tax most interspousal transfers, the problem won't arise on a federal level when creating a joint tenancy between a married couple (although some states may tax such gifts); the property is transferred to the surviving spouse tax free. Most couples don't have estates large enough to generate an estate tax and so, given that joint holding of major assets such as the home, autos, and bank accounts keeps things simple, joint tenancy is quite commonly used by married couples.

You should also be familiar with two other forms of ownership: *tenancy in common* and *community property*.

Tenancy in Common

tenancy in common
A form of co-ownership under which there is *no right of survivorship* and each co-owner can leave his or her share to whomever he or she desires.

A third common form of co-ownership is called **tenancy in common**. There is *no right of survivorship*, and each co-owner can leave his or her share to whomever he or she desires. Thus, the decedent owner's will controls the disposition of the decedent's partial interest in the asset. If the decedent dies without a will, then the intestate succession laws of the state where the property is located will determine who inherits the decedent's interest. Unlike joint tenancy, where all interests must be equal, tenancy in common interests can be unequal. Hence a property owned by three co-owners could be apportioned such that their respective shares are 50 percent, 30 percent, and 20 percent of the property.

Community Property

Tenancy by the entirety is a special form of marital property co-ownership that is found only in common-law states (i.e., states that trace their property law to England). In contrast, community property is a form of marital property co-ownership that is based on Roman law and is found primarily in the Southwestern states that had a Spanish or French influence.

community property
All marital property co-owned equally by both spouses while living in a community property state.

Community property is all property acquired by the effort of either or both spouses during marriage while they reside in a community property state. For example, wages and commissions earned and property acquired by either spouse while living in a community property state are automatically owned equally by both spouses, even if only one was directly involved in acquiring the additional wealth. Property acquired before marriage or by gift or inheritance can be maintained as the acquiring spouse's separate property.

By agreement, which typically must be in writing to be enforceable, the couple can change community property into separate property, and vice versa. Each spouse can leave his or her half of the community property to whomever he or she chooses, so there's *no right of survivorship* inherent in this form of ownership.

TEST YOURSELF

15-3   What is a *will*? Why is it important? Describe the consequences of dying *intestate*.

15-4   Describe the basic clauses normally included in a will and the requirements regarding who may make a valid will.

15-5   How can changes in the provisions of a will be made legally? In what four ways can a will be revoked?

15-6   Explain these terms: (a) *intestacy*, (b) *testator*, (c) *codicil*, (d) *letter of last instructions*.

15-7   What is meant by the *probate process*? Who is an *executor*, and what is the executor's role in estate settlement?

15-8   Describe briefly the importance of these documents in estate planning: (a) power of attorney, (b) living will, (c) durable power of attorney for health care, and (d) ethical will.

15-9   Define and differentiate between *joint tenancy* and *tenancy by the entirety*. Discuss the advantages and disadvantages of joint ownership. How does *tenancy in common* differ from joint tenancy?

15-10   What is the right of survivorship? What is community property, and how does it differ from joint tenancy with regard to the right of survivorship?

15-3 TRUSTS

Trusts facilitate the transfer of property and the income from that property to another party. Although trusts were once considered estate planning techniques only for the wealthy, today even those of modest means use trusts to their advantage in estate planning. This change is attributed to rising real estate values, bull financial markets, and marketing by estate planning attorneys. Also, as people live longer and are more likely to marry more than once, they need ways to protect and manage assets.

trust
A legal relationship created when one party transfers property to a second party for the benefit of third parties.

A **trust** is a legal relationship created when one party, the **grantor** (also called the *settlor*, *trustor*, or *creator*), transfers property to a second party, the

grantor

A person who creates a trust and whose property is transferred into it. Also called *settlor, trustor,* or *creator.*

trustee

An organization or individual selected by a *grantor* to manage and conserve property placed in trust for the benefit of the *beneficiaries.*

beneficiaries

Those who receive benefits—property or income—from a trust or from the estate of a decedent. A grantor can be a beneficiary of his own trust.

trustee (an organization or individual), for the benefit of third parties, the **beneficiaries**, who may or may not include the grantor. The property placed in the trust is called *trust principal* or *res* (pronounced "race"). The trustee holds the legal title to the property in the trust and must use the property and any income it produces solely for the benefit of trust beneficiaries. The trust generally is created by a written document.

The grantor spells out the substantive provisions (such as how to allocate the property in the trust and how to distribute income) and certain administrative provisions. A trust may be *living* (funded during the grantor's life) or *testamentary* (created in a will and funded by the probate process). It may be *revocable* or *irrevocable*. The grantor can regain property placed into a *revocable* trust and alter or amend the terms of the trust. The grantor cannot recover property placed into an *irrevocable* trust during its term.

Let's now look at how trusts solve various estate planning problems.

15-3a Why Use a Trust?

Trusts are designed for various purposes. The most common motives are to manage and conserve property over a long period of time and in some cases, to achieve income and estate tax savings.

Managing and Conserving Property

Minors, spendthrifts, and those who are mentally incompetent need asset management services for obvious reasons. However, busy executives and others who can't or don't want to spend the countless hours necessary to handle large sums of money and other property often use trusts to relieve themselves of those burdens. The trustee assumes the responsibility for managing and conserving the property on behalf of the beneficiaries. In some cases, management by the trustee is held in reserve in case a healthy and vigorous individual is unexpectedly incapacitated and becomes unable or unwilling to manage his or her assets.

Income and Estate Tax Savings

Under certain circumstances, a grantor who is a high-bracket taxpayer can shift the burden of paying taxes on the income produced by securities, real estate, and other investments to a trust or to its beneficiary, both of whom may be subject to lower income tax rates than the grantor is. Impressive *estate tax* savings are possible because the appreciation in the value of property placed into such a trust can be entirely removed from the grantor's estate and possibly benefit several generations of family members without incurring adverse federal estate tax consequences.

15-3b Selecting a Trustee

Five qualities are essential in a trustee. He or she must:

1. Possess sound business knowledge and judgment
2. Have an intimate knowledge of the beneficiary's needs and financial situation
3. Be skilled in investment and trust management
4. Be available to beneficiaries (specifically, this means that the trustee should be young enough to survive the trust term)
5. Be able to make decisions impartially

A corporate trustee, such as a trust company or bank that has been authorized to perform trust duties, may be best able to meet these requirements. A corporate trustee is likely to have investment experience and will not impose the problems created by the death, disability, or absence of the trustee. Unlike a family member, a corporate trustee is impartial and obedient to the directions of the trust instrument. Such objectivity adds value if there are several beneficiaries. On the other hand, a corporate trustee may charge high fees or be overly conservative in investments, be impersonal, or lack familiarity with and understanding of family problems and needs. A compromise often involves appointing one or more individuals and a corporate trustee as co-trustees.

15-3c Common Types and Characteristics of Trusts

Although there are various types of trusts, the most common ones are the *living trust,* the *testamentary trust,* and the *irrevocable life insurance trust,* each of which is described in the following sections. Exhibit 15.6 describes seven other popular trusts.

Living Trusts

living (inter vivos) trust
A trust created and funded during the grantor's lifetime.

A **living (inter vivos) trust** is one created and funded during the grantor's lifetime. It can be either revocable or irrevocable and can last for a limited period or continue long after the grantor's death. Such trusts come in two forms, revocable and irrevocable.

revocable living trust
A trust in which the grantor reserves the right to revoke the trust and regain trust property. The grantor can serve as the initial trustee.

Revocable Living Trust. The grantor reserves the right to revoke the trust and regain trust property in a **revocable living trust**. For federal income tax purposes, grantors of these trusts are treated as owners of the property in the trust—in other words, just as if they held the property in their own names—and are therefore taxed on any income produced by the trust.

FINANCIAL PLANNING TIPS

Reasons to Set up a Trust

Trusts can be used to achieve various financial objectives. Consider the key reasons that they are so commonly used:

- **Avoid probate.** A trust may be used to avoid the probate process, which can be cost as much as 5 percent of the value of an estate. However, the costs of setting up a trust should be compared with the expected cost of probate. It's important to keep in mind that a probated will is a public document, whereas trusts offer more privacy.

- **Protection in old age and disability.** You can set up a trust, name yourself as beneficiary, and then name yourself and another person as trustees. If you become gravely ill or mentally incapacitated, the other trustee can manage your assets and distribute them as you direct in the trust arrangement.

- **Provide for minors and young adults.** You can use a trust to leave assets to minors and young adults. The trustee will manage the trust until the beneficiary reaches the age that you designate is old enough to handle the assets responsibly.

- **Avoid estate taxes.** You can set up a trust to transfer assets to an irrevocable trust to avoid estate taxes. These assets are not included in your gross estate. However, it's important that the grantor trust is not also a beneficiary or there will be limits on distributions to shield from taxation. The possibility of gift taxes must be considered. And planning must recognize that if a grantor transfers a life insurance policy to an irrevocable trust within three years before the grantor's death, the policy may well be included in the estate.

- **Reduce income taxes.** Certain types of trusts may be used to transfer income to heirs in a lower income tax bracket, which can reduce overall taxes.

- **Benefit charity.** You can transfer assets to a trust, receive income from the trust, and distribute the assets to a charity upon death. Thus, trusts may be used to provide income and estate tax benefits to support your favorite charity.

EXHIBIT 15.6   **Seven Popular Trusts**

Trusts shift assets (and thus appreciation) out of one's estate while retaining some say in the future use of the assets. The drawback is that trusts can be cumbersome and expensive to arrange and administer. Here are brief descriptions of seven popular trusts:

- **Credit shelter trust.** The most common tax-saving trust for estate planning; couples with combined assets worth more than the applicable exclusion amount (AEA) can gain full use of each partner's exclusion by having that amount placed in a bypass trust—that is, one that bypasses the surviving spouse's taxable estate. It's called a *credit shelter trust* because, when one spouse dies, the trust receives assets from the decedent's estate equal in value to the estate AEA. So if the first death occurred in the year 2015, then the trust would be funded with assets worth exactly $5,430,000. This trust does not qualify for the marital deduction, but no tax is due because the tentative tax is equal to the available *unified credit*. The surviving spouse is usually given the right to all the trust income and, in an emergency, even has access to the principal. When the surviving spouse dies, the credit shelter trust is not included in his or her estate regardless of the trust's value, so it avoids having to pay a tax at both deaths. With the addition of the "portability" provision (discussed in this chapter), the need and usefulness of the credit shelter trust is reduced.

- **Qualified terminable interest property (QTIP) trust.** Usually set up in addition to a *credit shelter trust* to ensure that money stays in the family; it receives some or all of the estate assets over the applicable exclusion amount ($5,430,000 in 2015). Assets left outright to a spouse who remarries could be claimed by the new spouse. The survivor receives all income from the property until death, when the assets go to the persons chosen by the first spouse to die. Estate taxes on QTIP trust assets can be delayed until the second spouse dies. It is also useful for couples with children from prior marriages because the QTIP property can be distributed to the children of the grantor-spouse only after the death of the surviving spouse; hence, the survivor benefits from the trust's income, and the deceased spouse's children are assured that they will receive the remainder of the QTIP trust eventually.

- **Special needs trust.** An irrevocable trust established for the benefit of a person with disabilities. It is designed to provide extra help and life enrichment without reducing state and federal government help to the beneficiary.

- **Minor's section 2503(c) trust.** Set up for a minor, often to receive tax-free gifts. However, assets must be distributed to the minor before he or she turns 21.

- **Crummey trust.** Named after the first person to successfully use this trust structure, this is used to make tax-free gifts up to the annual exclusion amounts to children. Unlike a *minor's section 2503(c) trust,* these funds need not be distributed before age 21. However, the beneficiary can withdraw the funds placed into the trust for a limited time (e.g., for up to 30 days), after which the right to make a withdrawal ceases.

- **Charitable lead (or income) trust.** Pays some of or all its income to a charity for a period of time, after which the property is distributed to noncharitable beneficiaries; the grantor receives an immediate income tax deduction based on expected future payout to charity. If the grantor's children are the so-called remaindermen of the trust, then the value of the gift for gift or estate tax purposes is greatly reduced because their possession and enjoyment of the trust assets is delayed until the charitable interest terminates.

- **Charitable remainder trust.** Similar to a *charitable lead trust,* except that income goes to taxable beneficiaries (e.g., the grantor or the grantor's children) and the principal goes to a charity when the trust ends; the grantor gets an immediate income tax deduction based upon the value of the remainder interest that is promised to the charity.

Revocable living trusts have three basic advantages.

1. Management continuity and income flow are ensured even after the grantor's death. No probate is necessary because the trust continues to operate after the death of the grantor just as it did while he or she was alive.
2. The trustee assumes the burdens of investment decisions and management responsibility. For example, an individual may want to control investment decisions and

management policy as long as he is alive and healthy but sets up a trust to provide backup help in case he becomes unable or unwilling to continue managing the assets.

3. The details of the estate plan and the value of assets placed into the trust do not become public knowledge, as they would during the probate process.

The principal disadvantages of these trusts include the fees charged by the trustee for managing the property placed into the trust and the legal fees charged for drafting the trust instruments.

irrevocable living trust
A trust in which the grantor gives up the right to revoke or terminate the trust.

Irrevocable Living Trust. Grantors who establish an **irrevocable living trust** relinquish title to the property that they place in it and give up the right to revoke or terminate the trust. (The grantor may retain the income from certain types of irrevocable trusts.) Such trusts have all the advantages of revocable trusts plus the potential for reducing taxes. Disadvantages of such a trust relate to the fees charged by trustees for managing assets placed into it, possible gift taxes on assets placed into it, in some cases the grantor's complete loss of the trust property and any income it may produce, and the grantor's forfeiture of the right to alter the terms of the trust as circumstances change.

Living Trusts and Pour-Over Wills. A will can be written so that it "pours over" designated assets into a previously established revocable or irrevocable living trust. The trust may also be named the beneficiary of the grantor's insurance policies. The **pour-over will** generally contains a provision passing the estate—after debts, expenses, taxes, and specific bequests—to an existing living trust. The pour-over will ensures that the property left out of the living trust, either inadvertently or deliberately, will make its way into the trust (that is, "pour over" into it). The trust contains provisions for administering and distributing those assets (together with insurance proceeds payable to the trust). Such an arrangement provides for easily coordinated and well-administered management of estate assets.

pour-over will
A provision in a will that provides for the passing of the estate—after debts, expenses, taxes, and specific bequests—to an existing living trust.

Testamentary Trust

testamentary trust
A trust created by a decedent's will and funded through the probate process.

A trust created by a decedent's will is called a **testamentary trust**. Such a trust comes into existence only after the will is probated. A court order directs the executor to transfer the property to the trustee in order to fund the trust. The revocable living trust and the testamentary trust can have pretty much the same terms and long-range functions—for example, providing for asset management for the trustor's family long after the trustor has died. Indeed, the two main differences are: (1) only the living trust provides for management when and if the trustor becomes incapacitated; and (2) the living trust is funded by transfers to the trustee by assignment or deed during the trustor's life, whereas the funding mechanism for the testamentary trust is a court order distributing the property to the trustee at the end of the probate process.

irrevocable life insurance trust
An irrevocable trust in which the major asset is life insurance on the grantor's life.

Irrevocable Life Insurance Trust

A wealthy individual might want to establish an **irrevocable life insurance trust** in which the major asset of the trust is life insurance on the grantor's life. To avoid having the proceeds of the policy included in the grantor's estate, the independent trustee usually acquires the policy on the life of the wealthy person and names the trustee as the beneficiary. The terms of the trust enable the trustee to use the proceeds to pay the grantor's estate taxes and to take care of the grantor's spouse and children, and probably eventually to distribute the remainder of the proceeds to the children or other beneficiaries as specified in the trust document.

15-4 FEDERAL UNIFIED TRANSFER TAXES

gift tax
A tax levied on the value of certain gifts made during the giver's lifetime.

estate tax
A tax levied on the value of property transferred at the owner's death.

applicable exclusion amount (AEA)
Credit given to each person that can be applied to the amount of federal estate tax owed by that person at death. In 2015 the AEA was $5,430,000 per spouse.

unified rate schedule
A graduated table of rates applied to all taxable transfers; used for *both* federal gift and estate tax purposes.

The federal unified transfer tax is a tax on the right to transfer property from one individual to another. The tax affects two types of transfers: transfer by gift, referred to as the **gift tax**; and transfers through the estate, referred to as the **estate tax**. The tax base for both transfers is the fair market value of the property that is transferred. The amount that can pass tax-free, called the **applicable exclusion amount (AEA)**, is $5,430,000 in 2015. In addition, taxable gifts are reduced by an annual exclusion of $14,000 (adjusted for inflation over time) per donee. Thus, combined transfers of $5,430,000 plus the annual gift tax exclusion are not subject to the federal transfer tax. If the taxpayer is married, then the two married taxpayers each have an AEA of $5,430,000, or a total of $10,860,000, before any tax applies. The tax rate for gifts and estates is specified by the **unified rate schedule** (see the graduated table of rates in Exhibit 15.7). And if one of the spouses dies, then any unused applicable exclusion amount will carry over to the other spouse. This is referred to as the *portability* of the unified transfer tax credit. In order to benefit from the portability provision, it must be elected on the return of the first spouse to die, even if there is no taxable estate. Thus, if there is a chance that the combined estate will exceed $5,430,000, an estate tax return must be filed when the first spouse dies and the portability provision elected.

The applicable exclusion amount is high enough to remove transfer taxes from the concerns of estate planning for the middle-income taxpayer. For the upper-income taxpayer, however, the transfer tax is a major concern. For example, if a couple has a taxable estate of $20,000,000, then the transfer tax due is $3,656,000. That is a significant concern. The remainder of this section addresses these issues.

15-4a Gifts and Taxes

Gifting can be a good way to transfer property to a beneficiary before you die. However, very large transfers might be subject to gift taxes. The transfer tax applies to the fair market value of property transferred to a donee *less* the amount of compensation given to the donor. To determine the taxable gift, this amount is reduced by the annual exclusion ($14,000 in 2015). The annual exclusion applies to each donee who is given gifts. Thus, if the taxpayer gave three people $10,000 each, none of the transfers would be subject to the gift tax because the annual exclusion reduces each taxable gift to $0. The one requirement is that the transfer be a gift of *present interest*, not of a future interest. A typical example of the latter is the transfer of money to a trust with the provision that the trust's beneficiary must be 30 before withdrawing funds from the trust. This beneficiary has only a future interest, not a present interest.

There are two major exceptions to the present interest rule. Transfers to a minor trust—that is, a trust that allows no withdrawals until the minor is 21—qualify for the annual exclusions. A second exception is the Crummey provision, which

EXHIBIT 15.7   **Federal Unified Transfer Tax Rates**

This *unified rate schedule* defines the amount of federal gift and estate taxes that estates of various sizes would have to pay. It incorporates the rates passed in the *American Taxpayer Relief Act of 2012*, signed into law in 2013. Estates and gifts under the exclusion amount pay no federal tax. The estate exclusion amount increased annually from $2,000,000 in 2006 to $5,430,000 in 2015 (see Exhibit 15.8). From 2009 to 2015, the top tax rates decreased from 45% to 40%.

TAXABLE ESTATE VALUE		TENTATIVE TAX		
More Than	But Not More Than	Base Amount	+ Percent	On Excess Over
$ 0	$ 10,000	$ 0	18%	0
10,000	20,000	1,800	20%	$ 10,000
20,000	40,000	3,800	22	20,000
40,000	60,000	8,200	24	40,000
60,000	80,000	13,000	26	60,000
80,000	100,000	18,200	28	80,000
100,000	150,000	23,800	30	100,000
150,000	250,000	38,800	32	150,000
250,000	500,000	70,800	34	250,000
500,000	750,000	155,800	37	500,000
750,000	1,000,000	248,300	39	750,000
1,000,000		345,800	40	1,000,000

Source: Internal Revenue Code, Section 2001.

provides for withdrawal rights to the beneficiary for a specified period (e.g., 30 days). If the beneficiary does not ask for a withdrawal in that time period, the property must remain in the trust until it can be distributed according to the trust terms. Thus, with the Crummey withdrawal rights, transfers to the trust are considered a present interest and will qualify for the annual exclusion interest to the extent of the withdrawal right.

An essential first step to estate planning is making annual gifts to your potential heirs. Giving gifts reduce the taxable estate in two ways. First, any future appreciation of the gifted property is excluded from the estate because the decedent does not own the property on the date of death. Second, if the gift is so large that taxes are due, the money used to pay the tax is also removed from the estate. (There is an exception for gift taxes paid within three years of death.)

Another consideration when making gifts is their impact on the income taxes of the donee. If the gifted property is to be sold by the donee for a gain, it should be noted that property received by gift has a tax basis equal to its basis in the hands of the donor (i.e., a carryover basis). Property that is inherited has a basis equal to the fair market value on the date of death. For example, assume that a taxpayer owns a beach house that was purchased for $100,000 in 1990 and now has a value of $600,000. If the beach house is gifted, the basis to the donee will be $100,000. If passed through the estate, the basis to the heir will be $600,000. So long as the property is not sold or depreciated, the basis really does not matter. However, if it is sold, then there is a difference in income tax of $100,000 (20 percent capital gains rate multiplied by the difference in basis, which is $500,000) between receiving the property by gift rather than through the estate.

On December 17, 2010, the Tax Relief, Unemployment Insurance Reauthorization and Job Creation Act of 2010 was signed into law. The major features of the transfer tax provisions were to reinstate the transfer tax on estates, change the applicable exclusion amount for both gift transfers and estate transfers, and add the portability of the unified transfer tax credit. This table shows the recent history of the applicable exclusion amounts.

Year	Unified Tax Credit—Estates	Applicable Exclusion Amount—Estates	Unified Tax Credit—Gifts	Applicable Exclusion Amount—Gifts
2006	$780,800	$2,000,000	$345,800	$1,000,000
2007	$780,800	$2,000,000	$345,800	$1,000,000
2008	$780,800	$2,000,000	$345,800	$1,000,000
2009	$1,455,800	$3,500,000	$345,800	$1,000,000
2010	Estate tax repealed for 2010		$330,800	$1,000,000
2011	$1,730,800	$5,000,000	$1,730,800	$5,000,000
2012	$1,772,800	$5,120,000	$1,772,800	$5,120,000
2013	$2,045,800	$5,250,000	$2,045,800	$5,250,000
2014	$2,081,800	$5,340,000	$2,081,800	$5,340,000
2015	$2,117,800	$5,430,000	$2,117,800	$5,430,000

15-4b Is It Taxable?

Not everything that's transferred by an individual is subject to a gift tax. **Annual exclusions**, **gift splitting**, charitable deductions, and marital deductions are all means of reducing the total amount for tax purposes.

- **Annual exclusions:** The gift tax law allows a person to give gifts up to a specified annual amount per calendar year—$14,000 in 2015—to any number of recipients. For example, a person could give gifts of $14,000 each to 30 individuals, for a total of $420,000, without using up any of the recipient's AEA (and, of course, without paying any gift tax). Furthermore, the ability to give tax-free gifts of $14,000 per recipient renews annually. The amount is indexed for inflation over time but rounded down to the nearest thousand. This annual exclusion applies only for gifts given with "no strings attached" and generally only if the recipient is given a "present interest" in the gift, which was discussed previously.

- **Gift splitting:** Recall that donors may make gifts up to the annual exclusion ($14,000 in 2015) with no tax impact. Thus, a husband and wife may give a total of $28,000 to a single donee and incur no tax. Sometimes it is convenient for only one of the spouses to transfer property to a single donee. If the amount is over the annual exclusion, it may be taxable. In such cases, the donor's spouse may elect to split the donation of a gift. Thus, two annual exclusions apply and each spouse's unified transfer tax credit will apply to the transfer. Because this election by the spouse must be reported, gift tax returns must be filed.

- **Charitable deductions:** Many estate plans include a provision for charitable contributions. Transfers to charities are not subject to tax because of the deduction for charitable contributions. Once the decision has been made to make charitable contributions, the issue becomes whether to give now (during life) or later (at death) through bequests from the estate. There are many advantages to giving now rather than later. A lifetime gift results in an income tax deduction (namely, a tax savings of 39.6 percent at the top 2015 rate). In addition, such

annual exclusions
Under the federal gift tax law, the amount that can be given each year without being subject to gift tax—for example, $14,000 in 2015. This amount is indexed for inflation over time.

gift splitting
A method of reducing gift taxes; a gift given by one spouse, with the consent of the other spouse, can be treated as if each had given one-half of it.

gifts are removed from the estate and so there is an estate tax saving (40 percent top 2015 rate). Finally, a lifetime gift allows the donor to observe the effect of the gift on the charitable organization and to receive psychic income in the form of gratitude or other recognition. Another consideration is that you should not give so much of your wealth to charity that you no longer have enough to live on. You must provide for yourself and your family before charity. However, many large estates are able and desire to give lifetime charitable gifts.

- **Marital deductions:** Federal law permits an unlimited deduction for gift tax and estate tax purposes on property given or left to a spouse who is a U.S. citizen. The only qualification is that the property interest must be a nonterminable interest. Thus, an interest that terminates at the death of the spouse is not subject to the marital deduction. Special rules apply for transfers to a spouse who is not a U.S. citizen. These special rules prevent tax avoidance if the noncitizen spouse returns to his or her native country, where the bequest would then escape taxation in the United States.

15-4c Reasons for Making Lifetime Gifts

Estate planners recommend gift giving for the following tax-related reasons:

- **Gift tax annual exclusion:** As noted earlier, a single individual can give any number of donees up to $14,000 each year, with no tax costs to either the donees or the donor.
- **Gift tax exclusion escapes estate tax:** Property that qualifies for the annual exclusion is not taxable and thus is free from gift and estate taxes. Estate tax savings from this exclusion can be significant. Regardless of a gift's size—and even if it's made within three years of the donor's death—it's typically not treated as part of the donor's gross estate. However, the taxable portion of lifetime gifts (i.e., the amount above the annual exclusion) are called *adjusted taxable gifts* and these may push the donor's estate into a higher tax bracket.
- **Appreciation in value:** Generally, a gift's increase in value after it was given is excluded from the donor's estate.

> ### EXAMPLE: Excluding Appreciated Value from an Estate
>
> Suppose that Emilio gives his son, Diego, a gift of stock worth $35,000 in 2015. When Emilio dies two years later, the stock is worth $60,000. The amount subject to transfer taxes in 2015 will be $21,000 ($35,000 – $14,000)—the adjusted taxable gift amount. None of the subsequent appreciation is subject to the gift or estate tax.

- **Credit limit:** Because of the credit that's used to offset otherwise taxable gifts, gift taxes don't have to be paid on cumulative lifetime gifts up to the applicable gift exclusion amount of $5,430,000. To the extent that the credit is used against lifetime gift taxes, it's not available to offset estate taxes.
- **Impact of marital deduction:** The transfer tax marital deduction allows one spouse to give the other spouse an unlimited amount of property entirely transfer tax free without reducing the donor-spouse's AEA (i.e., the amount that can be transferred to others tax free). As mentioned before, the unlimited marital deduction is available only if the recipient spouse is a U.S. citizen. Since it is a deduction, a gift tax return is required to be filed.

TEST YOURSELF

15-14 What is a gift, and when is a gift made? Describe the following terms as they relate to federal gift taxes: (a) *annual exclusion*, (b) *gift splitting*, (c) *charitable deduction*, and (d) *marital deduction*.

15-15 Discuss the reasons estate planners cite for making lifetime gifts. How can gift giving be used to reduce estate shrinkage?

15-5 CALCULATING ESTATE TAXES

LG5 Estate taxes may be generated when property is transferred at the time of death, so one goal of effective estate planning is to minimize the amount of estate taxes paid. The federal estate tax is levied on the transfer of property at death. The tax base is measured by the fair market value of the property that the deceased transfers (or is deemed to transfer) to others. The phrase "deemed to transfer" is important because the estate tax applies not only to transfers that a deceased actually makes at death but also to certain transfers made during the person's lifetime. In other words, to thwart tax-avoidance schemes, the estate tax is imposed on certain lifetime gifts that essentially are the same as dispositions of property made at death.

TERRY VINE/GETTY IMAGES.

Although most gifts made during one's life are not part of the decedent's gross estate, there are some exceptions. A major exception pertains to life insurance if the owner is also the insured. If the owner-insured gives away the policy within three years of his or her death, the proceeds will be included in the insured's gross estate.

EXAMPLE: Use of Life Insurance in an Estate

In 2015, two years before his death, Neil gave his son, Simon, a $1 million term insurance policy on Neil's life. At the time of the gift, Neil was in good health, and the value of the term insurance policy for gift tax purposes was clearly less than the $14,000 annual exclusion amount. Therefore, Neil did not have to file a gift tax return. But because Neil died within three years of gifting the life insurance policy, the $1 million proceeds amount is included in his gross estate for estate tax purposes. Had Neil outlived the transfer by more than three years, the proceeds would not have been included in his gross estate.

15-5a Computing the Federal Estate Tax

The computation of federal estate taxes involves six steps:

1. Determine the *gross estate*, the fair market value of all property in which the decedent had an interest and that is required to be included in the estate.
2. Find the *adjusted gross estate* by subtracting from the gross estate any allowable funeral and administrative expenses, debts, and other expenses incurred during administration.

3. Calculate the *taxable estate* by subtracting any allowable marital deduction or charitable deduction from the adjusted gross estate.
4. Compute the *estate tax base*. After determining the value of the taxable estate, any "adjusted taxable gifts" (i.e., gifts above the annual exclusion) made after 1976 are added to the taxable estate. The unified tax rate schedule, shown in Exhibit 15.7, is applied to determine a *tentative tax* on the estate tax base.
5. After finding the tentative tax, subtract both the gift taxes the decedent paid on the adjusted taxable gifts and the **unified tax credit**. The result is total death taxes.
6. Determine the *federal estate tax due*. Some estates will qualify for additional credits—for example, the foreign tax credit (where different portions of the estate are taxed in the United States and in another country) and the prior transfer tax credit (where the decedent's estate includes property inherited from someone who died within the previous 10 years and the earlier estate had to pay an estate tax). These credits are fairly rare, but when available they result in a dollar-for-dollar reduction of the tax. After reducing the total death taxes by any eligible credits, the federal estate tax due is payable by the decedent's executor, generally within nine months of the decedent's death.

unified tax credit
The credit that can be applied against the *tentative tax on estate tax base*.

You can use Worksheet 15.2 to estimate federal estate taxes. The worksheet depicts the computations for a hypothetical situation involving a death in 2015, when the $5,430,000 estate AEA applies. Note that the AEA is not subtracted from the gross estate. The worksheet is useful in following the flow of dollars from the gross estate to the federal estate tax due.

Exhibit 15.8 shows the applicable exclusion amount for estates and the unified credit—the credit that's applied against the tentative tax. The worksheet factors the unified credit for the year 2015 into the calculation on line 9b. The $2,117,800 shown on that line is equal to the tentative tax on an estate tax base of $5,430,000, the AEA. Note the taxpayer is a surviving spouse and his wife elected the portability provision. Thus, the amount of unified transfer tax (UTT) credit is $4,235,600 less the credit used by his wife, the first to die spouse. If the tentative tax shown on line 8 is less than the unified credit available for the decedent's year of death, then no federal estate tax is due.

Financial Fact or Fantasy?

There are no federal taxes on estates of up to $5,340,000 for individuals. **Fact:** Such estates pass to their heirs and/or beneficiaries free from estates taxes. And this limit is doubled to $10,680,000 for married couples. Thus, only larger estates are subject to these taxes.

TEST YOURSELF

15-16 Explain the general nature of the federal estate tax. How does the unified tax credit affect the amount of estate tax owed? What is the portability concept?

15-17 Explain the general procedure used to calculate the federal estate tax due.

15-6 ESTATE PLANNING TECHNIQUES

Estate planning is the process of developing a plan to administer and distribute your estate after your death, in a manner consistent with your wishes and the needs of your survivors, while minimizing taxes. The primary taxes to consider are the income tax, the gift tax, and the estate tax. In developing a plan to distribute your estate, these three taxes must be taken into account. For 2015, the applicable exemption amount is $5,430,000, with a portability feature that allows

This worksheet is useful in determining federal estate tax due. Note that taxes are payable at the marginal tax rate applicable to the estate tax base (line 7), which is the amount that exists before the tax-free exemption is factored in by application of the unified credit.

COMPUTING FEDERAL ESTATE TAX DUE

Name Peyton Naylor   **Date** 9/5/2015

Line	Computation	Item	Amount	Total Amount
1		Gross estate		$ 7,850,000
2	Subtract sum of:	(a) Funeral expenses	$ 6,800	
		(b) Administrative expenses	75,000	
		(c) Debts	125,000	
		(d) Other expenses	0	
		Total		(206,800)
3	Result:	Adjusted gross estate		$ 7,643,200
4	Subtract sum of:	(a) Marital deduction	0	
		(b) Charitable deduction	180,000	
		Total		(180,000)
5	Result:	Taxable estate		$ 7,463,200
6	Add:	Adjusted taxable gifts (post-1976)		$ 0
7	Result:	Estate tax base		$ 7,463,200
8	Compute:	Tentative tax on estate tax base[a]		$ 2,931,080
9	Subtract sum of:	(a) Gift tax payable on post-1976 gifts	$ 0	
		(b) Unified tax credit[b]	2,117,800	
		Total		($ 2,117,800)
10	Result:	Total estate taxes[c]		813,280
10	Subtract:	Other credits		($ 0)
12	Result:	Federal estate tax due		$ 813,280

[a]Use Exhibit 15.7 to calculate the tentative tax.

[b]Use Exhibit 15.8 to determine the appropriate unified credit.

[c]Note that the amount shown on line 7 is a significant number, because most states use the same estate tax base as is used for the federal tax.

the surviving spouse to use the unified transfer tax credit not used by the deceased spouse. For a married couple, then, there is no transfer tax until $10,860,000 is transferred. In the balance of this section we discuss common estate planning techniques.

15-6a Gift Giving Program

With the annual exclusion of $14,000 and the ability to split gifts, a married couple may transfer $28,000 per year per donee. Giving gifts reduces the transfer tax and gives added joy to the donor. When selecting the property to give, the impact on income tax must be considered. Recall that the basis of gifted property is generally the cost of the property to the donor and that the basis of inherited property is the fair market value reported on the estate tax return. So if the property is expected to be sold, then there will be a higher gain for income tax purposes if the property is gifted (though only at the capital gains tax rate, at a top rate of 20 percent in 2015) than if the property is transferred at death through the estate. If the transfer will result in transfer taxes being paid, then the 40 percent transfer tax will probably be greater than the associated income tax relating to the property. In this case, it would be better to gift the property early, when the value is relatively low, even though the donee will have to pay tax on the gain when the property is sold.

15-6b Use of the Unified Transfer Tax Credit

Prior to 2011, the unified transfer tax (UTT) credit was unique to the individual. Thus, if an individual did not use it, then he or she would lose it. Beginning in 2011, Congress added portability to the credit, which allows the surviving spouse to use the unused deceased spouse's UTT credit. Because it is not certain that the portability feature will remain in the tax law, it is appropriate to take steps to ensure that the combination of the marital deduction and the UTT credit does not result in losing part of the credit. The common tools used are the "credit shelter trust" (also referred to as the *bypass trust*) and the QTIP trust, discussed earlier in this chapter. Property equal in value to the unused applicable exemption amount will be transferred at death to the credit shelter trust, resulting in tax for the first to die. The related unused UTT credit will reduce the estate tax to zero. The property in the credit shelter trust will bypass the surviving spouse's estate. The balance of the estate will be transferred either directly to the surviving spouse or to the QTIP and thereby qualify for the marital deduction resulting in no tax for the first to die. Thus, the full UTT credit has been used by both spouses, and no credit has been lost.

15-6c Life Insurance as an Estate Planning Tool

Life insurance can be a valuable component of your estate plan. A policy can be purchased for an annual premium of from 3 percent to 6 percent of the face (death) value of the policy. If someone other than the insured owns the policy, then the proceeds of such insurance can pass to the decedent's beneficiaries free of income tax, estate tax, inheritance tax, and probate costs. For example, the trustee of an irrevocable life insurance trust applies for and owns the policy. After the insured's death, the trustee uses the insurance proceeds for the benefit of the surviving family members, who in turn might use them to pay death taxes, debts, administrative expenses, or other family expenses such as college costs, mortgage balances, and other major expenditures. What's more, whole life and universal life insurance policies are an attractive form of loan collateral. As we pointed out in Chapters 7 and 8, some lending institutions and other creditors require borrowers to obtain enough life insurance to repay them if borrowers die before fully repaying their loans.

15-6d Charitable Contributions

If the taxpayer desires to make charitable contributions, the question to answer is whether the contribution should be made now (during life) or later (at death). If made now, the taxpayer gets an income tax deduction and the property is out of the estate. The added benefit of the income tax savings tips the charitable contribution timing question in favor of giving during life. Of course, if the funds are needed to support the taxpayer, then no contribution should be made until death. Transfers to charity at death are appropriate in such cases.

15-6e Trusts

One of the many uses of trusts is to split the income among family members and thereby reduce total income tax paid. However, the trust income tax rates are extremely compressed: in 2015, the top rate of 39.6 percent applied to income over $12,300. The trust income tax may be avoided by transferring income property to the beneficiaries. If the beneficiary is a minor, however, such income may be taxed at his or her parents' tax rate.

15-6f Valuation Issues

The tax base for the transfer tax is fair market value. When the estate includes closely held stocks, real estate, or large blocks of listed securities, there are discounts that apply to the value of the property. The following are the most used discounts.

- **Minority interest.** If the ownership of a closely held company is less than 50 percent of the outstanding stock, then it is a minority interest. Discounts of 25 percent to 30 percent are common. Thus, if the stock is considered to have a value of $100 per share, then a 30 percent minority interest discount will reduce the fair market value for inclusion in the taxable estate to $70 per share.
- **Marketability discount.** If a large amount of real estate is for sale in one market or area, the value will be reduced solely because of marketability factors. These discounts range from 10 percent to 30 percent.
- **Blockage discounts.** If a large block of stock of a listed company is sold, the market will react to reduce the price of the stock. For a publicly held company, 1 percent of the stock is a large enough block to reduce the value. So if that amount of stock is in the gross estate, then the value subject to the tax will be reduced by the blockage discount. Discounts of 5 percent to 15 percent are common.

15-6g Future of Estate Taxes

The Congress is always discussing changes to the income and transfer tax. Currently there are proposed laws to eliminate the estate tax, but keep the gift tax. The gift tax is seen as necessary to prevent splitting income among the family in order to minimize the family's income tax. There are proposals to reduce the AEA amount from the 2015 amount of $5,430,000 to $3,500,000. It is not known if any of these proposals will actually be enacted. Thus, when planning an estate, focus on flexibility so you can react when or if the law is changed. Obviously, the tax impact of your estate plan should be reviewed annually to insure the outcome is as you planned.

The transfer tax is a major concern to taxpayers with wealth over $10,680,000 but much less so for less wealthy taxpayers. However, estate planning is a concern to all, and the general issues discussed in this chapter apply to all estates, large and small.

TEST YOURSELF

15-18   Describe and discuss each of the techniques used in estate planning.

Planning Over a Lifetime: *Estate Planning*

Here are some key considerations for estate planning in each stage of the life cycle.

Independent Lifestyle (20s)	Family and Career Development (30s–40s)	Mature Lifestyle (50–60s)	Retirement (65+)
✓ While it might seem unnecessary when you're getting started, a will should be made.	✓ Update your will as your circumstances change. Specify who will care for your children if you and your spouse die prematurely.	✓ Start estate planning and consider trust arrangements for children.	✓ Establish a well-thought out estate plan. Update your will to be as specific as possible about the distribution of all property, especially personal property.
✓ A living will is a good idea as well as a durable power of attorney for health care. Make them available to your family and physicians.	✓ Make sure your will is available to family members.	✓ Revise your will as your children become adults and finish school.	✓ Consider explaining to your children what they will inherit and your rationale.
	✓ Prepare a durable power of attorney for financial matters.	✓ Review and revise as needed your durable power of attorney for financial matters and health care at least every few years.	✓ Make sure that a comprehensive list of your financial accounts is available to your spouse and family.
			✓ You and your spouse should make and fund your funeral arrangements to spare your family this burden.

Financial Impact of Personal Choices
The (Un)intended Effects of Corbin's Beneficiary Designations

Corbin Brenner died suddenly in 2015. He had amassed a significant estate and had an attorney write a will that would distribute his assets among his wife, Vanessa, and two grown daughters, Lydia and Gina, as he wished. Apart from his will, he had heard that it made sense to name beneficiaries on his investment accounts so those assets would go directly to his family and bypass the sometimes long and costly probate process. Corbin had been previously married to Patricia Brenner, who survived him.

Corbin named his wife, Vanessa, as the beneficiary to most of his investment accounts and designated one account to his daughter, Lydia, and one account to his daughter, Gina. He intended for his daughters to get equal amounts. While trying to be careful, Corbin forgot to change the beneficiary on one investment account from Patricia, his prior wife, to his current wife, Vanessa. That account was worth $50,000 at his death.

So what was the effect of Corbin's beneficiary designations? His wife Vanessa received most of the investment accounts as he intended. However, the $50,000 account that had not been updated to name Vanessa as the beneficiary went to Corbin's prior wife, Patricia, which is not what he intended. While it seemed fair to Corbin to designate one investment account to each of his daughters and the accounts had the same initial values, the accounts had grown to different values by the time of his death. Lydia's account had grown to $100,000 while Gina's account had grown to $200,000. Corbin had intended that his daughters receive equal amounts but they did not. Corbin could have achieved his objective by naming *both* of his daughters as beneficiaries on *both* of the accounts. And had Corbin reviewed his beneficiary designations at least once a year, he may well have discovered that he'd forgotten to make an important change.

Summary

LG1 **Describe the role of estate planning in personal financial planning, and identify the seven steps involved in the process, p. 599**
Estate planning involves accumulating, preserving, and distributing an estate in order to most effectively achieve an estate owner's personal goals. The seven major steps to estate planning are (1) assess the family situation and set estate planning goals, (2) gather comprehensive and accurate data, (3) list all assets and determine estate value, (4) designate beneficiaries of the estate's assets, (5) estimate estate transfer costs, (6) formulate and implement a plan, and (7) review the plan periodically and revise it as necessary.

LG2 **Recognize the importance of preparing a will and other documents to protect you and your estate, p. 606**
A person who dies without a valid will forfeits important privileges, including the right to decide how property will be distributed at death and the opportunity to select who will administer the estate and bear the burden of estate taxes and administrative expenses. The will should provide an explicit and unambiguous expression of the testator's wishes, be flexible enough to encompass possible changes in family circumstances, and give proper regard to minimizing income, gift, and estate taxes. A will is valid only if properly executed by a person of sound mind. Once drawn up, wills can be changed by codicil or be fully revoked. The executor, named in the will, is responsible for collecting the decedent's assets, paying his or her debts and taxes, and distributing any remaining assets to the beneficiaries in the prescribed fashion. In addition to the will, other important estate planning documents include the letter of last instructions, power of attorney, living will, durable power of attorney for health care, and an ethical will.

LG3 **Explain how trusts are used in estate planning, p. 617**
The trust relationship arises when one party, the *grantor* (also called the *trustor* or *settlor*), transfers property to a second party, the *trustee,* for the benefit of a third party, the *beneficiary.* There

are several types of trusts, but each is designed primarily for one or both of these reasons: to manage and conserve property over a long period, and to save income and estate taxes.

LG4 **Determine whether a gift will be taxable and use planned gifts to reduce estate taxes, p. 622**
Gifts of cash, financial assets, and personal or real property made during the donor's lifetime are subject to federal taxes. A gift, up to the annual exclusion amount, given to each recipient is excluded from the donor's gift tax calculation. Generally, donations to qualified charities and gifts between spouses are also excluded from the gift tax.

LG5 **Calculate federal taxes due on an estate, p. 626**
Federal estate taxes are a levy on the transfer of assets at death. They are unified (coordinated) with the gift tax—which imposes a graduated tax on the transfer of property during one's lifetime—so that the rates and credits are the same for both. Once federal estate taxes are computed and certain credits are allowed, the resulting amount is payable in full, generally within nine months of the decedent's death.

LG6 **Use effective estate planning techniques to minimize estate taxes, p. 627**
Well-defined estate plans seek to minimize income, gift, and estate taxes. Common estate planning techniques include gift giving, use of the unified transfer tax (UTT) credit, charitable contributions, life insurance, and trusts that split income among family members.

Key Terms

Answers to Test Yourself

You can find answers to these questions on this book's companion website. Look for it at *www.cengagebrain.com*. Search for this book by its title, and then add it to your dashboard.

Financial Planning Exercises

LG1, p. 599

1. **Estate planning objectives.** Generate a list of estate planning objectives that apply to your personal family situation. Be sure to consider the size of your potential estate as well as people planning and asset planning. Estate planning is not just about taxes.

LG2, p. 606

2. **Importance of writing a will.** Darrell and Karla Boykin are in their mid-30s and have two children, ages 8 and 5. They have combined annual income of $95,000 and own a house in joint tenancy with a market value of $310,000, on which they have a mortgage of $250,000. Darrell has $100,000 in group term life insurance and an individual universal life policy for $150,000. However, the Boykins haven't prepared their wills. Darrell plans to draw one up soon, but the couple thinks that Karla doesn't need one because the house is jointly owned. Explain why it's important for both Darrell and Karla to draft wills as soon as possible.

LG2, p. 606

3. **Will and last letter preparation.** Prepare a basic will for yourself, using the guidelines presented in the text; also prepare your brief letter of last instructions.

LG2, p. 606

4. **Topics in an ethical will.** State the topics you would cover in your ethical will. Would you consider recording it digitally?

LG2, p. 606

5. **Qualifications of estate executor.** Your best friend has asked you to be executor of his estate. What qualifications do you need, and would you accept the responsibility?

LG2,3,5, p. 606, 617, 626

6. **Trusts in estate planning.** Griffin West, 48 and a widower, and Hailey Burnette, 44 and previously divorced, were married five years ago. There are children from their prior marriages, two children for Griffin and one child for Hailey. The couple's estate is valued at $1.4 million, including a house valued at $475,000, a vacation home at the beach, investments, antique furniture that has been in Hailey's family for many years, and jewelry belonging to Griffin's first wife. Discuss how they could use trusts as part of their estate planning, and suggest some other ideas for them to consider when preparing their wills and related documents.

LG4,5, p. 622, 626

7. **Calculation of estate taxes. Use Worksheet 15.2.** When Jacob Kohler died unmarried in 2015, he left an estate valued at $7,850,000. His trust directed distribution as follows: $20,000 to the local hospital, $160,000 to his alma mater, and the remainder to his three adult children. Death-related costs and expenses were $16,800 for funeral expenses, $40,000 paid to attorneys, $5,000 paid to accountants, and $30,000 paid to the trustee of his living trust. In addition, there were debts of $125,000. Use Worksheet 15.2 and Exhibits 15.7 and 15.8 to calculate the federal estate tax due on his estate.

LG6, p. 627

8. **Recent estate taxes legislation.** Summarize important legislation affecting estate taxes, and briefly describe the impact on estate planning. Explain why getting rid of the estate tax doesn't eliminate the need for estate planning.

Applying Personal Finance

Prepare Your Will!

If you die without a valid will, the laws of your state will determine what happens to your property. That may be fine with people who have few assets, but it's not fine for people who care what happens to their property, and it's certainly not fine for people with dependents. In this project, you'll consider what your current will should contain and what changes you should make to your will based on your future circumstances.

Look back through this chapter and review the common features of a will. Then write your own will, based on the sample clauses and examples of a representative will given in the text. List the property that you currently have, or expect to have in the near future, and name a beneficiary for each. Be sure to name your personal representative, and charge him or her with disposing of your estate according to your wishes. If you have children or expect to have children, or if you have other dependents such as an elderly parent or a disabled sibling, be sure to name a guardian and a backup guardian for them. Also prepare a letter of last instructions to convey any personal thoughts or instructions that you feel cannot be properly included in your will. Remember, this exercise should help you think about the orderly disposition of your estate, which is the final act in implementing your personal financial plans.

CRITICAL THINKING CASES

LG2, p. 606

15.1 A Long-Overdue Will for Carsten

In the late 1980s, Carsten Richter, from Germany, migrated to the United States, where he is now a citizen. A man of many talents and deep foresight, he has built a large fleet of oceangoing oil tankers during his stay in the United States. Now a wealthy man in his 60s, he resides in Aspen, Colorado, with his second wife, Gabriela, age 50. They have two sons, one in junior high and one a high school freshman. For some time, Carsten has considered preparing a will to ensure that his estate will be properly distributed when he dies. A survey of his estate reveals the following:

Ranch in Colorado	$ 1,000,000
Condominium in Santa Barbara	800,000
House in Aspen	1,500,000
Franchise in ice cream stores	2,000,000
Stock in Google	5,000,000
Stock in Wal-Mart	1,000,000
Stock in Silver Mines International	3,000,000
Other assets	200,000
Total assets	$14,500,000

The house and the Silver Mines International shares are held in joint tenancy with his wife, but all other property is in his name alone. He desires that there be a separate fund of $1 million for his sons' education and that the balance of his estate be divided as follows: 40 percent to his sons, 40 percent to his wife, and 20 percent given to other relatives, friends, and charitable institutions. He has scheduled an appointment for drafting his will with his attorney and close friend, Forrest Gauthier. Carsten would like to appoint Forrest, who is 70 years old, and Carsten's 40-year-old cousin, Heinrich Richter (a CPA), as co-executors. If one of them predeceases Carsten, he'd like First National Bank to serve as co-executor.

Critical Thinking Questions

1. Does Carsten really need a will? Explain why or why not. What would happen to his estate if he were to die without a will?
2. Explain to Carsten the common features that need to be incorporated into a will.
3. Might the manner in which titles are held thwart his estate planning desires? What should be done to avoid problems?
4. Is a living trust an appropriate part of his estate plan? How would a living trust change the nature of Carsten's will?
5. How does the age of Carsten's children complicate the estate plan? What special provisions should he consider?
6. What options are available to Carsten if he decides later to change or revoke the will? Is it more difficult to change a living trust?
7. What duties will Forest Gauthier and Heinrich Richter have to perform as co-executors of Carsten's estate? If a trust is created, what should Carsten consider in his selection of a trustee or co-trustees? Might Forrest and Henrich, serving together, be a good choice?

15.2 Estate Taxes on Saul Schwab's Estate

Saul Schwab, of Knoxville, Tennessee, was 65 when he retired in 2010. Camille, his wife of 40 years, passed away the next year. Her will left everything to Saul. Although Camille's estate was valued at $2,250,000, there was no estate tax due because of the 100 percent marital deduction. Their only child, Eli, is married to Kathleen. They have four children, two in college and two in high school. In 2011, Saul made a gift of Apple stock worth $260,000 jointly to Eli and Kathleen. Because of the two $14,000 annual exclusions and the unified credit, no gift taxes were due. When Saul died in 2015, his home was valued at $850,000, his vacation cabin was valued at $485,000, his investments in stocks and bonds were valued at $1,890,000, and his pension funds were worth $645,000 (Eli was named beneficiary). Saul also owned a life insurance policy that paid proceeds of $700,000 to Eli. He left $60,000 to his church and $25,000 to his high school to start a scholarship fund in his wife's name. The rest of the estate was left to Eli. Funeral costs were $15,000. Debts were $90,000 and miscellaneous expenses were $25,000. Attorney and accounting fees came to $36,000. **Use Worksheet 15.2** to guide your estate tax calculations as you complete these exercises.

Critical Thinking Questions

1. Compute the value of Saul's *probate estate*.
2. Compute the value of Saul's *gross estate*.
3. Determine the total allowable deductions.
4. Calculate the *estate tax base;* taking into account the gifts given to Eli and Kathleen (remember that the annual exclusions "adjust" the taxable gifts).
5. Use Exhibit 15.7 to determine the *tentative tax on estate tax base.*
6. Subtract the appropriate *unified tax credit* (Exhibit 15.8) for 2015 from the *tentative tax on estate tax base* to arrive at the *federal estate tax due.*
7. Comment on the estate shrinkage experienced by Saul's estate. What might have been done to reduce this shrinkage? Explain.

APPENDIX A

Table of Future Value Factors

Instructions: To use this table, find the future value factor that corresponds to both a given time period (year) and an interest rate. For example, if you want the future value factor for 6 years and 10%, move across from year 6 and down from 10% to the point at which the row and column intersect: 1.772. Other illustrations: for 3 years and 15%, the proper future value factor is 1.521; for 30 years and 8%, it is 10.063.

INTEREST RATE

Period	1%	2%	3%	4%	5%	6%	7%	8%	9%	10%	11%	12%	13%	14%	15%	16%	17%	18%	19%	20%	25%	30%
1	1.010	1.020	1.030	1.040	1.050	1.060	1.070	1.080	1.090	1.100	1.110	1.120	1.130	1.140	1.150	1.160	1.170	1.180	1.190	1.200	1.250	1.300
2	1.020	1.040	1.061	1.082	1.103	1.124	1.145	1.166	1.188	1.210	1.232	1.254	1.277	1.300	1.323	1.346	1.369	1.392	1.416	1.440	1.563	1.690
3	1.030	1.061	1.093	1.125	1.158	1.191	1.225	1.260	1.295	1.331	1.368	1.405	1.443	1.482	1.521	1.561	1.602	1.643	1.685	1.728	1.953	2.197
4	1.041	1.082	1.126	1.170	1.216	1.262	1.311	1.360	1.412	1.464	1.518	1.574	1.630	1.689	1.749	1.811	1.874	1.939	2.005	2.074	2.441	2.856
5	1.051	1.104	1.159	1.217	1.276	1.338	1.403	1.469	1.539	1.611	1.685	1.762	1.842	1.925	2.011	2.100	2.192	2.288	2.386	2.488	3.052	3.713
6	1.062	1.126	1.194	1.265	1.340	1.419	1.501	1.587	1.677	1.772	1.870	1.974	2.082	2.195	2.313	2.436	2.565	2.700	2.840	2.986	3.815	4.827
7	1.072	1.149	1.230	1.316	1.407	1.504	1.606	1.714	1.828	1.949	2.076	2.211	2.353	2.502	2.660	2.826	3.001	3.185	3.379	3.583	4.768	6.275
8	1.083	1.172	1.267	1.369	1.477	1.594	1.718	1.851	1.993	2.144	2.305	2.476	2.658	2.853	3.059	3.278	3.511	3.759	4.021	4.300	5.960	8.157
9	1.094	1.195	1.305	1.423	1.551	1.689	1.838	1.999	2.172	2.358	2.558	2.773	3.004	3.252	3.518	3.803	4.108	4.435	4.785	5.160	7.451	10.604
10	1.105	1.219	1.344	1.480	1.629	1.791	1.967	2.159	2.367	2.594	2.839	3.106	3.395	3.707	4.046	4.411	4.807	5.234	5.695	6.192	9.313	13.786
11	1.116	1.243	1.384	1.539	1.710	1.898	2.105	2.332	2.580	2.853	3.152	3.479	3.836	4.226	4.652	5.117	5.624	6.176	6.777	7.430	11.642	17.922
12	1.127	1.268	1.426	1.601	1.796	2.012	2.252	2.518	2.813	3.138	3.498	3.896	4.335	4.818	5.350	5.936	6.580	7.288	8.064	8.916	14.552	23.298
13	1.138	1.294	1.469	1.665	1.886	2.133	2.410	2.720	3.066	3.452	3.883	4.363	4.898	5.492	6.153	6.886	7.699	8.599	9.596	10.699	18.190	30.288
14	1.149	1.319	1.513	1.732	1.980	2.261	2.579	2.937	3.342	3.797	4.310	4.887	5.535	6.261	7.076	7.988	9.007	10.147	11.420	12.839	22.737	39.374
15	1.161	1.346	1.558	1.801	2.079	2.397	2.759	3.172	3.642	4.177	4.785	5.474	6.254	7.138	8.137	9.266	10.539	11.974	13.590	15.407	28.422	51.186
16	1.173	1.373	1.605	1.873	2.183	2.540	2.952	3.426	3.970	4.595	5.311	6.130	7.067	8.137	9.358	10.748	12.330	14.129	16.172	18.488	35.527	66.542
17	1.184	1.400	1.653	1.948	2.292	2.693	3.159	3.700	4.328	5.054	5.895	6.866	7.986	9.276	10.761	12.468	14.426	16.672	19.244	22.186	44.409	86.504
18	1.196	1.428	1.702	2.026	2.407	2.854	3.380	3.996	4.717	5.560	6.544	7.690	9.024	10.575	12.375	14.463	16.879	19.673	22.901	26.623	55.511	112.455
19	1.208	1.457	1.754	2.107	2.527	3.026	3.617	4.316	5.142	6.116	7.263	8.613	10.197	12.056	14.232	16.777	19.748	23.214	27.252	31.948	69.389	146.192
20	1.220	1.486	1.806	2.191	2.653	3.207	3.870	4.661	5.604	6.727	8.062	9.646	11.523	13.743	16.367	19.461	23.106	27.393	32.429	38.338	86.736	190.050
21	1.232	1.516	1.860	2.279	2.786	3.400	4.141	5.034	6.109	7.400	8.949	10.804	13.021	15.668	18.822	22.574	27.034	32.324	38.591	46.005	108.420	247.065
22	1.245	1.546	1.916	2.370	2.925	3.604	4.430	5.437	6.659	8.140	9.934	12.100	14.714	17.861	21.645	26.186	31.629	38.142	45.923	55.206	135.525	321.184
23	1.257	1.577	1.974	2.465	3.072	3.820	4.741	5.871	7.258	8.954	11.026	13.552	16.627	20.362	24.891	30.376	37.006	45.008	54.649	66.247	169.407	417.539
24	1.270	1.608	2.033	2.563	3.225	4.049	5.072	6.341	7.911	9.850	12.239	15.179	18.788	23.212	28.625	35.236	43.297	53.109	65.032	79.497	211.758	542.801
25	1.282	1.641	2.094	2.666	3.386	4.292	5.427	6.848	8.623	10.835	13.585	17.000	21.231	26.462	32.919	40.874	50.658	62.669	77.388	95.396	264.698	705.641
26	1.295	1.673	2.157	2.772	3.556	4.549	5.807	7.396	9.399	11.918	15.080	19.040	23.991	30.167	37.857	47.414	59.270	73.949	92.092	114.475	330.872	917.333
27	1.308	1.707	2.221	2.883	3.733	4.822	6.214	7.988	10.245	13.110	16.739	21.325	27.109	34.390	43.535	55.000	69.345	87.260	109.589	137.371	413.590	1,192.533
28	1.321	1.741	2.288	2.999	3.920	5.112	6.649	8.627	11.167	14.421	18.580	23.884	30.633	39.204	50.066	63.800	81.134	102.967	130.411	164.845	516.988	1,550.293
29	1.335	1.776	2.357	3.119	4.116	5.418	7.114	9.317	12.172	15.863	20.624	26.750	34.616	44.693	57.575	74.009	94.927	121.501	155.189	197.814	646.235	2,015.381
30	1.348	1.811	2.427	3.243	4.322	5.743	7.612	10.063	13.268	17.449	22.892	29.960	39.116	50.950	66.212	85.850	111.065	143.371	184.675	237.376	807.794	2,619.996
35	1.417	2.000	2.814	3.946	5.516	7.686	10.677	14.785	20.414	28.102	38.575	52.800	72.069	98.100	133.176	180.314	243.503	327.997	440.701	590.668	2,465.190	9,727.860
40	1.489	2.208	3.262	4.801	7.040	10.286	14.974	21.725	31.409	45.259	65.001	93.051	132.782	188.884	267.864	378.721	533.869	750.378	1,051.668	1,469.772	7,523.164	36,118.865

Note: All factors are rounded to the nearest 1/1000 in order to agree with values used in the text.

APPENDIX B

Table of Future Value Annuity Factors

Instructions: To use this table, find the future value of annuity factor that corresponds to both a given time period (year) and an interest rate. For example, if you want the future value of annuity factor for 6 years and 10%, move across from year 6 and down from 10% to the point at which the row and column intersect: 7.716. Other illustrations: for 3 years and 15%, the proper future value of annuity factor is 3.473; for 30 years and 6%, it is 79.058.

INTEREST RATE

Period	1%	2%	3%	4%	5%	6%	7%	8%	9%	10%	11%	12%	13%	14%	15%	16%	17%	18%	19%	20%	25%	30%
1	1.000	1.000	1.000	1.000	1.000	1.000	1.000	1.000	1.000	1.000	1.000	1.000	1.000	1.000	1.000	1.000	1.000	1.000	1.000	1.000	1.000	1.000
2	2.010	2.020	2.030	2.040	2.050	2.060	2.070	2.080	2.090	2.100	2.110	2.120	2.130	2.140	2.150	2.160	2.170	2.180	2.190	2.200	2.250	2.300
3	3.030	3.060	3.091	3.122	3.153	3.184	3.215	3.246	3.278	3.310	3.342	3.374	3.407	3.440	3.473	3.506	3.539	3.572	3.606	3.640	3.813	3.990
4	4.060	4.122	4.184	4.246	4.310	4.375	4.440	4.506	4.573	4.641	4.710	4.779	4.850	4.921	4.993	5.066	5.141	5.215	5.291	5.368	5.766	6.187
5	5.101	5.204	5.309	5.416	5.526	5.637	5.751	5.867	5.985	6.105	6.228	6.353	6.480	6.610	6.742	6.877	7.014	7.154	7.297	7.442	8.207	9.043
6	6.152	6.308	6.468	6.633	6.802	6.975	7.153	7.336	7.523	7.716	7.913	8.115	8.323	8.536	8.754	8.977	9.207	9.442	9.683	9.930	11.259	12.756
7	7.214	7.434	7.662	7.898	8.142	8.394	8.654	8.923	9.200	9.487	9.783	10.089	10.405	10.730	11.067	11.414	11.772	12.142	12.523	12.916	15.073	17.583
8	8.286	8.583	8.892	9.214	9.549	9.897	10.260	10.637	11.028	11.436	11.859	12.300	12.757	13.233	13.727	14.240	14.773	15.327	15.902	16.499	19.842	23.858
9	9.369	9.755	10.159	10.583	11.027	11.491	11.978	12.488	13.021	13.579	14.164	14.776	15.416	16.085	16.786	17.519	18.285	19.086	19.923	20.799	25.802	32.015
10	10.462	10.950	11.464	12.006	12.578	13.181	13.816	14.487	15.193	15.937	16.722	17.549	18.420	19.337	20.304	21.321	22.393	23.521	24.709	25.959	33.253	42.619
11	11.567	12.169	12.808	13.486	14.207	14.972	15.784	16.645	17.560	18.531	19.561	20.655	21.814	23.045	24.349	25.733	27.200	28.755	30.404	32.150	42.566	56.405
12	12.683	13.412	14.192	15.026	15.917	16.870	17.888	18.977	20.141	21.384	22.713	24.133	25.650	27.271	29.002	30.850	32.824	34.931	37.180	39.581	54.208	74.327
13	13.809	14.680	15.618	16.627	17.713	18.882	20.141	21.495	22.953	24.523	26.212	28.029	29.985	32.089	34.352	36.786	39.404	42.219	45.244	48.497	68.760	97.625
14	14.947	15.974	17.086	18.292	19.599	21.015	22.550	24.215	26.019	27.975	30.095	32.393	34.883	37.581	40.505	43.672	47.103	50.818	54.841	59.196	86.949	127.913
15	16.097	17.293	18.599	20.024	21.579	23.276	25.129	27.152	29.361	31.772	34.405	37.280	40.417	43.842	47.580	51.660	56.110	60.965	66.261	72.035	109.687	167.286
16	17.258	18.639	20.157	21.825	23.657	25.673	27.888	30.324	33.003	35.950	39.190	42.753	46.672	50.980	55.717	60.925	66.649	72.939	79.850	87.442	138.109	218.472
17	18.430	20.012	21.762	23.698	25.840	28.213	30.840	33.750	36.974	40.545	44.501	48.884	53.739	59.118	65.075	71.673	78.979	87.068	96.022	105.931	173.636	285.01
18	19.615	21.412	23.414	25.645	28.132	30.906	33.999	37.450	41.301	45.599	50.396	55.750	61.725	68.394	75.836	84.141	93.406	103.74	115.27	128.117	218.045	371.52
19	20.811	22.841	25.117	27.671	30.539	33.760	37.379	41.446	46.018	51.159	56.939	63.440	70.749	78.969	88.212	98.603	110.28	123.41	138.17	154.740	273.556	483.97
20	22.019	24.297	26.870	29.778	33.066	36.786	40.995	45.762	51.160	57.275	64.203	72.052	80.947	91.025	102.444	115.380	130.033	146.628	165.418	186.688	342.945	630.165
21	23.239	25.783	28.676	31.969	35.719	39.993	44.865	50.423	56.765	64.002	72.265	81.699	92.470	104.768	118.810	134.841	153.139	174.021	197.847	225.026	429.681	820.215
22	24.472	27.299	30.537	34.248	38.505	43.392	49.006	55.457	62.873	71.403	81.214	92.503	105.491	120.436	137.632	157.415	180.172	206.345	236.438	271.031	538.101	1,067.280
23	25.716	28.845	32.453	36.618	41.430	46.996	53.436	60.893	69.532	79.543	91.148	104.603	120.205	138.297	159.276	183.601	211.801	244.487	282.362	326.237	673.626	1,388.464
24	26.973	30.422	34.426	39.083	44.502	50.816	58.177	66.765	76.790	88.497	102.174	118.155	136.831	158.659	184.168	213.978	248.808	289.494	337.010	392.484	843.033	1,806.003
25	28.243	32.030	36.459	41.646	47.727	54.865	63.249	73.106	84.701	98.347	114.413	133.334	155.620	181.871	212.793	249.214	292.105	342.603	402.042	471.981	1,054.791	2,348.803
26	29.526	33.671	38.553	44.312	51.113	59.156	68.676	79.954	93.324	109.182	127.999	150.334	176.850	208.333	245.712	290.088	342.763	405.272	479.431	567.377	1,319.489	3,054.444
27	30.821	35.344	40.710	47.084	54.669	63.706	74.484	87.351	102.723	121.100	143.079	169.374	200.841	238.499	283.569	337.502	402.032	479.221	571.522	681.853	1,650.361	3,971.778
28	32.129	37.051	42.931	49.968	58.403	68.528	80.698	95.339	112.968	134.210	159.817	190.699	227.950	272.889	327.104	392.503	471.378	566.481	681.112	819.223	2,063.952	5,164.311
29	33.450	38.792	45.219	52.966	62.323	73.640	87.347	103.966	124.135	148.631	178.397	214.583	258.583	312.094	377.170	456.303	552.512	669.447	811.523	984.068	2,580.939	6,714.604
30	34.785	40.568	47.575	56.085	66.439	79.058	94.461	113.283	136.308	164.494	199.021	241.333	293.199	356.787	434.745	530.312	647.439	790.948	966.712	1,181.882	3,227.174	8,729.985
35	41.660	49.994	60.462	73.652	90.320	111.435	138.237	172.317	215.711	271.024	341.590	431.663	546.681	693.573	881.170	1,120.713	1,426.491	1,816.652	2,314.214	2,948.341	9,856.761	32,422.868
40	48.886	60.402	75.401	95.026	120.800	154.762	199.635	259.057	337.882	442.593	581.826	767.091	1,013.704	1,342.025	1,779.090	2,360.757	3,134.522	4,163.213	5,529.829	7,343.858	30,088.655	120,392.883

Note: All factors are rounded to the nearest 1/1000 in order to agree with values used in the text.

APPENDIX C

Table of Present Value Factors

Instructions: To use this table, find the present value factor that corresponds to both a given time period (year) and an interest rate. For example, if you want the present value factor for 25 years and 7%, move across from year 25 and down from 7% to the point at which the row and column intersect: .184. Other illustrations: for 3 years and 15%, the proper present value factor is .658; for 30 years and 8%, it is .099.

INTEREST RATE

Period	1%	2%	3%	4%	5%	6%	7%	8%	9%	10%	11%	12%	13%	14%	15%	16%	17%	18%	19%	20%	25%	30%
1	0.990	0.980	0.971	0.962	0.952	0.943	0.935	0.926	0.917	0.909	0.901	0.893	0.885	0.877	0.870	0.862	0.855	0.847	0.840	0.833	0.800	0.769
2	0.980	0.961	0.943	0.925	0.907	0.890	0.873	0.857	0.842	0.826	0.812	0.797	0.783	0.769	0.756	0.743	0.731	0.718	0.706	0.694	0.640	0.592
3	0.971	0.942	0.915	0.889	0.864	0.840	0.816	0.794	0.772	0.751	0.731	0.712	0.693	0.675	0.658	0.641	0.624	0.609	0.593	0.579	0.512	0.455
4	0.961	0.924	0.888	0.855	0.823	0.792	0.763	0.735	0.708	0.683	0.659	0.636	0.613	0.592	0.572	0.552	0.534	0.516	0.499	0.482	0.410	0.350
5	0.951	0.906	0.863	0.822	0.784	0.747	0.713	0.681	0.650	0.621	0.593	0.567	0.543	0.519	0.497	0.476	0.456	0.437	0.419	0.402	0.328	0.269
6	0.942	0.888	0.837	0.790	0.746	0.705	0.666	0.630	0.596	0.564	0.535	0.507	0.480	0.456	0.432	0.410	0.390	0.370	0.352	0.335	0.262	0.207
7	0.933	0.871	0.813	0.760	0.711	0.665	0.623	0.583	0.547	0.513	0.482	0.452	0.425	0.400	0.376	0.354	0.333	0.314	0.296	0.279	0.210	0.159
8	0.923	0.853	0.789	0.731	0.677	0.627	0.582	0.540	0.502	0.467	0.434	0.404	0.376	0.351	0.327	0.305	0.285	0.266	0.249	0.233	0.168	0.123
9	0.914	0.837	0.766	0.703	0.645	0.592	0.544	0.500	0.460	0.424	0.391	0.361	0.333	0.308	0.284	0.263	0.243	0.225	0.209	0.194	0.134	0.094
10	0.905	0.820	0.744	0.676	0.614	0.558	0.508	0.463	0.422	0.386	0.352	0.322	0.295	0.270	0.247	0.227	0.208	0.191	0.176	0.162	0.107	0.073
11	0.896	0.804	0.722	0.650	0.585	0.527	0.475	0.429	0.388	0.350	0.317	0.287	0.261	0.237	0.215	0.195	0.178	0.162	0.148	0.135	0.086	0.056
12	0.887	0.788	0.701	0.625	0.557	0.497	0.444	0.397	0.356	0.319	0.286	0.257	0.231	0.208	0.187	0.168	0.152	0.137	0.124	0.112	0.069	0.043
13	0.879	0.773	0.681	0.601	0.530	0.469	0.415	0.368	0.326	0.290	0.258	0.229	0.204	0.182	0.163	0.145	0.130	0.116	0.104	0.093	0.055	0.033
14	0.870	0.758	0.661	0.577	0.505	0.442	0.388	0.340	0.299	0.263	0.232	0.205	0.181	0.160	0.141	0.125	0.111	0.099	0.088	0.078	0.044	0.025
15	0.861	0.743	0.642	0.555	0.481	0.417	0.362	0.315	0.275	0.239	0.209	0.183	0.160	0.140	0.123	0.108	0.095	0.084	0.074	0.065	0.035	0.020
16	0.853	0.728	0.623	0.534	0.458	0.394	0.339	0.292	0.252	0.218	0.188	0.163	0.141	0.123	0.107	0.093	0.081	0.071	0.062	0.054	0.028	0.015
17	0.844	0.714	0.605	0.513	0.436	0.371	0.317	0.270	0.231	0.198	0.170	0.146	0.125	0.108	0.093	0.080	0.069	0.060	0.052	0.045	0.023	0.012
18	0.836	0.700	0.587	0.494	0.416	0.350	0.296	0.250	0.212	0.180	0.153	0.130	0.111	0.095	0.081	0.069	0.059	0.051	0.044	0.038	0.018	0.009
19	0.828	0.686	0.570	0.475	0.396	0.331	0.277	0.232	0.194	0.164	0.138	0.116	0.098	0.083	0.070	0.060	0.051	0.043	0.037	0.031	0.014	0.007
20	0.820	0.673	0.554	0.456	0.377	0.312	0.258	0.215	0.178	0.149	0.124	0.104	0.087	0.073	0.061	0.051	0.043	0.037	0.031	0.026	0.012	0.005
21	0.811	0.660	0.538	0.439	0.359	0.294	0.242	0.199	0.164	0.135	0.112	0.093	0.077	0.064	0.053	0.044	0.037	0.031	0.026	0.022	0.009	0.004
22	0.803	0.647	0.522	0.422	0.342	0.278	0.226	0.184	0.150	0.123	0.101	0.083	0.068	0.056	0.046	0.038	0.032	0.026	0.022	0.018	0.007	0.003
23	0.795	0.634	0.507	0.406	0.326	0.262	0.211	0.170	0.138	0.112	0.091	0.074	0.060	0.049	0.040	0.033	0.027	0.022	0.018	0.015	0.006	0.002
24	0.788	0.622	0.492	0.390	0.310	0.247	0.197	0.158	0.126	0.102	0.082	0.066	0.053	0.043	0.035	0.028	0.023	0.019	0.015	0.013	0.005	0.002
25	0.780	0.610	0.478	0.375	0.295	0.233	0.184	0.146	0.116	0.092	0.074	0.059	0.047	0.038	0.030	0.024	0.020	0.016	0.013	0.010	0.004	0.001
26	0.772	0.598	0.464	0.361	0.281	0.220	0.172	0.135	0.106	0.084	0.066	0.053	0.042	0.033	0.026	0.021	0.017	0.014	0.011	0.009	0.003	0.001
27	0.764	0.586	0.450	0.347	0.268	0.207	0.161	0.125	0.098	0.076	0.060	0.047	0.037	0.029	0.023	0.018	0.014	0.011	0.009	0.007	0.002	0.001
28	0.757	0.574	0.437	0.333	0.255	0.196	0.150	0.116	0.090	0.069	0.054	0.042	0.033	0.026	0.020	0.016	0.012	0.010	0.008	0.006	0.002	0.001
29	0.749	0.563	0.424	0.321	0.243	0.185	0.141	0.107	0.082	0.063	0.048	0.037	0.029	0.022	0.017	0.014	0.011	0.008	0.006	0.005	0.002	*
30	0.742	0.552	0.412	0.308	0.231	0.174	0.131	0.099	0.075	0.057	0.044	0.033	0.026	0.020	0.015	0.012	0.009	0.007	0.005	0.004	0.001	*
35	0.706	0.500	0.355	0.253	0.181	0.130	0.094	0.068	0.049	0.036	0.026	0.019	0.014	0.010	0.008	0.006	0.004	0.003	0.002	0.002	*	*
40	0.672	0.453	0.307	0.208	0.142	0.097	0.067	0.046	0.032	0.022	0.015	0.011	0.008	0.005	0.004	0.003	0.002	0.001	0.001	0.001	*	*

*Present value factor is zero to three decimal places.

Note: All factors are rounded to the nearest 1/1000 in order to agree with values used in the text.

APPENDIX D

Table of Present Value Annuity Factors

Instructions: To use this table, find the present value of annuity factor that corresponds to both a given time period (year) and an interest rate. For example, if you want the present value of annuity factor for 30 years and 7%, move across from year 30 and down from 7% to the point at which the row and column intersect: 12.409. Other illustrations: for 3 years and 15%, the proper present value of annuity factor is 2.283; for 30 years and 8%, it is 11.258.

INTEREST RATE

Period	1%	2%	3%	4%	5%	6%	7%	8%	9%	10%	11%	12%	13%	14%	15%	16%	17%	18%	19%	20%	25%	30%
1	0.990	0.980	0.971	0.962	0.952	0.943	0.935	0.926	0.917	0.909	0.901	0.893	0.885	0.877	0.870	0.862	0.855	0.847	0.840	0.833	0.800	0.769
2	1.970	1.942	1.913	1.886	1.859	1.833	1.808	1.783	1.759	1.736	1.713	1.690	1.668	1.647	1.626	1.605	1.585	1.566	1.547	1.528	1.440	1.361
3	2.941	2.884	2.829	2.775	2.723	2.673	2.624	2.577	2.531	2.487	2.444	2.402	2.361	2.322	2.283	2.246	2.210	2.174	2.140	2.106	1.952	1.816
4	3.902	3.808	3.717	3.630	3.546	3.465	3.387	3.312	3.240	3.170	3.102	3.037	2.974	2.914	2.855	2.798	2.743	2.690	2.639	2.589	2.362	2.166
5	4.853	4.713	4.580	4.452	4.329	4.212	4.100	3.993	3.890	3.791	3.696	3.605	3.517	3.433	3.352	3.274	3.199	3.127	3.058	2.991	2.689	2.436
6	5.795	5.601	5.417	5.242	5.076	4.917	4.767	4.623	4.486	4.355	4.231	4.111	3.998	3.889	3.784	3.685	3.589	3.498	3.410	3.326	2.951	2.643
7	6.728	6.472	6.230	6.002	5.786	5.582	5.389	5.206	5.033	4.868	4.712	4.564	4.423	4.288	4.160	4.039	3.922	3.812	3.706	3.605	3.161	2.802
8	7.652	7.325	7.020	6.733	6.463	6.210	5.971	5.747	5.535	5.335	5.146	4.968	4.799	4.639	4.487	4.344	4.207	4.078	3.954	3.837	3.329	2.925
9	8.566	8.162	7.786	7.435	7.108	6.802	6.515	6.247	5.995	5.759	5.537	5.328	5.132	4.946	4.772	4.607	4.451	4.303	4.163	4.031	3.463	3.019
10	9.471	8.983	8.530	8.111	7.722	7.360	7.024	6.710	6.418	6.145	5.889	5.650	5.426	5.216	5.019	4.833	4.659	4.494	4.339	4.192	3.571	3.092
11	10.368	9.787	9.253	8.760	8.306	7.887	7.499	7.139	6.805	6.495	6.207	5.938	5.687	5.453	5.234	5.029	4.836	4.656	4.486	4.327	3.656	3.147
12	11.255	10.575	9.954	9.385	8.863	8.384	7.943	7.536	7.161	6.814	6.492	6.194	5.918	5.660	5.421	5.197	4.988	4.793	4.611	4.439	3.725	3.190
13	12.134	11.348	10.635	9.986	9.394	8.853	8.358	7.904	7.487	7.103	6.750	6.424	6.122	5.842	5.583	5.342	5.118	4.910	4.715	4.533	3.780	3.223
14	13.004	12.106	11.296	10.563	9.899	9.295	8.745	8.244	7.786	7.367	6.982	6.628	6.302	6.002	5.724	5.468	5.229	5.008	4.802	4.611	3.824	3.249
15	13.865	12.849	11.938	11.118	10.380	9.712	9.108	8.559	8.061	7.606	7.191	6.811	6.462	6.142	5.847	5.575	5.324	5.092	4.876	4.675	3.859	3.268
16	14.718	13.578	12.561	11.652	10.838	10.106	9.447	8.851	8.313	7.824	7.379	6.974	6.604	6.265	5.954	5.668	5.405	5.162	4.938	4.730	3.887	3.283
17	15.562	14.292	13.166	12.166	11.274	10.477	9.763	9.122	8.544	8.022	7.549	7.120	6.729	6.373	6.047	5.749	5.475	5.222	4.990	4.775	3.910	3.295
18	16.398	14.992	13.754	12.659	11.690	10.828	10.059	9.372	8.756	8.201	7.702	7.250	6.840	6.467	6.128	5.818	5.534	5.273	5.033	4.812	3.928	3.304
19	17.226	15.678	14.324	13.134	12.085	11.158	10.336	9.604	8.950	8.365	7.839	7.366	6.938	6.550	6.198	5.877	5.584	5.316	5.070	4.843	3.942	3.311
20	18.046	16.351	14.877	13.590	12.462	11.470	10.594	9.818	9.129	8.514	7.963	7.469	7.025	6.623	6.259	5.929	5.628	5.353	5.101	4.870	3.954	3.316
21	18.857	17.011	15.415	14.029	12.821	11.764	10.836	10.017	9.292	8.649	8.075	7.562	7.102	6.687	6.312	5.973	5.665	5.384	5.127	4.891	3.963	3.320
22	19.660	17.658	15.937	14.451	13.163	12.042	11.061	10.201	9.442	8.772	8.176	7.645	7.170	6.743	6.359	6.011	5.696	5.410	5.149	4.909	3.970	3.323
23	20.456	18.292	16.444	14.857	13.489	12.303	11.272	10.371	9.580	8.883	8.266	7.718	7.230	6.792	6.399	6.044	5.723	5.432	5.167	4.925	3.976	3.325
24	21.243	18.914	16.936	15.247	13.799	12.550	11.469	10.529	9.707	8.985	8.348	7.784	7.283	6.835	6.434	6.073	5.746	5.451	5.182	4.937	3.981	3.327
25	22.023	19.523	17.413	15.622	14.094	12.783	11.654	10.675	9.823	9.077	8.422	7.843	7.330	6.873	6.464	6.097	5.766	5.467	5.195	4.948	3.985	3.329
26	22.795	20.121	17.877	15.983	14.375	13.003	11.826	10.810	9.929	9.161	8.488	7.896	7.372	6.906	6.491	6.118	5.783	5.480	5.206	4.956	3.988	3.330
27	23.560	20.707	18.327	16.330	14.643	13.211	11.987	10.935	10.027	9.237	8.548	7.943	7.409	6.935	6.514	6.136	5.798	5.492	5.215	4.964	3.990	3.331
28	24.316	21.281	18.764	16.663	14.898	13.406	12.137	11.051	10.116	9.307	8.602	7.984	7.441	6.961	6.534	6.152	5.810	5.502	5.223	4.970	3.992	3.331
29	25.066	21.844	19.188	16.984	15.141	13.591	12.278	11.158	10.198	9.370	8.650	8.022	7.470	6.983	6.551	6.166	5.820	5.510	5.229	4.975	3.994	3.332
30	25.808	22.396	19.600	17.292	15.372	13.765	12.409	11.258	10.274	9.427	8.694	8.055	7.496	7.003	6.566	6.177	5.829	5.517	5.235	4.979	3.995	3.332
35	29.409	24.999	21.487	18.665	16.374	14.498	12.948	11.655	10.567	9.644	8.855	8.176	7.586	7.070	6.617	6.215	5.858	5.539	5.251	4.992	3.998	3.333
40	32.835	27.355	23.115	19.793	17.159	15.046	13.332	11.925	10.757	9.779	8.951	8.244	7.634	7.105	6.642	6.233	5.871	5.548	5.258	4.997	3.999	3.333

Note: All factors are rounded to the nearest 1/1000 in order to agree with values used in the text.

APPENDIX E

Using a Financial Calculator

Important Financial Keys on the Typical Financial Calculator

The important financial keys on a typical financial calculator are depicted and defined below. On some calculators the keys may be labeled using lowercase characters for "N" and "I". Also, "I/Y" may be used in place of the "I" key.

CPT — Compute key; used to initiate financial calculation once all values are input

 N — Number of periods

 I — Interest rate per period

PV — Present value

PMT — Amount of payment; used only for annuities

 FV — Future value

The handheld financial calculator makes it easy to calculate time value. Once you have mastered the time value of money concepts using tables, we suggest you use such a calculator. For one thing, it becomes cumbersome to use tables when calculating anything other than annual compounding. For another, calculators rather than tables are used almost exclusively in the business of personal financial planning.

You don't want to become overly dependent on calculators, however, because you may not be able to recognize a nonsensical answer in the event that you accidentally push the wrong button. The important calculator keys are shown and labeled above. Before using your calculator to make the financial computations described in this text, be aware of the following points.

1. The keystrokes on some of the more sophisticated and expensive calculators are menu-driven: after you select the appropriate routine, the calculator prompts you to input each value; a compute key (CPT) is not needed to obtain a solution.
2. Many calculators allow the user to set the number of payments per year. Most of these calculators are preset for monthly payments, or 12 payments per year. Because we work primarily with *annual* payments—one payment per year—it is important to make sure that your calculator is set for one payment per year. Although most calculators are preset to recognize that all payments occur at the end of the period, it is also important to make sure your calculator is actually in the END mode. Consult the reference guide that accompanies your calculator for instructions on these settings.

3. To avoid including previous data in current calculations, always clear all registers of your calculator before inputting values and making a new computation.
4. The known values can be punched into the calculator in any order; the order specified here and in the text simply reflects the authors' personal preference.

Calculator Keystrokes. Let's go back to the future value calculation on page 64, where we are trying to calculate the future value of $5,000 at the end of 6 years if invested at 5%. Here are the steps for solving the problem with a calculator:

1. Punch in 5000 and press PV.
2. Punch in 6 and press N.
3. Punch in 5 and press I.
4. To calculate the future value, press CPT and then FV. The future value of 6700.48 should appear on the calculator display.

Calculator

INPUTS	FUNCTIONS
5000	PV
6	N
5	I
	CPT
	FV
	SOLUTION
	6700.48

On many calculators, this value will be preceded by a minus sign, which is a way of distinguishing between cash inflows and cash outflows. For our purposes, this sign can be ignored.

To calculate the yearly savings (the amount of an annuity), let's continue with the example on page 64. For this example, the interest rate is 5%, the number of periods is 6, and the future value is $38,300. Your task is to solve the equation for the annuity. The steps using the calculator are:

1. Punch in 6 and press N.
2. Punch in 5 and press I.
3. Punch in 38300 and press FV.
4. To calculate the yearly payment or annuity, press CPT and then PMT.

Calculator

INPUTS	FUNCTIONS
6	N
5	I
38300	FV
	CPT
	PMT
	SOLUTION
	5630.77

The annuity of 5,630.77 should appear on the calculator display. Again, a negative sign can be ignored.

A similar procedure is used to find present value of a future sum or an annuity, except you would first input the FV or PMT before pressing CPT and then PV to calculate the desired result. To find the equal annual future withdrawals from an initial deposit, the PV would be input first; you solve for the PMT by pressing CPT and then PMT.

Index

exhibit = *e*, worksheet = *w*

A

ACA. *See* Patient Protection and Affordable Care Act and the Reconciliation Act of 2010
Accelerated benefits, 332
Accident policies, 357
Account executives, 429
Account reconciliation, 143–145
Accrued interest, 494–495
Accumulation period (annuity), 585
Active income, 92
Activities of daily living (ADLs), 366
Actual cash value, 383
Add-on method, 284–287
Adjustable-rate mortgages (ARMs)
    defined, 202
    features of, 202
Adjusted gross estate, 626
Adjusted gross income (AGI), 93–94
Adjustment period, 202
Adjustments to (gross) income, 93–94
Administrator, 614
Advanced directives for health care, 615
Aetna insurance, 352
Affinity cards, 229–230
Affordability ratio, 189–190
Affordable Care Act of 2010, 340, 348–349, 350
After-tax IRA, 581, 583*e*
Age
    education, income and, 35*e*
    median net worth by, 50*e*
Agency bonds, 489
Aggressive growth funds, 522
All-or-none order, 434
Allstate, 403
A.M. Best, 326–327, 328*e*
Amended return, 95, 108–109
American Association of Individual Investors (AAII), 447, 533
American Depository Receipts (ADRs), 478
Analysis
    lease *vs.* purchase, 175, 176*w*
    needs, life insurance, 291–296, 305–311
    rent-or-buy housing, 182
Anchoring, 168
Annual exclusions, 624
Annual percentage rate (APR), 244
Annual percentage yield (APY), 133
Annual renewable term life insurance premiums, 312*e*
Annual stockholders' reports, 437
Annuity
    contracts, 586*e*
    defined, 70, 585
    disposition of proceeds, 586–587
    does an annuity makes sense for you?, 589
    fixed *vs.* variable, 587–588
    future value of, 70–71

investment and income properties of, 588–590
    present value of, 71–72
    single premium/installments, 585–586
    sources of, 588
Annuity certain, 587
Antitheft devices (auto), 401
Apple Inc., 481
Applicable exclusion amount (AEA), 620*e*, **622**
Approximate expected yield, 468–469
April 15, tax filing deadline, 108
Arbitration, 431
Ask price, 424
Asset acquisition planning, 18
Asset allocation, 449–451, 465
Asset allocation funds, 526–527
Asset management account (AMA), 134–135
Asset planning, estate planning and, 601–602
Assets, 46–47
Audited returns, 109
Autobytel, 171
Auto loans, 262
Automated teller machines (ATMs), 135
Automatic investment plans, 528
Automatic reinvestment plans, 528–529
Automatic transfer program, 143
Automobile, buying, 263
    about, 164
    affordability, 165–169
    best car for you, 170*e*
    choosing a, 164–165
    closing the deal, 171–172
    decisions, 207
    fuel economy, 169
    gas, diesel, hybrid, 166–167
    key steps in, 165*e*
    leasing, 173–177
    new/used cars, 167
    operating costs, 166
    price, negotiating, 170–171
    purchase transaction, 169–172
    purchase *vs.* leasing, 175, 176*w*
    refinancing auto loans, 172
    reliability/warranties, 168–169
    safety, 169
    size/body style/features, 167–168
    trade ins, 169
Automobile, leasing
    about, 173
    checklist, 174
    ending the lease, 175–177
    leasing *vs.* purchase, 175
Automobile insurance
    buying, 401
    collision insurance, 398
    comprehensive, 398
    discounts, 401
    financial responsibility laws, 401–402